I0200035

Spurgeon's Sermons
Volume 17: 1871
By Charles Haddon Spurgeon
This Edition Edited by Anthony Uyl

Woodstock, Ontario, Canada 2017

Spurgeon's Sermons Volume 17: 1871

Charles Haddon Spurgeon (1834-1892)

This Edition Edited by Anthony Uyl

What kind of philosophies do you have?
Let us know!

Visit our online store: www.devotedpublishing.com
Contact us at: devotedpub@hotmail.com
Visit us on Facebook: @DevotedPublishing

Published in Woodstock, Ontario, Canada 2017

For bulk educational rates, please contact us at the above email address.

ISBN: 978-1-77356-169-1

Table of Contents

Life In Christ

A Sermon (No. 968)
Delivered on Lord's-day Morning, January 1st, 1871 by
C. H. SPURGEON,
At the Metropolitan Tabernacle, Newington

"Because I live, ye shall live also." - John 14:19.

THIS world saw our Lord Jesus for a very little time, but now it seeth him no more. It only saw him with the outward eye and after a carnal sort, so that when the clouds received him and concealed him from bodily vision, this spiritually blind world lost sight of him altogether. Here and there, however, among the crowds of the sightless there were a few chosen men who had received spiritual sight; Christ had been light to them, he had opened their blind eyes, and they had seen him as the world had not seen him. In a high and full sense they could say, "We have seen the Lord," for they had in some degree perceived his Godhead, discerned his mission, and learned his spiritual presence of its object, those persons who had seen Jesus spiritually, saw him after he had gone out of the world unto the Father. We who have the same sight still see him. Read carefully the words of the verse before us: "Yet a little while, and the world seeth me no more; but ye see me." It is a distinguishing mark of a true follower of Jesus that he sees his Lord and Master when he is not to be seen by the bodily eye; he sees him intelligently and spiritually; he knows his Lord, discerns his character, apprehends him by faith, gazes upon him with admiration as our first sight of Christ brought us into spiritual life, for we looked unto him and were saved, so it is by the continuance of this spiritual sight of Christ that our spiritual life is consciously maintained. We lived by looking, we live still by looking. Faith is still the medium by which life comes to us from the life-giving Lord. It is not only upon the first day of the Christian's life that he must needs look to Jesus only, but every day of that life, even until the last, his motto must be, "Looking unto Jesus, the author and finisher of our faith." The world sees him no more, for it never saw him aright; but ye have seen him and lived, and now, through continuing still to see him, you remain in life. Let us ever remember the intimate connection between faith and spiritual life. Faith is the life-look. we must never think that we live by works, by feelings, or by ceremonies. "The just shall live by faith." We dare not preach to the ungodly sinner a way of obtaining life by the works of the law, neither dare we hold up to the most advanced believer a way of sustaining life by legal means. We should in such a case expect to hear the apostle's expostulation, "Are ye so foolish? having begun in the Spirit, are ye now made perfect by the flesh?" Our glorifying is that our life is not dependent on ourselves, but is safe in our Lord, as saith the apostle, "I am crucified with Christ: nevertheless I live; yet not I, but Christ liveth in me: and the life which I now live in the flesh I live by the faith of the Son of God, who loved me, and gave himself for me." Because he lives, we live, and shall live for ever. God grant that our eye may ever be clear towards Jesus, our life. May we have no confidence but in our Redeemer; may our eyes be fixed upon him, that no other object may in any measure or degree shut out our view of him as our all in all.

The text contains in it very much of weighty truth, far more than we shall be able to bring forth from it this morning. First, we see in it a life; secondly, that life preserved; and thirdly, the reason for the preservation of that life: "Because I live, ye shall live also."

I. First, we have LIFE here spoken of.

We must not confound this with existence. It were indeed to reduce a very rich text to a poverty-stricken sentence if we read it, "Because I exist, ye shall exist also." We could not say of such a use of words that the water of ordinary speech was turned to wine, but rather that the wine was turned to water. Before the disciples believed in Jesus they existed, and altogether apart from him as their spiritual life their existence would have been continued; it was something far other and higher than immortal existence which our Lord was here dealing with.

Life, what is it? We know practically, but we cannot tell in words. We know it, however, to be a mystery of different degrees. As all flesh is not the same flesh, so all life is not the same life. There is the life of the vegetable, the cedar of Lebanon, the hyssop on the wall. There is a considerable advance when we come to animal life--the eagle or the ox. Animal life moves in quite a different world from that in which the plant vegetates--sensation, appetite, instinct, are things to which plants are dead, though they may possess some imitation of them, for one life mimics another. Animal life rises far above the experience and apprehension of the flower of the field. Then there is mental life, which we all of us possess, which introduces us into quite another realm from that which is inhabited by the mere beast. To judge, to foresee, to imagine, to invent, to perform moral acts, are not these new functions which the ox hath not? Now, let it be clear to you, that far above mental life there is another form of life of which the mere carnal man can form no more idea than the plant of the animal, or the animal of the poet. The carnal mind knoweth not spiritual things, because it has no spiritual capacities. As the beast cannot comprehend the pursuits of the philosopher, so the man who is but a natural man cannot comprehend the experience of the spiritually minded. Thus saith the Scripture: "The natural man receiveth not the things of the Spirit of God: for they are foolishness unto him: neither can he know them, because they are spiritually discerned. But he that is spiritual judgeth all things, yet he himself is judged of no man." There is in believers a life which is not to be found in other men--nobler, diviner for education cannot raise the natural man into it, neither can refinement reach it; for at its best, "that which is born of the flesh is flesh," and to all must the humbling truth be spoken, "Ye must be born again."

It is to be remarked concerning our life in Christ, that it is the removal of the penalty which fell upon our race for Adam's sin. "In the day that thou eatest thereof thou shalt surely die," was the Lord's threatening to our first parent, who was the representative of the race. He did eat of the fruit, and since God is true, and his word never fails, we may be sure of this, that in that selfsame day Adam died. It is true that he did not cease to exist, but that is quite another thing from dying. The threatening was not that he should ultimately die, but "In the day thou eatest thereof thou shalt surely die;" and it is beyond all doubt that the Lord kept his word to the letter. If the first threatening was not carried out we might take liberty to trifle with all others. Rest assured, then, that the threat was on the spot fulfilled. The spiritual life departed from Adam; he was no longer at one with God, no more able to live and breathe in the same sphere as the Lord. He fell from his first estate; he had need if he should enter into spiritual life to be born again, even as you and I must be. As he hides himself from his Maker, and uttersvain excuses before his God, you see that he is dead to the life of God, dead in trespasses and sins. We also, being heirs of wrath even as others, are through the fall dead, dead in trespasses and sins; and if ever we are to possess spiritual life, it must be said of us, "And you hath he quickened." We must be as "those that are alive from the dead." The world is the valley of dry bones, and grace raises the chosen into newness of life. The fall brought universal death, in the deep spiritual sense of that word, over all mankind; and Jesus delivers us from the consequences of the fall by implanting in us a spiritual life. By no other means can this death be removed: "He that believeth on the Son hath everlasting life: and he that believeth not the Son shall not see life; but the wrath of God abideth on him." The work of regeneration, in which the new life is implanted, effectually restores the ruin of the fall, for we are born again, "not of corruptible seed, but of incorruptible, by the word of God which liveth and abideth for ever." But you remind me that still sin remains in us after we have received the divine life. I know it does, and it is called "the body of this death;" and this it is which rages within, between the power of the death in the first Adam, and the power of the life in the second Adam; but the heavenly life will ultimately overcome the deadly energy of sin. Even to-day our inner life groans after deliverance, but with its groan of "O wretched man that I am! who shall deliver me from the body of this death?" it mingles the thankful song, "I thank God through Jesus Christ our Lord."

This life is of a purely spiritual kind. We find analogies and resemblances of it in the common mental life, but they are only analogies, the spiritual life is far and high above the carnal life, and altogether out of sight of the fleshly mind. Scarce are there words in which it can be described. To know this life you must have it; it must pulsate within your own bosom, for no explanations of others can tell you what this life is; it is one of the secrets of the Lord. It would not be possible for us with the greatest skill to communicate to a horse any conception of what imagination is; neither could we by the most diligent use of words, communicate to carnal minds what it is to be joined unto the Lord so as to be one spirit. One thing we know of it, namely, that the spiritual life is intimately connected with the indwelling of the Holy Spirit in the soul. When he comes we are "born again from above," "born of the Spirit." While he works in us mightily our life is active and powerful if he withdraws his active operations our new life becomes faint and sickly. Christ is our life, but he works in us through his Holy Spirit, who dwelleth in us evermore.

Further, we know that this life very much consists in union with God. "For to be carnally minded is death; but to be spiritually minded is life and peace. Because the carnal mind is enmity against God: for it is not subject to the law of God, neither again can be. So then they that are in the flesh cannot please God." Death as to the body consists in the body being separated from the soul; the death of the soul lies mainly in the soul's being separated form its God. For the soul to be in union with God is the soul's highest life; in his presence it unfolds itself like an opening flower;

away from him it pines, and loses all its beauty and excellence, till it is as a thing destroyed. Let the soul obey God, let it be holy, pure, gracious, then is it happy, an truly living; but a soul saundered from God is a soul blasted, killed, destroyed; it exists in a dreadful death; all its true peace, dignity, and glory, are gone; it is a hideous ruin, the mere corpse of manhood. The new life brings us near to God, makes us think of him, makes us love him, and ultimately makes us like him. My brethren, it is in proportion as you get near to God that you enter into the full enjoyment of life--that life which Jesus Christ gives you, and which Jesus Christ preserves in you. "In his favour is life." Psalm 30:5. "The fear of the Lord is a fountain of life." Prov. 14:27. To turn to God is "repentance unto life." To forget God is for a man to be "dead whilst he liveth." To believe the witness of God is to possess the faith which overcometh the world. "He that believeth on the Son of God hath the witness in himself: he that believeth not God hath made him a liar; because he believeth not the record that God gave of his Son. And this is the record, that God hath given to us eternal life, and this life is in his Son. He that hath the Son hath life; and he that hath not the Son of God hath not life."

This life within the soul bears fruit on earth in righteousness and true holiness. It blooms with sweetest of flowers of fellowship with God below, and it is made perfect in the presence of God in heaven. The life of glorified spirits above is but the life of justified men here below; it is the same life, only it is delivered from encumbrances, and has come to the fullness of its strength. The life of heaven is in every believer even now. The moment a sinner believes in Jesus he receives from God that selfsame life which shall look down serenely upon the conflagration of earth, and the passing away of those lower skies. Blessed is that man who hath everlasting life, who is made a partaker of the divine nature, who is born again from above, who is born of God by a seed which remaineth in him, for he is the man upon whom the second death hath no power, who shall enjoy life eternal when the wicked go away into everlasting punishment.

Thus much concerning this life. We have now to ask each of you whether you have received it. Have you been born, not of blood, nor of the will of the flesh, nor of the will of man, but of God? Was there a time with you when you passed from death unto life, or are you abiding in death? Have you the witness in yourself that you have been operated upon by a divinely spiritual power? Is there something in you which was not once there, not a faculty developed by education, but a life implanted by God himself? Do you feel an inward craving unknown to carnal minds, a longing desire which this world could neither excite nor gratify? Is there a strange sighing for a land as yet unseen, of which it is a native, and for which it yearns? Do you walk among the sons of men as a being of another race, not of the world, even as Christ was not of the world? Can you say, with the favoured apostle, "We know that the Son of God is come, and hath given us an understanding, that we may know him that is true, and we are in him that is true, even in his Son Jesus Christ. This is the true God, and eternal life." Oh! then, thank God for this, and thank God yet more that you have an infallible guarantee for this, and thank God yet more that you have an infallible guarantee that your life shall be continued and perfected, for so saith the text, "Because I live, ye shall live also."

II. Our second head treats of LIFE PRESERVED. "Because I life, ye shall live also." There stands the promise, " Ye shall live also. This heavenly life of yours which ye have received shall be preserved to you.

Concerning this sentence, let me draw your attention, first of all, to its fullness: "Ye shall live." I think I see in that much more than lies upon the surface. Whatever is meant by living shall be ours. All the degree of life which is secured in the covenant of grace, believers shall have. Moreover, all your new nature shall live, shall thoroughly live, shall eternally live. By this word it is secured that the eternal life implanted at regeneration shall never die out. As our Lord said so shall it be. "Whosoever drinketh of the water that I shall give him shall never thirst; but the water that I shall give him shall be in him a well of water springing up into everlasting life." We may not view this precious word as referring to all the essential spiritual graces which make up the new man? Not even, in part, shall the new man die. "Ye shall live," applies to all the parts of our new-born nature. If there be any believer here who has not lived to the full extent he might have done, let him lay hold upon this promise; and seeing that it secures the preservation of all his new nature, let him have courage to seek a higher degree of health. "I am come," saith Christ, "that ye might have life, and have it more abundantly." There is no reason, Christian, why your love to Jesus should not become flaming, ardent, conquering; for it lives, and ever must live. As to your faith, it also has immortal vitality in it, and even though it be just now weak, and staggering, lift up the hands that hang down and confirm the feeble knees, for your faith shall not die out. Here in your Lord's promise the abiding nature of the vital faculties of your spirit is guaranteed. There is no stint in the fullness of Christian life. Beneath the skies I would labour to attain it, but herein is my joy , that it shall be most surely mine, for this word is faithful and true. As surely as I have this day eternal life by reason of faith in Christ Jesus, so surely shall I reach its fullness when Christ who is my life shall appear. Even here on earth I have the permit to seek for the fullest development of this life; nay I have a precept in this promise bidding me to seek after it. "Ye shall live," means that the new life shall not be destroyed--no, not as to any of its essentials. All the members of the spiritual man shall be safe; we may say of it as of the Lord himself, "Not a bone of him shall be broken." The shield of Christ's own life covers all the faculties of our spiritual nature. We shall not enter into life halt or maimed; but he will present us faultless before the presence of his glory, not having spot or wrinkle, or any such thing, much less nay dead limbs or decayed faculties. It is a grand promise, and covers the spiritual nature as with the wings of God, so that we may apply to it the words of David, in the ninety-first Psalm: "Surely he shall deliver thee from the snare of the fowler, and from the noisome pestilence. He shall cover thee with his feathers, and under his wings shalt thou trust: his truth shall be thy shield and buckler. Thou shalt not be afraid for the terror by night; nor for the arrow that flieth by day; nor for the pestilence that walketh in darkness; nor for the destruction that wasteth at noonday. A thousand shall fall at thy side, and ten thousand at thy right hand; but it shall not come nigh thee."

The text secures that the death-penalty of the law shall never fall upon believers. The quickened man shall never fall back into the old death from which he has escaped; He shall not be numbered with the dead, and condemned either in this life or the next. Never shall the spiritually living become dead again in sin. As Jesus being raised form the dead dieth no more, death hath no more dominion over him; even so sin shall not have dominion over us again. Once, through the offense of one, death reigned in us; but now having received abundance of grace and of the gift of righteousness, we shall reign in life by one, Christ Jesus. Rom. 5:17. "For if, when we were enemies, we were reconciled to God by the death of his Son, much more, being reconciled, we shall be saved by his life." Rom. 5:10.

We are united to Christ this day by bands of spiritual life which neither things present nor things to come can separate. Our union to Jesus is eternal. It may be assailed; but it shall never be destroyed. The old body of this death may for awhile prevail, and like Herod it may seek the young child's life, but it cannot die. Who shall condemn to death that which is not under the law? Who shall slay that which abides under the shadow of the Almighty? Even as sin reigned unto death, even so must grace reign unto eternal life, by Jesus Christ our Lord.

Remark carefully the continuance insisted upon in this verse. Continuance is indeed the main element of this promise--"Ye shall live." It means certainly that during our abode in this body we shall live. We shall not be again reduced to our death-state during our sojourn here. Ten thousand attempts will be made to bring us under dominion to the law of sin and death, but this one word baffles all. Your soul may be so assailed that it shall seem as if you could not keep your hold on Christ, but Christ shall keep his hold on you. The incorruptible seed may be crushed, bruised, buried, but the life within it shall not extinguished, it shall yet arise. "Ye shall live." When ye see all around you ten thousand elements of death, think ye believers, how grand is this word, "Ye shall live." No falling from grace for you, no being cast out of the covenant, no being driven from the Father's house and left to perish. "Ye shall live."

Nor is this all, for when the natural death comes, which indeed to us is no longer death, our inner life shall suffer no hurt whatsoever; it will not even be suspended for a moment. It is not a thing which can be touched by death. The shafts of the last enemy can have no more effect upon the spiritual, than a javelin upon a cloud. Even in the very crisis, when the soul is separated from the body, no damage shall be done to the spiritual nature. And in the awful future, when the judgment comes, when the thrones are set, and the multitudes are gathered, and to the right the righteous, and to the left the wicked, let what may of terror and of horror come frothy, the begotten of God shall live. Onward through eternity, whatever may be the changes which yet are to be disclosed, nothing shall affect our God-given life. Like the life of God himself--eternal, and ever-blessed, it shall continue. Should all things else be swept away, the righteous must live on; I mean not merely that they shall exist, but they shall live in all the fullness of that far-reaching, much-comprehending word "life." Bearing the nature of God as far as the creature can participate in it, the begotten from the dead shall prove the sureness of the promise, "Ye shall live."

Let me further call to your notice that the fact here stated is univeral, in application to all spiritual life. The promise is, "Ye shall live," that is to say, every child of God shall live. Every one who sees Christ, as the world sees him not, is living and shall live. I can understand such a promised given to eminent saints who live near to God, but my soul would prostrate herself before the throne in reverent loving wonder when she hears this word spoken to the very least and meanest of the saints, "Ye shall live." Thou art not exempted, thou whose faith is but as a smoking flax, thou shalt live. The Lord bestows security upon the least of his people as well as upon the greatest. It is plain that the reason given for the preservation of the new life is as applicable to one saint as another. If it had been said, "Because your faith is strong, ye shall live" then weak faith would have perished; but when it is written, "Because I live," the argument is as powerful in the one case as in the other. Take it home to thyself, my brother, however heavy thy heart, or dim thy bone, Jesus lives, and you shall live.

Remark yet again that this text is exceeding broad. Mark its breadth and see how it meets everything to the contrary, and overturns all the hopes of the adversary. "Ye shall live." Then the inbred corruption which rides within us shall not stifle the new creature. Chained as the spirit seem to be to the loathsome and corrupt body of this death, it shall live in spite of its hideous companionship. Though besetting sins may be as arrows, and fleshly lusts like drawn swords, yet grace shall not be slain. Neither the fever of hasty passion, nor the palsy of timorousness, nor the leprosy of covetousness, nor any other disease of sin, shall so break forth in the old nature as to destroy the new. Nor shall outward circumstances overthrow the inner life. "For he shall give his angels charge over thee, to keep thee in all thy ways." They shall bear thee up in their hands, lest thou dash thy foot against a stone. If providence should cast you into a godless family, where you dwell as in a sepulcher, and the air you breathe is laden with the miasma of death, yet shall you live. Evil example shall not poison your spirit, you shall drink this deadly thing and it shall not hurt you, you shall be kept from giving way to evil. You shall not be decoyed by fair temptation, you shall not be cowed by fierce persecution: mightier is he that is in you than he which is in the world. Satan will attack you, and his weapons are deadly, but you shall foil him at all points. To you is it given to tread upon the lion and adder, the young lion and the dragon shall you trample under foot. If God should allow you for awhile to be sorely tried, as he did his servant Job, and if the devil should have all the world to help him in his attempt to destroy your spiritual life, yet even on the dunghill of poverty, and in the wretchedness of sickness, your spirit shall still maintain its holy life, and you shall prove it so by blessing and magnifying God, notwithstanding all. We little dream what may be reserved for us; we may have to climb steeps of prosperity, slippery and dangerous, but we shall live; we may be called to sink into the dark waters of adversity, all God's waves and billows may go over us, but we shall live. WE may traverse persilent swamps of error, or burning dewerts of unbelief, but the divine life shall live amid the domains of death. Let the future be bright or black, we need not wish to turn the page; that which we prize best, namely, our spiritual life, is hid with Christ in God, beyond the reach of harm, and we shall live. If old age shall be our portion, and our crown shall be delayed till we have fought a long and weary battle, yet nevertheless we shall live; or if sudden death should cut short the time of our trial here, yet we shall have lived in the fullness of that word.

III. Our third point is, THE REASON FOR THE SECURITY OF THE SPIRITUAL LIFE.

The reason assigned is this, "Because I live, ye shall live also." Christ has life essentially as God. Christ, as man, having fulfilled his life-work, having offered full atonement for human sin, dieth no more, death hath no more dominion over him. His life is communicated to us, and becomes the guarantee to us that we shall live also.

Observe, first, that this is the sole reason of the believer's spiritual life. "Because I live, ye shall live also." The means by which the soul is pardoned is found in the precious blood of Jesus; the cause of its obtaining spiritual life at first is found in Christ's finished work; and the only reason why the Christian continues still to live after he is quickened, lies in Jesus Christ, who liveth and was dead and is alive for evermore. When I first come to Christ, I know I must find all in him, for I feel I have nothing of my own; but all my life long I am to acknowledge the same absolute dependence; I am still to look for everything to him. " I am the vine, ye are the branches: he that abideth in me, and I in him, the same bringeth forth much fruit: for without me, yet can do nothing." the temptation is after we have looked to Jesus and found life there, to fancy that in future time we are to sustain ourselves in spiritual existence by some means within ourselves, or by supplies extra and apart from Christ. But it must not be so; all for the future as well as all for the past is wrapped up in the person and the work of the Lord Jesus. Because he died, ye are pardoned; because he lives, ye live; all your life still lies in him who is the way, the truth, and the life. Does not the Christian's life depend upon his prayerfulness? Could he be a Christian if he ceased to pray? We reply, the Christian's spiritual health depends upon his prayerfulness, but that prayerfulness depends on something else. The reason why the hands of the clock move may be found first in a certain wheel which operates upon them, but if you go to the primary cause of all, you reach the main-spring, or the weight, which is the source of all the motion. Many secondary causes tend to sustain spiritual life; but the primary cause, the first and foremost, is because Jesus Christ lives. "All my fresh springs are in thee." While Jesus lives, he sends the Spirit; the Spirit being sent, we pray; our payer becomes the evidence of our spiritual life. "But are not good works essential to the maintenance of the spiritual life?" Certainly, if there be no good works, we have no evidence of spiritual life. In its season the tree must bring forth its fruit and its leaves; if there be no outward sign we suspect that there is no motion of the sap within. Still, to the tree the fruit is not the cause of life, but the result of it, and to the life of the Christian, good works bear the same relationship, they are its outgrowth, not its root. If then my spiritual life is low, what am I to look to? I am not to look to my prayers, I am not to find comfort in my works. I may from these discover how declining I am; but if I want my life to be renovated, I must fly to the fountain of my life, even Jesus, for there, and there only, shall I find restoration. Do let us recollect this, that we are not saved because of anything that we are, or anything that we do; and that we do not remain saved because of anything we are or can be. A man is saved because Christ died for him he continues saved because Christ lives for him. The sole reason why the spiritual life abides is because Jesus lives. This is to get upon a rock, above the fogs which cover all things down below. If my life rests on something within me, then to-day I live, and to-morrow I die; but if my spiritual life rests in Christ, then in my darkest frames-ay, and when sin has most raged against my spirit- still I live in the ever-living One, whose life never changes.

Secondly, it is a sufficient cause for my life. "Because I live, ye shall live also." It must be enough to make believers live that Christ lives; for first, Christ's life is a proof that his work has accomplished the absolution of his people from their sins. He would have been in the tomb to this hour had he not made a complete satisfaction for their sins, but his rising again from the dead is the testimony of God that he has accepted the atonement of his dear Son; his resurrection is our full acquittal. Then if the living Christ be our acquittal, how can God condemn us to die for sins which he has by the fact of Christ's resurrection declared to be for ever blotted out? If Jesus lives, how can we die? Shall there be two deaths for one sin, the death of Christ and the death of those for whom he died? God forbid that there should be any such injustice with the Most High. The very fact that Jesus lives, proves that our sin has been atoned for, that we are absolved, and therefore cannot die.

Jesus is the representative of those for whom he is the federal head. Shall the representative live, and yet those represented die? How shall the living represent the dead? But in his life I see my own life, for as Levi was in the loins of Abraham, so is every saint in the loins of Christ, and the life of Christ is representatively the life of all his people.

Moreover, he is the surety for his people, under bonds and pledges to bring his redeemed safely home. His own declaration is, "I give unto my sheep eternal life, and they shall never perish, neither shall any pluck them out of my hands." Will he break his covenant bonds? Shall his suretyship be cast to the winds? It cannot be. The fact that if any of his people for whom he died, to whom he has given spiritual life, should after all die, Christ would be disappointed of his intent, which supposition involves the grossest blasphemy. What so many shall he have for his reward? The purchase-price shall not be given in vain; a redemption so marvelous as that which he has presented upon the tree, shall never in any degree become a failure. His life, which proves his labour to be over, guarantees to people. Know ye not, my brethren, that if one of those to whom Christ has given spiritual life should after all fall from it and die, it would argue either that he had a want of power to keep them, or a want of will to do so. Shall we conceive him to be devoid of power? Then how he is mighty God? Is he devoid of will to keep his people- is that conceivable? Cast out the traitorous thought! He must be as willing as he is able, and as able as he is willing. While he was in this world, he kept his people; having loved his own, he loved them to the end; he is "the same yesterday, to-day, and for ever," he will not suffer one of these little ones to perish.

Recollect, and this perhaps will cheer you most of all, that all who have spiritual life are one with Christ Jesus. Jesus is the head of the mystical body, they are the members. Suppose one of the members of the mystical body of Christ should die, then from that moment, with reverence be it spoken, Christ is not a complete Christ. What were the head without the body? A most ghastly sight. What were the head with only a part of the members? Certainly not perfect. There must be every member present to make a complete body. Therefore we gather that you, brother, though you think yourself the meanest part of the body, are nevertheless, essential to its perfection; and you, sister, though you fancy yourself to be one of the uncomely portions of the body, yet you must be there, or else the body cannot be perfect, and Christ cannot be a complete Christ. From him, the head, the life streams into all the members and while that head lives as a perfect head of a perfect body, all members must live also. As we have often said, as long as a man's head is above water you cannot drown his limbs; as long as our head is above the reach of spiritual death we also are the same-no weapons can hurt, no poison can destroy, not all hell's fires could burn, nor all earth's floods could drown, the spiritual life within us: it must be safe because it is indissolubly one with Jesus Christ the Lord. What comfort, then, lies in this, the sole but sufficient reason for the eternal maintenance of the new-born life within us, is this, "Because I live, ye shall live also."

And be it remembered, that this reason is an abiding reason--"Because I live, ye shall live also"--a reason which has as much force at one time as another. From causes variable the effects are variable; but remaining causes produce permanent effects. Now Jesus always lives. Yesterday, dear brother you were exalted in fellowship with him, and stood upon the mountain top; then your heart was glad, and your spirit rejoiced, and you could say, "I live in Christ." To-day darkness has intervened, you do not feel the motions of the inner life as you did yesterday, but do not therefore conclude that the life is not there. What is to be your sign; what is to be the rainbow of the covenant to you? Why, that Jesus lives. Do you doubt that he lives? You dare not. You trust him, doubt not then that you live, for your life is as sure as his. Believe also that you shall live, for that also is as sure as the fact that he lives. God gave to Noah, a token that he would not destroy the earth-it was the rainbow: but then the rainbow is not often seen; there are peculiar circumstances before the bow is placed in the cloud. You, brother, you have a token of God's covenant given you in the text which can always be seen, neither sun nor shower are needful to its appearance. The living Christ is the token that you live too. God gave to David the token of the sun and the moon; he said if the ordinances of day and night should be changed, then would he cast off the seed of David. But there are times when neither sun nor moon appear, but your token is plain when these are hidden. Christ at all times lives. When you are lowest, when you cannot pray, when you can hardly groan, when you do not seem to have spiritual life enough even to heave a desire, still if you cling to Jesus this life is as surely in you as there is life in Christ himself at the right hand of the Father.

And lastly, it is a most instructive cause. It instructs us in many ways: let us hint at three. It instructs us to admire the condescension of Christ. Look at the two pronouns, "ye" and "I"; shall they ever come into contact? yes, here they stand in close connection with each other. "I"--the I AM the Infinite; "ye" the creatures of an hour; yet I, the Infinite, come into union with you, the finite; I the Eternal, take up you the fleeting, and I make you live because I live. What? Is there such a bond between me and Christ? Is there such a link between his life and mine? Blessed be his name! Adored be his infinite condescension!

It demands of us next abundance of gratitude. Apart from Christ we are dead in trespasses and sins; look at the depth of our degradation! But in Christ we live, live with his own life. Look at the height of our exaltation, and let our thankfulness be proportioned to this infinity of mercy. Measure if you can from the lowest hell to the highest heaven, and so great let your thankfulness be to him who has lifted you from death to life.

Let the last lesson be see the all-importance of close communion with Jesus. Union with Christ makes you live; keep up your enjoyment of that union, that you may clearly perceive and enjoy your life. Begin this year with the prayer, "Nearer to thee, my Lord, nearer to thee." Think much of the spiritual life and less of this poor carnal life, which will be soon be over. Go to the source of life for an increase of spiritual life. Go to Jesus. Think of him more than you have done, pray to him more; use his name more believingly in your supplications. Serve him better, and seek to grow up into his likeness in all things. Make an advance this year. Life is a growing thing. Your life only grows by getting nearer to Christ; therefore, get under the beams of the Sun of the Righteousness. Time brings you nearer to him, you will soon be where he is in heaven; let grace bring you nearer also. You taste more of his love as fresh mercies come, give him more of your love, more of your fellowship. Abide in him, and may his word abide in you henceforth and for ever, and all shall be to his glory. Amen.

PORTION OF SCRIPTURE READ BEFORE SERMON--Colossians 3.

* This text has been sent us by a venerable clergyman of the Church of England, who has for many years selected a new year's text for us, and others of his friends. In the calm enjoyment of divine consolations, such as this verse affords, may his last days pass away in tranquility and rejoicing.

Rest, Rest

A Sermon (No. 969)
Delivered on Lord's-day Morning, January 8th, 1871, by
C. H. SPURGEON,
At the Metropolitan Tabernacle, Newington

"Come unto me, all ye that labor and are heavy laden, and I will give you rest. Take my yoke upon you, and learn of me; for I am meek and lowly in heart; and ye shall find rest unto your souls. For my yoke is easy, and my burden is light." - Matthew 11:28-30.

WE have oft repeated those memorable words, and they have brought us much comfort; but it is possible that we may never have looked deeply into them, so as to have seen the fulness of their meaning. The works of man will seldom bear close inspection. You shall take a needle which is highly polished, which appears to be without the slightest inequality upon its surface, and you shall put it under a microscope, and it will look like a rough bar of iron; but you shall select what you will from nature, the bark or the leaf of a tree, or the wing or the foot of an insect, and you shall discover no flaw, magnify it as much as you will, and gaze upon it as long as you please. So take the words of man. The first time you hear them they will strike you; you may hear them again and still admire their sentiment, but you shall soon weary of their repetition, and call them hackneyed and over-estimated. The words of Jesus are not so, they never lose their dew, they never become threadbare. You may ring the changes upon his words, and never exhaust their music: you may consider them by day and by night, but familiarity shall not breed contempt. You shall beat them in the mortar of contemplation, with the pestle of criticism, and their perfume shall but become the more apparent. Dissect, investigate, and weigh the Master's teaching word by word, and each syllable will repay you. When loitering upon the Island of Liddo, off Venice, and listening to the sound of the city's bells, I thought the music charming as it floated across the lagune; but when I returned to the city, and sat down in the centre of the music, in the very midst of all the bells, the sweetness changed to a horrible clash, the charming sounds were transformed into a maddening din; not the slightest melody could I detect in any one bell, while harmony in the whole company of noisemakers was out of the question. Distance had lent enchantment to the sound. The words of poets and eloquent writers may, as a whole, and heard from afar, sound charmingly enough; but how few of them bear a near and minute investigation! Their belfry rings passably, but one would soon weary of each separate bell. It is never so with the divine words of Jesus. You hear them ringing from afar and they are sweetness itself. When as a sinner, you roamed at midnight like a traveller lost on the wilds, how sweetly did they call you home! But now you have reached the house of mercy, you sit and listen to each distinct note of love's perfect peal, and wonderingly feel that even angelic harps cannot excel it.

We will, this morning, if we can, conduct you into the inner chambers of out text, place its words under the microscope, and peer into the recesses of each sentence. We only wish our microscope were of a greater magnifying power, and our ability to expound the text more complete; for there are mines of instruction here. Superficially read, this royal promise has cheered and encouraged tens of thousands, but there is a wealth in it which the diligent digger and miner shall alone discover. Its shallows are cool and refreshing for the lambs, but in its depths are pearls for which we hope to dive.

Our first head, this morning, is rest: "Come unto me, all ye that labor and are heavy laden, and I will give you rest." The second head is rest: "Take my yoke upon you, and learn of me, for I am meek and lowly in heart: and ye shall find rest unto your souls."

I. Let us begin at the beginning with the first REST, and here we will make divisions only for the sake of bringing out the sense more clearly.

1. Observe the person invited to receive this first rest: "Come unto me, all ye that labor and are heavy laden." The word "all" first demands attention: "All ye that labor." There was need for the insertion of that wide word. Had not the Saviour said a little before, "I thank thee, O Father, Lord of heaven and earth, because thou hast hid these things from the wise and prudent, and hast revealed them to babes?" Some one who had been listening to the Saviour, might have said, "The

Father, then, has determined to whom he will reveal the Christ; there is a number chosen, according to the Father's good pleasure, to whom the gospel is revealed; while from another company it is hidden!" The too hasty inference, which it seems natural for man to draw from the doctrine is, "Then there is no invitation for me; there is no hope for me; I need not listen to the gospel's warnings and invitations." So the Saviour, as if to answer that discouraging notion, words his invitation thus, "Come unto me, all ye that labor and are heavy laden." Let it not be supposed that election excludes any of you from the invitation of mercy; all of you who labor, are bidden to come. Whatever the great doctrine of predestination may involve, rest assured that it by no means narrows or diminishes the extent of gospel invitations. The good news is to be preached to "every creature" under heaven, and in this particular passage it is addressed to all the laboring and heavy laden.

The description of the person invited is very full. It describes him both actively and passively. "All ye that labor"--there is the activity of men bearing the yoke, and ready to labor after salvation; "heavy laden"--there is the passive form of their religious condition, they sustain a burden, and are pressed down, and sorely wearied by the load they bear. There are to be found many who are actively engaged in seeking salvation; they believe that if they obey the precepts of the law they will be saved, and they are endeavoring to the utmost to do them; they have been told that the performance of certain rites and ceremonies will also save them, they are performing those with great care; the yoke is on their shoulders, and they are laboring diligently. Some are laboring in prayer, some are laboring in sacraments, others in self-denials and mortifications, but as a class they are awakened to feel the need of salvation, and they are intensely laboring to save themselves. It is to these the Saviour addresses his loving admonition: in effect he tells them, "This is not the way to rest, your self-imposed labors will end in disappointment; cease your wearisome exertions, and believe in me, for I will at once give you rest--the rest which my labors have earned for believers." Very speedily those who are active in self-righteously working for salvation fall into the passive state, and become burdened; their labor of itself becomes a burden to them. Besides the burden of their self-righteous labor, there comes upon them the awful, tremendous, crushing burden of past sin, and a sense of the wrath of God which is due to that sin. A soul which has to bear the load of its own sin, and the load of divine wrath, is indeed heavily laden. Atlas with the world upon his back had a light load compared with a sinner upon whom mountains of sin and wrath are piled. Such persons frequently are burdened, in addition, by fears and apprehensions; some of them correct, others of them baseless, but anyhow the burden daily grows. Their active labors do not diminish their passive sufferings. The acute anguish of their souls will often be increased in proportion as their endeavors are increased; and while they hope at first that if they labor industriously they will gradually diminish the mass of their sin, it happens that their labor adds to their weariness beneath its pressure; they feel a weight of disappointment, because their labor has not brought them rest; and a burden of despair, because they fear that deliverance will never come. Now these are the persons whom the Saviour calls to himself--those who are actively seeking salvation, those who are passively bearing the weight of sin and of divine wrath.

It is implied, too, that these are undeserving of rest, for it is said, "Come unto me, and I will give you rest." A gift is not of merit but of grace; wages and reward are for those who earn, but a gift is a matter of charity. O you who feel your unworthiness this morning, who have been seeking salvation earnestly, and suffering the weight of sin, Jesus will freely give to you what you cannot earn or purchase, he will give it as an act of his own free, rich, sovereign mercy; and he is prepared, if you come to him, to give it to you now, for so has he promised, "Come unto me, all ye that labor and are heavy laden, and I will give you rest."

2. Notice next, the precept here laid down: "Come." It is not "Learn," it is not "Take my yoke"--that is in the next verse, and is intended for the next stage of experience-but in the beginning the word of the Lord is, "Come unto me," "Come." A simple word, but very full of meaning. To come is to leave one thing and to advance to another. Come, then, ye laboring and heavy laden, leave your legal labors, leave your self-reliant efforts, leave your sins, leave your presumptions, leave all in which you hitherto have trusted, and come to Jesus, that is, think of, advance towards, rely upon the Saviour. Let your contemplations think of him who bore the load of human sin upon the cross of Calvary, where he was made sin for us. Let your minds consider him who from his cross hurled the enormous mass of his people's transgressions into a bottomless sepulchre, where it was buried forever. Think of Jesus, the divinely-appointed substitute and sacrifice for guilty man. Then, seeing that he is God's own Son, let faith follow your contemplation; rely upon him, trust in him as having suffered in your stead, look to him for the payment of the debt which is due from you to the wrath of God. This is to come to Jesus. Repentance and faith make up this "Come"--the repentance which leaves that place where you now stand, the faith which comes into reliance upon Jesus.

Observe, that the command to "Come" is put in the present tense, and in the Greek it is intensely present. It might be rendered something like this: "Hither to me all ye that labor and are heavy laden!" It is a "Come" which means not "Come to-morrow or next year," but "Now, at once." Advance, ye slaves, flee from your task-master now! Weary ones recline on the promise now, and take your rest! Come now! By an act of instantaneous faith which will bring instantaneous peace, come and rely upon Jesus, and he will now give you rest. Rest shall at once follow the exercise of faith. Perform the act of faith now. O may the eternal Spirit lead some laboring heavy laden soul to come to Jesus, and to come at this precise moment!

It is "Come unto me." Notice that. The Christ in his personality is to be trusted in. Not "Come to John, and hear him say, "Repent, for the kingdom of heaven is at hand,'" for no rest is there. John commands a preparation for the rest, but he has no rest to give to the soul. Come not to the Pharisees, who will instruct you in tradition, and in the jots and tittles of the law; but go past these to Jesus, the man, the God, the mediator, the Redeemer, the propitiation for human guilt. If you want rest come to Christ in Gethsemane, to Christ on Calvary, to Christ risen, to Christ ascended. If you want rest, O weary souls, ye can find it nowhere until ye come and lay your burdens down at his dear pierced feet, and find life in looking alone to him. There is the precept then. Observe it is nothing but that one word, "Come." It is not "Do;" it is not even "Learn." It is not, "Take up my yoke," that will follow after, but must never be forced out of its proper place. To obtain the first rest, the rest which is a matter of gift--all that is asked of you is that you come to have it. Now, the least thing that charity itself can ask when it gives away its alms, is that men come for it. Come ye needy, come and welcome; come and take the rest ye need. Jesus saith to you, "Come and take what I freely give." Without money come, without merit come, without preparation come. It is just, come, come now; come as you are, come with your burden, come with your yoke, though the yoke be the yoke of the devil, and the burden be the burden of sin, yet come as you are, and the promise shall be fulfilled to you, "I will give you rest."

3. Notice next the promise spoken, "I will give you rest." "I will give." It is a rest that is a gift; not a rest found in our experience by degrees, but given at once. As I shall have to show you, the next verse speaks of the rest that is found, wrought out, and discovered; but this is a rest given. We come to Jesus; we put out the empty hand of faith, and rest is given us at once most freely. We possess it at once, and it is ours forever. It is a present rest, rest now; not rest after death; not rest after a time of probation and growth and advancement; but it is rest given when we come to Jesus, given there and then. And it is perfect rest too; for it is not said, nor is it implied, that the rest is incomplete. We do not read, "I will give you partial rest," but "rest," as much as if there were no other form of it. It is perfect and complete in itself. In the blood and righteousness of Jesus our peace is perfect.

I shall not stay except to ask you now, brethren and sisters, whether you know the meaning of this given rest. Have you come to Jesus and has he given you perfect and present rest? If so, I know your eye will catch joyously those two little words, "And I," and I would bid you lovingly remember the promiser who speaks. Jesus promises and Jesus performs. Did not all your rest, when first your sin was forgiven, come from him? The load was gone, but who took it? The yoke was removed, but who lifted it from off the shoulder? Do you not give to Jesus, this day, the glory of all your rest from the burden of guilt? Do you not praise his name with all your souls? Yes, I know you do. And you know how that rest came to you. It was by his substitution and your faith in that substitution. Your sin was not pardoned by a violation of divine justice; justice was satisfied in Jesus; he gave you rest. The fact that he has made full atonement is the rest of your spirit this morning. I know that deep down in your consciences, the calm which blesses you springs from a belief in your Lord's vicarious sacrifice. He bore the unrest that you might have the rest, and you receive rest this day as a free gift from him. You have done now with servile toils and hopeless burdens, you have entered into rest through believing; but all the rest and deliverance still comes to you as a gift from his dear hands, who purchased with a price this blessing for your souls. I earnestly wish that many who have never felt that rest, would come and have it; it is all they have to do to obtain it--to come for it; just where they now are, if God enables them to exercise a simple act of faith in Jesus, he will give them rest from all their past sins, from all their efforts to save themselves, a rest which shall be to his glory and to their joy.

II. We must now advance to our second head--REST.

It looks rather strange that after having received rest, the next verse should begin: "Take my yoke upon you." "Ah! I had been set free from laboring, am I to be a laborer again?" Yes, yes, take my yoke and begin. "And my burden is light." "Burden? Why, I was heavy laden just now, am I to carry another burden?" Yes. A yoke--actively and a burden--passively, I am to bear both of these. "But I found rest by getting rid of my yoke and my burden!" And you are to find a further rest by wearing a new yoke, and bearing a new burden. Your yoke galled, but Christ's yoke is easy; your burden was heavy, but Christ's burden is light. Before we enter into this matter more fully, let us illustrate it. How certain it is that a yoke is essential to produce rest, and without it rest is unknown! Spain found rest by getting rid of that wretched monarch Isabella; an iron yoke was her dominion upon the nation's neck, crushing every aspiration after progress by an intolerable tyranny. Up rose the nation, shook off its yoke, and threw aside its burden, and it had rest in a certain sense, rest from evil. But Spain has not fully rested yet, and it seems that she will never find permanent rest till she has voluntarily taken up another yoke, and found for herself another burden. In a word, she must have a strong, settled, recognized government, and then only will her distractions cease. This is just a picture of the human soul. It is under the dominion of Satan, it wears his awful yoke, and works for him; it bears his accursed burden, and groans under it; Jesus sets it free--but has it, therefore, a perfect rest? Yes, a rest from, but not a rest in. What is wanted now is a new government; the soul must have a sovereign, a ruling principle, a master-motive; and when Jesus has taken that position, rest is come. This further rest is what is spoken of in the second verse. Let me give you another symbol. A little stream flowed through a manufacturing town; an unhappy little stream it was, for it was forced to turn huge wheels and heavy machinery, and it wound its miserable way through factories where it was dyed black and blue, until it became a foul and filthy ditch, and loathed itself. It felt the tyranny which polluted its very existence. Now, there came a deliverer who looked upon the streamlet and said, "I will set thee free and give thee rest." So he stopped up the water-course, and said, "abide in thy place, thou shalt no more flow where thou art enslaved and defiled." In a very few days the brooklet found that it had but exchanged one evil for another. Its waters were stagnating, they were gathering into a great pool, and desiring to find a channel. It was in its very nature to flow on, and it foamed and swelled, and pressed against the dam which stayed it. Every hour it grew more inwardly restless, it threatened to break the barrier, and it made all who saw its angry looks tremble for the mischief it would do ere long. It never found rest until it was permitted to pursue an active course along a channel which had been prepared for it among the meadows and the corn fields. Then, when it watered the plains and made glad the villages, it was a happy streamlet, perfectly at rest. So our souls are made for activity, and when we are set free from the activities of our self-righteousness and the slavery of our sin we must do something, and we shall never rest until we find that something to do. Hence in the text you will be pleased to see that there is something said about a yoke, which is the ensign of working, and something about a burden, which is the emblem of enduring. It is in man's mortal nature that he must do or endure, or else his spirit will stagnate and be far from rest.

1. We will consider this second rest, and notice that it is rest after rest. "I will give you rest" comes before "Ye shall find rest." It is the rest of a man who is already at rest, the repose of a man who has received a given rest, and now discovers the found rest. It is the rest of a learner--"Learn of me, and ye shall find rest." It is not so much the rest of one who was aforetime laboring and heavy laden, as of one who is to-day learning at the Saviour's feet. It is the rest of a seeker evidently, for finding usually implies a search. Having been pardoned and saved, the saved man in the course of his experience discovers more and more reason for peace; he is learning, and seeking, and he finds. The rest is evidently lighted upon, however, as a thing unknown, which becomes the subject of discovery. The man had a rest from his burden; now he finds a rest, in Christ, which exceeds what he asked or even thought.

I have looked at this rest after rest as being a treasure concealed in a precious box. The Lord Jesus gives to his people a priceless casket, called the gift of rest; it is set with brilliants and inlaid with gems, and the substance thereof is of wrought gold; whosoever possesses it feels and knows that his warfare is accomplished and his sin is pardoned. After awhile the happy owner begins to examine his treasure. It is all his own, but he has not yet seen it all, for one day he detects a secret drawer, he touches a hidden spring, and lo! Before him lies a priceless Koh-i-noor surpassing all the rest. It had been given him it is certain, but he had not seen it at first, and therefore he finds it. Jesus Christ gives us in the gift of himself all the rest we can ever enjoy, even heaven's rest lies in him; but after we have received him we have to learn his value, and find out by the teaching of his Spirit the fulness of the rest which he bestows.

Now, I say to you who are saved, you who have looked to Jesus Christ, whether you looked this morning or twenty years ago, have you found out all that there is in the gift which Christ has given you? Have you found out the secret drawer yet? He has given you rest, but have you found the innermost rest which he works in your hearts? It is yours, for it is included in the one gift; but it is not yours enjoyed, understood, and triumphed in as yet unless you have found it, for the rest here meant is a rest after rest, a spiritual, experienced rest, which comes only to those who find it by experience.

2. Further observe that the rest in this second part of our text is a rest in service. It is coupled with a yoke, for activity--"Take my yoke;" it is connected with a burden, for endurance--"My burden is light." He who is a Christian will not find rest in being idle. There is no unrest greater than that of the sluggard. If you would rest take Christ's yoke, be actively engaged in his service. As the bullock has the yoke put upon its neck and then begins to draw, so have the yoke of Christ put on your neck and commence to obey him. The rest of heaven is not the rest of sleep; they serve him

day and night in his temple. They are always resting, and yet, in another sense, they rest not day nor night. Holy activity in heaven is perfect rest. True rest to the mind of the child of God is rest on the wing, rest in motion, rest in service, not rest with the yoke off, but with the yoke on. We are to enter upon this service voluntarily; we are to take his yoke upon us voluntarily. You observe, it does not say, "Bear my yoke when it is laid upon you, but take it." Do not need to be told by the minister, "My dear brother, such-and-such a work you are bound to do," but take up the yoke of your own accord. Do not merely submit to be the Lord's servant, but seek his service. Ask, "What can I do?" Be desirous to do it' voluntarily, cheerfully, do all that lieth in you for the extension of his kingdom who has given you rest, and you shall find that the rest of your soul shall lie in your doing all you can for Jesus. Every active Christian will tell you he is never happier than when he has much to do; and, on the whole, if he communes with Jesus, never more at rest than when he has least leisure. Look not for your rest in the mere enjoyments and excitements of religion, but find your rest in wearing a yoke which you love, and which, for that reason, is easy to your neck.

But, my dear brother, you must also be willing to bear Christ's burden. Now the burden of Christ is his cross, which every Christian must take up. Expect to be reproached, expect to meet with some degree of the scandal of the cross, for the offence of it never ceases. Persecution and reproach are a blessed burden; when your soul loves Jesus it is a light thing to suffer for him, and therefore never, by any cowardly retirement or refusal to profess your faith, evade your share of this honorable load. Woe unto those who say, "I will never be a martyr." No rest is sweeter than the martyr's rest. Woe unto those who say, "We will go to heaven by night along a secret road, and so avoid the shame of the cross." The rest of the Christian is found not in cowardice but in courage; it lies not in providing for ease but in the brave endurance of suffering for the truth. The restful spirit counts the reproach of Christ to be greater riches than all the treasures of Egypt; he falls in love with the cross, and counts the burden light, and so finds rest in service, and rest in suffering. Note that well.

3. The rest before us is rest through learning. Does a friend say, "I do not see how I am ever to get rest in working, and rest in suffering?" My dear brother, you never will except you go to school, and you must go to school to Christ. "Learn of me," saith he, "for I am meek and lowly in heart." Now, in order to learn of Christ it is implied that we lay aside all prejudices of the past. These things much prevent our finding peace. Have you any preconceived notions of what religion should be? Have you fashioned on your own anvil ideas of what the doctrines of the gospel ought to be? Throw them all away; learn of Jesus, and unlearn your own thoughts.

Then, when you are willing to learn, please to note what is to be learned. In order to get perfect rest of mind you have to learn of Jesus not only the doctrines which he teaches, but a great deal more than that. To go to school to be orthodox is a good enough thing, but the orthodoxy which brings rest is an orthodoxy of the spirit. Observe the text, "Take my yoke upon you, and learn of me." What? For I am wise and learned, and can teach you? No; you are to learn from his example to be "meek and lowly in heart," and in learning that you will "find rest unto your souls." To catch the spirit of Jesus is the road to rest. To believe what he teaches me is something, to acknowledge him as my religious leader and as my Lord is much, but to strive to be conformed to his character, not merely in its external developments but in its interior spirit, this is the grammar of rest. Learn to be like the meek and lowly-hearted One, and ye shall find rest.

He tells us the two points in which we are to learn of him. First, he is meek, then he says he is lowly in heart. Take the work "meek" first. I think that refers to the yoke-bearing, the active labor. If I actively labor for Christ I can only find rest in the labor by possessing the meek spirit of my Lord; for if I go forth to labor for Christ without a meek spirit, I shall very soon find that there is no rest in it, for the yoke will gall my shoulder. Somebody will begin objecting that I do not perform my work according to his liking. If I am not meek I shall find my proud spirit rising at once, and shall be for defending myself; I shall be irritated, or I shall be discouraged and inclined to do no more, because I am not appreciated as I should be. A meek spirit is not apt to be angry, and does not soon take offence, therefore if others find fault, the meek spirit goes working on, and is not offended; it will not hear the sharp word, nor reply to the severe criticism. If the meek spirit be grieved by some cutting censure and suffers for a moment, it is always ready to forgive and blot out the past, and go on again. The meek spirit in working only seeks to do good to others; it denies itself; it never expected to be well treated; it did not aim at being honored; it never sought itself, but purposed only to do good to others. The meek spirit bowed its shoulder to the yoke, and expected to have to continue bowing in order to keep the yoke in the right place for labor. It did not look to be exalted by yoke-bearing; it is fully contented if it can exalt Christ and do good to his chosen ones. Remember how meek and lowly Jesus was in all his service, and how calmly, therefore, he bore with those who opposed him? The Samaritans would not receive him, and therefore John, who felt the yoke a little galling to his unaccustomed shoulder, cried, "Master, call fire from heaven." Poor John! But Christ bore the yoke of service so well because of his meek spirit that he would do nothing of the kind. If one village would not receive him he passed on to another, and so labored on. Your labor will become very easy if your spirits are very meek. It is the proud spirit that gets tired of doing good if it finds its labors not appreciated; but the brave, meek spirit, finds the yoke to be easy. "Consider him who endured such contradictions of sinners against himself lest ye be weary and faint in your minds." If ye learn his meekness his yoke will be pleasant to your shoulder, and you will never wish to have it removed.

Then, as to the passive part of our rest-lesson, note the text, "I am lowly in heart." We shall all have to bear something for the truth's sake so long as we are here. The reproach is a part of the gospel. The rod is a blessing of the covenant. The lowly heart finds the burden very light because it acquiesces in the divine will. The lowly heart says, "Not my will but thine be done; let God be glorified in me, it shall be all I ask. Rich, poor, sick, or in health, it is all the same to me. If God the great One has the glory, what matters where such a little one as I am may be placed?" The lowly spirit does not seek after great things for itself, it learns in whatsoever state it is therewith to be content. If it be poor, "Never mind," says the lowly one, "I never aspired to be rich; among the great ones of this earth I never desired to shine." If it be denied honor, the humble spirit says, "I never asked for earthly glory, I seek not mine own honor but his that sent me. Why should I be honored, a poor worm like me? If nobody speaks a good word of me, if I get Christ to say, "Well done, good and faithful servant," that is enough. And if the lowly-hearted have little wordly pleasure, he says, "This is not my place for pleasure, I deserve eternal pain, and if I do not have pleasures here I shall have them hereafter. I am well content to abide my time." Our blessed Lord was always of that lowly spirit. He did not strive, nor cry, nor cause his voice to be heard in the streets. The baubles of empire had no charm for him. Had fame offered to sound her trumpet for none but him he would have cared not one whit for the offer. The kingdoms of this world and the glory thereof were offered him, and he repelled the tempter. He was gentle, unobtrusive, self-denying; hence he treated his burden of poverty and shame as a light thing. "He endured the cross, despising the shame." If we once learn Christ's spirit we shall find rest unto our souls.

4. But we must pass on to notice, that it is very evident that the rest which we are to find is a rest which grows entirely out of our spirits being conformed to the spirit of Christ. "Learn of me, and ye shall find rest." It is then a spiritual rest altogether independent of circumstances. It is a vain idea of ours, to suppose that if our circumstances were altered we should be more at rest. My brother, if you cannot rest in poverty, neither would you in riches; if you cannot rest in the midst of persecution, neither would you in the midst of honor. It is the spirit within that gives the rest, that rest has little to do with any thing without. Men have sat on thrones and have found them uneasy places, while others on the rack have declared that they were at rest. The spirit is the spring of rest, as for the outward surroundings they are of small account. Let but your mind be like the mind of Christ, and you shall find rest unto your souls: a deep rest, a growing rest, a rest found out more and more, an abiding rest, not only which you have found, but which you shall go on to find. Justification gave you rest from the burden of sin, sanctification will give you rest from molesting cares; and in proportion as it becomes perfect, and you are like your Saviour, your rest shall become more like that of heaven.

I desire one other thing to be called to your mind before I turn to the practical use of the text, and that is that here, as in the former rest, we are led to adore and admire the blessed person of our Lord. Observe the words, "For I." Oh! it all comes from him still, the second rest as much as the first, the casket and the treasure in the secret drawer. It all hinges there, "For I am." In describing the second rest there is more said concerning him than in the first. In the first part of our text it only says, "I will give you rest;" but in the second part his character is more fully explained--"For I am meek and lowly in heart;" as if to show that as believers grow in grace, and enjoy more rest, they see more of Jesus and know more of him. All they know when sin is pardoned is that he gives it, perhaps they hardly know how; but afterwards when they come to rest in him in sweet fellowship, they know more of his personal attributes, and their rest for that very reason becomes more deep and perfect.

Come we now to the practical use of all this. Read the chapter before us and find the clue. First, my dear brethren, if you find rest to your souls you will not be moved by the judgment of men. The children in the market-place were the type of our Lord's generation, who railed both at John the Baptist and at our Lord. The generation which now is follows the same course, men are sure to cavil at our service. Never mind; take Christ's yoke on you, live to serve him; take Christ's burden, make it a point to bear all things for his sake, and you will not be affected either by praise or censure, for you will find rest to your souls in surrendering yourself to the Father's will. If you learn of Jesus you will have rest from the fear of men. I recollect, before I came to London, being at a prayer-meeting where a very quaint brother prayed for me that I might be delivered from the "bleating of the sheep." I understood it after awhile, he meant that I might live above the fear of man, that when such a person said "How much we have been edified today," I might not be puffed

up; or if another said, "How dull the discourse was to-day," I might not be depressed. You will be delivered from "the bleating of the sheep" when you have the spirit of the Good Shepherd.

Next you will be delivered from fretfulness at want of success. "Then began he to upbraid the cities wherein most of his mighty works were done, because they repented not." He had wrought his mighty works, and preached the gospel, and they did not repent. Was Jesus discouraged? Was he, as we sometimes are, ready to quit the work? No; his heart rested even then. If we come to Jesus, and take his yoke and burden, we too shall find rest, though Israel be not gathered.

Then, too, our Lord denounced judgments upon those who repented not. He told them that those who had heard the gospel and rejected it would find it more tolerable for Sodom and Gomorrah in the day of judgment than for them. There are some who quarrel with the judgments of God, and declare that they cannot bear to think of the condemnation of the impenitent. Is not this because they do not bear the burden of the Lord, but are self-willed? The saints are described in the book of Revelation as singing "Hallelujah" while the smoke of Babylon goeth up for ever and ever. We shall never receive with humble faith the judgment of God in its terror until we take Christ's yoke, and are lowly in heart. When we are like Jesus we shall not feel that the punishment is too much for the sin, but we shall sympathize with the justice of God, and say "Amen" to it. When the mind is lowly it never ventures to sit in judgment upon God, but rests in the conviction that the Judge of all must do right. It is not even anxious to make apologies and smooth down the fact, for it feels, it is not mine to justify him, he can justify himself.

So, again, with regard to the divine sovereignty. Notice the rest of the Saviour's mind upon that matter: "I thank thee, O Father, Lord of heaven and earth, that thou hast hid these things from the wise and prudent." Learning of Jesus we too shall rest in reference to divine decrees; we shall rejoice in whatever the Lord determines; predestination will not cast a gloom over us, but we shall thank God for all he ordains.

What a blessed rest! As we open it up, does not its compass and depth surprise you? How sweet to lie passive in his hands, reconciled to every mystery, content with every dispensation, honored by every service satisfied in God!

Now, I do not know whether I am right, but it struck me, when considering this text from various points, that probably our Saviour meant to convey an idea of deeper fellowship than we have yet considered. Did not he mean this--that he carried a yoke on his shoulder, which he calls, "my yoke?" When bullocks are yoked, there are generally two. I have watched them in Northern Italy, and noticed that when two are yoked together, and they are perfectly agreed, the yoke is always easy to both of them. If one were determined to lie down and the other to stand up, the yoke would be very uncomfortable; but when they are both of one mind you will see them look at each other with those large, lustrous, brown eyes of theirs so lovingly, and with a look they read each other's minds, so that when one wants to lie down, down they go, or when one wishes to go forward, forward they both go, keeping step. In this way the yoke is easy. Now I think the Saviour says to us, "I am bearing one end of the yoke on my shoulder; come, my disciple, place your neck under the other side of it, and then learn of me. Keep step with me, be as I am, do as I do. I am meek and lowly in heart; your heart must be like mine, and then we will work together in blessed fellowship, and you will find that working with me is a happy thing; for my yoke is easy to me, and will be to you. Come, then, true yoke-fellow, come and be yoked with me, take my yoke upon you, and learn of me." If that be the meaning of the text, and perhaps it is, it invites us to a fellowship most near and honorable. If it be not the meaning of the text, it is at any rate a position to be sought after, to be laborers together with Christ, bearing the same yoke. Such be our lot. Amen.

PORTION OF SCRIPTURE READ BEFORE SERMON--Matthew 11.

The Lost Silver Piece

A Sermon (No. 970)
Delivered on Lord's-day Morning, January 15th, 1871 by
C. H. SPURGEON,
At the Metropolitan Tabernacle, Newington

"Either what woman having ten pieces of silver, if she lose one piece, doth not light a candle, and sweep the house, and seek diligently till she find it? And when she hath found it, she calleth her friends and her neighbours together, saying, Rejoice with me; for I have found the piece which I had lost. Likewise, I say unto you, there is joy in the presence of the angels of God over one sinner that repenteth." - Luke 15:8-10.

THIS CHAPTER IS FULL OF GRACE and truth. Its three consecutive parables have been thought to be merely a repetition of the same doctrine under different metaphors, and if that were so, the truth which it teaches is so important that it could not be rehearsed too often in our hearing. Moreover, it is one which we are apt to forget, and it is well to have it again and again impressed upon our minds. The truth here taught is just this--that mercy stretches forth her hand to misery, that grace receives men as sinners, that it deals with demerit, unworthiness, and worthlessness; that those who think themselves righteous are not the objects of divine compassion, but the unrighteous, the guilty, and the undeserving, are the proper subjects for the infinite mercy of God; in a word, that salvation is not of merit but of grace. This truth I say is most important, for it encourages penitents to return to their Father; but it is very apt to be forgotten, for even those who are saved by grace too often fall into the spirit of the elder brother, and speak as if, after all, their salvation depended on the works of the law.

But, my dear friends, the three parables recorded in this chapter are not repetitions; they all declare the same main truth, but each one reveals a different phase of it. The three parables are three sides of a vast pyramid of gospel doctrine, but there is a distinct inscription upon each. Not only in the similitude, but also in the teaching covered by the similitude, there is variety, progress, enlargement, discrimination. We have only need to read attentively to discover that in this trinity of parables, we have at once unity of essential truth and distinctness of description. Each one of the parables is needful to the other, and when combined they present us with a far more complete exposition of their doctrine than could have been conveyed by any one of them. Note for a moment the first of the three which brings before us a shepherd seeking a lost sheep. To whom does this refer? Who is the shepherd of Israel? Who brings again that which has gone astray? Do we not clearly discern the ever glorious and blessed Chief Shepherd of the sheep, who lays down his life that he may save them? Beyond a question, we see in the first parable the work of our Lord Jesus Christ. The second parable is most fitly placed where it is. It, I doubt not, represents the work of the Holy Spirit, working, through the church, for the lost but precious souls of men. The church is that woman who sweeps her house to find the lost piece of money, and in her the Spirit works his purposes of love. How the work of the Holy Spirit follows the work of Christ. As here we first see the shepherd seeking the lost sheep, and then read of the woman seeking the lost piece of money, so the great Shepherd redeems, and then the Holy Spirit restores the soul. You will perceive that each parable is thoroughly understood in its minute details when so interpreted. The shepherd seeks a sheep which has wilfully gone astray, and so far the element of sin is present; the lost piece of money does not bring up that idea, nor was it needful that it should, since the parable does not deal with the pardon of sin as the first does. The sheep, on the other hand, though stupid is not altogether senseless and dead, but the piece of money is altogether unconscious and powerless, and therefore all the fitter emblem of man as the Holy Ghost begins to deal with him, dead in trespasses and sins. The third parable evidently represents the divine Father in his abundant love receiving the lost child who comes back to him. The third parable would be likely to be misunderstood without the first and the second. We have sometimes heard it said--here is the prodigal received as soon as he comes back, no mention being made of a Savior who seeks and saves him. Is it possible to teach all truths in one single parable? Does not the first one speak of the shepherd seeking the lost sheep? Why need repeat what had been said before? It has also been said that the prodigal returned of his own free will, for there is no hint of the operation of a superior power upon his heart, it seems as if he himself spontaneously says, "I will arise, and go unto my Father." The answer is, that the Holy Spirit's work had been clearly described in the second parable, and needed not to be introduced again. If you put the three pictures in a line, they represent the whole compass of salvation, but each one apart sets forth the work in reference to one or other of the divine persons of the blessed Trinity. The shepherd, with much pain and self-sacrifice, seeks the reckless, wandering sheep; the woman diligently searches for the insensible but lost piece of money; the father receives the returning prodigal. What God has joined together, let no man put asunder. The three life-sketches are one, and one truth is taught in the whole three, yet each one is distinct from the other, and by itself instructive.

May we be taught of God while we try to discover the mind of the Spirit in this parable, which, as we believe, represents the work of the Holy Spirit in and through the church. The church is evermore represented as a woman, either the chaste bride of Christ, or the shameless courtesan of Babylon; as for good a woman sweeps the house, so for evil a woman takes the leaven and hides it in the meal till all is leavened. Towards Christ a wife and towards men a mother, the church is most fitly set forth as a woman. A woman with a house under her control is the full idea of the text, her husband away and herself in charge of the treasure: just such is the condition of the church since the departure of the Lord Jesus to the Father.

To bring each part of the text under inspection we shall notice man in three conditions--lost, sought, found.

I. First, the parable treats of man, the object of divine mercy, as lost.

Notice, first, the treasure was lost in the dust. The woman had lost her piece of silver, and in order to find it she had to sweep for it, which proves that it had fallen into a dusty place, fallen to the earth, where it might be hidden and concealed amid rubbish and dirt. Every man of Adam born is as a piece of silver lost, fallen, dishonored, and some are buried amid foulness and dust. If we should drop many pieces of money they would fall into different positions; one of them might fall into actual mire, and be lost there; another might fall upon a carpet, a cloth, or a clean, well-polished floor, and be left there. If you have lost your money, it is equally lost into whatever place it may have fallen. So all men are alike lost, but they have not all fallen into the like condition of apparent defilement. One man from the surroundings of his childhood and the influences of education, has never indulged in the coarser and more brutalising vices; he has never been a blasphemer, perhaps never openly even a Sabbath-breaker, yet he may be lost for all that. Another, on the other hand, has fallen into great excess of riot; he is familiar with wantonness and chambering, and all manner of evil; he is lost, he is lost with an emphasis: but the more decorous sinner is lost also. There may be some here this morning (and we wish always to apply the truth as we go on), who are lost in the very worst of corruption: I would to God that they would take hope and learn from the parable before us, that the church of God and the Spirit of God are seeking after them, and they may be among the found ones yet. Since, on the other hand, there are many here who have not dropped into such unclean places, I would affectionately remind them that they are nevertheless lost, and they need as much to be sought for by the Spirit of God as if they were among the vilest of the vile. To save the moral needs divine grace as certainly as to save the immoral. If you be lost, my dear hearer, it will be small avail to you that you perished respectably, and were accursed in decent company: if you lack but one thing, yet if the deficiency be fatal, it will be but a poor consolation that you had only one lack. If one leak sent the vessel to the bottom; it was no comfort to the crew that their ship only leaked in one place. One disease may kill a man; he may be sound everywhere else, but it will be a sorry comfort to him to know that he might have lived long had but that one organ been sound. If, dear hearer, thou shouldst have no sin whatever save only an evil heart of unbelief, if all thy external life should be lovely and amiable, yet if that one fatal sin be in thee, thou canst draw small consolation from all else that is good about thee. Thou art lost by nature, and thou must be found by grace, whoever thou mayst be.

In this parable that which was lost was altogether ignorant of its being lost. The silver coin was not a living thing, and therefore had no consciousness of its being lost or sought after. The piece of money lost was quite as content to be on the floor or in the dust, as it was to be in the purse of its owner amongst its like. It knew nothing about its being lost, and could not know. And it is just so with the sinner who is spiritually dead in sin, he is unconscious of his state, nor can we make him understand the danger and terror of his condition. When he feels that he is lost, there is already some work of grace in him. When the sinner knows that he is lost, he is no longer content with his condition, but begins to cry out for mercy, which is evidence that the finding work has already began. The unconverted sinner will confess that he is lost because he knows the statement to be scriptural, and therefore out of compliment to God's word he admits it to be true; but he has no idea of what is meant by it, else would he either deny it with proud indignation, or he would bestir himself to pray that he might be restored to the place from which he has fallen, and be numbered with Christ's precious property. O my hearers, this it is that makes the Spirit of God so needful in all our preachings, and every other soul-saving exercise, because we have to deal with insensible souls. The man who puts the fire-escape against the window of a burning house, may readily enough rescue those who are aware of their danger, and who rush to the front and help him, or at least are submissive to him in his work of delivering them; but if a man were insane, if he played with the flames, if he were idiotic and thought that some grand illumination were going on, and knew nothing of the danger but was only "glamoured by the glare," then would it be hard work for the rescuer. Even thus it is with sinners. They know not, though they profess to know, that sin is hell, that to be an alien from God is to be condemned already, to live in sin is to be dead while you live. The insensibility of the piece of money fairly pictures the utter indifference of souls unquickened by divine grace.

The silver piece was lost but not forgotten. The woman knew that she had ten pieces of silver originally; she counted them over carefully, for they were all her little store, and she found only nine, but she well remembered that one more was hers and ought to be in her hand. This is our hope for the Lord's lost ones, they are lost but not forgotten, the heart of the Savior remembers them, and prays for them. O soul, I trust you are one whom Jesus calls his own, if so he remembers the pangs which he endured in redeeming you, and he recollects the Father's love which was reflected on you from old eternity, when the Father gave you into the hands of his beloved Son. You are not forgotten of the Holy Spirit who seeks you for the Savior. This is the minister's hope, that there is a people whom the Lord remembers and whom he never will forget, though they forget him. Strangers to him, far-off, ignorant, callous, careless, dead, yet the everlasting heart in heaven throbs towards them with love; and the mind of the Spirit, working on earth, is directed to them. These, who were numbered and reckoned up of old are still in the inventory of the divine memory; and though lost they are earnestly remembered still. In some sense this is true of every sinner here. You are lost, but that you are remembered is evident, for I am sent to-day to preach the gospel of Jesus to you. God has thoughts of love concerning you, and bids you turn unto him and live. Have respect, I pray you, to the word of his salvation.

Next, the piece of silver was lost but still claimed. Observe that the woman called the money, "my piece which was lost." When she lost its possession she did not lose her right to it; it did not become somebody else's when it slipped out of her hand and fell upon the floor. Those for whom Christ hath died, whom he hath peculiarly redeemed, are not Satan's even when they are dead in sin. They may come under the devil's usurped dominion, but the monster shall be chased from his throne. Christ has received them of old of the Father, and he has bought them with his precious blood, and he will have them; he will chase away the intruder and claim his own. Thus saith the Lord, "Your covenant with death is disannulled, and your agreement with hell shall not stand." Ye have sold yourselves for nought; and ye shall be redeemed without money. Jesus shall have his own, and none shall pluck them from his hold; he will defend his claim against all comers.

Further, observe that the lost piece of money was not only remembered and claimed, but it was also valued. In these three parables the value of the lost article steadily rises. This is not very clear at first sight, because it may be said that a sheep is of more value than a piece of money; but notice that the shepherd only lost one sheep out of a hundred, but the woman lost one piece out of ten, and the father one son out of two. Now, it is not the value of the thing in itself which is here set forth, for the soul of a man, as absolutely valued in comparison with the infinite God, is of small esteem; but because of his love it is of great value to him. The one piece of money to the woman was a tenth part of all she had, and it was very valuable in her esteem. To the Lord of love a lost soul is very precious: it is not because of its intrinsic value, but it has a relative value which God sets at a high rate. The Holy Spirit values souls, and therefore the church prizes them too. The church sometimes says to herself, "We have but few conversions, few members; many are called, but few chosen." She counts over her few converts, her few members, and one soul is to her all the more precious because of the few there are who in these times are in the treasury of Christ, stamped with the image of the great Being, and made of the precious genuine silver of God's own grace. O dear friend, you think yourself of small value, you who are conscious that you have sinned, but the church does not think you of small value, and the Holy Spirit does not despise you. He sets a high price upon you, and so do his people. We value your souls, we only wish we knew how to save them; we would spare no expense or pains if we might but be the means of finding you, and bringing you once more into the great Owner's hand.

The piece of money was lost, but it was not lost hopelessly. The woman had hopes of recovering it, and therefore she did not despair, but set to work at once. It is a dreadful thing to think of those souls which are lost hopelessly. Their state reminds me of a paragraph I have cut from this week's newspaper:--"The fishing smack Veto, of Grimsby, S. Cousins, master, arrived in port from the Dogger Bank on Saturday night. The master reports that on the previous Wednesday, when about two hundred miles from Spurn, he sighted to the leeward what at first appeared to be a small schooner in distress, but on bearing down to her found her to be a full-sized lifeboat, upwards of twenty feet long, and full of water up to her corks. There was no name on the boat, which had evidently belonged to some large ship or steamer. It was painted white both inside and out, with a brown streak round the rim. When alongside, on closer examination, three dead sailors were perceived lying aft, huddled together, and a fourth athwart in the bow, with his head hanging over the rowlocks. They seemed from their dress and general appearance to be foreigners, but the bodies had been frightfully; washed about,' and were in a state of decomposition, and had evidently been dead some weeks. The water-logged waif drifted on with its ghastly cargo, and the horrible sight so shocked the crew of the Veto that afterwards they were almost too unnerved to attend to their trawling, and the smack, in consequence, returned to port with a comparatively small catch, and sooner than expected." Do you wonder at the men sickening in the presence of this mystery of the sea? I shudder as I think I see that Charon-like boat floating on and on; mercy need not follow it, she can confer no boon; love need not seek it, no deed of hers can save. My soul sees, as in a vision, souls hopelessly lost, drifting on the waves of eternity, beyond all hope or help. Alas! Alas! Millions of our race are now in that condition. Upon them has passed the second death, and powerless are we all to save them. Towards them even the gospel has no aspect of hope. Our joy is that we have to deal to-day with lost souls who are not yet hopelessly lost. They are dead in sin, but there is a quickening power which can make them live. O mariner of the sea of life, fisher of men upon this stormy sea, those castaways whom you meet with are accessible to your efforts of compassion, they can be rescued from the pitiless deeps; your mission is not a hopeless one. I rejoice over the ungodly man here to-day that he is not in torment, not in hell, he is not among those whose worm dieth not and whose fire is not quenched. I congratulate the Christian church too, that her piece of money has not fallen where she cannot find it. I rejoice that the fallen around us are not past hope; yea, though they dwell in the worst dens of London, though they be thieves and harlots, they are not beyond the reach of mercy. Up, O church of God, while possibilities of mercy remain! Gird up your loins, be soul-winners, and resolve by the grace of God that every hour of hope shall be well employed by you.

One other point is worthy of notice. The piece of silver was lost, but it was lost in the house, and the woman knew it to be so. If she had lost it in the streets, the probabilities are she would not have looked for it again, for other hands might have closed over it. If she had lost it in a river, or dropped it in the sea, she might very fairly have concluded that it was gone for ever, but evidently she was sure that she had lost it in the house. Is it not a consolation to know that those here, who are lost, are still in the house? They are still under the means of grace, within the sphere of the church's operations, within the habitation of which she is the mistress, and where the Holy Spirit works. What thankfulness there ought to be in your minds that you are not lost as heathens, nor lost amid Romish or Mohammedan superstition, but lost where the gospel is faithfully and plainly preached to you; where you are lovingly told, that whosoever believeth in Christ Jesus is not condemned. Lost, but lost where the church's business is to look after you, where it is the Spirit's work to seek and to find you.

This is the condition of the lost soul, depicted as a lost piece of silver.

II. Secondly, we shall notice the soul under another condition: we shall view it as sought.

By whom was the piece of silver sought? It was sought by its owner personally. Notice, she who lost the money lit a candle and swept the house, and sought diligently till she found it. So, brethren, I have said that the woman represents the Holy Spirit, or rather the church in which the Holy Spirit dwells. Now, there will never be a soul found till the Holy Spirit seeks after it. He is the great soul finder. The heart will continue in the dark until he comes with his illuminating power. He is the owner, he possesses it, and he alone can effectually seek after it. The God to whom the soul belongs must seek the soul. But he does it by his church, for souls belong to the church too; they are sons and daughters of the chosen mother, they are her citizens and treasures. For this reason the church must personally seek after souls. She cannot delegate her work to anybody. The woman did not pay a servant to sweep the house, but she swept it herself. Her eyes were much better than a servant's eyes, for the servant's eyes would only look after somebody else's money, and perhaps would not see it; but the mistress would look after her own money, and she would be certain to light upon it if it were anywhere within sight. When the church of God solemnly feels, "It is our work to look after sinners, we must not delegate it even to the minister, or to the City-missionary, or the Biblewoman, but the church as a church must look after the souls of sinners," then I believe souls will be found and saved. When the church recognizes that these lost souls belong to her, she will be likely to find them. It will be a happy day when every church of God is actively at work for the salvation of sinners. It has been the curse of Christendom that she has ventured to delegate her sacred duties to men called priests, or that she has set apart certain persons to be called the religious who are to do works of mercy and charity and of evangelization. We are, every one of us who are Christ's, bound to do our own share; nay, we should deem it a privilege of which we will not be deprived, personally to serve God, personally to sweep the house and search after the lost spiritual treasures. The church herself, in the power of the indwelling Spirit of God, must seek lost souls.

Note that this seeking became a matter of chief concern with the woman. I do not know what other business she had to do, but I do know that she put it all by to find the piece of money. There was the corn to be ground for the morning meal, perhaps that was done, at any rate, if not so, she left it unprepared. There was a garment to be mended, or water to be drawn, or the fire to be kindled, or the friends and neighbors to be conversed with--never mind, the mistress forgets everything else, she has lost her piece of money, and she must find it at once. So with the church of God, her chief concern should be to seek the perishing sons of men. To bring souls to know Jesus, and to be saved in him with a great salvation should be the church's great longing and concern. She has other things to do. She has her own edification to consider, she has other matters to be attended to in their place, but this first, this evermore and always first. The woman evidently said, "The money is lost, I must find that first." The loss of her piece of silver was so serious a matter that if she sat down to her mending, her hands would miss their nimbleness, or if any other household work demanded her attention, it would be an irksome task to her, for she was thinking of that piece of coin. If her friend came and talked with her, she would say to herself, "I wish she were gone, for I want to be looking after my lost money." I wish the church of God had such an engrossing love for poor sinners that she would feel everything to be an impertinence which hindered her from soul-saving. We have every now and then, as a church, a little to do with politics, and a little to do with finance, for we are still in the world, but I love to see in all churches everything kept in the background, compared with soul-saving work. This must be first and foremost. Educate the people--yes, certainly; we take an interest in everything which will do good to our fellow citizens, for we are men as well as Christians; but first and foremost our business is to win souls, to bring men to Jesus, to hunt up those who bear heaven's image, though lost and fallen. This is what we must be devoted to, this is the main and chief concern of believers, the very reason for the existence of a church; if she regard it not, she forgets her highest end.

Now note, that the woman having thus set her heart to find her money, she used the most fit and proper means to accomplish her end. First, she lit a candle. So doth the Holy Spirit in the church. In Eastern dwellings it would be necessary, if you lost a piece of money and wanted to find it, to light a candle at any time; for in our Savior's day glass was not used, and the windows of houses were only little slits in the side of the wall, and the rooms were very dark. Almost all the Oriental houses are very dark to this day, and if anything be dropped as small as a piece of silver, it must be looked for with a candle even at high noon. Now, the sphere in which the church moves here on earth is a dim twilight of mental ignorance, and moral darkness, and in order to find a lost soul, light must be brought to bear upon it. The Holy Spirit uses the light of the gospel; he convinces men of sin, of righteousness, and of judgment to come. The woman lit a candle, and even thus the Holy Spirit lights up some chosen man whom he makes to be a light in the world. He calls to himself whomsoever he wills, and makes him a lamp to shine upon the people. Such a man will have to be consumed in his calling, like a candle he will be burnt up in light-giving. Earnest zeal, and laborious self-sacrifice, will eat him up. So may this church, and every church of God, be continually using up her anointed men and women, who shall be as lights in the midst of a crooked and perverse generation, to find out lost souls.

But she was not content with her candle, she fetched her broom, she swept the house. If she could not find the silver as things were in the house, she brought the broom to bear upon the accumulated dust. Oh, how a Christian church, when it is moved by the Holy Spirit, cleanses herself and purges all her work! "Perhaps," saith she, "some of our members are inconsistent, and so men are hardened in sin; these offenders must be put away. The tone of religion is low--that may be hindering the conversion of souls, it must be raised. Perhaps our statements of truth, and our ways of proclaiming it, are not the most likely to command attention, we must amend them; we must use the best possible methods, we must in fact sweep the whole house." I delight to see an earnest house-sweeping by confession of sin at a prayer meeting, or by a searching discourse, a house-sweeping when every one is earnest to reform himself, and to get nearer to God himself by a revival of his own personal piety. This is one of the means by which the church is enabled to find the hidden ones. Besides this, all the neighborhood round the church (for the house is the sphere in which the church moves), must be ransacked, stirred, turned over, in a word "swept." A church that is really in earnest after souls will endeavor to penetrate the gloom of poverty and stir the heaps of profligacy. She will hunt high and hunt low if by any means she may rescue from destruction the precious thing upon which her heart is set.

Carefully note that this seeking after the lost piece of silver with fitting instruments, the broom and the candle, was attended with no small stir. She swept the house--there was dust for her eyes; if any neighbors were in the house there was dust for them. You cannot sweep a house without causing some confusion and temporary discomfort. We sometimes hear persons complain of certain Christians for making too much ado about religion. The complaint shows that something is being done, and in all probability some success being achieved. Those people who have no interest in the lost silver are annoyed at the dust; it is getting down their throats, and they cough at it; never mind, good woman, sweep again, and make them grumble more. Another will say, "I do not approve of religious excitement, I am for quiet and orderly modes of procedure." I dare say that this good woman's neighbor, when she came in to make a call, exclaimed in disgust, "Why, mistress, there is not a chair to sit down upon in comfort, and you are so taken up about this lost money that you scarce give me an answer. Why, you are wasting candle at a great rate, and seem quite in a fever." "Well," the good woman would answer, "but I must find my piece of silver, and in order to seek it out I can bear a little dust myself, and so must you if you wish to stop here while I am searching." An earnest church will be sure to experience a degree of excitement when it is soul-hunting, and very cautious, very fastidious, very critical people will find fault. Never mind them, my brethren, sweep on and let them talk on. Never mind making a dust if you find the money. If souls be saved irregularities and singularities are as the small dust of the balance. If men be brought to Jesus, care nothing what cavillers say. Sweep on, sweep on, even though men exclaim, "They that turn the world upside down are come hither also." Though confusion and stir, and even persecution be the present result, yet if the finding of an immortal soul be the ultimate effect, you will be well repaid for it.

It is to be remarked, also, that in the seeking of this piece of silver the coin was sought in a most engrossing manner. For a time nothing was thought of but the lost silver. Here is a candle: the good woman does not read by the light of it, nor mend her garments; no, but the candle-light is all spent on that piece of money. All its light is consecrated to the search. Here is a broom: there is other work for the broom to do, but for the present it sweeps for the silver and for nothing else. Here are two bright eyes in the good woman's head: ay, but they look for nothing but the lost money; she does not care what else may be in the house or out of it--her money she cares for, and that she must find; and here she is with candle, broom, strength, eyesight, faculties of mind, and limbs of body, all employed in searching for the lost treasure. It is just so when the Holy Ghost works in a church, the preacher, like a candle, yields his light, but it is all with the view of finding out the sinner and letting him see his lost estate. Whether it be the broom of the law or the light of the gospel, all is meant for the sinner. All the Holy Spirit's wisdom is engaged to find the sinner, and all the living church's talent and substance and power are put forth if by any means the sinner may be saved. It is a fair picture, may I see it daily. How earnestly souls are sought for when the Spirit of God is truly in his church!

One other thought only. This woman sought for her piece of silver continuously--"till she found it." May you and I, as parts of the church of God, look after wandering souls till we find them. We say they discourage us. No doubt that piece of silver did discourage the woman who sought it. We complain that men do not appear inclined to religion. Did the piece of money lend the housewife any help? Was it any assistance to her? She did the seeking, she did it all. And the Holy Ghost through you, my brother, seeks the salvation of the sinner, not expecting the sinner to help him, for the sinner is averse to being found. What, were you repulsed the other day by one whose spiritual good you longed for? Go again! Were your invitations laughed at? Invite again! Did you become the subject of ridicule through your earnest entreaties? Entreat again! Those are not always the least likely to be saved who at first repel our efforts. A harsh reception is sometimes only an intimation that the heart recognises the power of the truth, though it does not desire at present to yield to it. Persevere, brother, till you find the soul you seek. You who spend so much effort in your Sunday-school class, use still your candle, enlighten the child's mind still, sweep the house till you find what you seek; never give up the child till it is brought to Christ. You, in your senior class, dealing with that young man or young woman, cease not from your private prayers and from your personal admonitions, till that heart belongs to Jesus. You who can preach in the streets, or visit the lodging-houses, or go from door to door with tracts, I charge you all, for you can all do something, never give up the pursuit of sinners until they are safely lodged in Jesus' hands. We must have them saved! With all the intense perseverance of the woman who turned everything upside down, and counted all things but loss that she might but find her treasure, so may we also, the Spirit of God working in us, upset everything of rule and conventionality, and form and difficulty, if we may but by any means save some, and bring out of the dust those who bear the King's image, and are dear to the King's heart.

III. Time has fled, alas! too swiftly, and so I must close with the third point, which is the piece of silver FOUND.

Found! In the first place, this was the woman's ultimatum, and nothing short of it. She never stopped until the coin was found. So it is the Holy Spirit's design, not that the sinner should be brought into a hopeful state, but that he should be actually saved: and this is the church's great concern, not that people be made hearers, not that they be made orthodox professors, but that they be really changed and renewed, regenerated and born again.

The woman herself found the piece of money. It did not turn up by accident, nor did some neighbor step in and find it. The Spirit of God himself finds sinners, and the church of God herself as a rule is the instrument of their recovery. Dear brethren, a few years ago there was a kind of slur cast upon the visible church, by many enthusiastic but mistaken persons, who dreamed that the time was come for doing away with organised effort, for irregular agencies outside of the visible church were to do all the work. Certain remarkable men sprang up whose ferocious censures almost amounted to attacks upon the recognised churches. Their efforts were apart from the regular ministry, and in some cases ostentatiously in opposition to it. It was as much their aim to pull down the existing church as to bring in converts. I ask any man who has fairly watched these efforts, what they have come to? I never condemned them, nor will I; but I do venture to say to-day in the light of their history, that they have not superseded regular church work and never will. The masses were to be aroused, but where are the boasted results? What has become of many of these much-vaunted works? Those who have worked in connection with a church of God have achieved permanent usefulness; those who acted as separatist agencies, though they blazed for awhile before the public eye and filled the corners of the newspapers with spiritual puffery, are now either altogether or almost extinct. Where are the victories which were to be won by these freebooters? Echo answers, Where? We have to fall back on the old disciplined troops. God means to bless the church still, and it is through the church that he will continue to send a benediction upon the sons of men. I am glad to hear of anybody preaching the gospel if Christ is preached I therein do rejoice, yea, and will rejoice. I remember the Master's words, "Forbid them not! He that is not against us is for us." Still the mass of conversions will come through the church, and by her regular organised efforts. The woman who lights the candle and sweeps the house, to whom the silver belongs, will herself find it.

Now notice when she had found it what she did, she rejoiced. The greater her trouble in searching, the higher her joy in finding. What joy there is in the church of God when sinners are converted! We have our high holidays, we have our mirthful days downstairs in the lecture hall, when we hear of souls turned from the paths of the destroyer--and in the vestries behind, your pastors and elders often experience such joy as only heaven can equal, when we have heard the stories of souls emancipated from the slavery of sin, and led into the perfect liberty which Jesus gives. The church rejoices.

Next, she calls her friends and neighbors to share her joy. I am afraid we do not treat our friends and neighbors with quite enough respect, or remember to invite them to our joys. Who are they? I think the angels are here meant; not only the angels in heaven, but those who are watching here below. Note well, that when the shepherd took home the sheep, it is written, "There shall be joy in heaven over one sinner that repenteth;" but it does not mention heaven here, nor speak of the future, but it is written, "There is joy in the presence of the angels of God." Now, the church is on earth, and the Holy Spirit is on earth, at work; when there is a soul saved, the angels down below, who keep watch and ward around the faithful, and so are our friends and neighbors, rejoice with us. Know ye not that angels are present in our assemblies? for this reason the apostle tells us that the woman hath her head covered in the assembly. He saith, "Because of the angels, for they love order and decorum." The angels are wherever the saints are, beholding our orders and rejoicing in our joy. When we see conversions we may bid them rejoice too, and they will praise God with us. I do not suppose the rejoicing ends there; for as angels are always ascending and descending upon the Son of Man, they soon convey the tidings to the hosts above, and heaven rejoices over one repenting sinner.

The joy is a present joy; it is a joy in the house, in the church in her own sphere; it is the joy of her neighbors who are round about her here below. All other joy seems swallowed up in this: as every other occupation was suspended to find the lost silver, so every other joy is hushed when the precious thing is found. The church of God has a thousand joys--the joy of her saints ascending to the skies, the joy of her saints ripening for glory, the joy of such as contend with sin and overcome it, and grow in grace and receive the promise; but the chief Joy in the church, which swallows all others, as Aaron's rod swallowed up the other rods, is the joy over the lost soul which, after much sweeping and searching, is found at last.

The practical lesson to the unconverted is just this. Dear friend, see what value is set upon you. You think that nobody cares for you--why, heaven and earth care for you! You say, "I am as nothing, a castaway, and I am utterly worthless." No, you are not worthless to the blessed Spirit, nor worthless to the church of God--she longs for you.

See, again, how false that suspicion of yours is that you will not be welcome if you come to Christ. Welcome! welcome! why, the church is searching for you; the Spirit of God is searching for you. Do not talk of welcome, you will be a great deal more than welcome. Oh, how glad will Christ be, and the Spirit be, and the church be, to receive you! Ah! but you complain that you have done nothing to make you fit for mercy. Talk not so, what had the lost piece of money done? What could it do? It was lost and helpless. They who sought it did all; he who seeks you will do all for you. O poor soul, since Christ now bids thee come, come! If his Spirit draws thee, yield! Since the promise now speaks, "Come now, and let us reason together: though your sins be as scarlet, they shall be as white as snow; though they be red like crimson, they shall be as wool," accept the promise. Believe in Jesus. God bless you and save you, for Jesus' sake. Amen.

PORTION OF SCRIPTURE READ BEFORE SERMON--Psalm 136 and Luke 15.

The Open Fountain

A Sermon (No. 971)
Delivered on Lord's-day Morning, January 22nd, 1871 by
C. H. SPURGEON,
At the Metropolitan Tabernacle, Newington

"In that day there shall be a fountain opened to the house of David and to the inhabitants of Jerusalem for sin and for uncleanness." - Zechariah 13:1.

WE DO NOT GRUDGE to the seed of Israel after the flesh the first application of this very precious promise. There will be a day when those who have so long refused to acknowledge Jesus as the Messias shall discern the marks of his mission, and shall mourn that they have pierced him. When the tribes of Israel shall lament their sin with holy earnestness, there shall be no mourning to exceed it, they shall weep even as in the mourning of Hadadrimmon in the valley of Megiddo, when the wellbeloved Josiah was slain. Discovering that their nation rejected the Son of God, when they crucified Jesus of Nazareth their deeply religious spirit shall be filled with the utmost bitterness of repentance, and each man and each woman shall cry for pardon to the Lord of mercy. Then, close upon the heels of the weeping shall come the full and complete forgiveness; the transgression of the tribes shall be put away in one day; they shall perceive that the very side which they pierced has yielded a fountain to cleanse them from their sin; joyfully shall they behold on Calvary the brazen serpent lifted up for their healing, the Paschal Lamb slain for their redemption, the sin-offering sacrificed in their stead. What a blessed day will that be when "all Israel shall be saved: as it is written, There shall come out of Zion the Deliverer, and shall turn away ungodliness from Jacob." O that you and I might live to see that happy era when all the Jewish race shall behold their Messiahs; for then shall the fullness of the Gentiles be gathered in. Our history is wrapped up with theirs. "Through their fall salvation is come unto the Gentiles. Now if the fall of them be the riches of the world, and the diminishing of them the riches of the Gentiles; how much more their fullness?"

"Wake, harp of Zion, wake again,
Upon thine ancient hill,
On Jordan's long deserted plain,
By Kedron's lowly rill.
The hymn shall yet in Zion swell
That sounds Messiah's praise,
And thy loved name, Immanuel!
As once in ancient days.
For Israel yet shall own her King,
For her salvation waits,
And hill and dale shall sweetly sing
With praise in all her gates."

Having said thus much, however, we shall now take our text as belonging to ourselves in common with Israel, for in the gospel no promise is now set about with a hedge, and reserved for any race peculiarly; there is now "neither Jew nor Greek, there is neither bond nor free, there is neither male nor female: for ye are all one in Christ Jesus." This promise is our joy at this hour. O that I might be able so to speak of it that many anxious hearts might now see its meaning and appropriate its blessedness!

In order to explain the text we shall dwell upon three notes; if these three be clearly sounded we shall understand the passage--a fountain--opened--still open.

I. A FOUNTAIN.

What is this fountain which is said to be opened, and when and how was it opened? It is a fountain opened to the house of David, and the inhabitants of, for sin and for uncleanness. We observe, therefore, that the blessing here spoken of deals with the greatest evils to which mankind is subject--sin and uncleanness. We have all fallen; we have all proved our fall by our sinful practice. Sin has separated us from God and brought upon us the divine wrath; uncleanness, which is a tendency still to sin, a defilement of our nature, prevents our returning to our heavenly Father, and entering into renewed fellowship with aim. This great evil in its double form is, according to the text, distinctly recognized by God; it is not winked at, it is not treated as a trifle that may remain, and yet man may be beloved of God and be happy; no, but the evil being there, preparation is made for its removal. The text says, not that the filthiness is concealed, that the transgression is excused, but that there is a fountain opened for the effectual removal of sin and uncleanness. In the gospel God never trifles with human sin. We proclaim full, free, immediate forgiveness to the very chief of sinners, but it is not in a way which makes men think that sin is trivial in God's esteem, for there is coupled with the declaration of pardon a description of the way in which God by the sacrifice of his Son renders it possible for him to be merciful without being unjust. In the substitution of Christ Jesus we see justice and mercy peacefully embracing, and conferring double honor upon each other. I repeat the word, the uncleanness is not concealed, the sin is not winked at, but there is a fountain prepared for the purging away of the defilement, and it is opened to the house of David, for the great and mighty, and to the inhabitants of Jerusalem--the poor, common people of every class. Hear this, ye who feel yourselves sinners, God has provided means for delivering you from your sins.

The text recalls to your notice the double nature of the evil of sin, and the character of the provision which meets the double evil. The fountain is opened for sin, that refers, no doubt, to the guilt of sin, to sin as offending God and deserving punishment. There is a fountain opened in the atonement, by which the offense rendered to God's honor and dignity is put away. What if we have sinned, yet the Lord has punished that sin in the person of his own Son, he has thus fulfilled his threatening, and proven the truth of his word. In Jesus Christ, therefore, the guilt of those for whom he was a substitute is put away consistently with the righteousness of the great Lawgiver. God is just and yet the justifier of him that believeth in Jesus. But this would not be enough; there is a second mischief, namely, that our nature has become unclean and consequently estranged from God. Through our natural corruption and the effect of our past sin, we are diseased morally and spiritually, our mind is in itself biassed towards evil and averse from good. God does not pardon sin and leave the sinner as he was in other respects, but wherever forgiveness of the guilt is bestowed a renewal of the nature is wrought; the fountain opened for pardon is also opened for purification. The washing which takes away the offense before heaven removes also the love of offending. Herein is double joy, for does not every true penitent feel that mere pardon would be a poor boon to him if it allowed him to continue in sin? My God, deliver me from sin itself, for this is the great burden of my soul. Oh, could I have the past forgiven, and yet live an enemy to my God, enslaved by evil and a stranger to holiness--then were I still accursed! What if God ceases to punish wickedness, yet sin in itself is a curse; to love the wrong is the beginning of hell. Blessed be the Lord, when he opened the fountain to cleanse his sinful people, he made it "of sin the double cure," that it might at the same time cleanse us from its guilt and power. For our double need there is, according to the text, one only supply; no mention is made of two fountains, neither are there two methods for the putting away of sin. But the one method is divine, God himself has devised, ordained, and prepared it. Wouldst thou have sin forgiven thee? Wash, for there is a fountain opened. Wouldst thou have sin eradicated from thy nature, and thy heart made pure? Wash, for heaven declares that the fountain is opened for this also. Imagine not that God has proposed an ineffectual means of purgation. His arrangements are never failures. Man may through his poverty provide a feast which is so bare as to mock the hunger of those invited; his starveling hospitality may be an insult to the greatness of human necessity; but it is never so with God. For his banquet of mercy oxen and fatlings are killed, milk and wine run in rivers, fat things full of marrow are heaped up; no stint is found at Jehovah's board. When God appoints a supply for any need, we may be assured that it is a real and sufficient provision. O penitent souls, rest assured that in Jesus' sacrifice there is an effectual provision for the forgiveness of sin, and an infallible means for the purging of your nature from its tendency to sin. God in the covenant of grace provides no seeming, superficial semblance, but in very deed he satisfies the longing soul O men and women, there is provided for your sin and your uncleanness that which exactly meets your need.

According to the verse before us this provision is inexhaustible. There is a fountain opened; not a cistern nor a reservoir, but a fountain. A fountain continues still to bubble up, and is as full after fifty years as at the first; and even so the provision and the mercy of God for the forgiveness and the justification of our souls continually flows and overflows. There is a supply so large that when thousands of the sons of Adam come they find that there is enough for their demands, and as new generations continue still to come all along the centuries, they shall find that the supply has not in any degree been diminished. For the sin of Adam and Abel the atonement was sufficient, but it shall be equally so for the last repenting sinner. David saw the cleansing flood, and washed away his crimson sins, but he left the fountain undefiled, and it is as effectual for you and for me as it was for him. For sinners in the last days the fountain is as full, as cleansing, and as free, as for sinners in the first ages of the world.

Thus I have testified to you that for the great necessity of men in this double form, there is a divinely appointed and inexhaustible supply, and it is intended for high and low, rich and poor, for the royal and the ragged, the prince and the pauper.

When was this fountain opened? When was this divine and inexhaustible supply revealed to men? The answer may be given thus. The fountain was opened for sin and for uncleanness when the Lord Jesus died. God, the everlasting Word, was made flesh and dwelt among us, and in fullness of time the weight of human sin was laid on him. In order to put that sin away he must die, for death was the penalty for guilt; up to the cross he went through agonies unspeakable, and at the last he yielded up his soul; and when he did so sin was put away, and the fountain for the cleansing of sin was effectually opened. When the soldier with the spear pierced his side, and forthwith there came forth blood and water, then was it proven that this was he who came not with water only, but by water and by blood, a Savior who takes away the offense of sin as touching God, and the defilement of sin in human nature.

Furthermore, the fountain may be said to be opened to each one of us when the gospel is preached to us. "In that day there shall be a fountain opened," means secondarily, that whenever the gospel of Jesus Christ is fully and faithfully preached, then the cleansing efficacy of the atonement of Jesus which aforetime was as a sealed fountain, is opened to those who hear. And best of all, according to the connection of the text, this fountain is opened in the day when men repent of sin. Doth it not say that they shall mourn each family apart, and their wives apart, and in that day shall there be a fountain opened! The sinner does not find a Savior until he bewails his sin; when he sees his own filthiness then it is that the way to have that filthiness removed is made clear to him. God is always willing to forgive, but we are not always willing to be forgiven. The fountain is experimentally opened to each one of us when we spiritually discern it, believe in it, and are made partners of its cleansing power. Years ago a German prince who was entertained by the French Government, was taken to the galleys of Toulon, where a number of men were held as convicts on account of their crimes. The commandant decreed that in honor of the prince's visit, some prisoner whom he might choose should be set at liberty. The prince went round amongst the prisoners, and talked with them, they all knowing that he had the power to liberate some one of them. He found that according to their talk they were nearly all innocent, and had been condemned by mistake, or by flagrant injustice. He passed them all by, and spoke with one who talked in another style. He was guilty upon his own confession. "I certainly," said he, "have no reason to complain of my hard work in the galleys, for if I had my due I should have been put to death for my crimes." He went on to acknowledge with much humility the former evils of his life, and the justice of his sentence. The prince set him free, and said, "This is the only man in the whole of this place who is fit to be pardoned; he has a sense of his transgressions, he may be trusted in society." So too, the pardoning mercy of God passes by those who say each one in their souls, "I am not guilty, I have not been more sinful than other people, I see nothing very remarkable in my case, and if I were sent to hell the sentence would be too severe." Although there is a fountain for sin and uncleanness by Jesus Christ, it is not opened personally to your experience, you cannot see it, do not appreciate it, and will not participate in its benefits unless you know yourself to be a sinner; but if there be here one really guilty, one who feels his sin to be deserving the wrath of God, then this day I have authority from the Most High to say to him, there is a fountain opened for sin and uncleanness. You mourn your sin, you confess your guilt, you wish you could mourn it more, you feel yourself undeserving and unworthy--then you are the man to whom the mercy of heaven is this day freely proclaimed. Jesus has come forth on purpose to bind up the broken-hearted, to proclaim liberty to the captives, and the opening of the prison to them that are bound. The time for the actual opening of the cleansing fountain to us is the time when the heart confesses its guilt, and desires pardon of the Most High. Dear friend, has this time come to you? I pray you as you love your soul consider your ways, acknowledge your transgressions, and rest not till the blood of atonement has made you clear from guilt. Need the subject be pressed upon you? Surely your own reason should lead you to be anxious upon a matter so vital to your soul's eternal interests. How sad it will be if there be a fountain and yet you die unwashed! If there be a Savior, and you perish for ever, what wretchedness it will be!

II. My chief business, this morning, is to sound forth the second note of my text--it is a fountain OPEN.

The means by which sin and sinfulness can be put away are at this moment accessible to the sons of men. The atonement is not a fountain hid and concealed, and closed and barred and bolted, it is a fountain open. The doctrine I have to teach is very simple and plain; there is no room here for oratory and elocution, and polished periods; it is the plainest gospel doctrine in the world, and yet I am very, very happy to have to speak it to you, for I do trust God may bless it to many, that they may find the pardon of their sin, and the removal of their uncleanness. I would sooner tell you the good news from heaven in broken accents than anything else with the tongue of an angel.

The fountain which God has provided is open at this day. Now what is meant by this? It means partly that the gospel is so preached that you can understand it; the gospel at this day is not concealed in Latin, as it was before the days of Luther, it is not wrapped up in types and shadows, as it was in the old dispensation; the gospel is preached in many places in this country as plainly as words could deliver it, so plainly that he that runs may read it. I will tell it to you again. God must punish sin, but he has laid the punishment on Christ, and whosoever believeth in Christ Jesus is forgiven. Why do not men accept the Savior? Why do they not come and trust him? for when they trust him they are saved at once. Ah! my hearers, if any of you do not wash from your uncleanness it is not because you do not know how; if our gospel be hid it is not our fault, it is hid to them that are lost, in whom the God of this world hath blinded their eyes. God is our witness, we have never sought after excellency of speech, nor the gaudiness or elegance of language, but as of simplicity, we have set before your souls this fact that Jesus Christ is the substitute for sinners, and that you must simply trust in him and you shall be saved. At your own peril be it if you reject the gospel; but if you do so, at least bear us this witness, that we have set forth Christ visibly crucified among you, not hanging up veils of human speculation of our own spinning, or curtains embroidered with curious devices of logic and theology, or of ceremony and ritual. We have cried aloud in plain words--

"There is life in a look at the Crucified One."

We have bidden you look to Jesus, and have told you, in God's name, that as you look to the Crucified you shall find eternal life. Blessed are the people that know the joyful sound; more blessed still if they yield obedience thereto.

In the next place, it is meant that the provision made in Jesus is accessible to you all, and there is no barrier on account of uncircumcision or natural descent. When first Peter began to preach the gospel, if he had heard that there was a Gentile in the congregation I am afraid he would have put in a question as to whether a Gentile could be saved; it took some time to bring Peter's mind round to the belief that to the Gentiles also the gospel was to be preached. Paul seemed far more readily to imbibe that idea; but now to me, a Gentile preaching to you Gentiles, this difficulty does not arise, but how thankful we ought to be that it does not! "Is he the God of the Jews only? Is he not also the God of the Gentiles? Yes, of the Gentiles also." Our Lord Jesus, by his death, has rent the veil, and pulled down every wall of separation, so that the same Messiah who was sent to the seed of Abraham after the flesh is sent to us also who were sinners of the Gentiles, but who become of the seed of Abraham when we believe in Christ, for Abraham was the "father of the faithful." The fountain is open then in the removal of the barrier which divided the natural Israel from the rest of mankind.

So, too, at this day, when we read that the provision made for the removal of sin and sinfulness is open, we learn that it is personally approachable by us. Certain fanatics in our day will have it that grace comes to us through priests; there is the fountain, but you must not touch a drop of the purifying stream yourself; that venerable gentleman in white, or black, or blue, or scarlet, or violet, as the day of the month or the change of the moon may be, must stand at the fountain head and catch the water as it flows, and then after he has practiced upon it sundry manipulations you may drink from his hand, but you who are unordained must not go to the fountain for yourselves. Ah, my brethren, but we know better than to make gods of men, or saviours of sinners like ourselves. We dispense with priests, for we know that the fountain of salvation is open for us to come personally, and directly, and without any intervention. There is one Mediator between God and man, the Man Christ Jesus, but no other mediator is there. One of our colporteurs, some years ago abroad, was selling his Testaments, when the cure of a parish said to him, "Your books say a very great deal about pardon, but I do not see much in them about confession." The colporteur was about to reply, when a public notary, who was present, taking up the Testament, said to the priest, "Ah, my dear sir, what you say is very true, the New Testament does not say much about confession to priests; do you not remember that Jesus Christ saved the dying thief without the help of a priest, and that St. Stephen, when he was stoned was not shriven by a confessor, but entered glory without a priest!" "Ah," said the cur,--"but the rules of the church were very different in those days from what they are now." Full surely they were! We will go back however to the primitive times, and as the dying thief said, "Lord, remember me," so will we turn our eyes to that once crucified Savior, sitting in the highest heaven, and breathe the selfsame prayer, "Lord, remember me:" and as Stephen looked up directly into heaven, and found peace even amidst that stony shower, so on our dying bed, our glance shall be to the Christ in the open heaven; and we shall find rest in our last hours. Blessed be God, the doctrine of justification by faith is now so openly declared that priestcraft cannot hold us captives. The nations no longer need to crouch at the feet of shaveling impostors. Now that there is a fountain open, we can say, "Begone, ye priests, the whole herd of you, to whichever church ye belong; we who have believed are truly priests every one of us, and ye are mere pretenders. We have done with you; a plague and curse to humanity have ye been too long, and the gospel ends your detestable trade.

The text yet further signifies that the fountain is not marred by any amount of sin which we have already committed. If there be a fountain opened on purpose to remove filth, that man must be insane who shall say that his need of washing is a barrier to prevent his using it. Shall I stand outside the bath and say, "I am prevented from bathing because I am filthy"? everyone detects at once my illogical talk. If the fountain is open for sin, then sin is a qualification for washing in it. If Christ be a Savior for sinners, then no man may say that on the ground of sin Jesus cannot be his Savior; rather might he say, "The more truly I am a sinner the more surely is Christ Jesus suited to me." The exceeding heinousness of my sin, though I had been guilty of adultery, of murder, of crimes innumerable, cannot be a preventative to my being washed in the fount of atonement, because on account of my sin that fountain is provided, on purpose to put it away that cleansing flood was poured forth. Yet it ever is of the nature of sin, when the soul begins to know the bitterness of it, to make us fear that sin is a disqualification for mercy, and a reason why we should not believe in Christ Jesus the great propitiation for sin. O sinner, do not believe that sin unfits thee for a Savior, but believe that the Redeemer is come on purpose to save such as thou art. Some little time ago an earnest lady seeking the good of others, met with a poor girl some twenty years of age, who had most fearfully fallen and become a gross sinner, though still so young. She talked with her frequently, and at last saw in her tokens of repentance, but the poor girl's complaint was, "I can never be restored, I am so bad, nobody would ever take notice of me." "Have you not a mother?" "No," said the girl, "she died years ago." "Have you not a father?" "Yes, but I have not heard of him for years." "Does he know where you are?" "No, I do not want he should." "Do not you think he would receive you back into his house?" "No, that I know he would not, I could not expect him to do so; if I were in his place I would not receive such a one as I am." "Have you ever written to him since you have gone astray?" "No, I have kept out of the way of everybody that knew me; I do not want anybody to know what I am." "Have you tried your father whether he will receive you?" "No, I knew it was no good, pray do not mention it." "But," said the good sister, "who can tell? I think I will try and see if your father will receive you now that you are truly penitent for the past." "Oh, yes, I hate the sin, but my father would not receive me, it is of no use to ask him." "Well," said the visitor, "I will try;" and so she wrote a note to the father, giving him the daughter's address, telling him about her repentance, and entreating that she might be forgiven. What do you suppose was the reply? The next post brought the penitent girl a letter, on the envelope of which was written in large letters, "IMMEDIATE;" and when she opened it--well, I cannot tell you all her father said, but it just came to this, "Come and welcome, I am ready to forgive you; I have been praying night and day that you might be restored to me." Now, just what that father was to his poor lost girl, in tenderness and readiness to forgive, God is to sinners; if there be any unwillingness it is not on his part, it is all in their hearts, for the answer to every prayer for mercy is, God is ready, nay, he waiteth to be gracious, his heart yearneth over his erring ones. "How shall I give thee up?" saith he; "How shall I make thee as Adam how shall I set thee as Zeboim? mine heart is turned within me, my repentings are kindled together. I will not return to destroy Ephraim: for I am God, and not man." Our guilt therefore is no legitimate reason why we should not avail ourselves of the provisions of grace.

Neither is there any effectual barrier in the consideration of our inward sinfulness. If you say, "I could not be a Christian, I have such a bad disposition, I could not become holy it is impossible." This is true so far as you are concerned, but things impossible with men are possible with God. There is a fountain open for this very reason that this uncleanness of yours might be put away. Christ's blood will prove more than a match for the evil of your heart; his Spirit can renew you, make you a new creature, and from this day forward the things you hated you shall love, and the evil things you have delighted in shall become detestable to you. Is it not written, "Behold, I make all things new"?

The fountain of cleansing is not sealed by any demands in the gospel requiring one to prepare yourself for it before you come. The fountain is open, and if you are filthy, you are welcome to come to it. All that is asked of you is that you believe in Jesus; this he gives you, it is his own work in you. You must also repent and hate the sin which you have committed; this also he works in you, causing you by his Spirit to loathe the sin which aforetime you delighted in. Had there been a sort of purgatorial preparation, had there been a kind of quarantine through which the sinner had to pass before he could be renewed and forgiven, then were not the fountain completely open; but between you, a sinner, and acceptation before God, there need not be even a step of delay; believe now, and by believing you shall obtain the perfect pardon and the renewal of your soul.

Nor is there any other real barrier to shut up the fountain from the sinner. Some will say, "Perhaps I am not elected." My friend, read the text, the fountain is open; open for all ranks, "the house of David and the inhabitants of Jerusalem." The doctrine of election, true as it is, does not make my text a falsehood, or close the fount of grace upon any seeking soul. Can you think of any other doctrine? Does any other truth discourage you? Whatever it is I need only quote the text in order to answer your suspicion: The fountain is open for sin and for uncleanness, who dares say it is shut? If any theologian should say so, methinks I would push him into the fountain to make way for the sinner to come. There cannot be anything in theology, nor in nature, nor in heaven, nor earth, nor hell, which can shut what God declares to be open. If thou wiliest to be saved, if thou comest to Christ believing in him, there is nothing to shut up the fountain of life or prevent thee from being cleansed and healed. If there be any shutting and forbidding it is thy heart that is closed, and thy pride which forbids. No difficulties remain save only difficulties of thine own creating, there is none with God. There is a fountain opened by him for sin and for uncleanness, and thou hast enough of both, therefore come with them even as thou art. "I believe in the forgiveness of sins;" dost thou? It is an old doctrine of the Christian church--dost thou believe it? Methinks I hear thee say, "I believe in the forgiveness of everybody's sin but mine own." Brother, I believe in the forgiveness of thy sins. There was a time when it would not have troubled me to believe for thee, but it troubled me to believe for myself; now, can I believe for myself and for thee also. If thou desires forgiveness, take it; if thou desires a new heart and a right spirit, Jesus will give them to thee; the fountain is open, and none shall dare to deny access to the anxious heart. Jesus says, "Him that cometh unto me I will in no wise cast out." Would God that some were drawn of the Holy Spirit to come to-day and partake of the mercy which is so richly provided and so freely presented.

III. We have a rich consolation in the last point. The fountain is OPEN STILL.

The text says the fountain is opened, and I do not upon the closest inspection discover that it declares that it was afterwards shut; I find no intimation that the opening was for an occasion only; on the contrary, the opening is left as a fact accomplished. What a blessing is this to every child of God here; the fountain is still open for sin and uncleanness! What a comfort it is to that young man who but lately believed. Some little time after conversion there usually comes a period of surprising discoveries. The heart has believed in Jesus and found rest, and it has deluded itself into the idea that it is now so clean delivered from sin that it will never fall into it any more; but on a sudden it is tempted, it is overtaken in a fault, and then the devil cries, "You! Why, you are not saved, you are not a believer, see where you are now." Many remind me of a little girl who I trust was converted to God she in her simplicity quoted that sweet little hymn to her teacher, and said, "Teacher, I laid my sins on Jesus,' and now I love him so much that I never mean to do any more sins to lay on him." That is just what we thought when we were first pardoned; we did not quite say so, but we thought so. "All the past? Yes, that is all on him; now for the love we bear his name we will never sin again." So we thought; but, alas! we soon found that we were in the body still. When sin is seen to be still within us, how sweetly does the text ring out, like a silver bell, glad tidings of great joy--there is a fountain opened! You went at first to Jesus, young believer, go again. The fountain is not shut; you have washed in it once, it is not closed nor dried up, wash again; the same Christ you wanted when you first believed is there now as ready and willing as ever. His blood is equally efficacious, go, thou surprised one, and wash again:--

"This fountain from guilt not only makes pure,
And gives, soon as felt, infallible cure;
But if guilt removed return, and remain,
Its power may be proved again and again."

It will happen as we grow older and make progress in the Christian life, that we shall discover every day some fresh degree of defilement acquired by our pilgrimage through a sinful world. Do you ever go to rest a single night without feeling that you have been in many places during the day, and that there is fresh dust upon the garment, new soil upon the feet? Ah! bethink thee every night there is a fountain opened. To-day's sins can be as easily put away as yesterday's sins; and to-day's sinfulness, which I feel unconquerable for the moment, can be conquered still. I can go to Christ again and say, "Let thy blood kill this sin of mine, and soften my heart into tenderness and holiness once more." The fountain is still open, and no man can shut it.

I know that you in business, coming into contact with the world, must sometimes encounter some very trying circumstances. When perhaps you thought all would be plain sailing you meet with terrible storms. Though minded to live in peace, you fall into a sort of wrestling match with ungodly men; you are obliged to stand up for your own, and you try to do so with moderation of temper, yet your spirit becomes ruffled; and you have to say afterwards, when undergoing self-examination, "I do not know that I did exactly what I ought to have done; besides, my quiet walk with Christ has been broken by this strife with the sons of men; woe is me that I dwell in Mesech and tabernacle in the tents of Kedar." Beloved, there is a fountain open, go again by simple faith and look to Jesus once again and you will find fresh pardon, and the grace which restores the heart to its repose in Jesus. Your inner life will be again refreshed as you wash in the life-restoring fount prepared for you.

If you are at all like me you will at times feel your inner life to be sadly declining. I am ashamed to confess it, but even when I seek to live nearest to God, I feel an evil heart of unbelief struggling within me. There may come times when you will anxiously enquire, "Can I be a child of God at all? I cannot arouse my feelings towards God, my passions will not stir; even in holy duties I lack the living power; there is the wood, but where is the fire for the burnt offering? I would fain be zealous, earnest, intense, fervent, but I am sluggish, a very dolt in the Master's cause." At such times we are apt to say, "I must try to make myself somewhat better than this by some means, before I dare again to hope in God;" and then we go off to our own selves and our own works, and we sink in the deep mire where there is no standing. It is a happy thing if at such moments we turn again to Christ, end say, "O my Master, unworthy as I am to be thy follower, though vilest of all those those names are written on thy roll, yet I do believe in thee still. To thy cross I will cling, I will never let go my hope, for thou hast come to save sinners even such as I am, and on thee I will continue to trust. "My dear brethren, you will find that while this restores your peace, it at the same time excites you to seek after higher degrees of holiness. It is the idea of the worldling that if sin be pardoned so easily men will live in it, but it is not so; to the spiritual mind the great love displayed in the pardon of sin is the very highest motive for overcoming every unhallowed propensity. A sense of blood-bought pardon seals the death-warrant of the most favored sin. Ever shall we find our safest mode of battling with sin to be a new resort to the cross. Happy is it for us that the blood cleanseth from all sin; that is, it continues to do so every day. I should die in despair if it were not for this truth, that there is a fountain open still.

Some of us may have a long time to live possibly, but we shall never outlive that open fountain. Others may die soon, but, dear brother, in the last moment your eye may glance at the open fountain, and if the sins of all your life should rise before you, if in grim procession your transgressions should pass before your eyes each one accusing you, you may fly to the open fountain and they will disappear; and if the old Adam should rise even at the last, and some strong corruption should seek to prevail, there is the fountain open which will purge away the corruption of the flesh, and work in you the new nature yet more mightily, and preserve you to the Lord's eternal kingdom and glory.

I desire to close this sermon, all too poverty-stricken, with this thought. See here what our work is as a church. We have not to provide an atonement for the sinners round about us, but we have to point them to the fountain which is already opened. I want every one of you church members to be always telling others of the way of salvation. "It is so simple," you say; well, then you have no excuse if you do not tell it. Make your neighbors know the way of salvation, din it into their ears, constrain them to know it, so that if they die it shall not be for want of knowing the way of life.

I want to remind you as a church of one most important fact. Here is our preparation for the season of revival which I hope God is about to give us. The fountain open for the sinner is also open for the child of God. Let us all wash again. Have you grown cold? Come and get your spiritual life revived. Do any of you fear that you are becoming worldly and carnal? Come to Jesus, for where you first found life there you shall find it more abundantly. Come and wash again. I desire as your pastor to receive another baptism in the sacred atoning flood, and then to come and preach to you in its heavenly power. I pray God, that my dear brethren, the deacons and elders, may each one individually apart confess his sin, and apart receive the washing. And then I want every member, every Sunday-school teacher, and every worker, to prepare to serve God by receiving another of these blessed cleansings. In the old tabernacle there was a laver, and the priests washed their feet and their hands in it, which had to be filled up every now and then, because it was exhausted or foul; now we have not a brazen laver, but we have a fountain which never can be dried, and never becomes defiled. If you wash your feet in a little pool, the water is muddy directly, but if you wash in a running stream, as I have often done when climbing the Alps, or in a living fountain, you may wash, hundreds of you, and the water bears all defilement away and is just as bright as if it had never been touched by your feet. So there is here for all the church members a blessed flowing fountain; come and wash, I beseech you, even now.

I pray God backsliders may come hither, that those who have gone farther astray than in heart, and have wandered into outward actions of rebellion, may come to the fountain which is still open, and be cleansed anew. What sin it will be on our part if we neglect what God has provided! Though we have often come before, let us come again. I should like to suggest that this afternoon we each of us should spend a season alone, and pray for a renewed application of that blood which speaketh better things than that of Abel. The Master, after the last Supper, took a towel and girded himself, and went round with a basin and washed all his disciples' feet, and when he had done it said, "And ye are clean every whit." That is what I want him to do to all the members of this my beloved church now. You cannot serve God while you are defiled; you need fresh cleansing for successful service. O may he take the towel now in his infinite condescension, and visit each one and wash you one by one. Pastors, deacons, elders, members, may we all avail ourselves of the open fountain at this hour. O that the Holy Spirit might give to each one of us that cleansing which shall make us fit for service, O that we shall be useful during the coming months in the ingathering of his poor lost ones, to his praise and glory. May God grant it, for his name's sake. Amen.

PORTIONS OF SCRIPTURE READ BEFORE SERMON--Zechariah 12, and 13:1.

New Uses for Old Trophies

A Sermon (No. 972)
Delivered on Lord's-day Evening, November 20th, 1870 by
C. H. SPURGEON,
At the Metropolitan Tabernacle, Newington

"King David's spears and shields, that were in the temple of the Lord." - 2 Kings 11:10.

WHEN DAVID HAD FOUGHT with an adversary, and overcome him, he took away his armor and his weapons, and as other victorious heroes were wont to do, he bore them home as mementoes of his prowess, the trophies of the battle. These were placed in the house of the Lord. Perhaps David at the same time dedicated in like manner the shield and the sword which he had himself used in battle. After Solomon had built the temple, these trophies, which seem to have been very numerous, were hung up there. So they adorned the walls. So they illustrated the velour of noble sires. So they served to kindle emulation, I doubt not, in the breasts of true-hearted sons. Thus it was while generations sprung up and passed away; till at length other days dawned, darker scenes transpired, and sadder things filled up the chronicles of the nation. You will all of you remember the crisis to which my text refers. Athaliah, daughter of Ahab, wife of Jehoram, king of Judah, the usurping queen of Judah, had played the tyrant for well-nigh seven years. The endurance of the people had been tried to the uttermost; a just recompense was in store, and a well-concerted plan ready for execution. The time had come when she should be put to death, and the young prince who had been hidden away should be proclaimed king. It was arranged that he should be proclaimed in the temple court, yet the men that were to be the body-guard were not armed with weapons, for fear an alarm might be given, and the matter discovered too soon. But these weapons that were hung up of old in the temple were taken down, and the Levites and other friends were armed with them. When Athaliah came in and saw the young king surrounded by his body-guard, thus strangely equipped with the old weapons of former days ready to protect him, she rent her clothes, and cried, "Treason, Treason:" but her doom was sealed, escape was impossible, she was slain. To such good account there and then was the good old armor turned. This simple fact appears to me to suggest a striking moral.

The matter I shall speak to you about to-night will lie under four heads. We will give them to you as they occur to us.

I. And the first is this, IT IS WELL FOR US TO HANG ALL OUR TROPHIES IN THE HOUSE OF THE LORD.

We, too, are warriors. Every genuine Christian has to fight. Every inch of the way between here and heaven we shall have to fight, for as hitherto every single step of our pilgrimage has been one prolonged conflict. Sometimes we have victories, a presage of that final victory, that perfect triumph we shall enjoy with our Great Captain for ever.

"Oh! I have seen the day
When with a single word,
God helping me to say
'My trust is in the Lord,'
My soul has quelled a thousand foes,
Fearless of all that could oppose."

When we have these victories it behoves us to be especially careful that in all good conscience we hang up the trophies thereof in the house of the Lord. The reason for this lies here: it is to the Lord that we owe any success we have ever achieved. We have been defeated when we have gone in our own strength; but when we have been victorious it has always been because the strength of the Lord was put forth for our deliverance. You never fought with a sin, with a temptation, or with a doubt, and overthrew it, except by the Spirit's aid. You never won a soul for Jesus, you never spoke a valiant word that repelled an error, you never did an enterprising deed which really told well for the success of the kingdom, but God was in it all--virtually, nay, actually enabling you; and he did it of his own good will. What is it but a simple matter of justice that he who wrought the wonder should have the honor of it? It would have been a crying shame if Miriam had sung to the praise of Moses and Aaron at the Red Sea. They were but the outward instruments of the people's coming out of Egypt. As she took her timbre!, she rightly said, in the hymn that Moses had given her for the occasion: "Let us sing unto the Lord, for he hath triumphed gloriously." So in every struggle that transpires in our hearts, in every combat waged in the world, ascribe the power to him to whom it belongs, "The right hand of the Lord is exalted; the right hand of the Lord doeth valiantly." As before the fight in his name we set up our banner, so after the fight in his name again we give the conquering banner to the breeze. "All glory be unto him that won the victory."

This will save us from pride and self-sufficiency. Scarcely can God trust us with a victory, lest we begin fingering it with our own hands, as if our own ingenuity, our own wisdom, or our own strength had done marvels. As of old, Israel sacrificed to her net when a great draught of fish was taken, or to her drag when a great harvest had been threshed out, so are we too apt to sacrifice to our own ability, our own industry, our own superiority in one respect or another, and think that there is some virtue or merit in us to which the Almighty has awarded the palm. Instead of looking only to God we begin to look in some degree to ourselves. You cannot do otherwise than put the honor somewhere. If you do not ascribe it to God the temptation will be too strong for you, you will be sure to take it for yourself; and if you do this the most fatal consequences will follow, for they that walk in pride God will assuredly abase. No matter how dear you are to him, if pride be harboured in your spirit he will whip it out of you. They that go up in their own estimation must come down again by his discipline. You cannot be exalted in self without being by-and-by brought low before him. God will have it so; it is always the rule, "He hath put down the mighty from their seat, and hath exalted them of low degree." He goes forts with the axe, and this is the work he does among the thick trees--he cuts down the high tree and dries up the green tree, but he exalts the low tree, and makes the dry tree to flourish, that all the glory may be unto himself alone; for, saith he, I the Lord have spoken and have done it. Let us take care, however, that we ascribe the glory to God, and do not forget to honor him. We have received so many mercies, my brethren, that they come to us as common things. We receive them, and scarcely know, perhaps, that we have received them. According to the old proverb we do not know the value of our mercies till we miss them; but it ought not to be so. Must we be defeated in order to let us know that God gives us victory? Is it needful that you and I should suffer some great disaster in order to make us grateful for past success? Will you never prize health as one of the choicest boons of heaven till some grievous malady has sapped your strength, and made all the enjoyments of life tasteless or even nauseous? Well, if it be needful, it is a necessity of our own producing. The more the pity that we should challenge the ills we complain of, and incur the reverses we so bitterly deplore. O that we may never slight the good things we have, or trifle with the benefits we receive from the hand of the Lord! Especially, my dear brethren, let us bless God for every spiritual success achieved, and take care to make a record of it on the tablet of our grateful heart. If we should one day have to flee before the enemy, if our work for God should one day seem to be without success, we may look back with much smiting of heart upon those ungrateful times when God dealt so generously with us, and yet we did not take the trouble to sing him a psalm or offer up a vow, or do any act of homage to express our gratitude to him. Hang up Goliath's sword; do not put it by to rust. Hang up the shields and the spears of the Philistines. If by God's help you have taken them, set store by them, and make the world see what the Lord has done on your behalf, whereof you are glad. Hake the church to join your grateful song. There is too much of the cold silence of ingratitude amongst us. Too seldom do we chant forth our Te Deum laudamus with solemn, lively air. Stir the hearts of others because your own heart heaves with deep emotions of thankfulness to the Most High. I am persuaded, my brethren, that it is only in this way that we can secure for ourselves future success. David's life was a series of dilemmas and deliverances. With what sort of face, think you, could he have invoked rescue from fresh perils, had he failed to recognize God's help in past preservation? If, when flushed with victory, he had usurped the honor to himself, what assistance would he have received the next time he was curried with impending disaster? Or, had he not taught the Israelites in the hour of triumph to sing, "Non nobis, Domine"--"Not unto us, O Lord, not unto us, but unto thy name give glory;" how could he have engaged their hearts in the hour of trial to wail forth the litany of supplication--"The Lord hear thee in the day of trouble; the name of the God of Jacob defend thee, send thee help from the sanctuary, and strengthen thee out of Zion." Without consistency we cannot exert any moral influence with men, or obtain any spiritual prevalence with God. May not many of our barren seasons be ascribed to the fact that we did not thank God for fruitful ones? If the preacher has been honored in his ministry to win souls to Christ, but has not duly blessed his God for the enabling of the Holy Ghost granted to himself, and for the witness of the Holy Ghost given to the people; or, worse still if he has complimented himself on his own talents, and the use he makes of them; need he wonder if, when next he goes forth, as Samson of old, and shakes himself as aforetime, he finds his strength has departed from him? "Give unto the Lord, O ye mighty, give unto the Lord glory and strength. Give unto the Lord the glory due unto his name;" else when most you need him, you may find his strength is taken from you and your honors will have departed too. Hang up the shield, hang up the spear, let Jehovah's name be exalted. Bring forth the forgotten memorials of lovingkindness, expose them to public view, put them before your own mind's eye to-night, gratefully remember them, lovingly praise him and magnify his name. I am sure we, as a church whom God has blessed so long, ought not to be slow to hang up the trophies of his loving kindness in our midst. If God has done anything for you, tell it. If he has delivered you out of trouble, tell it. If he has fed your soul in the wilderness, tell it. If you have lately been converted, tell it. If you have found Christ precious to you, though just now you were a poor lost soul, tell it. Hang up the shields and spears. Let each individual do it, let the whole church do it; and often by our enlarged endeavors for the dear Savior's sake, by our consecrated self-denials, let us show that we do feel how much we owe to the infinite power of the God of victory, who maketh us strong in the day of battle. That is the first point. If we have any victories, let all the trophies be dedicated to the Lord.

II. The second is this: THESE TROPHIES MAY COME IN USEFUL AT SUCH TIMES AS WE CANNOT FORESEE, AND UNDER SUCH CIRCUMSTANCES AS WE WOT NOT OF.

Little could David have thought when he gave Abiathar the sword of Goliath, that he would ever go to the priests of Gad and ask them to lend him a sword, and that they should say, We have no sword here, save the sword of Goliath, the Philistine, whom thou slewest in the Valley of Elah, behold it is wrapped in a cloth behind the ephod. He gave it to God, but he did not think that he would ever have it back again with a priestly blessing on it, so that he should be able to say, "There is none like that: give it me." And when, in after years, he hung up the swords and shields which he had taken away from Philistine heroes, he did not surmise that one of his descendants, or the seed royal, would find the need to employ his own, his grandsire's, or, further back, from himself--his forefather's trophies--in order to establish himself on the throne. We never know, my brethren, when we praise God for mercies, but what the very praises might come back into our bosoms, and the offerings we make to God in the way of thankfulness may be our own enrichment in the days to come. The memorials we put up to record God's goodness, may be to us in after years among the most useful things in all our treasury. To ourselves and others the memorials of the victories we have won may be signally profitable, strangely opportune, seemingly indispensable.

Let me try to show this. Years ago you and I were fighting battles with unbelief. We were struggling after a Savior. Our sins rose up against us thick and furious. The fiery darts of the enemy rained upon us like hail. That conflict we never shall forget; we bear the scars of it to this very day. Glory be to God! by his grace we won the victory and overcame through the blood of the Lamb. We looked at Jesus Christ upon the cross, and in that moment our sins fled away. The whole host of them was defeated. A dying Savior was the symbol of victory. What then? Let us use the mementoes we laid up before the Lord of that day--the trophies that we took in that battle--for ourselves and for others.

For ourselves. If ever we have another struggle against sin--perhaps we shall have many--I mean such alarming assaults as involve severe struggles--let us recollect how Jesus met with us the first time, and "if, when we were enemies, we were reconciled to God by the death of his Son, much more, being reconciled, we shall be saved by his life." He saved us with a great salvation when we first came home as prodigals covered with rags, will he not help us now, when he come to him as his own children, clothed in his own righteousness, and say, "Abba, Father," being already accepted in the Beloved?

I do think it often proves a great blessing to a man that he had a terrible conflict, a desperate encounter, a hard-fought engagement in passing from the empire of Satan into the kingdom of God's dear Son. Sooner or later each saved man will have his hand-to-hand fight with the prince of darkness; and as a general rule, it is a great mercy to have it over on the outset of one's career, and be able afterwards to feel, "Whatever comes upon me, I never can suffer as I suffered when I was seeking Christ. Whatever staggering doubt, or hideous blasphemy, or ghastly insinuations, even of suicide itself, may assail my feeble heart, they cannot outdo the horror of great darkness through which my spirit passed when I was struggling after a Savior." Now I do not say that it is desirable that we should have this painful ordeal, much less that we should seek it as an evidence of regeneration, but when we have passed through it victoriously, we may so use it that it may be a perpetual armoury to us. If we can now defy all doubts and fears that come, because they cannot be so potent as those which already in the name of Jesus Christ our Savior we have overthrown, shall we not use that for ourselves? and can we not equally well use it for others? Full often have I found it good, when I have talked with a young convert in deep distress about his sin, to tell him something more of his anxious plight than he knew how to express and he wondered where I had found it, though he would not have wondered if he knew where I had been, and how much deeper in the mire than he; when he has talked about some horrible thought that he has had, with regard to the impossibility of his own salvation, and I have said, "Why, I have thought that a thousand times, and yet have overcome it through the help of God's Spirit." I know that a man's own experience is one of the very best weapons he can use in fighting with evil in other men's hearts. Often their misery and despondency, aggravated, as it commonly is by a feeling of solitariness, will be greatly relieved before it is effectually driven out when they find that a brother has suffered the same, and yet has been able to overcome. Do I show him how precious the Savior is to my soul he glorifies God in me. Right soon will he look into the same dear face and be lightened; and then he will magnify the Lord with me, and we shall exalt his name together. Thus good it is, you see, to take the old shields and spears away from the enemies and to use them again against new foes of the house of David.

Since that time, dear brethren, when we had the first struggle, we have had to fight with many evil passions and propensities. Perhaps we have had one besetting sin. We were a long time before we came up to beard that. We avoided it, and refrained from rising up against it, until at length we perceived that it must be killed or it would kill us. It was very like pulling out our eyes, but we saw it must be done; we stood foot to foot with it. A sharp time it was, for the sin threatened to prevail against us; if we threw it down it seemed to rise again, like the giant of old, strengthened by its fall. Did you ever have a personal, mental, moral conflict with some great dragon of besetting sin? If so be you have been enabled to smite it valiantly, and slay it utterly, I know you have gained trophies to hang in the house of God. To do so will be of no small advantage to ourselves, because you can take them down and use them in future; and you will find they are footholds of your strength to fight with the next sin that comes upon you. The strength which God has educated and fostered in the last struggle will greatly assist you in the next. The man who gives way to one sin will very readily give way to another, but a man who through God's grace has won a very high vantage ground by mastering one sin, will be very likely to win another. The spoils taken from the last Philistine will help us to go forth and win more, and in the name of God we shall get the victory. Many a man has had a hard struggle at first. He has been drawn to Christ, proved the grace of acceptance, and taken the vows of allegiance, and henceforth it behoves him to depart from iniquity, and not turn again to folly. Perhaps he has been addicted to swearing, and he has to get rid of that wicked habit at any cost. Perhaps he has been accustomed to frequent the public house, to sit in the seat of the scornful, and enliven his companions with jest and song, he has forthwith to relinquish that place, and take leave of that company for ever. Then perhaps there has been some other vice which he has cherished in secret, and clung to with the more tenacity because it so tenacious!, clung to him; of that evil he has purged himself, and from that bondage he has escaped. Is it not possible that there yet remains one transgression which lurks in the breast of such a one? Very likely at this time he has a passionate temper. Down with it, my brother. You slew the lion, and you slew the bear, and this uncircumcised Philistine shall be as one of them. Do not be afraid to grapple with it. Do not say, "I have a quick temper, and I cannot help it." There is no need for it. God's grace can drive it out even as the rest. Beard it in the name of the Most High, and use the trophies that you stole from past success--nay, fairly won them from the foes you have vanquished--use those with which to combat sins that now assail you.

To change the figure, it is the lot of some of us to be called to withstand great errors. We have been sorely harassed at times with doubts and misgivings about some established truth. I suppose no one is a firm believer who has not once been a doubter. He knows no faith who never had a fear; for candid enquiry must go before absolute credence. How can any one know the proofs and vouchers of his faith unless he has taken pains to dig into the volume of evidence that lies at its base? Now it is a fine, a noble thing, when you have had a conflict in your own soul with some plausible heresy, some seductive perversion of the truth, and have put it to flight with the sword of the Spirit, which is the word of God; it is a noble feat, I say, to capture the arms of your assailant and to use the very weapons of the adversary against him. You have detected his sophistry, you have found out his devices, and now for the future you will not be so readily carried away with every wind of doctrine. This time you are too old to be taken with his chaff. You were deceived once, but by God's grace you are not willing any longer to lend a ready ear to the fair speech which casts a mist over plain facts, but you henceforth resolve to prove the spirits whether they be of God. So from the spoils of past conflicts you are made strong to win present victories. Texts of Scripture are sometimes used by the adversaries of the gospel, and turned against us. I know some ministers who, when they meet with a passage that they cannot immediately reconcile with the orthodox faith, alter the reading, or put a fresh sense on the words, or twist it and turn it to suit their purpose. It is a bad plan, my brethren; the texts of Scripture are to be taken as they stand, and you may rest assured they will always defend, never overturn, the faith once delivered to the saints. When I have seen a text sometimes in the hand of the enemy made use of against the deity of Christ, or against the doctrine of election, or against some other important and vital doctrine, I have not felt at all inclined to give up the text or think lightly of it. I rather admire those Americans in the South, who when they had lost some guns, were asked by the commanding officer whether they had not spiked the guns before they gave them up to the foe? "Spiked them! no," said they, "we did not like to spoil such beautiful guns; we will take them again tomorrow." And so they did. I would not have a text touched. Grand old text! we honor thee even while we cannot keep the field, or ward thee from the aggression of the invader. But shall we spoil it, or give it up as lost? Never, we will take it out of the hand of the enemy, use it for the defense of the gospel, and show that it does not mean what they think, or answer the ends to which they would apply it. Are we baffled in attack, or do we lose ground in an argument, it is for us by more diligent study, and closer research, to take the guns, the good old guns, and use those which the enemy used against ourselves--to turn them round and use them against him. Depend upon it the great temple of truth is not like a house divided against itself. Nothing equivocal or prevaricating hath come forth at any time from the mouth of the Lord. As for our understanding, it is always weak, and as for our tactics in upholding the right, they are often at fault. But the word of God is steadfast; it does not change with the times or yield to suit any man's purpose. The weapons of our warfare are good, it is the hands that wield them that are so unskillful. Thus I might continue to show that in all the battles we fight, the trophies which we win should be stored; for they may come in for future use at some time or other. There is no experience of a Christian that will not have some ultimate service to render him. He may say to himself, "What can be the good of this feeling, what can be the practical advantage of that agony of mind through which I passed?" My brother, you know not what may be the history of your life, it is unfinished yet; if you did know you would see that in this present trial there is a preparation for some future emergency, which will enable you to come out of it in triumph. The shields and spears of David are hung up for future action.

III. In the third place, our text may mean that David hung up the spears and shields which he was accustomed to use himself; and if so, we shall remark that ANCIENT WEAPONS ARE GOOD FOR PRESENT USE.

I should like to show you this by taking you on to a battle-field. I did take you there just now, but you did not recognize it, perhaps, as a battle-ground. We will go to it. It is not Sadowa or Sedan, it is a grander arena far--the old seventy-seventh. Turn to the seventy-seventh Psalm, and you have a battle-field there. Should you ever have to fight the same battle, by looking through this Psalm, you will see David's shields and spears, and you will soon learn how to screen yourself with the one, and how to do exploits with the other. Here is David fighting with despondency--an old enemy of mine. I daresay some of you are afflicted with it. But observe how he fought with it. The first weapon he drew out of the scabbard was the weapon of all-prayer. And how grandly he used it! "I cried unto God with my voice, even unto God with my voice." Satan trembles when he hears the sound of prayer. They are the conquering legions that know how to pray. Despondency soon flies when a man knows how to ply this all-conquering and ever-useful weapon of petition to the Most High.

Then note how he used this weapon continually. "My hand was stretched out all night," saith he, according to the marginal reading of the second verse. If the first prayer did not help him, he prayed again; if an hour's prayer did not bring him peace, he would pray two hours; and all night long he kept at it. You will get a like result too, my brother, if you exercise a like perseverance, you must get a like result if you know how to linger at the mercy-seat.

When he had used the weapon of prayer, what did he do next? He took out another spear. It was that of remembering God. He had long enough pored in thought over himself and his present sinfulness and weakness, and now he remembered God's mercy, God's faithfulness, God's lovingkindness, God's power, God's covenant, God in the person of Christ. Oh! this is indeed to prepare a salvo against the enemy, and to fortify one's own position with fresh succours. He can win the battle that knows how to use this artillery of remembering God.

Going on with the strategy of war, what next? Why, in the fifth verse we read how he maintained his courage and his constancy--"I considered the days of old." He enquired of hoary fathers, and looked back upon the inspired traditions, if I may be allowed the expression, of the early church. He tamed to see whether God ever did forsake any of his people, rightly judging that if he never did he never would, and firmly resolving that till he could find a clear case of God's unfaithfulness he would not yield an inch of soil, nor give up a stone of any fortress, but would hold on and fight the battle out. That inward musing helped him much. The enemy began to weary, while he recruited his strength.

But now he used another weapon. He looked to his own experience--see the sixth verse. "I called to remembrance my song in the night." Past experience acknowledged gratefully, and taken as the index of what the future will be--this is another of David's shields and spears. And then he seemed to put a whole path of spears before the enemy, and hold up an entire wall of shields when he came to close quarters with him, and said, "Will the Lord cast off for ever? Will he be favorable no more? Is his mercy clean gone for ever? Doth his promise fail for evermore? Hath God forgotten to be gracious? Hath he in anger shut up his tender mercies?" Oh! this is how to win the battle. The next time, dear friend, you find yourself downcast in trouble, do not run away because Giant Despair is so strong. Though pressed by danger and beset by foes, feed not this frenzy of the soul with gloomy black forebodings. Armed with David's shield and spears, attack him; show a bold front, and so shall yet resist the devil and find that he flees from you, and you shall come back from the conflict with louder notes of victory than you had dreamed before.

There are some persons here, however, who are not yet far enough advanced to understand this battle of the seventy-seventh. I will take them to another battle, the battle of the fifty-first. That is the sinner's battle; we shall see David's shields and spears there. A tremendous battle it was with sin, with a guilty conscience, with despairing thoughts. Some of you, perhaps, are fighting such a battle to-night. I rather hope you are. I was preaching the other day, I think it was last Tuesday evening, at Acton. I went my way after service hopeful, prayerful that some fruits might be reaped from my labors. Not long after I received a letter from the minister to this effect: "My dear friend, I could not help writing to tell you that last Tuesday night when I was in bed and asleep, there was a knock at my door, and I came down and found a railway porter wanting to see me. "O sir," said he, "I cannot sleep; I was obliged to come and knock you up though it is late. I heard the sermon at your chapel to-night, and I want to know what I must do to be saved? It is time for me to seek the Lord, and I shall never get rest till I find him." Oh! it is good for us to be knocked up at night to answer any one that comes on such an errand as that. Would God it were every night in the year, if it were to hear a sinner saying, "What must I do to be saved?"

Now, if one here present be in such a condition as that, just let him follow me to this battle-field, and see how David fought. His shields and spears in such case consisted first in an appeal to God's mercy. Do not appeal to justice, sinner. That is against you; appeal to mercy. "Have mercy upon me, O God, according to thy lovingkindness!" Prayer he brings before God, but it is prayer tipped with a hope in the mercy in God. Go, sinner, and plead with God and fight your sins with hope in his mercy. When he had done that he then turns to confession: "I acknowledge my transgression, and my sin is ever before me." No weapon to drive away guilty fears like making a clean breast of your sins. Tell your Father you have offended; do not plead any extenuations or mitigations. Confess that you deserve his wrath. Put yourself before the throne of God's clemency. Confess that if it were turned to a throne of vengeance you deserve it well. Prayers, tears, pleas for mercy, and full confession--these are weapons to conquer with.

But note the master weapon! See where the battle began to turn into victory. It is here when he cries in the seventh verse, "Purge me with hyssop, and I shall be clean; wash me, and I shall be whiter than snow." You know that hyssop was a little bunch, a brush used to dip into the blood--a basin full of blood, and then with this brush of hyssop the priest sprinkled the guilty man, the unclean man, and he was counted clean. So the master argument in this verse is blood. Oh! how this destroys our sins, how this scatters all our doubts and fears--the almighty weapon of the cross, the divine weapon of the atonement. Let sins come on, and let them be more than the hairs of my head, loftier than mountains and deeper than the unfathomed ocean, let them come on--God's flaming wrath behind them, hell itself coming to devour me; yet if I can but take the cross and hold it up before me, if I can plead the precious blood I shall be safe, for I shall be saved and prove a conqueror, notwithstanding all. Beloved, then, see that in all your fights you use the old, old weapons of David himself--his shields and spears--by these same weapons shall you also win the day.

IV. And now, lastly, let me suggest to you a fourth version of the text. DID NOT DAVID HEREIN PREFIGURE HIM THAT WAS TO COME--DAVID'S SON AND DAVID'S LORD?

Jesus Christ, our King, has hung up many shields and spears in the house of the Lord. I shall not occupy many minutes, but I invite every believer's heart to look at the great temple that Christ has builded, and see how he has hung it round with trophies of his victory. Sin--Christ has borne it in himself, endured its penalty and overcome it; he has hung up the handwriting of ordinances that was against us as a trophy in the house of the Lord. He has nailed it to the cross. Satan--our great foe--he met him foot to foot in the wilderness and discomfited him--met him in the garden--overcame him on the cross. Now hell, too, is vanquished--Christ is Lord. The prince of the power of the air is but his serf. The King of kings hath led captivity captive, and all the crowns of this prince of the power of the air are hung up as trophies. Broken are their spears: their shields all battered and vilely cast away, hang up as memorials of what Christ has done. Death, too, the last enemy, Christ hath taken spoils from him when he rose again himself from his prison house, and ascended on high, leading captivity captive. And the enmity of the human heart, my brethren. Oh I how many of these enmities has Christ hung up in the hall, for he has conquered that enmity and made the hater into a lover. My heart, your heart, I hope that all our hearts, too, are trophies of what

Christ's love can do. There are some great sinners at this day who are wonderful tokens of the power of love. When we look round the temple and see the shields and spears hung up, we say, "Who did those shields and spears belong to?" One says, "Why, that is the shield and spear of John Newton, the old blasphemer!" Glory be to God, Christ conquered him. Whose shield and spears are those? Why, that is the shield and spear of John Bunyan, the blasphemer on the village green. God's mercy conquered him. Yes, there will be a pillar for many of us, and I do not know which will bring Christ most honor, for he had much ado to bring us down. I wonder whether there will be a place for you, you old sailor? These many year you have been living without God and without Christ. You have been a frequenter of every place of sin, every filthy haunt in London. I do trust God's grace will meet with you. The poor harlot, Mary, the woman that was a sinner--there hangs her shield and spear. She was a hard fighter, a very Amazon, but Christ conquered her, hung up her shield and spear, and there it shall hang for ever, to the praise of the glory of his grace, who vanquished even her, and made her his willing servant, nay, his beloved friend. What will heaven be when all of us shall be trophies of his power to save, and when our bodies shall be there as well as our souls! "O death, where is thy sting? O grave, where is thy victory?"--when not only souls, but bodies shall be in heaven too, all trophies of what Christ has done when he plucked his people from the jaws of the grave and delivered them from the grasp of the sepulcher.

I came just now, before I entered here, from a sight which did my very soul good. One of our dear and well-beloved sisters, lies very sick, I think sue is dying--in all human probability a few hours will see her in another world. I looked at her as one of the trophies of Christ's power to save. I would not have missed the visit for I know not what. She was not only calm, but joyous; nay, triumphant, expecting the time of her departure and longing for it, speaking of everlasting faithfulness, of sure promises, and of the presence of Christ as a reality, which she enjoyed even now, before the veil of flesh is rent that hides his blessed face from ours. I said to her, "How long is it since the cloud has broken away from you?" She said, "I have had a good deal of peace of mind, but never such joy as I have now. Now that I am going hence I shall soon see his face without a veil between." The victories of dying spirits substantiate the gospel. When Christian people have no motive to overrate their assurance, and certainly no inducement to play the hypocrite, when they have nothing in their present sensations to inspire courage, raise enthusiasm, or buoy them up with suspicious comfort--for heart and flesh fail--there is much to admire in their constancy, much to animate us in their faith:

"Our dying friends are pioneers to smoothe
Our rugged path to death, to break those bars
Of terror and abhorrence Nature throws
Cross our obstructed way, and thus to make
Welcome, as safe, our port from every storm."

When you can see the eye, soon to be closed, sparkling with ecstacy, and hear the voice feeble because the throat is choking, as brave, and braver still than ever it has been before, and when you mark the look of deep composure, nay, of heavenly expectancy, upon the pale, pale face--oh! this makes our soul, my brethren, to feel that we have a faith that is worth prizing, a Christ that is worth trusting. These are trophies; and these death-bed trophies are hung up in that part of the temple where we can see them.

Let us take care that we have good confidence, always walking by faith, be the path of our pilgrimage rough or smooth, arid ever maintaining the fight of faith, however fierce our temptations or fiery our trials. So when we come to die we may hang up our trophies too, saying to death and hell that we bid them defiance, for Christ is with us to the last, making our darkest moments to be bright with the light of his presence. God grant that all of us may be trophies of Christ, and hung up thus as memorials for ever. Amen.

PORTION OF SCRIPTURE READ BEFORE SERMON--Psalm 72.

The Power of Christ Illustrated by the Resurrection

A Sermon (No. 973)
Delivered on Lord's-day Morning, January 19th, 1871 by
C. H. SPURGEON,
At the Metropolitan Tabernacle, Newington

"For our conversation is in heaven; from whence we also we look for the Savior; the Lord Jesus Christ: who shall change our vile body, that it may be fashioned like unto his glorious body, according to the working whereby he is able even to subdue all things unto himself," - Philippians 3:20,21.

I SHOULD MISLEAD YOU if I called these verses my text, for I intend only to lay stress upon the closing expression, and I read the two verses because they are needful for its explanation. It would require several discourses to expound the whole of so rich a passage as this.

Beloved, how intimately is the whole of our life interwoven with the life of Christ! His first coming has been to us salvation, and we are delivered from the wrath of God through him. We live still because he lives, and never is our life more joyous than when we look most steadily to him. The completion of our salvation in the deliverance of our body from the bondage of corruption, in the raising of our dust to a glorious immortality, that also is wrapped up with the personal resurrection and quickening power of the Lord Jesus Christ. As his first advent has been our salvation from sin, so his second advent shall be our salvation from the grave. He is in heaven, but, as the apostle saith, "We look for the Savior, the Lord Jesus Christ: who shall change our vile body, that it may be fashioned like unto his glorious body." We have nothing, we are nothing, apart from him. The past, the present, and the future are only bright as he shines upon them. Every consolation, every hope, every enjoyment we possess, we have received and still retain because of our connection with Jesus Christ our Lord. Apart from him we are naked, and poor, and miserable. I desire to impress upon your minds, and especially upon my own, the need of our abiding in him. As zealous laborers for the glory of God I am peculiarly anxious that you may maintain daily communion with Jesus, for as it is with our covenant blessings, so is it with our work of faith and labor of love, everything depends upon him. All our fruit is found in Jesus. Remember his own words, "Without me ye can do nothing." Our power to work comes wholly from his power. If we work effectually it must always be according to the effectual working of his power in us and through us. Brethren, I pray that our eyes may be steadfastly turned to our Master at this season when our special services are about to commence. Confessing our dependence upon him, and resorting to him in renewed confidence, we shall proceed to our labor with redoubled strength. May we remember where our great strength lieth, and look to him and him alone, away from our own weakness and our own strength too--finding all in him in our work for others as we have found all in him in the matter of the salvation of our own souls. When the multitudes were fed, the disciples distributed the bread, but the central source of that divine commissariat was the Master's own hand. He blessed, he brake, he gave to the disciples, and then the disciples to the multitude. Significant also was one of the last scenes of our Lord's intercourse with his disciples before he was taken up. They had been fishing all the night, but they had taken nothing; it was only when he came that they cast the net on the right side of the ship, and then the net was filled with a great multitude of fishes. Ever must it be so; where he is souls are taken by the men-fishers, but nowhere else. Not the preaching of his servants alone, not the gospel of itself alone, but his presence with his servants is the secret of success. "The Lord working with them," his co-operating presence in the gospel, this is it which makes it "the power of God unto salvation." Lift up your eyes then, my brethren, confederate with us for the spread of the Redeemer's kingdom, to the Savior, the Lord Jesus, who is the Captain of our salvation, through whom and by whom all things shall be wrought to the honor of God, but without whom the most ardent desires, and the most energetic efforts must most certainly fail. I have selected this text with no less a design than this--that every eye may by it be turned to the omnipotent Savior before we enter upon the hallowed engagements which await us.

In the text notice, first of all, the marvel to be wrought by our Lord at his coming; and then gather from it, in the second place, helps to the consideration of the power which is now at this time proceeding from him and treasured in him; and then, thirdly, contemplate the work which we desire to see accomplished, and which we believe will be accomplished on the ground of the power resident in our Lord.

I. First, we have to ask you to CONSIDER BELIEVINGLY THE MARVEL WHICH IS TO BE WROUGHT BY OUR LORD AT HIS COMING.

When he shall come a second time he will change our vile body and fashion it like unto his glorious body. What a marvellous change! How great the transformation! How high the ascent! Our body in its present state is called in our translation a "vile body," but if we translate the Greek more literally it is much more expressive, for there we find this corporeal frame called "the body of our humiliation." Not "this humble body," that is hardly the meaning, but the body in which our humiliation is manifested and enclosed. This body of our humiliation our Lord will transform until it is like unto his own. Here read not alone "his glorious body," for that is not the most literal translation, but "the body of his glory;" the body in which he enjoys and reveals his glory. Our Savior had a body here in humiliation; that body was like ours in all respects except that it could see no corruption, for it was undefiled with sin; that body in which our Lord wept, and sweat great drops of blood, and yielded up his spirit, was the body of his humiliation. He rose again from the dead, and he rose in the same body which ascended up into heaven, but he concealed its glory to a very great extent, else had he been too bright to be seen of mortal eyes. Only when he passed the cloud, and was received out of sight, did the full glory of his body shine forth to ravish the eyes of angels and of glorified spirits. Then was it that his countenance became as the sun shining in its strength. Now, beloved, whatever the body of Jesus may be in his glory, our present body which is now in its humiliation is to be conformed unto it; Jesus is the standard of man in glory. "We shall be like him, for we shall see him as he is." Here we dwell in this body of our humiliation, but it shall undergo a change, "in a moment, in the twinkling of an eye, at the last trump: for the trumpet shall sound, and the dead shall be raised incorruptible, and we shall be changed." Then shall we come into our glory, and our body being made suitable to the glory state, shall be fitly called the body of glory. We need not curiously pry into the details of the change, nor attempt to define all the differences between the two estates of our body; for "it doth not yet appear what we shall be," and we may be content to leave much to be made known to us hereafter. Yet though we see through a glass darkly, we nevertheless do see something, and would not shut our eyes to that little. We know not yet as we are known, but we do know in part, and that part knowledge is precious. The gates have been ajar at times, and men have looked awhile, and beheld and wondered. Three times, at least, human eyes have seen something of the body of glory. The face of Moses, when he came down from the mount, shone so that those who gathered around him could not look thereon, and he had to cover it with a veil. In that lustrous face of the man who had been forty days in high communion with God, you behold some gleams of the brightness of glorified manhood. Our Lord made a yet clearer manifestation of the glorious body when he was transfigured in the presence of the three disciples. When his garments became bright and glistering, whiter than any fuller could make them, and he himself was all aglow with glory, his disciples sew end marvelled. The face of Stephen is a third window as it were through which we may look at the glory to be revealed, for even his enemies as they gazed upon the martyr in his confession of Christ, saw his face as it had been the face of an angel. Those three transient gleams of the morning light may serve as tokens to us to help us to form some faint idea of what the body of the glory of Christ and the body of our own glory will be.

Turning to that marvellous passage in the Corinthians, wherein the veil seems to be more uplifted than it ever had been before or since, we learn a few particulars worthy to be rehearsed. The body while here below, is corruptible, subject to decay; it gradually becomes weak through old age, at last it yields to the blows of death, falls into the ground, and becomes the food of worms. But the new body shall be incorruptible, it shall not be subject to any process of disease, decay, or decline, and it shall never, through the lapse of ages, yield to the force of death. For the immortal spirit it shall be the immortal companion. There are no graves in heaven, no knell ever saddened the New Jerusalem. The body here is weak, the apostle says "it is sown in weakness;" it is subject to all sorts of infirmities in life, and in death loses all strength. It is weak to perform our own will, weaker still to perform the heavenly will; it is weak to do and weak to suffer: but it is to be "raised in power, all infirmity being completely removed." How far this power will be physical and how far spiritual we need not speculate; where the material ends and the spiritual begins we need not define; we shall be as the angels, and we have found no difficulty in believing that these pure spirits "excel in strength," nor in understanding Peter when he says that angels are "greater in power and might." Our body shall be "raised in power."

Here, too, the body is a natural or soulish body--a body fit for the soul, for the lowest faculties of our mental nature but according to the apostle in the Corinthians, it is to be raised a spiritual body, adapted to the noblest portion of our nature, suitable to be the dwelling-place and the instrument of our new-born grace-given life. This body at present is no assistance to the spirit of prayer or praise; it rather hinders than helps us in spiritual exercises. Often the spirit truly is willing, but the flesh is weak. We sleep when we ought to watch, and faint when we should pursue. Even its joys as well as its sorrows tend to distract devotion: but when this body shall be transformed, it shall be a body suitable for the highest aspirations of our perfected and glorified humanity--a spiritual body like unto the body of the glory of Christ. Here the body is sinful, its members have been instruments of unrighteousness. It is true that our body is the temple of the Holy Ghost; but, alas! there are traces about it of the time when it was a den of thieves. The spots and wrinkles of sin are not yet removed. Its materialism is not yet so refined as to be an assistance to the spirit; it gravitates downwards, and it has a bias from the right line; but it awaits the last change, and then it shall be perfectly sinless, as alabaster white and pure, upon which stain of sin did never come; like the newly driven snow, immaculately chaste. "As we have borne the image of the earthy, we shall also bear the image of the heavenly."

Being sinless, the body when it shall be raised again shall be painless. Who shall count the number of our pains while in this present house of clay? Truly we that are in this tabernacle do groan. Does it not sometimes appear to the children of sickness as if this body were fashioned with a view to suffering; as if all its nerves, sinews, veins, pulses, vessels, and valves, were parts of a curious instrument upon which every note of the entire gamut of pain might be produced? Patience, ye who linger in this shattered tenement, a house not made with hands awaits you. Up yonder no sorrow and sighing are met with; the chastising rod shall fall no longer when the faultiness is altogether removed. As the new body will be without pain, so will it be superior to weariness. The glorybody will not yield to faintness, nor fail through languor. Is it not implied that the spiritual body does not need to sleep, when we read that they serve God day and night in his temple? In a word, the bodies of the saints, like the body of Christ, will be perfect; there shall be nothing lacking and nothing faulty. If saints die in the feebleness of age they shall not rise thus; or if they have lost a sense or a limb or are halt or maimed, they shall not be so in heaven, for as to body and soul "they are without fault before the throne of God." "We shall be like him," is true of all the saints, and hence none will be otherwise than fair, and beautiful, and perfect. The righteous shall be like Christ, of whom it is still true that not a bone of him shall be broken, so not a part of our body after its change shall be bruised, battered, or otherwise than perfect.

Put all together, brethren, and what a stretch it is from this vile body to the glorious body which shall be! yet when Christ comes this miracle of miracles shall be wrought in the twinkling of an eye. Heap up epithets descriptive of the vileness of this body, think of it in all its weakness, infirmity, sin, and liability to death; then admire our Lord's body in all its holiness, happiness, purity, perfection, and immortality; and know assuredly that, at Christ's coming, this change shall take place upon every one of the elect of God. All believers shall undergo this marvellous transformation in a moment. Behold and wonder! Imagine that the change should occur to you now. What a display of power! My imagination is not able to give you a picture of the transformation; but those who will be alive and remain at the coming of the Son of God will undergo it, and so enter glory without death. "For this corruptible must put on incorruption, and this mortal must put on immortality," and therefore the bodies of living believers shall in the twinkling of an eye pass from the one state into the other; they shall be transformed from the vile to the glorious, from the state of humiliation into the state of glory, by the power of the coming Savior.

The miracle is amazing, if you view it as occurring to those who shall be alive when Christ comes. Reflect, however, that a very large number of the saints when the Lord shall appear a second time will already be in their graves. Some of these will have been buried long enough to have become corrupt. If you could remove the mould and break open the coffin-lid, what would you find but foulness and putrefaction? But those mouldering relics are the body of the saint's humiliation, and that very body is to be transformed into the likeness of Christ's glorious body. Admire the miracle as you survey the mighty change! Look down into the loathsome tomb, and, if you can endure it, gaze upon the putrid mass; this, even this, is to be transformed into Christ's likeness. What a work is this! And what a Savior is he who shall achieve it! Go a little further. Many of those whom Christ will thus raise will have been buried so long that all trace of them will have disappeared; they will have melted back into the common dust of earth, so that if their bones were searched for not a vestige of them could be found, nor could the keenest searcher after human remains detect a single particle. They have slept in quiet through long ages in their lonely graves, till they have become absorbed into the soil as part and parcel of mother earth. No, there is not a bone, nor a piece of a bone left; their bodies are as much one with earth as the drop of rain which fell upon the wave is one with the sea: yet shall they be raised. The trumpet call shall fetch them back from the dust with which they have mingled, and dust to dust, bone to bone, the anatomy shall be rebuilded and then refashioned. Does your wonder grow? does not your faith accept with joy the marvel, and yet feel it to be a marvel none the less?

Son of man, I will lead thee into an inner chamber more full of wonder yet. There are many thousands of God's people to whom a quiet slumber in the grave was denied; they were cut off by martyrdom, were sawn asunder, or cast to the dogs. Tens of thousands of the precious bodies of the saints have perished by fire, their limbs have been blown in clouds of smoke to the four winds of heaven, and even the handful of ashes which remained at the foot of the stake their relentless persecutors have thrown into rivers to be carried to the ocean, and divided to every shore. Some of the children of the resurrection were devoured by wild beasts in the Roman ampitheatres or left a prey to kites and ravens on the gibbet. In all sorts of ways have the saints' bodies been hacked and hewn, and, as a consequence, the particles of those bodies have no doubt been absorbed into various vegetable growths, and having been eaten by animals have mingled with the flesh of beasts; but what of that? "What of that?" say you, how can these bodies be refashioned? By what possibility can the selfsame bodies be raised again? I answer it needs a miracle to make any of these dry bones live, and a miracle being granted, impossibility vanishes. He who formed each atom from nothing can gather each particle again from confusion. The omniscient Lord of providence tracks each molecule of matter, and knows its position and history as a shepherd knows his sheep; and if it be needful to constitute the identity of the body, to regather every atom, he can do it. It may not, however, be needful at all, and I do not assert that it will be, for there may be a true identity without sameness of material; even as this my body is the same as that in which I lived twenty years ago, and yet in all probability there is not a grain of the same matter in it. God is able then to cause that the same body which on earth we wear in our humiliation, which we call a vile body, shall be fashioned like unto Christ's body. No difficulties, however stern, that can be suggested from science or physical law, shall for a single instant stand in the way of the accomplishment of this transformation by Christ the King. What marvels rise before me! indeed, it needs faith, and we thank God we have it. The resurrection of Christ has for ever settled in our minds, beyond all controversy, the resurrection of all who are in him; "For if we believe that Jesus died and rose again, even so them also which sleep in Jesus will God bring with him." Still it is a marvel of marvels, a miracle which needs the fullness of the deity. Of whom but God, very God of very God, could it be said that he shall change our bodies, and make them like unto his glorious body?

I know how feebly I have spoken upon this sublime subject, but I am not altogether regretful of that, for I do not wish to fix your thoughts on my words for a single moment; I only desire your minds to grasp and grapple with the great thought of the power of Christ, by which he shall raise and change the bodies of the saints.

II. We will now pass on. Here is the point we aim at. Consider, in the second place, that THIS POWER WHICH IS TO RAISE THE DEAD IS RESIDENT IN CHRIST AT THIS MOMENT.

So saith the text, "according to the working whereby he is able to subdue all things unto himself." It is not some new power which Christ will take to himself in the latter days and then for the first time display, but the power which will arouse the dead is the same power which is in him at this moment, which is going forth from him at this instant in the midst of his church and among the sons of men. I call your attention to this, and invite you to follow the track of the text.

First notice that all the power by which the last transformation will be wrought is ascribed to our Lord Jesus Christ now as the Savior. "We look for the Savior, the Lord Jesus." When Christ raises the dead it will be as a Savior, and it is precisely in that capacity that we need the exercise of his power at this moment. Fix this, my brethren, in your hearts; we are seeking the salvation of men, and we are not seeking a hopeless thing, for Jesus Christ is able as a Savior, to subdue all things, to himself; so the text expressly tells us. It doth not merely say that as a raiser of the dead he is able to subdue all things, but as the Savior, the Lord Jesus Christ. His titles are expressly given, he is set forth to us as the Lord, the Savior, the Anointed, and in that capacity is said to be able to subdue all things to himself. Happy tidings for us! My brethren, how large may our prayers be for the conversion of the sons of men, how great our expectations, how confident our efforts! Nothing is too hard for our Lord Jesus Christ; nothing in the way of saving work is beyond his power. If as a Savior he wakes the dead in the years to come, he can quicken the spiritually dead even now. These crowds of dead souls around us in this area and in these galleries, he can awaken by his quickening voice and living Spirit. The resurrection is to be according to the working of his mighty power, and that same energy is in operation now. In its fullness the power dwells in him, let us stir him up, let us cry unto him mightily, and give him no rest till he put forth that selfsame power now. Think not, my brethren, that this would be extraordinary and unusual. Your own conversion, if you have truly been raised from your spiritual death, was by the same power that we desire to see exerted upon others. Your own regeneration was indeed as remarkable an instance of divine power as the resurrection itself shall be. Ay, and I venture to say it, your spiritual life this very day or any day you choose to mention, is in itself a display of the same working which shall transform this vile body into its glorious condition. The power of the resurrection is being put forth to-day, it is pulsing through the quickened portion of this audience, it is heaving with life each bosom that beats with love to God, it is preserving the life-courses in the souls of all the spiritual, so that they go not back to their former death in sin. The power which will work the resurrection will be wonderful, but it will be no new thing. It is everywhere to be beheld in operation in the church of God at this very moment by those who have eyes to see it; and herein I join with the apostle in his prayer "that the God of our Lord Jesus Christ, the Father of glory, may give unto you the spirit of wisdom and revelation in the knowledge of him: the eyes of your understanding being enlightened; that ye may know what is the hope of his calling, and what the riches of the glory of his inheritance in the saints, and what is the exceeding greatness of his power to us-ward who believe, according to the working of his mighty power, which he wrought in Christ, when he raised him from the dead, and set him at his own right hand in the heavenly places' far above all principality, and power, and might, and dominion, and every name that is named, not only in this world, but also in that which is to come: and hath put all things under his feet, and gave him to be the head over all things to the church, which is his body, the fullness of him that filleth all in all."

Note next that the terms of our text imply that opposition may be expected to this power, but that all resistance will be overcome. That word "subdue" supposes a force to be conquered and brought into subjection. "He is able even to subdue all things unto himself." Herein is a great wonder! There will be no opposition to the resurrection. The trumpet sound shall bring the dead from their graves, and no particle shall disobey the summons; but to spiritual resurrection there is resistance--resistance which only omnipotence can vanquish. In the conversion of sinners natural depravity is an opposing force; for men are set upon their sins, and love not the things of God, neither will they hearken to the voice of mercy. My brethren, to remove all our fears concerning our Lord's ability to save, the word is here used, "He is able," not only to raise all things from the dead, but "to subdue all things to himself." Here again I would bid you take the encouragement the text presents you. If there be opposition to the gospel, he is able to subdue it. If in one man there is a prejudice, if in another man the heart is darkened with error, if one man hates the very name of Jesus, if another is so wedded to his sins that he cannot part from them, if opposition has assumed in some a very determined character, does not the text meet every case? "He is able to subdue all things," to conquer them, to break down the barriers that interpose to prevent the display of his power, and to make I hose very barriers the means of setting forth that power the more gloriously. "He is able even to subdue all things." O take this to the mercy-seat, you who will be seeking the souls of men this month! Take it to him and plead this word of the Holy Spirit in simple, childlike faith. When there is a difficulty you cannot overcome, take it to him, for he is "able to subdue."

Note next, that the language of our text includes all supposable cases. He is able to "subdue all things unto himself," not here and there one, but "all things." Brethren, there is no man in this world so fallen, debased, depraved, and wilfully wicked, that Jesus cannot save him--not even among those who live beyond the reach of ordinary ministry. He can bring the heathen to the gospel, or the gospel to them. The wheels of providence can be so arranged that salvation shall be brought to the outcasts; even war, famine, and plague, may become messengers for Christ, for he, too, rides upon the wings of the wind. There lived some few years ago in Perugia, in Italy, a man of the loosest morale and the worst conceivable disposition. He had given up all religion, he loathed God, and had arrived at such a desperate state of mind that he had conceived an affection for the devil, and endeavored to worship the evil one. Imagining Satan to be the image and embodiment of all rebellion, free-thinking, and lawlessness, he deified him in his own mind, and desired nothing better than to be a devil himself. On one occasion, when a Protestant missionary had been in Perugia preaching, a priest happened to say in this man's hearing, that there were Protestants in Perugia, the city was being defiled by heretics. "And who do you think Protestants are?" said he. "They are men who have renounced Christ and worship the devil." A gross and outrageous lie was this, but it answered far other ends than its author meant. The man hearing this, thought, "Oh, then, I will go and meet with them, for I am much of their mind;" and away he went to the Protestant meeting, in the hope of finding an assembly who propagated lawlessness and worshipped the devil. He there heard the gospel, and was saved. Behold in this and in ten thousand cases equally remarkable, the ability of our Lord to subdue all things unto himself. How can any man whom God ordains to save escape from that eternal love which is as omnipresent as the deity itself? "He is able to subdue all things to himself." If his sword cannot reach the far off ones his arrows can, and even at this hour they are sharp in his enemy's hearts. No boastful Goliath can stand before our David; though the weapon which he uses to-day be but a stone from the brook, yet shall the Philistine be subdued. If there should be in this place a Deist, an Atheist, a Romanist, or even a lover of the devil, if he be but a man, mercy yet can come to him. Jesus Christ is able to subdue him unto himself. None have gone too far, and none are too hardened. While the Christ lives in heaven we need never despair of any that are still in this mortal life--"He is able to subdue all things unto himself."

You will observe, in the text that nothing is said concerning the unfitness of the means. My fears often are lest souls should not be saved by our instrumentality because of faultiness in us; we fear lest we should not be prayerful enough or energetic or earnest enough; or that it should be said, "He could not do many mighty works there because of their unbelief." But the text seems to obliterate man altogether--"He is able to subdue all things unto himself"--that is to say, Jesus does it, Jesus can do it, will do it all. By the feeblest means he can work mightily, can take hold of us, unfit as we are for service, and make us fit, can grasp us in our folly and teach us wisdom, take us in our weakness and make us strong. My brethren, if we had to find resources for ourselves, and to rely upon ourselves, our enterprise might well be renounced, but since he is able, we will cast the burden of this work on him, and go to him in believing prayer, asking him to work mightily through us to the praise of his glory, for "He is able even to subdue all things unto himself."

Note that the ability is said in the text to be present with the Savior now. I have already pointed that out to you, but I refer to it again. The resurrection is a matter of the future, but the working which shall accomplish the resurrection is a matter of the present. "According to the working whereby he is able even to subdue all things unto himself," Jesus is as strong now as he ever will be, for he changes not. At this moment he is as able to convert souls as at the period of the brightest revival, or at Pentecost itself. There are no ebbs and flows with Christ's power. Omnipotence is in the hand that once was pierced, permanently abiding there. Oh, if we could but rouse it; if we could but bring the Captain of the host to the field again, to fight for his church, to work his servants! What marvels should we see, for he is able. We are not straitened in him, we are straitened in ourselves if straitened at all.

Once more, for your comfort be it remembered that the fact of there having been, as it were, a considerable time in which few have been converted to Christ, is no proof that his power is slackening; for it is well known to you that very few have as yet been raised from the dead, only here and there one like Lazarus and the young man at the gates of Nain, but you do not therefore doubt the Lord's power to raise the dead. Though he tarrieth we do not mistrust his power to fulfill his promise in due time. Now the power which is restrained, as it were, so that it does not work the resurrection yet, is the same which may hare been restrained in the Christian church for awhile, but which will be as surely put forth ere long in conversion as it will be in the end of time to accomplish the resurrection. Let us cry unto our Lord, for he has but to will it and thousands of sinners will be saved; let us lift up our hearts to him who has but to speak the word and whole nations shall be born unto him. The resurrection will not be a work occupying centuries, it will be accomplished at once; and so it may be in this house of prayer, and throughout London, and throughout the world, Christ will do a great and speedy work to the amazement of all beholders. He will send forth the rod of his strength out of Zion, and rule in the midst of his enemies. He will unmask his batteries, he will spring his mines, he will advance his outworks, he will subdue the city of his adversaries, and ride victoriously through the Bozrah of his foes. Who shall stay his hand? Who shall say unto him, "What doest thou?"

I wish we had time to work out the parallel which our text suggests, between the resurrection and the subduing of all things. The resurrection will be worked by the divine power, and the subduing of sinners is a precisely similar instance of salvation. All men are dead in sin, but he can raise them. Many of them are corrupt with vice, but he can transform them. Some of them are, as it were, lost to all hope, like the dead body scattered to the winds, desperate cases for whom even pity seems to waste her sighs; but he who raises the dead of all sorts, with a word can raise sinners of all sorts by the selfsame power. And as the dead when raised are made like to Christ, so the wicked when converted are made like to Jesus too. Brilliant examples of virtue shall be found in those who were terrible instances of vice; the most depraved and dissolute shall become the most devout and earnest. From the vile body to the glory-body, what a leap, and from the sinner damnable in lust to the saint bright with the radiance of sanctity, what a space! The leap seems very far, but omnipotence can bridge the chasm. The Savior, the Lord Jesus Christ is able to do it; he is able to do it in ten thousand thousand cases, able to do it at this very moment. My anxious desire is to engrave this one thought upon your hearts, my brethren and sisters, yea, to write it on the palms of those hands with which you are about to serve the Lord, learn it and forget it not--almighty power lies with Jesus to achieve the purpose upon which our heart is set, namely, the conversion of many unto himself.

III. I said I would ask you to consider, in the third place, THE WORK WHICH WE DESIRE TO SEE ACCOMPLISHED. I will not detain you however, with that consideration farther than this.

Brethren, we long to see the Savior subduing souls unto himself. Not to our way of thinking, not to our church, not to the honor of our powers of persuasion, but "unto himself." "He is able even to subdue all things unto himself." O sinner, how I wish thou wert subdued to Jesus, to kiss those

dear feet that were nailed for thee, to love in life him who loved thee to the death. Ah! soul, it were a blessed subjection for thee. Never subject of earthly monarch so happy in his king as thou wouldst be. God is our witness, we who preach the gospel, we do not want to subdue you to ourselves, as though we would rule you and be lords over your spirits. It is to Jesus, to Jesus only that we would have you subdued. O that you desired this subjection, it would be liberty, and peace, and joy to you!

Notice that this subjection is eminently to be desired, since it consists in transformation. Catch the thought of the text. He transforms the vile body into his glorious body, and this is a part of the subjection of all things unto himself. But do you call that subjection? Is it not a subjection to be longed after with an insatiable desire, to be so subdued to Christ that I, a poor, vile sinner, may become like him, holy, harmless, undefiled? This is the subjection that we wish for you, O unconverted ones. We trust we have felt it ourselves, we pray you may feel it too. He is able to give it to you. Ask it of him at once. Now breathe the prayer, now believe that the Savior can work the transformation even in you, in you at this very moment. And, O my brethren in the faith, have faith for sinners now. While they are pleading plead for them that this subjection which is an uplifting, this conquering which is a liberating, may be accomplished in them.

For, remember again, that to be subjected to Christ is, according to our text, to be fitted for heaven. He will change our vile body and make it like the body of his glory. The body of the glory is a body fitted for glory, a body which participates in glory. The Lord Jesus can make you, sinner, though now fitted for hell, fitted for heaven, fitted for glory, and breathe into you now an anticipation of that glory, in the joy and peace of mind which his pardon will bring to you. It must be a very sad thing to be a soldier under any circumstances; to have to cut and hack and kill and subdue, even in a righteous cause, is cruel work; but to be a soldier of King Jesus is an honor and a joy. The service of Jesus is a grand service. Brethren, we have been earnestly seeking to capture some hearts that are here present, to capture them for Jesus. It has been a long and weary siege up till this hour. We have summoned them to surrender, and opened fire upon them with the gospel, but as yet in vain. I have striven to throw a few live shells into the very heart of their city, in the form of warning and threatening and exhortation. I know there have been explosions in the hearts of some of you, which have done your sins some damage, killed some of the little ones that would have grown up to greater iniquity. You have been carefully blockaded by providence and grace. Your hearts have found no provision for joy in sin, no helps to peace in unrighteousness. How I wish I could starve you out until you would yield to my Lord, the crown Prince, who again to-day demands that you yield to him. It is dreadful to compel a city to open its gates unwillingly to let an enemy come in; for however gentle be the enemy his face is an unwelcome sight to the vanquished. But oh! how I wish I could burst open the gates of a sinner's heart to-day, for the Prince Emmanuel to come in. He who is at your gates is not an alien monarch, he is your rightful prince, he is your friend and lover. It will not be a strange face that you will see, when Jesus comes to reign in you. When the King in his beauty wins your soul, you will think yourselves a thousand fools that you did not receive him before. Instead of fearing that he will ransack your soul, you will open all its doors and invite him to search each room. You will cry, "Take all, thou blessed monarch, it shall be most mine when it is thine. Take all, and reign and rule." I propound terms of capitulation to you, O sinner. They are but these: yield up yourself to Christ, give up your works and ways, both good and bad, and trust in him to save you, and be his servant henceforth and for ever. While I thus invite you, I trust he will speak through me to you and win you to himself. I shall not plead in vain, the word shall not fall to the ground. I fall back upon the delightful consolation of our text, "He is able to subdue all things unto himself." May he prove his power this morning. Amen and Amen.

PORTIONS OF SCRIPTURE READ BEFORE SERMON--Philippians 3.

Compassion for Souls

A Sermon (No. 974)
Delivered on Lord's-day Morning, February 5th, 1871 by
C. H. SPURGEON,
At the Metropolitan Tabernacle, Newington

"She went, and sat her down over against him a good way off, as it were a bowshot; for she said, Let me not see the death of the child. And she sat over against him, and lift up her voice, and wept." - Genesis 21:16.

BRIEFLY LET US REHEARSE the circumstances. The child Isaac was, according to God's word, to be the heir of Abraham. Ishmael, the elder son of Abraham, by the bondwoman Hagar, resided at home with his father till he was about eighteen years of age; but when he began to mock and scoff at the younger child whom God had ordained to be the heir, it became needful that he and his mother should be sent away from Abraham's encampment. It might have seemed unkind and heartless to have sent them forth, but God having arranged to provide for them sent a divine command which at once rendered their expulsion necessary, and certified its success. We may rest assured that whatever God commands he will be quite certain to justify. He knew it would be no cruelty to Hagar or Ishmael to be driven into independence, and he gave a promise which secured them everything which they desired. "Also of the son of the bondwoman will I make a great nation;" and again, "I have blessed him, and will make him fruitful, and will multiply him exceedingly; twelve princes shall he beget, and I will make him a great nation." Had they both been able to go forth from Abraham's tent in faith they might have trodden the desert with a joyous footstep, fully assured that he who bade them go, and he who promised that he would bless them, would be certain to provide all things needful for them. Early in the morning they were sent forth on their journey, with as much provision as they could carry, and probably they intended to make their way to Egypt, from which Hagar had come. They may have lost their way; at any rate, they are spoken of as wandering. Their store of food became exhausted, the water in the skin bottle was all spent; both of them felt the fatigue of the wilderness, and the heat of the pitiless sand; they were both faint and weary, and the younger utterly failed. As long as the mother could sustain the tottering, fainting footsteps of her boy, she did so; when she could do so no longer, he swooned with weakness, and she laid him down beneath the slight shade of the desert tamarisk, that he might be as far as possible screened from the excessive heat of the sun. Looking into his face and seeing the pallor of coming death gathering upon it, knowing her inability to do anything whatever to revive him, or even to preserve his life, she could not bear to sit and gaze upon his face, but withdrew just far enough to be able still to watch with all a mother's care. She sat down in the brokenness of her spirit, her tears gushed forth in torrents, and heartrending cries of agony startled the rocks around. It was needful that the high spirit of the mother and her son should be broken down before they received prosperity: the mother had been on a former occasion graciously humbled by being placed in much the same condition, but she had probably relapsed into a haughty spirit, and had encouraged her boy in his insolence to Sarah's son, and therefore she must be chastened yet again; and it was equally needful that the high-spirited lad should for little bear the yoke in his youth, and that he who would grow up to be the wild man, the father of the unconquerable Arab, should feel the power of God ere he received the fulfillment of the promise given to him in answer to Abraham's prayer. If I read the text aright while the mother was thus weeping, the child, almost lost to all around, was nevertheless conscious enough of his own helpless condition, and sufficiently mindful of his father's God to cry in his soul to heaven for help; and the Lord heard not so much the mother's weeping (for the feebleness of her faith, which ought to have been stronger in memory of a former deliverance, hindered her prayer), but the silent, unuttered prayers of the fainting lad went up into the ears of Elohim, and the angel of Elohim appeared, and pointed to the well. The child received the needed draught of water, was soon restored, and in him and his posterity the promise of God received and continues to receive a large fulfillment. I am not about to speak upon that narrative except as it serves me with an illustration for the subject which I would now press upon you.

Behold the compassion of a mother for her child expiring with thirst, and remember that such a compassion ought all Christians to feel towards souls that are perishing for lack of Christ, perishing eternally, perishing without hope of salvation. If the mother lifted up her voice arid wept, so also should we; and if the contemplation of her dying, child was all too painful for her, so may the contemplation of the wrath to come, which is to pass upon every soul that dies impenitent, become too painful for us, but yet it the same time it should stimulate us to earnest prayer and ardent effort for the salvation of our fellow men.

I shall speak, this morning, upon compassion for souls, the reasons which justify it, the sight it dreads, the temptation it must fight against, the paths it should pursue, the encouragement it may receive.

I. COMPASSION FOR SOULS--THE REASONS WHICH JUSTIFY IT, NAY, COMPEL IT.

It scarce needs that I do more than rehearse in bare outline the reasons why we should tenderly compassionate the perishing sons of men. For first, observe, the dreadful nature of the calamity which will overwhelm them. Calamities occurring to our fellow men naturally awaken in us a feeling of commiseration; but what calamity under heaven can be equal to the ruin of a soul? What misery can be equal to that of a man cast away from God, and subject to his wrath world without end! To-day your hearts are moved as you hear the harrowing details of war. They have been dreadful indeed; houses burnt, happy families driven as vagabonds upon the face of the earth, domestic circles and quiet households broken up, men wounded, mangled, massacred by thousands, and starved, I was about to say, by millions; but the miseries of war, if they were confined to this world alone, were nothing compared with the enormous catastrophe of tens of thousands of spirits accursed by sin, and driven by justice into the place where their worm dieth not, and their fire is not quenched. The edge of the sword grows blunt at last, the flame of war dies out for want of fuel, but, lo! I see before me a sword which is never quiet, a fire unquenchable. Alas! that the souls of men should fall beneath the infinite ire of justice. All your hearts have been moved of late with the thought of famine, famine in a great city. The dogs of war, and this the fiercest mastiff of them all, have laid hold upon the fair throat of the beautiful city which thought to sit as a lady for ever and see no sorrow; you are hastening with your gifts, if possible to remove her urgent want and to avert her starvation; but what is a famine of bread compared with that famine of the soul which our Lord describes when he represents it as pleading in vain for a drop of water to cool its tongue tormented in the flame? To be without bread for the body is terrible, but to be without the bread of life eternal, none of us can tell the weight of horror which lies there! When Robert Hall in one of the grand flights of his eloquence pictured the funeral of a lost soul, he made the sun to veil his light, and the moon her brightness; he covered the ocean with mourning and the heavens with sackcloth, and declared that if the whole fabric of nature could become animated and vocal, it would not be possible for her to utter a groan too deep, or a cry too piercing to express the magnitude and extent of the catastrophe. Time is not long enough for the sore lamentation which should attend the obsequies of a lost soul. Eternity must be charged with that boundless woe, and must utter it in weeping and wailing and gnashing of teeth. Not the tongues of prophets, nor of seraphs, could se forth all the sorrow of what it is to be condemned from the mouth of mercy, damned by the Savior who died to save, pronounced accursed by rejected love. The evil is so immense that imagination finds no place, and understanding utterly fails. Brethren, if our bowels do not yearn for men who are daily hastening towards destruction, are we men at all?

I could abundantly justify compassion for perishing men, even on the ground of natural feelings. A mother who did not, like Hagar, weep for her dying child--call her not "mother," call her "monster." A man who passes through the scenes of misery which even this city presents in its more squalid quarters, and yet is never disturbed by them, I venture to say he is unworthy of the name of man. Even the common sorrows of our race may well suffuse our eyes with tears, but the eternal sorrow, the infinite lake of misery--he who grieves not for this, write him down a demon, though he wear the image and semblance of a man. Do not think the less of this argument because I base it upon feelings common to all of woman born, for remember that grace does not destroy our manhood when it elevates it to a higher condition.

In this instance what nature suggests grace enforces. The more we become what we shall be, the more will compassion rule our hearts. The Lord Jesus Christ, who is the pattern and mirror of perfect manhood, what said he concerning the sins and the woes of Jerusalem? He knew Jerusalem must perish; did he bury his pity beneath the fact of the divine decree, and steel his heart by the thought of the sovereignty or the justice that would be resplendent in the city's destruction? Nay, not he, but with eyes gushing like founts, he cried, "O Jerusalem, Jerusalem, how often would I have gathered thy children together as a teen gathereth her chickens under her wings! and ye would not." If you would be like Jesus, you must be tender and very pitiful. Ye would be as unlike him as possible if we could sit down in grim content, and, with a Stoic's philosophy, turn all the flesh within you into stone. If it be natural, then, and above all, if it be natural to the higher gracegiven nature, I beseech you, let your hearts be moved with pity, do not endure to see the spiritual death of mankind. Be in agony as often as you contemplate the ruin of any soul of the seed of Adam.

Brethren, the whole ruin and current, and tenour and spirit of the gospel influences us to compassion. Ye are debtors, for what were ye if compassion had not come to your rescue? Divine compassion, all undeserved and free, has redeemed you from your vain conversation. Surely those who receive mercy should show mercy; those who owe all they have to the pity of God, should not be pitiless to their brethren. The Savior never for a moment tolerates the self-righteous isolation which would make you despise the prodigal, and cavil at his restoration, much less the Cainite spirit which cries, "Am I my brother's keeper?" No doctrine is rightly received by you if it freezes the genial current of your Christian compassion. You may know the truth of the doctrine, but you do not know the doctrine in truth if it makes you gaze on the wrath to come without emotions of pity for immortal souls. You shall find everywhere throughout the gospel that it rings of brotherly love, tender mercy, and weeping pity. If you have indeed received it in its power, the love of Christ will melt your spirit to compassion for those who are despising Christ, and sealing their own destruction.

Let me beseech you to believe that it is needful as well as justifiable that you should feel compassion for the sons of men. You all desire to glorify Christ by becoming soul-winners--I hope you do--and be it remembered that, other things being equal, he is the fittest in God's hand to win souls who pities souls most. I believe he preaches best who loves best, and in the Sunday-school and in private life each soul-seeker shall have the blessing very much in proportion to his yearning for it. Paul becomes a saviour of many because his heart's desire and prayer to God is that they may be saved. If you can live without souls being converted, you shall live without their being converted; but if your soul breaketh for the longing that it hath towards Christ's glory and the conversion of the ungodly, if like her of old you say, "Give me children, or I die," your insatiable hunger shall be satisfied, the craving of your spirit shall be gratified. Oh! I would to God there should come upon us a divine hunger which cannot stay itself except men yield themselves to Jesus; an intense, earnest, longing, panting desire that men should submit themselves to the gospel of Jesus. This will teach you better than the best college training how to deal with human hearts. This will give the stammering tongue the ready word; the hot heart shall burn the cords which held fast the tongue. You shall become wise to win souls, even though you never exhibit the brilliance of eloquence or the force of logic. Men shall wonder at your power--the secret shall be hidden from them, the fact being that the Holy Ghost shall overshadow you, and your heart shall teach you wisdom, God teaching your heart. Deep feeling on your part for others shall make others feel for themselves, and God shall bless you, and that right early.

But I stand not here any longer to justify what I would far rather commend and personally feel.

"Did Christ o'er sinners weep,
And shall our cheeks be dry?
Let floods of consecrated grief
Stream forth from every eye,"

Is God all love, and shall God's children be hard and cold? Shall heaven compassionate and shall not earth that has received hearer's mercy send back the echo of compassion? O God, make us imitators of thee in thy pity towards erring men.

II. We shall pass on to notice THE SIGHT WHICH TRUE COMPASSION DREADS.

Like Hagar, the compassionate spirit says, "Let me not see the death of the child," or as some have read it, "How can I see the death of the child?" To contemplate a soul passing away without hope is too terrible a task! I do not wonder that ingenious persons have invented theories which aim at mitigating the terrors of the world to come to the impenitent. It is natural they should do so, for the facts are so alarming as they are truthfully given us in God's word, that if we desire to preach comfortable doctrine and such as will quiet the consciences of idle professors, we must dilute the awful truth. The revelation of God concerning the doom of the wicked is so overwhelming as to make it penal, nay, I was about to say damnable, to be indifferent and careless in the work of evangelising the world. I do not wonder that this error in doctrine springs up just now when abounding callousness of heart needs an excuse for itself. What better pillow for idle heads than the doctrine that the finally impenitent become extinct? The logical reasoning of the sinner is, "Let us eat and drink, for to-morrow we die," and the professing Christian is not slow to feel an ease of heart from pressing responsibilities when he accepts so consolatory an opinion. Forbear this sleeping draught, I pray you, for in very deed the sharp stimulant of the truth itself is abundantly needful; even when thus bestirred to duty we are sluggish enough, and need not that these sweet but sleep-producing theories should operate upon us.

For a moment, I beseech you, contemplate that which causes horror to every tender heart; behold, I pray you, a soul lost, lost beyond all hope of restitution. Heaven's gates have shut upon the sanctified, and the myriads of the redeemed are there, but that soul is not among them, for it passed out of this world without having washed its robes in Jesus' blood. For it there are no harps of gold, no thrones of glory, no exultation with Christ; from all the bliss of heaven it is for ever excluded. This punishment of loss were a heavy enough theme for contemplation. The old divines used to speak much of the poena damni, or the punishment of loss; there were enough in that phase of the future to make us mourn bitterly, as David did for Absalom. My child shut out of heaven! My husband absent from the seats of the blessed! My sister, my brother not in glory! When the Lord counts up his chosen, my dear companion outside the gates of pearl, outside the jewelled battlements of the New Jerusalem! O God, tis a heartbreaking sorrow to think of this. But then comes the punishment added to the loss. What saith the Savior? "Where their worm dieth not, and the fire is not quenched." "These shall go away into everlasting punishment." And yet again, "And shall cut him asunder, and appoint him his portion with the hypocrites." And yet again, "Into outer darkness: there shall be weeping and gnashing of teeth." "Metaphors," say you. It is true, but not meaningless metaphors. There is a meaning in each expression--and rest assured though man's metaphors sometimes exaggerate, God's never do; his symbols everywhere are true; never is there an exaggeration in the language of inspiration. Extravagances of utterance! He uses them not; his figures are substantial truth. Terrible as the scriptural emblems of punishment are, they set forth matters of undoubted fact, which if a man could look upon this day, the sight might blanch his hair, and quench his eye. If we could hear the wailings of the pit for a moment, we should earnestly entreat that we might never hear them again. We have to thank God that we are not allowed to hear the dolorous cries of the lost, for if we did they would make our life bitter as gall. I cast a veil over that which I cannot paint; like Hagar I cannot bear to look at the dread reality which it breaks my heart to think upon.

How all this gathers intensity, when it comes to be our own child, our own friend! Hagar might perhaps have looked upon a dying child, but not upon her dying Ishmael. Can you bear now to think for a moment of the perdition of your own flesh and blood? Does not your spirit flinch and draw back with horror instinctively at the idea of one of your own family being lost? Yet, as a matter of stern fact, you know that some of them will be lost if they die as they are now living? At God's right hand they cannot stand unless they be made new creatures in Christ Jesus. You know that, do not try to forget it.

It will greatly add to your feeling of sorrow if you are forced to feel that the ruin of your child or of any other person may have been partly caused by your example. It must be a dreadful thing for a father to feel, "My boy learned to drink from me; my child heard the first blasphemous word from his father's lips." Or mother, if your dying daughter should say, "I was led into temptation by my mother's example," what a grief will this be! O parents, converted late in life, you cannot undo the evil which you have already done; God has forgiven you, but the mischief wrought in your children's characters is indelible, unless the grace of God step in. I want you to seek after that grace with great earnestness. As you must confess that you have helped to train your child as a servant of sin, will you not long to see your evil work undone before it ends in your child's eternal destruction?

If we shall have to feel that the ruin of any of our friends or relations is partly occasioned by our own personal neglect of religion, it will cause us bitter pangs. If our example has been excellent and admirable in all respects, but that we have forgotten the Lord and his Christ, it will have been none the less injurious to men's souls. I sometimes think that these examples are the very worst in their effect. Immoral, ungodly men can hardly work the same measure of mischief as moral but unchristian men. I will tell you why. The ungodly quote the orderly life of the moralist as an argument that there can be goodness apart from Christianity, and this often helps men to rest satisfied apart from Christ Jesus. And what, O moralist, though you never taught your child a vice, if you taught it unbelief, and if your example helped to harm its heart in bold rebellion against God! Ah! then, how will you blame yourself when you are converted, or curse yourself if both you and your child perish.

Dear friends, it makes a terrible addition to the sight of a soul being lost if we have to feel we were under responsibility concerning it, and have been in any measure unfaithful. I cannot bear the idea of any of my congregation perishing, for in addition to the compassion I hope I feel, I am influenced by a further additional consideration, for I am set as a watchman to your souls. When any die, I ask myself, "Was I faithful? Did I speak all the truth? And did I speak it from my very soul every time I preached?" John Walsh, the famous Scotch preacher, was often out of bed in the coldest night, by the hour together, in supplication; and when some one wondered that he spent so many hours upon his knees, he said, "Ah, man, I have three thousand souls to give account of in the day of judgment, and I do not know but what it is going very ill with some of them." Alas! I have more than that to give account of, and well may I cry to God that I may not see you perish. O may it never be that you shall go from these pews to the lowest hell. You, too, my fellow Christian, have your own responsibilities, each one in your measure--your children, your school classes, your servants, ay, and your neighbors, for if you are not doing any good and do not assume any responsibility towards the regions in which you dwell, that responsibility rests upon you none the less. You cannot live in a district without being responsible to God for doing something towards the bettering of the people among whom you reside. Can you endure it then, that your neighbors should sink into hell? Do not your hearts long for their salvation?

Is it not an awful thing that a soul should perish with the gospel so near? If Ishmael had died, and the water had been within bow-shot, and yet unseen till too late, it had been a dreadful reflection for the mother. Would she not have torn her hair with double sorrow? And yet many of you are being lost with the gospel ringing in your ears; you are perishing while Christ is lifted up before you; you are dying in the camp through the serpent's bite, though the brazen serpent is yonder before your eyes, and with many tears we cry to you, "Look unto Jesus Christ, and live!" Ah, woe is me, woe is me, if you perish when salvation is brought so close home to you. Some of you are very near the kingdom of God; you are very anxious, very concerned, but you have not believed in Jesus; you have much that is good, but one thing you lack. Will you perish for lack of only one thing? A thousand pities will it be if you make shipwreck in the harbour's mouth and go to hell from the gates of heaven.

We must add to all this, the remembrance that it is not one soul which is lost, but tens of thousands are going down to the pit. Mr. Beecher said in one of his sermons, "If there were a great bell hung high in heaven which the angels swung every time a soul was lost, how constantly would its solemn toll be heard!" A soul lost! The thunder would not suffice to make a knell for a lost spirit. Each time the clock ticks a soul departs out of this world, perhaps oftener than that, and out of those who make the last journey how few mount to the skies; what multitudes descend to endless woe! O Christians, pull up the sluices of your souls, and let your hearts pour out themselves in rivers of compassion.

III. In the third place, I said I would speak upon COMPASSION FOR THE SOULS OF MEN--THE TEMPTATION IT MUST RESIST.

We must not fall into the temptation to imitate the example of Hagar too closely. She put the child under the shrubs and turned away her gaze from the all too mournful spectacle. She could not endure to look, but she sat where she could watch in despair. There is a temptation with each one of us to try to forget that souls are being lost. I can go home to my house along respectable streets, and naturally should choose that way, for then I need not see the poverty of the lowest quarters of the city, but am I right if I try to forget that there are Bethnal Greens and Kent Streets, and such like abodes of poverty? The close courts, the cellars, the crowded garrets, the lodging-houses--am I to forget that these exist? Surely the only way for a charitable mind to sleep comfortably in London is to forget how one half of the population lives; but is it our object to live comfortably? Are we such brute beasts that comfort is all we care for; like swine in their stye? Nay, brethren, let us recall to our memories the sins of our great city, its sorrows and griefs, and let us remember also the sins and sorrows of the wide, wide world, and the tens of thousands of our race who are passing constantly into eternity. Nay, look at them! Do not close those eyes! Does the horror of the vision make your eyeballs ache? Then look until your heart aches too, and your spirit breaks forth in vehement agony before the Lord. Look down into hell a moment; open wide the door; listen, and listen yet again. You say you cannot, it sickens your soul; let it be sickened, and in its swooning let it fall back into the arms of Christ the Savior, and breathe out a cry that he would hasten to save men from the wrath to come. Do not ignore, I pray you, what does exist. It is a matter of fact that in this congregation many are going down to hell, that in this city there are multitudes who are hastening as certainly to perdition as time is hastening to eternity. It is no dream, no fiction of a fevered brain that there is a hell. If you think so, then why dare you call yourselves Christians? Renounce your Bible, renounce your baptism, renounce your profession if one spark of honesty remains in you. Call not yourselves Christians when you deny the teaching of your Master. Since assuredly there is a dreadful hell, shut not your eyes to it, put not the souls of your fellows away among the shrubs, and sit not down in supineness. Come and look, come and look, I say, till your hearts break at the sight. Hear the cries of dying men whose consciences are awakened too late. Hear the groans of spirits who are feeling the sure consequences of sin, where sin's cure will never avail them. Let this stir you, my brethren, to action--to action immediate and intense. You tell me I preach dreadful things; ay, and they are wanted, they are wanted. Was there ever such a happy age as this? Were there ever such sleepy persons as ourselves? Take heed lest you take sad precedence of all others in the accusations of conscience, because knowing the gospel, and enjoying it, you nevertheless use so little exertion in spreading it abroad among the human race. Let us shun the temptation which

Hagar's example might suggest.

IV. I will now speak upon THE PATH WHICH TRUE COMPASSION WILL BE SURE TO FOLLOW; and what is that?

First of all, true pity does all it can. Before Hagar sat down and wept, she had done her utmost for her boy; she had given him the last drop from the bottle; she had supported his tottering footsteps, she had sought out the place under the shrubs where he might be a little sheltered she had laid him down gently with soothing words, and then, but not till then, she sat herself down. Have we done all that it is possible for us to do for the unconverted around us? There are preventible causes of men's ruin. Some causes you and I cannot touch, but there are some we ought at once to remove. For instance, it is certain that many perish through ignorance. It ought never to be that a soul should perish of ignorance within a mile of where a Christian lives. I would even allot a wider area in regions where the people dwell not so thickly. It should at least be the resolve of each Christian, "Within this district where I live, so far as my ability goes, everybody shall know the gospel by some means or other. If I cannot speak to each one will send something for him to read; it shall not be said that a man lost his way for ever because he had no Bible. The Holy Ghost alone can lead men into the truth, but it is our part to put the letter of the word before all men's eyes.

Prejudice, too, is another preventible cause of unbelief. Some will not hear the gospel, or listen to it, because of their notions of its sternness, or of the moroseness of its professors. Such a prejudice may effectually close their hearts; be it yours to remove it. Be kind to the ungodly; be loving, be tender, be affable, be generous to them, so that you may remove all unnecessary antipathy to the gospel of Jesus. Do them all the good you can for their bodies, that they may be the more likely to believe in your love towards their souls. Let it be said by each one here, "If a soul perishes, I, at least, will have done all in my power to reclaim it."

But what next does compassion do? Having done all it can, it sits down and weeps over its own feebleness. I have not the pathos wherewith to describe to you the mother sitting there and pouring out her tears, and lifting up her plaintive voice over her child. The voice of a broken heart cannot be described, it must be heard. But, ah! there is wonderful power with God in the strong crying and tears of his people. If you know how to weep before the Lord, he will yield to tears what he will not yield to anything besides. O ye saints, compassionate sinners; sigh and cry for them; be able to say, as Whitfield could to his congregation, "Sirs, if ye are lost, it is not for want of my weeping for you, for I pour out my soul day and night in petitions unto God that ye may live." When Hagar's compassion had wailed itself out, she looked unto God, and God heard her. Take care that your prayers be abundant and continuous for those who are dying without hope.

And then what else doth Hagar teach us? She stood there ready to do anything that was needful after the Lord had interposed. The angel opened her eyes; until then she was powerless, and sat and wept, and prayed, but when he pointed to the well, did she linger for a minute? Was she unprepared with the bottle wherewith to draw water? Did she delay to put it to her child's lips? Was she slack in the blessed task? Oh, no! with what alacrity did she spring to the well; with what speed did she fill the bottle; with what motherly joy did she hasten to her child, and gave him the saving draught! And so I want every member here to stand ready to mark the faintest indication of grace in any soul. Watch always for the beginning of their conversion, be ready with the bottle of promise to carry a little comfort to their parched lips; watch with a mother's earnestness, watch for the opportunity of doing good to souls; yearn over them, so that when God shall work you shall work with him instanter, and Jesus shall not be hindered because of your carelessness and want of faith. This is the path which the true Christian should pursue. He is earnest for souls, and therefore he lays himself out for them. If we did really know what souls are, and what it is for them to be cast away, those of us who have done very little or nothing would begin to work for Christ directly. It is said in old classic story, that a certain king of Lydia had a son who had been dumb from his birth, but when Lydia was captured, a soldier was about to kill the king, when the young man suddenly found a tongue, and cried out, "Soldier, would you kill the king?" He had never spoken a word before, but his astonishment and fear gave him speech. And methinks if ye had been dumb to that moment, if ye indeed saw your own children and neighbors going down into the pit, you would cry out, "Though I never spoke before I will speak now. Poor souls, believe in Christ, and ye shall be saved." You do not know how such an utterance as that, however simple, might be blessed. A very little child once found herself in company with an old man of eighty, a fine old man who loved little children, and who took the child upon his knee to fondle it. The little one turning round to him said, "Sir, I got a grandpa just like you, and my grandpa love Jesus Christ, does you?" He said, "I was eighty-four years of age and had lived always among Christian people, but nobody ever thought it worth his while to say as much as that to me." That little child was the instrument of the old man's conversion. So have I heard the story. He knew he had not loved the Savior, and he began to seek him, and in his old age he found salvation. If as much as that is possible to a child it is possible to you. O dear brother, if you love Jesus, burst the bonds of timidity, or it may be of supineness; snap all fetters, and from this day feel that you cannot bear to think of the ruin of a soul, and must seek its salvation if there be in earth or heaven ways and means by which you can bring a blessing to it.

V. But I must close, and the last point shall be THE ENCOURAGEMENT WITH TRUE COMPASSION FOR SOULS WILL ALWAYS RECEIVE.

First take the case in hand. The mother compassionated, God compassionated too. You pity, God pities. The motions of God's Spirit in the souls of his people are the footfalls of God's eternal purposes about to be fulfilled. It is always a hopeful sign for a man that another man prays for him. There is a difficulty in getting a man to hell whom a child of God is drawing towards heaven by his intercessions. Satan is often defeated in his temptations by the intercession of the saints. Have hope then that your personal sense of compassion for souls is an indication that such souls God will bless. Ishmael, whom Hagar pitied, was a lad about whom promises had been made large and broad; he could not die; she had forgotten that, but God had not. No thirst could possibly destroy him, for God had said he would make of him a great nation. Let us hope that those for whom you and I are praying and laboring are in God's eternal purpose secured from hell, because the blood of Christ has bought them, and they must be the Lord's. Our prayers are ensigns of the will of God. The Holy Ghost leads us to pray for those whom he intends effectually to call.

Moreover, those we pray for, we may not know it, but there may be in their souls at this time a stirring of divine life. Hagar did not know that her son was praying, but God did. The lad did not speak, but God heard his heart cry. Children are often very reticent to their parents. Often and often have I talked with young lads about their souls, who have told me that they could not talk to their fathers upon such matters. I know it was so with me. When I was under concern of soul the last persons I should have elected to speak to upon religion would have been my parents, not out of want of love to them, nor absence of love on their part; but so it was. A strange feeling of diffidence pervades a seeking soul, and drives it from its friends. Those whom you are praying for may be praying too, and you do not know it; but the time of love will come when their secret yearnings will be revealed to your earnest endeavors.

The lad was preserved after all, the well of waters was revealed, and the bottle put to his lips. It will be a great comfort to you to believe that God will hear importunate prayers. Your child will be saved, your husband will be brought in yet, good woman, only pray on. Your neighbor shall be brought to hear the truth and be converted, only be earnest about it.

I do not know how to preach, this morning; the tongue cannot readily speak when the heart feels too much. I pray that we may have a great revival of religion in our midst as a church; my spirit longs and pants for it. I see a great engine of enormous strength, and a well-fashioned machine: the machine cannot work of itself, it has no power in it, but if I could get the band to unite the machine with the engine, what might be done! Behold, I see the omnipotence of God, and the organisation of this church. O that I could get the band to bind the two together! The band is living faith. Do you possess it? Brethren, help me to pass it round the fly wheel, and oh, how God will work, and we will work through his power, and what glorious things shall be done for Christ! We must receive power from on high, and faith is the belt that shall convey that power to us. The divine strength shall be manifest through our weakness. Cease not to pray. More than you ever have done, intercede for a blessing, and the Lord will bless us: he will bless us, and all the ends of the earth shall fear him. Amen.

PORTIONS OF SCRIPTURE READ BEFORE SERMON--Romans 10.; and Genesis 21:1-21.

The Parable of the Wedding Feast

A Sermon (No. 975)
Delivered on Lord's-day Morning, February 12th, 1871 by
C. H. SPURGEON,
At the Metropolitan Tabernacle, Newington

"The kingdom of heaven is like unto a certain king, which made a marriage for his son, and sent forth his servants to call them that were bidden to the wedding: and they would not come. Again, he sent forth other servants, saying, Tell them which are bidden, Behold, I have prepared my dinner: my oxen and my fatlings are killed and all things are ready: come unto the marriage." - Matthew 22:2,3,4.

IF GOD GRANT ME STRENGTH I hope to go through this parable, but at this present we shall confine our thoughts to the opening scene of the royal festival. Before, however, we proceed further, it is most fitting that we give expression to our deep gratitude, that it has pleased the infinite mind to stoop to our narrow capacities, and instruct us by parable. How tenderly condescending is God to devise similitudes, that his children may learn the mysteries of the kingdom! If it be sometimes marvelled at among men that great minds are ever ready to stoop, what a far greater marvel that God himself should bow the heavens and come down to meet our ignorance and slowness of comprehension! When the learned professor has been instructing his class in the hall in recondite matters of deep philosophy, and then goes home and takes his child upon his knee, and tries to bring down great truth to the grasp of his child's mind, then you see the great love of the man's heart: and when the eternal God, before whom seraphim are but insects of an hour, condescends to instruct our childishness and make us wise unto salvation, we may well say, "herein is love." Just as we give our children pictures that we may win the attention, and may by pleasing means fix truth upon their memories, so the Lord with loving inventiveness has become the author of many a charming metaphor, type, and allegory, by which he may gain our interest, and through his Holy Spirit enlighten our minds. If he who thunders till the mountains tremble, yet deigns to speak with us in a still small voice, let us gladly sit in Mary's place at his gracious feet, and willingly learn of him. O that God would give to each one a teachable spirit, for this is the greatest step towards understanding the mind of God. He who is willing to learn, in a childlike spirit, is already in a considerable measure taught of God. May we all so study this instructive parable as to be quickened by it to all that is well-pleasing in the sight of God, for after all true learning in godliness may be judged of by its result; upon our lives. If we are holier we are wiser, practical obedience to the will of the Lord Jesus is the surest evidence of an understanding heart.

In order to understand the parable before us we must first direct our attention to the design of the "certain king" here spoken of. He had a grand object in view; he desired to do honor to his son upon the occasion of his marriage. We shall then notice the very generous method by which he proposed to accomplish his purpose; he made a dinner, and bade many: there were other modes of honoring his son, but the great king elected the mode which would best display his bounty. We shall then observe, with sad interest, the serious hindrance which arose to the carrying out of his generous design--those who were bidden would not come. There was nothing to hinder the magnificence of the festival in the riches of the prince--he lavished out his stores for the feast; but here was a hindrance strange and difficult to remove, they would not come. Then our thoughts will linger admiringly over the gracious rejoinder which the king made to the opposers of his design; he sent other servants to repeat the invitation, "Come ye to the marriage." If we shall drink deep into the meaning of these three verses, we shall have more than enough for one meditation.

I. A certain king of wide dominions and great power designed to give a magnificent banquet, with a GRAND OBJECT in view. The crown prince, his well beloved heir, was about to take to himself a fair bride, and therefore the royal father desired to celebrate the event with extraordinary honors. From earth, look up to heaven. The great object of God the Father is to glorify his Son. It is his will "that all men should honor the Son, even as they honor the Father." (John 5:23.) Jesus Christ, the Son of God, is glorious already in his divine person. He is ineffably blessed, and infinitely beyond needing honor. All the angels of God worship him, and his glory fills all heaven.

He has appeared on the stage of action as the Creator and as such his glory is perfect, "For by him were all things created, that are in heaven, and that are in earth, visible and invisible, whether they be thrones, or dominions, or principalities, or powers: all things were created by him, and for him." He said, "Light be," and it flamed forth. He bade the mountains lift their heads, and their summits pierced the clouds. He created the water-floods, he bade them seek their channels, and he appointed their bounds. Nothing is lacking to the glory of the Word of God, who was in the beginning with God, who spake and it was done, who commanded, and it stood forth. He is highly exalted also as the preserver, for he is before all things, and by him all things consist. He is that nail fastened in a sure place, upon which all things hang. The keys of heaven, and death, and hell, are fastened to his girdle, and the government shall be upon his shoulders, and his name shall be called Wonderful. He hath a name which is above every name, before which all things shall bow, in heaven, and earth, and under the earth. He is God over all. He is blessed for ever. To him that is, and was, and is to come, the universal song goeth up.

But there is another relation in which the Son of God has graciously been pleased to stand towards us. He has undertaken to be a Savior, in order that he might be a bridegroom. He had enough glory before, but in the greatness of his heart, he would magnify his compassion even above his power, and he therefore condescended to take into union with himself the nature of man, in order that he might redeem the beloved objects of his choice from the penalty due to their sins, and might enter into the nearest conceivable union with them. It is as Savior that the Father seeks to honor the Son, and the gospel feast is not for the honor of his person merely, but for the honor of his person in this new, yet anciently purposed relationship. It is for the honor of Jesus as entering into spiritual union with his church, that the gospel is prepared as a royal entertainment.

Brethren, when I said that here was a grand occasion, it certainly is so in God's esteem, and it should be so in ours; we should delight to glorify the Son of God. To all loyal subjects in any realm, the marriage of one of the royal family is a matter of great interest, and it is usual and fitting to give expression to congratulations and sympathies by suitable rejoicings. In the instance before us the occasion calls for special joy from all the subjects of the great king of kings. For the occasion in itself is a subject for great delight and thankfulness to us personally. The marriage is with whom? With angels? He took not up angels. It is a marriage with our own nature, "he took up the seed of Abraham." Shall we not rejoice when heaven's great Lord is incarnate as a man, and stoops to redeem humanity from the ruin of the fall? Angels rejoice but they have no such share in the joy as we have. It is the highest personal joy to manhood that Jesus Christ who thought it not robbery to be equal with God, was made in the likeness of men that he might be one flesh with his chosen. Arise ye who slumber! If there was ever an occasion when ye should bestir your spirits and cry "wake up my glory, awake psaltery and harp" it is now, when Jesus comes to be affianced to his church, to make himself of one flesh with her, that he may redeem her, and afterwards exalt her to sit with him upon his throne. Here were abundant reasons why the invited guests should come with joyful steps, and count themselves thrice happy to be bidden to such a banquet. There is overwhelming reason wily mankind should rejoice in the glorious gospel of Jesus and hasten to avail themselves of it.

Beside that we must consider the royal descent of the Bridegroom. Remember that Jesus Christ our Savior is very God of very God. Are we asked to do him honor? It is right, for to whom else should honor be given? Surely we should glorify our Creator and Preserver! Wilful must be the disobedience which will not pay reverence to one so highly exalted and so worthy of all homage. It is heaven to serve such a Lord. His glory reacheth unto the clouds; let him be adored for ever and ever; O come let us worship and bow down, let us cheerfully obey those commands of God which aim at the honor of his Son.

Remember also the person of Immanuel, and you will desire his glory. This glorious Son, whose fame is to be spread abroad, is most certainly God--of that we have spoken, but he is also most assuredly man, our brother, bone of our bone, and flesh of our flesh. Do we not delight to believe that he, tempted in all points as we are, has never yet submitted to be stained by sin? Never such a man as he, head of the race, the second Adam, the everlasting Father--who among us would not do him reverence? Will we not seek his honor, seeing that now he lifts our race to be next to the throne of God.

Remember, too, his character. Was there ever such a life as his? I will not so much speak of his divine character, though that furnishes abundant reason for worship and adoration, but think of him even as a man. O beloved, what tenderness, what compassion, yet what holy boldness; what love for sinners, and yet what love for truth! Men who have not loved him have nevertheless admired him, and hearts in which we least expected to see such recognition of his excellence have nevertheless been deeply affected as they have studied his life. We must praise him, for He is "chief among ten thousand, and altogether lovely." It were treason to be silent when the hour has come to speak of him who is peerless among men and matchless among angels. Clap, clap your hands at the thought of the marriage of the King's Son, for whom his bride hath made herself ready.

Think, too, of his achievements. We take into reckoning whenever we do honor to a prince all that he may have done for the nation over which he rules. What, then, has Jesus done for us? Rather let me say what has he not done? Upon his shoulders were laid our sins; he carried them into the wilderness, and they are gone for ever. Against him came forth our foes; he met them in shock of battle, and where are they now? They are cast into the depths of the sea. As for death itself, that last of foes, he has virtually overcome it, and ere long the weakest of us through him shall say "O death, where is thy sting? O grave, where is thy victory?" He is the hero of heaven. He returned to his Father's throne amidst the acclamations of the universe. Do we not, for whom he fought, for whom he conquered, do we not desire to honor him? I feel I speak with bated breath upon a theme where all our powers of speech should be let loose. Bring forth the royal diadem and crown him! Is it not the universal verdict of all who know him? Ought it not to be the cry of all the sons of men? East and west, and north and south, ought they not to ring the joy bells and hang out streamers on his marriage day, for joy of him? Is the King's Son to be married, is there a festival in his honor? O then let him be great, let him be glorious! Long live the King! Let the maidens go forth with their timbrels, and the sons of music make sweet melody--yea, let all creatures that have breath break forth with his praises. "Hosanna! Hosanna! Blessed is he that cometh in the name of the Lord."

II. Secondly, here is a GENEROUS METHOD of accomplishing the design. A king's son is to be honored on the day of his marriage, in what way shall it be done? Barbarous nations have their great festivals, and alas, that men should have sunk so low; on such occasions rivers of human blood are made to flow. To this very day, on the borders of civilisation, there is found a wretched tyrant whose infernal customs, for I dare not call them by a less severe term, command the murder of hundreds of his fellow creatures in cold blood, on certain high days and festivals. Thus would the monster honor his son by acting like a fiend. No blood is poured forth to honor the Son of heaven's great King. I doubt not Jesus will have honor even in the destruction of men if they reject his mercy, but it is not so that God elects to glorify his Son. Jesus the Savior, on his wedding-day with manhood, is glorified by mercy, not by wrath. If blood be mentioned on such a day, it is his own by which he is glorified. The slaughter of mankind would bring no joy to him, he is meek and lowly, a lover of the sons of men. It has been the custom of most kings to signalise a princely wedding by levying a fresh tax, or demanding an increased subsidy from their subjects. In the case of the anticipated wedding of our beloved Queen's daughter, the dowry sought will be given with greater pleasure than upon any former occasion, and none of us would lift a whisper of complaint; but the parable shows that the King of kings deals with us not after the manner of man. He asks no dowry for his Son; he makes the marriage memorable not by demands but by gifts. Nothing is sought for from the people, but much is prepared for them, gifts are lavishly bestowed, and all that is requested of the subjects is, that they for awhile merge the subject in the more honorable character of the guest, and willingly come to the palace, not to labor or serve at the table, but to feast and to rejoice.

Observe, then, the generous method by which God honors Christ is set forth here under the form of a banquet. I noted Matthew Henry's way of describing the objects of a feast, and with the alliteration of the Puritans, he says, "A feast is for love and for laughter, for fullness and for fellowship." It is even so with the gospel. It is for love; in the gospel, sinner, you are invited to be reconciled to God, you are assured that God forgives your sins, ceases to be angry, and would have you reconciled to him through his Son. Thus love is established between God and the soul. Then it is for laughter, for happiness, for joy. Those who come to God in Christ Jesus, and believe in him, have their hearts filled with overflowing peace, which calm lake of peace often lifts up itself in waves of joy, which clap their hands in exultation.

It is not to sorrow but to joy that the great King invites his subjects, when he glorifies his Son Jesus. It is not that you may be distressed, but that you may be delighted that he bids you believe in the crucified Savior and live. A feast, moreover, is for fullness. The hungry famished soul of man is satisfied with the blessings of grace. The gospel fills the whole capacity of our manhood. There is not a faculty of our nature which is not made to feel its need supplied when the soul accepts the provisions of mercy; our whole manhood is satisfied with good things and our youth is renewed like the eagles. "For I have satisfied the weary soul, and I have replenished every sorrowful soul." To crown all, the gospel brings us into fellowship with the Father and his Son Jesus Christ. In Christ Jesus we commune with the sacred Trinity. God becomes our Father, and reveals his paternal heart. Jesus manifests himself unto us as he doth not unto the world, and the communion of the Holy Ghost abides with us. Our fellowship is like that of Jonathan with David, or Jesus with John. We feast on the bread of heaven, and drink wines on the lees well refined. We are brought into the heavenly banqueting house where the secret of the Lord is revealed to us, and our heart pours itself out before the Lord Very near is our communion with God; most intimate love and condescension does he show to us. What say you to this? Is there not here a rich repast worthy of him who prepares it. Here all your capacious powers can wish, O sinner, shall be given to you; all you want for time and for eternity God prepares in the person of his dear Son, and bids you receive it without money and without price.

I have already told you that all the expense lies with him. It was a very sumptuous festival, there were oxen, and there were fatlings, but none of these were taken from the pastures, or stalls of the guests. The gospel is an expensive business; the very heart of Christ was drained to find the price for this great festival; but it costs the sinner nothing, nothing of money, nothing of merit, nothing of preparation. You rosy come as you are to the gospel feast, for the only wedding dress required is freely provided for you. Just as you are, you are bidden to believe in Jesus. You have nothing to do but to receive of his fullness, for to "as many as received him, to them gave he power to become the sons of God, even to them that believe on his name." You are not asked to contribute to the provision, but to be a feaster at the divine banquet of infinite compassion.

How honorable, too, is the gospel to those who receive it. An invitation to a regal marriage was a high honor to those who were bidden. I do not suppose that many of us are likely to be invited to the Princess's wedding, and, if we were, we should probably be greatly elated, for we should most of us feel it to be one of the great events of our lives. So was it with these people. A king's son is not married every day, and it is not everybody that is bidden to the monarch's entertainment. All their lives long they would say, "I was at his wedding, and saw all the splendor of the marriage festival." Probably some of them had never before enjoyed such a feast as the luxurious potentate had prepared for that day, and had never before been in such good company. My brethren nothing so honors a man as for him to accept the gospel. While his faith honors Christ, Christ honors him. It is no mean thing to be a king's son, but those who come to the marriage feast of God's own Son shall become King's sons themselves--themselves participators in the glory of the great heir of all things. While I am speaking of this generous method my heart glows with sacred ardor, and my wonder rises that men do not come to the banquet of love which honors all its guests. When the banquet is so costly to the host, so free to the guests, and so honorable to all concerned, how is it that there should be found any so unwise as to refuse the favor. Surely here is an illustration of the folly of the unrenewed heart, and a proof of the deep depravity which sin has caused. If men turn their backs on Moses with his stony tables, I do not marvel, but to despise the loaded tables of grace, heaped up with oxen and fatlings--this is strange. To resist the justice of God is a crime, but to repel the generosity of heaven, what is this? We must invent a term of infamy with which to brand the base ingratitude. To resist God in majesty of terror is insanity but to spurn him in the majesty of his mercy is something more than madness. Sin reaches its climax when it resolves to starve sooner than owe anything to divine goodness. I feel I must anticipate the period for delivering my message, and as I have described to you the way in which God honors his Son, I must at once proclaim the invitation, and cry to you, "Come to the wedding feast. Come ye, and glorify Jesus by accepting the provisions of grace. Your works will not honor him, if you set them up as a righteousness in competition with his righteousness. Not even your repentance can glorify him, if you think to make it a rival to his precious blood. Come, guilty sinner, as you are, and take the mercy Jesus freely presents to you, and accept the pardon which his blood secures to those who believe in him." Methinks when the messenger went out from the King and first of all marked signs of neglect among those who were bidden, and saw that they would not come, he must have been mute with astonishment. He had seen the oxen, and seen the fatlings, and all the goodly preparations, he knew the King, he knew his Son, he knew what joy it was to be at such a feast; and when the bidden ones began to turn their backs on him, and go their way to their farms, the messenger, repeated his message over and over again with eagerness, wondering all the while at the treason which dared insult so good a Being. I think I see him, at first indignant for his Master's sake, and afterwards melted to pity as he saw what would surely come of such an extravagance of ingratitude, such a superfluity of insolence. We mourned that his fellow-citizens whom he loved should be such fools as to reject so good an offer, and spurn so blessed a proclamation. I, too, am tossed to and fro in soul, with mingled but vehement feelings. O, my God, thou hast provided the gospel, let none in this house reject it, and so slight thy Son and dishonor thee, but may all rejoice in thy generous way of glorifying Jesus Christ, the Bridegroom of his church, and may they come, and willingly grace the festival of thy love.

III. We now advance to our third point, and regretfully remember THE SERIOUS HINDRANCE which for awhile interfered with the joyful event.

The king had thought in his mind, "I will make a great feast, I will invite a large number. They shall enjoy all my kingdom can afford, and I shall thus show how much I love my son, and moreover all the guests will have sweet memories in connection with his marriage." When his messengers went out to intimate to those who had received previously an express invitation that the time was come, it is written, "They would not come;" not they could not, but they "would not come." Some for one reason, some for another, but without exception they would not come. Here was a very serious hindrance to the grand business. Cannot the king drag his guests to the table?

Yes, but then it would not accomplish his purpose. He wants not slaves to grace his throne. Persons compelled to sit at a marriage-feast would not adorn it. What credit could it be to a king to force his subjects to feast at his table? No for once, as I have said before, the subject must be merged in the guest. It was essential to the dignity of the festival that the guests should come with cheerfulness to the festival, but they would not come. Why? Why would they not come? The answer shall be such as to answer another question--Why do not you come and believe in Jesus! With many of them it was an indifference to the whole affair. They did not see what concern they had in the king or his son. Royal marriages were high things and concerned high people; they were plain-speaking men, farmers who went hedging and ditching, or tradesmen who made out bills and sold by the yard or pound. What cared they for the court, the palace, the king, the prince, his bride, or his dinner! They did not say quite that, but such was their feeling; it might be a fine thing, but it was altogether out of their line. How many run in the same groove at this hour? We have heard it said, "What has a working man to do with religion?" and we have heard others of another grade in life affirm that persons who are in business cannot afford time for religion, but had better mind the main chance. The Lord have mercy upon your folly! Here is one great obstacle to the gospel, the stolid indifference of the human mind concerning this grandest of all conceptions--God's glorifying his dear Son by having mercy upon sinners.

At the bottom the real reason for the refusal of those in the parable was that they were disloyal, they would not come to the supper because they saw an opportunity for the loyal to be glad, and not being loyal they did not wish to hear the songs and acclamations of others who were. By staying away they insulted the king, and declared that they cared not whether he was a king or not, whether his son was a prince or not. They determined to disavow their allegiance by refusing the invitation. They said in effect, "Anyhow, if he be a king and his son a prince, we will do him no honor, we will not be numbered with those who surround his board and show forth his splendor. No doubt a feast is worth having, and such a feast as there will be provided t'were well for us to participate in, but for once we will deny our appetites that we may indulge our pride. We proclaim a revolt. We declare we will not go." Ah, ye who believe not in Jesus, at the bottom of it your unbelief is enmity to your Maker, sedition against the great Ruler of the universe, who deserves your homage. "The ox knoweth his owner, and the ass his master's crib," but ye know not, neither do ye consider; ye are rebels against the Majesty of heaven.

Moreover, the refusal was a slight to the prince as well as to his father, and in some cases the gospel is refused mainly with this intent, because the unbeliever rejects the deity of Christ, or despises his atonement. O sirs, beware of this, I know of no rock more fatal than to dishonor Christ by denying his sonship and his deity. Split not upon it, I beseech you--"Kiss the Son, lest he be angry, and ye perish from the way when his wrath is kindled but a little." Indifference covered the refusal in the text, "they made light of it," but if you take off the film you will see that at the bottom there was treason against the majesty of the king, and distaste to the dignity of his son.

No doubt some of them despised the feast itself. They must have known that with such a king it could not be a starveling meal, but they pretended to despise the feast. How many there are who despise the gospel which they do not understand, I say which they do not understand, for almost invariably if you hear a man depreciate the gospel, you will find that he has scarcely even read the New Testament and is a utter stranger to the doctrines of grace. Listen to a man who is voluble in condemnation of the gospel, and you may rest assured that he is fond because he is empty. If he understood the subject better he would find, if he were indeed a man of candour, that he would be led at least to be silent in admiration if he did not become loyal in acceptance.

Beloved friends, the feast is such as you greatly need, let me tell you what it is. It is pardon for the past, renewal of nature for the present, and glory for the future. Here is God to be our helper, his Son to be our shepherd, the Spirit to be our instructor. Here is the love of the Father to be our delight, the blood of the Son to be our cleansing, the energy of the Holy Spirit to be life from the dead to us. You cannot want anything that you ought to want, but what is provided in the gospel, and Jesus Christ will be glorified if you accept it by faith. But here is the hindrance, men do not accept it, "they would not come." Some of us thought that if we put the gospel in a clear light, and if we were earnest in stating it our hearers must be converted, and God forbid we should ever try to do otherwise than make it plain and be earnest, but for all that the best ministry that ever was, or ever could be, will be unsuccessful in a measure; yea, and altogether so, unless the effectual work of the Spirit be present. Still will the cry go up, "Who hath believed our report?" Still will those who serve their Master best, have reason to mourn that they sow on stony ground, and cast their bread on thankless waters. Even the prince of preachers had to say, "Ye search the scriptures, for in them ye think ye have eternal life, but ye will not come to me that ye might have life." Alas, alas, that mercy should be rejected and heaven spurned.

IV. So now we must close with the most practical matter of consideration, THE GRACIOUS REJOINDER of the king to the impertinence which interfered with his plans. What did he say? You will observe that they had been bidden, and then called; after the Oriental custom, the call intimated that the festival was now approaching, so that they were not taken unawares, but knew what they did. The second invitation they rejected in cold blood, deliberately, and with intent. What did the monarch do? Set their city in a blaze, and at once root out the rebels? No, but in the first place, he winked at their former insolent refusal. He said in himself, "Peradventure they mistook my servants, peradventure they did not understand that the hour was come. Perhaps the message that was delivered to them was too brief, and they missed its meaning. Or, if perchance, they have fallen into some temporary enmity against me, on reconsideration, they will wish that they had not been so rude, and ungenerous to me. What have I done that they should refuse my dinner? What has my son done that they should not be willing to honor him by feasting at my table. Men lone feasting, my son deserves their honor--why should they not come? I will pass over the past and begin again." My hearers, there are many of you who have rejected Christ after many invitations, and this morning my Lord forgets your former unkindnesses, and sends me again with the same message, again to bid you "come to the wedding." It is no small patience which overlooks the past and perseveres in kindness, honestly desiring your good.

The King sent another invitation--"all things are ready, come ye to the marriage," but you will please to observe that he changed the messenger. "Again he sent forth other servants." Yes, and I will say it, for my soul feels it, if a change of messengers will win you, much as I love the task of speaking in my Master's name, I would gladly die now, where I am, that some other preacher might occupy this platform, if thereby you might be saved. I know my speech to some of you must be monotonous. I seek out images fresh and many, and try to vary my voice and manner, but for all that one man must grow stale to you when heard so often. Perhaps my modes are not the sort to touch your peculiarities of temperament--well, good Master, set thy servant aside, and consider him not. Send other messengers if perchance they may succeed. But to some of you I am another messenger, not a better, but another, since my brethren have failed with you. Oh, then, when my voice cries, "Come unto Jesus, trust in his atonement, believe in him, look to him and live," let the new voice be successful, where former heralds have been disregarded.

You notice, too, that the message was a little changed. At first it was very short. Surely if men's hearts were right, short sermons would be enough. A very brief invitation might suffice if the heart were right, but since hearts are wrong God bids his servants enlarge, expand, and expound. "Come, for all things are ready. I have prepared my dinner, my oxen and my fatlings are killed, all things are ready, come to the marriage." One of the best ways of bringing sinners to Christ is to explain the gospel to them. If we dwell upon its preparations, if we speak of its richness and freeness, some may be attracted whom the short message which merely tells the plan of salvation might not attract. To some it is enough to say, "Believe in the Lord Jesus Christ and thou shalt be saved," for they are asking, "Sirs, what must I do to be saved?" but others need to be attracted to the wedding feast by the description of the sumptuousness of the repast. We must try to preach the gospel more fully to you, but we shall never tell you of all the richness of the grace of God. As high as the heavens are above the earth, so high are his thoughts above your thoughts, and his ways above your ways. Forsake your sins and your thoughts and turn to the Lord, for he will abundantly pardon you. He will receive you to his heart of love, and give you the kiss of his affection at this hour, if, like prodigal children, you come back and seek your Father's face. The gospel is a river of love, it is a sea of love, it is a heaven of love, it is a universe of love, it is all love. Words there are none, fully to set forth the amazing love of God to sinners, no sin too big or too black, no crime too crimson or too cursed for pardon. If you do but look to his dear crucified Son all manner of sin and of blasphemy shall be forgiven you. There is forgiveness. Jesus gives repentance and remission. And then the happiness which will be brought to you here and hereafter are equally beyond description. You shall have heaven on earth and heaven in heaven; God shall be your God, Christ shall be your friend, and eternal bliss shall be your portion.

In this last message the "guests were pressed very delicately, but still in a way which if they had possessed any generosity of heart at all, must have touched them. You see how the evangelist puts it, he does not say, "Come, or else you will miss the feast; come, or else the king will be angry; come, come, or else you will be the losers." No, but--he puts it, as I read it, in a very remarkable way. I venture to say--if I be wrong, the Master forgive me so saying--the king makes himself the object of sympathy, as though he were an embarrassed host. See here, "My dinner is ready, but there is no one to eat it; my oxen and fatlings are all killed, but there are no guests." "Come, come," he seems to say, "for I am a host without guests." So sometimes in the gospel you will see God speaks as if he would represent himself as getting an advantage by our being saved. Now we know that herein he condescends in love to speak after the manner of men. What can he gain by us? If we perish what is he the loser? But he makes himself often in the gospel to be like a father who yearns over his child, longing for him to come home. He makes himself, the infinite God, turn beggar to his own creatures, and beseeches them to be reconciled. Wondrous stoop; for, like a chapman who sells his wares, he cries, "Ho, every one that thirsteth, come ye to the waters; and he that hath no money, let him come." Do you observe how Christ, as he wept over Jerusalem, seems to weep for himself as well as for them. "How often would I have gathered thy children together." And God, in the prophets, puts it as his own sorrow, "How can I set thee as Admah, how can I make thee as Zeboim," as if it were not the child's loss alone, but the father's loss also, if the sinner died. Do you not feel, as it were, a sympathy with God when you see his gospel rejected? Shall the cross be lifted high, and none look to it? Shall Jesus die, and men not be saved by his death? O blessed Lord, we feel, if nothing else should draw us, we must come when we see, as it were, thyself represented as a host under our embarrassment, for lack of guests. Great God, we come, we come right gladly, we come to participate of the bounties which thou hast provided, and to glorify Jesus Christ by receiving as needy sinners that which thy mercy has provided.

Brethren and sisters since Christ finds many loath to honor him, my exhortation is to you who love him, honor him the more since the world will not. You who have been constrained to come, remember to sing as you sit at his table, and rejoice and bless his name. Next go home and intercede for those who will not come, that the Lord will enlighten their understandings, and change their wills, that they may be yet constrained to believe in Jesus; and as for those of you who feel half inclined this morning by the soft touches of his grace to come and feast, let me bid you come. It is a glorious gospel--the feast is good. He is a glorious king--the Host is good. He is a blessed Savior, he who is married, he is good. It is all good, and you shall be made good too, if your souls accept the invitation of the gospel which is given to you this day. "He that believeth and is baptised shall be saved: he that believeth not shall be damned." "Believe on the Lord Jesus Christ and thou shalt be saved." The Lord send his Spirit to make the call effectual, for his dear Son's sake. Amen.

PORTION OF SCRIPTURE READ BEFORE SERMON--Matthew 21.

The Wedding Garment

A Sermon (No. 976)
Delivered on Lord's-day Morning, February 19th, 1871 by
C. H. SPURGEON,
At the Metropolitan Tabernacle, Newington

"And when the king came in to see the guests, he saw there a man which had not on a wedding garment: And he saith unto him, Friend, how camest thou in hither not having a wedding garment? And he was speechless. Then said the king to the servants, Bind him hand and foot, and take him away, and cast him into outer darkness; there shall be weeping and gnashing of teeth. For many are called, but few are chosen." - Matthew 22:11-14.

APPARENTLY the parable of the marriage feast would have been complete without this addition, but there was infinite wisdom in appending this sequel. This is seen practically in the experience of the church of God. Those who are permitted to see large additions to the church will find this parable of the wedding garment to be singularly appropriate and timely. Whenever there is a revival and many are brought to Christ, it seems inevitable that at the same time a proportion of unworthy persons should enter the church. However diligent may be the oversight there will be pretenders creeping in unawares who have no true part or lot in the matter, and hence, when the preacher is most earnest for the ingathering of souls to Christ, he needs to couple therewith a holy jealousy, lest those who come forward to make a profession of faith should be moved by carnal motives, and should not really have given their hearts to God. We must use the net to draw in the many, but all are not good fishes that are taken therein. On the threshing floor of Zion the heap is not all pure wheat, the chaff is mingled with the grain, and therefore the winnowing fan is wanted. God's furnace is in Zion, and there is good need for it, for the gold is yet in the ore and needs to be separated from the dross. Wood, hay, and stubble building is quick work, but it is a waste of effort; we need continually to examine our materials, and see that we use only gold, silver, and precious stones. It is most needful in times of religious excitement, to remind men that godliness does not consist in profession, but must be proved by inward vitality and outward holiness. Everything will have to be tested by a heart-searching God, and if, when he comes to search us, we are found wanting, we shall be expelled even from the marriage feast itself; for there is a way to hell from the very gates of heaven. In a word, it is well for all to be reminded that the enemies of the great King are not only outside the church, but they are even in it; while a part refuse to come to the wedding of his Son, others press into the banquet and are still his foes. May God grant that this subject may have a heart-searching effect. May it be as the north wind when it blows through the marrow of the bones. May it lead us to desire to be searched and tried of God, whether we are truly in the faith, or are reprobates in his esteem.

The parable may be discoursed upon under five heads. Here is an enemy at the feast; here is the king at the feast; that king becomes the judge at the feast; and hence the enemy becomes the criminal at the feast; and swiftly is removed by the executioner at the feast.

I. We see in the text AN ENEMY AT THE FEAST.

He came into the banquet when he was bidden, but he came only in appearance, he came not in heart. The banquet was intended for the honour of the son, but this man meant not so; he was willing to eat the good things, but he intended no respect to the prince. He did not, like others, say, "I will not come, for I will not have this man to reign over me"; but he said, "I will come, but it shall be in such a way that the royal purpose shall not be served, but rather hindered. I shall be present as an onlooker, but take no share in the ceremony; I will, on the contrary, show that I have no care for the business in hand, except so far as it serves my turn." The man came in full exercise of self-will and self-love. He resolved to yield no homage, but to assert his independent self-sovereignty. He would show the king even at his table, where his bounties were so largely dispensed, that he was not afraid to affront him. When he came to the door of the feast, he found the guests all putting on the garment suitable for the marriage banquet. As here, in our own country, at a funeral, each mourner is expected to put on the articles of mourning which are provided, so at the wedding feast each person was expected to wear the bridegroom's favours, the garment which, as a badge, marked him as an attendant at the wedding, and as one who rejoiced in it. While others cheerfully put on this wedding dress the traitor would not; he resolved to defy the rules of the palace, and to insult the king by appearing in his own garments. He scorned to wear the livery of respectful joy, he preferred to make himself conspicuous by his daring insolence. The badge was intended to show that the wearer was a real participator in the joy of the feast, and for that very reason he would not put it on. He did not acknowledge the king nor the prince, nor care one atom about the gladsome event. He had no objection to be there, to eat the dainties, or recline upon the seats, and see the pomp and the show, but he was only in it, and not of it; he was there in body, but not in spirit. Are there not crowds of people whose union to the church is nothing better than an insult to God? Custom sways them, and not sincere faith. They have no regard to the great Head of the church or to the heart-searching God. They treat church membership as a trifle, and have no tenderness of heart touching the matter. They, in effect, say, "The table of the Lord is contemptible." "Spots are they in our feasts, feeding themselves without fear."

Many a time the question has been asked: "What was the wedding garment?" It is a question which need not be curiously pried into. So many answers have been given that I conclude that if our Saviour had intended any one specific thing he would have expressed himself more plainly, so that we would have been able, without so much theological disputing, to have understood what he meant. It seems to me that our Lord intended much more than any one thing. The guests were bidden to come to the wedding to show their respect to the king and prince; some would not come at all, and so showed their sedition; this man came, and when he heard the regulation, that a certain garment should be put on, comely in appearance and suitable for the occasion, he determined that he would not wear it. In this act of rebellion, he went as far in opposition as they did who would not come at all, and he went a little further, for in the very presence of the guests and of the king he dared to declare his disloyalty and contempt. Alas, how many are willing enough to receive gospel blessings, but they are still at enmity with God and have no delight in the only Begotten Son. Such will dare to use the forms of godliness, and yet their hearts are full of rebellion against the Lord. The wedding garment represents anything which is indispensable to a Christian, but which the unrenewed heart is not willing to accept, anything which the Lord ordains to be a necessary attendant of salvation, against which selfishness rebels. Hence it may be said to be Christ's righteousness imputed to us, for alas, many nominal Christians kick against the doctrine of justification by the righteousness of the Saviour and set up their own self-righteousness in opposition to it. To be found in Christ, not having our own righteousness, which is of the law, but having the righteousness which is of God by faith, is a very prominent badge of a real servant of God, and to refuse it is to manifest opposition to the glory of God, and to the name, person, and work of his exalted Son. But we might with equal truth say that the wedding dress is a holy character, the imparted righteousness which the Holy Spirit works in us, and which is equally necessary as a proof of grace. If you question such a statement, I would remind you of the dress which adorns the saints in heaven. What is said of it? "They have washed their robes and made them white in the blood of the Lamb." Their robes therefore were such as once needed washing; and this could not be said in any sense of the righteousness of the Lord Jesus Christ; that was always perfect and spotless. It is clear then that the figure is sometimes applied to saints in reference to their personal character. Holiness is always present in those who are loyal guests of the great King, for "without holiness no man shall see the Lord." Too many professors pacify themselves with the idea that they possess imputed righteousness, while they are indifferent to the sanctifying work of the Spirit. They refuse to put on the garment of obedience, they reject the white linen which is the righteousness of saints. They thus reveal their self-will, their enmity to God, and their nonsubmission to his Son. Such men may talk what they will about justification by faith, and salvation by grace, but they are rebels at heart, they have not on the wedding dress any more than the self-righteous, whom they so eagerly condemn. The fact is, if we wish for the blessings of grace, we must in our hearts submit to the rules of grace without picking and choosing. It is idle to dispute whether the wedding garment is faith or love, as some have done, for all the graces of the Spirit and blessings of the covenant go together. No one ever had the imputed righteousness of Christ without receiving at the same time a measure of the righteousness wrought in us by the Holy Spirit. Justification by faith is not contrary to the production of good works: God forbid. The faith by which we are justified is the faith which produces holiness, and no one is justified by faith which does not also sanctify him and deliver him from the love of sin. All the essentials of the Christian character may be understood as making up the great wedding garment. In one word, we put on Christ, and he is "made of God unto us wisdom, righteousness, sanctification, and redemption."

The wedding garment is simply mentioned here as being a test of loyalty to those who came to the marriage feast, and as a mode by which rebellion was avowed and loyalty made apparent. Here was a man then who came into the gospel feast, and yet refused to comply with the command which related to that feast. He willfully preferred self to God, his heart was full of enmity and pride, he despised the gifts of grace, he scorned the rule of love, he stood a defiant rebel even at the banquet of mercy which his king had spread.

His sin lay, first of all, in coming in there at all without the wedding garment. If he did not mean to be of one heart with his fellow guests and his lord, why did he come? If a man does not intend to yield himself up to God's will, why does he profess to be of God's church? If a man is not saved by the righteousness of Christ, why does he profess to be a believer in Christ? If he will not be obedient to Christ's holy will, why does he pretend to be follower of Christ? It is a grave mistake for any person to imagine that he can be in the church of God to his own advantage unless his heart is renewed, unless he means what he declares, and sincerely loves the rule under which he professes to put himself.

The intruder's sin was aggravated by the fact that after he had unlawfully come into the feast he still continued there without the wedding robe. He does not appear to have had any compunction, or to have thought of amending his error. Only when the king came in and said, "Take him away," had the insolent rebel any idea of removing. Had he come in there, as I fear some of you have come into the church, under a mistake, thinking that there was no need of the wedding dress, when he looked around and saw all other persons wearing it, and observed that it was the peculiar mark of a guest, he would have felt uneasy and have gone to those who kept the royal wardrobe to get such a robe for himself; and then his sin in the matter would not have been laid to his charge. But he persisted in remaining where he was, and as he was. O my dear hearers, if you have already perpetrated the sin of union with the visible church of God without having the prerequisites, without being indeed submissive to God in heart and desirous to honour Christ, I entreat you, seek what is wanted, seek faith in God, seek a new heart, seek holiness of life, seek to become a loyal subject of the King, and be not content until you have these things, for the King will soon come in: he gives you time as yet, may he also give you grace to see to it that, being now where you ought never to have been, you may yet make your position a right one by obtaining that which will justify you in remaining where you are. The guest in his own clothes was a speckled bird amongst that company, it was possible for him even then to have become one of them; but he would not, he continued to defy the King.

This persistence he retained though he probably knew the fate of those who had refused to come. He knew that the king had sent forth his armies and destroyed those wicked men who had molested his messengers, and yet he dared to recline at his ease in the very teeth, and defying the terrible power of the monarch. He made his brow as brass and hardened his heart as adamant, and forced his way into a position where his seditious spirit would be able to display itself conspicuously. He said within his soul, "I care nothing for this marriage. I will make sport of it; I will intrude myself into that feast and show my contempt. I will take the provisions, but the son shall have no honour from me, and the king shall not find me bend my will to his command." Thus he had the audacity to disport himself as a willful rebel at the feast of mercy. Are there any such among you here? The tendency will be for those who are not so to begin to condemn themselves. I know already one who has said, "I am that guest that had not on a wedding garment." She is not that one, for she is not even a member of the church, and therefore it cannot concern her; but many like her write bitter things against themselves. Another will be saying, "I am that one," whereas, if there be one that lives near to God and whose desire is to be like Christ, and to be in all things conformed to the divine will, he is the man. You who are most assuredly right will probably be suspicious that you are not, and you who are insincere and have never submitted yourselves to the will of God will probably say, "What does it matter? I am doing as well as others, I give as much, I attend the means as much, surely there can be no cause for concern In me." God grant that you may feel anxiety and fear before the Lord.

II. We pass on to the next point--THE KING AT THE FEAST.

"The king came in to see the guests." What an honour and privilege this was to the poor creatures whom his royal munificence had brought together! Was it not indeed the chief point of the entire festival'? One of our greatest joys is to sing--

The king himself comes near
And feasts his saints today!

What would church fellowship be if it had not the fellowship of God with it? To sit with my dear brethren and rejoice in their love is exceedingly delightful; but the best wine is fellowship with the Father, and with his Son Jesus Christ. The king did not provide the banquet and leave his guests to eat by themselves, but he "came in," and into every gospel church gathered according to his command the King will come. I am sure the most fervent desire of this church is that the King may personally visit us. We trust he is with us, but we want him yet more fully to reveal himself. Our cry is, "Come, great King, with all thy glorious power, with thy Spirit and with thy glorious Son,

and manifest thyself to us as thou dost not unto the world."

When the king came into the banqueting chamber he saw the guests, and they also saw him. It was a mutual revelation. Ever sweet is this to the saints, that their God looks upon them; his look brings no terror to our minds when we are loyal and loving. "Thou God seest me" is sweet music. We desire to abide for ever beneath the divine inspection, for it is an inspection of unbounded love. He sees our faults, it is to remove them; he notes our imperfections, it is to cleanse them away. Behold me, O great King, and lift up thine eyes upon me, accepting me in the Beloved. What joy it is to us who are saved in Christ Jesus that we also can see him! "Through a glass darkly," I grant you we behold him, for as yet we are not fit to behold the full splendour of his Godhead! but yet how sweetly doth he reveal himself to our souls and unveil his eternal love. Then it is that the feast is most fully a banquet of wine, when the banner of love waves over us, and the king's voice fills us with unspeakable delight.

"The king came in to see his guests." This, I say, was the crowning point of the entire banquet. Observe that he came in after they were in their places. They did not see him before they had entered his halls. When an inferior entertains a superior he always advances to the door to meet him and waits until he comes. If her Majesty the Queen were entertained by one of her nobles, he would be in waiting, and at the threshold would meet her; but when a superior entertains an inferior the inferior may take his seat at the table, and when all is ready the noble host will come in. It is so in the banquet of mercy. You and I see nothing of God, by way of communion with him, until first we have been brought in by the message of mercy to the marriage-feast of the gospel; for, indeed, until then a sight of God would strike us with terror--

"Till God in human flesh I see,
My thoughts no comfort find;
The holy, just, and sacred Three
Are terrors to my mind;
But when Immanuel's face appear,
My hope, my joy, begins;
His name forbids my slavish fear,
His grace removes my sins."

When I get to the banquet of mercy, then it is that I can dare to look at the King of kings, but not until then. What a joyous sight, a vision of the God and Father of our Lord Jesus Christ, the Father of glory as he appears in the gospel, feasting us upon his fatlings. An incarnate God makes God visible to us and makes us happy in the sight. "How canst thou see my face and live?" was the old question, but, behold, it is answered this day. At the marriage union of Christ with his people we see the face of the King in his beauty, and our souls not only live, but we have life more abundantly.

Observe, dear brethren, that the King has special times for this. He is not always in the festal chamber; to our sorrow we sometimes miss the King's presence at his table. We have the ordinances always, but we do not always enjoy the God of ordinances. The means of grace are abiding, but the grace of the means will come and go according to the sovereign good pleasure of our God. The King has his times of coming in. These are glad times to his people, but they are trying times to the mass of professors. When are these times? So far as unworthy guests are concerned, the times of God's visitation are those seasons when character is manifested. All times and periods do not reveal character. A lion may lie all day asleep, you may scarce know but what it is tame; but when the night brings the time for it to go forth to its prey, then it howls, and displays its ferocity. And so an ungodly man may lie down in the church of God with the lambs of the flock, and nothing may lead you to suspect his true character, but when the time comes for him to make profit by sin, or to get pleasure by sin, or to escape from persecution by sin, then you find out what he is. These providences are the King's coming in to scrutinize the guests. Changes in the conditions of the church, changes in the condition of the individual, all sorts of providential events go to make up the great sieve by which the wheat and the chaff are separated.

A great and most solemn coming in of the King to see the guests is, when having looked over the church, unknown to us, he decides that such and such a hypocrite has had space enough for repentance and time enough for mischief, and must now be summoned to the dread tribunal by death. The time when the King comes in to see his guests is not the last judgment, for that is the coming of the Son and not of the Father, and if it were intended in the parable, we would read that the prince came in to see his guests. We are led to view the King himself as continually judging professors and detecting the rebels who place themselves among the saints; by this judgment of God men are taken away from the church in their transgressions, bound hand and foot, and cast into the outer darkness, where there is weeping and gnashing of teeth. I do not know, my dear brethren, when God may be visiting this church, and taking away the men that are rebels in our midst, but I do know that when professors die it is not certain that all of them sleep in Jesus; but some of them are rooted up, like tares from among the wheat, and are bound up in bundles to burn. The division is going on constantly. The King's presence is known to believers in the joy which they feel, but it is made known to hypocrites by his cutting them off and appointing them their portion in eternal woe.

If, however, there is any one time when we may be quite sure that the King comes in to see the guests, it is after large ingatherings from the world, for notice here, when the servants had gathered in guests in large numbers, it was then that the king came in. Now it will be after the time of revival which we are feeling just now, when I hope a great many will be added to the church, that the Lord will search and sift us. If there has been no visitation of the church before for purposes of love or judgment--for they go together--we shall be quite sure to have such a visit from the great Lord himself at this time.

III. Solemnly think of THE JUDGE AT THE FEAST.

To all the rest at the festival he was the king, the beloved monarch, the munificent donor of a splendid banquet, and all eyes feasted as they looked at him: it was joy enough to behold the king in his beauty, and to see his Son with all his royal jewels on, attired for the wedding feast; but he was a judge to the hypocritical intruder. The day of comfort to his saints is also the day of vengeance of our God. He who comes to comfort all that mourn comes at the same time to smite the rebellious with a rod of iron.

The judge begins, as you perceive, by seeing, "He saw there a man." What eyes are those of Omniscience! The parable represents but one such man as present, yet the All-seeing King saw him at once, he fixed his flaming eyes on that one. I suppose it was a greater crowd than this, but the king fixed his eyes on the solitary offender at once. Does the parable speak of only one because we may expect to find only one hypocrite in a church? Alas! there have been many such at the wedding feast, but one only is mentioned to show us that if there were but one, God would find him out; and, being many, the sinners in Zion may be the more sure that they will not escape. It is possible that none of the guests may have noticed the man's garments; the parable makes no remark upon any expostulations made to him by others; perhaps they were all so taken up with the sight of the king, and so glad to be at the feast themselves, that they had no heart to make remarks upon others. But this is certain, that the king detected at once the absence of what was requisite to the marriage feast. It was not the presence of anything offensive, but the absence of something which was requisite. He did not say to the unworthy guest, "Thou hast rags upon thee," or "thou art filthy." or "thou hast an unwashed face"; he enquired solely into the absence of the peculiar badge which denoted a loving guest. God will judge, and does continually judge his church upon this question, the absence of what is absolutely necessary to being a Christian, the absence of honouring the Son, and obeying the Father. O soul, if thou art a professor of religion, and yet dost not love Jesus, and dost not fear the great King of kings, thou lackest the wedding robe, and what dost thou here? The King will see at once that thou lackest it. Thy morality, thy generosity, thy high sounding prayers, ay, and even thine eloquent discoursings, these cannot conceal from him the fact that thy heart is not with him. The one thing needful is to accept loyally the Lord as King.

The king next began to deal with the rebel. Note how he spoke with him. He took him on his own ground. It was too high a day for the king to use rough speech; the man pretended to be a friend, and he addressed him as such, but though the word I doubt not was uttered softly, it must have stung him if he had any feeling left. Judas exemplified in his own person this character. When he gave the Saviour the traitor's kiss, our Lord addressed him as "friend." He pretended to be a friend. A friend, indeed, to insult his king at his own table, and to select for the insult the delicate occasion of the prince's marriage to which he had been hospitably invited! This was infamous! Friend indeed! Where will you find enemies if such shall be called friends? The king put it to him, "How camest thou in hither?" What business hast thou here? What could have induced thee so maliciously to defy me? To smite me in my tenderest point, and mock my guests, and trample on my son? Didst thou intend such daring insolence? "How camest thou in hither? In hither? Was there nowhere else to pour forth thy sedition, no other spot in which to play the traitor? Needest thou come into my palace, and to my table, and before my son on his wedding day to reveal thy enmity? Was there a need to do this?" So may the Lord say to some of us. "Were there no other ways to sin, but that you must profess to be my servant when you were not so? Were there no other bowls that you could drink from, that ye must profane the cups of my table? Was there no other bread that you could put into your wicked mouths but the bread that represents the body of my Son? Had you nowhere else to sin in that you must needs sin in the church? Could you do nothing else to show your spite but that you must make a lying profession of faith in my Son, who bled upon the cross to redeem the sons of men? Could you assail me nowhere else but through the wounds of my only-begotten Son? Could you vex my Spirit by no other means than by pretending to be my friend, and thrusting yourself in hither, while defiantly rejecting that which was necessary to do me honour, and to do my Son honour, at the festival of my grace?" I dare not dwell upon the topic. I give you the text; I pray that your conscience may preach the sermon.

Notice however, one thing, and that is, that the king, when he thus turned a judge, dealt with this man only about himself. "How camest thou in hither?" Did I hear a whisper in some one's mind, "Well, if I am unfit to be a church member, there are a great many others who are in the same condemnation." What is that to you? See to thyself! When the king came in to see the guests he did not say to this man, "How came yonder persons here without the wedding garment?" His dealings were personal with him alone: "How camest thou in hither, not having on the wedding garment?" Professor, look to thyself, look to thyself. Let thy charity begin at home. Cast out the beam from thine own eye, and then mayst thou see clearly to cast out the mote that is in thy brother's eye. He fixed on the one man, made him his entire audience, and directed to him the solemn question, "Friend, how camest thou in hither?" Ah, my dear hearers, as the pastor of this church it has been a very great joy to me to see our numbers increased; many have been added to us, and many have gone forth from us to form other churches; my joy has been constant in God concerning this matter. Our beloved brethren associated with me in office have done their best to keep any of you back who have sought membership in whom we could see no fruits corresponding. We have not used our office deceitfully; as in the sight of God we have tried to be neither too severe nor too lax, but for all that I cannot but know that there are some of you who are not Christians though you bear the name. Like those of old, you say you are Jews and are not, but do lie. I am not now speaking of any who have fallen into sin and have suffered our rebuke, or have been separated from us by excommunication and yet remain in the congregation; I mean others of you whose lives are all that could be desired openly, and yet there is a worm at the heart of your profession; you are not vitally godly, you have a name to live, and you keep that name untarnished as yet, but you are dead. Search ye yourselves; do not from this tabernacle descend into hell; let your prayer be, "Gather not my soul with sinners, nor my life with bloody men." I am as concerned about myself as about you, that I should be found "accepted in the Beloved;" lest after having preached to others I myself should be a castaway! Do let it be a matter of solemn anxiety with each one. If you have never come to Jesus, come now; if you have never sought holiness of life, seek it now. If you have never had the wedding garment, it is yet procurable; go ye to him who freely gives it, the Lord will not refuse you; go to-day and he will accept you.

IV. He who was the unworthy guest is now THE CRIMINAL AT THE FEAST. The king has now become a judge to him; the question has been personally put to him, and he is speechless. Why is he silent? Surely it was because he was convicted of open, undeniable disloyalty. No evidence was required; he had come there on set purpose with malice aforethought to display his disloyalty, and had done so in the presence of the King. I do not think he represents at all a person who enters the church through ignorance, with a sincere but ignorant intention, but he pourtrays one who makes a profession without care to make it true--willfully despising the Lord's commands. He is a man willing to be saved by grace, and professing to be so, but refusing to acknowledge his duty to God and his obligations to the Son. He was speechless; he could not have chosen a worse place, nor a more impertinent method of ventilating his disloyalty than that which he selected; there was nothing he could say in self-defense. At that moment, when the King looked him through and through, he saw the full horror of his position; his loins were loosed, like Belshazzar of old when he saw the handwriting on the wall; he saw now that his time to insult was over, and the day of retribution had come. He was taken in the very fact, and could not escape. He had been guilty of a superfluity of naughtiness, of an unnecessary extravagance of wickedness in coming into the feast to air his pride. He had committed a suicidal intrusion. He might have kept himself away at any rate, and not have thrust himself into the Judge's presence. He saw now that the cause of sedition was hopeless, the King was there and he was in his power and none could rescue him. Why did he not burst into tears? Why did he not confess the wrong? Why did he not say, "My king, I have insulted thee, have pity upon me"? His proud heart would not let him. Sin made him incapable of repentance. There is a verse in one of Hart's hymns which runs thus--

"Fixed is their everlasting state:
Could they repent, tis now too late."

That is true enough, but it supposes an impossibility, and I think it would have been far better to have said--

"Fixed is their everlasting state;
They can't repent, tis now too late."

Because the sinner goes on to sin he continues still to suffer; he will not turn, he cannot turn. As the Ethiopian cannot change his skin, nor the leopard his spots, so when sin has reached its height the man cannot bend, or bow, or retrace his steps. Oh, if he could have repented even then! But he could not; and the tears that came after the king had pronounced the sentence where no tears of penitence, but only of despairing pride. He stood speechless. It was not only that he had no excuse, but he would not confess his wrong. Have I anyone here in such a condition of heart, that while he has been sinning by making a false profession, and knows it, yet he sullenly refuses to confess his fault? Yield thee, man! Yield at once. Fall at the King's feet at once. Even if you are not a hypocrite, if you have any suspicion that you are, fall down and say, "My King, make me sincere; I submit myself to thy will, and am ready to put on the wedding badge; if there is any method by which I can honour thy Son, I cavil not at it; let me wear his colours, and be known by all men to be truly a lover of the great Prince."

But now, lastly, while he stood speechless in the king's presence, the king gave place to THE EXECUTIONER, for he uttered these words, "Bind him hand and foot." He was lawless, make him feel the law; he said, "I am free, and I will do as I like," let him never be free again; bind him, pinion him. Executioner, do your duty, prepare him for death. Alas, there are some who are bound and pinioned even before the breath is out of their bodies. In their dying hours false professors have often found that they could not pray, and could not repent; like dying Spira, that arch-hypocrite and apostate, they have been sensible of misery, but not penitent, and no gospel promise has availed to comfort them. Their hearts were seared, they were twice dead before they were dead. Then came the sentence, "Take him away," which is sometimes executed by the church in her excommunications--deceivers are taken away from the gospel feast by just discipline; but which is more fully carried out in the hour of death when the man's hope fails him. Ah, sirs, what will ye do if ye have no true grace in your hearts when you are taken away from the Lord's table, taken away from the baptism in which you gloried, taken away from the doctrines of the gospel which you understood so well by head, but which you did not know in your heart. John Bunyan's description of the man dragged by seven devils, bound with cords, comes up before my mind. "Bind him hand and foot and take him away." How thankful I am that the servants who brought them in are not the same who were commanded to take them away. The Douloi brought them in, the diakonoi took them away, the King has a special order of servants for the taking of deceivers away; his angels do that in the hour of death--they execute his vengeance. He gives us ministers a better office, he bids us be his heralds of mercy. Then the judge said, "Cast him," fling him like a useless, worthless thing. That wretch has dared pollute my marriage feast, cast him away, as men fling weeds over the garden wall or shake off vipers into the fire. There is none in heaven or earth thought more despicable, more fit to be thrown away as rubbish and offal, than a man who had a Christian name, but had not the essentials of the Christian nature. Cast him away. Where? "Into outer darkness" far from the banquet hall where torches flame and lamps are bright; drive him out into the cold, chilly midnight air. He has once seen the light, it will be all the darker now for him when he is driven into the dark. There is no darkness so dark as the darkness of the man who once saw light. Cast him into outer darkness. What will he do there? We are not told what would be done to him, it was not needful; we learn elsewhere as much as could be revealed to us, but we are told what he did, for "there shall be weeping," not the gush of tears which gives relief but the everlasting dropping of scalding tears which create fresh sorrow and enlarge their own source. The outcast shed no tears of regret, but of sullen disappointment, because he could not after all dishonour the king, and had even served to illustrate the royal justice and power, and so had brought glory to the king whom he hated in soul. Then came the "gnashing of teeth," caused by wrath and envy because he could do no more mischief. No sorrow is equal to that of a malicious spirit, that having attempted a daring deed of atrocious wickedness, has been defeated and has contributed to the triumph of the good and excellent. The misery of hell is not a misery which God arbitrarily creates, it is the necessary result of sin, it is sin itself come to ripeness. Here you see the picture of the man who was insolent enough to come into the church without being a Christian, and now for ever he gnashes with his teeth against that glorious Majesty of heaven which it will never be in his power to injure, but which it will always be in his heart to hate; and this will be his hell--that he hates God, this his darkness--that he cannot see beauty in God, and this the outerness of the darkness--that he cannot enter into God's will. "Depart ye cursed," is only love repelling that which is not lovely, it is only justice giving to man what his fallen nature craved after. "Get away from me, ye did not honour me; when ye did come to me it was with your lips only. Go where your hearts were; depart from me, you cursed." Oh, may God grant that not one here may come under the lash of this terrible parable, but may we be found of the Lord in peace in the day of his appearing. You see, then, how the Lord sifts us. First we are sifted by the preaching of the gospel, and many will not come--there is one heap of chaff: next, by the judgment of God in his church, and others are found wanting--there is another heap of chaff. Ah, when this is done, and the two great sieves are used, shall we be found among the wheat?

Do you say, "the sermon has nothing to do with me, I never made a profession, I shall go home easy enough." Come hither friend, I must not let you go. There is a vagabond brought before the magistrate accused of theft, he says he is perfectly innocent, but he is convicted and has to suffer for it; after him comes a bragging fellow, who says, "I do not make any profession of being honest, I rob anybody I can, and I mean to do so, I do not pretend to keep the law." Why, methinks the magistrate would say, "I condemned the one who did at least pretend to something decent, but to you I give double punishment, you are evidently incorrigible, and your case needs no consideration." You who do not say you are Christians, who confess you are not, you avow yourselves the enemies of Christ; get no comfort therefore out of this parable I pray you, but yield yourselves to the Saviour, and believe in him, for he that believeth and is baptized shall be saved.

PORTION OF SCRIPTURE READ BEFORE SERMON--Epistle of Jude.

The Master's Profession--The Disciple's Pursuit

A Sermon (No. 977)
Delivered on Thursday Evening, April 21st, 1870 by
C. H. SPURGEON,
At the Metropolitan Tabernacle, Newington.
In aid of the Baptist Young Men's Missionary Association.

"I have preached righteousness in the great congregation: lo, I have not refrained my lips, O Lord, thou knowest. I have not hid thy righteousness within my heart, I have declared thy faithfulness and thy salvation: I have not concealed thy lovingkindness and thy truth from the great congregation."
- Psalm 40:9,10.

WHO IS THE SPEAKER that gives utterance to these marvellous words? In the first instance they must be understood to proceed from our Lord Jesus Christ. By the Spirit of prophecy in the Old Testament they were spoken of him, and by the Spirit of interpretation in the New Testament they have been applied to him. Mark, then, how vehemently he here declares that he has fully discharged the work which he was sent to accomplish. When, in the days of his flesh, he was crying to his Father for preservation in a season of dire distress, he might well ask that he should then be helped, since all the previous strength he possessed had been laid out in his Father's service. But because this profession emphatically belongs to our Savior we need not suppose that it exclusively belongs to him. On the other hand, Christ being our forerunner and our example, we are encouraged to emulate the high calling and the dutiful obedience he so perfectly exhibited.

I. UNDOUBTEDLY OUR LORD JESUS CHRIST, AS WE READ HIS HISTORY IN THE FOUR EVANGELISTS, MOST GLORIOUSLY FULFILLED HIS LIFE-MISSION.

He was constantly testifying to the gospel of God, the gospel of his righteousness and of his grace. From the first moment when he, being full of the Holy Ghost, began to preach the gospel, until the day when he was taken up into heaven, while he blessed his disciples, he was instant in season and out of season. There were no waste moments of time, no neglected opportunities, no talents held in reserve. "I must work," was his motto. The zeal of God's house consumed him. It was his meat and his drink to do the will of him that sent him. A marvellous study is this life of Christ on earth; and as one looks at it thought begets thought, for--

"Kindred objects kindred thoughts inspire,
As summer clouds flash forth electric fire."

Mark ye not how he concentrated every attribute of his nature, ever faculty of his mind, and every power of his body in the one work he had undertaken--to do his Father's will? He seems all his life through to have challenged the enquiry, "Wist ye not that I must be about my Father's business?" He was continually preaching the gospel. "Never man spake as this man," may apply to the quantity as well as the quality of his utterances. All places seemed to be alike suitable to his ministry. Your gowns and your pulpits, your chancels and naves, your aisles and transepts were of no account with him. He wanted no toga or rostrum, nor did he need a preconcerted arrangement of the assembly to lend grace to his discourses when he made known the word of God to the people and astonished them with his doctrine. He could speak anywhere--even along the crowded thoroughfare, where the multitudes thronged him. He went down the lowest streets, and from the poorest beggars he didn't turn aside. He was not thwarted by the sneers, and sarcasms, and subtle questioning of the Pharisees and Sadducees. One thought possessed him, and he persistently wrought it out. His life-sermon as so thorough that nothing of earthly splendor could allure or distract him, or break the thread. He was always and everywhere either pleading with God for men, or else pleading with men for God. The reiterated expressions of these two verses are emphatically the truth: the asseverations are vehement, yet the effect is a noble vindication of integrity. "I have preached righteousness in the great congregation: lo, I have not refrained my lips, O Lord, thou

knowest. I have not hid thy righteousness within my heart; I have declared thy faithfulness and thy salvation: I have not concealed thy lovingkindness, and thy truth from the great congregation." He was the great Witness for God, the great Testifier, who went proclaiming everywhere the kingdom of God, and the good tidings of salvation to man.

Do not these words likewise suggest to you the thought that Christ testified frequently to the greatest crowds? "I have preached righteousness in the great congregation. . . . I have not concealed thy lovingkindness and thy truth from the great congregation." On the hill-top, where his disciples came unto him and he began with his benediction of "Blessed," the multitude that gathered together, when he sat down and taught them, was doubtless imposing. The people sometimes thronged to hear him in such numbers that the historian describes them as innumerable, and tells us that they trod one upon another. From the statement given us, that there were at one time five thousand and at another time four thousand men, besides women and children, collected together in the desert place and the wilderness, when he fed them, we might reasonably infer that in populous places the crowds assembled on a yet vaster scale. Of course, the whole population off Judea, scattered all over the land, was scarcely equal to the population of this city, and therefore greater crowds may be collected in London than could have been gathered in Jerusalem; yet the concourse there must at times have been exceedingly great and the spectacle unusually grand, especially when at the great feast our Lord stood up before the people, and rang out, in words clear and distinct--"If any man thirst, let him come unto me and drink." Why, for years afterwards, the very tones of his voice must have haunted the memories of those who stood and listened to him, if they rejected the message. It is not easy to stand up before a crowded assembly; let those who think so come and try. Oftentimes it tests a man's valor. It brings him many trials to his spirit to be prepared for the work. But our Lord Jesus Christ was fully equipped for his blessed ministry. He was a great preacher, with a great message, full of a great love, with a great Father by whom he was commissioned, sustained, cheered. All the qualities of his character and conduct were congruous. With a great assembly he was at home; for his sympathy was mighty in its aggregate and minute in its detail. At the same time, Christ did not want a great congregation to enable him to preach. The first verse of our text, if I catch the heart of its meaning, seems to me to intimate that he could speak personally to one or to two: "Lo, I have not refrained my lips, O Lord, thou knowest." From the court of human conscience to the court of divine omniscience the appeal is carried. Fame hath not heard of this private fidelity. Howbeit he that dwelleth in the heavens takes cognisance of it. "O Lord, thou knowest, and canst bear witness to it. When there was but one woman at the well's brink, I refrained not my lips." When there were but two--his disciples, as he was going to Emmaus--he opened his mouth. Whether they were those whom he had made or would make his disciples, he had a word for all at all times and at all seasons. In this we ought to imitate the Master. Be ready to tell of Christ not only when your heart is prepared for it at a set time, but at all times, whether you have prepared for it or not. Your spirit should be always on the alert; you should always be on the watch for souls. Fain would I be like the eagle that is on its way to the eyrie, and looks for it long before it comes in sight, and no sooner discerns it than, like a lightning-flash, it darts off and alights upon it. O for a heart that is set on winning souls, that is set on glorifying God, that is set on coming nearer to the model and being more conformed in this matter unto Christ our Head! Our Lord could truly assert that he had not kept back the gospel; he had preached it publicly to the crowds, and he had declared it privately, as opportunity allowed. That he never did seal his lips or stifle his testimony, he could call God to witness.

Does not the tenth verse, in its first clause, intimate that Christ's preaching was never heartless preaching? "I have not hid thy righteousness within my heart." As if he had said, "It is in my heart, but I have never concealed it there. What I have received of thee, O my Father, I have made known unto the people: forsooth, thy will, which I have observed in heaven, and engaged to fulfill on earth; thy righteousness, as it appears in the justice of thy throne and the benevolence of thy laws; thy faithfulness, as it is verified in the stability of thy covenant and the perpetuity of thine ordinances; thy salvation, as it was prepared in thy counsels of old, and is displayed when thou makes bare thy right hand and thy holy arm; thy lovingkindness which flows in one perpetual stream of mercy; and thy truth, which sets the final seal to thy testimonies;--all these have I treasured in my heart, not to hide them from the children of men, but to manifest them for the glory of thy name and the welfare of thy people." Is it so? Then this solemn protest before God is of vital interest to us. Henceforth every word, every statute, every precept of the gospel, comes to us distilled through the heart of Christ. I like the idea of pouring our sermons out of our own hearts. They must gone from our hearts, or they will not go to our hearers' hearts. But, oh, how full of gracious secrets our hearts ought to be, priceless secrets, which though hidden from the wise and prudent, are revealed unto babes! Jesus, we thank thee for this, that thou hast not concealed thy Father's lovingkindness and truth from us.

See, too, our Master kept always to vital matters. We notice here how he uses words which show that his teaching had a distinct reference to God. "I have not hid thy righteousness; I have declared thy faithfulness and thy salvation; I have not concealed thy lovingkindness and thy truth from the great congregation." Our Lord in his teaching never seems to have diverged from the great central truth. We are too apt to be taken up with the mere externals, and if we do not become mere sectarians, it is just possible that points of our creed of the least importance occupy the most prominent place in our thought and conversation. Our Lord, with eagle eye, descries what is most important for men to know, and upon that he dwells. Sinners must know of God's righteousness; they will never know their sinfulness else, or knowing it they will think it to be a little thing. The righteousness of God comes like a stream of light into the soul, and reveals its corruption. God's salvation, again, must be shown in its true colors. It does not owe its origin, its accomplishment, or its application to our works or our merits, but it proceeds from God's grace, and redounds to his glory. I hold that this should be the cherished motive of the gospel preacher, to glorify God! While it should be the chief end and aim of Christians ordinarily, it is to be the chief end and aim of the preacher extraordinarily. Beyond everyone else, he is concerned with that which, beyond everything else, brings glory to him who is first, last, midst, and without end. Jesus Christ preached God's righteousness, and showed God's righteousness even in salvation, and then he preached that salvation fully.

Nor, dear friends, did he withhold his testimony of the other attributes of God. Think for an instant of God's faithfulness. Oh, what a delightful theme! As immutability is a glory that belongs to all his attributes, so faithfulness pertains to all his purposes and promises. Well may his people everywhere rely upon his fidelity. Well may we tell that we serve no mutable God. "He is not a man that he should lie; neither the Soul of Man that he should repent. Hath he said, and shall he not do it? Or hath he spoken, and shall he not make it good?" Moreover he will rest in his love, "for the Lord will not forsake his people for his great name's sake." He is "the Father of lights, with whom is, no variableness, neither shadow of turning." His promises and his threatenings abide steadfast. Side by side with the faithfulness of God there is witness of his lovingkindness. Oh, what a glorious revelation! the God and Father of our Lord Jesus Christ is the God of pity and of pardon, the God of love. Not of love as with us, in a mere effeminate sense, as though it were only an impulse of human admiration that would wink at iniquities. He is Love, love in the essence, love essentially divine; love consistent with holiness, that hums like flames of fire. In justice deep and terrible is God; in majesty he doth ride on the wings of the wind. This God of tempest, is the God of God, and this is the God whom Jesus preached; and while he did not conceal the sterner attributes of the Almighty, yet he did not forget to depict the heart of mercy and the hand that is ready to help. The God whom he preached is full of gentleness and tenderness. May we learn to believe in the God and Father whom his only begotten Son Jesus Christ delighted to make known, and if called to testify of Him may we testify fully and heartily as Jesus did.

To sum up all, we may say that our Lord's three years' ministry was matchless in its perfection, such as he could look back upon without a single regret, but with unsullied complacency. It was matchless as to its doctrines, and as to its completeness it was unsurpassed. More might be said of his manner, which was full of tenderness to the men among whom he walked, and of his majestic oratory, which we may admire and seek to imitate, but which we can reach only at a distance, for it is peerless beyond all competition, it stands alone; "Never yet man spake like this man," shall be true of him to the world's end. All his life long there is no flaw, there is no excess. "I have finished the work which thou gavest me to do," he could truly say, as he laid down his earthly ministry, and ascended to exercise his ministrations before the throne. In the retrospect of his labors there was no occasion for self-reproach, no cause for a fault to be found, even by the accuser of the brethren. All was to be joy and rejoicing when he had completed his life-work.

Thus much concerning our Lord. I have only opened the door for you to enter. I wonder whether it will ever be given to us to be able to say, as Christians, in our humbler measure, what he said, as the very Christ in such exalted strains?

II. Let us now use the text IN REFERENCE TO OURSELVES.

It ought to be the ambition of every believer here, in a sense more or less extensive, to be able to say, "I have preached righteousness; I have not refrained my lips; I have not hid thy righteousness within my heart; I have declared thy faithfulness and thy salvation; I have not concealed thy and thy truth."

It is quite certain that many careless Christians will never be able to lay this unction to their heart. In all our churches there is a very large proportion of idle people. I hope they are saved; the Lord knows whether they are or not, but whatever else they are saved from, certainly they are not saved from laziness. We have in the visible church a large proportion of flesh that is not living, or if it is alive it gives very little indication of life. Now, I do like as pastor to be in fellowship with a living church, all alive, and everybody active. Though it may be our happy lot to have a goodly preponderance in this church of living men and women, I know there is a considerable portion of added flesh about it. Albeit, there are some portions of the body which may be said to be ornamental, it is equally true that they also have some distinct service; there is not one of them put there to do nothing. Some Christians seem to think themselves "a thing of beauty and a joy for ever" to the church, and that they have nothing to do in it for the common weal. They must imagine that they are ornaments, for certainly they are of no use, so far as any good offices are concerned. It used to be almost thought that the whole duty of man consisted in taking your sitting, paving your quarter's rent, filling up your place, and listening with more or less attention to the sermons that were preached. As to the idea of everybody doing something for Christ, and the exhortation to them as good soldiers of the cross not to shirk their duty, these people said that it was sheer madness. To do or dare, to labor or suffer in the cause of the Captain of our salvation, was no article of their creed. Sleepy souls, they presently become victims of their own infatuation. As men who habituate themselves to take opium, they grow soporific. Then their Christianity becomes like a dream. It may be they are filled with flattering illusions, but in full many a case they are scared with strange spectres that issue in the short sighs, weak cries, and dismal groans of doubt and fear. Alas for them! they will not be able to say, "I have preached righteousness; lo, I have not refrained my lips, O Lord, thou knowest. I have not hid thy righteousness within my heart; I have declared thy faithfulness and thy salvation; I have not concealed thy lovingkindness and thy truth." Nay, nay; when their conscience is awakened, they shall have poignant regrets that they have neglected so many glorious opportunities of bringing crowns to Christ.

Nor will cowardly people be able to make this protest. Many Christians are of a retiring disposition, and their retiring disposition is exemplified somewhat in the same way as that of the soldier who felt himself unworthy to stand in the front ranks. He felt that it would be too presumptuous a thing for him to be in front, where the cannon balls were mowing down men on the right hand and on the left, and therefore he would rather be in the van-guard. I always look upon those very retiring and modest people as arrant cowards, and I shall venture to call them so. I ask not every man and woman to rush into the front ranks of service, but I do ask every converted man and woman to take some place in the ranks, and to be prepared to make some sacrifice in that position they choose or think themselves fit to occupy. But ah! there are some who shrink back from any post that demands toil or vigilance. When they were young their ardor was never kindled, the spirit of enterprise was never stirred within them. Had they shown any mettle then, they might have been lion-hearted now; had they done Nothing then, their career of usefulness might have been in full vigor now. But alas for the man upon whom there is the rust of wasted years; he waits, he doubts, he parleys still, and shelters himself under a fictitious humility. Would God I had more courage myself, but I will tell you one thing, I dare not fold my arms, nor dare I hold my tongue; it seems to me so awful a thing not to be doing good, and it seems to me so dastardly a thing to shrink back when opportunities lie in one's path. I do wish that some of you would learn to imitate the character of the godly man--

"Who holds no parley with unmanly fears; Where duty bids, he confidently steers,
Faces a thousand dangers at her call
And, trusting in his God, surmounts them all."

The cowards will not be able to say, "I have preached righteousness: lo, I have not refrained my lips, O Lord, thou knowest. I have not hid thy righteousness within my heart; I have declared thy faithfulness and thy salvation: I have not concealed thy lovingkindness and thy truth."

Nor, again, will spasmodic people be able to adopt this language. There are some people who, if there is a revival, are so marvellously zealous and earnest that we are ready to clap our hands, but all on a sudden they stop. That Sunday-school class they were just getting into right order, but before there was an opportunity to reap the fruit they felt it was not precisely what they were called to. That Young Men's Bible Class--yes, that was a happy thought, the pastor was delighted; but, unfortunately, some little difficulty occurred that you had not foreseen, and that also has fallen through. So it has been in other cases. Know therefore that those who cannot, like the Master, look back upon a continuous and persevering testimony, will not be able to speak with a clear conscience as he did.

But although so many classes of those who profess and call themselves Christians will not be able to take a happy retrospect of their lives, yet there are not wanting those who could do so. I have known men of one talent who without any self-righteousness could say, "I have preached righteousness; I have not regained my lips, O Lord, thou knowest. I have not hid thy righteousness within my heart; I have declared thy faithfulness and thy salvation; I have not concealed thy lovingkindness and thy truth." Dear good men in many a country village whose Dames will never be known to fame have gathered just a few people together and have preached on, on, on for years, and when they come to die in the Lord and rest from their labors, their works will follow them, and their life-service will be as acceptable as the services of, many men with ten times the talents and ten times the scope for their exercise. Perhaps the Master will say to them, "Well done!" with a stronger emphasis than to some who were better known. That poor girl whose only work she could do for Christ was to teach those two little children who were entrusted to her, and that nursery maid with but one gift, and one only, may be able to say, "I have preached righteousness; lo! I have not refrained my lips: I have declared thy faithfulness and thy salvation; I have not concealed thy lovingkindness and thy truth." You one-talent servants, you have this within your reach.

And those, too, with an extremely narrow sphere may be able to say this. It is not, perhaps, the man who can stand and talk to thousands, but it may be you in the family--the housewife, the kitchen maid, the serving-man, or the woman who has been bed-ridden for years, whose only audience will be a few poor neighbors, or perhaps, now and then, a generous friend--it is you within these narrow spheres who may yet be able to say, "I have preached righteousness; I have not refrained my lips, O Lord, thou knowest; I have not hid thy righteousness within my heart; I have declared thy faithfulness and thy salvation; I have not concealed thy lovingkindness and thy truth." I have sat by a bedside where I have envied the poor woman despite the agonies and pains of body she suffered, because she yet could praise and magnify the lovingkindness revealed to her there.

But, brethren, we may be, able to quote these words, some of us to whom greater talents have been committed. Though we may feel that we have not preached as earnestly as we could have wished; that we have not done our utmost towards those whom we have taught; that in our house-to-house visitation we have not been so earnest with poor souls as we might have been in this respect, for alas! alas! we are all unprofitable servants; yet we can say, "I have preached righteousness; I have not refrained my lips, O Lord, thou knowest. I have not hid thy righteousness within my heart; I have declared thy faithfulness and thy salvation; I have not concealed thy lovingkindness and thy truth."

Fervently do I hope that those of you with the largest opportunities may yet be privileged to make this good profession with all sincerity. I am not afraid for those friends who have but narrow spheres--sometimes I wish that mine were such--I am not afraid for those in humbler fields, but oh, if with such spheres, and such churches as God here and there allots to some of his servants, they can thus give account of their stewardship, it will be grace indeed, and to grace alone will the honor be due. Yet let us hope that we too may be able to say, "I have preached righteousness in the great congregation; lo, I have not refrained my lips, O Lord, thou knowest. I have not hid thy righteousness within my heart; I have declared thy faithfulness and thy salvation; I have not concealed thy lovingkindness and thy truth from the great congregation."

III. It is with an overwhelming sense of the importance as well as the moral grandeur of this profession that I repeat it to you again and again; for when we are able to feel this, and to say it humbly and confidently, with good faith and without guile, IT CASTS MUCH COMFORTABLE LIGHT ON MANY SOLEMN subjects.

How awful to remember that every hour there are hundreds of men and women who are dying without Christ. Turn to the bills of mortality of this one city. Be our sentiments ever so charitable, let us judge with the utmost liberality, the dreadful fact fills our mind, and every knell speaks it to our heart, "They go out of this world unforgiven; they go before their Maker's bar without a hope!" I think our hearts would break with the dread recollection of this if we could not say, "I have preached righteousness in the great congregation; lo, I have not refrained my lips, O Lord, thou knowest. I have not hid thy righteousness within my heart; I have declared thy faithfulness and thy salvation: I have not concealed thy lovingkindness and thy truth from the great congregation."

And how many deaths there always are among our hearers! What comfort can any Christian who knows you have, if you die unsaved, unless he is able to appeal to God, and say, "My Father, I did all I could to teach that soul the way of salvation; I did all I could to persuade him to accept the Christ of God"?

Dear friends, whenever you see any of your neighbors, your relatives, your acquaintance die, can you forbear to ask yourselves, shall their blood be required at my hands? Are your skirts stained? Are there no blood drops there? Come, look them down, and say if you can ponder with a clear conscience the fact of a sinner dying in a Christless state without your being able to say, "I have done all I could to bring that soul to Christ"?

And as for that dreadful outlook--the hereafter of the lost--would that we could believe the softer theories which some so eagerly embrace! We would, but dare not. We believe that those who die in their sins when they pass from this life into the next, shall find that second death to be no extinction of existence, but an eternity of sin and of misery, Ah! how can any of us bear to think of this if we feel that we are morally responsible for any one soul that is damned? Yet are we so, I speak but the bare truth, until we have delivered ourselves from that responsibility by faithful earnestness. Is there a Cain here who says, "Am I my brother's keeper?" I shall not appeal to your most sympathetic soul, but leave you to your Judge. But to the Christian I say, "No man liveth to himself." When you think of a spirit in despair, cast out for ever from the presence of his God and from the glory of his power, may you, friends, be able to say, "Great God, though I understand not thy ways, for thy judgments are a great deep; yet I warned the sinner, I admonished him to lay hold on Christ, and if he perished it was not for want of preaching to or for praying over; my warnings and tears were never spared. I did what was in me to prevent his ruin." Put in that light, we may look at least with some degree of serenity upon the doctrine of divine sovereignty. I must confess that the sovereignty of God is a great mountain whose top we cannot scale. I often marvel at the coldness with which some men talk of the sovereignty of God, as though it were of small concern whether men were lost or saved. They seem to take these things as easily as if they were only talking of blocks of wood, or fields filled with tares. I do not think that we can equitably plead the divine sovereignty as a counterpart to our futile efforts, till we can say, "I have done all that was possible to bring that soul to God, I have prayed over him and wept over him, and now if he perish I must believe that this man wilfully rejected Christ, that his iniquities are upon his own head, and that in him, as a vessel of wrath, God will get glory as well as in vessels of mercy.

The doom of the heathen is a subject in like manner of which it were too painful for any of us to speak unless we can say, "I have, as far as lieth in me, sought to do something for them." This is a thing about which we ought not to think with any ease, unless we feel that we would fain save them, and give them the knowledge of the gospel of Jesus Christ; and to carry out this, our cherished purpose, we will do the best we can.

The uprisings of error often cause us dismay. Every now and then we see some old form of error spring up that was stamped out, as we supposed, in the days of our ancestors. Not unfrequently a foul old heresy is brought out as a brand new discovery, and all the world admires it, and wonders whence it came. Now, whenever these old heresies crop up, and are brought out as new, and lead men astray, it is a great comfort when you and I are able to say, "I have preached righteousness in the great congregation; lo, I have not refrained my lips, O Lord, thou knowest. I have not hid thy righteousness within my heart; I have declared thy faithfulness and thy salvation; I have not concealed thy lovingkindness and thy truth from the great congregation." Let men propagate whatever errors they choose, if we have no share in misleading the people, and are continually engaged in instructing them, we may wrap ourselves in our integrity, and lay the matter before our God to vindicate our righteous cause.

The apathy of the church, which has lasted so long, is truly disheartening. With many a deep-drawn sigh do we bewail it. O that we could get the church to awake! You might sound the trump of the archangel before you could rouse full many to the appalling destitution by reason of which the people perish for lack of knowledge. Even the cries of lost souls, and the shrieks of the sinners in this Metropolis, rushing headlong to the pit that is bottomless, do not startle some of us. Yes, but if we can say, "I have preached righteousness; I have not refrained my lips, O Lord, thou knowest. I have declared thy faithfulness and thy salvation," then we may take courage to work nobly and to persevere under terrible difficulties. Though for awhile we should see no conversions; and though for a season the ploughshare should break against the rock, or against even the very adamant itself, yet still if we can say, "I have preached righteousness, I have not refrained my lips, O Lord, thou knowest. I have not hid thy righteousness within my heart; I have declared thy faithfulness and thy salvation; I have not concealed thy lovingkindness and thy truth"--we are exonerated from blame; nay, more, we are unto God a sweet savor of Christ in the testimony we have delivered. Yes, brethren, I apprehend that amongst the sweetest dying-bed recollections, and amongst the minor comforts, in taking our farewell of the world as it is, not the least will be that of having been constant and faithful all our lives to the gospel of Jesus Christ.

Give me a few minutes longer while I turn this sermon into the special direction which it was intended to take. I do not know that there are many more "young men" present to-night than there are usually at our week-day lecture. I generally find when I preach a sermon for any of our societies it so happens that everybody connected with the society seems to stay away. They would be willing enough to come if it were for the Primitive Methodist, or any other denomination. They are in love with everybody else except their own relations. I do not say this by way of censure, but surely if there be a people under heaven without a grain of clannishness it is that denomination to which we belong. If it had been a sermon for Jews or Turks the building would have been crowded; but as it is for ourselves it does not signify. However, if they are not present for whom it was intended, they may probably read the sermon; so I will add a few words expressly for them.

Young man, it may be that you are one of those who ought to become a missionary; it may be that you ought to dedicate your life to some work for God either at home or abroad. Well, if it be so, do not mistake your path in life. We do not urge you to rush into the ministry, much less into the foreign ministry, unless you are called to it, for that is the very last place for a man to be in who is not called to the work. Act as a Christian young man for once in your life by asking whether it may not be your vocation to bear the cross of Christ into lands where as yet it is unknown. Surely, whatever answer you may feel called upon to give you will be ready for it. You will at least be willing to give yourself up to the very hardest form of service to which you maybe called. I should like you, then, to be sure about this on the outset lest you should in the turn of the road miss the path and so not be able to say at the last: "I have preached righteousness; lo, I have not refrained my lips, O Lord, thou knowest. I have not hid thy righteousness within my heart; I have declared thy faithfulness and thy salvation; I have not concealed thy lovingkindness and thy truth from the great congregation." I should not like you, if meant by the gifts of God for a great missionary, to die a millionaire. I should not like it, were you fitted to be a missionary, that you should drivel down into a king; for what are all your kings, what are all your nobles, what are all your stars, what are all your garters, what are all your diadems and your tiaras, when you put them all together, compared with the dignity of winning souls for Christ, with the special honor of building for Christ, not on another man's foundation, but preaching Christ's gospel in regions yet far beyond? I reckon him to be a man honored of men who can do a foreign work for Christ, but he who shall go farthest in self-annihilation and in the furtherance of the glory of Christ, he shall be a king among men, though he wear no crown that carnal eyes can see. Ask yourselves the question then, Christian young men, whether that is your vocation.

Should it happen that you feel convinced this is not your calling, remember you may still in your daily business be able to say these words. Some of my friends here never will be able to say them. They have been church members for twenty years, and during all those twenty years they have not preached righteousness, they have refrained their lips, they have hidden his righteousness, they have not declared his faithfulness and his salvation, they have concealed his lovingkindness and his truth. You, young men and women, have an opportunity of doing what is gone from them. Though they might publish Christ abroad from now till they die, there are twenty years they must ever regret and look back upon as waste land for which they will have to give an account at the last. You have, it may be, those twenty years before you, and it is a noble thing to begin working young, and so long as ever you live to go on building on that work. I have heard it said that you should not put young converts to work for which they are not qualified. Ah! say I, put the youngsters in; they will never learn to swim if they are not put in at once. Why should you, young men and women, be received as church members at all unless you are prepared to do something for Christ? Work becomes you as well as worship. I mean, of course, if not disqualified by sickness, and even then there is a sphere for testimony. You can make a sick bed a pulpit to preach Christ, while by patience and resignation you show forth his praise. No one should join a church without seeking out something to do for the glory of Jesus Christ. Do start your lives, young men, with high purpose, that you may close them with holy cheer.

In order to do this, you will need much more zeal than you are likely to possess by making resolutions, and much more grace than you will ordinarily get without much self-denial and devout consecration. You have need to be baptised into the Holy Ghost and in fire. I do like those converts who are thoroughly purged from the corruptions of the world, and thoroughly converted to God, every faculty of the mind and every member of the body being surrendered to Christ, all of them as instruments of righteousness. We seem to get some people who are not half converted. I hope their hearts are converted, but the effect is not to drain their pockets or to set their hands to work.

You need, dear friends, to go much to Jesus Christ, to live much in communion with him, for this life-service has many expenses, and you have no ready money. You must go to the great exchequer of the King of kings and draw from its inexhaustible treasury. Do so. Do resolve to live lavishly in the service of Christ, and the divine storehouse will supply all that you need, be your ambition as large as it may.

There are habits, it is true, to be acquired which must be the result of growth, for they cannot be matured without the manifold experience of sunshine and shower, summer and winter, heat and cold; to all of these you will be exposed. But when once you have yielded ourselves to those divine influences which foster life, you will prove that by all these things men live. To this I can bear you witness. Drudgery ceases to be irksome when the ruling passion of laboring for the Lord has begun to ferment in your breasts, and the sweet assurance that your labor is not in vain in the Lord has quickened a sacred enthusiasm in your spirit. It may be that in your apprenticeship you have to encounter many hardships, but it shall be that in the full discharge of your vocation you will reap a harvest of joy.

God help you never to refrain from preaching the truth, never to withhold any part of it; may you be clear in all these matters as before the living God.

Oh! yours will be cheerful dying if you familiarise yourselves with such noble living as this. You will have a welcome entrance into heaven if such has been your life on earth. The pastor, when he can preach no more the gospel, will say, "I preached when there was time, and now I will sing when sermons all are o'er." You Sunday-school teachers cannot teach any longer, but your Sabbath recreations below will prove the sweet prelude to your Sabbatic felicities above. Tract distributors, now that all your work is over, you will say, "I did but distribute the leaves of the tree of life for the healing of the people, but now I feed myself on all its luscious fruits."

I do not say that rewards are given as mere rewards of merit, but this I do assuredly know, there are rewards given in respect of service through the grace of our Lord Jesus Christ, and I pray you seek the prize. So run that you may obtain it. May you be able to say, "While I was down below where service could be done for my Master--

"In works which perfect saints above,
And holy angels cannot do,"

with all my might I labored to excel, and now I enter into the bliss of him who helped and strengthened me, who revealed his grace in me, and counted me worthy to put me into some part of the ministry of his church."

God bless you, dear friends, and make you earnest to tell to others those things he has made known unto you, for our Lord Jesus Christ's sake. Amen.

PORTION OF SCRIPTURE READ BEFORE SERMON--Psalm 40.

All Fulness in Christ

A Sermon (No. 978)
Delivered on Lord's-day Morning, February 26th, 1871 by
C. H. SPURGEON,
At the Metropolitan Tabernacle, Newington

"For it pleased the Father that in him should all fullness dwell." - Colossians 1:19.

THE PREACHER IS UNDER NO DIFFICULTIES this morning as to the practical object to be aimed at in his discourse. Every subject should be considered with an object, every discourse should have a definite spiritual aim; otherwise we do not so much preach as play at preaching. The connection plainly indicates what our drift should be. Read the words immediately preceding the text, and you find it declared that our Lord Jesus is in all things to have the pre-eminence. We would seer; by this text to yield honor and glory to the ever-blessed Redeemer, and enthrone him in the highest seat in our hearts. O that we may all be in an adoring frame of mind, and may give him the pre-eminence in our thoughts, beyond all things or persons in heaven or earth. Blessed is he who can do or think: the most to honor such a Lord as our Immanuel. The verse which succeeds the text, shows us how we may best promote the glory of Christ, for since he came into this world that he might reconcile the things in heaven and the things in earth to himself, we shall best glorify him by falling in with his great design of mercy. By seeking to bring sinners into a state of reconciliation with God, we are giving to the great Reconciler the pre-eminence. On gospel shall be the gospel of reconciliation on this occasion. May the reconciling word come home by the power of Christ's Spirit to many, so that hundreds of souls may from this day forth glorify the great Ambassador who has made peace by the blood of his cross.

The text is a great deep, we cannot explore it, but we will voyage over its surface joyously, the Holy Spirit giving us a favorable wind. Here are plenteous provisions far exceeding, those of Solomon, though at the sight of that royal profusion, Sheba's queen felt that there was no more spirit in her, and declared that the half had not been told to her.

It may give some sort of order to our thoughts if they fall under four heads. What is here spoken of--"all fullness." Where is it placed--"in him," that is, in the Redeemer. We are told why, because "it pleased the Father;" and we have also a note of time, or when, in the word "dwell." "It pleased the Father that in him should all fullness dwell." Those catch words, what, where, why, and when, may help you to remember the run of the sermon.

I. First, then, let us consider the subject before us, or WHAT--"It pleased the Father that in him should all fullness dwell." Two mighty words; "fullness a substantial, comprehensive, expressive word in itself, and "all," a great little word including everything. When combined in the expression, "all fullness," we have before us a superlative wealth of meaning.

Blessed be God for those two words. Our hearts rejoice to think that there is such a thing in the universe as "all fullness," for in the most of mortal pursuits utter barrenness is found. "Vanity of vanity all is vanity." Blessed be the Lord for ever that he has provided a fullness for us, for in us by nature there is all emptiness and utter vanity. "In me, that is, in my flesh, there dwelleth no good thing." In us there is a lack of all merit, an absence of all power to procure any, and even an absence of will to procure it if we could. In these respects human nature is a desert, empty, and void, and waste, inhabited only by the dragon of sin, and the bittern of sorrow. Sinner, saint, to you both alike these words, "all fullness," sound like a holy hymn. The accents are sweet as those of the angel-messenger when he sang, "Behold, I bring you glad tidings of great joy." Are they not stray notes from celestial sonnets? "All fullness." You, sinner, are all emptiness and death, you, saint, would be so if it were not for the "all fullness" of Christ of which you have received; therefore both to saint and sinner the words are full of hope. There is joy in these words to every soul conscious of its sad estate, and humbled before God.

I will ring the silver bell again, "all fullness," and another note charms us; it tells us that Christ is substance, and not shadow, fullness, and not foretaste. This is good news for us, for nothing but realities will meet our case. Types may instruct, but they cannot actually save. The patterns of the things in the heavens are too weak to serve our turn, we need the heavenly things themselves. No bleeding bird nor slaughtered bullock, nor running stream, nor scarlet wool and hyssop, can take away our sins.

"No outward forms can make me clean,
The leprosy lies deep within."

Ceremonies under the old dispensation were precious because they set forth the realities yet to be revealed, but in Christ Jesus we deal with the realities themselves, and this is a happy circumstance for us; for both our sins and our sorrows are real, and only substantial mercies can counteract them. In Jesus, we have the substance of all that the symbols set forth. He is our sacrifice, our altar, our priest, our incense, our tabernacle, our all in all. The law had "the shadow of good things to come," but in Christ we have "the very image of the things."Hebrews 10:1. What transport is this to those who so much feel their emptiness that they could not be comforted by the mere representation of a truth, or the pattern of a truth, or the symbol of a truth, but must have the very substance itself! "The law was given by Moses, but grace and truth came by Jesus Christ."John 1:16.

I must return to the words of the text again, for I perceive more honey dropping from the honeycomb. "All fullness" is a wide, far-reaching, all-comprehending term, and in its abundant store it offers another source of delight. What joy these words give to us when we remember that our vast necessities demand a fullness, yea, "all fullness," before they can be supplied! A little help will be of no use to us, for we are altogether without strength. A limited measure of mercy will only mock our misery. A low degree of grace will never be enough to bring us to heaven, defiled as we are with sin, beset with dangers, encompassed with infirmities, assailed by temptations, molested with afflictions, and all the while bearing about with us "the body of this death." But "all fullness," ay, that will suit us. Here is exactly what our desperate estate demands for its recovery. Had the Savior only put out his finger to help our exertions, or had he only stretched out his hand to perform a measure of salvation's work, while he left us to complete it, our soul had for ever dwelt in darkness. In these words, "all fullness," we hear the echo of his death-cry, "It is finished." We are to bring nothing, but to find all in him, yea, the fullness of all in him: we are simply to receive out of his fullness grace for grace. We are not asked to contribute, nor required to make up deficiencies, for there are none to make up--all, all is laid up in Christ. All that we shall want between this place and heaven, all we could need between the gates of hell, where we lay in our blood, to the gates of heaven, where we shall find welcome admission, is treasured up for us in the Lord Christ Jesus.

"Great God, the treasures of thy love
Are everlasting mines,
Deep as our helpless miseries are,
And boundless as our sins."

Did I not say well that the two words before us are a noble hymn? Let them, I pray you, lodge in your souls for many days; they will be blessed guests. Let these two wafers, made with honey, lie under your tongue; let them satiate your souls, for they are heavenly bread. The more you bemoan your emptiness the sweeter these words will be; the more you feel that you must draw largely upon the bank of heaven, the more will you rejoice that your drafts will never diminish the boundless store, for still will it retain the name and the quality of "all fullness."

The expression here used denotes that there is in Jesus Christ the fullness of the Godhead; as it is written, "In him dwelleth all the fullness of the Godhead bodily." When John saw the Son of Man in Patmos, the marks of Deity were on him. "His head and his hairs were white like wool, as white as snow"--here was his eternity; "His eyes were as a flame of fire"--here was his omniscience; "Out of his mouth went a sharp two-edged sword"--here was the omnipotence of his word; "And his countenance was as the sun shineth in his strength"--here was his unapproachable and infinite glory. He is the Alpha and Omega, the beginning and the end, the first and the last. Hence nothing is too hard for him. Power, wisdom, truth, immutability, and all the attributes of God are in him, and constitute a fullness inconceivable and inexhaustible. The most enlarged intellect must necessarily fail to compass the personal fullness of Christ as God; therefore we do no more than quote again that noble text: "In him dwelleth all the fullness of the Godhead bodily; and ye are complete in him."

Fulness, moreover, dwells in our Lord not only intrinsically from his nature, but as the result of his mediatorial world. He achieved by suffering as well as possessed by nature a wondrous fullness. He carried on his shoulders the load of our sin; he expiated by his death our guilt, and now he has merit with the Father, infinite, inconceivable, a fullness of desert. The Father has stored up in Christ Jesus, as in a reservoir, for the use of all his people, his eternal love and his unbounded grace, that it may come to us through Christ Jesus, and that we may glorify him. All power is put into his hands, and life, and light, and grace, are to the full at his disposal. "He shutteth and no man openeth, he openeth and no man shutteth." He has received gifts for men; yea, for the righteous also. Not only as the Mighty God, the Everlasting Father, is he the possessor of heaven and earth, and therefore filled with all fullness, but seeing that as the Mediator he has finished our redemption, "he is made of God unto us wisdom, and righteousness, and sanctification, and redemption." Glory be to his name for this double fullness.

Turn the thought round again, and remember that all fullness dwells in Christ towards God and towards men. All fullness towards God and--I mean all that God requires of man; all that contents and delights the eternal mind, so that once again with complacency he may look down on his creature and pronounce him "very good." The Lord looked for grapes in his vineyard, and it brought forth wild grapes, but now in Christ Jesus the great Husbandman beholds the true vine which bringeth forth much fruit. The Creator required obedience, and he beholds in Christ Jesus the servant who has never failed to do the Master's will. Justice demanded that the law should be kept, and, lo, Christ is the end of the law for righteousness to everyone that believeth. Seeing that we had broken the law, justice required the endurance of the righteous penalty, and Jesus has borne it to the full, for he bowed his head to death, even the death of the cross. When God made man a little lower than the angels, and breathed into his nostrils the breath of life, and so made him immortal, he had a right to expect singular service from so favored a being--a service perfect, joyful, continuous; and our Savior has rendered unto the Father that which perfectly contents him; for he cries, "This is my beloved Son in whom I am well pleased." God is more glorified in the person of his Son than he would have been by an unfallen world. There shines out through the entire universe a display of infinite mercy, justice, and wisdom, such as neither the majesty of nature nor the excellence of providence could have revealed. His work in God's esteem is honorable and precious; for his righteousness sake, God is well pleased. The Eternal mind is satisfied with the Redeemer's person, work, and sacrifice; for "unto the Son, he saith, Thy throne, O God, is for ever and ever: a scepter of righteousness is the scepter of thy kingdom. Thou hast loved righteousness, and hated iniquity; therefore God, even thy God, hath anointed thee with the oil of gladness above thy fellows."Hebrews 1:8,9.

What unspeakable consolations arise from this truth, for, dear brethren, if we had to render to God something by which we should be accepted, we should be always in jeopardy; but now since we are "accepted in the Beloved," we are safe beyond all hazard. And we to find wherewithal we should appear before the Most High God, we might still be asking, "Shall I come before him with burnt offerings, with calves of a year old? Will the Lord be pleased with thousands of rams, or with ten thousands of rivers of oil?" But now hear the voice which saith, "Sacrifice and offering and burnt offerings and offering for sin thou wouldest not, neither hadst pleasure therein:" we hear the same divine voice add, "Lo, I come to do thy will," and we rejoice as we receive the witness of the Spirit, saying, "By the which will ye are sanctified through the offering of the body of Jesus Christ once for all," for henceforth is it said, "Their sins and iniquities will I remember no more for ever."

The all-fullness of Christ is also man-ward, and that in respect of both the sinner and the saint. There is a fullness in Christ Jesus which the seeking sinner should behold with joyfulness. What dost thou want, sinner? Thou wantest all things, but Christ is all. Thou wantest power to believe in him--he giveth power to the faint. Thou wantest repentance--he was exalted on high to give repentance as well as remission of sin. Thou wantest a new heart: the covenant runs thus, "A new heart also will I give them, and a right spirit will I put within them." Thou wantest pardon--behold his streaming wounds wash thou and be clean. Thou wantest healing: he is "the Lord that healeth thee." Thou wantest clothing--his righteousness shall become thy dress. Thou wantest preservation--thou shalt be preserved in him. Thou wantest life, and he has said, "Awake, thou that sleepest, and arise from the dead, and Christ shall give thee life." He is come that we might have life. Thou wantest--but indeed, the catalogue were much too long for us to read it through at this present, yet be assured though thou pile up thy necessities till they rise like Alps before thee, yet the all-sufficient Savior can remove all thy needs. You may confidently sing--

"Thou, O Christ, art all I want,
More than all in thee I find."

This is true also of the saint as well as the sinner. O child of God, thou art now saved, but thy wants are not therefore removed. Are they not as continuous as thy heart-beats? When are we not in want, my brethren? The more alive we are to God, the more are we aware of our spiritual necessities. He who is "blind and naked," thinks himself to be "rich and increased in goods," but let the mind be truly enlightened, and we feel that we are completely dependent upon the charity of God. Let us be glad, then, as we learn that there is no necessity in our spirit but what is abundantly provided for in the all fullness of Jesus Christ. You seek for a higher platform of spiritual attainments, you aim to conquer sin, you desire to be plentiful in finis unto his glory, you are longing to be useful, you are anxious to subdue the hearts of others unto Christ; behold the needful grace for all this. In the sacred armoury of the Son of David behold your battle-ax and your weapons of war; in the stores of him who is greater than Aaron see the robes in which to fulfill your priesthood; in the wounds of Jesus behold the power with which you may become a living sacrifice. If you would glow like a seraph, and serve like an apostle, behold the grace awaiting you in Jesus. If you would go from strength to strength, climbing the loftiest summits of holiness, behold grace upon grace prepared for you if you are straitened, it will not be in Christ; if there be any bound to your holy attainments, it is set by yourself. The infinite God himself gives himself to you in the person of his dear Son, and he saith to you, "All things are yours." "The Lord is the portion of your inheritance and of your cup." Infinity is ours. Be who gave us his own Son has in that very deed given us all things. Bath he not said, "I am the Lord thy God, which brought thee out of the land of Egypt; open thy mouth wide, and I will fill it"?

Let me remark that this is not only true of saints on earth, but it is true also of saints in heaven, for all the fullness of the church triumphant is in Christ as well as that of the church militant. They are nothing even in heaven without him. The pure river of the water of life of which they drink, proceedeth out of the throne of God and of the Lamb. He hath made them priests and kings, and in his power they reign. Those snowy robes were washed and made white in his blood. The Lamb is the temple of heaven (Revelation 21:22), the light of heaven (Revelation 21:23), his marriage is the joy of heaven (Revelation 19:7), and the Song of Moses, the servant of God, and the song of the Lamb, is the song of heaven (Revelation 15:3). Not all the harps above could make a heavenly place if Christ were gone; for he is the heaven of heaven, and filleth all in all. It pleased the Father that for all saints and sinners all fullness should be treasured up in Christ Jesus.

I feel that my text overwhelms me. Men may sail round the world, but who can circumnavigate so vast a subject as this? As far as the east is from the west so wide is its reach of blessings.

"Philosophers have measured mountains,
Fathomed the depths of seas, of states, and kings,
Walked with a staff to Heaven, and traced fountains:
But there are two vast spacious things,
The which to measure it doth more behove:
Yet few there are that sound them: Grace and Love."

Who is he that shall be able to express all that is meant by our text? for here we have "all" and "fullness"--and in fullness and a fullness in all. The words are both exclusive and inclusive. They deny that there is any fullness elsewhere, for they claim all for Christ. They shut out all others. "It pleased the Father that in him should all fullness dwell." Not in you, ye pretended successors of the apostles, can anything dwell that I need. I can do well enough without you; nay, I would not insult my Savior by trading with, you, for since "all fullness" is in him, what call there be in you that I can require? Go to your dupes who know not Christ, but those who possess the exceeding riches of Christ's grace bow not to you. We are "complete in Christ" without you, O hierarchy of bishops; without you, ye conclave of cardinals; and without you, O fallible infallible, unholy Holiness of Rome. He who has all in Christ would be insane indeed if he looked for more, or having fullness craved for emptiness. This text drives us from all confidence in men, ay, or even in angels, by making us see that everything is treasured up in Jesus Christ. Brethren, if there be any good in what is called catholicism, or in ritualism, or in the modern philosophical novelties, let religionists have what they find there; we shall not envy them, for they can find nothing worth having in their forms of worship or belief but what we must have already in the person of the all-sufficient Savior. What if their candles burn brightly, the sun itself is ours! What if they are successors of the apostles, we follow the Lamb himself whithersoever he goeth! What if they be exceeding wise, we dwell with the Incarnate Wisdom himself! Let them go to their cisterns, we will abide by the fountain of living water. But indeed there is no light in their luminaries, they do but increase the darkness; they are blind leaders of the blind. They put their sounding emptinesses into competition with the all-fullness of Jesus, and preach another gospel which is not another. The imprecation of the apostle be upon them. They add unto the words of God, and he shall add to them its plagues.

While the text is exclusive it is also inclusive. It shuts in everything that is required for time and for eternity for all the blood-bought. It is an ark containing all good things conceivable, yea, and many that are as yet inconceivable; for by reason of our weakness we have not yet conceived the fullness of Christ. Things which ye yet have not asked nor even thought, he is able to give you abundantly. If you should arrive at the consecration of martyrs, the piety of apostles, the purity of angels, yet should you never have seen or be able to think of anything pure, lovely, and of good report, that was not already treasured up in Christ Jesus. All the rivers flow into this sea, for from this sea they, came. As the atmosphere surrounds all the earth, and all things live in that sea of air, so all good things are contained in the blessed person of our dear Redeemer. Let us join to praise him. Let us extol him with heart and voice, and let sinners be reconciled unto God by him. If all the good things are in him which a sinner can require to make him accountable with God, then let the sinner come at once through Such a mediator. Let doubts and fears vanish at the sight of the mediatorial fullness. Jesus must be able to save to the uttermost, since all fullness dwells in him. Come, sinner; come and receive him. Believe thou in him and thou shalt find thyself made perfect in Christ Jesus.

"The moment a sinner believes,
And trusts in his crucified God,
His pardon at once he receives,
Redemption in full through his blood."

II. Having thus spoken of what, we now turn to consider WHERE.

"It pleased the Father that in him should all fullness dwell." Where else could all fullness have been placed? There was wanted a vast capacity to contain "all fullness." Where dwells there a being with nature capacious enough to compass within himself all fullness? As well might we ask, "Who hath measured the waters in the hollow of his hand, and meted out heaven with the span, and comprehended the dust of the earth in a measure, and weighed the mountains in scales, and the hills in a balance?" To him only could it belong to contain "all fullness," for he must be equal with God, the Infinite. How suitable was the Son of the Highest, who "was by him, as one brought up with him," to become the grand storehouse of all the treasures of wisdom, and knowledge and grace, and salvation. Moreover, there was wanted not only capacity to contain, but immutability to retain the fullness, for the text says, "It pleased the Father that in him should all fullness dwell" that is, abide, and remain, for ever. Now if any kind of fullness could be put into us mutable creatures, yet by reason of our frailty we should prove but broken cisterns that can hold no water. The Redeemer is Jesus Christ, the same yesterday, to-day, and for ever: therefore was it meet that all fullness should be placed in him. "The Son abideth ever." "He is a priest for ever after the order of Melchisedec." "Being made perfect he became the author of eternal salvation unto all they that obey him." "His name shall endure for ever: his name shall be continued as long as the sun: and men shall be blessed in him: all nations shall call him blessed."

Perhaps the sweetest thought is, that the "all fullness" is fitly placed in Christ Jesus, because in him there is a suitability to distribute it, so that we may obtain it from him. How could we come to God himself for grace? for "even our God is a consuming fire." But Jesus Christ while God is also man like ourselves, truly man, of a meek lowly spirit, and therefore easily approachable. They who know him, delight in nearness to him. Is it not sweet that all fullness should be treasured up in him who was the friend of publicans and sinners: and who came into the world to seek and to save that which was lost? The Man who took the child up on his knee and said, "Suffer the little children to come unto me," the Man who was tempted in all points like as we are, the Man who touched the sick, nay, who "bore their sicknesses," the Man who gave his hands to the nails, and his heart to the spear; that blessed Man, into the print of whose nails his disciple Thomas put his finger, and into whose side he thrust his hand; it is he, the incarnate God, in whom all fullness dwells. Come, then, and receive of him, you who are the weakest, the most mean, and most sinful of men. Come at once, O sinner, and fear not.

"Why art thou afraid to come,
And tell him all thy ease?
He will not pronounce thy doom,
Nor frown thee from his face.
Wilt thou fear Immanuel?
Or dread the Lamb of (God,
Who, to save thy soul from hell,
Has shed his precious blood?"

Let it be noted here, however, very carefully, that while fullness is treasured up in Christ, it is not said to be treasured up in the doctrines of Christ; though they are full and complete, and we need no other teachings when the Spirit reveals the Son in us; nor is it said to be treasured up in the commands of Christ, although they are amply sufficient for our guidance; but it is said, "It pleased the Father that in him," in his person, "should all fullness dwell." In him, as God incarnate dwelleth in all the fullness of the godhead bodily;" not as a myth, a dream, a thought, a fiction, but as a living, real personality. We must lay hold of this. I know that the fullness dwells in him officially as Prophet, Priest, and King--but the fullness lies not in the prophetic mantle, nor in the priestly ephod, nor in the royal vesture, but in the person that wears all these. "It pleased the Father that in him should all fullness dwell." You must get to the very Christ in your faith and rest alone in him, or else you have not reached the treasury wherein all fullness is stored up. All fullness is in him radically; if there be fullness in his work, or his gifts, or his promises, all is derived from his person, which gives weight and value to all. All the promises are yea and amen in Christ Jesus. The merit of his death lies mainly in his person, because he was God who gave himself for us, and his own self bare our sins in his own body on the tree. The excellence of his person gave fullness to his sacrifice.Hebrews 1:3. His power to save at this very day lies in his person, for "he is able to save to the uttermost them that come unto God by him, seeing he ever liveth to make intercession for them." I desire you to see this, and feel it; for when your soul clasps the pierced feet of Jesus, and looks up into the face more marred than that of any man, even if you cannot understand all his works and offices, yet if you believe in him, you have reached the place wherein all fullness dwells, and of his fullness you shall receive.

Beloved, remember our practical aim. Praise his person, ye saints! Be ye reconciled to God through his person, ye sinners! Ye angels, lead us in the song! Ye spirits redeemed by blood, sing, "Worthy is the Lamb that was slain," and our hearts shall keep tune with yours, for we owe the same debt to him. Glory be unto the person of the blessed Lamb. "Blessing, and glory, and wisdom, and thanksgiving, and honor, and power, and might, be unto our God for ever and ever." Would God we could see him face to face, and adore him as we would. O sinners, will you not be reconciled to God through him, since all fullness is in him, and he stoops to your weakness, and holds forth his pierced hands to greet you? See him stretching out both his hands to receive you, while he sweetly woos you to come to God through him. Come unto him. O come with hasty steps, ye penitents; come at once, ye guilty ones! Who would not be reconciled unto God by such a one as this, in whom all fullness of grace is made to dwell?

III. The third question is, WHY? "It pleased the Father." That is answer enough. He is a sovereign, let him do as he wills. Ask the reason for election, you shall receive no other than this, "Even so, Father, for so it seemed good in thy sight." That one answer may reply to ten thousand questions, "It is the Lord, let him do what seemeth him good." Once "it pleased the Father to bruise him," and now "it pleased the Father that in him should all fullness dwell." Sovereignty may answer the question sufficiently, but hearken! I hear justice speak, should not be silent. Justice saith there was no person in heaven or under heaven so meet to contain the fullness of grace as Jesus.

None so meet to be glorified as the Savior, who "made himself of no reputation, and took upon himself the form of a servant, and being found in fashion as a man, humbled himself, and became obedient to death, even the death of the cross." It is but justice that the grace which he has brought to us should be treasured up in him. And while justice speaks wisdom will not withhold her voice. Wise art thou, O Jehovah, to treasure up grace in Christ, for to him men can come; and to him coming, as unto a living stone, chosen of God and precious, men find him precious also to their souls. The Lord has laid our hell, in the right place, for he has laid it upon one that is mighty, and who is as loving as he is mighty, as ready as he is able to save. Moreover, in the fitness of things the Father's pleasure is the first point to be considered, for all things ought to be to the good pleasure of God. It is a great underlying rule of the universe that all things were created for God's pleasure. God is the source and fountain of eternal love, and it is but meet that he should convey it to us by what channel he may elect. Bowing, therefore, in lowly worship at his throne, we are glad that in this matter the fullness dwells where it perpetually satisfies the decree of heaven. It is well that "it pleased the Father."

Now, brethren, if it pleased the Father to place all grace in Christ, let us praise the elect Savior. What pleases God pleases us. Where would you desire to have grace placed, my brethren, but in the Well-beloved? The whole church of God is unanimous about this. If I could save myself I would not; I would think salvation to be no salvation if it did not glorify Jesus. This is the very crown and glory of being saved, that our being saved will bring honor to Christ. It is delightful to think that Christ will have the glory of all God's grace; it were shocking if it were not so. Who could bear to see Jesus robbed of his reward? We are indignant that any should usurp his place, and ashamed of ourselves that we do not glorify him more. No joy ever visits my soul like that of knowing that Jesus is highly exalted, and that to him "every knee shall bow and every tongue confess that Jesus Christ is Lord, to the glory of God the Father." A sister in Christ, in her kindness and gratitude, used language to me the other day which brought a blush to my cheek, for I felt ashamed to be so undeserving of the praise. She said, "Your ministry profits me because you glorify Christ so much." Ah, I thought, if you knew how I would glorify him if I could, and how far I fall below what I fain would do for him, You would not commend me. I could weep over the best sermons I have ever preached because I cannot extol my Lord enough, and my conceptions are so low, and my words so poor. Oh, if one could but attain really to honor him, and put another crown upon his head, it were heaven indeed! We are in this agreed with the Father, for if it pleases him to glorify his Son, we sincerely feel that it pleases us.

Ought not those who are yet unrenewed, to hasten to be reconciled to God by such a Redeemer? If it pleases the Father to put all grace in Christ, O sinner, does it not please you to come and receive it through Christ? Christ is the meeting-place for a sinner and his God. God is in Christ, and when you come to Christ, God meets you, and a treaty of peace is made between you and the Most High. Are you not agreed with God in this--that Christ shall be glorified? Do you not say, "I would glorify him by accepting this morning all his grace, love, and mercy"? Well, if you are willing to receive Jesus, God has made you willing, and therein proved his willingness to save you. He is pleased with Christ. Are you pleased with Christ? If so, there is already peace between you and God, for Jesus "is our peace."

IV. We must close by dwelling upon the WHEN. When is all fullness in Jesus? It is there in all time, past, present, and to come. "It pleased the Father that in him should all fullness dwell." Fulness, then, was in Christ of old, is in Christ to-day, will be in Christ for ever. Perpetuity is here indicated; all fullness was, is, shall be in the person of Jesus Christ. Every saint saved under the old dispensation found the fullness of his salvation in the coming Redeemer, every saint saved since the advent is saved through the selfsame fullness. From the streaming fount of the wounds of Christ on Calvary, redemption flows evermore; and as long as there is a sinner to be saved, or one elect soul to be ingathered, Christ's blood shall never lose its power, the fullness of merit and grace shall abide the same.

While the expression "dwell" indicates perpetuity, does not it indicate constancy and accessibility? A man who dwells in a house is always to be found there, it is his home. The text seems to me to say that this fullness of grace is always to be found in Christ, ever abiding in him. Knock at this door by prayer, and you shall find it at home. If a sinner anywhere is saving, "God be merciful to me!" mercy has not gone out on travel, it dwells in Christ both night and day; it is there now at this moment. There is life in a look at the crucified One, not at certain canonical hours, but at any hour, in any place, by any man who looks. "From the end of the earth will I cry unto thee, when my heart is overwhelmed," and my prayer shall not be rejected. There is fullness of mercy in Christ to be had at any time, at any season, from any place. It pleased the Father that all fullness should permanently abide in him as in a house whose door is never shut.

Above all, we see here immutability. All fullness dwells in Christ--that is to say, it is never exhausted nor diminished. On the last day wherein this world shall stand before it is given up to be devoured with fervent heat, there shall be found as much fullness in Christ as in the hour when the first sinner looked unto him and was lightened. O sinner, the bath that cleanses is as efficacious to take out spots to-day as it was when the dying thief washed therein. O thou despairing sinner, there is as much consolation in Christ to-day as when he said to the woman, "Thy sins are forgiven thee, go in peace." His grace has not diminished. He is to-day as great a Savior as when Magdalen was delivered from seven devils. Till time shall be no more he will exercise the same infinite power to forgive, to renew, to deliver, to sanctify, to perfectly save souls.

Shall not all this make us praise Christ, since all fullness is permanent in him? Let our praises abide where the fullness abides. "All thy works praise thee, O God, but thy saints shall bless thee;" yea, they shall never cease their worship, because thou shalt never abate thy fullness This is a topic upon which we who love Christ, are all agreed. We can dispute about doctrines, and we have different views upon ordinances; but we have all one view concerning our Lord Jesus. Let him sit on a glorious high throne. When shall the day dawn that he shall ride through our streets in triumph? When shall England and Scotland, and all the nations become truly the dominions of the great King? Our prayer is that he may hasten the spread of the gospel, and his own coming as seemeth good in his sight. O that he were glorious in the eyes of men!

And surely if all fullness abides perpetually in Christ, there is good reason why the unreconciled should this morning, avail themselves of it. May the blessed Spirit show thee, O sinner, that there is enough in Jesus Christ to meet thy wants, that thy, weakness need not keep thee back, nor even the hardness of thy heart, nor the inveteracy of thy will; for Christ is able even to subdue all things to himself. If you seek him he will be found of you. Seek him while he may be found. Leave not the seat until your soul is bowed at his feet. I think I see him; cannot your hearts picture him, glorious to-day, but yet the same Savior who was nailed like a felon to the cross for guilty ones? Reach forth thy hand and touch the silver scepter of mercy which he holds out to thee, for those who touch it live. Look into that dear face where tears once made their furrows, and grief its lines; look, I say, and live. Look at that brow radiant with many a glittering gem, it once wore a crown of thorns; let his love melt you to repentance. Throw yourself into his arms now feeling, "If I perish I will perish there. He shall be my only hope." As the Lord liveth, before whom I stand, there shall never be a soul of you lost who will come and trust in Jesus. Heaven and earth shall pass away but this word of God shall never pass away. "He that believeth and is baptised shall be saved." God has said it; will he not do it? He has declared it, it must stand fast. "Whosoever believeth in him shall not perish, but have everlasting life." O trust ye him! I implore you by the mercy of God, and by the fullness of Jesus, trust him now, this day! God grant you may, for Christ's sake. Amen.

PORTION OF SCRIPTURE READ BEFORE SERMON--Colossians 1.

Faith and Regeneration

A Sermon (No. 979)
Delivered on Lord's-day Morning, March 5th, 1871 by
C. H. SPURGEON,
At the Metropolitan Tabernacle, Newington

"Whosoever believeth that Jesus is the Christ is born of God: and everyone that loveth him that begot loveth him also that is begotten of him." - 1 John 5:1.

FOR THE PREACHER of the gospel to make full proof of his ministry will be a task requiring much divine teaching. Besides much care in the manner and spirit, he will need guidance as to his matter. One point of difficulty will be to preach the whole truth in fair proportion, never exaggerating one doctrine, never enforcing one point, at the expense of another, never keeping back any part, nor yet allowing it undue prominence. For practical result will much depend upon an equal balance, and a right dividing of the word. In one case this matter assumes immense importance because it affects vital truths, and may lead to very serious results unless rightly attended to; I refer to the elementary facts involved in the work of Christ for us, and the operations of the Holy Spirit in us. Justification by faith is a matter about which there must be no obscurity much less equivocation; and at the same time we must distinctly and determinately insist upon it that regeneration is necessary to every soul that shall enter heaven. "Ye must be born again" is as much a truth as that clear gospel statement, "He that believeth and is baptized shall be saved." It is to be feared that some zealous brethren have preached the doctrine of justification by faith not only so boldly and so plainly, but also so baldly and so out of all connection with other truth, that they have led men into presumptuous confidences, and have appeared to lend their countenance to a species of Antinomianism very much to be dreaded. From a dead, fruitless, inoperative faith we may earnestly pray, "Good Lord, deliver us," yet may we be unconsciously, fostering it. Moreover to stand up and cry, "Believe, believe, believe," without explaining what is to be believed, to lay the whole stress of salvation upon faith without explaining what salvation is, and showing that it means deliverance from the power as well as from the guilt of sin, may seem to a fervent revivalist to be the proper thing for the occasion, but those who have watched the result of such teaching have had grave cause to question whether as much hurt may not be done by it as good. On the other hand, it is our sincere conviction that there is equal danger in the other extreme. We are most certain that a man must be made a new creature in Christ Jesus, or he is not saved; but some have seen so clearly the importance of this truth that they are for ever and always dwelling upon the great change of conversion, and its fruits, and its consequences, and they hardly appear to remember the glad tidings that whosoever believeth on Christ Jesus hath everlasting life. Such teachers are apt to set up so high a standard of experience, and to be so exacting as to the marks and signs of a true born child of God, that they greatly discourage sincere seekers, and fall into a species of legality from which we may again say, "Good Lord, deliver us." Never let us fail most plainly to testify to the undoubted truth that true faith in Jesus Christ saves the soul, for if we do not we shall hold in legal bondage many who ought long ago to have enjoyed peace, and to have entered into the liberty of the children of God.

It may not be easy to keep these two things in there proper position, but we must aim at it if we would be wise builders. John did so in his teaching. If you turn to the third chapter of his gospel it is very significant that while he records at length our Saviour's exposition of the new birth to Nicodemus, yet in that very same chapter he gives us what is perhaps the plainest piece of gospel in all the Scriptures: "And as Moses lifted up the serpent in the wilderness, even so must the Son of man be lifted up: that whosoever believeth in Him should not perish, but have everlasting life." So, too, in the chapter before us he insists upon a man's being born of God; he brings that up again and again, but evermore does he ascribe wondrous efficacy to faith; he mentions faith as the index of our being born again, faith as overcoming the world, faith as possessing the inward witness, faith as having eternal life--indeed, he seems as if he could not heap honour enough upon believing, while at the same time he insists upon the grave importance of the inward experience connected with the new birth.

Now, if such difficulty occurs to the preacher, we need not wonder that it also arises with the hearer, and causes him questioning. We have known many who, by hearing continually the most precious doctrine that belief in Jesus Christ is saving, have forgotten other truths, and have concluded that they were saved when they were not, have fancied they believed when as yet they were total strangers to the experience which always attends true faith. They have imagined faith to be the same thing as a presumptuous confidence of safety in Christ, not grounded upon the divine word when rightly understood, nor proved by any facts in their own souls. Whenever self-examination has been proposed to them they have avoided it as an assault upon their assurance, and when they have been urged to try themselves by gospel tests, they have defended their false peace by the notion that to raise a question about their certain salvation would be unbelief. Thus, I fear, the conceit of supposed faith in Christ has placed them in an almost hopeless position, since the warnings and admonitions of the gospel have been set aside by their fatal persuasion that it is needless to attend to them, and only necessary to cling tenaciously to the belief that all has been done long ago for us by Christ Jesus, and that godly fear and careful walking are superfluities, if not actually an offence against the gospel. On the other hand, we have known others who have received the doctrine of justification by faith as a part of their creed, and yet have not accepted it as a practical fact that the believer is saved. They so much feel that they must be renewed in the spirit of their minds, that they are always looking within themselves for evidences, and are the subjects of perpetual doubts. Their natural and frequent song is--

"Tis a point I long to know,
Oft it causes anxious thought;
Do I love the Lord, or no?
Am I his, or am I not?"

These are a class of people to be much more pitied than condemned. Though I would be the very last to spread unbelief, I would be the very first to inculcate holy anxiety. It is one thing for a person to be careful to know that he is really in Christ, and quite another thing for him to doubt the promises of Christ, supposing that they are really made to him. There is a tendency in some hearts to look too much within, and spend more time studying their outward evidences and their inward feelings, than in learning the fullness, freeness, and all sufficiency of the grace of God in Christ Jesus. They too much obscure the grand evangelical truth that the believer's acceptance with God is not in himself, but in Christ Jesus, that we are cleansed through the blood of Jesus, that we are clothed in the righteousness of Jesus, and are, in a word, "accepted in the Beloved." I earnestly long that these two doctrines may be well balanced in your souls. Only the Holy Spirit can teach you this. This is a narrow path which the eagle's eye has not seen, and the lions whelp has not trodden. He whom the Holy Ghost shall instruct will not give way to presumption and despise the Spirit's work within, neither will he forget that salvation is of the Lord Jesus Christ, "who of God is made unto us wisdom, and righteousness, and sanctification, and redemption." The text appears to me to blend these two truths in a very delightful harmony, and we will will try to speak of them, God helping us.

"He that believeth that Jesus is the Christ is born of God." We shall consider this morning, first of all, the believing which is here intended; and then, secondly, how it is a sure proof of regeneration; and then, thirdly, dwelling for awhile upon the closing part of the verse we shall show how it becomes an argument for Christian love: "Every one that loveth him that begat loveth him also that is begotten of him."

I. WHAT IS THE BELIEVING INTENDED IN THE TEXT? We are persuaded, first of all, that the believing here intended is that which our Lord and his apostles exhorted men to exercise, and to which the promise of salvation is always appended in the word of God; as for instance that faith which Peter inculcated when he said to Cornelius, "To him give all the prophets witness, that through his name whosoever believeth in him shall receive the remission of sins;" and which our Lord commanded when he came into Galilee, saying to men, "Repent ye, and believe the gospel" (Mark i. 15). Certain persons have been obliged to admit that the apostles commanded, and exhorted, and besought men to believe, but they tell us the kind of believing which the apostles bade men exercise was not saving faith. Now, God forbid we should ever in our zeal to defend a favorite position, be driven to an assertion so monstrous. Can we imagine for a moment apostles with burning zeal and ardor, inspired by the Spirit of God within them, going about the world exhorting men to exercise a faith which after all would not save them? To what purpose did they run on so fruitless an errand, so tantalizing to human need, so barren of results? When our Lord bade his disciples go into all the world and preach the gospel to every creature, and added, "he that believeth and is baptized shall be saved," the faith which was to be preached was evidently none other than a saving faith, and it is frivolous to say otherwise. I must confess that I felt shocked the other day to read in a certain sermon the remark that the words of Paul to the jailor "were spoken in a conversation held at midnight under peculiar circumstances, and the evangelist who wrote them was not present at the interview." Why, had it been at high noon, and had the whole world been present, the apostle could have given no fitter answer to the question, "What must I do to be saved?" than the one he did give, "Believe in the Lord Jesus Christ, and thou shalt be saved." It is, I repeat, a mere frivolity or worse, to say that the faith enjoined by the apostles was a mere human faith which does not save, and that there is no certainty that such faith saves the soul. That cause must be desperate that calls for such a defence.

Furthermore, the faith here intended is the duty of all men. Read the text again: "Whosoever believeth that Jesus is the Christ is born of God." It can never be less than man's duty to believe the truth; that Jesus is the Christ is the truth, and it is the duty of every man to believe it. I understand her by "believing," confidence in Christ, and it is surely the duty of men to confide in that which is worthy of confidence, and that Jesus Christ is worthy of the confidence of all men is certain, it is therefore the duty of men to confide in him.

Inasmuch as the gospel command, "Believe in the Lord Jesus Christ and thou shalt be saved," is addressed by divine authority to every creature, it is the duty of every man so to do. What saith John: "This is his commandment, That we should believe on the name of his Son Jesus Christ," and our Lord himself assures us, "He that believeth on him is not condemned: but he that believeth not is condemned already, because he hath not believed in the name of the only-begotten Son of God." I know there are some who will deny this, and deny it upon the ground that man has not the spiritual ability to believe in Jesus, to which I reply that it is altogether an error to imagine that the measure of the sinners moral ability is the measure of his duty. There are many things which men ought to do which they have now lost the moral and spiritual, though not the physical, power to do. A man ought to be chaste, but if he has been so long immoral that he cannot restrain his passions, he is not thereby free from the obligation. It is the duty of a debtor to pay his debts, but if he has been such a spendthrift that he has brought himself into hopeless poverty, he is not exonerated from his debts thereby. Every man ought to believe that which is true, but if his mind has become so depraved that he loves a lie and will not receive the truth, is he thereby excused? If the law of God is to be lowered according to the moral condition of sinners, you would have a law graduated upon a sliding- scale to suit the degrees of human sinfulness; in fact, the worst man would be under the least law, and become consequently the least guilty. God's requirements would be a variable quantity, and, in truth, we should be under no rule at all. The command of Christ stands good however bad men may be, and when he commands all men everywhere to repent, they are bound to repent, whether their sinfulness renders it impossible for them to be willing to so or not. In every case it is man's duty to do what God bids him.

At the same time, this faith, wherever it exists, is in every case, without exception, the gift of God and the work of the Holy Spirit. Never yet did a man believe in Jesus with the faith here intended, except the Holy Spirit led him to do so. He has wrought all our works in us, and our faith too. Faith is too celestial a grace to spring up in human nature till it is renewed: faith is in every believer "the gift of God." You will say to me, "Are these two things consistent?" I reply, "Certainly, for they are both true." "How consistent?" say you. "How inconsistent?" say I, and you shall have as much difficulty to prove them inconsistent as I to prove them consistent. Experience makes them consistent, if theory does not. Men are convinced by the Holy Spirit of sin--"of sin," saith Christ, "because they believe not on me;" here is one of the truths; but the selfsame hearts are taught the same Spirit that faith is of the operation of God. (Col. ii. 2) Brethren be willing to see both sides of the shield of truth. Rise above the babyhood which cannot believe two doctrines until it sees the connecting link. Have you not two eyes, man? Must you needs put one of them out in order to see clearly? Is it impossible to you to use a spiritual stereoscope, and look at two views of truth until they melt into one, and that one becomes more real and actual because it is made up of two? Man men refuse to see more than one side of a doctrine, and persistently fight against anything which is not on its very surface consistent with their own idea. In the present case I do not find it difficult to believe faith to be at the same time the duty of man and the gift of God; and if others cannot accept the two truths, I am not responsible for their rejection of them; my duty is performed when I have honestly borne witness to them.

Hitherto we have only been clearing the way. Let us advance. The faith intended in the text evidently rests upon a person--upon Jesus. "Whosoever believeth that Jesus is the Christ is born of God." It is not belief about a doctrine, nor an opinion, nor a formula, but belief concerning a person. Translate the words, "Whosoever believeth that Jesus is the Christ," and they stand thus: "Whosoever believeth that the Saviour is the Anointed is born of God." By which is assuredly not meant, whosoever professes to believe that he is so, for many do that whose lives prove that they are not regenerate; but, whosoever believes it to be the fact, as truly and in very deed to receive Jesus as God has set him forth and anointed him, is a regenerate man. What is meant by "Jesus is

the Christ," or, Jesus is the Anointed? First, that he is the Prophet; secondly, that he is the Priest; thirdly, that he is the King of the church, for in all these three senses he is the Anointed. Now, I may ask myself this question: Do I this day believe that Jesus is the great Prophet anointed of God to reveal to me the way of salvation? Do I accept him as my teacher and admit that he has the words of eternal life? If I so believe, I shall obey his gospel and possess eternal life. Do I accept him to be henceforth the revealer of God to my soul, the messenger of the covenant, the anointed prophet of the Most High? But he is also a priest. Now, a priest is ordained among men to offer sacrifices; do I firmly believe that Jesus was ordained to offer his one sacrifice for the sins of mankind, by the offering of which sacrifice once for all he has finished the atonement and made complete expiation? Do I accept his atonement as an atonement for me, and receive his death as an expiation upon which I rest my hope for forgiveness of all my transgressions? Do I in fact believe Jesus to be the one sole, only propitiating Priest, and accept him to act as priest for me? If so, then I have in part believed that Jesus is the Anointed. But he is also King, and if I desire to know whether I possess the right faith, I further must ask myself, "Is Jesus, who is now exalted in heaven, who once bled on the cross, is he King to me? Is his law my law? Do I desire to submit myself entirely to his government? Do I hate what he hates, and love what he loves? Do I live to praise him? Do I, as a loyal subject, desire to see his kingdom come and his will be done on earth as it is in heaven?" My dear friend, if thou canst heartily and earnestly say, "I accept Jesus Christ of Nazareth to be Prophet, Priest, and King to me, because God has anointed him to exercise those three offices; and in each of these three characters I unfeignedly trust him," then, dear friend, you have the faith of God's elect, for it is written, "He that believeth that Jesus is the Christ is born of God."

Now we go a little further. True faith is reliance. Look at any Greek lexicon you like, and you will find that the word pisteuein does not merely mean to believe, but to trust, to confide in, to commit to, entrust with, and so forth; and the marrow of the meaning of faith is confidence in, reliance upon. Let me ask, then, every professor her who professes to have faith, is your faith the faith of reliance? You give credit to certain statements, do you also place trust in the one who glorious person who alone can redeem? Have you confidence as well as credence? A creed will not save you, but reliance upon the Anointed Saviour is the way of salvation. Remember, I beseech you, that if you could be taught an orthodoxy unadulterated with error, and could learn a creed written by the pen of the Eternal God himself, yet a mere notional faith, such as men exercise when they believe in the existence of men in the moon, or nebulae in space, could not save your soul. Of this we are sure, because we see around us many who have such a faith, and yet evidently are not the children of God.

Moreover, true faith is not a flattering presumption, by which a man says, "I believe I am saved, for I have such delightful feelings, I have had a marvelous dream, I have felt very wonderful sensations;" for all such confidence may be nothing but mere assumption. Presumption, instead of being faith, is the reverse of faith; instead of being the substance of things hoped for, it is a mere mirage. Faith, is as correct as reason, and if her arguments are considered, she is as secure in her conclusions as though she drew them by mathematical rules. Beware, I pray you, of a faith which has no basis but your own fancy.

Faith, again, is not the assurance that Jesus died for me. I sometimes feel myself a little at variance with that verse--

"Just as I am--without one plea
But that thy blood was shed for me."

It is eminently suitable for a child of God, but I am not sure as to its being the precise way for putting the matter for a sinner. I do not believe in Jesus because I am persuaded that his blood was shed for me, but rather I discover that his blood was shed especially for me from the fact that I have been led to believe in him. I fear me there are thousands of people who believe that Jesus died for them, who are not born of God, but rather are hardened in their sin by their groundless hopes of mercy. There is no particular efficacy in a man's assuming that Christ has died for me; for it is a mere truism, if it true as some teach, that Jesus died for everybody. On such a theory every believer in a universal atonement would necessarily be born of God, which is very far from being the case. When the Holy Ghost leads us to rely upon the Lord Jesus, then the truth that God gave his only begotten Son that whosoever believeth in him might be saved, is opened up to our souls, and we see that for us who are believers, Jesus died with the special intent that we should be saved. For the Holy Spirit to assure us that Jesus shed his blood for us in particular is one thing, but merely to conclude that Jesus for us on the notion that he died for everybody is as far as the east is from the west, from being real faith in Jesus Christ.

Neither is it faith for me to be confident that I am saved, for it may be the case that I am not saved, and it can never be faith to believe a lie. Many have concluded rashly that they were saved when they were still in the gall of bitterness. That was not the exhibition of confidence in Christ but the exhibition of a base presumption destructive to the last degree. To come back to where we started from, faith, in a word, is reliance upon Jesus Christ. Whether the Redeemer died in special and particular for me or not, is not the question to be raised in the first place; I find that he came into the world to save sinners, under that general character I come to him, I find that whosoever trusteth him shall be saved, I therefore trust him, and having done so, I learn from his word that I am the object of his special love, and that I am born of God.

In my first coming to Jesus I can have no knowledge of any personal and special interest in the blood of Jesus; but since it is written, "God hath set him forth to be a propitiation for our sins: and not for ours only, but also for the sins of the whole world," I come and trust myself to that propitiation; sink or swim I cast myself on the Saviour. Great Son of God, thou hast lived and died, thou hast bled and suffered, and made atonement for sin for all such as trust thee, and I trust thee, I lean upon thee, I cast myself upon thee. Now, whoever has such faith as this is born of God, he has true faith which is proof positive of the new birth. Judge ye, therefore, whether ye have this faith or no.

Let me tarry just one minute longer over this. The true faith is set forth in Scripture by figures, and one or two of these we will mention. It was an eminent type of faith when the Hebrews father in Egypt slew the lamb and caught the warm blood in the basin, then took a bunch of hyssop and dipped it in the blood and marked the two posts of his door, and then struck a red mark across the lintel. That smearing of the door represented faith. The deliverance was wrought by the blood; and the blood availed through the householder's own personally striking it upon his door. Faith does that; it takes of the things of Christ, makes them its own, sprinkles the soul, as it were, with the precious blood, accepts the way of mercy by which the Lord passes over us and exempts his people from destruction. Faith was shown to the Jews in another way. When a beast was offered in sacrifice for sin, the priest and sometimes the representatives of the tribes or the individual laid their hands upon the victim in token that they desired their sins to be transferred to it, that it might suffer for them as a type of the great substitute. Faith lays her hands on Jesus, desiring to receive the benefit of his substitutionary death.

A still more remarkable representation of faith was that of the healing look of the serpent-bitten Israelites. On the great standard in the midst of the camp Moses lifted up a serpent of brass; high overhead above all the tents this serpent gleamed in the sun, and whoever of all the dying host would but look to it was made to live. looking was a very simple act, but it indicated that the person was obedient to God's command. He looked as he was bidden, and the virtue of healing came from the brazen serpent through a look. Such is faith. It is the simplest thing in the world, but it indicates a great deal more than is seen upon its surface:

"There is life for a look at the Crucified One."

To believe in Jesus is but to glance the eye of faith to him, to trust him with thy soul.

That poor woman who came behind our Saviour in the press offers us another figure of what faith is. She said, "If I may but touch the hem of his garment I shall be made whole." Taking no medicines, making no profession, and performing no ceremonies, she simply touched the ravelling of the Saviour's robe, and she was healed at once. O soul, if thou canst get into contact with Christ by simply trusting him, though that trust be ever so feeble, thou hast the faith of God's elect; thou hast the faith which is in every case the token of the new birth.

II. We must now pass on to show that WHEREVER IT EXISTS IT IS THE PROOF OF REGENERATION. There never was a grain of such faith as this in the world, except in a regenerate soul, and there never will be while the world standeth. It is so according to the text, and if we had no other testimony this one passage would be quite enough to prove it. "Whosoever believeth that Jesus is the Christ is born of God." "Ah!" I hear thee say, poor soul, "the new birth is a great mystery; I do not understand it; I am afraid I am not a partaker in it." You are born again if you believe that Jesus is the Christ, if you are relying upon a crucified Saviour you are assuredly begotten again unto a lively hope. Mystery or no mystery, the new birth is yours if you are a believer. Have you never noticed that the greatest mysteries in the world reveal themselves by the simplest indications. The simplicity and apparent easiness of faith is no reason why I should not regard its existence as an infallible indication of the new birth within. How know we that the new-born child lives except by its cry? Yet a child's cry--what a simple sound it is! how readily could it be imitated! a clever workman could with pipes and strings easily deceive us; yet was there never a child's cry in the world but what it indicated the mysteries of breathing, heart-beating, blood-flowing, and all the other wonders which come with life itself. Do you see yonder person just drawn out of the river? Does she live? Yes, life is there. Why? Because the lungs still heave. But does it not seem an easy thing to make lungs heave? A pair of billows blown into them, might not that produce the motion? Ah, yes, the thing is easily imitated after a sort; but no lungs heave except where life is. Take another illustration. Go into a telegraph office at any time, and you will see certain needles moving right and left with unceasing click. Electricity is a great mystery, and you cannot see or feel it; but the operator tells you that the electric current is moving along the wire. How does he know? "I know it by the needle." How is that? I could move your needles easily. "Yes; but do not you see the needle has made two motions to the right, one to the left, and two to the right again? I am reading a message." "But," say you, "I can see nothing in it; I could imitate the clicking and moving very easily." Yet he who is taught the art sees before him in those needles, not only electric action, but a deeper mystery still; he perceives that a mind is directing an invisible force, and speaking by means of it. Not to all, but to the initiated is it given to see the mystery hidden within the simplicity. The believer sees in the faith, which is simple as the movements of the needle, an indication that God is operating on the human mind, and the spiritual man discerns that there is an inner secret intimated thereby, which the carnal eye cannot decipher. To believe in Jesus is a better indicator of regeneration than anything else, and in no case did it ever mislead. Faith in the living God and his Son Jesus Christ is always the result of the new birth, and can never exist except in the regenerate. Whoever has faith is a saved man.

I beg you to follow me a little in this argument. A certain divine has lately said, "A man's act of believing is not the same as his being saved: it is only in the direction of being saved." This is tantamount to a denial that every believer in Christ is at once saved; and the inference is that a man may not conclude that he is saved because he believes in Jesus. Now, observe how opposed this is to Scripture. It is certain from the Word of God that the man who believes in Jesus is not condemned. Read John iii. 18, and many other passages. "He that believeth on Him is not condemned." Now is not every unregenerate man condemned? Is not a man who is not condemned a saved man? When you are sure on divine authority that the believer is not condemned, how in the name of everything that is rational can you deny that the believer is saved? If he is not condemned, what has he to fear? Will he not rightly conclude that being justified by faith, he has peace with God through our Lord Jesus Christ?

Note, secondly, that faith in the fourth verse of the chapter before us is said to "overcome the world." "This is the victory that overcomes the world, even our faith." What, then, does faith overcome the world in persons who are not saved? How can this be possible when the apostle saith that that which overcomes the world is born of God? Read the fourth verse: "Whatsoever is born of God overcometh the world:" but faith overcomes the world. therefore the man who has faith is regenerate; and what means that but that he is saved, and that his faith is the instrument by which he achieves victories.

Further, faith accepts the witness of God, and more, he that hath faith has the witness in himself to the truth of God. Read the tenth verse of the chapter: "He that believeth on the Son of God hath the witness in himself." It is not said, "He that does this or feels that," but "He that believeth hath the witness in himself," his heart bears witness to the truth of God. Has any unsaved man an experimental witness within? Will you tell me that a man's inner experience bears witness to God's gospel and yet the man is in a lost state, or only hopeful of being saved ultimately? No, sir, it is impossible. He that believeth has that change wrought in him which enables by his own consciousness to confirm the witness of God, and such a man must be in a state of salvation. It is not possible to say of him that he is an unsaved man.

Again, note in this chapter, at the thirteenth verse, that wherever there is faith there is eternal life; so run the words, "these things have I written unto you that believe on the name of the Son of God; that ye may know that ye have eternal life." Our Lord himself, and his apostles, in several places have declared, "He that believeth on him hath everlasting life." Do not tell me that a sinner who believes in Jesus is to make an advance before he can say he is saved, that a man who trusts Christ is only on his way to salvation, and must wait until he has used the ordinances, and has grown in grace, before he may know that he is saved. No, the moment that the sinner's trust in placed on the finished work of Jesus he is saved. Heaven and earth may pass away, but that man shall never perish. If only one second ago I trusted the Saviour I am safe; just as safe as the man who has believed in Jesus fifty years, and who has all the while walked uprightly. I do not say that the new born convert is as happy, nor as useful, nor as holy, nor as ripe for heaven, but I do say that the words, "he that believeth on him hath everlasting life," is a truth with general bearings, and relates as much to the babe in faith as does to the man who has attained to fullness of stature in Jesus Christ.

As if this chapter were written on purpose to meet the gross error that faith does not bring immediate salvation, it extols faith again and again, yea, and I may add, our Lord himself crowns faith, because faith never wears the crown, but brings all the glory to the dear Redeemer.

Now, let me say a word or two in reply to certain questions. But must not a man repent as well as believe? Reply: No man ever believed but what he repented at the same time. Faith and repentance go together. they must. If I trust Christ to save me from sin, I am at the same time repenting of sin, and my mind is changed in relation to sin, and everything else that has to do with its state. All the fruits meet for repentance are contained in faith itself. You will never find that a man who trusts Christ remains an enemy of God, or a lover of sin. The fact that he accepts the atonement provided is proof positive that he loathes sin, and that his mind is thoroughly changed in reference to God. Moreover, as to all the graces which are produced in the Christian afterwards, are they not all to be found in embryo in faith? "Only believe, and you shall be save," is the cry which many sneer at, and others misunderstand; but do you know what "only believe" means? Do you know what a world of meaning lies in that word? Read that famous chapter to the Hebrews, and see what faith has done and is still able to do, and you will see that it is no trifle. Wherever there is faith in a man let it but develop itself and there will be a purging of himself from sin, a separating himself from the world, a conflict with evil, and a warring for the glory of Christ, which nothing else could produce. Faith is in itself one of the noblest of graces; it is the compendium of all virtues; and as sometimes there will lie within one single ear enough seed to make a whole garden fertile, so, within that one word "faith," there lies enough of virtue to make earth blessed; enough of grace, if the Spirit make it to grow, to turn the fallen into the perfect. Faith is not the easy and light thing men think. Far are we from ascribing salvation to the profession of a mere creed, we loathe the idea; neither do we ascribe salvation to a fond persuasion, but we do ascribe salvation to Jesus Christ, and the obtaining of it to that simple, child like confidence which lovingly casts itself into the arms of him who gave both his hands to the nail and suffered to the death for the sins of his people. He who believes, then, is saved--rest assured of that. "Whosoever believeth that Jesus is the Christ is born of God."

III. Now what flows out of this? Love is the legitimate issue! We must love if we are begotten of God all those who are also born of God. It would be an insult to you if I were to prove that a brother should love his brother. Doth not nature herself teach us that? Those, then, who are born of God ought to love all those of the same household. And who are they? Why, all those who have believed that Jesus is the Christ, and are resting their hopes where we rest ours, namely, on Christ the Anointed One of God. We are to love all such. We are to do this because we are of the family. We believe, and therefore we have been begotten of God. Let us act as those who are of the divine family; let us count it our privilege we are received into the household, and rejoice to perform the lovely obligations of our high position. We look around us and see many others who have believed in Jesus Christ; let us love them because they are of the same kindred. "But they are some of them unsound in doctrine, they make gross mistakes as to the Master's ordinances." We are not to love their faults, neither ought we to expect them to love ours, we are nevertheless to love their persons, for "whosoever believeth that Jesus is the Christ is born of God," and therefore he is one of the family, and as we love the Father who begat we are to love all those who are begotten of him. First, I love God, and therefore I desire to promote God's truth and to keep God's gospel free from taint. But then I am to love all those whom God has begotten, despite the infirmities and errors I see in them, being also myself compassed about with infirmities. Life is the reason for love, the common life which is indicated by the common faith in the dear Redeemer is to bind us to each other. I must confess, though I would pay every deference to every brother's conscientious judgment, I do not know how I could bring my soul as a child of God to refuse any man communion at my Master's table, who believed that Jesus is the Christ. I have proof in his doing do, if he be sincere (and I can only judge of that by his life), that he is born of God; and has not every child a right to come to the Father's table? I know in the olden times, parent used to make their children go without meals as a punishment, but everybody tell us now this is cruel and unwise, for it injures the child's constitution to deprive it of necessary food. There are rods in the Lord's house, and there is no need to keep disobedient children away from supper. Let them come to the Lord's table, and eat and drink with the Lord Jesus and with all his saints, in the hope that when their constitution bestows stronger they will throw out the disease which now they labor under, and come to be obedient to the whole gospel, which saith, "He that believeth and is baptized shall be saved."

Let me beg the members of this church to exhibit mutual love to one another. Are there many feeble among you? Comfort them. Are there any who want instruction? Bring your knowledge to their help. Are there any in distress? Assist them. Are they backsliding? Restore them. "Little children, love one another," is the rule of Christ's family, may we observe it. May the love of God which has been she abroad in our hearts by the Holy Ghost which is given unto us, reveal itself by our love to all the saints. And, remember, other sheep he has which are not yet of this fold; them also he must bring in. Let us love those who are yet to be brought in, and lovingly go forth at once to seek them; in whatever other form of service God has given us, let us with loving eyes look after our prodigal brothers, and who knows, we may bring into the family this very day some for whom there will be joy in the presence of the angels of God, because the lost one has been found. God bless and comfort you, for Jesus Christ's sake. Amen.

PORTION OF SCRIPTURE READ BEFORE SERMON--1 John 5.

Hidden Manna

A Sermon (No. 980)
Delivered on Lord's-Day Morning, March 12th, 1871, by
C. H. SPURGEON,
At the Metropolitan Tabernacle, Newington

"Thy words were found, and I did eat them; and thy word was unto me the joy and rejoicing of mine heart: for I am called by thy name, O Lord God of hosts," - Jeremiah 15:16.

Jeremiah was a man of exceedingly sensitive temperament; the very reverse of Elijah. Yet he was sent of God to execute a duty which apparently required a person of great sternness and slender sensibility. It was his unhappy duty to denounce the judgments of God upon a people whom he dearly loved, but whom it was impossible to save; for even his deep anguish of heart and melting pathos were powerless with them, and rather excited their ridicule than their attention. Either they did not believe that he was sent of God at all, or else they neither cared for Jehovah nor for his prophet. Naturally mild and retiring, his strong sense of allegiance to God and love to Israel made him bear a fearless testimony for the truth; but the reproaches, insults, and threats, which were heaped upon him, sorely wounded his soul; and even deeper was his anguish, because he well knew that his rejected warnings were terribly true. He carried before his mind's eye at all times the picture of Jerusalem captured by her foes, and her wretched sons and daughters given up to the sword. There is no line in the whole of his prophecy more characteristic of him than that exclamation, "O that my head were waters, and mine eyes a fountain of tears, that I might weep day and night for the slain of the daughter of my people."

He was eminently the man that had seen affliction, and yet in the midst of a wilderness of woe he discovered fountains of joy. Like that Blessed One, who was "the man of sorrows" and the acquaintance of grief, he sometimes rejoiced in spirit and blessed the name of the Lord. It will be both interesting and profitable to note the root of the joy which grew up in Jeremiah's heart, like a lone palm tree in the desert. Here was its substance. It was an intense delight to him to have been chosen to the prophetic office; and when the words of God came to him, he fed upon them as dainty food. They were often very bitter in themselves, for they mainly consisted of denunciations, yet being God's words, such was the prophet's love to his God, that he ate every syllable, bitter or not. This also was evermore a consolation to him--that he was known by the people to be a prophet of Jehovah. This distinction, whatever persecution it brought upon him, was his joy "I am called by thy name." God's word received, God's name named upon him, and God's work entrusted to him, these were stars which cheered the midnight of his grief. However hard his lot might be, and none seem to have fallen upon worse times, there were secret sweetnesses of which none could deprive him. When he was "filled with bitterness, and drunken with wormwood," he still drank of that ever-flowing river, the streams whereof make glad the city of our God. The basis of faith's joy lies deeper than the water-floods of affliction; no torrents of misery can remove the firm foundations of our peace.

May our hearts be so moulded by divine grace that the words of the weeping prophet in this verse may be proper language for us to use. Especially do I speak to those who during the last few weeks have found a Savior; my prayer and cry to God for you, beloved friends, is that you may say sincerely, "Thy words were found, and I did eat them; and thy word was unto me the joy and rejoicing of mine heart: for I am called by thy name, O Lord God of hosts."

I. In considering these words, we shall begin by dwelling upon A MEMORABLE DISCOVERY--"Thy words were found." As Jeremiah meant them, they signified this: that certain messages came to him most clearly from God, and he recognised them as such; he ascertained how far the thoughts which passed through his mind were originated by the Spirit of God, and how far they were merely his own imaginings; he separated between the precious and the vile, and when he had found, discovered, and discerned God's word, then it was that he fed upon it.

But the words, as we may use them, may signify something more. Beloved, it is a great thing to find God's word, and discern it for ourselves. Many have heard it for years and yet have never found it. I may say of them as of the heathen gods, "Eyes have they, but they see not: ears have they, but they hear not." Content with the outward letter of the Scriptures, the inner meaning is hid from their eyes. O that they had known the life-giving truth! O that they had found the "treasure hid in the field!" The word of God to them might as well be the word of King James the First, whose name dishonors our authorised version, for they have never felt that its truths proceed immediately from the throne of God, and bear the sign-manual of the King of kings. Hence they have never felt the weight of authority with which its authorship impresses holy writ. What is meant by finding God's words! The expression suggests the mode. A thing found has usually been sought for. Happy is that man who reads the Scriptures and hears the word--searching all the while for the hidden spiritual sense, which is indeed the voice of God. The letter of the truth contains a kernel, which is the inner life of it. Like some tropical fruits, which are very large, but in which the actual life-germ is a comparatively small thing, so within the sacred volume are many words and books, but the living secret may be summed up in a few syllables. The mystery which was hid from ages, is a secret something which flesh and blood cannot reveal unto us. "Understandest thou what thou readest?" is a vital and heartsearching question, meaning more than appears at once. The chosen of God dig into the mines of revelation, believing that "Surely there is a vein for the silver, and a place for gold where they fine it;" therefore they give their hearts to meditation, and cry mightily unto God to reveal himself unto them. Such seekers winnow sermons as the husbandman winnows his corn; they care little for the chaff of fair speeches; they desire only the fine wheat of the Lord's own truth. Solomon tells us the method of finding the true wisdom, in that cheering word at the commencement of the second chapter of the Proverbs, "My son, if thou wilt incline thine ear to wisdom, and apply thine heart to understanding; yea, if thou criest after knowledge, and liftest up thy voice for understanding; if thou seekest her as silver, and searches for her as for hid treasures; then shalt thou understand the fear of the Lord, and find the knowledge of God." Though occasionally the Lord in his infinite sovereignty has been pleased to reveal his salvation to those who sought it not, according to his own word, "I am found of them that sought me not," yet there is no promise to this effect; the promise is to those who seek.

To find God's words, means that we have been made to understand them. A man may be well versed in Scripture, both in the English and in the original tongue; he may be accustomed to read the best of commentaries, and be acquainted with Eastern manners, and yet he may be quite ignorant as to the word of God. For the understanding of this Book, as to its depth of meaning, does not lie within the range of natural learning and human research; reason alone is blinded by the excess of light, and wanders in darkness at noon day; for "the natural man receiveth not the things of the Spirit of God: for they are foolishness unto him: neither can he know them, because they are spiritually discerned." Before my conversion I was accustomed to read the Scriptures, to admire their grandeur, to feel the charm of their history, and wonder at the majesty of their language; but I altogether missed the Lord's intent therein; but when the Spirit came with his divine life, and quickened all the page to my newly-enlightened soul, the inner meaning-shone forth with quickening glory. The Bible is to many carnal minds almost as dull a book for reading as an untranslated Latin work would be to an ignorant ploughman, because they cannot get at the internal sense, which is to the words as juice to the grape, or the kernel to the nut. It is a tantalising riddle till you get the key; but the clue once found, the volume of our Father's grace absorbs our attention, delights our intellect, and enriches our heart.

To find the word of God means not only to understand it, but to appropriate it as belonging to yourself. To read a will is not an interesting occupation--repetitions, legal phrases, tautologies multiplied to utter weariness; but if there be a legacy left to you in that will, no writing will be more fascinating; you will trip lightly over the lawyer's fences and five-barred gates, and rejoice as one that findeth spoil when you reach those clauses which leave certain "messages, tenements, and hereditaments" to yourself and heirs. In such a case every repetition becomes musical, and technical phrases sound harmoniously. After this manner we learn to enjoy the word of God by discovering that we have a part and lot in it. When we perceive that the Lord is calling us and blessing us, then have we found his word. When the divine promise assures us personally that our sin is forgiven, that our spirit is clothed in the righteousness of Christ, that heaven is for us, that we are accepted in the Beloved, then the word is found indeed. I will ask each hearer here, whether in this respect he has found God's word. Have you an ear to hear gospel truth as the voice of the Infinite God addressed to your own soul? The Dutch farmers at the Cape, at no very distant period, considered the hottentots around them to be little better than beasts, quite incapable of anything beyond mere eating, drinking, stealing, and lying. After our missionaries had labored among the natives for a time, one of them was found reading the Bible by the roadside. The Dutchman enquired of him, "What book are you reading?"--"The Bible." "The Bible! Why that book was never intended for you."--"Indeed it was," said the black man, "for I see my name here." "Your name: Where?" cried the farmer. "Show it to me."--"There," said the Hottentot, putting his finger on the word "sinners." "That's my name; I am a sinner, and Jesus Christ came to save me." It were well indeed if men would but read the Bible, saying, "In this volume the great God condescends to speak to me, and bids me come and reason with him that my scarlet sins may become white; therein he appeals to my weakness that he may remove it, to my wilfulness that he may subdue it, to my distance from him that he may bring me near!" Happy is that man who hears or reads the word of God for himself, feeling evermore a living power witnessing within his soul, and operating mightily upon him. Unapplied truth is useless. Unappropriated truth may condemn but cannot save. The word of God to an unregenerate heart is like a trumpet at the ear of a corpse: the sound is lost. Beloved, I pray that you may discern the truth, and then may grasp it as your own. May your interest and title to the promises be clearly made out, so that not presumptuously, but with the full approbation of your conscience, you may know yourself to be beloved of the Lord.

"Thy word was found." Yes, indeed, it has been found by many of us, and a blessed find it was! Recollect, my brethren, the time when you first found God's word. Recall the period of your conversion; let the remembrance kindle in you anew the flame of gratitude. Magnify the divine grace which revealed the heavenly word to you. What a removal of darkness, and bursting in of glory you then felt! It was a discovery far more memorable than the finding of a new continent by Columbus, or the discovery of gold mines in the southern continent--you found eternal life in God's word. May you who have never found the life-giving word, be led to desire it. We pray for you, that the Lord may open your eyes to see wondrous things in his law.

II. Secondly, our text testifies to AN EAGER RECEPTION. "Thy words were found, and I did eat them."

It is not "I did hear them," for that he might have done, and yet have perished. Herod heard John gladly, and yet became his murderer. He does not say, "I did learn them by heart"--hundreds have committed chapters to memory, and were rather wearied than benefited thereby. The Scribes fought over the jots and titles of the law, but were blind leaders of the blind not withstanding. It is not "Thy words were found, and I did repeat them," for that he might have done as a parrot repeats language it is taught: nor is it even, "Thy words were found, and I remembered them;" for though its an excellent thing to store truth in the memory, yet the blessed effect of the divine words comes rather to those who ponder them in their hearts. "Thy words were found, and I did eat them." What is meant by eating God's words? The phrase signifies more than any other word could express. It implies an eager study--"I did eat them." I could not have too much of them, could not enter too thoroughly into their consideration. He who loves the Savior desires to grow in knowledge of him; he cannot read or hear too much or too often concerning his great Redeemer. He turns to the holy page with ever new delight; he seeks the blessing of the man who meditates in God's law, both day and night. It is pleasing to notice the sharp-set, spiritual appetite of a new convert; he hungers and thirsts after righteousness; he will hear a sermon without fatigue, though he may have to stand in an uncomfortable position; and when one discourse is over, he is ready for another. O that we all had our first appetites back again! Some professors grow very squeamish and proudly delicate; they cannot feed on heavenly truth, because forsooth they see defects in the style of the preacher, or in the manner of the service. Some of you need a dose of bitters to keep you from quarrelling with your food. When the word was found by my soul I did not stand to remark upon an inelegant expression or a misplaced word, but I seized at once the marrow of the truth, and left the bones to the dogs. I drank in the expressed juice of the sacred clusters, and left the husks to the swine. I was greedy for the truth. My soul hungered even to ravenousness to be fed upon the bread of heaven.

The expression also implies cheerful reception. "I did eat them." I was so in love with thy word that I not merely held it, rejoiced in it, and embraced it, but I received it into my inner man. I was not in a frame of mind to judge God's word, but I accepted all without demur; I did not venture to sit in judgment upon my judge, and become the reviser of the unerring God. Whatever I found to be in his word I received with intense joy. The stamp of divine authority upon any teaching is enough for the believer. Proud self-will demands to have doctrines proved by reasoning, but faith lets the declaration of Jehovah stand in the place of argument. Others may cry, "Let us spin our creed out of our own bowels like the spiders; let us find in the easings of the great the grounds of our beliefs, or let us remain in a state of suspense, to be moulded by fresh discoveries;" but we are committed to revelation, our minds are made up; we confess that we have eaten God's word and intend still to feed upon it--upon the whole of it, and upon nothing else. Open your mouths, ye wild asses of the wilderness, and snuff up wind; our food is more substantial, and we will not leave it to wander with you.

The expression signifies also an intense belief. "Thy words were found, and I did eat them." He did not say, "Perhaps it is true, and if it be so it is of no great consequence," but he made practical use of it at once. He set about testing the power of the word to nourish his soul; he brought it into the most intimate contact with his being, and allowed it to operate upon his vital parts. We have heard that God's word is life; be it ours to possess that life abundantly. The truth makes men strong, free, pure, god-like. Let us then eat it, that it may purify, strengthen, liberate and elevate us.

Whatever God's word by his Spirit can do for man, it should be our desire to experience for ourselves. Blessed is that man who is so humbled as to become like a little child in the submission of his mind, his judgment, and all his faculties to the operation of the word of divine truth; he has eaten it, and shall live by it.

The language before us means besides both the diligent treasuring up of the truth and the inward digestion of the same. Food eaten does not long continue as it was; the juices of the body operate upon it, and the substance is dissolved and absorbed, so that it becomes a part of the man's body. So when we find God's truth, we delight to meditate, con template, and consider. We let it dwell in our hearts richly till at last its sustaining, upbuilding, nourishing influence is felt, and we grow thereby. It is not a hasty swallowing of the word which is blessed to us, but a deliberate eating of it. Our inward life acts upon the truth, and the truth acts upon our life. We become one with the truth, and the truth one with us. I would to God we were all more given to feeding and lying down in the green pastures of God's word; the sheep fattens as it chews the cud at peace, and so do we. Establishment in the gospel is the result of meditation, and nothing is more desirable at this present crisis than that all believers should more constantly study and weigh the word of God. Neglect in this matter has weakened, is weakening, and will weaken the church. We want at this time not merely persons who have been aroused by solemn exhortation, and led to give their hearts to Christ under the influence of deep emotion, but Christians well instructed in the things which are verily believed among us, rooted and grounded in gospel doctrines. Many professing Christians think very lightly of Scriptural knowledge, and especially of an experimental acquaintance with divine truth. Few nowadays have studied the doctrines of grace so as to be able to give a reason for the hope that is in them. Too often converts are made by excitement, and, as a consequence, when the excitement is gone, they grow cold; some of them go back to the world, and prove that they were never taught of God, and others linger on in a half-starved condition, because soul-sustaining truth is hidden from them. The man who knows the truth, and feels that the truth has made him free, is the man who will continue a free man at all hazards. There are enemies of the faith about nowadays; error is put in very tempting forms. Those who try to subvert the gospel are exceedingly dextrous, and know how to make every falsehood fascinating. These will rend and devour, but who will be their victims? Not the instructed saints, not those who can say "Thy words were found, and I did eat them," but the mixed multitude in nominal union with the church, who scarce know what they believe, or knowing it merely in the letter have no inward vital acquaintance therewith. We read in the word of God of certain deceivers who would, if it were possible, deceive the very elect, from which we gather that the elect cannot be deceived, and that for this reason--that the truth is not held in the hand of the elect man as a staff which can be wrenched from him, but he has eaten it: it has entered into his vital substance. You cannot tear away from a man what has become assimilated to himself. You might draw the silken thread out of a piece of tapestry, and in so doing injure the material, but you cannot remove the truth which is interwoven into the fabric of our new-born nature by the Holy Spirit. A Christian is dyed ingrain with the truth--he wears no flying nor fading colors; he can as soon cease to be as cease to believe what he has learned by the Spirit's teaching. In olden times, the fury of persecutors has failed to make the servants of Christ deny the faith. The saints were taken to the stake, but the fires which devoured their bodies only burned their testimonies into the hearts of other witnesses. They were faithful even unto death. This glorious firmness in the faith is greatly needed now to resist the insidiousness of error. Besides, dear friends, it may in the providence of God happen that some of you will be taken away from the ministry which now feeds you, and what will you do if the word of God be not in your inmost souls? I have observed many who did run well when under a gospel ministry, who, when they have been removed into a barren region, have lagged and loitered in the race. Some whose principles were never very deep have given them up when placed in society which despised them. I pray you get such a hold of the gospel, that you need not be dependent upon the preacher or upon earnest companions. Let not your faith stand in the wisdom of man, but in the power of God. No truth will be of any use to you unless it is branded into you; yea, and made to penetrate the marrow of your being. If you could give up truth you have never received it. He only has the truth of God who so holds it that he could never part with it. A person takes a piece of bread and eats it. He who gave it to him demands it back. If he had put that bread upon a shelf, or laid it in a cupboard, he can hand it down; but if he can reply, "I have eaten it," there is an end to the request; no human power can reproduce what is already eaten. "Give up justification by faith and trust in sacraments," says the Ritualist. "Give up faith and follow reason," cries the Infidel. We are utterly unable to do either. And why? Because our spiritual nature has absorbed the truth into itself, and none can separate it from us, or us from it. To live upon the truth is the sure method to prevent apostacy. "Be not carried about with divers and strange doctrines. For it is a good thing that the heart be established with grace; not with meats, which have not profited them that have been occupied therein." May you all be rooted and built up in Christ Jesus, and established in the faith as ye have been taught, abounding therein with thanksgiving.

Besides, good friend, you cannot be very useful to others if you are an unintelligent Christian. To do much good, we must have truth ready to hand, and be apt to teach. I desire that you may grow up, you who are new-born into the Christian family, to become fathers and mothers in Israel; but this cannot be, unless you as new-born babes desire the unadulterated milk of the word, that you may grow thereby. O for a race of Bible-reading Christians! We have long had a society for selling the Bible, but who shall found a society for getting the Bible read? A young man who never had read his Bible was tempted to do so, and led to conversion by the gift of a bookmarker, presented to him by a relative. The gift was made upon the condition that it should be put into his Bible, but should never stop two days in a place. He meant to shift it, and not to read the book, but his eye glanced on a text; after awhile he became interested, by-and-by he became converted, and then the bookmarker was moved with growing pleasure. I am afraid that even some professors cannot say that they shift their bookmark every day. Probably of all the books printed, the most widely circulated, and the least read volume, is the word of God. Books about the Bible are read, I fear, more than the Book itself. Do you believe we should see all these parties and sects if people studiously followed the teaching of inspiration? The Word is one; whence these many creeds? We cry, "the Bible, and the Bible alone, is the religion of Protestants;" but it is not true of half the Protestants. Some overlay the Bible with the Prayer-book, and kill its living meaning; others read through the spectacles of a religious leader, and rather follow man's gloss than God's text. Few indeed come to the pure fount of gospel undefiled. A second-hand religion suits most, for it spares them the trouble of thinking, which to many is a labor too severe while to be taught of man is so much easier than to wait upon the Holy Spirit for instruction. Remember ye, my beloved children in Christ, the words of David, and make them your own. "I will delight myself in thy statutes: I will not forget thy word." "How sweet are thy words unto my taste! yea, sweeter than honey to my mouth." "Thy testimonies have I taken as an heritage for ever: for they are the rejoicing of my heart." "Mine eyes prevent the night watches, that I might meditate in thy word." "My soul hath kept thy testimonies; and I love them exceedingly. I have kept thy precepts and thy testimonies: for all my ways are before thee."

III. Thirdly, the text tells us of HAPPY CONSEQUENCES. "Thy word was unto me the joy and rejoicing of mine heart." He who has spiritually found God's word, and consequently feeds upon it, is the happy man. But in order to get joy from God's word we must receive it universally. Jeremiah first speaks of God's "words," then he changes the number and speaks of God's "word." We are not only to receive parts of the gospel, but the whole of it, and then it will afford us great joy. That man's heart is right with God who can honestly say that all the testimonies of God are dear to him. "But," saith one, "that is impossible: parts of the Bible are full of terrible denunciations; can they afford us joy?" In this way, brethren. If God appoints that sin should be punished, we are not to rebel against his righteous ordinance, nor to close our minds to the consideration of divine justice: God's judgments are right, and what is right we must rejoice in. Moreover, by the threatenings of the word many are led to forsake their sin, and thus the warning itself is a means of grace. To tender-hearted Jeremiah I have no doubt it was a trial to say, "Your city will be destroyed, and your women and your children will be slain." But when he considered that some might be led to repentance he would with tearful vehemence deal out the thunder of the Lord. But, brethren, God's word is not all threatening. How much of it consists of exceeding great and precious promises? grace drops from it like honey from the comb. How would even Jeremiah brush away the falling tear, while that face usually so clouded would beam as the sun when he spoke of the Messiah? Surely, if there be anything in the whole range of truth which can make our hearts leap for joy, it is the part of it which touches upon the lovely person and finished work of our adorable Redeemer, to whom be honor and glory for ever. Receive the whole of God's word. Do not cut a single text out of Scripture or desire to pervert its meaning. Hold the truth in its entirety and harmony, and then as a matter of certainty it will become to you the joy and rejoicing of your spirit.

Allow me to interject another thought. No word of God to Jeremiah would have given him joy if he had not been obedient to it. If he had kept back a part of his Master's message, it would have been a burden intolerable to his conscience. What a wound it makes in the heart if we have inwardly to confess, "I have been unfaithful. I have neglected a command of the Host High." Never, I beseech you, allow any text of Scripture to accuse you of having neglected its teaching or denied its obvious meaning. There are ordinances to which some of you have not submitted yourselves which you know to be the will of Jesus Christ. How can the Scriptures be a joy and rejoicing to you when their pages accuse you of disobedience to your Master's will? In order to have the full joy of the testimony of God, your mind must yield itself to what God reveals as the plastic clay to the potter's touch, your willing spirit must be prompt to run as with winged feet in the ways of obedience to all that Christ commands. Then the word being found, and you having eaten it, it will be to you a song in the house of your pilgrimage.

Let me refresh your memories for a moment by reminding you of certain choice truths in God's word which are brimming with comfort. There is the doctrine of election: the Lord has a people whom he has chosen, and whom he loved before the foundations of the world. I will suppose that you have found it out for yourself, and have read the riddle, and like the apostle Paul, can say, "Whom he did foreknow, he also did predestinate to be conformed to the image of his Son; and whom he did predestinate, them he also called: and whom he called, them he also justified." I will suppose that you know yourself to be called, and therefore know yourself to be predestinated. Is not this the joy and rejoicing of your heart? Is it not to you a very heaven below to believe that ere the hills were made God loved you, ere sin was born or Satan fell, your name was in his book, and he regarded you with infinite affection? Could any doctrine be a more abundant table, spread for you in the presence of your enemies? Take the other doctrine, the doctrine of the immutability of divine love. Before you knew the secret of it, it was a mere dogma; but now you understand that Jesus never changes, and therefore the promises are yea and amen, you will, you must rejoice. Having loved his own, he loved them to the end. Is not this music to your ear? "I have loved thee with an everlasting love," is not this a heavenly assurance? As you sit down and consider for yourself, "God has loved me, for he has given me salvation in Jesus Christ, and the mountains may depart, and the hills be removed, but the covenant of his grace cannot depart from me;" will not your cup run over, and your soul dance before the ark of God? Of course it will not be so till you have found the word for yourself, and have eaten it, but then it shall be marrow and fatness to you. Thousands of God's people live in doubts and fears, because they have not eaten God's word as they should; they do not know the fullness of the blessings of the gospel of peace. How many are in bondage through the fear that after all though they have been for years believers they are not yet saved, whereas if they read the Scriptures, and received their meaning, they would know that the moment the sinner believes in Christ he is saved in that very instant he has passed from death into life, and shall never come into condemnation. If they read the Scriptures, would they endure such doubts about being left to perish after having believed? The thing is impossible. The people of his choice Jehovah cannot cast away. No members of Christ's body shall be suffered to perish, or else the body of Christ would be mangled, and he himself would be the head of a dismembered frame. To have a clear understanding of the gospel, to know the covenant which like a mighty rock underlies all gospel blessings, to know Christ and our union with him, to know his righteousness, his perfection and our perfection in him, to know the indwelling of the Holy Ghost, these things must inevitably make us strong in the joy of the Lord. Half our doubts and fears would vanish if we had more acquaintance with the Lord's statutes. Other knowledge brings sorrow, but this wisdom is the joy and rejoicing of the heart.

Beloved, if there is a quarrel between you and any text of Scripture, end the dispute by giving way at once, for the word of God is right, and you are wrong. Do not say, "We have always been of one way of thinking, and our parents were so before us." Have respect unto God, and sit at Jesus' feet. The Lord's teaching is in this Book, and may be opened to you by his Spirit. Test everything by the word; prove the spirits whether they be of God. Do not be such fools as to take your religion from fallible men when you may have it from the infallible God. Some who do so are not fools in other matters, but in this case it may be said of them as it was once said of the people of an Italian city, "They were not fools, but they acted as if they were." Persons who would not take the opinion of anybody else as to the goodness of a half-crown, will leave their religion to be settled by an Act of Parliament, or by convocation, or by conference. What are brains given to us for? Are we for ever to be the slaves of majorities and follow a multitude to do evil? God forbid! Stand upright, O Christian man, and be a man. God has given you a judgment, and his Spirit waits to enlighten it. Search the Scriptures! See whether the things handed down by tradition came from the devil or from God, for many an ancient maxim may be traced to the infernal pit. To the law and to the testimony, if they speak not according to this word it is because there is no light in them. May we have grace given us like Ezekiel to receive the roll from the Lord's hand, to eat it, and to find it in our mouth as honey for sweetness.

IV. The fourth point is A DISTINGUISHING TITLE. "I am called by thy name, O Lord God of hosts." This may not appear to some of you a very joyful thing--to Jeremiah it was pre-eminently so. In Jeremiah's day the name of the Lord God of hosts was despised. The God of hosts was the subject of derision among the rabble of Jerusalem, and the weeping prophet of mournful countenance, who spoiled their mirth, came in for his full share of scorn. Now. Jeremiah, instead of feeling it a hard thing to be associated with the Lord in this contempt of the wicked, was glad to be so honored. The reproaches of them that reviled the Lord fell upon his poor servant, and he was content to have it so. O you who love Jesus Christ, never shun the scandal of his cross! Count it glory to be despised for his sake. Let fear be far from you. Remember Moses, of whom it is written, "he esteemed the reproach of Christ to be greater riches than all the treasures of Egypt." It does not say he esteemed Christ to be greater riches, an ordinary believer would do that; but he reckoned the worst thing connected with Christ to be better than the best thing about the world. The reproach of Christ he esteemed above Pharaoh's crown. Disciples of Jesus, be willing to bear all the contumely the wicked pour upon you for your Lord's sake, for in so doing they help to make you blessed. Through the mire, and through the slough, march side by side with truth, for those who share her pilgrimage shall share her exaltation. Be content to abide with Christ in his humiliation, for only so may you be sure that you shall be with him in his glory. It was a comfort to Jeremiah that he bore the name of the despised God. It made him the object of very much persecution as well as contempt; the king put him in the dungeon; he was made to eat the bread of affliction, and was in tribulations oft, but he took it all joyfully for the Lord's sake. And if to serve Christ to-day, and bear his name, should entail suffering extreme, as in the days of Rome's tyranny, yet, my brethren, we ought to be cheerful in the bearing of it, and glad that we are counted worthy to suffer for the name of Jesus Christ.

Yet I am afraid I am speaking to some who do not count it a fair thing to bear the name of the Most High. I gather this from their conduct. They have a belief in Jesus, they hope they have, but they have never avowed Christ's name. You have missed, then, that which was a comfort to the prophet. Why have you missed it? Because you imagined that it would be a source of discomfort to you? Are you wiser than the prophet? To him it was consolation that he was called by God's name. Do you think it would be a sorrow to you? "Oh!" saith one, "I could not bear the world's rebuke." Can you bear Christ's rebuke, when he will say to those who did not confess him before men, "I never knew you"? But you say you could not live up to a profession; you are afraid your life might fall short of what it should be--a very salutary fear; but do you hope to improve your life by beginning with disobedience! If I own my Savior's name, it is Christ's business to keep me; but if I am so overwise that I think I am safer in the path of disobedience, then I cannot reckon upon grace to preserve me. The warfare is arduous, but we do enter upon it at our own charges, there is one who has promised to help us. Well, if you will be cowards, I will part company with you. If you were every one of you this day enemies of Christ, or if you were all of you lovers of Christ in secret, and none of you gloried in him, I, for my part, could not fire a moment without being an avowed Christian. I say not this in egotism, but as fact. My heart might sooner cease to beat than cease to own the Lord. It is a sneaking thing, and utterly degrading that my Lord should die upon the cross for me to save my soul from hell, and I should be ashamed to wear his livery; that he should honor me by redeeming me with his blood, and I should deny to him the little honor that my poor name could give when it is enrolled with his people. Nay, though least of all his followers, put down my name, O recording angel, and there let it stand, and if all men revile and devils rage so let it be. It shall be my heaven to suffer hell for Christ, if such must needs be. I cannot comprehend how so many believers remain outside the visible church of Christ. I would not question the safety of any man who has believed in Jesus, but I do avow that I would not run the risk that non-confessors run. For what is the gospel? "He that with his heart believeth, and with his mouth maketh confession of him should be saved." How dare you leave out one half of the gospel command? What was the gospel which according to the Evangelist Mark is to be preached to every creature? It runs thus: "He that believeth and is baptised shall be saved." I do not question the safety of the soul that has believed, but I do say again, I would not run the risk of the man who, having believed, refuses to be baptised. It is plainly his Master's will. I question the genuineness of his faith if he starts back from obedience to the known command of Jesus Christ. My dear brother, to confess Christ is so easy a burden, it involves so temporary a loss, and so real a gain, that I would have you say, "I have found God's word, and I have eaten it: it is the joy and rejoicing of my soul; and now from this day let others do as they will, but I will serve the Lord. I bow my willing back to his cross. I will be buried with him in baptism unto death, I would die to the world, and rise to newness of life through his Spirit." Blessed are they who go to their Lord without the camp, leaving the world's religion as well as its sin, in obedience to that sacred call: "Come out from among them, and be ye separate, and touch not the unclean thing; and I will receive you, and will be a Father unto you, and ye shall be my sons and daughters." The Lord deal graciously with you, beloved, and lead you in a plain path, because of your enemies, for his name's sake. Amen.

PORTION OF SCRIPTURE READ BEFORE SERMON--Jeremiah 15.

Carried by Four

A Sermon (No. 981)
Delivered on Lord's-day Morning, March 19th, 1871 by
C. H. SPURGEON,
At the Metropolitan Tabernacle, Newington

"And he withdrew himself into the wilderness, and prayed. And it came to pass on a certain day, as he was teaching, that there were Pharisees and doctors of the law sitting by, which were come out of every town of Galilee, and Judaea, and Jerusalem: and the power of the Lord was present to heal them. And, behold, men brought in a bed a man which was taken with a palsy: and they sought means to bring him in, and to lay him before him. And when they could not find by what way they might bring him in because of the multitude, they went upon the housetop, and let him down through the tiling with his couch into the midst before Jesus. And when he saw their faith, he said unto him, Man, thy sins are forgiven thee. And the scribes and the Pharisees began to reason, saying, Who is this which speaketh blasphemies? Who can forgive sins, but God alone? But when Jesus perceived their thoughts, he answering said unto them, What reason ye in your hearts? Whether is easier, to say, Thy sins be forgiven thee; or to say, Rise up and walk? But that ye may know that the Son of man hath power upon earth to forgive sins (he said unto the sick of the palsy), I say unto thee, Arise, and take up thy couch, and go into thine house. And immediately he rose up before them, and took up that whereon he lay, and departed to his own house, glorifying God. And they were all amazed, and they glorified God, and were filled with fear, saying, We have seen strange things to-day." - Luke 5:16-26.

YOU HAVE THIS SAME NARRATIVE in the ninth chapter of Matthew, and in the second chapter of Mark. What is three times recorded by inspired pens must be regarded as trebly important, and well worthy of our earnest consideration. Observe the instructive fact, that our Savior retired and spent a special time in prayer when he saw unusual crowd assembling. He withdrew into the wilderness to hold communion with his Father, and, as a consequence, to come forth clothed with an abundance of healing and saving power. Not but that in himself as God he always had that power without measure; but for our sakes he did it, that we might learn that the power of God will only rest upon us in proportion as we draw near to God. Neglect of private prayer is the locust which devours the strength of the church.

When our Lord left his retirement he found the crowd around him exceeding great, and it was as motley as it was great; for while here were many sincere believers, there were still more sceptical observers; some were anxious to receive his healing power, others equally desirous to find occasion against him. So in all congregations, however the preacher may be clothed with his Master's spirit and his Master's might, there will be a mixed gathering; there will come together your Pharisees and doctors of the law, your sharp critics ready to pick holes, your cold-blooded cavillers searching for faults; at the same time, chosen of God and drawn by his grace, there will be present some devout believers who rejoice in the power that is revealed among men, and earnest seekers who wish to feel in themselves the healing energy. It seems to have been a rule with our Savior to supply each hearer with food after his kind. The Pharisees soon found the matters to cavil at for which they were looking; the Savior so worded his expressions that they caught at them eagerly, and charged him with blasphemy; the enmity of their hearts was thus thrown out upon the surface that the Lord might have an opportunity of rebuking it; and had they been but willing, the power of the Lord was present to heal even them. Meanwhile, those poor tremblers who were praying for healing were not disappointed; the Good Physician passed not by a single case, and at the same time his disciples who were looking for opportunities of praising him anew, were also fully gratified, for with glad eyes they saw the paralytic restored, and heard sins forgiven.

The case which the narrative brings before us, is that of a man stricken down with paralysis. This sad disease may have been of long continuance. There is a paralysis which gradually kills the body, binding it more and more surely in utter helplessness. The nerve power is almost destroyed; the power of motion is entirely suspended; and yet the faculties of the mind remain, though greatly weakened, and some of them almost extinguished. Some have thought that this man may have been stricken with what is called the universal paralysis, which very speedily brings on death, which may account for the extreme haste of the four bearers to bring him near the Savior. We do not know the details of his case, but certain is it that he was paralyzed; and, as I look at the case, and study the three records, I think I perceive with equal clearness that this paralysis was in some way or other, at least in the man's own judgment, connected with his sin. He was evidently penitent, as well as paralytic. His mind was as much oppressed as his bodily frame. I do not know that he could be altogether called a believer, but it is most probable that being burdened with a sense of sin he had a feeble hope in divine mercy, which, like a spark in smoking flax, had hard work to exist, but yet was truly there. The affliction for which his friends pitied him was in his body, but he himself felt a far severer trouble in his soul, and probably it was not so much with the view of being healed bodily, as in the hope of spiritual blessing, that he was willing to be subjected to any process by which he might come under the Savior's eye. I gather that from the fact that our Savior addressed him in these words, "Be of good cheer;" intimating that he was desponding, that his spirit sunk within him, and, therefore, instead of saying to him at once, "Rise, take up thy bed," our tender-hearted Lord said, "Son, thy sins be forgiven thee." He gave him at the outset a blessing for which the patient's friends had not asked, but which the man, though speechless, was seeking for in the silence of his soul. He was a "son," though an afflicted one: he was ready to obey the Lord's bidding when power was given, though as yet he could neither lift hand nor foot. He was longing for the pardon of sin, yet could not stretch out his hand to lay hold upon the Savior.

I intend to use this narrative for practical purposes; may the Holy Spirit make it really useful. Our first remark will be this:

I. THERE ARE CASES WHICH WILL NEED THE AID OF A LITTLE BAND OF WORKERS BEFORE THEY WILL BE FULLY SAVED.

This man must needs be borne of four, so the evangelist, Mark, tells us; there must be a bearer at each corner of the couch whereon he lay. The great mass of persons who are brought into the kingdom of Christ are converted through the general prayers of the church by the means of her ministry. Probably three out of four of the members of any church will owe their conversion to the church's regular teaching in some form or other; her school, her pulpit, her press have been the nets in which they were taken. Private personal prayer has, of course, in many instances been mingled with all this; but still the most of cases could not be so distinctly traced out as to be attributable mainly to individual prayers or exertions. This is the rule, I think, that the Lord will have the many brought to himself by the sounding of the great trumpet of jubilee in the dispensation of the gospel by his ministers. There are some, again, who are led to Jesus by the individual efforts of one person; just as Andrew found his own brother Simon, so one believer by his private communication of the truth to another person becomes instrumental, by the power of God's Spirit, in his conversion. One convert will bring another, and that other a third. But this narrative seems to show that there are cases which will neither be brought by the general preaching of the word, nor yet by the instrumentality of one; they require that there should be two, or three, or four in holy combination, who, with one consent, feeling one common agony of soul, shall resolve to band themselves together as a company for this one object, and never to cease from their holy confederation until this object is gained and their friend is saved. This man could not be brought to Christ by one, he must have four to lend their strength for his carrying, or he cannot reach the place of healing. Let us apply the principle. Yonder is a householder as yet unsaved: his wife has prayed for him long; her prayers are yet unanswered. Good wife, God has blessed thee with a son who with thee rejoices in the fear of God. Hast thou not two Christian daughters also? O ye four, take each a corner of this sick man's coach and bring your husband, bring your father, to the Savior. A husband and a wife are here, both happily brought to Christ; you are praying for your children; never cease from that supplication: pray on. Perhaps one of your beloved family is unusually stubborn. Extra help is needed. Well, to you the Sabbath school teacher will make a third; he will take one corner of the bed; and happy shall I be if I may join the blessed quaternion, and make the fourth. Perhaps, when home discipline, the school's teaching, and the minister's preaching shall go together, the Lord will look down in love and save your child. Dear brother, you are thinking of one whom you have long prayed for; you have spoken to him also, and used all proper means, but as yet without effect. Perhaps you speak too comfortingly to him: it may be you have not brought that precise truth to bear upon him which his conscience requires. Seek yet more help. It may possibly be that a second brother will speak instructively, where you have only spoken consolingly; perhaps the instruction may be the means of grace. Yet may it possibly happen that even instruction will not suffice any more than consolation, and it may be needful for you to call in a third, who perhaps will speak impressively with exhortation, and with warning, which may possibly be the great requisite. You two, already in the field, may balance his exhortation, which might have been too pungent by itself, and might have raised prejudice in the person's mind if it had come alone. All three of you together may prove the fit instruments in the Lord's hand. Yet when you three have happily combined, it may be the poor paralysed one is not yet affected savingly; a fourth may be needed, who, with deeper affection than ail three of you, and perhaps with an experience more suited to the case than yours, may come in, and working with you, the result may be secured. The four fellow-helpers together may accomplish, by the power of the Spirit, what neither one, nor two, nor three were competent to have done. It may sometimes happen that a man has heard Paul preach, but his clear doctrine, though it has enlightened his intellect, has not yet convinced his conscience. He has heard Apollos, and the glow of the orator's eloquent appeals has warmed his heart, but not humbled his pride. He has later still listened to Cephas, whose rough cutting sentences have hewn him down, and convinced him of sin; but ere he can find joy and peace in believing, he will require to hear the sweet affectionate words of John. Only when the fourth shall grasp the bed and give a hearty lift will the paralysed person he laid in mercy's path. I anxiously desire to see in this church little bands of men and women bound to each other by zealous love to souls. I would have you say to one another, "This is a case in which we feel a common interest: we will pledge each other to pray for this person; we will unitedly seek his salvation." It may be that one of our seatholders, after listening to my voice these ten or fifteen years, is not impressed; it may be that another has left the Sabbath-school unsaved. Let brotherly quaternions look after these by God's help. Moved by one impulse, form a square about these persons, beset them behind and before, and let them not say, "No man careth for my soul." Meet together in prayer with the definite object before you, and then seek that object by the most likely ways. I do not know, my brethren, how much of blessing might come to us through this, but I feel certain that until we have tried it we cannot pronounce a verdict upon it; nor can we be quite sure that we are free from all responsibility to men's souls until we have tested every possible and probable method for doing them good.

I am afraid that there are not many, even in a large church, who will become sick-bearers. Many will say the plan is admirable, but they will leave it to others to carry it out. Remember that the four persons who join in such a labor of love ought all of them to be filled with intense affection to the persons whose salvation they seek. They must be men who will not shrink because of difficulty; who will put forth their whole strength to shoulder the beloved burden, and will persevere until they succeed. They need be strong, for the burden is heavy; they need be resolute, for the work will try their faith; they need be prayerful, for otherwise they labor in vain; they must be believing, or they will be utterly useless,--Jesus saw their faith, and therefore accepted their service; but without faith it is impossible to please him. Where shall we find quartettes such as these? May the Lord find them, and may he send them to some of you poor dying sinners who lie paralysed here to-day.

II. We now pass on to the second observation, that SOME CASES THUS TAKEN UP WILL NEED MUCH THOUGHT BEFORE THE DESIGN IS ACCOMPLISHED.

The essential means by which a soul is saved is clear enough. The four bearers had no question with each other as to what was the way to effect this man's cure: they were unanimous in this--that they must bring him to Jesus; by some means or other, by hook or by crook, they must place him in the Savior's way. That was undoubted fact. The question was, how to do this? There is an old worldly proverb, that "where there's a will there's a way;" and that proverb, I believe, may be safely imported into spiritual things, almost without a caution or grain of salt. "Where there's a will there's a way;" and if men be called of God's grace to a deep anxiety for any particular soul, there is a way by which that soul may be brought to Jesus; but that way may not suggest itself till after much consideration. In some cases the way to impress the heart may be an out-of-the-way way, an extraordinary way--a way which ordinarily should not be used and would not be successful. I dare say the four bearers in the narrative thought early in the morning, "We will carry this poor paralytic to the Savior, passing into the house by the ordinary door;" but when they attempted to do so the multitudes so blocked up the road that they could not even reach the threshold. "Make way; make way for the sick! Stand aside there, and give room for a poor paralysed man. For mercy's sake, give a little space, and let the sick man reach the healing prophet!" In vain their entreaties and commands. Here and there a few compassionate persons back out of the crowd, but the many neither can nor will remove; besides, many of them are engaged upon a similar business, and have equal reasons for pressing in. "See," cries one of the four, "I will make way;" and he pushes and elbows himself a little distance into the passage. "Come on you three!" he cries: "follow up, and fight for it, inch by inch." But they cannot do it; it is impossible; the poor patient is ready to die for fear; the bed is tossed about by the throng like a cockleshell boat on the sea-waves, the patient's alarm increases, the bearers are distressed, and they are quite glad to get outside again and consider. It is evidently quite impossible by ordinary means to get him in. What then? "We cannot burrow under the ground: can we not go over the heads of the people, and let the man down from above? Where is the staircase?" Frequently there is an external staircase to the top of an eastern house; we cannot be sure that there was one in this case; but if not, the next door house may have had such a convenience, and so the resolute bearers reached the top and passed from one roof to another.

Where we have no definite information much may he left to conjecture; but this much is clear: by some means they elevated their unhappy burden to the housetop, and provided themselves with the necessary tackle with which to let him down. The Savior was probably preaching in one of the upper rooms, unless the house was a poor one without an upper story. Perhaps the room was open to the courtyard, which was crowded. At any rate, the Lord Jesus was under cover of a roof, and a substantial roof too. No one who carefully reads the original will fail to see that there was real roofing to be broken through. It has been suggested as a difficulty, that the breaking up of a roof might involve danger to those below, and would probably make a great smother of dust; and to avoid this, there have been various suppositions--such as that the Savior was standing under an awning, and the men rolled up the canvas; or that our Lord stood under a verandah with a very light covering, which the men could readily uncover; others have even invented a trap-door for the occasion. But with all due deference to eminent travelers, the words of the evangelists cannot be so readily disposed of. According to our text, the man was let down through "tiling," not canvas, or any light material; whatever sort of tiling it was, it was certainly made of burnt clay, for that enters into the essence of the word. Moreover, according to Mark, after they had uncovered the roof, which, I suppose, means the removal of the "tiling," they broke it up, which looks exceedingly like breaking through a ceiling. The Greek word used by Mark, which is interpreted "breaking up," is a very emphatic word, and signifies digging through, or scooping up, which evidently conveys the idea of considerable labor for the removal of material. We are told that the roofs of Oriental houses are often made of big stones; that may be true as a general rule, but not in this case, for the house was covered with tiles; and as to the dust and falling rubbish, that may or may not be a necessary conclusion; but as clear as noonday is it that a substantial housetop, which required untiring and digging through, had a hole made in it, and through the aperture the man in his bed was let down. Perhaps there was dust, and possibly there was danger too, but the bearers were prepared to accomplish their purpose at all risks. They must get the sick man in somehow. There is no need, however, to suppose either, for no doubt the four men would be careful not to incommode the Savior or his hearers. The tiles or plaster might be removed to another part of the flat roof, and the boards likewise, as they were broken up; and as for the spars, they might be sufficiently wide to admit the narrow couch of the sick man without moving any of them from their places. Mr. Hartley, in his Travels, says: "When I lived at AEgina I used to look up not infrequently at the roof above my head, and contemplate how easily the whole transaction of the paralytic might take place. The roof was made in the following manner:--A layer of reeds, of a large species, was placed upon the rafters, on these a quantity of heather was strewed; on the heather earth was deposited, and beaten down into a solid mass. Now, what difficulty would there be in removing first the earth, next the heather, and then the reeds? Nor would the difficulty be increased, if the earth had a pavement of tiling laid upon it. No inconvenience could result to the persons in the house, from the removal of the tiles and earth; for the heather and reeds would stop anything that might otherwise fall down, and would be removed last of all." To let a man down through the roof was a device most strange and striking, but it only gives point to the remark which we have now to make here. If we want to have souls saved, we must not be too squeamish and delicate about conventionalities, rules, and proprieties, for the kingdom of heaven suffereth violence. We must make up our minds to this: "Smash or crash, everything shall go to pieces which stands between the soul and its God: it matters not what tiles are to be taken off, what plaster is to be digged up, or what boards are to be torn away, or what labor, or trouble, or expense we may be at; the soul is too precious for us to stand upon nice questions. If by any means we may save some, is our policy. Skin for skin, yea, all that we have is nothing comparable to a man's soul." When four true hearts are set upon the spiritual good of a sinner, their holy hunger will break through stone walls or house roofs.

I have no doubt it was a difficult task to carry the paralysed man upstairs; the breaking up of the roof, the removing the tiling with all due care, must have been a laborious task, and have required much skill, but the work was done, and the end was gained. We must never stop at difficulties; however stern the task, it must always be more difficult to us to let a soul perish than to labor in the most self-denying form for its deliverance.

It was a very singular action which the bearers performed. Who would have thought of breaking up a roof? Nobody but those who loved much, and much desired to benefit the sick. O that God would make us attempt singular things to save souls. May a holy ingenuity be excited in the church; a sacred inventiveness set at work for winning men's hearts. It appeared to his generation a singular thing when John Wesley stood on his father's tombstone and preached at Epworth. Glory be to God that he had the courage to preach in the open air. It seemed an extraordinary thing when certain ministers delivered sermons in the theatres; but it is matter of joy that sinners have been reached by such irregularities who might have escaped all other means. Let us but feel our hearts full of zeal for God, and love for souls, and we shall soon be led to adopt means which others may criticise, but which Jesus Christ will accept.

After all, the method which the four friends followed was one most suitable to their abilities. They were, I suppose, four strong fellows, to whom the load was no great weight, and the work of digging was comparatively easy. The method suited their capacity exactly. And what did they do when they had let the sick man down? Look at the scene and admire? I do not read that they said a single word, yet what they did was enough: abilities for lifting and carrying did the needful work. Some of you say, "Ah, we cannot be of any use; we wish we could preach." These men could not preach: they did not need to preach. They lowered the paralytic, and their work was done. They could not preach, but they could hold a rope. We want in the Christian church not only preachers, but soul-winners, who can bear souls on their hearts, and feel the solemn burden; men who, it may be, cannot talk, but who can weep; men who cannot break other men's hearts with their language, but who break their own hearts with their compassion. In the case before us there was no need to plead "Jesus, thou son of David, look up, for a man is coming down who needs thee." There was no need to urge that the patient had been so many years sick. We do not know that the man himself uttered a word. Helpless and paralysed, he had not the vigor to become a suppliant. They placed his almost lifeless form before the Savior's eye, and that was appeal enough; his sad condition was more eloquent than words. O hearts that love sinners lay their lost estate before Jesus; bring their cases as they are before the Savior; if your tongues stammer, your hearts will prevail; if you cannot speak even to Christ himself, as you would desire, because you have not the gift of prayer, yet if your strong desires spring from the spirit of prayer you cannot fail. God help us to make use of such means as are within our power, and not to sit down idly to regret the powers we do not possess. Perhaps it would be dangerous for us to possess the abilities we covet; it is always safe to consecrate those we have.

III. Now we must pass on to an important truth. We may safely gather from the narrative THAT THE ROOT OF SPIRITUAL PARALYSIS GENERALLY LIES IN UNPARDONED SIN.

Jesus intended to heal the paralysed man, but he did so by first of all saying, "Thy sins are forgiven thee." There are some in this house of prayer this morning who are spiritually paralysed; they have eyes and they see the gospel; they have ears and they have heard it, and heard it attentively too; but they are so paralysed that they will tell you, and honestly tell you, that they cannot lay hold upon the promise of God; they cannot believe in Jesus to the saving of their souls. If you urge them to pray, they say: "We try to pray, but it is not acceptable prayer." If you bid them have confidence, they will tell you, though not in so many words perhaps, that they are given up to despair. Their mournful ditty is:--

"I would, but cannot sing;
I would, but cannot pray
For Satan meets me when I try,
And frights my soul away.
I would, but can't repeat,
Though I endeavor oft;
This stony heart can never relent
Till Jesus makes it soft.
I would, but cannot love,
Though wooed by love divine;
No arguments have power to move
A soul so base as mine.
O could I but believe!
Then all would easy be;
I would, but cannot--Lord, relieve:
My help must come from thee."

The bottom of this paralysis is sin upon the conscience, working death in them. They are sensible of their guilt, but powerless to believe that the crimson fountain can remove it: they are alive only to sorrow, despondency, and agony. Sin paralyses them with despair. I grant you that into this despair there enters largely the element of unbelief, which is sinful; but I hope there is also in it a measure of sincere repentance, which bears in it the hope of something better. Our poor, awakened paralytics sometimes hope that they may be forgiven, but they cannot believe it; they cannot rejoice; they cannot cast themselves on Jesus; they are utterly without strength. Now, the bottom of it, I say again, lies in unpardoned sin, and I earnestly entreat you who love the Savior to be earnest in seeking the pardon of these paralysed persons. You tell me that I should be earnest; so I should; and so I desire to be: but, brethren, their cases appear to be beyond the minister's sphere of action; the Holy Spirit determines to use other agencies in their salvation. They have heard the public word; they now need private consolation and aid, and that from three or four. Lend us your help, ye earnest brethren; form your parties of four; grasp the couches of these who wish to be saved, but who feel they cannot believe. The Lord, the Holy Spirit, make you the means of leading them into forgiveness and eternal salvation. They have been lying a long time waiting; their sin, however, still keeps them where they are; their guilt prevents their laying hold on Christ; there is the point, and it is for such cases that I earnestly invoke my brethren's aid.

IV. Let us proceed to notice, fourthly, that JESUS CAN REMOVE BOTH THE SIN AND THE PARALYSIS IN A SINGLE MOMENT. It was the business of the four bearers to bring the man to Christ; but there their power ended. It is our part to bring the guilty sinner to the Savior: there our power ends. Thank God, when we end, Christ begins, and works right gloriously. Observe that he began by saying: "Thy sins be forgiven thee." He laid the axe at the root; he did not desire that the man's sins might be forgiven, or express a good wish in that direction, but he pronounced an absolution by virtue of that authority with which he was clothed as the Savior. The poor man's sins there and then ceased to be, and he was justified in the sight of God. Believest thou this, my hearer, that Christ did thus for the paralytic man? Then I charge you believe something more, that if on earth Christ had power to forgive sins before he had offered an atonement, much more hath he power to do this, now that he hath poured out his blood, and hath said, "It is finished," and hath gone into his glory, and is at the right hand of the Father. He is exalted on high, to give repentance and remission of sin. Should he send his Spirit into thy soul to reveal himself in thee, thou wouldst in an instant be entirely absolved. Does blasphemy blacken thee? Does a long life of infidelity pollute thee? Hast thou been licentious? Hast thou been abominably wicked? A word can absolve thee--a word from those dear lips which said, "Father forgive them, for they know not what they do." I charge thee ask for that absolving word. No earthly priest can give it thee; but the great High Priest, the Lord Jesus, can utter it at once. Ye twos and fours who are seeking the salvation of men, here is encouragement for you. Pray for them now, while the gospel is being preached in their hearing; pray for them day and night, and bring the glad tidings constantly before them, for Jesus is still able "to save to the uttermost them that come unto God by him."

After our blessed Lord had taken away the root of the evil, you observe he then took away the paralysis itself. It was gone in a single moment. Every limb in the man's body was restored to a healthy state; he could stand, could walk, could lift his bed, both nerve and muscle were restored to vigor. One moment will suffice, if Jesus speaks, to make the despairing happy, and the unbelieving full of confidence. What we cannot do with our reasonings, persuadings, and entreaties, nor even with the letter of God's promise, Christ can do in a single instant by his Holy Spirit, and it has been our joy to see it done. This is the standing miracle of the church, performed by Christ to-day even as aforetime. Paralysed souls who could neither do nor will, have been able to do valiantly, and to will with solemn resolution. The Lord has poured power into the faint, and to them that had no might he hath increased strength. He can do it still. I say again to loving spirits who are seeking the good of others, let this encourage you. You may not have to wait long for the conversions you aim at; it may be ere another Sabbath ends, the person you pray for may be brought to Jesus; or if you have to wait a little, the waiting shall well repay you, and meanwhile remember he has never spoken in secret in the dark places of the earth; he has not said to the seed of Jacob, "Seek ye my face in vain."

V. Passing on, and drawing to a conclusion: WHEREVER OUR LORD WORKS THE DOUBLE MIRACLE IT WILL BE APPARENT. He forgave the man's sin and took away his disease at the same time. How was this apparent? I have no doubt the pardon of the man's sin was best known to himself; but possibly those who saw that gleaming countenance which had been so sad before, might have noticed that the word of absolution sunk into his soul as the rain into the thirsty earth. "Thy sins be forgiven thee," fell on him as a dew from heaven; he believed the sacred declaration, and his eyes sparkled. He might almost have felt indifferent whether he remained paralysed or not, it was such joy to be forgiven, forgiven by the Lord himself. That was enough, quite enough for him; but it was not enough for the Savior, and therefore he bade him take up his couch and walk, for he had given him strength to do so. The man's healing was proved by his obedience. Openly to all onlookers an active obedience became indisputable proof of the poor creature's restoration. Notice, our Lord bade him rise--he rose; he had no power to do so except that power which comes with divine commands. He rose, for Christ said "Rise." Then he folded up that miserable palliasse--the Greek word used shows us that it was a very poor, mean, miserable affair--he rolled it up as the Savior bade him, he shouldered it, and went to his home. His first impulse must have been to throw himself down at the Savior's feet, and say, "Blessed be thy name;" but the Master said, "Go to thy house;" and I do not find that he stayed to make one grateful obeisance, but elbowing the crowd, jostling the throng with his load on his back, he proceeded to his house just as he was told, and that without deliberation, or questioning. He did his Lord's bidding, and he did it accurately, in detail, at once, and most cheerfully. Oh! how cheerfully; none can tell but those in like case restored. So, the true sign of pardoned sin, and of paralysis removed from the heart, is obedience. If thou art really saved thou wilt do what Jesus bids thee; thy request will be, "Lord, what wilt thou have me to do?" and that once ascertained, thou wilt be sure to do it. You tell me Christ has forgiven you, and yet you live in rebellion to his commands; how can I believe you? You say you are a saved man, and yet you wilfully set up your own will against Christ's will; what evidence have I of what you say? Have I not, rather, clear evidence that you speak not the truth? Open, careful, prompt, cheerful obedience to Christ, becomes the test of the wonderful work which Jesus works in the soul.

VI. Lastly, ALL THIS TENDS TO GLORIFY GOD.

Those four men had been the indirect means of bringing much honor to God and much glory to Jesus, and they, I doubt not, glorified God in their very hearts on the housetop. Happy men to have been of so much service to their bedridden friend! Who else united in glorifying God? Why, first the man who was restored. Did not every part of his body glorify God? I think I see him! He sets one foot down to God's glory, he plants the other to the same note, he walks to God's glory, he carries his bed to God's glory, he moves his whole body to the glory of God, he speaks, he shouts, he sings, he leaps to the glory of God. When a man is saved his whole manhood glorifies God; he becomes instinct with a new-born life which glows in every part of him, spirit, soul and body. As an heir of heaven, he brings glory to the Great Father who has adopted him into the family, he breathes and eats and drinks to God's praise. When a sinner is brought into the church of God we are all glad, but we are none of us so joyous and thankful as he; we would all praise God, but he must praise him the loudest, and he will.

But who next glorified God! The text does not say so, but we feel sure that his family did, for he went to his own house. We will suppose that he had a wife. That morning when the four friends came and put him on the bed, and carried him out, it may be she shook her head in loving anxiety, and I dare say she said, "I am half afraid to trust him with you. Poor, poor creature, I dread his encountering the throng. I am afraid it is madness to hope for success. I wish you Godspeed in it, but I tremble. Hold well the bed; be sure you do not let him fall. If you do let him down through the roof hold fast the ropes, be careful that no accident occurs to my poor bedridden husband; he is bad enough as he is, do not cause him more misery." But when she saw him coming home, walking with the bed on his back, can you picture her delight? How she would begin to sing, and praise and bless the Lord Jehovah Rophi, who had healed her beloved one. If there were little children about, playing before the house, how they would shout for glee, "Here's father; here's father walking again, and come home with the bed on his back; he is made whole again, as he used to be when we were very little." What a glad house! They would gather round him, all of them, wife and children, and friends and neighbors, and they would begin to sing, "Bless the Lord, O my soul: and all that is within me, bless his holy name. Bless the Lord, O my soul, and forget not all his benefits: who forgiveth all thine iniquities: who healeth all thy diseases." How the man would sing those verses, rejoicing in the forgiveness first, and the healing next, and wondering how it was that David knew so much about it, and had put his case into such fit words.

Well, but it did not end there. A wife and family utter but a part of the glad chorus of praise, though a very melodious part. There are other adoring hearts who unite in glorifying the healing Lord. The disciples who were around the Savior, they glorified God, too. They rejoiced, and said one to another, "We have seen strange things to-day." The whole Christian church is full of sacred praise when a sinner is saved; even heaven itself is glad.

But there was glory brought to God, even by the common people who stood around. They had not yet entered into that sympathy with Christ which the disciples felt, but they were struck by the sight of this great wonder, and they, too, could not help saying that God had wrought great marvels. I pray that onlookers, strangers from the commonwealth of Israel, when they see the desponding comforted, and lost ones brought in, may be compelled to bear their witness to the power of divine grace, and be led themselves to be partakers in it. There is "Glory to God in the highest, and on earth peace, good-will towards men," when a paralysed soul is filled with gracious strength.

Now, shall I need to stand here, and entreat for the four to carry poor souls to Jesus? Shall I need to appeal to my brethren who love their Lord, and say, band yourselves together to win souls? Your humanity to the paralytic soul claims it, but your desire to bring glory to God compels it. If you are indeed what you profess to be, to glorify God must be the fondest wish and the loftiest ambition of your souls. Unless ye be traitors to my Lord as well as inhuman to your fellow-men, you will catch the practical thought which I have striven to bring before you, and you will seek out some fellow Christians, and say, "Come, let us pray together, for such an one," and if you know a desperate case you will make up a sacred quaternion, to resolve upon its salvation. May the power of the Highest abide upon you, and who knoweth what glory the Lord may gain through you? Never forget this strange story of the bed which carried the man, and the man who carried his bed.

PORTION OF SCRIPTURE READ BEFORE SERMON--Luke 5:1-26.

The Ascension of Christ

A Sermon (No. 982)
Delivered on Lord's-day Morning, March 26th, 1871 by
C. H. SPURGEON,
At the Metropolitan Tabernacle, Newington

"Unto every one of us is given grace according to the measure of the gift of Christ. Wherefore he saith, when he ascended up on high, he led captivity captive and gave gifts unto men. (Now that he ascended, what is it, but that he also descended first into the lower parts of the earth? He that descended is the same also that ascended up far above all heavens, that he might fill all things.) And he gave some, apostles; and some, prophets; and some, evangelists; and some, pastors and teachers; for the perfecting of the saints, for the work of the ministry, for the edifying of the body of Christ." - Ephesians 4:7-12.

OUR blessed Lord and Master has gone from us. From the mount of Olives, the place where in dread conflict his garments were rolled in blood, he has mounted in triumph to his throne. After having shown himself for forty days amongst his beloved disciples, giving them abundant evidence that he had really risen from the dead, and enriching them by his divine counsels, he was taken up. Slowly rising before them all, he gave them his blessing as he disappeared. Like good old Jacob, whose departing act was to bestow a benediction on his twelve sons and their descendants, so ere the cloud received our Lord out of our sight, he poured a blessing upon the apostles, who were looking upward, and who were the representatives of his church. He is gone! His voice of wisdom is silent for us, his seat at the table is empty, the congregation on the mountain hears him no more. It would be very easy to have found reasons why he should not have gone. Had it been a matter of choice to us, we should have entreated him to tarry with us till the dispensation closed. Unless, peradventure, grace had enabled us to say: "Not as we will! but as thou wilt," we should have constrained him, saying, "Abide with us." What a comfort to disciples to have their own beloved teacher visibly with them! What a consolation to a persecuted band to see their leader at their head; difficulties would disappear, problems would be solved, perplexities removed, trials made easy, temptations averted! Let Jesus himself, their own dear Shepherd be near, and the sheep will lie down in security. Had he been here we could have gone to him in every affliction, like those of whom it is said, "they went and told Jesus."

It seemed expedient for him to stay, to accomplish the conversion of the world. Would not his presence have had an influence to win by eloquence of gracious word and argument of loving miracle? If he put forth his power the battle would soon be over, and his rule over all hearts would be for ever established. "Thine arrows are sharp in the heart of the king's enemies; whereby the people fall under thee." Go not from the conflict, thou mighty bowman, but still cast thine all-subduing darts abroad. In the days of our Lord's flesh, before he had risen from the dead, he did but speak, and those who came to take him fell to the ground; might we but have him near us no persecuting hand could seize us; at his bidding, the fiercest enemy would retire. His voice called the dead out of their graves; could we but have him still in the church his voice would awaken the spiritually dead. His personal presence would be better to us than ten thousand apostles, at least, so we dream; and we imagine that with him visibly among us the progress of the church would be like the march of a triumphant army.

Thus might flesh and blood have argued, but all such reasoning is hushed by our Lord's declaration, "It is expedient for you that I go away: for if I go not away, the Comforter will not come unto you." He might have told us that his majestic presence was expected by the saints in heaven to complete their felicity; he might have said that for himself it was fitting that after so long an exile and the performance of such stupendous labors, he should rise to his reward; he might also have added that it was due to his Father that he should return into the bosom of his love; but, as if he knew that their trembling at his departure was mainly occasioned by fear for their own personal interests, he puts the consoling word into this form: "It is expedient for you that I go away." He has gone then, and whether our weak understandings are able to perceive it or not, it is better for us that Jesus should be at the right hand of God than here corporeally in our assemblies below. Fain would a hundred Bethanies entertain him, a thousand synagogues would rejoice to see him open the Scriptures; women there are among us who would kiss his feet, and men who would glory to unloose the latchets of his shoes; but he has gotten him away to the mountains of myrrh and the hills of frankincense. He no more sits at our tables, or walks with us on our highways; he is leading another flock to living fountains of waters, and let not his sheep below imagine that he has injured them by his removal; unerring wisdom has declared that it is expedient for us that he is gone.

This morning, instead of standing here gazing up into heaven; like the men of Galilee, deploring that we have lost our Lord, let us sit down in quiet contemplation, and see if we cannot gather profitable redactions from this great thing which has come to pass. Let our meditations ascend the yet glowing trackway of our Lord's ascension,--

"Beyond, beyond this lower sky,
Up where eternal ages roll."

We shall, by the Holy Spirit's aid, first consider, with a view to practical good, the fact of his ascension; secondly, the triumph of that ascension; thirdly, the gifts of that ascension; and then we shall conclude by noticing the bearings of that ascension upon the unconverted.

I. First, then, let our earnest thoughts gaze upward, viewing THE FACT OF THE ASCENSION. We lay aside all controversy or attempt at mere doctrinal definition, and desire to meditate upon the ascension with a view to comfort, edification, and soul profit.

It should afford us supreme joy to remember that he who descended into the lower parts of the earth has now "ascended up far above all heavens." The descent was a subject of joy to angels and men, but it involved him in much humiliation and sorrow, especially when, after having received a body which, according to the psalmist, was "curiously wrought in the lowest parts of the earth," he further descended into the bowels of the earth, and slept as a prisoner in the tomb. His descent on earth, though to us the source of abounding joy, was full of pain, shame, and humiliation to him. In proportion, then, ought to be our joy that the shame is swallowed up in glory, the pain is lost in bliss, the death in immortality. Did shepherds sing at his descent, let all men sing at his rising. Well deserves the warrior to receive glory, for he has dearly won it. Our love of justice and of him compels us to rejoice in his rejoicing. Whatever makes the Lord Jesus glad makes his people glad. Our sympathy with him is most intense; we esteem his reproach above all wealth, and we set equal store by his honor. As we have died with him, were buried with him in baptism, have also risen with him through the faith of the operation of God who raised him from the dead, so also have we been made to sit together in the heavenly places, and have obtained an inheritance. If angels poured forth their sweetest minstrelsy when the Christ of God returned to his royal seat, much more should we. Those celestial beings had but slight share in the triumphs of that day compared with us; for it was a man who led captivity captive, it was one born of woman who returned victoriously from Bozrah. We may well say with the psalmist, in the sixty-eighth Psalm, to which our text refers, "Let the righteous be glad; let them rejoice before God: yea, let them exceedingly rejoice. Sing unto God, sing praises to his name: extol him that rideth upon the heavens by his name JAH, and rejoice before him." It was none other than Christ, bone of our bone and flesh of our flesh; it was the second Adam who mounted to his glory. Rejoice, O believers, as those who shout because of victory, divide ye the spoil with the strong.

"Bruised is the serpent's head,
Hell is vanquished, death is dead,
And to Christ gone up on high,
Captive is captivity.
All his work and warfare done,
He into his heaven is gone,
And beside his Father's throne,
Now is pleading for his own:
Sing, O heavens! O earth, rejoice!
Angel harp and human voice,
Round him, in his glory, raise
Your ascended Savior's praise."

Reflect yet again that from the hour when our Lord left it, this world has lost all charms to us. If he were in it, there were no spot in the universe which would hold us with stronger ties; but since he has gone up he draws us upward from it. The flower is gone from the garden, the first ripe fruit is gathered. Earth's crown has lost its brightest jewel, the star is gone from the night, the dew is exhaled from the morning, the sun is eclipsed at noon. We have heard of some who, when they lost a friend or favourite child never smiled again, for nothing could supply the dreary vacuum. To us it could not be that any affliction should bring us such grief, for we have learned to be resigned to our Father's will; but the fact that "Jesus, our all, to heaven is gone," has caused something of the same feeling in our souls; this world can never be our rest now, its power to content us is gone. Joseph is no more in Egypt, and it is time for Israel to be gone. No, earth, my treasure, is not here with thee, neither shall my heart be detained by thee. Thou art, O Christ, the rich treasure of thy people, and since thou art gone thy people's hearts have climbed to heaven with thee.

Flowing out of this is the great truth that "our conversation is in heaven; from whence also we look for the Savior, the Lord Jesus Christ." Brethren, inasmuch as Christ is gone our life is hid with him in God. To the glory-land our Head is gone, and the life of the members is there. Since the head is occupied with things celestial, let not the members of the body be grovelling as slaves to terrestrial things. "If ye then be risen with Christ, seek those things which are above, where Christ sitteth on the right hand of God. Set your affection on things above, not on things on the earth." Our Bridegroom has gone into the ivory palaces, he dwelleth in the midst of his brethren; do we not hear him calling us to commune with him? Hear ye not his voice, "Rise up my love, my fair one, and come away"? Though awhile our bodies linger here, let our spirits even now walk the golden streets, and behold the King in his beauty. Begin, O faithful souls, to-day the occupation of the blessed, praising God even while ye linger yet below, and honoring him if not by the same modes of service as the perfect ones above, yet with the same obedient delight. "Our conversation is in heaven." May you and I know what that means to the full. May we take up our celestial burgess-rights, exercise our privileges and avocations as heavenly citizens, and live as those that are alive from the dead, who are raised up together and made partakers of his resurrection life. Since the head of the family is in the glory, let us by faith perceive how near we are to it, and by anticipation live upon its joys and in its power. Thus the ascension of our Lord will remind us of heaven, and teach us the holiness which is our preparation for it.

Our Lord Jesus Christ has gone from us. We return again to the thought. We cannot speak into his ear and hear his voice reply in those dear accents with which he spoke to Thomas and to Philip. He no longer sits at feasts of love with favored friends, such as Mary and Martha and Lazarus. He has departed out of this world unto the Father, and what then? Why he has taught us by this the more distinctly, that we must henceforth walk by faith and not by sight. The presence of Jesus Christ on earth would have been, to a great extent, a perpetual embargo upon the life of faith. We should all have desired to see the Redeemer; but since, as man, he could not have been omnipresent, but could only have been in one spot at one time, we should have made it the business of our lives to provide the means for journey to the place where he might be seen; or if he himself condescended to journey through all lands, we should have fought our way into the throng to feast our eyes upon him, and we should have envied each other when the turn came for any to speak familiarly with him. Thank God we have no cause for clamor or strife or struggle about the mere sight of Jesus after the flesh; for though once he was seen corporeally by his disciples, yet now after the flesh know we even him no more. Jesus is no more seen of human eyes; and it is well, for faith's sight is saving, instructing, transforming, and mere natural sight is not so. Had he been here we should have regarded much more the things which are visible, but now our hearts are taken up with the things which are not seen, but which are eternal. This day we have no priest for eyes to gaze upon, no material altar, no temple made with hands, no solemn rites to satisfy the senses; we have done with the outward and are rejoicing in the inward. Neither in this mountain nor in that do we worship the Father, but we worship God, who is a Spirit, in spirit and in truth. We now endure as seeing him who is invisible; whom, having not seen, we love; in whom, though now we see him not, yet believing, we rejoice with joy unspeakable and full of glory. In the same fashion as we walk towards our Lord, so walk we towards all that he reveals; we walk by faith, not by sight. Israel, in the wilderness, instructed by types and shadows, was ever prone to idolatry; the more there is of the visible in religion, the more is there of difficulty in the attainment of spirituality. Even baptism and the Lord's Supper, were they not ordained by the Lord himself, might be well given up, since the flesh makes a snare of them, and superstition engrafts on them baptismal regeneration and sacramental efficacy. Our Lord's presence might thus have become a difficulty to faith, though a pleasure to sense. His going away leaves a clear field for faith; it throws us necessarily upon a spiritual life, since he who is the head, the soul, the center of our faith, hope, and love is no more within the range of our bodily organs. It is poor believing which needs to put its finger into the nail-prints; but blessed is he that hath not seen and yet hath believed. In an unseen Savior we fix our trust, from an unseen Savior we derive our joy. Our faith is now the substance of things hoped for, the evidence of things not seen.

Let us learn this lesson well, and let it never be said to us, "Are ye so foolish? Having begun in the Spirit, are ye now made perfect by the flesh?" Let us never attempt to live by feeling and evidence. Let us banish from our soul all dreams of finding perfection in the flesh, and equally let

us discard all cravings for signs and wonders. Let us not be like the children of Israel, who only believed while they saw the works of the Lord. If our Beloved has hidden himself from our sight, let him even hide everything else, if so it pleases him. If he only reveals himself to our faith, the eye which is good enough to see him with is good enough to see everything else with, and we will be content to see his covenant blessings, and all else with that one eye of faith, and no other, till the time shall come when he shall change our faith to sight.

Beloved, let us further reflect how secure is our eternal inheritance now that Jesus has entered into the heavenly places. Our heaven is secured to us, for it is in the actual possession of our legal representative, who can never be dispossessed of it. Possession is nine points of the law, but it absolutely secures completely our tenure under the gospel. He who possesses a covenant blessing shall never lose it, for the covenant cannot be changed, nor its gifts withdrawn. We are heritors of the heavenly Canaan by actual hold and sure title, for our legal representative, appointed by the highest court of judicature, has entered into possession and actual occupancy of the many mansions of the great Father's house. He has not merely taken possession, but he is making all ready for our reception and eternal inhabitation. A man who enters a house and claims it, if he has any question about his rights, will not think of preparing it for the inhabitants, he will leave any expenditure of that kind till all doubts are cleared up: but our good Lord has taken such possession of the city of the new Jerusalem for us, that he is daily preparing it for us, that where he is we may be also. If I could send to heaven some mere human being like myself to hold my place for me till my arrival, I should fear that my friend might lose it: but since my Lord, the King of heaven and the Master of angels, has gone thither to represent all his saints and claim their places for them, I know that my portion is secure. Rest content, beloved, and sing for joy as the apostle's heart did when he wrote "In whom also we have obtained an inheritance."

Further, if Jesus has gone into the glory, how successful must our prayers be. You send a petition to court, and you hope for its success, for it is drawn up in proper style, and it has been countersigned by an influential person; but when the person who has backed your plea for you is himself at court, to take the petition and present it there, you feel safer still. To-day our prayers do not only receive our Savior; imprimatur, but they are presented by his own hand, as his own requests. "Seeing then that we have a great high priest, that is passed into the heavens, Jesus the Son of God," "let us come boldly unto the throne of grace, that we may obtain mercy, and find grace to help in time of need." No prayer which Jesus urges can ever be dismissed unheard, that case is safe for which he is advocate.

"Look up, my soul, with cheerful eye
See where the great Redeemer stands;
The glorious Advocate on high,
With precious incense in his hands.
He sweetens every humble groan,
He recommends each broken prayer;
Recline thy hope on him alone,
Whose power and love forbid despair."

Once more, though I feel this theme might detain us long, we must leave it, and remark further that, as we consider Christ ascended, our hearts burn within us at the thought that he is the type of all his people. As he was, so are we also in this world; and as he is, so shall we also be. To us also there remain both a resurrection and an ascension. Unless the Lord come very speedily, we shall die as he did, and the sepulcher shall receive our bodies for awhile; there is for us a tomb in a garden, or a rest in the Machpelah of our fathers. For us there are winding-sheets and grave-clothes; yet like our Lord we shall burst the bonds of death, for we cannot be holden of them. There is a resurrection morning for us, because there was a rising again for him. Death could as soon have held the head as the members; the prison doors once taken away, post and bar and all, the captives are set free. Then when we have risen from the dead at the blast of the archangel's trumpet, we shall ascend also, for is it not written that we shall be caught up together with the Lord in the air, and so shall be for ever with the Lord? Have courage, brother; that glittering road up to the highest heavens, which Christ has trodden, you too must tread; the triumph which he enjoyed shall be yours in your measure. You, too, shall lead your captivity captive, and amidst the acclamations of angels you shall receive the "well done" of the ever-blessed Father, and shall sit with Jesus on his throne, even as he has overcome and sits with the Father upon his throne.

I have rather given you suggestions for meditation than the meditations themselves. May the Holy Spirit bless them to you; and as you in imagination sit down on Olivet and gaze into the pure azure, may the heavens open to you, and, like Stephen, may you see the Son of Man at the right hand of God.

II. Let us advance to the second point, and dwell upon it very briefly--THE TRIUMPH OF THE ASCENSION. Psalmists and apostles have delighted to speak upon our Lord's triumphal ascension to the hill of the Lord. I shall not attempt to do more than refer to what they have said. Call to your minds how the Psalmist in vision saw the Savior's ascension, and, in the twenty-fourth Psalm, represented the angels as saying: "Lift up your heads, O ye gates; and be ye lift up, ye everlasting doors; and the King of glory shall come in. Who is this King of glory? The Lord strong and mighty, the Lord mighty in battle." The scene is described in rich poetic imagery of the most sublime kind, and it evidently teaches us that when our Savior left the sight of mortals, he was joined by bands of spirits, who welcomed him with acclamations and attended him in solemn state as he entered the metropolis of the universe. The illustration which has usually been given is, I think, so good that we cannot better it. When generals and kings returned from war, in the old Roman ages, they were accustomed to celebrate a triumph; they rode in state through the streets of the capital, trophies of their wars were carried with them, the inhabitants crowded to the windows, filled the streets, thronged the house-tops, and showered down acclamations and garlands of flowers upon the conquering hero as he rode along. Without being grossly literal, we may conceive some such a scene as that attending our Lord's return to the celestial seats. The sixty-eighth Psalm is to the same effect: "The chariots of God are twenty thousand, even thousands of angels: the Lord is among them, as in Sinai, in the holy place. Thou hast ascended on high, thou hast led captivity captive: thou hast received gifts for men; yea, for the rebellious also, that the Lord God might dwell among them." So also in Psalm forty-seven: "God is gone up with a shout, the Lord with the sound of a trumpet." Angels and glorified spirits, saluted our returning champion; and, leading captivity captive, he assumed the mediatorial throne amidst universal acclamations. "having spoiled principalities and powers, he made a show of them openly triumphing over them in it."

Our Lord's ascension was a triumph over the world. He had passed through it unscathed by its temptations; he had been solicited on all hands to sin, but his garments were without spot or blemish. There was no temptation which had not been tried upon him, the quivers of the earth had been emptied against him, but the arrows had glanced harmlessly from his armor of proof. They had persecuted him relentlessly; he had been made to suffer all that cruel scorn could invent, but he came forth from the furnace with not the smell of fire upon him. He had endured death itself with love unquenched and courage invincible. He had conquered by enduring all. As he rose he was infinitely beyond their reach; though they hated him no less than before, he had been forty days amongst them, and yet no hand was outstretched to arrest him. He had shown himself openly in divers places, and yet not a dog dare move his tongue. In the clear air, from far above the hills of Salem, he who was once tempted in the desert, looked down upon the kingdoms of the earth, which had been shown him by Satan as the price of sin, and reserved them all as his own by right of merit. He rises above all, for he is superior to all. As the world could not injure his character by its temptations, so no longer could it touch his person by its malice. He has defeated altogether this present evil world.

There, too, he led captive sin. Evil had assailed him furiously, but it could not defile him. Sin had been laid upon him, the weight of human guilt was borne upon his shoulders, it crushed him down, but he rose from the dead, he ascended into heaven, and proved that he had shaken off the load, and left it buried in his sepulcher. He has abolished the sins of his people; his atonement has been so efficacious that no sin is upon him, the Surety, and certainly none remains upon those for whom he stood as substitute. Though once the Redeemer stood in the place of the condemned, he has so suffered the penalty that he is justified now, and his atoning work is finished for ever. Sin, my brethren, was led captive at our Immanuel's chariot-wheels when he ascended.

Death also was led in triumph. Death had bound him, but he snapped each fetter, and bound death with his own cords.

"Vain the stone, the water, the seal,
Christ has burst the gates of hell;
Death in vain forbids his rise,
Christ hath opened paradise.
Lives again our glorious King!
'Where, O death, is now thy sting?'
Once he died our souls to save;
'Where's thy victory, boasting grave?'"

Our Savior's ascension in that same body which descended into the lower parts of the earth, is so complete a victory over death, that every dying saint may be sure of immortality, and may leave his body behind without fear that it shall for ever abide in the vaults of the grave.

So, too, Satan, was utterly defeated! He had thought that he should overcome the seed of the

woman when he had bruised his heel, but lo! as the conqueror mounts aloft, he breaks the dragon's head beneath his feet. See ye not the celestial coursers as they drag the war chariot of the Prince of the house of David up the everlasting hills! He comes who has fought the prince of darkness! Lo! he has bound him in iron fetters. See how he drags him at his chariot wheels, amidst the derision of all those pure spirits who retained their loyalty to the almighty King! Oh, Satan! thou wast worsted then! Thou didst fall like lightning from heaven when Christ ascended to his throne.

Brethren in Christ, everything that makes up our captivity Christ has led captive. Moral evil he has defeated, the difficulties and trials of this mortal life he has virtually overcome. There is nothing in heaven, or earth, or hell, that can be thought to be against us which now remaineth, he hath taken all away. The law he hath fulfilled; its curse he hath removed: the handwriting against us, he hath nailed to his cross. All foes of ours he hath made a show of openly. What joy there is to us in this triumph! What bliss to be interested in it by the gift of faith in him!

III. We may now turn to consider THE GIFTS OF THE ASCENSION. Our Lord ascended on high, and gave gifts to men. What were these gifts which he both received from God and gave to men? Our text says that he ascended that he might fill all things. I do not think this alludes to his omnipresence--in that respect he does fill all things; but allow me to explain, as I receive it, the meaning of the passage, by a very simple figure. Christ descended into the lowest parts of the earth, and thereby he laid the foundations of the great temple of God's praise: he continued in his life laboring, and thereby he built the walls of his temple: he ascended to his throne, and therein he laid the topstone amidst shoutings. What remained then? It remained to furnish it with inhabitants, and the inhabitants with all things necessary for their comfort and perfection. Christ ascended on high that he might do that. In that sense the gift of the Spirit fills all things, bringing in the chosen, and furnishing all that is necessary for their complete salvation. The blessings which come to us through the ascension, are "for the perfecting of the saints, for the work of the ministry, for the edifying of the body of Christ: till we all come in the unity of the faith, and of the knowledge of the Son of God, unto a perfect man, unto the measure of the stature of the fullness of Christ."

Observe next, that these filling blessings of the ascension are given to all the saints. Does not the first verse of our text say: "Unto every one of us is given grace according to the measure of the gift of Christ." The Holy Spirit is the particular benediction of the ascension, and the Holy Spirit is in measure given to all truly regenerated persons. You have all, my brethren, some measure of the Holy Spirit; some more; some less but whatever you have of the Holy Spirit comes to you, because Christ, when he ascended up on high, received gifts for men, that the Lord God might dwell among them. Every Christian having the gift of Christ in his measure, is bound to use it for the general good; for in a body no joint or member exists for itself, but for the good of the whole. You, brother, whether you have much grace or little, must, according to the effectual working in you, supply your part to the increase of the body unto the edifying of itself in love. See that ye regard your gifts in this light; trace them to Christ, and then use them for the object for which he designed them.

But to some persons the Holy Spirit is given more largely. As the result of the ascension of Christ into heaven the church received apostles, men who were selected as witnesses because they had personally seen the Savior--an office which necessarily dies out, and properly so, because the miraculous power also is withdrawn. They were needed temporarily, and they were given by the ascended Lord as a choice legacy. Prophets, too, were in the early church. They were needed as a link between the glories of the old and new covenant; but each prophetic gift came from the Spirit through the Redeemer's ascent to glory. There remain rich gifts among us still, which I fear we do not sufficiently prize. Among men God's richest gifts are men of high vocation, separated for the ministry of the gospel. From our ascended Lord come all true evangelists; these are they who preach the gospel in divers places, and find it the power of God unto salvation; they are founders of churches, breakers of new soil, men of a missionary spirit, who build not on other men's foundations, but dig out for themselves. We need many such deliverers of the good news where as yet the message has not been heard. I scarcely know of any greater blessing to the church than the sending forth of earnest, indefatigable, anointed men of God, taught of the Lord to be winners of souls. Who among us can estimate the value of George Whitfield to the age in which he lived? Who shall ever calculate the price of a John Williams or a William Knibb? Whitfield was, under God, the salvation of our country, which was going down straight to Pandemonium; Williams reclaimed the islands of the sea from cannibalism, and Knibb broke the negro's chains. Such evangelists as these are gifts beyond all price. Then come the pastors and teachers, doing one work in different forms. These are sent to feed the flock; they abide in one place, and instruct converts which have been gathered--these also are invaluable gifts of the ascension of Jesus Christ. It is not given unto all men to be pastors, nor is it needed; for if all were shepherds, where were the flock? Those to whom this grace is especially given are fitted to lead and instruct the people of God, and this leading is much required. What would the church be without her pastors? Let those who have tried to do without them be a warning to you.

Wherever you have pastors or evangelists they exist for the good of the church of God. They ought to labor for that end, and never for their own personal advantage. Their power is their Lord's gift, and it must be used in his way.

The point I want to come at is this. Dear friends, since we all, as believers, have some measure of the Spirit, let us use it. Stir up the gift that is in thee. Be thou not like to him in the parable who had but one talent and hid it in a napkin. Brother, sister, if thou be in the body the least known joint, rob not the body by indolence or selfishness, but use the gift thou hast in order that the body of Christ may come to its perfection. Yet since thou hast not great personal gifts, serve the church by praying the Lord who has ascended to give us more evangelists, pastors, and teachers. He alone can give them; any that come without him are imposters. There are some prayers you must not pray, there are others you may pray, but there are a few you must pray. There is a petition which Christ has commanded us to offer, and yet I very seldom hear it. It is this one. "Pray ye therefore the Lord of the harvest, that he will send forth laborers into his harvest." We greatly lack evangelists and pastors. I do not mean that we lack muffs, who occupy the pulpits and empty the pews. I believe the market has for many years been sufficiently supplied therewith; but we lack men who can stir the heart, arouse the conscience, and build up the church. The scatterers of flocks may be found everywhere; the gatherers of them, how many have we of such? Such a man at this day is more precious than the gold of Ophir. The Queen can make a bishop of the Established Church, but only the ascended Lord can send a bishop to the true church. Prelates, popes, cardinals, vicars, prebends, canons, deans, the Lord has nothing to do with. I see not even the name of them in his word, but the very poorest pastor whom the Lord ordains is a gift of his ascending glory. At this moment we are deploring that in the mission field our good men are grey. Duff, Moffat, and the like, are passing from the stage of action. Where are their successors? I was almost about to say, Echo answers, Where? We want evangelists for India, for China, for all the nations of the earth; and though we have many godly fathers among us, who are instructors in the faith, yet have we in all our pastorates few of eminence, who could be mentioned in the same day as the great Puritanic divines. If the ministry should become weak and feeble among us, the church richly deserves it, for this, the most important part of her whole organisation, has been more neglected than anything else. I thank God this church has not only prayed for ministers, but has proved the sincerity of her prayer by helping such as God has called, by affording them leisure and assistance for understanding the way of God more perfectly. We have thought that Christ's gifts were valuable enough for us to treasure up and improve them. Our College has now received and sent forth, in the name of Jesus, more than two hundred ministers of the word. Look around you and see how few churches care to receive the ascension gifts of Christ, and how few pastors encourage young men to preach. I read the other day, with unutterable horror, the complaint that our churches were like to have too many ministers; an almost blasphemous complaint, impugning the value of Christ's ascension gifts. O that God would give us ten times the number of men after his own heart, and surely there would be then great lack of more! But there are too many, say they, for the present pulpits. Oh, miserable soul is it come to this, that a minister of Christ must have a pulpit ready to hand? Are we all to be builders on other men's foundations? Have we none among us who can gather their own flocks? In a three million city like this can any man say that laborers for Christ are too many? Loiterers are too many, doubtless; and when the church drives out the drones, who shall pity them? While there remain hundreds of towns and villages without a Baptist church, and whole districts of other lands without the gospel, it is idle to dream that of evangelists and teachers we can have too many. No man is so happy in his work as he who presides over a flock of his own gathering, and no pastor is more beloved than he who raised from ruin a destitute church and made it to become a joy and praise in the earth. Pray the Lord to send true pastors and true evangelists. Christ procured them by his ascension. Let us not forget this. What! shall it be thought that the blessings of the crucifixion are worth the having, and the blessings of the resurrection worth receiving, but the blessings of the ascension are to be regarded with indifference or even with suspicion? No; let us prize the gifts which God gives by his Son, and when he sends us evangelists and pastors, let us treat them with loving respect. Honour Christ in every true minister; see not so much the man as his Master in him. Trace all gospel success to the ascended Savior. Look to Christ for more successful workers. As they come receive them from his hands, when they come treat them kindly as his gifts, and daily pray that the Lord will send to Zion mighty champions of the faith.

IV. We shall conclude by noticing THE BEARING OF OUR LORD'S ASCENSION UPON sinners.

We will utter few words, but full of comfort. Did you notice in the sixty-eighth Psalm the words: "He received gifts for men; yea, for the rebellious also"? When the Lord went back to his throne he had thoughts of love towards rebels still. The spiritual gifts of the church are for the good of the rebels as well as for the building up of those who are reconciled. Sinner, every true minister exists for thy good, and all the workers of the church have an eye to you.

There are one or two promises connected with our Lord's ascension which show his kindness to you: "I, if I be lifted up from the earth, will draw all men unto me." An ascended Savior draws you--run after him. Here is another word of his: "He is exalted on high." To curse? No; "to give repentance and remission of sins." Look up to the glory into which he has entered; ask for repentance and remission. Do ye doubt his power to save you? Here is another text: "He is able also to save them to the uttermost that come unto God by him, seeing he ever liveth to make intercession for them." Surely he has gone to heaven for you as well as for the saints. You ought to take good heart, and put your trust in him at this happy hour.

How dangerous it will be to despise him! They who despised him in his shame perished. Jerusalem became a field of blood because it rejected the despised Nazarene. What will it be to reject the King, now that he has taken to himself his great power? Remember, that this same Jesus who is gone up to heaven, will so come in like manner as he was seen to go up into heaven. His return is certain, and your summons to his bar equally certain; but what account can you give if you reject him? O come and trust him this day. Be reconciled to him lest he be angry, and ye perish from the way while his wrath is kindled but a little. The Lord bless you, and grant you a share in his ascension. Amen, and Amen.

PORTIONS OF SCRIPTURE READ BEFORE Sermon--Psalm 68:1-19; Ephesians 4:1-16.

Moab Is My Washpot

A Sermon (No. 983)
by C. H. SPURGEON,
At the Metropolitan Tabernacle, Newington

"Moab is my washpot." - Psalm 60:8.

MOAB, which had threatened Israel, was to be so completely subdued, and become so utterly contemptible as to be likened to a washpot or basin in which men wash their feet. More than this, however, may have been intended--nay, we feel sure was intended by the expression. Let us explain exactly what the language literally means. In the East the general mode of washing the hands and the feet is with a basin and ewer; water is poured upon the hands or feet from the ewer, and it falls into the basin. No Oriental, if he can help it, will wash in standing water; he prefers to have it clear and running. He puts his feet into the washpot, into the bath, into the basin, and then the clear, cool liquid is poured upon his feet; the washpot answering the sole purpose of holding the dirty water which has already passed over the man's flesh. Wearing no completely covering shoes, as we do, but only sandals, the feet of an eastern traveler in a long journey become very much defiled; the water, therefore, when it runs off from them, is far from clean, and the washpot is thus put to a very contemptible use by being only the receptacle of dirty water. When Moab thus became a washpot, it was far other than when it was said, "Moab hath been at ease from his youth, and he hath settled on his lees, and hath not been emptied from vessel to vessel, neither hath he gone into captivity: therefore his taste remained in him, and his scent is not changed." "We have heard the pride of Moab (he is exceeding proud), his loftiness, and his arrogancy, and his pride, and the haughtiness of his heart."

What does Moab represent to you and to me? We are the children of Israel by faith in Christ, and in him we have obtained by covenant a promised land. Our faith may cry, "I will divide Shechem, and mete out the valles of Succoth." All things are ours in Christ Jesus; "Gilead is mine, and Manasseh is mine." Now Moab was outside of Canaan. It was not given to Israel as a possession, but in course of time it was subdued in warfare, and became tributary to the Jewish king. Even thus our faith overcometh the world, and enables us to say, "this world is ours"--ours for a useful, needful purpose. We set but small store by it; it is nothing but our washpot, but we are content to use it as far as we may make it subserve a holy end. The best possessions we have outside of the spiritual heritage we put under our feet, desiring to keep them in their proper inferior position; they are not the crown of our head, nor the comfort of our heart, nor the girdle of our loins, nor the staff of our support; they are put to baser uses far. They yield us some comfort, for which we are grateful to God, but it is only for our feet or lower nature; our head and heart find nobler joys. The whole world put together, with all its wealth, is but a mess of potage for Esau, and nothing more. God's Jacob has a better portion, for he has the birthright. Our worst is better than the world's best, for the reproach of Christ is greater riches than all the treasures of Egypt.

"We trend the world beneath our feet,
With all that earth calls good or great."

"Moab is my washpot," nothing more--a thing contemptible and despicable as compared with the eternal realities of covenant blessings; yet, for all that, there was a use for Moab, a use to be rightly understood. A washpot has its necessary function; and even this base world may be made by faith, in the hands of God, to be the means of aiding the purity of the saints; its afflictions and troubles may work our present and lasting good. The world and its trials can never be compared to the water which cleanses our feet; for that purifying stream we look to a far higher source; but it may be likened to the basin in which our feet are placed while they are being washed.

If we regard Moab as representative of the unregenerate people among whom we dwell, we do well, like the children of Israel, on their march to Canaan, to let them alone, for their heritage is not our heritage, neither are their joys our joys. The less communion we have with them the better. If we ask of them, as Israel did of Moab, simply to be allowed to go on our way in peace, it is all we need. Moses sent his messenger, who said, "Let me pass through thy land: I will go along by the highway, I will neither turn unto the right hand nor to the left. Thou shalt sell me meat for money, that I may eat; and give me water for money, that I may drink: only I will pass through on my feet; until I shall pass over Jordan into the land which the Lord our God giveth us." Like the pilgrims in Vanity Fair, we only ask a clear passage through the place, for we have no inheritance in it, no, not so much as we can set our foot upon. Yet, inasmuch as we cannot altogether separate ourselves from the sinful, for then must we needs go out of the world, we are compelled to feel the influence of their conduct, and it will become our wisdom to watch that this become not injurious to us, but be made under God rather to be of service to us than a hindrance.

My object will be to show that, contrary to the ordinary course of nature, but not contrary to faith, even this ungodly world may be made to assist our advance in holiness. As of old the men of Israel went down to the Philistines to sharpen every man his axe and his courter, so may we derive some sharpening from our enemies. We may gather honey from the lion, take a jewel from the toad's head, and borrow a star from the brow of night. Moab may become our washpot.

While this is contrary to nature, it is also unusual in history. In the Book of Numbers we read that Balak, son of Zippor, desired to vanquish Israel, and therefore he sent for Balaam, the son of Beor, saying, "Curse me Israel, and peradventure I shall prevail against them." Balaam was not able to curse Israel by word of mouth, but he cursed them in very deed when he counselled the king to make them unclean in God's sight by sending the daughters of Moab among them, who not only led them into lasciviousness, but invited them to the sacrifices of their gods. Then the anger of the Lord was kindled against Israel, and the plague would have devoured them, had not the holy zeal of Phinehas turned away the divine anger. Thus it is clear that Moab of old was foremost in polluting and defiling Israel. It is a great feat of faith when the thing which naturally defiles is turned into a washpot. Behold the transformations of grace! This ungodly world outside the church, the world of wicked men, would naturally pollute us, but faith turns them into a washpot, and finds in them motives for watchfulness and holiness. We sigh, in the words of the old psalm--

"Woe's me that I in Mesech am
A sojourner so long;
That I in tabernacles dwell
To Kedar that belong."

As we cannot sing the Lord's song in a strange land, so neither can we very readily keep our garments unspotted in a land deluged with uncleannees. With difficulty do we save ourselves from this untoward generation. And yet faith learns the secret of overcoming the ordinary tendency of things, and of making that which might injure us subsidiary to our advantage; fulfilling that ancient promise, "And strangers shall stand and feed your flocks, and the sons of the alien shall be your plowmen and your vinedressers."

The defiling world may be made helpful to us in the following ways.

I. First of all, ungodly men, if we are in a gracious spirit, may be of solemn service to us, because WE SEE IN THEM WHAT SIN IS. They are beacons upon the rocks to keep us from danger. The lives of many men are recorded in Scripture, not as excuses for our sins, much less as examples, but the very reverse. Like murderers in the olden times hung in chains, they are meant to be warnings. Their lives and deaths are danger-signals, bidding those who are pursuing a career of sin, to come to a pause, and reverse the engine forthwith. They are our washpot in that respect, that they warn us of pollution, and so help to prevent our falling into it. When we learn that pride turned angels into devils, we have a lesson in humility read to us from heaven and hell. When we read of profane Esau, obstinate Pharaoh, disobedient Saul, apostate Judas, or vacillating Pilate, we are taught thereby to shun the rocks upon which they made eternal shipwreck. Trangressors of our own race are peculiarly suitable to act as warnings to us, for we ought ever to remember when we see the sins of ungodly men, that "such were some of us." Whenever thou seest a drunkard, if thou wast once such, it will bring the tears to thine eyes to remember when thou too wast a slave to the ensnaring cup, and thou wilt thank God that his grace has changed thee. Not as the Pharisee wilt thou pretend to thank God, whilst thou art flattering thine own self, but with deep humiliation thou wilt confess what grace has done. When we read in the newspaper a sad case of lasciviousness, or any other breach of the laws of God and man, if we were aforetime guilty of the like and have now been renewed in heart, it will make us blush; it will humble us, and cause us to admire the power and sovereignty of divine grace. Now the blush of repentance, the shamefacedness of humility, and the tear of gratitude, are three helpful things, and all tend under God's grace to set us purging out the old leaven. Remember, O believer, that there is no wretch upon earth so bad, but what thou wast once his equal in alienation from God and death in sin. In untoward acts there may have been much difference, but in the inner man how little! The seed of all the sin which thou seest in him lies in thy corrupt nature, and needs only a fit season to bring forth and bud. Thou wast once in that fire of sin, in which he is consumed by his passions; thou hast been plucked as a brand from the burning, else hadst thou been there still. Yonder is a prodigal, all bespattered from head to foot, but we also once were plunged into the ditch, until our own clothes abhorred us, and we should be sinking in the mire even now, if the mighty hand of grace had not lifted us up from the horrible pit, and washed us in the Savior's blood. We were "heirs of wrath even as others." "All have sinned and come short of the glory of God." Our sins are different, but we were all without exception shapen in iniquity, and as in water, face answereth unto face, so the heart of man to man.

When you see the wickedness of an ungodly man, make him your washpot, by remembering that you also, though you are regenerate, are encompassed with "the body of this death." Remember the words of the Apostle: "For I know that in me (that is, in my flesh,) dwelleth no good thing: for to will is present with me; but how to perform that which is good I find not. For the good that I would I do not: but the evil which I would not, that I do. I find then a law, that, when I would do good, evil is present with me. For I delight in the law of God after the inward man: but I see another law in my members, warring against the law of my mind, and bringing me into captivity to the law of sin which is in my members." The old nature so remains in us, that, if we were to be deserted by God, we should even yet become such as the ungodly are. Need I quote to you the speech of John Bradford, one of the godliest of men? When he saw a wretch taken out to Tyburn to be hanged, the tears were in his eyes, and when they asked him why, he said, "There goes John Bradford, but for the grace of God." Ah, and when we see a prodigal plonging into excess of riot, there goes the best among us, if we are not preserved in Christ Jesus. Ay, and when the damned go down to hell, there must I go, unless the same grace which restrains me now from sin, shall uphold me to my last day; and keep me from falling. Brother Christian, you carry much combustible matter in your nature, be warned when you see your neighbour's house on fire. When one man falls, the next should look to his steps. You are a man of like passions, remember yourself, lest you also be tempted. In these days of epidemics, if we knew that a certain house was tainted with disease, and if we saw a person who had come from it with the marks of the disease in his face; what should we feel? Should we not take it as a warning to keep clear, both of the house and of him; because we ourselves are as likely to take the disease as He was? So when we see a sinner transgressing we should say to ourselves, "I also am a man, and a fallen man, let me abhor every evil way, and guard myself jealously, lest I also fall into sin." In this way Moab may be a washpot. By remembering what we are, and what we were, we may, by taking warning from the evil courses of others, avoid the like condemnation.

There are certain sins which we readily detect in others, which should serve as loud calls to us to us to correct the same things in ourselves. When a man sees the faults of others, and congradulates himself that he is far superior to such, he evidently knows not how to extract good from evil; he is proud, and knows nothing. But when we perceive errors in others, and immediately set a diligent watch against falling into the like, then Moab is rightly used, and becomes our washpot. For instance, as to the matter of bodily indulgence? The sinner is a man who puts his body before his soul, and his head where his feet should be; he is therefore a monster in nature. Instead of the world being under his feet, as it is with every good man, he inverts himself, and places his head and his heart in the dust. He lives for the body which is to die, and forgets the soul which lives for ever. When therefore you see a drunkard, or an unchaste person, say to yourself, "I must mortify my members, and give my Spiritual nature the predominance. For this I must cry mightily to God, the Eternal Spirit, lest the body of this death prevail over me. I must keep under my body, as the Apostle saith, and bring it into subjection, lest I too become a prey to the same animal passions, which lead sinners captives."

I see the ungodly man putting this poor fleeting world before the eternal world to come; therein he is a fool; but let me take heed that I in no measure imitate him. Let me never in my business live as though to make money; to get a competence, to earn the wherewithal to eat and drink, were the first thing with me. Let me not fall into his error, but ever seek first the kingdom of God and his righteousness, and believe that other things shall be added to me. The ungodly man disregards God. God is not in all his thoughts. He saith in his heart, "No God." Now when I know that the ungodly man does that, it should be a warning to me not to forget the Lord, or depart from him in any measure. Alas, we are all of us more or less atheistic. How little of our life is given to God! You who love and fear him are not always near to him, though he is always near to you. Do you never enter upon your enterprises without him? When you begin your business with him, are you not apt to forget him in the middle passage of it? Or when you have gone on to the very center of a work with him, are you not liable to leave him ere you close? Is not this to learn the way of the wicked and to be like them in wandering away from the living God? To have God always with us, to lean hourly upon him, and to feel each moment that he is all in all to us--this is the true condition in which our minds ought to be continually. The atheism of the outside world should warn us against the inward godlessness of our naturally atheistic hearts.

We select these sins as specimens of the general principle, but it is applicable to all forms of evil. Did you ever meet with a vain man, who boasted loudly, and evermore talked about his own beloved self? Was not that a lesson for you? Surely it will help to preserve you from acting so ridiculous a part. Did not I hear you, the other night, laughing at the boaster for his folly? Let us hope, then, you will never set others laughing at yourself. You know another person who is morose, he always speaks sharply, and makes enemies. Be you of another spirit; be courteous, cultivate the grace of cheerfulness and good temper as a Christian. The moroseness of the churl should enforce upon you the duty of godly gentleness. Moab will be your washpot. You know a certain person whose hands appear to be paralysed if they are required to bestow a contribution. How unlovely his meanness makes him! Will not the miserable exhibition of stinginess, which he presents, lead you to avoid all covetousness? Another person of your acquaintance is very soon irritated. You can hardly say a word to displease him but he makes a crime of it immediately, and falls into the temporary insanity of anger. Well, then, learn yourself to be slow to wrath. Seek that charity which is not easily provoked, thinketh no evil. May be your friend's blood is warmer than yours, and there is some excuse for him; but since you see how unwise and wicked it is in him, seek much grace wherewith to overcome the propensity in your own case. If a man should fall into a pit through walking unwarily along a dangerous path, his fall should be my safety, his experience should be my instruction; there can be no need for me to roll over the same precipice in order to know experimentally how dangerous it is. How sad a fact it is that very few of us ever do learn by the experience of other people! Dame Experience must take each one of us into her school, and make us personally smart under her rod--we will not learn else. Warnings are neglected by the foolish. The young slaggard sees the huge thorns and thistles in the older sluggard's garden and yet he follows the same lazy habits. One step follows another into the shambles. Flies see their brethren perishing, in the sugared trap, and yet rush into it themselves. The Lord make us wise and prudent, and from the errors of others may we learn to steer our own course aright; then may we truly say, "Moab is my washpot."

II. Another illustration of this practical principle lies in the fact, that WE SEE IN THE UNGODLY THE PRESENT EVIL RESULTS OF SIN. We frequently have the opportunity of beholding in them, not only sin, but some of its bitter fruits, and this should still further help us to shun it, by God's grace. Evil is now no longer an unknown seed of doubtful character; we have seen it planted, and have beheld sinners reaping the first sheaves of its awful harvest. This poison is no longer an uncertain drug, for its deadly effects are apparent in those around us. If we sin, it is no longer through the want of knowing what sin will lead to, for its mischief is daily before our eyes.

First, are you not very certain, those of you who watch unconverted and ungodly people, that they are not solidly happy? What roaring boys they are sometimes! How vociferous are their songs! How merry their dances! How hilarious their laughter! You would think that there were no happier people to be found under the sun; but as, on many a face, beauty is produced by art rather than by nature, and a little paint creates a transient comeliness, so, often the mirth of this world is a painted thing, a base imitation, not so deep even as the skin. Ungodly men know nothing of heart-laughing; they are strangers to the deep, serene happiness which is the portion of believers. Their joy comes and goes with the hour. See them when the feast is over--"Who hath woe? Who hath redness of the eyes? They that tarry long at the wine; the men of strength to mingle strong drink." Mark them when alone: they are ready to die with dulness. They want to kill time, as if they had an overplus of it and would be glad to dispose of the superfluity. A man's face must be very ugly when he never cares to look at it, and a man's state must be very bad indeed in when he is ashamed to know what it is; and yet in the case of tens of thousands of people, who say they are very happy, there is a worm inside the apple; the very foundation-stone has been removed from the edifice; and you may be sure it is so, for they dare not examine into matters. Ungodly men at bottom are unhappy men. "The way of trangressors is hard." "There is no peace, saith my God, to the wicked." Their Marah is never dry, but flows with perennial waters of bitterness. What says their great poet Byron:--

"Count o'er the joys thine hours have seen,
Count o'er the days from anguish free;
And know whatever thou hast been,
Tis something better not to be."

Now then, if things be so--if sin brings after all an unsatisfactory result to the mind, if a man is not rendered happy by an evil course--then let me choose another path, and, by God's grace, keep to wisdom's ways of pleasantness and paths of peace, into which my Lord by his love has drawn me and by his grace has led me. I am happy in his bosom, I drink living waters out of his fountain. Why should I go to those broken cisterns, which I clearly see can hold no water? Why should I wish to wander over the dreary waste of waters? Noah's hand is warm, and the peaceful ark is near: "Return unto thy rest, O my soul, for the Lord hath dealt bountifully with thee." When I read of aching hearts, and hear that great worldling, who had all the world could give him, sum it all up with this sentence, "Vanity of vanities, all is vanity," does not my heart say at once, "Oh, empty world, thou temptest me in vain, for I see through the cheat." Madam Bubble we have seen with her mask off, and are not to be fascinated by so ugly a witch. We follow not after yonder green meads and flowing brooks, because they are not real, and are only a mirage mocking the traveler. Wherefore should we pursue a bubble or chase the wind? We spend our money no more for that which is not bread. Moab is our washpot; if others have found earthly things to be unsatisfactory, we wash our hands of their disappointing pursuits. Dear Savior, we would follow thee whithersoever thou goest, till we come to dwell with thee for ever.

But it is not merely that ungodly men are not happy; there are times when they are positively wretched through their sins. Sometimes fear cometh upon them as a whirlwind, and they have no refuge or way of escape. I have been now and then called to witness the utter anguish of a man who has lost his gods. His great idols have been broken, and he has been in despair. His darling child is dead, or his wife is a corpse, and he knows not how to endure life. Did you ever see a godless man when he had lost all his money in a speculation which once promised fair? Did you mark his woe? Did you ever see the countenance of a gambler who had staked his last and lost his all? See him in an agony which can find no alleviation. He rises from the table, he rushes to imbrue his hands in his own blood. Poor soul, he has lost his all! That never happens to a Christian--never! If all he had on earth were gone, it would be only like losing a little of his spending-money, but his permanent capital would be safe in the Imperial exchequer, where Omnipotence itself stands guard.

Even when no very great calamity puts out the candle of the worldling, Yet, as years revolve, a gathering cloud darkens his day. Hear again the world's master songster. The confession will suit many:--

"My days are in the yellow leaf,
The flowers and fruits of love are gone;
The worm, the canker, and the grief--
Are mine alone.
The fire that in my bosom plays
Alone as some volcanic isle;
No torch is kindled at its blaze--
A funeral pile."

This is the world's treatment of its old servants: it dishonors them in old age; but it is not so with aged believers: "they shall still bring forth fruit in old age; they shall be fat and flourishing, to show that the Lord is upright." When all our wealth on earth is gone, our treasure is still safe in heaven, where moth corrupts not, and thieves break not through nor steal. When we think of the despair of men, of blasted hopes, Moab may become our washpot, and may keep us from setting our affection upon their fleeting joys.

Here and there, in the Moab of sin, you meet with men who are in their garments, their trembling limbs, their penury, and their shame, living monitors and standing proves that the way of transgressors in hard. There are sins whose judgment hastens as a whirlwind--sins of the flesh, which eat into the bones and poison the blood; sins of appetite, that degrade and destroy the frame. If young men knew the price of sin, even in this life, they would not be so but to purchase pleasurable moments at the price of painful years. Who would coin his life into iniquity to have it returned to him in this life, red-hot from the mint of torment! Mark well the spendthrift, void of understanding! I have seen him at my door. I knew his relatives; people of reputable character and good estate. I have seen him in rags which scarcely covered him, piteously weeping for a piece of bread. Yet a few short years ago he inherited a portion which most men would have thought wealth. In a mad riot, into which he could not crowd enough of debauchery, he spent all that he had. He was soon penniless, and then loathsome and sore sick. He was pitied by his friends, but pity has been lost on him, and now none of his kith or kin dare own him. I too fed him, clothed him, and found him a place of labor. The garments which charity had supplied him, within the next few hours, were sold for drink, and he was wallowing in drunkenness. The work was deserted almost as soon as attempted. He will die of starvation, if he be not already dead, for he has abandoned himself to every vicious excess, and already trembles from head to foot, and looks to be on the borders of the grave. Nothing keeps him sober but want of another penny to buy drink; not even that can restrain him from uncleanness. Hunger, and cold, and nakedness he knows full well, and prefers to endure them rather than earn honest bread and abandon his licentiousness. Tears have been wept over him in vain, and many must have been his own tears of misery when he has been in want. The workhouse is his best shelter and its pauper clothing his noblest livery. Away from that retreat he is a mass of rags and indescribable filth. Young Christian professor, if you are tempted by the strange woman, or by the wine which moveth itself aright in the cup, look on the victims of these destroyers ere you dally with them. See the consequences of sin even in this life, and avoid it, pass not by it, look not on it, but flee youthful lusts which war against the soul. Thus make filthy Moab to become your washpot from this time forth.

The unconverted when they go not thus far may yet be beacons to us. Observe, for instance, the procrastinating hearer of the gospel, how certainly he becomes hardened to all rebukes. Early sensibility gives way to indifference. Let us also beware lest we, by trifling with convictions and holy impulses, lose tenderness of conscience. They advance in evil, and at last commit with impunity sins which, years ago, would have struck them with unaffected horror; let us be cautious lest a similarly blunting process should be carried on upon our hearts. But time would fail me to show you in detail how readily the evil results of sin in others may preserve us from falling into the like; how, in a word, Moab may be our washpot.

III. A third point suggests itself. Men of this world are made useful to us since they DISCOVER IN US OUR WEAK PLACES. Their opposition, slander, and persecution, are a rough pumice-stone, to remove some of our spots. When young men come to college, one of the chief benefits they obtain is the severe criticism to which they are subjected from their tutors and fellow students. Sharp ears hear their slips of speech, and they are made conscious of them. Now in a certain sense the outside world often becomes a college to the Christian. When we are with our dear Christian brethren, they do not look for our faults--at least, they should not--neither do they irritated us and so bring our infirmities to the surface, but they treat us so lovingly and gently that we do not know our weak side. Young Christians would be like plants under glass cases in a conservatory, and become tender and feeble, but the rough world tries them, and is over-ruled by God to their strengthening and general benefit. Men's lynx eyes see our shortcomings, and their merciless tongues inform us of them; And, for my part, I see much advantage brought out of this maliciousness of theirs; they are our monitors, and help to keep us humble, and make us careful. If we cannot bear a little shake from men, how shall we bear the shaking of heaven and earth at the last day?

The world often tries us as with fire, and the things which we reckoned to be gold and silver perish in the ordeal it they are but counterfeit, but we are gainers by such a loss. In the world our temper is tried, and too often we become irritated. What then? Why just this; if sanctification has regulated our emotions, patience will have her perfect work, and charity will suffer long; but if we are soon angry and find it hard to forgive, let us not so much find fault with those who try us as with ourselves, because we cannot bear the ordeal. Our pride must go down, we must become slow to wrath, we must be content to be as our Lord, the meek and lowly Savior. These irritations show us how far we are from the model, and should excite in us a desire for progress towards his complete image. Perhaps you had fondly said in your heart, "I could bear a great deal. I could act the Christian under the worst abuse;" but now you sing another song, and find how great your weakness is. Moab thus again becomes your washpot, for now you will go to God in prayer, and ask to be subdued to his will.

Do not worldly men in some cases frighten professors out of their testimony for Christ? I mean, has it never happened that our cheek has blanched, and our tongue failed us in the presence of cavillers, and blasphemers, and sceptics, and have we not been silent when we ought to have avowed our Lord? That also shows how cowardly we are at heart, and how cold is our love. We are to blame for not having more courage; for if we were strong in the Lord and in the power of his might, as we ought to be, we should be ready to go with Christ to prison and to death, and never think of shunning his service.

Do you not find that ungodly men, when you are obliged to be in their company in business, will occasionally utter remarks which shake your faith about truths which you imagined you firmly believed? Too many are content with a superficial creed. Their faith is not rooted deep in their hearts, and therefore a little wind rocks the tree to and fro, but ere long the very motion of the tree tends to root it, and it becomes all the more firm. God over-rules for good the evilness of men against the truth. Besides, do not ungodly men drive us from loving the world! We might think of finding our rest here below, but when we hear their tongues cruelly and unkindly slandering us, there we are sick of their company.

"My soul distracted mourn and pines
To reach that peaceful shore,
Where all the weary are at rest,
And troubles vex no more."

An extreme case of the way in which evil treatment may tend to our sanctification, may be found in the life of one of the old ministers in the north of Scotland. "A cold, unfeeling, bold, unheeding, worldly woman was the wife of Mr. Fraser, one of the ministers of Ross-shire," writes my beloved friend, Mr. John Kennedy, in his interesting book, entitled, "The Days of the Fathers in Ross-shire." "Never did her godly husband sit down to a comfortable meal in his own home, and often would he have fainted but for the considerate kindness of some of his parishioners. She was too insensate to try to hide her treatment of him, and well was it for him, on one account, that she was. His friends thus knew of his ill-treatment, and were moved to do what they could for his comfort. A godly acquaintance arranged with him to leave a supply of food in a certain place, beside his usual walk, of which he might avail himself when starved at home. Even light and fire in his study were denied to him on the long, cold winter evenings; and as his study was his only place of refuge from the cruel scourge of his wife's tongue and temper, there, shivering and in the dark, he used to spend his winter evenings at home. Compelled to walk in order to keep himself warm, and accustomed to do so when preparing for the pulpit, he always kept his hands before him as feelers in the dark, to warn him of his approaching the wall at either side of the room. In this way he actually wore a hole through the plaster at each end of his accustomed beat, on which some eyes have looked that glistened with light from other fire than that of love, at the remembrance of his cruel wife. But the godly husband had learned to thank the Lord for the discipline of this trial. Being once at a Presbytery dinner, alone, amidst a group of moderates, one of them proposed, as a toast, the health of their wives, and turning to Mr. Fraser, said, as he winked at his companions, You, of course, will cordially join in drinking to this toast.'--So I will, and so I ought,' Mr. Fraser said, for mine has been a better wife to me than any of yours has been to you.' How so?' they all exclaimed.--She has sent me,' was his reply, seven times a day to my knees, when I would not otherwise have gone, and that is more than any of you can say of yours.'" Ah, this is the way to make Moab our washpot, that is to say, to make those who grieve us most, act but as rough waves to hurry us on to the rock, or as biting winds that drift as the faster into port. If the birds of paradise will keep to the nest, their ungodly relatives or neighbors shall be a thorn therein to make them mount into their native element--the heaven of God.

The attacks of the ungodly upon the church have been overruled by God to make his people leave the camp and foresake ungodly associations, so as to be separate. I know a beloved sister in Christ who was baptised; she had moved in high circles, but they told me that after her baptism she received the cold shoulder. When I heard it, I said, "Thank God for it," for half her temptations are gone. If the world has turned its back upon her, she will be all the more sure to turn her back on the world and live near to her Lord. The friendship of the world is enmity to God--why should we seek it? "If any man love the world, the love of the Father is not in him." If any man will follow Christ he must expect persecution, and one of the cardinal precepts of the Christian faith runs thus: "Come ye out from among them, and be ye separate, saith the Lord, and I will be a Father unto you, and ye shall be my sons and daughters." "Let us go forth, therefore, unto him, without the camp, bearing his reproach."

IV. Lastly, IN REFERENCE TO THE WORLD TO COME, the terrible doom of the ungodly is a most solemn warning to us. My heart fails me to speak concerning the destiny of the ungodly in another world. Dying without hope, without a Savior, they go before the throne uncleansed, unforgiven, to hear that awful sentence, "Depart, ye cursed, into everlasting fire, prepared for the devil and his angels." Pursue them for a moment in your thoughts, down to the deeps of wrath, whither God's judgment shall pursue them. My Lord, I pray thee of thy grace, save me from the sin which brings such a result at the end of it. If the wages of sin be such a death as this, Lord save me from so accursed a service. Will not the sight of their destruction drive us to watchfulness, and cause us to make our calling and election sure? Will it not make us anxious lest we also come into this place of torment? O the wrath to come! The wrath to come whereof this Book speaks in so many terrible tones and dreadful images! Remember Lot's wife "I will therefore put you in remembrance, though ye once knew this, how that the Lord, having saved the people out of the land of Egypt, afterward destroyed them that believed not. And the angels which kept not their first estate, but left their own habitation, he hath reserved in everlasting chains under darkness unto the judgment of the great day. Even as Sodom and Gomorrha, and the cities about them in like manner, giving themselves over to fornication, and going after strange flesh, are set forth for an example, suffering the vengeance of eternal fire."

In this way Moab becomes our washpot, by showing us what sin grows to when it has developed itself. This consideration will surely cause us more heartily to love the Savior, who can deliver us from it.

Dear friends, if you are not in Christ, much of what I have said bears upon you. Bethink yourself, and pray to escape from the wrath to come. I would not have you be made a mere washpot to be used and broken as a potter's vessel. Neither should you wish to be a vessel without honor, a thing of no esteem; but may you have faith in Jesus--life in him, and then you shall be a royal diadem, a crown of glory in the hand of our God. May you have a heritage among those who fear the Lord, and are reconciled to him by faith in the total sacrifice of our Lord Jesus Christ.

PORTION OF SCRIPTURE READ BEFORE SERMON--Psalm 60.

The Church As She Should Be

A Sermon (No. 984)
Delivered by
C. H. SPURGEON,
At the Metropolitan Tabernacle, Newington

"Thou art beautiful, O my love as Tirzah, comely as Jerusalem, terrible as an army with banners."
- Song of Solomon 6:4.

THERE are various estimates of the Christian church. Some think everything of her; some think nothing of her; and probably neither opinion is worth the breath which utters it. Neither Ritualists, who idolise their church, nor sceptics, who vilify all churches, have any such knowledge of the true spiritual church of Jesus Christ as to be entitled to give an opinion. The king's daughter is all glorious within, with a beauty which they are quite unable to appreciate. What is usually the most correct character which is obtainable of a woman? Shall we be guided by the praises of those neighbors who are on good terms with her, or by the scandal of those who make her the subject of ill-natured gossip? No; the most accurate judgment we are likely to get is that of her husband. Solomon saith in the Proverbs concerning the virtuous woman, "Her husband also riseth up, and he praiseth her." Of that fairest among women, the church of Christ, the same observation may be made. It is to her of small consequence to be judged of man's judgment, but it is her honor and joy to stand well in the love and esteem of her royal spouse, the Prince Emmanuel. Though the words before us are allegorical, and the whole song is crowded with metaphor and parable, yet the teaching is plain enough in this instance; it is evident that the Divine Bridegroom gives his bride a high place in his heart, and to him, whatever she may be to others, she is fair, lovely, comely, beautiful, and in the eyes of his love without a spot. Moreover, even to him there is not only a beauty of a soft and gentle kind in her, but a majesty, a dignity in her holiness, in her earnestness, in her consecration, which makes even him say of her that she is "terrible as an army with banners," "awful as a bannered army." She is every inch a queen: her aspect in the sight of her beloved is majestic. Take, then, the words of our text as an encomium upon Christ's church, pronounced by him who knows her best, and is best able to judge concerning her, and you learn that to his discerning eye she is not weak, dishonorable, and despicable, but bears herself as one of highest rank, consciously, joyously strong in her Lord's strength.

On this occasion let us note, first of all, WHY IT IS THAT THE CHURCH OF GOD IS SAID TO BE AN ARMY WITH BANNERS. That she is an army is true enough, for the church is one, but many; and consists of men who march in order under a common leader, with one design in view and that design a conflict and a victory. She is the church militant here below, and both in suffering and in service she is made to prove that she is in an enemy's country. She is contending for the truth against error, for the light against darkness: till the day break and the shadows flee away, she must maintain her sentinels and kindle her watch fires; for all around her there is cause to guard against the enemy, and to descend the royal treasure of gospel truth against its deadly foes. But why an army with banners? Is not this, first of all, for distinction? How shall we know to which king an army belongs unless we can see the royal standard? In times of war the nationality of troops is often declared by their distinguishing regimentals. The grey coats of the Russians were well known in the Crimea; the white livery of the Austrians was a constant eyesore in bygone days to the natives of Lombardy. No one mistook the Black Brunswickers for French Guards, or our own Hussars for Garibaldians. Quite as effectively armies have been distinguished by the banners which they carried. As the old knights of old were recognised by their plume and helmet, and escutcheon, so an army is known by its standard and the national colors. The tricolor of the French readily marked their troops as they fled before the terrible black and white of the German army. The church of Christ displays its banners for distinction's sake. It desires not to be associated with other armies, or to be mistaken for them, for it is not of this world, and its weapons and its warfare are far other than those of the nations. God forbid that followers of Jesus should be mistaken for political partisans or ambitious adventurers. The church unfurls her ensign to the breeze that all may know whose she is and whom she serves. This is of the utmost importance at this present, when crafty men are endeavoring to palm off their inventions. Every Christian church should know what it believes, and publicly avow what it maintains. It is our duty to make a clear and distinct declaration of our principles, that our members may know to what intent they have come together, and that the world also may know what we mean. Far be it from us to join with the Broad Church cry, and furl the banners upon which our distinctive colors are displaced. We hear on all sides great outcries against creeds. Are these clamours justifiable? It seems to me that when properly analysed most of the protests are not against creeds, but against truth, for every man who believes anything must have a creed, whether he write it down and print it or no; or if there be a man who believes nothing, or anything, or everything by turns, he is not a fit man to be set up as a model. Attacks are often made against creeds because they are a short, handy form by which the Christian mind gives expression to its belief, and those who hate creeds do so because they find them to be weapons as inconvenient, as bayonets in the hands of British soldiers have been to our enemies. They are weapons so destructive to theology that it protests against them. For this reason let us be slow to part with them. Let us day hold of God's truth with iron grip, and never let it go. After all, there is a Protestantism still worth contending for; there is a Calvinism still worth proclaiming, and a gospel worth dying for. There is a Christianity distinctive and distinguished from Ritualism, Rationalism, and Legalism, and let us make it known that we believe in it. Up with your banners, soldiers of the cross! This is not the time to be frightened by the cries against conscientious convictions, which are nowadays nicknamed sectarianism and bigotry. Believe in your hearts what you profess to believe; proclaim openly and zealously what you know to be the truth. Be not ashamed to say such-and-such things are true, and let men draw the inference that the opposite is false. Whatever the doctrines of the gospel may be to the rest of mankind, let them be your glory and boast. Display your banners, and let those banners be such as the church of old carried. Unfurl the old primitive standard, the all-victorious standard of the cross of Christ. In very deed and truth--in hoc signo vinces--the atonement is the conquering truth. Let others believe as they may, or deny as they will, for you the truth as it is in Jesus is the one thing that has won your heart and made you a soldier of the cross.

Banners were carried, not merely for distinctiveness, but also to serve the purposes of discipline. Hence an army with banners had one banner as a central standard, and then each regiment or battalion displayed its own particular flag. The hosts of God, which so gloriously marched through the wilderness, had their central standard. I suppose it was the very pole upon which Moses lifted up the brazen serpent (at any rate, our brazen serpent is the central ensign of the church); and then, besides that, each tribe of the twelve had its own particular banners, and with these uplifted in the front, the tribes marched in order, so that there was no confusion on the march, and in time of battle there was no difficulty in marshalling the armed men. It was believed by the later Jews that "the standard of the camp of Judah represented a lion; that of Reuben, a man; that of Joseph, an ox; and that of Dan, an eagle. The Targumists, however, believe that the banners were distinguished by their colors, the color for each tribe being analogous to that of the precious stone for that tribe, in the breastplate of the high priest; and that the great standard of each of the four camps combined the three colors of the tribes which composed it." So, brethren, in the church of God there must be discipline--the discipline not only of admission and of dismission in receiving the converts and rejecting the hypocrites, but the discipline of marshalling the troops to the service of Christ in the holy war in which we are engaged. Every soldier should have his orders, every officer his troop, every troop its fixed place in the army, and the whole army a regularity such as is prescribed in the rule, "Let all things be done decently and in order." As in the ranks each man has his place, and each rank has its particular phase in the battalion, so in every rightly constituted church each may, each woman, will have, for himself or herself, his or her own particular form of service, and each form of service will link in with every other, and the whole combined will constitute a force which cannot be broken. A church is not a load of bricks, remember: it is a house builded together. A church is not a bundle of cuttings in the gardener's hand: it is a vine, of which we are the branches. The true church is an organised whole; and life, true spiritual life, wherever it is paramount in the church, without rules and rubrics, is quite sure to create order and arrangement. Order without life reminds us of the rows of graves in a cemetery, all numbered and entered in the register: order with life reminds us of the long lines of fruit trees in Italy, festooned with fruitful vines. Sunday-school teachers, bear ye the banner of the folded lamb; sick visitors, follow the ensign of the open hand; preachers, rally to the token of the uplifted brazen serpent; and all of you, according to your sacred calling, gather to the name of Jesus, armed for the war.

An army with banners may be also taken to represent activity. When an army holds up its colors the fight is over. Little is being done in military, circles when the banners are put away; the troops are on furlough, or are resting in barracks. An army with banners is exercising, or marching, or fighting; probably it is in the middle of a campaign, it is marshalled for offense and defense, and there will be rough work before long. It is to be feared that some churches have hung up their flags to rot in state, or have encased them in dull propriety. They do not fool; to do great things, or to see great things. They do not expect many conversions; if many did happen, they would be alarmed and suspicious. They do not expect their pastor's ministry to be with power; and if it were attended with manifest effect they would be greatly disturbed, and perhaps would complain that he created too much excitement. The worst of it is, that do-nothing churches are usually very jealous lest any should encroach on their domain. Our churches sometime ago appeared to imagine that a whole district of this teeming city belonged to them to cultivate or neglect, as their monopolising decree might be. If anybody attempted to raise a new interest, or even to build a preaching station, within half a mile of them, they resented it as a most pernicious poachings upon their manor. They did nothing themselves, and were very much afraid lest anybody should supplant them. Like the lawyers of old, who took away the key of knowledge, they entered not in themselves, and them that were entering in they hindered. That day, it is to be hoped, has gone once for all; yet too much of the old spirit lingers in certain quarters. It is high time that each church should feel that if it does not work, the sole reason for its existence is gone. The reason for a church being a church dies its mutual edification and in the conversion of sinners; and if these two ends are not really answered by a church, it is a mere name, a hindrance, an evil, a nuisance; like the salt which has lost its savor, it is neither fit for the land nor yet for the dunghill. May we all in our church fellowship be active in the energy of the Spirit of God. May none of us be dead members of the living body, mere impediments to the royal host, baggage to be dragged rather than warriors pushing on the war. May we, every one of us, be soldiers filled with vigor to the fullness of our manhood, by the eternal power of the Holy Spirit; and may we be resolved that any portion of the church which does not uplift its banner of service shall not long number us among its adherents. Be it ours to determine that whether others will or will not serve God and extend the kingdom of his dear Son, we will, in his name and strength, contend even to the death. Unsheath our swords, ye soldiers of the cross; arise from your slumbers, ye careless ones, gird on your swords and prepare for the war. The Lord has redeemed you by his blood, not that you might sleep, but that you might fight for the glory of his name.

Does not the description, "an army with banners," imply a degree of confidence? It is not an army retiring from the foe, and willing enough to hide its colors to complete its escape. An army that is afraid to venture out into the open, keeps its banners out of the gleam of the sun. Banners uplifted are the sign of a fearlessness which rather courts than declines the conflict. Ho! warriors of the cross, unfurl the gospel's ancient standard to the breeze; we will teach the foeman what strength there is in hands and hearts that rally to the Christ of God. Up with the standard, ye brave men at arms; let all eyes see it; and it the foemen glare like lions on it, we "will call upon the Lion of the tribe of Judah to lead the van, and we will follow with his word like a two-edged sword in our hands:--

"Stand up! stand up for Jesus!
Ye soldiers of the cross!
Lift high hits royal banner;
It must not suffer loss:
From victory unto victory
His army shall he lead
Till every foe is vanquished
And Christ is Lord indeed."

We cannot place too much reliance in the gospel; our weakness is that we are so diffident and so apt to look somewhere else for strength. We do not believe in the gospel as to its power over the sons of men as we should believe in it. Too often we preach it with a coward's voice. Have I not heard sermons commencing with abject apologies for the preacher's daring to open his mouth; apologies for his youth, for his assertions, for his venturing to intrude upon men's consciences, and I know not what else? Can God own ambassadors of this cowardly cringing breed, who mistake fear of men for humility! Will our Captain honor such carpet-knights, who apologise for bearing arms? I have heard that of old the ambassadors of Holland, and some other states, when introduced to his celestial majesty, the brother of the son and cousin of the moon, the Emperor of China, were expected to come crawling on their hands and knees up to the throne; but when our ambassadors went to that flowery land, they declined to pay such humiliating homage to his impertinent majesty, and informed him that they would stand upright in his presence, as free men should do, or else they would decline all dealings with him, and in all probability his majesty would hear from a cannon's mouth far less gentle notes than he would care for. Even thus, though we may well humble ourselves as men, yet as ambassadors of God we cannot crouch to the sons of men, to ask them what message would suite them best. It must not, shall not, be that we shall smoothe our tongues and tone our doctrines to the taste of the age. The gospel that we preach, although the worldly wise man despises it, in God's gospel for all that. "Ah," says he, "there is nothing in it: science has overthrown it." "And," says another, "this gospel is but so much platitude; we have heard it over and over again." Ah, sir, and though it be platitude to you, and you decree it to be contemptible, you shall hear it or nothing else from us; "for it is the power of God, and the wisdom of God." In its simplicity lies its majesty and its power. "We are not ashamed of the gospel of Christ. "God forbid that we should glory, save in the cross of our Lord Jesus Christ." We will proclaim it again with confidence; We will bring forth once more the selfsame truth as of old; and as the barley loaf smote the tent of Midian, so that it lay along, so shall the gospel overturn its adversaries. The broken pitcher, and the flaming torches, and the old war cry, "The sword of the Lord, and of Gideon" shall yet fill the foeman with dismay. Let us but be bold for Jesus, and we shall see what his arm can do. The gospel is the voice of the eternal God, and has in it the same power as that which brought the world out of nothing, and which shall raise the dead from their graves at the coming of the Son of Man. The gospel, the word of God, can no more return to him void than can the snow go back to heaven, or the rain-drops climb again the path by which they descended from the clouds. Have faith in God's word, faith in the presence of the Holy Ghost, faith in the reigning Savior, faith in the fulfillment of the everlasting purposes, and you will be full of confidence, and like an army with banners.

Once more, an army with banners may signify the constancy and perseverance in holding the truth. We see before us not an army that has lost its banners, that has suffered its colors to be rent away from it, but an army which bears aloft its ancient standard and swears by it still. Let us be very earnest to maintain the faith once delivered to the saints. Let us not give up this doctrine or that, at the dictates of policy or fashion; but whatsoever Jesus saith unto us, let us receive it as the word of life. Great injury may be done to a church ere it knows it, if it shall tolerate error here and there; for false doctrine, like the little leaven, soon leavens the whole lump. If the church be taught of the Spirit to know the voice of the Good Shepherd, a stranger it will not follow; for it knows not the voice of strangers. This is part of the education which Christ gives to his people: "All thy people shall be taught of the Lord." They shall know the truth, and the truth shall make them free. May we, as a church, hold fast the things which we have learned and have been taught of God; and may we be preserved from the philosophies and refinings of these last days. If we give up the things which are verily believed among us we shall lose our pourer, and the enemy alone will be pleased; but if we maintain them, the maintenance of the old faith, by the Spirit of God, shall make us strong in the Lord and in the power of his might. Wrap the colors round you, ye standard bearers, in the day of danger, and die sooner than give them up. Life is little compared with God's lovingkindness, and that is the sure heritage of the brave defender of the faith. Thus resolute for truth, the church becomes an army with banners.

II. Secondly, the church is said to be TERRIBLE. To whom is she terrible? She should be amiable, and she is. May God grant that our church may never be terrible to young converts by moroseness and uncharitableness. Whenever I hear of candidates being alarmed at coming before our elders, or seeing the pastor, or making confession of faith before the church, I wish I could say to them: "Dismiss your fears, beloved ones; we shall be glad to see you, and you will find your intercourse with us a pleasure rather than a trial." So far from wishing to repel you, if you really do love the Savior, we shall be glad enough to welcome you. If we cannot see in you the evidence of a great change, we shall kindly point out to you our fears, and shall be thrice happy to point you to the Savior; but be sure of this, if you have really believed in Jesus, you shall not find the church terrible to you. Harsh judgments are contrary to the spirit of Christ and the nature of the gospel; where they are the rule, the church is despicable rather than terrible. Bigotry and uncharitableness are indications of weakness, not of strength.

To what and to whom is the church terrible? I answer, first, in a certain sense she is terrible to all ungodly men. A true church in her holiness and testimony is very terrible to sinners. The ungodly care not a rush about a mock church, nor about sham Christians; but a really earnest Christian makes the ungodly abashed. We have known some who could not use the foul language which they were accustomed to when they were in the presence of godly men and women, though these persons had no authority or position or rank. Even in the most ribald company, when a Christian of known consistency of character has wisely spoken the word of reproof, a solemn abashment comes over the majority of those present; their consciences have borne witness against them, and they have felt how awful goodness is. Not that we are ever to try and impress others with any dread of us; such an attempt would be ridiculed, and end in deserved failure; but the influence which we would describe flows naturally out of a godly light. Majesty of character never lies in affectation of demeanor, but in solidity of virtue. If there be real goodness in us--if we really, fervently, zealously love the right, and hate the evil--the outflow of our life almost without a word will judge the ungodly--and condemn them in their heart of hearts. Holy living is the weightiest condemnation of sin. We have heard of an ungodly son who could not bear to dive in the house where his departed father had in his lifetime so devoutly prayed; every room, and every piece of furniture reproved him for forsaking his father's God. We have read of others who were wont to dread the sight of certain godly men whose holy lives held them more in check than the laws of the land. The bad part of this is that the terror of the ungodly suggests to them an unhallowed retort upon their reprovers, and becomes the root out of which springs persecution. Those whom the ungodly fear because they condemn them by their character, they try to put out of the world if they can, or to bespatter them with slander if they cannot smite them with the hand of cruelty. The martyrdom of saints is the result of the darkness hating the light, because the light makes manifest its evil deeds. There will be always in proportion to the real holiness, earnestness, and Christ likeness of a church something terrible in it to the perverse generation in which it is placed; it will dread it as it does the all-revealing day of judgment.

So is there something terrible in a living church to all errorists. Just now two armies have encamped against the host of God, opposed to each other, but confederates against the church of God. Ritualism, with its superstition, its priestcraft, its sacramental efficacy, its hatred of the doctrines of grace; and on the other side Rationalism, with its sneering unbelief and absurd speculations. These, like Herod and Pilate, agree in nothing but in opposition to Christ; they have one common dread, although they may not confess it. They do not dread those platform speeches in which they are so furiously denounced at public meetings, nor those philosophical discussions in which they are overthrown by argument; but they hate, but they fear, and therefore abuse and pretend to despise, the prayerful, zealous, plain simple preaching of the truth as it is in Jesus. This is a weapon against which they cannot stand--the weapon of the odd gospel. In the days of Luther it did marvels; it wrought wonders in the days of Whitfield and Wesley: it has often restored the ark of the Lord to our land, and it will again. It has lost none of its ancient power, and therefore is it the terror of the adversaries of Christ.

"Thine aspect's awful majesty
Doth strike thy foes with fear;
As armies do when banners fly,
And martial flags appear.
How does thine armor, glitt'ring bright,
Their frighted spirits quell!
The weapons of thy warlike might
Defy the gates of hell."

Even to Satan himself the church of God is terrible. He might, he thinks, deal with individuals, but when these individuals strengthen each other by mutual converse and prayer, when they are bound to each other in holy love, and make a temple in which Christ dwells, then is Satan hard put to it. O brethren and sisters, it is not every church that is terrible thus, tent it is a church of God in which there is the life of God, and the love of God; a church in which there is the uplifted banner, the banner of the cross, high-held amid those various banners of truthful doctrine and spiritual grace, of which I have just now spoken.

III. We will take a third point; and that is, WHY IS THE CHURCH OF CHRIST TERRIBLE AS AN ARMY WITH BANNERS? Why is it terrible because of its banners? The whole passage seems to say that the church is terrible as an army, but that to the fullest degree she owes her terribleness to her banners. "Terrible as an army with banners." I believe the great banner of the Christian church to be the uplifted Savior. "I, if I be lifted up from the earth, will draw all men unto me." Around him then we gather. "Unto him shall the gathering of the people be." As the brazen serpent in the midst of the camp in the wilderness, so is the Savior lifted high, our banner. The atoning, sacrifice of Christ is the great central standard of all really regenerate men, and this is the main source of dismay to Israel's foes.

But we shall take the thoughts in order. The church herself is terrible, and then terrible because of her banners. Brethren, the army itself is terrible. Why? First, because it consists of elect people. Remember how Haman's wife enquired concerning Mordecai whether he belonged to the seed of the Jews; for if he did, then she foretold that her husband's scheme would prove a failure. "If Mordecai be of the Seed of the Jews, before whom thou hast begun to fall, thou shalt not prevail against him, but shalt surely fall before him." Now, the church of God as made up of men and women is nothing more than any other organisation. Look at its exterior, and you see in it few persons of great education and a great many of no education; here and there a wealthy and powerful person, but hundreds who are poor and despised. It does not possess in itself, naturally, the elements of strength, according to ordinary reckoning. Indeed, its own confession is that in itself it is perfect weakness, a flock of sheep among wolves; but here lies its strength, that each of the true members of the church are of the seed royal; they are God's chosen ones, the seed of the woman ordained of old to break the head of Satan and all his serpent seed. They are the weakness of God, but they are stronger than men; he has determined with the things that are not to bring to nought the things that are. As the Canaanites feared the chosen race of Israel because the rumor of them had gone forth among the people, and the terror of Jehovah was upon them; so is it with the hosts of evil. They have dreamed their dreams, as the Midianite did, and valiant men like Gideon can hear them telling it; the barley cake shall fall upon the royal tent of Gideon and smite it till it lies along; the sword of the Lord, and of Gideon, shall rout the foe. The elect shall overcome through the blood of the Lamb, and none shall say them nay. Ye are a royal priesthood, a peculiar people, a chosen generation; and in you the living God will gloriously declare his sovereign grace.

The church, again, consists of a praying people. Now prayer is that which links weakness with infinite strength. A people who can pray can never be overcome, because their reserve forces can never be exhausted. Go into battle, my brother; and if you be vanquished with the strength you have, prayer shall call up another legion. Yea, twenty legions of angels, and the foe shall marvel to see undefeated adversaries still holding the field. If ten thousand saints were burned to-morrow, their dying prayers would make the church rise like a phoenix from her ashes. Who, therefore, can stand against a people whose prayers enlist God in their quarrel? "The Lord of hosts is with us; the God of Jacob is our refuge." We cry unto the Lord, and he heareth us; he breaketh through the ranks of the foe; he giveth us triumph in the day of battle: therefore, terrible as an army with banners are those who wield the weapon of all-prayer.

Again, a true church is based upon eternal truth. I need not quote to you the old Latin proverb which says that truth is mighty and must prevail. Truth is, and truth shall be. It alone is substance, and must outlast the lapse of ages. Falsehoods are soon swollen to their perfection of development, like the bubbles with rainbow hues which children blow, but they are dispersed as easily as they are fashioned; they are children of the hour, while truth is the offspring and heir of eternity. Falsehood dies, pierced through the heart by the arrows of time, but truth, in her impenetrable mail bids defiance to all foes. Men who love the truth are building gold and silver, and precious stones; and though their architecture may progress but slowly, it is built for eternity. Ramparts of truth may often be assailed, but they will never be carried by the foe. Establish a power among men of the most ostentatious and apparently stable kind, but rest assured that if untruth be at the root of it, it must perish, sooner or later; only truth is invincible, eternal, supreme. The fear of the true church and the dread thereof falls upon the enemy, because they have wit enough left to know that truth has an abiding and indestructible power. I was very much amused, the other day, to read a criticism by an eminent infidel, whose name would be well known if I were to mention it, in which he speaks very highly of the exceeding great skill and wisdom, and common sense, always exhibited in the arrangements of the Roman Catholic Church in opposition to Infidelity, and of the imbecility and childishness manifested by Christian ministers in assailing Rationalism with their dogmatism, etc. I was very glad to receive information so valuable, and I thought: "I see, my friend, what kind of warfare you like best. You admire the Roman Catholic kind of fighting, but you do not admire that which evangelical ministers have adopted. It is no aim of ours to please our enemies in our mode of warfare, but the reverse; and if we have discovered a weapon which galls you, we will use that same arm more freely than ever." There is a story of an officer who was rather awkward in his manners, and, upon some great occasion, almost fell over his sword in his haste. His majesty remarked, "Your sword seems to be very much in the way." "So your majesty's enemies have very often felt," was the reply. So, when the enemies of the truth are finding fault with our procedure, we accept their verdict when we have turned it the other way upwards. If they do not admire our mode of warfare, we think; it is in all probability about the best method we could adopt. We would still, God granting us help, continue preaching the "foolishness" of the gospel, and deliver again and again the old truth, that God was in Christ reconciling the world unto himself, not imputing their trespasses unto them. Instead of lifting up a new banner (which would better please our adversaries) it shall be the old banner still--"None but Christ." "By grace are ye saved through faith; and that out of yourselves: it is the gift of God." Salvation is by free favor, through the expiatory sacrifice of Jesus Christ our Lord.

We are now to observe, that the chief glory and majesty of the church lies mainly in the banner which she carries. What cause for terror is there in the banner? We reply, the enemies of Christ dread the cross, because they know what the cross has done. Wherever the crucified Jesus has been preached, false systems have tottered to their fall. Dagou has always fallen before the ark of the Lord. Rage the most violent is excited by the doctrine of the atonement, a rage in which the first cause for wrath is fear.

The terribleness of the church lies in her banners, because those banners put strength into her. Drawing near to the standard of the cross the weakest soldier becomes strong: he who might have played the coward becomes a hero when the precious blood of Jesus is felt with power in his soul. Martyrs are born and nurtured at the cross. It is the blood of Jesus which is the life-blood of self-denial; we can die because our Savior died. The presence of Alexander made the Greeks more than giants: the presence of our Redeemer makes believers swifter than eagles, and stronger than lions.

Moreover, the powers of evil tremble at the old standard, because they have a presentiment of its future complete triumph. It is decreed of God, and fixed by his predestinating purpose, that all flesh shall see the salvation of God. Jesus must reign; the crucified One must conquer. The hands nailed to the wood must sway the scepter of all kingdoms. Like potters' vessels dashed to pieces, must all the might and majesty of men be, that shall oppose the crown and scepter of Christ's kingdom. In Christ preached lies the battle-axe and weapons of war, with which the Lord will work out his everlasting decrees. The church with the name of Immanuel emblazoned on her banner, which it is her duty to keep well displayed, and lifted high, is sure to be terrible to all the powers of darkness.

We will close with one or two reflections. Will each one here say to himself: "An army, a company of warriors, am I one of them? Am I a soldier? I have entered the church; I make a profession; but am I really a soldier? Do I fight? Do I endure hardness? Am I a mere carpet-knight, a mere lie-a-bed soldier, one of those who are pleased to put on regimentals in order to adorn myself with a profession without ever going to the war?"

"Am I a soldier of the cross--a follower of the Lamb?"

Pass the question round, my dear brethren and sisters: Are you soldiers who engage in actual fighting for Jesus, under his banner? Do you rally round it? Do you know the standard? Do you love it? Could you die in defense of it? Is the person of Jesus dearest of all things to you? Do you value the doctrine of the atoning substitution? Do you feel your own energy and power awakened in the defense of that, and for the love of that? Let not one go away without making the searching question.

And then "terrible." Am I in any way terrible through being Christian? Is there any power in my life that would condemn a sinner? my holiness about me that would make a wicked man feel ill at ease in my company? Is there enough of Christ about my life to make me like a light in the midst of the darkness? or is it very likely that if I were to live in a house the inhabitants would never see any difference between me and the ungodly? Oh, how many Christians there are who need to wear a label round their necks: you would never know that they were Christians without it! They make long prayers and great pretences, but they are Christians in nothing but the name. May your life and mine never be thus despicable, but may we convince gainsayers that there is a power in the gospel of Jesus Christ, and make them confess, that they, not having it, are losing a great blessing.

One other thought. If I am not a soldier, if I am not a servant of Christ in very truth, and yet I come to the place of worship where Christians meet, and where Christ is preached, the day will be when the church of God will be very terrible to me. I will suppose that there is a person listening to this sermon who has been hearing the preaching of the word in this place now for many years. Imagine that the last day is come. You are brought before the great judgment-seat, and this is the question:--"Did this sinner hear the gospel faithfully preached? He is ungodly, he has rejected Christ: does he deserve to be cast away? Did he really bear the gospel, and did he reject it?" If I am asked to give my witness, I must say, "To the best of my ability, I tried to tell him the gospel of Jesus Christ." "Was this sinner prayed for by the church?" There are many of the members of this church who would feel bound to declare "Yes, Lord, we did pray for him." Yes, and all of us should say, "If we did not pray for him by name, we included him in the general company of those who attended upon the means of grace, for whom we made a constant intercession." Is there any member of the church who would be able to make an apology for the rejector of Christ? He has willfully rejected the Savior, he knowingly continued in sin. Will anybody be an advocate for him? Not one tongue would be able to excuse you at the judgment, or to argue against the righteous sentence of God. When the great Judge condemns the sinner to be taken away to execution, the whole church with whom that sinner has worshipped, and in whose presence that sinner has rejected Christ, will become "terrible as an army with banners;" for all its voices will say, "Amen, Amen, Amen! Thou art righteous, O Lord."

This is no picture drawn from fancy. Know ye not that the saints shall judge the world? They shall sit as co-assessors with the Son of God at the last great assize, and shall say, "Amen!" to every verdict which proceedeth from his mouth. O that the thought of this might be blessed of God's Spirit, so as to lead many of you to be reconciled to God. Jesus is still the loving Mediator, and a full surrender of yourselves to him will assuredly save you. Whosoever believeth on him is not condemned; and this is to believe on him--that ye trust in him, and know that God hath given unto us eternal life--and this life is in his Son who suffered in the stead of sinners, that whosoever believeth in him might not perish, but have everlasting life. The Lord bless you, for the Lord Jesus' sake. Amen.

MR. SPURGEON has been laid aside by sickness for two Sabbaths, but is now recovering and hopes to be again in the pulpit next Lord's-day. He earnestly beg the prayers of loving friends that his frequent infirmities may be sanctified to the glory of God and the profit of the church; and then, if it were the Lord's will, eventually removed.

The Touchstone of Godly Sincerity

A Sermon (No. 985)
Delivered by
C. H. SPURGEON,
At the Metropolitan Tabernacle, Newington

"Will he always call upon God?" - Job 27:10.

WHEN Job resumes his address in this chapter, he appeals to God in a very solemn matter as to the truth of all that he had spoken. No less vehemently does he assert his innocence of any signal crime, or his consciousness of any secret guile, which could account for his being visited with extraordinary suffering. I do not know that his language necessarily implies any culpable self-righteousness; it appears to me rather that he had good cause to defend himself against the bitter insinuations of his unfriendly friends. Possibly his tone was rash, but his meaning was right. He might well feel the justice of vindicating his character before men: but it was a pity if in so doing he seemed to utter a protest of complete purity in the sight of God. You may remember how Paul under equal, if not exactly similar, provocation, tempered his speech and guarded against the danger of misconstruction. Thus he wrote to the Corinthians: "With me it is a very small thing that I should be judged of you, or of man's judgment: yea, I judge not mine own self. For I know nothing by myself [or myself, as though he should say, My conscience does not accuse me of wrong']; yet am I not hereby justified." But the two holy men are very like in one respect, for just as Paul, in the struggles of the spirit against the flesh, faced the peril and mounted guard against it, "lest that by any means, when I have preached to others, I myself shall be a castaway;" so Job lays bare before his own eyes, and points to the view of those who heard him, the features of a hypocrite, lest by any means he should turn out to be such. In terrible language he describes and denounces the hypocrite's flattering hope and withering doom. The suspicion that he himself could harbour a vain presence in his own breast, or would pretend to be what he was not, was utterly abhorrent to Job's honest heart. He placed himself at the bar, he laid down the law with rigour, he weighed his case with exactness; and so forestalled his adversaries' verdict, by judging himself that he might not be judged.

Who, then, is this "wicked man," thus portrayed before us? And what are the first symptoms of his depravity? We ask not the question idly, but in order that we take heed against the uprise of such an evil in ourselves.

"Beneath the saintly veil the votary of sin
May lurk unseen; and to that eye alone
Which penetrates the heart, may stand revealed."

The hypocrite is very often an exceedingly neat imitation of the Christian. To the common observer he is so good a counterfeit that he entirely escapes suspicion. Like base coins which are cunningly made, you can scarcely detect them by their ring; it is only by more searching tests that you are able to discover that they are not pure gold, the current coin of the realm. It would be difficult to say how nearly any man might resemble a Christian, and yet not be "in Christ a new creature;" or how closely he might imitate all the virtues, and yet at the same time possess none of the fruits of the Spirit as before the judgment of a heart-searching God. In almost all deceptions there is a weak point somewhere. Never is a lying story told but, if you be keen enough, you may from internal evidence somewhere or other detect the flaw. Though Satan himself has been engaged in the manufacture of impostures for thousands of years, yet whether through the lack of skill on his part, or through the folly of his agents, he always leaves a weak point; his clattering statements are a little too strongly scented and smell of a lie; and his mimic Christians are so overdone in one place, and slovenly in another, that their falsehood betrays itself. Now, in discriminating between saints and hypocrites, one great test-point is prayer. "Behold, he prayeth," was to the somewhat sceptical mind of Ananias demonstration enough that Paul was really converted. If he prays, it may be safely inferred that the breath of prayer arises from the life of faith. The process of spiritual quickening has at least begun. Hence the hypocrite feigns to possess that vital action. If the Christian prays, he will betake himself to the like exercise: if the Christian calls upon God the deceiver takes care that he will likewise make mention of the name of the Lord. And yet, between the prayer of the truly converted man and the prayer of the hypocrite there is a difference as radical as between life and death, although it is not apparent to everybody. No one, it may be, at first can be aware of it except the man himself, and sometimes even he scarcely perceives it. Many are deceived by the fine expressions, by the apparent warmth, and by the excellent natural disposition of the hypocrite, and they think when they hear him call upon God that his supplications are sufficient evidence that he is truly a quickened child of God. Prayer is always the tell-tale of spiritual life. No right prayer, then is there no grace within. Slackened prayer, then is there a decrease of grace. Prayer stronger, thee the whole man also is stronger. Prayer is as good a test of spiritual life and health as the pulse is of the condition of the human frame. Hence I say the hypocrite imitates the action of prayer while he does not really possess the spirit of prayer.

Our text goes deeper than the surface, and enquires into vital matters. Prayer is a test, but here is a test for the test--a trial even for prayer itself. "Will he always call upon God?" There is the point. He does call upon God now, and he appears to be intensely devout; he says he was converted in the late revival; he is very fervid in expression, and very forward in manner at present. But will it wear? Will it wear? Will it last? His prayerfulness has sprung up like Jonah's gourd in a night. Will it perish in a night? It is beautiful to look upon, like the early dew that glistens in the sunlight as though the morning had sown the earth with orient pearl; will it pass away like that dew? or will it always abide? "Will he always call upon God?" There is the point. O that each one of us now may search ourselves, and see whether we have those attributes connected with our prayer which will prove us not to be hypocrites, or whether, on the contrary, we have those sad signs of base dissembling and reckless falsehood which will before long discover us to be dupes of Satan, impostors before heaven.

"Will he always call upon God?" This question, simple as it is, I think involves several pertinent enquiries. The first point which it raises is that of CONSISTENCY. Is the prayer occasional, or is it constant? Is the exercise of devotion permanent and regular, or is it spasmodic and inconstant? Will this man call upon God in all seasons of prayer? There are certain times when it is most fit to pray, and a genuine Christian will and must pray at such periods. Will this hypocrite pray at all such times, or will he only select some of the seasons for prayer? Will he only be found praying at certain times and in selected places? Will he always, in all fit times, be found drawing near to God? For instance, he prayed standing at the corners of the streets where he was seen of men: he prayed in the synagogue, where everybody could mark his fluency and his fervor, but will he pray at home? Will he enter into his closet and shut to the door? Will he there speak unto the Father who heareth in secret? Will he there pour forth petitions as the natural outflow of his soul? Will he walk the field at eventide, in lonely meditation, like Isaac, and pray there? Will he go to the housetop with Peter, and pray there? Will he seek his chamber as Daniel did, or the solitude of the garden as did our Lord? Or is he one who only prays in public, who has the gift of prayer rather than the spirit of prayer, who is fluent in utterance rather than fervent in feeling? Oh, but this, this is one of the surest of tests, by which we may discern between the precious and the vile. Public prayer is no evidence of piety: it is practiced by an abundance of hypocrites; but private prayer is a thing for which the hypocrite has no heart--and if he gives himself to it for a little time he soon finds it too hot and heavy a business for his soulless soul to persevere in, and he lets it drop. He will sooner perish than continue in private prayer. O for heart searchings about this! Do I draw near to God alone? Do I pray when no eye sees, when no ear hears? Do I make a conscience of private prayer? Is it a delight to pray? For I may gather that if I never enjoy private prayer I am one of those hypocrites who will not always call upon God.

The true Christian will pray in business; he will pray in labor; he will pray in his ordinary calling: like sparks out of the smithy chimney short prayers fly up all day long from truly devout souls. Not thus is it with the mere pretender. The hypocrite prays at prayer-meetings, and his voice is heard in the assembly, sometimes at tedious length; but will he pray with ejaculatory prayer? Will he speak with God at the counter? Will he draw near to God in the field? Will he plead with his Lord in the busy street with noiseless pleadings? When he finds that a difficultly has occurred in his daily life, will he without saving a word breathe his heart into the ear of God? Ah, no! hypocrites know nothing of what it is to be always praying, to abide in the spirit of prayer. This is a choice part of Christian experience with which they do not meddle. But be sure of this--where there is genuine religion within, it will be more or less habitual to the soul to pray. Some of us can say that to be asking blessings from God in brief, wordless prayers, comes as natural to us as to eat and drink, and breathe. We never encounter a difficulty now but we resolve it by appealing to the wisdom of God--never meet with any opposition but what we overcome it by leaning upon the power of God. To wait upon the Lord and speak with him has become a habit with us--not because it is a duty--we have left legal bondage far behind--but because we cannot help it, our soul is inwardly constrained thereto. The nature within as naturally cries to God as a child cries after its mother. The hypocrite prays in his fashion because it is a task allotted to him: the Christian because it is a part of his very life. Herein is an everstanding mark of distinction by which a man may discern himself. If your prayer is only for certain hours, and certain places, and certain times, beware lest it turn out to be an abomination before the Lord. The fungus forced by artificial heat is a far different thing from the rosy fruit of a healthy tree, and the unreal devotions of the unspiritual differ widely from the deep inward groanings of renewed hearts. If you pray by the almanac, observing days and weeks, you may well fear that your religion never came from the great Father of Lights, with whom are no changing moons. If you can pray by the clock, your religion is more mechanical than vital. The Christian does not fast because it is Lent; if his Lord reveals his face he cannot fast merely because a church commands him. Neither can he therefore feast because it happens to be a festival in the calendar. The Spirit of God might make his soul to be feasting on Ash-Wednesday, or his soul might be humbled within him at Easter; he cannot be regulated by the dominical letter, and the new moons and days of the month. He is a spiritual character, and he leaves those who have no spiritual life to yield a specious conformity to such ecclesiastical regulations, his new-born nature spurns such childish bonds. The living soul prays evermore with groanings that cannot be uttered, and believingly rejoices evermore with joy unspeakable and full of glory.

A second point in debate is that of CONTINUANCE. "Will he always call upon God?" There are trying periods and sifting seasons; those who hold on through these are the true, but those who suspend prayer at these test intervals are the false. Now times of joy and sorrow are equally critical seasons. Let us look at them in turn. Will the hypocrite call upon God in times of pleasure? No; if he indulges himself in what he calls pleasure, he dares not pray at night when he comes home. He goes to places where he would think it a degradation of prayer to think of praying. The genuine Christian prays always, because if there be any spot where he dares not pray, just there he dares not be found; or if there be any engagement about which he could not pray, it is an engagement that shall never ensnare him. Some one once proposed to write a collect to be said by a pious young lady when attending a theater, and another to be repeated by a Christian gentleman when shuffling a pack of cards. There might he another form of prayer to be offered by a pious burglar when he is breaking open a door, or by a religious assassin when he is about to commit murder. There are things about which you cannot pray: they have nothing to do with prayer. Many tolerated amusements lead to outrages upon the morals of earth, and are an insult to the holiness of heaven. Who could think of praying about them? Herein is the hypocrite discerned; he does that which he could not ask a blessing upon. Poor as is the conscience he owns, he knows it is ridiculous to offer prayer concerning certain actions which, notwithstanding, he has the hardihood to perform. The Christian avoids things which he could not pray about; and so he feels it a pleasure to pray always.

Equally trying is the opposite condition of depression and sorrow. There, too, we try the question, "Will he always call upon God?" No; the hypocrite will not pray when in a desponding state. He breathed awhile the atmosphere of enthusiasm. His passions were stirred by the preacher, and fermented by the contagious zeal of the solemn assembly. But now a damp cold mist obscures his view chills his feelings, settles in his heart. Others are growing cold, and he is among the first to freeze. He is down-hearted and discouraged. Forthwith, like King Saul, he succumbs to the evil spirit. Were he a Christian indeed, he would follow in the wake of David, and say: "Why art thou cast down, O my soul? and why art thou disquieted within me? hope in God: for I shall yet praise him, who is the health of my countenance, and my God;" but he has no heart to hope on in ill weather. He built up his hopes tastefully, and he admired the structure which was of his own piling, but the rain descended, the floods came, and the winds blew, and down it all went; and therefore, being a hypocrite, he said within himself: "Now I have no enjoyment of religion: it has lost its novelty; I have worn out its delights; I have now no comfort from it; I will give it up." Thus in the trying hour the deceiver is laid bare. Look at the real Christian when a storm bursts over him which shakes his confidence and spoils his joy: what does he do? He prays more than ever he did. When his mountain stood firm, and he said, "I shall not be moved," he perhaps grew too slack in prayer; but now, when all God's waves and billows are going over him, and he hardly knows whether he is a child of God or not, and questions whether he has any part or lot in the matter, he proves that all is right within, by crying unto God in the bitterness of his soul, "O God, have mercy upon me, and deliver me from going down into the pit." A Christian's despair makes him pray; it is a despair of self. A worldling's despair makes him rave against God, and give up prayer. Mark then, how in the opposite seasons of joy and sorrow prayer is put into the crucible and tested. All our times of pleasure ought to be times of prayer; Job accounted his family festivities opportune for calling his children together for special devotion. No less should our periods of despondency become incentives to prayer; every funeral knell should ring us to our knees. The hypocrite cannot keep the statutes and ordinances, but the true Christian follows them out; for he is alike at home in seeking the Lord, calling upon his name, and asking counsel and guidance at his mercy-seat, in any variety of experience, and every diversity of circumstance.

"Will he always call upon God?" Here is the question of CONSTANCY. Will he pray constantly? It seems to most men a very difficult thing to be praying always, to continue in prayer, to pray without ceasing. Yes; and herein again is there a great distinction between the living child of God and the mere pretender. The living child of God soon finds that it is not so much his duty to pray, as his privilege, his joy, a necessity of his being. What moment is there when a Christian is safe without prayer? Where is there a place wherein he would find himself secure if he ceased to pray? Just think of it. Every moment of my life I am dependent upon the will of God as to whether I shall draw another breath or not. Nothing stands between me and death but the will of God. An angel's arm could not save me from the grave, if now the Lord willed me to depart. Solemn, then, is the Christian's position: ever standing by an open tomb. Should not dying men pray? We are always dying. As life is but a long dying, should it not be also a long praying? Should we not be incessantly acknowledging to God in prayer and praise the continuance of our being, which is due to his grace? Brethren, every moment that we live we are receiving favors and benefits from God. There is never a minute in which we are not recipients of his bounty. We are wont to thank God for his mercies as if we thought they came at certain set times; so in truth they do: they are new every morning; great is his faithfulness; and they soothe us night by night, for his compassion faileth not, but there are mercies streaming on in one incessant flow. We never cease to need; he never ceases to supply. We want constant protection, and he that keepeth Israel neither slumbers nor sleeps. Lest any hurt us, he keeps us night and day. The river of God rolls on with undiminished volume and unimpeded velocity. How greatly doth he enrich us thereby! Should we not be ever careful to secure his gifts, to reap the harvest be provides, and as his people to take these good things from his gracious hands? But, oh! let us take heed to mingle prayer with all our thanksgiving, lest he should curse the boon over which we have asked no blessing; blight the crops, of which we have dedicated to him no firstfruits; or smite us with the rod of his anger, while the food is yet in our mouth. Our cravings know no abatement, our dependence on God knows no limit; therefore our prayers should know no intermission. Speak of beggars, we are always beggars. Is it not better for us, then, to be regular pensioners than mere casuals? Whatever God has given us we are as needy still; we are always, if taken apart from him, naked, and poor, and miserable, altogether dependent upon him, as well for the soul as for the body; for good thoughts, for spiritual aspirations, for holy graces, ay, and for the breath of our nostrils and the bread of our mouths; always needing temporals, always needing spirituals. If we are always needing, we should be always pleading. Besides that, dear friends, we are always in danger; we are in an enemy's country, behind every bush there is a foe; we cannot reckon ourselves to be secure in any place. The world, the flesh, and the devil constantly assail us. Arrows are shot from beneath us, and from around us, while the poison of our own corruption rankles within us. At any moment temptation may get the mastery over us, or we ourselves may go astray and be our own tempters. Storms may drive us, whirlpools suck us down, quicksands engulf us, and if none of these accomplish our shipwreck we may founder of ourselves, or perish of spiritual dry-rot. We need, then, each hour to watch, and each separate moment to pray, "Hold thou me up, and I shall be safe." Are ye wealthy? Pray God that your silver and your gold bring no spiritual plague with them! Do not let your money stick to your hand or your heart, for in proportion as it glues itself to you it poisons you. Pray God to sanctify your abundance, so that you may know how to abound; a difficult piece of knowledge to attain. Are ye poor? Then ask to be kept from envy, from discontent, and all the evils that haunt the narrow lanes of poverty. Pray that as you are each in danger one way or another, you may all be kept hour by hour by the constant grace of God. If we knew what poor, weak, helpless creatures we are, we should not want to be told always to pray; we should wonder how we could think of living without prayer. How can I, whose legs are so feeble, try to wall: without leaning on my Father's hand? How can I, who am so sickly, wish to be a day without the Good Physician's care? The hypocrite does not see this; he does not discern these perpetual needs and perpetual gifts, these perpetual dangers and perpetual preservations--not be. He thinks he has prayed enough when he has had his few minutes in the morning and his few minutes at night. He trots through his form of morning devotion just as he takes his morning wash, and has he not settled the business for the day? If at evening he says his prayers with the same regularity with which he puts on his slippers, is it not all he needs? He almost thinks that little turn at his devotions to be a weariness. As to his heart going up in prayer to God, he does not understand it; if he be spoken to concerning it, it sounds like an idle tale, or mere cant.

Dear brethren, "we ought always to pray, and not to faint," because we are always sinning. If I were not evermore sinning, if I could pause in that constant aberration of mind from the pure, the unselfish, the holy, perhaps I might suspend confession, and relax supplication awhile; but if unholiness stains even my holy things--if in my best endeavors there is something of error, something of sin--ought I not to be continually crying to God for pardon, and involving his grace? And are we not constantly liable to new temptations? May we not fall into grosser sins than we have hitherto committed, unless we are preserved by a power beyond our own? O pray perpetually, for you know not what temptations may assail you. Pray that ye enter not into temptation. If perchance in some favored moment we could imagine ourselves to have exhausted all the list of our needs, were we enjoying complete pardon and full assurance, did we stand upon the mountain's brow, bathing our foreheads in the sunlight of God's favor, if we had no fear, no care, no trouble of our own to harass us, yet we might not therefore cease to pray. The interests of others, our kindred, our neighbors, our fellow creatures might--ah! must--then start up before us, and claim that we should bear upon our breasts their memorial. Think of the sinners around you hardening in transgression, some of them dying, seared with guilt or frenzied with despair. O brethren, how could you cease to intercede for others, were it possible, which it is not, that you should have no further need to supplicate for yourselves? The grand old cause which we have espoused, and the Christ who hath espoused our cause--both these demand our prayers. By the truth whose banner waves above us, by the king who has ennobled us, love to whose person fires us this day with ardor for his cross, and zeal for his gospel, we are constrained to unwavering devotion. So spake the gospel of old, and so doth the Spirit of God prompt us now. "Prayer also shall be made for him continually; and daily shall he be praised." O that in our case the prediction might be verified, the promise fulfilled! Not so the hypocrite: he will not have it on this fashion. Enough for him to have prayers on the Sunday; enough to get through family prayers at any rate, and if that does not please you, the morning prayer and the evening prayer shall be said by rote at the bedside; will not these suffice? Praying all day long, why he considers that it would be almost as bad as heaven, where they are singing without ceasing. So he turns on his heel, and saith he will have none of it. Nor shall he; for where God is he shall not come, but the Lord will tell him, "I never knew you: depart from me, thou worker of iniquity."

"Will he always call upon God?" The question may be an enquiry as to IMPORTUNITY. Will the hypocrite pray importunately? He will do no such thing. I have heard farmers talk about the why to know a good horse. It will serve me to illustrate the way to tell a good Christian. Some horses when they get into the traces pull, and when they feel the load move they work with all their might, but it they tug and the load does not stir, they are not for drawing any longer. There is a breed of really good horses in Suffolk which will tug at a dead weight, and if they were harnessed to a post, they would pull till they dropped though nothing stirred. It is so with a lively Christian. If he is seeking a great favor from God, he prays, whether he gets it or not, right on: he cannot take a denial; if he knows his petition to be according to God's will and promise, he pleads the blood of Jesus about it; and if he does not get an answer at once, he says, "My soul, wait"--wait! a grand word--"wait thou only upon God; for my expectation is from him." As for the hypocrite, if he gets into a church and there is a prayer-meeting and he feels, "Well, there is a fire kindling and an excitement getting up"--ah! how that man can pray, the waggon is moving behind him, and he is very willing to pull. But the sincere believer says, "I do not perceive any revival yet. I do not hear of many conversions. Never mind, we have prayed that, God will glorify his dear Son: we will keep on praying. If the blessing does not come in one week, we will try three; if it does not come in three weeks, we will try three months; if it does not come in three months, we shall still keep on for three years; and if it does not come in three years, we will plead on for thirty years: and if it does not; come then, we will say, Let thy work appear unto thy servants, and thy glory unto their children.' We will plead on until we die, and mingle with those who beheld the promise afar off, were persuaded of it, prayed for it, and died believing it would be fulfilled." Such prayer would not be wasted breath. It is treasure put out to interest; seed sown for a future harvest; rather it is the aspiration of saints kindled by the inspiration of God. The genuine believer knows how to tug. Jacob, when he came to Jabbok, found that the angel was not easily to be conquered. He laid hold of him, but the angel did not yield the blessing; something more must be done. Had Jacob been a hypocrite he would have let the angel loose at once, but being one of the Lord's own, he said, "I will not let thee go, except thou bless me." When the angel touched him in the hollow of his thigh and made the sinew shrink, had he been a hypocrite he would have thought, "I have had enough of this already; I may be made to shrink all over; I cannot tell what may happen next. I will have no more of this midnight encounter with an unknown visitor. I will get me back to my tent." But no; he meant to prevail, and though he felt the pain, Yet he said--

"With thee all night I mean to stay,
And wrestle till the break of day."

He did so, and became a prince from that night. Will you take a denial from God, you shall have it; but if you will not be denied, neither shall you. O importunate Christian, you are he whom

God loves! Alas for those who only give, as it were, runaway knocks at the door of heaven, like boys in the street that knock and run away--they shall never find the blessing. Oh, to continue in prayer! it is the very test of sincerity. Hence of the hypocrite it is said, "Will be always call upon God?" A hypocrite leaves off praying in either case; he leaves off if he does not get what he asks for, as I have shown you; and he leaves off if he does get what he asks for. Has he asked to be recovered from sickness when ill? If he gets well, what cares he for praying again? Did he pray that he might not die? Oh, what a long face he drew, and what drawling professions of repentance he groaned out! But when his health is regained, and his nerves braced, his spirits are cheered, and his manly vigor has come back to him; where are his prayers? where are the vows his soul in anguish made? He has forgotten them all. That he is a hypocrite is palpable, for he leaves oft praying if he does not get heard, and if he does. There is no keeping this man up to God's statute or his own promise; he has not the heart for true devotion, and soon fails in the attempt to exercise it.

"Will He always call upon God?" Here is the trial of PERSEVERANCE. Will he always continue to pray in the future? Will he pray, in years to come, as he now professes to do? I call to see him, and he is very sick; the doctor gives a very poor account of him; his wife is weeping; all over the house there is great anxiety. I sit down by his bedside; I talk to him, and he says, "Oh, yes, yes, yes;" he agrees with all I say, and he tells me he believes in Jesus. And when he can sit up, he cries, "God be merciful to me." His dear friends are godly people; they feel so pleased; they look torward to his recovery, and reckon upon seeing him a new creature, a disciple of Christ. Besides, he has told them, when he gets up, how earnest he will be in a life of faith and obedience to the Lord. He will not be a mere professor, he means to throw his whole soul into the Master's service. Now mark him. He recovers; and when he breaks forth from that sick chamber, and can dispense with the ministry of those gentle patient women who nursed him and prayed for him, what does the hypocrite do? Oh, he says he was a fool to think and speak as he did. He admits he was frightened, but he disclaims every pious expression as an infirmity of his distracted brain, the delirium of his malady, not the utterance of his reason; and he recants all his confessions like the atheist in Addison's "Spectator." Addison tells us that certain sailors heard that an atheist was on board their vessel: they did not know what an atheist was, but they thought it must be some odd fish; and when told it was a man who did not believe in God, they said, "Captain, it would be an uncommonly good thing to pitch him overboard." Presently a storm comes on, and the atheist is dreadfully sick and very fearful; there, on the deck, he is seen crying to God for mercy, and whining like a child that he is afraid he will be lost and sink to hell. This is the usual courage of atheism! But when the coward reached the shore, he begged the gentlemen who heard him pray to think nothing of it, for indeed he did not know what he was saying, he had no doubt uttered a great deal of nonsense. There are plenty of that sort--who pray in danger, but brag when they get clear of the tempest. Hereby the hypocrite is discovered. Once take away from him the trouble and you do away with the motive for which he put on the cloak of religion. He is like a boy's top, which will spin as long as you whip it. The man will pray while he smarts, but not one whit longer. The hypocrite will pray to-day in society congenial for prayer, but he will discard prayer to-morrow when he gets laughed at for it in his business. Some old friend of his drops in, who has heard that he has been converted, and he begins to ridicule him. He asks him whether he has really turned a Methodist? The next thing he expects to hear is, that he is dipped. He makes some coarse remarks rather to the chagrin of our courageous friend, till he, who set out so boldly to heaven with his prayers, feels quite small in the presence of the sceptic. It he were right in heart, he would not only have a proper answer to give to the mocker, but in all probability he would carry the war into the enemy's country, and make his antagonist feel the folly of his sins and the insanity of his conduct in living without a God and without a Savior. The meet object of ridicule and contempt is the godless, the Christless man. The Christian need never be ashamed or lower his colors. The hypocrite may well blush and hide his head, for if there is any creature that is contemptible, it is a man who has not his heart where he professes it to be.

Neither will such a one always call upon God if he gets into company where he is much flattered; he feels then that he has degraded himself somewhat by associating with such low, mean people as those who make up the church of God. And if he prospers in business, then he considers that the people he once worshipped with are rather inferior to himself: he must go to the world's church: he must find a fashionable place where he can hear a gospel that is not for the poor and needy, but for those who have the key of aristocratic drawing-rooms and the select assemblies. His principles--well, he is not very particular--he swallows them; probably his nonconformity was a mistake. The verities which his fathers suffered martyrdom to defend, for which they were mulcted of their possessions, driven as exiles from their country, or cast into prison, he flings away as though they were of no value whatever. Many have fallen from us through the temptations of prosperity who stood firmly enough under persecution and adversity. It is another form of the same test, "Will he always call upon God?"

Besides, if none of these things should occur the man who is not savingly converted and a genuine Christian, generally gives up his religion after a time because the novelty of it dies off. He is like the stony ground that received the seed, and because there was no depth of earth the sun could play upon it with great force, and up it sprang in great haste, but because there was no depth of earth, therefore it soon was scorched. So this man is easily impressible, feels quickly, and acts promptly under the influence of a highly emotional nature. Says he, "Yes, I will go to heaven," as he inwardly responds to the appeal of some earnest minister. He thinks he is converted, but we had better not be quite so sure as he is. "Wait a bit, wait a bit." He cools as fast as he was heated. Like thorns under a pot that crackle and blaze and die out, leaving but a handful of ashes, so is it with all his godliness. Ere long he gets tired of religion, he cannot away with it--what a weariness it is. If he perseveres awhile, it is no more pleasure to him than a pack is to a pack horse. He keeps on as a matter of formality: he has got into it and he does not see how to break away, but he likes it no better than an owl loves daylight. He holds on to his forms of prayer with no heart for prayer--and what a wretched thing that is! I have known people who felt bound to keep up their respectability when they had little or no income. Their debts were always increasing, their respectability was always tottering, and the strain upon their dignity was exhausting their utmost resources. Such persons I have considered to be the poorest of the poor. An unhappy life they lead, they never feel at ease. But what an awful thing it is to have to keep up a spiritual respectability with no spiritual income; to overflow with gracious talk when there is no well of living water springing up within the soul; to be under the obligation to pay court to the sanctuary while the heart is wandering on the mountain; to be bound to speak gracious words and yet possess no gracious thoughts to prompt their utterance. O man, thou art one of the devil's double martyrs, because thou hast to suffer for him here in the distaste and nausea of thy hypocritical profession, and then thou will be made to suffer hereafter also for having dared to insult God, and ruin thy soul by being insincere in thy profession of faith in Jesus Christ!

I may be coming very close home to some persons before me: I am certainly pressing my own conscience very severely. I suppose there is no one amongst us who does not feel that this is a very searching matter. Well, dear friends, if our hearts condemn us not, then have we peace towards God; but if our hearts condemn us, God is greater than our hearts and knoweth all things. Let us confess to him all past failures, and though we may not be conscious of hypocrisy (and I trust we are not so), yet, let us say, "Lord, search and try me, and know my ways; see if there be any wicked way in me, and lead me in the way everlasting." I was speaking with a gentleman last night, and I said to him, "You are a director of such a Life Assurance Company, are you not?" "Yes," he said. "Well," I said, "yours is a poor society, is it not?" "It is a very good one," he replied; "a very good one." "But it is very low down in the list." "What list is that?" "Why, the list that has been sent round by certain persons to let the public see the condition of the life assurance companies." "Well," said he, "where is it to be seen?" "Oh, never mind where it is to be seen: is it true?" "No, it is not true; our society stands well--admirably well." "How so?" "Well, you know such a man, he is an excellent actuary and a man of honor." "Yes." "Well, when we employed him to go over our accounts, we said just this to him: Take the figures, examine them thoroughly, sift our accounts, and tell us where the figures land you; tell us just that, neither less nor more, do not shirk the truth in the slightest degree. If we are in a bankrupt state, tell us; if we are flourishing, tell us so.'" My friend has convinced me that his office is not what I feared it was. I have much confidence in any man's business when he wishes to know and to publish the unvarnished truth. I have great confidence in the sincerity of any Christian man who says habitually and truthfully, "Lord, let me know the very worst of my case, whatever it is. Even if all my fair prospects and bright ideals should be but dreams--the fabric of a vision; if yonder prospect before me of green fields and flowing hills should be but an awful mirage, and on the morrow should change into the hot burning desert of an awful reality; so be it, only let me know the truth; lead me in a plain path; let me be sincere before thee, O thou heart-searching, rein-trying God!" Let us, with such frank candour, such ingenuous simplicity, come before the Lord. Let as many of us as fear the Lord and distrust ourselves, take refuge in his omniscience against the jealousies and suspicions which haunt our own breasts. And let us do better still, let us hasten anew to the cross of Jesus, and thus end our difficulties by accepting afresh the sinners' Savior. When I have a knot to untie as to my evidence of being a child of God, and I cannot untie it, I usually follow Alexander's example with the Gordian knot, and cut it. How cut it? Why, in this way. Thou sayest, O conscience, this is wrong, and thus is wrong. Thou sayest, O Satan, thy faith is a delusion, thy experience a fiction, thy profession a lie. Be it so then, I will not dispute it, I end that matter; if I am no saint, I am a sinner; there can be no doubt about that! The devil himself is defied to question that. Then it is written that "Jesus Christ came into the world to save sinners," and to sinners is the gospel preached, "He that believeth on him is not condemned." I do believe on him; if I never did before I will now, and all my transgressions are therefore blotted out. And now, Lord, grant me grace to begin again, and from this time forth let me live the life of faith, the life of prayer; let me be one of those who will pray always, let me be one of those who will pray when they are dying, having prayed all their lives. Prayer is our very life: ceasing prayer we cease to live. As long as we are here preserved in spiritual life we must pray. Lord, grant it may be so with each one here present, through the power of thy Spirit, and the merit of Jesus' blood. Amen, and Amen.

PORTION OF SCRIPTURE READ BEFORE SERMON--Job 27.

Victor Emmanuel, Emancipator

A Sermon (No. 986)
Delivered by
C. H. SPURGEON,
At the Metropolitan Tabernacle, Newington

"To open the blind eyes, to bring out the prisoners from the prison, and them that sit in darkness out of the prison house." - Isaiah 42:7.

ON A FORMER occasion we contemplated the unconverted man as being bound by the cords of his sins. It was a very solemn and sorrowful topic. I trust it humbled us all, and made those of us whom the Son has made free, feel renewed gratitude for the glorious liberty of the children of God. Sad was the spectacle of the dungeon and the fetters, and the felon bound therewith, a man, a brother, the image of ourselves. It is a great relief to turn to another subject akin to that, but full of cheerfulness and joy. We showed you the prisoner: we have now to speak of him who came to set the prisoners free. We decribed the captive's cords and bonds; we have now to tell you of him whose mighty touch liberates the bond-slaves, and signs the Magna Carta of eternal emancipation. The case of manhood bound like Prometheus to the rock, and preyed upon by the vulture of hell, appeared utterly hopeless, and the more so because the prisoner was his own fetter, and disdained to be free. After all that has been done for man, by the tenderness of God, the simplicity of the gospel, and the clear and plain command; yes, and after all the thunders of threatening, followed by the wooing notes of mercy, the captive continues still the willing slave of sin, and his liberation appears utterly hopeless. But things impossible with men are possible with God, and where human agency fails, divine agency delights to illustrate its own extraordinary energy. We gladly survey at this time the effectual operations of Jesus the Savior, the true Victor Emmanuel, who comes to set men free from the bondage of their sins, to whose name be honor and glory world without end.

I. Looking at the first verses of this chapter, we shall consider WHO IT IS THAT SENDS JESUS CHRIST TO ACCOMPLISH THE LIBERATION OF THE SONS OF MEN, because much will depend upon the liberator's credentials, the authority by which he is warranted, and the power by which he is backed.

We sing for joy of heart as we see that the Infinite God himself commissioned the Lord Jesus to be the deliverer of men; and he did this, first, in his capacity as Creator. Read the fifth verse, and behold the great author of the Redeemer's commission: "Thus saith Jehovah, he that created the heavens, and stretched them out; he that spread forth the earth, and that which cometh out of it." He, then, who spared not his own Son, but sent him forth on the embassage of love, is Jehovah, who has made the heavens a pavilion of azure, gilded with the sun, and bedecked with stars; the self-same all-sustaining One who bears up the pillars of the universe, and impels the earth in its majestic circuit. He who gave its lustre to every precious stone from the mine, its life to every blade of grass, its fruit to every tree, its motion to every beast and winged fowl--for all these may be said to come out of the earth; he it is who sent the Incarnate God to open the two-leaved gates, and cut the bars of iron asunder, that the slaves of Satan might escape from the thraldom of their sins. Jesus, the Son of God, comes armed with the power of the Creator himself. Rejoice, then, ye that are lost, for surely the power which spake all things out of nothing, can new create you, though there be nought of good within you to aid the godlike work. Rejoice, ye that are marred and broken, like vessels spoiled upon the potter's wheel, your great Creator puts his hand a second time to the work, and resolves to form you for himself that you may show forth his praise. He by whom you were made in secret, and curiously wrought in the lowest parts of the earth, is able by his mysterious working to create in you a new heart, and infuse into you a right spirit. Is there not hope for the dark chaos of your fallen nature, and that heart of yours which is now without form and void? Is anything too hard for the Lord? Is there any restraint of his power? It is true your fellow-creatures, be they exalted never so highly by office or character, cannot regenerate you, the very idea is blasphemy against the prerogative of him who alone can create or destroy; but where the will of man, and blood, and birth all fail, the Spirit of the Lord achieves the victory. Thus saith the Lord, "Behold, I create new heavens and a new earth: and the former shall not be remembered, nor come into mind. But be ye glad and rejoice for ever in that which I create: for, behold, I create Jerusalem a rejoicing, and her people a joy." What has John written in the book of his vision? Is it not to the same purpose? He that sat upon the throne saith, "Behold, I make all things new." He who made the light can open your eyes. He who bade the rivers flow, can open springs of penitence within your souls. He who clothed the earth with verdure, can make your barren minds fruitful to his praise. If he piled yon Alpine summits, balanced the clouds which float about them, and formed the valleys which laugh at their feet, he can yet create within the little world of man thoughts that aspire to heaven, desires that ascend to the realms of purity, and good works which are the fair products of his Spirit. Has the Creator sent forth a liberator to captive men? Then is there hope indeed!

He who sent forth the Lord Jesus as his Elect One to restore our fallen race, also describes himself as the life giver; for returning to the fifth verse of the chapter before us, we read, "He that giveth breath unto the people upon it, and spirit to them that walk therein!" The Lord creates animal life: he puts breath into the nostrils of men and beasts; he gives also mental life--the life which thinks, imagines, doubts, fears, understands, desires. All life comes from the central fountain of self-existence in the great I Am, in whom we live, and move, and have our being. This Eternal One, who has life in himself, has sent forth his Son to give life to those who are dead in trespasses and sins, and he has girded him with his own power, "For as the Father hath life in himself; so hath he given to the Son to have life in himself." It is by the word of Jesus that the dead shall rise, "for the hour is coming, in the which all that are in the graves shall hear his voice, and shall come forth." Arrayed in such life-giving power no case of human corruption can be beyond the Redeemer's skill even those who rot, like Lazarus, shall come forth when he calls them, and the bonds of death and hell shall be loosed. Thus saith the Lord of life: "Verily, verily, I say unto you, He that heareth my word, and believeth on him that sent me, hath everlasting life, and shall not come into condemnation; but is passed from death unto life." The vision of Ezekiel's valley has become a fact since Jesus has appeared; and it is no marvel that it should be so, since the Eternal and Ever-living God has sent him. He can breathe the Holy Spirit into the dead soul, and give the heart that palpitates with penitence, and leaps with desires after God. He can give eyes to the blind and feet to the lame. All that belongs to life he can bestow--the hearing ear, the speaking tongue, the grasping hand. The great obstacle in his way is spiritual death, and as with a word he can remove it, the salvation of man is no longer a difficulty. Rejoice, ye heavens; and be glad, O earth; for among the graves of our sins, and into the very charnel-house of our corruption, the Quickener has descended, and is quickening whomsoever he will.

Nor is this all for he who sent the Redeemer is represented in the sixth verse as the faithful God. "I the Lord have called thee in righteousness;" that is to say, the God who sends Christ the Savior is not one who plays with words, and having given a promise to-day, retracts it to-morrow. "He is not a man, that he should lie; neither the son of man, that he should repent." Immutable are his promises and purposes, for they are founded in righteousness. He who has commissioned his chosen messenger is not unrighteous to forget his word. Hath he said, and shall he not do it? Hath he spoken, and shall it not come to pass? Hence, thy dear brethren, every gospel promise has the stamp of the divine righteousness upon it, that you may know it to be true. Jesus assures us that, if we believe in him, we shall be delivered. God, who cannot lie, sets his seal to the promise. "He that believeth and is baptised shall be saved," is not only the declaration of Christ, but God himself confirms it. Then, "Amen, so let it be!" The vilest sinner that believeth shall find life and pardon, acceptance and blessedness in Christ Jesus. Thou hast not to deal, O trembler, with one who will interpret his promise at a lower point than thou dost understand it at; but thou hast to deal with One who means more than words can express, whose thoughts are as high above your thoughts, even when enlightened by his Word, as the heavens are above the earth. "Come now, and let us reason together, saith the Lord: though your sins be as scarlet, they shall be as white as snow; though they be red like crimson, they shall be as wool." He who utters these words is the Lord, the faithful Promiser, who has sent forth Christ, not to deceive you with specious presences, but in very deed and truth to bring abundance of grace to those who trust him.

Reading further in the same verse, you will perceive that the everblessed sender of the Lord Jesus is omnipotent, for is it not added, "And will hold thine hand, and will keep thee"? By which is meant that God will give to the Mediator all his power. Christ is the power of God. Omnipotence dwells in him who once was slain, but now ever liveth, and he is able to save unto the uttermost them that come unto God by him. In the gospel of Christ there is a putting forth of divine power as manifest as in the creation and in the upholding of the world. Here is our comfort under all the assaults with which the Christian faith is threatened, and under all the disappointments which the Christian church has hitherto undergone; Emmanuel, God with us, is still our strength. We are persuaded that the ultimate victory of the cross is absolutely certain, for "the glory of the Lord shall be revealed, and all flesh shall see it together: for the mouth of the Lord hath spoken it." The creation was a work of omnipotence, and yet it was not accomplished all at once. The Lord could, if he had so willed it, have fashioned this habitable globe in one second of time, and have furnished all its chambers by a single word of his mouth. Instead of this, we have reason to believe that he lingered in the first formation of it, in the beginning, when he created the heavens and the earth; and arranged and disarranged it many times before he came to the final constitution of it in the first six days of time, wherein he modeled it to be a fit abode for man. Even then when he came to the final work, not in one day did he build up chaos into the beautiful house of humanity. Not at first did the firmament divide the waters, or the dry land appear above the seas. Not till the third day did the earth bring forth grass and the herb yielding seed, nor did sun and moon divide the empire of day and night till the fourth day had dawned; while the fowl that fly in the open firmament of heaven, and the living creatures that move in the waters, owned a yet later birth. Everything was gradual. Step by step the Maker advanced, get was there never anything less than omnipotence in every step of his progress. So, my brethren, the Lord might as easily have converted the whole world to Christ on the day of Pentecost as not, but not so had his decrees appointed. A step was taken in apostolic times, and the light shone forth in darkness; further on, the great division between the heavenly and the earthly became marked and clear, and the church rose like the dry land above the seas of sin, while the plants of the Lord's right-hand planting brought forth their seed and their fruit. Even now the appointed lights make glad the sky, and the time hastens on when the Lord shall more evidently bless his living ones, and say, "Be fruitful, and multiply, and fill the earth;" but all is done by degrees as he appoints. Our impatience would fain stand at the Eternal elbow, and say, "Master, complete thy work, and let our eyes behold the Second Adam in a world restored into a second Eden." But he tarries for awhile, and waits while his great appointed evenings and mornings fill up his week of glorious work. He delights in this noblest labor of his hands, and is not as the hireling who earnestly desireth the shadow that his toilsome task may be ended. He lingers lovingly, and his long suffering is salvation. The Lord's decrees tarry not so long but what in the divine reckoning, and according to the Lord's own estimate, the end will come quickly, but to the presumptuous who dare to say, "where is the promise of his coming?" he seems to linger long. How blessed will be the grand finale of redemption work; then shall the morning stars sing together, and all the sons of God shout for joy. The seventh day of redemption shall eclipse the Sabbath of nature, even as the new heavens and the new earth shall outshine the former: a river purer than Hiddekel shall water the new Eden, the tree of life of richer fruit shall grow in the midst of the garden, and then shall be fulfilled the saying which is written, "Sing, O ye heavens; for the Lord hath done it: shout, ye lower parts of the earth: break forth into singing, ye mountains, O forest, and every tree therein: for the Lord hath redeemed Jacob, and glorified himself in Israel." As we read the promise, "I will hold thine hand, and will keep thee," we see the certainty that the Savior girt with the allsufficiency of divine strength, will accomplish the work of human salvation. Be of good cheer, O children of God, and comfort yourselves with the belief, "that he shall see his seed, he shall prolong his days, and the pleasure of the Lord shall prosper in his hand." His church has no reason for fear, but every ground of confidence as to her future. Rejoice, O daughter of Zion; for great is the Holy One of Israel in the midst of thee.

"Fear not, though many a mighty foe
Against thy walls advance;
Jehovah's arm will lay them low
For thy deliverance.
Oh, take him at his royal word
That word which cannot lie
Thy shield and sword is Israel's Lord,
Almighty sovereignty."

I know you will tell me, "most men say that the world will end in a few years; is it not written that the Bridegroom cometh quickly?" Yes, but remember that eighteen hundred years ago it was written that he would come quickly, and there have been prophets in all ages who have concluded from this that the end was near, while many believers have been like the Thessalonians, to whom Paul wrote: "Now we beseech you, brethren, by the coming of our Lord Jesus Christ, and by our gathering together unto him, that ye be not soon shaken in mind, or be troubled, neither by spirit, nor by word, nor by letter as from us, as that the day of Christ is at hand." We have been instructed by certain pretended expositors to expect the time of the end for the last seven years, and yet it is possible that it may not arrive for the next seventy thousand years. Perhaps human history, as yet written, is but the first stanza of a wondrous poem, which shall be unfolded page by page for many an age to come, and it may be possible far more rapturous strains of divine mercy and grace in the conversion of men are yet to be read by angels and glorified spirits. If it be so it will still be true that he comes quickly, for what will time be compared with eternity? Even if the space taken up by the world's history be not a brief six thousand years, but sixty thousand times six thousand years, yet will it be but as a drop of a bucket compared with the years of the right hand of the Most High, the lifetime of the Ancient of Days. Fight on hopefully, my brethren, and be not distressed with rumors of times and seasons, but believe ye this, that God is, in Christ Jesus, reconciling the world unto himself, and all the ends of the earth shall see the salvation of our God. Watch daily for the Lord's coming, but yet struggle to advance his empire, for "he shall have dominion also from sea to sea, and from the river unto the ends of the earth." The Lord has not withdrawn his hand from his "elect, in whom his soul delighteth." He will subdue nations before him, he will loose the loins of kings, to open before him the two-leaved gates. With such a deliverer so gloriously upheld, there is no room for fear of failure. Our hope and faith joyfully rest in him to whom the Eternal gives his almightiness wherewith to subdue all things unto himself.

II. We will now advance a little further, the Lord helping us. Having contemplated the glorious One who sent Jesus to the work of man's emancipation, let us, in the second place, consider the SENT ONE HIMSELF.

We have him described in the first verse of this chapter, and the first words which we will select from the description inform us that Jesus is a chosen one. "Mine elect, in whom my soul delighteth." God has been pleased to set apart his well-beloved Son to be the Savior of sinners, and in every way he is most suitable. As man he is supremely adapted for the work; no other of woman born was fitted for the enterprise. Born in a peculiar manner, without taint or blemish, he alone of human kind possessed the holy nature needful to make him God's messenger of love. I tried to show just now that God has girded our Lord with his omnipotence, and this ought to lead every sinner to feel that Christ can save him, for what cannot Omnipotence do? We may not talk of impossibilities or even difficulties when we have almightiness before us. No sinner can be difficult to save, no bonds hard to remove, when God, the Almighty One, comes forth to save. Now look at the other side of the picture, and remember that Christ Jesus was the most suitable person in whom the Father could place the fullness of his saving power. In his complex person he is every way adapted to stand as mediator between God and man. He who laid help upon one that is mighty, and exalted one chosen out of the people, was guided by infallible wisdom in his choice. None other was so fit as he; in fact there was no other. "Other foundation can no man lay than that is laid." Other door of hope can no man open than that which God has opened in the person of Christ. O sinner, I beseech thee accept what God has wisely chosen. Let God's choice be thy willing choice. At this hour, constrained by the grace of God, say, "If God has chosen the Lord Jesus to be a propitiation for sin, my heart accepts him as the atonement for my sin, feeling that he alone can save me." If thus thou dost elect the Lord's elect One, thou shalt find him precious.

But we are also told in the first verse that the Lord Jesus is anointed to this work, as well as a choice one for it. "I have put my Spirit upon him." Now, the Holy Spirit is the greatest of all actors in the world of mind. He it is who can illuminate, persuade, and control the spirits of men. He doeth as he wills with mind, even as in the first creation the Lord wrought as he willed with matter. Now, if Jesus Christ has the fullness of the Holy Spirit resting upon him, it is not supposable that any sinner shall be so desperately enslaved that he cannot set him free. We are about to speak of blind eyes to be opened, but in the light of the Holy Spirit what eye need remain blind? We shall speak of captives to be liberated, but with God's free Spirit to loose him what soul need be bound? Bold men have taught doctrines which have emancipated the minds of their fellows from the slavery of superstition, but the Holy Ghost's teachings deliver minds from bondage of every kind, and make men free before the living God. Trembling sinner, accept Christ as your Savior; God appoints him; God anoints him. Are not these two reasons sufficient to make him acceptable to your soul?

Furthermore, the Redeemer is spoken of as being gentle and lowly of heart, which should commend him much to every lowly and contrite spirit. "A bruised reed shall he not break, and the smoking flax shall he not quench." We need a Savior who can be touched with the feeling of our infirmities, and Jesus is such. Souls conscious of sin are very tender, and agitated with many fears; to cure a wounded conscience is no fool's work, but fit labor for the most experienced physician. See you, then, how fitted Christ is. He never yet said an unkind word to a soul that desired to find mercy at his hands. In the records of his life you may find him try, but you shall never see him repel, an anxious spirit. When feeble faith could only touch the hem of his garment, yet virtue flowed from him. When the leper said, "Lord, if thou wilt, thou canst make me clean," it was but poor faith, but that faith saved him. Though you cannot yet believe as you would, yet say, "Lord, I believe; help thou mine unbelief," and he will not reject you. Look at the smoking candle-wick which yields no light, but makes much offensive smoke; yet, perchance, a living fire lingers in it, and therefore the tender Savior will not quench it, but will even fan it to a flame. And that bruised reed, how it mars the music of the pipes; draw it out and break it. So would men do, but not so the sinner's Friend. He makes it perfect yet again, and pours the music of his love through it. O thou who art in thine own esteem utterly worthless, only fit to be thrown away, unfit to live and unfit to die; Jesus Christ, the gentle One, will give thee mercy, if thou seek him, and in giving he will not upbraid thee. O wandering child, Jesus will introduce thee to his Father, who will kiss thee with the kisses of his love, and take off thy rags of sin, and clothe thee with glorious robes of righteousness. Only come thou to him, for he is such an one that he cannot reject thee. "How can I come?" saith one. A prayer will bring thee; an anxious desire will be as a chariot to thee. A trust in him hath brought thee, and Christ is thine, if thou dost now accept him. If thy soul is truly willing to have Christ, Christ hath made thee willing, and has already begun to set thee free. May these thoughts concerning the great Emancipator cheer thee on to confidence in him.

One point more in this direction. The Christ who has come to save the sons of men is persevering to the last degree. "He shall not fail, nor be discouraged, till he have set judgment in the earth: and the isles shall wait for his law." Men are unwilling to be saved; they do not desire to be brought out of their prison-houses; but Jesus Christ will not cease to teach, nor cease to seek, nor cease to save, till every one of his elect is redeemed from the ruin of the fall, and until a multitude beyond all count shall surround the Father's throne. I tell thee, soul, if Christ wills to save thee, he will save thee. He will track thy footsteps, wander where thou mayst. If thou shouldest escape time after time, from the arrows of conviction, and plunge again and again into sin, yet will he seek thee out and find thee yet. O delay not, but yield to his power! I pray that he may stretch out his sovereign arm at this moment, and rescue thee from thyself. If thy heart were as adamant, or as the nether millstone, he can dissolve it with a touch. O that the rock-breaking hammer would come down upon thee now! He is mighty to save; may he prove his mightiness in thee!

III. It is time that we expound the text itself, and review THE WORK ITSELF.

According to the text, the Messiah's work of grace is divided into three parts, of which the first is, to open the blind eyes. Here is a notable work which brings much glory to our Lord. Man's understanding is perverted from the knowledge of God, from a true sense of sin, from a realisation of divine justice, from a right estimate of salvation. The understanding, which is the eye of the soul, is darkened. But when the anointed Savior comes, he removes the scales of our mental ophthalmia, and in the light of God we see light, and then the sinner is humbled and bowed down, for he perceives his guilt and the justice of God. Moreover, he is filled with alarm, for he sees the bleeding Savior bearing Jehovah's wrath, and rightly judges that in every case sin must receive a recompense of wrath; for if sin laid on Christ was punished, how much more must personal sin involve banishment from the presence of the Most High? The sinner is then made to see that the only way in which sin can be removed is through the expiatory sufferings of a substitute. He is led to see that the atonement avails for him upon his believing. He is led to understand what believing is. He does believe; he trusts, and then in trusting he is made to see the completeness of pardon, and the glory of the justification which comes to us by faith in Jesus Christ. You may think that this is an easy thing for men to see, trained in the doctrine of it from their childhood, and hearing it incessantly from the pulpit; but, believe me, simple as it seems to he, no man receives it unless it has been given him from heaven. We may say to each one who has seen all this, "Blessed art thou, for flesh and blood hath not revealed it unto thee." Many of us heard the gospel from our childhood, but until the Holy Spirit explained to us what it was to be a sinner, and what it was to believe in Jesus, we did not know even the rudiments of the gospel. We were in darkness ourselves, though the light shone round about us; and well might we be, for our eyes were not opened. When Jesus came we saw it all, and we understood the mystery. Our once blind eyes clearly saw ourselves lost, and Christ suffering instead of us; we believed in him, our sins disappeared, and we were accepted in the Beloved. My dear friend, if thou art seeking rest, I pray the Lord to open thine eyes to see the simplicities of the gospel. One touch of his finger will make thee wise unto salvation. There is no need for thee to study the twenty-one folio volumes of Albertus Magnus, or even the fifty-two volumes of John Calvin, for the whole secret of the gospel lies in these few words, "Believe and live;" yet thou canst not open the casket unless the Lord give thee the secret key. It needs an opened eye to see even through a glass window; the clear witness of the gospel is dark to blind eyes.

The next work of the Messiah, according to the text, is to bring out the prisoners front the prison. This, I think, relates to the bondage under which a man lies to his sins. Habits of sin, like iron nets, surround the sinner, and he cannot escape their meshes. The man sins, and imagines that he cannot help sinning. How often do the ungodly tell us that they cannot renounce the world, cannot break off their sins by righteousness, and cannot believe in Jesus? Let all men know that the Savior has come on purpose to remove every bond of sin from the captive, and to set him free from every, chain of evil. I have known men strive against the habit of blasphemy, others against unchaste passions, and many more against a haughty spirit, or an angry temper; and when they have strived manfully but unsuccessfully in their own strength, they have been filled with bitter chagrin that they should have been so betrayed by themselves. When a man believes in Jesus his resolve to become a freeman is to a great extent accomplished at once. Some sins die the moment we believe in Jesus, and trouble us no more; others hang on to us, and die by slow degrees, but they are overcome so as never again to get the mastery over us. O struggler after mental, moral, spiritual liberty, if thou wouldst be free, thine only possible freedom is in Christ. If thou wouldst shake off evil habits or any other mental bondage, I shall prescribe no remedy to thee but this, to commit thyself to Christ the Liberator.

"The gates of brass before him burst,
The iron fetters yield."

Love him, and thou shalt hate sin. Trust him, and thou shalt no more trust thyself. Submit thyself to the sway of the incarnate God, and he will break the dragon's head within thee, and hurl Satan beneath thy feet. Nothing else can do it. Christ must have the glory of thy conquest of self. He can set thee free from sin's iron yoke. He never failed yet, and he never shall. I earnestly entreat any man who desires to break off his sins (and we must break them off or perish by them), to try this divine remedy, and see if it does not give him holy liberty. Ask the thousands who have already believed in Jesus, and their testimony will confirm my doctrine. Faith in the Lord Jesus is the end of bondage and the dawn of freedom.

The last part of this divine work is, bringing them that sit in darkness out of the prison-house. This we will refer to those who are truly emancipated, and yet by reason of despondency sit down in the dark dungeon. We have in our pastoral duties constantly to console persons who are free from their sins, having by divine grace got the mastery over them, but yet they are in sadness. The door is open, the bars are broken, but with strange obstinacy of despondency they remain in the cell of fear, in which there is no necessity for them to continue for a moment. They cannot believe that these good things are true to them. They forgiven? They could believe everybody else to be pardoned but themselves. They made the children of God? Nay, they could hope for their sisters; they have joy in knowing that their father is a child of God, but as to themselves--can such blessings really fall to the lot of such unworthy ones? We have talked with hundreds of such and tried to console them, but we have only learned our own unskilfulness in the art of consolation. They are rich in inventions for self-torture, ingenious in escaping comfort. But, ah! the blessed Master of our souls, whose business it has been since Adam fell to bind up broken hearts, is never foiled. When his eternal Spirit comes to anoint with the oil of joy, he soon gives beauty for ashes. The mournful sentinel of the night-watches must rejoice when the day breaketh and the Sun of righteousness shines forth.

Although I speak to you in very common-place language, yet the theme is rich. This one thought alone ought to make our hearts dance for joy, to think that the Christ of God undertakes to lift up desponding and despairing spirits into hope and joy once more. I know who will rejoice to hear this. It is yonder good woman, who these many years has been in spiritual bondage. It is yonder young man, who has carried a secret burden month after month. It is yonder aged man, who longs to find Christ ere he gathers up his feet in his dying bed, and who thinks that his hour of grace has passed. Man, it is not so. Christ is still mighty to save. Still doth the message run: "He that believeth on him is not condemned." "Whosoever will, let him take the water of life freely." "Go, every one that thirsteth, come ye to the waters, and he that hath no money; come ye, buy, and eat; yea, come, buy wine and milk without money and without price." Prisoners of hope, your liberator is near at hand. Trust him and be free. Though it seem a venturesome believing, yet venture on him. He cannot, will not reject you; he will proclaim a jubilee, and set each bondslave free.

See, then, how the great Redeemer blessed us: Jesus the Christ does all things well; he clears the understanding; he breaks the power of sinful habits; he removes the load of despondency; he doth it all. Christ Jesus, Mary's son and Jehovah's son man, bone of our bone and flesh of our flesh, yet God over all, blessed for ever; he who died on Calvary, whose precious blood is the panacea for all human ills, he it is, and he only, who is the Liberator of our fallen race.

IV. WHAT IS THE DESIGN OF GOD IN ALL THIS?

This question is answered in the next verse to the text: "I am the Lord: that is my name: and my glory will I not give to another." The great end of God in Christ was the manifestation of his own glorious attributes--a simple truth, but big with comfort, for should the sinner who has been an atrocious offender against laws human and divine conceive himself to be an improper subject for the grace of God, I would take him by the hand, and lest despair drive him to further sin, I would put this truth clearly before him. Where is mercy most glorified? Is it not in passing by the greatest offenses? Thou hast great offenses; there is room in thee for mercy to be greatly displaced. Where is grace glorified? Is it not in conquering the most violent passions? Thou hast such; grace may therefore be glorified in thee. Why, great sinner, instead of not being a fit subject for grace, I will venture to say that thou art in all respects one of the most suitable. There is elbow-room in thee for grace to work. There is room in thine emptiness for God's fullness. There is a clear stage in thy sinfulness for God's superabounding grace. But you have been a ringleader in the devil's army. Yes, and how can God strike a more telling blow against the hosts of darkness than by capturing you? But you tell me that you are an enormous sinner. How will the Lord of love encourage other sinners to come better than by calling you? For it will be rumoured about among your fellow-sinners:- "Have you heard that such an one is saved?" I know they will jeer, but still, in their secret hearts, they will think it over, and they will say, "How is this?" and they will be led to enquire into the ways of God's grace. A brother told the church, a short time since, a little of his history, and it caused us all to rejoice in sovereign grace. He had lived in all manner of sin and iniquity; his profession had been for some years that of a public runner, and in that course of life he was brought into collision with the scum of society. He was practiced, also, in the pugilistic art, and that, we all know, is the very reverse of having an elevating tendency. But he came to the Tabernacle, and here Jesus met with him, and he rejoices now to teach to others the gospel which he once rejected. But what, think you has he been accustomed to do these three years? Some of our brethren preach in the streets, and he goes with them, and after they have told of what the grace of God can do, he humbly and yet boldly rises and says, "I am a living witness to what grace can do; I can declare to you what God's love has done for me." If the sermon which precedes his little speech has not interested the people, they are quite certain to be struck with his personal testimony, for in some localities many of the street folk know him, and as they look at him they say, "Why, that is old so-and-so. I knew him when he was this and that, and here he is converted;" and his witness-bearing works mightily among his old friends and acquaintances. I say, then, if now I speak to any other who has been a great offender, a drunkard, or what not, if my Master does but set you free and enlist you in his army, there will be such a shout go up in the hosts of Israel as shall make heaven ring, while the Philistines shall tremble, for their Goliath shall be slain, and a new champion raised up from his dead body to fight for the Lord of hosts. If the Lord saved men because of their merits, there would be no hope for great sinners, nor indeed for any one; but if he saves us for his own glory, that he may magnify his grace and his mercy among the sons of men, then none need despair. Up to the very gates of hell would I preach the gospel, and between the jaws of death would I proclaim it. God to glorify his grace sets free the captives, then why should not the most hell-deserving sinner, whose heart is like hardened steel, yet become a monument of Christ's power to save? I remember one who used to say that if God would but have mercy on him he should never hear the last of it, and it may well be the resolve of all of us, that earth and heaven shall never hear the last of our praises if grace shall but save us. As one of our hymns puts it

"Then loudest of the crowd I'll sing,
While heaven's resounding mansions ring
With shouts of sovereign grace."

Yes, we will each sing loudest, each owing most, each desiring, therefore, to bend the lowest and to praise the most heartily, the grace which has set us free.

Time flies with us; days are rushing past; years are hastening away. How long shall it be ere Christ shall gain your hearts? How long shall ye hear of him, and continue to refuse his grace? How long, ye unconverted ones, will ye hug your chains and kiss your fetters? "Turn ye, turn ye from your evil ways; for why will ye die, O house of Israel?" "Seek ye the Lord while he may be found, call ye upon him while he is near: let the wicked forsake his way, and the unrighteous man his thoughts: and let him return unto the Lord, and he will have mercy upon him; and to our God, for he will abundantly pardon."

PORTION OF SCRIPTURE READ BEFORE SERMON--Isaiah 42.

*Metropolitan Tabernacle Pulpit, No. 915. "Sinners Bound with the Cords of Sin."

Marah; or, The Bitter Waters Sweetened

A Sermon (No. 987)
Delivered On Lord's-day Morning, April 23rd, 1871, by
C. H. SPURGEON,
At the Metropolitan Tabernacle, Newington

"And when they came to Marah, they could not drink of the waters of Marah for they were bitter: therefore the name of it was called Marah. And the people murmured against Moses, saying, What shall we drink? And he cried unto the Lord, and the Lord showed him a tree, which when he had cast into the waters, the waters were made sweet." - Exodus 15:23-25.

WHAT A SUDDEN CHANGE from the sound of the timbrel to the voice of murmuring! You saw the maidens dancing three days ago, and you little dreamed that they would make part of yonder clamorous throng who surround the servant of God, and cry, "What shall we drink?" Such are the changes of our outward conditions and of our inward feelings, so fickle and so mutable is man. What is there that can be rested upon in this mortal life? We say to-day, "My mountain standeth firm, I shall never be moved;" to-morrow, terra firma there is none, and we are tossed upon a stormy sea. Our life is like an April day, the sunshine alternates with the shower; or like each day of all the year, the morning and the evening are needful to complete it. Quick on the heels of light treads the darkness, followed with equal haste by light again. The sun's rule, at this golden hour, is but temporary; he must abdicate in favor of the usurping stars, but they, in their turn, must give way before his lordly presence yet again. This world, which is our inn, owns to the sign of the "chequers"--the blacks and whites are everywhere. We can be sure of nothing between here and heaven of the things which are seen; but of this we may be certain, that underneath all the outward change there is the immutable love of God towards his people, and that, after all, the change lies only in the seeming things, not in the things which truly are; for the things which are not seen are eternal and changes come not there; it is but in the things which are seen that the change occurs. Let us set the less store by earth, because its fashion abides not. Let us prize heaven more, because it cannot fade.

I. The text directs your attention, first of all, to THE EVILS OF THE WILDERNESS. We need not spend much time in thinking of these evils, because they throw themselves in our way often enough; and the tendency of our mind is unduly to exaggerate them. Notice that the perils and trials of the wilderness occur very early in the pilgrim life. It is a notion, I have no doubt, of very young Christians who still have the shell upon their heads and are scarce hatched, that their trials are over now that they have become winged with faith; they had far better have reckoned that their trials have begun with tenfold force, now that they are numbered with the servants of the Most High. Whatever else comes not to thee, O servant of God, this will surely be fulfilled, "In the world ye shall have tribulation." "What son is he whom the Father chasteneth not?" Some privileges are not common to ail the adopted, but the privilege of chastisement is universal to all true sons. It is the token of bastardy if the rod be escaped, but scourging, is the sure pledge of paternal love. I say, however, that these trials come very soon. Israel was no sooner across the Red Sea than they went three days into the wilderness of Shur, but found no water; and on the third day, when they did arrive at a fountain, they found worse than no water, for it was so brackish, so altogether unfit for drinking, that though they thought they would have drunk anything, they could not possibly drink this. What, in three days, must they that sang unto the Lord because he triumphed gloriously, nauseate the water for which their thirst makes them pant? In three days shall they be reduced to such straits that they must drink or die, and yet feel that they should die if they were to drink of such nauseous streams? Ah yes, with some of us our delight at conversion was very great, our exhilaration at finding the Savior was something never to be forgotten, and yet only a day or so after we were stumbled with great temptation, amazed at the discovery of the evil of our hearts, or tried by the coldness of our fellow Christians, or the cruelty of the outside world, so that we found we had come to Marah. And this was all the severer trial, because some of us had found a degree of pleasure in the ways of sin, and now it stumbled us to find sorrow in the ways of God. When Israel was in Egypt, they drank of the river Nile. No ordinary water that. To this day the dwellers on the banks of the Nile assert that the water has a peculiar taste not to be discovered in any other stream, and they prefer the waters of the Nile to all the waters in the world besides. What a change from the sweetness of the Nile to the bitterness of Marah! Did not the suggestion rise in their hearts, "It was better with us in the bondage of Egypt, with water in abundance, than it is now in the liberty of the wilderness with the bitterness of Marah?" The devil tempted some of us at the very first by saying: "See what you have got by being a Christian. While you were as others are, your mind had mirth; now you have come out and followed the Crucified, you have lost the liveliness of your spirits, the brightness of your wit--that which made life worth having is taken away from you." Young Christian, is that your case to-day? Be not stumbled, neither believe the enemy. Man, it were better to die at Marah free, than live a slave by the sweet Nile. Even men that know not the Spirit of God have felt it were better to die free than live slaves, and truly to be a slave to Satan is so degrading a thing, that if this mouth were for ever filled with Marah's bitterness, yet were it better to be so than to be enchanted with the pleasures of sin. Yet these early trials are very severe, and need much grace lest they cause us great mischief.

Secondly, these evils assume varied shapes. You noticed that for the first three days in the wilderness they found no wafer; that is one trial. But the next day, or at the end of the third day, they found water. Now they thought their trial was over: alas! it had only changed its shape. They found water, but it was too bitter to drink. Do not be in a hurry to change your trials, dear friends. We have heard of some who have repined that they had no children, and, like Rachel, their cry was, "Give me children, or else I die." Ere long they have had children who proved to be far worse than none. Better no son than an Absalom. We have known those who were in good health, but discontented because they had no wealth; they have gained wealth at last, but with an injured constitution, they have had no power to enjoy it. If we could choose our trials, we might well remember the wisdom of the old philosopher, who told the people oppressed by a tyrant to be content with his tyranny, "for," said he, "it is with oppressors as with mosquitoes, let those suck which are now upon you, for if you drive those off, the fresh ones which will succeed them will be hungrier than those that are there now: better be content with the tyranny you have, than seek a new one." It is much the same with the trials we now feel you will get used to them by degrees: they will spend their force. Desire for a change of trials may only be a wish for a worse affliction, for whether was the worse, to have no water, or to have the water and to find it to bitter that you could not drink it?

Yet when God changes the trial be well satisfied that it should be changed. You may anticipate, Christian, that you will have your trial changed: indeed, you must reckon that it is so. I mean, that if today it is smooth sailing with you, though yesterday waves rolled mountains high, it is only a change of trial you are now tried by prosperity, which may prove to be a more severe test for you than adversity. Is the wind balmy, blows it from the south? Is it but another trial for thee, be sure of that, for they who have withstood the northern blast and grown the ruddier and stronger for its influence, have often grown faint and weary under softer airs. Watch thou in all things, thy trials are with thee constantly; the crucible is changed, the fire still burns.

Note again, that as the trials of the wilderness came soon, and assumed various shapes, so often do the trials of the Christ touch very vital matters. They found no water, or finding it, it was bitter. It is not said they found no wine--a small trial indeed; it is not said they found no milk, yet might the infant children have been sorely troubled by such a want; but they found no drinkable water. Here was a denial of an essential of life. They must have water, it was no luxury, it was a necessity; with the hot, burning sand beneath them reflecting the fierce heat of a cruel sun, not to have water in the wilderness is to feel an urgent necessity producing a terrible pain. God may touch us, and probably has done so or will, in points most vital. To be tried in the loss of some of your superfluities, my brethren, is but little; but to lose even the little that you had to live upon, to be brought to straitness of bread, this is real tribulation. To have the hand put forth to touch your bone and your flesh, this is affliction. Believe me, our virtues and graces look very fine, and we think much of them until they undergo that ordeal, but that test often takes from them their gloss and beauty; we find how great our weakness is when the very marrow of our bones seems to be a den in which pains, like robbers, hide themselves. God may touch you in the most beloved object of your heart. It is not one child that is taken out of many, but the only one; it is not a friend, or distant relative, but the partner of your bosom is laid low. Do not wonder if the trial affects you greatly, and comes home to your soul and heart. It is one of God's determinations that trials shall not be mock trials with his servants, and the grace given shall not be imaginary, but true. God never plays at chastening his children. No trial for the present seemeth to be joyous, but grievous. By the blueness of the wound the heart is made better; if it do not bruise, it doth not benefit. Very much in proportion to the bitterness felt will be the benefit that will come of it. They found no water. O my God, to what straits dost thou reduce thine own people; thine own people who carry with them the title-deeds of a land that flows with milk and honey! Jordan and Kishon are theirs, and yet they find only Marah to drink while they are here; thine own people for whom thou hast appointed that they shall dwell in a land of brooks and rivers of water, where they shall sit every man under his vine and fig-tree; these, thy darlings, whom thou hast brought out with a high hand and an outstretched arm, are brought to the extreme of poverty, and the little that they have has often a bitter taste infused into it.

Notice once again, there is a reason why the earthly mercies which supply our necessities must be more or less bitter. When Israel received water out of the rock it was not bitter, but this water came out of the sand. To this day in the desert water is found in different places, but where it oozes up from a sandy bed it is almost without exception so brackish and bitter, by reason of the sand, that it is not fit for human drinking; and even the camels, unless they are sore pressed, turn away from it with great aversion. The sand has tainted it, the flavour of earth has got into the blessing. So it is with most of our blessings; by reason of our sin and infirmity too much of the flavour of earth enters into the gift of heaven. Our common mercies, when we receive them direct from heaven as God gives them, are mercies indeed--cool, flowing streams that gush from the rock of his favor; but we are so apt to trace them to the creature, so ready to look upon them as derived from earth instead of coming from heaven; and just in that proportion may we expect to find bitterness in them. What can you hope for in a wilderness, but productions congruous to it? Canaan! who looks for bitterness there? Is it not the land that flows with milk and honey? Sweet land, when shall we reach thee? Thy sweetness is but congruous to thyself: But here, in this wilderness, where we have no continuing city, who looks for the streams of Lebanon? who hopes to find Canaan's fruits in the wilderness of Sin? As well seek to gather from the briny sea the sweet fruits of the palm or the luscious clusters of the vine, as hope to find, amidst these changing scenes, comforts that shall be all comfortable and joys that shall be all joyous. No, they will be comforts, but they will be often embittered; they will be joyous somewhat, but the earthy flavour in them will make us remember that this is not our rest.

I know not that I ought to detain you longer with these evils of the wilderness. I do not feel it is wrong to speak of them, for we do not mention them with any view of discouraging those who have set out on pilgrimage; we are not like those who hold up their hands and say, "The lions, the giants, the dragons; young pilgrim, you will never reach the land of promise;" but yet we would imitate the Savior, who said to the follower who thought he could follow him whithersoever he might go, "Sit down, and count the cost." There are trials for you, ye followers of Christ, if there are none for others--peculiar trials for you, peculiar joys ten thousand times outweighing them, but yet peculiar griefs, new griefs of a new life of which it will be a blessed thing to have been a participant; but there they are, and we will not deceive you. For you there will be Marahs that others may not know, and for you there will be long thirsts where others drink to the full; nevertheless, we will take Christ and his reproach, Christ and his Marah, rather than the world with its sweetness, for with every drawback that is supposable to Christ Jesus, he is better than the world with all the additions that can be invented by the sons of mirth.

II. Thus much on the first point, the evils of the wilderness. Now, secondly, THE TENDENCY OF HUMAN NATURE. The people murmured against Moses, saying, "What shall we drink?" Do not say "human nature," says one; say, "the tendency of Jewish nature." Ah, but if anything, I would prefer the people in the wilderness to any other: rest assured that they were no worse than we are. They are an example to us of what our heart is; and whatever we see in them we have but to watch a little, and we shall see it all in ourselves. It was not Jewish nature that God proved in the wilderness so much as human nature at its very best estate. Assuredly, the tendency of human nature is to murmur. They murmured, complained, found fault. A very easy thing, for the very word "murmur," how simple it is, made up of two infantile sounds--mur mur. No sense in it, no wit in it, no thought in it: it is the cry rather of a brute than of a man--murmur--just a double groan. Easy is it for us to kick against the dispensations of God, to give utterance to our griefs, and what is worse, to the inference we drew from them that God has forgotten to be gracious. To murmur is our tendency; but, my dear brethren and sisters in Christ, do we mean to let the tendencies of the old nature rule us? Will we murmur? O that we might have grace rather to say with Job, "Though he slay me, yet will I trust in him!" Shall a living man complain? Have we not received so much good from the hands of the Lord that we may well receive evil without rebellion? Will we not disappoint Satan, and overrule the tendency of the flesh, by saying in the might of God's Spirit, "The Lord gave, and the Lord hath taken away; blessed be the name of the Lord." I know we are apt to say, "Well, that is human nature," and when we have said it is human nature, we suppose we have given a very excellent excuse for doing it. But is human nature to rule the divine nature? You, believer, profess to be a partaker of the divine nature. Let the superior force govern, let that which cometh from above be uppermost, and put the lower nature down; let us eschew murmurings and complainings, and magnify and adore the God who lays our comforts low.

Observe--and this is worthy of note--that the murmuring was not ostensibly against God.

They murmured against Moses. And have you ever noticed how the most of us, when we are in a murmuring vein, are not honest enough to murmur distinctly against God. No: the child is dead, and we form a conjecture that there was some wrong treatment on the part of nurse, or surgeon, or ourselves; we lay our hold on that for which there may not be a shadow of proof, and the murmuring is upon that point. Or we have lost money, and have been brought down from opulence to almost poverty; then some one person was dishonest, a certain party betrayed us in a transaction by failing to fulfill his part; all the murmuring is heaped on that person. We deny, perhaps indignantly, that we murmur against God; and to prove it we double the zeal with which we murmur against Moses. To complain of the second cause is about as sensible as the conduct of the dog, which bites the stick with which it is beaten. It owes no anger to the stick, but to the person who uses it. Is there evil in the city and the Lord hath not done it? Whoever is the instrument, the Lord overrules. In our heart of hearts our rebellion is against the Lord himself. We have not quite honesty enough to rail against God openly and avowedly, and so we hypocritically cover up our repining against him by murmuring against some person, occasion, or event. "If I had not happened to go out on such an occasion I might not have had that cold and been laid aside." Thus we blame an accidental circumstance, as if it were not part of the divine arrangement. Is this complaining of the second cause better than railing against God? I trow not, for, in very deed, it is railing against God, and it is, in addition, an injustice to the second cause, so made a butt of. When Pharaoh bade the Israelites make bricks, and gave them no straw, there was injustice; but when the Israelites gathered around Moses and virtually told him that he ought to supply them with water, it was much the same thing. Whence should this man have water to give them to drink? How could he sweeten Marah? They knew right well that it was not possible for him to open a well for them in the wilderness; they complained, I say, in their hearts, really against God, but they added to this the hypocrisy and the injustice of veiling their murmuring against the Most High by an unjust and clamourous complaint against his servant Moses. Stop thy tongue, my brother; cease thy cavilling against this and that, against him or her; for be sure that thou art doing injustice to thy fellowman as well as a wrong to thy God.

Once more, while we speak of this tendency in human nature, I want you to observe how they betrayed an utter unbelief of God. They said unto Moses, "What shall we drink?" They meant by it, "By what means can God supply our want of water?" What a question! They were at the Red Sea, and God cleft the intervening gulf in twain, through the depths thereof they marched dryshod; there is Marah's water--shall it be more difflcult for God to purify than to divide? To sweeten a fountain--is that more difficult than to cleanse a sea? Is anything too hard for the Lord? A great miracle had been wrought; had they but considered it, and exercised even the lowest degree of faith, they must have seen that he who could work such a miracle as they had seen could work yet another; and they might joyously have stood at Marah's brink, and have sung, "He who cast Pharaoh and his chosen captains into the Red Sea, and delivered his people, can give his chosen drink, therefore sing we, Spring up, O well, and let thy waters be sweet and clean." O that they had faith in God but as a grain of mustard seed, and they would have seen great things, and glorified his name. Do you blame them? Do so; blame them much, but include yourselves in the censure. How often has it been so with us? We have said, "I will never distrust my God after this memorable deliverance, this singular display of his power has slain my unbelief;" yet a new trial has occurred, and our faith, where was it? Had the Son of Man himself been on the earth with those quick eyes to discern the faith which he himself creates, could he find faith in us in the hour of tribulation? Be humbled as ye see yourselves in this mirror. Behold your instability, which is as water. How like to reeds shaken with the wind are we; or like to meteors, which flash across the brow of night, to leave the darkness denser than before. How soon is the glory of our confidence spent, and the excellence of our faith withered. Hold thou our feet in life, great God, or we shall soon be silent in darkness.

III. Now, thirdly--and may divine help, the help of the Holy Ghost be given me--I will speak upon THE REMEDY OF GRACE. I have shown you the evils of the wilderness and the tendency of nature: it is delightful to behold the remedy of grace. First, if thou wouldst have Marah's bitterness healed, take the case in prayer to God. God begins by making us begin. The people complained to Moses; Moses took the complaint to his Master. In all trials, the surest way to a remedy is prayer. In heavenly pharmacy, prayer is a catholicon; it healeth all things. Prayer, which overcomes heaven, will certainly never be overmatched on earth. Neither men nor devils can stand against prayer: it smites them hip and thigh like another Samson. The bow of prayer returns not empty; it is swifter than an eagle, it is stronger than a lion. Take thy case to God, O heir of trouble; unroll Rabshakeh's letter before the Host High, and the Lord will silence his revilings. Half the work is done when it is brought before God in supplication.

Note, next, that as soon as we have a prayer God has a remedy. The remedy is near at hand; but we do not perceive it till it is shown us. "The Lord showed him a tree." The tree had been growing for years on purpose to be used. God has a remedy for all our troubles before they happen

to us. A delightful employment it is to notice how God forestalls himself; how long before we reach the encampment, if there be the bitter well, there is also the healing tree. All is ready between here and heaven. He that has gone to prepare a place for us by his presence, has prepared the way to that place for us by his providence. But, brethren, though for every trouble in this mortal life there is a remedy, you and I do not always discern it. "The Lord showed him a tree." I am persuaded that for every lock in Doubting Castle there is a key, but the promises are often in great confusion to our minds, so that we are perplexed. If a blacksmith should bring you his great bundle of picklocks, you would have to turn them over, and over, and over; and try half of them, perhaps two-thirds, before you would find the right one; ay, and perhaps the right one would be left to the last. It is always a blessing to remember that for every affliction there is a promise in the word of God; a promise which meets the case, and was made on purpose for it. But you may not be always able to find it--no, you may go fumbling over the Scriptures long before you get the true word; but when the Lord shows it to you, when it comes with power to the soul, when the heart can grasp it, and cry, "Ay, that is the word, my Master; indeed and of a truth that is the precious truth which can sweeten my sad discomforts," oh, what a bliss it is! All glory be unto the Holy Ghost, who to this day is ever ready to show unto his praying servants the sweetening tree when they come to the bitter streams.

Now that remedy for the healing of Marah's water was a very strange one. Why should a tree sweeten the waters? I do not suppose there was any natural efficacy in the tree, although that would not be altogether impossible, since there are trees, so travelers tell us, which have been used in the sweetening of waters. There is in South Africa a certain river, which water cannot be drunk until branches of a certain tree are placed in it, and then the bitterness which is in the stream is deposited at the bottom, and the water becomes drinkable. The thing is not unnatural nor altogether necessarily supernatural, though I think in this case it was supernatural, for there are no trees found now in the wilderness of Shur that would have the effect of sweetening brackish waters. This was no doubt a miraculous incident, and it was also meant to teach us something. The fruit of the tree of knowledge of good and evil was eaten by our first parents and embittered all; there is a tree of life, the leaves of which are for the healing of the nations. Blessed is he that eats of this tree of life; it shall take away from him the bitterness which the first forbidden fruit brought into the world. A tree is a living thing: may we not learn that there are living principles in true religion which will sweeten our adversities? Mere doctrines may not, but living principles will; these cast into our troubles will assuage our grief.

Best of all, may not this tree cut down be an emblem of the Savior? A glorious tree indeed was he, with spreading branches, and top reaching to heaven--but he must suffer the axe for our sakes; and now, to-day, contemplating his atoning sacrifice, and by faith resting in him, the troubles of life and the troubles of death are sweetened by his dear cross, which, though it be a bitter tree in itself, is the antidote for all the bitterness that comes upon us here and hereafter.

That remedy was most effective. When they cut down the tree, and put it into the water, it turned the water sweet--they could drink of it; and let me assure you, that in the case of our trouble, the cross is a most effective sweetener. Shall I put the tree into the water for a minute, and then ask you to drink Have you been suffering pain, or any other form of tribulation? I will lay the cross asoak in it for a minute, and your first reflection will be--"In all this that I am called to suffer there is not even a single particle of punishment for my sin; God has punished Christ, consequently he cannot punish me: to punish two for one offense would be unjust, therefore there is nothing penal in all that I am suffering." I do not know of any reflection more consoling than this, that my sorrow is not laid on me by a judge, nor inflicted on me as the result of divine anger. There is not a drop of wrath in a riverful of a believer's grief. Does not that take the bitterness out of affliction and make it sweet? And then the reflection goes further. Since Christ has died for me, I am God's dear child; and now if I suffer, all my suffering comes from my Father's hand--nay, more, from my Father's heart. He loves me, and therefore makes me suffer; not because he does not love, but because he does love does he thus afflict me. In every stripe I see another token of paternal love. This it is to sweeten Marah's waters indeed.

Then will come the next reflection--that a Father's love is joined with infinite wisdom, and that, therefore, every ingredient in the bitter cup is measured out drop by drop, and grain by grain, and there is not one pang too many ever suffered by an heir of heaven. The cross is not only weighed to the pound but to the ounce ay, to the lowest conceivable grain. You shall not have one half a drop of grief more than is absolutely needful for your good and God's glory. And does not this also sweeten the cross, that it is laid on us by infinite wisdom, and by a Father's hand?

Ravishing, indeed, is the reflection in the midst of all our grief and suffering, that Jesus Christ suffers with us. In all thine affliction, O member of the body, the Head is still a sharer. Deep are the sympathies of the Redeemer, acute, certain, quick, infallible; he never forgets his saints.

All the while the Lord lays his chastening hand upon his servants they may be cheered by this reflection, that in this he is making them conformable unto Christ. What should they know of

Gethsemane if they had no sweat of pain? What should they know of the passion if they never had to cry, "I thirst," or "My God, my God, why hast thou forsaken me?" They were poor scholars in the school of Christ's sufferings if they endured no sufferings themselves; and it is a blessed thing, a sweet thing to drink of his cup, and to be baptised with his baptism.

Moreover, when the child of God is in his right state, it is always enough for him that his condition is the result of his Father's will. Is it God's will? Is it Christ's will? Then it is my will. How could I dare to wish anything to be otherwise than divine love appoints?

I do not know but what it will become sometimes to the Christ a subject of joy that Marah is bitter. For suppose Marah had been sweet, then, Moses had not prayed to God, and then the tree had not been cut down, and they had never known the power of God to sweeten bitter waters. It must be an awful thing to live an unafflicted life on earth. You say it must be a very delightful thing. I have no doubt it may be from some aspects; but a person who has had no sickness, how can he have a sympathetic heart? What service can he render in cheering the people of God? If you never had any trials, I should suppose, unless something very extraordinary happened, that you would become harsh, and untender; I am afraid some would grow brutal, coarse, hard of heart. Who wishes, where others have to suffer, to claim an immunity from a blessing which brings rich consolations with it, and works eternal benefits? Beloved, this is ever one thing that sweetens Marah that it afterwards bringeth forth the comfortable fruits of righteousness. Our trials are not sent to us alone and by themselves; there is a quantum suff. grace sent with them, by which they are made available as means to sanctify us, and make us meet to be partakers of the inheritance of the saints in light.

I will not keep you much longer upon this point, but I must notice, that while I have shown you that the remedy is very efficacious, it is something more than efficacious: it is transcendant. The water was bitter, but it became absolutely sweet. The same water that was bitter became sweet, and the grace of God, by leading us into contemplations that spring out of the cross of Christ, can make our trials themselves to become pleasant to us. It is a triumph of grace in the heart when we not only acquiesce in trouble, but even rejoice in it. "We glory in tribulations also: knowing that tribulation worketh patience." It is a grand thing when we can truly say that as to the rod of the covenant we would not escape it if we might. It becomes in the judgment of wisdom so good a thing to be tried, that though we would not seek it yet we accept it with something more than readiness, and the bitter thing becomes sweet to us.

Let me say, and have done with this part of the subject, that the remedy which is suggested to us by a spiritualizing of text, is efficacious for all trials, and will be found especially so for the bitter waters of death at the last. With all that can be said about death it is not a pleasant subject for contemplation, and needs to be viewed in connection with covenant consolations. Certain brethren buoy themselves up with the hope of escaping death by the second Advent. I am not certain that they are wiser than David who did not hope to omit the valley of the shadow of death, but trusted that he should fear no evil therein, because the rod and staff would be his stay. The death of Christ robs death of its terrors. The prospect of the resurrection and the certainty of immortality make us say, "Surely the bitterness of death is past!"

Be it remembered, that if the cross avails to sweeten all the bitterness of our mortal life, and even the last bitterness of death, it is assuredly available this morning to sweeten the bitterness of our present sorrow. Did you drink the quassia-cup this morning before you came here? Do you feel desponding at this moment, my brother, my sister? Go to your Savior at once, view him suffering on your behalf, behold the completion of your reconciliation to God, mark the security of your soul through the finished work of your glorious Surety, take down your harps from the willows, put away your ashes, ask the Lord to anoint you with the oil of joy instead of mourning, and even at the waters of Marah lift up your song again, and let the timbrel still be heard. "Sing unto the Lord, for he hath triumphed gloriously: Marah's bitterness hath he turned to sweetness, he hath cut down the mighty tree which he gave for us, and which yielded itself to the axe for us, and into the bitter stream the tree is cast, and now henceforth, O Marah, thou art sweet indeed." Did you come here this morning as Naomi when she returned to her city and said, "Call me not Naomi, call me Mara: for the Almighty hath dealt very bitterly with me." Ah, when she dandled on her knee and held in her fond bosom the child of Ruth and Boaz, the joy of her old age, she was glad to think the neighbors had not changed her name, and she was willing enough to be called Naomi still. Call not yourself Marah, but remember the new name which the Lord hath named upon you. The bitter pool itself call it not Marah; be not so ready to affix names of sad memorials, your griefs are apt enough to gall your memory; do not aid them to sting you. Call the well by another name; forget Marah, and remember Jehovah Rophi, the Lord that healeth both thee and the waters. Record the mercy rather than the sorrow, and give thanks unto the Most High.

Now, in closing, somebody will say, "This is a very curious missionary sermon." Yes, but you see I did not appoint the missionary sermon for to-day: my brethren did that, and certainly I did not arrange my own sickness, so as to make it fall on this day. How can I dance to the sound of the timbrel when I am feeble and sad? If I had the choosing of my own state of health and mind, I would have the choosing of my own texts, and make them always suitable to the occasions as they arise; but I am obliged to preach what I can preach, and as I know pretty well the flavor of Marah, and a little about the sweetness which the healing tree can give it, I can only tell you what I know by experience.

But it is a good missionary sermon for all that. Let us show you how. Here is A SUGGESTION OF COMPASSION.

Brethren, all the world over, the heathen have trials, bitternesses, woes. I said that Christ have peculiar woes, but the dark places of the earth have direr sorrows. Some nations are devastated with war; others are tormented with diabolical customs and rites: their actions even towards themselves through their superstition are brutal. I may well liken the world that lieth in darkness to a thirsty caravan gathered around Marah's well where the water is too bitter to drink. Oh, the woes, the woes of mankind! High are the Andes, lofty the Himalayas, but the woes of the sons of Adam are higher, huger still. The Ganges and the Indus, and other mighty streams, pour their floods into the ocean; but what mighty deep could contain the torrents of human grief? A very deluge is the sorrow as well as the sin of man. And, my brethren, the heathen know nothing of the healing tree, the tree cut down of old, which still hath power to sweeten mortal misery. You know it, you have your trials, and you surmount them by the appeals you make to your Lord, and by the power of his consolations; but alas! these sons of darkness have your griefs, and more, but they have not your Comforter. For them the deluge, but not the ark; for them the tempest, but not the refuge. And you are so sure that you have that which would cheer them: no doubt passes across your mind as to the gospel. These are wavering times in which some professors, and even some teachers, almost believe, that the gospel is but one theory of many, and will have to stand its test, and, in all probability, will fail as many human systems of thought have done. You think not so; you believe that God's gospel is a verity, a revelation of Jehovah Heaven and earth may pass away, but not his word, his Christ, his decree, his covenant. You know that you have a tree that can heal the bitter fountains. No doubt comes across your mind as to that: what then? By common humanity, much more by the tender movements of the grace of God upon your souls, I conjure you present this remedy to those who need it, and who need it so much. Will anything suffice as a substitute for it? Is there anywhere on earth another healing tree beside that which fell beneath the axe at Calvary? Are there other leaves for the healing of the nations? On the seven-hilled city of Rome, grows there a tree that can heal man's diseases? No; it is a deadly upas. Cut it down, and burn the very roots thereof. Amongst the fancies of idolatry are there any inventions of man that can cool his fevered brow and sooth his griefs? Does Mohammedanism offer hopes for eternity that can light up the grave to an awakened sinner? Are there thoughts of bliss in idolatry calculated to cheer the sepulcher? All religions answer, "Comforts are not in us." It is only at the cross, it is only by Jesus crucified that the world can be healed. Hitherto little has been accomplished compared with our desires; and in contrast to our ambitions, next to nothing; but faith, darting beyond the things that are seen, flying into the presence-chamber of God, can behold him writing with the eternal pen, "All flesh shall see the salvation of God;" and she is sure that the tree will sweeten the waters yet. Come, brethren, let your faith prove itself by your works. Help to-day--to-day, by your gifts; help to-morrow--to-morrow, by your prayers. Help, some of you, by consecrating yourselves to mission labor. There is a prayer I mean to continue to offer until it is answered, that God would pour out on this church a missionary spirit. I want to see our young men devoting themselves to the work, some that will not be afraid to venture and preach Jesus Christ in the regions beyond. I have not much faith in missionary societies; it gets less, I must protest, each year; yet we must never put aside one instrumentality until we have a better ready. If the Lord would send the living fire through the churches of England, if he would send from on high a divine impulse, we should see starting up here and there men who would say: "Here are we: send us." The Spirit of God will say, "Separate me Paul and Barnabas for the work," and when this is done I look to see far happier days.

We have sweetened the waters a little; no more the suttee burns; the African is free; the slave-ship crosses no more the deep. In some regions exterminating wars have ceased; the white dove of peace flies where the raven of war was seen. Glory be to God. A few leaves cast into the waters have done this. Let us bear a whole Christ and a whole gospel amongst the nations, and lay the tree in this Marah, until at last the whole world shall drink of the sweet waters of divine love, and God shall be all in all. God bless you, beloved, for Jesus' sake. Amen.

PORTION OF SCRIPTURE READ BEFORE SERMON--Exodus 15.

The Pastor's Parting Blessing

A Sermon (No. 988)
Delivered by
C. H. SPURGEON,
At the Metropolitan Tabernacle, Newington
BEFORE LEAVING HOME FOR A JOURNEY

"The grace of our Lord Jesus Christ be with you all. Amen." - Romans 16:24.

THE CHRISTIAN IS A MAN of generous actions, but his wishes go far beyond his deeds. Where he cannot be beneficent he is benevolent. If he cannot actually accomplish good for all, yet he anxiously desires it. If it be not in his power to confer grace upon any, yet he prays that God would give his grace to all the brotherhood. His heart entertains thousands, though his house might be overfull with ten; his liberal desires feed nations, even though his purse be so scant that he cannot afford more than a penny for a poor child. God, whose providence limits our ability, has set no measure to our willingness. Our wishes may be boundless though our powers are contracted, and this will be good for ourselves and not useless to others.

Christianity never came into the world to make individual professors of it isolated, like the icebergs which float away on the wide sea in solitary terribleness; neither is it intended that we should be so anxious for our own salvation as to be indifferent to the welfare of others. True religion is not a separating and repelling force, but rather, like attraction, it draws individual atoms into one body and holds them together. It does not shiver to fragments, but welds into one. It is a loadstone, not a whirlwind. God in his grace gathers together in one body in Christ Jesus all his scattered ones, and the same Spirit who constrains us to love God leads us to love our brother also.

A loving spirit, when it can actually do no more, naturally seizes upon the ever open outlet of good wishes, benedictions, and intercessions. Thus the great heart of the apostle relieved itself; though he would have been willing to lay down his life for the brethren, yet he did not think it idle to give them his blessing, nor did they reject it as worthless because it cost him nothing. It was meet that he who had in so many ways proved his sincere love to the saints should in his letter give utterance to it by pronouncing inspired blessings upon them Thus wrote the apostle of the Gentiles to those he longed to serve; "The grace of our Lord Jesus Christ be with you all."

We have dropped, to a great extent, the custom of having the benediction pronounced by the minister upon the people. The minister, as a rule, rather turns it into a prayer than pronounces it as his own personal blessing. I am not certain that it is a great improvement. The dread of anything like priestism has led us to this custom. It may be, however, that in avoiding an evil we have missed a good. Are benedictions sinful or vain? Are the blessings of good men of no value? Can we no more say, "Peace be to this house," and hope that our peace shall rest upon it? May no Jacob nowadays bless the two sons of a beloved Joseph? Will it be a mere form if an Isaac should invoke a blessing on his descendants, or a departing servant of God, like Moses, pronounce a benediction on his people? I confess I would not treat lightly my father's blessing or the benediction of my mother; and though neither father nor mother can by their mere wish confer anything upon us, yet who would wish them to depart this life without having bequeathed us the legacy of their blessing? Like Joseph, you may bring your lads to receive their grandsire's blessing if the old man be yet alive, nor need you suspect yourself of being superstitious. Many there are who have had no other heritage than a father's blessing, and have counted themselves rich therein. Now, if the blessing of a natural father and mother may be considered valuable without attributing too much to men, so I think may the blessing of those spiritual parents who have been made useful to our souls. I was reading in the life of Caesar Malan an incident which touched my heart, and I feel no scruple in quoting it in this connection. In travelling through one of the valleys of Switzerland he met with a woman who told him that her father was dying, but that he was comforted and cheered by reading a little book. Being unknown by any one in the village, Malan stepped into the room and sat by the dying man's bed, and was delighted to find that the book which had led to the man's conversion was written by himself. His son, who was his companion, thus describes the scene:--"The old man exclaimed, Ah! had I not been aged and infirm, I should long ago have gone there to see the good

Mr. Malan. Look here, sir, you cannot think how earnestly I have entreated the Lord that I might see him before I died. For a long time I thought he would grant my desire, but I'm afraid I shall have to give it up.' I stole a glance at my father, who was sitting silently looking at his hands. What is the name of the book you refer to?' he suddenly enquired as he raised his head. Stay,' was the reply, here it is, it's always by me,' and he drew from under his pillow a well-worn copy of one of the earliest editions of my father's hymns, and handed it to my father. Do you sing any of these, then?' asked my father as he turned over the leaves. Oh, Jeannette knows some of them; she often sings them to me, and I derive pleasure and profit whenever I hear them,' adding, as though speaking to himself, If I could only see the dear gentleman who wrote those beautiful hymns; he must be a good Christian.' Listen, brother,' said my father, this young gentleman and I have just come from Geneva.' You have come from Geneva? then perhaps you have seen Mr. Malan?' Certainly, I have; we all know him well and I can assure you that if he were here he would remind you that he has only been a feeble and imperfect instrument of good to you; and he would speak to you, above all, not of himself, a poor sinner as you are, but of the eternal grace and perfection of our blessed Lord.' The conversation lasted a few moments longer; my father prayed; then, when we had sung together one of the hymns which Jeannette knew, he prepared to leave, telling her that he was to preach the next day, Sunday, at Motiers. When he had got to the door, however, he stopped; and returning once more to the bed where the old man was lying with folded hands, said to him with emotion, My Father, God himself, to whom you will so soon depart, has granted your prayer. I am Malan of Geneva; your brother in the faith of the blessed Savior.' The poor old man, fixing his streaming eyes upon him in a long and ardent gaze, and slowly raising his trembling hands, exclaimed, Bless me, bless me before I die! You, whom I have so long prayed God to send to me, bless me now that I have had the joy of seeing you.' Falling on his knees at the bedside, my father replied, in tones which betrayed his deep feeling, You ought rather to bless me, for you are old enough to be my father; but all blessing comes from God alone; let us once more ask it of him together.' And folding in his arms the lowly brother, whom he felt he should never see again till they met in the better country, he invoked upon him the peace which Jesus gives,' and we left the hamlet."

I am ready to confess that there are those to whom I fool: with the same respect; without the slightest worship of men or care about mental attainments, or mere office, I recognize those from whom I would fain receive a blessing. Priestcraft assumes to be the divinely appointed channel of communicating with heaven, and this monstrous presence is so abominable that we would sooner have the curse than the blessing of a man hardened to such imposture; but men who live near to God, and have power with him in prayer, do, without assuming it, become by their prayers and fervent wishes the means of procuring many blessings for those whom they bear upon their hearts. I have even now ringing in my ears the fervent benediction of a venerable minister whose daily prayers for me, and reading of my sermons, constrained him to make a considerable journey that he might in person pronounce a blessing upon my head. Job thought it no little thing that the blessing of him that was ready to perish came upon him, and that when the eye saw him then it blessed him. Good men in their benedictions are moved to give us something more than words, for they mean what they say; and they appeal to heaven to make true their wishes, and their wishes being prayers minted in another form become current coin of the realm, and greatly enrich us, for they bear the approving stamp of heaven upon them.

I look upon the apostle's words, though they are venerable with years, as dropping heaven's own dew upon us to-night. I hear their mellow tones ringing all along the centuries and scattering blessings right through the ages. Their music is not silent, nor is it impotent at this hour: "The grace of our Lord Jesus Christ be with you all" is Paul's present and ever new blessing; he being dead yet sneaketh, and his Lord yet hears his holy prayer. Long has the benediction lain in the epistle like the wheat in the Egyptian catacomb, but there is a vitality in it yet.; lo, it buds and brings forth good to us after the lapse of eighteen centuries. May every one of us feel an unction from the Lord attending these words. May the apostle bless us now, yea, better may the apostle and High Priest of our profession pronounce anew this benediction over us.

Let us now analyse the text itself. The first thing we will speak upon is this,--what is meant by the grace of our Lord Jesus Christ? secondly, with whom is it to be?--the apostle says, "Be with you all;" and thirdly, and what will be the effect if it be with us all?

I. Let us first enquire WHAT IS THE GRACE OF OUR LORD JESUS CHRIST WHICH THE APOSTLE WOULD HAVE TO BE WITH US ALL? He repeats the expression verbatim in his epistles to the Corinthians, and to the Philippians, and also in his second letter to the Thessalonians. He closes each of these epistles with precisely the same benediction, therefore he felt it to be fitting and weighty. Does he mean by this "grace of our Lord Jesus Christ," the grace which was revealed in Christ the Savior; that grace of God which shone in the gift of a Savior to the sons of men, that grace which was displayed in the coming of Christ to be bone of our bone, and flesh of our flesh, which was manifested in the whole life of Christ on earth, was revealed especially in the death of Christ, and which is still to be seen since his resurrection and ascension in his intercession, and in his standing as our representative before the Father's throne? Grace was gloriously revealed in the person of Christ when he became the incarnate God, and none can consider him as uniting in one person God and man without discerning much love, and perceiving that it was meant to make way for still more clear displays of mercy. Does not the benediction desire for us a part in the blessing which lies couched in the Messiah's person, in whom all nations are blessed?

Does the apostle mean the grace which comes to us through Christ as well as that which is shown to us in Christ? Our Lord, as it were, took out of the river-bed of grace the great rock which blocked up the water courses, and now along the wide and open channel--

"Immortal joys come streaming down,
Joys like his griefs, immense, unknown."

Christ did not create the Father's love to us, the elect were loved of God before all worlds, and Christ is the gift of that love, not the cause of it. Calvary did not procure the Father's love to us, but the love of God towards us could not, by reason of our sins, and the penalty due thereto, come to us so as to be enjoyed by us. It could not bring to us the blessings which we now possess until Jesus had finished transgression, and made an end of sin. Both the grace implied in the sending of the Messiah, and the grace which flows to us through him, are here intended.

Does the apostle also mean the grace which comes to us WITH Christ?--by which I mean those peculiar blessings which come to souls who abide in Christ, who commune with him, walk with him, work for him, and are raised up together, and made to sit together in heavenly places in him; who are not only saved, but something more; who are not drowning men barely landed on the shore, and hardly possessed of life, but who have life abundantly, walk in the light of God's countenance, and go from strength to strength. If so, there is an exquisite sweetness of meaning in his benediction. May it be richly fulfilled in each of us. May our union to Jesus be so clearly apprehended that we may experience no stinted measure of vital energy, but the rather may be filled with all the fullness of God. Surely Paul means nothing less than this.

But he intended more yet, for his is no niggardly invocation. Grace in Christ, grace through Christ, and grace with Christ--put these together, and even then you have not grasped the whole. He desires for us all the grace that is in anyway connected with Christ; for you will have remarked that in the close of the second of Corinthians, where he gives the same benediction, he extends it, "The grace of the Lord Jesus Christ, and the love of God, and the communion of the Holy Ghost, be with you all." Here he gives it the shorter form, but he doubtless intended it to comprehend all the rest. He really wishes that the one comprehensive blessing of the divine unity, even all the triple blessing of the sacred Trinity, may abide with all those who by faith were one with Christ, and therefore were beloved of the apostolic soul. "The grace of our Lord Jesus Christ" then includes all the grace secured to us in the eternal covenant. In many of his epistles, the apostle sums up with a shorter word than our text, and yet in some respects a fuller one, "grace be with you all." You have this in the Colossians, in the first epistle to Timothy, in Titus, and in the Hebrews. He says, "Grace be with you all," without mentioning any person of the Godhead. So that "the grace of our Lord Jesus Christ" is synonymous with grace as such; and comprehends all the various displays of grace which are in other passages of Scripture referred to the various persons of the Godhead. He wishes the saints all the grace they need, all the grace they can desire; all the grace the Infinite God can give. How truly do I echo his great prayer that all grace may be with you all.

Coming to particulars more closely. When it is the desire of our heart that the grace of our Lord Jesus Christ may be with you all, we mean, first, may the love of Jesus Christ be with you, and may you know that you have it. May it be so with you that you may distinctly and beyond all doubt know that Jesus loves you, and the fact being ascertained, may you drink deep into the fullness of its meaning. May you be ravished with the assurance that the ever-blessed Son of God has set his affection upon you, has loved you from before the foundation of the world, loves you now even as the Father loves him, and will love you when heaven and earth shall, like a scroll, be rolled up, and like an outworn vesture be put away. O that you all might he in such a condition, that the love of Christ might shine full into your souls, a noon-tide without a solitary cloud, a summer without a single blight. May you know of a surety, by the witness of the Holy Ghost, that you have passed from death unto life, and that the love of God is shed abroad within your souls. What a happy church would it be were all the members in such a condition! But, alas, we see one fearful, another doubting, and a third declining; here is one living at a distance from Christ, and another saying,, "O that I knew where I might find him!" May the grace of our Lord Jesus Christ, in the sense of a conscious enjoyment of his love be the habitual possession of your hearts and minds.

Paul intends also as much as this,--may the mercy as well as the love of our Lord Jesus Christ be with you! May that mercy be shown to you by the full pardon of all your sins, and your knowledge that they are pardoned. May your conscience be purged from dead works, and not merely cleansed, but cleansed so that you may know it to be clean. The great mercy is to have no suspicion that sin is left upon you, but to be certain that every transgression of every sort has been for ever put away through the precious blood which cleanses from all sin. Alas! there are many Christians who even in their prayers do not appear to understand or distinguish between themselves and the unconverted. I believe it to be our duty to ask for pardon every day. Our Lord in the model prayer teaches us to say, "Forgive us our trespasses as we forgive them that trespass against us;" but we should not confound that petition of a child to its father with the first supplication for pardon which befitted us as aliens before we were brought nigh. As guilty sinners we stood before the judge, but now we are no longer criminals, for there is now no condemnation to them that are in Christ Jesus. We need not say with Peter in his enthusiastic folly, "Wash not my feet only, but also my hands and my head," for the Master tells us that we have been washed and are clean, and therefore we need only to wash our feet, for we are, in him, clean every whit. May you not, therefore, come before him with what is too often used as a mere parrot cry, "Lord, have mercy upon us miserable sinners." If you believers are miserable sinners you ought not to be. You are sinners, but you ought not to be miserable. You have been forgiven; you are justified by faith in Christ Jesus. Is all this nothing? How can you ignore it, and speak of yourself still as you would have spoken before you were saved? Is the Lord's pardon nothing that you complain still of being condemned? Do you despise the divine forgiveness? You are a child of God, and do you still use the language of a slave, and feel no liberty in your soul? I fear that what is imagined to be humility is a mingle-mangle of hypocrisy and unbelief. If you are saved it is sheer cant to call yourself a miserable sinner; you ought to be one of the happiest of beings, and rejoice that the mercy of our Lord Jesus Christ abides with you.

Furthermore, beloved, may you be the subjects of Christ's work constantly. That will give yet another meaning to this benediction. The Lord Jesus Christ, by his Spirit, is carrying on in believers daily a purifying work; for he sits as a refiner and he purifies the sons of Levi. He is like a refiner's fire, and like fullers' soap. Let us pray that, however trying it may be to us, and whatever rough providences it may involve, the grace of our Lord Jesus Christ may be with us all in this respect. May our prayer be, "Refining fire, go through my heart!" Let the winnowing fan be used; let our chaff be driven away, there is not a particle of it we would wish to retain. We desire to be sanctified--spirit, soul, and body--through him who leads his people without the camp that they may be separated unto himself. May we walk in the light as he is in the light, and so have fellowship one with another, and may the blood of Jesus Christ, God's dear Son, cleanse us from all sin.

May the benediction rest upon you also in another manner. May you brethren, be possessors of Christ's peace. One of the benedictions frequently used by the apostle expressly mentions peace. "Grace, mercy, and peace be with you." Where Christ is, peace reigns within; he is the peacemaker, yea, peace itself. Conscience is quieted, the heart rests in God, the whole man casts anchor, the barque has reached its haven when it has come to the Well-beloved. O that you may enjoy this grace of Christ, for it was his prerogative to say, "Peace I leave with you, my peace I give unto you." It was his delight to pronounce upon his disciples the word, "Peace be unto you." May the peace of God, which passeth all understanding, keep your hearts and minds by Christ Jesus. If you are troubled with family concerns, may you roll your burden upon the Lord and find rest; or if you are vexed about your past transgressions, may you confess the sin unto the Lord and hear his blood speak peace to your soul. Whatever it is that troubles you, may he comfort you and give you his peace, the deep, unruffled calm which reigns in his own bosom. If there be one gem of grace which beyond all others especially belongs to the Lord Jesus, it is the lovely pearl of peace. He is the Lord and giver of peace, the Prince of Peace, and the messenger of the covenant of peace. Brethren, may we live in peace with God, with men, and with ourselves. We all say "Amen" to that prayer.

Would not Paul also desire for us that we may exhibit in ourselves the grace which shone so brightly in Christ, and was seen by men and angels to the glory of God the Father? You will never have grace, dear friends, in the same measure as the Lord Jesus had it (rather let me correct myself, for he had grace without measure), but you may receive and exhibit the same grace in your measure. O that you and I may have a high degree of it! Grace displayed itself in the Lord Jesus in a character absolutely perfect, in which not one of the virtues was absent or exaggerated, and in which not a single fault could be found. You can depict the character of John, for a prominent excellence is visible; you can describe the characteristics of Peter; you can give an idea of Paul for each of these is like a separate gem, and each one has its own especial brightness and color, and I may add each one has its own peculiar flaw; but when you come to the altogether lovely One your descriptive powers fail you, for he is like the high priest's breastplate in which all the jewels met in harmony. The excellences of all the excellent are in him, and none of the flaws. In him all perfections meet to make up one perfection. All the spices, the myrrh, the aloes, the cassia, the sweet cinnamon, and whatever else may be grateful to God and to holy men--all these divinely compounded with the art of the apothecary, and well-balanced as to the proportions are to be found in one rare anointing oil upon the person of our Well-beloved. O may that grace be with you which was poured upon our glorious Head and continues to distil to the skirts of his priestly garments. May his sacred unction anoint and perfume us all! It was poured on Jesus that it might drop on us. He received this fullness that we might receive out of him grace for grace. He does not possess grace that he may store it up for himself, for he needs it not; but he has all fullness in himself on purpose for us, that we may partake thereof both now and for ever. O that we may manifest it in our lives both public and private, in the emotions of our hearts, and the words of our mouths. May men in all the actions of our lives observe that we are heirs of grace by our gracious conversation, knowing us as a tree is known by its fruit. May this grace be in you, and abound that you may not be barren nor unprofitable.

I am far from having brought out all the various shades of meaning which lie within this ancient benediction; for as the Holy Spirit, like the sun, shines on this crystal text, it flashes with all the colors of the rainbow. It is a very full, rich, and large benediction. Even Aaron himself could not pronounce a fuller blessing. The Lord fulfill it to every one of you, according to the riches of his glory by Christ Jesus!

II. Secondly, WITH WHOM IS THIS GRACE TO BE? "With you all." The apostle meant with all the saints. He did not actually limit it in words to the saints, but he evidently intended to be so understood; for he was writing "to all that be in Rome, beloved of God, called to be saints," and to them he said, "grace be with you all." We will not go beyond the apostolic wish, neither will we stop short of it. This moment I say to you, "the grace of our Lord Jesus Christ be with you all"--with all the members of this church, and all my fellow-servants in Christ Jesus. The like grace be with all the churches, with all the chosen of God in every land; but at this present I may be permitted to utter this as my personal and especial wish for you my beloved flock at this time, when for a season I shall be absent from you. The demands of health call me away, and what shall I leave with you, my dear companions, my own children, my reverend elder brethren, my beloved fellow soldiers? What better word shall be the last to salute your ear from my lips till I return to you? How can my affection frame a fitter utterance than that which fell from Paul's pen, when he added to the apostolic benediction his own personal love, and wrote to the Corinthians, "The grace of our Lord Jesus Christ is with you; my love be with you all in Christ Jesus?"

Now, why with you all? Is it not because you all need it? There is not one among you who can do without the grace of our Lord Jesus Christ. You experienced Christians are greatly in danger when you think your mountain stands firm and will never be moved. You wise and intelligent believers are in sore peril when you dream that you can battle with error apart from your Master. Conscious weakness is our true strength. "When I am weak then am I strong." The boldest, bravest, wisest, most judicious, and most experienced among you, need the grace of our Lord Jesus Christ, and certainly the babes in grace and the weaklings of the flock require it no less.

More delightful still, is it to remember that you all may have it. You all, having believed in Jesus, have him to be your own, and you may surely have his grace. He who gave you Christ has virtually given you all the grace that is in Christ Jesus. Indeed we know from the best authority that grace was given us in Christ Jesus ere the world began.

And, beloved, there is no grace which you may not have, no grace which you ought to be content to go without. If a line should be drawn in Christian experience, and a decree should be passed that such and such a Christian should never advance beyond that mark, you might feel very unhappy, and yet some of you have drawn such a line for yourselves, and you are not unhappy. It is grievous to see how we stunt and dwarf ourselves, and appear to be content with a very poor and feeble form of spiritual life. May the Holy Spirit breathe into your hearts a higher ambition, for rest assured if you do not possess the whole land of Canaan, it is because you are too idle to drive out the Hivites and Jebusites, for there is not one of all the clan but what you may conquer, though they have chariots of iron. There is not a brook that cows with milk and honey but you may drink of it, if you have but faith and prayer enough to win it for yourselves. He giveth more grace; seek to enjoy it.

My dear brethren in office, my esteemed deacons and elders, I pray that you may have the grace of our Lord Jesus Christ abundantly, so that you may walk before us as becometh fathers in Israel, that you may be ensamples to the flock, that none of the weaker sort may see in you any occasion of stumbling, but much that may lead them forward in the divine life. You who are especially the workers among us, you Sabbath-school teachers, you who have the conduct of our adult classes, you who preach for the Master in the streets, or go from house to house with your tracts, I pray that the grace of our Lord Jesus be with you all. Whatever your form of work may be, it will come to nought without his grace; but you may have it, and I pray you be not content unless you possess it abundantly.

Among you there are members of the church who are very poor; there are in proportion probably more poor among us than in another church of our order and standing, and for this I devoutly thank God, for I can hardly conceive a church to be rich in grace which has not in it many of the Lord's poor. But this I pray, that the grace of our Lord Jesus Christ may be with you, who are the sons and daughters of poverty, to enable you to be patient, to sanctify your trials, to make your homes bright with the presence of the Lord, and to keep you from envy and murmuring. May your rooms be palaces to you, because the King visits you and feast you with his love.

May that same grace, however, be with the few among us who may be said to be rich, for how much grace do the wealthy require, that they may be kept from the temptations which beset their position, and may be delivered from the cankering influence of riches! May the grace of our Lord Jesus Christ be with you, my brethren and sisters, that, consecrating your substance habitually to Christ, it may bring with it many comforts to your souls as well as to your bodies.

May the grace of our Lord Jesus Christ be with you, dear brethren and sisters, who are ripening for heaven; may it be light with you at eventide, and may your rest be glorious. Though near to glory, you know right well that you are still dependent upon grace, and I trust you will abundantly enjoy it. May the grace of our Lord Jesus Christ be with you, young beginners, who have just put on the harness. May you live long in the Christian Church, and serve your Master well. Amidst the temptations of youth, and the trials of manhood, may you stand fast and glorify your Lord.

Some of you are strong in the Lord, and in the power of his might. May the grace of our Lord Jesus Christ be with you to keep you strong. If you have trodden down strength, and have had the hind's feet with which you have stood upon your high places, may you never lose your position, but maintain your joy. And as for you who are doubting and fearing, the timid ones of the flock, may the grace of our Lord Jesus Christ be with you too, for he carrieth the lambs in his bosom, and doth gently lead those that are with young. A bruised reed he will not break, and the smoking flax he will not quench.

While I make the benediction thus as large as the apostle did, let me remind you very affectionately that there is a limit to it. He is speaking to the saints, and to none else. Have you noticed the form this benediction takes in the epistle to Philemon, and in the epistle to the Galatians? There the apostle puts it thus, "The grace of our Lord Jesus Christ be with your spirit." It is only meant, then, for spiritual-minded men, for such as have been born again of the Holy Spirit. Jesus Christ cannot be with the carnal. He will not give the blessing of his presence to those who mind earthly things. When ye have been born again ye can understand the grace of our Lord Jesus Christ, but not till then. May that gracious work of regeneration be wrought in every soul here. The apostle limits it again in his Epistle to the Ephesians. He there utters a desire that the grace of our Lord Jesus Christ may be with "all them that love our Lord Jesus Christ in sincerity." You cannot expect the blessing of Christ to abide with you if you are hypocritical, or formal, or self-deceived. Sincerity is a needful index of the grace of Christ being with you. Do you, dear hearer, in sincerity love Jesus Christ? If you do, may his grace be with you.

One other limit the apostle gives. Let me read it to you. I can never read these words either in public or in private without a conscious shudder, but they demand an attentive consideration by us all. You will find them at the close of the first Epistle to the Corinthians. "The salutation of me Paul with mine own hand. If any man love not the Lord Jesus Christ, let him be Anathema Maran-atha. The grace of our Lord Jesus Christ be with you." What a limitation is this! He pronounces a solemn curse upon those whom he feels he cannot bless, because they are so base as not to love the infinitely loving Jesus. "If any man love not the Lord Jesus Christ, let him be accursed when the Lord cometh," for that is the meaning of the words, "Anathema Maran-atha," "cursed when the Lord cometh," or "As surely cursed as the Lord cometh." Whoever, then, loves not Christ is cursed. Oh! God, save us all from a curse so well deserved; for not to love such a generous Savior, not to love one so lovely and so gracious, not to love one who loved his enemies, and laid down his life for sinners, is in itself to be accursed. That spirit is withered already, Savior, that loves not thee! To be able to withhold its affections from so lovely an object is in itself a doom. God save you from it! May there not be one among you here upon whom that curse may come, but "may the grace of our Lord Jesus Christ be with you all."

III. And now as this must serve for my parting word for some little time, let me explain, in the third place, what will be THE RESULT TO YOU IF THE GRACE OF OUR LORD JESUS CHRIST BE WITH YOU ALL.

First, there will be a blessed consequence to you Godward. As you have this grace of Christ in you you will love God better, you will seek his face oftener; you will pray with more confidence, and more vehemence. You could not have the grace of Christ without being much in prayer, for this eminently distinguished his character. If you have the grace of Christ you will walk with God, even as he did. Your communion with the Father will be closer then heretofore; it will be less interrupted; it will become thorough. O that I might see a church made up wholly of saints who live in habitual intercourse with God! I know it is not so with all in this church. I know there are many out of our four thousand members who walk with God, but I mourn that there are others who follow afar off. May this affectionately-intended remark raise in each heart the personal enquiry, "Lord, is it I?" And if your hearts condemn any of you, may the grace of our Lord Jesus Christ be with you most effectually, that you may amend your ways.

The next beneficial effect will extend to your fellow church-members. If you have the grace of our Lord Jesus Christ with you, you will love each other with a pure heart fervently. You will have compassion one towards another. No one will seek his own, but every man his brother's benefit. Suspicion, harsh judgment, envy, and jealousy will cease. Gossipping and foolish talking will come to an end. Alas! how much these things abound, and what sorrow they cause. When the grace of our Lord Jesus Christ is with us our speech will be to edification. We shall esteem others better than ourselves. We shall rather see their excellences than their faults, while we shall each strive which can be of most service to the rest. "Behold, how good and how pleasant it is for brethren to dwell together in unity!" By this shall all men know that ye are Christ's disciples, if ye have love one towards another. May we be mutually enriched in all spiritual gifts and graces by loving communion in the grace which is in Christ Jesus. Eighteen years and more have we now dwelt together in union and prosperity, and that this same grace may continue with us through twice another eighteen years, if the Lord spare us so long, is my soul's most fervent prayer.

Another admirable result will follow towards your families and yourselves. If the grace of our Lord Jesus Christ be with you, you will personally be much the happier. Your troubles will sit lightly upon you when grace is fully within you. Your joys will have a mellower taste in them than now when they are seasoned with grace. The family altar will become a reality. The servants will find the house a home, and the children will become children of God, when the master and mistress are filled with the grace of our Lord Jesus. Gracious men are a sure blessing to the neighbourhoods in which they live; the sweet perfume of their family piety will blow out at the doors and windows, and spread a balmy influence around. As trades of an ill savor make a whole district nauseous, so saints, who have the sweet savor of Christ in them, render a region fragrant.

Thus a blessing will flow out to the world which lieth in darkness. If the grace of our Lord Jesus Christ be with us, we shall have all our thoughts and feelings towards sinners materially changed. We shall mourn over them with intense compassion. Parents, you will not be able to look upon your unconverted children as you now do, holy sorrow will mingle with natural pleasure. Ah! he is a fine young man; he is growing up, and is quite his mother's joy. Mother, if his soul is unsaved, do not so much as look at him without a tear. "Ah!" says the father, "there is my girl--what a lovely creature she is!" Is she converted? If not, think what a fallen creature she is. Employers, if you have grace you will not go into your factories as you have done, and think of the "hands," but you will have pity on the "souls" therein. Many sensations pass through a man's mind if he stands at a window in Cheapside and sees the rush of the living river. It strikes me that the flow of our crowded streets is one of the most wonderful sights in the whole world. There go the thousands, tramp, tramp, tramp, on, on, on, without a pause. Thoughtful men watch the stream and calculate this and that, according to the manner of statistics; but the right-minded Christian, contemplating the scene, has this consideration uppermost, "All these are immortal. How many, or how few of them, are on the road to bliss, and how many are heaping up wrath against the day of wrath." Then will he breathe the prayer involuntarily, "Lord, have mercy upon this guilty city; save the myriads of this modern Nineveh, and let transgressors learn thy ways." Oh! if the grace of our Lord Jesus Christ were with us, we should, like the Savior, often burst into tears over London, as he did over Jerusalem. We should not trifle, as we now do, with opportunities of doing good. We should speak to ones and twos if we could reach no more, and Jesus' love would be our theme.

Time compels me to cease, but ere I leave you, my beloved flock, I solemnly pronounce this benediction upon you:--"The peace of our Lord Jesus Christ be with you all." And my heart says, Amen, Amen, Amen.

PORTION OF SCRIPTURE READ BEFORE SERMON--Romans 16.

P.S.--During our absence, we trust our ever-affectionate friends, both hearers and readers, will care for our various works and see that they do not lack pecuniary means. The College, the Orphanage, and the Colportage are always at work, and expending considerable sums. Mr. Blackshaw, Secretary, Tabernacle, Newington, will receive and acknowledge any aid rendered. To the God of Providence, who supplies our needs through the willing offerings of his people, we look confidently. There will be no alteration in the publication of the Sermons during our absence. We have arranged that a Sermon shall appear each week, as usual.

A Last Look-Out

A Sermon (No. 989)
Delivered by
C. H. SPURGEON,
At the Metropolitan Tabernacle, Newington

"The time of my departure is at hand." - 2 Timothy 4:6.

SO NEAR, SO VERY NEAR THE CHANGE--his removal from this to another world; and so very conscious of it; yet Paul looked back with calm satisfaction; he looked forward with sweet assurance; and he looked round with deepest interest on the mission that had engaged his life. As you must have noticed while we were reading the chapter, in his case "the ruling passion was strong in death." Writing what he well knows is the last letter he shall ever write, its main topic is care for the church of God--anxiety for the promotion of the truth--zeal for the furtherance of the gospel. When he is dead, and gone from the post of service, the scene of suffering, the field of enterprise, on whom shall his mantle fall? He desires that in Timothy he may find a worthy successor, strong in the faith, sincere of heart, and having dauntless courage withal, one who will wield the sword and hold the banner when his hand is palsied in death. Men have usually shown us what lies at the bottom of their heart when they have come to die. Often their last expiring expressions have been indicative of their entire character. Certainly you have before you in the last sentences of Paul's pen a fair epitome of his entire life. He is trusting in the Savior; he is anxious to show his love for that Savior. The welfare of the Christian church and the advancement of the holy cause of the gospel are uppermost in his mind. May it be yours and mine to live wholly for Christ, and to die also for him. May this ever be foremost in our thoughts, "How can I advance the kingdom of our Lord and Savior? By what means can I bless his church and people?" It is very beautiful to observe the way in which Paul describes his death in this verse. According to our translation he speaks of it as an offering. "I am now ready," saith he, "to be offered." If we accept this version he may be supposed to mean that he felt as one standing like a bullock or a lamb, ready to be laid on an altar. He foresaw he would die a martyr's death. He knew he could not be crucified as his brother Peter had been, for a Roman citizen was, as a rule, exempt from that ignominious death. He expected to die in some other manner. Probably he guessed it would be by the sword, and so he describes himself as waiting for the sacrificial knife to be used, that he might be presented as a sacrifice. So I say the words of our translation would lead us to think. But the original is far more instructive. He here likens himself, in the Greek, not to an offering, but to the drink-offering. Every Jew would know what that meant. When there was a burnt-sacrifice offered, the bullock or the victim then slain was the main part of the sacrifice. But sometimes there was a little, what if I say an unimportant, supplement added to that sacrifice--a little oil and a little wine were poured on to the altar or the bullock, and thus a drink-offering was said to be added to the burnt-offering. Now, Paul does not venture to call himself an offering,--Christ is his offering. Christ is, so to speak, the sacrifice on the altar. He likens himself only to that little wine and oil poured out as a supplement thereto, not necessary to its perfection, but tolerated in performing a vow, or allowed in connection with a free will offering, as you will find if you refer at leisure to the fifteenth chapter of Numbers, from the fourth to the eighth verses. The drink-offering was thus a kind of addendum, by which the person who gave it showed his thankfulness. So Paul is resolved to show his thankfulness to Christ, the great sacrifice, and he is willing that his blood should be poured as a drink-offering on the altar where his Lord and Master was the great burnt-offering. He rejoices when he can say, "I am ready to be presented as a drink-offering unto God."

We have mainly to do with the second description which he gives of his death. What does he say when the hour that this grim monster must be grappled with is at hand? I do not find him sad. Those who delight in gloomy poetry have often represented death in terrible language. "It is hard," says one--

To feel the hand of death arrest one's steps,
Throw a chill blight on all one's budding hopes,
And hurl one's soul untimely to the shades."

And another exclaims--

"O God, it is a fearful thing
To see the human soul take wing,
In any shape, in any mood!
I've seen it rushing forth in blood,
I've seen it on the breaking ocean,
Strive with a swollen convulsive motion."

Not so the apostle Paul. I do not even hear him speak of flying through the gate as our grand old poet has described death. He does not say, "The hour of my dissolution is at hand"--a very proper word if he had used it; but he is not looking so much at the process as at the result of his dying. He does not even say, "The hour of my death is at hand," but he adopts a beautiful expression, "The time of my departure"--words which are used sometimes to signify the departure of a vessel from the port; the pulling up of the anchor so that it looses its moorings, when about to put out to sea--so he feels himself like a ship lying at the harbor for awhile--but he says, "The time for pulling up the anchor, the time for letting loose the cable, and cutting from the mooring is at hand; I shall soon be launched upon my voyage." And he knew right well where that voyage would end, in the fair havens of the port of Peace in the better country, whither his Lord had gone before him.

Now we will proceed very briefly to say a word about departure; and then a shorter word still about the time of our departure; and then a little more about the time of our departure being at hand--trying here, especially, to bring forward some lessons which may be of practical usefulness to each one of us.

I. First, then, dear brethren, let us think a little about OUR DEPARTURE.

It is quite certain we shall not dwell here for ever: we shall not live here below as long as the first man did, or as those antediluvian fathers, who tarried some eight or nine hundred years. The length of human life then led to greatness of sin. Monstrosities of evil were ripened through the long continuance of physical strength, and the accumulating force of eager passions. All things considered, it is a mercy that life is abridged and not prolonged to a thousand years. Amidst the sharp competition of man with man, and class with class, there is a bound to every scheme of personal aggrandisement, a limit to all the spoils of individual despotism, a restraint upon the hoardings of any one's avarice. It is well, I say, that it should be so. The narrow span of life clips the wings of ambition, and baulks it of its prey. Death comes in to deprive the mighty of his power, to stay the rapacity of the invader, to scatter abroad the possessions of the rich. The most reprobate men must end their career after they have had their three score years and ten, or their four score years of wickedness. And as for the good and godly, though we mourn their exit, especially when we think that they have been prematurely taken from us, we remember how the triumphs of genius have been for the most part achieved in youth, and how much the world has been enriched by the heads and hearts of those who have but sown the seeds of faith and left others to reap the fruits. If into less than the allotted term they have crowded the service of their generation, we may save our tears, for our regrets are needless. The summons will reach each one of us ere long. We cannot stop here as long as the grey fathers of our race: we expect, and it is meet that we should prepare, to go. The world itself is to be consumed one day. "The elements shall melt with fervent heat." The land on which we stand we are wont to call terra firma, but beneath it is probably an ocean of fire, and it shall itself feel the force of the ocean. We must not marvel, the house being so frail, that the tenants are unsettled and migratory. Certainly, whether we doubt it or not, we shall have to go. There will be a departure for us. Beloved believer in Christ Jesus, to you the soft term, "Departure" is not more soft than the truth it represents. To die is to depart out of this world unto the Father. What say you about your departure? What say you of that from which you go, and what think you of that land to which you go? Well, of the land from which we go, my brethren, we might say many hard things if we would, but I think we had better not. We shall speak more correctly, if we say the hard things of ourselves. This land, my brethren, has been a land of mercy to us: there have been sorrows in it; but in bidding it farewell we will do it justice and speak the truth concerning it. Our sorrows have usually sprung up in our own bosoms, and those that have come from the soil itself would have been very light if it had not been for the plague of our hearts, which made us vex, and fret over them. Oh, the mercy you and I have enjoyed even in this life! It has been worth while to live for us who are believers. Even had we to die like a dog dieth, it has been worth while to live for the joy

and blessedness which God has made to pass before us. I dare not call that an evil country in which I have met my Savior, and received the pardon of my sin. I dare not call that an ill life in which I have seen my Savior, though it be through a glass darkly. How shall I speak ill of that lamb where Zion is built, beautiful for situation, the joy of the whole earth, the place of our solemn assemblies, where we have worshipped God? No; cursed of old as the earth was to bring forth the thorn and the thistle, the existence of the church of God in that land seems to a great degree to have made reparation for the blight to such as know and love the Savior. Oh, have we not gone up to the house of God in company with songs of ecstatic joy, and have we not when we have gathered round the table of the Lord--though nothing was upon it but the type and emblem--have we not felt it a joyous thing to be found in the assembly of the saints, and in the courts of the Lord's house even here? When we loose our cable, and bid farewell to earth, it shall not be with bitterness in the retrospect. There is sin in it, and we are called to leave it; there has been trial in it, and we are called to be delivered from it; there has been sorrow in it, and we are glad that we shall go where we shall sorrow no more. There have been weakness, and pain, and suffering in it, and we are glad that we shall be raised in power; there has been death in it, and we are glad to bid farewell to shrouds and to knells; but for all that there has been such mercy in it, such lovingkindness of God in it, that the wilderness and the solitary place have been made glad, and the desert has rejoiced and blossomed as a rose. We will not bid farewell to the world, execrating it, or leaving behind us a cold shudder and a sad remembrance, but we will depart, bidding adieu to the scenes that remain, and to the people of God that tarry therein yet a little longer, blessing him whose goodness and mercy have followed us all the days of our life, and who is now bringing us to dwell in the house of the Lord for ever.

But, dear brethren, if I have had to speak in a somewhat apologetic manner of the land from which we depart, I shall need to use many apologies for my own poor talk about the land to which we are bound. Ah, whither goest thou, spirit loosened from thy clay--dost know? Whither goest thou? The answer must be, partly, that we know not. None of us have seen the streets of gold of which we sang just now; those harpings of the harpers, harping with their harps, have never fallen on these ears; eye hath not seen it, ear hath not heard it: it is all unrevealed to the senses; flesh and blood cannot inherit it, and, therefore, flesh and blood cannot imagine it. Yet it is not unknown, for God hath revealed it unto us by his Spirit. Spiritual men know what it is to feel the spirit, their own new-born spirit, living, glowing, burning, triumphing within them. They know, therefore, that if the body should drop off they would not die. They feel there is a life within them superior to blood and bone, and nerve and sinew. They feel the life of God within them, and none can gainsay it. Their own experience has proven to them that there is an inner life. Well, then, when that inner life is strong and vigorous, the spirit often reveals to it what the world of spirits will be. We know what holiness is, do we not, brethren? Are we not seeking it? That is heaven--perfect holiness is heaven. We know what peace means; Christ is our peace. Rest--he gives us rest: we find that when we take his yoke. Rest is heaven. And rest in Jesus tells us what heaven is. We know, even to-day, what communion with God is. If any one should say, "I do not know it," I should reply to him thus: Suppose I said to you, "You know not what it is to eat and drink:" the man would tell me that I belied him, for he knew, as he knew his own existence, what it was to eat and drink; and, as surely as I live, I have communion with God. I know it as certainly as you know that I have declared it to you. Well, friends, that is heaven. It has but to be developed from the germ to the produce, and there is heaven in its full development.

Communion with saints in like manner--know we not what that is? Have we not rejoiced in each other's joys, been made glad with the experience of our brethren? That, too, carried to perfection, will be heaven. Oh, to throw yourself into the bosom of the Savior and lie there taken up with his mind and his love, yielding all things to his supremacy, beholding your King in him! When you have been in that state you have had an antepast of heaven. Your view may have been but as one seeing a man's face in shadow yet you would know that man again even by the shadow; so know we what heaven is. We shall not be strangers in a strange land when we get there. Though, like the Queen of Sheba, we shall say, "The half has not been told me," yet we shall reflect on it thus: "I did surmise there would be something of this sort. I did know from what I felt of its buddings in my soul below that the full-blown flower would be somewhat of this kind." Whither away, then, spirit that art departing to soar through backs to thyself unknown? Thine answer is, "I am away: away to the throne of him whose cross first gave me life, and light, and hope. I am away to the very bosom of my Savior, where I hope to rest and to have fellowship with the church of the firstborn, whose names are written in heaven." This is your departure that you have in near prospect.

Suppose, dear friend, the thought of departing from this world to the glory-world should ever startle you, let me remind you that you are not the first that ever went that way. Your vessel is in the pool, as it were, or in the dock; she is going out on her voyage; oh, but you will not go alone, nor have to track your course through paths unnavigated or unknown before! When the Portuguese captain first went by the Cape of Storms it was a venturous voyage, and he called it the Cape of Good Hope when he had rounded it. When Columbus first went in search of the New World, his was a brave spirit that dared cross the unnavigated Atlantic. But oh, there are tens of thousands that have gone whither you go. The Atlantic that severs us from Canaan is white with the sails of the vessels that are on voyage thither. Fear not, they have not been wrecked; we hear good news of their arrival there is good hope for you. There are no icebergs on the road, no mists, no counter currents, and no sunken vessels or quicksands; you have but to cut your moorings, and with Christ on board you shall be at your desired haven at once.

Remember, too, your Savior went that way. Have you to depart? So Christ departed too. Some of my brethren are always so pleased--pleased as some children are with a new toy--at the idea that they shall never die; that Christ will come, it may be before the time of their decease; for, "we shall not all sleep, but we shall all be changed." Well, let him come, ay, let him come; come quickly. But if I had my choice, were it permitted me to choose, I would prefer to pass through the portals of the grave. Those that are alive and remain unto the coming of the Lord will not prevent, go before, or steal a march on them which are asleep. But surely they will lack one point of conformity to their Lord, for he disdained not to sojourn awhile in the tomb, though it was impossible that he should be holden of death. Let the seal of death, then, be set upon this face of mine, that my fate in the matter may be like his. Enoch and Elias were exempt from this privilege--privilege, I call it--of conformity to his death. But it is safe to go by the beaten track, and desirable to travel by the ordinary route to the heavenly city. Jesus died. Through the valley of shadows, the vale of death-shades, there are the foot-prints of Immanuel all the way along: go down into it and fear not. Bethink you, too, dear brethren and sisters, that we may well look forward to our departure, and look forward to it comfortably too? Is it not expedient by reason of nature? Is it not desirable by reason of grace? Is it not necessary by reason of glory? I say, is not our departure needful by reason of nature? Men are not, when they come to hoary age, what they were in the prime of their days. The staff is needed for the foot, and the glass is wanted for the eye; and after a certain number of years, even those on whom Time hath gently laid his hand, find the taste is gone. They might proclaim, like old Barzillai, that they know not what they eat or drink. The hearing fails, the daughters of music are silent, the whole tenement gets very crazy. Oh, it were a melancholy thing if we had to continue to live! Perhaps there is no more hideous picture than that which the satirist drew of men who lived on to six or seven hundred years of age--that strange satirical man, Swift. Be thankful that we do not linger on in imbecility. Kind Nature says we may depart; she gives us notice, and makes it welcome by the decays that come upon us. Besides, grace desires it; for it were a poor experience of his kindness as our best and truest friend that did not make us long to see our Savior's face. It is no mere drivelling sentiment, I hope, when we join to sing--

"Father, I long, I faint to see
The place of thine abode;
I'd leave thy earthly courts, and flee
Up to thy seat, my God!"

I must confess there was one verse in the hymn we sung just now which I could not quite chime in with. I am not eagerly wishing to go to heaven this night. I have a great deal more to do here; therefore I do not want to take a hasty leave of all below. To full many of us, I suppose, there are times of quiet contemplation and times of rapt devotion, when our thoughts surmount these lower skies, and look within the veil and then, Oh, how we wish to be there! Yet there are other times; times of strenuous activity when we buckle on the armor and press to the front; and then we see such a battle to be waged, such a victory to be won, such a work to be wrought, that we say: "Well to abide in the flesh, to continue with you all for the joy and furtherance of your faith, seems more loyal to Christ, more needful for you, and more in accord with our present feelings." I think it is idle for us to be crying, to go home; it is too much like the lazy workman, that wants Saturday night to come when it is only Tuesday morning. Oh, no; if God spare us to do a long life's work, so much the better. At the same time, as a spark flies upward to the sun, the central source of flame, so does the newborn spirit aspire towards heaven, towards Jesus, by whom it was kindled. And, I add, that glory demands it, and makes our departure needful. Is not Christ in heaven praying that we may be with him where he is? Are there not the saints in heaven, of whom it is said, they without us cannot be perfect? The circle of the skies cannot be completed until all the redeemed be there. The grand orchestra of glory misses some notes as yet. What if the bass be full, there are wanting still some trebles and tenors! There are some sopranos that will be requisite to swell the enchanting melodies, and consummate the worship of the Eternal! What, therefore, nature prepares for, grace desires, and glory itself demands, we have no just cause to shudder at. Our departure need not make

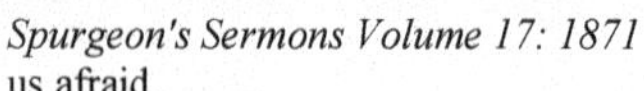
us afraid.

II. Having thus occupied so much time on this first point, I have little or no room to enlarge on the second.

THE TIME OF OUR DEPARTURE, though unknown to us, is fixed by God, unalterably fixed; so rightly, wisely, lovingly settled, and prepared for, that no chance or haphazard can break the spell of destiny. The wisdom of divine love shall be proven by the carefulness of its provision. Perhaps you will say: "It is not easy to discern this; the natural order of things is so often disturbed by casualties of one kind or another." Let me remind you, then, that it is through faith, only through faith, we can understand these things; for it is as true now of the providence of God as it was of old of the creation of God that "things which are seen were not made of things which do appear." Because the mode of your departure is beyond your own ken, it does not follow that the time of your departure is not foreseen by God. "Ah! but," say you, "it seems so shocking for any one to die suddenly, unexpectedly, without warning, and so come to an untimely end!" I answer you thus. If you take counsel with death your flesh will find no comfort; but if you trust in God your faith will cease to parley with these feverish anxieties, and your spirit will enjoy a sweet calm. Dire calamities befell Job when he was bereaved of his children and his servants, his herds and his flocks. Yet he took little heed of the different ways in which his troubles were brought about; whether by an onslaught of the Sabeans or by a raid of the Chaldeans; whether the fire fell from heaven, or the wind came from the wilderness; it mattered little. Whatever strange facts broke on his ear, one thought penetrated his heart, and one expression broke from his lips. "The Lord gave, and the Lord hath taken away; blessed be the name of the Lord." So, too, beloved, when the time of your departure arrives--be it by disease or decay, be it by accident or assault, that your soul quits its present tenement--rest assured that "thy times are in his hand;" and know of a surety that "all his saints are in his hand" likewise. Besides this, dear friends, since the time of our departure must come, were the manner of it at our own disposal, I think we should most of us say, "What I shall choose, I wot not." Fevers and agues, the pangs and tortures of one malady and another, or the delirium incident to sickness, are not so much to be preferred to the shock of a disaster, or the terror of a wreck at sea, because one is the prolonging of pain, and the other the despatch of fate, that we need to covet, and desire weeks or months spent in the vestibule of the grave. Rather should we say, Let the Lord do with me as seemeth him good. To live in constant communion with God is a sure relief from all these bitter frettings. Those who have walked with him have often been favored with such presentiments of their departure as no physician could give them. Survivors will tell you that though death seemed to come suddenly to the godly merchant, he had in the last acts of his life appeared to expect and prepare for it, and even to have taken an affecting farewell of his family while in the vigor of health, as though he were aware that he was setting out on his last journey, which a few hours afterwards it proved to be. So, too, the minister of Christ has sometimes fallen, expiring in his pulpit with a nunc dimittis, "Now lettest thou thy servant depart in peace" on his lips; secretly, but surely, made ready to depart and to be with his Lord. There is a time to depart; and God's time to call me is my time to go.

III. Now, to our third point--the THE TIME AT HAND. "The time of my departure is at hand."

In a certain sense, every Christian here may say this; for whatever interval may interpose between us and death, how very short it is! Have you not all a sense that time flows faster than it did? In our childish days, we thought a year was quite a period of time, a very epoch in our career; now as for weeks--one can hardly reckon them! We seem to be travelling by an express train, flying along at such a rate that we can hardly count the months. Why, the past year only seemed to come in at one door and go out at the other; it was over so soon. We shall soon be at the terminus of life, even if we live for several years; but in the case of some of us, God knows of whom, this year, perhaps this month, will be our last. I think to-morrow night we shall have to report at the church meeting the deaths of nine members of this church within the last eight or nine days. Since these have gone, some of us may expect to follow them. There are those who will evidently go; disease has set in upon them. Some of those disorders that in this land seem to be always fatal, tell these dear friends that the time of their departure is undoubtedly at hand. And then old age, which comes so gracefully and graciously to many of our matrons and our veterans, shows, past all dispute, "the time of your departure is at hand." The lease of your life is almost up. Not indeed that I would address myself to such special cases only. I speak to every brother and sister in Christ here. "The time of our departure is at hand." What then, dear friends?

Is not this a reason for surveying our condition again? If our vessel is just launching, let us see that she is seaworthy. It would be a sad thing for us to be near departing, and yet to be just as near discovering that we are lost. Remember, dear friends, it is possible for any one to maintain a decent Christ profession for fifty years, and be a hypocrite after all; possible to occupy an office in the church of God, and that of the very highest, and yet to be a Judas; and one may not only serve

Christ, but suffer for him too, and yet, like Demas, may not persevere to the end; for all that looks like grace is not grace. Where true grace is, there it will always be; but where the semblance of it is, it will ofttimes suddenly disappear. Search thyself, good brother; set thine house in order, for thou must die and not live. Hast thou the faith of God's elect? Art thou built on Christ? Is thy heart renewed? Art thou verily an heir of heaven? I charge every man and woman within this place, since the time of his departure may be far nearer than he thinks, to take stock, and reckon up, and see whether he be Christ's or no.

But if the time of my departure be at hand, and I am satisfied that it is all right with me, is there not a call for me to do all I can for my household? Father, the time of your departure is at hand; is your wife unsaved? Will you pass another night without lovingly speaking to her of her soul? Are those dear boys unregenerate? Is that girl still thoughtless? The time of your departure is at hand. You can do little more for the lads and lasses; you can do little more for the wife and the brother. Oh! do what you can now. Sister, you are consumptive; you will soon be gone. You are the only Christ in the family. God sent you there to be a missionary. Do not have to say, when you are dying, "The last hope of my family is going out, for I have not cared for their souls." Masters, you that have servants about you, you must soon be taken away. Will you not do something for their souls? I know if there were a mother about to go to Australia, and she had to leave some of her children behind, she would fret if she thought, "I have not done all that needs to be done for those poor children. Who will care for them now their mother is gone?" Well, but to have neglected something necessary for their temporal comfort would be little in comparison with not having cared for their souls! Oh, let it not be so! Let it not be a thorn in your dying pillow that you did not fulfill the relations of life while you had the opportunity. "The time of my departure is at hand."

Then there is a third lesson. Let me try to finish all my work, not only as regards my duty to my family, but in respect to all the world so far as my influence or ability can reach. Rich men, be your own executors. Do what you can with your substance while it is your own. Men of talent, speak for Jesus before your tongue has ceased to articulate, and becomes a piece of clay. George Whitfield may supply us with a fine model of this uniform consistency. He was so orderly and precise in his habits, and so scrupulous and holy in his life, that he used to say he would not like to go to bed if there were a pair of gloves out of place in the house, much less were his will not made, or any part of his duty unfulfilled to the best of his knowledge. He wished to have all right, and to be fully prepared for whatever might happen, so that, if he never woke again from the slumbers of the night, nobody would have cause to reflect upon anything he had left undone, entailing needless trouble on his wife or his children. Such care bestowed on what some account to be trifles is a habit; worthy of our imitation. The main work of life may be sadly spoiled by negligence in little things. This is a striking test of character. "He that is faithful in that which is least is faithful also in much: and he that is unjust in the least is unjust also in much." Oh, then! time is fleeting, despatch is urgent; gather up your thoughts, quicken your hands, speed your pace, for God commandeth thee to make haste. If you have ought to do, you must do it soon. The wheels of eternity are sounding behind you. Press on! If you are to run a race you must run it fast, for Death will soon overtake you. You may almost feel the hot breath of the white horse of Death upon your cheeks already. O God, help us to do something ere we go hence and be no more seen. It was grand of the apostle that in the same breath, when he said, "The time of my departure is at hand," he could also say, "I have fought a good fight, I have finished my course, I have kept the faith." So may we be able to say when the time of our departure has arrived.

If the time of our departure is at hand, let it cheer us amid our troubles. Sometimes, when our friends go to Liverpool to sail for Canada, or any other distant region, on the night before they sail they get into a very poor lodging. I think I hear one of them grumbling, "What a hard bed! What a small room! What a bad look-out" "Oh," says the other, "never mind, brother; we are not going to live here; we are off to-morrow." Bethink you in like manner, ye children of poverty, this is not your rest. Put up with it, you are away tomorrow. Ye sons of sorrow, ye daughters of weakness, ye children of sickness, let this cheer you:--

"The road may be rough,
But it cannot be long
And I'll smooth it with hope,
And cheer it with song."

Oftentimes when I have been travelling on the Continent I have been obliged to put up at an hotel that was full, where the room was so inconvenient, that it scarcely furnished any accommodation at all. But we have said, "Oh, never mind: we are off in the morning! What matters it for one night?" So, as we are soon to be gone, and the time of our departure is at hand, let us not be ruffling our tempers about trifles, nor raise evil spirits around us by cavilling and finding fault.

Take things as you find them, for we shall soon be up and away.

And if the time of my departure is at hand, I should like to be on good terms with all my friends on earth. Were you going to stop here always, when a man treated you badly, apart from a Christ spirit, you might as well have it out with him; but as we are going to stop such a little while, we may well put up with it. It is not desirable to be too ready at taking an offense. What if my neighbor has an ugly temper, the Lord has to put up with him, and so I may. There are some people with whom I would rather dwell in heaven for ever than abide with them half an hour on earth. Nevertheless, for the love of the brethren, and for the peace of the church, we may tolerate much during the short time we have to brook with peevish moods and perverse humors. Does Christ love them, and shall not we? He covers their offenses; why, then, should we disclose them or publish them abroad? If, any of you have any grievances with one another, if there is any bickering, or jealousy between you, I should like you to make it up to-night, because the time of your departure is at hand. Suppose there is some one you spoke harshly to, you would not like to hear to-morrow that he was dead. You would not have minded what you said to him if he had lived, but now that the seal is set upon all your communications one with another, you could wish that the last impress had been more friendly. There has been a little difference between two brothers--a little coldness between two sisters. Oh, since one or other of you will soon be gone, make it up! Live in love, as Christ loved you and gave himself for you. If one of you were going to Australia to-morrow, never to come back again, and you had had a little tiff with your brother, why I know before you started you would say, "Come, brother, let us part good friends." So now, since you are so soon to depart, end all strife, and dwell together in blessed harmony till the departure actually occurs.

If the time of my departure is at hand, then let me guard against being elated by any temporal prosperity. Possessions, estates, creature comforts dwindle into insignificance before this out-look. Yes, you may have procured a comfortable house and a delightful garden, but it is not your rest: your tenure is about to expire. Yes, you may say, "God did prosper me last year, the bank account did swell, the premises were enlarged, and the business thrived beyond all expectation." Ah! hold them loose. Do not think that they are to be your heaven. Be very jealous lest you should get your good things here, for if you do you will not have them hereafter. Be not lifted up too much when you grasp the pain, of which you must so soon quit your hold. As I said of the discomfort of the hotel, we did not think much of it, because we were going away. So, if it happens to be very luxurious, do not be enamoured of it, for you must go to-morrow. "These are the things," said one, when he looked at a rich man's treasures, "that make it hard to die." But it need not be so, if you hold them as gifts of God's kindness, and not as gods to be worshipped with self-indulgence, you may take leave of them with composure; "knowing in yourselves that ye have in heaven a better and an enduring substance."

Lastly, if the time of our departure is at hand, let us be prepared to bear our testimony. We are witnesses for Christ. Let us bear our testimony before we are taken up and mingle with the cloud of witnesses who have finished their course and rested from their labors. Dost thou say, "I hope to do that on my dying bed?" Brother, do it now: do it now, for you may never have opportunity to do it then. Mr. Whitfield was always desirous that he might bear a testimony for Christ in the hour of death; but he could not do so at that momentous crisis, for as you well know, he was suddenly taken ill after preaching, and very soon expired. Was this to be grievously deplored? Ah, no. Why, dear friends, he had borne so many testimonies for his Lord and Master while he was alive, there was no need to add anything in the last few moments before his death, or to supply the deficiencies of a life devoted to the proclamation of the gospel. Oh, let you and I bear our testimony now! Let us tell to others wherever we can what Christ hath done for us. Let us help Christ's cause with all our might while it is called to-day. Let us work for Jesus while we can work for him. As to thinking we can undo the effect of our idleness by the spasmodic effort of our dying breath, that were a vain hope indeed compared with living for Jesus Christ. Your dying testimony, if you are able to bear it, will have the greater force if it is not a sickly regret, but a healthy confirmation of your whole career.

I only wish these words about departure were applicable to all here. "Precious in the sight of the Lord is the death of his saints." But, "As I live, saith the Lord God, I have no pleasure in the death of the wicked, but that the wicked turn from his ways, and live." O unconverted man, the time for letting loose your cable draws nigh; it is even at the door. You must shortly, set sail for a far country. Alas! then yours is not the voyage of a passenger, with a sweeter clime, a happier home, a brighter prospect in view. Your departure is the banishment of a convict, with a penal settlement looming in the distance; fear all rife, and hope all blank, for the term of your banishment is interminable. I fear there are some of you who may depart ere long full of gloom with a fearful looking for of judgment and of fiery indignation. I seem to see the angel of death hovering over my audience. He may, perhaps, select for his victim an unconverted soul. If so, behind that death-angel attends there something far more grim. Hell follows death to souls that love not Christ. Oh, make haste, make haste! Seek Christ. Lay hold on eternal life; and may infinite mercy save you, for Jesus

Christ's sake. Amen and Amen.

Self-Humbling and Self-Searching

A Sermon (No. 990)
Delivered by
C. H. SPURGEON,
At the Metropolitan Tabernacle, Newington

"Look not upon me, because I am black, because the sun hath looked upon me: my mother's children were angry with me, they made me the keeper of the vineyards; but mine own vineyard have I not kept." - Song of Solomon 1:6.

WHENCE DO I DRAW MY TEXT but from the very fountain of love? And to whom shall I address my discourse but to the friends of the bridegroom? Ye must have warm hearts, quick sensibilities, lively emotions to interpret the sayings and sympathise the tender notes of this most sacred song.

I suppose that the history of the statues in St. Paul's Cathedral, from year to year, would not be remarkably interesting. They are placed upon their pedestals; they stand there quietly; and unless some terrible convulsion should occur, probably that will be the whole of their history for many years to come, as it has been for many years past. During the time in which any one of those statues has stood there, however, the history of any one human person has been checkered with all sorts of incidents, happy and sorrowful. Aches and pains, joys and rejoicings' depressions and exultations, have alternated in the living; but in the cold marble there has been no such change. Many of you in this house know little of what are the experiences of God's people. If you hear of their anxieties and encouragements, their temptations and deliverances, their inward conflicts and spiritual triumphs, their gloomy depressions and cheerful exultations--all those things seem to you as an idle tale. The living, the living, shall know the secret; but unto the mere professor this thing is not revealed.

My subject, which will be mainly addressed to God's working people--to such as are really serving him--will appear to have very little bearing upon any here present who do not understand the spiritual life, and they will probably think that the evening to them is wasted. Just this word on the outset, however, I would drop in your ears. If you do not know anything of spiritual life, what will you do in the end of your natural life? If there be no work of God's Spirit upon your soul, and you are a stranger to the living experience of God's children, what will be your portion for ever? It must be divided to you with the unbelievers. Are you prepared to receive it? Are you willing that this should be your eternal destiny? Are you not, rather, alarmed? Are you not made anxious and desirous if by any means you may pass into that better, truer, state of life? Considering its boundless interests, notwithstanding all the present struggles and sorrows it may entail on you, do you not wish to know and prove what spiritual life means? I pray God you may. Let me remind you that the gospel preached to you is still available for your quickening; and whosoever believeth in Christ Jesus is born of God, and is possessor of that spiritual life.

Now, in conducting the people of God to a special survey of our text, "Look not upon me, because I am black," our first remark shall be this: the fairest Christians are the most shamefaced with regard to themselves. The person who says, "Look not upon me, because I am black," is described by some one else in the eighth verse as the "fairest among women." Others, who thought her the fairest of the fair, spoke no less than the truth when they affirmed it; but in her own esteem she felt herself to be so little fair, and so much uncomely, that she besought them not even to look upon her. Why is it that the best Christians depreciate themselves the most?

Is it not because they are most accustomed to look within? They keep their books in a better condition than those unsafe tradesmen, the counterpart of mere professors, who think themselves "rich and increased in goods," when they are on the very verge of bankruptcy. The Christian in his right state tests himself to see whether he be in the faith. He values too much his own soul to go on blindly. He knows that Heedless and Toobold are always bad pilots, so he sets Caution and Self-examination at the helm. He cries to God, "Search me, and know my heart." He is accustomed to examine his actions and his motives--to pass his words and his thoughts in review. He does not live the life of one who goes recklessly on; but he stops and considers his ways; and looks well to the state of everything within him "to have always a conscience void of offense toward God and toward men." Solomon says, "The wise man looks to the state of his flocks and his herds;" and it is no marvel if any one suffer loss who neglects the counsel. But he also says, "Keep thy heart with all diligence, for out of it are the issues of life;" and it is quite certain that he who fails in this exercise is liable to every kind of moral disorder. In his anxiety to be pure from evil, the godly man will be eager to notice and quick to detect the least particle of defilement; and for this reason he discovers more of his blackness than any other man is likely to see. He is no blacker, but he looks more narrowly, and therefore he sees more distinctly the spots on his own character.

The genuine Christian, also, tries himself by a higher standard. The professor, if he be as good as another professor, is well content. He estimates himself by a comparison with his neighbors. He has no standard but that of ordinary commonplace Christianity. Par otherwise is it with the believer who walks near to God; he asks himself "What manner of persons ought we to be, in all holy conversation and godliness?" He knows the law to be spiritual, and therefore he judges many things to be sinful which others wink at; and he counts some things to be important duties which others regard as trifles. The genuine Christian sets up no lower standard than perfection. He does not judge himself by others, but by the exact measure of the divine requirements, by the law of God, and especially by the example of his Lord and Master; and when he thus sets the brightness of the Savior's character side by side with his own, then it is that he cries out, "Look not upon me, for I am black." The mere professor never does this: he neither scrutinises himself nor observes his Master with close heed and strained attention, desiring to ascertain the truth; but he flatters himself in his own eyes, and goes on presumptuously. Not so the genuine Christian; he hides his face, sighs in secret, and cries before God, because he is not what he wants to be; not what his Lord was; not fully conformed to Christ in all things; and just because these short-comings grieve and vex his righteous soul, he cries, "Look not upon me, for I am black." All the while he may be of the highest type of Christian, yet he is not so in his own esteem. He may be a star to others, but he is a blot, as he thinks, to himself. In God's esteem he is "accepted in the Beloved," but in his own esteem he seems to himself to be full of all manner of evil, and he cries out against it before his Lord.

Another reason why the fairest Christ are generally those that think themselves the blackest, is that they have more light. A person may seem to be very fair in the dark, very fair in the twilight; but when the light gets strong, and the eye is strengthened to perceive, then it is that spots that were not noticed before are soon discovered. You have, perhaps, a handkerchief that has looked to you extremely white; so it has been in comparison with other linen: but one day, when there has been a fall of snow, you have laid your handkerchief side by side with the snow, and you have seen that it was very far from the whiteness which you imagined. When the light of God comes into the soul, and we see what purity really is, what holiness really is, then it is the contrast strikes us. Though we might have thought we were somewhat clean before, when we see God in his light we see light, and we abhor ourselves in dust and ashes. Our defects so appall our own heart, that we marvel they do not exhaust his patience.

The better Christ a man is, the more abashed he always feels; because to him sin is so exceedingly hateful, that what sin he sees in himself he loathes himself for far more than others do. The ungodly man would condone very great sin in himself; though he might know it to be there; it would not disturb him; but the Christian being another sort, having a love for holiness and a hatred for sin, cannot bear to see the smallest speck of sin upon himself: He knows what it is. There are persons living before the public eye, and jealous of popularity, who appear quite indifferent to the good opinion of the sovereign in whose kingdom they dwell there are other persons favourites at court, who would lie awake at night tossed to and fro in fear if they thought that something had been reported to the sovereign's ear that was disloyal. A man who fears not God, will break all his laws with an easy conscience, but one who is the favorite of heaven, who has been indulged to sit at royal banquets, who knows the eternal love of God to him, cannot bear that there should be any evil way in him that might grieve the Spirit and bring dishonor to the name of Christ. A very little sin, as the world calls it, is a very great sin to a truly awakened Christian. I will ask you now, dear hearers (most of on are members of this or of other churches), do you know what it is to fret because you have spoken an unadvised word? Do you know what it is to smite upon your breast, because you were angry?--justly provoked, perhaps, but still, being angry, you spoke unadvisedly. Have you ever gone to a sleepless couch, because in business you have let fall a word, or have done an action which, upon mature deliberation, you could not justify? Does the tear never come from your eye because you are not like your Lord, and have failed where you hoped to succeed? I would give little for your godliness, if you know nothing of this. Repentance is as much a mark of a Christian as faith itself. Do not think we have done with repenting when we come to Christ and receive the remission of our sins by the blood that did once atone. No; we shall repent as long as we sin, and as long as we need the precious blood for cleansing. While there is sin, or a proneness to any kind of sin, lurking in us, the grace of God will make us loathe the sin and humble ourselves before the Most High on account of it.

Now, I think our text seems to say just this: there were some that admired the church. They said she was fair. She seemed to say, "Don't say it; you don't know what I am, or you would not praise me." Oh, there is nothing that brings a blush to a genuine Christian's face like praising him; for he feels--"Praise such a heap of dirt as I am? Give any credit to such a worthless worm as I am? No; do not cast admiring glances at me! Do not say, That man has many virtues and many excellences!' Look not upon me, for I am black.'" Are there not some who will imitate any Christian--and be very right in so doing--any Christian who is eminently godly and holy? There will be many who will follow in his footsteps. I think I see such a man turn round to his followers, and say: "Do not look at me; do not copy me. I am black. Copy a better model even Jesus. If I follow in his footsteps, follow me; but inasmuch as I have gone astray like a lost sheep, follow the shepherd; do not follow my example." Every Christian, in proportion as he lives near to God, will feel this self-abasement, this lowliness of heart; and if others talk of admiring or of imitating him, he will say, "Look not upon me, for I am black." And as he thus, in deep humility, begs that he be not exalted, he will often desire others that they would not despise him. It will come into his mind, "Such-and-such a man of God is a Christian indeed; as he sees my weakness, he will contemn me. Such-and-such a disciple of Christ is strong; he will never be able to bear with my weakness. Such-and-such a Christian woman does, indeed, adorn the doctrine of God her Savior; but as for me, alas! I am not what I ought to be, nor what I would be. Christ of God, do not look upon me with scorn. I will not say that you have motes in your own eyes. I have a beam in mine. Look not upon me too severely. Judge me not harshly. If you do look at me, look to Christ for me, and pray that I may be helped; for I am black, because the sun hath looked upon me.'" Still I would have you beware of affecting aught that you do not feel. Humility itself may be counterfeited with much ostentation. Wherever there is anything like cant, as it is practiced by some people who depreciate themselves but do not mean it, it is loathsome to the last degree. I recollect a very proud man, certainly twice as proud as he was high, who used to pray for himself as "God's poor dust." There was nothing, I am sure, about his conduct and conversation that entitled him to use any such expression. I have heard of a monk who said he was full of sin--he was as bad as Judas; and when somebody said, "That is true," he turned round, and said, "What did I ever do that you should say so?" The effrontery of the arrogant is not more odious than the servility of the sycophant. There is a great deal of self-abnegation which is not genuine; it is the offspring of self-conceit, and not of self-knowledge. Much that we say of ourselves would mightily offend our vainglory if anybody else said the same of us. Oh, let us beware of mock humility! At the same time, the more of the genuine article we have the better, and the more truthfully we can cry out to God's people, "Look not upon me, because I am black," the more clear will it be that we are, after all, amongst the fairest.

But I pass on. The most diligent Christian--let this stand for the second observation--the most diligent Christian will be the man most afraid of the evils connected with his work. "Evils connected with his work!" says one. "Does work for God have evils contingent upon it?" Yes; but for every evil connected with the work of God, there are ten evils connected with idleness. Nay, all you professors who are doing, nothing, are wearing yourselves out faster by rust than you could have done by honest wear. But, you see, in the case of our text, there was evil connected with work. She had been made a keeper of the vineyards, and having to trim the vines, the sun had shone upon her; and she says, "Look not upon me, because I am black, because the sun hath looked upon me." The blackness that she confessed was a blackness occasioned by her having to bear the burden and heat of the day.

And now I speak to such as live in active service, doing the work of God. Dear brethren, there are certain evils connected with our lifework coming of the sun that looks upon us, which we should confess before our heavenly Father. I speak now only to the workers. I have known some whom the sun has looked upon in this respect; their zeal has grown cold through non-success. You went out, first of all, as a Christian, full of fire and life. You intended to push the church before you, and drag the world after you. Peradventure you thought that you were going to work a Reformation almost as great as that of Luther. Well, much of that was of the flesh, though beneath the surface there was an earnest zeal for God which was eating you up. But you have been mixed up with Christians for some years of a very cool sort. Use the thermometer to-night. Has not the spiritual temperature gone down in your own soul? Perhaps you have not seen many conversions under your ministry? or in the class which you conduct you have not seen many children brought to Jesus? Do you feel you are getting cool? Then wrap your face in your mantle to-night! and say: "Look not upon me, for in losing my zeal I am black, for the sun hath looked upon me." Perhaps it has affected you in another way, for the sun does not bring freckles out on all faces in the same place. Perhaps it is your temper that is grown sour? When you joined the church you felt all love, and you expected, as you had a right to do, that everybody would reciprocate the same feeling; it may be that since then you have had to do battle against contentions. You have been in a part of the church where there has been a strife, not altogether for the faith once delivered to the saints, but something of a party feeling was mixed with it, and you have had to take some share in it. And perhaps you have gradually acquired a carping, critical habit, so that where you used to enjoy the word, you are now all for judging the preacher. You are not so much a feeder upon the word, as a mere taster of the dishes, to see if you cannot find some fault with their flavour. Wrap your face again, I beseech you, in your mantle. Again bow before God, and say: "Look not upon me, because I am black; the sun hath looked upon me. In my service for God I have been impaired." Perhaps, dear friend, you have suffered in another way! I sometimes suffer in this respect very materially. The Christian's walk ought to be calm, peaceful, quiet, unruffled. Leaving everything with the Lord, and waiting his will, our peace should be like a river. But you know that, when there is much to be done in God's service, there is a very strong temptation to want to push this and that thing forward with undue haste. Or if it does not move quickly at the rate you would wish, there is a temptation to be sad, careful, and anxious; to be, in fact, like Martha, cumbered with much service. When you get into that condition it is an injury to yourself and really prejudicial to your own work; for they serve Christ best who commune with him most, and broken fellowship means broken strength. Yet this is often our trouble; our energies are exhausted by worry more than by work. Part of our duty is neglected through unexpected cares that have distracted our thoughts. Pardon me, if I transfer the thing to myself in a figure. Say that this Tabernacle wants all my vigilance concentrated upon its welfare. Then there is another matter that wants instant attention at the same time. Here is a soul seeking Christ; here is another backsliding; here is a brother falling to ears with a brother. Innumerable things crowd upon one's view and clamor for immediate investigation till one gets disturbed and troubled. "Look not upon me, because I am black; because the sun hath looked upon me. The work I have engaged in for thee hath brought me into the sun, and burnt my face." It ought to be bright and fair with fellowship; it is soiled and begrimed with service.

Sometimes this evil of sun-burning will come in the shape of joy taken away from the heart by weariness. I do not think, dear brethren, any of us are weary of God's work. If so, we never were called to it. But we may get weary in it. You recollect, some of you here--I speak to such as often preach the gospel--how happy you were when first you were permitted to open your mouth for Christ! Oh, what a joy it was! What a pleasure! How you threw your whole soul into it! There was no sleepiness and dulness in your sermon then. But now, year after year, year after year, your brain gets weary, and though the spirit is willing, the flesh is weak; the joy you once had in the service was your strength, and it has some what gone from you. The toil is more irksome when the spirits are less buoyant. Well, I would advise you to confess this before God, and ask for a medicine to heal you. You had need get your joy back, but first you must acknowledge that you have lost it. Say, "I am black, because the sun hath looked upon me."

On the other hand, it is a bad result of a good work when our humility is injured thereby. Place a Christian man in a position where he has to do much for Christ, and is much thought of and set by: let him have great success: and the tendency will be for him to compliment himself as though he were some great one. You cannot reap great sheaves for the Master without this temptation coming over your soul. What a glorious workman you are, and what a great reward will your soul have for having done so well! It is the sun looking upon you; taking away the fairness of your humility, freckling and blackening your face with a pride that is obnoxious to God. This ought to be confessed at once and heartily repented of.

I do not think I shall attempt to go through the list of all the matters that might come out of Christian service. It will suffice me to say, I am afraid that in many cases our motives get mixed. Pure and simple at first in our service, we may get at last to serve Christ only because it is our office to do so. Woe to the man that preaches only because he is a minister, and does not preach because he loves Christ! We may get also to be self-reliant. It is a great mercy for God's ministers when they tremble on going into the pulpit, even though they have been accustomed to preach for twenty years. Martin Luther declares that he never feared the face of man; and all who knew him could bear witness that it was even so; yet he said he never went up the stairs of the pulpit at Wittenburg but he felt his knees knock together with fear lest he should not be faithful to God and his truth. When we begin to rely upon ourselves' and think we can do it, and our experience and our practice will suffice to bear us safely through the next discourse without help from on high, then the sun has looked upon us, and blackened our face indeed, and the time of our usefulness draws to a close. Come, Christian people, brethren and sisters, thankful though I am that I can address so large a number who are engaged in the Master's work, I beseech you, let us go together to the footstool of the heavenly grace, confess there our blackness, and own that much of it has come upon us even while we were engaged in the service of God.

In the third place, the most watchful Christian is conscious of the danger of self-neglect. That is the next part of our text. "they made me the keeper of the vineyards; but mine own vineyard have I not kept."

Solemnly, let me speak again to my brethren who are seeking to glorify Christ by their lives. I met some time ago with a sermon by that famous divine, Mr. Henry Melvill, which consists all through of one solitary thought, and one only image well worked out. I will give you the pith of what took some eight pages to get through. He supposes a man to be a guide in Switzerland. It is his duty to conduct travelers in that country through the sublime passes, and to point out to them the glories of the scenery, and the beauties of the lakes, and streams, and glaciers, and hills. This man, as he continues in his office, almost inevitably gets to repeat his descriptions as a matter of course; and everybody knows how a guide at last comes to "talk book," and just iterate words which do not awaken any corresponding feeling in his own mind. Yet when he began, perhaps it was a sincere love of the sublime and the beautiful that led him to take up the avocation of a guide; and at first it really was to him a luxury to impart to others what he had felt amidst the glories of nature; but as, year after year, to hundreds of different parties, he had to repeat much the same descriptions, call attention to the same sublimities, and indicate the same beauties, it is almost impossible but that he should get to be at last a mere machine. Through the hardening tendency of custom, and the debasing influence of gain, his aptest descriptions and most exquisite eulogies come to be of no greater account than the mere language of a hireling. This thought I will not work out in extenso as that famous preacher has done, but I give it to you as a cutting, which may germinate if planted in the garden of your heart. Every worker for Christ is deeply concerned in the application of this parable; because the peril of self complacency increases in precisely the same ratio as the zeal of proselytising. When counselling others, you think yourself wise. When warning others, you feel yourself safe. When judging others, you suppose yourself above suspicion. You began the work with a flush of ardor; it may be with a fever of enthusiasm; a sacred instinct prompted, a glowing passion moved you. How will you continue it? Here is the danger--the fearful danger--lest you do it mechanically, fall into a monotony, continue in the same train, and use holy words to others with no corresponding feeling in your own soul. May we not stir others up to devout emotions, and yet our own hearts fail to burn with the sacred fire? Oh, may it not be easy for one to stand as a signpost on the road to heaven, and never stir himself? Every preacher who judges himself aright knows that this is the risk he incurs; and I believe the same danger in a measure threatens Christ in every form of work in which they occupy themselves for Christ. Dear friends, beware of reading the Bible for other people. Get your own text--your own morsel of marrow and fatness--out of Scripture; and do not be satisfied to be sermon-making or lesson-making for your class in the Sunday-school. Feed on the word yourselves, or else your own vineyard will not be kept. When you are on your knees in prayer, pray for others by all means; but, oh, let private prayer be kept up with a view to your own edification and your own growth in grace as well. Preach not the Savior's blood, and yet be without the blood mark on yourselves. Tell not of the fountain, and yet go unwashed. Do not point to heaven, and then turn your back to it and go down to hell. Fellow-workers, look to yourselves, lest after having preached to others ye yourselves should be cast away. Your neighbors certainly, but yourselves also; the children in your class certainly, your own children at home certainly, but look to yourselves also, oh, ye that are workers in God's house, lest ye keep the vineyards of others and your own vineyards be not kept. It is very possible for a man to get to dislike the very religion which he feels bound still by force of custom to go on teaching to others. "Is that possible?" says one. Alas! that it is. Have you never heard of the flower-girl in the streets? What is her occupation! I dare say some girls like her have passed by and seen her with a great basket full of violets, and said: "What a delightful occupation, to have that fragrant smell for ever near to one!" Yes, but there was one girl who sold them, and said she hated the smell of violets. She had got to loathe them, and to think that there was no smell in the world so offensive, because they were always under her nostrils all day, and taken home to her little scanty room at night, and having nothing but violets around her, she hated them altogether. And I do believe that there are persons without the grace of Christ in their hearts who keep on talking about grace, and mercy, and practicing prayer, and yet in their heart of hearts they hate the very fragrance of the name of Jesus, and need that there should come upon them an awakening out of their sleep of presumption and hypocrisy, to make them know that though they thought they were the friends of God, they were, after all, his enemies. They were mere keepers of other men's vineyards, but their own vineyards had gone to ruin.

Our last reflection is of the deepest importance. The most conscientious Christian will be the first to enquire for the antidote, and to use the cure.

What is the cure? The cure is found in the verse next to my text. "Look not upon me, because I am black, because the sun hath looked upon me. They made me the keeper of the vineyards; but mine own vineyard have I not kept." What next? "Tell me, O thou whom my soul loveth, where thou feedest, where thou makest thy flock to rest at noon: for why should I be as one that turneth aside by the flocks of thy companions?" See, then, you workers, if you want to keep up your freshness, and not to get blackened by the sun under which you labor, go to your Lord again--go and talk to him. Address him again by that dear name, "Thou whom my soul loveth." Ask to have your first love rekindled; strive after the love of your espousals. There are men in married life who seem to have forgotten that they ever loved their wives; but there are others concerning whom the hymn is true--

"And as year rolls after year,
Each to other still more dear."

So there are some Christians who seem to forget that they ever loved the Savior; but I trow there are others in whom that love deepens and becomes more fervent as each year passes over their heads. If any of you are at fault in this, do not give sleep to your eyelids to-night till you have renewed your espousal love. Thy Lord recollects it, if thou dost not, for he says: "I remember thee, the kindness of thy youth, the love of thine espousals, when thou wentest after me in the wilderness, in a land that was not sown." You did some wild things in those early days. You were a great deal more zealous than wise; but, though you look back upon that with censure, Christ regards it with delight. He wishes you were now as you were then. Perhaps to-day you are not quite cold to him. Do not flatter yourself on that account; for he has said, "I would thou wert cold or hot." It is just lukewarmness that he loathes most of all, and he has threatened to spue the lukewarm out of his mouth. Oh, to be always full of love to him! You will never get any hurt by working for him then; your work will do you good. The sweat of labor will even make your face the fairer. The more you do for souls, the purer, and the holier, and the more Christ will you be, if you do it with him. Keep up the habit of sitting at his feet, like Mary, as well as serving him with Martha. You can keep the two together; they will balance each other, and you shall not be barren or unfruitful, neither shall you fall into the blackness which the sun is apt to breed. O for more nearness to Christ, more love to Christ, and closer communion with him! Did you notice what the spouse said: "Tell me, O thou whom my soul loveth, where thou feedest?" I suppose her object was to go and feed with him. Look to the feeding of your own soul, Christian. When a man says, "I have a hard day's work to do, I shall have no time to eat," you know full well that he is losing time where he thinks he gains it; for if he does not keep himself in good repair he will sicken by-and-by, and in the long run he will do less than if he gave himself due pause. So is it with your soul. You cannot give out a vital energy which you have not got in you healthy and vigorous; and if you have not got power from God in your own soul, power cannot come out of you, for it is not there. Do, therefore, feed upon Christ. Or do you feel yourself like that guide of whom we spoke just now? Has the routine of service blunted your sensibilities, till you gaze unmoved on those objects of beauty and marvel that should awaken every passion and thrill every nerve of your being? Ask then in what way he might keep up his interest in the lakes and the mountains? Would it not be well for him, occasionally, at any rate, to take a lonely journey to find out new features in the gorgeous scenery or to stand in solitude, and see the hills in a fresh light, or mark the forest trees in different states of the weather; so that he might again renew his own sensations of admiration, and of gratitude to God for having created such sublimities? Then I can readily believe his enthusiasm would increase rather than abate by an increasing familiarity with the landscape. And you, worker for God, you must go to God alone; feed on precious truth for yourself; dig into the deep things of God and enrich your own spirit. Thus you may serve God as much as ever you will: you will get no hurt therefrom. Did you notice that she also asked: "Tell me where thou makest thy flock to rest at noon?" Rest is what the worker wants. Where is the rest of Christ's flock but in his own dear bosom? Where is there repose, but in his own fidelity, in the two immutable things wherein it is impossible for God to lie--the oath and the promise? Oh, never turn away from that rest! Turn into it again, to-night, beloved. As for me, I feel I want my Savior more than ever I did. Though I have preached his gospel now these five-and-twenty years and more, I need still to come and cling to his cross as a guilty sinner, and find "life for a look at the crucified One," just as I did at first. O that God's grace may ever keep the most ardent among us always faithful with our own soul, abiding in the Lord, and rejoicing in him!

I have done. This is my word to workers. Let me only say to you for whom there has seemed nothing in the sermon, if you are not workers for Christ, you are workers against him. "He that is not with me is against me; and he that gathereth not with me scattereth abroad." O souls, why should you stand out against the Savior? Why should you resist him? Bleeding out his life for his enemies, the mirror of disinterested love, what is there in him that can make you fight against him? Drop your weapons, man! Drop them to-night, I charge you by the living God! And come now, ask pardon through the precious blood, and it shall be given you. Seek a new heart, and a right spirit. The Holy Ghost will work it. From this night be a worker for Christ. The church wants you. The armies of Christ need recruiting. Take the proffered blessing, and become a soldier of the cross; and may the Lord build up his Zion by many of you who were not his people aforetime, but of whom it is said: "They were not my people, but they shall be the people of the living God."

The Fourfold Treasure

A Sermon (No. 991)
Delivered on Thursday Evening, April 27th, 1871, by
C. H. SPURGEON,
At the Metropolitan Tabernacle, Newington

"But of him are ye in Christ Jesus, who of God is made unto us wisdom, and righteousness, and sanctification, and redemption: that, according as it is written, he that glorieth, let him glory in the Lord." - 1 Corinthians 1:30, 31.

WE MEET SOMEWHERE IN THE OLD TESTAMENT with the expression "salt without prescribing how much." Beyond all question the name, person, and work of Jesus are the salt and savor of every true gospel ministry, and we cannot have too much of them. Alas! that in so many ministries there is such a lack of this first dainty of the feast, this essence of all soul-satisfying doctrine. We may preach Christ without prescribing how much, only the more we extol him the better. It would be impossible to sin by excess in preaching Christ crucified. It was an ancient precept, "With all thine offerings thou shalt offer salt;" let it stand as an ordinance of the sanctuary now: "With all thy sermonisings and discoursings thou shalt ever mingle the name of Jesus Christ, thou shalt ever seek to magnify the alpha and omega of the plan of redemption." The apostle in the first chapter of this epistle was anxious to speak to the Corinthians about their divisions and other serious faults; but he could not confine himself to that unpleasant theme; as naturally as possible his heart bounded over the mountains of division to his Lord and Master. Divisions did but remind him of the great uniting one who has made all his people one, and human follies did but drive him nearer to the infallible Christ who is the wisdom of God. Though Paul had to write many sharp things to those ancient Plymouth Brethren at Corinth, yet how sweetly did he prevent all bitterness by dipping his pen in the honeyed ink of love to the Lord Jesus, and admiration of his person and work! Let us, dear friends, if we have to preach, preach Christ crucified; and if we are private persons, let us in our household life, and in all our conversation, make his name to be as ointment poured forth. Let your life be Christ living in you. May you be like Asher, of whom it is said, he dipped his foot in oil may you be so anointed with the Spirit of your Lord that wherever you put down your foot, you may leave an impression of grace. The balmy south wind bears token of having passed over sunny lands; may the ordinary bent and current of your life bear evidence in it that you have communed with Jesus.

To-night we have before us a text which is extraordinarily comprehensive, and contains infinitely more of meaning than mind shall grasp, or tongue shall utter at this hour. Considering it carefully, let us observe, first, that the apostle here attributes the fact that we are in Christ Jesus to the Lord alone. He shows that there is a connection between our very being as Christians, and the love and grace of God in Christ. "Of him" (that is of God) "are ye in Christ Jesus." So we will first speak about our spiritual existence. Then Paul goes on to write of our spiritual wealth, which he sums up under four heads: wisdom, righteousness, sanctification, and redemption; but which indeed, I might say, he sums up under one head, for he declares that Christ is made of God unto us all these four things: and then he closes the chapter by telling us where our glorying ought to go--it should return to the source of our spiritual existence and heavenly wealth. "He that glorieth, let him glory in the Lord."

I. To begin, then, where God began with us--OUR SPIRITUAL EXISTENCE.

"Of him are ye in Christ Jesus." Different translators have read this passage in divers ways. "Of him," they think properly should be "Through him:" that is, "Through God we are in Christ Jesus." Are you this day united to Christ--a stone in that building, of which he is both foundation and topstone--a limb of that mystical body, of which he is the head? Then you did not get there of yourself. No stone in that wall leaped into its place; no member of that body was its own creator. You come to be in union with Christ through God the Father. You were ordained unto this grace by his own purpose, the purpose of the Infinite Jehovah, who chose you, or ever the earth was. "Ye have not chosen me, but I have chosen you." The first cause of your union with Christ lies in the purpose of God who gave you grace in Christ Jesus from before the foundation of the world. And as to the purpose, so to the power of God is your union with Christ to be attributed. He brought you into Christ; you were a stranger, he brought you near; you were an enemy, he reconciled you. You had never come to Christ to seek for mercy if first of all the Spirit of God had not appeared to you to show you your need, and to lead you to cry for the mercy that you needed. Through God's operation as well as through God's decree you are this day in Christ Jesus. It will do your souls good, my brethren, to think of this very common-place truth. Many days have passed since your conversion, it may be, but do not forget what a high day the day of your new birth was; and do not cease to give glory to that mighty power which brought you out of darkness into marvellous light. You did not convert yourself; if you did, you still have need to be converted again. Your regeneration was not of the will of man, nor of blood, nor of birth; if it were so, let me tell you the sooner you are rid of it the better. The only true regeneration is of the will of God and by the operation of the Holy Ghost. "By the grace of God I am what I am." He "has begotten us again unto a lively hope." "He that hath wrought us to the selfsame thing is God." "Of him are ye in Christ Jesus." Through the operation and will and purpose of God are you this day a member of Christ's body and one with Jesus. Give all the glory, then, to the Lord alone.

But suppose we read it as we have it in the text, and then we shall not have an allusion to the source of our spiritual life, but to the dignity of it. "Of God are ye in Christ Jesus." Being in Christ you are of God. Not of the earth earthy now, not of Satan, not of the bondage of the law, not of the powers of evil, but of God are you; God's husbandry, God's people, God's children, God's beloved ones. "Ye are of God," little children, "and the whole world lieth in wickedness." On you hath God's light shone, to you hath God's life come, in you God's love is made manifest, and in you shall God's glory be fully revealed. What a dignity is this to be "of God!" Some have thought it a great thing to have it said, "These are they which are of the prince's household," and others have been yet more boastful when they have been pointed at as parts of an imperial court; but you are of the divine family, descended from him who only hath immortality. "they shall be mine, saith the Lord, in the day when I make up my jewels." "For the Lord's portion is his people, Jacob is the lot of his inheritance." Of God, are you, every one of you who are in Christ Jesus: ye are Christ's, and Christ is God's. The Creator, the Upholder, the Sublime, the Invisible, the Infinite, the Eternal claims you. You have a part and lot with him, and you are herein uplifted to the highest degree of exaltation because you are in Christ.

Here, then, you have the dignity of the Christ life--it is of God, as its source is through God.

But note the essence of the Christ life. "Of God are ye in Christ Jesus." You have no life before the Lord, except as you are in Christ Jesus. Apart from him, you are as the branch that is severed from the vine--dead, withered, useless, obnoxious, rotten. Men gather these branches, and cast them into the fire, and they are burned. A ghastly sight it must be on the battle-field, to see on all sides arms, legs, and various portions of limbs torn away from the bodies to which they belonged, and scattered in hideous disorder! Once of the utmost service, these severed limbs are useless now. Every one knows that they are dead, for they cannot live divided from the vital regions: even thus if you and I could be separated from Christ, our vital head, death--spiritual death--must be the inevitable result. Our life hinges upon union to our Lord. "Because I live, ye shall live also." Out of Christ we abide in death, but in Christ we live, and we are of God. Our spiritual being, and the fact that our spiritual being is an exalted one, both hang upon this--that we are in Christ. Beloved Christian friends, I can congratulate you upon your being able to know that you are in Christ, and that so you are of God; but I must not speak so broadly to all this congregation. I must rather put a grave enquiry, and ask each of my hearers: Are you all in Christ Jesus? could the apostle write to you, and say: "Of God are you in Christ Jesus." Have you ever been the subject of a work of God, putting you into Christ Jesus?" Are you now of God in Christ Jesus so as to be depending for everything upon him, dwelling in him, and he in you; feeling his life within you, and that your life is hid with him in God? Beloved hearer, there is no joy in this world like union with Christ. The more we can feel it, the happier we are, whatever our circumstances may be. But if you are without Christ, you are without hope. Joy comes not where Jesus comes not. No Savior, then no peace in life or death. Oh remember, beloved hearer, that you will soon die. Where, where will you look for consolation in your last moments? Your soul will soon have to fly through tracks unknown, and face the burning throne of judgment. What will you do then, without the hand of love to guide you and the righteousness of Christ to cover you? He who wraps himself about with Christ's matchless robe can say--

"Bold shall I stand in that great day,
For who aught to my charge shall lay?
While through thy blood absolved I am
From sin's tremendous curse and shame."

But he that hath no Savior, it were better for him that he had never been born. That day is cursed, and hath no blessing, on which he first saw the light. Jesus Christ is willing to receive you if you desire to come to him. Noah's ark was shut, but not until the flood came, it was open till then; Christ is the ark of the covenant, and the door is not shut yet. Let not this, however, cause you to delay, for the flood will rise, and the rains will fall, and then to those who shall knock at the door, it will be said, "Too late! too late! Ye cannot enter now."

Of him, beloved believers in Christ, are ye in Christ Jesus. All you are, even to your bare existence as Christians, you have to trace to "the God and Father of our Lord Jesus Christ, which according to his abundant mercy hath begotten us again unto a lively hope by the resurrection of Jesus Christ from the dead, to au inheritance incorruptible and undefiled, and that fadeth not away."

II. Now let us turn to the second part of our subject, and contemplate OUR SPIRITUAL WEALTH. Christ Jesus is of God made unto us wisdom, righteousness, sanctification, and redemption. Here are four things--only it is to be noticed that in the original Greek the second and third have a peculiar connecting link, which the others have not. The wisdom stands alone, and the redemption, but the righteousness and sanctification have a special link, as though we should be taught that they always go together, that they should always be considered as united--a warning to modern theology, which so often divideth what God hath joined together.

Let us take the first blessing first, asking to be partakers of it at this very moment. Jesus Christ is made unto us wisdom. You noticed when we read the chapter that the apostle had been speaking of some other wisdom which he treated somewhat roughly. It had set itself up in opposition to the cross of Christ, and the apostle handled it with no gentle handling. There have always been those in the world who have conceived that wisdom would come to them as the result of the exercise of their own thoughts assisted by culture; that is to say, they hoped to know divine truth by their own thoughts and the additional light arising from the thoughts of other men. They fancied that wisdom would rise out of the human mind, and would not need to be taught us from above. There were those in Paul's days who were always ruminating, considering, contemplating with themselves, and then disputing, dialoguing, and conversing with others. These were the philosophers of the time. They looked for wisdom through man, and expected to find it in the shallow brain of a poor son of Adam. They so believed that they themselves were wise; that though they affected modesty and did not call themselves "the Sophoi, or wise;" but "the Philosophoi," or lovers of wisdom, yet for all that, in their innermost hearts they esteemed themselves to be an inner circle of instructed persons, and they looked upon the rest of mankind as the unilluminated and the ignorant. They had found a treasure which they kept to themselves, and virtually said to their fellow-men, "You are almost without exception hopelessly ignorant." Now, the apostle, instead of pointing to his own brain, or pointing to the statue of Socrates or Solon, says Jesus Christ is made of God unto us wisdom. We look no more for wisdom from the thoughts that spring of human mind, but to Christ himself; we do not expect wisdom to come to us through the culture that is of man, but we expect to be made wise through sitting at our Master's feet and accepting him as wisdom from God himself. Now, as it was in the apostle's day, so is it very much at this present. There are those who will have it that the gospel--the simple gospel--such as might have been preached by John Bunyan or Whitfield, or Wesley, and others, was very well for the many, and for the dark times in which they lived--the great mass of mankind would be helped and improved by it; but there is wanted, according to the wiseacres of this intensely luminous century, a more progressive theology, far in advance of the Evangelism now so generally ridiculed. Men of mind, gentlemen of profound thought, are to teach us doctrines that were unknown to our fathers; we are to go on improving in our knowledge of divine truth till we leave Peter and Paul, and those other old dogmatists far behind. Nobody knows how wise we are to become. Brethren, our thoughts loathe this; we hate this cant about progress and deep thought; we only wish we could know as much of Christ as the olden preachers did. We are afraid that instead of getting into greater light through the thinkings of men, the speculations and contemplations of the scribes, ancient and modern, and the discoveries of the intellectual and eclectic, have made darkness worse, and have quenched some of the light that was in the world. Again has it been fulfilled: "I will destroy the wisdom of the wise, and will bring to nothing the understanding of the prudent. Where is the wise? where is the scribe? where is the disputer of this world? hath not God made foolish the wisdom of this world?" It seemeth to me to be greater wisdom to believe what Christ hath said than to believe what my deepest thoughts have discovered; and though I have thought long upon a subject, and turned it over and over, and think I know more of it than another man, yet, in one simple word of Christ there is more wisdom than in all my thoughts and ruminatings. I am never to look to myself for wisdom, and to fancy that I am the creator of truth or the revealer of it; but ever to go to him, my Lord, my teacher, my all, and to believe that the highest culture, the best results of the highest education are to be found by sitting at his feet, and the best results of the deepest meditation, too, are to be gained in lying down in the green pastures, beside the still waters, where he, as the good Shepherd, leads me. Brethren, when we read that Christ is made of God unto us wisdom, let us recollect what wisdom is. Wisdom is, I suppose, the right use of knowledge. To know is not to be wise. Many men know a great deal, and are all the more fools for what they know. There is no fool so great a fool as a knowing fool. But to know how to use knowledge is to have wisdom. Now, that man is wise in three respects who has Christ for his wisdom. Christ's teaching will make him wise of thought, and wise of heart. All you want to know of God, of sin, of life, of death, of eternity, of predestination, of man's responsibility, Christ has either personally, or by his Spirit in the word of God, taught you. Anything that you find out for yourself, anything over and above revelation, is folly, but whatever he has taught is wisdom; and he has so taught it that if you learn it in the spirit in which he would have you learn it, it will not be dry, dead doctrine to you, but spirit and life; and his teaching will endow you with wisdom as well as knowledge. Scholars at the cross-foot let us always be. Never let us go to any other school than Schola crucis, for the learners of the cross are the favourites of wisdom. Let Corpus Christi be the college in which we study. To know Jesus, and the power of his resurrection, this is wisdom.

But, in addition to profiting by our Lord's instruction, the Christian learns wisdom through his Master's example. "Wherewithal shall a young man cleanse his way?" How shall I be made wise in action? Policy says, "Adopt this expedient and the other;" and the mass of mankind at this age are guided by the policy of the hour; but policy is seeming wisdom and real folly. Remember it is always wisest to act in any condition as Jesus would have acted, supposing him to have been in that condition. Never did he temporise. Principlo guided him, not fashion nor personal advantage. You shall never be a fool if you follow Christ, except in the estimation of fools; and who wishes to be wise in a fool's esteem? But sometimes it may be said: "To do as Christ would have done would involve me in present difficulty or loss." It is true; but there is no man that loseth aught in this life for Christ's sake who shall remain a loser, for he shall receive tenfold in this life, and in the world to come life everlasting. The wisest action is not always the most pecuniarily profitable. It is wise sometimes for men to be poor, ay, even to lose their lives. Truest wisdom--not sham wisdom, not temporary wisdom--you shall manifest by following the example of Christ, though it lead you to prison or to death. His teachings and his example, together, will give you the wisdom which cometh from above.

Above all, if you have the Redeemer's presence, he will be made of God unto you wisdom in a very remarkable sense. Never forget or doubt that Jesus is still with his people. They who know how to enter into the secret place of the tabernacles of the Most High, find him still at the mercy-seat. He feedeth among the lilies, and they who know the lilies know where to find him; and those who live with him, and catch his spirit, have their garments perfumed as his are with myrrh, and aloes, and cassia. These may be thought to be mad by some, and others may call them fanatical enthusiasts; but these are the wisest of mankind. O happy men that live at the gates of heaven while yet on earth, that sit at the feet of the blessed in the heavenly places in Christ Jesus while they are toiling along through the pilgrimage of this life! This is to be wise, to have Christ's teaching, Christ's example and above all, Christ's presence; so may the poorest find the Lord Jesus made of God unto them wisdom.

Pause just a minute. Let none of us ever be so foolish as to suppose that when we have received Jesus and his gospel, we have occasion to blush when we are in the company of the very wisest of the present day. Carry a bold face when you confront the brazen faced philosophy which insults your Lord. The man who does not believe the Bible does not know so much as thou dost. Blush not, though with mimic wisdom the unbeliever tries to laugh or argue thee down. He who knows; not Christ, though he propounds wonderful theories as to the creation of mankind and the formation of the world, and though he has a glib tongue, is only an educated fool, a learned idiot, who thinks his own rushlight brighter than God's own sun. "Ah I but he has been to college, and he has a degree, and he is esteemed by men; for he has written books that nobody can comprehend." "The fool hath said in his heart, There is no God;" and I do not care even if he be a Solon, if he has said that there is no God, he is a fool. Do not blush, then, if you find yourself in his company, do not make yourself the blushing one because the fool is there. Self-conceit were to be avoided and loathed; but this is not self-conceit, but a holy courage in a case which demands of you to be courageous. To know Christ is the best of all philosophy, the highest of all sciences. Angels desire to look into this; but I do not know that they care a fig for half the sciences so valued among men. If you know Christ you never need be afraid of being ashamed and confounded whatever company you may be in. If you stood in a senate of emperors, or amidst a parliament of philosophers, and only told them of the God that came in human flesh, and loved, and lived, and died to redeem mankind, you would have told them a greater mystery and a profounder secret than reason could discover. Be not ashamed, then, amid the intellectual pride of this boastful age.

At the same time let me remind you of another evil: do not seek to complete your wisdom at any other source: be satisfied that in keeping close to Christ you have the highest and truest wisdom. As I would not have you cowed before the pretender, neither would I have you envy him, or seek to supplement the wisdom that is in Christ Jesus by the wisdom that is of man. Are you so foolish, having begun with Jesus, will you end with a German neologian, or a French wit, or a Puseyite dreamer? Have you taken Christ's word to be your guide, and will you go and tack on to that some decree of Convocation, some rubric of a church, some minute of Conference, or other invention of human brain and fallen fancy? God forbid! Array yourself solely in this armor of gold, and go forth and gleam in the sun, and angels themselves shall marvel at you as they see your brightness. "Jesus Christ is made of God unto you wisdom."

It is high time for us to proceed to review the next blessing. He is made of God unto us righteousness. This was a great want of ours, for naturally we were unrighteous, and to this hour in ourselves we are the same. Righteous we must be to be acceptable with God, but righteous we certainly are not personally, and by merit. All our righteousnesses are as filthy rags, and we are unable to stand before the great King; but there is one who says: "Take away his filthy garments from him," and that same Deliverer, even the Lord Jesus Christ, is made of God unto us righteousness. You know how we usually speak of this as a double work. His blood cleanseth us from all guilt; by it pardon is bestowed upon the believer. He that looks to Christ is absolved from all sin--completely so. Then, in addition to that cleansing, which we call pardon, there is the clothing, the arraying in the righteousness of Christ--in a word, there is justification by faith. The doctrine of imputed righteousness seems to me to be firmly established in the word of God. Yet I have sometimes fancied I have heard a little too much stress put upon the word "imputed," and scarcely enough upon the word "righteousness;" for though I know that righteousness is imputed to us, yet I believe it is not all the truth that we are righteous by imputation. It is true, most true, but there is something true beyond it. Not only is Christ's righteousness imputed to me, but it is mine actually, for Christ is mine. He who believes in Jesus, has Jesus Christ to be his own Christ, and the righteousness of Christ belongs to that believer, and is his. We are not merely imputedly righteous, but the righteousness of our substitute is legally, actually, truly our righteousness. I am not now speaking of nature--that would have to do with sanctification--but I am speaking of repute before God. He reckons us to be righteous in Christ, and he does not reckon wrongly; the imputation is not a legal fiction or a charitable error. We are righteous. Depend upon it, God's imputation is not like human imputation, which makes a thing to be what it is not: we are in Christ made actually righteous, because we are one with him. Do you think that there is an unrighteous member of Christ's body? God forbid! Do you think Christ mystical to be a building with an unholy stone in it? Is Christ a vine with branches, which bear deadly fruit? As he is, so are we also in this respect. His salt has seasoned the whole lump. In the mystical body, every member is made righteous before God, because joined to the living head. Here is an actual righteousness given to us through the righteousness of Jesus Christ our Lord. He is made of God unto us righteousness. Consider this, O believer--you are to-night righteous before God. You are a sinner in yourself worthy to be condemned, but God does not condemn you, nor ever will he do so, for before the eye of his justice you are arrayed in perfect righteousness. Your sin is not upon you: it was laid upon the Scapegoat's head of old. All your iniquities were made to meet upon the head of the Crucified Savior: he bore your transgressions in his own body on the tree. Where are your sins now? You may ask the question without fear, for they have ceased to be. "As far as the east is from the west, so far hath he removed our transgressions from us." "He hath cast our iniquities into the depths of the sea." Glory be to his name, there is no sin in existence against a believer. Is it not written: "He hath finished transgression, made an end of sin [what stronger expression can there be?], and brought in everlasting righteousness"? And that is true of you to-night, Christian, as true of you to-night as it will be when you are in heaven. You are not so sanctified to-night as you will be in the glory land, but you are as righteous as you can be even there. In God's sight you are as much "accepted in the Beloved," as you will be when you stand on the sea of glass mingled with fire. You are beloved of God, and dear to him and justified, so that even to-night you can say: "Who shall lay anything to the charge of God's elect? It is God that justifieth. Who is he that condemneth?" You cannot lift up a louder boast than that, even when you shall see your Savior, and shall be like him because you see him as he is. By faith this righteousness is yours at this present moment, and will always be yours without a change; yours when your spirit is cast down, as much as when your joys abound. You are accepted not because of anything in yourself, but because you stand in the Lord your righteousness.

I remarked some time ago that the next blessing in our text is pinned on to this one. I need not not say much about that fact, but just note it. Righteousness and sanctification must always go together, and though they are two different things, or else there would not have been two different words, yet they blend into each other most remarkably, hence the Greek joins the two words by a close link. Our sanctification is all in Christ; that is to say, it is because we are in Christ that we have the basis of sanctification, which consists in being set apart. A thing was sanctified of old, under the law, when it was set apart for God's service. We were sanctified in Christ Jesus when we were set apart by the divine Spirit to be the Lord's own peculiar people for ever. Election is the basis of sanctification. Moreover, the power by which we are sanctified comes to us entirely by virtue of our union with Christ. The Holy Spirit who sanctifies us through the truth, works in us by virtue of our union with Jesus. That which becomes holy in us is the new life. The old nature never changes into a holy thing; the carnal mind is not reconciled to God, neither, indeed, can be. The old man is not sent to the hospital to be healed, but to the cross to be crucified. It is not transformed and improved, but doomed to die and to be buried. The ordinance of baptism, which is placed at the outset of Christ life, is meant to show, by our immersion in the liquid tomb, that it is by death and burial that we pass into life by the power of resurrection. If any man be in Christ, he is not an old creature mended up: he is a new creature. "Old things are passed away; behold all things are become new." Now, it is because this new life is the great, the true matter of sanctification, and because it comes to us by virtue of our oneness with Christ, that Jesus Christ is made to us the power and the life by which we are sanctified. Beloved, let your hearts add another meaning: let Jesus always be the motive for your sanctification. Is it not a strange thing that some professors should look to Christ alone for pardon and justification, and run away to Moses when they desire sanctification? For instance, you will hear persons preach this doctrine: "The Christian is to be holy, because if he be not holy he will fall from grace and perish." Do you not hear the crack of the old legal whip in all that? What is that but the yoke of that covenant which none of our fathers were able to bear? It is the bondage of Egypt, not the freedom of the children of God. Christ talks not so, nor his gospel. Think not to make thyself holy by motives of that kind. They are not right motives for a child of God. How then should we urge the child of God to holiness? Should it not be in this way: "Thou art God's child: walk worthy of him who is thy Father"? His love to thee will never cease. He cannot cast thee away: he is faithful and never changes, therefore love him in return. This is a motive fit for the child of the free woman, and it moves his heart. The child of the bond woman is driven by the whip, but the child of the free woman is drawn by cords of love. "The love of Christ constraineth us;" not fear of hell, but love of Christ; not fear that God will cast us away, for that he cannot do, but the joy that we are saved in the Lord with an everlasting salvation constrains us to cling to him with all our heart and soul, for ever and ever. Rest assured, if motives fetched from the gospel will not kill sin, motives fetched from the law never will. If you cannot be purged at Calvary, you certainly cannot be cleansed at Sinai. If "the water and the blood, from the riven side which flowed," are not sufficient to purify thee, no blood of bulls or of goats--I mean, no argument from the Jewish law, or hope of salvation by your own efforts--will ever furnish motives sufficiently strong to cast out sin. Let your reasons for being holy be found in Christ, for he is made of God unto you sanctification! I have ever found, and I bear my witness to it, that the more entirely for the future as well as for the present, I lean upon my Lord, the more conscious I am of my own emptiness and unworthiness; and the more completely I rest my whole salvation upon the grace of God in Christ Jesus, the more carefully do I walk in my daily life. I have always found that self-righteous thoughts very soon lead to sinful actions; but that, on the other hand, the very faith which leads to assurance, and makes the heart rest in the faithfulness of God in Christ, purifies the soul. "He that hath this hope in him purifieth himself, even as he is pure." Jesus, the Savior, saves us from our sins, and is made of God to us "sanctification."

Now the last item of our boundless wealth catalogued in the text is "redemption." Somebody says: "That ought to have come first; because redemption, surely, is the first blessing that we enjoy." Ay, but it is the last as well. It is the alpha blessing, I grant you that--but it is the omega blessing too. You are not yet redeemed altogether. By price you are--for he that redeemed you on the tree did not leave unpaid a penny of your ransom; but you are not yet altogether redeemed by power. In a measure, you are set free by divine power; for you have been brought up out of the Egypt of your sin, you have been delivered from the galling bondage of your corruption, and led through the Red Sea, to be fed upon the heavenly manna; but you are not altogether redeemed by power as yet. There are links of the old chains yet to be snapped from off you, and there is a bondage still about you from which you are ere long to be delivered. You are "waiting for the adoption, to wit, the redemption of the body." You will fall asleep, rejoicing that you were redeemed; but you will not, even when you die, have received the full redemption. When will that come--the full redemption? Only at the second advent of the Lord Jesus; for when the Lord shall descend from heaven with a shout, then the bodies of his saints, which have long been lying in the prison-house of the sepulcher, shall be redeemed by a glorious redemption from the power of death. "I know that my redeemer liveth." The bodies of the saints shall come again from the land of the enemy. Then their body, soul, and spirit--their entire manhood, which Christ hath bought, shall be altogether free from the reign of the enemy. Then will redemption be completed. Remember the saints in heaven without us cannot be made perfect, that is to say, they wait till we arrive among them, and when all the rest of the chosen ones shall be gathered in, and the fullness of time has come, then shall the bodies of the dead arise; and then, in body and soul made perfect, the year of the redeemed shall have fully come. "Lift up your heads; for your redemption draweth nigh." Here, then, is my joy, that Christ is my redemption. My soul is free from slavery, but my poor trembling and much suffering body feels the chains of death. Weakened by pain, my body shall in all probability bow before the stroke of death's sword. Unless the Lord soon come, it must be the portion of this frame to feed the worm and mingle with the dust: but, O my body, thou art redeemed, and thou shalt rise in power and incorruption; thou shalt yet adore the Lord without weariness, and without pain shalt thou serve him day and night in his temple. Even thou, O my weary body; even thou shalt be made glorious like unto the Lord himself: Thou shalt rise and live in the brightness of his presence.

All, then, that you can possibly want, O Christian, is in Christ. You cannot conceive a need which Jesus does not supply. "Wisdom, righteousness, sanctification, redemption," you have all in him. Some gather a flower here; some gather another there; some will go farther, and pluck another there; and some will go yet beyond to grasp a fourth; but when we win Christ we have a posey; we have all sweet flowers in one.

"All human beauties, all divine,
In my Beloved meet and shine
Thou brightest, sweetest, fairest one,
That eyes have seen or angels known."

But we cannot stay on this tempting subject, though even amid my present pain I would fain talk on by the hour together; and therefore I must finish with the last point; and on that only a word.

You see then, brethren, our very existence as Christians, and all that we possess as Christians, we get from God by Jesus Christ; let all our glory then be unto him. What insanity it is to boast in any but in our Lord Jesus! How foolish are they that are proud of the beauty of their flesh-worms' meat at the best! How foolish are they who are proud of their wisdom! The wisdom of which a man is proud, is but folly in a thin disguise. How foolish are they that are vain of their wealth! He must be a poor man who can think much of gold. He must be a beggar indeed who counts a piece of dirt a treasure. They that know Christ, always value these things at their right estimate, and that is low indeed. If any glory--and I suppose it is natural to us to glory, there is a boasting bump on all our heads--let us glory in the Lord; and here is a wide field and ample sea-room. Now, put out every stitch of canvas, run up the topgallants, seek as stiff a breeze as you will, there is no fear of running on a lee shore here, or striking a rock, or drifting on a quicksand! O men, O angels, O cherubim, O seraphim, boast in Jesus Christ! Wisdom, righteousness, sanctification, and redemption is he, therefore ye may boast and boast, and boast again! You will never exaggerate. You cannot exceed his worth, or reach the tithe of it. You can never go beyond the truth, you do not even reach beyond the skirts of his garments. So glorious is God that all the angels' harps cannot sound forth half his glory. So blessed is Christ that the orchestra of the countless multitudes of the redeemed, though it continue for ever and for ever its pealing music, can never reach to the majesty of his name or the glory of his work. "Give unto the Lord, O ye mighty, give unto the Lord glory and strength. Give unto the Lord the glory due unto his name." Let time and space become great mouths for song; let the infinite roll up its waves; let all creatures lift up their voices in praise of him that liveth and was dead; but chiefly, O my soul, since to him thou owest in a double sense thine existence, give thy praise to him from whom all blessing comes. Give thou the homage of thine intellect to him who is thy wisdom. Let thy conscience and love of rectitude adore him who has made thee righteous. Give the tribute of thy soul to him who sanctifies thee; let thy sanctified nature consecrate itself continually; and to him that hath redeemed thee give thou never-ceasing praise. I wish it were possible for me to rise to the height of my text, but my wings flag; I cannot ascend as the eagle, and face the full blaze of the sun; I can but mount a little as the lark, and sing my song, and then return to my nest. God grant you to know the Lord Jesus in his fullness in your personal experience.

O you to whom Christ is no wisdom, how foolish are you! O you to whom he is no righteousness, you are condemned sinners! O you to whom he is no sanctification, the fire of God's wrath will consume you! O you to whom he is no redemption, you are slaves in hopeless bondage! God deliver you! May you be led to put your trust in Jesus even now.

PORTION OF SCRIPTURE READ BEFORE SERMON--1 Corinthians 1.

Mr. Spurgeon earnestly requests the prayers of the Lord's people for his restoration to health. He has now been laid aside for eight most painful weeks, and at present there are very feeble signs of recovery.

A New Order of Priests and Levites

A Sermon (No. 992)
Delivered by
C. H. SPURGEON,
At the Metropolitan Tabernacle, Newington

"And I will also take of them for priests and for Levites, saith the Lord." - Isaiah 66:21.

THIS chapter is surrounded with critical difficulties, and yet it is full of spiritual instruction. The verse before us is by some referred to Gentiles, and supposed to mean that the Lord promises that he will take out of the heathen nations a people whom he will make into priests and Levites. Others would say it points to the Jews, rejected for their unbelief and dispersed in judgment among all nations. When their own Messiah came, it was not with a devout faith, but with a profane imprecation, they said, "His blood be on us, and on our children." The curse they invoked did come upon them. The retribution they challenged has been meted out to them in full measure. To the letter it was verified. Have you never read how, when Titus was besieging Jerusalem, five hundred Jews were sometimes crucified in a day? Do you not remember that Josephus, speaking as an eye-witness, said, "There wanted room for crosses, and crosses for bodies"? To this day their children are scattered in all lands, and have found no rest for the soles of their feet. But they are to be restored; they are to be brought back to their own land, and to worship God in his holy mountain; and in the latter days, when they are restored, then will God take of them for priests and Levites. To me it appears of very small consequence to which this verse refers, for in Christ Jesus there is neither Gentile nor Jew, circumcision nor uncircumcision; and this promise seems to me to stand good to the whole human race considered in its fallen state. "I will take of them for priests and for Levites, saith the Lord." Under the gospel dispensation God will select both out of Jews and Gentiles a chosen people, who shall stand before him spiritually as the priests and the Levites stood before him typically.

Think for a minute of the compass of this great promise. Evidently a high honor is here conferred. The connection leads us to see that not only a great promise but likewise a great privilege is herein implied. What is this privilege? It is that we shall be priests and Levites. Now, the priests or Levites were persons set apart to be God's peculiar property. When the firstborn were spared in Egypt, God claimed the firstborn to be his own, and he took the tribe of Levi to represent the firstborn; they were to be the Lord's. Though all Israel belonged to God, yet the tribe of Levi was especially selected and particularly appointed to do the service of the tabernacle of the congregation; and of this tribe of Levi, chief among them the house of Aaron, to minister in the sanctuary as priests. So now, glory be to God, he takes out of all nations a people that are to be peculiarly his own--his own by election, as he chose them--his own by redemption, as he bought them--his own by endowment through the regenerating and sanctifying operations of the Holy Spirit. "They shall be mine, saith the Lord of hosts, in that day when I make up my jewels;" his own, therefore, before time, and after time shall close. "I will take of them for priests and for Levites, saith the Lord." Being thus set apart as the Lord's property, the priests and Levites lived only for divine service. While others were engaged with their trade or upon their farm, the Levites were attending to the tabernacle or temple, and the priests in their courts were slaughtering bullocks and lambs, and offering them to God; or they had other duties of a kindred order, by reason of the charge given them of all the hallowed things of the children of Israel. Anyhow, it was in sacred things that they were occupied; so now, it is the duty of every man to serve the Lord; but, alas! man will not; and therefore God takes unto himself a people out of all nations, and kindreds, and tongues, and he ordains them to stand before him continually, to wait on his commands, and to do his bidding. Thus he puts upon their shoulders his easy yoke and weights them with his light burden, and they become his willing servants--that their life may be for his glory, and that their desire, as well as their duty, may be to serve him with heart and strength so long as they have any being. In this sense, then, happy is the man who is set apart to the divine service, a priest and a Levite unto God.

Further than this, the priests and the Levites enjoyed the privilege of drawing near to God--

nearer than the rest of the people in that typical dispensation. While the people stood without, the Levites are busy inside. One of them, the chief of the tribe, and the High Priest before the Lord for all the tribes, was permitted and commanded to go into the most holy place within the veil; and you know that the holy places made with hands are figures of the true, even of heaven itself. In like manner there is a people to be found on earth at this day whom God has chosen to draw near unto him. In Christ Jesus they who sometimes were afar off, are made nigh by the blood of Christ. The same precious blood that is applied to their conscience is sprinkled on the mercy-seat; therefore they have access to the Father. Oh! happy they, who, like the priests and Levites, love dwelling in the Lord's house, and praising him, who can say--

"Here, Lord, I find settled rest
While others go and come;
No more a stranger or a guest,
But like a child at home."

Lord, thou hast been our dwelling-place in all generations: we are a people near unto thee made nigh by affinity with the Son of God, brought nigh by the blood, led nigh by the Spirit of God, kept nigh, and rejoicing to be nigh--for herein is our honor and comfort, to be near unto God; made priests and Levites, because claimed as God's portion, prepared for God's service, and admitted to a near familiarity with him. There are some such to be found in this place to-day, whom God has taken from among the Gentiles to be priests and Levites unto him. But priests and Levites had two works to do: something to do towards God for men, and something to do towards men for God. They were engaged to do something towards God for men, and so they offered the sacrifices that were brought to the door of the tabernacle, whether according to the general ordinances, or to any special vows. Spiritually minded, they were much engaged in intercession for the rest of Israel. So there is a people to be found this day who offer unto God acceptable prayer and praise, and in answer to their prayer, unnumbered blessings come down upon the sons of men. I trust there are some here that have power with God in prayer. Ye are the king's remembrancers; ye make mention of his name, and keep not silence; ye cry to God for Sodom, and yet more hopefully ye cry to God for Jerusalem: your prayer ceaseth not, and God's grace and favor always follow it. In this sense God is constantly taking out, even from amongst the vilest of the vile, a people whom he makes to be priests and Levites for men towards himself. Another part of their office consisted in speaking for God to the people; "For the priest's lips should keep knowledge." As for the Levites, they were as ushers in the schools and tutors in the families of Israel. Amongst the Levites were found those scribes who became the instructors of the people, the copyists of the law, and the expounders of its statutes and ordinances; ministers who opened up to the people, as Ezra did, the knotty points of the old covenant, and expounded the word. So not all of us in the same degree, but all of us in a measure, are to be teachers of God's revealed truth, even as he has taught us; and he has in this place, and throughout the world, taken out a certain company whom he has made to speak as his mouth to the sons of men--men of his own choosing, and his own sending, who are as priests and Levites for his name. They claim no priestly office as though they could absolve the sinner: they leave that with Christ, the firstborn of his Father's house, and the chief rabbi of all the Lord's chosen seed, but as teachers and instructors; they are in the midst of the world the priests and Levites of God. I have thus shown what the promise means. God will take out of the Jews and Gentiles a people whom he will bring very near to himself, and make use of for his own sacred purposes. The great point is this. It seems to be mentioned here as a matter of surprise that God should take any of them--of the persons here mentioned--of the sinful, backsliding, tranegressing Jews, or of the blinded, dark, benighted, heathen Gentiles--that he should take them, and make them to be priests and Levites before him. Now, that is parallel to the fact that God does take some of the most unlikely persons, who seem to be the most unsuitable of all, and make these to be his faithful and honored servants among the sons of men.

Now, I shall first notice that fact; then, the reason for it; and then, the lessons from it.

I. First, I notice that God does, to the astonishment of men, TAKE SOME WHOM HE MAKES BE PRIESTS AND LEVITES TO HIMSELF. This is a fact. How, there are priests and Levites that God never took. There have been such in all ages. There were those in the days of Aaron who said: "Ye take too much upon you, ye sons of Levi;" and when they stood before the Lord with their censers, "the earth opened her mouth and swallowed them up." There were those in the days of Elias. When he stood by the altar of the Lord, the priests of Baal, in great numbers, stood by their altar, offering prayer to Baal. Ye know how God had no regard to their sacrifice. They were the church established by law; but, for all that, Elias the Nonconformist, put them to the rout, and maintained the worship of the invisible God of Israel firm and faithful to the end. So in our Savior's days there were priests and Levites--men taught and instructed in the law, and these were the very men who conspired together against him, who took counsel how they might put him to death, and who stirred up the people to say, "Not this man, but Barabbas." And on down to this present day there are those legitimate priests and Levites--at least, those who call themselves so--whom God hath never taken, upon whom he hath never laid his hand, upon whom his Holy Spirit hath never descended; who speak, but he speaks not by them; and who administer ordinances, but he gives not grace to the ordinances by their hands. And such there always will be, doubtless, till Christ cometh, but they are not spoken of in the text, for the text says, "I will take," and it is only those whom God himself takes and chooses among men that are the real priests and Levites that serve him.

Observe, according to the text, men have nothing to do with the selection; for here it is said, "I will also take of them"--not "their parents shall bring them up to it;" not "those who shall be looked out as the most fit and proper men on account of some natural bent and bias, or gift and talent, but I will take." God's priesthood in the world is a priesthood of his own choosing of his own setting apart, of his own anointing. "He hath made us kings and priests unto God." The church is a royal priesthood, not of man, neither by man, nor of the will of man, nor of blood, nor of birth: it is of God's choosing. This sacred and consecrated band of priests and Levites, and all that serve God effectually and acceptably, are men whom he has himself chosen to the work. He himself hath done it, and only his own will as been consulted in the matter. In their case, it appears from the text, that whatever was unfit in their character has been overcome by divine grace. "I will also take of them for priests and for Levites, saith the Lord." If God takes them for Levites, he makes them Levites; if he chooses them for priests, he makes them priests. So, glory be to his name, when he chose you, my dear brother, when he chose you, my dear sister, to be his servants, to be his priests and his Levites, he gave you the grace you wanted. He found in you no natural fitness, no suitability, but in fitness for sin, a suitability to go astray, and to become a brand for the burning; but if there be a fitness in you to serve him on earth and in heaven, it is his grace that has done it. It is his grace speaking in all its wondrous majesty--"I will take of them for priests and for Levites"--which has effected in you the great transformation, making in you all things new, and thus qualifying you to become the servants of the Most High. In some persons this natural inaptitude and unfitness for the Lord's work has been more apparent than in others. They have been men of rough exterior, unhallowed life; their education neglected, their passions wild and lawless, their tastes low and grovelling; yet, for all that, God has taken from amongst such men some who in an especial manner, even beyond the rest of God's servants have become as priests and Levites unto him. He has sometimes selected women, in whom there seemed to be no suitability for his grace, to make them matrons in the church; and men, who seemed to be ringleaders in the service of Satan, to make them very captains of the Lord's hosts. They had no inbred faculty, no natural genius that qualified them to become the instruments of righteousness: as I have said before, it was the reverse of this. Their career was not foreshadowed by any instinct with which they were born; nor was it aided by any training they received in childhood. The God who chose them gave the grace they required at their second birth, and subdued all the evil that was in them by the rich discipline of his spiritual operations, in order to qualify them for efficient service. I thank God, I do remember in my soul some dear brethren who have been made eminent ministers of the gospel, of whom, if any one had said they would ever have preached the gospel, none would have believed it. Not to mention the living, the men of to-day, go back to the early days of John Newton, an earnest preacher, a famous evangelist, not to add a sweet poet. Almost a model for the ministry was John Newton, but once a blasphemer and injurious. Turn farther back, to John Bunyan, on the village green, with his tip-cat on the Sabbath-day, with all a drunkard's vices and sins, and foul-mouthed in his profanity: yet John Bunyan becomes an eminent proclaimer of the gospel, and the author of a matchless allegory which has served to guide many a pilgrim to heaven. Turn farther back, to Luther, most earnest as a Romanist for all the letter of the law, diligent in every ceremony, superstitious to a high degree, yet afterwards the bold proclaimer of the gospel of the grace of God. Turn to Augustine, in youth of corrupt and vicious propensities, according to his own confession, to the grief of his mother Monica, yet called by sovereign grace to be one of the fathers of the church, and a notable exponent of sound doctrine. Look yet farther back to the apostle Paul, breathing out threatenings and slaughter against the disciples of the Lord, like a huge wild beast, making havoc of the church, but suddenly struck down, and almost as suddenly raised up a new man, and ordained (not of men, neither by man, but by Jesus Christ and God the Father) to be a chosen vessel unto Christ, to bear his name unto the Gentiles. "I will also take of them," the most unlikely and unfit, according to human judgment. "I will also take of them for priests and for Levites unto me." And where the service has not taken the form of preaching, we can remember some whom God hath made eminent in prayer. Never account prayer second to preaching. No doubt prayer in the Christian church is as precious as the utterance of the gospel. To speak to God for men is a part of the Christian priesthood that should never be despised. Surely I have heard some prayers of those whom none would ever have expected to pray, such as I have not heard from those who, from their youth up, have been accustomed to the language of devotion--moved with energy and full of fervor, like Elijah. Or, shall I say it, they have become in spiritual force nerved as Samson was with physical strength. In their prayers they have seemed to take hold of the pillars of the temple of Satan, and pull it down upon their enemies; they have been so mighty as to wrestle with God and prevail. God has taken of them--that is, even of the prayerless, and the careless, and the blaspheming--and he has made these to be priests and Levites unto him. And in all other holy service I think I can recollect eminent men who out of weakness were made strong, from simpletons they were changed into sages, or, rescued from the dregs of infamy, they became paragons of virtue. In their unregeneracy as bitter fruit, apples of Sodom, that crumbled into dust and turned to ashes, yet so transformed by the renewing of their minds, that they bore the richest clusters of choicest fruit to the praise and glory of the Great Husbandman. "I will also take of them for priests and for Levites, saith the Lord." There is the fact. You need not that I enlarge upon it. While a false priesthood still lives (and always will), God has his elect people, who are his royal priesthood among the sons of men, who are discharging regal functions and sacred offices among the sons of men in his name, and before his face; and these he oftentimes takes out from the least likely of mankind.

II. And now, secondly, as to THE REASON OF THE FACT. Does not he do this to display his mercy--his great and infinite mercy? that those who have provoked him to wrath should become the men in whom he should show forth his lovingkindness--men to be pardoned, men to be washed, to be sanctified--and then men to be put in trust of the gospel of Jesus Christ--does not this reveal and illustrate the high prerogative of sovereign grace? "Unto me," saith the apostle, "who am less than the least of all saints, is this grace given, that I should preach among the Gentiles the unsearchable riches of Christ." It is a great grace to be permitted to preach the gospel. I have sometimes said to you that when the prodigal came back to his father, and was received into his father's house, no earthly parent, though he had quite forgiven him all the wildness of his son's adventure, could wholly forget the waywardness of his disposition. He might condone the past without confiding in him for the future. If it were needful to send one of the sons to market with a bag of money, the good old father would, in all probability, say to himself, "I will send the elder son with it: he is better to be trusted; I would hardly like to put such a responsibility upon the young lad who has so lately been reclaimed." I can fancy, without uttering a word to his younger son he would, discreetly (as you would say), trust the other with any weighty concerns. But our heavenly Father--oh, how he forgives us! He leaves no back reckonings, for though we used to be such sinners, some of us, and so injurious, after he forgave us, he committed to our charge not merely silver and gold, the perishable resources of time, but the priceless treasure of the gospel of Jesus Christ: he allowed us to go and tell to others "the unsearchable riches of Christ." See ye not the impure giving, lessons on chastity, the intemperate teaching chastity? and mark ye not how he who persecuted the disciples in times past, now preacheth the faith he once destroyed? Oh, what deep mercy there is in Jesus! What wonderful grace there is in giving his commissions, that those that cursed him themselves should intercede with him for others; that those that despised him should be permitted to honor him; that those who broke his Sabbaths should nevertheless be helpful to his people in hallowing the Lord's-day; that those who despised his word, and put it behind their back, should be the men to open it, and display the sweetness of it to their fellow men! Is not this grace? Methinks every time Paul preached Jesus Christ he would say to himself: "I used to call him the Nazarene; I abhorred him and used opprobrious language, but herein is great mercy, boundless mercy, that he should take me to be his servant, permit me to labor for his people and suffer for his sake."

Next to this, do you not think that the Lord loves to display his power? Men who are tamers of wild beasts, will frequently, when they have subdued a lion, take a delight in showing to the people how obedient that lion will be to them, and how every word that the lion-tamer chooses to say, it will regard and pay attention to. Thus, when the Lord takes a great sinner, after he has tamed him, removed his heart of stone, and given him a heart of flesh, he desires to show how, without the use of the whip, without a threatening look or an angry word, he causes his enemy to become his diligent servant, his earnest friend. O brethren, it shows the power of love on a man when he is so broken down that the things he sneered at he now preaches with all his might. Surely it showed the power of divine grace when Paul avowed Christ openly, and vehemently preached--exposing himself to persecution and death--that same gospel which his soul had previously nauseated; yea, which his zeal, full of bitterness, had kindled to exterminate. God takes great sinners, and then appoints and qualifies them to be priests and Levites, in order that he might show the exceeding greatness of his power to usward who believe.

Again, does not God do this to show his sovereignty? Can we ever forget that attribute of the Almighty? Divine grace, while it comes freely to us, is dispensed freely by God, according to the good pleasure of his will. I should like to hear that text thundered throughout Christendom: "I will have mercy on whom I will have mercy, and I will have compassion on whom I will have compassion." No man hath any right to the mercy of God. We have all sinned ourselves into outlaw: all the rights we have are the right to be condemned, and the right to be cast into hell; all the rights of man that he can appeal to God for in equity are merged in the wrongs for which he is responsible. If the Lord have mercy, it is his own will to do it: he can withhold it if it pleases him; so he selects the most degraded, those that have gone farthest from him, and takes them into his church; nay, more, advances them into eminent positions of service in that church, that all his people may know that the Most High ruleth in the armies of heaven and Amongst the inhabitants of this earth, and none can stay his hand, or say unto him, "What doest thou?" He lifteth up the poor from the dunghill, and setteth him among princes, even among the princes of his people. His mercy, power, and sovereignty are displayed when he takes of them to be priests and Levites.

But does he not thereby secure to himself the most loving service? I have sometimes thought (I hope I am not censorious) as I have observed with pain the superficiality of a great deal of what is called ministry in these days--that kind of superficiality, I mean, in which little is said about the corruption and depravity of the heart; little about the experience of the child of God when under the law; little, far too little, about the glory of that grace that takes such worms of the dust to make them one with Christ. I have often thought that this avoidance of, not to say this aversion to, deep ploughing, may be accounted for by the fact that the preachers themselves probably had not been suffered to go very far into outward sin; had never had any very deep law-work upon their souls; never had much awakening of conscience, nor felt much of the powers of the world to come. They got their religion very easily; and so knowing little of soul-humbling sensations themselves, they could not go very deeply into the experience of the children of God. When the Lord calls a grievous sinner, to make a gracious example of him, it is not so. The man who has done business in deep waters knows what sin means; tortured with a sense of his own crimes, he has been like those wretched culprits who surrender themselves to justice, because their conscience makes liberty chafe them. He knows what pardon means, for he has found peace after great bitterness, and got remission after the gnawings of despair; he knows what the conflicts of God's people are, for he has had many fierce encounters with the lusts that beset him within, and the temptations that assailed him from without. And now, when he opens his mouth, the testimony he bears is from an inwrought experience: he speaks of things which he has tasted and handled of the good Word of God. John Newton, to whom I referred just now, could not do otherwise than livingly and lovingly preach the Word of God. You could not have brooked from him a dainty essay or a flowery sermon, because nothing else would have consorted and accorded with his experience, but a faithful tale of the way the Lord had led him, and a forcible exposition of what the Lord had taught him. He had been such a sinner, that it must be grace which saved him; and he would have belied all his inward feelings if he had not proclaimed the grace of God. And so with Bunyan: if he had not tearfully wept over sinners and preached Jesus Christ in his fullness, as the Savior of Jerusalem sinners, he would have been opposing all that animated his own breast, and all that burned and glowed for utterance. God, therefore, takes some of these men who have gone far astray, that he might have warm-hearted, intensely earnest men, who must proclaim the gospel, because they have felt its power; who love much because they have had much forgiven; who preach of grace, because they need much grace, and lift up high the brazen serpent amongst the sin-bitten hosts of men, because they have been sin-bitten themselves and do remember it; they have looked and been cured, and they still remember the cure, and rejoice in it.

Another reason why the Lord takes the vilest of men to make them the saintliest is, that he might openly triumph over Satan. How the devil must feel defeated when such a man as Saul is taken straight away from persecuting to preaching! Surely, it makes Satan bite his chains and gnash his teeth when he loses his servants so. Just when he has trained them up, and got them into fine condition for doing mischief, in comes the officer of divine grace, arrests them, and changes their hearts. You know none ever do the devil so much mischief as those who once did him service. They know the ins and outs of his castle--where to attack it. They understand so much of his devices and tactics, that they become all the more powerful adversaries when they are converted. All heaven rings with rapture when a great sinner is saved; and all hell howls with dismay when one of the arch host bows down to kiss the feet of Christ, and receive the mercy of God. Glory be to God when he takes those that would have been deepest damned, and sets them highest among the saved on earth to be priests and Levites unto him. By these means also he secures another end: he encourages poor penitents; for when a sinner, under a sense of sin, meets with a brother in Christ, who was like himself once, but is now living near to God and serving him acceptably, he is much encouraged. "Why," he thinks to himself, "is this how God receives sinners when they turn to him? Perhaps he will receive me." And if he gets into conversation with one of those whom God has made priests and Levites, he says, "Tell me what the Lord has done for thy soul." And the minister being a man of like passions, and having had like experience, delights to describe the works and ways of God with hardened sinners and old offenders and then the man who is seeking finds in the other a guide who is touched with the feeling of his infirmity, is very helpful to him, and much blessed of God to enter into the secrets of his heart, and lead him to the cross. If there be here some great rebel against God, I think he ought to take encouragement thence to turn unto the Lord and live, for surely, when God so treats his most defiant enemies as to make them his most honored ministers, there should be some comfort for the great sinner to seek the Lord while yet he waits to be gracious.

And do not you think this is done very much for the encouragement of the church of God? I know, as myself one of its humble members I often need to be solaced by seeing what God's hand can do. We ought to walk by faith, and so I trust we do; but when we see sinners converted, it gives zest to our fellowship and zeal to our enterprise. We all of us feel the happier for it. I hardly expect to see so many converts in the Tabernacle as there used to be. We have had so very many brought to God, that those of you who are left, I almost fear, have resisted overmuch the wooings and warnings of love divine. Indeed, there are so few comparatively left, that we have not the opportunities we once had when the mass of the congregation was not converted. Peradventure there are few of you whom God has not blessed. But I do long to see a fresh ingathering of converts: it would make my heart glad, and it would make all the church glad if we heard of some great sinners being saved.

I pray God sometimes that he would save a great multitude of the priests of the church of Rome and the church of England. Be did in the olden times bring a great multitude of the priests to believe the gospel, and why should he not yet again? If he wills to call to himself some of the lowest of the low, and the vilest of the vile, and make them wonders of his grace, his omnipotent fiat shall be instantly obeyed. Why should he not? Why should he not? He has done so: why should he not again? He has done so, I say, and the text says, "I will take of them for priests and for Levites." Why should he not go on to take from strange quarters still a people that shall serve him? Does he not say "I will"? Suppose it should ever come to this, as some say it will, that the churches, many of them, should desert the old truths, and the ministers become dumb dogs that cannot bark, and one by one their testimony should be silent, and every candlestick should be taken out of its place, and the whole head should be sick, and the whole heart faint, and Zion be under a cloud, and there should be none to help her, and none to lift up the banner for the truth? What then? Why, then God would arise, and take again from the fishermen in their boats new apostles, and from the lowest dens of iniquity, and the worst haunts of vice, from the saloons of frivolity where the rich resort, and from the chambers of commerce and the palaces of merchandise where buyers and sellers make their contracts, he would take a fresh staff of men. Out of the roughest material he can make the finest fabric, out of the newest recruits he can raise the noblest regiment, to show forth his praise, to do his work, and to secure victory for his cause. If some were unworthy holders of his vineyard, and brought him no revenue, he would put aside these wicked men, and send forth fresh laborers, and give his vineyard unto others, for he will get glory unto his name; he "will take of them for priests and for Levites." Never say it is a dark day; never say God has forgotten his church; never give way to despairing fits, and dream of horrible times coming, that yet are not to come. Verily, "all flesh shall see the salvation of God," and the glory of God shall be revealed, and all flesh shall see it; for the mouth of the Lord hath spoken it. He shall arise, and have mercy upon Zion; he will build up her walls, heal all her breaches, and once again shall she be the joy of the whole earth. Take heart and comfort, God can find his servants anywhere. Omnipotence hath instruments where we see them not. He "will take of them for priests and for Levites."

III. Lastly, WHAT IS THE LESSON FROM THIS? I address myself to those of you especially, my dear brethren and sisters, whom the grace of God has taken to make priests and Levites unto God. You are near to him: you serve him. What effect should this have upon you? First, remember what state you where in before God's grace took you in hand. Then consider what you are called to be; you are made priests and Levites. Then ask yourself what you would soon become if his grace were to depart from you? Why, as you were before, only with this difference, that the evil spirit in you would take unto himself seven other spirits more wicked than the first, and enter in and dwell there, and your last state would be worse than the first. Watch then, watch! watch! God, his grace enabling you to watch, will preserve you to the end. Am I a priest and Levite--a holy vessel set apart before God, serving at his altar, bringing prayers and praises to him? Ah! yes, I may be a priest and a Levite, but I should be a devil if his grace did not prevent. O watch, watch, watch! "What I say unto you I say unto all, Watch."

And oh, what humility this vocation of God should produce! However high we may be raised, we must remember whence the honor cometh. For this promotion cometh neither from the east nor from the west--it is God's gift. Thou, a blasphemer and injurious; thou, a careless, godless, Christless man, now raised to be a servant of God, to wait in his courts, and honor his name, be thankful that thou art lifted so high, but wonder, and fear and tremble, for all the goodness that God has made to pass before thee. What am I, and what is my father's house, that thou hast brought me hitherto; to pray and my prayer to be heard, yet not worthy to lift mine eyes to the place where thine honor dwelleth; to have thy holy Spirit dwelling in me, and yet not worthy that thou shouldst come under my roof! Be humble brother: it will help you to watch. Watching is done best in a lowly manner.

And since he hath taken us for priests and for Levites, let us do every office heartily as unto the Lord. If others in this world can serve God coldly, yet, my brethren and sisters, you and I cannot afford to do so. We were such sinners, that if we have been forgiven, we must love him. Those that had little sin to be cleansed may not have much love to lavish on their Redeemer. Not so with me or thee:

"Love I most; I've more forgiven;
I'm a miracle of grace."

Those that had some good principles instilled into them by early training or some sort of preparation to receive the gospel, may not feel their deep indebtedness to the wonderful working of the Spirit; but those of us who were steeped in sin, and hardened in heart, when we are saved must magnify the power of God, and moved by that feeling we must serve him heartily with our whole spirit, soul, and body. A man that feels what grace has done for him cannot help throwing his whole soul into it. I used to know a man whom I often heard swear--on the other side of the river, in the town where I was--and when converted I recollect his prayers. They used to trouble us rather: they were so loud. It was not everybody that knew the reason why. He had been so accustomed to swear loud that he could not help praying loud; and when a man has been very loud for the devil, he cannot help being loud for Christ. Some of those dear Methodist brethren who cry out, "Amen!" so stentoriously, do it, I hope, because they feel the love of God in Christ on account of what great things have been done for them. Let those go the common track of service that have gone the common track of sin, but let those serve the Lord with all their heart, and mind, and strength, that have been unusual sinners. Bring your alabaster box, O great sinner, break it on his blessed head that pardoned you. Wash his feet with your tears, and wipe them with the hairs of your head, for where extraordinary love has been experienced, extraordinary love ought to be the outgrowth, and extraordinary service ought to be the consequence.

Once again, if the Lord has taken of us to be his priests and Levites, let us serve him with great thankfulness and joy. If any people should be glad, I am sure it is those people that feel the aboundings of his mercy in forgiveness, having heard those glad tidings, as it were, from the lips of Jesus himself. "Thy sins which are many are all forgiven thee: go in peace." They have something always to stimulate their gratitude and regale them with sunshine. "I am very poor," saith one, "but, never mind, poor as I am, I am not a drunkard or a swearer now; I feel weak and sickly in body, it may be; never mind that; I have not the burden of sin upon my soul." Or, "I am unknown, quite unknown. I have nobody to come and see me. Never mind that; I am known to God. I am poor and needy, yet the Lord thinketh upon me. My great wounds have been healed in Jesus' precious blood." Why, you have always cause to be glad, my dear brother and sister, if you have had your sins forgiven: you have a fountain opened in your soul of love to Christ and joy in God, quite as surely as there is a fountain open for the cleansing of your sin in the side of Jesus.

So let me close, by saying, surely we ought to serve God with great confidence in him. If he has made us priests and Levites to him, why then we may trust him to do anything. "He that spared not his own Son, but delivered him up for us all, how shall he not with him also freely give us all things?" He that has done so much for us, as to take us out of the miry clay, and set our feet upon a rock, and put his gospel into our hearts, may be trusted for the rest. Suppose a man owed you ten thousand pounds and a trifling sum besides for a small promissory note he had given you; if he paid you the ten thousand pounds, you might trust him to meet the little bill when it fell due. And when the Lord has given us so much, so infinitely much, the little that remains--for it is comparatively little--ought to cause us no anxieties or doubts, no fears or misgivings. "Because thou hast been my help, therefore in the shadow of thy wings will I rejoice." He who found me a sinner, made me a pardoned sinner, put me among his children, and numbered me among his honored servants, has not done all this to desert me at last and put me to shame. He has not been at this expense with his poor servant to fling him away after all. No, glory be to his name: he will continue his work till he has perfected it. He is the God that performeth all things for me, and in him will I rest, and not be ashamed, world without end. Amen.

PORTION OF SCRIPTURE READ BEFORE SERMON--Isaiah 66.

The Northern Iron and the Steel

A Sermon (No. 993)
Delivered by
C. H. SPURGEON,
At the Metropolitan Tabernacle, Newington

"Shall iron break the northern iron and the steel?" - Jeremiah 15:12.

THE prophet Jeremiah was, as we saw upon a former occasion, a man of exquisitely sensitive character; not a prophet of iron, like Elijah, but nearer akin to him who was a man of sorrows and acquainted with grief. He lived in times which were peculiarly trying to him, and in addition was called to exercise an office which involved him in perpetual sorrow. He loved the people among whom he dwelt, yet was he commissioned by God to pronounce judgments upon them; this in itself was a hard task to such a nature as his. As a loving father, fearful of Eli's doom, uses the rod upon his child, but feels each stroke in his own heart far more acutely than the child does upon his back, so every threatening word which the prophet uttered lashed his own soul, and cost his heart the direst panics. He went, however, to his work with unstaggering firmness; hopeful, perhaps, that when his countrymen heard the divine threatening, they would repent of their sin, seek mercy, and find it. Surely if anything can add weight to the prophecy of the judgments of God, it is the trembling love, the anxious fear with which such a messenger as Jeremiah would deliver his warning. The deep sorrow of him who warned them ought to have driven the sinful nation to a speedier repentance; instead of which they rejected his warnings, they despised his person, and defied his God. As they thus heaped wrath upon themselves, they also increased his sorrow. He was a delicate, sensitive plant, and felt an inward shudder as he marked the tempest gathering overhead. Though a most loyal servant of his God, he was sometimes very trembling, and though he never ventured, like Jonah, to flee unto Tarshish, yet he cried in the bitterness of hie soul, "O that I had in the wilderness a lodging-place of wayfaring men; that I might leave my people, and go from them!" The Jews treated him so harshly and unjustly, that he feared they would break his heart; they smote him ae with an iron rod, and he felt like one crushed beneath their unkindness. To silence his fear, the Lord assures him that he will renew his strength. "Behold," saith he, "I have made thee this day a defenced city and an iron pillar, and brazen walls against the whole land, against the kings of Judah, against the princes thereof, against the priests thereof, and against the people of the land. And they shall fight against thee; but they shall not prevail against thee; for I am with thee, saith the Lord, to deliver thee." Thus the Lord promised to his servant the divine support which his trials demanded He never did and never will place a man in a trying position and then leave him to perish. David dealt thus treacherously with Uriah, but the Lord acts not thus with his servants. If the rebellious seed of Israel were iron, the Lord declared that his prophet should be hardened by sustaining grace into northern iron and steel. If they beat upon him like hammers on an anvil, he should be made of such strong, enduring texture, that he should be able to resist all their blows. Iron in the olden times amongst the Israelites was very coarsely manufactured, but the best was the iron from the north. So bad was their iron generally, that an admixture of brass, which among us would be thought rather to deteriorate the hardness, was regarded as an improvement; so the Lord puts it, "Shall iron--the common iron--break the most firm and best prepared iron?" It cannot do so: and if the people acted like iron against Jeremiah, God would make his spirit indomitably firm, that they should no more be able to put him down than common iron could break the northern iron and the steel.

That being the literal meaning, we shall draw from our text a general principle. It is a proverbial expression, no doubt, and applicable to many other matters besides that of the prophet and the Jews; it is clearly meant to show, that in order to achieve a purpose, there must be a sufficient force. The weaker cannot overcome the stronger. In a general clash the firmest will win. There must be sufficient firmness in the instrument or the work cannot be done. You cannot cut granite with a pen-knife, nor drill a hole in a rock with an auger of silk. Some forces are inadequate for the accomplishment of certain purposes. If you would break the best iron, you will be foiled if you strike it with a metal less hard.

I. We shall first of all apply this proverb to the PEOPLE OF GOD INDIVIDUALLY. Shall any power be able to destroy the saints?

We are sent into the world, if we are believers in Christ, like sheep in the midst of wolves, defenseless, and in danger of being devoured, yet no power on earth can destroy the chosen disciples of Christ. Weak as they are, they will tread down the strength of their foes. There are more sheep in the world now than wolves. There are parts of the world where wolves once roamed in troops where not a wolf can now be found; yet tens of thousands of sheep feed on the hillside: one would not be very bold to say that the day will come when the wolf will only be known as an extinct animal, while as long as the world lasts the sheep will continue to multiply. In the long run, the sheep has gained the victory over the wolf. And it is so with Christ's people. They appear to be weak, but there is a force about them which cannot be put down: they will overcome the ungodly yet, for the day will come when mighty truth shall prevail. God hasten that blessed and long-expected day. Till then, when persecuted we are not forsaken, when cast down we are not destroyed. Many Christians, are placed in positions where they are subject to very great temptations and persecutions; they are mocked, laughed at, ridiculed, called by evil names. Persecuted one, will you deny the faith? Are you going to put aside your colors, and relinquish the cross of Christ? If so, I can only tell you, you are not made of the same stuff as the true disciples of Jesus-Christ; for when the grace of God is in them, if the world be iron, they are northern iron and steel; they can bear all the blows which the world may possibly choose to lay upon them, and as the anvil breaks the hammers in the long run, so will they, by their patient endurance for Christ's sake, break the force of all persecution, and triumph over it. Do I speak to a young Christian, who has come up to London, and finds himself placed where he is continually ridiculed? Will you shrink in the day of trial? Do you mean to play the coward? Shall the iron break the northern iron and the steel! Let it not be so. Be strong. Quit you like men; and in the energy of the Holy Spirit, endure as seeing him that is invisible. There is no need that we should fear, for amid all dangers the love of God shall live within us as a fire unquenchable. "Who shall separate us from the love of Christ? shall tribulation, or distress, or persecution, or famine, or nakedness, or peril, or sword?" "Nay, in all these things we are more than conquerors through him that loved us."

Besides persecution, we are called frequently to serve the Lord under great difficulties. There are supreme difficulties connected with the evangelisation of this city. To stand here and preach to such a congregation as this, so large and so eager for the word, is a pleasure; but every sphere of labor is not equally cheering. Some of you who go to the lodging-houses to speak, or who visit the alleys, or stand up in the low neighbourhoods to preach the word of life, I know full well find it anything but child's play to serve your Lord under such conditions. Yours is rough hedging and ditching work, with very little in it of rosewater and gentility, and very much of annoyance and disappointment. What, then, is your resolution? I trust it is this: that as much strength is needed, you will wait more than ever upon the strong One till the needed power is given you. I trust you are not of that craven spirit which shrinks at difficulty or toil. Will you give way before the labors demanded of you? Do the redeemed of the Lord consent to give London up to Satan's rule? Do they say in despair that its darkest parts cannot be enlightened? Will the church of God despair of any race or country? Will it say: "There is no converting the Romanist; there is no convincing the literate and crafty Brahmin?" Is the iron to break the northern iron and the steel? Will we not rather take a firmer grip upon Omnipotence, and draw down almighty help by the blessed vehemence of prayer? What are we at? What aileth us that we are so soon dispirited? Is the Lord's arm waxed short? The apostles never thought of defeat; they believed that the gospel could break everything in pieces that stood in its way: and they went without hesitation to the work which the Lord sent them to do. Twas theirs to dare and die; questions and forebodings were not theirs. Into the bloody jaws of death those champions of Christendom rode on with dauntless courage, and won the victory. And are we to give way under difficulties? Are we to be as reeds shaken of the wind? You, Sunday-school teacher, are you going to give up your class because the boys are unruly? You in the Ragged-school, are you thinking of closing the doors, because as yet the children have not come in great numbers, or because the young Arabs are as wild as unbroken colts? You, who stood in the corner of the street the other night to preach, did you determine never to stand up and preach again, because of the rough reception you received? O man, be of different metal from this! If God has called you to do anything, do it, if you die in doing it. To a man for whom Jesus died, no work should seem hard, no sacrifice grievous. All things are possible to those who burn with the love of God. There is nothing but what you can make a way through if you can find something harder to bore it with. Look at the Mont Cenis Tunnel, made through one of the hardest of known rocks; with a sharp tool, edged with diamond, they have pierced the heart of the Alps, and made a passage for the commerce of nations. As St. Bernard says: "Is thy work hard? set a harder resolution against it; for there is nothing so hard that it cannot be cut by something harder still." May the Spirit of God work in thee invincible resolution and unconquerable perseverance. Let not the iron break the northern iron and the steel. Under persecutions and difficulties, let God's people resolve on victory, and by faith they shall have it, for according to our faith so shall it be unto us.

One of the greatest trials to which the people of God are subject, in trying to serve their Master, is non-success. The seven lean kine, as they eat up the seven fat kine, sorely try the believer's faith. Alas! our disappointments seldom come alone, but like Job's messengers, follow close upon each other's heels. When a man succeeds, he continues to succeed, as a rule; he derives encouragement from what God has already done by him, and goes from strength to strength. Probably, however, there is more grace exhibited by the Christian, who, without present success, realises the things not seen as yet, and continues still to work on. To labor is not easy, but to labor and to wait is harder far. It is a grand thing to continue patiently in well doing, confident that in the end the reward is sure. He is a man indeed who under long-continued disappointment will not--

"Bate a jot
Of heart or hope, but still bear up and steer
Right onward."

Such a man "plucks success even from the spear-proof crest of rugged danger." The well-annealed steel within him ere long breaks in shivers the common iron which strikes him so severely. To him, to overcome by grace is glory indeed.

Some of the greatest works that were ever performed by Christian people were not immediate in their results. The husbandman has waited long for the precious fruits of the earth. The question has been asked, again and again, "Watchman, what of the night?" Some, no doubt, have had to labor all their lives, and have bequeathed to their heirs the promise whose fulfillment they had not personally seen. They laid the underground courses of the temple, and others entered into their labors. You know the story of the removal of old St. Paul's by Sir Christopher Wren. A very massive piece of masonry had to be broken down, and the task, by pick and shovel, would have been a very tedious one, so the great architect prepared a battering-ram for its removal, and a large number of workmen were directed to strike with force against the wall with the ram. After several hours of labor, the wall, to all appearances, stood fast and firm. Their many strokes had been apparently lost, but the architect knew that they were gradually communicating motion to the wall, creating an agitation throughout the whole of it, and that, by-and-by, when they had continued long enough, the entire mass would come down beneath a single stroke. The workmen, no doubt, attributed the result to the one crowning concussion, but their master knew that their previous strokes had only culminated in that one tremendous blow and that all the nonresultant work had been necessary to prepare for the stroke which achieved the purpose. O Christian people, do not expect always to see the full outgrowth of your labors! Go on, serve your God, testify of his truth, tell of Jesus' love, pray for sinners, live a godly life, serve God with might and main, and if no harvest spring up to your joyous sickle, others shall follow you and reap what you have sown, and since God will be glorified, it shall be enough for you. Let no amount of nonsuccess daunt you. Be uneasy about it, but do not be discouraged; let not even this iron break the resolution of your soul; let your determination to honor Jesus be as the northern iron and the steel.

I might thus enlarge, but I have so many other things to speak of, that I shall pass on. The pith of what I want to say is this: if any dear brother here, as a Christian, is put to very severe trials, he may depend upon it there is nothing that happens to him but what is common to men, and that there is grace enough to be had to enable him to bear up under all. There is no need for any one soldier of God to turn his back in the day of battle. It is not right that any one of us should consider himself doomed to be defeated. The Holy Spirit giveth power to the weak, and lifts the common warriors into the ranks of the mightiest. Fulness of grace is provided for us in Christ Jesus, and if we draw from it by faith we shall not need to fail. Let us not be slow to arm ourselves with the divine might. Let us ask the Captain of our salvation to make us as tough in the day of battle as the northern iron was beneath the blow of the common iron; that having done and suffered all, we may still stand, and none may be able to rob us of our crown.

II. But we shall now make a second use of this same proverb. It is applicable to the cause of God in the world--to THE CHURCH. I shall speak but little upon this, for time would fail me. What power, however like to iron, shall suffice to break the kingdom of Jesus, which is comparable to steel? We every now and then hear the babyish talk of persons who say that the gospel will die out in England--that Romanism will return in all its darkness, gospel light will be extinguished, and the candle which Latimer helped to light will be blown out. Atrocious nonsense, if not partial blasphemy. If this thing were of men it would come to nought; but if it be of God, who shall overthrow it? It has sometimes happened that fear has been the father of the thing it feared: let it not be so in this case; let us not court defeat by anticipating it. As surely as the Lord liveth the end of the Romish Anti-Christ will come, and the long-expected angel shall cry with a loud voice,

"Babylon the great is fallen, is fallen, and is become the habitation of devils, and the hold of every foul spirit, and a cage of every unclean and hateful bird." "Rejoice over her, thou heaven, and ye holy apostles and prophets; for God hath avenged you on her." Revelation 18:2, 20. Other desponding prophets foretell that infidelity will so spread through all the churches and the fabric of society, that at last we shall see this country without a gospel ministry, and perhaps, through the spread of revolutionary principles, bereft of all respect for law and order. We are to go down by way of Paris to the foulness of Sodom, and thence into Pandemonium. Brethren, let those who will believe these evil tidings, I am not greatly moved thereby; for there are eternal principles and immutable decrees which uphold my joyful hopes. Consider for a moment what is involved in these gloomy forebodings. Then the gates of hell are to prevail against the church, are they? Then Christ is to be defeated by anti-Christ, is he? Then the pleasure of the Lord is not to prosper in his hand? Who said that? Who but a lying spirit that would lay low the faith and confidence of the people of God? It is no more possible for the truth of God and the church of God to be defeated, than for God himself to be overcome in conflict. Lo! Jehovah girds his church like a buckler on his arm: this is his battle-axe; this his weapons of war; and if you can wrench from his hand the weapons of his choice, then may you lift up the shout of triumph over the Eternal himself. But it never can be, for who shall stand against the Lord and prosper? My brethren, we may well fear the crafty machinations of the church of Rome, for all the subtlety of the old serpent is within her; but with the wisdom of God to meet it, there can be no alarm. He taketh the wise in their own craftiness: there is no device nor counsel against the Lord. We may well be dismayed at the insidious attacks of scepticism; but while there remains a Holy Ghost to create and sustain faith in the world, we need not fear that the faithful will utterly cease out of the land. The thousands will still be reserved whose knees have never bowed to Baal. Infidelity and Socinianism have ready tongues, but every tongue that rises against the church in judgment she will condemn. The forges of hell are busy in fashioning new weapons with which to assail us, but the Lord will break their bows and cut their spears in sunder. They may and will defeat the dogmas of superstition, but the truths of revelation and the people who believe them they can never overthrow. The iron will never break the northern iron and the steel. The church can bear the blows of Ritualism and Infidelity, and survive them all, and be the better for them too. See what the cause of Christ is. It is truth: therein is victory. Who knows not that the truth must prevail? There is in the church of God, moreover, life, and life is a thing you cannot overcome. A dead thing may be cut in pieces, and strewn to the winds of heaven; but the life in Christ's church is that which has defied and overcome Satan a thousand times already. In the dark ages the enemy thought he had destroyed the church, but life came into the monk in his cell, and Luther shook the world. The church in England fell into a deadly slumber in the days of Whitfield and Wesley; but she was not dead, and therefore a time of awakening came. The flame burned low but the heavenly fire still lingered among the ashes, and only needed the Holy Spirit to blow upon it, and cause a hallowed conflagration. Six young men in Oxford were found guilty of meeting to pray: their offense was contagious, and soon there sprang up hundreds glorying in the same blessed crime. Earnest servants of the living God were forthcoming and no man knew whence they came; like the buds and blossoms which come forth at the bidding of spring, a people made willing in the day of God's power came forward at once. Seeing that there is life in the church of God, you can never calculate what will happen within its bounds to-morrow, for life is an unaccountable thing, and scorns the laws which bind the formal and inanimate. The statues in St. Paul's Cathedral stand fixed on their pedestals, and the renowned dead in Westminster Abbey never raise a riot; but who can tell what the living may next conceive or attempt? Men have said: "We will put down the troublesome religion of these gospellers. Build prisons enough, forge chains enough, make racks enough, concoct tortures infernal enough, slay enough victims, and stamp out the plague." But their designs have never been accomplished. They hatched the cockatrice's egg, but that which came of it died. They burnt the gospel out in Spain, did they not? And in the Low Countries they erased the memory thereof. How is it now? Has not Spain achieved her liberty at a blow? Is not also Belgium free to the preacher of the word? Not even Italy or Rome itself is safe against the obnoxious heretic. Everywhere the gospel penetrates. Even the earth helps the woman, and swallows up the flood which the dragon casts out of his mouth to drown the man child: political rulers restrain the violence of those who otherwise would slay the saints in one general massacre. It shall be so, right on through all the ages till Christ comes--the iron shall not break the northern iron and the steel. Glory be to God, we have confidence in this, and in the name of God we set up our banner. This, too, is a pleasing theme; but we must leave it and pass on to another.

III. We may apply the principle to a very different matter indeed--THE SELF-RIGHTEOUS EFFORTS WHICH MEN MAKE FOR THEIR OWN SALVATION. We may remind them that the iron will never break the northern iron and the steel. The bonds of guilt are not to be snapped by a merely human power. Here is a man with the fetters of his transgressions about him, but "he will get them off," he says: prayer shall be his file; tears shall be the aquafortis to dissolve the metal, and his own resolutions shall, like a hammer, dash the links in fragments. But it cannot be: the iron shall never break this northern iron and the steel. Habits of sin yield not to raspings of the unregenerate resolves. You are condemned, and only Christ the Son of God can set you free from the fetters which hold you in the condenmed cell. All your efforts apart from Jesus are utterly useless. He must bring liberty--you cannot emancipate yourselves. You say that you will break off the chains of evil habit. There are some you can break off, but can you alter your nature? "Can the Ethiopian change his skin, or the leopard his spots?" That were an easy task compared with a man renewing his own heart. The imaginations of the thoughts of your heart are evil, only evil, and that continually, and do what you will they will remain so. The dead cannot give themselves life: it needs superior power to hew off the fetters which hold you prisoner in the sepulcher of your natural death. Your iron can never break the northern iron and the steel which bind you to the slavery of hell. Do you think to force your way to heaven by ceremony? Do you imagine that baptism can wash away your sin, that confirmation can convey to you grace, that outward ceremonies of man's devising, or of God's instituting can deliver you from wrath? Believe no such thing; there is no potency in all these to deliver you from the bonds which hold you. The iron cannot break the northern iron and the steel. Come, sinner, with thy fetters, and day thy Christ here at the cross-foot, where Christ can break the iron at once. Come, bring thyself, chained as thou art, to him, or if thou canst not stir an inch, cry out to him! Ask him to deliver thee! He can do it. Trust in him, for trust in his precious blood and reliance upon his perfect sacrifice will make thee a free man in a moment, never to be a bondslave again. But, oh, let not thy puny strength be wasted on so futile an effort as that which aims at self-salvation; how shall weakness achieve the labor of omnipotence, or death accomplish the sublimes miracle of the Immortal? Remember the work of salvation think how great it is, how worthy of a God; and then cease utterly from all self-reliance, for it is madness and blasphemy. Where were the need of the Holy Ghost, if you could regenerate yourself? Where would there be room for a display of the power of sovereign grace, if man's will and effort could accomplish all? But I leave that topic, also, and pass on to another consideration.

IV. This same text is applicable to the case of any persons who are making SELF-RELIANT EFFORTS FOR THE GOOD OF OTHERS. How painfully are we made to feel, my brethren, after every series of our special services at this Tabernacle, that we of ourselves can do nothing! How are we driven to the conclusion that it is not by might nor by power, but by the Spirit of God, and by the Spirit of God alone! Man's heart is very hard; it is like the northern iron and the steel. Our preaching--we try to make it forcible, but how powerless is it of itself! The preacher seeks goodly words and illustrations; he brings forth the law of God, he gives forth threatenings in God's name; he reasons concerning judgment to come, and flinches not from declaring the eternal punishment of sin; he preaches the love of God, and the infinite mercy of Christ Jesus, and he blends all this with an affection which longs for conversion, and he prays for God's blessing; but in many many hearts there is no change, the northern iron and the steel remain unmovable. We call spirits from the vasty deep of their lost estate, but they come not at our bidding. We plead with sinners to be reconciled to God, and we beseech them as though God himself besought them by us; but they remain unreconciled; they are even the more obdurate in iniquity. The cries and tears of a Whitfield would not avail. Though all the apostles reasoned with them they would turn to them a deaf ear. Herein the best adapted means cannot break the northern iron and the steel. With some of you an instrumentality has been used which ought to have been more prolific of results. A mother's tears, to your knowledge, have been shed for you. How affectionately has she spoken to you of the Savior, whom she loves: but powerful as your mother's pleadings would be on any other point, you reject them in the matter of your soul. How would it make you gray-headed man, your father, rejoice if he might see you saved! In other matters this also would have weight with you, but it has none in this. You have had the gospel, too, some of you, put to you very, very tenderly by those whom you love best, but you are unsaved still. There could be no better means than human love sanctified and strengthened by indwelling grace; it has been strong as iron, and would have broken any ordinary heart, but it has not crushed yours, for it is hard as the northern iron and the steel. Ay, and you have been sick; you have been stretched upon the bed with fever, within a hair's breadth of hell; or you have been at sea, and escaped as with the skin of your teeth from shipwreck; but even the judgments of God have not aroused you. The iron has not broken the northern iron and the steel. This month, to some of you, there have been addresses delivered pointedly, plaintively, which should have moved a rock. I have been present at some of the meetings, when I have heard certain of our brethren speak in a way that made me inwardly say, "Surely these careless ones will yield to that." There has been much sighing and crying for your souls; and you have been spoken with personally, many of you; a kind hand has been put upon your wrist, and with tearful eye, brother and sister have looked into your face, and told you of your danger and of your remedy. Oh I if this does not save you, what will? "What shall I do unto thee?" "O Ephraim, what shall I do unto thee?"

What other instrumentality can be employed? The iron will not break the northern iron and the steel. Children of God, you are driven to this, that here is a case in which you are powerless. You might as well reverse the wind, or move a star, or create a world, as soften these hardened hearts. What are you then to do? Certainly, you are to continue the effort; nothing must tempt you to relinquish it, or even to relax your zeal. If you cannot break the heart, truly it is no business of yours to do so; commit that work to him who is fully equal to the miracle, keep to your work, and fear not that the Lord will work with you. God bids you continue prayer, warning instruction, and invitation. If you knew that every soul you preached to or talked with would be lost, it were no less your duty to preach the gospel; for the duty to tell out the gospel is not influenced by our success, but is based upon the commission of Christ: "Go ye into all the world, and preach the gospel to every creature." It is not Ezekiel's duty to make the dry bones live; but whether they live or not, it is his duty to prophesy upon them. Noah was none the less a preacher of righteousness because none, save his own family, listened to his appeals and sought shelter with him in the ark. Go on with your work; but let a sense of your personal inability make you fall back upon your God. Let it keep you from one self-reliant prayer or word, much more from one self-confident sermon or address. Every time we try to do good in our own strength, the effort bears the certainty of defeat in its own bowels. You shoot pointless darts; you wield a blunted sword when you go to work for God without God. It is only when we go in God's power that we can save souls. "Except the Lord build the house, they labor in vain that build it: except the Lord keep the city, the watchman waketh but in vain." Lo, spiritual children are a heritage of the Lord, and the fruit of our soul's womb is his reward. Feel your weakness, my brethren, and then you shall know your strength. Go to the sinner in God's strength, and then shall you see the divine operation; but certainly not till then. What a blessing it has been to some of us at times to be made to lie very low in the dust, and see what unworthy creatures we are! I have often noticed that when God intends to give a great blessing upon my ministry, and to let me know it, he usually makes me feel as if I had rather die than dive, because I feel myself so utterly unworthy to preach his word, and am made to bemoan my wretched unfitness to be used at all by my gracious Master. Let the stone lie in the brook, and let it be rounded, and made smooth by trituration of the water--it will do nothing of itself; but when it has been worn away enough by the brook, and David slings it, and smites the giant's brow, the stone cannot say, "I slew the giant by my own force;" but all men will give glory to the champion who hurled it at the giant's forehead. Yes, God will have the glory, and he will take means to prevent us from usurping it. He will make us feel that the iron cannot break the northern iron and the steel, and then he will send us forth to victory. Truly my inmost heart confesses that if one heart has been won for my Lord Jesus by me, I am less than nothing in it, and he is all in all. My soul dares not touch the glory, but loathes every thought of self-praise. He hath done it, and to him be everlasting songs.

V. But now I must close--time warns me to do so--by remarking that this text has A VERY SOLEMN APPLICATION TO ALL THOSE WHO ARE REBELS AGAINST GOD. Men sometimes think themselves of very great consequence. I spoke with one some years ago who had professed to be a Christian, who addressed me very indignantly after some little argument, and said that ere long he intended to produce a pamphlet which would extinguish Christianity. I remember making the remark, that I dared to say that the world would hear as much about it as when a fly fell into a pail of water and was drowned, and not much more. And then he was more indignant still; but I told him I had seen many a moth dash against my gas-burner in the evening, but I had never seen the light put out, though I had seen the wretched insect fall with singed wings upon my table, to suffer for its fatal folly; and I feared that such a fate would happen to him. So rest assured it will be to you, O blasphemer of God, or hater of his Christ. Fight against God, would you? Measure your adversary, I charge you. The wax is about to wrestle with the flame: the tow is about to contend with the fire. It is too unequal a warfare. If you are wise, you will select another adversary, and not attempt to go to war with the omnipotent King, with such a puny force as yours. "Hast thou an arm like God? or canst thou thunder with a voice like him?" You may be like iron: go and break the potsherds of the earth; they are fair game for you; but do not contend against the northern iron and the steel, for these will break you. You will not be able to deprive Christ of a single atom of his glory. You may blaspheme, but even that shall, somehow or other by a holy alchemy, be turned to his glory. You cannot thwart his decrees. The great wheels of his providence grind on, and woe to him who throws himself in their track; they will surely grind him to powder. The huge Matterhorn lilts its colossal head above the clouds. Who will may speak against it; but it bows not its giant form; and no matter what of snow and sleet may dash against its ramparts, there it stands, still the same; emblem herein of the great throne of the Eternal, firm and immutable, though all the universe storm at its foot. To resist God is to strike with naked feet against a goad. "It is hard for thee to kick against the pricks." You will hurt yourself; you cannot injure him, nor change his purposes by so much as the turning of a hair. God will have his way: None shall resist his will. Everlasting and eternal are his decrees; and fast and fixed they ever must remain, though all earth and hell should unite in one great conspiracy. He thrusts a bit into the tempest's mouth, and rides upon the wings of the wind. Confusion there is none to him. Adversaries, what are they? They are utterly consumed as the stubble. But take ye heed that God come not out against you, ye who are rebels; for if he once put on the war-harness and fight against you, woe unto you! Have you not heard? Hath no one told you of the arrows of his quiver? They are sharp, heart-piercing, infallible. Sickness can shake you till every nerve shall become a road for pain to carry on its dreadful traffic. Poverty can come upon you, and want, like an armed man. Death shall strike down ail your lovers, and your acquaintances shall sink into the abyss. Let God but come forth in judgment against a man, or a people, and what can he not do? Look at the nation across the Channel, and see how God hath dealt with it. Turn to any other nation against whom his fiat has gone forth, and read the story of its overthrow. What can emperors do, and what their imperial guards, and what their novel instruments of war, and what their death-dealing machines, that were to mow down thousands in an hour? He that sitteth in the heavens doth laugh; the Lord doth have them in derision. He hath broken the bow and cut the spear in sunder; he hath burned the chariot in the fire. Contend no more against the Almighty: put back thy sword into the scabbard, and submit thyself to the inevitable; for remember, ere long, O rebel against God, he will deal with thee in another fashion than he doth now. Let that breath which is in thy nostrils go forth from thee, and where art thou then? I will quote one passage of Scripture and leave it to your thoughts. "Beware, ye that forget God"--that is, the very mildest form of rebellion--"Beware, ye that forget God, lest I tear you in pieces, and there be none to deliver." O may you never know what that means! Cast down your weapons. Come now, and ask for reconciliation. The ambassador of peace invites you. I point you no longer to his burning throne, but to yonder cross. See there God in human flesh--bleeding, suffering, dying. Those wounds are fountains of mercy. Look to them, and you shall live. Wrath is appeased by the death of Jesus. Fury is no more in Jehovah! Trust in Jesus, the crucified, and your transgression shall be forgiven you. That precious blood shall make reconciliation: there shall be peace between you and God; but O resist no longer, for the iron cannot break the northern iron and the steel.

The Lord bless you for Jesus' sake. Amen.

PORTION OF SCRIPTURE READ BEFORE SERMON--Isaiah 40. 9-31.

LETTER.
CLAPHAM, JUNE 5TH.

TO MY FRIENDS EVERYWHERE,

I HAVE now endured ten silent Sabbaths, and as I know that many of you are anxious to have accurate information as to my state of health, and as I have now something cheerful to communicate, I feel bound to add the present note to this week's sermon. The pain of my disease, which has been intense, has now ceased for a week or more. I have had a succession of good nights, in which sweet sleep has so refreshed me that I felt each morning to be far in advance of the previous day. I am now very weak--weak as a little child--but by the same mercy which allayed the pain strength will be restored, and I shall have the pleasure of being again at my delightful labor. Please pray for me that I may be speedily and lastingly restored to health, if it be the Lord's will. Ask also that the furnace heat which I have suffered may produce its full effect upon me in my own soul and in my ministry. My heart's inmost desire, as the Lord knoweth, is the salvation of sinners and the building up of his people in their most holy faith, to the glory of the Lord Jesus: hence it has been very grievous to me to have been debarred my pulpit and shut out from other means of usefulness. Nevertheless, no work has flagged at the Tabernacle because of my illness; pecuniary help has been furnished just when it was needed, and spiritual help has been given by the Lord of Hosts. We desire to accomplish more and to receive more blessing when our health is restored to us. Surely the Master has some great design to be answered by laying his servants aside: we trust it will prove to be so. Let our prayers be more fervent, our zeal more ardent and our labors for the spread of the truth more abundant, and "God will bless us, and all the ends of the earth shall fear him."

I have one great favor to ask of all readers of the sermons, and that is, that they will try to spread them abroad, and increase the number of regular subscribers. What has been good to you will be good for others if the Lord bless it. If you cannot preach yourself, you can distribute the word spoken by others.

I hope to be able to occupy the pulpit again by June 25th, if the Lord will; but all things are uncertain to us, especially when one is slowly recovering from severe affliction.

Yours to serve till death,

The Prayer of Jabez

A Sermon (No. 994)
Delivered by
C. H. SPURGEON,
At the Metropolitan Tabernacle, Newington

"Oh that thou wouldest bless me indeed!" - 1 Chron. 4:10.

WE know very little about Jabez, except that he was more honorable than his brethren, and that he was called Jabez because his mother bare him with sorrow. It will sometimes happen that where there is the most sorrow in the antecedents, there will be the most pleasure in the sequel. As the furious storm gives place to the clear sunshine, so the night of weeping precedes the morning of joy. Sorrow the harbinger; gladness the prince it ushers in. Cowper says:--

"The path of sorrow, and that path alone,
Leads to the place where sorrow is unknown."

To a great extent we find that we must sow in tears before we can reap in joy. Many of our works for Christ have cost us tears. Difficulties and disappointments have wrung our soul with anguish. Yet those projects that have cost us more than ordinary sorrow, have often turned out to be the most honorable of our undertakings. While our grief called the offspring of desire "Benoni," the son of my sorrow, our faith has been afterwards able to give it a name of delight, "Benjamin," the son of my right hand. You may expect a blessing in serving God if you are enabled to persevere under many discouragements. The ship is often long coming home, because detained on the road by excess of cargo. Expect her freight to be the better when she reaches the port. More honorable than his brethren was the child whom his mother bore with sorrow. As for this Jabez, whose aim was so well pointed, his fame so far sounded, his name so lastingly embalmed--he was a man of prayer. The honor he enjoyed would not have been worth having if it had not been vigorously contested and equitably won. His devotion was the key to his promotion. Those are the best honors that come from God, the award of grace with the acknowledgment of service. When Jacob was surnamed Israel, he received his princedom after a memorable night of prayer. Surely it was far more honorable to him than if it had been bestowed upon him as a flattering destinction by some earthly emperor. The best honor is that which a man gains in communion with the Most High. Jabez, we are told, was more honorable than his brethren, and his prayer is forthwith recorded, as if to intimate that he was also more prayerful than his brethren. We are told of what petitions his prayer consisted. All through it was very significant and instructive. We have only time to take one clause of it--indeed, that one clause may be said to comprehend the rest: "Oh that thou wouldest bless me indeed!" I commend it as a prayer for yourselves, dear brethren and sisters; one which will be available at all seasons; a prayer to begin Christian life with, a prayer to end it with, a prayer which would never be unseasonable in your joys or in your sorrows.

Oh that thou, the God of Israel, the covenant God, would bless me indeed! The very pith of the prayer seems to lie in that word, "indeed." There are many varieties of blessing. Some are blessings only in name: they gratify our wishes for a moment, but permanently disappoint our expectations. They charm the eye, but pall on the taste. Others are mere temporary blessings: they perish with the using. Though for awhile they regale the senses, they cannot satisfy the higher cravings of the soul. But, "Oh that thou wouldest bless me indeed!" I wot whom God blesseth shall be blessed. The thing good in itself is bestowed with the good-will of the giver, and shall be productive of so much good fortune to the recipient that it may well be esteemed as a blessing "indeed," for there is nothing comparable to it. Let the grace of God prompt it, let the choice of God appoint it, let the bounty of God confer it, and then the endowment shall be something godlike indeed; something worthy of the lips that pronounce the benediction, and verily to be craved by every one who seeks honor that is substantial and enduring. "Oh that thou wouldest bless me indeed!" Think it over, and you will see that there is a depth of meaning in the expression.

We may set this in contrast with human blessings: "Oh that thou wouldest bless me indeed!"

It is very delightful to be blessed by our parents, and those venerable friends whose benedictions come from their hearts, and are backed up by their prayers. Many a poor man has had no other legacy to leave his children except his blessing, but the blessing of an honest, holy, Christian father is a rich treasure to his son. One might well feel it were a thing to be deplored through life if he had lost a parent's blessing. We like to have it. The blessing of our spiritual parents is consolatory. Though we believe in no priestcraft, we like to live in the affections of those who were the means of bringing us to Christ, and from whose lips we were instructed in the things of God. And how very precious is the blessing of the poor! I do not wonder that Job treasured that up as a sweet thing. "When the ear heard me, then it blessed me." If you have relieved the widow and the fatherless, and their thanks are returned to you in benediction, it is no mean reward. But, dear friends, after all--all that parents, relatives, saints, and grateful persons can do in the way of blessing, falls very far short of what we desire to have. O Lord, we would have the blessings of our fellow-creatures, the blessings that come from their hearts; but, "Oh that Thou wouldest bless me indeed!" for thou canst bless with authority. Their blessings may be but words, but thine are effectual. They may often wish what they cannot do, and desire to give what they have not at their own disposal, but thy will is omnipotent. Thou didst create the world with but a word. O that such omnipotence would now bespeak me thy blessing! Other blessings may bring us some tiny cheer, but in thy favor is life. Other blessings are mere tittles in comparison with thy blessing; for thy blessing is the title "to an inheritance incorruptible" and unfading, to "a kingdom which cannot be moved." Well therefore might David pray in another place, "With thy blessing let the house of thy servant be blessed for ever." Perhaps in this place, Jabez may have put the blessing of God in contrast with the blessings of men. Men will bless thee when thou doest well for thyself. They will praise the man who is successful in business. Nothing succeeds like success. Nothing has so much the approval of the general public as a man's prosperity. Alas! they do not weigh men's actions in the balances of the sanctuary, but in quite other scales. You will find those about you who will commend you if you are prosperous; or like Job's comforters, condemn you if you suffer adversity. Perhaps there may be some feature about their blessings that may please you, because you feel you deserve them. They commend you for your patriotism: you have been a patriot. They commend you for your generosity: you know you have been self-sacrificing. Well, but after all, what is there in the verdict of man? At a trial, the verdict of the policeman who stands in the court, or of the spectators who sit in the court-house, amounts to just nothing. The man who is being tried feels that the only thing that is of importance at all will be the verdict of the jury, and the sentence of the judge. So it will little avail us whatever we may do, how others commend or censure. Their blessings are not of any great value. But, "Oh that thou wouldest bless me," that thou wouldest say, "Well done, good and faithful servant." Commend thou the feeble service that through thy grace my heart has rendered. That will be to bless me indeed.

Men are sometimes blessed in a very fulsome sense by flattery. There are always those who, like the fox in the fable, hope to gain the cheese by praising the crow. They never saw such plumage, and no voice could be so sweet as yours. The whole of their mind is set, not on you, but on what they are to gain by you. The race of flatterers is never extinct, though the flattered usually flatter themselves it is so. They may conceive that men flatter others, but all is so palpable and transparent when heaped upon themselves, that they accept it with a great deal of self-complacency, as being perhaps a little exaggerated, but after all exceedingly near the truth. We are not very apt to take a large discount off the praises that others offer us; yet, were we wise, we should press to our bosom those who censure us; and we should always keep at arm's length those who praise us, for those who censure us to our face cannot possibly be making a market of us; but with regard to those who extol us, rising early, and using loud sentences of praise, we may suspect, and we shall very seldom be unjust in the suspicion, that there is some other motive in the praise which they render to us than that which appears on the surface. Young man, art thou placed in a position where God honors thee? Beware of flatterers. Or hast thou come into a large estate? Hast thou abundance? There are always flies where there is honey. Beware of flattery. Young woman, art thou fair to look upon? There will be those about thee that will have their designs, perhaps their evil designs, in lauding thy beauty. Beware of flatterers. Turn thou aside from all these who have honey on their tongue, because of the poison of asps that is under it. Bethink thee of Solomon's caution, "meddle not with him that flattereth with his lips." Cry to God, "Deliver thou me from all this vain adulation, which nauseates my soul." So shalt thou pray to him the more fervently, "Oh that thou wouldest bless me indeed!" Let me have thy benediction, which never says more than it means; which never gives less than it promises. If you take then the prayer of Jabez as being put in contrast with the benedictions which come from men, you see much force in it.

But we may put it in another light, and compare the blessing Jabez craved with those blessings that are temporal and transient. There are many bounties given to us mercifully by God for which we are bound to be very grateful; but we must not set too much store by them. We may accept them with gratitude, but we must not make them our idols. When we have them we have great need to cry, "Oh that thou wouldest bless me indeed, and make these inferior blessings real blessings;" and if we have them not, we should with greater vehemence cry, "Oh that we may be rich in faith, and if not blessed with these external favors, may we be blessed spiritually, and then we shall be blessed indeed."

Let us review some of these mercies, and just say a word or two about them.

One of the first cravings of men's hearts is wealth. So universal the desire to gain it, that we might almost say it is a natural instinct. How many have thought if they once possessed it they should be blessed indeed! but there are ten thousand proofs that happiness consists not in the abundance which a man possesseth. So many instances are well known to you all, that I need not quote any to show that riches are not a blessing indeed. They are rather apparently than really so. Hence, it has been well said, that when we see how much a man has we envy him; but could we see how little he enjoys we should pity him. Some that have had the most easy circumstances have had the most uneasy minds. Those who have acquired all they could wish, had their wishes been at all sane, have been led by the possession of what they had to be discontented because they had not more.

"Thus the base miser starves amidst his store,
Broods o'er his gold, and griping still at more,
Sits sadly pining, and believes he's poor."

Nothing is more clear to any one who chooses to observe it, than that riches are not the chief good at whose advent sorrow flies, and in whose presence joy perennial springs. Full often wealth cozens the owner. Dainties are spread on his table, but his appetite fails, minstrels wait his bidding, but his ears are deaf to all the strains of music; holidays he may have as many as he pleases, but for him recreation has lost all its charms: or he is young, fortune has come to him by inheritance, and he makes pleasure his pursuit till sport becomes more irksome than work, and dissipation worse than drudgery. Ye know how riches make themselves wings; like the bird that roosted on the tree, they fly away. In sickness and despondency these ample means that once seemed to whisper, "Soul, take thine ease," prove themselves to be poor comforters. In death they even tend to make the pang of separation more acute, because there is the more to leave, the more to lose. We may well say, if we have wealth, "My God, put me not off with these husks; let me never make a god of the silver and the gold, the goods and the chattels, the estates and investments, which in thy providence thou hast given me. I beseech thee, bless me indeed. As for these worldly possessions, they will be my bane unless I have thy grace with them." And if you have not wealth, and perhaps the most of you will never have it, say, "My Father, thou hast denied me this outward and seeming good, enrich me with thy love, give me the gold of thy favor, bless me indeed; then allot to others whatever thou wilt, thou shalt divide my portion, my soul shall wait thy daily will; do thou bless me indeed, and I shall be content."

Another transient blessing which our poor humanity fondly covets and eagerly pursues is fame. In this respect we would fain be more honorable than our brethren, and outstrip all our competitors. It seems natural to us all to wish to make a name, and gain some note in the circle we move in at any rate, and we wish to make that circle wider if we can. But here, as of riches, it is indisputable that the greatest fame does not bring with it any equal measure of gratification. Men, in seeking after notoriety or honor, have a degree of pleasure in the search which they do not always possess when they have gained their object. Some of the most famous men have also been the most wretched of the human race. If thou hast honor and fame, accept it; but let this prayer go up, "My God, bless thou me indeed, for what profit were it, if my name were in a thousand mouths, if thou shouldest spue it out of thy mouth? What matter, though my name were written on marble, if it were not written in the Lamb's Book of Life? These blessings are only apparently blessings, windy blessings, blessings that mock me. Give me thy blessing: then the honor which comes of thee will make me blessed indeed." If you happen to have lived in obscurity, and have never entered the lists for honors among your fellow-men, be content to run well your own course and fulfill truly your own vocation. To lack fame is not the most grievous of ills; it is worse to have it like the snow, that whitens the ground in the morning, and disappears in the heat of the day. What matters it to a dead man that men are talking of him? Get thou the blessing indeed.

There is another temporal blessing which wise men desire, and legitimately may wish for rather than the other two--the blessing of health. Can we ever prize it sufficiently? To trifle with such a boon is the madness of folly. The highest eulogiums that can be passed on health would not be extravagant. He that has a healthy body is infinitely more blessed than he who is sickly, whatever his estates may be. Yet if I have health, my bones well set, and my muscles well strung, if I scarcely know an ache or pain, but can rise in the morning, and with elastic step go forth to labor, and cast myself upon my couch at night, and sleep the sleep of the happy, yet, oh let me not glory in my strength! In a moment it may fail me. A few short weeks may reduce the strong man to a skeleton. Consumption may set in, the cheek may pale with the shadow of death. Let not the strong man glory in his strength. The Lord "delighteth not in the strength of the horse: he taketh not pleasure in the legs of a man." And let us not make our boast concerning these things. Say, thou that are in good health, "My God, bless me indeed. Give me the healthy soul. Heal me of my spiritual diseases. Jehovah Rophi come, and purge out the leprosy that is in my heart by nature: make me healthy in the heavenly sense, that I may not be put aside among the unclean, but allowed to stand amongst the congregation of thy saints. Bless my bodily health to me that I may use it rightly, spending the strength I have in thy service and to thy glory; otherwise, though blessed with health, I may not be blessed indeed." Some of you, dear friends, do not possess the great treasure of health. Wearisome days and nights are appointed you. Your bones are become an almanac, in which you note the changes of the weather. There is much about you that is fitted to excite pity. But I pray that you may have the blessing indeed, and I know what that is. I can heartily sympathise with a sister that said to me the other day, "I had such nearness to God when I was sick, such full assurance, and such joy in the Lord, and I regret to say I have lost it now; that I could almost wish to be ill again, if thereby I might have a renewal of communion with God." I have oftentimes looked gratefully back to my sick chamber. I am certain that I never did grow in grace one half so much anywhere as I have upon the bed of pain. It ought not to be so. Our joyous mercies ought to be great fertilizers to our spirit; but not unfrequently our griefs are more salutary than our joys. The pruning knife is best for some of us. Well, after all, whatever you have to suffer, of weakness, of debility, of pain, and anguish, may it be so attended with the divine presence, that this light affliction may work out for you a far more exceeding and eternal weight of glory, and so you may be blessed indeed.

I will only dwell upon one more temporal mercy, which is very precious--I mean the blessing of home. I do not think any one can ever prize it too highly, or speak too well of it. What a blessing it is to have the fireside, and the dear relationships that gather round the word "Home," wife, children, father, brother, sister! Why, there are no songs in any language that are more full of music than those dedicated to "Mother." We hear a great deal about the German "Fatherland"--we like the sound. But the word, "Father," is the whole of it. The "land" is nothing: the "Father" is key to the music. There are many of us, I hope, blessed with a great many of these relationships. Do not let us be content to solace our souls with ties that must ere long be sundered. Let us ask that over and above them may come the blessing indeed. I thank thee, my God, for my earthly father; but oh, be thou my Father, then am I blessed indeed. I thank thee, my God, for a mother's love; but comfort thou my soul as one whom a mother comforteth, then am I blessed indeed. I thank thee, Savior, for the marriage bond; but be thou the bridegroom of my soul. I thank thee for the tie of brotherhood; but be thou my brother born for adversity, bone of my bone, and flesh of my flesh. The home thou hast given me I prize, and thank thee for it; but I would dwell in the house of the Lord for ever, and be a child that never wanders, wherever my feet may travel, from my Father's house with its many mansions. You can thus be blessed indeed. If not domiciled under the paternal care of the Almighty, even the blessing of home, with all its sweet familiar comforts, does not reach to the benediction which Jabez desired for himself. But do I speak to any here that are separated from kith and kin? I know some of you have left behind you in the bivouac of life graves where parts of your heart are buried, and that which remains is bleeding with just so many wounds. Ah, well! the Lord bless you indeed! Widow, thy maker is thy husband. Fatherless one, he hath said, "I will not leave you comfortless: I will come to you." Oh, to find all your relationships made up in him, then you will be blessed indeed! I have perhaps taken too long a time in mentioning these temporary blessings, so let me set the text in another light. I trust we have had human blessings and temporary blessings, to fill our hearts with gladness, but not to foul our hearts with worldliness, or to distract our attention from the things that belong to our everlasting welfare.

Let us proceed, thirdly, to speak of imaginary blessings. There are such in the world. From them may God deliver us. "Oh that thou wouldest bless me indeed!" Take the Pharisee. He stood in the Lord's house, and he thought he had the Lord's blessing, and it made him very bold, and he spoke with unctuous self-complacency, "God, I thank thee, that I am not as other men are," and so on. He had the blessing, and well indeed he supposed himself to have merited it. He had fasted twice in the week, paid tithes of all that he possessed, even to the odd farthing on the mint, and the extra halfpenny on the cummin he had used. He felt he had done everything. His the blessing of a quiet or a quiescent conscience; good, easy man. He was a pattern to the parish. It was a pity everybody did not live as he did; if they had, they would not have wanted any police. Pilate might have dismissed his guards, and Herod his soldiers. He was just one of the most excellent persons that ever breathed. He adored the city of which he was a burgess! Ay; but he was not blessed indeed. This was all his own overweening conceit. He was a mere wind-bag, nothing more and the blessing which he fancied had fallen upon him, had never come. The poor publican whom he thought accursed, went to his home justified rather than he. The blessing had not fallen on the man who thought he had it. Oh, let every one of us here feel the sting of this rebuke, and pray: "Great God, save us from imputing to ourselves a righteousness which we do not possess. Save us from wrapping ourselves up in our own rags, and fancying we have put on the wedding garments. Bless me indeed. Let me have the true righteousness. Let me have the true worthiness which thou canst accept, even that which is of faith in Jesus Christ."

Another form of this imaginary blessing is found in persons who would scorn to be thought self-righteous. Their delusion, however, is near akin. I hear them singing--

"I do believe, I will believe
That Jesus died for me,
And on his cross he shed his blood,
From sin to set me free."

You believe it, you say. Well, but how do you know? Upon what authority do you make so sure? Who told you? "Oh, I believe it." Yes, but we must mind what we believe. Have you any clear evidence of a special interest in the blood of Jesus? Can you give any spiritual reasons for believing that Christ has set you free from sin? I am afraid that some have got a hope that has not got any ground, like an anchor without any fluke--nothing to grasp, nothing to lay hold upon. They say they are saved, and they stick to it they are, and think it wicked to doubt it; but yet they have no reason to warrant their confidence. When the sons of Kohath carried the ark, and touched it with their hands, they did rightly; but when Uzzah touched it he died. There are those who are ready to be fully assured; there are others to whom it will be death to talk of it. There is a great difference between presumption and full assurance. Full assurance is reasonable: it is based on solid ground. Presumption takes for granted, and with brazen face pronounces that to be its own to which it has no right whatever. Beware, I pray thee, of presuming that thou art saved. If with thy heart thou dost trust in Jesus, then art thou saved; but if thou merely sayest, "I trust in Jesus," it doth not save thee. If thy heart be renewed, if thou shalt hate the things that thou didst once love, and love the things that thou didst once hate; if thou hast really repented; if there be a thorough change of mind in thee; if thou be born again, then hast thou reason to rejoice: but if there be no vital change, no inward godliness; if there be no love to God, no prayer, no work of the Holy Spirit, then thy saying, "I am saved," is but thine own assertion, and it may delude, but it will not deliver thee. Our prayer ought to be, "Oh that thou wouldest bless me indeed, with real faith, with real salvation, with the trust in Jesus that is the essential of faith; not with the conceit that begets credulity. God preserve us from imaginary blessings!" I have met with persons who said, "I believe I am saved, because I dreamt it." Or, "Because I had a text of Scripture that applied to my own case. Such and such a good man said so and so in his sermon." Or, "Because I took to weeping and was excited, and felt as I never felt before." Ah! but nothing will stand the trial but this, "Dost thou abjure all confidence in everything but the finished work of Jesus, and dost thou come to Christ to be reconciled in him to God?" If thou dost not, thy dreams, and visions, and fancies, are but dreams, and visions, and fancies, and will not serve thy turn when most thou needest them. Pray the Lord to bless thee indeed, for of that sterling verity in all thy walk and talk there is a great scarcity.

Too much I am afraid, that even those who are saved--saved for time and eternity--need this caution, and have good cause to pray this prayer that they may learn to make a distinction between some things which they think to be spiritual blessings, and others which are blessings indeed. Let me show you what I mean. Is it certainly a blessing to get an answer to your prayer after your own mind? I always like to qualify my most earnest prayer with, "Not as I will, but as thou wilt." Not only ought I to do it, but I would like to do it, because otherwise I might ask for something which it would be dangerous for me to receive. God might give it me in anger, and I might find little sweetness in the grant, but much soreness in the grief it caused me. You remember how Israel of old asked for flesh, and God gave them quails; but while the meat was yet in their mouths the wrath of God came upon them. Ask for the meat, if you like, but always put in this: "Lord, if this is not a real blessing, do not give it me." "Bless me indeed." I hardly like to repeat the old story of the good woman whose son was ill--a little child near death's door--and she begged the minister, a Puritan, to pray for its life. He did pray very earnestly, but he put in, "If it be thy will, save this child." The woman said, "I cannot bear that: I must have you pray that the child shall live. Do not put in any ifs or buts." "Woman," said the minister, "it may be you will live to rue the day that ever you wished to set your will up against God's will." Twenty years afterwards, she was carried away in a fainting fit from under Tyburn gallows-tree, where that son was put to death as a felon. Although she had lived to see her child grow up to be a man, it would have been infinitely better for her had the child died, and infinitely wiser had she left it to God's will. Do not be quite so sure that what you think an answer to prayer is any proof of divine love. It may leave much room for thee to seek unto the Lord, saying, "Oh that thou wouldest blessed me indeed!" So sometimes great exhilaration of spirit, liveliness of heart, even though it be religious joy, may not always be a blessing. We delight in it, and oh, sometimes when we have had gatherings for prayer here, the fire has burned, and our souls have glowed! We felt at the time how we could sing--

"My willing soul would stay
In such a frame as this,
And sit and sing herself away
To everlasting bliss."

So far as that was a blessing we are thankful for it; but I should not like to set such seasons up, as if my enjoyments were the main token of God's favor; or as if they were the chief signs of his blessing. Perhaps it would be a greater blessing to me to be broken in spirit, and laid low before the Lord at the present time. When you ask for the highest joy, and pray to be on the mountain with Christ, remember it may be as much a blessing; yea, a blessing indeed to be brought into the Valley of Humiliation, to be laid very low, and constrained to cry out in anguish, "Lord, save, or I perish!"

"If to-day he deigns to bless us
With a sense of pardon'd sin,
He to-morrow may distress us,
Make us feel the plague within,
All to make us
Sick of self, and fond of him."

These variable experiences of ours may be blessings indeed to us, when, had we been always rejoicing, we might have been like Moab, settled on our lees, and not emptied from vessel to vessel. It fares ill with those who have no changes; they fear not God. Have we not, dear friends, sometimes envied those persons that are always calm and unruffled, and are never perturbed in mind? Well, there are Christians whose evenness of temper deserves to be emulated. And as for that calm repose, that unwavering assurance which comes from the Spirit of God, it is a very delightful attainment; but I am not sure that we ought to envy anybody's lot because it is more tranquil or less exposed to storm and tempest than our own. There is a danger of saying, "Peace, peace," where there is no peace, and there is a calmness which arises from callousness. Dupes there are who deceive their own souls. "They have no doubts," they say, but it is because they have little heart searching. They have no anxieties, because they have not much enterprise or many pursuits to stir them up. Or it may be they have no pains, because they have no life. Better go to heaven, halt and maimed, than go marching on in confidence down to hell. "Oh that thou wouldest bless me indeed!" My God, I will envy no one of his gifts or his graces, much less of his inward mood or his outward circumstances, if only thou wilt "bless me indeed." I would not be comforted unless thou comfortest me, nor have any peace but Christ my peace, nor any rest but the rest which cometh from the sweet savor of the sacrifice of Christ. Christ shall be all in all, and none shall be anything to me save himself. O that we might always feel that we are not to judge as to the manner of the blessing, but must leave it with God to give us what we would have, not the imaginary blessing, the superficial and apparent blessing, but the blessing indeed!

Equally too with regard to our work and service, I think our prayer should always be, "Oh that thou wouldest bless me indeed!" It is lamentable to see the work of some good men, though it is not ours to judge them, how very pretentious, but how very unreal it is. It is really shocking to think how some men pretend to build up a church in the course of two or three evenings. They will report, in the corner of the newspapers, that there were forty-three persons convinced of sin, and forty-six justified, and sometimes thirty-eight sanctified; I do not know what besides of wonderful statistics they give as to all that is accomplished. I have observed congregations that have been speedily gathered together, and great additions have been made to the church all of a sudden. And what has become of them? Where are those churches at the present moment? The dreariest deserts in Christendom are those places that were fertilised by the patent manures of certain revivalists. The whole church seemed to have spent its strength in one rush and effort after something, and it ended in nothing at all. They built their wooden house, and piled up the hay, and made a stubble spire that seemed to reach the heavens, and there fell one spark, and all went away in smoke; and he that came to labor next time--the successor of the great builder--had to get the ashes swept away before he could do any good. The prayer of every one that serves God should be, "Oh that thou wouldest bless me indeed." Plod on, plod on. If I only build one piece of masonry in my life, and nothing more, if it be gold, silver, or precious stones, it is a good deal for a man to do; of such precious stuff as that, to build even one little corner which will not show, is a worthy service. It will not be much talked of, but it will last. There is the point: it will last. "Establish thou the work of our hands upon us; yea, the work of our hands establish thou it." If we are not builders in an established church, it is of little use to try at all. What God establishes will stand, but what men build without his establishment will certainly come to nought. "Oh that thou wouldest bless me indeed!" Sunday-school teacher, be this your prayer. Tract distributer, local preacher, whatever you may be, dear brother or sister, whatever your form of service, do ask the Lord that you may not be one of those plaster builders using sham compo that only requires a certain amount of frost and weather to make it crumble to pieces. Be it yours, if you cannot build a cathedral, to build at least one part of the marvellous temple that God is piling for eternity, which will outlast the stars.

I have one thing more to mention before I bring this sermon to a close. The blessings of God's grace are blessings indeed, which in right earnest we ought to seek after. By these marks shall ye know them. Blessings indeed, are such blessings as come from the pierced hand; blessings that come from calvary's bloody tree, streaming from the Savior's wounded side--thy pardon, thine acceptance, thy spiritual life: the bread that is meat indeed, the blood that is drink indeed--thy oneness to Christ, and all that comes of it--these are blessings indeed. Any blessing that comes as the result of the Spirit's work in thy soul is a blessing indeed; though it humble thee, though it strip thee, though it kill thee, it is a blessing indeed. Though the harrow go over and over thy soul, and the deep plough cut into thy very heart; though thou be maimed and wounded, and left for dead, yet if the Spirit of God do it, it is a blessing indeed. If he convinceth thee of sin, of righteousness, and of judgment, even though thou hast not hitherto been brought to Christ, it is a blessing indeed. Anything that he does, accept it; do not be dubious of it; but pray that he may continue his blessed operations in thy soul. Whatsoever leads thee to God is in like manner a blessing indeed. Riches may not do it. There may be a golden wall between thee and God. Health will not do it: even the strength and marrow of thy bones may keep thee at a distance from thy God. But anything that draws thee nearer to him is a blessing indeed. What though it be a cross that raiseth thee? Yet if it raise thee to God it shall be a blessing indeed. Anything that reaches into eternity, with a preparation for the world to come, anything that we can carry across the river, the holy joy that is to blossom in those fields beyond the swelling flood, the pure cloudless love of the brotherhood which is to be the atmosphere of truth for ever--anything of this kind that has the eternal broad arrow on it--the immutable mark--is a blessing indeed. And anything which helps me to glorify God is a blessing indeed. If I be sick, and that helps me to praise him, it is a blessing indeed. If I be poor, and I can serve him better in poverty than in wealth, it is a blessing indeed. If I be in contempt, I will rejoice in that day and leap for joy, if it be for Christ's sake--it is a blessing indeed. Yea, my faith shakes off the disguise, snatches the vizor from the fair forehead of the blessing, and counts it all joy to all into divers trials for the sake of Jesus and the recompense of reward that he has promised. "Oh that we may be blessed indeed!"

Now, I send you away with these three words: "Search." See whether the blessings are blessings indeed, and be not satisfied unless you know that they are of God, tokens of his grace, and earnests of his saving purpose. "Weigh"--that shall be the next word. Whatever thou hast, weigh it in the scale, and ascertain if it be a blessing indeed, conferring such grace upon you as causeth you to abound in love, and to abound in every good word and work. And lastly, "Pray." So pray that this prayer may mingle with all thy prayers, that whatsoever God grants or whatever he withholds thou mayest be blessed indeed. Is it a joy-time with thee? O that Christ may mellow thy joy, and prevent the intoxication of earthly blessedness from leading thee aside from close walking with him! In the night of sorrow, pray that he will bless thee indeed, lest the wormwood also intoxicate thee and make thee drunk, lest thy afflictions should make thee think hardly of him. Pray for the blessing, which having, thou art rich to all the intents of bliss, or which lacking, thou art poor and destitute, though plenty fill thy store. "If thy presence go not with me, carry us not up hence." But "Oh that thou wouldest bless me indeed!"

Letter from Mr. Spurgeon, read at the Tabernacle on Lord's-day, June 11th:--

BELOVED FRIENDS,--Whom I have in constant and affectionate remembrance I am obliged again to take up the note of mourning, for I have been all the week suffering, and the most of it confned to my bed. The severe weather has driven me back, and caused a repetition of all my pains.

Nevertheless, the Lord's will be done. Let Him have his way with me, for he is Love. I have been wearying to preach again, but it may be my dumb Sabbaths are appointed for my chastisement, and their number is not yet fufilled. We must work for God while we can, for not one of us knows how soon he may be unable to take a share in the service. At the same time, how unimportant we are! God's work goes on without us. We all need him, but he needs no one of us.

Beloved, hitherto I have had much solace in hearing that the Lord's work among you goes on. I pray you make earnest intercession that this may continue. I hope week-night services will not droop. If you stay away, let it be when I am there, but not now. May the Deacons and Elders find themselves at every meeting for worship surrounded by an untiring band of helpers.

May abundance of grace rest on you all, especially on the sick, the poor, and the bereaved. Pray for me, I entreat you. Perhaps if the church met for prayer I should be speedily restored. I know thousands do pray, but should not the church do so as a church? I fear I must give up all hope of preaching on the 25th; but I trust the Lord will be merciful to me, and send me among you on the first Sabbath of July.

Next Sunday there should be a collection for the Association, an object very dear to me. With deep Christian love,

Your suffering Pastor,

C.H. Spurgeon

The Sheep and Their Shepherd

A Sermon (No. 995)
Delivered by
C. H. SPURGEON,
At the Metropolitan Tabernacle, Newington

"My sheep hear my voice, and I know them, and they follow me." - John 10:27.

CHRISTIANS ARE HERE compared to sheep. Not a very flattering comparison you may say; but then we do not wish to be flattered, nor would our Lord deem it good to flatter us, While far from flattering, it is, however, eminently consoling, for of all creatures there are not any more compassed about with infirmity than sheep. In this frailty of their nature they are a fit emblem of ourselves; at least, of so many of us as have believed in Jesus and become his disciples. Let others boast how strong they are; yet if there be strong ones anywhere, certainly we are weak. We have proved our weakness, and day by day we lament it. We do confess our weakness; yet may we not repine at it, for, as Paul said, so we find, when we are weak then are we strong. Sheep have many wants, yet they are very helpless, and quite unable to provide for themselves. But for the shepherd's cure they would soon perish. This, too, is our case. Our spiritual needs are numerous and pressing, Yet we cannot supply any of them. We are travelers through a wilderness that yields us neither food nor water. Unless our bread drop down from heaven, and our water flow out of the living rock, we must die. Our weakness and our want we keenly feel: still we have no cause to murmur, since the Lord knows our poor estate, and succours us with the tenderest care. Sheep, too, are silly creatures, and in this respect likewise we are very sheepish. We meekly own it to him who is ready to guide us. We say, as David said, "O God, thou knowest my foolishness;" and he says to us as he said to David, "I will instruct thee and teach thee in the way which thou shalt go." If Christ were not our wisdom, we should soon fall a prey to the destroyer. Every grain of true wisdom that we possess we have derived from him; of ourselves we are dull and giddy; folly is bound up in our heart. The more conscious you are, dear brethren, of your own deficiencies, your lack of stamina, discretion, sagacity, and all the instincts of self-preservation, the more delighted you will be to see that the Lord accepts you under these conditions, and calls you the people of his pasture and the sheep of his hand. He discerns you as you are, claims you as his own, foresees all the ills to which you are exposed, yet tends you as his flock, sets store by every lamb of the fold, and so feeds you according to the integrity of his heart, and guides you by the skilfulness of his hands. "I will feed my flock, and I will cause them to lie down, saith the Lord God." Oh, what sweet music there is to us in the name which is given to our Lord Jesus Christ of "the good Shepherd"! It not only describes the office he holds, but it sets forth the sympathy he feels, the aptness he shows, and the responsibility he bears to promote our well-being. What if the sheep be weak, yet is the shepherd strong to guard his flock from the prowling wolf or the roaring lion. If the sheep suffer privation because the soil is barren, yet is the shepherd able to lead them into pasturage suitable for them. If they be foolish, yet he goes before them, cheers them with his voice, and rules them with the rod of his command. There cannot be a flock without a shepherd; neither is there a shepherd truly without a flock. The two must go together. They are the fullness of each other. As the church is the fullness of him that filleth all in all, so we rejoice to remember that "of his fullness have all we received, and grace for grace." That I am like a sheep is a sorry reflection; but that I have a shepherd charms away the sorrow and creates a new joy. It even becomes a gladsome thing to be weak, that I may rely on his strength; to be full of wants, that I may draw from his fullness; to be shallow and often at my wit's end, that I may be always regulated by his wisdom. Even so doth my shame redound to his praise. Not to you, ye great and mighty, who lift your heads high, and claim for yourselves honor: not for you is peace, not to you is rest; but unto you, ye lowly ones, who delight in the valley of humiliation, and feel yourselves to be taken down in your own esteem--to you it is that the Shepherd becomes dear; and to you will he give to lie down in green pastures beside the still waters.

In a very simple way, we shall speak about the proprietor of the sheep. "My sheep," says Christ. Then, we shall have a little to say about the marks of the sheep. After that I propose to talk awhile about the privileges of the sheep. "I know my sheep:" they are privileged to be known of Christ. "My sheep hear my voice."

I. Who is the proprietor of the sheep? They are all Christ's. "My sheep hear my voice." How came the saints to be Christ's?

They are his, first of all, because he chose them. Ere the worlds were made, out of all the rest of mankind he selected them. He knew the race would fall, and become unworthy of the faculties with which he endowed them, and the inheritance he had assigned them. To him belonged the sovereign prerogative that he might have mercy on whom he would have mercy; and he, out of his own absolute will, and according to the counsel of his own good pleasure, made choice severally and individually of certain persons, and he said, "These are mine." Their names were written in his book: they became his portion and his heritage. Having chosen them of old so many ages ago, rest assured he will not lose them now. Men prize that which they have long had. If there is a thing that was mine but yesterday, and it is lost today, I might not fret about it; but if I have long possessed it, and called it my patrimony, I would not willingly part with it. Sheep of Christ, ye shall be his for ever, because ye have been his from ever. They are Christ's sheep, because his Father gave them to him. They were the gift of the Father to Christ. He often speaks of them in this way. "As many as thou hast given me:" "Thou hast given them me," saith he, over and over again. Of old, the Father gave his people to Christ. Separating them from among men, he presented them to him as a gift, committed them into his hand as a trust, and ordained them for him as the lot of his inheritance. Thus they become a token of the Father's love to his only begotten Son, a proof of the confidence he reposed in him, and a pledge of the honor that shall be done unto him. Now, I suppose we most of us know how to value a gift for the donor's sake. If presented to us by one whom we love, we set great store by it. If it has been designed to be a love-token, it awakens in our minds many sweet memories. Though the intrinsic worth may be of small account, the associations make it exceedingly precious. We might be content to lose something of far greater value in itself rather than that which is the gift of a friend, the offering of his love. I like the delicate sentiment of the poet, as it is expressed in that pretty verse--

"I never cast a flower away,
The gift of one who cared for me;
A little flower--a faded flower,
But it was done reluctantly."

Yet, oh, how weak the words of human passion! but, oh, how strong the expressions of divine ardor, when Jesus speaks to the Father of "the men whom thou gavest me out of the world"! "Thine they were," he says, "and thou gavest them me; and those that thou gavest me I have kept." Ye sheep of Christ, rest safely; let not your soul be disturbed with fear. The Father gave you to his Son, and he will not lightly lose what God himself has given him. The infernal lions shall not rend the meanest lamb that is a love-token from the Father to his best Beloved. While Christ stands defending his own, he will protect them from the lion and the bear, that would take the lambs of his flock; he will not suffer the least of them to perish.

"My sheep," says Christ. They are his, furthermore, because, in addition to his choice and to the gift, he has bought them with a price. They had sold themselves for nought; but he has redeemed them, not with corruptible things as with silver and gold, but with his precious blood. A man always esteems that to be exceedingly valuable which he procured with risk--with risk of life and limb. David felt he could not drink the water that the brave warriors who broke through the host of the Philistines brought to him from the well at Bethlehem, because it seemed to him as though it were the blood of the men that went in jeopardy of their lives; and he poured it out before the Lord. It was too precious a draught for him, when men's lives had been hazarded for it. But the good Shepherd not only hazarded his life, but even laid it down for his sheep. Jacob exceedingly valued one part of his possessions, and he gave it to Joseph: he gave him one portion above his brethren. Now, you may be sure he would give, Joseph that which he thought most precious. But why did he give him that particular portion? Because, he says, "I took it out of the hand of the Amorite with my sword and with my bow." Now, our blessed Shepherd esteems his sheep because they cost him his blood. They cost him his blood--I may say, he took them out of the hand of the Amorite with his sword and with his bow in bloody conflict, where he was victor, but yet was slain. There is not one sheep of all his flock but what he can see the mark of his blood on him. In the face of every saint the Savior sees, as in a glass, the memorial of his bloody sweat in Gethsemane, and his agonies at Golgotha. "Ye are not your own, for ye are bought with a price." That stands as a call to duty, but it is at the same time a consolation, for if he has bought me, he will have me. Bought with such a price, he will not like to lose me, nor suffer any foe to take me out of his hand. Think not that Christ will suffer those to perish for whom he died. To me the very suggestion seems to draw near to the verge of blasphemy. If he has bought me with his blood, I cannot conceive he cares nothing for me, will take no further concern about me, or will suffer my soul to be cast into the pit. If he has suffered in my stead, where is justice gone that the substitute should bear my guilt, and I should bear it too? and where is mercy fled, that God should execute twice the punishment for one offense! Nay, beloved, those whom he hath bought with blood are his, and he will keep them.

"My sheep," says Christ. They are his, or in due time they shall become so, through his capturing them by sacred power. As well by power are we redeemed as by price, for the blood-bought sheep had gone astray even as others. "All we like sheep have gone astray; we have turned every one to his own way," but, my brethren, the good shepherd has brought many of us back with infinite condescension: with boundless mercy he followed us when we went astray. Oh, what blind slaves we were when we sported with death! We did not know then what his love had ordained for us: it never entered our poor, silly heads that there was a crown for us; we did not know that the Father's love had settled itself on us, or ever the day-star knew its place. We know it now, and it is he that has taught us; for he followed us over mountains of vanity, through bogs and miry places of foul transgression; tracked our devious footsteps on and on, through youth and menhood, till at last, with mighty grace, he grasped us in his arms and laid us on his shoulder, and is this day carrying us home to the great fold above, rejoicing as he bears all our weight and finds us in all we need. Oh, that blessed work of effectual grace! He has made us his own, he has defeated the enemy, the prey has been taken from the mighty, and the lawful captive has been delivered. "He hath broken the gates of brass, and cut the bars of iron asunder," to set his people free. "O that men would praise the Lord for his goodness, and for his wonderful works to the children of men!"

"My SHEEP," saith Christ, as he stands in the midst of his disciples. "My Shepherd," let us one and all reply. All the sheep of Christ who have been redeemed by his power, become his by their own willing and cheerful surrender of themselves to him. We would not belong to another if we might; nor would we wish to belong to ourselves if we could; nor, I trust, do we want any part of ourselves to be our own property. Judge ye whether this be true of you or not. In that day when I surrendered my soul to my Savior, I gave him my body, my soul, my spirit; I gave him all I had, and all I shall have for time and for eternity. I gave him all my talents, my powers, my faculties, my eyes, my ears, my limbs, my emotions, my judgment, my whole manhood, and all that could come of it, whatever fresh capacity or new capability I may be endowed with. Were I at this good hour to change the note of gladness for one of sadness, it should be to wail out my penitent confession of the times and circumstances in which I have failed to observe the strict and unwavering allegiance I owe to my Lord. So far from regretting, I would fain renew my vows and make them over again. In this I think every Christian would join.

"Tis done!
the great transaction's done:
I am my Lord's, and he is mine:
He drew me, and I follow'd on,
Charm'd to confess the voice divine.
Now rest, my long-divided heart;
Fix'd on this blissful center, rest:
With ashes who would grudge to part,
When call'd on angels' bread to feast?
High heaven, that heard the solemn vow,
That vow renew'd shall daily hear:
Till in life's latest hour I bow,
And bless in death a bond so dear."

And yet, brethren, though our hearts may now be all in a glow, lest they should presently grow cold, or the bleak atmosphere of this evil world should chill our devotion, let us never cease to think of the good Shepherd in that great, good act, which most of all showed his love when he laid down his life for the sheep. You have heard the story told by Francis de Sales. He saw a girl carrying a pail of water on her head, in the midst of which she had placed a piece of wood. On asking her why she did this, she told him it was to prevent the motion of the water, for fear it might be spilt. And so, said he, let us place the cross of Christ in the midst of our hearts to check the movement of our affections, that they may not be spilt in restless cares or grievous troubles.

"My sheep," says Christ, and thus he describes his people. They are Christ's, his own, a peculiar property. May I hope that this truth will be henceforth treasured up in your soul! It is a common truth, certainly; but when it is laid home by the Holy Spirit it shines, it beams, not merely as a lamp in a dark chamber, but as the day-star rising in your hearts. Remember this is no more our shame that we are sheep, but it is our honor that we are Christ's sheep. To belong to a king carries some measure of distinction. We are the sheep of the imperial pastures. This is our safety: he will not suffer the enemy to destroy his sheep. This is our sanctity: we are separated, the sheep of the pasture of the Lord's Christ. This is sanctification in one aspect of it: for it is the making of us holy, by setting us apart to be the Lord's own portion for ever. And this is the key to our duty: we are his sheep: then let us live to him, and consecrate ourselves to him who loved us and gave himself for us. Christ is the proprietor of the sheep; and are the property of the good Shepherd.

II. Now, let us commune together awhile upon the marks of the sheep. When there are so many flocks of sheep, it is necessary to mark them. Our Savior marks us. It has been very properly observed, that there are two marks on Christ's sheep. One is on their ear, the other is on their foot. These are two marks of Christ's sheep not to be found on any other; but they are to be found on all his own--the mark on the ear: "My sheep hear my voice."--the mark on the foot: "I know them, and they follow me."

Think of this mark on their ear. "My sheep hear my voice." They hear spiritually. A great many people in Christ's day heard his voice who did not hear it in the way and with the perception that is here intended. They would not hear; that is to say, they would not hearken or give heed, neither would they obey his call or come unto him that they might have life. These were not always the worst sort of people: there were some of the best that would not hear Christ, of whom he said, according to the original, as translated by some, "Ye search the Scriptures; for in them ye think ye have eternal life: and they are they which testify of me. And ye will not come to me, that ye might have life." They would get as far as curiosity or criticism might allure them; but they would not go any farther: they would not believe in Jesus. Now, the spiritual ear listens to God. The opening of it is the work of the Holy Spirit, and this is a mark of Christ's chosen blood-bought people, that they hear not only the hollow sound, but the hidden sense; not the bare letter, but the spiritual lesson; and that too not merely with the outward organ, but with the inward heart. The chief point is that they hear his voice. Oh, if all that heard my voice heard Christ's voice, how would I wander down every street in this city to proclaim the gospel of Jesus Christ; but, alas! the voice of the minister is utterly ineffectual to save a soul, unless the voice of Christ reach the conscience and rouse its dormant powers. "My sheep hear my voice;" the voice of Jesus, his counsel, his command, clothed with the authority of his own sacred sovereign utterance. When the gospel comes to you as Christ's gospel, with demonstration of the Spirit, the invitation is addressed to you by him. You can look upon it in no other light; so you must accept and receive it. When his princely power comes with it--being mighty to save, he puts saving power into the word--then you hear Christ's voice as a fiat that must be obeyed, as a summons that must be attended to, as a call to which there must be a quick response. O beloved, do not ever rest satisfied with hearing the voice of the preacher. We are only Christ's speaking-trumpets: there is nothing in us: it is only his speaking through us that can do any good. O children of God, some of you do not always listen to Christ's voice in the preaching. While we comment on the word, you make your comments on us. Our style, or our tone, or even our gesture, is enough to absorb--I might rather say, to distract--your thoughts. "Why look ye so earnestly on us?" I beseech you, give less heed to the livery of the servant, and give more care to the message of the Master. Listen warily, if you please; but judge wisely, if you can. See how much pure grain, and how much of Christ, there is in the sermon. Use your sieve; put away all the chaff; take only the good wheat; hear Christ's voice. Well were it if we could obscure ourselves that we might manifest him. I could wish so to preach that you could not see even my little finger; might I but so preach that you could get a full view of Jesus only. O that you could hear his voice drowning ours! This is the mark, the peculiar mark of those who are Christ's peculiar people: they hear his voice. Sometimes, truly it sounds in the ministry; sometimes it thrills forth from that book of books, which is often grossly neglected; sometimes it comes in the nightwatches. His voice may speak to us in the street. Silent as to vocal utterance, but like familiar tones that sometimes greet us in our dreams, the voice of Christ is distinctly audible to the soul. It will come to you in sweet or in bitter providences; yea, there is such a thing as hearing Christ's voice in the rustling of every leaf upon the tree, in the moaning of every wind, in the rippling of every wave. And there be those that have learned to lean on Christ's bosom, till they have looked for all the world as though they were a shell that lay in the ocean of Christ's love, listening for ever to the sonorous cadence of that deep, unfathomed, all-mysterious main. The billows of his love never cease to swell. The billowy anthem still peals on with solemn grandeur in the ear of the Christian. O may we hear Christ's voice each one of us for ourselves! I find that language fails me, and metaphors are weak to describe its potent spell.

One point is worth noticing, however. I think our Lord meant here that his sheep, when they hear his voice, know it so well that they can tell it at once from the voice of strangers. The true child of God knows the gospel from the law. It is not by learning catechisms, reading theological books, or listening to endless controversies, that he finds this out. There is an instinct of his regenerate nature far more trustworthy than any lessons he has been taught. The voice of Jesus!

Why there is no music like it. If you have once heard it, you cannot mistake it for another, or another for it. Some are babes in grace: others are of full age, and by reason of use, have their senses exercised; but one sense is quickly brought out--the sense of hearing. It is so easy to tell the joy-bells of the gospel from the death-knell of the law; for the letter killeth, but the Spirit giveth life. "Do, or die," says Moses. "Believe, and live," says Christ: you must know which is which. Yes; and I think they are equally shrewd and quick to discriminate between the flesh and the Spirit. Let some of the very feeblest of God's people sit down under a fluent ministry, with all the beauties of rhetoric, and let the minister preach up the dignity of human nature, and the sufficiency of man's reason to find out the way of righteousness, and you will hear them say: "It is very clever; but there is no food for me in it." Bring, however, the best and most instructed, and most learned Christian man, and set him down under a ministry that is very faulty as to the gift of utterance, and incorrect even in grammar; but if it is full of Jesus Christ, I know what he will say: "Ah! never mind the man, and never mind the platter on which he brought the meat; it was food to my soul that I fed upon with a hearty relish; it was marrow and fatness, for I could hear Christ's voice in it." I am not going to follow out these tests; but certain it is, that the sheep know Christ's voice, and can easily distinguish it. I saw hundreds of lambs the other day together, and there were also their mothers; and I am sure if I had had the task of allotting the proper lamb to each, or to any of them, it would have kept me till now to have done it. But somehow the lambs knew the mothers, and the mothers knew the lambs; and they were all happy enough in each other's company.

Every saint here, mixed up as he may be at times with parties and professors of all sorts, knows Christ, and Christ knows him, and he is therefore bound to his owner. That is the mark on the ear. You have seen sometimes in the country two flocks together on the road, and you say: "I wonder how the shepherds will manage to keep them distinct? They will get mixed up." They do not; they go this way and that way; and after a little commingling they separate, for they know their master's voice; "and a stranger will they not follow." You will go to-morrow, many of you, out into the world, some to the Exchange, others to the market, and others again into the factory: you are all mixed. Yes; but the seeming confusion of your company is temporary, not real and permanent. You will come right again, and you will go to your own home and your own fellowship. And at the last, when we shall have ended our pilgrimage, the one shall wend his way to the glory land, and the other to the abyss of woe. There will be no mistake. You will hear the Master's call, and obey. There is a mark on the ear which identifies every saint.

Christ's sheep hear his voice obediently. This is an important proof of discipleship. Indeed, it may serve as a reproof to many. Oh, I would that you were more careful about this! "He that hath my commandments, and keepeth them," said Jesus, "he it is that loveth me." "He that loveth me not keepeth not my sayings." How comes it to pass, then, that there are certain commands of Christ which some Christians will suffer to lie in abeyance? They will say, "The Lord commands this, but it is not essential." Oh, unloving spirit, that can think anything unessential that thy Bridegroom bids thee do! They that love, think little things of great moment, especially when they are looked upon as tokens of the strength or the tenderness of one's regard. It may not be essential, in order to prove the relation in which a wife stands to her husband, that she should study his tastes, consult his wishes, or attend to his comfort. But will she the less strive to please, because love, not fear, constrains her? I trow not. And can it be that any of you, my brethren, would harbour such a thought as your negligence implies? Do you really suppose that after the choice of Christ has been fixed on you, and the love of Christ has been plighted to you, you may now be as remiss or careless as you like? Nay, rather, might we not expect that a sacred passion, an ardent zeal, a touch of inspiration would stir you up, put you on the alert, make you wake at the faintest sound of his voice, or keep you listening to do his will? Be it ours, then, to act out with fidelity that verse we have often sung with enthusiasm:--

"In all my Lord's appointed ways
My journey I'll pursue."

However little the precept may appear in the eyes of others; however insignificant as compared with our salvation, yet--doth the Lord command it?--then his sheep hear his voice, and they follow him.

Christ has marked his sheep on their feet as well as their ears. They follow him: they are gently led, not harshly driven. They follow him as the Captain of their salvation; they trust in the power of his arm to clear the way for them. All their trust on him is stayed; all their hope on him they lean. They follow him as their teacher; they call no man "Rabbi" under heaven, but Christ alone. He is the infallible source of their creeds; neither will they allow their minds to be ruled by conclaves, councils, nor decrees. Hath a Christ said it? It is enough. If not, it is no more for me than the whistling of the wind. They follow a Christ as their teacher.

And the sheep of Christ follow him as their example; they desire to be in this world as he was. It is one of their marks, that to a greater or less degree they have a Christ-like spirit; and if they could they would be altogether like their Lord.

They follow him, too, as their Commander, and Lawgiver, and Prince. "Whatsoever he saith unto you, do it," was his mother's wise speech; and it is the children's wise rule: "Whatsoever he saith unto you, do it." Oh, blessed shall they be above many of whom it shall be said, "These are they that have not defiled their garments." "These are they which follow the Lamb whithersoever he goeth." Some of his followers are not very scrupulous. They love him. It is not for us to judge them. Rather we place ourselves among them and share in the censure. But happiest of all the happy are they who see the footprint--the print of that foot that once was pierced with the nail--and put their foot down where he placed it, and then again, in the selfsame mark, follow where he trod, till they climb at last to the throne. Keep close to Christ; take care of his little precepts unto the end. Remember, "Whosoever shall break one of these least commandments, and shall teach men so, he shall be called the least in the kingdom of heaven." Do not peril being least in the heavenly kingdom though it is better to be that than to be greatest in the kingdom of darkness. O seek to be very near him, to be a choice sheep in his chosen flock, and to have the mark distinctly upon your foot!

I will not stay to apply these truths, but leave each one of you to make such self-searching enquiries as the text suggests. Have I the ear mark? Have I the foot mark? "My sheep hear my voice," "and they follow me." I hope that I am among the number.

III. The last point, with which we now proceed to close, is--THE PRIVILEGE OF CHRIST'S SHEEP. It does not look very large, but if we open it we shall see an amazing degree of blessedness in it. "I know them," "I know them." What does it mean?

I have not time now to tell you all it means. "I know them." What is the reverse of this but one of the most dreadful things that is reserved for the day of judgment? There will be some who will say, "Lord, Lord, have we not prophesied in thy name, and in thy name cast out devils?" And he shall say, "Verily, verily, I say unto you, I never knew you; depart from me, ye cursed." Now measure the height of that privilege by the depth of this misery. "I never knew you." What a volume of scorn it implies! What a stigma of infamy it conveys! Change the picture. The Redeemer says, "I know them," "I know them." How his eyes flash with kindness; how their cheeks burn with gratitude, as he says, "I know them "! Why, if a man had a friend and acquaintance that he used to know, and some years after he found him a disreputable, abandoned, wicked, guilty criminal, I feel pretty sure he would not say much about having known such a fellow, though he might be driven to confess that he had some years ago a passing acquaintance with him. But our Lord Jesus Christ, though he knows what poor, unworthy ones we are, yet when we shall be brought up before the Lord, before the great white throne, he will confess he knew us. He does know us, we are old acquaintances of his, and he has known us from before the foundation of the world, "For whom he did foreknow, he also did predestinate to be conformed to the image of his Son, that he might be the firstborn among many brethren. Moreover whom he did predestinate, them he also called." There are riches of grace in this; but we will consider it in another way. Our Savior knows us, our Shepherd knows us. Beloved, he knows your person and all about you. You, with that sick body, that aching head, he knows you and he knows your son with all its sensitiveness; that timidity, that anxiety, that constitutional depression--he knows it all. A physician may come to see you, and be unable to detect what the disease is that pains or prostrates you, but Christ knows you through and through; all the parts of your nature he understands. "I know them," saith he; he can therefore prescribe for you. He knows your sins. Do not let that dismay you, because he has blotted them all out; and he only knows them to forgive them, to cover them with his righteousness. He knows your corruptions; he will help you to overcome them; he will deal with you in providence and in grace, so that they shall be rooted up. He knows your temptations. Perhaps you are living away from your parents and Christian friends, and you have had an extraordinary temptation, and you wish you could go home and tell your mother. Oh, he knows it, he knows it; he can help you better than your mother can. You say: "I wish the minister knew the temptation I have passed through." Do not tell it; God knows it. As Daniel did not want Nebuchadnezzar to tell him the nature of his dream, but gave him the dream and the interpretation at the same time, so God can send you comfort. There will be a word as plainly suited to your case as though it were all printed and the preacher had known it all. It must be so. Depend upon it, the Lord know's your temptation, and watches your trial; or be it a sick child, or be it a bad matter of business that has lately occurred; or be it a slander that has wounded your heart, there is not a pang you feel but God as surely sees it as the weaver sees the shuttle which he throws with his own hand. He knows your trial, and he knows the meaning of your groans: he can read the secret desire of your heart, you need not write it nor speak it: he has understood it all. You were saying: "O that my child were converted! O that I grew in grace!" He knows it: he knows it every whit. There is not a word on your tongue, nor a wish in your heart, but he knoweth it altogether. O dear heart, he knows your sincerity! Perhaps you want to join the church, and your proposal has been declined, because you could not give satisfactory testimony. If you are sincere, he knows it; he knows, moreover, what your anxiety is. You cannot tell another what it is that is bitter to you--the heart knoweth its own bitterness--he knows it. As his secret is with you, so your secret is with him. He knows you: he knows what you have been trying to do. That secret gift--that offering dropped so quietly where none could see it--he knows it. And he knows that you love him. "Yes," you are saying in your soul, "if ever I loved thee, my Jesus, tis now." No, you cannot tell him, nor tell others; but he knows it all.

So, now, in closing, let us say that in the text there is mutual knowledge. "I know them, but they also know me, because they hear my voice, and recognize it." Here is mutual confession. Christ speaks, else there would be no voice: they hear, else were the voice not useful. "I know them;" that is his thoughts go towards them. "They follow me;" that is, their thoughts go towards him. He leads the way, else they could not follow. They follow, however, whom he leads the way. Being the counterpart of each other, what the one does the other returns through grace; and what grace puts into the sheep the shepherd recognises, and makes a return to them. Christ and his church become an echo of each other: his the voice, theirs is but a faint echo of it; still it is a true echo, and you shall know who are Christ's by this. Do they echo what Christ saith? Oh, how I wish we were all sheep! How my soul longs that we may many of us who are not of his fold be brought in. The Lord bring you in, my dear hearers. The Lord give you his grace, and make you his own, comfort you, and make you to follow him. And if you are his, show it. These, dear brethren and sisters, here at this time, desire to confess Christ in your presence. If they are doing right, and you are not doing as they do, then you are doing wrong. If it is the duty of one, it is the duty of all; and if one Christian may neglect making a profession, all may do so, and then there will be no visible church whatever, and the visible ordinances must die out. If you know him, own him, for he hath said: "Whosoever therefore shall confess me before men, him will I confess also before my Father which is in heaven. But whosoever shall deny me before men, him will I also deny before my Father which is in heaven." God bless you, for Christ's sake. Amen.

Letter from Mr. Spurgeon, read at the Tabernacle on Lord's-day, June 18th:--

MY BELOVED FRIENDS,--

As soon as the church had resolved to meet for special prayer for me, I began rapidly to recover. It pleased God to turn the wind at the beginning of this week, and the change in the temperature has worked wonders. We may truthfully say of the Wednesday meeting for prayer, that the Lord fulfilled his word: "Before they call, I will answer; and while they are yet speaking, I will hear." For all this great goodness I pray you to unite with me in sincere and intense gratitude to the Lord our God.

I feel bound publicly to express my happiness of heart. This week has furnished me with the liveliest proofs of your true love. I have been deeply touched with the various ways in which the affection of so many of you has sought to find expression. I value this not only for my own sake, though it is very sweet to be the object of such hearty love, but because I see in it the evidence that our union has been cemented by years, and the earnest of future years of united effort, if God spares us. The absence of unity is weakness: its indisputable presence is strength.

On the closing day of my thirty-seventh year, I find myself the pastor of a beloved flock, who have borne the test of twelve Sabbaths of their minister's absence, and the severer test of more than seventeen years of the same ministry, and are now exhibiting more love to him than ever. I bless God, but I also thank you, and assure you that I never felt happier in the midst of my people than I do now in the prospect of returning to you.

I am still weak, but the improvement in strength has been this week very surprising. I hardly dare speak of the future; but I earnestly hope we shall look each other in the face on the first Sabbath of July.

The collection to-day is to enable the London Baptist Association to build a new chapel in the Wandsworth Road. We are to carry out the project, so that it will not become us to be slack in our collection. London grows so rapidly, that much must be done to keep pace with its spiritual needs. Our Association does something, but ten times more would be little enough. You will I am sure give as God has prospered you. The College, of course, will be less helped; but I must beg to thank you for the continued series of noble contributions which have made each week remarkable.

Peace be with you and the Lord's own anointing. May those who speak to you to-day be filled with the Spirit. May the soft south wind of the Spirit's love be among you, and may you pour forth praise as flowers breathe perfume.

Yours very truly,

C.H. Spurgeon

The Alarum

A Sermon (No. 996)
Delivered by
C. H. SPURGEON,
At the Metropolitan Tabernacle, Newington

"I myself will awake early." - Psalms 42:8.

The proper subject to treat upon with such a text would be the propriety and excellence of early rising, especially when we are desirous of praising or serving God. The dew of dawn should be consecrated to devotion. The text is a very remarkable expression, and might fitly be made the early riser's motto. It is, in the original, a highly poetical phrase, and milton and others have borrowed or imitated it. "I will awaken in the morning." So early would the psalmist arise for the praise of God that he would call up the day, and bid the sun arise from the chambers of the east, and proceed upon his journey. "I will awaken the morning." Early rising has the example of Old Testament saints to recommend it, and many modern saints having conscientiously practiced it, have been loud in its praise. It is an economy of time and an assistance to health, and thus it doubly lengthens life. Late rising is the token of indolence, and the cause of disorder throughout the whole day. Be assured that the best hours are the first. Our City habits are to be deplored, because by late hours of retirement at night we find early rising difficult if not impossible. If we are able to escape the shackles of custom, and secure for devotion and contemplation the hour when the dew is on the grass, we may count ourselves thrice happy. If we cannot do all we would in this matter, at least let us do all we can.

That is not, however, the topic upon which I now desire to speak to you. I come at this time, not so much to plead for the early as for the awakening. The hour we may speak of at another time--the fact is our subject now. It is bad to awake late, but what shall be said of those who never awake at all? Better late than never: but with many it is to be feared it will be never. I would take down the trumpet and give a blast, or ring the alarm-bell till all the faculties of the sluggard's manhood are made to bestir themselves, and he cries with new born determination, "I myself will awake."

"Will awake." This is a world in which most men nowadays are alive to their temporal interests. If in these pushing times any man goes about his business in a sleepy, listless fashion, he very soon finds himself on an ebb-tide, and all his affairs aground. The wideawake man seizes opportunities or makes them, and thus those who are widest awake usually come to the front. Years ago affairs moved like the broad-wheel wagon, very sleepily, with sober pause and leisurely progression, and then the son of the snail had a chancel but now, when we almost fly, if a man would succeed in trade he must be all alive, and all awake. If it be so in temporals, it is equally so in spirituals, for the world, the flesh, and the devil are all awake to compete with us; and there is no resolution that I would more earnestly commend to each one of the people of God than this one: "I will awake; I will awake at once; I will awake early, and I will pray to God that I may be kept awake, that my Christian existence may not be dreamy, but that I may be to the fullest degree useful in my Master's service." If this were the resolve of each, what a change would come over the Christian church! I long to see the diligence of the shop exceeded by the closet, and the zeal of the market excelled by the church. Each Christian is alive: but is he also awake? He has eyes, but are they open? He has lofty possibilities of blessing his fellow men, but does he exercise them? My heart's desire is that none of us may feel the dreamy influence of this age, which is comparable to the enchanted ground; but that each of us may be watchful, wakeful, vigorous, intense, fervent. Trusting that the Holy Spirit may bless or meditations to our spiritual quickening, we shall briefly turn our thoughts to the consideration of two or three things.

I. Our text is connected with the duty of praise, and therefore our first point shall be--IT IS MOST NECESSARY THAT OUR MINDS SHOULD BE IN A STATE OF WAKEFULNESS WHEN WE ARE PRAISING GOD. Therefore, as we ought to be always praising him, our mind ought always to be wakeful. It is a shame to pray with the mind half asleep: it is an equal shame to attempt to praise God till all the powers of the mind are thoroughly aroused. David is herein a most fit example, for he sings, "My heart is fixed, O God, my heart is fixed: I will sing and give praise.

Awake up, my glory; awake, psalter and harp: I myself will awake early."

We should be fully awake when engaged in private thanksgiving; the song of our solitude should be full of living joy. I am afraid there is very little private singing nowadays. We often hear discourse concerning private prayer, but very seldom of private praise: and yet ought there not to b as much private praise as private prayer? I fear from the seldomness of its being mentioned, that private thanksgiving has grown to be a sleepy affair. Then as to public worship, how earnest ought it to be! Yet how seldom is it hearty and real! How often do we hear half-awake singing. Sometimes a sort of musical box, consisting of pipes, keys, and bellows, is set to do all the adoration. The heathens of Tibet turn the wind to account religiously, by making it turn their windmills and pray for them; and our brethren in England, by an ingenious adjustment of pipes, make the same motive power perform their praise. Where this machinery is not adopted, still the Lord is robbed of his praise by other methods, Sometimes half a dozen skilled voices of persons who would be equally as much at home at the opera or the theater as in the house of God, are formed into a choir to perform the psalmody; and it is supposed that God accepts their formal notes as the praise of the entire assembly. How far different is the genuine song of gracious men who lift up their voices to the Lord because their hearts adore him! Oh, I love to hear every voice pouring out its note, especially if I can but hope that with every voice there is going forth a fervent heart. This warm hearted, joyful singing--why, it makes the congregation on earth to be like the assembly of the skies; and causes the meeting-place of the saints to be a faint type of the gathering of the angels and glorified spirits before the throne of God. To drone or to whisper in such a delightful exercise is criminal. If ever we should exhibit the angels' wakefulness, it should be when we are emulating their employment.

Our praise ought to be performed with a fully awakened mind: first, that we may recollect what we are praising God for. We should have a vivid sense of the mercies we have received, or we cannot bless God aright for them. You who have not yet received spiritual blessings, should not be forgetful of his temporal mercies: it is surely sufficient cause for lively thanksgiving that you are not upon a bed of sickness; that you are not in the lunatic asylum; that you are not in the workhouse; that you are not on the borders of the grave; that you are not in hell; that you still have food and raiment, and that you are where the gospel is graciously presented to you. Should not all this be thought of? Should not this be fuel for the flame of gratitude? As for us who have tasted spiritual blessings, if our minds were awake, we should think of eternal love and its going forth from eternity; of redeeming love, and the streams that flow from the fount of Calvary; of God's immutable love, and his patience with our ill-manners in the wilderness; of covenant mercy, of mercies yet to come, of heaven, and the bliss hereafter. Such recollections should call up our whole man to praise the Lord. If the innumerable benefits which we receive were thought of and dwelt upon, the contemplation would put a force, a volume, a body into our song, and make it far more than the flaming ethereal thing which it ought to be.

We want our souls awakened, next, so that we may remember to whom our praise is offered. Before no mean kind do we bow the knee of homage. To praise God is to stand in the immediate presence of the blessed and only Potentate. Do not even seraphs veil their faces in that august presence? With what lowliness ought we boy! With what earnestness of spirit should we praise! "Put off thy shoes from off thy feet, for the place whereon thou standest is holy ground." Courtiers are not expected to nod with drowsiness in the presence of their king; and if they came to present thanksgiving, it would seem strange if they were to yawn as men half asleep. Surely. it would be hypocritical congratulation and insulting behavior if they should be detected in a sleepy condition! If we come together to praise God, let us really do it. If we cannot praise him, let us know and mourn that we cannot do it, and let us be sure that the spirit is willing, even if the flesh is weak. Let all sleepiness be put away in the presence of the ever-wakeful Jehovah, before whose eyes all things are naked and open. He never slumbereth nor sleepeth, so as to make a pause in his mercy to us: let not our slumbering spirits cause an omission of our grateful song.

We need that we should be awake in praise, that our whole hearts may be thoroughly warm in the exercise. Under Christ and the power of the Holy Spirit, the acceptableness of our praise depends very much upon the warmth of it. As cold prayers virtually ask God to deny them, so cold praises ask God to reject them. Cold praises are a sort of semi-blasphemy: they do, as it were, say, "Thou art not worthy to be ardently praised. O God, we bring thee these poor thanksgivings: they are good enough for thee." Surely if we treated our heavenly Father as we should, every sacred passion would glow in our hearts like a furnace: our whole heart would catch fire, and as Elijah went up into heaven with horses of fire and chariots of fire, so, too, our souls , as we thought upon the goodness and the graciousness of God, would ascend to heaven in vehement joy of adoration. Our praises would not be like the incense in the censer, sweet, but cold; but coals of fire would be put in with the incense, and then, like a holy cloud of smoke, our gratitude would ascend to heaven. Mark with what exhilaration the psalmist rendered praise unto God, and imitate him therein. See him dancing before the ark, and hear him cry aloud, "Sing praises to God, sing praises: sing praises unto our King, sing praises."

Brethren, we have need to wake up our souls in praise, or else we shall at all times fail altogether in the duty. Only the wakeful are praiseful. Sleeping birds sing now., The very best praises God receives from earth are from his troubled saints; but then they are awake; the strokes of the rod have aroused them. When the three holy children sung in the fire, their song was sweet indeed; yet had they not been thoroughly in earnest, they had poured forth no holy hymn. When martyrs have magnified God standing on the burning fagot, they have given God better praise than even the angels can. It was the old fable, that the nightingale was made to sing by the thorn that pricked her breast: and many a child of God has poured forth his sweetest music when the thorn of affliction has pierced his heart. Wake up your souls--you that are desponding, you that are depressed, you that have a dead child at home, you that are expecting soon to go to the grave with those you love, you that have been losing your property, you that are pinched with poverty--wake up your souls to praise God still, for unless well awake you will forget to extol him. Remember what Job did. When he sat on the dunghill, scraping himself with a bit of broken pot, yet he praised God and said, "The Lord gave and the Lord hath taken away; blessed be the name of the Lord." It was grand of thee, O patriarch of Uz, to be able thus to able thus to extol thy Lord: then was thy soul fully awake. Beloved friends, may our inmost souls be so energetic with the power of grace that we may spontaneously and earnestly bless the Lord at all times and under all circumstances.

Do you believe, my brethren, that amongst all the throng of those who see Jehovah face to face, there is one dull, cold, careless worshipper? Look through the seraphim and cherubim: they are flaming ones, burning with intense desire and fervent adoration. Look through the hosts of angels: they are all his minsters that do his pleasure, and bless him while they do it. Search through all those sanctified and glorified hands of spirits, and you shall not find one with half-closed eye wearily praising his Maker. Heaven consists in joyful praise. Look at the very birds on earth how they shame us! Dear little creatures, if you watch them when they are singing, you will sometimes wonder how so much sound can come out of such diminutive bodies. How they throw their whole selves into the music, and seem to melt themselves away in song! How the wing vibrates, the throat pulsates, and every part of their body rejoices to assist the strain! This is the way in which we ought to praise God. IF birds that are sold at three for two farthings yet render God such praise, how much more heartily ought we to sing before him? Let it be a resolution with us at this hour that we will praise God more; that we will sing to him more at home, about our business, and in all proper places; and that whenever we do sing we will do it heartily, waking up our tongue and all the powers of our mind and body to bless and praise the name of God.

II. Now, secondly, we shall notice that WAKEFULNESS IS A GREAT NEED IN THE ENTIRE SPIRITUAL LIFE. I believe it to be one of the great wants of the church now. I question whether most of us are awake spiritually. I question whether I am. I wish to be wakened far more to a sensibility of the power of the world to come, and a tenderness in regard to spiritual truth. Slumber is so natural to us. "Well," says one, "but we talk about the things of God." Yes, but people talk when they are asleep, and a good deal of Christian conversation is very much like the talk of sleepers. There is not the force in it--the life in it that there would be in conversation if we were really awakened to feel the power of eternal verities. "Yet," says one, "I hope we act consistently." I trust you do, but there are many people who walk in their sleep, and, alas!I know some Christian professors who appear to be trying very hazardous feats of sleep-walking just now. Some somnambulists have been able to walk on places where, had they been awake, they never would have been able to endure the dizzy height; and I see some Christians, if indeed they be Christians, running awful risks which I think they would never venture upon unless they had fallen into the deep sleep of carnal security. Speak of a man slumbering at the mast-head, it is nothing to a professor of religion at ease while covetousness is his master, or worldly company his delight. If professors were awake, they would see their danger, and avoid sinful amusements and ungodly associations, as men fly from fierce tigers or deadly cobras. "Well, but we are doing much good and useful work," says one: "teaching in Sabbath schools, distributing religious tracts, or labouring in some other form of service; we are spending our time in commendable engagements." I am glad to hear it; but people can do a great deal in their sleep. We have heard many strange instances of how habit at last has enabled persons to pursue their callings, to answer signals, and keep up all the appearance of industry, and yet they have been at the time asleep. Oh, it is a very shocking thing that so many of our churches in England are in a deep sleep! Dissenting churches I know best about, and there are many where the minister preaches in his sleep, where the people sing in their sleep, where prayer is offered in sleep, and even the communion is celebrated amid a profound spiritual slumber. Have you never been at a prayer-meeting where half, if not all, both of those who prayed vocally and those who listened, were in a lethargy as rigid as death? Talk of sleeping women who have been in a swoon by the month together, the wonder may be a lying one in the natural world, but in the spiritual world it is as common as daisies in the meadows. Adam slept soundly when the taking away of his rib did not wake him, but what shall we say of those who startle not though they are losing all the strength and glory of their souls? Alas! for some congregations, it is long since they had a revival, they have lost the very idea of vigorous piety and vital energy. All the week round they are all asleep, and if a real, earnest, living, stirring sermon were preached among them, it would be almost as if the King of Prussia's Krupp guns had dropped a live shell into their midst. I wish a spiritual live shell could fall into some congregations, and burst among them, killing their conventionality, and wounding their self satisfaction with a deadly wound. Men may attend to outward worship with unimpeachable decorum and correctness and yet there may be no wakefulness in it, and consequently no acceptableness with God Most High.

Come, ourselves, and we must do so because we are in an enemy's country; it will not do to sleep here. This side of heaven we are in every place and at all hours surrounded by foes. What did the Master say? "What I say unto you I say unto all, Watch!" Be like sentries at your post, for otherwise the enemy will soon betray you. Will you not grieve the Holy Spirit if you are lethargic? Will you not dishounor your Master if you fall asleep? Remember also, that the devil seeks your destruction, and can never do you so much mischief awake as he can if he finds you sleeping. Let the growling of the old lion arouse you. If nothing else will bestir you, remember the fiery darts of the wicked one. Saul would not have lain so quiet if he had known that Abishai was holding the spear over him, and longing to pin him to the earth: yet this is the condition of professors who are given to slumber. Samson would have scarcely slept on Delilah's lap if he had foreseen that his hair would be cut, and his eyes put out by the Philistines. Up, then, ye drowsy professors, for the Philistines are upon you!

Moreover, brethren, slumber impoverishes us. The sluggard, and the thistle and thorn, always go together, and rags and poverty follow close behind. You may miss by your sleep great spiritual profit., You cannot expect sleepy Christians to grow in grace. They will miss many instructive things in God's word, many precious promises meant only for the wakeful. They will lose high enjoyments and spiritual banquetings, for the king's entertainments are not for those who fold their arms, and toss upon the bed of indolence. Wealth lies in the field of the wakeful, but the lover of ease shall have want come upon him as an armed man. I blow the trumpet in Zion, and sound an alarm in God's holy mountain, for it is high time to awake out of sleep.

Awaken too, my brother, for you are losing opportunities for usefulness. While you sleep men are dying. See how the cemeteries are becoming crowded, how the area of them has to be enlarged. Day by day you see wending through the streets the funeral procession: men gone beyond the reach of your instructions and your warnings are carried to their long homes. Awake then, awake, for death is busy everywhere. Meanwhile, those who do not die before you may be removed beyond the sphere of your usefulness; they go where at least you cannot reach them, where perhaps no one ever will, and their blood may lie upon your head, and that for ever. Awake, for perhaps while you are asleep another heart that is now accessible to the gospel may become finally hardened. Conscience will soon become seared, and then there is nothing for zeal and earnestness to work upon. It will be too late for you to put the seal upon the wax when once it is cool. Quick, sir; while the wax is soft put the seal down! How many opportunities for good we all miss! But those who are asleep lose all their opportunities, and they will be surely required of them when the Master comes.

Awake! I pray you, because you will insensibly lose the power, the joy of your spiritual life. Communion with God will become more and more scarce with you as you become more sleepy. Awake, lest you backslide, lest you all become apostate, and prove yourself not to be a child of God. Awake, for your power with others will certainly depart from you as your wakefulness departs. A sleepy preacher never wins the souls of men. A dull, formal servant of God is of little or no use in the church of God. I think I said years ago, "Give me half a dozen thorough red hot Christians, and I will do more, by God's grace, with them, than with a half a dozen hundred of ordinary professors." I am sure it is so. Crowds of professors are past all cure. I would as soon hunt with dead dogs, as try to work with them. They cannot be trained into heroes: they are dolts both by nature and by practice; much slothfulness has drained out their souls' life. The most you can hope for them is that they will remain decently Christianized, so as not altogether to disgrace us. But, O for thoroughly wideawake men, men who feel the life of God in their souls, and are, therefore, more than ordinarily earnest. Band together half a dozen such, and the Holy Spirit being with them, they will make all London feel their presence before long. O may God awaken all of us, for our spiritual life absolutely requires it.

III. Thirdly, I am going to mention CERTAIN WAYS OF KEEPING YOURSELVES AWAKE. "How can I be kept awake?" says one. Answer, first, make it a matter of prayer with the Lord to awaken you. No one can give you spiritual power and watchfulness but the Spirit of God. "All my fresh springs are in thee." Where life first comes from, there more life must be obtained. Christ has come that we may have life, and that we may have it more abundantly. He who first called us from the dead, must also arouse us from among the slumbering. He who brought us from the grave of our depravity must bring us from the couch of our indolence. Pray about the matter; make it a point with God: ask him to arouse you. On your knees is the posture in which to conquer sloth.

Next, means are to be used. We are not to leave the matter with God, and think there is nothing to be done by ourselves. Act towards yourselves about spiritual wakefulness as you would with natural wakefulness. Set your inventive faculties to work, and devise means for chasing away the sleep dragon. What would you do if you required to be awakened early? Perhaps you would set an alarum; a good thing, no doubt. Take care you set a spiritual alarum. Every Christian ought to keep one, and it should be so well set as to keep exact time, and so powerful as to arouse the most slumbering. A tender conscience, quick as the apple of the eye, is a precious preservative against sinful sleep; but it must never be tampered with, or its usefulness will soon end. When once the hour has come, down runs the alarum, the man starts up all at once, and says, "It is time to rise;" so should my conscience be so well regulated, that when a temptation is near, or a sinner is near me whom I ought about warn, my soul should at once take the alarm and say, "Here is work to do--a sin to be conquered, or a soul to be instructed: now, therefore, perform the doing of it with all thy might! I hear the alarum, and I must bestir myself!" May we always maintain and retain such a special wakefulness that we may be at our post of duty or in our place of conflict with a punctuality which none can gainsay. O for the alarum of a tender conscience!

Many of our friends who have to be up early in the morning ask the policeman to call them at the appointed hour. I may not compare the Christian minister with a policeman in some respects; but yet he is one of God's officers, and it is part of his business to stir up drowsy professors. It is well to attend an earnest gospel ministry, where the minister's voice, under God's blessing, will be likely to wake you up. Faithful preachers are among God's best gifts. Cherish them, and be obedient to their admonitions. I have known persons become offended when a minister is "too personal;" but wise men always prize a ministry in proportion as it is personal to themselves. He who never tells me of my faults, nor makes me feel uneasy, is not likely to be the means of good to my soul. What is the use of a dog that never barks? Why have a doctor, and grow angry with him if he points out the source of your disease? Did God send us, as his messengers, to pander to your taste or flatter your vanity? We seek not your approval if it be not founded on right. I have often felt pleased when I have heard people confess, after their conversion, "I came to the Tabernacle, and at the first I could not endure the preaching. I hated the preacher, and raged at his doctrine; but I could not help coming again." Just so. Conscience makes men respect the gospel, even when their depravity makes them loathe it. They are held fast by the cords which they fain would cast from them. May it often be so, O my unregenerate believers, that while my plain dealing excites your anger, it may nevertheless have a power over you; and may every man and woman here, whether saved or unsaved, feel that the preaching is the truth of God to his or her soul; and, whether liked or not liked, may it become the permanent means of arousing from sleep, and ultimately bringing to Christ every one of you to whom these words shall come. Be sure and attend an arousing ministry, and pray God to make the ministry which you now listen to more and more an arousing ministry to your own soul. Pray for the preacher, for he is in the same danger as yourselves, for he is too compassed with infirmity. The minister soon goes to sleep unless God wakens him; and what is more sad than to see the professed messenger of God become a traitor both to his Master and to men's souls by a lack of zealous affection? It is ill for the sheep if the shepherd himself be asleep. Woe to the camp where the sentry is given to slumber! May God deliver our country from being overrun with preachers whose souls are insensible concerning their grand work, and who love the bread of their office better than the glory of God or the good of their hearers.

I have known some persons adopt a plan for awaking in the morning which I can recommend spiritually at any rate. They have drawn up the blinds in the direction of the morning sun, that the sun might shine on their face and wake them. I know of no better way of waking for your soul, than letting the light, and the life, and the love of God shine full into your face. When the Sun of Righteousness arises he brings healing beneath his wings, and he brings awakening too. A man cannot think much of Christ, and love Christ much, and walk much in Christ's fellowship, and yet be asleep. The two who went to Emmaus in Immanuel's company, were their hearts cold? Nay, do not think so. "Did not our heart burn within us?" Yes, and your hearts will burn too, and your whole spiritual system will flame and glow if you walk in the company of Jesus. I can recommend constant fellowship with God as one of the best remedies for spiritual sloth, the surest provocative of holy zeal.

Many time people are awakened in the morning by the noise of the street in which they live. "I cannot sleep after such an hour," says one, "for I hear the tramp of those who are going into the city, and the grind of the street traffic." At a certain time you hear the hammer of the blacksmith, the scream of an engine, or the heaving of machinery, and after that sleep is gone. The activities of the world ought about awaken Christians. Are worldlings active? How active ought we to be! Do they labour and spend their sweat for earthly wages? How much more ought I to put forth my entire strength to serve so good a Master, whose reward of grace is everlasting bliss? The world is all astir to-day: let the church be all awake too.

We ought to be stimulated to supreme efforts by the activity of our fellow Christians. I find it does me much service about read the biographies of eminent servants of Christ, such as martyrs, missionaries, and reformers. I rise from reading their memorials feeling ashamed to be of so dwarfish a stature compared with these spiritual giants. What a humbling effect such a reflection ought to have on the do-nothings who swarm in the churches! but alas! these are not soon moved to judge themselves. With this one word we leave them: think of what some are doing, and be ashamed that you are doing so little in proportion to what they accomplish.

There are many ways of waking, but here is one, with which I will close my observations on this point. Hear the trumpet of the second coming. "Behold the bridegroom cometh; go ye out to meet him," was the cry that awakened the virgins when they all slumbered and slept: may it have the like arousing power at this moment. We know not when Christ will come, nor is it for us to utter prophecies about it: the times and seasons are hidden from us. "Of that day and that hour knoweth no man." Whether it will be before the Millennium or after the Millennium, let those judge who can. I have no judgement upon it. I think, as you carefully read the Scriptures, you will feel more and more convinced that only this is clearly and certainly revealed--that the Lord will personally come in such an hour as we look not for him. Let that awaken us; let it keep us always watchful, with loins girt and lamps trimmed, proving our faithful love to our blessed Master.

These are, it is clear, very many ways by which Christians may be awakened. God grant that they may be effective to each and all. I think it was Sydney Smith who was once preaching a sermon about sleeping in church, and when he had done, he said, "Now, what good have I done? All those who sleep have been asleep through my sermon, and only those who are wakeful have heard me, and they did not need my rebukes and advice." I often feel that this is very much the preacher's case. Earnest people, when the congregation is exhorted to earnestness, take it home to themselves; but those persons who do nothing, and are most indolent, are the very ones who say, "I don not see the need of it; I do not want to be disturbed." Of course not! It is not only the mark of the sluggard to sleep, but it is another characteristic of him that he is wrath with those who would compel him to rise. "A little more sleep," says he, "a little more slumber;" he turns his heavy head upon the pillow once again, and wishes no blessings upon those who knock at his door so heavily. You sleepy professors are likely to do the same, but I will not refrain from knocking till you refrain from dozing. I pray God that there may be very few in this church of the incorrigible order, whose life is one long dream, a dream of self-aggrandizement, meanness, and littleness. May you and I, and all of us, be thoroughly earnest in the service of our Master, and if we cannot arouse others by our precept, at least let us not fail to try the force of our example.

IV. I must close with a word upon that fourth point, which is this--THE GREAT AND URGENT NEED THAT THE UNCONVERTED SINNER SHOULD AWAKE. Hitherto I have spoken to the converted man: now let me address myself to the ungodly, and may the voice which shall call the dead to judgement now awaken him. You, you unconverted man, are asleep; a deep and horrible sleep holds you fast. If it were not so, you would perceive your danger, and you would be alarmed. You have broken God's law; the fact is certain and solemn, though you treat it lightly. Punishment must follow every breach of that law, for God will not be mocked nor suffer his government to be treated with contempt. For every transgression there is an appointed recompense of reward. The retribution which is your lawful due will not long be withheld: it is on its road towards you. The feet of justice are shod with wool: you hear not its coming, but it is as sure as it is silent. Its steps are swift, and its stroke overwhelming. Awaken, O man, and listen to this text: "God is angry with the wicked every day. If he turn not, he will whet his sword; he hath bent his bow, and made it ready." No peril of plague, battle, shipwreck, or poison, can equal the hazard of an unpardoned soul. Beware, yet that forget God, for his terrors are past conception, and his wrath burneth as an oven.

If you were awakened, O sin-stricken transgressor, you would also perceive that there is a remedy for your disease, a rescue from your present danger. "God was in Christ, reconciling the world unto himself, not imputing their trespasses unto them;" and "Whosoever believeth in Jesus Christ hath everlasting life." Forgiveness of sin is guaranteed to every one that rests in the work of Jesus, and all other necessary blessings are secured to him. If thou wert awake, thou wouldst not remain an unconverted sinner another hour, but thou wouldst turn unto God with full purpose of heart. If God would awaken thee, thou wouldst tremble at the jaws of hell which are open to receive thee; thou wouldst turn to Christ, and say, "Jesus, save me! Save me now!" You are asleep, sinner--you are asleep, or you would not take matters so coolly. I am afraid for you, and bowed down with amazement and dread. The mercy is that you may be awakened: you are not yet among the slain that go down into the pit. O that that almighty grace would awaken you at this present moment, ere your doom is sealed and your damnation executed! Here I offer my fervent prayers for you, believing that he to whom I pray is able to bring to holy sensibility the most stolid of mankind.

Strange ways God has of awakening his elect ones from their deadly slumbers. Awake them he will, and he will shake heaven and earth sooner than let any one of them perish in unfeeling security. He will strike them down as he did Paul, or send an earthquake to shake them, as he did to the gaoler at Philippi; in his own way and time he will make them come to themselves and then to Christ. Remember the story of Augustine. To the grief of his dear mother, Monica, he had been leading a wicked life; but God's time had come, and as Augustine walked in the garden he heard a little child say, "Take! Read! Take! Read!" This induced him to take the Bible and read it. He no sooner read, than a passage came before his eyes which awakened him, and he sought a Saviour, and found him. Perhaps it will be a death in your house that will wake you--sad means, but often most effectual. A mother's death-bed has been a soul-saving sermon to many a family. Some sleepers need a thunderclap to arouse them. Pray, you dear people of God that are awake, that the sinner may be awakened, for there is this awful danger that he may sleep himself into hell. Spiritual sleep deepens, the slumberer becomes more heavy still, the stupor more dense, till the conscience grows seared, and the soul is unimpressionable; the flesh is turned into stone, the heart is harder than steel. It may be that some of those who hear these words of warning may never wake to think about their souls till in hell they lift up their eyes. What an awful lifting up of the eyes will that be! O you who are now peaceful and secure, what a change awaits you! Hurled from vainglorious security to blank despair in a moment! You took it all so easily: you said, "Let me alone; do not worry me; there's time enough. The preacher ought not to frighten us with these bugbears; we all have a great deal else to do besides listening to horrible stories of hell and damnation;" and so you wrapped it up, and so you smoothed it over, but the end thereof who shall describe? Have you never heard of the Indian in his boat upon one of the great rivers of America? Somehow his moorings had broken, and his canoe was in the power of the current. He was asleep, while his canoe was being borne rapidly along by the stream. He was sound asleep, and yet had good need to have been awake, for there was a tremendous cataract not far ahead. Persons on shore saw the canoe--saw that there was a man in it asleep; but their vigilance was of no use to the sleeper: it needed that he himself should be aware of his peril. The canoe quickened its pace, for the waters of the river grew more rapid as they approached the cataract; persons on the shore began to cry our, and raise alarm on all sides and at last the Indian was aroused. He started up, and began to use his paddle, but his strength was altogether insufficient for the struggle with the gigantic force of the waters around him. He was seen to spring upright in the boat and disappear--himself and the boat--in the fall. He had perished, for he woke too late! Some persons on their dying beds just wake up in time to see their danger, but not to escape from it: they are carried right over the cataract of judgement and wrath. They are gone, for ever gone, where mercy is succeeded by justice, and hope forbidden to enter. Let much prayer go up from believing hearts that God would awaken sinners now, and begin with those who come to the place of worship, and remain at ease in Zion. Ask for the arm of God to be revealed while the heavenly message is delivered; for his is our message: "Awake thou that sleepest, and arise from the dead, and Christ shall give thee light." There is a man before me now asleep in his sins, whom God means to make a minister of Christ: he knows not the divine purpose, but there are lines of love in it for him. Arise oh slumberer, for Jesus calls thee! Awake, thou Saul of Tarsus, thou art a chosen vessel unto the Lord! Turn thou from thy sin: seek thou thy Saviour. There is one here who has been a great sinner but the Lord intends to wash him in the cleansing fount, and clothe him in the righteousness of Christ. Come, thou guilty one, awake! for mercy waits for thee. There is a poor weeping woman here who has gone far in sin; but Jesus says, "Neither do I condemn thee: go, and sin no more." Sister awake! Come and receive the mercy which Jesus Christ is ready to bestow upon thee! God give thee waking grace, and saving grace.

May you and I, beloved brethren in Christ, awake to the most earnest and intense form of life in Christ and life for Christ. At once let us bestir ourselves: we may think it early, but it will be none too early; may we awake now, for Jesus' sake. Amen.

PORTIONS OF SCRIPTURE READ BEFORE SERMON--Psalm 108; 1 Thessalonians 5:1-11.

Prosperity Under Persecution

A Sermon (No. 997)
Delivered by
C. H. SPURGEON,
At the Metropolitan Tabernacle, Newington

"Come on let us deal wisely with them; lest they multiply, and it come to pass, that, when there falleth out any war, they join also unto our enemies, and fight against us, and so get them up out of the land. Therefore they did set over them taskmasters to afflict them with their burdens. And they built for Pharaoh treasure cities, Pithom and Raamses. But the more they afflicted them, the more they multiplied and grew." - Exodus 1:10-12.

THE children of this world are wise in their generation. Their policy may be short-sighted and their stratagems crooked, nevertheless the world admires the wisdom of their counsels, and makes light of the craftiness of their projects. In their opposition to the Christian church, the men of the world might certainly have been as well able to outwit her by the variety of their manoeuvres as to overwhelm her by the force of their numbers, were it not that there is an unseen One in her midst, who is more than a match for the guile of their hearts and the might of their hosts. Looking back at the early struggles of the Hebrew race to gain a footing among the nations, it is very clear that had the contest been merely between Pharaoh and Israel, the Egyptian king could exercise power and policy enough to defeat the sons of Jacob and reduce them to serfdom; but when a new name is brought in, and the contest appears to be truly between Pharaoh and Jehovah the God of Israel, it is quite another matter, and a far different issue may be counted upon. There is one behind the curtain that takes Israel's part. He sees through all Pharaoh's plots. Or ever his thoughts have ripened into plans they are forestalled; fast as they are set up they are upset; for every intrigue there is a reprisal. Thus he taketh the wise in their own craftiness. The whole history of the long feud between the seed of the woman and the seed of the serpent illustrates the subtlety of the serpent's seed, and the simplicity of the woman's seed; but still more does it bring to light the infinite wisdom of him who rules the seed of the woman; and who will in the end bruise the serpent's head, and give unto his people and the cause they have espoused a complete triumph. Whatever has been done by the enemies in rage or in recklessness, God has always met it calmly and quietly. He has shown himself ready for every emergency. And he has not only baffled and utterly defeated all the inventions of wicked men, but he has turned their strange devices to good account, for the development of his own sovereign purposes. Be has made his enemies work for him, aiding the enterprise they eschewed: he has turned their curse into a blessing: he has made evil productive of good: he has extracted sweetness out of their bitter spleen, and distilled healthful medicine out of their deadly animosity. He hath his way in the whirlwind: the clouds are the dust of his feet. He does not only meet evil with good, but he takes the evil, and subjects it to his own eternal purpose, and from it brings forth a course of events that results in his own glory, the benefit of his children, and the fulfillment of their destiny.

Of this general principle we shall now proceed to consider three special illustrations. First, the circumstances of the children of Israel; secondly, the history of the church of Christ; thirdly, the experience of individual Christians.

I. IN THE CASE OF ISRAEL, it did seem to be a deep-laid plot, very politic and crafty indeed, that as the kings of Egypt, themselves of an alien race, had subdued the Egyptians, they should prevent the other alien race, the Israelites, from conquering them. Instead of murdering them wholesale, it did seem a wise though a cruel thing to make them slaves; to divide them up and down the country; to subject them to toil till their spirits were broken; to appoint them to the most menial work in the land, that they might be crushed down and their spirits become so base that they would not dare to rebel. Thus we may suppose it was hoped that their physical strength would be so relaxed, and their circumstances so reduced, that the clan would soon be insignificant if not utterly extinct. But God met and overruled this policy in various ways. "The more they afflicted them, the more they multiplied." The census proved the error of their calculation. The cause looked likely, but it was not productive of the consequence expected. Had it been another people, the tactics might have been successful; but they were God's people, endeared to him by their ancestry, ennobled in his sight by their covenant destiny, and encompassed with his favor as with a shield. No conspiracy formed against them could thrive. And so it came to pass, that like certain herbs which spring up when trodden down, or like certain trees that grow taller if loaded with weights, Israel rose superior to all her disadvantages. "The more they afflicted them, the more they multiplied and grew."

The glory of God shines forth conspicuously in the use to which he turned the persecutions they endured. The severe treatment they had to bear from the enemy became to them a salutary discipline. This cometh of the Lord of Hosts, who is wonderful in counsel and excellent in working. From that time the children of Israel began to feel a disgust with Egypt. They had settled down very quietly in Goshen, and thought that it was their rest. They had imbibed much of the manners and customs of the Egyptians. We have it on record that they worshipped the gods of Egypt. They seemed greatly to have appreciated what they afterwards called the luxuries of the land--the leeks, the garlics, the onions, the melons, and the cucumbers. They appear to have been almost naturalised to that country. They were little better than Egyptians. Perhaps persons travelling, except by certain tones of language and contour of countenance, would scarcely have known but what they were descendants of Ham. But now their masters treat them cruelly, and they loathe the Egyptians. They are scattered up and down throughout the land, and Goshen is no longer dear to them. The, are treated like strangers, and they feel they are strangers. Now that they hear from morning till night the taskmaster's oath, and the crack of the cruel whip, and are subjected to incessant toil and bondage, they think far less of Egypt than they used to do. This is what the Lord designed. He never intended that his people Israel should be absorbed into any other family. He never meant them to be other than sojourners on that soil. He had some better thing for them than that they should dwell in that land, and be as the heathen were. God was thus answering one purpose. And he did more than this. Now they began to remember, as their bondage waxed more and more severe, the God of their fathers whom they had forgotten. I have reminded you that they had fallen into the worship of the gods of Egypt; but now they turn with abhorrence from the gods of their oppressors, and they bethink themselves of the covenant which Jehovah had made with Abraham, and with Isaac and Jacob, and they betook themselves to their knees. In secret, they utter their groanings before the Most High, and when their taskmasters make them smart, they lift their eyes, suffused with bitter tears, and silently appeal to heaven, to the God of their fathers, that he would have mercy upon them. They had forgotten to pray until then. The mass of them had been unused to call upon the name of the Lord; but now the scourge drives them to seek help from above. Their terrors, their pains, their griefs, and their vexations compel them to lift up that cry to heaven which came into the ears of Jehovah, and moved his hand to help them.

More than that, remember that it was necessary for this people to be altogether rescued from that land which for many a year had taxed their labor and bounded their enterprise, because it was not the land which had been promised them as an inheritance. It was God's intention and covenant purpose to give them the Land of Canaan, a land that flowed with milk and honey. But it is not very easy to induce a nation, numbering some millions, to leave a country in which they have been born and nourished and found a home. Only some very fearful evil can induce them to expatriate themselves. Had Moses gone to the children of Israel before the time of their bondage, and said, "Up I get you hence unto the land which the Lord swears that he will give it to you," he would have seemed to them as one that mocked: they would have laughed him to scorn. In order to cut loose the bonds that bound them to Egypt, the sharp knife of affliction must be used; and Pharaoh, though he knew it not, was God's instrument in weaning them from the Egyptian world, and helping them as his church to take up their separate place in the wilderness, and receive the portion which God had appointed for them.

Once more--and here you may see the wisdom of God--the very means which Pharaoh devised for the effectual crushing of the people--the destruction of the male children--became the direct, nay, the divine provision for educating a deliverer for them. Moses had never been, in all probability, trained in the courts of Pharaoh if he had not been put in the basket of bulrushes on the brink of the Nile; and his mother would certainly never have put him there if there had not been a pitiless edict that the male children should be put to death. Moved by maternal instinct to save her child, and moved by faith in God not to obey the king's command, she places her child in the ark. Pharaoh's daughter finds the child, compassionates its cry, extricates it from peril, loves it fondly, adopts it capriciously, and educates it in the very court of Pharaoh. That child grows up to be the man who should vex the fields of Zoan--the man of God, who with a high hand and an outstretched arm, would lead forth the slaves of Egypt to become a great nation, which God should bless. So you see the Lord in all points meets Pharaoh and foils him. This Pharaoh was the great representative in those days of the power of evil, and he stands still to the Christian church as the type of the seed of the serpent. But the Lord withstands him, despoils him of his purpose, and turns all he does to the very highest and best end. Such the narrative, full of instruction, and charged with portent, that serves as a type of the Lord's doing when he makes bare his arm for the salvation of his own heritage.

II. Let us now carry the same thought a stage farther, and take a brief survey of THE HISTORY OF THE CHILDREN OF GOD. The like means will appear in manifold operation. Men meditate mischief, but it miserably miscarries. God grants protection to the persecuted, and provides an escape from the most perilous exposure. Full often the darkest conspiracy is brought to the direst confusion. No sooner does Christ gather a church in any place, be it a renowned empire or a paltry village, than opposition is stirred up. "If ye were of the world, the world would love his own: but because ye are not of the world, but I have chosen you out of the world, therefore the world hateth you." "I will put enmity between thee and the woman, and between thy seed and her seed," is the first check for the serpent's wiles, the first ray of hope for his helpless victims; and the prediction will continue to be fulfilled till at last, according to the word of the Lord, the tares are bound in bundles to burn them, and the wheat is gathered into his garner.

Whenever there has been a great persecution raised against the Christian church, God has overruled it, as he did in the case of Pharaoh's oppression of the Israelites, by making the aggrieved community more largely to increase. The early persecutions in Judea promoted the spread of the gospel; hence, when after the death of Stephen the disciples were all scattered abroad throughout the regions of Judea and Samaria, except the apostles, the result is thus given: "Therefore they that were scattered abroad went everywhere preaching the word." So, too, when Herod stretched forth his hands to vex certain of the church, and killed James, the brother of John, with the sword; what came of it? Why Luke tells us in almost the same words that Moses had used: "The word of God grew and multiplied." Those terrible and bloody persecutions under the Roman Emperor by no means stayed the progress of the gospel; but strangely enough seemed to press forward for the crown of martyrdom. The church probably never increased at a greater ratio than as when her foes were most fierce to assail and most resolute to destroy her. It was so in after times. The Reformation in this country and throughout Europe never went on so prosperously as when it was most vigorously opposed. You shall find in any individual church that wherever evil men have conspired together, and a storm of opposition has burst forth against the saints, the heart of the Lord has been moved with compassion, and the hand of the Lord has been raised to succor, till we have come to look upon opposition as an omen of good, and persecution for righteousness' sake as a tearful seed-time, quickly to be followed by a harvest of joy. We have looked on our adversaries, though they seemed like stormy petrels, as being the index of a favorable wind to the good barque of Christ's church. Persecution seems to be the wave that, when it leaps up around her, speeds her course. Let the mountains be removed, and cast into the midst of the sea; but after long experience of Jehovah's faithfulness towards his people, we are confident that his church shall not be moved: in quietude shall she possess her soul. Persecution has evidently aided the increase of the church by the scattering abroad of earnest teachers. We are very apt to get hived--too many of us together--and our very love of one another renders it difficult to part us and scatter us about. Persecution therefore is permitted to scatter the hive of the church into various swarms, and each of these swarms begins to make honey. We are all like the salt if we be true Christians, and the proper place for the salt is not massed in a box, but scattered by handfuls over the flesh which it is to preserve. We are of good service when we are kept together in great bands: happy we certainly are in the presence of each other; but we are to separate and scatter, and we shall conquer as we are scattered abroad. You remember the days of our Puritan forefathers, when the dominant church of the day determined to crush out pure evangelism. To what extent did it succeed? Did it destroy their faith and their confidence? Nay, my brethren; by driving them out of an apostate church, and compelling them to take up their stand as separated believers without the camp, bearing Christ's reproach and cross, an everlasting testimony for pure truth was enshrined. Was the crisis prolonged? Were deeds of violence legalised? By the increasing rigour of such persecution, our forefathers were constrained to leave their native shores, and they had to pass in the May Flower, and afterwards in some succeeding vessels, across the blue Atlantic, sadly but surely to found another center for the proclamation of the gospel, and upon the wide continent of a new world they became the progenitors of another nation holding fast the fundamentals of the faith, and rejoicing in the liberty wherewith Christ has made us free. There might have been no church in the United States if it had not been that our sires were driven to the wilds amongst the Red Indians, there to establish themselves, and set up a banner for the truth as it is in Jesus. It will always be so. I could almost wish that in this island, though I dread calamity, I could almost wish, for the Master's honor, that some irresistible impulse should force his disciples to go abroad to the regions beyond our present sphere of life and labor. I rejoice, though I love not to miss my friends, when I find them led or driven, it may be, to emigration, whether it be to Australia, Canada or anywhere else, because I trust that if they are living seed they will be as a handful of corn sown in the land, the fruit whereof shall shake like Lebanon. Christian men are sometimes called to leave positions of great comfort and to occupy stations of great hardship. They may account it a reverse of fortune, while God designs it as an appointment to especial service. If they bear Christ's gospel with them to a people sitting in darkness, that will be great gain in the long run to the church. Your being sent to a village, though you like it not, may be a lasting blessing to the hamlet. Your residing among strangers, when you would far rather find a more congenial home among your own kindred, may be for the good of that neighborhood. Who knows? Where should lamps be set up but in dark places? Where should we have a guard for Christ's army, but where the enemy is most likely to make the assault? Be patient, then, my brethren, amidst the persecutions or trials you may be called upon to bear; and be thankful that they are so often overruled for the growth of the church, the spread of the gospel, and the honor of Christ.

Moreover, beloved, persecution in the church--even when it does not take the form of burning or imprisonment, but of slander, of cruel mockings, jesting, jeering, and venomous spite--in whatever form it is sent, persecution helps to keep up the separation between the church and the world. I fear most the rich when they bring gifts. I loathe the world most when it fawns and flatters. When I heard of a lady who had put on Christ by baptism, that the cold shoulder was given her in all the circles in which she moved; did I, think you, feel more disposed to condole or to congratulate? It was said that now she had but few invitations to such places and such society as she had previously frequented; and I rejoiced, and thanked God for it. I was glad of it, for I felt she was farther removed from temptation. When I heard of a young man that, after he joined the church, those in his workshop met him at once with loud laughter and reproached him with bitter scorn. I was thankful, because now he could not take up the same position with themselves. He was a marked man: they who knew him discovered that there was such a thing as Christianity, and such a one as an earnest defender of it. It is no evil to the church, depend upon it, to have a great gulf fixed between her and the world. The worst thing that ever could happen for us is, when affinities are made between the sons of God and the children of Belial. This brought on the Deluge; and if it could ever be carried out thoroughly again, it would bring on judgments terrible to think of. It is ill for the worldly, since "they that are far from God shall perish;" but it is a thousand times worse for the professing when they play foul with their profession, for so it is written, "Thou hast destroyed all them that go a whoring from thee." Summary vengeance is their lot. "Come out from among them, and be ye separate, and touch not the unclean thing; and I will receive you, and will be a Father unto you, and ye shall be my sons and daughters." This is a text that needs to be thundered in trumpet tone. What says the great King unto the spouse? "Forget also thine own people, and thy father's house; so shall the King greatly desire thy beauty: for he is thy Lord; and worship thou him." "Be not conformed to this world: but be ye transformed by the renewing of your mind." Too much laxness, giving way to the world a friendship foil of fascination brings on leanness of spirit, and causes us to be scarcely known as Christians, weakens our testimony, and in every way promotes Satan's ends. But when persecution breaks forth, barriers are set up, and distinctive colors are worn, so the two camps are kept in open hostility, and when brought to battle with each other, the church is kept pure with armor bright; victory waits her march, and her champions win their laurels.

Again, persecution in the Christian church acts like a winnowing fan to the heaps gathered on the threshing-floor. In these soft and silken days any man may be a Christian professor. Oftentimes it pays well to make a profession of godliness. Men think the better of you: it brings customers to the shop. No one knows how many conveniences may attach to the profession of religion: albeit, if it be pretense without pretext, everlasting destruction awaits such violation of truth, for God will surely avenge hypocrisy. But in days of persecution, to profess Christ is very inconvenient. Then to be baptised in water may involve a baptism of blood. Then for the soul to burn with zeal for Christ would probably be followed with the body being burnt at the stake. Then a word for Jesus would bring a word of conviction from the judge's mouth, and, close at the heels of that word, death. Then they who loved not Christ betook themselves to the other side; the cowards and the spies shrunk away. Demas went, and Judas went, and all of that brood, to their own company, and then only the true and the brave, the regenerate, the elect of God were left. They stood fast and firm--all the stronger for losing such ill company. Then in those days the church was like a heap of golden wheat, all winnowed and clean grain, fit for a burnt offering to the Most High, to be offered up as a meat offering upon his altar. Her martyrs were amongst her noblest sons, the very glory of the church and of the Lord Jesus Christ. So you see persecution is overruled for this great good. It ought never to be, while there are sinners in this world--it ought never to be that the Christian escapes opposition. I take it that if a man makes an advance in life, comes to a position of fame, he ought to win it, ought to fight for it. Men ought not to be crowned until first of all they have striven for the mastery; and it should be so in the church of God that we must fight if we would reign. It should not be that we should think it an easy thing and a light matter to be a follower of him whose life was sorrow, and whose death was the death of the cross. If we are to be conformed to him, it cannot be by ease and sloth. Not the downy couch, but the crown of thorns; not the triumph, but the shame, must be the portion of the imitators of the Crucified.

Persecution has a further beneficial use in the church of God, and it is this. It may be that the members of the church want it. It is a sorrowful thing that slander should be so often used against God's people; it is a grievous thing that their little faults should be severely criticised and magnified; but, on the whole, it is good and profitable. It is a great blessing to be made to walk carefully. The Roman who professed that he would like to have a window in his bosom, that everybody might see his heart, would have wished, I should think, before long for a shutter to that window; yet it is no slight stimulus to a man's own circumspection for him to know that he is observed by unfriendly eyes. Our life ought to be such as will bear criticism. As Christian men we serve a jealous God, and our works will have to stand the test of fire at the last great day. The wood, and the hay, and the stubble that we have builded will be consumed, and only the gold, the silver, and the precious stones will remain. Are we, therefore, to be afraid of the ordinary ordeal of human censure and malignity? If we run with the footmen and they weary us, what shall we do when we contend with horses? And if in this land of comparative peace we are weary, what shall we do in the swelling of Jordan? This is the opposition appointed for us. It is through much tribulation we are to inherit the kingdom; and if we be sincere, and honest and true, we shall not flinch at this: we shall feel that God will overrule it for our sanctification, by making us take heed unto our ways, because the wicked watch our paths.

And this persecution, dear brethren, has a further usefulness. Often does it happen that the enmity of the world drives the Christian nearer to his God. How many prayers have been offered up as the result of persecution that would never have been offered else, heaven alone can tell! How many a groan, and sigh, and tear, acceptable to God, have been forced from true hearts by their sufferings, God alone knows! Ah! in the soft days, the summer days of peace and prosperity, we are apt to gad abroad after vain delights; but when the winter comes, with its keen and cutting blast, we haste to our own abode, we cleave to our own hearth, we love to dwell with our own kindred. Even so right frequently, with hearts all chill and cheerless, we have sought the house of our Father and our God, drawn near to his altar, and found a refreshment we fain could wish that we might never leave. Why, oh! why, are we so fickle? If we could find succor and solace apart from the Rock, away from the Sun, absent from our Lord, our wayward hearts would do so; but when the waters of affliction have covered all the earth, then we fly back to our Noah, our ark, and find rest for the sole of our foot. The friendship of this world is enmity to God. It rivals God's friendship, it deceives and deludes many hearts; but when the world frowns, it is a blessed frown that makes me seek my Savior's smile. Anything that drives me to my knees is good. Anything that makes me trust in the promise, and wait only upon God because my expectation is from him, is healthful to my soul, infuses courage, and inspires confidence, and invests her with fresh strength. O brethren, the very glory of the church is to live nearer to God. The more she thinks of her great and glorious Head, and the more she leans upon the invisible arm of the Eternal, the more invincible she is persecution in driving her to her stronghold is overruled to her help.

And yet, further, the dark days of fiendish persecution have witnessed bright deeds of Christian heroism never to be forgotten. How often have the richest and the ripest fruits of the Spirit been put forth by the Lord's people when they have been most grieved and smitten! Then the saints have been like clusters thrown into the winepress; but who shall bring forth the red wine? Whose but the feet of God's enemies shall tread the grapes? And as with exultation they bruise and trample down, they shall crush nothing in the dust but husks: the living wine shall flow, and God shall receive the whole of it. They work--these foes work--and think that with axes they can break down our carved work, and cast fire into the sanctuary of God, but all the while they burn not the true sanctuary: they burn but the base wooden erection with which man has defaced the living temple. Let them burn on: they do no hurt, but good ensues. If you read "Foxe's Book of Martyrs," or any of the martyrologies of earlier ages, you will find there patience, self-denial, consecration, confidence in God, and all the finer graces of temper in full bloom, perfuming the air with their fragrance. One is astonished at what our poor, weak humanity has been able to endure for the truth, when strengthened by the Spirit of God. Verily, humble and weak, and timid women have shown true mettle, waxing valiant, and cheering on men of muscle and sinew, whose hearts had grown faint. We could mention the names of many saints, if this were the time, who have endured torment as severe as inquisitors could devise, or relentless executioners could inflict, and yet they have not denied their Lord. This is the patience of the saints, I think, when the martyrs perished in the Roman Amphitheatre, and the cruel crowd looked down to watch their agonies as their bones were crushed between the jaws of wild beasts; angels gathered in tiers, invisible multitudes of them gathered, and looked on with eyes of admiration at the spectacle of mortal men ravished with the love of God, waving the banner of immortal truth, while from frightful wounds and horrid gashes their life-blood streamed. Oh! what God can do by us when he works in us! Perhaps heaven itself, save when it gazed upon the cross, never saw a nobler spectacle than when men and women, who bore the cross of Christ in their hearts, gave themselves up wholly as living sacrifices unto him. The church looks fairer and shines brighter when she is in the furnace. Not the smell of fire doth pass upon her. Her Lord is with her, and if the fire be heated seven times hotter, his glory is seven times the brighter. Thus, again, the principle of the text is brought out: "the more they afflicted them, the more they multiplied." Their enemies try to deal wisely with them to put them down, but their wisdom is folly. God has blessed the church by her persecution.

And do you not think that persecution and opposition--such little oppositions as we meet with now; little indeed, compared with those of olden times--are permitted for our good, as in Israel's case, to make us feel that this is not our rest, and cause us to long for the better land? Perhaps, dear Christian, if you lived in a Christian household, where all the wonted order helped your piety, if you were put into the conservatory of a gracious providence, you might be content to dwell below always. We soon take root in this soil, for we are earthy by nature, and we cling to earth--like to its like. But when there comes the jeer, the unkind remark, the cruel innuendo, the bitter sarcasm, then we feel, "This is not my rest: I must seek better company than this, a better land, and a better portion than I shall find this side of Jordan." And then we long for the home-bringing, when the King, the Husband, shall fetch home his spouse, and the marriage shall be consummated in the skies. Oh! how sometimes, when the world has been very very cold you have longed for the warm bosom of your Savior! You would have nestled in the world's bosom if you could, but when she would not receive you but thrust you forth, then you came to your true self, and exercised your right senses, and you said, "I will return unto my husband. It was better with me then than now." O that our hearts were always set on heaven! There is our treasure: there let our hearts be also. There is our Lord and King: to him should our hearts fly. There are the best ones of our families, our relations, who are everlastingly our associates, brethren and sisters whose brotherhood and sisterhood no death can bring to an end--

"There my best friends my kindred dwell,
There God my Savior reigns."

We ought to long for that land: and I say the whip of persecution is helpful, because it makes us learn that this is the house of bondage, and moves us to long after and seek for the land of liberty--the land of joy.

III. And now I close this address by just very briefly hinting that THIS GREAT GENERAL TRUTH APPLIES TO ALL BELIEVERS; but I will make a practical use of it. Dear brother, dear sister, are you passing through great trials? Very well then, to meet them I pray that God's grace may give you greater faith; and if your trials increase more and more, so may your strength increase. You will be acting after God's manner, guided by his wisdom, if you seek to get more faith out of more trial, for that trial does strengthen faith, through divine grace, experience teaches us, and as we make full proof of the faithfulness of God, our courage, once apt to waver, is confirmed. Do pray the Lord that when the trials multiply you may get faith wherewith to meet them; that out of the eater you may get meat; and out of the strong find strength.

So, too, if you know the truth of God to be at any time assailed, and your own mind is beset with doubt about any doctrine, always ask God so to open that particular truth to your understanding, and endear it to your heart, that by the assaults you are enabled to repel your faith may be the more confirmed. Oh! there is a light way of holding truth, and there is a tenacious way of grasping it. I have held doctrines, as it were, in my hand, like a boy's ball, that might be thrown away. But it is another thing when the King prints the mark of the doctrine right into your very soul, so that you could no more part with it than you could part with life itself. Trials often burn doctrines into us, and heresies and infidelities make the good confession dear in our sight as a prize which we could never part with. Thus opposition to the truth leads to the multiplication of evidences in its support, and the more we are assailed with the arguments of science, falsely so-called, the firmer we adhere to the oracles of God.

Or it may be, dear Christian worker, that of late you have met with a great many discouragements. You seem to have labored in vain, and spent your strength for nought. Ask then, in prayer, and act accordingly, that the more you are defeated the less you may be disposed to yield; but rather that you may be endowed with fresh energy for the service, and strive with increased assurance for the victory. When you feel "I am foiled in that point," say, "Nevertheless, I cannot be beaten: I belong to a seed that cannot be vanquished. If I did not belong to the house of Israel, I might have been destroyed and overcome; but none can stand against the Hebrew race, against true Israelites--they must win the day." Therefore, settle it in your mind that if you do not win souls one day, you will another; and if you cannot press into your enemies' territory in one part you will in another; and if he defeats you at any time, then multiply your efforts to do good. Always take revenge on Satan if he defeats you, by trying to do ten times more good than you did before. It is in some such way that a dear brother now preaching the gospel, whom God has blessed with a very considerable measure of success, may trace the opening of his career to a circumstance that occurred to myself. Sitting in my pulpit one evening, in a country village, where I had to preach, my text slipped from my memory, and with the text seemed to go all that I had thought to speak upon it. A rare thing to happen to me; but I sat utterly confounded. I could find nothing to say. With strong crying I lifted up my soul to God to pour out again within my soul of the living water that it might gush forth from me for others; and I accompanied my prayer with a vow that if Satan's enmity thus had brought me low, I would take so many fresh men whom I might meet with during the week, and train them for the ministry, so that with their hands and tongues I would avenge myself on the Philistines. The brother I have alluded to came to me the next morning. I accepted him at once as one whom God had sent, and I helped him, and others after him, to prepare for the service, and to go forth in the Savior's name to preach the gospel of the grace of God. Often when we fear we are defeated, we ought to say, "I will do all the more. Instead of dropping from this work, now will I make a general levy, and a sacred conscription upon all the powers of my soul, and I will gather up all the strength I ever had in reserve, and make from this moment a tremendous life-long effort to overcome the powers of darkness, and win for Christ fresh trophies of victory." After this fashion you will have an easier time of it, for if you do more good the more you are tempted, Satan will not so often tempt you. When he knows that all the more you are afflicted so much the more you multiply, very likely he will find it wiser to let you alone, or try you in some other method than that of direct and overt opposition. So whenever you have a trial, take it as a favor; whenever God holds in one hand the rod of affliction, he has a favor in the other hand; he never strikes a child of his but he has some tender blessing in store. If he visits you with unwonted affliction, you will have unusual delight; the Lord will open new windows for you, and show his beauty as he shows it not to others recording as your tribulations abound, so also shall your consolations abound in Christ Jesus. In the deeper waters you shall find him nearer, for he has said, "When thou passest through the waters, I will be with thee." He will be with you always, but he has promised to come to you specially and peculiarly, and, as it were, by appointment, when you are driven out into the wilderness, or harassed by the foe. He comforteth those that are cast down. Rejoice, therefore, in your afflictions, if so be you have faith to believe that they shall be blessed for your good.

What is all this to the unconverted? Ah, sirs! while the men of God flourish in adversity, the men of this world are ruined by their prosperity. Even the cup of pleasure and sensual enjoyment, of which ye delight to drink, has its bitter dregs which ye shall be compelled to swallow. Yet even now all your days are not passed in sunshine. You have your troubles; but you have no God to resort to. You will have many sorer plagues than you have ever yet been visited with; but if you continue in unbelief, you will still have no God to trust in. Perhaps you go to some friends in any emergency now, but no friend can help you in the dying hour. No brother can go with you through the swellings of Jordan. O friendless one, O Christless sinner! dost thou not want God to be thy helper, and Christ to be thy friend? If thou dost, then on the cross behold the Savior. Turn to him thine eye: penitently trust him: rely upon him, and he is ours, and then henceforth the Lord of Hosts shall be with you, and God of Jacob shall be your refuge, and your afflictions also shall work your good. May God bless each one of you, for Jesus' sake. Amen.

MR. SPURGEON hopes to be permitted to preach on July 2. He is most thankful to inform all friends that be is better in health, and trusts be may be able again to occupy the pulpit of the Tabernacle from Sabbath to Sabbath.

More and More

A Sermon (No. 998)
Delivered on Lord's-day Morning, July 2nd, 1871, by
C. H. SPURGEON,
At the Metropolitan Tabernacle, Newington

"But I will hope continually, and will yet praise thee more and more." - Psalm 71:14.

WHEN sin conquered the realm of manhood, it slew all the minstrels except those of the race of Hope. For humanity, amid all its sorrows and sins, hope sings on. To believers in Jesus there remains a royal race of bards, for we have a hope of glory, a lively hope, a hope eternal and divine. Because our hope abides, our praise continues--"I will hope continually, and will yet praise thee." Because our hopes grow brighter, and are every day nearer and nearer to their fulfillment, therefore the volume of our praise increases. "I will hope continually, and yet praise thee more and more." A dying hope would bring forth declining songs; as the expectations grew more dim, so would the music become more faint; but a hope immortal and eternal, flaming forth each day with intenser brightness, brings forth a song of praise which, as it shall always continue to arise, so shall it always gather new force. See well, my brethren, to your faith, and your faith and hope, for otherwise God will be robbed of his praise. It will be in proportion as you hope for the good things which he has promised to your faith, that you will render to him the praise which is his royal revenue, acceptable to him by Jesus Christ, and abundantly due from you.

David had not been slack in praise: indeed, he was a sweet singer in Israel, a very choir-master unto the Lord yet he vowed to praise him more and more. Those who do much already, are usually the people who can do more. He was old. Would he praise God more when he was infirm than he had done when he was young and vigorous? If he could not excel with loudness of voice, yet would he with eagerness of heart; and what his praise might lack in sound, it should gain in solemn earnestness. He was in trouble too, yet he would not allow the heyday of his prosperity to surpass in its notes of loving adoration the dark hour of his adversity. For him on no account could there be any going back. He had adored the Lord when he was but a youth and kept his father's flock. Harp in hand, beneath the spreading tree, he had worshipped the Lord his Shepherd, whose rod and staff were his comfort and delight. When an exile he had made the rocky fastnesses of Adullam and Engedi resound with the name of Jehovah. In after time, when he had become king in Israel, his psalms had been multiplied, and his harpstrings were daily accustomed to the praises of the God of his salvation. How could that zealous songster make an advance in praise? See him yonder dancing before the ark of the Lord with all his might: what more of joy and zeal can be manifest? Yet he says: "I will yet praise thee more and more." His troubles had been multiplied of late, and his infirmities too, yet for all that, no murmuring escapes him, but he resolved that his praise should rise higher and higher till he continued it in better lands for ever and ever.

Beloved, it is an intense joy to me to address you this morning after so long and sad an absence, and I pray that the Holy Spirit may make my word stimulating to you all. Our subject is that of our praising God more and more. I do not intend to exhort you to praise God; but shall take it for granted that you are doing so, though I fear it will be a great mistake in the case of many. We must, however, take that fact for granted in those to whom we address ourselves upon our particular topic; for those who do not praise God at all cannot be exhorted to praise him more and more. To those I direct my speech who now love to praise God; these would I charge to resolve with the psalmist: "I will yet praise thee more and more."

I. Our first business shall be, to URGE OURSELVES TO THIS RESOLUTION. Why should we praise God more and more? Here I am embarrassed with the multitude of arguments which beset me. So many crowd around me that I cannot number them in order, but must seize them somewhat at random.

It is humbling to remember that we may very well praise God more than we have done, for we have praised him very little as yet. What we have done, as believers, in glorifying God Mls far, far short of his due. Personally, upon consideration, we shall each own this. Bethink thee, my dear brother, or sister, what the Lord has done for thee. Some years ago thou wast in thy sin, and death, and ruin; he called thee by his grace. Thou wast under the burden and curse of sin; he delivered thee. Didst thou not expect in the first joy of pardon to have done more for him, to have loved him more, to have served him better? What are the returns which thou hast made for the boons which thou hast received? Are they at all fitting or adequate? I look at a field loaded with precious grain and ripening for the harvest: I hear that the husbandman has expended so much in rent, so much upon the ploughing, so much upon enriching the soil, so much for seed, so much more for needful weeding. There is the harvest, and it yields a profit: he is contented. But I see another field: it is my own heart; and, my brother, thine is the same. What has the Husbandman done for it? He has reclaimed it from the wild waste, by a power no less then omnipotent. He has hedged it, ploughed it, and cut down the thorns. He has watered it as no other field was ever watered, for the bloody sweat of Christ has bedewed it, to remove the primeval curse. God's own Son has given his whole self that this barren waste may become a garden. What has been done it were hard to sum: what more could have been done none can say. Yet what is the harvest? Is it adequate to the labor expended? Is the tillage remunerative? I am afraid if we cover our faces, or if a blush shall serve us instead of a veil, it will be the most fit reply to the question. Here and there a withered ear is a poor recompense for the tillage of infinite love. Let us, therefore, be shamed into a firm resolve, and say with resolute spirit: "By the good help of infinite grace, I, at any rate, having been so great a laggard, will quicken my pace; I will yet praise thee more and more."

Another argument which presses upon my mind is this: that wherein we have praised God up till now, we have not found the service to be a weariness to ourselves, but it has ever been to us both a profit and a delight. I would not speak falsely even for God, but I bear my testimony that the happiest moments I have ever spent have been occupied with the worship of God. I have never been so near heaven as when adoring before the eternal throne. I think every Christian will bear like witness. Among all the joys of earth, and I shall not depreciate them, there is no joy comparable to that of praise. The innocent mirth of the fireside, the chaste happinesses of household love, even these are not to be mentioned side by side with the joy of worship, the rapture of drawing near to the Most High. Earth, at her best, yields but water, but this divine occupation is as the wine of Cana's marriage feast. The purest and most exhilarating joy is the delight of glorifying God, and so anticipating the time when we shall enjoy him for ever. Now, brethren, if God's praise has been no wilderness to you, return to it with zest and ardor, and say: "I will yet praise thee more and more." If any suppose that you grow weary with the service of the Lord, tell them that his praise is such freedom, such recreation, such felicity, that you desire never to cease from it. As for me, if men call God's service slavery, I desire to be such a bondslave for ever, and would fain be branded with my Master's name indelibly. I would have my ear bored to the door-post of my Lord's house, and go no more out. My soul joyfully sings--

"Let thy grace, Lord, like a fetter,
Bind my wandering heart to thee."

This to me shall be ambition--to be more and more subservient to the divine honor. This shall be gain--to be nothing for Christ's sake. This my all in all--to praise thee, my Lord, as long as I have any being.

A third reason readily suggests itself. We ought surely to praise God more to-day than at any other previous day, because we have received more mercies. Even of temporal favors we have been large partakers. Begin with these, and then rise higher. Some of you, dear brethren and sisters, may well be reminded of the great temporal mercies which have been lavished upon you. You are to-day in a similar state with Jacob when he said: "with my staff I passed over this Jordan, and now I am become two bands." When you first left your father's house to follow a toilsome occupation, you had a scant enough purse, and but poor prospects; but where are you now as to temporal circumstances and position? How highly God has favored some of you! Joseph has risen from the dungeon to the throne, David has gone up from the sheepfolds to a palace. Look back to what you were, and give the Lord his due. He lifts up the poor from the dust, and sets them among princes. You were unknown and insignificant, and now his mercy has placed you in prominence and esteem. Is this nothing? Do you despise the bounty of heaven? Will you not praise the Lord more and more for this? Surely, you should do so, and must do so, or else feel the withering curse which blasts ingratitude wherever it dwells. Perhaps divine providence has not dealt with you exactly in that way but with equal goodness and wisdom has revealed itself to you in another form. You have continued in the same sphere in which you commenced life, but you have been enabled to pursue your work, have been preserved in health and strength, have been supplied with food and raiment and what is best, have been blessed with a contented heart and a gleaming eye. My dear friend, are you not thankful? Will you not praise your heavenly Father more and more? We ought not to over estimate temporal mercies so as to become worldly; but I am afraid there is a greater likelihood of our under estimating them, and becoming ungrateful. We must beware of so under estimating them as to lessen our sense of the debt in which they involve us before God. We speak sometimes of great mercies. Come now, I will ask you a question: Can you count your great mercies? I cannot count mine. Perhaps you think the numeration easy! I find it endless. I was thinking the other day, and I will venture to confess it publicly, what a great mercy it was to be able to turn over in bed. Some of you smile, perhaps. Yet I do not exaggerate when I say, I could almost clap my hands for joy when I found myself able to turn in bed without pain. This day, it is to me a very great mercy to be able to stand upright before you. We carelessly imagine that there are but a score or two of great mercies, such as having our children about us, or enjoying health and so on; but in trying times we see that innumerable minor matters are also great gifts of divine love, and entail great misery when withdrawn. Sing ye, then, as ye draw water at the nether springs, and as the brimming vessels overflow, praise ye the Lord yet more and more.

But ought we not to praise God more and more when we think of our spiritual mercies! What favors have we received of this higher sort! Ten years ago you were bound to praise God for the covenant mercies you had even then enjoyed; but now, how many more have been bestowed upon you; how many cheerings amid darkness; how many answers to prayer; how many directions in dilemma; how many delights of fellowship; how many helps in service; how many successes in conflict; how many revelations of infinite love! To adoption there has been added all the blessings of heirship; to justification, all the security of acceptance; to conversion, all the energies of indwelling. And, remember, as there was no silver cup in Benjamin's sack the Joseph put it there, so there was no spiritual good in you till the Lord of mercy gave it. Therefore, praise ye the Lord. Louder and louder yet be the song. Praise him on the high-sounding cymbals. Since we cannot hope to measure his mercies, let us immeasurably praise our God. "I will yet praise thee more and more."

Let us now go on a little farther. We have been proving through a series of years the faithfulness, immutability, and veracity of our God--proving these attributes by our sinning against God, and their bearing the strain of our misbehaviour--proving them by the innumerable benefits which the Lord has bestowed upon us. Shall all this experience end in no result? Shall there be no advance in gratitude where there is such an increase of obligation? God is so good that every moment of his love demands a life of praise.

It should never be forgotten that every Christian as he grows in grace should have a loftier idea of God. Our highest conception of God falls infinitely short of his glory, but an advanced Christian enjoys a far clearer view of what God is than he had at the first. Now, the greatness of God is ever a claim for praise. "Great is the Lord, and"--what follows?--"greatly to be praised." If, then, God is greater to me than he was, let my praise be greater. If I think of him now more tenderly as my Father--if I have a clearer view of him in the terror of his justice--if I have a clearer view of the splendors of his wisdom by which he devised the atonement--if I have larger thoughts of his eternal, immutable love--let every advance in knowledge constrain me to say: "I will yet praise thee more and more." I heard of thee by the hearing of the ear, but now mine eye seeth thee: therefore while I abhor myself in dust and ashes, my praise shall rise yet more loftily; up to thy throne shall my song ascend. I did but see as it were the skirts of thy garment, but thou hast hidden me in the cleft of the rock Christ Jesus, and made thy glory pass before me, and now will I praise thee even as the seraphs do, and vie with those before the throne in magnifying thy name. We learn but little in Christ's school, if the practical result of it all be not to make us cry: "I will yet praise thee more and more."

Still culling here and there a thought out of thousands, I would remind you that it is a good reason for praising God more that we are getting nearer to the place where we hope to praise him, world without end, after a perfect sort. Never have we made these walls ring more joyously than when we have united in singing of our Father's house on high, and the tents pitched--

"A day's march nearer home."

Heaven is indeed the only home of our souls, and we shall never feel that we have come to our rest till we have reached its mansions. One reason why we shall be able to rest in heaven, is because we shall there be able perpetually to achieve the object of our creation. Am I nearer heaven? then I will be doing more of the work which I shall do in heaven. I shall soon use the harp: let me be carefully tuning it: let me rehearse the hymns which I shall sing before the throne; for if the words in heaven shall be sweeter and more rich than any that poets can put together here, yet the essential song of heaven shall be the same as that which we present to Jehovah here below.

"they praise the Lamb in hymns above,
And we in hymns below."

The essence of their praise is gratitude that he should bleed: it is the essence of our praise too. They bless Immanuel's name for undeserved favors bestowed upon unworthy ones, and we do the same. My aged brethren, I congratulate you, for you are almost home; be yet more full of praise than ever. Quicken your footsteps as the glory land shines more brightly. You are close to the gate of pearl; sing on, dear brother, though infirmities increase, and let the song grow sweeter and louder until it melts into the infinite harmonies.

Shall I need to give another reason why we should praise God more and more? If I must, I would throw this one into the scale, that surely at this present juncture we ought to be more earnest in the praise of God, because God's enemies are very earnest in laboring to dishonor him. These are times when scoffers are boundlessly impudent. Did it not make your blood chill when you heard revolutionists in unhappy Paris talk of having "demolished God"? It struck me as almost a sadder thing when I read the proposition of one of their philosophers who would have them become religious again, that they should bring God back again for ten years at least--an audacious recommendation as blasphemously impertinent as the insolence which had proclaimed the triumph of atheism. But we need not look across the Channel; perhaps they speak more honestly on that side than we do here; for among ourselves we have abounding infidelity, which pretends to reverence Scripture while it denies its plainest teachings; and we have what is quite as bad, a superstition which thrusts Christ aside for the human priest, and makes the sacraments everything, and simple trust in the great atonement to be as nothing. Now, my brethren, those who hold these views are not sleepers, nor do they relax their efforts. We may be very quiet and lukewarm about religion (alas! that we should be); but these persons are earnest propagators of their faith, or no faith--they compass sea and land to make one proselyte. As we think of these busy servants of Satan, we ought to chide ourselves and say: "Shall Baal be diligently served, and Jehovah have such a sleepy advocate? Be stirred, my soul! Awake, my spirit! Arouse thee at once, and praise thy God more and more!"

But, indeed, while I give you these few arguments out of many that come to my mind, the thought cheers my spirit that with those of you who know and love God, there is little need for me to mention reasons, for your own souls are hungering and thirsting to praise him. If you are debarred for a little time from the public service of God, you pant for the assemblies of God's house, and envy the swallows that build their nests beneath the eaves. If you are unable to accomplish service which you were accustomed to perform for Christ's church, the hours drag very wearily along. As the Master found it his meat and his drink to do the will of him that sent him, so when you are unable to do that will, you are like a person deprived of his meat and drink, and an insatiable hunger grows upon you. O Christian brother, do you not pant to praise God? I am sure you feel now: "O that I could praise him better!" You are perhaps in a position in which you have work to do for him, and your heart is saying, "How I wish I could do this work more thoroughly to his praise!" Or possibly you are in such a condition of life that it is little you can do, and you often wish if God would make a change for you, not that it should be one more full of comfort, but one in which you could be more serviceable. Above all, I know you wish you were rid of sin, and everything which hinders your praising God more and more. Well, then, I need not argue, for your own heart pleads the holy cause.

Suffer me to conclude this head with a fact that illustrates the point. I know one, who has been long privileged to lift his voice in the choir of the great King. In that delightful labor none more happy than he. The longer he was engaged in the work the more he loved it. Now, it came to pass that on a certain day, this songster found himself shut out of the choir; he would have entered to take his part, but he was not permitted. Perhaps the King was angry; perhaps the songster had sung carelessly; perhaps he had acted unworthily in some other matter; or possibly his master knew that his song would grow more sweet if he were silenced for awhile. How it was I know not, but this I know, that it caused great searching of heart. Often this chorister begged to be restored, but he was as often repulsed, and somewhat roughly too. I think it was more than three months that this unhappy songster was kept in enforced silence, with fire in his bones and no vent for it. The royal music went on without him; there was no lack of song, and in this he rejoiced, but he longed to take his place again. I cannot tell you how eagerly he longed. At last the happy hour arrived, the king gave his permit, he might sing again. The songster was full of gratitude, and I heard him say--you shall hear him say it: "My Lord, since I am again restored, I will hope continually, and will yet praise thee more and more."

II. Now let us turn to another point. Let us in the Spirit's strength DRIVE AWAY THAT WHICH HINDERS US FROM PRAISING GOD MORE AND MORE.

One of the deadliest things is dreaminess, sleepiness. A Christian readily falls into this state. I notice it even in the public congregation. Very often the whole service is gone through mechanically. That same dreaminess falls upon many professors and abides with them, and instead of praising God more and more, it is as much as ever they can do to keep up the old strain--and barely that. Let us shake ourselves from all such sleep. Surely if there were any service in which a man should be altogether and wholly awake, it is in praising and magnifying God. A sleepy seraph before the throne of Jehovah, or a cherub nodding during sacred song, it were ridiculous to imagine. And shall such an insult to the majesty of heaven be seen on earth? No! Let us say to all that is within us, "Awake! awake!"

The next hindrance would be divided objects. We cannot, however we may resolve, praise God more and more, if, as we grow older, we allow this world to take up our thoughts. If I say, "I will praise God more and more," and yet I am striking out right and left with projects of amassing wealth, or I am plunging myself into greater business cares unnecessarily, my actions belie my resolutions. Not that we would check enterprise. There are periods in life when a man may be enabled to praise God more and more by extending the bounds of his business; but there are persons whom I have known who have praised God right well in a certain condition, but they have not been content to let well alone, and they have been for aggrandising themselves, and they have had to give up their Sabbath-school class, or the village station, or attendance at the visiting committee, or some other form of Christian service, because their money-getting demanded all their strength. Beloved, you shall find it small gain if you gain in this world, but lose in praising God. As we grow older, it is wise to concentrate more and more our energies upon the one thing, the only thing worth living for--the praise of God.

Another great obstacle to praising God more is, self-content; and this, again, is a condition into which we may very easily fall. Our belief is, only we must not avow it when we may be overheard, we are all very fine fellows indeed. We may confess when we are praying, and at other times, that we are miserable sinners--and I daresay we have some belief that it is so--but for all that, there is within our minds the conviction that we are very respectable people, and are doing exceedingly well upon the whole; and comparing ourselves with other Christians, it is much to our credit that we are praising God as well as we are. Now, I have put this very roughly, but is it not what the heart has said to us at times? Oh, loathsome thought! that a sinner should grow content with himself. Self-satisfaction is the end of progress. Dear friend, why compare yourself with the dwarfs around you? If you must compare yourself with your fellow men, look at the giants of other days; but, better still, relinquish the evil habit altogether; for Paul tells us it is not wise to compare ourselves among ourselves. Look to our Lord and Master, who towers so high above us in peerless excellence. No, no, we dare not flatter ourselves, but with humble self-condemnation we resolve to praise the Lord more and more.

To rest on the past is another danger as to this matter. We did so much for God when we were young. I occasionally meet with drones in the Christian hive, whose boast is that they made a great deal of honey years ago. I see men lying upon their oars to-day, but they startle me with a description of the impetus they gave to the boat years ago. You should have seen them when they were master-rowers, in those former times. What a pity that these brethren cannot be aroused to do their first works; it would be a gain to the church, but it would be an equal benefit to themselves. Suppose God should say, "Rest on the past. I gave you great mercies twenty years ago; live on them." Suppose the eternal and ever beloved Spirit should say, "I wrought a work in you thirty years ago; I withdraw myself, and I will do no more." Where were you then? Yet, my dear brother, if you still have to draw afresh upon the eternal fountains, do, I beseech you, praise the ever-blessed source of all.

May God help us then to shake off all those things which would prevent our praising him! Possibly there is some afflicted one here, in so low a state, so far pressed by poverty or bodily pain, that he is saying: "I cannot praise God more and more: I am ready to despair." Dear brother, may God give you full resignation to his will, and the greater your troubles the sweeter will be your song. I met in an old divine a short but sweet story, which touched my heart. A poor widow and her little child were sitting together in great want, both feeling the pinch of hunger, and the child looked up into the mother's face, and said: "Mother, God won't starve us, will he?" "No, my child," said the mother; "I do not think he will." "But, mother," said the child, "if he does, we will still praise him as long as we live, won't we, mother?" "May those who are grey headed be able to say what the child said, and to carry it out. "Though he slay me, yet will I trust in him." We have received good at the hands of the Lord; shall we not also receive evil? "The Lord gave, and the Lord hath taken away; blessed be the name of the Lord." "I will yet praise thee more and more."

III. Very briefly LET US APPLY OURSELVES TO THE PRACTICAL CARRYING OUT OF THIS RESOLUTION. I have given you arguments for it, and tried to move away impediments. Now for a little help in the performance of it. How shall I begin to praise God more and more?

Earnestness says: "I shall undertake some fresh duty this afternoon." Stop, dear brother, just a minute. If you want to praise God, would not it be as well first to begin with yourself? The musician said: "I will praise God better;" but the pipes of his instrument were foul; he had better look to them first. If the strings have slipped from their proper tension, it will be well to correct them before beginning the tune. If we would praise God more, it is not to be done as boys rush into a bath--head first. No; prepare yourself; make your heart ready. Thou needest the Spirit's aid to make thy soul fit for praising God. It is not every fool's work. Go then to thy chamber, confess the sins of the past, and ask the Lord to give thee much more grace that thou mayst begin to praise him.

If we would praise God more and more, let us improve our private devotions. God is much praised by really devout prayer and adoration. Preachings are not fruits: they are sowings. True song is fruit. I mean this, that the green blade of the wheat may be the sermon, but the wheat-ear is the hymn you sing, the prayer in which you unite. The true result of life is praise to God. "The chief end of man," says the catechism, and I cannot put it better, "is to glorify God, and enjoy him for ever;" and wherein we glorify God in our private devotion, we are answering the true end of our being. If we desire to praise God more, we must ask grace that our private devotions may rise to a higher standard. I am more and more persuaded from my own experience, that in proportion to the strength of our private life with God will be the force of our character, and the power of our work for God amongst men. Let us look well to this.

Again, however, I hear the zealous young man or woman saying: "Well, I will attend to what you have said. I will see to private prayer and to heart work, but I mean to begin some work of usefulness." Quite right; but stay a little. I want to ask you this question: Are you sure that your own personal conduct in what you call your everyday life has as much of the praise of God in it as it might have? It is all a mistake to think that we must come here to praise God. You can praise God in your shops, and in your kitchens, and in your bedrooms. It is all a mistake to suppose that Sunday is the only day to praise God in. Praise him on Mondays, Tuesdays, Wednesdays, every day, everywhere. All places are holy to holy people, and all engagements holy to holy men, if they do them with holy motives, lifting up their hearts to God; and whether a man swings the blacksmith's hammer, or lays his hand upon the ploughtail, that is true worship which is done as unto the Lord and not unto men. I like the story of the servant-maid, who, when she was asked on joining the church, "Are you converted?" "I hope so, sir." "What makes you think you are really a child of God?" "Well, sir, there is a great change in me from what there used to be." "What is that change?" "I don't know, sir, but there is a change in all things; but there is one thing, I always sweep under the mats now." Many a time she had hidden the dust under the mat. It was not so now; it is a very excellent reason for believing that there is a change of heart when work is conscientiously done. There is a set of mats in all our houses where we are accustomed to put the dirt away; and when a man gets in his business to sweep from under the mats--you merchants have your mats, you know, when you avoid the evils which custom tolerates but which God condemns, then you have marks of grace within. Oh, to have a conduct moulded by the example of Christ! If any man lived after a holy sort, though he never preached a sermon or even sung a hymn, he would have praised God; and the more conscientiously he acted, the more thoroughly would he have done so.

These inner matters being considered, let us go on to increase our actual and direct service of God. Let us do what we have been doing of Christian teaching, visiting, and so on; but in all let us do more, give more, and labor more. Who among us is working at his utmost, or giving at his utmost? Let us quicken our speed. Or suppose we are already doing so much that all the time we can possibly spare is fully occupied, let us do what we do better. In some Christian churches they do not want more societies, but they want more force put into them. You may trip over the sand of the sea-shore and scarcely leave an impression, but if you take heavy steps there is a deep foot-mark each time. May we in our service of God tread heavily, and leave deep foot-prints on the sands of time. Whatsoever ye do, do it heartily; throw yourselves into it; do it with thy might. "Thou shalt love the Lord thy God with all thine heart, and with all thy soul, and with all thy might." Oh, to be enabled to serve God after this fashion--this would be to praise him more and more! Though I do not say that you can always tell how far a man praises God by the quantity of work that he does for God, yet it is not a bad gauge. It was an old aphorism of Hippocrates, the old physician, that you could judge of a man's heart by his arm; by which he meant that by his pulse he judged of his heart: and as a rule, though there may be exceptions, you shall tell whether a man's heart beats truly to God, by the work that he does for God. You who are doing much, do more; and you who are doing little, multiply that little, I pray you, in God's strength, and so praise him more and more.

We should praise God much more if we threw more of his praise into our common conversation--if we spoke more of him when we are by the way or when we sit in the house. We should praise him more and more if we fulfilled our consecration, and obeyed the precept, "Whether therefore ye eat, or drink, or whatsoever ye do, do all to the glory of God." We should do well if we added to our godly service more singing. The world sings: the million have their songs; and I must say the taste of the populace is a very remarkable taste just now as to its favourite songs. They are, many of them, so absurd and meaningless as to be unworthy of an idiot. I should insult an idiot if I could suppose that such songs as people sing nowadays would really be agreeable to him. Yet these things will be heard from men, and places will be thronged to listen to hear the stuff. Now, why should we, with the grand psalms we have of David, with the noble hymns of Cowper, of Milton, of Watts--why should not we sing as well as they? Let us sing the songs of Zion they are as cheerful as the songs of Sodom any day. Let us drown the howling nonsense of Gomorrha with the melodies of the New Jerusalem.

But to conclude, I would that every Christian here would labor to be impressed with the importance of the subject which I have tried to bring before you. And when I say every Christian, I may correct myself and say, every person here present. "I will yet praise thee more and more." Why some of you present have never praised God at all! Suppose you were to die to-day, and soon you must: where should you go? To heaven? Where would heaven be to you? There can be no heaven for you. They praise God in the only heaven I have ever heard of. The element of heaven is gratitude, praise, adoration you do not know anything of this, and therefore it would not be possible for God to make a heaven for you. God can do all things except make a sinful spirit happy, or violate truth and justice. Thou must either praise God or be wretched. O my hearer, there is a choice for thee: thou must either worship the God that made thee, or else thou must be wretched. It is not that he kindles a fire for thee, nor that he casts upon it the brimstone of his wrath, though that be true; but thy wretchedness will begin within thyself, for to be unable to praise is to be full of hell. To praise God is heaven. When completely immersed in adoration, we are completely filled with felicity; but to be totally devoid of gratitude is to be totally devoid of happiness. O that a change might come over you who have never blessed the Lord, and may it happen this morning! May the work of regeneration take place now! There is power in the Holy Spirit to change thy heart of stone in a moment into a heart of flesh, so that instead of being cold and lifeless, it shall palpitate with gratitude. Seest thou not Christ on the cross dying for sinners? Canst thou look on that disinterested love, and not feel some gratitude for such love as is there exhibited? Oh, if thou canst look to Jesus and trust him, thou shalt feel a flash of life come into thy soul, and with it shall come praise, and then shalt thou find it possible to begin the happy life, and it shall be certain to thee that as thou shalt praise God more and more, so shall that happy life be expanded, be perfected in bliss.

But Christians, the last word shall be to you. Are you praising God more and more? If you are not, I am afraid of one thing, and that is, that you are probably praising him less and less. It is a certain truth that if we do not go forward in the Christian life, we go backward. You cannot stand still; there is a drift one way or the other. Now he that praises God less than he did, and goes on to praise him less to-morrow, and less the next day, and so on--what will he get to? and what is he? Evidently he is one of those that draw back unto perdition, and there are no persons upon whom a more dreadful sentence is pronounced, often spoken of by Paul, and most terribly by Peter and Jude. Those "Trees twice dead, plucked up by the roots;" the "Wandering stars for whom is reserved the blackness of darkness for ever." It would have been infinitely better for them not to have known the way of righteousness, than having known it, after a fashion, to have turned aside! Better never to have put their hand to the plough, than having done so, after a sort, to turn back from it.

But, beloved, I am persuaded better things of you, and things that accompany salvation, though I thus speak. I pray that God will lead you on from strength to strength, for that is the path of the just. May you grow in grace, for life is proven by growth. May you march like pilgrims towards heaven, singing, all the way. The lark may serve us as a final picture, and an example of what we all should be. We should be mounting: our prayer should be, "Nearer, my God, to thee." We should be mounting: our motto might well be, "Higher! higher! higher!" As we mount, we should sing, and our song should grow louder, clearer, more full of heaven. Upward, brother I sing as thou soarest. Upward, sing till thou art dissolved in glory. Amen.

PORTION OF SCRIPTURE READ BEFORE SERMON--Psalm 71.

The Withering Work of the Spirit

A Sermon (No. 999)
Delivered on Lord's-day Morning, July 9th, 1871, by
C. H. SPURGEON,
At the Metropolitan Tabernacle, Newington

"The voice said, Cry. And he said, What shall I cry? All flesh is grass, and all the goodliness thereof is as the flower of the field: the grass withereth, the flower fadeth: because the Spirit of the Lord bloweth upon it surely the people is grass. The grass withereth, the flower fadeth: but the word of our God shall stand for ever." - Isaiah 40:6-8.

"Being born again, not of corruptible seed, but of incorruptible, by the word of God, which liveth and abideth for ever. For all flesh is as grass, and all the glory of man as the flower of grass. The grass withereth, and the flower thereof falleth away: but the word of the Lord endureth for ever. And this is the word which by the gospel is preached unto you." - 1 Peter 1:23-25.

THE passage in Isaiah which I have just read in your hearing may be used as a very eloquent description of our mortality, and if a sermon should be preached from it upon the frailty of human nature, the brevity of life, and the certainty of death, no one could dispute the appropriateness of the text. Yet I venture to question whether such a discourse would strike the central teaching of the prophet. Something more than the decay of our material flesh is intended here; the carnal mind, the flesh in another sense, was intended by the Holy Ghost when he bade his messenger proclaim those words. It does not seem to me that a mere expression of the mortality of our race was needed in this place by the context; it would hardly keep pace with the sublime revelations which surround it, and would in some measure be a digression from the subject in hand. The notion that we are here simply and alone reminded of our mortality does not square with the New Testament exposition of it in Peter, which I have also placed before you as a text. There is another and more spiritual meaning here beside and beyond that which would be contained in the great and very obvious truth that all of us must die.

Look at the chapter in Isaiah with care. What is the subject of it? It is the divine consolation of Zion. Zion had been tossed to and fro with conflicts; she had been smarting under the result of sin. The Lord, to remove her sorrow, bids his prophets announce the coming of the long-expected Deliverer, the end and accomplishment of all her warfare and the pardon of all her iniquity. There is no doubt that this is the theme of the prophecy; and further, there is no sort of question about the next point, that the prophet goes on to foretell the coming of John the Baptist as the harbinger of the Messiah. We have no difficulty in the explanation of the passage, "Prepare ye the way of the Lord, make straight in the desert a highway for our God;" for the New Testament again and again refers this to the Baptist and his ministry. The object of the coming of the Baptist and the mission of the Messiah, whom he heralded, was the manifestation of divine glory. Observe the fifth verse: "The glory of the Lord shall be revealed, and all flesh shall see it together: for the mouth of the Lord hath spoken it." Well, what next? Was it needful to mention man's mortality in this connection? We think not. But there is much more appropriateness in the succeeding verses, if we see their deeper meaning. Do they not mean this? In order to make room for the display of the divine glory in Christ Jesus and his salvation, there would come a withering of all the glory wherein man boasts himself: the flesh should be seen in its true nature as corrupt and dying, and the grace of God alone should be exalted. This would be seen under the ministry of John the Baptist first, and should be the preparatory work of the Holy Ghost in men's hearts, in all time, in order that the glory of the Lord should be revealed and human pride be for ever confounded.

The Spirit blows upon the flesh, and that which seemed vigorous becomes weak, that which was fair to look upon is smitten with decay; the true nature of the flesh is thus discovered, its deceit is laid bare, its power is destroyed, and there is space for the dispensation of the ever-abiding word, and for the rule of the Great Shepherd, whose words are spirit and life. There is a withering wrought by the Spirit which is the preparation for the sowing and implanting by which salvation is wrought.

The withering before the sowing was very marvellously fulfilled in the preaching of John the Baptist. Most appropriately he carried on his ministry in the desert, for a spiritual desert was all around him; he was the voice of one crying in the wilderness. It was not his work to plant, but to hew down. The fleshly religion of the Jews was then in its prime. Phariseeism stalked through the streets in all its pomp; men complacently rested in outward ceremonies only, and spiritual religion was at the lowest conceivable ebb. Here and there might be found a Simeon and an Anna, but for the most part men knew nothing of spiritual religion, but said in their hearts: "We have Abraham to our father," and this is enough. What a stir he made when he called the lordly Pharisees a generation of vipers! How he shook the nation with the declaration, "Now also the axe is laid unto the root of the trees"! Stern as Elias, his work was to level the mountains, and lay low every lofty imagination. That word, "Repent," was as a scorching wind to the verdure of self-righteousness, a killing blast for the confidence of ceremonialism. His food and his dress called for fasting and mourning. The outward token of his ministry declared the death amid which he preached, as he buried in the waters of Jordan those who came to him. "Ye must die and be buried, even as he who is to come will save by death and burial." This was the meaning of the emblem which he set before the crowd. His typical act was as thorough in its teaching as were his words; and as if that were not enough, he warned them of a yet more searching and trying baptism with the Holy Ghost and with fire, and of the coming of one whose fan was in his hand, thoroughly to purge his floor. The Spirit in John blew as the rough north wind, searching and withering, and made him to be a destroyer of the vain goryings of a fleshly religion, that the spiritual faith might be established.

When our Lord himself actually appeared, he came into a withered land, whose glories had all departed. Old Jesse's stem was bare, and our Lord was the branch which grew out of his root. The scepter had departed from Judah, and the lawgiver from between his feet, when Shiloh came. An alien sat on David's throne, and the Roman called the covenant-land his own. The lamp of prophecy burned but dimly, even if it had not utterly gone out. No Isaiah had arisen of late to console them, nor even a Jeremiah to lament their apostacy. The whole economy of Judaism was as a worn-out vesture; it had waxed old, and was ready to vanish away. The priesthood was disarranged. Luke tells us that Annas and Caiaphas were high priests that year--two in a year or at once, a strange setting aside of the laws of Moses. All the dispensation which gathered around the visible, or as Paul calls it, the "worldly" sanctuary, was coming to a close; and when our Lord had finished his work, the veil of the temple was rent in twain, the sacrifices were abolished, the priesthood of Aaron was set aside, and carnal ordinances were abrogated, for the Spirit revealed spiritual things. When he came who was made a priest, "not after the law of a carnal commandment, but after the power of an endless life," there was "a disannulling of the commandment going before for the weakness and unprofitableness thereof."

Such are the facts of history; but I am not about to dilate upon them: I am coming to your own personal histories--to the experience of every child of God. In every one of us it must be fufilled that all that is of the flesh in us, seeing it is but as grass, must be withered, and the comeliness thereof must be destroyed. The Spirit of God, like the wind, must pass over the field of our souls, and cause our beauty to be as a fading flower. He must so convince us of sin, and so reveal ourselves to ourselves, that we shall see that the flesh profiteth nothing; that our fallen nature is corruption itself, and that "they who are in the flesh cannot please God." There must be brought home to us the sentence of death upon our former legal and carnal life, that the incorruptible seed of the word of God, implanted by the Holy Ghost, may be in us, and abide in us for ever.

The subject of this morning is the withering work of the Spirit upon the souls of men, and when we have spoken upon it, we shall conclude with a few words upon the implanting work, which always follows where this withering work has been performed.

I. Turning then to THE WORK OF THE SPIRIT IN CAUSING THE GOODLINESS OF THE FLESH TO FADE, let us, first, observe that the work of the Holy Spirit upon the soul of man in withering up that which is of the flesh, is very unexpected. You will observe in our text, that even the speaker himself, though doubtless one taught of God, when he was bidden to cry, said, "What shall I cry?" Even he did not know that in order to the comforting of God's people, there must first be experienced a preliminary visitation. Many preachers of God's gospel have forgotten that the law is the schoolmaster to bring men to Christ. They have sown on the unbroken fallow ground and forgotten that the plough must break the clods. We have seen too much of trying to sew without the sharp needle of the Spirit's convincing power. Preachers have labored to make Christ precious to those who think themselves rich and increased in goods: and it has been labor in vain. It is our duty to preach Jesus Christ even to self-righteous sinners, but it is certain that Jesus Christ will never be accepted by them while they hold themselves in high esteem. Only the sick will welcome the physician. It is the work of the Spirit of God to convince men of sin, and until they are convinced of sin, they will never be led to seek the righteousuess which is of God by Jesus Christ. I am persuaded, that wherever there is a real work of grace in any soul, it begins with a pulling down:

the Holy Ghost does not build on the old foundation. Wood, hay, and stubble will not do for him to build upon. He will come as the fire, and cause a conflagration of all proud nature's Babels. He will break our bow and cut our spear in sunder, and burn our chariot in the fire. When every sandy foundation is gone, then, but not till then, behold he will lay in our souls the great foundation stone, chosen of God, and precious. The awakened sinner, when he asks that God would have mercy upon him, is much astonished to find that, instead of enjoying a speedy peace, his soul is bowed down within him under a sense of divine wrath. Naturally enough he enquires: "Is this the answer to my prayer? I prayed the Lord to deliver me from sin and self, and is this the way in which he deals with me? I said, Hear me,' and behold he wounds me with the wounds of a cruel one. I said, Clothe me,' and lo! He has torn off from me the few rags which covered me before, and my nakedness stares me in the face. I said, Wash me,' and behold he has plunged me in the ditch till mine own clothes do abhor me. Is this the way of grace?" Sinner, be not surprised: it is even so. Perceivest thou not the cause of it? How canst thou be healed while the proud flesh is in thy wound? It must come out. It is the only way to heal thee permanently: it would be folly to film over thy sore, or heal thy flesh, and leave the leprosy within thy bones. The great physician will cut with his sharp knife till the corrupt flesh be removed, for only thus can a sure healing work be wrought in thee. Dost thou not see that it is divinely wise that before thou art clothed thou shouldst be stripped! What, wouldst thou have Christ's lustrous righteousness outside whiter than any fuller can make it, and thine own filthy rags concealed within? Nay, man; they must be put away; not a single thread of thine own must be left upon thee. It cannot be that God should cleanse thee until he has made thee see somewhat of thy defilement; for thou wouldst never value the precious blood which cleanses us from all sin if thou hadst not first of all been made to mourn that thou art altogether an unclean thing.

The convincing work of the Spirit, wherever it comes, is unexpected, and even to the child of God in whom this process has still to go on, it is often startling. We begin again to build that which the Spirit of God had destroyed. Having begun in the spirit, we act as if we would be made perfect in the flesh; and then when our mistaken upbuilding has to be levelled with the earth, we are almost as astonished as we were when first the scales fell from our eyes. In some such condition as this was Newton when he wrote:--

"I asked the Lord that I might grow
In faith and love and every grace,
Might more of his salvation know,
And seek more earnestly his face.
Twas he who taught me thus to pray,
And he, I trust, has answered prayer;
But it has been in such a way
As almost drove me to despair.
I hop'd that in some favour'd hour,
At once he'd answer my request,
And by his love's constraining power
Subdue my sins, and give me rest.
Instead of this, he made me feel
The hidden evils of my heart.
And let the angry powers of hell
Assault my soul in ev'ry part."

Ah, marvel not, for thus the Lord is wont to answer his people. The voice which saith, "Comfort ye, comfort ye my people," achieves its purpose by first making them hear the cry, "All flesh is grass, and all the goodliness thereof is as the flower of the field."

2. Furthermore, this withering is after the usual order of the divine operation. If we consider well the way of God, we shall not be atonished that he beginneth with his people by terrible things in righteousness. Observe the method of creation. I will not venture upon any dogmatic theory of geology, but there seems to be every probability that this world has been fitted up and destroyed, refitted and then destroyed again, many times before the last arranging of it for the habitation of men. "In the beginning God created the heaven and the earth;" then came a long interval, and at length, at the appointed time, during seven days, the Lord prepared the earth for the human race. Consider then the state of matters when the great architect began his work. What was there in the beginning? Originally, nothing. When he commanded the ordering of the earth how was it? "The earth was without form and void; and darkness was upon the face of the deep." There was no trace of another's plan to interfere with the great architect. "With whom took he counsel, and who instructed him, and taught him in the path of judgment, and taught him knowledge, and showed to

him the way of understanding." He received no contribution of column or pillar towards the temple which he intended to build. The earth was, as the Hebrew puts it, Tohu and Bohu, disorder and confusion--in a word, chaos. So it is in the new creation. When the Lord new creates us, he borrows nothing from the old man, but makes all things new. He does not repair and add a new wing to the old house of our depraved nature, but he builds a new temple for his own praise. We are spiritually without form and empty, and darkness is upon the face of our heart, and his word comes to us, saying, "Light be," and there is light, and ere long life and every precious thing.

To take another instance from the ways of God. When man has fallen, when did the Lord bring him the gospel? The first whisper of the gospel, as you know, was, "I will put enmity between thee and the woman, between thy seed and her seed. He shall bruise thy head." That whisper came to man shivering in the presence of his Maker, having nothing more to say by way of excuse; but standing guilty before the Lord. When did the Lord God clothe our parents? Not until first of all he had put the question, "Who told thee that thou wast naked?" Not until the fig-leaves had utterly failed did the Lord bring in the covering skin of the sacrifice, and wrap them in it. If you will pursue the meditation upon the acts of God with men, you will constantly see the same thing. God has given us a wonderful type of salvation in Noah's ark; but Noah was saved in that ark in connection with death; he himself, as it were, immured alive in a tomb, and all the world besides left to destruction. All other hope for Noah was gone, and thee the ark rose upon the waters. Remember the redemption of the children of Israel out of Egypt: it occurred when they were in the saddest plight, and their cry went up to heaven by reason of their bondage. When no arm brought salvation, then with a high hand and an outstretched arm the Lord brought forth his people. Everywhere before the salvation there comes the humbling of the creature, the overthrow of human hope. As in the back woods of America before there can be tillage, the planting of cities, the arts of civilization, and the transactions of commerce, the woodman's axe must hack and hew: the stately trees of centuries must fall: the roots must be burned, the odd reign of nature disturbed. The old must go before the new can come. Even thus the Lord takes away the first, that he may establish the second. The first heaven and the first earth must pass away, or there cannot be a new heaven and a new earth. Now, as it has been outwardly, we ought to expect that it would be the same within us and when these witherings and facings occur in our souls, we should only say "It is the Lord, let him do as seemeth him good."

3. I would have you notice, thirdly, that we are taught in our text how universal this process is in its range over the hearts of all those upon whom the Spirit works. The withering is a withering of what? Of part of the flesh and some portion of its tendencies? Nay, observe, "All flesh is grass; and all the goodliness thereof"--the very choice and pick of it--"is as the flower of the field," and what happens to the grass? Does any of it live? "The grass withereth," all of it. The flower, will not that abide? So fair a thing, has not that an immortality? No, it fades: it utterly falls away. So wherever the Spirit of God breathes on the soul of man, there is a withering of everything that is of the flesh, and it is seen that to be carnally minded is death. Of course, we all know and confess that where there is a work of grace, there must be a destruction of our delight in the pleasures of the flesh. When the Spirit of God breathes on us, that which was sweet becomes bitter; that which was bright becomes dim. A man cannot love sin and yet possess the life of God. If he takes pleasure in fleshly joys wherein he once delighted, he is still what he was: he mince the things of the flesh, and therefore he is after the flesh, and he shall die. The world and the lusts thereof are to the unregenerate as beautiful as the meadows in spring, when they are bedecked with flowers, but to the regenerate soul they are a wilderness, a salt land, and not inhabited. Of those very things wherein we once took delight we say, "Vanity of vanities; all is vanity." We cry to be delivered from the poisonous joys of earth, we loathe them, and wonder that we could once riot in them. Beloved hearers, do you know what this kind of withering means? Have you seen the lusts of the flesh, and the pomps and the pleasures thereof all fade away before your eyes? It must be so, or the Spirit of God has not visited your soul.

But mark, wherever the Spirit of God comes, he destroys the goodliness and flower of the flesh; that is to say, our righteousness withers as our sinfulness. Before the Spirit comes we think ourselves as good as the best. We say, "All these commandments have I kept from my youth up," and we superciliously ask, "What lack I yet?" Have we not been moral? Nay, have we not even been religious? We confess that we may have committed faults, but we think them very venial, and we venture, in our wicked pride, to imagine that, after all, we are not so vile as the word of God would lead us to think. Ah, my dear hearer, when the Spirit of God blows on the comeliness of thy flesh, its beauty will fade as a leaf, and thou wilt have quite another idea of thyself thou wilt then find no language too severe in which to describe thy past character. Searching deep into thy motives, and investigating that which moved thee to thine actions, thou wilt see so much of evil, that thou wilt cry with the publican, "God be merciful to me, a sinner!"

Where the Holy Ghost has withered up in us our self-righteousness, he has not half completed his work; there is much more to be destroyed yet, and among the rest, away must go our boasted power of resolution. Most people conceive that they can turn to God whenever they resolve to do so. "I am a man of such strength of mind," says one, "that if I made up my mind to be religious, I should be without difficulty." "Ah," saith another volatile spirit, "I believe that one of these days I can correct the errors of the past, and commence a new life." Ah, dear hearers, the resolutions of the flesh are goodly flowers, but they must all fade. When visited by the Spirit of God, we find that even when the will is present with us, how to perform that which we would we find not; yea, and we discover that our will is averse to all that is good, and that naturally we will not come unto Christ that we may have life. What poor frail things resolutions are when seen in the light of God's Spirit!

Still the man will say, "I believe I have, after all, within myself an enlightened conscience and an intelligence that will guide me aright. The light of nature I will use, and I do not doubt that if I wander somewhat I shall find my way back again." Ah, man! thy wisdom, which is the very flower of thy nature, what is it but folly, though thou knowest it not? Unconverted and unrenewed, thou art in God's sight no wiser than the wild ass's colt. I wish thou wert in thine own esteem humbled as a little child at Jesus' feet, and made to cry, "Teach thou me."

When the withering wind of the Spirit moves over the carnal mind, it reveals the death of the flesh in all respects, especially in the matter of power towards that which is good. We then learn that word of our Lord: "Without me ye can do nothing." When I was seeking the Lord, I not only believed that I could not pray without divine help, but I felt in my very soul that I could not. Then I could not even feel aright, or mourn as I would, or groan as I would. I longed to long more after Christ; but, alas! I could not even feel that I needed him as I ought to feel it. This heart was then as hard as adamant, as dead as those that rot in their graves. Oh, what would I at times have given for a tear! I wanted to repent, but could not; longed to believe, but could not; I felt bound, hampered, and paralysed. This is a humbling revelation of God's Holy Spirit, but a needful one; for the faith of the flesh is not the faith of God's elect. The faith which justifies the soul is the gift of God and not of ourselves. That repentance which is the work of the flesh will need to be repented of. The flower of the flesh must wither; only the seed of the Spirit will produce fruit unto perfection. The heirs of heaven are born not of blood, nor of the will of the flesh, nor of man, but of God. If the work in us be not the Spirit's working, but our own, it will droop and die when most we require its protection; and its end will be as the grass which to-day is, and tomorrow is cast into the oven.

4. You see, then, the universality of this withering work within us, but I beg you also to notice the completeness of it. The grass, what does it do? Droop? nay, wither. The dower of the field: what of that? Does it hang its head a little? No, according to Isaiah it fades; and according to Peter it falleth away. There is no reviving it with showers, it has come to its end. Even thus are the awakened led to see that in their flesh there dwelleth no good thing. What dying and withering work some of God's servants have had in their souls! Look at John Bunyan, as he describes himself in his "Grace Abounding!" For how many months and even years was the Spirit engaged in writing death upon all that was the old Bunyan, in order that he might become by grace a new man fitted to track the pilgrims along their heavenly way. We have not all endured the ordeal so long, but in every child of God there must be a death to sin, to the law, and to self, which must be fully accomplished ere he is perfected in Christ and taken to heaven. Corruption cannot inherit incorruption; it is through the Spirit that we mortify the deeds of the body, and therefore live. But cannot the fleshly mind be improved? By no means; for "the carnal mind is enmity against God: for it is not subject to the law of God, neither indeed can be." Cannot you improve the old nature? No; "ye must be born again." Can it not be taught heavenly things? No. "The natural man receiveth not the things of the Spirit of God: for they are foolishness unto him: neither can he know them, because they are spiritually discerned." There is nothing to be done with the old nature but to let it be laid in the grave; it must be dead, and buried, and when it is so, then the incorruptible seed that liveth and abideth for ever will develop gloriously, the fruit of the new birth will come to maturity, and grace shall be exalted in glory. The old nature never does improve, it is as earthly, and sensual, and devilish in the saint of eighty years of age as it was when first he came to Christ; it is unimproved and unimprovable; towards God it is enmity itself: every imagination of the thoughts of the heart is evil, and that continually. The old nature called "the flesh lusteth against the Spirit, and the Spirit against the flesh: and these are contrary the one to the other," neither can there be peace between them.

5. Let us further notice that all this withering work in the soul is very painful. As you read these verses do they not strike you as having a very funereal tone? "All flesh is grass, and all the goodliness thereof is as the flower of the field: the grass withereth, the flower fadeth." This is mournful work, but it must be done. I think those who experience much of it when they first come to Christ have great reason to be thankful. Their course in life will, in all probability, be much brighter and happier, for I have noticed that persons who are converted very easily, and come to

Christ with but comparatively little knowledge of their own depravity, have to learn it afterwards, and they remain for a long time babes in Christ, and are perplexed with masters that would not have troubled them if they had experienced a deeper work at first. No, sir; if grace has begun to build in your soul and left any of the old walls of self-trust standing, they will have to come down sooner or later. You may congratulate yourself upon their remaining, but it is a false congratulation, your glorying is not good. I am sure of this, that Christ will never put a new piece upon an old garment, or new wine in old bottles: he knows the rent would be worse in the long run, and the bottles would burst. All that is of nature's spinning must be unravelled. The natural building must come down, lath and plaster, roof and foundation, and we must have a house not made with hands. It was a great mercy for our city of London that the great fire cleared away all the old buildings which were the lair of the plague, a far healthier city was then built; and it is a great mercy for a man when God sweeps right away all his own righteousness and strength, when he makes him feel that he is nothing and can be nothing, and drives him to confess that Christ must be all in all, and that his only strength lies in the eternal might of the ever-blessed Spirit. Sometimes in a house of business an old system has been going on for years, and it has caused much confusion, and allowed much dishonesty. You come in as a new manager, and you adopt an entirely new plan. Now, try if you can, and graft your method on to the old system. How it will worry you! Year after year you say to yourself, "I cannot work it: if I had swept the whole away and started afresh, clear from the beginning, it would not have given me one-tenth of the trouble." God does not intend to graft the system of grace upon corrupt nature, nor to make the new Adam grow out of the old Adam, but he intends to teach us this: "Ye are dead, and your life is hid with Christ in God." Salvation is not of the flesh but of the Lord alone; that which is born of the flesh is only flesh at the best; and only that which is born of the Spirit is spirit. It must be the Spirit's work altogether, or it is not what God will accept.

Observe, brethren, that although this is painful it is inevitable. I have already entrenched upon this, and shown you how necessary it is that all of the old should be taken away; but let me further remark that it is inevitable that the old should go, because it is in itself corruptible. Why does the grass wither? Because it is a withering thing. "Its root is ever in its we, and it must die." How could it spring out of the earth, and be immortal? It is no amaranth: it blooms not in Paradise: it grows in a soil on which the curse has fallen. Every supposed good thing that grows out of your own self, is like yourself, mortal, and it must die. The seeds of corruption are in all the fruits of manhood's tree; let them be as fair to look upon as Eden's clusters, they must decay.

Moreover, it would never do, my brother, that there should be something of the flesh in our salvation and something of the Spirit; for if it were so there would be a division of the honor. Hitherto the praises of God; beyond this my own praises. If I were to win heaven partly through what I had done, and partly through what Christ had done, and if the energy which sanctified me was in a measure my own, and in a measure divine, they that divide the work shall divide the reward, and the songs of heaven while they would be partly to Jehovah must also be partly to the creature. But it shall not be. Down, proud flesh! Down! I say. Though thou cleanse and purge thyself as thou mayst, thou art to the core corrupt though thou labor unto weariness, thou buildest wood that will be burned, and stubble that will be turned to ashes. Give up thine own self-confidence, and let the work be, and the merit be where the honor shall be, namely, with God alone. It is inevitable, then, that there should be all this withering.

7. This last word by way of comfort to any that are passing through the process we are describing, and I hope some of you are. It gives me great joy when I hear that you unconverted ones are very miserable, for the miseries which the Holy Spirit works are always the prelude to happiness. It is the Spirit's work to wither. I rejoice in our translation, "Because the Spirit of the Lord bloweth upon it." It is true the passage may be translated, "The wind of the Lord bloweth upon it." One word, as you know, is used in the Hebrew both for "wind" and "Spirit," and the same is true of the Greek; but let us retain the old translation here, for I conceive it to be the real meaning of the text. The Spirit of God it is that withers the flesh. It is not the devil that killed my self-righteousness. I might be afraid if it were: nor was it myself that humbled myself by a voluntary and needless self-degradation, but it was the Spirit of God. Better to be broken in pieces by the Spirit of God, than to be made whole by the flesh! What doth the Lord say? "I kill." But what next? "I make alive." He never makes any alive but those he kills. Blessed be the Holy Ghost when he kills me, when he drives the sword through the very bowels of my own merits and myself-confidence, for then he will make me alive. "I wound, and I heal." He never heals those whom he has not wounded. Then blessed be the hand that wounds; let it go on wounding; let it cut and tear; let it lay bare to me myself at my very worst, that I may be driven to self-despair, and may fall back upon the free mercy of God, and receive it as a poor, guilty, lost, helpless, undone sinner, who casts himself into the arms of sovereign grace, knowing that God must give all, and Christ must be all, and the Spirit must work all, and man must be as clay in the potter's hands, that the Lord may do

with him as seemeth trim good. Rejoice, dear brother, how ever low you are brought, for if the Spirit humbles you he means no evil, but he intends infinite good to your soul.

II. Now, let us close with a few sentences concerning THE IMPLANTATION.

According to Peter, although the flesh withers, and the flower thereof falls away, yet in the children of God there is an unwithering something of another kind. "Being born again, not of corruptible seed, but of incorruptible, by the word of God, which liveth and abideth for ever." "The word of the Lord endureth for ever. And this is the word which by the gospel is preached unto you." Now, the gospel is of use to us because it is not of human origin. If it were of the flesh, all it could do for us would not land us beyond the flesh; but the gospel of Jesus Christ is super-human, divine, and spiritual. In its conception it was of God; its great gift, even the Savior, is a divine gift; and all its teachings are full of deity. If you, my hearer, believe a gospel which you have thought out for yourself, or a philosophical gospel which comes from the brain of man, it is of the flesh, and will wither, and you will die, and be lost through trusting in it. The only word that can bless you and be a seed in your soul must be the living and incorruptible word of the eternal Spirit. Now this is the incorruptible word, that "God was made flesh and dwelt among us;" that "God was in Christ, reconciling the world unto himself, not imputing their trespasses unto them." This is the incorruptible word, that "Whosoever believeth that Jesus is the Christ is born of God." "He that believeth on him is not condemned: but he that believeth not is condemned already, because he hath not believed in the name of the only begotten Son of God." "God hath given to us eternal life, and this life is in his Son." Now, brethren, this is the seed; but before it can grow in your soul, it must be planted there by the Spirit. Do you receive it this morning? Then the Holy Spirit implants it in your soul. Do you leap up to it, and say, "I believe it! I grasp it! On the incarnate God I fix my hope; the substitutionary sacrifice, the complete atonement of Christ is all my confidence; I am reconciled to God by the blood of Jesus." Then you possess the living seed within your soul.

And what is the result of it? Why, then there comes, according to the text, a new life into us, as the result of the indwelling of the living word, and our being born again by it. A new life it is; it is not the old nature putting out its better parts; not the old Adam refining and purifying itself, and rising to something better. No; have we not said aforetime that the flesh withers and the flower thereof fades? It is an entirely new life. Ye are as much new creatures at your regeneration, as if you had never existed, and had been for the first time created. "Old things are passed away; behold, all things are become new." The child of God is beyond and above other men. Other men do not possess the life which he has received. They are but duplex--body and soul have they. He is of triple nature--he is spirit, soul, and body. A fresh principle, a spark of the divine life has dropped into his soul; he is no longer a natural or carnal man, but he has become a spiritual man, understanding spiritual things and possessing a life far superior to anything that belongs to the rest of mankind. O that God, who has withered in the souls of any of you that which is of the flesh, may speedily grant you the new birth through the Word.

Now observe, to close, wherever this new life comes through the word, it is incorruptible, it lives and abides for ever. To get the good seed out of a true believer's heart and to destroy the new nature in him, is a thing attempted by earth and hell, but never yet achieved. Pluck the sun out of the firmament, and you shall not even then be able to pluck grace out of a regenerate heart. It "liveth and abideth for ever," saith the text; it neither can corrupt of itself nor be corrupted. "It sinneth not, because it is born of God." "I give unto them eternal life, and they shall never perish, neither shall any man pluck them out of my hand." "The water that I shall give him shall be in him a well of water springing up into everlasting life." You have a natural life--that will die, it is of the flesh. You have a spiritual life--of that it is written: "Whosoever liveth and believeth in me shall never die." You have now within you the noblest and truest immortality: you must live as God liveth, in peace and joy, and happiness. But oh, remember, dear hearer, if you have not this you "shall not see life." What then--shall you be annihilated? Ah! no, but "the wrath of the Lord is upon you." You shall exist, though you shall not live. Of life you shall know nothing, for that is the gift of God in Christ Jesus; but of an everlasting death, full of torment and anguish, you shall be the wretched heritor--"the wrath of God abideth on him." You shall be cast into "the lake of fire, which is the second death." You shall be one of those whose "worm dieth not, and whose fire is not quenched." May God, the ever-blessed Spirit, visit you! If he be now striving with you, O quench not his divine flame! Trifle not with any holy thought you have. If this morning you must confess that you are not born again, be humbled by it. Go and seek mercy of the Lord, entreat him to deal graciously with you and save you. Many who have had nothing but moonlight have prized it, and ere long they have had sunlight. Above all, remember what the quickening seed is, and reverence it when you hear it preached, "for this is the word which by the gospel is preached unto you." Respect it, and receive it. Remember that the quickening seed is all wrapped up in this sentence: "Believe in the Lord Jesus Christ, and thou shalt be saved." "He that believeth and is baptised shall be saved; but he that believeth not shall be damned."

The Lord bless you, for Jesus' sake. Amen.

PORTION OF SCRIPTURE READ BEFORE SERMON--Isaiah 40:1-11; Luke 3:1-17; and 1 Peter 1:17-25.

Number One Thousand; Or, "Bread Enough and To Spare"

A Sermon (No. 1000)
Delivered on Lord's-day Morning, July 16th, 1871, by
C. H. SPURGEON,
At the Metropolitan Tabernacle, Newington

"And when he came to himself, he said, How many hired servants of my father's have bread enough and to spare, and I perish with hunger!" - Luke 15:17.

HE came to himself." The word may be applied to one waking out of a deep swoon. He had been unconscious of his true condition, and he had lost all power to deliver himself from it; but now he was coming round again, returning to consciousness and action. The voice which shall awaken the dead aroused him; the visions of his sinful trance all disappeared; his foul but fascinating dreams were gone; he came to himself. Or the word may be applied to one recovering from insanity. The prodigal son had played the madman, for sin is madness of the worst kind. He had been demented, he had put bitter for sweet and sweet for bitter, darkness for light and light for darkness; he had injured himself, and had done for his soul what those possessed of devils in our Savior's time did for their bodies, when they wounded themselves with stones, and cut themselves with knives. The insane man does not know himself to be insane, but as soon as he comes to himself he painfully perceives the state from which he is escaping. Returning then to true reason and sound judgment, the prodigal came to himself. Another illustration of the word may be found in the old world fables of enchantment: when a man was disenthralled from the magician's spell he "came to himself." Classic story has its legend of Circe, the enchantress, who transformed men into swine. Surely this young man in our parable had been degraded in the same manner. He had lowered his manhood to the level of the brutes. It should be the property of man to have love to his kindred, to have respect for right, to have some care for his own interest; this young man had lost all these proper attributes of humanity, and so had become as the beast that perisheth. But as the poet sings of Ulysses, that he compelled the enchantress to restore his companions to their original form, so here we see the prodigal returning to manhood, looking away from his sensual pleasures, and commencing a course of conduct more consistent with his birth and parentage. There are men here to-day perhaps who are still in this swoon; O God of heaven arouse them! Some here who are morally insane; the Lord recover them, the divine Physician put his cooling hand upon their fevered brow, and say to them: "I will; be thou made whole." Perhaps there are others here who have allowed their animal nature to reign supreme may he who destroys the works of the devil deliver them from the power of Satan, and give them power to become the sons of God. He shall have all the glory!

It appears that when the prodigal came to himself he was shut up to two thoughts. Two facts were clear to him, that there was plenty in his father's house, and that he himself was famishing. May the two kindred spiritual facts have absolute power over all your hearts, if you are yet unsaved; for they were most certainly all-important and pressing truths. These are no fancies of one in a dream; no ravings of a maniac; no imaginations of one under fascination: it is most true that there is plenty of all good things in the Father's house, and that the sinner needs them. No where else can grace be found or pardon gained; but with God there is plenitude of mercy; let none venture to dispute this glorious truth. Equally true is it that the sinner without God is perishing. He is perishing now; he will perish everlastingly. All that is worth having in his existence will be utterly destroyed, and he himself shall only remain as a desolation; the owl and the bittern of misery and anguish shall haunt the ruins of his nature for ever and for ever. If we could shut up unconverted men to those two thoughts, what hopeful congregations we should have. Alas! they forget that there is mercy only with God, and fancy that it is to be found somewhere else; and they try to slip away from the humbling fact of their own lost estate, and imagine that perhaps there may be some back door of escape; that, after all, they are not so bad as the Scripture declares, or that perchance it shall be right with them at the last, however wrong it may be with them now. Alas! my brethren, what shall we do with those who wilfully shut their eyes to truths of which the evidence is overwhelming, and the importance overpowering? I earnestly entreat those of you who know how to approach the throne of God in faith, to breathe the prayer that he would now bring into captivity the unconverted heart, and put these two strong fetters upon every unregenerate soul; there is abundant grace with God, there is utter destitution with themselves. Bound with such fetters, and led into the presence of Jesus, the captive would soon receive the liberty of the children of God.

I intend only to dwell this morning, or mainly, upon the first thought, the master thought, as it seems to me, which was in the prodigal's mind--that which really constrained him to say, "I will arise and go to my father." It was not, I think, the home-bringing thought that he was perishing with hunger, but the impulse towards his father found its mainspring in the consideration, "How many hired servants of my father's have bread enough and to spare!" The plenty, the abundance, the superabundance of the father's house, was that which attracted him to return home; and many, many a soul has been led to seek God when it has fully believed that there was abundant mercy with him. My desire this morning shall be to put plainly before every sinner here the exceeding abundance of the grace of God in Christ Jesus, hoping that the Lord will find out those who are his Sons, and that they may catch at these words, and as they hear of the abundance of the bread in the Father's house, may say, "I will arise and go to my Father."

I. First, then, let us consider for a short time THE MORE THAN ABUNDANCE OF ALL GOOD THINGS IN THE FATHER'S HOUSE. What dost thou need this morning, awakened sinner? Of all that thou needest, there is with God an all-sufficient, a superabounding supply; "bread enough and to spare." Let us prove this to thee. First, consider the Father himself, and whosoever shall rightly consider the Father, will at once perceive that there can be no stint to mercy, no bound to the possibilities of grace. What is the nature and character of the Supreme? "Is he harsh or loving?" saith one. The Scripture answers the question, not by telling us that God is loving, but by assuring us that God is love. God himself is love; it is his very essence. It is not that love is in God, but that God himself is love. Can there be a more concise and more positive way of saying that the love of God is infinite? You cannot measure God himself; your conceptions cannot grasp the grandeur of his attributes, neither can you tell the dimensions of his love, nor conceive the fullness of it. Only this know, that high as the heavens are above the earth, so are his ways higher than your ways, and his thoughts than your thoughts. His mercy endureth for ever. He pardoneth iniquity, and passeth by the transgression of the remnant of his heritage. He retaineth not his anger for ever, because he delighteth in mercy. "Thou, Lord, art good, and ready to forgive: and plenteous in mercy unto all them that call upon thee." "Thy mercy is great above the heavens." "The Lord is very pitiful, and of tender mercy."

If divine love alone should not seem sufficient for your salvation, remember that with the Father to whom the sinner returns, there is as much of wisdom as there is of grace. Is thy case a very difficult one? He that made thee can heal thee. Are thy diseases strange and complex? He that fashioned the ear, can he not remove its deafness? He that made the eye, can he not enlighten it if it be blind? No mischief can have happened to thee, but what he who is thy God can recover thee from it. Matchless wisdom cannot fail to meet the intricacies of thy case.

Neither can there be any failure of power with the Father. Dost thou not know that he who made the earth, and stretched out the heavens like a tent to dwell in, hath no bound to his strength, nor limit to his might? If thou needest omnipotence to lift thee up from the slough into which thou hast fallen, omnipotence is ready to deliver thee, if thou cry to the strong for strength. Though thou shouldest need all the force with which the Creator made the worlds, and all the strength with which he bears on the pillars of the universe, all that strength and force should be laid out for thy good, if thou wouldst believingly seek mercy at the hand of God in Christ Jesus. None of his power shall be against thee, none of his wisdom shall plan thy overthrow; but love shall reign in all, and every attribute of God shall become subservient to thy salvation. Oh, when I think of sin I cannot understand how a sinner can be saved; but when I think of God, and look into his heart, I understand how readily he can forgive. "Look into his heart," saith one; "how can we do that?" Hath he not laid bare his heart to you? Do you enquire where he has done this? I answer, yonder, upon Calvary's cross. What was in the very center of the divine heart? What, but the person of the Well-beloved, his only begotten Son? And he hath taken his only begotten and nailed him to the cross, because, if I may venture so to speak, he loved sinners better than his Son. He spared not his Son, but he spares the sinner; he poured out his wrath upon his Son and made him the substitute for sinners, that he might lavish love upon the guilty who deserved his anger. O soul, if thou art lost, it is not from any want of grace, or wisdom, or power in the Father; if thou perish, it is not because God is hard to move or unable to save. If thou be a castaway, it is not because the Eternal refused to hear thy cries for pardon or rejected thy faith in him. On thine own head be thy blood, if thy soul be lost. If thou starve, thou starvest because thou wilt starve; for in the Father's house there is "bread enough and to spare."

But, now, consider a second matter which may set this more clearly before us. Think of the Son of God, who is indeed the true bread of life for sinners. Sinner, I return to my personal address. Thou needest a Savior; and thou mayst well be encouraged when thou seest that a Savior is provided--provided by God, since it is certain he would not make a mistake in the provision. But consider who the Savior is. He is himself God. Jesus who came from heaven for our redemption was not an angel, else might we tremble to trust the weight of our sin upon him. He was not mere man, or he could but have suffered as a substitute for one, if indeed for one; but he was very God of very God, in the beginning with the Father. And does such a one come to redeem? Is there room to doubt as to his ability, if that be the fact? I do confess this day, that if my sins were ten thousand times heavier than they are, yea, and if I had all the sins of this crowd in addition piled upon me, I could trust Jesus with them all at this moment now that I know him to be the Christ of God. He is the mighty God, and by his pierced hand the burden of our sins is easily removed; he blotteth out our sins, he casts them into the depths of the sea.

But think of what Jesus the Son of God has done. He who was God, and thus blessed for ever, left the throne and royalties of heaven and stooped to yonder manger. There he lies; his mother wraps him in swaddling clothes, he hangs upon her breast; the Infinite is clothed as an infant, the Invisible is made manifest in flesh, the Almighty is linked with weakness, for our sakes. Oh, matchless stoop of condescension! If the Redeemer God does this in order to save us, shall it be thought a thing impossible for him to save the vilest of the vile? Can anything be too hard for him who comes from heaven to earth to redeem?

Pause not because of astonishment, but press onward. Do you see him who was God over all, blessed for ever, living more than thirty years in the midst of the sons of men, bearing the infirmities of manhood, taking upon himself our sicknesses, and sharing our sorrows: his feet weary with treading the acres of Palestine; his body faint often times with hunger and thirst, and labor; his knees knit to the earth with midnight prayer; his eyes red with weeping (for ofttimes Jesus wept), tempted in all points like as we are? Matchless spectacle! An incarnate God dwells among sinners, and endures their contradiction! What glory flashed forth ever and anon from the midst of his lowliness! a glory which should render faith in him inevitable. Thou who didst walk the sea: thou who didst raise the dead, it is not rational to doubt thy power to forgive sins! Didst thou not thyself put it so when thou badest the man take up his bed and walk? "Whether is easier, to say, Thy sins be forgiven thee; or to say, Rise up and walk?" Assuredly he is able to save to the uttermost them that come unto God by him: he was able even here on earth in weakness to forgive sins, much more now that he is seated in his glory. He is exalted on high to be a Prince and a Savior, to give repentance and remission of sins.

But, ah! the master proof that in Christ Jesus there is "bread enough and to spare," is the cross. Will you follow me a moment, will you follow him, rather, to Gethsemane? Can you see the bloody sweat as it falls upon the ground in his agony? Can you think of his scourging before Herod and Pilate? Can you trace him along the Via Dolorosa of Jerusalem? Will your tender hearts endure to see him nailed to the tree, and lifted up to bleed and die? This is but the shell; as for the inward kernel of his sufferings no language can describe it, neither can conception peer into it. The everlasting God laid sin on Christ, and where the sin was laid there fell the wrath. "It pleased the Lord to bruise him; he hath put him to grief." Now he that died upon the cross was God's only begotten Son. Can you conceive a limit to the merit of such a Savior's death? I know there are some who think it necessary to their system of theology to limit the merit of the blood of Jesus: if my system of theology needed such a limitation, I would cast it to the winds. I cannot, dare not, allow the thought to find a lodging in my mind; it seems so near akin to blasphemy. In Christ's finished work I see an ocean of merit; my plummet finds no bottom, my eye discovers no shore. There must be sufficient efficacy in the blood of Christ, if God had so willed it, to have saved not only all this world, but ten thousand worlds, had they transgressed the Maker's law. Once admit infinity into the matter, and limit is out of the question. Having a divine person for an offering, it is not consistent to conceive of limited value; bound and measure are terms inapplicable to the divine sacrifice. The intent of the divine purpose fixes the application of the infinite offering, but does not change it into a finite work. In the atonement of Christ Jesus there is "bread enough and to spare;" even as Paul wrote to Timothy, "He is the Savior of all men, specially of those that believe."

But now let me lead you to another point of solemnly joyful consideration, and that is the Holy Spirit. To believe and love the Trinity is to possess the key of theology. We spoke of the Father, we spoke of the Son; let us now speak of the Holy Spirit. We do him all too little honor, for the Holy Spirit condescends to come to earth and dwell in our hearts; and notwithstanding all our provocations he still abides within his people. Now, sinner, thou needest a new life and thou needest holiness, for both of these are necessary to make thee fit for heaven. Is there a provision for this? The Holy Spirit is provided and given in the covenant of grace; and surely in him there is "enough and to spare." What cannot the Holy Spirit do? Being divine, nothing can be beyond his power. Look at what he has already done. He moved upon the face of chaos, and brought it into order; all the beauty of creation arose beneath his moulding breath. We ourselves must confess with Elihu, "The Spirit of God hath made me, and the breath of the Almighty hath given me life." Think of the great deeds of the Holy Spirit at Pentecost, when men unlearned spake with tongues of which they knew not a syllable aforetime, and the flames of fire upon them were also within them, so that their hearts burned with zeal and courage to which they hitherto had been strangers. Think of the Holy Spirit's work on such a one as Saul of Tarsus. That persecutor foams blood, he is a very wolf, he would devour the saints of God at Damascus and yet, within a few moments, you hear him say, "Who art thou, Lord?" and yet again, "Lord, what wilt thou have me to do?" His heart is changed; the Spirit of God has new created it; the adamant is melted in a moment into wax. Many of us stand before you as the living monuments of what the Holy Ghost can do, and we can assure you from our own experience, that there is no inward evil which he cannot overcome, no lustful desire of the flesh which he cannot subdue, no obduracy of the affections which he cannot melt. Is anything too hard for the Lord? Is the Spirit of the Lord straitened? Surely no sinner can be beyond the possibilities of mercy when the Holy Spirit condescends to be the agent of human conversion. O sinner, if thou perish, it is not because the Holy Spirit wants power, or the blood of Jesus lacks efficacy, or the Father fails in love; it is because thou believest not in Christ, but dost abide in wilful rebellion, refusing the abundant bread of life which is placed before thee.

A few rapid sentences upon other things, which will go to show still further the greatness of the provision of divine mercy. Observe well that throughout all the ages God has been sending one prophet after another, and these prophets have been succeeded by apostles, and these by martyrs and confessors, and pastors and evangelists, and teachers; all these have been commissioned by the Lord in regular succession; and what has been the message they have had to deliver? They have all pointed to Christ, the great deliverer. Moses and the prophets all spoke of him, and so have all truly God-sent ambassadors. Dost thou think, sinner, that God has made all this fuss about a trifle? Has he sent all these servants to call thee to a table insufficiently furnished? Has he multiplied his invitations through so long a time to bid thee and others come to a provision which is not, after all, sufficient for them? Oh, it cannot be! God is not mocked, neither does he mock poor needy souls. The stores of his mercy are sufficient for the utmost emergencies.

"Rivers of love and mercy here
In a rich ocean join;
Salvation in abundance flows,
Like floods of milk and wine.
Great God, the treasures of thy love
Are everlasting mines,
Deep us our helpless miseries are,
And boundless as our sins."

Recollect, again, that God has been pleased to stake his honor upon the gospel. Men desire a name, and God also is jealous of his glory. Now, what has God been pleased to select for his name? Is it not the conversion and salvation of men? When instead of the brier shall come up the myrtle-tree, and instead of the thorn shall come up the fir-tree, it shall be to the Lord for a name, for an everlasting sign that shall not be cut off. And dost thou think God will get a name by saving little sinners by a little Savior? Ah! his great name comes from washing out stains as black as hell, and pardoning sinners who were foulest of the foul. Is there one monstrous rebel here who is qualified to glorify God greatly, because his salvation will be the wonder of angels and the amazement of devils? I hope there is. O thou most degraded, black, loathsome sinner, nearest to being a damned sinner, if this voice can reach thee, I challenge thee to come and prove whether God's mercy is not a match for thy sin. Thou Goliath sinner, come thou hither; thou shalt find that God can slay thine enmity, and make thee yet his friend, and the more his loving and adoring servant, because great forgiveness shall secure great love. Such is the greatness of divine mercy, that "where sin abounded, grace doth much more abound."

Dost thou think, again, O sinner, that Jesus Christ came out of heaven to do a little deed, and to provide a slender store of mercy? Dost thou think he went up to Calvary, and down to the grave, and all, that he might do a commonplace thing, and provide a stinted, narrow, limited salvation, such as thine unbelief would imagine his redemption to be? No. We speak of the labors of Hercules, but these were child's play compared with the labors of Christ who slew the lion of hell, turned a purifying stream through the Augean stables of man's sin, and cleansed them, and performed ten thousand miracles besides: and will you so depreciate Christ as to imagine that what he has accomplished is, after all, little, so little that it is not enough to save you? If it were in my power to single out the man who has been the most dishonest, most licentious, most drunken, most profane--in three words, most earthly, sensual, devilish--I would repeat the challenge which I gave just now, and bid him draw near to Jesus, and see whether the fountain filled with Christ's atoning blood cannot wash him white. I challenge him at this instant to come and cast himself at the dear Redeemer's feet, and see if he will say, "I cannot save thee, thou hast sinned beyond my power." It shall never, never, never be, for he is able to the uttermost to save. He is a Savior, and a great one. Christ will be honored by the grandeur of the grace which he bestows upon the greatest of offenders. There is in him pardon "enough and to spare."

I must leave this point, but I cannot do so without adding that I think "BREAD ENOUGH AND TO SPARE" might be taken for the motto of the gospel. I believe in particular redemption, and that Christ laid down his life for his sheep; but, as I have already said, I do not believe in the limited value of that redemption; how else could I dare to read the words of John, "He is the propitiation for our sins: and not for ours only, but also for the sine of the whole world." There is a sure portion for his own elect, but there is also over and above "to spare." I believe in the electing love which will save all its objects--"bread enough;" but I believe in boundless benevolence, "Bread enough and to spare." We, when we have a purpose to accomplish, put forth the requisite quantity of strength and no more, for we must be economical, we must not waste our limited store; even charity gives the poor man no more than he absolutely needs; but when God feeds the multitude, he spreads the board with imperial bounty. Our water-cart runs up and down the favored road, but when heaven's clouds would favor the good man's fields, they deluge whole nations, and even pour themselves upon the sea. There is no real waste with God; but at the same time there is no stint. "BREAD ENOUGH AND TO SPARE;" write that inscription over the house of mercy, and let every hungry passer-by be encouraged thereby to enter in and eat.

II. We must now pass on to a second consideration, and dwell very briefly on it. According to the text, there was not only bread enough in the house, but THE LOWEST IN THE FATHER'S HOUSE ENJOYED ENOUGH AND TO SPARE.

We can never make a parable run on all fours, therefore we cannot find the exact counterpart of the "hired servants." I understand the prodigal to have meant this, that the very lowest menial servant employed by his father had bread to eat, and had "bread enough and to spare." Now, how should we translate this? Why, sinner, the very lowest creature that God has made, that has not sinned against him, is well supplied and has abounding happiness. There are adaptations for pleasure in the organisations of the lowest animals. See how the gnats dance in the summer's sunbeam; hear the swallows as they scream with delight when on the wing. He who cares for birds and insects will surely care for men. God who hears the ravens when they cry, will he not hear the returning penitent? He gives these insects happiness; did he mean me to be wretched? Surely he who opens his hand and supplies the lack of every living thing, will not refuse to open his hand and supply my needs if I seek his face.

Yet I must not make these lowest creatures to be the hired servants. Whom shall I then select among men? I will put it thus. The very worst of sinners that have come to Christ have found grace "enough and to spare," and the very least of saints who dwell in the house of the Lord find love "enough and to spare." Take then the most guilty of sinners, and see how bountifully the Lord treats them when they turn unto him. Did not some of you, who are yourselves unconverted, once know persons who were at least as bad, perhaps more outwardly immoral than yourselves? Well, they have been converted, though you have not been; and when they were converted, what was their testimony? Did the blood of Christ avail to cleanse them? Oh, yes; and more than cleanse them, for it added to beauty not their own. They were naked once; was Jesus able to clothe them? Was there a sufficient covering in his righteousness? Ah, yes! and adornment was superadded; they received not a bare apparel, but a royal raiment. You have seen others thus liberally treated, does not this induce you also to come? Some of us need not confine our remarks to others, for we can speak personally of ourselves. We came to Jesus as full of sin as ever you can be, and felt ourselves beyond measure lost and ruined; but, oh, his tender love! I could sooner stand here and weep than speak to you of it. My soul melts in gratitude when I think of the infinite mercy of God to me in that hour when I came seeking mercy at his hands. Oh! why will not you also come? May his Holy Spirit sweetly draw you! I proved that there was bread enough, mercy enough, forgiveness enough, and to spare. Come along, come along, poor guilty one; come along, there is room enough for thee.

Now, if the chief of sinners bear this witness, so do the most obscure of saints. If we could call forth from his seat a weak believer in God, who is almost unknown in the church, one who sometimes questions whether he is indeed a child of God, and would be willing to be a hired servant so long as he might belong to God, and if I were to ask him, "How after all how has the Lord dealt with you?" what would be his reply? You have many afflictions, doubts and fears, but have you any complaints against your Lord? When you have waited upon him for daily grace, has he denied you? When you have been full of troubles, has he refused you comfort? When you have been plunged in distress, has he declined to deliver you? The Lord himself asks, "Have I been a wilderness unto Israel?" Testify against the Lord, ye his people, if ye have aught against him. Hear, O heavens, and give ear, O earth, whosoever there be in God's service who has found him a hard task-master, let him speak. Amongst the angels before Jehovah's throne, and amongst men redeemed on earth, if there be any one that can say he hath been dealt with unjustly or treated with ungenerous churlishness, let him lift up his voice! But there is not one. Even the devil himself when he spoke of God and of his servant Job, said, "Doth Job serve God for nought?" Of course he did not: God will not let his servants serve him for nought; he will pay them superabundant wages, and they shall all bear witness that at his table there is "bread enough and to spare." Now, if these still enjoy the bread of the Father's house, these who were once great sinners, these who are now only very commonplace saints, surely, sinner, it should encourage you to say, "I will arise and to my Father," for his hired servants "have bread enough and to spare."

III. Notice in the third place, that the text dwells upon THE MULTITUDE OF THOSE WHO HAVE "BREAD ENOUGH AND TO SPARE." The prodigal lays an emphasis upon that word, "How many hired servants of my father's!" He was thinking of their great number, and counting them over. He thought of those that tended the cattle, of those that went out with the camels, of those that watched the sheep, and those that minded the corn, and those that waited in the house; he ran them over in his mind: his father was great in the land, and had many servants; yet he knew that they all had of the best food "enough and to spare." "Why should I perish with hunger? I am only one at any rate; though my hunger seem insatiable, it is but one belly that has to be filled, and, lo, my father fills hundreds, thousands every day; why should I perish with hunger?" Now, O thou awakened sinner, thou who dost feel this morning thy sin and misery, think of the numbers upon whom God has bestowed his grace already. Think of the countless hosts in heaven: if thou wert introduced there to-day, thou wouldst find it as easy to tell the stars, or the sands of the sea, as to count the multitudes that are before the throne even now.

They have come from the east and from the west, and they are sitting down with Abraham, with Isaac, and with Jacob, and there is room enough for thee. And beside those in heaven, think of those on earth. Blessed be God, his elect on earth are to be counted by millions, I believe, and the days are coming, brighter days than these, when there shall be multitudes upon multitudes brought to know the Savior, and to rejoice in him. The Father's love is not for a few only, but for an exceeding great company. A number that no man can number will be found in heaven; now, a man can number a very great amount. Set to work your Newtons, your calculators, they can count great numbers, but God and God alone can tell the multitude of his redeemed. Now, sinner, thou art but one at any rate, great sinner as thou art, and the mercy of God which embraces millions must have room enough in it for thee. The sea which holds the whales and creeping things innumerable, dost thou say, "It will overflow its banks if I bathe therein"? The sun which floods the universe with light, canst thou see "I should exhaust his beams if I should ask him to enlighten my darkness"? Say not so. If thou comest to thyself thou wilt not tolerate such a thought, but thou wilt remember with hope the richness of the Father's grace, even though thine own poverty stare thee in the face.

Let us add a few words to close with, close grappling words to some of you to whom God has sent his message this morning, and whom he intends to save. O you who have been long hearers of the gospel, and who know it well in theory, but have felt none of the power of it in your hearts, let me now remind you where and what you are! You are perishing. As the Lord liveth, there is but a step between you and death; but a step, nay, but a breath between you and hell. Sinner, if at this moment thy heart should cease its beating, and there are a thousand causes that might produce that result ere the clock ticks again, thou wouldst, be in the flames of divine wrath canst thou bear to be in such peril? If you were hanging over a rock by a slender thread which must soon break, and if you would then fall headlong down a terrible precipice, you would not sleep, but be full of alarm. May you have sense enough, wit enough, grace enough, to be alarmed until you escape from the wrath to come.

Recollect, however, that while you are perishing, you are perishing in sight of plenty; you are famishing where a table is abundantly spread; what is more, there are those whom you know now sitting at that table and feasting. What sad perversity for a man to persist in being starved in the midst of a banquet, where others are being satisfied with good things!

But I think I hear you say, "I fear I have no right to come to Jesus." I will ask you this: have you any right to say that till you have been denied! Did you ever try to go to Christ? Has he ever rejected you? If then you have never received a repulse, why do you wickedly imagine that he would repel you? Wickedly, I say, for it is an offense against the Christ who opened his heart upon the gross, to imagine that he could repel a penitent. Have you any right to say, "But I am not one of those for whom mercy is provided"? Who told you so? Have you climbed to heaven and read the secret records of God election? Has the Lord revealed a strange decree to you, and said, "Go and despair, I will have no pity on you"? If you say that God has so spoken, I do not believe you. In this sacred book is recorded what God has said, here is the sure word of testimony, and in it I find it said of no humble seeker that God hath shut him out from his grace. Why hast thou a right to invent such a fiction in order to secure thine own damnation? Instead thereof, there is much in the word of God and elsewhere to encourage thee in coming to Christ. He has not repelled one sinner yet; that is good to begin with: it is not likely that he would, for since he died to save sinners, why should he reject them when they seek to be saved? You say, "I am afraid to come to Christ." Is that wise? I have heard of a poor navigator who had been converted, who had but little education, but who knew the grace of our Lord Jesus Christ, and when dying, very cheerfully and joyful longed to depart. His wife said to him, "But, mon, ain't ye afeared to stand before the judge?" "Woman," said he, "why should I be afeared of a man as died for me?" Oh, why should you be afraid of Christ who died for sinners? The idea of being afraid of him should be banished by the fact that he shed his blood for the guilty. You have much reason to believe from the very fact that he died, that he will receive you. Besides, you have his word for it, for he saith, "Him that cometh to me I will in no wise cast out"--for no reason, and in no way, and on no occasion, and under no presence, and for no motive. "I will not not cast him out," says the original. "Him that cometh to me I will in no wise cast out." You say it is too good to be true that there can be pardon for you: this is a foolish measuring of God's corn with your bushel, and because it seems too good a thing for you to receive, you fancy it is too good for God to bestow. Let the greatness of the good news be one reason for believing that the news is true, for it is so like God.

"Who is a pardoning God like thee?
Or who hath grace so rich and free?"

Because the gospel assures us that he forgives great sins through a great Savior, it looks as if it were true, since he is so great a God.

What should be the result of all this with every sinner here at this time? I think this good news should arouse those who have almost gone to sleep through despair. The sailors have been pumping the vessel, the leaks are gaining, she is going down, the captain is persuaded she must be a wreck. Depressed by such evil tidings, the men refuse to work; and since the boats are all stove in and they cannot make a raft, they sit down in despair. Presently the captain has better news for them. "She will float," he says; "the wind is abating too, the pumps tell upon the water, the leak can be reached yet." See how they work; with what cheery courage they toil on, because there is hope! Soul, there is hope! There is hope! THERE IS HOPE! To the harlot, to the thief, to the drunkard.

"There is no hope," says Satan. Liar that thou art, get thee back to thy den; for thee there is no hope; but for fallen man, though he be in the mire of sin up to his very neck, though he be at the gates of death, while he lives there is hope. There is hope for hopeless souls in the Savior.

In addition to arousing us this ought to elevate the sinner's thoughts. Some years ago, there was a crossing-sweeper in Dublin, with his broom, at the corner, and in all probability his highest thoughts were to keep the crossing clean, and look for the pence. One day, a lawyer put his hand upon his shoulder, and said to him, "My good fellow, do you know that you are heir to a fortune of ten thousand pounds a year?" "Do you mean it?" said he. "I do," he said. "I have just received the information; I am sure you are the man." He walked away, and he forgot his broom. Are you astonished? Why, who would not have forgotten a broom when suddenly made possessor of ten thousand a year? So, I pray that some poor sinners, who have been thinking of the pleasures of the world, when they hear that there is hope, and that there is heaven to be had, will forget the deceitful pleasures of sin, and follow after higher and better things.

Should it not also purify the mind? The prodigal, when he said, "I will arise and go to my father," became in a measure reformed from that very moment. How, say you? Why, he left the swine-trough: more, he left the wine cup, and he left the harlots. He did not go with the harlot on his arm, and the wine cup in his hand, and say, "I will take these with me, and go to my father." It could not be. These were all left, and though he had no goodness to bring, yet he did not try to keep his sins and come to Christ. I shall close with this remark, because it will act as a sort of caveat, and be a fit word to season the wide invitations of the free gospel. Some of you, I fear, will make mischief even out of the gospel, and will dare to take the cross and use it for a gibbet for your souls. If God is so merciful, you will go therefore and sin the more; and because grace is freely given, therefore you will continue in sin that grace may abound. If you do this, I would solemnly remind you I have no grace to preach to such as you. "Your damnation is just;" it is the word of inspiration, and the only one I know that is applicable to such as you are; but every needy, guilty soul that desires a Savior is told to-day to believe in Jesus, that is, trust in the substitution and sacrifice of Christ, trust him to take your sin and blot it out; trust him to take your soul and save it. Trust Christ entirely, and you are forgiven this very moment; you are saved this very instant, and you may rejoice now in the fact that being justified by faith you have peace with God through Jesus Christ our Lord. O come ye, come ye, come ye; come and welcome; come ye now to the Redeemer's blood. Holy Spirit, compel them to come in, that the house of mercy may be filled. Amen, and Amen.

THE reader, if a believer in Christ, is requested to unite with the preacher in praising the Lord for grace abundantly given in connection with these sermons. This is the thousandth of the series of sermon which we have published consecutively week by week, and of which the circulation has continued to increase. These discourses have many of them been reprinted in the United States, and have also been translated into German, French, Swedish, Dutch, Italian, and Welsh. Some of them have also been issued in the Hungarian, Russian, Danish, Spanish Telugu, Malagasay, Maori, and Gaelic tongues. Of their effect by the blessing of God's Spirit, thousands in heaven, and in all parts of the earth, are joyful witnesses. If we did not praise God for such mercy the stones would cry out.

Altogether Lovely

A Sermon (No. 1001)
Delivered on Lord's-day Morning, July 23rd, 1871, by
C. H. SPURGEON,
At the Metropolitan Tabernacle, Newington

"Yea, he is altogether lovely." - Song of Solomon 5:16.

WHEN THE OLD PURITAN MINISTER had delivered his discourse, and dwelt upon firstly, and secondly, and thirdly, and perhaps upon twenty-fifthly, before he sat down he usually gave a comprehensive summary of all that he had spoken. Every one who carefully noted the summary would carry away the essence of the sermon. The summary was always looked upon by the Puritan hearer as one of the most valuable helps to memory, and consequently a most important part of the discourse. In these five words the spouse here gives you her summary. She had delivered a tenfold discourse concerning her Lord; she had described in detail all his various beauties, and when she had surveyed him from head to foot, she gathered up all her commendations in this sentence: "Yea, he is altogether lovely." Remember these words, and know their meaning, and you possess the quintessence of the spouse's portion of the Song of Songs. Now, as in this allegorical song, the bride sums up her witness in these words, so may I say that all the patriarchs, all the prophets, all the apostles, all the confessors, yea, and the entire body of the church have left us no other testimony. They all spoke of Christ, and they all commended him. Whatever the type, or symbol, or obscure oracle, or open word in which they bore witness, that witness all amounted to this: "Yea, He is altogether lovely." Yes, and I will add, that since the canon of inspiration has closed, the testimony of all saints, on earth and in heaven, has continued to confirm the declaration made of old. The verdict of each particular saint and of the whole elect host as a body, still is this, "Yea, he is altogether lovely." From the sighs and the songs which mingle on the dying beds of saints, I hear this note supreme above all others, "He is altogether lovely;" and from the songs unmingled with groans, which perpetually peal forth from immortal tongues before the presence of the Most High, I hear this one master note. "Yea, he is altogether lovely." If the whole church desired to say with the apostle, "Now of the things which we have spoken this is the sum," she need not wait for a brief and comprehensive summary, for it lies before her in this golden sentence, "Yea, he is altogether lovely."

Looking at my text in this light I felt much humbling of spirit, and I hesitated to preach upon it, for I saith in my heart, "It is high, I cannot attain unto it." These deep texts show us the shortness of our plumb-line; these ocean verses are so exceeding broad that our skiffs are apt to be driven far out of sight of land where our timid spirits tremble to spread the sail. Then I comforted myself by the thought that though I could not comprehend this text in a measure, nor weigh its mountains in scales, or its hills in a balance, yet it was all mine own, by the gift of divine grace, and therefore I need not fear to enter upon the meditation of it. If I cannot grasp the ocean in my span, yet may I bathe therein with sweet content; if I cannot describe the king in his beauty, yet may I gaze upon him, since the old proverb saith, "A beggar may look at a prince." Though I pretend not so to preach from such a heavenly word as that before us, as to spread before you all its marrow and fatness, yet may I gather up a few crumbs which fall from its table. Poor men are glad of crumbs, and crumbs from such a feast are better than loaves from the tables of the world. Better to have a glimpse of Jesus, than to see all the glory of the earth all the days of our life. If we fail on this subject we may do better than if we succeeded upon another; so we will pluck up courage, seek divine help, and draw near to this wondrous text, with our shoes from off our feet like Moses when he saw the bush aglow with God.

This verse has been translated in another way: "He is all desires;" and so indeed Jesus is. He was the desire of the ancients, he is the desire of all nations still. To his own people he is their all in all; they are complete in him; they are filled out of his fullness.

"All our capacious powers can wish,
In him doth richly meet."

He is the delight of his servants, and fills their expectations to the full. But we will not dispute about translations, for, after all, with such a text, so full of unutterable spiritual sweetness, every man must be his own translator, and into his own soul must the power of the message come, by the enforcement of the Holy Ghost. Such a test as this is very like the manna which fell in the wilderness, of which the rabbis say it tasted after each man's liking. If the flavour in a man's mouth was very sweetness, the angel's food which fell around the camp was luscious as any dainty he had conceived; whatever he might be, the manna was to him as he was. So shall this text be. To you with low ideas of Christ the words shall but glide over your ears, and be meaningless; but if your spirit be ravished with the precious love of Jesus there shall be songs of angels, and more than that, the voice of God's own Spirit to your soul in this short sentence, "Yea, he is altogether lovely."

I am an engraver this morning, and I seek somewhat whereon I may engrave this heavenly line. Shall I take unto me ivory or silver? Shall I borrow crystal or gold? These are too common to bear this unique inscription: I put them all aside. Shall I spell my text in gems, with an emerald, a sapphire, a ruby, a diamond, or a pearl for each single letter? Nay, these are poor perishable things: we put them all away. I want an immortal spirit to be the tablet for my writing; nay, I must lay aside my graving tool, and ask the Spirit of God to take it: I want a heart prepared of the Holy Ghost, upon whose fleshy tablets there shall be written this morning no other sentence than this, and this shall suffice for a right royal motto to adorn it well: "Yea, he is altogether lovely." Spirit of God, find out the prepared heart, and with thy sacred hand write in eternal characters the love of Christ, and all his inimitable perfections.

In handling our text this morning we shall note three points of character, and then we shall show three uses to which we may profitably turn it.

I. We shall consider THREE POINTS OF CHARACTER which are very noticeable in these words, and the first which suggests itself is this: the words are evidently uttered by one who is under the influence of overwhelming emotion. The words are rather a veil to the heart than a glass through which we see its emotions. The sentence labors to express the inexpressible; it pants to utter the unutterable. The person writing these words evidently feels a great deal more than any language can possibly convey to us. The spouse begins somewhat calmly in her description: "My beloved is white and ruddy." She proceeds with due order, commencing at the head, and proceeding with the divers parts of the person of the Beloved but she warms, she glows, she flames, and at last the heat which had for awhile been repressed is like fire within her bones, and she bursts forth in flaming words. Here is the live coal from off the altar of her heart: "Yea, he is altogether lovely." It is the utterance of a soul that is altogether overcome with admiration, and therefore feels that in attempting to describe the Well-beloved, it has undertaken a task beyond its power. Lost in adoring wonder, the gracious mind desists from description, and cries with rapture, "Yea, he is altogether lovely." It has often been thus with true saints; they have felt the love of Jesus to be overpowering and inebriating. Believers are not always cool and calm in their thoughts towards their Lord: there are seasons with them when they pass into a state of rapture, their hearts burn within them, they are in ecstacy, they mount up with wings as eagles, their souls become like the chariots of Amminadib, they feel what they could not tell, they experience what they could not express though the tongues of men and of angels were perfectly at their command. Favored believers are altogether enraptured with the sight they have of their all-beauteous Lord. It is to be feared that such raptures are not frequent with all Christians, though I should gravely question his saintship, who has never experienced any degree of holy rapture: but there are some saints to whom a state of overwhelming adoration of their Lord has been by no means an unusual thing. Communion with Jesus has not only entranced them now and then, but it has perfumed all their life with holiness; and if it has not caused their faces literally to shine like the face of Moses, it has made the spiritual glory to flash from their countenances, and elevated them among their fellow Christians to be leaders of the host of God, whereat others have admired and wondered. Peradventure, I speak to children of God who know very little of what I mean by the overwhelming emotions created by a sight of our Lord; they have not so seen the Lord as to have felt their souls melting within them while the Beloved spake with them; to such I shall speak with sorrowful sympathy, being, alas! too much like unto them, but my prayer shall go up all the while, "Lord, reveal thyself to us, that we also may be compelled to say, Yea, he is altogether lovely.' Show us thy hands and thy side till we exclaim with Thomas, My Lord and my God.'"

Shall I tell you why it is, my brethren, that many of you but seldom enjoy the exceeding bliss of Jesus' presence? The cause may lie partly in what is, alas! too common among Christians, a great degree of ignorance of the person of the Lord Jesus. Every soul that sees Jesus by faith is saved thereby. If I look to Christ with a bleared eye, that is ever so weak and clouded with tears, and if I only catch a glimpse of him through clouds and mists, yet the sight saves me. But who will remain content with such a poor gleam of his glory as that? Who wishes to see only "through a glass, darkly"? No, let my eyes be cleansed till they become as doves by the rivers of waters, and I can see my Lord as he is seen by his bosom friends, and can sing of those beauties which are the light and crown of heaven itself. If you do but touch the hem of Jesus' garment, you shall be made whole; but will this always satisfy you? Will you not desire to get beyond the hem and beyond the garment, to himself, and to his heart, and there for ever take up your abode? Who desires to be for ever a babe in grace, with a half-awakened dreamy twilight consciousness by the Redeemer? Brethren, be diligent in the school of the cross, therein is enduring wisdom. Study your Savior much. The science of Christ crucified is the most excellent of sciences; and to know him and the power of his resurrection, is to know that which is best worth knowing. Ignorance of Jesus deprives many saints of those divine raptures which carry others out of themselves, therefore let us be among those children of Zion who are taught of the Lord.

Next to this you shall find the want of meditation to be a very serious robber of the wealth of renewed hearts. To believe a thing is, as it were, to see the cool crystal sparkling in the cup; but to meditate upon it is to drink thereof. Reading gathers the clusters, contemplation squeezes forth their generous juice. Meditation is of all things the most soul-fattening when combined with prayer. The spouse had meditated much in this chapter, for otherwise she had not been able to speak in detail concerning her Lord. O saintly hearts, imitate ye her example! Think, my brethren, of our Lord Jesus: he is God, the Eternal, the Infinite, the ever blessed; yet he became man for us--man of the substance of his mother, like ourselves. Meditate upon his spotless character; review the sufferings which he endured on Calvary; follow him into the grave, and from the grave to the resurrection, and from the resurrection up the starry way to his triumphant throne. Let your souls dwell upon each of his offices, as prophet, priest, and king; pore over each one of his characters, and every scriptural title; pause and consider every phase of him, and when you have done this, begin again and yet again. It is good to chew the cud by meditation, then shall the sweetness and fatness of divine truth come to your soul, and you shall burst forth with such rapturous expressions as that of the text, "Yea, he is altogether lovely." The most of you are too busy, you have too much to do in the world; but; what is it all about? Scraping together dust, loading yourselves with thick clay. O that you were busy after the true riches, and could step aside awhile to enrich yourselves in solitude, and make your hearts vigorous by feeding upon the person and work of your ever blessed Lord! You miss a heaven below by a too eager pursuit of earth. You cannot know these joyful raptures if meditation be pushed into a corner.

Another reason why little of the Lord's beauty is discerned, is the low state of the spiritual life in many a Christian. Many a believer is just alive and no more. Do you not know such starveling souls? May you not be one such yourself! His eyes are not delighted with the beauties of Christ, he is purblind, and cannot see afar off; he walks not with Jesus in the garden of pomegranates, he is too feeble to rise from the couch of weakness; he cannot feed upon Christ, his appetite is gone--sure sign of terrible decline. For him there are no climbings to the top of Amana, no leaping for joy in the temple, no dancing before the ark with David; no, if he be but carried to the feet of Jesus in an ambulance as a sick man borne of four, it is as much as he has yet received. To be strong in the Lord, and in the power of his might, to have the wings of eagles with which to mount above the clouds of earth, to this many are strangers. But beloved, there are noble spirits and better taught, who know something of the life of heaven even while here below. The Lord strengthen us with grace in our inner man, and then shall we drink deeper draughts of the wines on the lees well refined, and then also our eyes being open, we shall see Jesus more clearly, and bear fuller witness that he is "fairer than the children of men."

I am afraid that the visits of Christ to our souls have been disesteemed, and the loss of those visits has not caused us corresponding sorrow. We did not sufficiently delight in the beauty of the Bridegroom when he did come to us; when our hearts were somewhat lifted up with his love we grew cold and idle and then he withdrew his conscious presence; but, alas! we were not grieved, but we wickedly tried to live without him. It is wretched work for a believer to try and live without his Savior. Perhaps, dear brethren, some of you have tried it until at last you have almost succeeded. You were wont to mourn like doves if you had no word from your Master in the morning, and without a love-token before you went to rest you tossed uneasily upon your bed; but now you are carnal and worldly, and careless, and quite content to have it so. Jesus hides his face, the sun is set, and yet it is not night with you. O may God be pleased to arouse you from this lethargy, and make you mourn your sad estate! Even if an affliction should be needful to bring you back from your backsliding it would be a cheap price to pay. Awake, O north wind, with all thy cutting force, if thy bleak breath may but stir the lethargic heart! May the Lord grant us grace so to love Christ that if we have not our fill of him, we may be ready to die with hungering and thirsting after him. May we never be able to find a place to build our nest upon while our wing wanders away from the tree of life. Like the dove of Noah, may we drop into the water and be drowned sooner than find rest for the sole of our foot except upon the ark, Christ Jesus, our Savior.

Beloved, if none of these suggestions should hit the mark, and reveal the cause why so little is known of rapturous love to Christ, let me suggest another. Very often professors' hearts are vain and frivolous; they are taken up during the week with their business. This might plead some excuse; but when they have little spaces and intervals these are filled up with very vanity. Now, if the soul has come to look at the mere trifles of this world as all-important, is it any marvel that it should be unable to perceive the exceeding preciousness of Christ Jesus? Who will care for the wheat when he dotes on the chaff? And with this it will often happen that the professor's mind has grown proud as well as vain; he does not remember his natural poverty and meanness, and consequently does not value the riches of Christ Jesus. He has come to think himself an established, experienced Christian; he fancies that he is not like those foolish beginners who are so volatile and so readily led astray; he has acquired the wisdom of years and the stability of experience. O soul, if thou art great, Christ will be little; thou canst never see him on the throne until thou hast been on the dunghill thyself. If thou be anything, so much the less is Christ; for if he be all in all, then there is no room for anything else and if thou be something, thou hast stolen just so much from the glory of thy Lord Jesus. Lie low in the dust, it is the place for thee.

"The more thy glories strike my eyes,
The humbler I shall lie."

The humbler I am in myself, the more shall I be capable of seeing the enchanting beauties of Christ.

Let me just say these two or three words. I believe those are the happiest saints who are most overwhelmed with a sense of the greatness, goodness, and preciousness of Christ. I believe these to be the most useful saints, also, and to be in the Christian church as a tower of strength. I pray that you and I, walking with God by faith, may nevertheless often have our festival days, our notable seasons, when he shall specially bless us with the kisses of his love, and we shall drink larger draughts of his love, which is better than wine. Oh! to be carried right away with the divine manifestation of the chief among ten thousand, so that our souls shall cry out in rapture, "Yea, he is altogether lovely." This is one characteristic of the text: may it be transferred to us.

2. A second is this, and very manifest it is upon the surface of the verse--here is undivided affection. "He is altogether lovely." Note that these words have a world of meaning in them, but chiefly they tell us this, that Jesus is to the true saint the only lovely one in the world. "He is altogether lovely;" then there is no loveliness anywhere else. It is as though the spouse felt that Christ had engrossed all the beauty and all the loveworthiness in the entire universe. Who among us will say that she erred? Is not Jesus worthy of all the admiration and love of all intelligent beings? But may we not love our friends and kinsfolk? Ay but in him, and in subservience to him; so, and so only, is it safe to love them. Did not our Lord himself say, "If any man love father or mother more than me, he is not worthy of me"? Yea, and in another place he put it more strongly still, for he said, "Except a man hate father and mother," or love them not at all in comparison with me, "he is not worthy of me." Except these are put on a lower stage than Jesus is we cannot be his disciples. Christ must be monarch in the breast; our dear ones may sit at his footstool, and we may love them for his sake, but he alone must fill the throne of our hearts. I may see excellences in my Christian brethren, but I must not forget that there would be none in them if they were not derived from him; that their loveliness is only a part of his loveliness, for he wrought it in them by his own Spirit. I am to acknowledge that Jesus is the monopoliser of all loveliness, the engrosser of all that is admirable in the entire universe; and I am, therefore, to give him all my love, for "he is altogether lovely."

Our text means, again, that in Jesus loveliness of all kinds is to be found. If there be anything that is worthy of the love of an immortal spirit, it is to be seen in abundance in the Lord Jesus. Whatsoever things are true, whatsoever things are honest, whatsoever things are just, whatsoever things are pure, whatsoever things are lovely, whatsoever things are of good report; if there be any virtue, and if there be any praise, all can be found without measure in Christ Jesus. As all the rivers meet in the sea, so all beauties unite in the Redeemer. Take the character of any gracious man, and you shall find a measure of loveliness, but it has its bounds and its mixtures. Peter has many virtues, but he has not a few failings. John, too, excels, but in certain points he is deficient; but herein our Lord transcends all his saints, for all human virtues, all divine, are harmoniously blended in him. He is not this flower or that, but he is the Paradise of perfection. He is not a star here or a constellation there, he is the whole heaven of stars, nay, he is the heaven of heavens; he is all that is fair and lovely condensed in one.

When the text says again that Jesus "is altogether lovely," it declares that he is lovely in all views of him. It generally happens that to the noblest building there is an unhappy point of view from which the architecture appears at a disadvantage; the choicest piece of workmanship may not be equally complete in all directions; the best human character is deformed by one flaw, if not with more; but with our Lord all is lovely, regard him as you will. You shall contemplate him from all points, and only find new confirmation of the statement that "he is altogether lovely." As the everlasting God before the world was made, angels loved him and adored; as the babe at Bethlehem or as the man at Bethany; as walking the sea or as nailed to the cross; in his grave, dead, and buried, or on his throne triumphant; rising as forerunner, or descending a second time to judge the world in righteousness; in his shame, despised and spit upon, or in his glory, adored and beloved; with the thorns about his brow and the nails piercing his hands, or with the keys of death and hell swinging at his girdle; view him as you will, and where you will, and when you will, "he is altogether lovely." Under all aspects, and in all offices and in relations, at all times and all seasons, under all circumstances and conditions, anywhere, everywhere, "he is altogether lovely."

Nor is he in any degree unlovely; the commendation forbids the idea it he be "altogether lovely," where could you find room for deformity? When Apelles painted Alexander, he laid the monarch's finger on an unsightly scar; but there are no scars to conceal when you pourtray the countenance of Immanuel. We say of our country--and who among us will not say it?--"With all her faults we love her still;" but we love Jesus, and find no strain put upon our heart, for trace of fault he has none. There is no need of apologies for Jesus, no excuses are required for him. But what is that I see upon his shoulder? It is a hard rough cross; and if I follow him I must carry that cross for his sake. Is not that cross unsightly? Oh, no! he is altogether lovely, cross and all. Whatever it may involve to be a Christian, we count even the reproach of Christ to be greater riches than the treasures of Egypt. The world will honor a half Christ, but a whole Christ it will not acknowledge. The bat's-eyed Socinian saith, "I admire the man Christ, but I will not adore Jesus the God." To him the eternal word is but half lovely, if lovely at all. Some will have Christ the exemplar, but they will not accept him as the vicarious sacrifice for sin, the substitute for sinners. Many will have Christ in silver slippers--my lord archbishop's religion--but they would not listen to the gospel from a poor gracious Methodist, or think it worth their while to join the unlettered throng whose devout songs rise from the village green. Alas! how much we see of crosses of gold and ivory, but how little do men love the lowly cross of Jesus! Brethren, we think Jesus "altogether lovely" even in poverty, or when hanging naked on the cross, deserted and condemned. We see unspeakable beauty in Jesus in the grave, all fair with the pallor of death. Jesus bruised as to his heel by the old serpent is yet comely. His love to us makes him evermore "white and ruddy" to our eye. We adore him anywhere and everywhere, and in any place, for we know that this same Christ whose heel is bruised breaks also the serpent's head, and he who was naked for our sakes, is now arrayed in glory. We know that the despised and rejected is also King of kings, and Lord of lords, the "Wonderful, Counsellor, The Mighty God, The Everlasting Father. The Prince of Peace." "Yea, he is altogether lovely." There are no flaws in him.

The text intends us to know that Jesus is lovely in the highest degree: not lovely positively and then failing comparatively, but lovely superlatively, in the highest possible sense. But I leave this for your hearts to enlarge upon. I will close this point by saying, every child of God acknowledges that Christ Jesus is lovely altogether to the whole of himself. He is lovely to my judgment; but many things are so, and yet are not lovely to my affections; I know them to be right, and yet they are not pleasant: but Jesus is as lovely to my heart as to my head, as dear as he is good. He is lovely to my hopes: are they not all in him? Is not this my expectation--to see him as he is? But he is lovely to my memory too: did he not pluck me out of the net? Lovely to all my powers and all my passions, my faculties and feelings. As David puts it, "My heart and my flesh crieth out for the living God"--the whole of the man seeking after the whole of the Savior; the whole Savior sweet and inexpressibly precious to the man's entire being. May it be so with you and with me. But is it so? Do you not set up idols in your hearts? Men of God, do you not need to take the scourge of small cords, and purge the temple of your souls this morning? Are there not; buyers and sellers where Christ alone ought to be? Oh, to love him wholly, and to love him only, so that we have no eyes for other beauty, no heart for other loveliness since he fills our souls, and is to us "altogether lovely."

3. The third characteristic of the text is that to which I desire to draw the most attention, and that is ardent devotion. I called the text a live coal from off the altar and surely it is so. If it should drop into our hearts to set them on a blaze, it would be an unspeakable mercy. Ardent devotion flames from this sentence. It is the language of one who feels that no emotion is too deep when Jesus moves the heart. Do any chide you and say you think too much of your religion? It cannot be, it cannot be. If the zeal of God's house should eat us up until we had no existence except for the Lord's glory, we should not have gone too far. If there be corresponding knowledge to balance it, there cannot be too much of zeal for God. The utterance is that of one whose heart is like a furnace, of which love is the fire. "He is altogether lovely"--it is the exclamation of one who feels that no language is too strong to commend the Lord. The spouse looked through the Hebrew tongue to find an intense expression, and our translators ransacked the English language for a forcible word, and they have put it in the most weighty way--"He is altogether lovely." There is no fear of

exaggeration when you speak of Christ; hyperboles are only sober truth when we depict his excellences. We have heard of a portrait painter who owed his popularity to the fact that he never painted truthfully, but always gave a flatteringly touch or two; here is one who would defy his art, for it is impossible to flatter Jesus. Lay on, ye men of eloquence, spare no colors, ye shall never depict him too bravely. Bring forth your harps, ye seraphs; sing aloud, ye blood-washed ones; all your praises fall short of the glory which is due to him.

It is the language of one who feels that no service would be too great to render to the Lord. I wish we felt as the apostles and martyrs and holy men of old did, that Jesus Christ ought to be served at the highest and richest rate. We do little, very little: what if I had said we do next to nothing for our dear Lord and Master nowadays? The love of Christ doth not constrain us as it should. But those of old bore poverty and dared reproach, marched weary leagues, passed tempestuous seas, bore perils of robbers and of cruel men, to plant the cross in lands where as yet Jesus was not known; labors that nowadays could not be expected of men, were performed as daily matters of commonplace by the Christians of the earliest times. Is Christ less lovely, or is his church less loyal? Would God she estimated him at his right rate, for then she would return to her former mode of service. Brethren, we want to feel, and we shall feel if this text is deeply engraven on our hearts, that no gift is too great for Christ, though we give him all we have, and consecrate to him all our time and ability, and sacrifice our very lives to him. No suffering is too great to bear for the sake of the Crucified, and it is a great joy to be reproached for Christ's sake. "He is altogether lovely." Then, my soul, I charge thee think nothing hard to which he calls thee, nothing sharp which he bids thee endure. As the knight of the olden time consecrated himself to the Crusade, and wore the red cross on his arm, fearing not to meet death at the hands of the Infidel, if he might be thought a soldier of the Lord, so we too would face all foes for Jesus' sake. We want, only refined and purified, and delivered from its earthly grossness, we want the chivalrous spirit once again in the church of God. A new crusade fain would I preach: had I the tongue of such a one as the old hermit to move all Christendom, I would say, "This day Christ, the altogether lovely one, is dishonored: can ye endure it? This day idols stand where he should be and men adore them; lovers of Jesus, can ye brook it? This day Juggernaut rides through the streets on his bloody way, this day God's Christ is still unknown to millions, and the precious blood cleanses not the nations, how long will ye have it so? We, in England, with ten thousand Christian hearts, and as many tongues endowed with eloquence, and purses weighted with gold, shall we refuse our gifts, withhold our witness, and suffer the Lord to be dishonored? The church is doing next to nothing for her great Lord, she falls short both of her duty and of the grim need of a perishing world. O for a flash of the celestial fire! Oh, when shall the Spirit's energy visit us again! When shall men put down their selfishness and seek only Christ? When shall they leave their strifes about trifles to rally round his cross! When shall we end the glorification of ourselves, and begin to make him glorious, even to the world's end? God help us in this matter, and kindle in our hearts the old consuming heart-inflaming fire, which shall make men see that Jesus is all in all to us.

II. Thus I have shown you the characteristics of the text, and now I desire to USE IT IN THREE WAYS FOR PRACTICAL PURPOSES. As time flies, we must use it briefly.

The first word is to you, Christians. Here is very sweet instruction. The Lord Jesus "is altogether lovely." Then if I want to be lovely, I must be like him, and the model for me as a Christian is Christ. Have you ever noticed how badly boys write at the bottom of the pages in their copy-books? There is the copy at the top; and in the first line they look at that; in the second line, they copy their own imitation; in the third line, they copy their imitation of their imitation, and so the writing grows worse and worse as it descends the page. Now, the apostles followed Christ; the first fathers imitated the apostles; the next fathers copied the first fathers, and so the standard of holiness fell dreadfully; and now we are too apt to follow the very lees and dregs of Christianity, and we think if we are about as good as our poor, imperfect ministers or leaders in the church, that we shall do well and deserve praise. But now, my brethren, cover up the mere copies and imitations, and live by the first line. Copy Jesus; "he is altogether lovely;" and if you can write by the first line, you will write by the truest and best model in the world. We want to have Christ's zeal, but we must balance it with his prudence and discretion we must seek to have Christ's love to God, and we must feel his love to men, his forgiveness of injury, his gentleness of speech, his incorruptible truthfulness, his meekness and lowliness, his utter unselfishness, his entire consecration to his Father's business. O that we had all this, for depend upon it whatever other pattern we select, we have made a mistake; we are not following the true classic model of the Christian artist. Our master model is the "altogether lovely" one. How sweet it is to think of our Lord in the double aspect as our exemplar and our Savior! The laver which stood in the temple was made of brass: in this the priests washed their feet whenever they offered sacrifices; so does Christ purify us from sin; but the tradition is that this laver was made of very bright brass, and acted as a mirror, so that as often as the priests came to it they could see their own spots in it. Oh, when I come to my Lord Jesus, not only do I get rid of my sins as to their guilt, but I see my spots in the light of his perfect character, and I am humbled and taught to follow after holiness.

The second use to which we would put the verse is this, here is a very gentle rebuke to some of you. Though very gentle, I beseech you to let it sink deep into your hearts. You do not see the lowliness of Christ, yet "he is altogether lovely." Now, I will not say one hard word! but I will tell you sorrowfully what pitiable creatures you are. I hear enchanting music, which seems more a thing of heaven than of earth: it is one of Handel's half-inspired oratorios. Yonder sits a man, who says, "I hear nothing to commend." He has not the power to perceive the linked sweetnesses, the delicious harmonies of sounds. Do you blame him? No, but you who have an ear for music, say, "How I pity him: he misses half the joy of life!" Here, again, is a glorious landscape, hills and valleys, and flowing rivers, expansive lakes and undulating meadows. I bring to the point of view a friend, whom I would gratify, and I say to him, "Is not that a charming scene?" Turning his head to me, he says, "I see nothing." I perceive that he cannot enjoy what is so delightful to me; he has some little sight, but he sees only what is very near, and he is blind to all beyond. Now, do I blame him? Or if he proceed to argue with me, and say, "You are very foolish to be so enthusiastic about a non-existent landscape, it is merely your excitement," shall I argue with him? Shall I be angry until him? No, but I shed a tear, and whisper to myself, "Great are the losses of the blind." Now, you who have never heard music in the name of Jesus, you are to be greatly pitied, for your loss is heavy. You who never saw beauty in Jesus, and who never will for ever, you need all our tears. It is hell enough not to love Christ! It is the lowest abyss of Tartarus, and its fiercest flame, not to be enamoured of the Christ of God. There is no heaven that is more heaven than to love Christ and to be like him, and there is no hell that is more hell than to be unlike Christ and not to want to be like him, but even to be averse to the infinite perfections of the "altogether lovely." The Lord open those blind eyes of yours, and unstop those deaf ears, and give you the new and spiritual life, and then will you join in saying, "Yea, he is altogether lovely."

The last use of the text is, that of tender attractiveness. "Yea, he is altogether lovely." Where are you this morning, you who are convinced of sin and want a Savior, where have you crept to? Are you hidden away where my eyes cannot reach you? At any rate, let this sweet thought reach you. You need not be afraid to come to Jesus, for "he is altogether lovely." It does not say he is altogether terrible--that is your misconception of him; it does not say he is somewhat lovely, and sometimes willing to receive a certain sort of sinner; but "he is altogether lovely," and therefore he is always ready to welcome to himself the vilest of the vile. Think of his name. It is Jesus, the Savior. Is not this lovely? Think of his work. He is come to seek and to save that which was lost. This is his occupation. Is not that lovely? Think of what he has done. He hath redeemed our souls with blood. Is not that lovely? Think of what he is doing. He is pleading before the throne of God for sinners. Think of what he is giving at this moment--he is exalted on high to give repentance and remission of sins. Is not this lovely? Under every aspect Christ Jesus is attractive to sinners who need him. Come, then, come and welcome, there is nothing to keep you away, there is everything to bid you come. May this very Sabbath day in which I have preached Christ, and lifted him up, be the day in which you shall be drawn to him, never again to leave him, but to be his for ever and for ever. Amen.

PORTION OF SCRIPTURE READ BEFORE SERMON--Solomon's Song 5.

MR. SPURGEON begs earnestly to thank a friend, who desires to be anonymous, for £500 towards buildings for the Pastors' College, to commemorate the thousandth Sermon, as also Mr. Thomas Ness for £10, and a Sermon-reader for a guinea. This last donor believes that at least a thousand readers might send a guinea each at once, to celebrate the occasion, and to aid in erecting rooms in which preachers would be trained, whose theme would be the gospel of Jesus. Mr. Spurgeon is thankful for the timely aid. Some £3,000 more will probably be required for the buildings.

Now, and Then

A Sermon (No. 1002)
Delivered by
C. H. SPURGEON,
At the Metropolitan Tabernacle, Newington

"For now we see through a glass, darkly; but then face to face." - 1 Corinthians 13:12.

IN THIS CHAPTER the apostle Paul has spoken in the highest terms of charity or love. He accounts it to be a grace far more excellent than any of the spiritual gifts of which he had just before been speaking. It is easy to see that there were good reasons for the preference he gave to it. Those gifts you will observe, were distributed among godly men, to every man his several portion, so that what one had another might have lacked; but this grace belongs to all who have passed from death unto life. The proof that they are disciples of Christ is found in their love to him and to the brethren. Those gifts, again, were meant to fit them for service, that each member of the body should be profitable to the other members of the body; but this grace is of personal account: it is a light in the heart and a star on the breast of every one who possesses it. Those gifts, moreover, were of temporary use: their value was limited to the sphere in which they were exercised; but this grace thrives at all times and in all places, and it is no less essential to our eternal future state than it is to our present welfare. By all means covet the best gifts, my dear brother, as an artist would wish to be deft with all his limbs and quick with all his senses; but above all, cherish love, as that same artist would cultivate the pure taste which lives and breathes within him--the secret spring of all his motions, the faculty that prompts his skill. Learn to esteem this sacred instinct of love beyond all the choicest endowments. However poor you may be in talents, let the love of Christ dwell in you richly. Such an exhortation as this is the more needful, because love has a powerful rival. Paul may have noticed that in the academies of Greece, as indeed in all our modern schools, knowledge was wont to take all the prizes. Who can tell how much of Dr. Arnold's success, as a schoolmaster, was due to the honor in which he held a good boy in preference to a clever boy? Most certainly Paul could discern in the church many jealousies to which the superior abilities of those who could speak foreign tongues, and those who could prophecy or preach well, gave rise. So, then, while he extols the grace of love, he seems rather to disparage knowledge; at least, he uses an illustration which tends to show that the kind of knowledge we pride ourselves in, is not the most reliable thing in the world. Paul remembered that he was once a child. A very good thing for any of us to bear in mind. If we forget it, our sympathies are soon dried up, our temper is apt to get churlish, our opinions may be rather overbearing, and our selfishness very repulsive. The foremost man of his day in the Christian church, and exerting the widest influence among the converts to Christ, Paul thought of the little while ago when he was a young child, and he thought of it very opportunely too. Though he might have hinted at the attainments he had made or the high office he held, and laid claim to some degree of respect, he rather looks back at his humble beginnings. If there is wisdom in his reflection, there is to my mind a vein of pleasantry in his manner of expressing it. "When I was a child I spake as a child, I understood as a child, I thought as a child: but when I became a man, I put away childish things." Thus he compares two stages of his natural life, and it serves him for a parable. In spiritual knowledge he felt himself to be then in his infancy. His maturity, his thorough manhood, lay before him in prospect. He could easily imagine a future in which he should look back on his present self as a mere tyro, groping his way amidst the shadows of his own fancy. "For now," he says, "we see through a glass, darkly; but then face to face: now I know in part; but then shall I know even as also I am known." Here he employs one or two fresh figures. "Through a glass!" What kind of a glass he alluded to, we may not be able exactly to determine. Well; we will leave that question for the critics to disagree about. It is enough for us that the meaning is obvious. There is all the difference between viewing an object through an obscure medium, and closely inspecting it with the naked eye. We must have the power of vision in either case, but in the latter case we can use it to more advantage. "Now we see through a glass, darkly." Darkly--in a riddle! So weak are our perceptions of mind, that plain truths often puzzle us. The words that teach us are pictures which need explanation. The thoughts that stir us are visions which coat in our brains and want rectifying. Oh, for clearer vision! Oh, for more perfect knowledge! Mark you, brethren, it is a matter of congratulation that we do see; though we have much cause for diffidence, because we do but "see through a glass, darkly." Thank God we do know; but let it cheek our conceit, We know only in part. Beloved, the objects we look at are distant, and we are near-sighted. The revelation of God is ample and profound, but our understanding is weak and shallow.

There are some things which we count very precious now, which will soon be of no value to us whatever. There are some things that we know or think we know, and we pride ourselves a good deal upon our knowledge; but when we shall become men we shall set no more value upon that knowledge than a child does upon his toys when he grows up to be a man. Our spiritual manhood in heaven will discard many things which we now count precious, as a full grown man discards the treasures of his childhood. And there are many things that we have been accustomed to see that, after this transient life has passed, we shall see no more. Though we delighted in them, and they pleased our eyes while sojourning on earth, they will pass away as a dream when one awaketh; we shall never see them again, and never want to see them; for our eyes in clearer light, anointed with eye-salve, shall see brighter visions, and we shall never regret what we have lost, in the presence of fairer scenes we shall have found. Other things there are that we know now and shall never forget; we shall know them for ever, only in a higher degree, because no longer with a partial knowledge; and there are some things that we see now that we shall see in eternity, only we shall see them there in a clearer light.

So we shall speak upon some things that we do see now, which we are to see more fully and more distinctly hereafter; then enquire how it is we shall see them more clearly; and finish up by considering what this fact teaches us.

I. Among the things that we see now, as many of us as have had our eyes enlightened by the Holy Spirit, is OURSELVES.

To see ourselves is one of the first steps in true religion. The mass of men have never seen themselves. They have seen the flattering image of themselves, and they fancy that to be their own facsimile, but it is not. You and I have been taught of God's Holy Spirit to see our ruin in the fall; we have bemoaned ourselves on account of that fall; we have been made conscious of our own natural depravity; we have been ground to the very dust by the discovery; we have been shown our actual sinfulness and how we have transgressed against the Most High. We have repented for this, and have fled for refuge to the hope set before us in the gospel. Day by day we see a little more of ourselves--nothing very pleasing, I grant you--but something very profitable, for it is a great thing for us to know our emptiness. It is a step towards receiving his fullness. It is something to discover our weakness; it is a step essential towards our participation of divine strength. I suppose the longer we live the more we shall see ourselves; and we shall probably come to this conclusion: "Vanity of vanities; all is vanity:" and cry out with Job, "I am vile." The more we shall discover of ourselves, the more we shall be sick of ourselves. But in heaven, I doubt not, we shall find out that we never saw even ourselves in the clearest light, but only as "through a glass, darkly," only as an unriddled thing, as a deep enigma; for we shall understand more about ourselves in heaven than we do now. There we shall see, as we have not yet seen, how desperate a mischief was the Fall, into what a horrible pit we fell, and how fast we were stuck in the miry clay. There shall we see the blackness of sin as we have never seen it here, and understand its hell desert as we could not till we shall look down from yonder starry height whither infinite mercy shall bring us. When we shall be singing, "Worthy is the Lamb that was slain," we shall look at the robes that we have washed in his blood, and see how white they are. We shall better understand then than now how much we needed washing--how crimson were the stains and how precious was that blood that effaced those scarlet spots. There, too, shall we know ourselves on the bright side better than we do now. We know to-day that we are saved, and there is therefore now no condemnation to them that are in Christ Jesus; but that robe of righteousness which covers us now, as it shall cover us then, will be better seen by us, and we shall discern how lustrous it is, with its needlework and wrought gold--how much better than the pearls and gems that have decked the robes of monarchs are the blood and righteousness of Jehovah Jesus, who has given himself for us. Here we know that we are adopted. We feel the spirit of sonship; "we cry, Abba, Father;" but there we shall know better what it is to be the sons of God, for here it doth not yet appear what we shall be; but when we shall be there, and when Christ shall appear, we shall be like him, for we shall see him as he is, and then we shall understand to the full what sonship means. So, too, I know to-day that I am a joint-heir with Christ, but I have a very poor idea of what it is I am heir to; but there shall I see the estates that belong to me; not only see them, but actually enjoy them. A part shall every Christian have in the inheritance undefiled and that fadeth not away, that is reserved in heaven for him, because he is in Christ Jesus; one with Christ--by eternal union one. But I am afraid that is very much more a riddle to us than a matter of understanding. We see it as an enigma now, but there our oneness with Christ will be as conspicuous to us and as plain as the letters of the alphabet. There shall we know what it is to be a member of his body, of his flesh, and of his bones; there shall I understand the mystical marriage bond that knits the believer's soul to Christ; there shall I see how, as the branch springs from the stem, my soul stands in union, vital union, with her blessed Lord Jesus Christ. Thus, one thing that we see now which we shall see in a much clearer light hereafter, is "ourselves."

Here, too, we see the CHURCH, but WE SHALL SEE THE CHURCH MUCH MORE CLEARLY BY-AND-BY.

We know there is a church of God. We know that the Lord has a people whom he hath chosen from before the foundation of the world: we believe that these are scattered up and down throughout our land, and many other lands. There are many of them we do not know, many that we should not particularly like, I daresay if we did know them, on account of their outward characteristics; persons of very strange views, and very odd habits perhaps; and yet, for all that, the people of the living God; Now, we know this church, we know its glory, moved with one life, quickened with one Spirit, redeemed with one blood, we believe in this church, and we feel attachment to it for the sake of Jesus Christ, who has married the church as the Bride. But, oh! when we shall get to heaven, how much more we shall know of the church, and how we shall see her face to face, and not "through a glass, darkly." There we shall know something, more of the numbers of the chosen than we do now, it may be to our intense surprise. There we shall find some amongst the company of God's elect, whom we in our bitterness of spirit had condemned, and there we shall miss some who, in our charity, we have conceived to be perfectly secure. We shall know better then who are the Lord's and who are not than we ever can know here. Here all our processes of discernment fail us. Judas comes in with the apostles, and Demas takes his part among the saints, but there we shall know the righteous, for we shall see them; there will be one flock and one Shepherd, and he that on the throne doth reign for evermore shall be glorified. We shall understand then, what the history of the church has been in all the past, and why it has become so strange a history of conflict and conquest. Probably, we shall know more of the history of the church in the future. From that higher elevation and brighter atmosphere we shall understand better what are the Lord's designs concerning his people in the latter day; and what glory shall redound to his own name from his redeemed ones, when he shall have gathered together all that are called and chosen and faithful from among the sons of men. This is one of the joys we are looking for, that we shall come to the general assembly and church of the firstborn whose names are written in heaven; and have fellowship with those who have fellowship with God through Jesus Christ our Lord.

Thirdly. Is it not possible, nay, is it not certain, that in the next state WE SHALL KNOW MORE OF THE PROVIDENCE OF GOD THAN WE DO NOW?

Here we see the providence of God, but it is in a glass, darkly. The apostle says "through" a glass. There was glass in the apostles' days, not a substance such as our windows are now made of, but thick dull coloured glass, not much more transparent than that which is used in the manufacture of common bottles, so that looking through a piece of that glass you would not see much. That is like what we now see of divine providence. We believe all things work together for good to them that love God; we have seen how they work together for good in some cases, and experimentally proved it to be so. But still it is rather a matter of faith than a matter of sight with us. We cannot tell how "every dark and bending line meets in the center of his love." We do not yet perceive how he will make those dark dispensations of trials and afflictions that come upon his people really to subserve his glory and their lasting happiness; but up there we shall see providence, as it were, face to face; and I suppose it will be amongst our greatest surprises, the discovery of how the Lord dealt with us. "Why," we shall some of us say, "we prayed against those very circumstances which were the best that, could have been appointed for us." "Ah!" another will say, "I have fretted and troubled myself over what was, after all, the richest mercy the Lord ever sent." Sometimes I have known persons refuse a letter at the door, and it has happened, in some cases, that there has been something very valuable in it, and the postman has said, afterwards, "You did not know the contents, or else you would not have refused it." And often God has sent us, in the black envelope of trial, such a precious mass of mercy, that if we had known what was in it, we should have taken it in, and been glad to pay for it--glad to give it house room, to entertain it; but because it looked black we were prone to shut our door against it. Now, up there we shall know not only more of ourselves, but perceive the reasons of many of God's dealings with us on a larger scale; and we shall there perhaps discover that wars that devasted nations, and pestilences that fill graves, and earthquakes that make cities tremble, are, after all, necessary cogs in the great wheel of the divine machinery; and he who sits upon the throne at this moment, and rules supremely every creature that is either in heaven, or earth, or hell, will there make it manifest to us that his government was right. It is good to think in these times when ever; thing seems loosening, that "the government shall be upon his shoulder: and his name shall be called Wonderful, Counsellor, The mighty God, The everlasting Father, The Prince of Peace." It must come out right in the long run; it must be well; every part and portion must work together with a unity of design to promote God's glory and the saint's good. We shall see it there! and we shall lift up our song with new zest and joy, as fresh displays of the wisdom and goodness of God, whose ways are past finding out, are unfolded to our admiring view.

Fourthly. It is surely no straining of the text to say, that, though here we know something of THE DOCTRINES OF THE GOSPEL, AND THE MYSTERIES OF THE FAITH, by-and-by, in a few months or years at the longest, we shall know a great deal more than we do now. There are some grand doctrines, brethren and sisters, we dearly love, but though we love them, our understanding is too feeble to grasp them fully. We account them to be mysteries; we reverently acknowledge them, yet we dare not attempt to explain them. They are matters of faith to us. It may be that in heaven there shall be counsels of eternal wisdom into which no saints or angels can peer. It is the glory of God to conceal a matter. Surely, no creature will ever be able, even when exalted to heaven, to comprehend all the thoughts of the Creator. We shall never be omniscient--we cannot be. God alone knoweth everything, and understandeth everything. But how much more of authentic truth shall we discern when the mists and shadows have dissolved; and how much more shall we understand when raised to that higher sphere and endowed with brighter faculties, none of us can tell. Probably, things that puzzle us here will be as plain as possible there. We shall perhaps smile at our own ignorance. I have fancied sometimes that the elucidations of learned doctors of divinity, if they could be submitted to the very least in the kingdom of heaven, would only cause them to smile at the learned ignorance of the sons of earth. Oh! how little we do know, but how much we shall know! I am sure we shall know, for it is written, "Then shall I know even as also I have known." We now see things in a mist--"men as trees, walking"--a doctrine here, and a doctrine there. And we are often at a loss to conjecture how one part harmonizes with another part of the same system, or to make out how all these doctrines are consistent. This knot cannot be untied, that gnarl cannot be unravelled, but--

"Then shall I see, and hear and know
All I desired or wish'd below;
And every power find sweet employ
In that eternal world of joy."

But, my dear brethren and sisters, having kept you thus far in the outer courts, I would fain lead you into the temple; or, to change the figure, if in the beginning I have set forth good wine, certainly I am not going to bring out that which is worse; rather would I have you say, as the ruler of the feast did to the bridegroom, "thou has kept the good wine until now." HERE WE SEE JESUS CHRIST, BUT WE DO NOT SEE HIM AS WE SHALL SEE HIM SOON. We have seen him by faith in such a way, that we have beheld our burdens laid on him, and our iniquities carried by him into the wilderness, where, if they be sought for, they shall not be found. We have seen enough of Jesus to know that "he is altogether lovely;" we can say of him, he "is all my salvation, and all my desire." Sometimes, when he throws up the lattice, and shows himself through those windows of agate and gates of carbuncle, in the ordinances of his house, at the Lord's Supper especially, the King's beauty has entranced us even to our heart's ravishment; yet all we have ever seen is somewhat like the report which the Queen of Sheba had of Solomon's wisdom. When we once get to the court of the Great King we shall declare that the half has not been told us. We shall say, "mine eyes shall behold, and not another." Brethren, is not this the very cream of heaven? There have been many suggestions of what we shall do in heaven, and what we shall enjoy, but they all seem to me to be wide of the mark compared with this one, that we shall be with Jesus, be like him, and shall behold his glory. Oh, to see the feet that were nailed, and to touch the hand that was pierced, and to look upon the head that wore the thorns, and to bow before him who is ineffable love, unspeakable condescension, infinite tenderness! Oh, to bow before him, and to kiss that blessed face! Jesu, what better do we want than to see thee by shine own light--to see thee, and speak with thee, as when a man speaketh with his friend? It is pleasant to talk about this, but what will it be there when the pearl gates open? The streets of gold will have small attraction to us, and the harps of angels will but slightly enchant us, compared with the King in the midst of the throne. He it is who shall rivet our gaze, absorb our thoughts, enchain our affection, and move all our sacred passions to their highest pitch of celestial ardor. We shall see Jesus.

Once again (and here we come into the deep things), beyond a doubt WE SHALL ALSO SEE GOD. It is written that the pure in heart shall see God. God is seen now in his works and in his word. Little indeed could these eyes bear of the beatific vision, yet we have reason to expect that, as far as creatures can bear the sight of the infinite Creator, we shall be permitted to see God. We read that Aaron and certain chosen ones saw the throne of God, and the brightness as it were of sapphire stone--light, pure as jasper. In heaven it is the presence of God that is the light thereof. God's more immediately dwelling in the midst of the new Jerusalem is its peerless glory and peculiar bliss. We

shall then understand more of God than we do now; we shall come nearer to him, be more familiar with him, be more filled with him. The love of God shall be shed abroad in our hearts; we shall know our Father as we yet know him not; We shall know the Son to a fuller degree than he has yet revealed himself to us, and we shall know the Holy Spirit in his personal love and tenderness towards us, beyond all those influences and operations which have soothed us in our sorrows and guided us in our perplexities here below. I leave your thoughts and your desires to follow the teaching of the Spirit. As for me, I cower before the thought while I revel in it. I, who have strained my eyes while gazing at nature, where the things that are made show the handiwork of God; I, whose conscience has been awe-struck as I listened to the voice of God proclaiming his holy law; I, whose heart has been melted while there broke on my ears the tender accents of his blessed gospel in those snatches of sacred melody that relieve the burden of prophecy; I, who have recognised in the babe of Bethlehem the hope of Israel; in the man of Nazareth, the Messiah that should come; in the victim of Calvary, the one Mediator; in the risen Jesus, the well-beloved Son--to me, verily, God incarnate has been so palpably revealed that I have almost seen God, for I have, as it were, seen him in whom all the fullness of the Godhead bodily doth dwell. Still I "see through a glass, darkly." Illumine these dark senses, waken this drowsy conscience, purify my heart, give me fellowship with Christ, end thee bear me up, translate me to the third heavens; so I may, so I can, so I shall see God. But what that means, or what it is, ah me! I cannot tell.

II. We proposed to enquire, in the second place, HOW THIS VERY REMARKABLE CHANGE SHALL BE EFFECTED? WHY IS IT THAT WE SHALL BE MORE CLEARLY THEN THAN NOW? We cannot altogether answer the question, but one or two suggestions may help us. No doubt many of these things will be more clearly revealed in the next state. Here the light is like the dawn: it is dim twilight. In heaven it will be the blaze of noon. God has declared somethings of himself by the mouth of his holy prophets and apostles. He has been pleased, through the lips of his Son, whom he hath appointed heir of all things, to speak to us more plainly, to show us more openly the thoughts of his heart and the counsel of his will. These are the first steps to knowledge. But there the light will be as the light of seven days, and there the manifestation of all the treasures of wisdom shall be brighter and clearer than it is now; for God, the only-wise God, shall unveil to us the mysteries, and exhibit to us the glories of his everlasting kingdom. The revelation we now have suits us as men clad in our poor mortal bodies; the revelation then will suit us as immortal spirits. When we have been raised from the dead, it will be suitable to our immortal spiritual bodies. Here, too, we are at a distance from many of the things we long to know something of, but there we shall be nearer to them. We shall then be on a vantage ground, with the entire horizon spread out before us. Our Lord Jesus is, as to his personal presence, far away from us. We see him through the telescope of faith, but then we shall see him face to face. His literal and bodily presence is in heaven, since he was taken up, and we need to be taken up likewise to be with him where he is that we may literally behold him. Get to the fountain-head, and you understand more; stand in the center, and things seem regular and orderly. If you could stand in the sun and see the orbits in which the planets revolve round that central luminary, it would become clear enough; but for many an age astronomers were unable to discover anything of order, and spoke of the planets as progressive, retrograde, and standing still. Let us get to God, the center, and we shall see how providence in order revolves round his sapphire throne. We, ourselves, too, when we get to heaven, shall be better qualified to see than we are now. It would be an inconvenience for us to know here as much as we shall know in heaven. No doubt we have sometimes thought that if we had better ears it would be a great blessing. We have wished we could hear ten miles off; but probably we should be no better off; we might hear too much, and the sounds might drown each other. Probably our sight is not as good as we wish it were, but a large increase of ocular power might not be of any use to us. Our natural organs are fitted for our present sphere of being; and our mental faculties are, in the case of most of us, properly adapted to our moral requirements. If we knew more of our own sinfulness, we might be driven to despair; if we knew more of God's glory, we might die of terror; if we had more understanding, unless we had equivalent capacity to employ it, we might be filled with conceit and tormented with ambition. But up there we shall have our minds and our systems strengthened to receive more, without the damage that would come to us here from overleaping the boundaries of order, supremely appointed and divinely regulated. We cannot here drink the wine of the kingdom, it is too strong for us; but up there we shall drink it new in our heavenly Father's kingdom, without fear of the intoxications of pride, or the staggerings of passions. We shall know even as we are known. Besides, dear friends, the atmosphere of heaven is so much clearer than this, that I do not wonder we can see better there. Here Here is the smoke of daily care; the constant dust of toil; the mist of trouble perpetually rising. We cannot be expected to see much in such a smoky atmosphere as this; but when we shall pass beyond, we shall find no clouds ever gather round the sun to hide his everlasting brightness. There all is clear. The daylight is serene as the noonday. We shall be in a clearer atmosphere and brighter light.

III. The practical lessons we may learn from this subject demand your attention before I close. Methinks there is an appeal to our gratitude. Let us be very thankful for all we do see. Those, who do not see now--ah, not even "through a glass, darkly"--shall never see face to face. The eyes that never see Christ by faith shall never see him with joy in heaven. If thou hast never seen thyself a leper, defiled with sin and abashed with penitence, thou shalt never see thyself redeemed from sin, renewed by grace, a white-robed spirit. If thou hast no sense of God's presence here, constraining thee to worship and love him, thou shalt have no sight of his glory hereafter, introducing thee to the fullness of joy and pleasure for evermore. Oh! be glad for the sight you have, dear brother, dear sister. It is God that gave it to thee. Thou art one born blind; and "Since the world began was it not heard that any man opened the eyes of one that was born blind." This miracle has been wrought on thee; thou canst see, and thou canst say: "One thing I know, that whereas I was blind, now I see."

Our text teaches us that this feeble vision is very hopeful. You shall see better by-and-by. Oh, you know not how soon--it may be a day or two hence--that we shall be in glory! God may so have ordained it, that betwixt us and heaven there may be but a step.

Another lesson is that of forbearance one with another. Let the matters we have spoken of soften the asperity of our debates; let us feel when we are disputing about points of difficulty, that we need not get cross about them, because after all there are limits to our present capacity as well as to our actual knowledge. Our disputes are often childish. We might as well leave some questions in abeyance for a little while. Two persons in the dark have differed about a color, and they are wrangling about it. If we brought candles in and held them to the color, the candles would not show what it was; but if we look at it to-morrow morning, when the sun shines, we shall be able to tell. How many difficulties in the word of God are like this! Not yet can they be justly discriminated; till the day dawn, the apocalyptic symbols will not be all transparent to our own understanding. Besides, we have no time to waste while there is so much work to do. Much time is already spent. Sailing is dangerous; the winds are high; the sea is rough. Trim the ship; keep the sails in good order; manage her and keep her off quicksands. As to certain other matters, we must wait till we get into the fair haven, and are able to talk with some of the bright spirits now before the throne. When some of the things they know shall be opened unto us, we shall confess the mistakes we made, and rejoice in the light we shall receive.

Should not this happy prospect excite our aspiration and make us very desirous to be there? It is natural for us to want to know, but we shall not know as we are known till we are present with the Lord. We are at school now--children at school. We shall go to the college soon--the great University of Heaven--and take our degree there. Yet some of us, instead of being anxious to go, are shuddering at the thought of death--the gate of endless joy we dread to enter! There are many persons who die suddenly; some die in their sleep, and many have passed out of time into eternity when it has scarcely been known by those who have been sitting at their bedsides. Depend upon it, there is no pain in dying; the pain is in living. When they leave off living here, they have done with pain. Do not blame death for what it does not deserve; it is life that lingers on in pain: death is the end of it. The man that is afraid of dying ought to be afraid of living. Be content to die whenever the Master's will shall bid thee. Commit thy spirit to his keeping. Who that hath seen but the glimpses of his beaming countenance doth not long to see his face, that is as the sun shining in his strength? O Lord! thy will be done. Let us speedily behold thee, if so it may be--only this one word, if so it may be. Do we now see, and do we expect to see better? Let us bless the name of the Lord, who hath chosen us of his mercy and of his infinite lovingkindness. On the other hand, let it cause us great anxiety if we have not believed in Jesus, for he that hath not believed in him, dying as he is, will never see the face of God with joy. Oh! unbeliever, be concerned about your soul, and seek thou after him, repair thou to him. Oh! that God would open thy eyes now in this very house of prayer. Blessed for thee to know in part. Thrice blessed, I say; for as surely as thou knowest in part now, thou shalt fully know hereafter. Be it your happy lot to know him, whom to know is life eternal. God grant it, for Jesus' sake. Amen.

PORTION OF SCRIPTURE READ BEFORE SERMON--2 Corinthians 5.

Your Own Salvation

A Sermon (No. 1003)
Delivered on Lord's-day Morning, July 30th, 1871, by
C. H. SPURGEON,
At the Metropolitan Tabernacle, Newington

"Your own salvation." - Philippians 2:12.

WE SELECT THE WORDS, "your own salvation," as our text this morning, not out of any singularity, or from the slightest wish that the brevity of the text should surprise you; but because our subject will be the more clearly before you if only these three words are announced. If I had nominally taken the whole verse I could not have attempted to expound it without distracting your attention from the topic which now weighs upon my heart. O that the divine Spirit may bring home to each one of your minds the unspeakable importance of "your own salvation"!

We have heard it said by hearers that they come to listen to us, and we talk to them upon subjects in which they have no interest. You will not be able to make this complaint to-day, for we shall speak only of "your own salvation;" and nothing can more concern you. It has sometimes been said that preachers frequently select very unpractical themes. No such objection can be raised to-day, for nothing can be more practical than this; nothing more needful than to urge you to see to "your own salvation." We have even heard it said that ministers delight in abstruse subjects, paradoxical dogmas, and mysterious surpassing comprehension; but, assuredly, we will keep to plain sailing this morning. No sublime doctrines, no profound questions shall perplex you; you shall only be called on to consider "your own salvation:" a very homely theme, and a very simple one, but for all that, the most weighty that can be brought before you. I shall seek after simple words also, and plain sentences, to suit the simplicity and plainness of the subject, that there may be no thought whatever about the speaker's language, but only concerning this one, sole, only topic, "your own salvation." I ask you all, as reasonable men who would not injure or neglect yourselves, to lend me your most serious attention. Chase away the swarming vanities which buzz around you, and let each man think for himself upon his "own salvation." O may the Spirit of God set each one of you apart in a mental solitude, and constrain you each one, singly, to face the truth concerning his own state! Each man apart, each woman apart; the father apart, and the child apart: may you now come before the Lord in solemn thought, and may nothing occupy your attention but this: "your own salvation."

I. We will begin this morning's meditation by noting THE MATTER UNDER CONSIDERATION--Salvation!

Salvation! a great word, not always understood, often narrowed down, and its very marrow overlooked. Salvation! This concerns every one here present. We all fell in our first parent; we have all sinned personally; we shall all perish unless we find salvation. The word salvation contains within it deliverance from the guilt of our past sins. We have broken God's law each one of us, more or less flagrantly; we have all wandered the downward road, though each has chosen a different way. Salvation brings to us the blotting out of the transgressions of the past, acquital from criminality, purging from all guiltiness, that we may stand accepted before the great Judge. What man in his sober senses will deny that forgiveness is an unspeakably desirable blessing!

But salvation means more than that: it includes deliverance from the power of sin. Naturally we are all fond of evil, and we run after it greedily; we are the bondslaves of iniquity, and we love the bondage. This last is the worst feature of the case. But when salvation comes it delivers the man from the power of sin. He learns that it is evil, and he regards it as such, loathes it, repents that he has ever been in love with it, turns his back upon it, becomes, through God's Spirit, the master of his lusts, puts the flesh beneath his feet, and rises into the liberty of the children of God. Alas! there are many who do not care for this: if this be salvation they would not give a farthing for it. They love their sins; they rejoice to follow the devices and imaginations of their own corrupt hearts. Yet be assured, this emancipation from bad habits, unclean desires, and carnal passions is the main point in salvation, and if it be not ours, salvation in its other branches is not and cannot be enjoyed by us. Dear hearer, dost thou possess salvation from sin? hast thou escaped the corruption which is in the world through lust? If not, what hast thou to do with salvation? To any right-minded man deliverance from unholy principles is regarded as the greatest of all blessings. What thinkest thou of it?

Salvation includes deliverance from the present wrath of God which abides upon the unsaved man every moment of his life. Every person who is unforgiven is the object of divine wrath. "God is angry with the wicked every day. If he turn not, he will whet his sword." "Be that believeth not is condemned already, because he hath not believed in the name of the only begotten Son of God." I frequently hear the statement that this is a state of probation. This is a great mistake, for our probation has long since passed. Sinners have been proved, and found to be unworthy; they have been "weighed in the balances," and "found wanting." If you have not believed in Jesus, condemnation already rests upon you: you are reprieved awhile, but your condemnation is recorded. Salvation takes a man from under the cloud of divine wrath, and reveals to him the divine love. Be can then say, "O God, I will praise thee, though thou wast angry with me, thine anger is turned away, and thou comfortest me." Oh, it is not hell hereafter which is the only thing a sinner has to fear, it is the wrath of God which rests upon him now. To be unreconciled to God now is an awful thing: to have God's arrow pointed at you as it is at this moment, even though it fly not from the string as yet, is a terrible thing. It is enough to make you tremble from head to foot when you learn that you are the target of Jehovah's wrath: "he hath bent his bow, and made it ready." Every soul that is unreconciled to God by the blood of his Son is in the gall of bitterness. Salvation at once sets us free from this state of danger and alienation. We are no longer the "children of wrath, even as others," but are made children of God and joint heirs with a Christ Jesus. What can be conceived more precious than this?

And then, we lastly receive that part of salvation which ignorant persons put first, and make to be the whole of salvation. In consequence of our being delivered from the guilt of sin, and from the power of sin, and from the present wrath of God, we are delivered from the future wrath of God. Unto the uttermost will that wrath descend upon the souls of men when they leave the body and stand before their Maker's bar, if they depart this life unsaved. To die without salvation is to enter into damnation. Where death leaves us there judgment finds us; and where judgment finds us eternity will hold Us forever and ever. "He which is filthy, let him be filthy still," and he that is wretched as a punishment for being filthy, shall be hopelessly wretched still. Salvation delivers the soul from going down into the pit of hell. We, being justified, are no longer liable to punishment, because we are no longer chargeable with guilt. Christ Jesus bore the wrath of God that we might never bear it. He has made a full atonement to the justice of God for the sins of all believers. Against him that believeth there remaineth no record of guilt; his transgressions are blotted out, for a Christ Jesus hath finished transgression, made an end of sin, and brought in everlasting righteousness. What a comprehensive word then is this--"salvation"! It is a triumphant deliverance from the guilt of sin, from the dominion of it, from the curse of it, from the punishment of it, and ultimately from the very existence of it. Salvation is the death of sin, its burial, its annihilation, yea, and the very obliteration of its memory; for thus saith the Lord: "their sins and their iniquities will I remember no more."

Beloved hearers, I am sure that this is the weightiest theme I can bring before you and therefore I cannot be content unless I see that it grasps you and holds you fast. I pray you give earnest heed to this most pressing of all subjects. If my voice and words cannot command your fullest attention, I could wish to be dumb, that some other pleader might with wiser speech draw you to a close consideration of this matter. Salvation appears to me to be of the first importance, when I think of what it is in itself, and for this reason I have at the outset set it forth before your eyes; but you may be helped to remember its value if you consider that God the Father thinks highly of salvation. It was on his mind or ever the earth was. He thinks salvation a lofty business, for he gave his Son that he might save rebellious sinners. Jesus Christ, the only Begotten, thinks salvation most important, for he bled, he died to accomplish it. Shall I bide with that which cost him his life? If he came from heaven to earth, shall I be slow to look from earth to heaven? Shall that which cost the Savior a life of zeal, and a death of agony, be of small account with me? By the bloody sweat of Gethsemane, by the wounds of Calvary, I beseech you, be assured that salvation must be worthy of your highest and most anxious thoughts. It could not be that God the Father, and God the Son, should thus make a common sacrifice: the one giving his Son and the other giving himself for salvation, and yet salvation should be a light and trivial thing. The Holy Ghost thinks it no trifle, for he condescends to work continually in the new creation that he may bring about salvation. He is often vexed and grieved, yet he continues still his abiding labors that he may bring many sons unto glory. Despise not what the Holy Ghost esteems, lest thou despise the Holy Ghost himself. The sacred Trinity think much of salvation; let us not neglect it. I beseech you who have gone on trifling with salvation, to remember that we who have to preach to you dare not trifle with it. The longer I live the more I feel that if God do not make me faithful as a minister, it had been better for me never to have been bow. What a thought that I am set as a watchman to warn your souls, and if I warn you not aright, your blood will be laid at my door! My own damnation will be terrible enough, but to have your blood upon my skirts as well--! God save any one of his ministers from being found guilty of the souls of men. Every preacher of the gospel may cry with David, "Deliver me from bloodguiltiness, O God, thou God of my salvation."

Bethink you, O careless hearers, that God's church does not consider salvation to be a little matter? Earnest men and women, by thousands, are praying day and night for the salvation of others, and are laboring too, and making great sacrifices, and are willing to make many more, if they may by any means bring some to Jesus and his salvation. Surely, if gracious men, and wise men, think salvation to be so important, you who have hitherto neglected it ought to change your minds upon the matter, and act with greater care for your own interests.

The angels think it a weighty business. Bowing from their thrones, they watch for repenting sinners; and when they hear that a sinner has returned to his God, they waken anew their golden harps and pour forth fresh music before the throne, for "there is joy in the presence of the angels of God over one sinner that repenteth." It is certain also that devils think salvation to be a great matter, for their arch-leader goeth about seeking whom he may devour. They never tire in seeking men's destruction. They know how much salvation glorifies God, and how terrible the ruin of souls is; and therefore they compass sea and land, if they may destroy the sons of men. Oh, I pray you, careless hearer, be wise enough to dread that fate which your cruel enemy, the devil, would fain secure for you! Remember, too, that lost souls think salvation important. The rich man, when he was in this world, thought highly of nothing but his barns, and the housing of his produce; but when he came into the place of torment, then he said: "Father Abraham, send Lazarus to my father's house: for I have five brethren; that he may testify unto them, lest they also they come into this place of torment." Lost souls see things in another light than that which dazzled them here below; they value things at a different rate from what we do here, where sinful pleasures and earthly treasures dim the mental eye. I pray you then, by the blessed Trinity, by the tears and prayers of holy men, by the joy of angels and glorified spirits, by the malice of devils and the despair of the lost, arouse yourselves from slumber, and neglect not this great salvation!

I shall not depreciate anything that concerns your welfare, but I shall steadfastly assert that nothing so much concerns any one of you as salvation. Your health by all means. Let the physician be fetched if you be sick; care well for diet and exercise, and all sanitary laws. Look wisely to your constitution and its peculiarities; but what matters it, after all, to have possessed a healthy body, if you have a perishing soul? Wealth, yes, if you must have it, though you shall find it an empty thing if you set your heart upon it. Prosperity in this world, earn it if you can do so fairly, but "what shall it profit a man, if he shall gain the whole world, and lose his own soul?" A golden coffin will be a poor compensation for a damned soul. To be cast away from God's presence, can that misery be assuaged by mountains of treasure? Can the bitterness of the second death be sweetened by the thought that the wretch was once a millionaire, and that his wealth could affect the polities of nations? No, there is nothing in health or wealth comparable to salvation. Nor can honor and reputation bear a comparison therewith. Truly they are but baubles, and yet for all that they have a strange fascination for the soul of men. Oh, sirs, if every harpstring in the world should resound your glories, and every trumpet should proclaim your fame, what would it matter if a louder voice should say, "Depart from me, ye cursed, into everlasting fire, prepared for the devil and his angels"? Salvation! salvation! SALVATION! Nothing on earth can match it, for the merchandise of it is better than silver, and the gain thereof than fine gold. The possession of the whole universe would be no equivalent to a lost soul for the awful damage it has sustained and must sustain for ever. Pile up the worlds, and let them fill the balance: ay, bring as many worlds as there are stars, and heap up the scale on the one side; then in this other scale place a single soul endowed with immortality, and it outweighs the whole. Salvation! nothing can be likened unto it. May we feel its unutterable value, and therefore seek it till we possess it in its fullness!

II. But now we must advance to a second point of consideration, and I pray God the Holy Spirit to press it upon us, and that is, WHOSE MATTER IS IT? We have seen what the matter is--salvation; now, consider whose is it. "Your own salvation." At this hour nothing else is to occupy your thoughts but this intensely personal matter, and I beseech the Holy Spirit to hold your minds fast to this one point.

If you are saved it will be "your own salvation," end you yourself will enjoy it. If you are not saved, the sin you now commit is your own sin, the guilt your own guilt. The condemnation under which you fire, with all its disquietude and fear, or with all its callousnees and neglect is your own--all your own you may share in other men's sins, and other men may become participators in yours, but a burden lies on your own back which no one besides can touch with one of his fingers. There; is a page in God's Book where your sins are recorded unmingled with the transgressions of your fellows. Now, beloved, you must obtain for all this sin a personal pardon, or you are undone for ever. No other can be washed in Christ's blood for you; no one can believe and let his faith stand instead of your faith. The very supposition of human sponsorship in religion is monstrous. You must yourself repent, yourself believe, yourself be washed in the blood, or else for you there is no forgiveness, no acceptance, no adoption, no regeneration. It is all a personal matter through and through: "your own salvation" it must be, or it will be your own eternal ruin.

Reflect anxiously that you must personally die. No one imagines that another can die for him. No man can redeem his brother or give to God a ransom. Through that iron gate I must pass alone, and so must you. Dying will have to be our own personal business; and in that dying we shall have either personal comfort or personal dismay. When death is past, salvation is still our "own salvation;" for if I am saved, mine "eyes shall see the king in his beauty: they shall behold the land that is very far off." Mine eyes shall see him, and not another on my behalf. No brother's head is to wear your crown; no stranger's hand to wave your palm; no sister's eye to gaze for you upon the beatific vision, and no sponsor's heart to be filled as your proxy with the ecstatic bliss. There is a personal heaven for the personal believer in the Lord Jesus Christ. It must be if you possess it, "your own salvation." But if you have it not, reflect again, that it will be your own damnation. No one will be condemned for you; no other can bear the hot thunder bolts of Jehovah's wrath on your behalf. When you shall say, "Hide me, ye rocks! Conceal me, O mountains!" No one will spring forward, and say, "You can cease to be accursed, and I will become a curse for you." A substitute there is to-day for every one that believeth--God's appointed substitute, the Christ of God; but if that substitution be not accepted by you, there can never be another; but there remains only for you a personal casting away to suffer personal pangs in your own soul and in your own body for ever. This, then, makes it a most solemn business. O be wise, and look well to "your own salvation."

You may be tempted to-day, and very likely you are to forget your own salvation by thoughts of other people. We are all so apt to look abroad in this matter, and not to look at home. Let me pray you to reverse the process, and let everything which has made you neglect your own vineyard be turned to the opposite account, and lead you to begin at home, and see to "your own salvation." Perhaps you dwell among the saints of God, and you have been rather apt to find fault with them, though for my part, I can say these are the people I desire to live with and desire to die with: "thy people shall be my people, and thy God my God." But, O if you live among the saints ought it not to be your business to see to "Your own salvation"? See that you are truly one of them, not written in their church-book merely, but really graven upon the palms of Christ's hands; not a false professor, but a real possessor; not a mere wearer of the name of Christ, but a bearer of the nature of Christ. If you live in a gracious family be afraid lest thou should be divided from them for ever. How could you endure to go from a Christian household to the place of torment! Let the anxieties of saints lead you to be anxious. Let their prayers drive you to prayer. Let their example rebuke your sin, and their joys entice you to their Savior. O see to this! But perhaps you live most among ungodly men, and the tendency of your converse with the ungodly is to make you think as they do of the trifles and vanities, and wickednesses of this life. Do not let it be so; but, on the contrary, say, "O God, though I am placed among these people, yet gather not my soul with sinners, nor my life with bloody men. Let me avoid the sins into which they fall, and the impenitence of which they are guilty. Save me, I pray thee, O my God, save me from the transgressions which they commit."

Perhaps to-day some of your minds are occupied with thoughts of the dead who have lately fallen asleep. There is a little one unburied at home, or there is a father not get laid in the grave. Oh, when you weep for those who have gone to heaven, think of "your own salvation," and weep for yourselves, for you have parted with them for ever unless you are saved. You have said, "Farewell" to those beloved ones, eternally farewell, unless you yourselves believe in Jesus. And if any of you have heard of persons who have lived in sin and died in blasphemy, and are lost, I pray you think not of them carelessly lest you also suffer the same doom: for what saith the Savior: "Suppose ye that these were sinners above all the sinners?" "I tell you, Nay: but, except ye repent, ye shall all likewise perish." It seems to me as if everything on earth and everything in heaven, and everything in hell, yea, and God himself, calls upon you to seek "your own salvation," first, and foremost, and above all other things.

It may be profitable to mention some persons upon whom this theme needs much pressing. I will begin at home. There is great need to urge this matter upon official Christians, such as I am, such as my brethren, the deacons and elders, are. If there are any persons who are likely to be deceived, it is those who are called by their office to act as shepherds to the souls of others. Oh, my brethren I it is so easy for me to imagine because I am a minister, and have to deal with holy things, that therefore I am safe. I pray I may never fall into that delusion, but may always cling to the cross, as a poor, needy sinner resting in the blood of Jesus. Brother ministers, co-workers, and officials of the church, do not imagine that office can save you. The son of perdition was an apostle, greater than we are in office, and yet at this hour he is greater in destruction. See to it, ye that are numbered amongst the leaders of Israel, that you yourselves be saved.

Unpractical doctrinalists are another class of persons who need to be warned to see to their own salvation. When they hear a sermon, they sit with their mouths open, ready to snap at half a mistake. They make a man an offender for a word, for they conclude themselves to be the standards of orthodoxy, and they weigh up the preacher as he speaks, with as much coolness as if they had been appointed deputy judges for the Great King himself. Oh, sir, weigh yourself! It may be a great thing to be sound in the head, in the faith, but it is a greater thing to be sound in the heart. I may be able to split a hair between orthodoxy and heterodoxy, and yet may have no part nor lot in the matter. You may be a very sound Calvinist, or you may happen to think soundness lies in another direction; but, oh, it is nought, it is less than nought, except your souls feel the power of the truth, and ye yourselves are born again. See to "your own salvation," O ye wise men in the letter, who have not the Spirit.

So, too, certain persons who are always given to curious speculations need warning. When they read the Bible it is not to find whether they are saved or no, but to know whether we are under the third or fourth vial, when the millenium is going to be, or what is the battle of Armageddon. Ah, sir, search out all these things if thou hast time and skill, but look to thine own salvation first. The book of Revelation, blessed is he that understands it, but not unless, first of all, he understands this, "He that believeth and is baptised shall be saved." The greatest doctor in the symbols and mysteries of the Apocalypse shall be as certainly cast away as the most ignorant, unless he has come to Christ, and rested his soul in the atoning work of our great substitute.

I know some who greatly need to look to their own salvation. I refer to those who are always criticising others. They can hardly go to a place of worship but what they are observing their neighbour's dress or conduct. Nobody is safe from their remarks, they are such keen judges, and make such shrewd observations. Ye faultfinders and talebearers, look to "your own salvation." You condemned a minister the other day for a supposed fault, and yet he is a dear servant of God, who lives near his Master; who are you, sir, to use your tongue against such a one as he? The other day a poor humble Christian was the object of your gossip and your slander, to the wounding of her heart. Oh, see to yourself, see to yourself. If those eyes which look outward so piercingly would sometimes look inward they might see a sight which would blind them with horror. Blessed horror if it led them to turn to the Savior who would open those eyes afresh, and grant them to see his salvation.

I might also say that in this matter of looking to personal salvation, it is necessary to speak to some who have espoused certain great public designs. I trust I am as ardent a Protestant as any man living, but I know too many red-hot Protestants who are but little better than Romanists, for though the Romanists of old might have burnt them, they would certainly withhold toleration from Romanists to-day, if they could; and therein I see not a pin to choose between the two bigots. Zealous Protestants, I agree with you, but yet I warn you that your zeal in this matter will not save you, or stand in the stead of personal godliness. Many an orthodox Protestant will be found at the left hand of the Great Judge. And you, too, who are for ever agitating this and that public question, I would say to you, "Let politics alone till your own inward politics are settled on a good foundation." You are a Radical Reformer, you could show us a system of political economy which would right all our wrongs and give to every man his due; then I pray you right you own wrongs, reform yourself, yield yourself to the love of Jesus Christ, or what will it signify to you, though you knew how to balance the affairs of nations, and to regulate the arrangement of all classes of society, if you yourself shall be blown away like chaff before the winnowing fan of the Lord. God grant us grace, then, whatever else we take up with, to keep it in its proper place, and make our calling and election sure.

III. And now, thirdly, and O for grace to speak aright, I shall try to ANSWER CERTAIN OBJECTIONS. I think I hear somebody say, "Well, but don't you believe in predestination? What have we to do with looking to our own salvation? Is it not all fixed?" Thou fool, for I can scarce answer thee till I have given thee thy right title; was it not fixed whether thou shouldst get wet or not in coming to this place? Why then did you bring your umbrella? Is it not fixed whether you shall be nourished with food to-day or shall go hungry? Why then will you go home and eat your dinner? Is it not fixed whether you shall live or not to-morrow; will you therefore, cut your throat? No, you do not reason so wickedly, so foolishly from destiny in reference to anything but "your own salvation," and you know it is not reasoning, it just mere talk. Here is all the answer I will give you, and all you deserve.

Another says, "I have a difficulty about this looking to our own salvation. Do you not believe in full assurance? Are there not some who know that they are saved beyond all doubt? Yes, blessed be God, I hope there are many such now present. But let me tell you who these are not. These are not persons who are afraid to examine themselves. If I meet with any man who says, "I have no need to examine my self any more, I know I am saved, and therefore have no need to take any further care," I would venture to say to him, "Sir, you are lost already. This strong delusion of yours has led you to believe a lie." There are none so cautious as those who possess full assurance, and there are none who have so much holy fear of sinning against God, nor who walk so tenderly and carefully as those who possess the full assurance of faith. Presumption is not assurance, though, alas! many think so. No fully assured believer will ever object to being reminded of the importance of his own salvation.

But a third objection arises. "This is very selfish," says one. "You have been exhorting us to look to ourselves, and that is sheer selfishness." Yes, so you say; but let me tell you it is a kind of selfishness that is absolutely needful before you can be unselfish. A part of salvation is to be delivered from selfishness, and I am selfish enough to desire to be delivered from selfishness. How can you be of any service to others if you are not saved yourself? A man is drowning. I am on London Bridge. If I spring from the parapet and can swim, I can save him; but suppose I cannot swim, can I render any service by leaping into sudden and certain death with the sinking man? I am disqualified from helping him till I have the ability to do so. There is a school over yonder. Well, the first enquiry of him who is to be the master must he, "Do I know myself that which I profess to teach?" Do you call that enquiry selfish? Surely it a most unselfish selfishness, grounded upon common sense. Indeed, the man who is not so selfish as to ask himself, "Am I qualified to act as a teacher?" would be guilty of gross selfishness in putting himself into an office which he was not qualified to fill. I will suppose an illiterate person going into the school, and saying, "I will be master here, and take the pay," and yet he cannot teach the children to read or write. Would he not be very selfish in not seeing to his own fitness? But surely it it is not selfishness that would make a man stand back and say, "No, I must first go to school myself, otherwise it is but a mockery of the children for me to attempt to teach them anything." This is no selfishness, then, when looked at aright, which makes us see to our own salvation, for it is the basis from which we operate for the good of others.

IV. Having answered these objections, I shall for a minute attempt to RENDER SOME ASSISTANCE to those who would fain be right in the best things.

Has the Holy Spirit been pleased to make any one here earnest about his own salvation? Friend, I will help you to answer two questions. Ask yourself, first, "Am I saved?" I would help thee to reply to that very quickly. If you are saved this morning, you are the subject of a work within you, as saith the text, "Work out your own salvation; for it is God which worketh in you." you cannot work it in, but when God works it in you work it out. Have you a work of the Holy Ghost in your soul? Do you feel something more than unaided human nature can attain unto? Have you a change wrought in you from above? If so, you are saved. Again, does your salvation rest wholly upon Christ? He who hangs anywhere but upon the cross, hangs upon that which will deceive him. If thou standest upon Christ, thou art on a rock; but if thou trustest in the merits of Christ in part, and thy own merits in part, then thou hast one foot on a rock but another on the quicksand; and thou mightest as well have both feet on the quicksand, for the result will be the same.

"None but Jesus, none but Jesus
Can do helpless sinners good."

Thou art not saved unless Christ be all in all in thy soul, Alpha and Omega, beginning and ending, first and last. Judge by this, again: if you are saved, you have turned your back on sin. You have not left off sinning--would to God we could do so--but you have left off loving sin; you sin not wilfully, but from infirmity; and you are earnestly seeking after God and holiness. You have respect to God, you desire to be like him, you are longing to be with him. Your face is towards heaven. You are as a man who journeys to the Equator. You are feeling more and more the warm influence of the heavenly heat and light. Now, if such be your course of life, that you walk not after the flesh, but after the Spirit, and bring forth the fruits of holiness, then you are saved. May your answer to that question he given in great honesty and candour to your own soul. Be not too partial a Judge. Conclude not that all is right because outward appearances are fair. Deliberate before you return a favorable verdict. Judge yourselves that ye be not judged. It were better to condemn yourself and be accepted of God, than to acquit yourself and find your mistake at the last.

But suppose that question should have to be answered by any here in the negative (and I am afraid it must be), then let those who confess that they are not saved, hear the answer to another enquiry: "How can I be saved?" Ah, dear hearer, I have not to bring a huge volume nor a whole armful of folios to you, and to say, "It will take you months and Years to understand the plan of salvation." No, the way is plain, the method simple. Thou shalt be saved within the next moment if thou believest. God's work of salvation is, as far as its commencement and essence is concerned, instantaneous. If thou believes "that Jesus is the Christ, thou art born of God now. If thou dost now stand in spirit at the foot of the cross, and view the incarnate God suffering, bleeding, and dying there, and if as thou dost look at him, thy soul consents to have him for her Savior, and casts herself wholly on him, thou art saved. How vividly there comes before my memory this morning the moment when I first believed in Jesus! It was the simplest act my mind every performed, and yet the most wonderful, for the Holy Spirit wrought it in me. Simply to have done with reliance upon myself, and have done with confidence in all but Jesus, and to rest alone, my undivided confidence in him, and in what he had done. My sin was in that moment forgiven me, and I was saved, and may it all be so with you, my friend, even with you if you also, trust the Lord Jesus. "Your own salvation" shall be secured by that one simple act of faith; and henceforward, kept by the power of God through faith unto salvation, you shall tread the way of holiness, till you come to be where Jesus is in everlasting bliss. God grant that not a soul may go out of this place unsaved. Even you, little children, who are here, you youngsters, you young boys and girls, I pray that you may in early life attend to "your own salvation." Faith is not a grace for old people only, nor for your fathers and mothers only; if your little hearts shall look to him who was the holy child Jesus, if you know but little yet, if you trust him salvation shall be yours. I pray that to you who are young, "your own salvation" may become, while you are yet in your youth, a matter of joy, because you have trusted it in the hands of your Redeemer.

Now I must close: but one or two thoughts press me. I must utter them ere I sit down. I would anxiously urge each person here to see to this matter of his own salvation. Do it, I pray you, and in earnest, for no one can do it for you. I have asked God for your soul, my hearer, and I pray I may have an answer of peace concerning you. But unless you also pray, vain are my prayers. You remember your mother's tears. Ah! you have crossed the ocean since those days, and you have gone into the deeps of sin, but you recollect when you used to say your prayers at her knee, and when she would lovingly say "Amen," and kiss her boy and bless him, and pray that he might know his mother's God. Those prayers are ringing in the ears of God for you, but it is impossible that you can ever be saved unless it is said of you, "Behold, he prayeth." Your mother's holiness can only rise up in judgment to condemn your wilful wickedness unless you imitate it. Your father's earnest exhortations shall but confirm the just sentence of the Judge unless you hearken to them, and yourselves consider and put your trust in Jesus. Oh I bethink you each one of you, there is but one hope, and that one hope lost, it is gone for ever. Defeated in one battle, a commander attempts another, and hopes that he may yet win the campaign. Your life is your one fight, and if it be lost it is lost for aye. The man who was bankrupt yesterday commences again in business with good heart, and hopes that he may yet succeed; but in the business of this mortal life, if you are found bankrupt, you are bankrupt for ever and ever. I do therefore charge you by the living God, before whom I stand, and before whom I may have to give an account of this day's preaching ere another day's sun shall shine, I charge you see to your own salvation. God help you, that you may never cease to seek unto God till you know by the witness of the Spirit that you have indeed passed from death unto life. See to it now, now, NOW, NOW. This very day the voice of warning comes to certain of you from God, with special emphasis, because you greatly need it, for your time is short. How many have passed into eternity during this week! You may yourself be gone from the land of the living before next Sabbath-day. I suppose, according to the calculation of probabilities, out of this audience there are several who will die within a month. I am not conjecturing now, but according to all probabilities these thousands cannot all meet again, it all have a mind to do so. Who then among us will be summoned to the unknown land? Will it be you, young woman, who have been laughing at the things of God? Shall it be yonder merchant, who has not time enough for religion? Shall it be you, my foreign friend, who have crossed the ocean to take a holiday? Will you be carried back a corpse? I do conjure you bethink yourselves, all of you. You who dwell in London will remember years ago when the cholera swept through our streets, some of us were in the midst of it, and saw many drop around us, as though smitten with an invisible but deadly arrow. That disease is said to be on its way hither again; it is said to be rapidly sweeping from Poland across the Continent, and if it come and seize some of you, are you ready to depart? Even if that form of death do not afflict our city, as I pray it may not, yet is death ever within our gates, and the pestilence walketh in darkness every night, therefore consider your ways. Thus saith the Lord, and with his word I conclude this discourse: "Prepare to meet thy God, O Israel."

PORTION OF SCRIPTURE READ BEFORE SERMON--Hebrews 10:23-39.

"Bought with a Price"

A Sermon (No. 1004)
Delivered on Lord's-day Morning, August 6th, 1871, by
C. H. SPURGEON,
At the Metropolitan Tabernacle, Newington

"Ye are not your own: for ye are bought with a price: therefore glorify God in your body, and in your spirit, which are God's." - 1 Corinthians 6:19-20.

OUR BELOVED BROTHER, Thomas Cook, who has for so long a time served this church as an honored deacon, has fallen asleep in Christ. We have laid his earthly remains in the tomb: his spirit rejoices before the throne of God. This day we thank God for his useful life, and ask for grace to imitate it. Before he closed his eyes in death he left a text of Scripture for the pastors: "Christ is all, and in all;" and he left another for his fellow church members, for all of you this day who are members of the body of Christ; and this is the legacy, which now, as a spiritual executor, I present to you: "Ye are not your own: for ye are bought with a price: therefore glorify God in your body and in your spirit, which are God's." I have no doubt the intention of our departed brother was to promote God's glory by speaking to us even after he was dead concerning our sanctification, that so we might be stirred up to a greater consecration to the Lord our Savior.

You will notice that in this chapter the apostle Paul has been dealing with sins of the flesh, with fornication and adultery. Now, it is at all times exceedingly difficult for the preacher either to speak or to write upon this subject; it demands the strictest care to keep the language guarded, so that while we are denouncing a detestable evil we do not ourselves promote it by a single expression that should be otherwise than chaste and pure. Observe how well the apostle Paul succeeds, for though he does not mask the sin, but tears the veil from it, and lets us know well what it is that he is aiming at, yet there is no sentence which we could wish to alter. Herein he is a model for all ministers, both in fidelity and prudence.

Be sure also to note that the apostle, when he is exposing sin, does not trifle with it, but like a mighty hunter before the Lord, pursues it with all his might; his hatred to it is intense; he drags it forth to the light; he bids us mark its hideous deformity; he hunts it through all its purlieus, hotfoot, as we say. He never leaves it breathing time; argument after argument he hurls like javelins upon it; he will by no means spare the filthy thing. He who above all others speaks most positively of salvation by grace, and is most clear upon the fact that salvation is not by the works of the law, is at the same time most intensely earnest for the holiness of Christians, and most zealously denounces those who would say, "Let us do evil, that good may come." In this particular instance he sets the sin of fornication in the light of the Holy Spirit; he holds up, as it were, the seven-branched candlestick before it, and lets us see what a filthy thing it is. He tells us that the body is the temple of the Holy Ghost, and therefore ought not to be profaned; he declares that bodily unchastity is a sacrilegious desecration of our manhood, a violation of the sacred shrine wherein the Spirit takes up its dwelling-place; and then, as if this were not enough, he seizes the sin and drags it to the foot of the cross, and there nails it hand and foot, that it may die as a criminal; for these are his words: "Ye are not your own: for ye are bought with a price:" the price being the blood of Jesus. He finds no sharper weapon, no keener instrument of destruction than this. The redemption wrought on Calvary by the death of Jesus must be the death of this sin, and of all other sins, wherever the Spirit of God uses it as his sword of execution. Brethren and sisters, it is no slight thing to be holy. A man must not say, "I have faith," and then fall into the sins of an unbeliever; for, after all, our outer life is the test of our inner life; and if the outer life be not purified, rest assured the heart is not changed. That faith which does not bring forth the fruit of holiness is the faith of devils. The devils believe and tremble. Let us never be content with a faith which can live in hell, but rise to that which will save us--the faith of God's elect, which purifies the soul, casting down the power of evil, and setting up the throne of Jesus Christ, the throne of holiness within the spirit.

Noticing this as being the run of the chapter, we now come to the text itself, and in order to discuss it we must take it to pieces, and I think we shall see in it at once three things very clearly. The first is a blessed fact, "Ye are," or as it should be rendered, "Ye were bought with a price;" then comes a plain consequence from that fact, a consequence of a double character, negative and positive: "Ye are not your own;" "your body and your spirit are God's;" and out of that there springs inevitably a natural conclusion: "Therefore, glorify God in your body, and in your spirit."

I. Let us begin, then, first of all, with this BLESSED FACT--"Ye are bought with a price." Paul might, if his object were to prove that we are not our own, have said: "Ye did not make yourselves." Creation may well furnish motives for obedience to the great Lawgiver. He might also have said, "Ye do not preserve yourselves: it is God who keeps you in life; you would die if he withdrew his power." The preservation of divine providence might furnish abundant arguments for holiness. Surely he who feeds, nourishes, and upholds our life should have our service. But he prefers, for reasons known to himself, which it would not be hard to guess, to plead the tenderer theme, redemption. He sounds that note, which if it do not thunder with that crash of power which marked the six days' labor of Omnipotence, yet has a soft, piercing, subduing tone in it, which, like the still small voice to which Elias listened, has in it the presence of God.

The most potent plea for sanctity is not "Ye were made," or, "Ye are nourished," but "Ye are bought." This the apostle selects as a convincing proof of our duty, and as a means to make that duty our delight. And truly, beloved, it is so. If we have indeed experienced the power of redemption we fully admit that it is so. Look ye back to the day when ye were bought, when ye were bondslaves to your sins, when ye were under the just sentence of divine justice, when it was inevitable that God should punish your transgressions; remember how the Son of God became your substitute, how he bared his back to the lash that should have fallen upon you, and laid his soul beneath the sword which should have quenched its fury in your blood. You were redeemed then, redeemed from the punishment that was due to you, redeemed from the wrath of God, redeemed unto Christ to be his for ever.

You will notice the text says, "Ye were bought with a price." It is a common classical expression to signify that the purchase was expensive. Of course, the very expression, "Ye were bought," implies a price, but the words "with a price" are added, as if to show that it was not for nothing that ye were purchased. There was a something inestimably precious paid for you; and ye need scarcely that I remind you that "ye were not redeemed with corruptible things, as silver and gold;" "but with the precious blood of Christ, as of a lamb without blemish and without spot." Ah! those words slip over our tongue very glibly, but we may well chide ourselves that we can speak of redemption with dry eyes. That the blood of Christ was shed to buy our souls from death and hell is a wonder of compassion which fills angels with amazement, and it ought to overwhelm us with adoring love whenever we think of it, glance our eye over the recording pages, or even utter the word "redemption." What meant this purchasing us with blood? It signified pain. Have any of you lately been racked with pain? Have you suffered acutely? Ah! then at such times you know to some degree what the price was which the Savior paid. His bodily pains were great, hands and feet nailed to the wood, and the iron breaking through the tenderest nerves. His soul-pains were greater still, his heart was melted like wax, he was very heavy, his heart was broken with reproach, he was deserted of God, and left beneath the black thunder-clouds of divine wrath, his soul was exceeding sorrowful, even unto death. It was pain that bought you. We speak of the drops of blood, but we must not confine our thoughts to the crimson life-floods which distilled from the Savior's veins; we must think of the pangs which he endured, which were the equivalent for what we ought to have suffered, what we must have suffered had we endured the punishment of our guilt for ever in the flames of hell. But pain alone could not have redeemed us; it was by death that the Savior paid the ransom. Death is a word of horror to the ungodly. The righteous hath hope in his death; but as Christ's death was the substitute for the death of the ungodly, he was made a curse for us, and the presence of God was denied him. His death was attended with unusual darkness; he cried, "My God, my God, why hast thou forsaken me?" O think ye earnestly on this. The Ever-living died to redeem us; the Only Begotten bowed his head in agony, and was laid in the grave that we might be saved. Ye are bought then "with a price"--a price incalculable, stupendous, infinite, and this is the plea which the apostle uses to urge upon us that we should "be holiness to the Lord."

I desire upon this theme, which is a very simple and every-day one, but which is nevertheless of the weightiest consideration, to remind you, dearly beloved, who profess to be followers of Christ, that this matter of your being "bought with a price" is an indisputable fact to every Christian. To every person here present it either is a fact or not. I scarcely need to ask whether any of you are prepared to abjure your redemption; and yet, professor of the faith of Christ, I shall put it to you now: Are you willing to have the negative put upon this? will you deny that you were "bought with a price?" Will you now confess that you were not redeemed on Calvary? You dare not, I am sure. You would sooner die than abjure your belief of it. Well, then, as certain as is your redemption, so certain is it that you "are not your own," but belong to God, and should glorify him. It is inevitable that if you be "bought with a price," you have ceased to be your own property, and belong to him who bought you. Holiness, therefore, is necessary to all the redeemed. If you cast off your responsibility to be holy, you at the same time cast away the benefit of redemption. Will you do this? As I am sure you could not renounce your salvation, and cast away your only hope, so I charge you by the living God be not so inconsistent as to say: "I am redeemed, and yet I will live as I list." As redeemed men, let the inevitable consequences follow from the fact, and be ye evidently the servants of the Lord Jesus.

Remember, too, that this fact is the most important one in all your history. That you were redeemed "with a price" is the greatest event in your biography. Even your birth, what was it unless a second birth had been yours! Might you not say: "Let the day perish wherein I was born and the night in which it was said, there is a man child conceived"? Would it not have been to you the direst calamity to be born into the world if you had not been rescued from the wrath of which you were the heir? You left your father's house, and it was an important step in life; perhaps you crossed the great and wide sea; it may be you aspired to high office in the state and you obtained it; it is possible you have been sore sick, or it may be you have sunk from affluence to poverty. Such events leave their impress upon the memory; men cannot forget these great changes in their lives; but they all shrivel into less than nothing compared with this fact that you were "bought with a price." Your connection with Calvary is the most important thing about you. Oh, I do beseech you then, if it be so, prove it; and remember the just and righteous proof is by your not being your own, but consecrated unto God. If it be the most important thing in the world to you, that you were "bought with a price," let it exercise the most prominent influence over your entire career. Be a man, be an Englishman, but be most of all Christ's man. A citizen, a friend, a philanthropist, a patriot: all these you may be, but be most of all a saint redeemed by blood.

Recollect, again, that your being "bought with a price" will be the most important fact in all your future existence. What say they in heaven when they sing? They would naturally select the noblest topic and that which most engrosses their minds, and yet in the whole range of their memory they find no theme so absorbing as this: "Thou wast slain, and hast redeemed us to God by thy blood." Redeeming love is the theme of heaven. When you reach the upper realms your most important memory will not be that you were wealthy or poor in this life, nor the fact that you sickened and died, but that you were "bought with a price." We do not know all that may occur in this world before the close of its history, but certainly it will be burnt up with fire, and you in yonder clouds with Christ may witness the awful conflagration. You will never forget it. There will be new heavens and new earth, and you with Christ may see the new-born heavens, and earth, laughing in the bright sunlight of God's good pleasure; you will never forget that joyous day. And you will be caught up to dwell with Jesus for ever and ever; and there will come a time when he shall deliver up the kingdom to God, even the Father and God shall be all in all. You will never forget the time of which the poet sings--

"Then the end, beneath his rod
Man's last enemy shall fall.
Hallelujah, Christ in God,
God in Christ is all in all."

All these divinely glorious events will impress themselves upon you, but not one of them will make an impression so lasting, so clear, so deep as this, that you were "bought with a price." High over all the mountain tops, Calvary, that was but a little mount in human estimation, shall rise; stars shall the events of history be; but this event shall be the sun in whose presence all others hide their diminished heads. "Thou wast slain," the full chorus of heaven shall roll it forth in thundering accents of grateful zeal. "Thou wast slain, and hast redeemed us to God by thy blood;" the saints shall remember this first and foremost; and amidst the cycles of eternity this shall have the chief place in every glorified memory. What then, beloved? Shall it not have the chief place with you now? It has been the fact of your life hitherto, it will be the fact of your entire eternal existence: let it saturate your soul, let it penetrate your spirit, let it subdue your faculties, let it take the reins of all your powers and guide you whither it will. Let the Redeemer, he whose hands were pierced for you, sway the scepter of your spirit and rule over you this day, and world without end.

If I had the power to do it, how would I seek to refresh in your souls a sense of this fact that you are "bought with a price." There in the midnight hour, amidst the olives of Gethsemane, kneels Immanuel the Son of God; he groans, he pleads in prayer, he wrestles; see the beady drops stand on his brow, drops of sweat, but not of such sweat as pours from men when they earn the bread of life, but the sweat of him who is procuring life itself for us. It is blood, it is crimson blood; great gouts of it are falling to the ground. O soul, thy Savior speaks to thee from out Gethsemane at this hour, and he says: "Here and thus I bought thee with a price." Come, stand and view him in the agony of the olive garden, and understand at what a cost he procured thy deliverance. Track him in all his path of shame and sorrow till you see him on the Pavement; mark how they bind his hands and

fasten him to the whipping-post; see, they bring the scourges and the cruel Roman whips; they tear his flesh; the ploughers make deep furrows on his blessed body, and the blood gushes forth in streams, while rivulets from his temples, where the crown of thorns has pierced them, join to swell the purple stream. From beneath the scourges he speaks to you with accents soft and low, and he says, "My child, it is here and thus I bought thee with a price." But see him on the cross itself when the consummation of all has come; his hands and feet are fountains of blood, his soul is full of anguish even to heartbreak; and there, ere the soldier pierces with a spear his side, bowing down he whispers to thee and to me, "It was here and thus, I bought thee with a price." O by Gethsemane, by Gabbatha, by Golgotha, by every sacred name collected with the passion of our Lord, by sponge and vinegar, and nail and spear, and everything that helped the pang and increased the anguish of his death, I conjure you, my beloved brethren, to remember that ye were "bought with a price," and "are not your own." I push you to this; you either were or were not so bought; if you were, it is the grand fact of your life; if you were, it is the greatest fact that ever will occur to you: let it operate upon you, let it dominate your entire nature, let it govern your body, your soul, your spirit, and from this day let it be said of you not only that you are a man, a man of good morals and respectable conduct, but this, above all things, that you are a man filled with love to him who bought you, a man who lives for Christ, and knows no other passion. Would God that redemption would become the paramount influence, the lord of our soul, and dictator of our being; then were we indeed true to our obligations: short of this we are not what love and justice both demand.

II. Now let us pass on to the second point. Here is A PLAIN CONSEQUENCE arising from the blessed fact. Ye were "bought with a price." Then first it is clear as a negative, that "Ye are not your own," and secondly, it is clear as a positive, that "Your body and spirit are God's."

Take first the negative: if bought, you are not your own. No argument is needed for this, and indeed it is so great a boon in itself that none of us could find it in our hearts to demur to it. It is a great privilege not to be one's own. A vessel is drifting on the Atlantic hither and thither, and its end no man knoweth. It is derelict, deserted by all its crew; it is the property of no man; it is the prey of every storm, and the sport of every wind: rocks, quicksands, and shoals wait to destroy it: the ocean yearns to engulf it. It drifts onward to no man's land, and no man will mourn its shipwreck. But mark well yonder barque in the Thames which its owner surveys with pleasure. In its attempt to reach the sea, it may run ashore, or come into collision with other vessels; or in a thousand ways suffer damage; but there is no fear, it will pass through the floating forest of "the Pool;" it will thread the winding channel, and reach the Nore because its owner will secure it pilotage, skillful and apt. How thankful you and I should be that we are not derelict to-day! we are not our own, not left on the wild waste of chance to be tossed to and fro by fortuitous circumstances; but there is a hand upon our helm; we have on board a pilot who owns us, and will surely steer us into the Fair Havens of eternal rest. The sheep is on the mountain side, and the winter is coming on; it may be buried in the snow; perhaps the wolf may seize it, or by-and-by, when the summer crops have been eaten, there may be little fodder for it, and it may starve; but the sheep's comfort if it could think at all, would be this: it is not its own, it belonged to the shepherd, who will not willingly lose his property; it bears the mark of its owner, and is the object of his care. O happy sheep of God's pasture, what a bliss it is to you that you are not your own! Does any man here think it would be a pleasure to be his own? Let me assure him that there is no ruler so tyrannical as self. He that is his own master, has a fool and a tyrant to be his lord. No man ever yet governed himself after the will of the flesh but what he by degrees found the yoke heavy and the burden crushing. Self is a fierce dictator, a terrible oppressor; imperious lusts are cruel slavedrivers. But Christ, who says we are not our own, would have us view that truth in the light in which a loving wife would view it. She, too, is not her own. She gave herself away on a right memorable day, of which she bears the golden token on her finger. She did not weep when she surrendered herself and became her husband's; nor did they muffle the bells, or bid the organ play the "Dead March" in Saul: it was a happy day for her; she remembers it at this moment with glowing joy. She is not her own, but she has not regretted the giving herself away: she would make the same surrender again to the self-same beloved owner, if it were to be done. That she is her husband's does not bespeak her slavery, but her happiness; she has found rest in her husband's house, and to-day, when the Christian confesses that he is not his own, he does not wish that he were. He is married to the Savior; he has given himself up, body, soul, and spirit, to the blessed Bridegroom of his heart; it was the marriage-day of his true life when he became a Christian, end he looks back to it with joy and transport. Oh, it is a blissful thing not to be our own, so I shall not want arguments to prove that to which every gracious spirit gives a blissful consent.

Now, if it be true that we are not our own, and I hope it is true to many here present, then the inference from it is, "I have no right to injure myself in any way." My body is not my own, I have no right then, as a Christian man, to do anything with it that would defile it. The apostle is mainly arguing against sins of the flesh, and he says, "the body is not for fornication, but for the Lord; and the Lord for the body." We have no right to commit uncleanness, because our bodies are the members of Christ and not our own. He would say the same of drunkenness, gluttony, idle sleep, and even of such excessive anxiety after wealth as injures health with carking care. We have no right to profane or injure the flesh and blood which are consecrated to God; every limb of our frame belongs to God; it is his property; he has bought it "with a price." Any honest man will be more concerned about an injury done to another's property placed under his care, than if it were his own. When the son of the prophet was hewing wood with Elisha, you remember how he said, when the axe head flew off into the water, "Alas! master, for it was borrowed." It would be bad enough to lose my own axe, but it is not my own, therefore I doubly deplore the accident. I know this would not operate upon thievish minds. There are some who, if it was another man's, and they had borrowed it, would have no further care about it: "Let the lender get it back, if he can." But we speak to honest men, and with them it is always a strong, argument: Your body is another's, do it no injury. As for our spirit too, that is God's, and how careful we should be of it. I am asked sometimes to read an heretical book: well, if I believed my reading it would help its refutation, and might be an assistance to others in keeping them out of error, I might do it as a hard matter of duty, but I shall not do it unless I see some good will come from it. I am not going to drag my spirit through a ditch for the sake of having it washed afterwards, for it is not my own. It may be that good medicine would restore me if I poisoned myself with putrid meat, but I am not going to try it: I dare not experiment on a mind which no longer belongs to me. There is a mother and a child, and the child has a book to play with, and a blacklead pencil. It is making drawings and marks upon the book, and the mother takes no notice. It lays down one book and snatches another from the table, and at once the mother rises from her seat, and hurriedly takes the book away, saying: "No, my dear, you must not mark that, for it is not ours." So with my mind, intellect, and spirit; if it belonged to me I might or might not play tomfool with it, and go to hear Socinians, Ritualists, Universalists, and such like preach, but as it is not my own, I will preserve it from such fooleries, and the pure word shall not be mingled with the errors of men. Here is the drift of the apostle's argument--I have no right to injure that which does not belong to me, and as I am not my own, I have no right to injure myself.

But, further, I have no right to let myself lie waste. The man who had a talent, and went and dug in the earth and hid it, had not he a right to do so? Yes, of course, if it was his own talent, and his own napkin. If any of you have money and do not put it out to interest, if it is all your own, nobody complains. But this talent belonged to the man's master, it was only intrusted to him as a steward, and he ought not to have let it rust in the ground. So I have no right to let my faculties run to waste since they do not belong to me. If I am a Christian I have no right to be idle. I saw the other day men using picks in the road in laying down new gas-pipes; they had been resting, and just as I passed the clock struck one, and the foreman gave a signal. I think he said, "Blow up;" and straightway each man took his pick or his shovel, and they were all at it in earnest. Close to them stood a fellow with a pipe in his mouth, who did not join in the work, but stood in a free-and-easy posture. It did not make any difference to him whether it was one o'clock or six. Why not? Because he was his own: the other men were the master's for the time being. He as an independent gentlemen might do as he liked, but those who were not their own fell to labor. If any of you idle professors can really prove that you belong to yourselves, I have nothing more to say to you, but if you profess to have a share in the redeeming sacrifice of Christ, I am ashamed of you if you do not go to work the very moment the signal is given. You have no right to waste what Jesus Christ has bought "with a price."

Further than that, if we are not our own, but "are bought with a price," we have no right to exercise any capricious government of ourselves. A man who is his own may say, "I shall go whither I will, and do what I will;" but if I am not my own but belong to God who has bought me, then I must submit to his government; his will must be my will, and his directions must be my law. I desire to enter a certain garden, and I ask the gardener at the gate if I may come in. "You should be very welcome, sir, indeed," says he, "if it were mine, but my master has told me not to admit strangers here, and therefore I must refuse you." Sometimes the devil would come into the garden of our souls. We tell him that our flesh might consent, but the garden is not ours, and we cannot give him space. Worldly ambition, covetousness, and so forth, might claim to walk through our soul, but we say, "No, it is not our own; we cannot, therefore, do what our old will would do, but we desire to be obedient to the will of our Father who is in heaven." Thy will be done, my God, in me, for so should it be done where all is thine own by purchase.

Yet, again, if we are not our own, then we have no right to serve ourselves. The man who is living entirely for himself, whose object is his own ease, comfort, honor, or wealth, what knows he concerning redemption by Christ? If our aims rise no higher than our personal advantages, we are false to the fact that we "are bought with a price," we are treacherous to him in whose redemption we pretend to share.

But time would fail me if I dwelt upon this, or, indeed, at any length upon the positive side of this blessed fact: I will therefore only say a word or two concerning it. Our body and our spirit are God's; and, Christian, this is certainly a very high honor to you. Your body will rise again from the dead at the first resurrection, because it is not an ordinary body, it belongs to God: your spirit is distinguished from the souls of other men; it is God's spirit, and he has set his mark upon it, and honored you in so doing. You are God's, because a price has been paid for you. According to some, the allusion price here is to the dowry that was paid by a husband for his wife in ancient days. According to the Rabbis there were three ways by which a woman became the wife of a man, and one of these was by the payment of a dowry. This was always held good in Jewish law; the woman was not her own from the moment when the husband had paid to her father or natural guardian the stipulated price for her. Now, at this day, you and I rejoice that Jesus Christ has espoused us unto himself in righteousness or ever the earth was; we rejoice in that language which he uses by the prophet Hosea, "I will betroth thee unto me for ever;" but here is our comfort, the dowry money has been paid, Christ has redeemed us unto himself, and Christ's we are, Christ's for ever and ever.

Remember that our Lord has paid all the price for us; there is no mortgage or lien upon us; we have therefore no right to give a portion of ourselves to Satan. And he has bought us entirely from head to foot, every power, every passion, and every faculty, all our time, all our goods, all that we call our own, all that makes up ourselves in the largest sense of that term; we are altogether God's. Ah! it is very easy for people to say this, but how very difficult it is to feel it true and to act as such! I have no doubt there are many persons here who profess to be willing to give God all they have, who would not actually give him five shillings. We can sing--

"Here, Lord, I give myself away;"

and yet if it comes to yielding only a part of ourselves, if it requires self-denial, or self-sacrifice, straightway there is a drawing back. Now, was the cross a fiction? Was the death of Christ a fable? Were you only fancifully "bought with a price," and not in deed and in truth? If redemption be a fable, then return a fabled consecration; if your purchase be a fiction, then lead the fictitious lives that some of you do lead with regard to consecration to Christ. If it be only an idea, a pretty something that we read of in books, then let our belonging unto God be a mere idea and a piece of sentiment; but a real redemption demands real holiness. A true price, most certainly paid, demands from us a practical surrendering of ourselves to the service of God. From this day forth even for ever, "ye are not your own," ye are the Lord's.

III. And now I must close, and oh, may God give power to his word while I beg to speak upon the last point, namely, THE NATURAL CONCLUSION: "Therefore glorify God in your body, and in your spirit." I am not clear that the last few words are in the original. A large number of the old manuscripts and versions, and some of the more important of them, finish the verse at the word "body"--"Therefore glorify God in your body." It was the body the apostle was speaking about, and not the spirit, and there is no necessity for the last words: still we will not further raise the question, but take them as being the inspired word of God: but still. I must make the remark, that according to the connection the force of the apostle's language falls upon the body; and perhaps it is so, because we are so apt to forget the truth, that the body is redeemed and is the Lord's, and should be made to glorify God.

The Christian man's body should glorify God by its chastity. Pure as the lily should we be from every taint of uncleanness. The body should glorify God by temperance also; in all things, in eating drinking, sleeping in everything that has to do with the flesh. "Whether ye eat or drink, or whatsoever ye do, do all to the glory of God," or as the apostle puts it elsewhere, "whatsoever ye do in word or deed, do all in the name of the Lord Jesus, giving thanks to God and the Father by him." The Christian man can make every meal a sacrament, and his ordinary avocations the exercise of his spiritual priesthood. The body ought to glorify God by its industry. A lazy servant is a bad Christian. A working man who is always looking for Saturday night, a man who never spends a drop of sweat except when the master is looking on, does not glorify God in his body. The best Christian is the man who is not afraid of hard work when it is due, who works not as an eye-servant or man pleaser, but in singleness of heart seeks to glorify God. Our bodies used to work hard enough for the devil; now they belong to God we will make them work for him. Your legs used to carry you to the theater; be not too lazy to come out on a Thursday night to the house of God. Your eyes have been often open upon iniquity, keep them open during the sermon: do not drop asleep! Your ears have been sharp enough to catch the word of a lascivious song let them be quick to observe the word of God. Those hands have often squandered your earnings in sinfulness, let them give freely to the cause of Christ. Your body was a willing horse when it was in the service of the devil, let it not be a sluggish hack now that it draws the chariot of Christ. Make the tongue speak his praises, make the mouth sing of his glory, make the whole man bow in willing subservience to the will of him who bought it.

As for your spirit, let that glorify God too. Let your private meditations magnify God; let your songs be to him when no one hears you but himself, and let your public zeal, let the purity of your conversation, let the earnestness of your life, let the universal holiness of your character, glorify God with your body and with your spirit.

Beloved Christian friends, I want to say these few things and have done. Because you are God's, you will be looked at more than others, therefore, glorify him. You know it is not always the thing itself, but the ownership that causes curiosity. If you were to go to a cattle-show and it were said "such and such a bullock belongs to Her Majesty," it may be it is no better than another, but it would be of interest to thousands as belonging to royalty. See here, then, such and such a man belongs to God; what manner of person ought he to be? If there be any one in this world who will not be criticised, depend upon it, Christian, it is not the Christian; sharp eyes will be upon him, and worldly men will find faults in him which they would not see if he were not a professor. For my part I am very glad of the lynx eyes of the worldlings. Let them watch if they will. I have heard of one who was a great caviller at Christian people, and after having annoyed a church a long time, he was about to leave, and therefore, as a parting jest with the minister, he said, "I have no doubt you will be very glad to know that I am going a hundred miles away?" "No," said the pastor, "I shall be sorry to lose you." "How? I never did you any good." "I don't know that, for I am sure that never one of my flock put half a foot through the hedge but what you began to yelp at him, and so you have been a famous sheep-dog for me." I am glad the world observes us. It has a right to do so. If a man says, "I am God's," he sets himself up for public observation. Ye are lights in the world, and what are lights intended for but to be looked at? A city set on a hill cannot be hid.

Moreover, the world has a right to expect more from a Christian than from anybody else. He says he is "bought with a price," he says he is God's, he therefore claims more than others, and he ought to render more. Stand in fancy in one of the fights of the old civil war. The Royalists are fighting desperately and are winning apace, but I hear a cry from the other side that Cromwell's Ironsides are coming. Now we shall see some fighting. Oliver and his men are lions. But, lo! I see that the fellows who come up hang fire, and are afraid to rush into the thick of the fight; surely these are not Cromwell's Ironsides, and yonder captain is not old Noll? I do not believe it: it cannot be. Why, if they were what they profess to be, they would have broken the ranks of those perfumed cavaliers long ago, and have made them fly before them like chaff before the wind. So when I hear men say, "Here is a body of Christians", What! those Christians? Those cowardly people, who hardly dare speak a word for Jesus! Those covetous people who give a few cheese-parings to his cause! Those inconsistent people whom you would not know to be Christian professors if they did not label themselves! What! such beings followers of a crucified Savior? The world sneers at such pretensions; and well it may. With such a leader let us follow bravely; and bought with such a price, and being owned by such a Master, let us glorify him who condescends to call such poor creatures as we are his portion, whom he hath set apart for himself.

And let us remember that by men who profess to be "bought with a price," the name of Christ is compromised if their behavior is unseemly. If we are not holy and gracious, ungodly men are sure to say, "That is one of your believers in God; that is one of your Christians." Do not let it be so. Every soldier in a regiment ought to feel that the renown of the whole army depends upon him, and he must fight as if the winning of the battle rested upon himself. This will cause every man to be a hero. Oh, that every Christian felt as if the honor of God and the church rested upon him, for in a measure it certainly does!

May we so seek God, that when we come to die we may feel that we have lived for something; that although our hope has rested alone in what Jesus did, yet we have not made that an excuse for doing nothing ourselves. Though we shall have no good works in which to glory, yet may we bring forth fruit that shall be for the glory of our Lord. I feel I so desire to glorify God, body, soul, and spirit while I breathe, that I would even do so on earth after I am dead. I would still urge my brethren on in our Lord's cause. Old Zizka, the Hussite leader, when about to die, said to his soldiers: "Our enemies have always been afraid of my name in the time of battle, and when I am dead take my skin, and make a drum-head of it, and beat it whenever you go to battle. When the foemen hear the sound they will tremble, and you will remember that Zizka calls on his brethren to fight valiantly." Let us so live that when we die, we live on, like Abel, who being dead yet speaketh. The only way to do this is to live in the power of the Immortal God, under the influence of his Holy Spirit: then out of our graves we shall speak to future generations. When Doctor Payson died, he desired that his body should be placed in a coffin, and that his hearers should be invited to come and see it. Across his breast was placed a paper bearing these words, "Remember the words which I spake unto you, being yet present with you." May our lives be such that even if we are not public speakers, yet others may remember our example, and so may hear what our lives spake while we were yet on earth. Your bodies and your spirits are God's: oh, live to God, and glorify him in the power of his Spirit as long as you have any breath below, that so when the breath is gone, your very bones, like those of Joseph, shall be a testimony. Even in the ashes of the saints their wonted fires live on. In their hallowed memories they rise like a phoenix from their ashes.

The Lord make us more and more practically his own, and may his name be glorious, for ever and ever. Amen, and amen.

PORTION OF SCRIPTURE READ BEFORE SERMON--1 Peter 1.

Lessons From Nature

A Sermon (No. 1005)
Delivered on Lord's-day Morning, August 13th, 1871, by
C. H. SPURGEON,
At the Metropolitan Tabernacle, Newington

"Where the birds make their nests: as for the stork, the fir trees are her house. The high hills are a refuge for the wild goats, and the rooks for the conies." - Psalm 104:17-18.

THIS PSALM IS ALL through a song of nature, the adoration of God in the great outward temple of the universe. Some in these modern times have thought it to be a mark of high spirituality never to observe nature; and I remember sorrowfully reading the expressions of a godly person, who, in sailing down one of the most famous rivers in the world, closed his eyes, lest the picturesque beauties of the scene should divert his mind from scriptural topics. This may be regarded by some as profound spirituality; to me it seems to savor of absurdity. There may be persons who think they have grown in grace when they have attained to this; it seems to me that they are growing out of their senses. To despise the creating work of God, what is it but, in a measure, to despise God himself? "Whoso mocketh the poor despiseth his Maker." To despise the Maker, then, is evidently a sin; to think little of God under the aspect of the Creator is a crime. We should none of us think it a great honor to ourselves if our friends considered our productions to be unworthy of admiration, and rather injurious to their minds than improving. If when they passed our workmanship they turned their eyes away, lest they should suffer injury by looking at it, we should not regard them as very respectful to ourselves; surely the despising of that which is made is somewhat akin to the despising of the Maker himself. David tells us that "The Lord shall rejoice in his works." If he rejoices in what he has made, shall not those who have communion with him rejoice in his works also? "The works of the Lord are great, sought out of them that have pleasure therein." Despise not the work, lest thou despise the worker.

This prejudice against the beauties of the material universe reminds me of the lingering love to Judaism, which acted like a spell upon Peter of old. When the sheet knit at the four corners descended before him, and the voice said, "Rise, Peter; kill, and eat," he replied that he had not eaten anything that was common or unclean. He needed that the voice should speak to him from heaven again and again before he would fully learn the lesson, "What God hath cleansed that call not thou common." The Jew thinks this and that unclean, though Christ has cleansed it; and certain Christians appear to regard nature as unclean. The birds of the air, and the fish of the sea, the glorious sunrise and sunset, the snow-clad Alps, the ancient forests, the mysterious glaciers, the boundless ocean, God hath cleansed them: call them not common. Here on this earth is Calvary where the Savior died, and by his sacrifice, offered not within walls and roofs, he made this outer world a temple wherein everything doth speak of God's glory. If thou be unclean, all things will be unclean to thee; but if thou hast washed thy robe and made it white in the blood of the Lamb, and if the Holy Spirit hath overshadowed thee, then this world is but a nether heaven; it is but the lower chamber of which the upper story glows with the full splendor of God, where angels see him face to face, and this lower story is not without glory, for in the person of Christ Jesus we have seen God, and have communion and fellowship with him even now.

It appears to me that those who would forbear the study of nature, or shun the observation of its beauties, are conscious of the weakness of their own spirituality. When the hermits and monks shut themselves out from the temptations of life, foolish persons said, "These are strong in grace." Not so, they were so weak in grace that they were afraid to have their graces tried. They ran away from the battle like the cowards they were, and shut themselves up because they knew their swords were not of the true Jerusalem metal, and they were not men who could resist valiantly. Monasticism was the confession of a weakness which they endeavored to cover with the vain show of humility, and the presence of superior sanctity. If my graces are strong, I can look upon the outward world, and draw forth its good without feeling its evil, if evil there be; but if my religion is mainly fictitious, then hypocrisy dictates to me the affectation of unusual spirituality, or at any rate I have not grace enough to rise from a contemplation of the works of God to a nearer fellowship with God himself. It cannot be that nature of itself debases me, or diverts me from God; I ought to suspect a deficiency in my self when I find that the Creator's handiworks have not a good effect upon my soul.

Moreover, rest assured brethren, that he who wrote the Bible, the second and clearest revelation of his divine mind, wrote also the first book, the book of nature; and who are we that we should derogate from the worth of the first because we esteem the second. Milton's "Paradise Regained" is certainly inferior to his "Paradise Lost," but the Eternal God has no inferior productions, all his works are master-pieces. There is no quarrel between nature and revelation, fools only think so: to wise men the one illustrates and establishes the other. Walking in the fields at eventide, as Isaac did, I see in the ripening harvest the same God of whom I read in the word that he covenanted that seed-time and harvest should not cease. Surveying the midnight skies, I remember him who, while he calls the stars by their names, also bindeth up the broken in heart. Who will may neglect the volume of creation, or the volume of revelation, I shall delight in them both as long as I live.

Let us, then, follow David this morning, for when he wrote our text, he evidently traveled amongst the works of God, admiring and adoring. Let us go with him, and see if there be not something to be learned among the birds and storks, the wild goats and the conies.

I. Our first observation from our text shall be this: FOR EACH PLACE GOD HAS PREPARED A SUITABLE FORM OF LIFE. For the fir trees, the stork; for the high hills, the wild goat, or steinbock; for the rocks, the conies, or rabbits. Almost every part of God's world was meant to be the abode of some creature or another. On earth, a countless company wait upon the Lord for meat; and as for the sea, it contains "creeping things innumerable, both small and great beasts." Among the trees which shade the brooks, the birds are singing; in the tall sombre pine, the silent storks are building their nests; on the lofty crags, virgin as yet to human foot, the chamois leaps from ledge to ledge; and away, where human voice was never heard, the marmot, the mouse, and the rabbit (whichever creature the Hebrew may mean) find their dwelling-place among the rocks. The teaching of this fact is clear. We shall find that for all parts of the spiritual universe God has provided suitable forms of divine life. Think out that thought a moment. Each age has its saints. The first age had its holy men, who walked with God: and when the golden age had gone, and men everywhere had polluted themselves, God had his Noah. In after days, when men had again multiplied upon the face of the earth, and sin abounded, there was Job in the land of Uz, and Abraham, and Isaac, and Jacob dwelling in tents in the land which had been given to them by promise. On whatever period of the world's history you choose to place your finger you may rest assured that as God is there, so is there also some form of the divine life extant; some of God's twice born creatures are to be found even in the most barren ages. If you come to a period like that of Ahab, when a lonely Elijah bitterly complains, "I, only I am left, and they seek my life to destroy it," you shall hear a still small voice that saith, "Yet have I reserved unto myself seven thousand men that have not bowed the knee to Baal." God has still his elect remnant in the most wicked times to whom he has given a banner, because of the truth. When the light was almost gone from Israel, and formalism had eclipsed the sun of Judaism, there were still a Simeon and an Anna waiting for the coming of the Messiah. Times of fearful persecution, when to mention the name of Christ was to sentence yourself to death, have not been devoid of saints, but rather in the hottest times of oppression God has brought forth heroes equal to the emergency. The fiercer the trial the stronger the men. The church of God, like the fabled Salamander, has lived and flourished amid the flames, and has seemed to feed upon the flames that threatened to devour her. As on the crags where it appears impossible for life to exist God places wild goats, so on the high crags of persecution he upholds men whose feet are like hind's feet, and who glory as they tread upon their high places. Oppression brings out the heavenly manhood of the saints and lets the devil see what strength God can put into the weakness of man. There have been times of heresy too--such as the age of rampant Arianism, but saints have outlived it. God has provided for such an emergency brave defenders of the faith. What a man was Athanasius, when standing upright and alone he said, "I know that Jesus Christ is very God, and if all the world believe the contrary, I, Athanasius, stand against the world." Sardis may have a name to live and be dead, but the Lord saith, "thou hast a few names even in Sardis which have not defiled their garments, and they shall walk with me in white, for they are worthy." Is not this an encouraging truth, for as it has been in the past it is in the present, and it will be in the future. Do not give way to gloomy forebodings as to the church's future welfare. Whine not with those who deplore these evil days, and prognosticate overwhelming ills. We are told that we are passing through a crisis, but I recollect that it was a crisis twenty years ago, and our grandsires could tell us of a crisis every year of the last fifty. The fact is there is no such crisis as is talked of. The crisis is past, for Christ said, "Now; is the crisis of this world, now shall the prince of this world be cast out." When Jesus went to Golgotha and bled and died, the crisis of the church and of the world was over; the victory of truth and of Christ was secured beyond all hazard. Even if times should darken and the night should grow thicker and thicker, rest assured that he who has the conies for the rocks, and goats for the high hills, and finds for the forests the stork, will find for every age a suitable form of Christian life that shall bring glory to his name.

As it has been in every age, so is it in every position in which men are found. Go into all classes of society, and you shall find that the Christian religion, if received in truth, is equally well adapted for all conditions. Here and there upon the throne have been found those that have feared God, and have gone from a crown on earth to a crown in heaven. There can be no better qualification for swaying a kingdom than obedience to the King of kings. Go straight down from the palace to the poor-house, little enough of comfort there, but the richest consolation which can be found for the meanest pauper, will be brought by that hand which was nailed to the tree. He it is that can console the sorrows of poverty as well as sanctify the risks of wealth. Go ye where ye will amongst the busy, whose cares buzz around them, and you shall find no relief for aching heads like a contemplation of the love of Christ: or go amongst those who have leisure, and spend it in solitude, no meditation can be so sweet to while away their hours as the meditation which springs out of the Gospel of Jesus Christ. Glory be to God, no man need say, "My trade does not permit me to be a Christian;" if it be so, you have no business to follow that trade, for no lawful calling is without its saint. Up there among the precipices the wild goat finds safe footing, and so amid dignity and honor saints can survive, and in the dark rock-rifts of this sin-smitten city, as conies live among the rocks, so Christian men are useful and happy. Where the believer is persecuted on every side, he shall not be forsaken, and where, through the example of the wicked, his heart is grieved, he shall be preserved like righteous Lot. As God maintains life in every region, so doth he maintain spiritual life in every position and every calling. Have comfort in this you who are placed in circumstances unfavourable to grace.

Again, you shall find spiritual life in every church. I know it is the notion of the bigot, that all the truly godly people belong to the denomination which he adorns. Orthodoxy is my doxy; heterodoxy is anybody else's doxy who does not agree with me. All the good people go to little Bethel, and nowhere else: they all worship at Zoar, and they sing out of such-and-such a selection, and as for those who cannot say Shibholeth, and lay a pretty good stress on the "h," but who pronounce it "Sibboleth;"let the fords of the Jordan be taken, and let them be put to death. True, it is not fashionable to roast them alive, but we will condemn their souls to everlasting perdition, which is the next best thing, and may not appear to be quite so uncharitable. Many suppose that because there is grievous error in a church, concerning an ordinance or a doctrine, therefore no living children of God are there. Ah, dear brethren, this severe opinion arises from want of knowing better. A mouse had lived in a box all its life, and one day crawled up to the edge of it, and looked round on what it could see. Now the box only stood in a lumber room, but the mouse was surprised at its vastness, and exclaimed: "How big the world is!" If some bigots would get out of their box, and only look a little way round them, they would find the realm of grace to be far wider than they dream. It is true that these pastures are a most proper place for sheep, but yet upon yonder hill-tops wild goats are pastured by the Great Shepherd. It is true that yonder plains covered with verdure are best fitted for cattle, but the Lord of all has his beasts in the forest, and his conies among the rocks. You may have to look a long while before you find these living things, but he sees them when you do not, and it is a deal more important to a cony for God to see it, than it is for a man to see it; and so it is an infinitely more weighty matter for a child of God for his Father to know that he is his child, than for his brother to know it. If my brother will not believe me to be a Christian, he cannot help being my brother; he may do what he will in his unkindness, but if I am one of God's children, and he also is one, the tie of brotherhood cannot be broken between us. I love to think that the Lord has his hidden ones--even in churches that have sadly degenerated from the faith; and, although it is yours and mine to denounce error unsparingly, and with the iconoclastic hammer to go through the land and break the idols of all the churches in pieces as far as God gives us strength, yet there is not a lamb amongst Christ's flock that we would disdain to feed--there is not the least of all his people, however mistaken in judgment, whom our soul would not embrace an ardent love. God, in nature, has placed life in singular spots, and so has he put spiritual life into strange out-of-the-way places, and has his own chosen where least we should look for them.

Once more, there are to be found God's people in every city. Some of you are going away, it may be, to the ends of the earth, and this word may be comfortable to you. The Lord has an elect people everywhere. The wild goats are on the rocks, and the conies amongst the stones, and the storks in the trees. Go you where you will, you shall find that God has a living people; or if you should be sent to a country where as yet there are no converted men or women, let not that discourage you, but rather say, "I am sent with the purpose of finding out God's elect, who as yet are hidden in sin. I am to be the instrument of finding out the Lord's own blood-bought but hidden ones here." When thou goest into a city that is given to idolatry, thou shalt hear it said to thee, "I have much people in this city;" go, therefore, and labor to find out the much people. Introduce the gospel, tell of the love of Jesus, and you shall soon find that your efforts are rewarded by the discovery of those who shall love your Savior, and delight in the same truth which now charms your heart. Do not believe that there is a rock without its wild goat; do not think that there is a fir-forest without its stork; or that there are to be found trees by the brook without their birds. Expect to find where God dwells that there are some who are sojourners with him, as all their fathers were.

I shall leave the first point, repeating the sentence, for each place there a form of life.

II. Secondly, the text teaches us plainly that EACH CREATURE HAS ITS APPROPRIATE PLACE. Birds with their nests for the cedars of Lebanon, storks for the fir trees, wild goats for the high hills, and conies for the rocks. Each of these creatures looks most beautiful at home. Go into the Zoological Gardens, and see the poor animals there under artificial conditions, and you can little guess what they are at home. A lion in a cage is a very different creature from a lion in the wilderness. The stork looks wretched in his wire pen, and you would hardly know him as the same creature if you saw him on the housetops or on the fir trees. Each creature looks best in its own place. Take that truth, now, and use it for yourself. Each man has by God a providential position appointed to him, and the position ordained for each Christian is that in which he looks best; it is the best for him and he is the best for that; and if you could change his position, and shift him to another, he would not be half as happy, nor half as useful, nor half so much himself. Put the stork on the high hills, put the wild goat on the fir trees--what monstrosities! Take my dear brother who has been a working-man this last twenty years, and always been a spiritually-minded man, and make him Lord Mayor of London, and you would spoil him altogether. Take a good hearer and set him preaching, and he would make a sorry appearance. A man out of place is not seen to advantage, you see the wrong side of him, the gracious side is hidden. The position in which God has placed me is the best for me. Let me remember this when I am grumbling and complaining. It may be I have got past that foolish discontent which is altogether selfish, but perhaps I repine because I think, if I were in a different position, I could glorify God more. This species of discontent is very insinuating, but let us beware of it. It is foolish to cry, "if I were placed in a different position, I could do so much more for God!" You could not do so much as you can do now. I am sure the goat would not show the wisdom of God so well in a fir tree, as he would up on a high hill; and you would not display the grace of God so well anywhere else as you can do where you are. Ah, says the young Christian, "I am only an apprentice; if I were a master man, I think I could then glorify God." Sir, if you cannot magnify him in your apprenticeship, you will not do so when you become a journeyman. "Oh, but my shop is so little, my trade brings me in such a small amount, I can give but little, and I have such few opportunities of doing good." Be slow to leave your calling till you have plain indications from providence that you ought to do so, for many a man in moving from his place has been as a bird that has wandered from her nest. God knows better than you what is best for you; bow your soul to his sovereign will. God appoints our position infinitely better than we could appoint it, even it we could have the choosing of it.

My beloved friends, it is not only that each form of life has its own best position as to providence, but it is so as to experience. God has not made two creatures precisely alike. You shall gather leaves from a tree, and you shall not find two veined in precisely the same way. In Christian experience it is the same. Wherever there is living Christian experience, it is different from everybody else's experience in some respect. In a family of children each child may be like its father, and yet each child shall be different from each other child; and amongst the children of God, though they all have the likeness of Christ in a measure, yet are they not all exactly the one like the other. You read the other day the life of John Bunyan, and you said, "Oh, if I had experience like John Bunyan, then I should know I was a child of God." This was foolish. The biographies that are published in our magazines in many cases do some good, but more mischief; for there are Christian people who begin at once to say, "Have I felt precisely thus? Have I felt exactly that?--If not, I am lost." Hast thou felt thyself a sinner and Christ a Savior? Art thou emptied of self and dost thou look to Christ alone? Well, if no other soul hath trod the same path as thou hast done, thou art in a right path; and though thy experience may have eccentricities in it that differ from all others, it is right it should be so. God has not made the wild goat like the cony, nor has he made the stork like any other bird, but he has made each to fit the place it is to occupy, and he makes your experience to be suitable to the bringing out some point of his glory, which could not be brought out otherwise. Some are full of rejoicing, others are often depressed; a few keep the happy medium; many soar aloft, and then dive into the deeps again; let these varied experiences, as they are all equally clear phases of the same divine lovingkindness, be accepted, and let them be rejoiced in.

The same holds good as to individuality of character. Each creature has its appropriate place, and I believe that each constitution is meant, under the power of grace, to be suitable for a man's position. I might wish to be of a different temperament from what I am--I sometimes think so, but in wiser moments, I would not wish to alter anything in myself but that which is sinful. Martin Luther might have wished that he had been as gentle as Melancthon, but then we might have had no reformation: Melancthon might certainly sometimes have wished that he had been as energetic as Martin Luther, but then Luther might have lacked his most tender comforter, if Melancthon had been as rough as he. Peter might have been improved if he had not been so rough, and John might possibly have been improved if he had been somewhat more firm; but after all, when God makes Peter he is best as Peter, and when he makes John he is best as John, and it is very foolish when Peter wants to be John, and when John pines to be Peter. Dear brethren, the practical matter is, be yourselves in your religion. Never attempt to counterfeit another's virtues, nor try to square your experience according to another man's feelings, nor endeavor to mould your character so that you may look as if you were like a certain good man whom you admire. No, ask the Lord, who made a new man of you, to let your manhood come out as he meant it, and whichever grace he meant to be prominent, let it be prominent. If you are meant to play the hero and rush into the thick of the battle, then let courage be developed; or if he designed you to lie in the hospital and suffer, then let patience have its perfect work; but ask the Lord to mould you after his own mind, that as he finds a stork for a fir tree and a fir tree for a stork; a hill for a wild goat, and a wild goat for a hill; he will find a place for you, the man, and find for you, the man, the place that he has created for you, There his name shall be most glorified, and you shall be safest. Kick not against the pricks, but take kindly to the yoke, and serve your day and generation till your Master calls you home.

III. Now, briefly, a third point. It appears from the text that EVERY CREATURE THAT GOD HAS MADE IS PROVIDED WITH SHELTER. Birds fly to the trees, and the stork to the fir, the wild goat to the high hills, and the cony to the rocks. There is a shelter for every one of these creatures, great and small. Think a moment, then, if God has made each creature happy, and given a place of refuge to each creature, then, depend upon it, he has not left man's soul without a shelter. And here is an important truth, for every man is certainly in danger, and every thinking man knows it. My God, dost thou shield and shelter the cony in the rock, and is there no rock for me to shelter in? Assuredly thou hast not made man and left him without a refuge; when thou givest to the rock-rabbit the cleft in which he may hide himself, there must be a shelter for man. This must certainly be true, because you and I, if we have observed our inner life, must have felt conscious that nothing here below can fill an immortal soul. You have prospered in business, and have enjoyed good health; but for all that, in quiet moments of reflection, you feel a craving for something not to be found beneath the sun. Have you not felt yearnings after the Infinite,--hungerings which bread cannot satisfy; thirstings which a river could not quench? And are you never conscious--I know I am as a man, I speak not as a Christian now--of cold shiverings of fear, which make the entire manhood to tremble? The mind looks forward and considers, "And shall I live for ever? When my body moulders, shall I continue? Am I a vessel launched upon the river of existence, and shall I be borne onward to a shoreless and mysterious sea? And what will be that sea, and will it be a calm, or tossed with storms?" Or, to change the figure, "I shall sleep, but in that sleep of death, what dreams may come?" Have you never felt all that, and said within yourself, "O that there were a place where I could hide myself, never to tremble more! O that I could grasp something that would satisfy my insatiable lodgings! O that I could get my foot upon a rook, and no longer feel that a quicksand is beneath me! O that I knew of truth sure and indisputable, and possessed a treasure that would enrich me for ever." Well, then, if you have such longings as these, surely there must be a provision to meet them. The stork has an instinct for building a nest of a certain sort; it is too large a nest to be placed on a bush, she needs a tree; there is a tree somewhere then, for God never made a stork for a tree but he made also a tree for the stork. Here is a wild goat: you put it down on a flat meadow, and it is not happy. Give it the greenest pasture, it looks up and pines. Rest assured that since those little feet are meant to traverse rocks and crags, there are rocks and crags that are meant for those feet to leap upon. A chamois argues an Alps, and the conclusion is verified by fact. Yonder little cony cannot live anywhere but among the stones; it delights to conceal itself in the fissures of the rock; then be assured there are rocks meant for conies. So for me, with my thirstings, my longings, my pipings, my mysterious instincts--there is a God somewhere, there is a heaven somewhere, there is an atonement somewhere, there is a fullness somewhere to meet my emptiness. Man wants a shelter, there must be a shelter; let us show you what it is.

Beloved, there is a shelter for man from the sense of past guilt. It is because we are guilty that we are fearful: we have broken our Maker's law, and therefore we are afraid. But our Maker came from heaven to earth; Jesus, the Christ of God, came here, and was made man, and bore that we might never bear his Father's righteous wrath, and whosoever believeth in Jesus shall find perfect rest in those dear wounds of his. Since Christ suffered for me, my guilt is gone, my punishment was endured by my Substitute, therefore do I hear the voice that saith, "Comfort ye, comfort ye my people! Say unto them, that their warfare is accomplished; for they have received at the Lord's hand double for all their sins." And as for future fears, he who believes in Jesus finds a refuge from them in the Fatherhood of God. He who trusts Christ, says: "Now I have no fear about the present, nor about the future. Let catastrophe follow catastrophe, let the world crash, and all the universe go to ruin; beneath the wings of the Eternal God I must be safe. All things must work together for my good, for I love God, and have been called according to his purpose." What a blessed shelter this is! The little conies in their rock-clefts are perfectly at ease, and so we, when we enter fully into the truth of our adoption of God, are filled with unutterable peace. And as for the present, with its cares, and griefs, and heart-throbs, there is the Holy Ghost abiding in us, the Comforter, and we fly to him, and receive consolations so rich and powerful, that this day we feel at peace in the midst of discomforts, and if perplexed we are not in despair. Brethren, there is a shelter in the atonement of Christ, in the Fatherhood of God, in the abiding presence of the Comforter--there is a shelter for man--would God that all of us had found it!

IV. And now just a moment of your attention will be wanted for the fourth observation, that FOR EACH CREATURE THE SHELTER IS APPROPRIATE. The tree for the bird; the fir tree, a particular and special tree, for the stork; a high hill for the steinbock or ibex, and the rocks for the hyrax or rabbit. Whatever creature it may be, each shall have his own suitable shelter. But you will reply to me, is there a shelter, then, for each individual man? Did you not say that there was only one shelter for manhood? If I did not say it, I certainly will say it now. There is only one shelter under heaven or in heaven for any man of woman born, but yet there is a shelter suitable for each. Christ Jesus suits all sorts of sinners, all sorts of sufferers. He is a Savior as suitable for me as if he came to save me and no one else; but he is a Redeemer as remarkably suitable to every other of his redeemed ones. Note, then, that there is a refuge in Christ Jesus for those simple trustful natures that take the gospel at once and believe it. These are like the little birds that fly to the trees and build their nests and begin to sing. These are the commonest sort of Christians, but in some respects they are the best. They hear the gospel, believe it to be God's word, accept it, and begin to sing. Jesus Christ exactly suits them, he is a shelter for those chosen birds of the air, whom your heavenly Father daily feed. But there are others of larger intellect, who require unusual support ere they can build their nest and be at ease. These, like the stork, need a special support, and they find it in the gospel. Since they are more weighty with doubt and perplexity, they need substantial verities to rest on; these find great fir-tree doctrines and cedar-like principles in the Bible, and they rest in them. Many of us this day are resting on the immutable things wherein it is impossible for God to lie. We rest upon the substitution of Christ, and repose in the completeness of the atonement. Some get hold of one great principle and some another in connection with the grace of God; and God has been pleased to reveal strong, immovable, eternal, immutable principles in his Word which are suitable for thoughtful and troubled minds to rest on. Moreover, we have in the church of God persons of great reasoning powers: these love the craggy paths of thought, but when they come to Christ and trust in him, though they are like the wild goat and love the high places, they find in the Scriptures good ground for them. The doctrine of election, and all the mysteries of predestination, the deep and wonderful doctrines that are spoken of by the apostle Paul; where is the man of thought who will not be at home among these if he loves sublimity? If you have that turn of mind which delights to deal with the high things of God, which have been the perplexity of men and angels, you shall find yourself at home, and what is better, safe with the gospel. If you are in Christ, you shall have good, solid, safe material for the profoundest meditations. Perhaps, instead of being bold and daring and thoughtful, you are not comparable to the wild goat but you are "a very timid trembling little creature like the cony. If anyone claps his hands, away runs the cony; he fears always. But there is a shelter for conies; and so in the grace of God for very timid trembling people, there is a suitable refuge. Here is a delightful shelter for some of you to run into. "Fear not, I am with thee; be not dismayed, I am thy God." Here is another--"Him that cometh to me I will in no wise cast out." Many a poor trembler has hidden under that condescending word. If I cannot find shelter in one text, what a blessing it is the Bible is full of promises, and there are promises in the Bible which seem made for a certain form of mind, as if the Holy Ghost cast his thoughts and his words into all sorts of moulds to suit the habits of thought and mind of all whom he would bless. O trembling soul, though thou art half afraid to say that thou belongest to Jesus, yet come and rest in him, hide in the rift of his side, and thou art safe.

V. Now we must close, and we do so with this observation, that EACH CREATURE USES ITS SHELTER, for the storks have made their nests in the fir trees, and the wild goats climb the high hills, and the conies hide among the rocks. I never heard of one of these creatures that neglected its shelter--they love their natural abodes; but I have heard of men who have neglected their God, I know women who have forgotten Christ. We say, "silly sheep." Ah, if the sheep knew all about us, they would wonder we should call them silly. The cony in danger which does not seek its rock is foolish; but the soul in danger which does not seek its Savior is insane--insane, nay, if there can be a madness which is as much beyond madness, as madness is beyond sanity, then such is the raving lunacy of a man who neglects the Savior. I have never heard of any of these creatures that they despise the shelter provided. The birds are satisfied with the trees, and the stork with the firs, and even the cony with its rock-hole; but, alas! there are men who despise Christ. God himself becomes the shelter of sinners, and yet sinners despise their God. The Son of God opens his side and lays bare his heart that a soul may come and shelter there in the crimson cleft, and yet that soul for many a day refuses to accept the shelter. Oh, where are tears? Who shall give us fit expressions for our sorrow that men should be such monsters to themselves, and to their God? The ox knoweth its owner, and the ass its master's crib; but men know not God. The stork knows its fir tree, the wild goat its crag, and the cony knows its cleft, but the sinner knows not his Christ. Ah, manhood, what has befallen thee? What strange wine of Gomorrah hast thou drank which has thus intoxicated thee!

One other thing, I never heard of a stork that when it met with a fir tree demurred as to its right to build its nest there, and I never heard of a cony yet that questioned whether it had a permit to run into the rock. Why these creatures would soon perish if they were always doubting and fearing as to whether they had a right to use providential provisions. The stork says to himself, "ah, here is a fir tree;" he consults with his mate--"Will this do for the nest in which we may rear our young?" "Ay" says she, and they gather the materials, and arrange them. There is never any deliberation, "May we build here?" but they bring their sticks and make their nest. So the wild goat on the crag does not say, "Have I a right to be here?" No! he must be somewhere, and there is a crag which exactly suits him; and he springs upon it. Yet though these dumb creatures know the provision of their God, the sinner does not recognize the provisions of his Savior. He quibbles and questions, "May I?" and "I am afraid it is not for me," and "I think it cannot be meant for me; and I am afraid it is too good to be true." And yet nobody ever said to the stork, "Whosoever buildeth on this fir tree shall never have his nest pulled down." No inspired word has ever said to the cony, "Whosoever runs into this rock-cleft shall never be driven out of it;" if it had been so, it would make assurance doubly sure. And yet here is Christ provided for sinners, just the sort of a Savior sinners need, and the encouragement is added, "Him that cometh unto me I will in no wise cast out;" "Whosoever will let him come, and take the water of life freely." O dear brothers and sisters, do not be standing out against the generosity of a sin-pardoning God, who bids the sinner come and welcome. Come, believe in Jesus, and find salvation now. O that you would come, it is what God has provided for your wants. Come, take it, for he bids you come. "The Spirit and the bride say come, and whosoever will let him come and take the water of life freely." To believe is to trust Jesus, to trust his suffering, to trust his atonement, and rely upon him alone for salvation. May God enable you to do it for Christ's sake. Amen.

PORTION OF SCRIPTURE READ BEFORE SERMON--Psalm 104.

Christ Is All

A Sermon (No. 1006)
Delivered on Lord's-day Morning, August 20th, 1871, by
C. H. SPURGEON,
At the Metropolitan Tabernacle, Newington

"Christ is all in all." - Colossians 3:11.

THE APOSTLE WAS ARGUING for holiness. He was earnestly contending against sin and for the maintenance of Christian graces, but he did not, as some do, who would like to be thought preachers of the gospel, resort to reasons inconsistent with the gospel of free grace. He did not bring forward a single legal argument; he did not say, "This do, and ye shall merit reward;" or, "This do not, and ye shall cease to be the beloved of the Lord." He knew that he was writing to believers, who are not under the law but under grace, and be therefore used arguments fetched from grace, and suitable to the character and condition of "the elect of God, holy and beloved." He fed the flame of their love with suitable fuel, and fanned their zeal with appropriate appliances.

Observe in this chapter that he begins by reminding the saints of their having risen with Christ. If they indeed have risen with him, he argues that they should leave the grave of iniquity and the graveclothes of their sins behind, and act as those who are endowed with that superior life, which accounts sin to be death and corruption. He then goes on to declare that the believer's life is in Christ, "for ye are dead, and your life is hid with Christ in God." He infers holiness from this also. Shall those who have Christ for their life defile themselves with guilt! Is it not inevitable that, if the Holy One of Israel be in them as their life, their life should be fraught with everything that is virtuous and good? And then he brings forward the third argument that in the Christian church Christ is the only distinguishing mark. In the new birth we are created in the image of Jesus, the second Adam, and in consequence all the distinctions that appertain to the old creation are rendered valueless; "there is neither Greek nor Jew, circumcision nor uncircumcision, Barbarian, Sythian, bond nor free: but Christ is all, and in all": the argument from this fact being, that since the only abiding distinction in the new creation is Christ, we should take care that his image is most clearly stamped upon us so that we may not only confess with our tongues that we are Christians, but our conversation and our entire character shall bespeak us to be such. As you may recognize the Jew by his physiognomy, the Greek by his gracefulness, and the barbarian by his uncouthness; so should the Christian be known by his Christliness, by the light, love, and life of Christ streaming forth from him. This is the seal of God which is set upon the forehead of the faithful, and this is the mark of election which is in due season graven in the right hand of all the elect.

Now, as the only distinction which marks the Christian from other men, and the only essential distinction in the new world of grace, is Christ, we are led to see beneath this fact a great underlying doctrine. In the realm of grace, things are what they seem. Christ is apparently all, because he is actually all. The fact of a man's possessing Christ is all in all in the church, because in very deed Christ is all in all. All that is real in the Christian, all that is holy, heavenly, pure, abiding, and saving, is of the Lord Jesus. This great granite fact lies at the basis of the whole Christian system, Christ is really and truly all in all in his church, and in each individual member of it.

We shall, this morning, in trying to open up this precious subject, by the help of the Divine Spirit, first, notice by whom this truth is recognised; secondly we shall consider what this truth includes; thirdly, what it involves; and fourthly, what it requires of us; for if you observe, the text is followed by a "Therefore;" there is a conclusion logically drawn from it.

I. First, then, BY WHOM IS THIS TRUTH RECOGNISED? Paul does not say that Christ is all in all to all men, but he tells us that there is a new creation, in which the man is "renewed in knowledge after the image of him that created him," where all national and ceremonial distinctions cease, and Christ is all and in all. It is not to every man that Christ is all and in all. Alas! there are many in this world to whom Christ is nothing; he scarcely enters into their thoughts. Some of the baser sort only use his name to curse by; and as to many others, if they have a religion, it is a proud presumption which excludes a Savior. The creed of the self-righteous has no room in it for the sinner's Savior; the justifier of the ungodly is nothing to them. The worldly, the frivolous, the unchaste, the licentious, these do not permit themselves to think of the Holy Redeemer. Perchance some such are now present, and though they will hear about him this morning, and of nothing else but him, they will say, "what a weariness it is," and be glad when the discourse is ended. Jesus is a root out of a dry ground to multitudes, to them he hath no form nor comeliness, and in him they see no beauty that they should desire him. Ah, what will they do when he is revealed in the glory of his power? They thought it nothing to them as they passed by his cross, but they will not be able to despise him as they stand convicted before his throne. O ye who make Jesus nothing, kiss the Son lest he be angry, and ye perish from the way, when his wrath is kindled but a little. Without Christ, you are to-day without peace, and will be for ever without hope! Nothing remains for Christless souls at the last, but a fearful looking for of judgment and of fiery indignation. I could well pause here, and say, let us pray for those who are unbelievers, and so are living without a Savior, that they may not remain any longer in this state of condemnation.

There are others in this world to whom Christ is something, but not much. They are anxious to save themselves, but since they must confess some imperfections they use the merits of Christ as a sort of makeweight for their slight deficiencies. Their robe is almost long enough, and by adding a little fringe of the Redeemer's grace it becomes all they can wish. To say prayers, to go to church, to take the sacrament to observe Good Friday, these are the main reliances of many a religionist, and then if the coach sticks a little in a deeper rut than usual they call in the help of the Lord Jesus, and hope that he will put his shoulder to the wheel. They commonly say, "Well, we must do our best, then Christ will be our Savior, and God is very merciful." They allow the blessed and all-sufficient work and sacrifice of the Savior to fill up their failures; and imagine that they are extremely humble in allowing so much as that. Jesus is to them a stopgap, and nothing more. I know not whether the condition of such people is one whit more desirable than that of those to whom Jesus is nothing at all, for this is a vile contempt and despising of Christ indeed, to think that he came to help you to save yourselves, to dream that he is a part Savior, and will divide the world; and honor of salvation with the sinner. Those who yoke the sinner and the Savior together as each doing a part rob Christ of all his glory; and this is robbery indeed, to pilfer from the bleeding Lamb of God the due reward of his agonies. "He trod the winepress alone, and of the people there was none with him." In the work of salvation Jesus stands alone. Salvation is of the Lord. It Christ is not all to you he is nothing to you. He will never go into partnership as a part Savior of men. If he be something he must be everything, and if he be not everything he is nothing to you.

There are many who, unconsciously to themselves, think Jesus Christ to be much, but yet they do not understand that he is all in all. I allude to many seeking souls, who say, "I would put my trust in Jesus this morning, but I do not feel as I ought." I see, thou thinkest that there is at least a little of thy feeling to be added to the Savior's work ere it can avail for thee. "But I am not as penitent as I should be, and, therefore, I cannot rest in Jesus." I see, thy penitence is to add the topstone to the Savior's yet unfinished work. Perhaps it is one of the hardest works in the world, so hard as to be impossible except to the Holy Spirit himself, to drive a man away from the idea that he is to do something, or to be something, in order to his own salvation. Sinner, thou art the emptiness, and Christ the fullness; thou art the filthiness, and he the cleansing; thou art nothing, and he is all in all; and the sooner thou consentest to this the better. Have done with saying, "I would come to the Savior if this, and if that," for this quibbling will delude, delay, and destroy thee. Come as thou art, just now, even at this moment, for Christ is not almost all, but all in all.

There are some, too, who think that Christ is all in some things, but they have not yet seen the full teaching of the text; for it saith: "Christ is all, and in all." He is all, "say they, in justification; he it is that pardons all our sins and covers us with his righteousness, but as to our sanctification, surely, we are to effect that ourselves; and as to our final perseverance, it must depend wholly upon our own watchfulness. Are we not in jeopardy still? Are there not some points which depend upon our own virtue and goodness?" Beloved, God forbid I should say a word against the most earnest watchfulness, against the most diligent endeavors, but I beseech you do not place them in a wrong position, or speak us though the ultimate salvation of the believer were based upon such shifting sand. We are saved in Christ. We are complete in him. We are sanctified in Christ Jesus: "And he is made of God unto us wisdom, righteousness, sanctification, and redemption." Christ is all, not in my justification only, but in my sanctification too. He is all, not only in the first steps of my faith, but in the last. "He is Alpha and Omega; he is the beginning and the ending, saith the Lord." There is no point between the gates of hell and the gates of heaven where a believer shall have to say, "Christ fails me here, and I must rely upon my own endeavors. From the dunghill of our corruption up to the throne of our perfection there is no point left to hazard, or set aside for us to supply; our salvation has Christ to begin with, Christ to go on with, and Christ to finish with, and that in all points, at all times, for every man of woman born that ever shall be saved. There is no point in which the creature comes in to claim merit, or to bring strength, or to make up for that which was lacking. "Christ is all, and in all." The saints are "perfect in Christ Jesus." He said, "it is finished," and finished it is. He is not the author of our faith only, but the finisher of it too. He is all in all, and man is nothing at all.

This is a truth which every believer has recognised. There are a great many differences among believers, but there is no difference as to this essential point. Unhappily, the Christian church has been divided into sections, but those divisions do not affect our agreement upon this one point, that Christ is all. It is no uncharity if I say that the man who does not accept this is no Christian, nor is it too wide a liberality to affirm that every man who is sound in heart upon this point is most certainly a believer. He who trusts alone in Christ, who submits to him as his sole teacher, king, and Savior, is already a saved man; but he who gives not Christ the glory, though he should speak with the tongues of men and of angels, though he should have the gift of prophecy, and all knowledge, and though he should have all faith, and could remove mountains, and he should appear to have all virtue, yet he is no Christian if Christ be held in light esteem by him, or be anything less than all in all; for in the new creation this one thing stands as the mark of the newly created, that "Christ is all, and in all" to them, whatever he may be to others.

II. Having thus shown where this truth is recognised, we pass on to notice WHAT THIS TRUTH INCLUDES.

It was the advice of an aged tutor to a young student not to take too magnificent a text. I have sounded that warning in my own ears this morning. This little text is yet one of the greatest in the whole Bible, and I feel lost in its boundless expanse. It is like one of those rare gems which are little to look upon, and yet he who carries them bears the price of empires in his hand. It would not be within the compass of arithmetic to set down the value of this sapphire test. I might as soon hope to carry the world in my hand as to grasp all that is contained in these few words. I cannot navigate so huge a sea, my skiff is too small, I can only coast along the shore. Who can compress "all things" into a sermon? I will warrant you that my discourse this morning will be more remarkable for its omissions than for what it contains, and I shall hope indeed that every Christian here will be remarking upon what I do not say; for then I shall have done much good in exciting meditations and reflections. If I were to try to tell you all the meaning of this boundless text, I should require all time and eternity, and even then all tongues, human and angelic, could not avail me to compass the whole. We will swim in this sea though we cannot fathom it, and feast at this table though we cannot reckon up its costliness.

1. According to the connection, Christ is all by way of national distinction, subject for glorying, and ground for custom. Observe, "there is neither Greek nor Jew, circumcision nor uncircumcision, barbarian, Scythian, bond nor tree," in the new creation, but "Christ is all, and in all." In the new world there is no difference between Jew and Gentile; barbarian simplicity and Greek cultivation are as nothing. I suppose as long as we are in the flesh we shall set some store by our nationality, and like Paul shall somewhat glory that we were free born: but surely the less of this the better. Within the gates of the Christian church we are cosmopolitan, or rather we are citizens of the New Jerusalem only. As a man, I rejoice that I am an Englishman, but not with the same holy joy which fills me when I remember that I am a Christian. When I meet another man who fears God, I do not want him to think me an Englishman, nor do I desire to regard him as an American, a Frenchman, or a Dutchman; for we are no longer strangers and foreigners but fellow-citizens. If any man be a Christian and a foreigner after the flesh, he is yet in spirit ten thousand times more allied to me than if he were an Englishman and an unbeliever. Greatly is it to be deplored whenever the convulsions of nations drag Christian men into opposition to one another on the ground of politics. One part of the body of Christ cannot be at war with another. It is a shameful thing whenever we suffer our earthly nationality to dominate over our heavenly citizenship. Queen Victoria and President Grant are well enough in their places, but King Jesus is Lord of all; we are above all things subjects of his Imperial Highness the Prince of Peace. Nobody comes into the church as a Jew or a Gentile, nor does he remain there as a Greek or a Scythian, whatever he may have been before; when he becomes a Christian, Christ is all. Earthly distinctions of rank, if they still exist, as they must while we are in this world, are brought to a minimum within the church, they are almost obliterated, and what remains is sanctified to sacred ends.

Christ is all in the church by way of glorying. The Greek said, "The Hellenes are a race of heroes; remember Sparta and Athens. Are we not foremost in civilisation, and were we not chief in war? Who set bounds to the Persian tyrant, and bade the boastful monarch bite the dust? We hold our heads erect when we think of Marathon and Salamis." But when the Greek joined the Christian church, he forgot his national boastings, and henceforth gloried only in the cross of him whose single arm defeated the hosts of Satan, and led captivity captive. The Jew when despised returned scorn for scorn, and said to Greek and Roman, "You may speak of Marathon, but I sing of the Red Sea; you may boast of Persia broken, but I tell of Egypt vanquished, mine are the glories of the Lord of hosts in the far off ages. We were a people when you were as get unknown, and we are the chosen favourites of Jehovah." The moment the Jew sat down at the gospel supper, he laid aside his hereditary pride and bigotry, and recognised the fact that the Greek was a, much a brother as the believing Hebrew at his side. So the Sythian, when he came into the Christian church, was no longer a Barbarian, he spoke the language of Canaan as correctly as his Grecian fellow Christian. The slave no sooner breathed the air of the Christian church than his shackles fell from him. He might be a slave at home with his master, but he was no slave there. While the freeman, though he had been born free, or with a great price had obtained his freedom, never in the Christian church looked down upon the slave. Bond and free were one in Christ Jesus. Nobody had any personal ground for glory; neither race, nor pedigree, nor rank, nor position, were of any account, but Christ was all. "Christianus sum," I am a Christian was and is the universal glorying of all saints.

This at the same time obliterated all their sinful national customs. The Greek said originally, "I may certainly indulge in this vice, because the Lacedaemonians have always observed this custom;" and the Jew, perhaps, might have said, "I will eat nothing common or unclean, neither will I consort with Gentiles, because our fathers did not so." The Barbarian said, "I cannot submit to the laws of civilised life; my father ranged the desert;" and the Sythian said, "I shall rob, and pillage, and kill, for I am a wild man; why should I not? Did not my fathers do so from generation to generation?" When the various tribes came into the Christian church, down went all separating and evil customs at once. What hath Christ said? What hath Christ done? What hath he bidden us? These are law to us and nothing else.

Thus the distinctions of race, the gloryings of the nationality, and the habitudes and customs of various nations, all sank into nothing, for Jesus Christ in the Christian church became all in all. That, I doubt not, is the meaning of the text in its connection. Christ all and in all by way of distinction.

2. Secondly, Christ is all in all to us in another three-fold way--to God, before our enemies, within ourselves. Happy art thou, O child or God, that in all thy relationships to the Great Judge of all the earth, Christ is all in all to thee. Thou needest a mediator to stand between thee and God; Christ is that. Thou wantest a high Priest to present with his own sacrifice thy prayers and praises; Christ is that. Thou wantest a representative to stand at all times before God, an intercessor to plead for thee, one who shall be a daysman akin to thee and akin to God, who can put his hand upon both; Christ is that to thee. Whenever God looks upon thee in Christ, he sees in thee all that ought to be there. Did he look upon thee apart from Christ, he would see in thee nothing he could commend: but thou art "accepted in the Beloved." Even the omniscient eye of God detects nothing for which to condemn the soul which is covered with the righteousness of Christ. "Who shall lay anything to the charge of God's elect? It is God that justifieth." Without spot, or wrinkle, or any such thing, is the entire church as seen in the person of Christ Jesus, her representative and head. Christ is all for us before the throne of God.

But, alas! we need some one to stand between us and our enemies. There is Satan; how shall I meet him? He will accuse me; Who shall plead my case? Christ is all in all for that. Whatever fiery darts Satan may shoot, Christ is the shield that can quench those darts. If Satan tempt me, Christ shall plead for me before the temptation comes. Whenever I have to contend with Satan, this is the weapon with which I should arm myself: If I reason with him, if I bring forward any strength of my own to oppose him, he may well say to me: "Jesus I know; but who art thou?" But if I bring Jesus into the conflict, and wield the merit of his blood, and the faithfulness of his promise, the destroying angel cannot overcome the sprinkled blood. We overcome through the blood of the Lamb. Christ Jesus is both shield and sword to us, armor and weapons of war.

So in our conflict with the world. Whatever trials you have, my dear brother, Christ is all in all to meet them. Are you poor? He will make you rich in your poverty by his consoling presence. Are you sick? He will make your bed in your sickness, and will so make your sick-bed better than the walks of health. Are you persecuted? Be it for his sake, and you may even leap for joy. Are you oppressed? Remember how he also was oppressed and afflicted; and you will have fellowship with him in his sufferings. Amidst all the vicissitudes of this present life, Christ is all that the believer wants to bear him up, and bear him through. No wave can sink the man who clings to this life-buoy; he shall swim to glory on it.

So, too, within myself Christ is all. If I look into the chambers of my inner nature, I see all manner of deficiencies and deformities, and I may well be filled with dismay; but when I see Christ there, my heart is comforted, for he will both destroy the works of the devil, and perfect that which he has begun in me. I am a sinner, but my heart rests on its Savior; I am burdened with this body of sin and death but behold my Savior is formed in me the hope of glory. I am by nature an heir of wrath, even as others, but I am born into the second Adam's household, and therefore I am beloved of the Most High, and a joint-heir with Christ. Is there Christ in thy heart beloved? Then everything that is there that would make thee sorrow may also suggest to thee a topic for joy. The saint is grieved to think that he has sin to confess, but he is glad to think that he is enabled to confess sin. The saint is vexed that he should have so much infirmity, yet he glories in infirmity because the power of Christ doth rest upon him. He is grieved day by day to observe his wanderings, but he is also rejoiced to see how the Good Shepherd follows him and restores his soul. So that all the evils and short comings in me which make me weep, also make me glad when Jesus is seen within. For all I see within myself lacking or sinful, I see a sufficient remedy in Christ who is all in all.

Thus I have given you a second way of meditating upon our text. Christ is not only all by way of distinction, but he is all to God, all between us and our enemies, and all within ourselves.

3. We may see another phase of the same meaning if we take a third division. Christ is all for us, he is all to us, he is all in us.

Christ is all for us, the surety, the substitute in our stead to bear our guilt; "For the Lord hath laid on him the iniquity of us all." "The chastisement of our peace was upon him." "He hath made him to be sin for us who knew no sin, that we might be made the righteousness of God in him." He is also the worker standing in our place to fulfill all righteousness for us. He is the end of the law for righteousness to every one that believeth. All that God requires us to be, Christ is for us. He has not presented to God a part of what was done, but has to the utmost farthing paid all that his people owed. Acting as our forerunner in heaven, he has taken possession of our inheritance, and as our surety he secures to us our entrance there. For us all Jesus is all.

And this day he is all to us. We trust wholly in him. I often question myself upon many Christian graces, but there is one thing I never can doubt about, and that is I know I have no other hope but in the blood and righteousness of Jesus Christ. If a soul can perish relying with all its power upon the finished work of the Savior, then I shall perish; but if saving faith be an entire reliance upon Him whom God hath sent forth to be a propitiation for sin, then I can never perish until God's word be broken. Can you not say that, dear brethren, and will it not yield you comfort? Have you anything else you could trust to? Have you one good work that you could rely upon? Is there a prayer you have ever offered, an emotion you have ever felt, that you would dare to use as a buttress, or as in some degree a prop, to your hope of salvation? I know you reply, "I have nothing, nothing, nothing, nothing; but Christ my Savior is all my salvation and all my desire, and I abhor the very idea of putting anything side by side with him as a ground of my dependence before God." Oh, then, assuredly you have the mark of Christ's sheep, for to all of them Christ is all.

I said also that Christ is all in us, and so he is. Whatever there is in us that is not of Christ and the work of his Spirit, will have to come out of us, and blessed be the day in which it is ejected. If I am growing and advancing, but it is a growth in the flesh and an advance in self, it is a spurious fungus growth; and, like Jonah's gourd, it will perish in a night. Wood, hay, stubble, are quick building, but they are also quick burning; only that which belongs to "Christ formed in me the hope of glory," will prove to be gold, silver, precious stones, this may seem slow building, but it will abide the fire. O Christian, pray much and labor much to have Christ in thee, for he is all that is worth having in thee. He is only the husk of a Christian who has not the precious kernel of Christ in his heart. Christ on the cross saves us by becoming Christ in the heart. Jesus is indeed all for us, all to us, all in us.

4. Shift the kaleidoscope, and take the same truth in another way Christ is the channel of all, the pledge of all, the sum of all.

The channel of all. All love and mercy flow from God through Christ the mediator. We get nought apart from him. "No man cometh unto the Father but by me." Other conduits are dry, but this channel is always full. "He is able to save them to the uttermost that come unto God by him, seeing he ever liveth to make intercession for them."

Christ is the pledge of all. When God gave us Christ, he did as much as say, "I have given you all things." "He that spared not his own Son, but freely delivered him up for us all, how shall he not with him also freely give us all things?" He is a covenant to us, the title-deeds of the promised rest.

And, indeed, Christ is not only the channel of all, and the pledge of all, but the apostle says he is all; so I take it he is the sum of all. If you are going to travel on the Continent, you need not carry a bed with you, nor a house, nor a table, nor medicine, nor food; if you only have gold in your purse, you have these condensed. Gold is the representative of everything it can buy, it is a kind of universal talisman, producing, what its owner wishes for. I have never yet met with a person in any country who did not understand its meaning. "Money answereth all things," says the wise man, and this is true in a limited sense; but he that has Christ, has indeed all things: he has the essence, the substance of all good. I have only to plead the name of Jesus before the Father's throne, and nothing desirable shall be denied me. If Christ is yours, all things are yours. God, who gave you Christ, has in that one gift summed up the total of all you will want for time and for eternity, to obliterate the sin of the past, to fulfill the needs of the present, and to perfect you for all the work and bliss of the future.

5. Once more let us view our text in another light. Christ is all we need, all we desire, and all of good that we can conceive. He is all I need. Jesus is the living water to quench my thirst, the heavenly bread to satisfy my hunger, the snow-white robe to cover me, the sure refuge, the happy

home of my soul, my meat and my medicine, my solace and my song, my light and my delight.

He is all I desire, and when most covetous I only covet more of his presence; when most ambitious, it is my ambition to be like him; when most insatiable in desire, I only long to be with him where he is. He is all I can conceive of good. When my imagination stretches all her wings to take a flight into realms beyond where the eagle's wing hath been, yet even then she reacheth not the height of the glory which Christ Jesus hath promised her; she cannot conceive with her most expanded powers of anything more rich and precious than Christ, her Christ, herself Christ's, and Christ all her own. Oh, if you want to know what heaven is, know what Christ is, for the way to spell heaven is with those five letters that make up the word Jesus. When you get him he shall be all to you that your glorified body shall need, and all your glorified spirit can conceive. O precious Christ, thou art all in all.

III. I have shown you then, in a very hurried way, what it is that this truth includes, now, with greater brevity still, WHAT DOES THIS TRUTH INVOLVE? It involves a great many things. First, it involves the glory and excellence of Christ. Of whom else could it be said that be is all in all? There are many things in this world that are good, but there is nothing that is good for everything. Some plants may be a good medicine, but not a good cordial; the plant of renown is good every way. Good clothing is not able to stay your hunger, but Christ the bread of heaven is also the Father's best robe. You cannot expect any finite thing to be good for all things, but Christ is infinite goodness. This tree of life bears all manner of fruits, and the leaves are for the healing of the nations. He is strength and beauty, safety and sanctity, peace and plenty healing and help, comfort and conquest, life here, and life for ever. Glory be to the Lord Jesus Christ! What can he be less than God, if he be all? "All." Is it not a synonym for God? We say there cannot be two Gods, because the one God is everywhere, and fills all space; and who then can he be who is called "all in all," but "very God of very God?" Worship him, my brethren, with all your hearts, rejoice in him, bless him from day to day. Let not the world think you poor who are so rich in him. Never suffer men to think you unhappy, who have perfect happiness in the ever blessed Immanuel.

See, in the next place, the safety and the blessedness of the believer. Christ is all; but the believer can add, "And Christ is mine." Then the believer has all things--all that he will want, as well as all he does want. No emperor that has not Christ is half as rich as he that has Christ and is a beggar. He that hath Christ, being a pauper, hath all things; and he that hath not Christ, possessing a thousand worlds, possesses nothing for real happiness and joy. Oh, the blessedness of the man who can say, "Christ is mine." On the other hand, see the wretchedness of the man who has not the Savior: for if Christ is all, you who believe not on him are devoid of all, in being destitute of Christ. But you say, "I try my best, I attend public worship, I do a great deal that is good;" you have nothing if you have not Christ. Do not flatter yourself that you are getting on and adding goods to goods in spiritual things; if you have not a Savior you are naked and poor and miserable; you are without all if you are without Christ, who is all. The Christian, then, is rich, but everyone who is destitute of Christ is poor to the extreme of poverty.

See, too, in the truth before us a rebuke for the doubts of many seekers. They will say, "I have not this, I have not that." Suppose thou hast it not, Christ has it, if it be good for anything. "I would fain cast myself upon the mercy of God in Christ this day, but,"--Ah, away with thy "buts." What dost thou want? "I want true belief," saith one. Come to Christ for it then. "I want a broken heart," says another. If you cannot come with a broken heart to Christ, come for a broken heart.

"True belief, and true repentance
Every grace that brings us nigh,
Without money
Come to Jesus Christ and buy."

We have an odd proverb about the folly of taking coals to Newcastle; but what folly must that be which makes a man think that he can take something to Christ, when Christ is all. Come, come, come, come to him, poor sinner, and let him be all in all to thee. Simply rely upon him and be at peace.

How this, again, rebukes the coldness of saints. If Christ be all in all, then how is it we love him so little? If he is so precious, how is it we prize him so little? Oh! my dull, dead, cold heart, what art thou at? Art thou harder than adamant, and baser than brutish, that thou art not much more moved with ardor and fervent affection towards such a Lord us this? Christ is all, my brethren, yet look how little we offer to him--of our substance how scant a portion--of our time how slender a part--of our talents how small a parcel! God stir us to holy fervency, that if Christ be all for us, we may be all for Christ. May we lay ourselves out without reservation to the utmost stretch of our power, asking fresh strength from him, that we may do all that can be done by mortal men, and that all may be done with us by God, that he shall see it to be compatible with his glory to do.

Again, by our text another lesson is furnished us. We learn here how to measure young converts. We ought not to expect them to be philosophers or divines; Christ is all. If they know Christ, and are resting in him, we are bound to say, "Come, and welcome." Be they poor, be they unlettered, if Jesus Christ be formed in their hearts, even though we can see him there only as a dim outline, we are to open wide the gate, and receive them as Jesus received us.

Here is a measure, too, by which to measure ministers. The fashion of the world is to admire him most who shall speak most rhetorically. Accursed be the day in which oratory was tolerated in the Christian pulpit. It has been the bane and plague of the church of God. This labor after flowery speech, this seeking after polished periods and gaudy sentences, what is it but a pandering to the world, and a prostitution of the ministry of reconciliation. Had men learned what the apostle meant when he said, "I brethren, came not with excellency of speech or of wisdom," they would have preached far other wise than they have done. We should strive to speak the gospel simply from our hearts, and then men's hearts will be impressed with the truth. Alas, this toying with fair words, and seeking after pleasing expressions, this dressing up of truth in the flaunting finery of falsehood, degrades rather than adorns the gospel, and it has done incalculable damage to souls, and to the advance of truth. Measure ministers by this, What is there of Christ about them? That ministry which hath no savor of Christ in it, be it what it may, is a ministry which the Lord will not own, and that you ought not to own; it is not God-sent, and ought not to be received by you. Give me Christ Jesus, though the speech in which he be set forth be of the most uncouth kind, rather than the choicest inventions of the most ingenious thinkers, from which Jesus Christ is absent, or in which he is not exalted.

Brother, this will also help you to estimate your own devotions. You came to the communion table the other day, but you did not enter into fellowship with Christ. Ah! then there was a lost opportunity. You were in your closet this morning in prayer, but you did not plead the name of Jesus. Ah! then again there was a lost season of devotion. You are a Bible reader, and your eye glances over the holy words but you do not see Jesus in each page; then your reading has failed. You have been giving to the poor of late; but have you done it for Christ's sake? You have sought to win souls: have you done it in Christ's strength? If Jesus be absent, you have offered a sacrifice from which the heart is gone; and among the Romans, no omen was supposed to be so damaging as the absence of the heart from the sacrifice. No Christ, then there can be no acceptance, but a fullness of Christ proves a fullness of acceptance with God.

IV. There are many other things which I could have said, but time has failed me, and therefore I must close by noticing WHAT THIS TRUTH REQUIRES OF US. Christ is all in all; therefore "put on, as the elect of God, holy and beloved, bowels of mercies, kindness, humbleness of mind, meekness, longsuffering." The exhibition of the Christ-life in the saints is the legitimate inference from the fact that Christ is all to them. If Christ is all, and yet I being a Christian am not like Christ, my Christianity is a transparent sham, I am nothing but a base pretender, and my outward religiousness is a pompous pageantry for my soul to be carried to hell in--nothing more. It is a gilded coffin for a lifeless spirit. I shall perish with a double destruction, if I have dared to profane the name of Christ by taking it upon me, when I have not the essence of the Christian religion within me. Orthodoxy, though it be of the most assured sort, is vanity of vanities, unless there be with it an orthodoxy of life: and experience, whatever man may say about it, is but a dream, a fiction of his own imagining, if it does not display itself in shaking off the sins of the flesh, and putting on the adornments of holiness. O brethren, these are searching things to everyone of us. Who amongst us lives as he should at home? Could you bear that the angel who visits your house should publish, before the great cloud of witnesses, all that he has seen there? In your shops, in your businesses, you professors, are you always upright and straightforward as Christians should be! You merchants on the Exchange, are not some of you, who profess to be Christians, as greedy and as overreaching as others? I charge you, if you have any respect for Christ, lay down his name if you will not endeavor to honor it you will be lost, you covetous money-grubbers, you earth-scrapers, who live only for this world, you will be lost; you need not doubt of that, you will be lost sure enough; but why need you make the assurance of your condemnation doubly sure by the base imposture of calling yourselves Christians. Meanwhile, let the Ethiopian call himself white, if he will; let the leopard declare that he has no spots; these things shall not matter; but the falsehood of a man who lives without Christ, while calling himself a Christian, brings such dishonor upon him who was nailed to the tree, and whose religion is that of holiness, that I beseech you, by the living God, give up your profession, if you do not endeavor to make it true. If you are not living as you should, do not pretend to be what you are not. Seek ye unto God, that the life of Christ being in you, you may manifest it in your conversation.

Without Christ ye are nothing, though ye be baptised, though ye be members of churches, though ye be highly esteemed as deacons, elders, pastors. Oh, then, have Christ everywhere in all things, and constrain men to say of you, "To that man Christ is all in all: I have marked him; he has been with Jesus, he has learned of him, for he acts as Jesus did. God grant a blessing on these words, for Christ's sake. Amen.

PORTIONS OF SCRIPTURE READ BEFORE SERMON--Colossians 3, and 4:1-6.

Sermon Readers are respectfully reminded that the 200 boys at the Stookwell Orphanage are supported by voluntary contributions, and that these are always thankfully received by C. H. Spurgeon, Clapham.

North and South

A Sermon (No. 1007)
Delivered by
C. H. SPURGEON,
At the Metropolitan Tabernacle, Newington

"I will say to the north, Give up; and to the south, keep not back." - Isaiah 43:6.

IN THE FULLNESS of the promised days when the Jews shall be restored from their wanderings, and all the seed of Jacob shall again meet in their own land, God in his mighty providence will speak to all the nations, saying: "To the north, Give up; and to the south, Keep not back;" and at the divine bidding free passage shall be given, all lets and hindrances shall be removed, and his own people shall come to their own land. Entailed on Abraham's seed by a covenant of salt, the Holy Land shall receive again its rightful heritors, the banished shall come to their own again, and no nation or people shall keep them back. So much for the literal meaning. I am unable to indulge you with fuller details, for I have no skill in guessing at the meaning of dark passages, but leave such things to those to whom it is given, or who think it is given to them. We shall now pursue the spiritual teaching of the passage.

At this moment, my brethren and sisters, we who follow the footsteps of King Jesus are soldiers of an army which has invaded this world. This land belongs to our great Leader, for he made it. It was right that everywhere, all round the globe, his name should he honored, for he is the King among the nations, and the governor thereof: But our race has revolted, set up another monarch, and bowed its strength to support another dynasty--the dynasty of darkness and death. Our race has broken the good and wholesome laws of the great Lord, the rightful King, and set up new laws and new customs altogether opposed to right and truth. This is the Great Rebellion the Revolt of Manhood, the Sedition of Sinners. Now, no king will willingly lose his dominions, and therefore the Great King of kings has sent his son to conquer this world by force of arms, though not by arms of steel, or weapons that cut and kill, and wound, yet by arms more mighty far; and this earth is to be yet subdued to the kingdom of the Crown Prince, the Prince Imperial of heaven, Jesus Christ, the Lord. We, his regenerated people, form part of the army of occupation. We have invaded the land. Hard and stern hath been the battle up to this point. We have had to win every inch of ground by sheer push of pike. Effort after effort has been put forth by the church of God under the guidance of her heavenly leader, and none has been in vain. Hitherto the Lord hath helped us, but there is much yet to be done. Canaanites and Hivites, and Jebusites have to be driven out; yea, in fact, the whole world seems still to lie in darkness, and under the dominion of the wicked one. We do but hold here and there a sacred fortress for truth and holiness in the land; but these we must retain till the Lord Jesus shall send us more prosperous times, and the battle shall be tamed against the foe, and the kingdom shall come unto our prince. Nor is there any fear but that such a time will come, therefore let us have courage. Soldiers of the cross, have faith; have faith in your great leader, for behold he is still at the head of you, and is still omnipotent. The hour of his weakness is past. His sun set once in blood, but it has risen to go down no more. Once was it eclipsed at noon day; but now the Sun of Righteousness ariseth with healing beneath his wings. He who died once for all, is now life's source, center, and Lord. The living Christ is present among us as the commander-in-chief of the church militant. Let us refresh our souls by drawing, near to him by the power of the Holy Ghost.

The text has two grand matters in it:--First, here is the royalty of the word--where the word of this king is there is power. Secondly, here is the word of royalty, and that word we may well consider, for where the word of this king is there is wisdom.

I. First, here is THE ROYALTY OF THE WORD. It is more than an imperial edict; it is the fiat of onmipotence. Jesus Christ saith to the north, "Give up," and it does give up; and to the south, "Keep not back," and it cannot keep back.

I understand from reading this declaration, that there is a general opposition in the world to the cause and kingdom of God; for until he saith, "Give up,"' and "Keep not back," men do not crowd to Immanuel's feet, and even the chosen of God do not come forth from their hiding places.

All the world over there is a general opposition to the cause of Christ, to the doctrine of truth, to the throne of God. Go where you may, in the highest places of the earth, you shall find true religion despised; among the lowest of the land you shall find that same religion blasphemed; and in the middle classes, where some seem to fancy that all virtue resides, you shall find carelessness about the things of the world to come, and carking carefulness about the selfishness of this present life. Jesus Christ is everywhere despised in comparison with the things that perish. They will not have this man to reign over them. The trees of the wood reject heaven's cedar, and choose hell's bramble. Even the eleven sell the true Joseph into Egypt, nor is there one found who will defend the chosen of God. Go amongst savage nations, and there the idol is worshipped, but Jesus is not known. Go among civilised nations, and, lo, they have only changed their idols; they have rebaptised their imates, given new names to the objects of their superstitious reverence, but the true Christ is misunderstood and rejected. Go you to the swarthy Hindoo, the man of deep philosophy and sophistry, and you shall find his heart set against the gospel of Jesus of Nazareth; and then sail over the blue sea to the islands of the deep, and man in his simplicity worships he knows not what, but not the incarnate God. Traverse the central parts of continents where as yet civilization has scarcely reached, and you shall find that man is still opposed to his Maker, and hates the name of the only begotten Son of God. Nor need we travel or even look abroad; the opposition is universal among ourselves, among the old, among the young. Striking is that text, "They go astray from the womb, speaking lies." An old Puritan puts it; "They go astray before they go: they speak lies before they speak;" and so it is. Before it comes to acts, the evil propensity is in the heart; and before the lips can frame the falsehood, there is the lie within the soul. From the earliest infancy to palsied age, nothing seems to cure manhood of its rebellious disposition; the carnal mind is enmity against God, and is not reconciled to God, neither indeed while it remains what it is can it be. There is a general opposition to the cause and kingdom of Christ.

But the text seems to hint that there is a particular form of that opposition in each case. There is a word to the north, a different word from that which is given to the south. The north holds fast, and therefore the word is, "Give up:" the south retires, is despairing, therefore it is said, "Keep not back." The opposition takes different shapes, and there is a different word to meet its ever varying forms. How true is Dr. Watts's verse--

"We wander each a different way,
But all the downward road."

As each land has its own tribes of wild animals, so has each heart its indigenous sins. All land will grow weeds, but you will not find the same sort of weed equally abundant in every soil: so in one heart the deadly nightshade of ignorance chokes the seed, and in another the prickly thistle of malice crowds out the wheat. There are difficulties in reaching the heart of any man, but not the same difficulties in all men. Some, for instance, cannot be influenced because of their want of intelligence; others because of their supposed learning. Some cannot be come at because of their presumption; others because of their despondency. Some spend their all upon the pleasures of this world, others spend nothing, but find their pleasure simply in hoarding, yet are they equally averse to heavenly things. Whatever form sin takes, it is the same opposition, but yet it may need a different mode of treatment, and by a different weapon will it have to be overcome. My dear brother in Christ, you perhaps have a different personal, spiritual difficulty from mine. I have no wish to change with you, and I should not advise you to change with me. The same is true with our trials in winning souls. We have each our difficulties, but they are not precisely alike in detail. You have to fight the north perhaps, and I the south; but the same Lord and Master can make us victorious, and without him we shall be equally defeated. The opposition which we encounter in serving our Lord is the same, depend upon it. You need not say, "Mine is a peculiarly hard task," or if you do, I may say the same of mine. After all, both tasks are impossibilities without God, and both labors shall be readily performed if Jesus speaks the divine fiat, and saith "to the north, Give up; arid to the south, Keep not back."

Further, as there is in all an opposition, and as there is in each a distinct opposition, so no power can in any case subdue any part of the world to Christ apart from him. It is possible that you may fall in with a family which seems to be naturally religious: you may even meet with tribes of people who appear to he spontaneously inclined to godliness; but if you bring the religion of Christ to them, you will find that their very religiousness is the greatest difficulty you have to deal with. Some, on the other hand, never could be superstitious: the conformation of their mind is that of practical, sound, common sense; but do not deceive yourself with the idea that their conversion is any the easier. You may preach the gospel in the most forcible way to them, and you will find that this very common sense of theirs will be the main difficulty to be overcome. Believe me, however intent you may be in winning souls to Christ, you shall never meet with one who can be subdued to

him by any persuasions of yours apart from the working of his own power. I know the preacher has thought within himself, "I have only to put the truth in a reasonable way, and the man will see it." Ah! sir, but sinners are not reasonable: they are the most unreasonable of all creatures: none are so senseless, none act so madly us they do. "But," saith one, "if I were to tell them of the love of Christ in an affectionate loving way, that would reach them." Yes; but you will find that all your affection and your tears, and earnest delineation of the love of Jesus, will be powerless against human hearts, unless the Eternal Spirit shall drive home your appeals. We know some who have been reasoned with, and if logic could win them, they ought to have been won long ago: they have also been persuaded, and if rhetoric could reach them, they ought to have turned away from their evil ways years ago; but all human art has been tried and tried, and tried in vain; yet there is no room for despair, for Jesus can conquer the unconquerables, and heal the incurables. Do not be disappointed, dear brother, if you have hitherto failed in your efforts; you have but proved that "vain is the help of man." You see now by experience that "it is not of him that willeth, nor of him that runneth, but of God that showeth mercy." It is yours to try and bring that soul to Jesus; but it lies with him to perform the work. Duty is ours, the result is God's. If the soil of the field committed to me will never yield a harvest, I am yet bound to plough it, if my Lord commands. If I could foresee that my child would never turn to the Lord, yet I ought not to slacken my efforts for its conversion. I have to do with my Master's command, and what he bids me do I am bound to do. Never let us be surprised when we are defeated, for we ought to know that old Adam is far too strong for us, if we assail him single-handed. We cannot expect to cast out the devil: he laughs us to scorn if we attempt to exorcise him in our own name. We may speak as we will, but if it is only we that speak, the devil will say, "Jesus I know, and the Holy Ghost I know--but who are ye? I do not yield to you. I will not go out of this sinner, through all your persuasions and all your talkings." Do not forget then that there is a general opposition to the kingdom of Christ--such opposition as no human power can by any possibility overcome.

But, my brethren, here is the point of the text. That opposition, whatever form it assumes, though not to be subdued by our agency alone, shall assuredly yield before the fiat of our great King, when he saith "to the north, Give up; and to the south, Keep not back." His word is a word of power wherever it comes. Let us rejoice then, whatever place we dwell in, that we have only to ask the King himself to come there, and to speak with power, and we shall see conversions, conversions most numerous, that shall glorify his name. I fully believe that the darkest time of any true Christian church is just the period when it ought to have most hope, for when the Lord has allowed us to spin ourselves out till there is no more strength in us, then it is that he will come to our rescue. What could have been lower than the condition into which we, as a church, had sunk some seventeen years ago? But a little faithful band used to meet in that dreary chapel in Park Street, and cry unto the Lord, never ceasing their prayers. And, oh! how soon the house began to fill, and how speedily our tent was too strait for us, and we broke forth on the right hand and on the left, and God made the desolate places to be inhabited. Members of other churches, you have the same God to go to. Go to him, for he can work the same wonders for you. Look to the Most High, and not to man, or ministers, or modes, or methods, but only to him, and the guidance of his Spirit. "Well, but ours is a village," saith one. And is not he the Lord of the villages? Is he the Lord of the cities, and not the Lord of the hamlets? "But our chapel is ugly, and built in a back street," saith one. "Nobody knows of its existence. We shall never get the people within its obscure and dreary walls." Is God the God of the wide thoroughfares and not of the lanes? Does not the Lord know the back streets as well as the broad ones? Was not that the question in dispute of old? Is he the God of the hills, and not the God of the valleys? I have already put it in another shape to you. In his name I ask you, can anything be too hard for the Lord? Perhaps in your sphere of service you have grown so dispirited that you are inclined to say, "I may as well give up all further effort; no good will result from my endeavors." But what have you told the Master, and what have you sought at his hand? Have you told him all your discouragements? Have you asked him to speak with power, and has he refused you? If so, then give it up, but not till then, for he can even now "say to the north, Give up; and to the south, Keep not back;" and as when he said to the thick primaeval darkness, "Let there be light," and the light leaped into being, and the darkness fled, so can he, amid the gross darkness of our huge city, or the not less dense darkness of our villages, create light to our astonishment and to his glory. It is the king's word we want--nothing short of it, and nothing more. We must get that by prayer: we must wait upon him with importunity. If there be only two or three whose hearts break over the desolations of the church, if we have only half a dozen that resolve to give the Lord no rest till he establish and make Jerusalem a praise in the earth, we shall see great things yet. A handful of people who resolve if a blessing is to be had they will have it, and that if souls are not saved it shall be the sovereignty of God that prevents it and nothing else: such a mere handful shall win the day. If they will have souls saved; if so they plead and agonize, oh! then the Lord will turn his gracious hand, and send a plenteous stream of blessing upon their district; for where he wills it the blessing must come, and he always wills to display his grace where and when he leads his people to pray for it.

Before I leave this point, let me say the power of the King's word is always exercised in full consistence with the free agency of man. You must not think when we say that Christ has his will, and works omnipotently in men's hearts, that we imagine that he violates the free agency which he has created. He says to the north, "Give up," and that word does it; for a word is a suitable instrument by which to rule a free agent. The way to make blocks of timber move would be to drag them, and if we wish to shape them we must hew them with the axe, or cut them with a saw; but the way to deal with men is to speak with them. That is how Jesus operates. His power is exerted in conformity with the laws of human mind. He does not violate the free agency of man, though he does as he wills with man: His word is an instrument consistent with our mental nature, and he uses that word wisely. He says to the north, "Give up:" he says to the south, "Keep not back." His word touches the secret spring, and sets all in motion. No man is ever taken to heaven against his will, though I do not believe any man ever went there of his own free will till God's sovereign grace enlightened him and made him willing. You must not suppose that Christ conquers human hearts by physical compulsion, such as the King of Prussia used, for instance, in subduing France, or such as a man uses in driving a horse. The Lord knows how to leave us free, and yet to make us do his bidding, and therein lies the beauty of gospel influences. Suppose man's will to be a room; if you and I want to open it, we break in the lock; we do not understand the true method; but the Lord has the key, and knows how to open the door without a wrench. Without violating even the most delicate spring in the watch, the maker knows how to regulate it. Grace draws, but it is with hands of a man; it rules, but it is with a scepter of love. The fact is, the great dispute between Calvinists and Arminians has arisen very much through not understanding one another, and from one brother saying, "What I hold is the truth"--and the other saying, "What I hold is truth, and nothing else." The men need somebody to knock both their heads together, and fuse their beliefs into one. They need one capacious brain to hold both the truths which their two little heads contain; for God's word is neither all on one side nor altogether on the other: it overlaps all systems, and defies all formularies. It lays the full responsibility of his ruin on man, but all the power and glory of grace it ascribes to God; and it is wise of us to do the same. The great King doeth as he wills among men as well as among the armies of heaven. Who shall stay his hand or say unto him, "What doest thou?" He rules men as men, and not as inanimate stones. He has a scepter which is adapted to mind and spirit. The weapons of his warfare are not carnal: his forces rule the heart, the mind, the whole manhood as he has made it; and so he conquers, and becomes the happy king of willing subjects, who, though subdued by power, are happy to own his sway. Thus much on the first point--the royalty of the word.

II. How we will consider THE WORD OF ROYALTY. The King saith "to the north, Give up; and to the south, Keep not back."

We will not spend many minutes over these words, but just briefly hint at what meaning may be drawn from them. There are some persons to whom, when the powerful word of grace comes, it speaks in this way--"Give up; give up." There are other persons in another state of mind to whom, whenever the word of salvation comes, it says, "Keep not back; keep not back." Now, to some we find that it comes in this way: "Give up; give up." You say, "I am righteous; I am no worse than others. I have broken the law, but not much; my sins are trivial. I cannot deserve to be cast into hell for my small offenses. I have been--not perfect, but as righteous as most. I have done this, I have done that, I have done the other." Ah, dear friend, the sword of divine grace will kill all this; and the message that God's mercy sends to you to-day is, "Give up." Renounce your fancied goodness and deceitful self-esteem. Oh, give up that spinning; it is a poor trade to spin cobwebs. Give it up. Your father, Adam, taught you to make aprons of fig-leaves; but it was after he had fallen. It is a bad business: give it up. Your own works will never cover you as you should be covered; there is a better righteousness than yours to be had; there is a better footing to stand before God upon than anything you have done. Your refuges are all refuges of lies; give them up. That pretty righteousness of yours, which fools so white, is only white because your eyes are blind; if you could see it, it is all as black as filth can make it. You conceive your robe to be new and fair, but it is all riddled through and through with holes. The worms have devoured it; it is all moth-eaten and decayed. Give it up. Oh, give up that Pharisaic mouthful, "God, I thank thee," and betake thyself to the publican's prayer, "God be merciful to me, a sinner." Give up thy selftrust; it is a painted lie, a rotten plank, a foul deception, a false traitor; it promises salvation, but it brings sure damnation. Jesus is the sinner's only hope. Give up every other reliance.

Then, too, you have an opposition in your hearts to the gospel. Concerning that also the word saith to you, "Give up." Perhaps you were prejudiced against it foolishly and ignorantly; before you ever heard it you felt persuaded you should not like it. Possibly you have been brought up to a religion of forms; you hardly think that salvation can be by simple faith in Jesus Christ; you feel a great deal of attachment to that regeneration of yours which was wrought in your baptism, and to that confirmation of yours bestowed by the bishop's fingers. Besides, you have been so regular in your religion up till now, that you can hardly brook to be told that the whole bundle of it is mere rubbish, not worth the time you have spent on it. You cannot endure to be told that--

"None but Jesus can do helpless sinners good."

But rest assured, the sooner you give up all those flattering reliances of yours, the better for you, for there is nothing in them. Even ceremonies that God has commanded are only of spiritual use to spiritual men, and since you are not a spiritual man they cannot profit you. Have you in your heart an opposition to Christ? Can you not yield to him as God? Can you not stoop to be saved entirely by his merits, and acknowledge him for your Lawgiver, and Teacher, and Guide? Then as, the text saith so would I say, and may the Lord apply the word: "Give up; give up." There is no salvation for thee till thou "give up" all ceremonial hopes and formal confidences. Strike the colors, man, before a broadside goes through thee; for depend upon it, if thou yield not in one way thou wilt in another. Thou shalt either break or bow; thou shalt either turn or burn; that is the alternative to every man of woman born: he must turn away from his enmity to Christ, and yield himself up to his love, or else he shall find the power of God in Christ to be his destruction.

It is possible, dear friends, that your opposition to Jesus Christ has taken the form of the love of a favourite sin. Now, there is nothing more certain than this, that you cannot be saved and keep your sins: they must be parted with. No man can carry fire in his bosom and yet be safe from burning. While you drink the poison, it must and will work death in you. The thief cannot expect mercy while he keeps the goods he has stolen. John Bunyan says that one day, when he was playing "cat" on a Sunday, on the village green, he thought he heard a voice saying to him: "Wilt thou have thy sins and go to hell, or leave thy sins and go to heaven?" That question is put to every man who hears the gospel faithfully preached. Most men in their heart of hearts would like to have their sins and go to heaven too. But that cannot be; while God is just, and heaven is holy, and truth is precious, it cannot be. What then? "Let the wicked forsake his way, and the unrighteous man his thoughts: and let him return unto the Lord, and he will have mercy upon him; and to our God, for he will abundantly pardon." Give up, give up; give up your sin. What is the sin? The drunkards cup? Away with the bewitching draught. Is it the drunkard's company? That is as damnable as his cup; renounce such society at once. Is it blaspheming? O man, God rinse thy mouth our of such black stuff as that! Have done with a sin for which there cannot be any excuse, for it cannot bring thee any pleasure or profit, nor can there be any necesssity for it: it is a degrading, useless, senseless. God-provoking crime. Is it some secret sin that must not be named lest the cheek of modesty be reddened? Give it up, friend; it will be much better for thee to lose it though it were as precious as thy right arm or thy right eye, than to keep it and be cast into hell fire. The chamber of wantonness is the gate of death, flee from it without delay. The sins of the flesh are a deep ditch, and the abhorred of the Lord fall therein; but as thou lovest thy soul, O young man, escape like a bird from the fowler's snare. Here is the message of God to thee: "Give up, give up thy sin." Perhaps though you hear the summons, you trifle with it, and reply, "Yes; I mean to give them all up, and I hope by so doing I shall find my way to heaven. I shall deserve well of my Maker when I have denied myself all sinful pleasures." But stop; let me not deceive you: this is not all. I fear that some men are not improved in their hearts when they are altered in their outward behavior. I am glad of the outward improvement, but I have sometimes fancied that they have only changed their sins, but not given them up. They show no leprosy in their skin, but it dies in their bone and their flesh. It is little use merely to shift the region in which sin sets up its throne if its dominion is still undestroyed. It reminds one of the verse--

"So when a raging fever burns,
We shift from side to side by turns;
And tis a poor relief we gain
To shift the place but keep the pain."

What if the man does not go to hell as a drunkard, it will not mend it if he is ruined by being self-righteous: so long as he is lost I do not see that it materially matters how. Many and many a man has given up outward sins and set up a self-righteousness of his own, and said, "These be thy gods, O Israel;" and so he fled from a bear, and a lion slew him; he leaned on a wall, and a serpent bit him. All sin must be cast out of the throne of the heart, and whatever righteousness that is not Christ's righteousness must go with it. I would fain put the sword-point to thy heart, O sinner, and say, "Give up all that opposes Christ;" for if thou do not give it up, thy soul will be lost.

In fine, dear friends, speaking to the children of God as well as to such as are not converted, I say, give up all and have Christ; give up all attempts to save yourself, and let Christ save you. Work afterwards, because he worketh in you to will and to do, but now do nothing either great or small, to make yourself righteous, for Jesus did it, did it all, long, long ago. Do nothing by way of straining for merit, but begin to do everything by way of gratitude. "Give up;" that is, give up yourself to Christ, whatever his will may be. If it be his will that you be sick, that you be poor, that you die, give all up, and say, "Thy will be done. I resign all to thee, my God." Doth Jesus command you to do anything? Let it not be irksome to you. Whatsoever he saith unto you, do it. Let there be no back-stair by which to play the truant; no keeping back of part of the price as though you would not do Christ's will, except in some points. Give up unreservedly, and make no provision for the flesh. Let his will be your will. Yield entirely; and if you have anything in this world of substance, of talent, of opportunity, "Give up." Begin with resignation, go on to obedience, and finish with consecration. "Give up, give up" till all is given up, body, soul, and spirit, a reasonable sacrifice to him, till you can say:

"Now Lord I would be thine alone,
And wholly live to thee."

I perceive that my text has grown from a word to the sinner who has to be conquered into a word directed to Christ's nearest and dearest friends, even to those who are the soldiers of his army. It is in effect a lofty, far-reaching precept, and would to God we could live up to it, by presenting our all to Jesus our Lord.

Let us now spend a minute or two on the second word of the King: "Keep not back." Is there some person within this assembly who feels within his heart, the desire to come and confess his sins to his God? Standing at the filthy swine-trough, does the prodigal say within himself: "I will arise and go unto my Father, and say unto him, Father, I have sinned"? "Keep not back:" quench not that holy flame. If thou hast a desire to come and acknowledge thy transgressions unto the pardoning Savior, let nothing keep thee back--neither fear, nor shame, nor procrastination, but rest not till thou hast reached the bosom of thy God and acknowledged all thy guilt before him. A repulse need not be feared, nor even an upbraiding--a rich, free, loving welcome is sure. "Keep not back."

But is there another who has confessed his sin, but yet has found no peace? Dost thou see yonder Christ on the cross? "Yes," sayest thou; "I know there is life in a look at him, but may I look?" My Master's message to thee is, "Keep not back; keep not back," for whosoever looketh shall be made whole, and none are forbidden to look. Does the crowd around the Savior hinder thee, thou sick and dying soul? Be not baffled by difficulty, but persevere. Press into the thickest of the throng for if thou do but touch the hem of his garment thou shalt be made whole. "Keep not back; keep not back." Thou mayst believe in Jesus now! Mayst! Nay, thou art commanded to do it; and thou art threatened if thou do not, which proves that thou hast permission and something more. It is written: "He that believeth not shall be damned." O man, it is but another way of saying thou hast a full permission to do it, for thou art threatened if thou do it not. Come thou, then, come thou, now, right joyfully. "Keep not back." Confess thy sin with repentance, and lay it on Christ by faith, and thou shalt be saved.

Dear brethren and sisters, many of you have come to Christ and have been saved, and to you the text says, "Keep not back," in another sense. Do not keep back from confessing Christ. If you have the love of Jesus Christ in your soul, confess it, tell it to others. Never be ashamed of your Lord and Master. Come and unite with his church and people. It is due to the church; it is due to the preacher who was the means of your conversion, it is due especially to your Lord and Master that you "keep not back." I have heard of some who keep back because the church is not perfect. And you are very perfect I dare say! Why, if the church were perfect we should not endure you in it, my captious friend. I have no doubt whatever that you will find the church quite as perfect as you are. There are others who keep aloof from the people of God because they feel they are not perfect themselves. My dear friend, if you were perfect we should not want you, because you would be the only perfect member among us, and having a very imperfect pastor, I do not know what we should do with you; we should find you such a speckled bird among us, that we should probably pray the Lord to take you home to heaven at once. I should like to have you become perfect, and the nearer perfection the better--but still if you make no profession of faith till you are sinless, it will not be this side the grave. Nay, confess Christ, for is it not written: "He that with his heart believeth, and with his mouth maketh confession of him, shall he be saved"? Do not forget the confession of the mouth. "Keep not back." And when you have done that, if there be any Christian excellency that can be reached, do not despair of reaching it. "Keep not back." And if perfection itself be attainable, never be content till you get it. If you are a child of God you never will be self-satisfied, you will be always crying: Not as though I had already attained, either were already perfect: but I follow after, if that I may apprehend that for which also I am apprehended of Christ Jesus." O that you may never be content with yourself! Self-satisfaction is the death of progress. You have come into the lowest seat at the feast, but Jesus saith: "Friend, come up higher;" and when you get into a higher room, and enter into closer communion with him, he will say to you, "Friend, come up higher." Do not hesitate to climb higher in grace and fellowship. Let your prayer be, "Nearer to thee, my God, nearer to thee." Be insatiable in the longings of your soul; hunger and thirst after righteousness; covet earnestly the best gifts. Grow in grace, and in the knowledge of your Lord and Savior Jesus Christ. "Keep not back." There is no point in grace which we are prohibited from aiming at. We ought none of us to say, "I am all I can ever be." Oh, no, let us reach to the front ranks by God's grace; for he says, "Keep not back."

Let me add if there be a brother who could do more for Christ than he is doing, let him "keep not back." Could you preach? Well, there are plenty of places needing occasional minister, and others that are quite destitute. I do not know a nobler occupation for a man who is in business in London than for him to be maintaining himself by his shop, or whatever else his calling may be, and going out to suburban villages on the Sabbath to preach. I often wonder more persons do not imitate the example of some good brethren, whom I could name, who are in their business diligent, and who are also fervent in spirit in their Master's work. What reason can there be that for every little church there should be a pastor specially set apart for the work? It is a very desirable thing wherever there are enough Christian people to be able to support the minister that there should be such; but I believe we very much hamper ourselves in our Christian work through always imagining that a paid person set apart to preach is necessary for every Christian church. There ought to be more farmers who educate themselves, and preach in their own barns or on the village greens. There ought to be more men of business in London who seek to improve their minds, that they may preach acceptably anywhere the gospel of Jesus Christ; and I hope the time will come when our dear friends, the members of churches in London, will not be so backward as they are, but will come forward and speak to the honor of the Lord Jesus. If you cannot edify a thousand, perhaps you can influence ten; if you cannot with a regular congregation continue to find fresh matter year after year (and believe me that is a very difficult thing), yet you can preach a sermon here and a sermon there, and tell to different companies the same story of the Savior's love. I do not know what special work you can do, but something is within your power, and from that "Keep not back." Besides, there are all our street corners. In spring and summer, how delightful to stand in the thick of the throng and uplift the Crucified One! Of course, you are sure to have a congregation out of doors, and a congregation that is rather attentive, and sometimes rather inquisitive, and do not need to be so inconveniently crowded as we are in this Tabernacle. Take the wide sweep, cast the big net, and hope for fish. If you have any grace or gift, "Keep not back." "Alas!" murmurs the glowworm, "I mean to shut up my lamp, and hide under those damp weeds, and never shine again." What is the matter with you? "Why," says he, "I have seen the sun; I shall never shine again after seeing the sun." That glowworm is stupid. If it were wise, it would say, "I have looked upon the sun; and I perceive with shame that my lamp is but a poor light, but for that reason I must use it the more diligently. The sun may well hide its light after twelve hours are over; but I must try to glimmer during the whole twenty-four hours, and so give as much light as I can, little though it be." You complain that you have but one talent; that is the reason for being doubly diligent with it. If you had five, they ought to be fully used; but if you have only one, you must put all your wits to work to make something more of it. At any rate, "Keep not back."

"Well," says one, "I think I could do something, but I am of a retiring disposition." I am afraid if I had been in the French army in the late war, I should be very much of the same disposition; but in a soldier, as a rule, a retiring disposition in the hour of battle is not much commended by his captain. You who are so modest (shall I say so cowardly?) that you cannot do for Christ what you ought to do, will have an account to settle with your consciences one of these days, which will cost you a world of sorrow. Break through this bashfulness, this laziness (for it comes to that in the long run), this silly, wicked, shame. Pride must also be slain, for this hinders many. They cannot be so prominent as others, and therefore shun the work altogether. Get rid of all that cripples you, shake all off by the power of the Holy Spirit, my dear brethren, and "Keep not back," for who knows but that you may yet bring sinners to Jesus, may save a soul from death, and hide a multitude of sins, through God's eternal Spirit. May it be so, for Christ's sake. Amen.

PORTION OF SCRIPTURE READ BEFORE SERMON--Isaiah 43.

Love's Logic

A Sermon (No. 1008)
Delivered on Lord's-day Morning, August 27th, 1871, by
C. H. SPURGEON,
At the Metropolitan Tabernacle, Newington

"We love him because he first loved us." - 1 John 4:19.

THIS is a great doctrinal truth, and I might with much propriety preach a doctrinal sermon from it, of which the sum and substance would be the sovereign grace of God. God's love is evidently prior to ours: "He first loved us." It is also clear enough from the text that God's love is the cause of ours, for "We love him because he first loved us." Therefore, going back to old time, or rather before all time, when we find God loving us with an everlasting love, we gather that the reason of his choice is not because we loved him, but because he willed to love us. His reasons, and he had reasons (for we read of the counsel of his will), are known to himself, but they are not to be found in any inherent goodness in us, or which was foreseen to be in us. We were chosen simply because he will have mercy on whom he will have mercy. He loved us because he would love us. The gift of his dear Son, which was a close consequent upon his choice of his people, was too great a sacrifice on God's part to have been drawn from him by any goodness in the creature. It was not possible for the highest piety to have deserved so vast a boon as the gift of the Only-begotten; it was not possible for any thing in man to have merited the incarnation and the passion of the Redeemer. Our redemption, like our election, springs from the spontaneous self-originating love of God. And our regeneration, in which we are made actual partakers of the divine blessings in Jesus Christ, was not of us, nor by us. We were not converted because we were already inclined that way, neither were we regenerated because some good thing was in us by nature; but we owe our new birth entirely to his potent love, which dealt with us effectually turning us from death to life, from darkness to light and from the alienation of our mind and the enmity of our spirit into that delightful path of love, in which we are now travelling to the skies. As believers on Christ's name we "were born not of blood, nor of the will of the flesh, nor of the will of man, but of God." The sum and substance of the text is that God's uncaused love, springing up within himself, has been the sole means of bringing us into the condition of loving him. Our love to him is like a trickling rill, speeding its way to the ocean because it first came from the Ocean. All the rivers run into the sea, but their floods first arose from it: the clouds that were exhaled from the mighty main distilled in showers and filled the water-brooks. Here was their first cause and prime origin; and, as if they recognised the obligation, they pay tribute in return to the parent source. The ocean love of God, so broad that even the wing of imagination could not traverse it, sends forth its treasures of the rain of grace, which drop upon our hearts, which are as the pastures of the wilderness; they make our hearts to overflow, and in streams of gratitude the life imparted flows back again to God. All good things are of thee, Great God; thy goodness creates our good; thine infinite love to us draws forth our love to thee.

But, dear friends, I trust after many years of instruction in the doctrines of our holy faith, I need not keep to the beaten doctrinal track, but may lead you in a parallel path, in which the same truth may be from another point. I purpose to preach an experimental sermon, and possibly this will be even more in accordance with the run of the passage and the mind of its writer, than a doctrinal discourse. We shall view the text as a fact which we have tested and proved in our own consciousness. Under this aspect the statement of the text is this:--a sense of the love of God to us is the main cause of our love to him. When we believe, know, and feel that God loves us, we, as a natural result, love him in return; and in proportion as our knowledge increases, our faith strenthens, our conviction deepens that we are really beloved of God; we, from the very constitution of our being, are constrained to yield our hearts to God in return. The discourse of this morning, therefore, will run in that channel. God grant it may be blessed to each of us by his Holy Spirit.

I. At the outset we will consider THE INDISPENSABLE NECESSITY OF LOVE TO GOD IN THE HEART.

There are some graces which in their vigor are not absolutely essential to the bare existence of spiritual life, though very important for its healthy growth; but love to God must be in the heart, or else there is no grace there whatever. If any man love not God, he is not a renewed man. Love to God is a mark which is always set upon Christ's sheep, and never set upon any others. In enlarging upon this most important truth, I would all your attention to the connection of the text. You will find in the seventh verse of this chapter, that love to God is set down as being a necessary mark of the new birth. "Every one that loveth is born of God, and knoweth God." I have no right, therefore, to believe that I am a regenerated person unless my heart truly and sincerely loves God. It is vain for me, if I love not God, to quote the register which records an ecclesiastical ceremony, and say that this regenerated me; it certainly did no such thing, or the sure result would have followed. If I have been regenerated I may not be perfect, but this one thing I can say, "Lord thou knowest all things, thou knowest that I love thee." When by believing we receive the privilege to become the sons of God, we receive also the nature of sons, and with filial love we cry, "Abba, Father." There is no exception to this rule; if a man loves not God, neither is he born of God. Show me a fire without heat, then show me regeneration that does not produce love to God; for as the sun must give forth its light, so must a soul that has been created anew by divine grace display its nature by sincere affection towards God." "Ye must be born again," but ye are not born again unless ye love God. How indispensable, then, is love to God.

In the eighth verse we are told also that love to God is a mark of our knowing God. True knowledge is essential to salvation. God does not save us in the dark. He is our "light and our salvation." We are renewed in knowledge after the image of him that created us. Now, "he that loveth not knoweth not God, for God is love." All you have ever been taught from the pulpit, all you have ever studied from the Scriptures, all you hove ever gathered from the learned, all you have collected from the libraries, all this is no knowledge of God at all unless you love God; for in true religion, to love and to know God are synonymous terms. Without love you remain in ignorance still, ignorance of the most unhappy and ruinous kind. All attainments are transitory, if love be not as a salt to preserve them; tongues must cease and knowledge most vanish away; love alone abides for ever. This love you must have or be a fool for ever. All the children of the true Zion are taught of the Lord, but you are not taught of God unless you love God. See then that to be devoid of love to God is to be devoid of all true knowledge of God, and so of all salvation.

Further, the chapter teaches us that love to God is the root of love to others. The eleventh verse says, "Beloved, if God so loved us, we ought also to love one another. If we love one another, God dwelleth in us, and his love is perfected in us." Now no man is a Christian who does not love Christians. He, who, being in the church, is yet not of it heart aud soul, is but an intruder in the family. But since love to our brethren springs out of love to our one common father, it is plain that we must have love to that father, or else we shall fail in one of the indispensable marks of the children of God. "We know that we have passed from death unto life, because we love the brethren;" but we cannot truly love the brethren unless we love the father; therefore, lacking love to God, we lack love to the church, which is an essential mark of grace.

Again, keeping to the run of the passage, you will find by the eighteenth verse, that love to God is a chief means of that holy peace which is an essential mark of a Christian. "Being justified by faith, we have peace with God through Jesus Christ our Lord," but where there is no love there is no such peace, for fear, which hath torment, distresses the soul; hence love is the indispensable companion of faith, and when they come together, peace is the result. Where there is fervent love to God there is set up a holy familiarity with God, and from this flow satisfaction, delight, and rest. Love must co-operate with faith and cast out fear, so that the soul may have boldness before God. Oh! Christian, thou canst not have the nature of God implanted within thee by regeneration, it cannot reveal itself in love to the brotherhood, it cannot blossom with the fair flowers of peace and joy, except thine affection be set upon God. Let him then be thine exceeding joy. Delight thyself also in the Lord. O love the Lord ye his saints.

We also see, if we turn again to St. John's epistle and pursue his observations to the next chapter and the third verse, that love is the spring of true obedience. "This is the love of God, that we keep his commandments." Now a man who is not obedient to God's commandments is evidently not a true believer; for, although good works do not save us, yet, being saved, believers are sure to produce good works. Though the fruit be not the root of the tree, yet a well rooted tree will, in its season, bring forth its fruits. So, though the keeping of the commandments does not make me a child of God, yet, being a child of God, I shall be obedient to my heavenly Father. But this I cannot be unless I love God. A mere external obedience, a decent formal recognition of the laws of God, is not obedience in God's sight. He abhors the sacrifice where not the heart is found. I must obey because I love, or else I have not in spirit and in truth obeyed at all. See then, that to produce the indispensable fruits of saving faith, there must be love to God; for without it, they would be unreal and indeed impossible.

I hope it is not necessary for me to pursue this argument any further. Love to God is as natural to the renewed heart as love to its mother is to a babe. Who needs to reason a child into love? As certainly as you have the life and nature of God in you, you will seek after the Lord. As the spark, because it has in it the nature of fire, ascends aloft to seek the sun, so will your new-born spirit seek her God, from whom she has derived her life. Search yourselves, then, and see whether you love God or no. Put your hands on your hearts, and as in the sight of him, whose eyes are us a flame of fire, answer to him; make him your confessor at this hour; answer this one question: "Lovest thou me?" I trust very many of you will be able to say--

"Yes, we love thee and adore;
Oh, for grace to love thee more."

This much was necessary to bring us to the second step of our discourse. May the Holy Spirit lead us onward.

II. You see the indispensable importance of love to God: let us now learn THE SOURCE AND SPRING OF TRUE LOVE TO GOD. "We love him because he first loved us." Love to God, wherever it really exists, has been created in the bosom by a belief of God's love to us. No man loves God till he knows that God loves him; and every believer loves God for this reason first and chiefly, that God loves him. He has seen himself to be unworthy of divine favour, yet he has believed God's love in the gift of his dear Son, and he has accepted the atonement that Christ has made as a proof of God's love, and now being satisfied of the divine affection towards him, he of necessity loves his God.

Observe, then, that love to God does not begin in the heart from any disinterested admiration of the nature of God. I believe that, after we have loved God because he first loved us, we may so grow in grace as to love God for what he is. I suppose it is possible for us to be the subjects of a state of heart in which our love spends itself upon the loveliness of God in his own person: we may come to love him because he is so wise, so powerful, so good, so patient, so everything that is lovable. This may be produced within us as the ripe fruit of maturity in the divine life, but it is never the first spring and fountain of the grace of love in any man's heart. Even the apostle John, the man who had looked within the veil and seen the excellent glory beyond any other man, and who had leaned his head upon the bosom of the Lord, and had seen the Lord's holiness, and marked the inimitable beauty of the character of the incarnate God, even John does not say, "We love him because we admire him," but "We love him because he first loved us." For see, brethren, if this kind of love which I have mentioned, which is called the love of disinterested admiration, were required of a sinner, I do not see how he could readily render it. There are two gentlemen of equal rank in society, and the one is not at all obliged to the other; now, they, standing on an equality, can easily feel a disinterested admiration of each other's characters, and a consequent disinterested affection; but I, a poor sinner, by nature sunk in the mire, full of everything that is evil, condemned, guilty of death, so that my only desert is to be cast into hell, am under such obligations to my Saviour and my God, that it would be idle for me to talk about a disinterested affection for him, since I owe to him my life, my all. Besides, until I catch the gleams of his mercy and his loving-kindness to the guilty, his holy, just, and righteous character are not loveable to me, I dread the purity which condemns my defilement, and shudder at the justice which will consume me for my sin. Do not, O seeker, trouble your heart with nice distinctions about disinterested love, but be you content with the beloved disciple to love Christ because be first loved you.

Again, our love to God does not spring from the self-determining power of the will. I greatly, question whether anything does in the world, good or bad. There are some who set up the will as a kind of deity,--it doeth as it wills with earth and heaven; but in truth the will is not a master but a servant. To the sinner his will is a slave; and in the saint, although the will is set free, it is still blessedly under bonds to God. Men do not will a thing because they will it, but because their affections, their passions, or their judgments influence their wills in that direction. No man can stand up and truly say, "I, unbiassed and unaided, will to love God and I will not to love Satan." Such proud self-assuming language would prove him a liar; the man would be clearly a worshipper of himself. A man can only love God when he has perceived some reasons for so doing; and the first argument for loving God, which influences the intellect so as to turn the affections, is the reason mentioned in the text, "We love him because he first loved us."

Now, having thus set the text in a negative light, let us look at it in a more positive manner.

It is certain, beloved brethren, that faith in the heart always precedes love. We first believe the love of God to us before we love God in return. And, Oh what an eneouraging truth this is. I, a sinner, do not believe that God loves me because I feel I love him; but I first believe that he loves me, sinner as I am, and then having believed that gracious fact, I come to love my Benefactor in return. Perhaps some of you seekers are saying to yourselves, "Oh, that we could love God, for then we could hope for mercy." That is not the first step. Your first step is to believe that God loves you, and when that truth is fully fixed in your soul by the Spirit, a fervent love to God will spontaneously issue from your soul, even as flowers willingly pour forth their fragrance under the influence of the dew and the sun. Every man that ever was saved had to come to God not as a lover of God, but as a sinner, and to believe in God's love to him as a sinner. We all wish to take money in our sacks when we go down hungry to this Egypt to buy the bread of life; but it must not be, heaven's bread is given to us freely, and we must accept it freely without money and without price. Do you say, "I do not feel in my heart one good emotion; I do not appear to possess one good thought; I fear I have no love to God at all." Do not remain in unbelief until you feel this love, for if you do, you will never believe at all. You ought to love God, it is true, but you never will till you believe him, and especially believe in his love as revealed in his only begotten Son. If you come to God in Christ, and believe this simple message. "God was in Christ reconciling the world unto himself, not imputing their trespasses unto them," you shall find your heart going out after God. "Whosoever believeth in Jesus Christ shall not perish, but have everlasting life;" believest thou this? Canst thou now believe in Jesus; that is, trust him? Then, Christ died for thee; Christ the Son of God, in thy stead, suffered for thy guilt. God gave his only Son to die for thee. "Oh," saith one, "if I believed that, how I would love God !" Yes, indeed, thou wouldst, and that is the only consideration which can make thee do so. Thou, a sinner, must take Christ to be thy Saviour, and then love to God shall spring up spontaneously in thy soul, as the grass after showers. Love believed is the mother of love returned. The planet reflects light, but first of all it receives it from the sun; the heliotrope turns its face to the orb of day, but first the sunbeams warm and woo it. You shall turn to God, and delight in God, and rejoice in God; but it must be because you first of all believe, and know, and confide in the love of God to you. "Oh," saith one, "it cannot be that God should love an unloving sinner, that the pure One should love the impure, that the Ruler of all should love his enemy." Hear what God saith: "My thoughts are not your thoughts, neither are my ways your ways, for the heavens are higher than the earth; so are my ways higher than your ways, and my thoughts than your thoughts." You think that God loves men because they are godly, but listen to this: "God commendeth his love towards us, in that, while we were yet sinners Christ died for us." "He came not to call the righteous, but sinners to repentance." "While we were yet without strength, in due time Christ died for the ungodly." Think of his "great love wherewith he loved us, even when we were dead in trespasses and sins." God has love in his heart towards those who have nothing in them to love. He loves you, poor soul, who feel that you are most unloveable; loves you who mourn over a stony heart, which will not warm or melt with love to him. Thus saith the Lord: "I have blotted out, as a thick cloud, thy transgressions, and, as a cloud, thy sins; return unto me; for I have redeemed thee." O that God's gracious voice this morning might so call some of his poor wandering ones that they may come and believe his love to them, and then cast themselves at his feet to be his servants for ever.

Brethren, rest assured that in proportion as we are fully persuaded of God's love to us, we shall be affected with love lo him. Do not let the devil tempt you to believe that God does not love You because your love is feeble; for if he can in any way weaken your belief in God's love to you, he cuts off or diminishes the flow of the streams which feed the sacred grace of love to God. If I lament that I do not love God as I ought, that is a holy regret; but if I, therefore, conclude that God's love to me is the less because of this, I deny the light because my eye is dim, and I deprive myself also of the power to increase in love. Let me rather think more and more of the greatness of God's love to me, as I see more and more my unworthiness of it; the more a sinner I am, let me the more fully see how great must be that love which embraces such a sinner as I am; and then, as I receive a deeper sense of the divine mercy, I shall feel the more bound to gratitude and constrained to affection. O for a great wave of love, to carry us right out into the ocean of love.

Observe, beloved brethren, day by day the deeds of God's love to you in the gift of food and raiment, and in the mercies of this life, and especially in the covenant blessings which God gives you, the peace which he sheds abroad in your hearts, the communion which he vouchsafes to you with himself and his blessed Son, and the answers to prayer whieh he grants you. Note well these things, and if you consider them carefully, and weigh their value, you will be accumulating the fuel on which love feeds its consecrated flame. In proportion as you see in every good gift a new token of your Father's love, in that proportion will you make progress in the sweet school of love. Oh, it is heavenly living to taste God's love in every morsel of bread we eat; it is blessed living to know that we breathe an atmosphere purified and made fragrant with divine love, that love protects us while we sleep, changing like a silken curtain all around our bed, and love opens the eyelids of the morning to smile upon us when we wake. Ah, even when we are sick, it is love that chastens us; when we are impoverished, love relieves us of a burden; love gives and love takes; love cheers and love smites. We are compassed about with love, above, beneath, around, within, without. If we could but recognise this, we should become as flames of fire, ardent and fervent towards our God. Knowledge and observation are admirable nurses of ourn infant love.

And, ah, the soul grows rich in love to God when she rests on the bosom of divine lovingkindness. You, who are tossed about with doubts and fears as to whether you are now accepted or shall persevere to the end, you call scarcely guess the ardours of heart which inflame those saints who have learned to cast themselves wholly upon Jesus, and know beyond a doubt his love immutable. Whether I sink or swim, I have no hope but in Christ, my life, my all.

"I know that safe with him remains,
Protected by his power,
What I've committed to his hands
Till the decisive hour:"

And in proportion as I am thus scripturally confident, and rest in my Lord, will my love to him engross all my heart, and, consecrate my life to the Redeemer's glory.

Beloved, I desire to make this very clear, that to feel love to God we must tread along the road of faith. Truly, this is not a hard or perilous way but one prepared by infinite wisdom. It is a road Suitable for sinners, and indeed saints must come that way too. If thou wouldst love God, do not look within thee to see whether this grace or that be as it ought to be, but look to thy God, and read his eternal love his boundless love, his costly love, which gave Christ for thee; then shall thy love drink in fresh life and vigour.

Remember wherever there is love to God in the soul it is an argument that God loves that soul. I recollect meeting once with a Christian woman who said she knew she loved God, but, she was afraid God did not love her. That is a fear so preposterous that it ought never to occur to anybody. You would not love God in deed and in truth unless he had shed abroad his love in your heart in a measure. But on the other hand, our not loving God is not a conclusive argument that God does not love us; else might the sinner be afraid to come to God. O loveless sinner, with heart unquickened and chill, the voice of God calls even thee to Christ. Even to the dead in sin, his voice saith "Live." Whilst thou art yet polluted in thy blood, cast out in the open field, to the loathing of thy person, the Lord of mercy passes by, and says "live." His mighty sovereignty comes forth dressed in robes of love, and he touches thee the unloveable, the loveless, the depraved, degraded sinner, at enmity with God,--he touches thee in all thine alienation and he lifts thee out of it and makes thee to love him, not for thine own sake, but for his name sake and for his mercy sake. Thou hadst no love at all to him, but all the love lay in him alone; and therefore he began to bless thee, and will continue to bless thee world without end, if thou art a believer in Jesus. In the bosom of the Eternal are the deep springs of all love.

III. This leads us, in the third place, to consider for a moment THE REVIVAL OF OUR LOVE. It is sadly probable that there are in this house some who once loved God very earnestly, but now they have declined and become grievously indifferent; God's love to us never changes, but ours too often sinks to a low ebb. Perhaps some of you have become so cold in your affections, that it is difficult to be sure that you ever did love God at all. It may be that your life has become lax, so as to deserve the censure of the Church. You are a backslider and you are in a dangerous condition; yet, if there be indeed spiritual life in you, you will wish to return. You have gone astray like a lost sheep, but your prayer is, "seek thy servant, for I do not forget thy commandments." Now, note well, that the cause which originated your love is the same which must restore it. You went to Christ as a sinner at first, and your first act was to believe the love of God to you when there was nothing in you that evidenced it. Go the same way again. Do not stop, my dear brother, to pump up love out of the dry well within yourself! Do not think it possible that love will come at your bidding. If a man would give all the substance of his house for love, it would utterly be contemned. Think of the Lord's unchanging grace, and you will feel the spring-time of love returning to your soul. Still doth the Lord reserve mercy for the sinful, still he waiteth to be gracious; he is as willing to receive you now that you have played the prodigal, as he was to have retained you at home in the bosom of his 1ove. Many considerations ought to aid you, a backslider, to believe more in the love of God than ever you did. For think what love it must be that can invite you still to return, you, who after knowing so much have sinned against light and knowledge; you, who after having experienced so much, have given the lie to your profession. He might justly have cut you down, for you have cumbered the ground long enough. Surely, when Israel went astray from God, it was a clear proof to her of Jehovah's love when he graciously said, "They say if a man put away his wife, or she go from him, and become another man's, shall he return to her again?" Why, the answer in every bosom is "No !" Who would love a wife who had so polluted herself? But thus saith the Lord, "Thou hast played the harlot with many lovers, yet return unto me." What matchless love is this.

Hear yet more of these gracious words, which you will find in the third chapter of Jeremiah's prophecy. "Go and proclaim these words toward the north, and say, Return, thou backsliding Israel, saith the Lord; and I will not cause mine anger to fall upon you: for I am merciful, saith the Lord, and I will not keep anger for ever." "Turn, O backsliding children, saith the Lord , for I am married unto you: and I will take you one of a city, and two of a family, and I will bring you to Zion." "Return, ye backs1iding children, and I will heal your backslidings." Can you hear these words without emotion? Backslider! I pray thee take the wings of God's love to fly back to him with. But I hear you enquiring, Will he still receive me? Shall I be once more--

"To the Father's bosom pressed,
Once again a child confessed."

It shall be so. Does he not declare that he is God and changes not, and therefore you are not consumed? Rekindled are the flames of love in the backslider's bosom when he feels all this to be true; he cries, "Behold, we come to thee for thou art the Lord our God." I pray you, then, any of you who are conscious of gross derelictions of duty, and wanderings of heart, do not ask Moses to lead you back to Christ, he knows the way to Sinai's flames, but not to Calvary's pardoning blood. Go to Christ himself at once. If you go to the law and begin to judge yourself, if you get the notion that you are to undergo a sort of spiritual quarantine, that you must pass through a mental purgatory before you may renew your faith in the Saviour, you are mistaken. Come just as you are, bad as you are, hardened, cold, dead as you feel yourselves to be, come even so, and believe in the boundless love of God in Christ Jesus. Then shall come the deep repentance; then shall come the brokenness of heart; then shall come the holy jealousy, the sacred hatred of sin, and the refining of the soul from all her dross; then, indeed, all good things shall come to restore your soul, and lead you in the paths of righteousuess. Do not look for these first; that would be looking for the effects before the cause. The great cause of love in the restored backs1ider must still be the love of God to him, to whom he clings with a faith that dares not let go its hold.

"But," saith one, "I think it is very dangerous to tell the backslider to believe in God's love, surely it will be gross presumption for him so to believe," It is never presumptuous for a man to believe the truth: whether a statement be comfortable or unconmfortable, the presumption does not lie in the matter itself: but in its untruthfulness. I say again, it is never presumptuous to believe the truth. And this is the truth, that the Lord loves his prodigal sons still, and his stray sheep still, and he will devise means to bring his banished back again, that they perish not. "If any man sin, we have an advocate with the Father, Jesus Christ the righteous."

Remember here that the motive power which draws back the backslider again, is the cord of love, the band of a man, which makes him feel he must go back to God with weeping and repentance, because God loves him still. What man among you this morning hath a son who has disobeyed him and gone from him, and is living in drunkenness, and in all manner of lust? If you have in anger told him, so that he doubts it not, that you have struck his name out of your family, and will not regard him as a child any longer, do you think that your severity will induce him to return to you in love? Far from it. But suppose instead thereof, you still assure him that you love him; that there is always a place at your table for him, and a bed in your house for him, ay, and better still, a warm place in your heart for him; suppose he sees your tears and hears your prayers for him, will not this draw him? Yes, indeed, if be be a son. It is even thus between thy God and thee, O backslider. Hear ye the Lord as he argues thy case within his own heart. "My people are bent to backsliding from me; though they called them to the most High, none at all would exalt him. How shall I give thee up, Ephraim? how shall I deliver thee, Israel? how shall I make thee as Admah? how shall I set thee as Zeboim? mine heart is turned within me, my repentings are kindled together. I will not execute the fierceness of mine anger, I will not return to destroy Ephraim; for I am God, and not man." Surely, if anything will draw you back, this will. "Ah !' saith the wandering son, "my dear father loves me still. I will arise and go to him. I will not vex so tender a heart. I will be his loving son again. God does not say to you prodigals, who once professed his name, "I have unchilded you, I have cast you away," but he says, "I love you still; and for my name's sake will I restrain my wrath that I cut you not off." Come to your offended Father, and you shall find that he has not repented of his love, but will embrace you still.

IV. Time fails, but I must speak for a little, time or no time, upon the fourth point--THE PERFECTING OF OUR LOVE TO GOD.

Beloved, there are few of us who know much of the deeps of the love of God; our love is shallow; ah, how shallow! Love to God is like a great mountain. The majority of travellers view it from afar, or traverse the valley at its base: a few climb to a halting place on one of its elevated spurs, whence they see a portion of its sublimities: here and there an adventurous traveller climbs a minor peak, and views glacier and alp at closer range; fewest of all are those who scale the topmost pinnacle and tread the virgin snow. So in the Church of God. Every Christian abides under the shadow of divine love: a few enjoy and return that love to a remarkable degree: but there are few in this age sadly few, who reach to seraphic love, who ascend into the hill of the Lord, to stand where the eagle's eye hath not seen, and walk the path which the lion's welp hath never trodden, the high places of complete consecration and ardent self-consuming love. Now, mark you, it may be difficult to ascend so high, but there is one sure route, and only one, which the man must follow who would gain the sacred elevation. It is not the track of his works, nor the path of his own actions, but this, "We love him because he first loved us." John and the apostles confessed that thus they attained their love. For the highest love that ever glowed in human bosom there was no source but this--God first loved that man. Do you not see how this is? The knowledge that God loves me casts out my tormenting dread of God: and when this is expelled, there is room for abounding love to God. As fear goes out, love comes in at the other door. So the more faith in God the more room there is for soul-fllling love.

Again, strong faith in God's love brings great enjoyment; our heart is glad, our soul is satisfied with marrow and fatness when we know that the whole heart of God beats towards us as forcibly as if we were the only creatures he had ever made, and his whole heart were wrapt up in us. This deep enjoyment creates the flaming love of which I have just now spoken.

If the ardent love of some saints often takes the shape of admiration of God, this arises from their familiarity with God, and this familiarity they never would have indulged in, unless they had know that he was their friend. A man could not speak to God as to a friend, unless he knew the love that God hath toward him. The more true his knowledge and the more sure, the more close his fellowship.

Brethren beloved, if you know that God has loved you, then you will feel grateful; every doubt will diminish your gratitude, but every grain of faith will increase it. Then as we advance in grace, love to God in our soul will excite desire after him. Those we love we long to be with; we count the hours that separate us; no place so happy as that in which we enjoy their society. Hence love to God produces a desire to be with him; a desire to be like him, a longing to be with him eternally in heaven, and this breaks us away from worldliness; this keeps us from idolatry, and thus has a most blessedly sanctifying effect upon us, producing that elevated character which is now so rare, but which wherever it exists is powerful for the good of the church and for the glory of God. Oh that we had many in this church who had reached the highest platform of piety. Would God we had a band of men full of faith and of the Holy Ghost; strong in the Lord and in the power of his might. It may help those who aspire to mount high in grace, if they keep in mind that every step they climb they must use the ladder which Jacob saw. The love of God to us is the only way to climb to the love of God.

And now I must spend a minute in putting the truth of my text to the test. I want you not to listen to me so much as to listen to your own hearts, and to God's word, a minute, if you are believers. What is it we have been talking about? It is God's love to us. Get the thought into your head a minute: "God loves me--not merely bears with me, thinks of me, feeds me, but loves me. Oh, it is a very sweet thing to feel that we have the love of a dear wife, or a kind husband; and there is much sweetness in the love of a fond child, or a tender mother; but to think that God loves me, this is infinitely better! Who is it that loves you? God, the Maker of heaven and earth, the Almighty, All in all, does he love me? Even he? If all men, and all angels, and all the living creatures that are before the throne loved me, it were nothing to this--the Infinite loves me! And who is it that he loves? Me. The text saith, "us." "We love him because he first loved us." But this is the personal point--he loves me, an insignificant nobody, full of sin--who deserved to be in hell; who loves him so little in return--God loves me. Beloved believer, does not this melt you? Does not this fire your soul? I know it does if it is really believed. It must. And how did he love me? He loved me so that he gave up his only begotten Son for me, to be nailed to the tree, and made to bleed and die. And what will come of it? Why, because he loved me and forgave me,--I am on the way to heaven, and within a few months, perhaps days, I shall see his face and sing his praises. He loved me before I was born; before a star begun to shine he loved me, and he has never ceased to do so all these years. When I have sinned he has loved me; when I have forgotten him he has loved me; and when in the days of my sin I cursed him, yet still he loved me; and he will love me when my knees tremble, and my hair is grey with age, "even to hoar hairs" he will bear and carry his servant; and he will love me when the world is on a blaze, and love me for ever, and for ever. Oh, chew the cud of this blessed thought; roll it under your tongue as a dainty morsel; sit down this afternoon, if you have leisure, and think of nothing but this--his great love wherewith he loves you; and if you do not feel your heart bubbling with a good matter, if you do not feel your soul yearning towards God, and heaving big with strong emotions of love to God, then I am much mistaken. This is so powerful a truth, and you are so constituted as a Christian as to be wrought upon by this truth, that if it be believed and felt, the consequence must be that you will love him because he first loved you. God bless you, brethren and sisters, for Christ's sake. Amen.

PORTION OF SCRIPTURE READ BEFORE SERMON--John 4:1-5.

Travailing for Souls

A Sermon (No. 1009)
Delivered on Lord's-day Morning, September 3rd, 1871, by
C. H. SPURGEON,
At the Metropolitan Tabernacle, Newington

"As soon as Zion travailed, she brought forth her children." - Isaiah 66:8.

ISRAEL had fallen into the lowest condition, but an inward yearning of heart was felt in the midst of God's people for the return of the divine blessing; and no sooner had this anxious desire become intense, than God heard the voice of its cry, and the blessing came. It was so at the time of the restoration of the captives from Babylon, and it was most evidently so in the days of our Lord. A faithful company had continued still to expect the coming of the Lord's anointed messenger; they waited till he should suddenly come in his temple; the twelve tribes, represented by an elect remnant, cried day and night unto the Most High, and when at last their prayers reached the fulness of vehemence, and their anxiety wrought in them the deepest agony of spirit, then the Messiah came; the light of the gentiles, and the glory of Israel. Then began the age of blessedness in which the barren woman did keep house and become the joyful mother of children. The Holy Ghost was given, and multitudes were born to the church of God, yea we may say, a nation was born in a day. The wilderness and the solitary place were glad for them, and the desert rejoiced and blossomed as the rose. We are not, however, about to enter into the particular application of our text as Isaiah uttered it: the great declarations of revelation are applicable to all cases, and, once true, they stand fast for ever and ever. Earnestly desiring that God may give a large spiritual blessing to his church this morning, through the subject to which my mind has been directed, I shall first ask you to note that in order to the obtaining of an increase to the church, there must be travail, and that, secondly, this travail is frequently followed by surprising results. I shall then have to show why both the travail and the result are desirable, and pronounce woe on those who stand back and hinder it, and a blessing on such as shall be moved by God's own Spirit to travail for souls.

I. It is clear from the text, "As soon as Zion travailed, she brought forth her children," that THERE MUST BE THE TRAVAIL before there will be the spiritual birth.

Let me first establish this fact from history. Before there has fallen a great benediction upon God's people, it has been preceded by great searchings of heart. Israel was so oppressed in Egypt, that it would have been very easy, and almost a natural thing, for the people to become so utterly crushed in spirit as to submit to be hereditary bond-slaves, making the best they could of their miserable lot; but God would not have it so; he meant to bring them out "with a high hand and an outstretched arm." Before, however, he began to work, he made them begin to cry. Their sighs and cries came up into the ears of God, and he stretched out his hand to deliver them. Doubtless, many a heart-rending appeal was made to heaven by mothers when their babes were torn from their breasts to be cast into the river. With what bitterness did they ask God to look upon his poor people Israel, and avenge them of their oppressors. The young men bowed under the cruel yoke and groaned, while hoary sires, smarting under ignominious lashes from the taskmaster, sighed and wept before the God of Israel. The whole nation cried, "O God visit us; God of Abraham, of Isaac, and of Jacob, remember thy covenant, and deliver us." This travail brought its result; for the Lord smote the field of Zoan with mighty plagues, and forth from under the bondage of the sons of Misraim, the children of Israel marched with joy.

As we shall not have time to narrate many instances, let us take a long leap in history to the days of David. The era of the son of Jesse was evidently a time of religious revival. God was honored and his service maintained in the midst of Judea's land in the days of the royal bard; but it is clear to readers of the Scriptures that David was the subject of spiritual throes and pangs of the most intense kind. His bosom throbbed and heaved like that of a man made fit to be the leader of a great revival. What yearnings he had! He thirsted after God, after the living God! What petitions he poured forth that God would visit Zion, and make the vine which he had planted to flourish once again. Even when his own sins pressed heavily upon him, he could not end his personal confession without entreating the Lord to build the walls of Jerusalem, and to do good in his good pleasure unto Zion. Now, David was only the mouth of hundreds of others, who with equal fervency cried unto God that the blessing might rest upon his people. There was much soul-travail in Israel and Judah, and the result was that the Lord was glorified, and true religion flourished.

Remember also the days of Josiah, the king. You know well now the book of the law was found neglected in the temple, and when it was brought before the king, he rent his clothes, for he saw that the nation had revolted, and that wrath must come upon it to the uttermost. The young king's heart, which was tender, for he feared God, was ready to break with anguish to think of the misery that would come upon his people on account of their sins. Then there came a glorious reformation which purged the land of idols, and caused the passover to be observed as never before. Travails of heart among the godly produced the delightful change.

It was the same with the work of Nehemiah. His book begins with a description of the travail of his heart. He was a patriot, a man of nervous, excitable temperament, and keen sensibility for God's honor, and when his soul had felt great bitterness and longing, then he arose to build, and a blessing rested on his efforts.

In the early dawn of Christian history, there was a preparation of the church before it received an increase. Look at the obedient disciples sitting in the upper room, waiting with anxious hope; every heart there had been ploughed with anguish by the death of the Lord, each one was intent to receive the promised boon of the Spirit. There, with one heart and one mind, they tarried, but not without wrestling prayer, and so the Comforter was given, and three thousand souls were given also.

The like living zeal and vehement desire have always been perceptible in the Church of God before any season of refreshing. Think not that Luther was the only man that wrought the Reformation. There were hundreds who sighed and cried in secret in the cottages of the Black Forest, in the homes of Germany, and on the hills of Switzerland. There were hearts breaking for the Lord's appearing in strange places, they might have been found in the palaces of Spain, in the dungeons of the Inquisition, among the canals of Holland, and the green lanes of England. Women, as they hid their Bibles, lest their lives should be forfeited, cried out in spirit, "O God, how long?" There were pains as of a woman in travail, in secret places there were tears and bitter lamentations, on the high places of the field there were mighty strivings of spirit, and so at length there came that grand revulsion which made the Vatican to rock and reel from its foundation to its pinnacle. There has been evermore in the history of the church, the travail before there has been the result.

And this, dear friends, while it is true on the large scale, is true also in every individual case. A man with no sensibility or compassion for other men's souls, may accidentally be the means of a conversion; the good word which he utters will not cease to be good because the speaker had no right to declare God's statutes. The bread and meat which were brought to Elijah were not less nourishing because the ravens brought them, but the ravens remained ravens still. A hard-hearted man may say a good thing which God will bless, but, as a rule, those who bring souls to Christ are those who first of all have felt an agony of desire that souls should be saved. This is imaged to us in our Master's character. He is the great Saviour of men; but before he could save others, he learned in their flesh to sympathize with them. He wept over Jerusalem, he sweat great drops of blood in Gethsemane; he was, and is, a high priest who is touched with the feeling of our infirmities. As the Captain of our salvation, in bringing many sons unto glory he was made perfect by sufferings. Even Christ went not forth to preach until he had spent nights in intercessory prayer, and uttered strong cryings and tears for the salvation of his hearers. His ministering servants who have been most useful, have always been eagerly desirous to be so. If any minister can be satisfied without conversions, he shall have no conversions. God will not force usefulness on any man. It is only when our heart breaks to see men saved, that we shall be likely to see sinners' hearts broken. The secret of success lies in all-consuming zeal, all-subduing travail for souls. Read the sermons of Wesley and of Whitfield, and what is there in them? It is no severe criticism to say that they are scarcely worthy to have survived, and yet those sermons wrought marvels, and well they might, for both preachers could truly say--

"The love of Christ doth me constrain
To seek the wandering souls of men;
With cries, entreaties, tears, to save,
To snatch them from the fiery wave."

In order to understand such preaching, you need to see and hear the man, you want his tearful eye, his glowing countenance, his pleading tone, his bursting heart. I have heard of a great preacher who objected to having his sermons printed, "Because," said he, "you cannot print me." That observation is very much to the point. A soul-winner throws himself into what he says. As I have sometimes said, we must ram ourselves into our cannons, we must fire ourselves at our hearers, and when we do this, then, by God's grace, their hearts are often carried by storm. Do any of you desire your children's conversions? You shall have them saved when you agonize for them. Many a parent who has been privileged to see his son walking in the truth, will tell you that before the blessing came he had spent many hours in prayer and in earnest pleading with God, and then it was that the Lord visited his child and renewed his soul. I have heard of a young man who had grown up and left the parental roof, and through evil influences, had been enticed into holding skeptical views. His father and mother were both earnest Christians, and it almost broke their hearts to see their son so opposed to the Redeemer. On one occasion they induced him to go with them to hear a celebrated minister. He accompanied them simply to please them, and for no higher motive. The sermon happened to be upon the glories of heaven. It was a very extraordinary sermon, and was calculated to make every Christian in the audience to leap for joy. The young man was much gratified with the eloquence of the preacher, but nothing more; he gave him credit for superior oratorical ability, and was interested in the sermon, but felt none of its power. He chanced to look at his father and mother during the discourse, and was surprised to see them weeping. He could not imagine why they, being Christian people, should sit and weep under a sermon which was most jubilant in its strain. When he reached home, he said, "Father, we have had a capital sermon, but I could not understand what could make you sit there and cry, and my mother too?" His father said, "My dear son, I certainly had no reason to weep concerning myself, nor your mother, but I could not help thinking all through the sermon about you, for alas, I have no hope that you will be a partaker in the bright joys which await the righteous. It breaks my heart to think that you will be shut out of heaven." His mother said, "The very same thoughts crossed my mind, and the more the preacher spoke of the joys of the saved, the more I sorrowed for my dear boy that he should never know what they were." That touched the young man's heart, led him to seek his father's God, and before long he was at the same communion table, rejoicing in the God and Saviour whom his parents worshiped. The travail comes before the bringing forth; the earnest anxiety, the deep emotion within, precede our being made the instruments of the salvation of others.

I think I have established the fact; now for a minute or two let me show you the reason for it. Why is it that there must be this anxiety before desirable results are gained? For answer, it might suffice us to say that God has so appointed it. It is the order of nature. The child is not born into the world without the sorrows of the mother, nor is the bread which sustains life procured from the earth without toil: "In the sweat of thy face shalt thou eat bread," was a part of the primeval curse. Now, as it is in the natural, so is it in the spiritual; there shall not come the blessing we seek, without first of all the earnest yearning for it. Why, it is so even in ordinary business. We say, "No sweat no sweet," "no pains no gains," "No mill no meal." If there be no labor there shall be no profit. He that would be rich must toil for it; he that would acquire fame must spend and be spent to win it. It is ever so. There must ever be the travail and then the desire cometh. God has so appointed it: let us accept the decree.

But better still, he has ordained this for our good. If souls were given us without any effort, anxiety or prayer it would be our loss to have it so, because the anxieties which throb within a compassionate spirit exercise his graces; they produce grateful love to God; they try his faith in the power of God to save others; they drive him to the mercy-seat; they strengthen his patience and perseverance, and every grace within the man is educated and increased by his travail for souls. As labor is now a blessing, so also is soul-travail; men are fashioned more fully into the likeness of Christ thereby, and the whole church is by the same emotion quickened into energy. The fire of our own spiritual life is fanned by that same breath which our prayers invite to come from the four winds to breath upon the slain. Besides, dear friends, the zeal that God excites within us is often the means of effecting the purpose which we desire. After all, God does not give conversions to eloquence, but to heart. The power in the hand of God's Spirit for conversions is heart coming in contact with heart. This is God's battle-axe and weapons of war in his crusade. He is pleased to use the yearnings, longings, and sympathies of Christian men, as the means of compelling the careless to think, constraining the hardened to feel, and driving the unbelieving to consider. I have little confidence in elaborate speech and polished sentences, as the means of reaching men's hearts; but I have great faith in that simple-minded Christian woman, who must have souls converted or she will weep her eyes out over them; and in that humble Christian who prays day and night in secret, and then avails himself of every opportunity to address a loving word to sinners. The emotion we feel, and the affection we bear, are the most powerful implements of soul-winning. God the Holy Ghost usually breaks hard hearts by tender hearts.

Besides, the travail qualifies for the proper taking care of the offspring. God does not commit his new-born children to people who do not care to see conversions. If he ever allows them to fall into such hands, they suffer very serious loss thereby. Who is so fit to encourage a new-born believer as the man who first anguished before the Lord for his conversion? Those you have wept over and prayed for you will be sure to encourage and assist. The church that never travailed, should God send her a hundred converts, would be unfit to train them; she would not know what to do with little children, and would leave them to much suffering. Let us thank God, brethren, if he has given us any degree of the earnest anxiety and sympathy, which marked soul-wining men and women, and let us ask to have more for, in proportion as we have it, we shall be qualified to be the instruments in the hand of the Spirit, of nursing and cherishing God's sons and daughters.

Once more, there is a great benefit in the law which makes travail necessary to spiritual birth, because it secures all the glory to God. If you want to be lowered in your own esteem, try to convert a child. I would like those brethren who believe so much in free will, and the natural goodness of the human heart, to try some children that I could bring to them, and see whether they could break their hearts and make them love the Saviour. Why, sir, you never think yourself so great a fool as after trying in your own strength to bring a sinner to the Saviour. Oh! How often have I come back defeated from arguing with an awakened person whom I have sought to comfort: I did think I had some measure of skill in handling sorrowful cases, but I have been compelled to say to myself, "What a simpleton I am! God the Holy Ghost must take this case in hand, for I am foiled." When one has tried in a sermon to reach a certain person who is living in sin, you learn afterwards that he enjoyed the sermon which he ought to have smarted under; then, you say, "Ah, now I see what a weak worm I am, and if good be done, God shall have the glory." Your longing, then, that others should be saved, and your vehemence of spirit, shall secure to God all the glory of his own work; and this is what the Lord is aiming at, for his glory he will not give to another, nor his praise to an arm of flesh.

And now, having established the fact, and shown the reasons for it, let us notice how this travail shows itself.

Usually when God intends greatly to bless a church, it will begin in this way:--Two or three persons in it are distressed at the low state of affairs, and become troubled even to anguish. Perhaps they do not speak to one another, or know of their common grief, but they begin to pray with flaming desire and untiring importunity. The passion to see the church revived rules them. They think of it when they go to rest, they dream of it on their bed, they muse on it in the streets. This one thing eats them up. They suffer great heaviness and continual sorrow in heart for perishing sinners; they travail in birth for souls. I have happened to become the centre of certain brethren in this church; one of them said to me the other day, "O sir, I pray day and night for God to prosper our church; I long to see greater things; God is blessing us, but we want much more." I saw the deep earnestness of the man's soul, and I thanked him and thanked God heartily, thinking it to be a sure sign of a coming blessing. Sometime after, another friend, who probably now hears me speak, but who did not know any thing about the other, felt the same yearning, and must needs let me know it; he too is anxious, longing, begging, crying, for a revival; and thus from three or four quarters I have had the same message, and I feel hopeful because of these tokens for good. When the sun rises the mountain tops first catch the light, and those who constantly live near to God will be the first to feel the influence of the coming refreshing. The Lord give me a dozen importunate pleaders and lovers of souls, and by his grace we will shake all London from end to end yet. The work would go on without the mass of you, Christians; many of you only hinder the march of the army; but give us a dozen lion-like, lamb-like men, burning with intense love to Christ and souls, and nothing will be impossible to their faith. The most of us are not worthy to unloose the shoe-latches of ardent saints. I often feel I am not so myself, but I aspire and long to be reckoned among them. Oh, may God give us this first sign of the travail in the earnest ones and twos.

By degrees the individuals are drawn together by sacred affinity, and the prayer-meetings become very different. The brother who talked twenty minutes of what he called prayer, and yet never asked for a single thing, gives up his oration and falls to pleading with many tears and broken sentences: while the friend who used to relate his experience and go through the doctrines of grace, and call that a prayer, forgets that rigmarole and begins agonizing before the throne. And not only this, but little knots here and there come together in their cottages, and in their little rooms cry mightily to God. The result will be that the minister, even if he does not know of the feeling in the hearts of his people, will grow fervent himself. He will preach more evangelically, more tenderly, more earnestly. He will be no longer formal, or cold, or stereotyped; he will be all alive. Meanwhile, not with the preacher only will be the blessing, but with his hearers who love the Lord. One will be trying a plan for getting in the young people; another will be looking after the strangers in the aisles, who come only now and then. One brother will make a vehement attempt to preach the gospel at the corner of the street; another will open a room down a dark court; another will visit lodging-houses and hospitals; all sorts of holy plans will be invented, and zeal will break out in many directions. All this will be spontaneous, nothing will be forced. If you want to get up a revival, as the term is, you can do it, just as you can grow tasteless strawberries in winter, by artificial heat. There are ways and means of doing that kind of thing but the genuine work of God needs no such planning and scheming; it is altogether spontaneous. If you see a snowdrop next

February in your garden, you will feel persuaded that spring is on the way; the artificial-flower maker could put as many snow-drops there as you please, but that would be no index of coming spring. So you may get up an apparent zeal which will be no proof of God's blessing; but when fervor comes of itself, without human direction or control, then is it of the Lord. When men's hearts heave and break, like the mould of the garden under the influence of the reviving life which lay buried there, then in very deed a benediction is on the way. Travail is no mockery, but a real agony of the whole nature. May such be seen in this our church, and throughout the whole Israel of God.

II. Now, with great brevity, let us consider that THE RESULT IS OFTEN VERY SURPRISING. It is frequently surprising for rapidity. "As soon as Zion travailed, she brought forth her children." God's works are not tied by time. The more spiritual a force is the less it lies within the chains of time. The electric current, which has a greater nearness to the spiritual than the grosser forms of materialism, is inconceivably rapid from that very reason, and by it time is all but annihilated. The influences of the Spirit of God are a force most spiritual, and more quick than any thing beneath the sun. As soon as we agonize in soul the Holy Spirit can, if he pleases, convert the person for whom we have pleaded. While we are yet speaking he hears, and before we call he answers. Some calculate the expected progress of a church by arithmetic; and I think I have heard of arithmetical sermons in which there have been ingenious calculations as to how many missionaries it would take to convert the world, and how much cash would be demanded. Now, there is no room here for the application of mathematics; spiritual forces are not calculable by an arithmetic which is most at home in the material universe. A truth which is calculated to strike the mind of one man to-day may readily enough produce a like effect upon a million minds to-morrow. The preaching which moves one heart needs not be altered to tell upon ten thousand. With God's Spirit our present instrumentalities will suffice to win the world to Jesus; without him, ten thousand times as much apparent force would be only so much weakness. The spread of truth, moreover, is not reckonable by time. During the ten years which ended in 1870, such wondrous changes were wrought throughout the world that no prophet would have been believed had he foretold them. Reforms have been accomplished in England, in the United States, in Germany, in Spain, in Italy, which according to ordinary reckoning, would have occupied at least one hundred years. Things which concern the mind cannot be subjected to those regulations of time which govern steamboats and railways; in such matters God's messengers are flames of fire. The Spirit of God is able to operate upon the minds of men instantaneously: witness the case of Paul. Between now and to-morrow morning he could excite holy thought in all the minds of all the thousand millions of the sons of Adam; and if prayer were mighty enough, and strong enough, why should it not be done on some bright day? We are not straitened in him, we are straitened in our own bowels. All the fault lies there. Oh for the travail that would produce immediate results.

But the result is surprising, not only for its rapidity, but for the greatness of it. It is said, "Shall a nation be born at once?" As soon as ever Zion was in distress concerning her children, tens of thousands came and built up Jerusalem, and re-established her fallen state. So, in answer to prayer, God not only bestows speedy blessings, but great blessings. There were fervent prayers in that upper room "before the day of Pentecost had fully come," and what a great answer it was when, after Peter's sermon, some three thousand were ready to confess their faith in Christ, and to be baptized. Shall we never see such things again? Is the Spirit straitened? Has his arm waxed short? Nay, verily, but we clog and hinder him. He cannot do any mighty work here because of our unbelief; and, if our unbelief were cast out, and if prayer went up to God with eagerness, and vehemence, and importunity, then would a blessing descend so copious as to amaze us all.

But enough of this, for I must needs pass on to the next point.

III. THIS TRAVAIL AND ITS RESULT ARE ABUNDANTLY DESIRABLE; pre-eminently desirable at this hour. The world is perishing for a lack of knowledge. Did any one among us ever lay China on his heart? Your imagination cannot grapple with the population of that mighty empire, without God, without Christ, strangers to the commonwealth of Israel. But it is not China alone; there are other vast nations lying in darkness; the great serpent hath coiled himself around the globe, and who shall set the world free from him? Reflect upon this one city with its three millions. What sin the moon sees! What sin the Sabbath sees! Alas for the transgressions of this wicked city. Babylon of old could not have been worse than London is, nor so guilty, for she had not the light that London has received. Brethren, there is no hope for China, no hope for the world, no hope for our own city, while the church is sluggish and lethargic. Through the church the blessing is usually bestowed. Christ multiplies the bread, and gives it to the disciples; the multitudes can only get it through the disciples. Oh, it is time, it is high time that the churches were awakened to seek the good of dying myriads. Moreover, brethren, the powers of evil are ever active. We may sleep, but Satan sleepeth never. The church's plough lies yonder, rusting in the furrow; do you not see it to your shame? But the plough of Satan goes from end to end of his great field, he leaves no headland, but he ploughs deep while sluggish churches sleep. May we be stirred as we see the awful activity of evil spirits and persons who are under their sway. How industriously pernicious literature is spread abroad, and with what a zeal do men seek for fresh ways of sinning. He is eminent among men who can invent fresh songs to gratify the lascivious tongue, or find new spectacles to delight unclean eyes. O God, are thine enemies awake, and only thy friends asleep? O Sufferer, once bathed in bloody sweat in Gethsemane, is there not one of the twelve awake but Judas? Are they all asleep except the traitor? May God arouse us for his infinite mercy's sake.

Besides this, my brethren, when a church is not serving God, mischief is brewing withing herself. While she is not bringing others in, her own heart is becoming weak in its pulsations, and her entire constitution is a prey to decline. The church must either bring forth children unto God, or else die of consumption: she has no alternative but that. A church must either be fruitful or rot, and of all things, a rotting church is the most offensive. Would God we could bury our dead churches out of our sight, as Abraham buried Sarah, for above ground they breed a pestilence of scepticism; for men say, "Is this religion?" and taking it to be so, they forego true religion altogether.

And then, worst of all is, God is not glorified. If there be no yearning of heart in the church, and no conversions, where is the travail of the Redeemer's soul? Where, Immanuel, where are the trophies of thy terrible conflict? Where are the jewels for thy crown? Thou shalt have thine own, thy Father's will shall not be frustrated; thou shalt be adored; but as yet we see it not. Hard are men's hearts, and they will not love thee; unyielding are their wills, and they will not own thy sovereignty. Oh! weep because Jesus is not honored. The foul oath still curdles our blood as we hear it, and blasphemy usurps the place of grateful song. Oh! by the wounds and bloody sweat, by the cross and nails, and spear, I beseech you followers of Christ, be in earnest, that Jesus Christ's name may be known and loved through the earnest agonizing endeavors of the Christian church.

IV. And now I must come near to a close, by, in the fourth place, noticing THE WOE WHICH WILL SURELY COME TO THOSE WHO HINDER THE TRAVAIL OF THE CHURCH, and so prevent the bringing forth of her children. An earnest spirit cannot complete its exhortations to zeal without pronouncing a denunciation upon the indifferent. What said the heroine of old who had gone forth against the enemies of Israel, when she remembered coward spirits? "Curse ye Meroz, saith the angel of the Lord, curse ye bitterly the inhabitants thereof; because they came not to the help of the Lord against the mighty." Some such curse will assuredly come upon every professing Christian who is backward in helping the church in the day on her soul's travail. And who are they that hinder her? I answer, every worldly Christian hinders the progress of the gospel. Every member of a church who is living in secret sin, who is tolerating in his heart any thing that he knows to be wrong, who is not seeking eagerly his own personal sanctification, is to that extent hindering the work of the Spirit of God. "Be ye clean that bear the vessels of the Lord," for to the extent that we maintain known unholiness, we restrain the Spirit. He cannot work by us as long as any conscious sin is tolerated. It is not over breaking of commandments that I am now speaking of, brethren, but I include worldliness also--a care for carnal things, and a carelessness about spiritual things, having enough grace just to make us hope that you are a Christian, but not enough to prove you are; bearing a shriveled apple here and there on the topmost bough, but not much fruit; this I mean, this partial barrenness, not complete enough to condemn, yet complete enough to restrain the blessing, this robs the treasure of the church, and hinders her progress. O brethren, if any of you are thus described, repent and do your first works; and God help you to be foremost in proportion as you have been behind.

They are also guilty who distract the mind of the church from the subject in hand. Anybody who calls off the thoughts of the church from soul-saving is a mischief maker. I have heard it said of a minister, "He greatly influences the politics of the town." Well, it is a very doubtful good in my mind, a very doubtful good indeed. If the man, keeping to his own calling of preaching the gospel, happens to influence these meaner things, it is well, but any Christian minister who thinks that he can do two things well, is mistaken. Let him mind soul-winning, and not turn a Christian church into a political club. Let us fight out our politics somewhere else, but not inside the church of God. There our one business is soul-winning, our one banner is the cross, our one leader is the crucified King. Inside the church there may be minor things that take off the thoughts of men from seeking souls,--little things that can be made beneath the eye that is microscopical, to swell into great offences. Oh, my brethren, let us, while souls are perishing, waive personal differences. "It must need be that offences come, but woe unto him by whom the offence cometh;" but, after all, what can there be that is worth taking notice of, compared with glorifying Christ. If our Lord and Master would be honored by your being a doormat for his saints to wipe their feet on, you would be honored to be in the position; and if there shall come glory to God by your patient endurance, even of insult and contumely, be glad in your heart that you are permitted to be nothing that Christ may be all in all. We must by no means turn aside to this or that; not even golden apples must tempt us in this race! There lies the mark, and until it is reached, we must never pause, but onward press, for Christ's cause and crown.

Above all, my brethren, we shall be hindering the travail of the church if we do not share in it. Many church members think that if they do nothing wrong, and make no trouble, then they are all right. Not at all, sir; not at all. Here is a chariot, and we are all engaged to drag it. Some of you do not put out your hands to pull; well, then, the rest of us have to labor so much the more; and the worst of it is we have to draw you also. While you do not add to the strength which draws, you increase the weight that is to be drawn. It is all very well for you to say, "But I do not hinder;" you do hinder, you cannot help hindering. If a man's leg does not help him in walking, it certainly hinders him. Oh, I cannot bear to think of it. That I should be a hindrance to my own sou's growth is bad indeed; but that I should stand in the way of the people of God and cool their courage, and damp their ardor--my Master, let it never be! Sooner let me sleep among the clods of the valley, than be a hindrance to the meanest work that is done for thy name.

V. And now I shall close, not with this note of woe, but with A WORD OF BLESSING. Depend upon it there shall come a great blessing to any of you who feel the soul travail that brings souls to God. Your own heart will be watered. You know the old illustration, so often used that it is now almost hackneyed, of the two travelers, who passed a man frozen in the snow, and thought to be dead; and the one said, "I have enough to do to keep myself alive, I will hasten on;" but the other said, "I cannot pass a fellow-creature while there is the least breath in him." He stooped down and began to warm the frozen man by rubbing him with great vigor; and at last the poor fellow opened his eyes, came back to life and animation, and walked along with the man who had restored him to life; and what think you was one of the fist sights they saw? It was the man who so selfishly took care of himself frozen to death. The good Samaritan had preserved his own life by rubbing the other man; the friction he had given had caused the action of his own blood, and kept him in vigor. You will bless yourselves if you bless others.

Moreover, will it not be a joy to feel that you have done what you could? It is always well on a Sunday evening for a preacher to feel when he gets home, "Well, I may not have preached as I could wish, but I have preached the Lord Jesus, and poured forth all my heart and I could do no more." He sleeps soundly on that. After a day spent in doing all the good you can, even if you have met with no success, you can lean your head on Christ's bosom and fall asleep, feeling that if souls be not gathered, yet you have your reward. If men are lost, it is some satisfaction to us that they were not lost because we failed to tell them the way of salvation. But what a comfort it will be to you supposing you should be successful in bringing some to Christ. Why it will set all the bells of your soul ringing. There is no greater joy except the joy of our own communion with Christ, than this of bringing others to trust the Saviour. Oh seek this joy and pant after it. And what if you should see your own children converted? You have long hoped for it, but your hopes have been disappointed; God means to give you that choice blessing when you live more nearly to him yourself. Yes, wife, the husband's heart will be won when your heart is perfectly consecrated. Yes, mother, the girl shall love the Saviour when you love him better. Yes, teacher, God means to bless your class, but not until first of all he has made you fit to receive the blessing. Why, now, if your children were to be converted through your teacher, you would be mightily proud of it: God knows you could not bear such success, and does not mean to give it until he has laid you low at his feet, and emptied you of yourself, and filled you with himself.

And now I ask the prayers of all this church, that God would send us a time of revival. I have not to complain that I have labored in vain, and spent my strength for nought; far from it. I have not even to think that the blessing is withdrawn from the preaching of the word, even in a measure, for I never had so many cases of conversion in my life as I have known since I have been restored from sickness; I have never before received so many letters in so short a time, telling me that the sermons printed have been blest, or the sermons preached here; yet I do not think we ever had so few conversions from the regular congregation. I partly account for it from the fact, that you cannot fish in one pond always and catch as many fish as at first. Perhaps the Lord has saved all of you he means to save; sometimes, I am afraid he has; and then it will be of little use for me to keep on preaching to you, and I had better shift quarters and try somewhere else. It would be a melancholy thought if I believed it:--I do not believe it, I only fear it. Surely it is not always to be true that strangers, who drop in here only once, are converted, and you who are always hearing the gospel remain unaffected. Strange, but may it not be strangely, lamentably true of you? This very day may the anxiety of your Christian friends be excited for you, and then may you be led to be anxious for yourselves, and give your eyes no slumber till you find the Saviour. You know the way of salvation; it is simply to come with your sins and rest them on the Saviour; it is to rely upon or trust in the atoning blood. Oh that you may be made to trust this morning, to the praise of the glory of his grace. The elders mean to meet together tomorrow evening to have a special hour of prayer; I hope, also, the mothers will meet and have a time wrestling, and that every member of the church will try to set apart a time for supplication this week, that the Lord may visit again his church, and cause us to rejoice in his name. We cannot go back; we dare not go back. We have put our hand to the plough, and the curse will be upon us if we turn back. Remember Lot's wife. It must be onward with us; backward it cannot be. In the name of God the Eternal, let us gird up our loins by the power of his Spirit, and go onward conquering through the blood of the Lamb. We ask it for Jesus' sake. Amen.

PORTIONS OF SCRIPTURE READ BEFORE SERMON--Isaiah 66.

Of this sermon, a copy was sent to every Baptist and Congregational minister in Great Britain, and several letters have been received, acknowledging the quickening thereby received. May the like result be far more abundant in the New World.

Light for Those Who Sit in Darkness

A Sermon (No. 1010)
Delivered on Lord's-day Morning, September 10, 1871, by
C. H. SPURGEON,
At the Metropolitan Tabernacle, Newington

"The land of Zabulon, and the land of Nephthalim, by the way of the sea, beyond Jordan, Galilee of the Gentiles; the people which sat in darkness saw great light; and to them which sat in the region and shadow of death light is sprung up," - Matthew 4:15-16.

FULL OF LOVE to the place where he had been brought up, our Lord had gone to Nazareth, and in the Synagogue he had preached the gladdest tidings; but, alas, the greatest of prophets end the Lord of prophets, received no honor in his own country. "He came unto his own and his own received him not." Expelled the city by violence, the patient one turned his footsteps another way, yet, even when justly angry, love guided his footsteps. He must go for the Nazarenes had proved themselves unworthy, but whither shall he go? He will go to the outcasts, to that part of his country which was most neglected, to that region where the population was mixed and degenerate so as to be called, not Galilee of the Jews, but Galilee of the Gentiles, where from distance from Jerusalem little was known of the worship of the temple, where error was rampant, where men's minds were enveloped in darkness, and their hearts in the gloom of deathshade. The loss of Nazareth shall be the gain of Galilee. Even his judgment upon a place is overruled in mercy, and even thus to day there are some in this house who have often had Jesus preached to them from their very childhood, but until this hour they have refused obedience to the gospel's command. What if he should now turn away from them; I pray he may not have done so already. Yet, in turning away from them, he will deal with others in mercy. As the casting away of the Jews was the salvation of the Gentiles, so the leaving of these privileged ones shall open a door of mercy and hope to those who have not enjoyed the privilege aforetime. To you who are not familiar with the gospel sound, to you who count yourselves more unworthy than the rest of mankind, to you desponding and despairing ones who write bitter things against yourselves, to you is the gospel sent. As aforetime, the Lord preached to Zabulon and Nephthalim, and the people who sat in darkness saw a great light, even so is he this day proclaimed among you.

From the text it appears that some are in greater darkness than others; and that, secondly, for such there is a hope of light; but that, thirdly, the light which will come to them lies all in Christ; and, fourthly (joyful news!) that light is already sprung up all around them: they have but to open their eyes to delight in it.

I. SOME SOULS ARE IN GREATER DARKNESS THAN OTHERS. It appears from the text that it was so in Christ's days, and certainly it is so now. Divine sovereignty runs through all God's dealings. He does not even distribute the privilege of hearing the gospel to all alike, for some lands are as yet untrodden by the missionary's foot, while here at the corner of all our streets the gospel is preached to us. Some, from the very circumstances of their birth and parentage, have never attended the worship of God, while others, even before they had the discretion to choose, were carried in their parents' arms to the place where prayer is wont to be made. God distributeth his grace and privileges even as he wills.

In the text, those persons who were more deplorably circumstanced than others are described first as being in darkness--"The people that sat in darkness;" by which is meant, first, ignorance. The Galileans were notoriously ignorant: few teachers of the law had been among them; they did not know even the letter of the law. So are there many, to whom the gospel, even in the theory of it, is a thing scarcely known. They may have gone to places of worship in this country from their youth up, and have never heard the gospel, for the gospel is a rare thing in some synagogues; you shall hear philosophy, you shall hear ceremonialism and sacramentarianism cried up, but the blessed truth, "Believe, and live," is kept in the background, so that men may come to full age, ay, and even to old age, in Christian England, and yet the plan of salvation by the righteousness of Jesus Christ may be an unknown thing to them. They sit in the darkness of ignorance.

The consequence is, that another darkness follows, the darkness of error. Men who know not the truth, since they must have some faith, seek out many inventions; for, if they are not taught of God, they soon become taught of Satan, and apt scholars are they in his school. Galilee was noted for the heresies which abounded there. But what a mercy it is that God can save heretics. Those who have received false doctrine, and added darkness to darkness in so doing, can yet be brought into the glorious light of truth. Though they may have denied the Deity of Christ, though they may have doubted the inspiration of Scripture, though they may have fallen into many traps and pitfalls of false doctrine, yet the Divine Shepherd, when he seeks his lost sheep, can find them out and bring them home again.

In consequence of being in the darkness of ignorance and error, these people were wrapt in the gloom of discomfort and sorrow. Darkness is an expressive type of sorrow. The mind that knows not God, knows not the heart's best rest. There is no solace for our griefs like the gospel of Jesus Christ, and those who are ignorant of it are tossed about upon a stormy sea, without an anchorage. Glory be to God; when sorrow has brought on a midnight, grace can transform it into noon.

This darkness of sorrow was no doubt attended with much fear. We love not darkness because we cannot see what is before us, and therefore we are alarmed by imaginary dangers; and, in the same way, those who are ignorant of the light of Christ will frequently be the victims of superstitious dread; ay, and true and well founded fears will arise too, for they will dread death, and the bar of God, and the sentence of justice. Believe me, there is no darkness so black as the horror which surrounds many an awakened conscience when it sees its ruin, but cannot find a Savior; feels its sin, and cannot see the way by which it may be expiated.

Here, then, we have considered one part of this sad condition; perhaps it describes some of you.

It is said next that they "sat in darkness." Matthew did not quote from Isaiah correctly; I think he purposely alters it. Isaiah speaks, in his ninth chapter, of a people that "walked in darkness;" but here the evangelist speaks of a people who "sat in darkness." That is a state of less hopefulness. The man who walks is active, he has some energy left, and may reach a brighter spot; but a man sitting down is inactive, and will probably abide where he is. "The people that sat in darkness"--as if they had been there a long while, and would be there longer yet. They sat as though they had been turned to stone. They "sat in darkness," probably through despair; they had, after a fashion, striven for the light, but had not found it, and so they gave up all hope. Their disappointed hearts told them that they might as well spare those fruitless efforts, and therefore down they sat with the stolidity of hopelessness. Why should they make any more exertion? If God would not hear their prayers, why should they pray any longer? Being ignorant of his abounding grace, and of the way of salvation by his Son, they considered themselves as consigned to perdition. They "sat in darkness." Perhaps they sat there so long that they reached a state of insensibility and indifference, and this is a horrible condition of heart; but, alas! a very common one. They said, "What matters it, since there is no hope for us? Let it be as fate appoints, we will sit still, we will neither cry nor pray." How many have I met with who are not only thus in darkness, but are half-content to dare the terrible future, and sullenly to wait till the storm-cloud of wrath shall burst over them. It is a most sad and wretched condition, but what a blessing it is that this day we have a gospel to preach to such.

Our description is not complete, for the text goes on to speak of them as sitting "in the region of death;" that is to say, these people lived in a territory that appeared to be ruled by death, and to be death's haunt and natural abode. Many at this time, and in this City, are truly living in the domain of spiritual death. All around them is death. If they have stepped into this house this morning, their position is an exception to their general one. They will go home to a Sabbath-breaking household; they hear habitually oaths, profane language, and lascivious songs; and thus they breathe the reek of the charnel-house. If they have a good thought, it is ridiculed by those about them. They dwell as among the tombs, with men whose mouths are open sepulchres, pouring forth all manner of offensiveness. How sad a condition! It seems to such poor souls, perhaps, being now a little awakened, that everything about them is prophetic of death. They are afraid to take a step lest the earth should open a door to the bottomless pit. I remember well, when I was under conviction, how all the world seemed in league against me, the beasts of the field and the stones thereof. I wondered then the heavens could refrain from falling upon me, or the earth from opening her mouth to swallow me up. I was under sentence of divine wrath, and felt as if I were in a condemned cell, and all creation were but the walls of my dungeon. "They sat in the region of death."

But it is added that they sat "in the shadow of death;" that is, under its cold, poisonous, depressing shade; as though grim death stood over them in all they did, and his shadow kept from them the light of heaven. They are sitting there this morning: they are saying to themselves, "Preach, sir, as you may, you will never comfort me: you may tell me of love and mercy, but I shall never be cheered thereby: I am chilled through my very marrow, as though the frost of death had smitten me: I am unable now to hope, or even to pray, even my desires are all but dead. Like a frozen corpse is my soul."

And it is implied, too, that to such death itself is very near, for those who are in the shadow of a thing are near to the thing itself; and the sinner, bewildered and amazed at the guilt of his sin, is only sure of one thing, and that is, that he is in immediate danger of being cast into hell. I have known some afraid to shut their eyes at night, lest they should open them in torments; others have been afraid to go to their beds, lest their couch should become their coffin; they have not known what to do, by reason of depression of spirit. Job's language has been theirs, "My soul is weary of my life." It is clear to me that the description of the text very accurately pictures many of the sons of men. I pray God that none of you poor darkened souls may be so foolish as to try to exclude yourself from it, though such is the perversity of despondency that I greatly fear you may do so. However small we make the meshes of the gospel net, there are certain little fish that will find a way of escaping from its blessed toils, though we try to meet the character, we miss it through the singular dexterity of despair. The fact is that when a man is sin-sick, his soul abhorreth all manner of meat, and unless the beloved physician shall interpose, he will die of famine with the bread of life spread out before him. Dear friends, may the Lord visit you with his saving health, and give to the saddest of you joy and peace in believing.

II. Having given the description of those in the darkness, let us now pass on to the second point. FOR THOSE WHO ARE IN A WORSE CONDITION THAN OTHERS THERE IS HOPE AND LIGHT.

To the benighted land of Zabulon and Naphtali the gospel came, and evermore to souls enwrapt in gloom the gospel has come as a cheering and guiding light; and there are good reasons why it should be so. For, first, among such people the gospel has reaped very rich fruit. Among barbarous nations Christ has won great trophies. The poor Karens are wonders of grace, the cannibals of the South Sea Islands are miracles of mercy, and among the once enslaved Ethiopians there are warm and loving hearts which rejoice in Jesus' name. In this city, I will venture to say, that no churches reflect more honor upon the Master's name than those which have been gathered from among the destitute districts. What wonders God has done by that blessed church in Golden Lane, under our dear brother Orsman? What conversions have taken place in connection with the mission churches of St. Giles' and Whitechapel? churches made of the poorest of the poor and the lowest of the low. God is glorified when the thief and the harlot are washed and cleansed and made obedient to the law of Christ. When those who are healed stand at the pastor's side, even ribald tongues are silent, or are made to exclaim, "What hath God wrought?" The same is true of persons mentally depressed, who are despairing of themselves; many such have been converted. Some of us were brought very low before we found the Savior; lower we could not well have been: we were emptied like a dish that a man wipes and turns upside down; we had not even a drop of hope left in us; but we rejoice in Christ to-day, and we say to despairing souls, we are personal witnesses that Christ has saved such as you are, he has in our case caused light to shine on those who sat in darkness, and out of death's cold shade into life's full light he has brought us as prisoners of hope; and, therefore, he can do the same with you. Be of good courage, there is hope for you.

It is a further consolation to sad hearts, that many promises are made to such characters, even to those who are most dark. How precious is that word, "Come unto me, all ye that labor and are heavy laden, and I will give you rest." Is not that made for you, ye burdened and laboring sinners? What say you to that gracious word--"When the poor and needy seek water, and there is none, and their tongue faileth for thirst, I the Lord will hear them, I the God of Jacob will not forsake them?" Is there no light in that word of love--"Let the wicked forsake his way, and the unrighteous man his thoughts: and let him return unto the Lord, and he will have mercy upon him; and to our God, for he will abundantly pardon?" Is there no music in this passage--"Who is a God like unto thee, that pardoneth iniquity, and passeth by the transgression of the remnant of his heritage? he retaineth not his anger for ever, because he delighteth in mercy. He will turn again, he will have compassion upon us; he will subdue our iniquities; and thou wilt cast all their sins into the depths of the sea?" I recollect when my soul was stayed for weeks on that one short word, "Whosoever calleth upon the Lord, shall be saved." I knew I did call on his name, and therefore I hoped to see his salvation. Many have laid hold and rested themselves on this faithful saying, "Him that cometh to me, I will in no wise cast out." He will receive any "him" or "her" in all the world that comes, be he or she ever so defiled. That also is a rich word, "He is able to save them to the uttermost that come unto God by him, seeing he ever liveth to make intercession for them." What a word was that of our Master when he commanded his disciples to preach the gospel to every creature, beginning at Jerusalem. They were to commence their labors amongst his murderers, amongst hypocritical Pharisees and proud Herodians; they were to begin where the devil reigned most supreme, and to present Christ to the worst sinners first. See you, then, that great sinners, so far from being excluded, are just those to whom the good news is to be first published. Be of good comfort, then, ye that sit in darkness: there are special promises for you.

Moreover, remember, that the conversion of the more deplorably dark and despairing brings the highest degree of glory to God. When his glory passes by great sin, then it is mercy indeed. Where it is greatly displaced, it is greatly extolled. Many are saved by Christ, in whom the change is not very apparent, and consequently but little fame is brought to the good Physician through it; but, oh, if he will have mercy upon yonder mourner, who has been these ten years in despair; if he will say, "Woman, thou art loosed from thine infirmities," the whole parish will ring with it! If Jesus will come and save that black, ignorant sinner, whom everybody knows because he has become a pest and a nuisance to the town; if such a demoniac has the devil cast out of him, how all men will say. "This is the finger of God." Yes, a poor wretch brought back again, as the sixty-eighth Psalm has it, "from Bashan, and from the depths of the sea," is a splendid trophy to the conquering power of Almighty grace. God's great object is to glorify his great name; and, as this is best accomplished when his mercy delivers the worst cases, there is surely hope for those who sit in darkness, bound in affliction and iron.

Moreover, when they happily behold the light, such persons frequently become eminently useful to others. Their experience aids them in counseling others, and their gratitude makes them eager to do so. O sweet light, how precious art thou to blind eyes, when they are newly opened. You do not know what it is to be blind: thank God that you do not: there are some here, however, who painfully know what constant darkness is; it is a grievous privation: but when their eyes are opened, as they will be in another state, and they see that best of sights, the King in his beauty, how sweet will light be to them!

"Nights and days of total blindness
Are their portion here below;
Beams of love from eyes of kindness,
Never here on earth they know.
But on high they shall behold
Angels tuning harps of gold;
Rapture to the new-born sight;
Jesus in celestial light!"

So, when the spiritual eye has long been dim, and we have mourned and wept for sin, but could not beheld a Savior, light is sweet beyond expression. And, because it is so sweet, there is a necessity within the enlightened soul to tell out the joyful news to others. When a man has deeply felt the evil of sin, and has at length obtained mercy, he cries with David, "Then will I teach transgressors thy ways, and sinners shall be converted unto thee." John Bunyan's impulse when he found the Savior was to tell the crows on the ploughed ground about it, and he lived to do better than talk to crows, for day by day, from generation to generation, his works proclaim the Friend of sinners, who leads them from the City of Destruction to the Celestial glory. Zealous saints are usually those who once were in great darkness; they see what grace has done for them, and for that very reason they feel an attachment to their dear Lord and Master, which they might never had felt if they had not once sat in the valley of the shadow of death. So, poor troubled ones, for these reasons, and fifty more I might bring if time did not fail me, there is hope for you.

III. But now, the best part of our discourse comes under the third head. THE TRUE LIGHT FOR A SOUL IN DARKNESS IS ALL IN CHRIST. Hear ye the text. "The people which sat in darkness saw great light." Now Christ is not only light, but great light; he reveals great things, he manifests great comforts, saves us from great sin and great wrath, and prepares us for great glory. He is, however, a Savior that must be seen. "The people that sat in darkness saw great light." Light is of no use unless it be seen. Faith must grasp the blessings which the Savior brings. "Look unto me, and be ye saved, all ye ends of the earth." We must see the Savior with a glance of faith, then have we light. Let us consider how clearly Christ Jesus himself is the light of every believing eye, and delivers the most troubled soul from its misery. In him is light, and the light is the light of men. Jesus personally is the day-dawn and the morning without clouds.

First, there is light in Christ's name for a troubled sinner. What is it? Jesus. Jesus, a Savior. I am a sinner lost and ruined, but I rejoice, for Jesus has come to seek and to save that which was lost. My sins trouble me, but he shall save his people from their sins. Satan annoys me, but he has come to destroy the works of the devil. He is not a nominal, but a real Savior. We know captains and colonels who have no troops, and never saw fighting, but not so the Captain of our salvation; he brings many sons unto glory. If a man is called a builder, we expect him to build; if a merchant, we expect him to trade; and as Jesus is a Savior, he will carry on his sacred business, he will save multitudes. Why, surely there is comfortable hope here. Do you not see the dawning in the name of Savior? Surely if he comes to save, and you need saving, there is a blessed suitability in you for one another. A prisoner at the bar is glad to meet one who is by profession an advocate, a ship out of its track welcomes a pilot; a traveler lost on the moors is delighted if he meets one who is by trade a guide; and so a sinner should rejoice at the bare mention of a Savior.

There is similar encouragement in the second name, Christ, for it means anointed. Our Lord Jesus is not an amateur Savior, who has come here without a commission from God; he is not an adventurer, who sets up on his own account to do a kind of work for which he is not qualified: no, the Spirit of the Lord is upon him, for the Lord hath anointed him to this work of saving souls. He is Jesus Christ, whom God hath sent. Him hath God the Father sealed. He spake not of himself, but God was with him, and in him. Why, beloved friend, now that I am in the light I can see a whole sunful of splendor in that double name Jesus Christ, and yet I fear that those who are in darkness may not perceive it. Whom God anoints to save, must surely be both able and willing to save the guilty. This name is as the morning star; look at it, and know that day is near. It has such joy in it that misery itself ought to leap with holy mirth at the sound of it.

It is our delightful task to add that there is light for those who sit in darkness in our Lord's person and nature. Mark right well who this Jesus Christ is. He is in the constitution of his person both God and man, divine and human, equal with God and fellow with man. Do you not see in this fact the love of God, that he should be willing to take humanity into union with himself? If God becomes man, he does not hate men, but has love towards them. Do you not see the suitability of Christ to deal with you, for he is like yourself a man, touched with the feeling of your infirmities; of a human mother born, he hung at a woman's breast, he suffered hunger and thirst and weariness, and, dead and buried in the tomb, he was partaker in our doom as well as our sorrow? Jesus of Nazareth was most truly a man, he is bone of our bone and flesh of your flesh. O sinner, look into the face of the man of sorrows and you must trust him. Since he is also God, you therein see his power to carry on the work of salvation. He touches you with the hand of his humanity, but he touches the Almighty with the hand of his Deity. He is man, and feels your needs; he is God, and is able to supply them. Is anything too tender for his heart of love? Is anything too hard for his hand of power? When the Lord himself, that made the heavens and digged the foundations of the earth, comes to be your Savior, there remains no difficulty in your being saved. Omnipotence cannot know a difficulty, and, O sinner, to an omnipotent Savior it is not hard to save even you. A look of faith will give you perfect pardon. A touch of the hem of the Redeemer's garment will heal you at once. Come, then, and trust the incarnate God. Cast yourself into his arms at once.

There is light, moreover, in his offices, and, indeed, a brightness of glory which a little thought will soon perceive. What are his offices? I cannot stay to mention a tithe of them, but one of them is that of Mediator. Your soul longs to speak to God and find acceptance with him, but you are afraid to venture into his terrible presence. I wonder not at your fear, for "even our God is a consuming fire." But be of good comfort, the way of access is open, and there is One who will go in unto the King with you, and open his mouth on your behalf. Jesus has interposed and filled the great gulf which yawned between the sinner and his righteous judge. His blood has paved the crimson way; his cross has bridged each stream; his person is the highway for those who would draw near to God. Now, as Christ Jesus is the Mediator between God and man, and you want one, take him and you will have light at once.

You desire, also, this day a sacrifice, to make atonement for your iniquities; that also you will find in Christ. God must punish sin, every transgression must receive its just recompense of reward; but, lo, Christ has come, and as the scape-goat he has carried sin away; as the sin-offering he has removed transgression. Is not this good news? But I hear you say that your sins are too many and great. Do you then foolishly think that Christ is a sin-bearer for the innocent? That would be ridiculous. Do you suppose that Christ bore little sins only? That is to make him a little Savior. Beware of this. Nay, but mountain sins, heaven-defying sins, were laid on him when he hung upon the tree, and for these he made effectual atonement. Is there no light in all this?

Moreover, to mention only one other office, our Lord is an Intercessor. Perhaps, one of your greatest difficulties is that you cannot pray. You say, "I cannot put a dozen words together; if I groan, I fear I do not feel in my heart what I ought to feel." Well, there is One who can pray for you if you cannot for yourself. Give him your cause to plead, and do not doubt but that it shall succeed. God grant you grace, as you see each office of Christ, to perceive that it has a bright side for sinners. I doubt not, light streams continually from every part of the sun to cheer the worlds that revolve around it; so, from the whole of Christ, there issues forth comfort for poor and needy souls. He delighteth in mercy. He is a Savior and a great one. He is all love, all tenderness, all pity, all goodness; and the very chief of sinners, if they do but see him, shall see light.

Once again, if you want light, think of his character, as the meek and lowly Savior. Little children loved him; he called them and they willingly came, for he was meek and lowly of heart. O sinner, could he refuse thee? Do you think he could give you a hard word and send you about your business, if you were to seek mercy to day? It could not be; it is not in the nature of him, who was both the Son of God and the Son of Man, ever to repel a heart that fain would cling to him. Until he has once acted harshly to a coming sinner, you have no right to dream of his rejecting you, if you come to him.

Think for a minute of his life. He was "separate from sinners," we are told, and yet it is elsewhere said of him, "this man receiveth sinners, and eateth with them." Friend of sinners was his name, and is still. Think of that self-denying life spent among the sick and the sinful for their good. And then think of his death, for here the light of grace is focused; the cross, like a burning-glass, concentrates the light and heat of Christ's love upon the sinner. See him agonizing in the garden for sins that were not his own: see him scourged with awful flagellations for transgressions in which he had no share: behold him bleeding and dying on the tree for his enemies; sufferer for iniquities in which he never was a participator, for in him was no sin. It must be true that God can save me, if Christ has died in the stead of the guilty. This argument has killed my unbelief. I cannot disbelieve, when I see incarnate God suffering for the guilty, the just for the unjust, to bring them to God.

"Sinners! come, the Savior see,
Hands, feet, side, and temples view;
See him bleeding on the tree,
See his heart on fire for you!
View awhile, then haste away,
Find a thousand more, and say:
Come, ye sinners! come with me,
View him bleeding on the tree."

I wish it were in my power to convey the light which I see in the cross into the mental eyeballs of all my hearers, but I cannot; God the Holy Ghost must do it. Yet, beloved, if ever you get light, it will be in this way: Christ must be a great light to you. Nobody ever found light by raking in his own inward darkness; that is indeed seeking the living among the dead. You may rake as long as ever you will among the embers of your depravity before you will find a spark of good there. Away from self, away from your own resolutions, away from your own prayers, repentances, and faith; away to Christ on the cross must you look. All your hope and help are laid on Immanual's shoulders. You are nothing. Not a rag nor a thread of your own righteousness will do; Christ's robe of righteousness must cover you from head to foot. Blow out your paltry candles, put out the sparks which you have vainly kindled, for behold the Sun is risen! "Arise, shine; for thy light is come, and the glory of the Lord is risen upon thee." Ye want no other light than that of Jesus: dream of no other. Give up self, give up self-hope, be in utter despair of anything that you can do, and now, whether you sink or swim, throw yourself into the sea of Christ's love: rest in him and you shall never perish, neither shall any pluck you from his hands.

"Cast your deadly doing' down,
Down at Jesus' feet,
Stand in him, in him alone,
Gloriously complete."

IV. But, lastly, we would say to every poor soul in darkness, you need be in darkness no longer; for LIGHT IS ALL AROUND YOU: it has already "sprung up."

What a mercy, my dear despairing hearer, that you are not in hell! You might have been there: many no worse than you are there; and yet here you are in the land of hope. This day God does not deal with you according to the law, but after the gospel fashion; you are not come to Sinai this morning, no burning mountain is before you, and no tones of thunder peal from it; you are come unto Mount Zion, where the mediator of the new covenant speaks peace and pardon. I have no commission to curse you, but I have distinct authority from my Master to bid you come and receive his blessing. On Zion's top to-day ye have come to the blood of sprinkling; you might have been called to the blood of your own execution! No devils are around you, but an innumerable company of angels, who wish you well. See that ye refuse not him that speaketh. Remember, dear hearers, that to-day the gospel command is sent to you all; you that are most despairing, you are bidden to believe in the Lord Jesus Christ. "Prove that," say you. I prove it thus: he bade his disciples go into all the world and preach the gospel to every creature; you are a creature, therefore we preach it to you. And what was the gospel? Why, just this: "He that believeth and is baptised, shall be saved: he that believeth not shall be damned." That gospel, then, comes to you--God commandeth all men, everywhere, to repent. O what mercy it is that the light of the gospel shines around you still! Will you shut your eyes to it? I beseech you, do not so wickedly.

Moreover, the provisions of the gospel, which are full of light and love, are all around you at this moment. If you will now believe in Christ Jesus, every sin that you have committed shall be forgiven you for his namesake; you shall be to God as though you had never sinned; the precious blood shall make you as white as snow. "But that will not suffice," says one, "for God righteously demands obedience to his holy law, and I have not kept his commandments, and therefore am weighed in the balances and found wanting." You shall have a perfect righteousness in one moment if you believe in Jesus, "even as David also describeth the blessedness of the man unto whom God imputeth righteousness without works." Happy is the man to whom Jesus Christ is made wisdom and righteousness, and he is so to every one that believeth." There is therefore now no condemnation to them which are in Christ Jesus." "Ah," say you, "but I have a bad heart and an evil nature." If thou believest, thy nature is changed already, "A new heart also will I give them, and a right spirit will I put within them." "They shall also walk in my judgments, and observe my statutes, and do them." He can change you so that you shall scarcely know yourself; you shall be a new creature in Christ Jesus; old things shall pass away and all things shall become new. He will take away the heart of stone, and give you a heart of flesh. "Alas," say you, "even this is not enough, for I shall never hold on in the ways of righteousness, but shall go back unto perdition." Hear, O thou trembler, these gracious words: "I will put my fear in their hearts, and they shall not depart from; me." And what saith our Lord himself? He saith, "They shall never perish, neither shall any pluck them out of my hand." "The water that I shall give him shall be in him a well of water springing up unto everlasting life." "But what, if I go astray," says one. Then he will heal your backslidings, receive you graciously, and love you freely. "He restoreth my soul." He will not suffer even his wandering sheep to perish, but once again will he put them in the right way. "Ah, but my soul-poverty is deep, and my wants will be too great." How can you say this? Is he not the God all sufficient? Has the arm of the Lord waxed short! Did he not furnish a table in the wilderness? Is it not written, "My God shall supply all your need?" He shall cause all grace to abound towards you. "Fear not thou worm Jacob, I will help thee, saith the Lord." "Ah, but," saith one, "I shall surely be afraid to die, for I am afraid of it even now." "He that liveth and believeth in me, though he were dead, yet shall he live." "When thou passest through the rivers, I will be with thee." Death is swallowed up in victory. Having loved his own which are in the world, he will love them to the end. Thou shalt have such faith in dying moments that thou shalt say: "O death, where is thy sting? O grave, where is thy victory?" "But you do not mean me," saith one. I mean you that sit in darkness, you that are ignorant, you that are depressed, you that have no good thing of your own, you that cannot help yourselves, you lost ones, you condemned ones, I mean you. And this is God's message to you: "God sent not his Son into the world to condemn the world, but that the world through him might be saved." "Whom God hath set forth to be a propitiation through faith in his blood, to declare his righteousness for the remission of sins that are past, through the forbearance of God; to declare, I say, at this time his righteousness: that he might be just, and the justifier of him which believeth in Jesus." "He that believeth on him is not condemned." Oh, come, ye guilty; for he is ready to forgive you. Come, ye filthy; the fountain is ready for your cleansing. Come, ye sorrowful, since joy is prepared; his oxen and fatlings are killed, for all things are ready; come to the feast of love. But I hear you say, "I must surely do something." Have done with your doings, and take Christ's doings. "Oh, but I do not feel as I should." Have done with your feelings: Christ's feelings on the cross must save you, not your own feelings. "Oh, but I am so vile." He came to save the vile.

"Come, in all thy filthy garments,
Tarry not to cleanse or mend;
Come, in all thy destitution,
As thou art, and he'll befriend.
By the tempter's vain allurements,
Be no longer thou beguiled:
God the Father waits to own thee
As his dear adopted child."

"But I have been an adulterer, I have been a thief, I have been a whoremonger, and everything that is bad." Be it so, yet it is a faithful saying, and worthy of all acceptation, that Christ Jesus came into the world to save sinners. All manner of sin and of blasphemy shall be forgiven unto men. It is true that you are much worse then you think you are: you may tell me you are horribly bad, but you have no idea how bad you are: the hottest place in hell is your desert; but it is to you the mercy is sent; to you, O man, to you, O woman, to you who have defiled yourself with all manner of unmentionable enormities, even to you, thus saith the Lord, "I have blotted out thy sins like a cloud and like a thief; cloud thy transgressions; return unto me and I will have mercy upon thee." I cannot say more. I wish I had the power to speak, I was about to say, with the tongues of men and of angels, but I have such a blessed message to deliver to you, that I feel it need not goodly words, the message itself is all that is needed if the Spirit bless it. Oh, do not reject it, I beseech you, you guilty ones! you despairing ones, do not turn from it, put not away from you the kingdom lest you prove yourselves unworthy, and bring upon yourselves wrath unto the uttermost.

If ye be willing and obedient, ye shall eat the good of the land. Receive the Lord Jesus as your Savior, now on the spot. May God the Holy Spirit lead you to do this, for Jesus' sake. Amen.

PORTIONS OF SCRIPTURE READ BEFORE SERMON--Matthew 4:12-25; and 5:1-12.

Job's Regret and Our Own

A Sermon (No. 1011)
Delivered on Lord's-day Morning, September 17th, 1871, by
C. H. SPURGEON,
At the Metropolitan Tabernacle, Newington

"Oh that I were as in months past, as in the days when God preserved me when his candle shined upon my head, and when by his light I walked through darkness; as I was in the days of my youth, when the secret of God was upon my tabernacle." - Job 29:2,3,4.

IF Job here refers to the temporal prosperity which he had lost, we cannot condemn him for his complaint, neither can we commend him. It is but the expression of a natural regret, which would be felt by any man who had experienced such great reverses. But there is everywhere in the expressions which he uses such a strain of spirituality, that we are inclined to believe that he had more reference to the condition of his heart than to the state of his property. His soul was depressed; he had lost the light of God's countenance; his inward comforts were declining, his joy in the Lord was at a low ebb, this he regretted far more than anything besides. No doubt he deplored the departure of those prosperous days when, as he words it, his root was spread out by the waters, and the dew lay all night upon his branch; but, much more did he bemoan that the lamp of the Lord no more shone upon his head, and the secret of God was not upon his tabernacle. As his spiritual regrets are far more instructive to us than his natural ones, we will turn all our attention to them. We may, without violence, appropriate Job's words to ourselves; for I fear that many of us can with great propriety take up our wailing and mourn for the days of our espousals, the happy days of our first love. I shall have to trouble you with many divisions this morning; but I shall be brief upon each one, and I hope that our thoughts may be led onward, and rendered practically serviceable to us, by the blessing of God's Spirit.

I. Let us begin by saying, that regrets such as those expressed in the text are and ought to be very BITTER. If it be the loss of spiritual things that we regret, then may we say from the bottom of our hearts, "Oh that I were as in months past."

It is a great thing for a man to be near to God; it is a very choice privilege to be admitted into the inner circle of communion, and to become God's familiar friend. Great as the privilege is, so great is the loss of it. No darkness is so dark as that which falls on eyes accustomed to the light. The poor man who was always poor is scarcely poor, but he who has fallen from the summit of greatness into the depths of poverty is poor indeed. The man who has never enjoyed communion with God knows nothing of what it must be to lose it; but he who has once been pressed upon the Savior's bosom will mourn, as long as he liveth, if he be deprived of the sacred enjoyment. The mercies which Job deplored in our text are no little ones. First, he complains that he had lost the consciousness of divine preservation. He says, "Oh that I were as in months past, as in the days when God preserved me." There are days with Christians when they can see God's hand all around them, checking them in the first approaches of sin, and setting a hedge about all their ways. Their conscience is tender, and the Spirit of God is obeyed by them; they are, therefore, kept in all their ways, the angels of God watching over them, lest they dash their foot against a stone. But when they fall into laxity of spirit, and walk at a distance from God, they are not so preserved. Though kept from final and total apostasy, yet they are not kept from very grievous sin; for, like Peter who followed afar off, they may be left to deny their Master, even with oaths and cursings. If we have lost that conscious preservation of God, which once covered us from every fiery dart; if we no longer abide under the shadow of the Almighty, and feel no longer that his truth is our shield and buckler, we have lost a joy worth worlds, and we may well deplore it with anguish of heart.

Job had also lost divine consolation, for he looks back with lamentation to the time when God's candle shone upon his head, when the sun of God's love was as it were in the zenith, and cast no shadow; when he rejoiced without ceasing, and triumphed from morning to night in the God of his salvation. The joy of the Lord is our strength, the joy of the Lord is Israel's excellency; it is the heaven of heaven, it is heaven even upon earth; and, consequently, to lose it, is a calamity indeed. Who that has once been satisfied with favor, and full of the blessing of the Lord, will be content to go into the dry and thirsty land, and live far off from God? Will he not rather cry out with David, "My soul thirsteth for God; when shall I come and appear before God?" Surely his agonising prayer will be, "Restore unto me the joy of thy salvation, and uphold me with thy free Spirit." Love to God will never be content if his face be hidden. Until the curtain be drawn aside and the King's face be seen through the lattices, the true spouse will spend her life in sighing; mourning like a dove bereaved of its mate.

Moreover, Job deplored the loss of divine illumination. "By his light," he says, "I walked through darkness," that is to say, perplexity ceased to be perplexity; God shed such a light upon the mysteries of providence, that where others missed their path, Job, made wise by heaven, could find it. There have been times when, to our patient faith, all things have been plain. "If any man will do his will, he shall know of the doctrine;" but, if we walk far off from God, then, straightway, even the precious truth of God is no more clear to us, and the dealings of God with us in providence appear to be like a maze. He is wise as Solomon who walks with God, but he is a very fool who trusts his own understanding. All the wit that we have gathered by observation and experience will not supply us with sufficiency of common sense, if we turn away from God. Israel, without consulting God, made a league with her enemies; she thought the case most plain when she entered into hasty alliance with the Gibeonites, but she was duped by cunning because she asked not counsel of the Lord. In the simplest business we shall err, if we seek not direction from the Lord; yet, where matters are most complicated, we shall walk wisely, if we wait for a voice from the oracle, and seek the good Shepherd's guidance. We may bitterly lament, therefore, if we have lost the Holy Spirit's light. If now the Lord answereth us not, neither by his word, nor by his providence, if we wander alone, crying Oh that I knew where I might find him, we are in an evil case, and may well sigh for the days, when by his light we walked through darkness.

Moreover, Job had lost divine communion: so it seems, for he mourned the days of his youth, when the secret of God was upon his tabernacle. Who shall tell to another what the secret of God is? Believing hearts know it, but they cannot frame to pronounce aright the words that could explain it, nor can they convey by language what the secret is. The Lord manifests himself unto his people as he doth not unto the world. We could not tell the love passages that there are between believers and their Lord; even when they are set to such sweet music as the Song of Solomon, carnal minds cannot discern their delights. They cannot plough with our heifer, and therefore they read not our riddle. As Paul in heaven saw things which it were unlawful for a man to utter, so the believer sees and enjoys in communion with Christ what it would not only be unlawful but impossible for him to tell to carnal men. Such pearls are not for swine. The spiritual discerneth all things, but he himself is discerned of no man. Now, it is a high privilege, beyond all privileges, to enter into familiar intercourse with the Most High, and the man who has once possessed it, and has lost it, has a bitterer cause for regret than if, being rich, he had lost his wealth; or being famous, he had lost esteem; or being in health, he were suddenly brought to the bed of languishing. No loss can equal the loss of thee, my God! No eclipse is so black as the hiding of thy face! No storm is so fierce as the letting forth of thine indignation! It is grief upon grief to find that thou art not with me as in the days of old. Wherever, then, these regrets do exist, if the men's hearts are as they should be, they are not mere hypocritical or superficial expressions, but they express the bitterest experiences of our human existence. "Oh that I were as in months past" is no sentimental sigh, but the voice of the innermost spirit in anguish, as one who has lost his firstborn.

II. But, secondly, let me remind you that these regrets are NOT INEVITABLE; that is to say, it is not absolutely necessary that a Christian man should ever feel them, or be compelled to express them. It has grown to be a tradition among us, that every Christian must backslide in a measure, and that growth in grace cannot be unbrokenly sustained. It is regarded by many as a law of nature, that our first love must grow cold, and our early zeal must necessarily decline. I do not believe it for a moment. "The path of the just is us the shining light, which shineth more and more unto the perfect day;" and were we watchful and careful to live near to God, there is no reason why our spiritual life should not continuously make progress both in strength and beauty. There is no inherent necessity in the divine life itself compelling it to decline, for is it not written, "It shall be in him a well of water, springing up unto everlasting life;" "out of his belly shall flow rivers of living water." Grace is a living and incorruptible seed that liveth and abideth for ever, and there is nowhere impressed upon the divine life a law of pining and decay. If we do falter and faint in the onward path, it is our sin, and it is doubly sinful to forge excuses for it. It is not to be laid upon the back of some mysterious necessity of the new nature that it should be so, but it is to be brought as a charge against ourselves. Nor do outward circumstances ever furnish a justification to us if we decline in grace; for, under the worst conditions, believers have grown in grace: deprived of the joys of Christian fellowship, and denied the comforts of the means of grace, believers have nevertheless been known to attain to a high-degree of likeness to Christ Jesus: thrown into the midst of wicked companions, and forced to hear, like righteous Lot, the filthy conversation of the ungodly, yet

Christian men have shone all the brighter for the surrounding darkness, and have been able to escape from a wicked and perverse generation. Certain is it, that a man may be an eminent Christian, and be among the poorest of the poor: poverty need not, therefore, make us depart from God; and, it is equally certain, that a man may be rich, and for all that may walk with God and be distinguished for great grace. There is no lawful position of which we may say, "It compels a man to decline in grace."

And, brethren, there is no period of our life in which it is necessary for us to go back. The young Christian, with all the strength of his natural passions, can by grace be strong and overcome the Wicked One; the Christian in middle life, surrounded with the world's cares, can prove that "this is the victory which overcometh the world, even our faith." The man immersed in business may still be baptised of the Holy Ghost. Assuredly, old age offers no excuse for decline: "they shall still bring forth fruit in old age; they shall be fat and flourishing; to show that the Lord is upright." No, brethren as Christ said to his disciples, when they would fain have sent the multitude away to buy meat, "they need not depart;" so would he say to the whole company of the Lord's people, "ye need not depart;" there is no compulsion for decline in grace." Your sun need not stand still, your moon need not wane. If you cannot add a cubit to your spiritual stature, at any rate, it need not decrease. There are no reasons written in the book of your spiritual nature why you, as a believer, should lose fellowship with God, and, if you do so, take blame and shame to yourself, but do not ascribe it to necessity. Do not gratify your corruptions by supposing that they are licensed to prevail occasionally, neither vex your graces by conceiving that they are doomed to inevitable defeat at a certain season. The spirit that is in us lusteth to evil, but the Holy Spirit is able to subdue it, and will subdue it, if we yield ourselves to him.

III. But, now, I am compelled Lo say that the regrets expressed in our test are exceedingly COMMON, and it is only here and there that we meet with a believer who has not had cause to use them. It ought not to be so, but it is so. How grievously often will the pastor hear this among the other bleatings of the sheep: "Oh that I were as in months past, as in the days when God preserved me:"

"What peaceful hours I then enjoy'd,
How sweet, their memory still;
But they have left an aching void
The world can never fill."

The commonness of this lamentation may be somewhat accounted for, by the universal tendency to undervalue the present and exaggerate the excellence of the past. Have you never noticed this in natural things, we are prone to cast a partial eye upon some imaginary "good old times?" It is gone, and therefore it was good; it is here, and therefore it is dubious. In the middle of the summer, we feel that the heat is so relaxing that a frost would be the most delightful thing conceivable; we love, we say, the bracing air of winter; we are sure it is much healthier for us: yet, usually, when winter arrives, and the extreme cold sets in, we are all most anxious for the advent of spring, and we feel that somehow or other the frost is more trying to us than the heat. Personally, I met with an illustration of this tendency the other day. I went down a steep cliff to the sea shore, and during the descent every step tried my weak knees, and I felt that going down hill was the most difficult travelling in the world. Soon I had to return from the sands, and climb the steep path again; and, when I began to pant and puff with the difficult ascent, I changed my opinion, and felt that I would a great deal sooner go down than come up. The fact is that whatever is with us we think to be the worse, and whatever was with us we conceive to be the better. We may, therefore, take some discount from our regrets; for, peradventure, were we more conscious of the benefit of the present state, and did we make less prominent the difficulty of it, we should not sigh to be as we were in months past.

Then, again, regrets may in some cases arise from a holy jealousy. The Christian, in whatever state he is, feels his own imperfection much, and laments his conscious shortcomings. Looking back, he observes with joy the work of grace in his soul, and does not perhaps so readily recollect the then existing deficiencies of nature; hence, he comes to think that the past was better than the present. He is afraid of backsliding, and therefore he jealously fears that he is so; he is so anxious to live nearer to God, so dissatisfied with his present attainments, that he dares not believe that he advances, but fears that he has lost ground. I know this in my own experience, for when lying sick I have frequently lamented that pain has distracted my mind, and taken off my attention from the word of God, and I have longed for those seasons of health when I could read, meditate, and study with pleasure; but, now that I have risen up from the sick bed, and am growing strong again, I frequently look back to the long nights and quiet days spent in my sick chamber, and think that it was better with me then than now, for now I am apt to be cumbered with much serving, and then I was shut in with God. Many a man is really strong in Christ; but, because he does not feel all the juvenile vivacity of his early days, he fears that ritual decreptitude has come upon him. He is now far more solid and steadfast, if not quite so quick and impulsive; but, the good man in his holy jealousy marks most the excellencies of his juvenile piety, and forgets that there were grave deficiencies in it; while, in his present state, he notes the deficiencies, and fears to hope that he possesses any excellencies. We are poor judges of our own condition, and usually err on one side or the other. All graces may not flourish at the same time, and defalcations in one direction may be more than balanced by advantages in another. We may be deeper in humility if we are not higher in delight. We may not glitter so much, and yet there may be more real gold in us. The leaf may not be so green, but the fruit may be more ripe. The way may be rougher, and yet be nearer heaven. Godly anxiety, then, may be the cause of many regrets which are, nevertheless, not warranted by any serious declension.

And, let me add, that very often these regrets of ours about the past are not wise. It is impossible to draw a fair comparison between the various stages of Christian experience, so as to give a judicious preference to one above another. Consider, as in a parable, the seasons of the year. There are many persons who, in the midst of the beauties of spring, say, "Ah, but how fitful is the weather! These March winds and April showers come and go by such fits and starts, that nothing is to be depended upon. Give me the safer glories of summer." Yet, when they feel the heat of summer, and wipe the sweat from their brows, they say, "After all, with all the full-blow of beauty around us, we admire more the freshness, verdure, and vivacity of spring. The snowdrop and the crocus, coming forth as the advance guard of the army of flowers, have a superior charm about them." Now it is idle to compare spring with summer; they differ, and have each its beauties. We are in autumn now, and very likely, instead of prizing the peculiar treasures of autumn, some will despise the peaceful Sabbath of the year, and mournfully compare you fading leaves to funeral sermons replete with sadness. Such will contrast summer and autumn, and exalt one above another. Now, whoever shall claim precedence for any season, shall have me for an opponent. They are all beautiful in their season, and each excels after its kind. Even thus it is wrong to compare the early zeal of the young Christian with the mature and mellow experience of the older believer, and make preferences. Each is beautiful according to its time. You, dear young friend, with your intense zeal, are to be commended and imitated; but very much of your fire I am afraid arises from novelty, and you are not so strong as you are earnest; like a newborn river, you are swift in current, but neither deep nor broad. And you, my more advanced friend, who are much tried and buffeted, to you it is not easy to hold on your way under great inward struggles and severe depressions, but your deeper sense of weakness, your firmer grasp of truth, your more intense fellowship with the Lord Jesus in his sufferings, your patience, and your steadfastness, are all lovely in the eyes of the Lord your God. Be thankful each of you for what you have, for by the grace of God you are what you are.

After making all these deductions, however, I cannot conceive that they altogether account for the prevalence of these regrets; I am afraid the fact arises from the sad truth that many of us have actually deteriorated in grace, have decayed in spirit, and degenerated in heart. Alas! in many cases, old corruptions have fought desperately, and for awhile caused a partial relapse. Grace has become weak, and sin has seized the occasion for attack; so that for a time the battle is turned, and Israel's banner is trailed in the mire. With many professors, I am afraid, prayer is neglected, worldliness is uppermost, sin has come to the front, nature leads the van, and grace and holiness are in the background. It should not be so, but I am afraid, ah, sadly afraid it is so.

IV. I will more fully speak upon this matter under the fourth head. Since these regrets are exceedingly common, it is to be feared that in some cases they are very sadly NEEDFUL. Now, let the blast of the winnowing fan be felt through the congregation. Behold, the Lord himself winnows this heap. Are there not many among us who once walked humbly with God, and near to him, who have fallen into carnal security? Have we not taken it for granted that all is well with us, and are we not settled upon our lees like Moab of old? How little of heart-searching and self-examination are practiced now-a-days! How little enquiry as to whether the root of the matter is really in us! Woe unto those who take their safety for granted, and sit down in God's house and say, "The temple of the Lord, the temple of the Lord are we." Woe unto them that are at ease in Zion. Of all enemies, one of the most to be dreaded is presumption. To be secure in a Christ is a blessing, to be secure in ourselves is a curse. Where carnal security reigns, the Spirit of God withdraws. He is with the humble and contrite, but he is not with the proud and self-sufficient. My brethren, are we all clear in this respect? Do not many of God's people also need to bemoan their worldliness? Once Christ was all with you, brethren; is it so now? Once you despised the world, and contemned alike its pleasures and its frowns; but now, my brethren, are not the chains of worldly custom upon you? Are you not many of you enslaved by fashion, and eaten up with frivolity? Do you not, some of you, run as greedily as worldlings after the questionable enjoyments of this present life? Ought these things to be so? Can they remain so and your souls enjoy the Lord's smile? "Ye cannot serve

God and mammon." "If any man love the world, the love of the Father is not in him." You cannot be Christ's disciples, and be in fellowship with the ungodly. Come ye out from among them; be ye separate; touch not the unclean thing; then shall ye know right joyfully that the Lord is a Father to you, and that you are his sons and daughters. But, brethren, have ye gone unto Jesus without the camp, and do ye abide there with him? Is the line of your separation visible--ay, is it existing? Is there any separation at all? Is it not often the case that the professed people of God are mixed up with the sons of men so that you cannot discern the one from the other? If it be so with anyone of us, let him humble himself, and let him cry in bitterness, "Oh that I were as in months past."

Brethren and sisters feel ye the breath of the winnowing fan again. How is it with you as to private prayer? Are there not believers, and we hope true believers too, who are lax in devotion? The morning prayer is brief, but alas! it is not fervent; the evening prayer is too often sleepy; ejaculations are few and far between; communion with heaven is distant, suspended, almost non-existent in many cases. Look ye to this, my brethren; let each man commune with his own heart, and be still. Think not of others just now, but let each one consider his ways. How is it with your love to the souls of sinners? There was a time when you would have done anything to bring a man to Christ, when any exertion you could have put forth would have been made spontaneously, without the need of incessant exhortations; are you as ready to speak for Jesus now as you once were? Do you watch to bring souls to him? Does the tear tremble in your eye, now, as it once did for lost souls, perishing without Christ? Alas, upon how many has a hardening influence operated. Ah, and this is true even of us, ministers. We have grown professional in our service, and now we preach like automatons, wound up for a sermon, to run down when the discourse is over, and we have little more care for the souls of men than if they were so much dirt. Trifles of criticism, fancies of speculation, or fopperies of oratory, fascinate too many who should be wise to win smile. God forgive us if we have fallen into so deplorable a state.

Ah, and how many of God's people must confess that their conscience is not so tender now as it used be. The time was when, if you said half a word amiss, you would hide away to weep over it; when, in business, if there had been a little mistake, and anything that might be construed into want of integrity, you would have felt ashamed for a week that such a thing had happened; but now ah, professors hear ye this--some of you can be dishonest and speak words that border on lasciviousness, and be as others are, yet your heart does not smite you, but you come to the communion table and feel you have a right to be there, and listen to the Word of God, and take comfort from it, when rather you should be ashamed and confounded.

Let me enquire whether there are not many of us whose zeal is almost gone? We once loved the Savior intensely, and his cause we eagerly sought to serve, but now we take matters easily, and do not travail in birth for souls. Some rich men were wont to give most freely to the cause of God, but now covetousness has palsied the hand of generosity. Even poor Christians are not always so ready with their two mites as they were in better days. You were wont to labor, too, but that Sunday School class sees you no longer; no street preaching now; no tract distributing now; all forms of Christ's service you have renounced, for you fancy you have done enough. Alas, poor sluggard! Has the sun shone long enough? Has God given you your daily bread long enough? Oh, cease not working, brethren, till God ceases to be merciful to you. "On, on, on," "forward, forward, forward," is the very motto of the Christian life. Let none of us talk of finality, for we have not yet attained. Till life is over, our zeal should still glow, and our labors for Christ should multiply.

Are there but other signs of declension, that some of us might, with but a very slight examination, discover in ourselves? Is not brotherly love, in many Christians, very questionable? Have they not forgotten, altogether, the family ties which bind all Christians to one another? And, with brotherly love, has not love to the Gospel gone too, so that now with many, one doctrine is almost as good as another? If a man can talk well, and is an orator, they enjoy his ministry whether he advocates truth or error. Once they could go to the little meeting house, where Christianity was preached faithfully though in an uncouth style, but now they must have the help of organs or they cannot praise God; and there must be millinery and genuflexions, or else they cannot pray to him; and they must listen to oratory and elocution, or else they cannot accept God's word. He is sickly who cannot dine without made dishes and spiced meats, but he is a healthy man of God who can eat heaven's bread and heaven's meat, even when it is not served on a lordly dish. Might not many of us blush, if we were to think how low our graces are, how weak our faith, how few our good works, and our gracious words with which we should bear testimony to his name. Yes, in thousands of cases, Christians need not be stopped if they were to commence this mournful cry, "Oh that I were as in the days of my youth, when the secret of God was upon my tabernacle."

V. But, I must pass on to observe that these regrets BY THEMSELVES ARE USELESS. It is unprofitable to read these words of Job, and say, "Just so, that is how I feel," and then continue in the same way. If a man has neglected his business, and so has lost his trade, it may mark a turn in his affairs when he says, "I wish I had been more industrious;" but if he abides in the same sloth as before, of what use is his regret? If he shall fold his arms and say, "Oh that I had dug that plot of land; oh that I had sown that field;" no harvest will come because of his lamentations. Up, man, up and labor, or you will have the sluggard's reward, rags and poverty will still be your portion. If a man be in declining health, if drunkenness and riot have broken down his constitution, it may mark a salutary reform in his history if he confesses his former folly; but if his regrets end in mere expressions, will these heal him? I trow not. So neither will a man, affected by spiritual decline, be restored by the mere fact of his knowing himself to be so. Let him go to the beloved physician, drink of the waters of life again, and receive the leaves of the tree which are for the healing of the nations. Inactive regrets are insincere. If a man really did lament that he had lost communion with God, he would seek to regain it. If he doth not seek to be restored he is adding to all his former sins this of lying before God, in uttering regrets that he does not feel in his soul.

I have known some, I fear who even satisfied themselves with expressions of regrets. "Ah," say they, "I am a deep experienced man, I can go where Job went; I can mourn and lament as Job did." Remember, many have been on Job's dunghill, who knew nothing of Job's God; many have imitated David in his sins, who never followed him, in his repentance. They have gone from their sin into hell by the way of presumption, whereas David went from it to heaven by the road of repentance and forgiveness. Never let us; merely because we feel some uneasiness within, conclude that this suffices. If in the dead of the night you should hear thieves in your house, you would not congratulate yourself because you were awake to hear them. You would waive all such comfortable reflections till the rogues were driven out and your property was safe; and so, when you know things are amiss with you, do not say "I am satisfied, because I know it is so." Up, men, and with all the strength that God's Holy Spirit can give you, strive to drive out these traitors from your bosom, for they are robbing your soul of her best treasures.

VI. Brethren, these regrets when they are necessary are very HUMBLING. Meditate now for a minute. Think, dear brother, what was thy position in thy happiest times, in those days that are now past. Had you any love to spare then? You were zealous; were you too zealous? You were gracious; were you too gracious? Nay, in our best estate, we were very far short of what we ought to be, and yet we have gone back from even that. It was a poor attainment at the best, have we fallen even from that. During the time we have been going back, we ought to have gone forward. What enjoyments we have lost by our wanderings! What progress we have missed! As John Bunyan well puts it, when Christian fell asleep and lost his roll, he had to go back for it, and he found it very hard going back, and, moreover, he had to go on again, so that he had to traverse three times the road he need only have traveled once, and then he came in late at the gates of the palace Beautiful, and was afraid of the lions, of which he would have had no fear had not the darkness set in. We know not what we lose, when we lose growth in grace.

Alas, how much the church has lost through us, for if the Christian becomes poor in grace, he lessens the church's wealth of grace. We have a common exchequer as a church, and every one who takes away his proportion from it robs the whole. Dear brethren, how accountable are many of us for the low tone of religion in the world, especially those of us who occupy the foremost ranks. If grace be at a low ebb with us, others say, "Well, look at so and so; I am as good as he." So much in the church do we take the cue from one another, that each one of us is in a measure responsible for the low state of the whole. Some of us are very quick to see the faults of others; may it not be that these faults are our own children? Those who have little love to others generally discover that there is little love in the church, and I notice that those who complain of the inconsistencies of others, are usually the most inconsistent persons themselves. Shall I be a robber of my fellow Christians? Shall I be an injury to the cause of Christ? Shall I be a comfort unto sinners in their sin? Shall I rob Christ of his glory,--I, who was saved from such depths of sin,--I, who have been favored with such enjoyments of his presence,--I, that have been on Tabor's top with him, and seen him transfigured,--I, that have been in his banqueting house, and have drunk out of the flagons of his love,--shall I be so devoid of grace, that I shall even injure his children, and make his enemies to blaspheme? Wretch that I am, to do this! Smite your breast, my brother, if such has been your sin; go home and smite your breast again, and ask God to smite it, till, with a broken heart, you cry repentingly for restoration, and then again go forth as a burning and a shining light, to serve your Master better than before.

VII. These regrets, then, are humbling, and they may be made very PROFITABLE in many other ways. First, they shew us what human nature is. Have we gone back so far? O, brethren, we might have gone back to perdition: we should have done so, if it had not been for the grace of God. What a marvel it is that God has borne with our ill manners, when he might justly have laid the reins on our necks, and suffered us to rush on in the road which we so often hankered after. See you not, dear brethren, what a body of death we carry with us, and what a terrible power it possesses? When you see the mischief that corruption has already done, never trust yourself, but look for new grace every day.

Learn again to prize what spiritual blessings yet remain. If you have such bitter regrets for what you have lost, hold fast what is still yours. Slip back no further, for if these slips have cost you so much, take heed that they do not ruin you. To continue presumptuous may be a proof that our profession is rotten throughout: only a holy jealousy can remove the suspicion of insincerity. Let your previous failings teach you to walk cautiously for the future. Be jealous, for you serve a jealous God. Since grey hairs may come upon you, here and there, and you may not know it, search, watch, try yourself day by day, lest you relapse yet more.

This should teach us to live by faith, since our best attainments fail us. We rejoice to-day, but we may mourn to-morrow. What a mercy it is that our salvation does not depend on what we are or what we feel. Christ has finished our salvation; no man can destroy what he has completed. Our life is hid with Christ in God, and is safe there; none can pluck us out of Jehovah's hands. Since we so frequently run aground, it is clear that we should be wrecked altogether, if we went to sea in a legal vessel with self for our pilot; let us keep to the good ship of free grace, steered by immutable faithfulness, for none other can bring us to the desired haven. But oh, let that free grace fill us with ardent gratitude. Since Christ has kept us, though we could not keep ourselves, let us bless his name, and, overwhelmed with obligations, let us rise with a solemn determination that we will serve him better than we have ever done before; and may his blessed Spirit help us to make the determination a fact.

VIII. So, to close; these regrets OUGHT NOT TO BE CONTINUAL: they ought to be removed, decidedly, removed, by an earnest effort, made in God's strength, to get back to the position which we occupied before, and to attain something better still.

Dear brethren and sisters, if any of you desire now to come into the higher life, and to feel anew your first love, what shall I say to you? Go back to where you started. Do not stay discussing whether you are a Christian or not. Go to Christ as a poor guilty sinner. When the door to heaven seems shut to me as a saint, I will get through it as a sinner, trusting in the precious blood of Jesus. Come and stand again, as though all your sins were on you still, at the cross's foot, where still may be seen the dropping blood of the infinitely precious atonement. Savior, I trust thee again: guilty, more guilty than I was before, a sinful child of God, I trust thee: "wash me thoroughly from mine iniquities, and purge me from my sin." You will never have your graces revived, unless you go to the cross. Begin life again. The best air for a man to breathe when he is sickly is said to be that of his birthplace: it was at Calvary we were born; it is only at Calvary we can be restored when we are declining. Do the first works. As a sinner, repair to the Savior, and ask to be restored. Then, as a further means of health, search out the cause of your declension. Probably it was a neglect of private prayer. Where the disease began, there must the remedy be applied. Pray more earnestly, more frequently, more importunately. Or, was it a neglect of hearing the word? Were you enticed by novelty or cleverness away from a really searching and instructive ministry? Go back, and feed on wholesome food again perhaps that may cure the disease. Or, have you been too grasping after the world? Brother, you loved God when you had but one shop, you have two now, and are giving all your time and thoughts to business, and your soul is getting lean. Man alive, strike off some of that business, for it is a bad business that makes your soul poor. I would not check industry or enterprise for a single moment; let a man do all he can, but not at the expense of his soul. Push, but do not push down your soul. You may buy gold too dear, and may attain a high position in this world at a cost which you may have to rue all your days. Where the mischief began, there apply the remedy. And oh, I urge upon you, and most of all upon myself, do not make excuses for yourselves; do not palliate your faults; do not say it must be so; do not compare yourselves among yourselves, or you will be unwise; but to the perfect image of Christ let your hearts aspire, to the ardor of your divine Redeemer, who loved not himself, but loved you; to the intense fervor of his apostles, who laid themselves upon the altar of God for his sake, for Christ's sake, and for yours. Aspire to this, and may we as a church live near to God, and grow in grace, then shall the Lord add to us daily of such as shall be saved.

There are some here who will say, "I do not comprehend this sermon: I have no cause to look back with regret. I have always been much the same as I am. I know nothing of religion." The day shall come when you will envy the least and most trembling believer. To you careless, Christless sinners, the day shall come when you will cry to the rocks for mercy, and beg them to conceal you from the eyes of him whom now you dare despise. I beseech you be not high minded, lift not up your horn on high, speak not so exceeding proudly, bow before the Christ of God, and ask him to give you the new life; for even if that new life have declined and become sickly, it is better than the death in which you dwell. Go and seek grace of him who alone can give it, and he will grant it to you this day, for his infinite mercy's sake. Amen.

PORTIONS OF SCRIPTURE READ BEFORE SERMON--Revelation 2; 3:1-6.

MR. SPURGEON takes occasion to inform his weekly readers that the funds in hand for sustaining the Orphans under his care at Stockwell are gradually diminishing, and assistance will be very seasonable. About 200 fatherless boys are in the Orphanage.

The Unbeliever's Unhappy Condition

A Sermon (No. 1012)
Delivered on Lord's-day Morning, September 24th, 1871, by
C. H. SPURGEON,
At the Metropolitan Tabernacle, Newington

"He that believed, not the Son shall not see life; but the wrath of God abideth on him." - John 3:36.

THIS IS A PART of a discourse by John the Baptist. We have not many sermons by that mighty preacher, but we have just sufficient to prove that he knew how to lay the axe at the root of the tree by preaching the law of God most unflinchingly; and also that he knew how to declare the gospel, for no one could have uttered sentences which more clearly contain the way of salvation than those in the text before us. Indeed, this third chapter of the gospel according to the evangelist John is notable among clear and plain Scriptures--notable for being yet clearer and plainer than almost any other. John the Baptist was evidently a preacher who knew how to discriminate--a point in which so many fail--he separated between the precious and the vile, and therefore he was as God's mouth to the people. He does not address them as all lost nor as all saved, but he shows the two classes, he keeps up the line of demarcation between him that feareth God and him that feareth him not. He plainly declares the privileges of the believer, he saith he hath even now eternal life; and with equal decision he testifies to the sad state of the unbeliever--"he shall not see life; but the wrath of God abideth on him." John the Baptist might usefully instruct many professedly Christian preachers. Although he that is least in the kingdom of heaven is greater than John the Baptist, and ought, therefore, more clearly to bear witness to the truth; yet, there are many who muddle the gospel, who teach philosophy, who preach a mingle-mangle, which is neither law nor gospel; and these might well go to school to this rough preacher of the wilderness, and learn from him how to cry, "Behold the Lamb of God which taketh away the sin of the world." I desire this morning to take a leaf out of the Baptist's lesson book; I would preach as he did the gospel of the Lord Jesus, "whose shoes I am not worthy to bear." It is my earnest desire to enjoy the delight of expounding to you the deep things of God; I feel a profound pleasure in opening up the blessings of the covenant of grace, and bringing forth out of its treasury things new and old. I should be happy to dwell upon the types of the Old Testament, and even to touch upon the prophecies of the New; but, while so many yet remain unsaved, my heart is never content except when I am preaching simply the gospel of Jesus Christ. My dear unconverted hearers, when I see you brought to Christ, I will then advance beyond the rudiments of the gospel; but, meanwhile, while hell is gaping wide, and many of you will certainly help to fill it, I cannot turn aside from warning you. I dare not resist the sacred impulse which constrains me to preach over and over again to you the glad tidings of salvation. I shall, like John, continue laying the axe at the root of the trees, and shall not go beyond crying, "Repent ye, for the kingdom of heaven is at hand." As he did, we shall now declare the sad estate of him who believeth not the Son of God.

This morning, with the burden of the Lord upon us, we shall speak upon the words of the text. Our first point shall be a discovery of the guilty one, "he that believeth not the Son." Next, we shall consider his offense; it lies in "not believing the Son;" thirdly, we shall lay bare the sinful causes which create this unbelief; and, fourthly, we shall show the terrible result of not believing in the Son: "he shall not see life, but the wrath of God abideth on him." May the Spirit help us in all.

I. To begin, then, who is THE GUILTY ONE? Who is then unhappy man here spoken of? Is he a person to be met with only once in a century? Must we search the crowds through and through to find out an individual in this miserable plight? Ah! no; the persons who are here spoken of are common; they abound even in our holy assemblies; they are to be met with by thousands in our streets. Alas, alas! they form the vast majority of the world's population. Jesus hath come unto his own and his own have not received him, the Jewish race remain unbelieving; while the Gentiles, to whom he was to be a light, prefer to sit in darkness and reject his brightness. We shall not be talking this morning upon a recondite theme, with only a remote relation to ourselves, but there are many here of whom we shall be speaking, and we devoutly pray that the word of God may come with power to their souls.

The persons here spoken of are those who believe not the Son of God. Jesus Christ, out of infinite mercy, has come into the world, has taken upon himself our nature, and in that nature has suffered the just for the unjust, to bring us to God. By reason of his sufferings, the gospel message is now proclaimed to all men, and they are honestly assured that "whosoever believeth in him shall not perish, but have everlasting life." The unhappy persons in this text will not believe in Jesus Christ, they reject God's way of mercy; they hear the gospel, but refuse obedience to its command. Let it not be imagined that these individuals are necessarily avowed sceptics, for many of them believe much of revealed truth. They believe the Bible to be the word of God; they believe there is a God; they believe that Jesus Christ is come into the world as a Savior; they believe most of the doctrines which cluster around the cross. Alas! they may do this, but yet the wrath of God abideth on them, if they believe not the Son of God. It may surprise you to learn that many of these persons are very much interested in orthodoxy. They believe that they have discovered the truth, and they exceedingly value those discoveries, so that they frequently grow very warm in temper with those who differ from them. They have read much, and they are matters of argument in the defense of what they consider to be sound doctrine. They cannot endure heresy, and yet sad is the fact, that believing what they do, and knowing so much, they have not believed the Son of God. They believe the doctrine of election, but they have not the faith of God's elect: they swear by final perseverance, but persevere in unbelief. They confess all the five points of Calvinism, but they have not come to the one most needful point of looking unto Jesus, that they may be saved. They accept in creed the truths that are assuredly believed among us, but they have not received that faithful saying, worthy of all acceptation, that Christ Jesus came into the world to save sinners; at any rate, they have not received it personally and practically for their souls' salvation.

It must be admitted that not a few of these persons are blameless as to their morals. You could not, with the closest observation, find either dishonesty, falsehood, uncleanness, or malice in their outward life; they are not only free from these blots, but they manifest positive excellences. Much of their character is commendable. They frequently are courteous and compassionate, generous and gentle-minded. Often times, they are so amiable and admirable that, while looking upon them, we understand how our Lord, in a similar case, loved the young man who asked "what lack I yet?" The one thing needful they are destitute of, they have not believed in Christ Jesus, and loath as the Savior was to see them perish, yet it cannot be helped, one doom is common to all who believe not; they shall not see life, but the wrath of God abideth on them.

In many cases these persons are, in addition to their morality, religious persons after a fashion. They would not absent themselves from the usual service of the place of worship. They are most careful to respect the Sabbath, they venerate the Book of God, they use a form of prayer, they join in the songs of the Sanctuary, they sit as God's people sit, and stand as God's people stand, but, alas, there is a worm in the center of that fair fruit, they have missed the one essential thing, which, being omitted, brings certain ruin; they have not believed on the Son of God. Ah, how far a man may go, and yet, for lack of this one thing the wrath of God may still abide upon him. Beloved of parents who are hopeful of the conversion of their boy, esteemed by Christians who cannot but admire his outward conversation, yet for all that, the young man may be under the frown of God, for "God is angry with the wicked every day." The wrath of God abideth on the man, whoever he may be, that hath not believed in Jesus.

Now, if our text showed that the wrath of God was resting on the culprits in our jails, most persons would assent to the statement, and none would wonder at it. If our text declared that the wrath of God abides upon persons who live in habitual unchastity and constant violation of all the laws of order and respectability, most men would say "Amen;" but the text is aimed at another character. It is true that God's wrath does rest upon open sinners; but, oh sirs, this too is tree, the wrath of God abideth upon those who boast of their virtues but have not believed in Jesus his Son. They may dwell in palaces; but, if they are not believers, the wrath of God abideth on them. They may sit in the senate house and enjoy the acclamations of the nation; but, if they believe not on the Son, the wrath of God abideth on them. Their names may be enrolled in the peerage, all they may possess countless wealth, but the wrath of God abideth on them. They may be habitual in their charities, and abundant in external acts of devotion; but, if they have not accepted the appointed Savior, the word of God bears witness, that "the wrath of God abideth on them."

II. Now let us, with our hearts awakened by God's Spirit, try to think upon THEIR OFFENCE.

What is this peculiar sin which entails the wrath of God upon these people? It is that they have not believed the Son of God. What does that amount to? It amounts to this, first of all, that they refuse to accept the mercy of God. God made a law, and his creatures were bound to respect and obey it. We rejected it, and turned aside from it. It was a great display of the heart's hatred, but it was not in some respects so thoroughly and intensely wicked a manifestation of enmity to God as when we reject the gospel of grace. God has now presented not the law but the gospel to us, and he has said: "My creatures, you have broken my law, you have acted very vilely towards me. I must punish for sin, else I were not God, and I cannot lay aside my justice; but I have devised a way by which, without any injury to any of my attributes, I can have mercy upon you. I am ready to forgive the past, and to restore you to more than your lost position, so that you shall be my sons and my daughters. My only command to you is, believe in my Son. If this command be obeyed, all the blessings of my new covenant shall be yours. Trust him, and follow him; for, behold, I give him as a leader and commander to the people. Accept him as making atonement by his substitution, and obey him." Now, to reject the law of God shows an evil heart of unbelief; but who shall say what a depth of rebellion must dwell in that heart which refuses not only the yoke of God but even the gift of God. The provision of a Savior for lost men is the free gift of God, by it all our wants are supplied, all our evils are removed, peace on earth is secured to us, and glory for ever with God: the rejection of this gift cannot be a small sin. The all-seeing One, when he beholds men spurning the supreme gift of his love, cannot but regard such rejection as the worst proof of the hatred of their hearts against himself. When the Holy Spirit comes to convince men of sin, the especial sin which he brings to light is thus described: "Of sin, because they believed not on me." Not because the heathen were licentious in their habits, barbarians in their ways, and bloodthirsty in their spirit. No: "Of sin, because they believe not on me." Condemnation has come upon men, but what is the condemnation? "That light is come into the world, and men love darkness rather than light, because their deeds are evil." Remember, also, that expressive text: "He that believeth not is condemned already;" and what is he condemned for! "Because he hath not believed in the name of the only-begotten Son of God."

Let me remark, further, that in the rejection of divine mercy as presented in Christ, the unbeliever has displayed an intense venom against God, for observe how it is. He must either receive the mercy of God in Christ, or he must be condemned--there is no other alternative. He must trust Christ whom God has set forth to be the propitiation for sin, or else he must be driven from the presence of God into eternal punishment. The unbeliever in effect says, "I had sooner be damned than I would accept God's mercy in Christ." Can we conceive a grosser insult to the infinite compassion of the great Father? Suppose a man has injured another, grossly insulted him, and that repeatedly, and yet the injured person, finding the man at last brought into a wretched and miserable state, goes to him, and simply out of kindness to him, says, "I freely forgive you all the wrong you ever did me, and I am ready to relieve your poverty, and to succor you in your distress." Suppose the other replies, "No, I would sooner rot than take anything from you;" would not you have in such a resolve a clear proof of the intense enmity that existed in his heart? And so when a man saith, and everyone of you unbelievers do practically say so, "I would sooner lie for ever in hell than honor Christ by trusting him," this is a very plain proof of his hatred of God and his Christ. Unbelievers hate God. Let me ask for what do you hate him? He keeps the breath within your nostrils; he it is that gives you food and rainment, and sends fruitful seasons. For which of these good things do you hate him? You hate him because he is good. Ah, then, it must be because you yourself are evil, and your heart very far removed from righteousness. May God grant that this great and crying sin may be clearly set before your eyes by the light of the Eternal Spirit, and may you repent of it, and turn from your unbelief, and live this day.

But yet further, the unbeliever touches God in a very tender place by his unbelief. No doubt, it was to the great Maker a joyous thing to fashion this world, but there are no expressions of joy concerning it at all equal to the joy of God in the matter of human redemption. We would be guarded when we speak of him; but, as far as we can tell, the gift of his dear Son to men, and the whole scheme of redemption, is the master work even of God himself. He is infinite in POWER, and wisdom, and love; his ways are as high above our ways as the heavens are above the earth; but Scripture, I think, will warrant me in saying--

"That in the grace which rescued man
His brightest form of glory shines;
Here on the cross tis fairest writ,
In precious blood and crimson lines."

Now, the man who saith, "There is no God" is a fool, but he who denies God the glory of redemption, in addition to his folly, has robbed the Lord of the choicest jewel of his regalia, and aimed a deadly blow at the divine honor. I may say of him who despises the great salvation, that, in despising Christ, he touches the apple of God's eye. "This is my beloved Son," saith God, "hear ye him." Out of heaven he saith it, and yet men stop their ears and say, "We will not have him." Nay, they wax wrath against the cross, and turn away from God's salvation. Do you think that God will always bear this? The times of your ignorance he hath winked at, but "now commandeth all men every where to repent." Will ye stand out against his love? His love that has been so inventive in ingenious plans by which to bless the sons of men? Shall his choicest work be utterly contemned by you? If so, it is little wonder that it is written, "The wrath of God abideth on him."

I must, still further, unveil this matter by saying that the unbeliever perpetrates an offense against every person of the blessed Trinity. He may think that his not believing is a very small business, but, indeed, it is a barbed shaft shot against the Deity. Take the Persons of the blessed Trinity, beginning with the Son of God who comes to us most nearly. It is to me the most surprising thing I ever heard of that "the word was made flesh and dwelt among us." I do not wonder that in Hindostan the missionaries are often met with this remark: "It is too good to be true that God ever took upon himself the nature of such a thing as man!" Yet, more wonderful does it seem to be that, when Christ became man, he took all the sorrows and infirmity of man, and, in addition, was made to bear the sin of many. The most extraordinary of all facts is this: that the infinitely Holy should be "numbered with the transgressors," and, in the words of Esaias, should "bear their iniquities." The Lord hath made him, who knew no sin, to be made sin for us. Wonder of wonders! It is beyond all degree amazing that he who distributes crowns and thrones should hang on a tree and die, the just for the unjust, bearing the punishment due to sinners for guilt. Now, knowing this, as most of you do, and yet refusing to believe, you do, in effect, say, "I do not believe that the incarnate God can save." "Oh no," you reply, "we sincerely believe that he can save." Then, it must be that you feel, "I believe he can, but I will not have him to save me." Wherein I excuse you in the first place, I must bring the accusation more heavily in the second. You answer that "you do not say you will not believe him." Why do you then remain in unbelief? The fact is you do not trust him; you do not obey him. I pray you account for the fact. "May I believe him?" saith one. Have we not told you ten thousand times over that whosoever will may take the water of life freely. If there be any barrier it is not with God, it is not with Christ, it is with your own sinful heart. You are welcome to the Savior now, and if you trust him now he is yours for ever. But oh, unbeliever, it appears to be nothing to you that Christ has died. His wounds attract you not. His groans for his enemies have no music in them to you. You turn your back upon the incarnate God who bleeds for men, and in so doing you shut yourselves out of hope, judging yourselves unworthy of eternal life.

Furthermore, the wilful rejection of Christ is also an insult to God the Father. "He that believeth not hath made God a liar, because he hath not believed the record that God gave of his Son." God has himself often borne testimony to his dear Son. "Him hath God the Father set forth to be a propitiation for our Sins." In rejecting Christ, you reject God's testimony and God's gift. It is a direct assault upon the truthfulness and lovingkindness of the gracious Father, when you trample on or cast aside his priceless, peerless gift of love.

And, as for the blessed Spirit, it is his office here below to bear witness to Christ. In the Christian ministry, daily the Holy Spirit cries to the sons of men to come to Jesus. He has striven in the hearts of many of you, given you a measure of conviction of sin, and a degree of knowledge of the glory of Christ, but you have repressed it, you have labored to your utmost to do despite to the Spirit of God. Believe me, this is no slight sin. An unbeliever is an enemy to God the Father, to God the Son, and God the Holy Ghost. Against the blessed Trinity in Unity, O unbeliever, your sin is a standing insult: you are now to God's face insulting him, by continuing an unbeliever.

And, I must add, that there is also in unbelief an insult against every attribute of God. The unbeliever in effect declares, "If the justice of God is seen in laying the punishment of sin upon Christ--I do not care for his justice, I will bear my own punishment." The sinner seems to say, "God is merciful in the gift of Christ to suffer in our stead--I do not want his mercy, I can do without it. Others may be guilty, and they may trust in the Redeemer, but I do not feel such guilt and I will not sue for pardon." Unbelievers attack the wisdom of God, for, whereas the wisdom of God is in its fullness revealed in the gift of Jesus, they say, "It is a dogma, unphilosophical, and worn-out." They count the wisdom of God to be foolishness, and thus cast a slight upon another of the divine attributes. I might in detail mention every one of the attributes and prerogatives of God, and prove that your nonacceptance of the Savior is an insult to every one of them, and to God himself: but the theme is too sad for us to continue upon it, and, therefore, let us pass to another phase of the subject, though I fear it will be equally grievous.

III. Thirdly, let us consider THE CAUSES OF THIS UNBELIEF.

In a great many, unbelief may be ascribed to a careless ignorance of the way of salvation. Now, I should not wonder if many of you imagine that, if you do not understand the gospel, you are therefore quite excused for not believing it. But, sirs, it is not so. You are placed in this world, not as heathens in the center of Africa, but in enlightened England, where you live in the full blaze of gospel day. There are places of worship all around you, which you can without difficulty attend. The book of God is very cheap; you have it in your houses; you can all read it or hear it read. Is it so, then, that the king has been pleased to reveal himself to you, and tell you the way to salvation, and yet you, at the age of twenty, thirty, or forty, do not know the way of salvation? What, do you mean, sir? What can you mean? Has God been pleased to reveal himself in Scripture, and tell you how to escape from hell and fly to heaven, and yet have you been too idle to inquire into that way? Dare you say to God, "I do not think it worth my while to learn what thou hast revealed, neither do I care to know of the gift which thou hast bestowed on men." How can you think that such ignorance is an excuse for your sin? What could be a more gross aggravation of it? If you do not know, you ought to know; if you have not learned the gospel message, you might have learned it, for there are, some of us whose language it is not difficult for even the most illiterate to understand, and who would, if we caught ourselves using a hard word, retract it, and put it into little syllables, so that not even a child's intellect need be perplexed by our language. Salvation's way is plain in the book; those words, "Believe and live," are in this Christian England almost as legible and as universally to be seen as though they were printed on the sky. That trust in the Lord Jesus saves the soul is well-known news. But, if you still say you have not known all this, then I reply, "Dear sir, do try to know it. Go to the Scriptures, study them, see what is there. Hear, also, the gospel, for it is written, "Incline your ear to come unto me; hear, and your soul shall live." Faith cometh by hearing, and hearing by the word of God." For your soul's sake I charge you, be no longer ignorant of that which you must know, or else must perish.

In some others, the cause is indifference. They do not think the matter to be of any very great consequence. They are aware that they are not quite right, but they have a notion that somehow or other they will get right at last; and, meanwhile, it does not trouble them. Oh man, I pray thee as thy fellow creature let me speak with thee a word of expostulation. God declares that his wrath abides upon you as an unbeliever, and do you call that nothing? God says, "I am angry with you," and you say to him, "I do not care, it is of very small importance to me. The rise or fall of the consols is of much more consequence than whether God is angry with me or not. My dinner being done to a turn concerns me a great deal more than whether the infinite God loves me or hates me." That is the English of your conduct, and I put it to you whether there can be a higher impertinence against your Creator, or a direr form of arrogant revolt against the eternal Ruler. If it does not trouble you that God is angry with you, it ought to trouble you; and it troubles me that it does not trouble you. We have heard of persons guilty of murder, whose behavior during the trial has been cool and self-possessed. The coolness with which they pleaded "not guilty" has been all of a piece with the hardness of tears which led them to the bloody deed. He who is capable of great crime is also incapable of shame concerning it. A man who is able to take pleasure and be at ease while God is angry with him shows that his heart is harder than steel.

In certain cases, the root of this unbelief lies in another direction. It is fed by pride. The person who is guilty of it does not believe that he needs a Savior. His notion is that he will do his very best, attend the church or the meeting-house very regularly, subscribe occasionally or frequently, and go to heaven partly by what he does, and partly by the merits of Christ. So that not believing in Christ is not a matter of any great consequence with him, because he is not naked, and poor, and miserable; but he is rich, and increased in goods in spiritual things. To be saved by faith is a religion for harlots, and drunkards, and thieves; but for respectable persons such as he is, who have kept the law from their youth up, he does not see any particular need of laying hold upon Christ. Such conduct reminds me of the words of Cowper:--

"Perish the virtue, as it ought, abhorr'd,
And the fool with it that insults his Lord."

God believed it needful, in order to save man, that the Redeemer should die; yet you self-righteous ones evidently think that death a superfluity: for if a man could save himself, why did the Lord descend and die to save him? If there be a way to heaven by respectability and morality without Christ, what is the good of Christ? It is utterly useless to have an expiator and a meditator, if men are so good that they do not require them. You tell God to his face that he lies unto you, that you are not so sinful as he would persuade you, that you do not need a substitute and sacrifice as he says you do. Oh, sirs, this pride of yours is an arrogant rebellion against God. Look at your fine actions, you that are so good--your motives are base, your pride over what you have done has defiled, with black fingers, all your acts. In as much as you prefer your way to God's way, and prefer your righteousness to God's righteousness, the wrath of God abideth on you.

Perhaps I have not hit the reason of your unbelief, therefore let me speak once more. In many love of sin rather than any boasted self-righteousness keeps them from the Savior. They do not believe in Jesus, not because they have any doubt about the truths of Christianity, but because they have an enslaving love for their favourite sin. "Why," saith one, "if I were to believe in Christ, of course, I must obey him--to trust and to obey go together. Then I could not be the drunkard I am, I could not trade as I do, I could not practice secret licentiousness, I could not frequent the haunts of the ungodly, where laughter is occasioned by sin, and mirth by blasphemy. I cannot give up these my darling sins." Perhaps, this sinner hopes that one day, when he cannot any longer enjoy his sin, he will meanly sneak out of it, and try to cheat the devil of his soul; but, meanwhile, he prefers the pleasures of sin to obedience to God, and unbelief to acceptance of his salvation. O sweet sin! O bitter sin! How art thou murdering the souls of men! As certain serpents before they strike their prey fix their eyes upon it and fascinate it, and then at last devour it, so does sin fascinate the foolish sons of Adam; they are charmed with it, and perish for it. It yields but a momentary joy, and the wage thereof is eternal misery, yet are men enamoured of it. The ways of the strange woman, and the paths of uncleanness lead most plainly to the chambers of death, yet are men attracted thereto as moths by the blaze of the candle, and so are they destroyed. Alas! that men wantonly dash against the rocks of dangerous lasts, and perish wilfully beneath the enchantment of sin. Sad pity it is to prefer a harlot to the eternal God, to prefer a few pence made by dishonesty to heaven itself, to prefer the gratification of the belly to the love of the Creator, and the joy of being reconciled and saved. It was a dire insult to God when Israel set up a golden calf, and said, "These be thy gods, O Israel." Shall the image of an ox that eateth grass supplant the living God! He that had strewn the earth with manna, had made Sinai to smoke with his presence, and the whole wilderness to tremble beneath his marchings, is he to be thrust aside by the image of a bullock that hath horns and hoofs? Will men prefer molten metal to the infinitely holy and glorious Jehovah? But, surely, the preference of a lust to God is a greater insult still: to obey our passions rather than his will, and to prefer sin to his mercy; this is the crime of crimes. May God deliver us from it, for his mercy's sake.

IV. We have heavy tidings in the last head of my discourse, THE TERRIBLE RESULT of unbelief. "He shall not see life, but the wrath of God abideth on him." "The wrath of God!" No words can ever fully explain this expression. Holy Whitfield, when he was preaching, would often hold up his hands, and, with tears streaming down his eyes, would exclaim, "Oh, the wrath to come! the wrath to come!" Then would he pause because his emotions checked his utterance. The wrath of God! I confess I feel uneasy if anybody is angry with me, and yet one can bear the auger of foolish, hot-tempered persons with some equanimity. But the wrath of God is the anger of one who is never angry without a cause, one who is very patient and long suffering. It takes much to bring the choler into Jehovah's face, yet is he wroth with unbelievers. He is never wroth with anything because it is feeble and little, but only because it is wrong. His anger is only his holiness set on fire. He cannot bear sin; who would wish that he should? What right-minded man would desire God to be pleased with evil? That were to make a devil of God. Because he is God, he must be angry with sin wherever it is. This makes the sting of it, that his wrath is just and holy anger. It is the anger, remember, of an Omnipotent Being, who can crush us as easily as a moth. It is the anger of an Infinite Being, and therefore infinite anger, the heights and depths and breadths and lengths of which no man can measure. Only the incarnate God ever fully knew the power of God's anger. It is beyond all conception, yet the anger rests on you my hearer. Alas, for you, if you are an unbeliever, for this is your state before God. It is no fiction of mine, but the word of inspired truth: "the wrath of God abideth on him."

Then notice the next word, it "abideth," this is to say, it is upon you now. He is angry with you at this moment,--and always. You go to sleep with an angry God gazing into your face, you wake in the morning, and if your eye were not dim, you would perceive his frowning countenance. He is angry with you, even when you are singing his praises, for you mock him with solemn sounds, upon a thoughtless tongue; angry with you on your knees, for you only pretend to pray, you utter words without heart. As long as you are not a believer, he must be angry with you every moment. "God is angry with the wicked every day."

That the text saith it abideth, and the present tense takes a long sweep, for it always will abide on you. But may you not, perhaps, escape from it, by ceasing to exist? The test precludes such an idea. Although it says, that you "shall not see life," it teaches that God's wrath is upon you, so that the absence of life is not annihilation. Spiritual life belongs only to believers; you are now without that life, yet you exist, and wrath abides on you, and so it ever must be. While you shall not see life, you shall exist in eternal death, for the wrath of God cannot abide on a non-existent creature. You shall not see life, but you shall feel wrath to the uttermost. It is horror enough that wrath should be on you now, it is horror upon horrors, and hell upon hell, that it shall be upon you for ever.

And notice that it must be so, because you reject the only thing that can heal you. As George Herbert says, "Whom oils and balsams kill, what salve can cure?" If Christ himself has become a savor of death unto death unto you, because you reject him, how can you be saved? There is but one door, and if you close it by your unbelief, how can you enter heaven? There is one healing medicine, and, if you refuse to take it, what remains but death? There is one water of life, but you refuse to drink it; then must you thirst for ever. You put from you, voluntarily, the one only Redeemer; how then shall you be ransomed? Shall Christ die again, and in another state be offered to you once more? O sirs, you would reject him then as you reject him now. But there remaineth no more sacrifice for sin. On the cross, God's mercy to the sons of men was fully revealed, and will you reject God's ultimatum of grace; his last appeal to you. If so, it is at your own peril: Christ being raised from the dead, dieth no more; he shall come again, but without a sin offering unto the salvation of his people.

Remember, sirs, that the wrath of God will produce no saving or softening effect. It has been suggested that a sinner, after suffering God's wrath awhile, may repent, and so escape from it. But our observation and experience prove that the wrath of God never softened anybody's heart yet, and we believe it never will: those who are suffering divine wrath will go on to harden, and harden, and harden, the more they suffer, the more they will hate: the more they are punished, the more will they sin. The wrath of God abiding on you will produce no good results to you, but rather you shall go from evil to evil, further and further from the presence of God.

The reason why the wrath of God abides on an unbeliever is partly because all his other sins remain on him. There is no sin that shall damn the man who believes, and nothing can save the man who will not believe. God removes all sin the moment we believe; but while we believe not, fresh cords fasten upon us our transgressions. The sin of Judah is written as with an iron pen, and graven with a point of a diamond. Nothing can release you from guilt while your heart remains at enmity with Jesus Christ your Lord.

Remember that God has never taken an oath, that I know of, against any class of persons, except unbelievers. "To whom sware he that they should not enter into his rest, but to them that believed not?" Continued unbelief God never will forgive, because his word binds him not to do so. Doth he swear an oath, and shall he go back from it? It cannot be. O that you might have grace to relinquish your unbelief, and close in with the gospel, and be saved.

Now, I hear some one object, "You tell us that certain people are under the wrath of God, but they are very prosperous." I reply, that yonder bullock will be slaughtered. Yet it is being fattened. And your prosperity, O ungodly man, is but a fattening of you for the slaughter of justice. Ay, but you say, "They are very merry, and some of those who are forgiven are very sad." Mercy lets them be merry while they may. We have heard of men who, when driven to Tyburn in a cart, could drink and laugh as they went to the gallows. It only proved what bad men they were. And so, whereas the guilty can yet take comfort, it only proves their guiltiness.

Let me ask what ought to be your thoughts concerning these solemn truths which I have delivered to you? I know what my thoughts were; they made me go to my bed unhappy. They made me very grateful because I hope I have believed in Jesus Christ; yet they made me start in the night, and wake this morning with a load upon me. I come here to say to you, must it be so that you will always remain unbelievers, and abide under the wrath of God? If it must be so, and the dread conclusion seems forced upon me, at any rate, do look it in the face, do consider it. If you are resolved to be damned, know what you are at. Take advise and consider. O sirs, it cannot need an argument to convince you that it is a most wretched thing to be now under the wrath of God. You cannot want any argument to show that it must be a blessed thing to be forgiven--you must see that. It is not your reason that wants convincing, it is, your heart that wants renewing.

The whole gospel lies in this nutshell. Come, thou guilty one, just as thou art, and rest thyself upon the finished work of the Savior, and take him to be thine for ever. Trust Jesus now. In your present position it may be done. God's Holy Spirit blessing your mind, you may at this moment say, "Lord, I believe, help thou mine unbelief." You may now confide in Jesus, and some who came in here unforgiven, may make the angels sing because they go down yonder steps saved souls, whose transgressions are forgiven, and whose sins are covered. God knoweth one thing, that if I knew by what study and what art I could learn to preach the gospel so as to affect your hearts I would spare no cost or pains. For the present, I have aimed simply to warn you, not with adornment of speech, lest the power should be the power of man; and now I leave my message, and commit it to him who shall judge the quick and the dead. But this know, if ye receive not the Son, I shall be a swift witness against you. God grant it be not so, for his mercy's sake. Amen.

PORTIONS OF SCRIPTURE READ BEFORE SERMON--Hebrews 2:14-18; Hebrews 3.

Our Watchword

A Sermon (No. 1013)
Delivered on Lord's-day Morning, October 1st, 1871, by
C. H. SPURGEON,
At the Metropolitan Tabernacle, Newington

"Let such as love thy salvation say continually, Let God be magnified." - Psalm 70:4.

THESE WORDS OCCUR at least three times in the book of Psalms, and therefore we may regard them as especially important. When God speaks once, twice, thrice, he doth as it were awaken us to peculiar attention, and call for prompt obedience to what he saith. Let us not be deaf to the divine voice, but let each one say, "Speak Lord, for thy servant heareth."

You will observe that in this, and in the fortieth Psalm, this holy saying is put in opposition to the ungodly speeches of persecutors. The wicked say, "Aha, aha," therefore let those who love God's salvation have a common watchword with which to silence the malicious mockeries of the ungodly; let them say, "LET GOD BE MAGNIFIED." The earnestness of the wicked should be a stimulus to the fervency of the righteous. Surely, if God's enemies do not spare blasphemy and profanity, if they are always upon the watch to find reasons for casting reproach upon the name and church of Christ, we ought to be more than equally vigilant and diligent in spreading abroad the knowledge of the gospel, which magnifies the name of the Lord. Would to God his church were half as earnest as the synagogue of Satan! Oh that we had, in our holy cause, a tithe of the indefatigable spirit of those Scribes and Pharisees, who compass sea and land to make one proselyte! Even the archfiend shames us by his preserving industry, for he goeth up and down in the earth seeking whom he may destroy!

The clause which we have selected for our text also follows immediately after another which may be looked upon as a stepping-stone to it. Before we can love God's salvation, we must be seekers of it; hence we read, "Let all those that seek thee rejoice and be glad in thee." There is a duty peculiar to seekers, let them see to it; and then there follows a further obligation peculiar to those who have found what they sought for. Let joy and rejoicing be first realised by the seeker through his receiving personally the grace of God, and then let us go on to a stage further. The fresh convert has his business mainly within; it will be well for him if his heart can, in sincerity, be glad in the Lord. When believers are young and feeble they are not fit for the battle; therefore, let them tarry at home awhile, and under their vine and fig-tree eat the sweet fruits of the gospel, none making them afraid. We do not send our children to hard service; we wait till their limbs are developed, and then appoint them their share in life's labors. Let the newly called be carried like lambs in the Savior's bosom, and borne as on eagles' wings. "Let all those that seek thee rejoice and be glad in thee." But when men have advanced beyond the earliest stage, when they are persuaded that Christ is theirs, and that they have been adopted into the family of God, then let them cheerfully accept active service. Let it not be now the main concern with them to possess a joyous experience on their own account, but let them studiously seek the good of their fellow creatures, and the glory of God. Strong men have strength given them that they may bear burdens and perform labors; light is this burden and blessed is this labor. Let them "say continually, Let God be magnified." I shall, therefore, hope that anything of earnest exhortation which shall be addressed to believers at this time, will come with double power to those of you who are advanced in the divine life. The more you know of God's salvation the more you will love it, and the more you love it the more are you bound to recognize the sacred duty and privilege of saying continually, "Let God be magnified." May each one of you here be willing to take up the obligation if you have enjoyed the benefit.

It may simplify our discourse this morning if we arrange it under three heads. Here is, first, the character: "They that love thy salvation. Here is secondly, the saying: "Let them say continually, Let God be magnified. And here is, thirdly, the wish, the wish of the psalmist and of the psalmist's master, that all who answer to the character shall use the watchword, and say continually, Let God be magnified."

I. We will begin, then, by discriminating THE CHARACTER.

The individuals here spoken of are those who love God's salvation. Then it is implied that they are persons who are saved, because it is not according to nature to love a salvation in which we have no part. We may admire the salvation which is preached, but we shall only love the salvation which is experienced. We may hold orthodox views as to salvation, though not ourselves saved; but we shall not have earnest affection towards it unless we are ourselves redeemed by it from the wrath to come. Saved ones, then, are meant here, and we may add that they are so saved as to be assured of it, and consequently to feel the warm glow of ardent, grateful love. They love God's salvation because they have grasped it; they possess it, they know they possess it, and, therefore, they prize it, and their hearts are wedded to it. Beloved, I hope that the large proportion of this congregation could say before the heart searching God, "We are saved; we have come all guilty and heavy laden to the foot of the cross; we have looked up, we have seen the flowing of the Savior's precious blood, we have trusted in him as our atoning sacrifice, and by faith we have received full pardon through his precious blood." Happy people who have this blessing and know it! May no doubts ever becloud your sky! May you clearly read your titles to the mansions in the skies, written legibly and indelibly in the precious blood of Jesus Christ your Savior. You are the persons to whom we speak to-day; you know, and therefore love the salvation of God.

But, more than this, to sustain and bring to perfection in the renewed heart an ardent affection towards the divine salvation of a sort that will continue, and become practically fruitful, there must be an intelligent consideration, and an instructed apprehension as to the character of this salvation. It is a great pity that so many professors have only a religion of feeling, and are quite unable to explain and justify their faith. They live by passion, rather than by principle. Religion is in them a series of paroxysms, a succession of emotions. They were stirred up at a certain meeting, excited, and carried away, and let us hope they were really and sincerely converted: but they have failed to become to the fullest extent disciples or learners. They do not sit at Jesus' feet, they are not Bereans who search the Scriptures daily to see whether these things be so: they are content with the mere rudiments, the simple elements: they are still little children and have need to be fed with milk, for they cannot digest the strong meat of the kingdom. Such persons do not discern so many reasons for admiring and loving the salvation of God, as the intelligent enlightened Spirit-taught believer. I would to God that all of us, after we have received Christ, meditated much upon his blessed person, and the details of his work, and the various streams of blessings which leap forth from the central fount of Calvary's sacrifice. All Scripture is profitable, but especially those Scriptures which concern our salvation. Some things lose by observation, they are most wondered at when least understood; but the gospel gains by study: no man is ever wearied in meditating upon it, nor does he find his admiration diminished, but abundantly increased. Blessed is he who studies the gospel both day and night, and finds his heart's delight in it. Such a man will have a steadier and intenser affection for it, in proportion as he perceives its excellence and surpassing glory. The man who receives the gospel superficially, and holds it as a matter of impression and little more, being quite unable to give a reason for the hope that is in him, lacks that which would confirm and intensify his love.

Now, let me show you, beloved, what it is in salvation that the thoughtful believer loves; and I may begin by saying that he loves, best of all, the Savior himself. Often our Lord is called Salvation, because he is the great worker of it, the author and finisher, the Alpha and the Omega of it. He who has Christ has salvation; and, as he is the essence of salvation, he is the center of the saved ones' affection. Have you, beloved, carefully considered that Jesus is divine, that he counts it not robbery to be equal with God, being our Creator and Preserver, as well as our Redeemer? Do you fully understand that our Lord is infinite, eternal, nothing less than God; and yet for our sakes he took upon himself our nature, was clothed in that nature with all its infirmities, sin alone excepted, and in that nature agonized, bled, and died, the just for the unjust, that he might bring us to God. Oh, marvel of marvels, miracle of miracles! The immortal Lord stoops to death; the Prince of glory bows to be spit upon. Shame and dishonor could not make him start back from his blessed purpose, but to the death of the cross he surrendered himself. O, you who are saved, do you not love Christ, who is your salvation ? Do you not feel a burning desire to behold him as he is ? Is not his presence, even now, a nether heaven to you ? Will not a face to face view of his glory be all the heaven that your utmost stretch of imagination can conceive ? I know it is so. Your heart is bound to Jesus, his name is set as a seal upon it; therefore, I charge you to say continually, "Let God be magnified." Glory be to the Father who gave his Son, to the Son who gave himself, to the Spirit who revealed all this to us. Triune God, be thou extolled for ever and ever.

But you love not only the Savior's person, but I am sure you delight in the plan of salvation. What is that plan? It is summed up in a single word--substitution.

"He bore, that we might never bear,
His Father's righteous ire."

Sin was not pardoned absolutely, else justice had been dishonored; but sin was transferred from the guilty to the innocent One. "The Lord hath laid on him the iniquity of us all." When our iniquity was found upon the innocent Lamb of God, he was "smitten of God and afflicted," as if he had been a sinner; he was made to suffer for transgressions not his own, as if they had been his own; and thus mercy and justice met together, righteousness and grace kissed each other. Alas! there are many who fight against this plan, but I rejoice that I am surrounded by warm hearts who love it, and would die for it. As for me, I know no other gospel, and let this tongue be dumb rather than it should ever preach any other. Substitution is the very marrow of the whole Bible, the soul of salvation, the essence of the gospel, we ought to saturate all our sermons with it, for it is the life-blood of a gospel ministry. We must daily show how God the Judge can be "just, and yet the justifier of him that believeth." We must declare that God has made the Redeemer's soul a sacrifice for sin, making him to be sin for us, who knew no sin, that we might be made the righteousness of God in him. Our plain testimony must be, that "he was made a curse for us;" that "he his own self bare our sins in his own body on the tree;" that "he was once offered to bear the sins of many;" and that "he was numbered with the transgressors, and he bare the sin of many." About this we must never speak with bated breath, lest we be found unfaithful to our charge. And why, brethren, should we not joyfully proclaim this doctrine? for is it not the grandest, noblest, most divine, under heaven. The plan so adorns all the attributes of the Godhead, and furnishes such a safe footing for a trembling conscience to rest upon, such a fortress, castle, and high tower for faith to rejoice in, that we cannot do otherwise than love it. The very way and plan of it is dearer to our souls than life itself. Oh, then let us always say, "Let God be magnified," since he devised, arranged, and carried out this Godlike method of blending justice with mercy.

But, beloved, we also love God's salvation when we consider what was the object of it. The object of it towards us was to redeem unto Christ a people who should be zealous for good works. The sinner loves a salvation from hell, the saint loves a salvation from sin. Anybody would desire to be saved from the pit, but it is only a child of God who pants to be saved from every false way. We love the salvation of God because it saves us from selfishness, from pride, from lust, from worldliness, bitterness, malice, sloth, and uncleanness. When that salvation is completed in us we shall be "without spot or wrinkle or any such thing," and shall be renewed in holiness after the image of Christ Jesus our Lord. That its great aim is our perfection in holiness is the main beauty of salvation. We would be content to be poor, but we cannot be content to be sinful; we could be resigned to sickness, but we could not be satisfied to remain in alienation from God. We long for perfection and nothing short of it will content us, and, because this is guaranteed to the believer in the gospel of Christ, we love his salvation, and we would say continually, "Let God be magnified."

I might thus enlarge upon every part of this salvation, and say that it endears itself to us under every aspect, and from every point of view.

We love his salvation because of one or two characteristics in it which especially excite our delight. Foremost is the matchless love displayed in it. Why should the Lord have loved men, such insignificant creatures as they are, compared with the universe? Why should he set his heart upon such nothings? But more, how could he love rebellious men who have wantonly and arrogantly broken his laws? Why should he love them so much as to give up his only begotten? These are things we freely speak of, but who among us knows what is their weight.; "God commendeth his love toward us, in that while we were yet sinners, Christ died for us." I believe that even in heaven, with enlarged faculties, it will be a subject of perpetual wonder to us that ever God could love and save us. And shall we not love the salvation which wells up from the deep fount of the Father's everlasting affection? O brethren, our hearts must be harder than adamant, and made of hell-hardened steel, if we can at once believe that we are saved and yet not love, intensely love the salvation which was devised by Jehovah's heart.

We love his salvation, again, because, in addition to the display of wondrous love, it is so safe a salvation, so real, so true: we have not given heed to cunningly devised fables; we have not chanced our souls upon a fiction. We run no risk when we trust the Savior. Though one of our hymns puts it:--

"Venture on Him, venture wholly,
Let no other trust intrude."

This is only a condescension to the feelings of trembling unbelievers, for there is no venture in it; it is sure and certain. Did God lay on Christ my sin? Was it really punished in him? Then there cannot exist a reason why I should be condemned, but there are ten thousand arguments why I should for ever be "accepted in the beloved." "Who shall lay anything to the charge of God's elect? It is God that justifieth. Who is he that condemneth? It is Christ that died, yea rather, that is risen again, who is even at the right hand of God, who also maketh intercession for us." Substitution is a basis for intelligent confidence; it satisfies both the demand of the law and the fears of conscience; and gives to believers a deep, settled, substantial peace, which cannot be broken. We love this salvation because we feel that it places a foundation of granite beneath our feet instead of the quicksand of human merit. Justice being satisfied is as much our friend as even mercy herself; in fact, all the attributes unite to guarantee our safety.

We love God's salvation, too, because it is so complete. Nothing remains unfinished which is necessary to remove sin from the believer and give him righteousness before God. As far as atonement for sin is concerned, the expiation is most gloriously complete. Remember that remarkable expression of the apostle, where he describes the priests as continually standing at the altar, offering sacrifice year by year, and even day by day, because atonement by such means could never be finished. Such sacrifices could never take away sin; therefore must they be perpetually offered, and the priest must always stand at the altar. "But," saith the apostle, "this man (our great Melchisedec), after he had offered one sacrifice for sin for ever, sat down (for the work was accomplished), sat down at the right hand of God." Jesus has performed what the Aaronic priesthood, in long succession, had failed to do. Though streams of blood might flow from bullock, and from goat, like Kishon's mighty river, and though incense might smoke till the pile thereof was high as Lebanon, with all her goodly cedars, what was there in all this to make propitiation for sin? The work was but shadowed, the real expiation was not offered; it was a fair picture, but the substance itself was not there. But, when our Divine Lord went up to Calvary, and on the cross gave up his body, his soul, his spirit, a sacrifice for sin, he finished transgression, made an end of sin, and brought in everlasting righteousness. Herein, my brethren, we have strong consolation, the immutable things wherein it is impossible for God to lie, his word and oath, are our immovable security. By the atonement we are infallibly, effectually, eternally saved, for he has become the "author of eternal salvation, unto all them that obey him." How we love this salvation! Our inmost heart rejoines in it! I rejoice to preach it, brethren, and I delight to muse upon it, appropriating it to myself by faith in solitary thought. How it makes the tears stream down one's cheeks with joy, to think "He loved me, and gave himself for me: he took my sins, and he destroyed them, they have ceased to be, they are annihilated, they are blotted out like a cloud, and like a thick cloud have they vanished." Surely, we should have lost sanity, as well as grace, if we did not love this salvation, beyond the choicest joys of earth.

II. Thus I have described the character, and now, secondly, we will meditate on THE SAYING. Every nation has its idiom, every language has its shibboleth, almost every district has its proverb. Behold the idiom of gracious souls, listen to their household word, their common proverb,--it is this, "Let God be magnified! Let God be magnified!"

Let us proceed at once to the consideration of it, I trust it belongs to us, it certainly does if we love his salvation.

Observe that this is a saying which is founded upon truth and justice. "Let God be magnified," for it is he that saved us, and not we ourselves. We trace our salvation not to our ministers, nor to any pretentious priesthood. None can divide the honors of grace, for the Lord alone hath turned our captivity. He decreed our salvation, planned it, arranged it, executed it, applied it, and secures it. From beginning to end salvation is of the Lord, therefore, let God be magnified. Moreover, the Lord wrought salvation that he might be magnified thereby. It was God's object in salvation to glorify his own name. "Not for your sakes do I this, O house of Israel." Truly we desire that the Lord's end and purpose should be fully subserved, for it is his well-deserved due. O thou who hast bled upon the cross, may thy throne be glorious! O thou who wast despised and rejected of men, be thou extolled, and be thou very high. Thou deservest all glory, great and merciful God. Such a gift, such a sacrifice, such a work; thou oughtest indeed to be lauded and had in honor by all the intelligent universe. The saying is settled deep in truth, and established in right.

This saying is naturally suggested by love. It is because we love his salvation that we say, "The Lord be magnified." You cannot love God without desiring to magnify him, and I am sure that you cannot know that you are saved without loving him. For here is a wonder, a central wonder of wonders to many of us, that ever we in particular were saved. I do not think I could be so wonder-struck and amazed at the salvation of you all as at my own. I should know it to be infinite mercy that saved any one of you, or all of you, I say I should know it, but in my own case I feel it is an unspeakable and inconceivably great mercy which has saved me; and I suppose each brother here, each sister here will feel a special love to Christ from the fact of being himself or herself an object of his love. We never sing, I am sure, with warmer hearts any hymn in our hymn-book than that one--

]

"What was there in us that could merit esteem,
Or give the Creator delight?
Twas even so Father, we ever must sing,
For so it seemed good in thy sight."

The Lord might have left as he has left others to carry out their own wills, and wilfully to reject the Savior, but since he has made us willing in the day of his power, we are for ever beyond measure under obligations to him. Let us say continually, "The Lord be magnified, which hath pleasure in the prosperity of his servants."

Moreover, this saying of our text is deeply sincere and practical. I am sure David did not wish to see hypocrites multiplied; but such would be the case if men merely said, "Let God be magnified," and did not mean it. No doubt there is a great deal among professors of mere expression without meaning; it is sadly evident that much godly talk is only talk, but it ought not so to be. You know, how often charity is assumed, and men say to the naked and hungry, "Be ye warmed, and be ye filled;" but they give nothing to the poor, except vain words, which cannot profit them. So, too, often professors will sing:--

"Fly abroad, thou mighty gospel,
Win and conquer, never cease;
May thy lasting wide dominion
Multiply and still increase."

and so on; but there it ends; they have said it, but they have done nothing for it. Now, as he is condemned as a hypocrite who merely utters words of charity without deeds, so is he who shall say, "Let God be magnified," but who does not put forth his hand and throw in all his energies to promote that which he professes to desire. The wish must be, and oh! if we are saved by grace, it will be sincere, intense, and fervent in every believing heart.

Moreover, it must not only be sincere, but it must be paramount. I take it that there is nothing which a Christian man should say continually, except this, "Let God be magnified." That which a man may say continually is assuredly the master-thought of his mind. Listen to the cherubim and seraphim; they continually do cry, "Holy! Holy! Holy! Lord God of Hosts!" Why cry they thus continually? Is it not because it is their chief business, their highest delight? So should it be with us; our end and aim should ever be to glorify him who redeemed us by his most precious blood. You are a citizen, but you are more a Christian. You are a father, but you are more a child of God. You are a laborer, but you are most of all a servant of the Most High. You are wealthy, but yet more enriched by his covenant. You are poor, but you are most emphatically rich if Christ is yours. The first, chief, leading, lordly, master-thought within you must be this, "Let God be magnified."

And, brethren, the text tells us this must be continual. How earnest you feel about the cause of Christ when you have heard an inspiriting sermon, but how long does it last? Ah, those old days of mission enterprise, when Exeter Hall used to be crowded because missionaries had interesting stories to tell of what God was doing--what enthusiasm there used to be--where is it now? Where is it now? Echo might well answer "where is it now?" To a great degree it has departed. The zeal of many rises and falls like a barometer. They are hot as fire, and cold as ice, in the shortest space; their fervor is as transient as the flame of thorns, and hence it is very hard to turn it to any practical account. Oh, for more of the deep-seated principle of intense love to God's salvation, steady and abiding, which shall make a man say continually, "Let God be magnified." We would desire to wake up in the morning with this on our lips. We would begin with the enquiry, "What can I do to magnify God this day?" We would be in business in the middle of the day, and yet never lose the one desire to magnify God. We would return to our family at night, urged by the same impulse, "How can I magnify God in my household?" If I lie sick, I would feel that I must magnify God by patience; if I rise from that bed, I would feel the sweet obligation to magnify him by gratitude; if I take a prominent position, I am doubly bound to magnify him who makes me a leader to his dock, and, if I be unknown and obscure in the church, I must with equal zeal magnify him by a conscientious discharge of the duties of my position. Oh, to have one end always before us, and to press forward towards it, neither turning to the right hand nor to the left. As though we were balls shot out of a rifled cannon we would rush on, never hesitating or turning aside, but flying with all speed towards the center of the target. May our spirits be impelled by a divine energy towards this one only thing. The Lord be magnified! whether I live or die, may God be glorified in me!

According to the text, this saying should be universal among the saints. It should be the mark of all those that love God's salvation, pertaining not to a few who shall be chosen to minister in public, but to all those whom grace has renewed. All of us, women as well as men, illiterate as well as learned, poor as well as rich, silent as well as eloquent, should after our own ability say, "Let

God be magnified." Oh, would to God we were all stirred up to this! Our churches seem to be half alive. It is a dreadful thing to read of the punishment practiced by ancient tyrants when they tied a living man to a corpse, and he had to go about with this corpse strapped to him, and rotting under his nostrils, and yet that is too often the condition of the living ones in our churches: they are bound by ties of church union to a portion of the church which is spiritually dead, though not so manifestly corrupt as to render it possible for us to cut it off. The tares, which we may not root up, hamper and dwarf the wheat. O God, the Holy Ghost, make the church alive right through, from the crown of its head to the sole of its foot, so that the whole church may cry continually, "Let God be magnified."

You will notice that the cry is an absolute one. It does not say, let God be magnified by me if he will please to make me successful in business, and happy, and healthy, but it leaves it open. Only let God be magnified, and he may do what he wills with me. As a poor soldier in the regiment of Christ, I only care for this that HE may win the day, and if I see him riding on his white horse and know that he is conquering, though I lie bleeding and wounded in a ditch, I will clap my hands and say, "Blessed be the name of the Lord." Though I be poor, and despised, and reproached, this shall compensate for all, if I can only hear that "him hath God highly exalted, and given him a name that is above every name; that at the name of Jesus every knee should bow, of things in heaven, and things in earth, and things under the earth; that every tongue should confess that Jesus Christ is Lord, to the glory of God the Father." I would close my eyes in death, and say, my soul is satisfied with favor and hath all she wants if Jesus be exalted. Remember how David put it: when he had said "Let the whole earth be filled with his glory," he added, "Amen and amen. The prayers of David, the son of Jesse, are ended." He desired no more than that; that was the ultimatum of his wishes. Beloved, I trust it is the same with us.

Nor is there any limit as to place or persons. My heart says, "Let God be magnified among the Wesleyans! The Lord be magnified among the Independents! The Lord be magnified among the Episcopalians! The Lord be magnified among the Baptists!" We pray very earnestly, "Let God be magnified in the Tabernacle," but we would not forget to cry, "Let God be magnified in all parts of London, in all counties of England, and Scotland, and Ireland." We desire no restriction as to race--let God be magnified both in France and in Prussia; in Turkey and in Italy; in the United States and in Australia; among any and every people! So that God's name be magnified, what matters it how or where? We know no politics but this, "Let God be magnified." All nationalities sink before our relation to our God. Christians are cosmopolitan; we are burgesses of the New Jerusalem--there is our citizenship; we are freemen of the entire new creation. What is all else to God's glory! So long as the Lord is glorified, let the empires go and the emperors with them; let nations rise or fall, so long as he comes whose right it is to reign; let ancient dynasties pass away, if his throne is but exalted. We would never dictate to the God of history; let him write out as he pleases the stanzas of his own august poem, but let this always be the close of every verse, "The Lord be magnified! The Lord be magnified! The Lord be magnified!" This is the continual saying of all them that love his salvation.

III. We had much to say under our second head, but time will not tarry for us; therefore we must proceed to the last, which is THE WISH. Holy David, and David's perfect Lord both wish that we may say, "Let God be magnified." This wish is promoted by an anxiety for God's glory; it is a most holy wish, and it ought to be fulfilled. I shall ask your attention only for a minute or two to the reasons of the wish. Why should it be wished?

First, because it always ought to be said, "Let God be magnified." It is only right, and according to the fitness of things, that God should be magnified in the world which he himself created. Such a handiwork deserves admiration from all who behold it. But when he new-made the world, and especially when he laid the foundation of his new palace in the fair colors of Jesus' blood, and adorned it with the sapphires of grace and truth; he had a double claim upon our praise. He gave his Son to redeem us, and for this let his praise be great and endless. Things are out of joint if God the Redeemer be not glorified. Surely the wheels of nature revolve amiss, if God the loving and gracious be not greatly magnified. As every right-hearted man desires to see right and justice done, therefore does he wish that those who love God's salvation may say continually, "Let God be magnified."

But, we wish it next, because it always needs saying. The world is dull and sleepy, and utterly indifferent to the glory of God in the work of redemption. We need to tell it over and over and over again, that God is great in the salvation of his people. There are many, Who will rise up and deny God's Glory; revilers of all sorts abound in rage; but over and above their clamor, let the voice of truth be heard, "Let God be magnified." They cry, "the Bible is worn out." They doubt its inspiration, they question the deity of Christ, they set up new gods that have lately come up, that our fathers knew not. Let us confront them with the truth, let us oppose them with the gospel, let us overcome them through the blood of the Lamb, using this one only war-cry, "Let God be magnified." Everywhere in answer to all blasphemy, in direct conflict with profanity, let us lift up this voice with heart and soul. "Let God be magnified."

And, again, we desire this, because the saying of this continually does good to the sayers. He who blesses God blesses himself. We cannot serve God with the heart without serving ourselves most practically. Nothing, brethren, is more for your benefit than to spend and be spent for the promotion of the divine honor.

Then, again, this promotes the welfare of God's creatures. We ought to desire to spread the knowledge of God, because the dark places of the earth will never cease to be the habitation of cruelty till they become the temple of the Lord of hosts. Myriads are dying, while we are sitting complacently here souls are passing into eternity unforgiven. The wrath of God is abiding still upon the sons of men, for they know not Christ. What stronger motive could there be for desiring that God's name should continually be magnified. I have been told, and I believe it is the general impression, that at this particular time there is a great cessation of the zealous spirit which once ruled among Christians. We have passed over the heroic age, the golden period of missions, and we have come to the time in which the church rests upon her oars, takes matters quietly, what if I say regards them hopelessly? Very few young men are now coming forward, at least in our denomination, to offer themselves for missionaries; the funds are barely sustained and nothing more. I fear there is among those who conduct the affairs of missions too little of faith, and too much of bastard prudence, which last had better be banished to the bottomless pit at once, for it has long been the clog upon the chariot wheels of the gospel. Faith is too much cast into the background, and the work is viewed in a mercantile light, as though it were a rule of three sum--so much money and so many men, and then so many conversions, whereas it is not so. God worketh not according to arithmetical rules and calculations. There is, I fear, on the whole, a general backsliding from the right state; and what a sad thing it is that it should be so, since at our best we were never too zealous. Few can bring the charge of fanaticism against the English Baptists: we have been too solid, if not stolid, for that. I almost wish it were possible for us to err in that direction, for if an evil it would at any rate be a novelty, if not an improvement.

Why is this, and whence comes it? Years ago our fathers compassed this Jericho, they passed round it according to the Master's bidding, and are we about, after having done the same these many years, to relinquish the task, and lose the result? Do we fear that the walls will never fall to the ground? Brethren, I believe it is the duty of the Christian church to go on working quite as earnestly and zealously and believingly, if there be no conversions, as if half the world were transformed in a twelve month. Our business is not to create a harvest but to sow the seed; if the wheat does not come up, if we have sown it aright, our Master does not hold us responsible. If missions had been an utter failure it would be no sort of reason why we should give them up. There was a great failure when the hosts of Israel, on the first occasion, went round Jericho; a dreadful failure when they marched round the city twice, and the walls shook not; it was an aggravated failure when they had compassed it four times; it was a most discouraging defeat when they had tramped round it five times; and, on the whole, a breakdown, almost enough to drive them to despair, when they had performed the circuit six times and not a single brick had stirred in the wall. Yes; but then the seventh day made amends, when the people shouted and all the walls fell flat to the ground. Brethren, it is not yet time to shout, but we must continue marching and say, "Let God be magnified." The longer the walls stand, and the longer we wait, the louder will be our shout when they lie prostrate before us, as they shall; for, "Verily, verily, I say unto you there shall not be one stone left upon another that shall not be cast down." Remember the Greeks when they attacked old Troy: ye have the record in ancient story. They waited many years till their ships had well nigh rotted on the seas, but the prowess of Hector and the armed men of Troy kept back the "King of men," and all the hosts of the avengers. Suppose that after nine years had dragged along their weary length, the chiefs of the Greeks had said, "It is of no avail, the city is impregnable! O Pelasgi, back to your fair lands washed by the blue Aegean, you will never subdue the valor of Ilium." No.; but they persevered in the weary siege, with feats of strength and schemes of art, till at last they saw the city burned and heard the dire lament: "Troy was, but is no more"

Let us still continue to attack the adversary. We are few, but strength lies not in numbers. The Eternal One has used the few where he has put aside the many. In our weakness lies part of our adaptation to the divine work; only let us gather up fresh faith, and renew our courage and industry, and we shall see greater things than these. "Pshaw," says one, "Protestant Christianity is in a miserable minority, it is ridiculous to suppose it will ever be the dominant religion of the world." We reply, that it is ridiculous, nay blasphemous, to doubt when God has sworn with an oath that "all flesh shall see the salvation of God." God's oath is better evidence than appearances; for, in a moment, if he wills it, he can give such an impetus to the Christian church, that she shall in her enthusiasm spread the gospel, and at the same time he can give such a turn to the human mind, that it shall be as ready to accept the gospel as the church is to spread it. Observe how the church grew during the first few centuries. After the apostles had died you do not find in the next century the name of any very remarkable man, but all Christians then were earnest, and the good cause advanced. They were mostly poor, they were generally illiterate, but they were all missionaries, they were all seeking to glorify God, and, consequently, before long, down went Jupiter, Saturn lost his throne, even Venus was abjured, and the cross, at least nominally, became supreme throughout all Europe. It shall be done again. In the name of the Eternal, let us set up our banners. Oh, ye that love the Lord and his salvation, vow it in your souls, determine it in your hearts, and, God the Holy Spirit being with you, if you have but faith in him, it will be no empty boast, no vain vaunting. God shall speak and it shall be done. The Lord of hosts is with us, the God of Jacob is our refuge; and such being the case, nothing is impossible to us.

May the Lord stir us up with these thoughts, and fling us like firebrands into the midst of his church and the world, to set both on a blaze with love through the love that burns in our hearts. "Let God be magnified." Amen and Amen.

PORTION OF SCRIPTURE READ BEFORE SERMON--Psalm 40.

"Nunc Dimittis"

A Sermon (No. 1014)
Delivered on Lord's-day Morning, October 8th, 1871, by
C. H. SPURGEON,
At the Metropolitan Tabernacle, Newington

"Lord, now lettest thou thy servant depart in peace, according to thy word: for mine eyes have seen thy salvation." - Luke 2:29-30.

BLESSED WERT THOU, O Simeon, for flesh and blood had not revealed this unto thee; neither had it enabled thee so cheerfully to bid the world farewell. The flesh clings to the earth--it is dust, and owns affluity to the ground out of which it was taken; it loathes to part from mother earth. Even old age, with its infirmities, does not make men really willing to depart out of this world. By nature we hold to life with a terrible tenacity; and even when we sigh over the evils of life, and repine concerning its ills, and fancy that we wish ourselves away, it is probable that our readiness to depart lies only upon the surface, but down deep in our hearts we have no will to go. Flesh and blood had not revealed unto Simeon that he saw God's salvation in that babe which he took out of the arms of Mary, and embraced with eager joy. God's grace had taught him that this was the Savior, and God's grace at the same time loosened the cords which bound him to earth, and made him feel the attractions of the better land. Blessed is that man who has received thy grace a meekness for heaven, and a willingness to depart to that better land: let him magnify the Lord who has wrought so great a work in him. As Paul says, "Thanks be unto the Father who hath made us meet to be partakers of the inheritance of the saints in light." Certainly none of us were meet by nature--not even Simeon; the fitness of the venerable man was all the handiwork of God, and so, also, was his anxiety to obtain the inheritance for which God had prepared him. I trust, brethren, while we consider this morning the preparedness of the saints for heaven, and turn over in our mind those reflections which will make us ready to depart, God's Holy Spirit, sent forth from the Father, may make us also willing to leave these mortal shores, and launch upon the eternal sea at the bidding of our Father, God.

We shall note, this morning, first, that every believer may be assured of departing in peace; but that, secondly, some believers feel a special readiness to depart now: "Now lettest thou thy servant depart in peace;" and, thirdly, that there are words of encouragement to produce in us the like readiness: "according to thy word." There are words of Holy Writ which afford richest consolation in prospect of departure.

I. First, then, let us start with the great general principle, which is full of comfort; namely, this, that EVERY BELIEVER MAY BE ASSURED OF ULTIMATELY DEPARTING IN PEACE. This is no privilege peculiar to Simeon, it is common to all the saints, since the grounds upon which this privilege rests are not monopolised by Simeon, but belong to us all.

Observe, first, that all the saints have seen God's salvation, therefore, should they all depart in peace. It is true, we cannot take up the infant Christ into our arms, but he is "formed in us, the hope of glory." It is true, we cannot look upon him with these mortal eyes, but we have seen him with those eyes immortal which death cannot dim--the eyes of our own spirit which have been opened by God's Holy Spirit. A sight of Christ with the natural eye is not saving, for thousands saw him and then cried, "Crucify him, crucify him." After all, it was in Simeon's case the spiritual eye that saw, the eye of faith that truly beheld the Christ of God; for there were others in the temple who saw the babe; there was the priest who performed the act of circumcision, and the other officials who gathered round the group; but I do not know that any of them saw God's salvation. They saw the little innocent child that was brought there by its parents, but they saw nothing remarkable in him; perhaps, Simeon and Anna, alone of all those who were in the temple, saw with the inward eye the real Anointed of God revealed as a feeble infant. So, though you and I miss the outward sight of Christ, we need not regret it, it is but secondary as a privilege; if with the inner sight we have seen the Incarnate God, and accepted him as our salvation, we are blessed with holy Simeon. Abraham saw Christ's day before it dawned, and even thus, after it has passed, we see it, and with faithful Abraham we are glad. We have looked unto him, and we are lightened. We have beheld the

Lamb of God which taketh away the sins of the world. In the "despised and rejected of men" we have seen the anointed Savior; in the crucified and buried One, who afterwards rose again, and ascended into glory, we have seen salvation, full, free, finished. Why, therefore, should we think ourselves less favored than Simeon? From like causes like results shall spring: we shall depart in peace, for we have seen God's salvation.

Moreover, believers already enjoy peace as much as ever Simeon did. No man can depart in peace who has not lived in peace; but he who has attained peace in life shall possess peace in death, and an eternity of peace after death. "Being justified by faith we have peace with God through our Lord Jesus Christ." Jesus has bequeathed us peace, saying, "Peace I leave with you, my peace I give unto you." "For he is our peace," and "the fruit of the Spirit is peace." We are reconciled unto God by the death of his Son. Whatever peace flowed in the heart of Simeon, I am sure it was not of a diviner nature than that which dwells in the bosom of every true believer. If sin be pardoned, the quarrel is ended; if the atonement is made, then is peace established, a peace covenanted to endure for ever. We are now led in the paths of peace; we walk the King's highway, of which it is written, "no lion shall be there;" we are led beside the still waters, and made to lie down in green pastures. We feel no slavish fear of God, though he be "a consuming fire" even to us; we tremble no longer to approach into his presence, who deigns to be our Father. The precious blood upon the mercy-seat has made it a safe place for us to resort at all times; boldness has taken the place of trembling. The throne of God is our rejoicing, though once it was our terror.

"Once twas a seat of dreadful wrath,
And shot devouring flame;
Our God appear'd consuming fire,'
And vengeance was his name."

Therefore, brethren, having peace with God, we may be sure that we shall "depart in peace." We need not fear that the God of all consolation, who has already enriched us in communion with himself, and peace in Christ Jesus, will desert us at the last. He will help us to sing a sweet swan-song, and our tabernacle shall be gently taken down, to be rebuilt more enduringly in the fair country beyond Jordan.

Furthermore, we may rest assured of the same peace as that which Simeon possessed, since we are, if true believers, equally God's servants. The text says, "Lord, now lettest thou thy servant depart in peace." But, in this case, one servant cannot claim a privilege above the rest of the household. The same position towards God, the same reward from God. Simeon, a servant; you also, my brother, a servant; he who saith to Simeon, "depart in peace," will say also the same to you. The Lord is always very considerate towards his old servants, and takes care of them when their strength faileth. The Amalekite of old had a servant who was an Egyptian, and when he fell sick he left him, and he would have perished if David had not had compassion on him; but our God is no Amalekite slave-owner, neither doth he cast off his wornout servants. "Even to your old age I am he; and even to hoar hairs will I carry you: I have made, and I will bear; even I will carry, and will deliver you." David felt this, for he prayed to God, and said, "Now, also, when I am old and gray-headed, O God, forsake me not." If thou hast been clothed in thy Lord's livery of grace, and taught to obey his will, he will never leave thee, nor forsake thee; he will not sell thee into the hands of thine adversary, nor suffer thy soul to perish. A true master counts it a part of his duty to protect his servants, and our great Lord and Prince will show himself strong on the behalf of the very least of all his followers, and will bring them every one into the rest which remaineth for his people. Do you really serve God? Remember, "his servants ye are to whom ye obey." Are ye taught of the Spirit to obey the commandments of love? Do you strive to walk in holiness? If so, fear not death; it shall have no terrors to you. All the servants of God shall depart in peace.

There is also another reflection which strengthens our conviction that all believers shall depart in peace, namely, this: that up till now all things in their experience have been according to God's word. Simeon's basis of hope for a peaceful departure was "according to thy word;" and, surely, no Scripture is of private interpretation, or to be reserved for one believer to the exclusion of the rest? The promises of God, which are "Yea and amen in Christ Jesus," are sure to all the seed: not to some of the children is the promise made, but all the grace-born are heirs. There are not special promises hedged round and set apart for Simeon and a few saints of old time, but with all who are in Christ, their federal head, the covenant is made, and stands "ordered in all things and sure." If, then, Simeon, as a believer in the Lord, had a promise that he should depart in peace, I have also a like promise if I am in Christ. What God hath said in his word Simeon lays hold of, and none can say him nay; but if, with the same grace-given faith, I also grasp it for myself, who shall challenge my right? God will not violate his promise to one of his people any more than to another, and, consequently, when our turn shall come to gather up our feet in the bed and to resign our spirit, some precious passage in sacred writ shall be as a rod and a staff to us that we may fear no evil.

These four considerations, gathered out of the text itself, may give fourfold certainty to the assurance that every believer, at the hour of his departure, shall possess peace.

For a moment, review attentively the words of the aged saint: they have much instruction in them. Every believer shall in death depart in the same sense as Simeon did. The word here used is suggestive and encouraging: it may be applied either to escape from confinement, or to deliverance from toil. The Christian man in the present state is like a bird in a cage: his body imprisons his soul. His spirit, it is true, ranges heaven and earth, and laughs at the limits of matter, space, and time; but for all that, the flesh is a poor scabbard unworthy of the glittering soul, a mean cottage unfit for a princely spirit, a clog, a burden, and a fetter. When we would watch and pray, we find full often that the spirit is willing but the flesh is weak. "We that are in this body do groan." The fact is, we are caged birds; but the day cometh when the great Master shall open the cage door, and release his prisoners. We need not dread the act of unfastening the door, for it will give to our soul the liberty for which it only pines, and then, with the wings of a dove, covered with silver, and its feathers with yellow gold, though aforetime it had lien among the pots, it will soar into its native air, singing all the way with a rapture beyond imagination. Simeon looked upon dying as a mode of being let loose--a deliverance out of durance vile, an escape from captivity, a release from bondage. The like redemption shall be dealt unto us. How often does my soul feel like an unhatched chick, shut up within a narrow shell, in darkness and discomfort! The life within labors hard to chip and break the shell, to know a little more of the great universe of truth, and see in clearer light the infinite of divine love. Oh, happy day, when the shell shall be broken, and the soul, complete in the image of Christ, shall enter into the freedom for which she is preparing! We look for that, and we shall have it. God, who gave us to aspire to holiness and spirituality and to likeness to himself, never implanted those aspirations in us out of mockery. He meant to gratify these holy longings, or, else, he would not have excited them. Ere long we, like Simeon, shall depart--that is, we shall be set free to go in peace.

I said that the word meant also a release from toil. It is as though Simeon had been standing at the table of his Master like a servant waiting on his Lord. You know the parable in which Christ says that the master does not first bid his servant sit down and eat bread, but commands him thus, "Gird thyself and serve me." See then, Simeon stands yonder, girt and serving his Master; but by-and-by, when the Master sees fit, he turns round and says to Simeon, "Now thou mayest depart, and take thine own meat, thy work is done." Or, we may use another simile, and picture Simeon sitting at the King's gate, like Mordecai, ready for any errand which may be appointed him, but at length his time of attendance expires, and the great monarch bids him depart in peace. Or, yet again, we may view him as a reaper toiling amid the harvest beneath a burning sun, parched with thirst and wearied with labor, and lo! the great Boaz came into the field, and, having saluted his servant, says to him, "Thou hast fulfilled like an hireling thy day: take thou thy wage, and depart in peace." The like shall happen to all true servants of Christ; they shall rest from their labors where no weariness shall vex them, "neither shall the sun light on them, nor any heat." They shall enter into the joy of their Lord, and enjoy the rest which remaineth for them. There is much of comfortable thought if we meditate upon this.

But, note the words again. You perceive that the departure of the child of God is appointed of the Lord. "Now lettest thou thy servant depart." The servant must not depart from his labor without his Masters permission, else would he be a runaway, dishonest to his position. The good servant dares not stir till his Master says, "Depart in peace." Simeon was content to wait till he received permission to depart, and it becomes us all to acquiesce cheerfully in the Lord's appointment, whether he lengthens or shortens, our life. It is certain that without the Lord's will no power can remove us. No wind from the wilderness shall drive our souls into the land of darkness, no fiends with horrid clamor can drag us down to the abyss beneath, no destruction that wasting at noonday, or pestilence waiting in darkness can cut short our mortal career. We shall not die till God shall say to us, "My child, depart from the field of service, and the straitness of this thy tabernacle, and enter into rest." Till God commands us we cannot die, and when he bids us go it shall be sweet for us to leave this world.

Note, further, that the words before us clearly show that the believer's departure is attended with a renewal of this divine benediction. "Depart in peace," saith God. It is a farewell, such as we give to a friend: it is a benediction, such as Aaron, the priest of God, might pronounce over a suppliant whose sacrifice was accepted. Eli said unto Hannah, "Go in peace, and the God of Israel grant thee thy petition that thou hast asked of him." Around the sinner's death-bed the tempest thickens, and he hears the rumblings of the eternal storm: his soul is driven away, either amid the thunderings of curses loud and deep, or else in the dread calm which evermore forebodes the hurricane. "Depart, ye cursed," is the horrible sound which is in his ears. But, not so the righteous. He feels the Father's hand of benediction on his head, and underneath him are the everlasting arms.

The best wine with him is kept to the last. At eventide it is light; and, as his sun is going down, it grows more glorious, and lights up all the surroundings with a celestial glow, whereat bystanders wonder, and exclaim "Let me die the death of the righteous, and let my last end be like his." That pilgrim sets out upon a happy journey to whom Jehovah saith, "Depart in peace." This is a sole finger laid upon the closing eyelid by a tender father, and it ensures a happy waking, where eyes are never wet with tears.

I cannot detain you longer over these words: suffice it to add, that whatever belonged to Simeon in this benediction must not be regarded as peculiar to him alone, but as, in their measure, the possession of all believers. "This is the heritage of the servants of the Lord, and their righteousness is of me, saith the Lord."

II. But now, secondly, we remind you, that SOME BELIEVERS ARE CONSCIOUS OF A SPECIAL READINESS TO DEPART IN PEACE.

When do they feel this? Answer: first, when their graces are vigorous. All the graces are in all Christians, but they are not all there in the same proportion, nor are they at all times in the same degree of strength. In certain believers faith is strong and active. Now, when faith becomes "the evidence of things not seen," and "the substance of things hoped for," then the soul is sure to say, "Lord, now lettest thou thy servant depart in peace." Faith brings the clusters of Eschol into the desert, and makes the tribes long for the land that floweth with milk and honey. When the old Gauls had drunk of the wines of Italy, they said, "Let us cross the Alps, and take possession of the vineyards, which yield such generous draughts." So, when faith makes us realize the joy's of heaven, then it is that our soul stands waiting on the wing, watching for the signal from the glory-land.

The same is true of the grace of hope, for hope peers into the things invisible. She brings near to us the golden gates of the Eternal City. Like Moses, our hope climbs to the top of Pisgah, and beholds the Canean of the true Israel. Moses had a delightful vision of the promised land when he gazed from Nebo's brow, and saw it all from Dan to Beersheba: so also hope drinks in the charming prospect of the goodly fund and Lebanon, and then she exclaims exultingly, "Lord, now lettest thou thy servant depart in peace." Heaven realised and anticipated by hope renders the thought of departure most precious to the heart.

And the like, also, is the effect of the grace of love upon us. Love puts the heart, like a sacrifice, on the altar, and then she fetches heavenly fire, and kindles it; and, as soon as ever the heart begins to burn and glow like a sacrifice, what is the consequence? Why, it ascends like pillars of smoke up to the throne of God. It is the very instinct of love to draw us nearer to the person whom we love; and, when love towards God pervades the soul, then the spirit cries, "Make haste, my beloved, be thou like a roe or a young hart upon the mountains of separation." Perfect love, casting out all fear, cries, "Up, and away."

"Let me be with thee, where thou art,
My Savior my eternal rest!
Then only will this longing heart
Be fully and for ever blest."

I might thus mention all the graces, but suffer one of them to suffice! one which is often overlooked, but is priceless as the gold of Ophir--it is the grace of humility. Is it strange that the lower a man sinks in his own esteem the higher does he rise before his God? Is it not written, "Blessed are the poor in spirit, for theirs is the kingdom of heaven?" Simeon had no conceit of his own importance in the world, else he would have said, "Lord, let me stay, and be an apostle. Surely I shall be needed at this juncture to lend my aid in the auspicious era which has just commenced?" But no, he felt himself so little so inconsiderable, that now that he had attained his heart's wish and seen God's salvation, he was willing to depart in peace. Humility by making us lie low helps us to think highly of God, and, consequently, to desire much to be with God. O to have our graces always flourishing, for then shall we always be ready to depart, and willing to be offered up. Lack of grace entangles us, but to abound in grace is to live in the suburbs of the New Jerusalem.

Another time, when believers are thus ready to go, is when their assurance is clear. It is not always so with even the most mature Christians, and some true saints have not yet attained to assurance; they are truly saved, and possess a genuine faith, but as assurance is the cream of faith, the milk has not stood long enough to produce the cream; they have not yet come to the flower of assurance, for their faith is but a tender plant. Give a man assurance of heaven and he will be eager to enjoy it. While he doubts his own security, he wants to linger here. He is like the Psalmist when he asked that God would permit him to recover his strength before he went hence, and was no more. Some things were not yet in order with David, and he would stay awhile till they were. But, when the ship is all loaded, the crew on board, and the anchor heaved, the favoring breeze is desired that the barque may speed on its voyage. When a man is prepared for his journey, ready to depart, he does not care to linger long in these misty valleys, but pants for the sunny summits of the mount of God, whereon standeth the palace of the Great King. Let a man know that he is resting upon the precious blood of Christ, let him by diligent self-examination perceive in himself the marks of regeneration, and by the witness of his own spirit and by the infallible witness of the Holy Ghost bearing witness with his own spirit, let him be certified that he is born of God, and the natural consequence will be that he will say, "Now let me loose from all things here below and let me enter into the rest which is assuredly my own." O you that have lost your assurance by negligent living, by falling into sin, or by some other form of backsliding, I do not wonder that you hug the world, for you are afraid you have no other portion; but with those who read their titles clear to mansions in the skies it will be otherwise. They will not ask to linger in this place of banishment, but will sing in their hearts, as we did just now:

"Jerusalem my happy home,
Name ever dear to me;
when shall my labors have an end,
In joy and peace and thee?"

Beloved, furthermore, saints feel most their readiness to go when their communion with Christ is near and sweet; when Christ hides himself we are afraid to talk of dying, or of heaven; but, when he only shows himself through the lattices, and we can see those eyes which are "as the eyes of doves by the rivers of water, washed with milk and fitly set;" when our own soul melteth even at that hazy sight of him, as through a glass darkly. Oh then we fain would be at home, and our soul crieth out for the day when her eyes shall see the King in his beauty, in the land that is very far off. Have you never felt the heavenly homesickness? Have you never pined for the home-bringing? Surely, when your heart has been full of the bridegroom's beauty, and your soul has been ravished with his dear and ever precious love, you have said: "When shall the day break, and the shadows flee away? Why are his chariots so long in coming?" You have swooned, as it were, with love-sickness for your precious Savior, thirsting to see him as he is, and to be like him. The world is black when Christ is fair; it is a poor heap of ashes when he is altogether lovely to us. When a precious Christ is manifested to our spirits, we feel that we could see Jesus and die. Put out these eyes, there is nothing more for them to see when they have seen him. "Black sun," said Rutherford, "black moon, black stars, but inconceivably bright and glorious Lord Jesus." How often did that devout man write words of this sort: "Oh if I had to swim through seven hells to reach him, if he would but say to me, like Peter, Come unto me,' I would go unto him not only on the sea, but on the boiling floods of hell, if I might but reach him, and come to him." I will pause here and give you his own words: "I profess to you I have no rest, I have no ease, till I be over head and ears in love's ocean. If Christ's love (that fountain of delight) were laid as open to me as I would wish, Oh, how I would drink, and drink abundantly.! I half call his absence cruel; and the mask and veil on Christ's face a cruel covering that hideth such a fair, fair face from a sick soul. I dare not upbraid him, but his absence is a mountain of iron upon my heavy heart. Oh, when shall we meet? Oh, how long is it to the dawning of the marriage day? O sweet Lord Jesus, take wide steps; O my Lord, come over the mountains at one stride! O my Beloved, be like a roe, or a young hart, on the mountains of separation. Oh, if he would fold the heavens together like an old cloak, and shovel time and days out of the way, and make ready in haste the Lamb's wife for her Husband! Since he looked upon me my heart is not mine; he hath run away to heaven with it." When these strong throes, these ardent pangs of insatiable desire come upon a soul that is fully saturated with Christ's love, through having been made to lean its head upon his bosom, and to receive the kisses of his mouth, then is the time when the soul saith, "Lord, now lettest thou thy servant depart in peace."

So again, beloved, saints have drawn their anchor up and spread their sails, when they have been made to hold loose by all there is in this world; and that is generally when they hold fastest by the world to come. To many this world is very sweet, very fair, but God puts bitters into the cup of his children; when their nest is soft, he fills it with thorns to make them long to fly. Alas, that it should be so, but some of God's servants seem as if they had made up their minds to find a rest beneath the moon. They are moon-struck who hope to do so. All the houses in this plague-stricken land are worm-eaten and let in the rain and wind: my soul longeth to find a rest among the ivory palaces of thy land, O Immanuel.

Brethren, it often happens that the loss of dear friends, or the treachery of those we trusted, or bodily sickness, or depression of spirit, may help to unloose the holdfasts which enchain us to this life; and then we are enabled to say with David in one of the most precious little Psalms in the whole Book, the 131st, "I have behaved and quieted myself as a child that is weaned of his mother, my soul is even as a weaned child." I have often thought that if David had said, "my soul is even as a weaning child," it would have been far more like most of God's people. But to be weaned, quite weaned from the world, to turn away from her consolations altogether, this it is which makes us cry, "Lord, now lettest thou thy servant depart in peace." Even as the psalmist when he said, "And now, Lord, what wait I for? my hope is in thee."

Again, saints are willing to depart when their work is almost done. This will not be the case with many here present, perhaps, but it was so with Simeon. Good old man! He had been very constant in his devotions, but on this occasion he came into the temple, and there, it is said, he took the child in his arms, and blessed God. Once more he delivered his soul of its adoration--once more he blended his praise with the songs of angels. When he had done that, he openly confessed his faith: another important work of every believer--for he said, "Mine eyes have seen thy salvation." He bore public testimony to the child Jesus, and declared that he should be "a light to lighten the Gentiles." Having done that, he bestowed his fatherly benediction upon the child's parents, Joseph and his mother; he blessed them, and said unto Mary "Behold, this child is set for the fall and rising again of many in Israel." Now, we read that David, after he had served his generation, fell on sleep; it is time for man to sleep when his life's work is finished. Simeon felt he had done all: he had blessed God; he had declared his faith; he had borne testimony to Christ; he had bestowed his benediction upon godly people; and so he said, "Now, Lord, lettest thou thy servant depart in peace." Ah, Christian people, you will never be willing to go if you are idle. You lazy lie-a-beds, who do little or nothing for Christ, you sluggish servants, whose garden is overgrown with weeds, no wonder that you do not want to see your master! Your sluggishness accuses you, and makes you cowards. Only he who has put out his talents to good interest will be willing to render an account of his stewardship. But when a man feels, without claiming any merit, that he has fought a good fight, finished his course, and kept the faith, then will he rejoice in the crown which is laid up for him in heaven, and he will long to wear it. Throw your strength into the Lord's work, dear brethren--all your strength; spare none of your powers: let body, soul, and spirit be entirely consecrated to God, and used at their utmost stretch. Get through your day's work, for the sooner you complete it, and have fulfilled like an hireling your day, the more near and sweet shall be the time when the shadows lengthen, and God shall say to you, as a faithful servant, "Depart in peace!"

One other matter, I think, helps to make saints willing to go, and that is when they see or foresee the prosperity of the church of God. Good old Simeon saw that Christ was to be a light to lighten the Gentiles, and to be the glory of his people Israel; and, therefore, he said, "Lord, lettest now thy servant depart in peace." I have known many a godly deacon who has seen a church wither and decay, its ministry become unprofitable, and its membership become divided; the dear old man has poured out his soul in agony before God, and when at last the Lord has sent a man to seek the good of Israel, and the church has been built up, he has been overjoyed, and he has said, "now lettest thou thy servant depart in peace." It must have reconciled John Knox to die when he had seen the reformation safely planted throughout all Scotland. It made dear old Latimer, as he stood on the fagot, feel happy when he could say, "Courage, brother, we shall this day light such a candle in England as shall never be blown out." "Pray for the peace of Jerusalem," Ay, that we do, and we vehemently desire her prosperity, and if we can see Christ glorified, error defeated, truth established, sinners saved, and saints sanctified our spirit feels she has all she wishes. Like dying, David, when we have said, "Let the whole earth be filled with his glory," we can fall back upon the pillows and die, for our prayers like those of David the son of Jesse are ended. Let us pray for this peace and this prosperity, and when we see it come, it shall bring calm and rest to our spirits, so that we shall be willing to depart in peace.

III. I shall call your attention now, for a little while, to the third point, that THERE ARE WORDS TO ENCOURAGE US TO THE LIKE READINESS TO DEPART. "According to thy word." Now let us go to the Bible, and take from it seven choice words all calculated to cheer our hearts in the prospect of departure, and the first is Psalm 33:4; "Yea, though I walk through the valley of the shadow of death, I will fear no evil: for thou art with me; thy rod and thy staff they comfort me." "We walk"--the Christian does not quicken his pace when he dies; he walked before, and he is not afraid of death, so he calmly walks on. It is a walk through a "shadow." There is no substance in death, it is only a shade. Who needs fear a shadow? It is not a lonely walk--"Thou art with me." Neither is it a walk that need cause us terror; "I will fear no evil:" not only is there no evil, but no fear shall cloud my dying hours. It shall be a departure full of comfort: "Thy rod and thy staff"--a duplicate means shall give us a fullness of consolation. "Thy rod and thy staff they comfort me."

Take another text, and so follow the direction, "According to thy word." Psalm 37:37: "Mark the perfect man, and behold the upright: for the end of that man is peace." If we are perfect, that is sincere; if we are upright, that is honest in heart; our end then assuredly be peace.

Take another word, Psalm 116:15: "Precious in the sight of the Lord is the death of his saints." It is no ordinary thing for a saint to die; it is a spectacle which the eyes of God are delighted with. As king's delight in their pearls and diamonds, and count them precious, so the death-beds of the saints are God's precious things.

Take another, Isaiah 57:2: "He shall enter into peace: they shall rest in their beds, each one walking in his uprightness." Here is an entrance into peace for the saint, rest on his dying, bed, rest for his body in the grave, rest for his spirit in the bosom of his Lord, and a walking in his uprightness in the immortality above. "According to thy word." Oh, what force there is in these few syllables! When you can preach the word of God you must prevail. Nothing has such marrow and fatness in it as a text of Scripture. It has a force of comfort all its own. Consider also 1 Corinthians 3:22: "For all things are your's: whether Paul, or Apollos, or Cephas, or the world, or life, or death, or things present, or things to come; all are your's." Now, if death is yours, there can be no sort of reason why you should be afraid of that which is made over to you as a part of your inheritance.

Take the fifteenth chapter and fifty-fourth verse of the same epistle: "So when this corruptible shall have put on incorruption, and this mortal shall have put on immortality, then shall be brought to pass the saying that is written, Death is swallowed up in victory. O death, where is thy sting? O grave, where is thy victory? The sting of death is sin; and the strength of sin is the law. But thanks be to God, which giveth us the victory through our Lord Jesus Christ." With such a text we need not fear to depart.

And so that other word, the seventh we shall quote, and in that number seven dwelleth perfection of testimony. Revelation 14:13: "And I heard a voice from heaven saying unto me, Write, Blessed are the dead which die in the Lord from henceforth: yea, saith the Spirit, that they may rest from their labors; and their works do follow them."

Now, I dare say, many of you have said, "I wish I had a word from God, just like Simeon had, to cheer me in my dying moments." You have it before you; here are seven that I have read to you, most sure words of testimony, unto which you do well to take heed, as unto a light shining in a dark place. These promises belong to all believers in our precious Lord and Savior, Jesus Christ. Fear not, then, be not afraid, but rather say, "How lettest thou thy servant depart in peace."

I have done the sermon, but we must put a rider to it. Just a word or two to those of you who cannot die in peace because you are not believers in Christ: you have never seen God's salvation, neither are you God's servants. I must deal with you as I have dealt with the saints. I have given them texts of Scripture, for the text saith, "according to thy word;" and I will give you also two passages of Scripture, which will show you those who may not hope to depart in peace.

The first one is negative: it shows who cannot enter heaven, and, consequently, who cannot depart in peace. 1 Corinthians 6:9: "Know ye not that the unrighteous shall not inherit the kingdom of God?" the unjust, the oppressive, cheats, rogues, "the unrighteous shall not inherit the kingdom of God." I will read these words. I need not explain them, but let every one here who comes under their lash submit to God's word. "Be not deceived: neither fornicators,"--plenty of them in London--"nor idolaters,"--and ye need not worship a God of wood and stone to be idolaters, worship anything but God, you are an idolater--"nor adulterers, nor effeminate, nor abusers of themselves with mankind, nor thieves, nor covetous, nor drunkards,"--alas, some of these come to this house regularly,--"nor revilers," that is, backbiters!, cavillers, tale-bearers, swearers, and such like, "nor extortioners,"--you fine twenty percent gentlemen! You who grind poor borrowers with usurious interest. None of you shall inherit the kingdom of God, not one of you. If you come within this list, except God renew your hearts and change you, the holy gates of heaven are shut in your face.

Now, take another text, of a positive character, from the Book of Revelation 21:7: "He that overcometh shall inherit all things; and I will be his God, and he shall be my son. But the fearful,"--that means the cowardly, those that are ashamed of Christ, those that dare not suffer for Christ's sake, those who believe everything, and nothing, and so deny the truth, because they cannot endure to be persecuted; "the fearful and unbelieving,"--that is, those who do not trust a Savior--"and the abominable,"--and they are not scarce, some among the poor are abominable, and there are Right Honourables who ought to be called Right Abominables; ay, and greater than that, too, whose vices make them abominable to the nation: and "murderers,"--"he that hateth his brother is a murderer;" and "whoremongers and sorcerers;" "those who have or pretend to have dealings with devils and spirits, your spirit rappers, the whole batch of them; "and idolaters, and all liars," and these swarm everywhere, they lie in print, and they lie with the voice; "all liars shall have their part in the lake which burneth with fire and brimstone, which is the second death."

Now, these are no words of mine, but the words of God; and if they condemn you, you are condemned; but, if you be condemned, fly to Jesus. Repent and be converted, as saith the gospel, and forgiveness shall be yours, through Jesus Christ. Amen.

PORTIONS OF SCRIPTURE READ BEFORE SERMON--Luke 1:46-55;1:67-75;2:25-35.

Our usual Penny Almanack is now ready, and we hope it will be as much approved of as its predecessors have been. We have also with no small labor, written an Almanack for the walls, which is called John Ploughman's Sheet Almanack. Our friends tells us that it will have an unprecedented sale, and we only hope it may, but not to the detriment of the older one. They are quite distinct things, and very different in all respects, except that they are by the same author, cost the same price--one penny, and can be had of the same publishers, Messrs. Passmore and Alabaster.--C. H. S.

The One Thing Needful

A Sermon (No. 1015)
Delivered on Lord's-day Morning, October 15th, 1871 by
C. H. SPURGEON,
At the Metropolitan Tabernacle, Newington

"But one thing is needful." - Luke 10:42.

WE HAVE no difficulty whatever in deciding what the one thing is. We are not allowed to say that it is the Saviour, for he is not a thing; and we are not permitted to say that it is attention to our own salvation, for although that would be true, it is not mentioned in the context. The one thing needful evidently is that which Mary chose--that good part which should not be taken away from her. Very clearly this was to sit at Jesus' feet and hear his word. This and nothing less, this and nothing more.

The mere posture of sitting down and listening to the Saviour's word was nothing in itself: it was that which it indicated. It indicated, in Mary's case, a readiness to believe what the Saviour taught, to accept and to obey--nay to delight in, the precepts which fell from his lips. And this is the one thing needful--absolutely needful; for no rebel can enter the kingdom of heaven with the weapons of rebellion in his hands. We cannot know Christ while we resist Christ: we must be reconciled to his gentle sway, and confess that he is Lord, to the glory of God the Father.

To sit at Jesus' feet implies faith as well as submission. Mary believed in what Jesus said, and, therefore, sat there to be taught by him. It is absolutely necessary that we have faith in the Lord Jesus Christ, in his power as God and man, in his death as being expiatory, in his crucifixion as being a sacrifice for our sins. We must trust him for time and eternity, in all his relationships as Prophet, Priest, and King. We must rely on him; he must be our hope, our salvation, our all in all. This one thing is absolutely necessary: without it we are undone. A believing submission, and a submissive faith in Jesus we must have, or perish.

But sitting at Jesus' feet implies, also, that having submitted and believed, we now desire to be his disciples. Discipleship is too often forgotten; it is as needful as faith. We are to go into all the world and disciple all nations, baptizing them in the name of the Father, the Son and of the Holy Ghost. A man cannot be saved unless he has become a learner in the school of Christ, and a learner, too, in a practical sense, being willing to practice what he learns. Only he who does the Master's will knows his doctrines. We are, if we have chosen the good part, sitters at the feet of Jesus, just as Saul of Tarsus sat at the feet of Gamaliel; Christ is to us our great Instructor, and we take the law from his lips. The believer's position is that of a pupil, and the Lord Jesus is his teacher. Except we be converted and become as little children, we can in no wise enter the kingdom of heaven. Sitting at the feet of Jesus indicates the child-like spirit of true discipleship; and this is the one thing needful: there is no salvation apart from it.

It meant, also, service, for though Mary was not apparently engaged in waiting upon Christ as Martha was, yet she was, in very truth, ministering unto him in a deeper and truer sense. No one gives greater joy to a public speaker than an attentive listener; no one serves a teacher better than he who is an apt and attentive scholar. The first duty, indeed, of the student to the tutor is that he be cheerful in accepting, and diligent in retaining, what is taught: in this sense, Mary was really waiting upon Christ in one of his loftiest capacities, namely--that of a teacher and prophet in the midst of Israel. In that same spirit, had the Master only intimated it, she would have risen to wash his feet, or anoint his head, or wait at table, as Martha did; but she would, while she was performing these active duties, have continued spiritually in her first posture; she could not, of course, have continued literally sitting at the feet of the Saviour, but her heart would have remained in the condition which that posture indicates. She was in the fittest position for service, for she waited to hear what her Lord would have her to do. We must all be servants, too; as we have been servants of unrighteousness, we must by grace submit ourselves unto the rules of Jesus, and become servants of righteousness, or, else, we miss the one thing that is indispensable for entrance into heaven.

Sitting at the feet of Jesus, also, signifies love. She would not have been sitting there at ease and happy in mind, if she had not loved him. There was a charm in the very tone of his words to her. She knew how he had loved her, and, therefore, each syllable was music to her soul. She looked up again and again, I doubt not, into that dear face, and often caught the meaning of the words more readily as she read his countenance, marked his eyes ofttimes suffused with tears, and ever bright with holy sympathy. Her love to his person made her a willing learner, and we must be the same. We must not learn of Christ like unwilling truant boys, who go to school and must needs have learning flogged into them; we must be eager to learn; we must open our mouth wide that he may fill it, like the thirsty earth when it needs the shower, our soul must break for the longing it hath towards his commandments at all times. We must rejoice in his statutes more than gold, yea, than much fine gold. When we are moved by this spirit, we have found the one thing needful.

Having laid before you the meaning of the text, that to sit at Jesus' feet is the one thing necessary, for a literal translation of the text would be--"of one thing there is a necessity;" let us take the text as it stands and notice in it four things. The first is a word of consideration: the disjunctive conjunction, "but." The Saviour bids us to make a pause. He says, "but one thing is needful." Then there comes a word of necessity:"one thing is needful." thirdly, a word of concentration: "one thing is needful;" and then a word of immediateness "one thing is needful--needful now, at once.

I.--To begin, then, here is a word of CONSIDERATION, which, as I have already said, is interjected into the middle of our Lord's brief word to Martha. Martha is very busy; she is rather quick tempered also, and so she speaks to the Saviour somewhat shortly; and the Master says, "Martha, Martha,"--very tenderly, kindly, gently, with only the slightest tinge of rebuke in his tone--"Martha, Martha, thou art careful and troubled about many things--but, but, but, but, but, wait a while and hear." That wise and warning but may be very useful to many here. You are engaged to-day in business; very diligent you are in it. You throw your whole energy into your trading, as you must, if you would succeed. You rise up wearily, and you sit up late. Shall I say a word that should discourage your industry? I will not; but, but is there nothing else?--is this life all? Is making money everything? Is wealth worth gaining merely for the sake of having it said, "He died worth fifty thousand pounds?" Is it so?

Perhaps, you are a very hard-working man. You have very little rest during the week, and in order to bring up your family comfortably, you strain every nerve; you live as you should, economically, and you work diligently; from morning to night the thought with you is, "How shall I fill these many little mouths? How shall I bring them up properly? How shall I, as a working man, pay my way?" Very right; I wish all working men would be equally thoughtful and economical, and that there were fewer of those foolish spendthrifts who waste their substance when they have it, and who, the moment there is a frost, or they are out of employ, become paupers, loafing upon the charity of others. I commend your industry, but, but, but, at the same time, is that all? Were you made only to be a machine for digging holes, laying bricks, or cutting out pieces of wood? Were you created only to stand at a counter and measure or weigh out goods? do you think your God made you for that and that only? Is this the chief end of man--to earn shillings a week, and try to make ends meet therewith? is that all immortal men were made for? As an animal like a dog, nor a machine like a steam engine, can you stand up and look at yourself, and say, "I believe I am perfectly fulfilling my destiny"? I beg this morning to interject that quiet "but," right into the middle of your busy life, and ask from you space for consideration, a pause for the voice of wisdom, that a hearing may be granted her. Business? Labour? Yes, but there is a higher bread to be earned, and there is a higher life to be considered. Hence the Lord puts it, "Labour not for the meat that perisheth," that is to say, not for that first and foremost; "but for that which endureth unto life eternal." God hath made man that he may glorify him; and whatever else man accomplishes, if he fail to reach that end, and make eternal shipwreck, unless he comes to sit at Jesus' feet; there and there only can he learn how to sanctify his business and to consecrate his labour, and so bring forth unto God; through his grace, that which is due to him.

Now, I have spoken thus to the busy, but I might speak, and I should have certainly as good a claim to do so, to those who are lovers of pleasure. They are not cumbered with much serving; rather, they laugh at those who cumber themselves about anything. They are merry as the birds, their life is as the flight of a butterfly, which lightly floats from flower to flower, according to its own sweet will; with neither comb to make, nor hive to guard. Now, thou gay young man, what doth solomon say to thee? "Rejoice, O young man, in thy youth; and let thy heart cheer thee in the days of thy youth; but"--there comes in a pause, and the cool hand of wisdom is laid upon the hot brow of folly, and the youth is asked to think awhile--"but know thou, that for all these things, God will bring thee into judgement." It cannot be that an immortal spirit was made of frivolities; a soul immortal spending all her fires on the playthings of the world, "resembles ocean into tempest toss'd, to waft a feather, or to drown a fly." So great a thing as an immortal soul could not have been made by God with no higher object than to spend itself upon trifles light as air. Oh, pause a while, thou careless, godless one, and hear the voice that saith unto thee, "but." There is something more than the fool's hell; and should not life be? The charms of music, the merriment of the gay assembly, the beauties of art, and the delights of banqueting--there must be something more for thee than these; and something more must be required of thee than that thou shouldst waste from morn to night thy precious time upon nothing but to please thyself. Stop, stop, and let this admonitory "but" sound in thine ears.

I take liberty, moreover, to address the same word to religious people, who, perhaps, need it as much as the others. They will, of course, agree with anything I can say about the mere worldling or the profligate; but, will they listen to me when I say to them, "You are very diligent in your religion, you are attentive to all its outward rites and ceremonies, you believe the articles of your church, you practice the ceremonies ordained by its rulers; but, but, do you know that all this is nothing , unless you sit at Jesus' feet?" we may do what the church tells us, and never do what Christ tells us, for these may be different things; and the church is not our Saviour, but Christ. We may believe what a certain creed tells us, but not believe what Jesus teaches; for our creed and Christ may be two very different things. Ay, and we may believe even what the Bible itself teaches to us, or think we believe it; but, if our heart has never made submission to the Teacher himself, so as to sit at his feet, and receive the truth obediently from him, our religion is altogether vain. Traditional religion is not submission to Christ, but to custom. Obedience to a denomination is not obedience to Jesus himself. How I wish that all professing Christians would bring themselves to an examination and enquire, "Do I really believe in the person of my Lord, and accept him as my Teacher? Do I study the Word of God to learn the truth from him, and not accept it blindly and at second hand from my minister, or my parents, or the church of the nation, or the creed of my family?" We go to Jesus for teaching, desiring in our hearts to be taught by his book and his Spirit, cheerfully agreeing in all things to shape our faith to his declaration, and our life to his rule. For us, there must be no spiritual law-giver, and no infallible Rabbi, but the Blessed One, whom Magdalene called "Rabboni," and whom Thomas saluted as, "My Lord and my God."

Yes, and let me say, even to those of you who can honestly declare that Christ is your sole confidence, it is possible for you to forget the necessity of sitting at his feet. You, dear brethren, are looking to his precious blood alone for your salvation, and his name is sweet to you, and you desire all things to be conformed to his will. So far it is well with you, for in this you have a measure of sitting at his feet; but so had Martha; she loved her Lord, and she knew his word, and she was a saved soul, for "Jesus loved Mary, and Martha, and lazarus;" but you have not perhaps so much of this needful thing as Mary had, and as you ought to have. You have been very busy this week, and have been drifted from your moorings; you have not lived with your Lord in conscious fellowship; you have been full of care and empty of prayer; you have not committed your sorrows to your loving friend; you have blundered on in duty without asking his guidance or assistance, you have not maintained, in your Christian service, the communion of your spirit with the Well-Beloved, and, if such has been the case, let me say "but" to you, and ask you, as you sit here this morning, to make a little stop in your Sunday-school teaching or your street preaching, or whatever else it is that you are so laudably engaged in, and say to yourself: "To me, as a worker, the one thing needful is to keep near my Lord, and I must not so suffer the watering of others to occupy me, as to neglect my own heart, lest I should have to say woe is me, they made me keeper in the vineyards, but my own vineyard have I not kept.'" To the saints, as well as to others, the one thing needful is to sit at Jesus' feet. We are to be always learners and lovers of Jesus. Departure from him, and independence of him, let them not once be named among you. It is weakness, sickness, sin, and sorrow for a believer to leave his Lord and become either his own leader or reliance. We are only safe while we remain humbly and gladly subservient to him. You see, then, that this word "but" suggests a very useful and salutary pause to us all. May God help us to benefit thereby.

II. Secondly, our text speaks of NECESSITY--one thing is a necessity. If this be proven, it overrides all other considerations. We are nearly right when we say proverbially, "Necessity has no law." If a man steal, and it be found that he was dying of hunger, he is always half forgiven, and charity has been known to excuse him altogether. Necessity has been frequently accepted as a good excuse for what else might not have been tolerated; and when a thing is right, and necessity backs it, then indeed the right become imperative, and pushes to the front to force its way. Necessity, like hunger breaks through stone walls. The text claims for sitting at Jesus' feet that it is the first and only necessity. Now, I see all around me a crowd of things alluring and fascinating. Pleasure calls to me I hear her syren song--but I reply, "I cannot regard thee, for necessity presses upon me to hearken to another voice." Philosophy and learning charm me, fain would I yield my heart to them; but, while I am yet unsaved, the one thing needful demands my first care, and wisdom bids me give it. Not that we love human learning less, but eternal wisdom more. Pearls? Yes. Emeralds? Yes; but bread, in God's name--bread at once, when I am starving in the desert! What is the use of ingots of gold, or bars of silver, or caskets of jewels, when food is wanting? If one thing be needful, it devours, like Aaron's rod, all the matters which are merely pleasurable. All the fascinating things on earth may go, but the needful things we must have. If you are wise, you will evermore prefer the necessary to the dazzling.

About us are a thousand things entangling. This world is very much like the pools we have heard of in India, in which grows a long grass of so clinging a character that, if a man once falls into the water, it is almost certain to be his death, for only with the utmost difficulty could he be rescued from the meshes of the deadly, weedy net, which immediately wraps itself around him. This world is even thus entangling. All the efforts of grace are needed to preserve men from being ensnared with the deceitfulness of riches and the cares of this life. The ledger demands you, the day-book wants you, the shop requires you, the warehouse bell rings for you; the theater invites, the ball-room calls: you must live, you say, and you must have a little enjoyment, and , consequently, you give your heart to the world. These things, I say, are very entangling; but we must be disentangled from them, for we cannot afford to lose our souls. "What shall it profit a man if he gain the whole world and lose his own soul?" If a ship is going down, and a passenger has his gold in a bag about him, and he has upon him a costly cloak, see how he acts. Off goes the garment when he knows that he cannot possibly swim with it upon him. No matter though it be lined with miniver and be made of costliest stuff, off he throws it; and, as for his bag of treasure, with many a regret he flings them down upon the deck, for his life is dearer than they. If he may but save his life, he is willing to lose all beside. Oh sirs! for the one thing needful, all entangling things must be give up. You must lay aside every weight, and the sin that doth so easily beset you, if by any means the one thing needful may be yours.

There are many things very puzzling, and some people have a strange delight in being bewildered. It is astonishing the many letters I receive and interviews I am asked to give, in order to adjust in people's minds the doctrine of predestination and the fact of free agency; and equally remarkable is the way in which young people, and old people too, will pick out extremely difficult texts, perhaps relating to the Second Advent, or to the battle of Armageddon, and they must needs have these opened up to them before they will believe the gospel. I think it utterly useless to begin upon such things with those who are unsaved. One thing is needful, sir, and that is by no means a puzzling matter; it is plainly this, that thou submit thyself to Jesus Christ and sit at his feet. That is needful: as for the doctrines of election and the second advent, they are important, but they are neither the most essential nor the most pressing. The one thing needful for a seeking soul is that it receives Jesus and become submissive to him, sitting as a disciple at his feet and as a servant doing his will. It is true there is the ninth chapter of Romans in the Bible, and a precious chapter it is: but the seeking sinner should take care to read first the third chapter of John, and till he has mastered that, he had better let the Romans alone. Go first to the business which concerns your salvation; attend to that, and when all is right with you, then, at Jesus' feet, you will be in the best possible position to learn all that can be learned of the higher mysteries and the deeper truths.

Moreover, there is much that is desirable, very desirable--desirable in the highest spiritual sense; but it must be second to that which is needful. If I read the experience of men who have known their own hearts and mourned before the Lord, I wish that I had as deep a sense of sin as they had; or, I read the story of saints who have lived the angelic life, and even here on earth have dwelt with Christ and walked the golden streets in fellowship with him, I wish I could rise to all their heights; but for all that, if my soul is still polluted with sin, for me the one thing needful is cleansing by the Redeemer's blood; I must at once believingly yield to Jesus, for this is of necessity, and the desirable things will come to me afterwards, if I sit down at Jesus' feet. So near the source of all good things, it will be easy to be enriched with all knowledge and grace, but our first business is to get there, and by the Holy Spirit's blessing we may come there without either the deep experience or the elevated feelings we have described; we may come just as we are, all guilty and lost, and submit ourselves to the Saviour. Having done that, we are in the best position for spiritual attainments--yea, they shall surely be ours. Let the heart yield itself to our sole reliance and sure confidence, it is well with us: we have all that is needful, and the pledge of all that is desirable.

Tell us it is a necessity, and everything else must give way: necessity overrules all else. Now, what is it that sitting at Jesus' feet is a necessity? It is so, because it is needful for us to have our sins forgiven; but Jesus will never forgive the unhumbled rebel. If he will not take Jesus to be a Master, the sinner cannot have him to be a Saviour. As long as we rebel against him, we cannot be saved by him. Submission, by repentance and faith, we must have, or our transgressions will remain upon us to our everlasting ruin. It is necessary, because we must have our inbred sins overcome; but none can stay corruption in a many but Christ, who has come to destroy the work of the devil, and to save his people from their sins. Jesus, the seed of the woman, is the only power that can crush the serpent's head. Only at the feet of Jesus can the divine power be gained which works in us holiness and sanctifies us practically; therefore, as you must be purified or you cannot enter heaven, you must come to Jesus' feet. Moreover, it is at the feet of Jesus that the soul's ignorance is removed; and since ignorance concerning ourselves and our God must be taken from us, we must be taught of him. God is "our light and our salvation;" our light first, and our salvation in consequence. We must have the light. The spiritually blind man cannot enter heaven, he must have his eyes opened, but Jesus alone can work that miracle of grace. Neither can we receive true light except from him, for he is "the true light, that lighteth every man that cometh into the world;" none are ever enlightened, except by him. "In him is light--all light; and the light is the light of men." As God is the mind of the world, he who has not God is demented; and as Christ is the light of the world, he that believes not in him abideth in darkness even until now. We must come, then, and yield ourselves unreservedly to Jesus, worshipping him, trusting him, and obeying him--in a word, we must sit at his feet, and hear his word; otherwise, we shall abide in darkness and death.

In order to enter heaven, it is necessary that our nature should become like the nature of Christ. This earth is for those who bear the image of the first Adam; but the new heaven and the new earth are for those who bear the image of the second Adam.. We must, by some means, acquire the nature of the second and heavenly Adam, and this must be wrought in us by regeneration, and developed by acquaintance with him. By sitting at his feet, and beholding him, we become changed into the same image from glory to glory even as by the Spirit of the Lord. If we reject the Lord Jesus as our trust, teacher, and exemplar, we have no new life, we are not new creatures in Christ, and we can never be admitted within the holy gates where those alone dwell who are fashioned after his likeness. We must, then, sit at his feet; it is absolutely necessary, and, without it, our whole life will be a complete failure; we may make money, but we shall lose our souls; we may gain honour, but shall have come short of the glory of God; we may enjoy pleasure, but we shall forfeit the pleasure which are at God's right hand for evermore; we may have done our country some service, but to our God, and the higher country, we shall have rendered no service, for we cannot serve God if we will not obey Christ. "He that honoureth not the Son, honoureth not the Father which hath sent him." This life is a blank, a long rebellion, to the man who submits not to Jesus, and the life for ever hereafter will be darkness and confusion; as darkness itself, a land of sorrow, and of weeping, and of wailing, and of gnashing of teeth, a land of despair, upon which no star shall ever shine, or sun shall ever rise. Woe, woe, woe, woe to the Godless, Christless spirit that passeth across the river of death without a hope. Woe, woe, woe, woe eternally to the soul that will not sit at the feet of Jesus! he shall be trodden beneath his feet in his anger, and crushed in his hot displeasure. God grant that may never be our portion. To sit at Jesus' feet is the one thing needful then.

And, brethren, let me just say, and leave this point, it is needful to every one of you. It is not some of us who must be there, but all. The wisest must become fools to learn of him, or fools they are; the most educated and cultured mind must submit to this further culture, or else it is nothing but a barren waste in his sight. One thing is a necessity to you all, high or low, rich or poor, queen or beggar--you must sit at Jesus' feet; and all alike must accept his teaching, or you know nothing that can save you.

Some things in this world are necessary, after a measure, but this is necessary without measure; infinitely needful is it that you sit at Jesus' feet, needful now, needful in life; needful in life for peace, in death for rest, and in eternity for bliss. This is needful always. Many things have their uses for youth, others come not into value till old age; but one thing, the one thing, is needful for childhood, and needful for palsied age; it is needful for the ruddy cheek, and the active limb, and needful everywhere and always. In the highest and most emphatic sense, "one thing is needful."

III. Thus much about the necessity, the next word is CONCENTRATION: "One thing is needful." I am glad it says "one thing," because a division of ends and objects is always weakening. A man cannot follow two things well. Our life-flood suffices not to fill two streams or three; there is only enough water, as it were, in our life's brooklet, to turn one wheel. It is a great pity when a man fritters away his energies by being "everything by turns, and nothing long;" trying all things, and mastering nothing. Oh soul, it is well for thee that there is only one thing in this world that is absolutely necessary, give thy whole soul to that. If other things are necessary in a secondary place, "Seek first the kingdom of God and his righteousness, and all these shall be added unto you."

One thing is needful, and this is well arranged, for we cannot follow two things. If Christ be one of them, we cannot follow another. Is it not written, "No man can serve two masters, either he will hate the one and love the other, or cleave to the one and despise the other. Ye cannot serve God and mammon." Not only would it be very weakening to you to attempt to serve both, but it is absolutely impossible that you should do so. Jesus Christ is a monopolizer of human hearts, he will never accept a portion of our manhood. He bought us altogether, and he will have the whole of our personality. Christ must be everything, or he will be nothing. He does not love Christ who loves anything as well as Christ, neither does he trust him who trusts in anything besides. Christ must reign alone. "Jesus only," must be the motto of our spirits. It is well for us, therefore, that only one thing is necessary, for only one thing is possible.

It is an unspeakable mercy that the one thing needful is a very simple one. Little child, thou couldst not climb the mountain, but thou canst sit down at Jesus' feet; thou canst not understand hard doctrine, but thou canst love him who said, "Suffer the little children to come unto me, and forbid them not, for of such is the kingdom of heaven." Unlearned man, thou who hast no time to acquire earthly lore, if the one thing needful were something that belonged only to the learned, alas for thee; but if thou canst not teach, it is not needful that thou shouldst, it is only needful that thou shouldst learn. Take the Incarnate Wisdom to be thy Master, and sit as a little child at his feet to learn with all thine heart. That is all he asks of thee. Men will have it that they must do something to be saved. They must fret and worry like Martha, but after all, the right way is to end your doing and fretting by sitting down content with Jesus' doing, satisfied with his righteousness and with the merit of his precious blood. The one thing needful is very easy, except to proud hearts, which cannot brook to accept everything gratis, and to be beholden to sovereign mercy. To the poor in spirit it is not only simple but sweet to sit at Jesus' feet. I would be nothing but what he makes me, I would have nothing but what he gives me, I would ask nothing but what he promises me, I would trust in nothing but what he has done for me, and I would desire nothing but what he has prepared for me. To sit at Jesus's feet in humble submission and quiet rest, he the master and I the little child, I the vessel waiting to be filled, and he my fulness, I the mown grass, and he the falling dew, I the rain drop, and he the sun that makes me glisten in life with diamond brilliance, and then exhales me in death to be absorbed in him; this is all in all to me.

Let us remark that, though this is only one thing, and so concentrated, yet it is also comprehensive and contains many things. Imagine not that to sit at Jesus' feet is a very small, unmeaning thing. It means peace, for they who submit to Jesus find peace through his precious blood. It means holiness, for those who learn of Jesus learn no sin, but are instructed in things lovely and of good repute. It means strength, for they that sit with Jesus, and feed upon him, are girded with his strength; the joy of the Lord is their strength. It means wisdom, for they that learn of the Son of God understand more than the ancients because they keep his statutes. It means zeal, for the love of Christ fires hearts that live upon it, and they that are much with Jesus become like Jesus, so that the zeal of the Lord's house eats them up. If we say that in an army the one thing needful is loyalty to the sovereign, we know what that means; for the loyal solider will be sure to be obedient to his officers, and if attached to his queen, he will be brave in the day of battle, and do his duty well. If we said that the one thing needful in a family was love, we should not have required a small thing; for love will place husband and wife in their true position; love will produce obedience in children, and diligence in servants. Let love permeate everything, and other virtues will grow out of it, as flowers spring from the soil. So when we say that sitting at Jesus' feet is the one thing needful, we have not uttered a mere truism: it comprehends a world of blessings.

And here would I address a word to the church of God in this country at this present time. She, too, is as Martha, cumbered with much serving. It were her wisdom, and her strength, if she would become more like Mary, and sit at Jesus' feet. Just now we need revival. Oh that God would send it! Oh for a mighty flood of spiritual influences, that would bear the stranded churches right out into a sea of usefulness. But how can we get revival? We shall have it, brethren, when we commune with Christ. When the saints habitually sit at Jesus' feet they will be revived, and of necessity the revival will spread from them, and the hearts of sinners will be touched.

There is great talk now-a-days of union; the walls of the various churches are to be broken down, and the denominations are to be blended. Think not of it in such a fashion; the only union possible, or desirable, is that we all unite to sit at Jesus' feet. It is not allowable that we concede one truth and you another; that is not natural charity, but common treason to Christ. We have no right to yield an atom of the truth of God, under the pretence of charity. Truth is no property of ours; we are only God's stewards, and it behooves us to be faithful to our trust. Neither one church nor another has any right to bate its testimony one jot, if it be true. To alter the statute-book of Christ is blasphemy. True union will come when all the churches learn of Christ, for Christ does not teach two things opposed to each other. There are not two baptisms in the Bible; we shall not find two sets of dogmas diametrically opposite to each other. If we give up the various things that are of man, and hold fast each of us only that which is of God, we shall be united in principle and in doctrine; and "One Lord, one faith, one baptism" will once again be emblazoned upon the banners of the church of God. Sit at Jesus' feet, O thou church of Christ, and true unity will come to thee.

We hear a great deal about the necessity of controversy. We ought to be ready to answer all that infidels object, so wise men say. Every absurdity of every fool we are to sit down and reply to, and when this labour of Hercules is accomplished, we are to begin again, for by that time new whimsies will be in men's brains, and new lies will have been begotten. Is this so? Am I to do nothing in winning souls and glorifying God, but to spend all my time in finding wind for the nostrils of the wild asses of the desert? Well, let those do it who please, we believe that the settlement of all controversy in the church and for the church would come from the Lord himself, if we believed more fully in him, and waited more upon him for guidance, and if we preached the gospel more in his own strength, and in his own Spirit.

And, as for missions: we appoint our committees, we amend our plans, and suggest schemes.. All very well and good; but missions will never flourish till the church, with regard to missions, sits at Jesus' feet. She will never convert the heathen in her own way: God will give success only when we work in his way. It may be very useful to make translations, and exceedingly beneficial to keep schools; but if I read my Bible right, it is not Christ's way. "Go ye into all the world, and preach the gospel to every creature," is the law of Jesus Christ, and when the church everywhere, at home and abroad, takes more earnestly to preaching, when the testimony of the truth is perpetual and incessant, in simple language, and popular speech, then Christ the Lord will look upon the church that, like Mary, sits at his feet, and say "Thou hast done thy part," and blessing shall follow. "Thy work is done, and I will give thee thy reward."

For us all, beloved, saints and sinners, one thing is needful: that we always sit, like Mary, at the Master's feet.

IV. The last word is IMMEDIATENESS, and there is no need that we say much upon it. One thing is a necessity, a necessity not of the future only, but of to-day. It is not written, "it shall be needful," on certain coming days, to sit at Jesus's feet; but it is so now. Young man, one thing is necessary to you while yet young; do not postpone it till advanced years. Christian, it is needful for thee to-day to have communion with Christ; do not think of it as indispensable to-morrow or to-night at the communion table; it is needful now. There are dangers thou canst not see, which can only be warded off by present and immediate fellowship with Christ. "One thing is needful." It is not that it was needful in the past, indeed it was so; but it is needful now. It was needful for me in the days of my sinfulness to submit to Christ, it is equally needful for me now. However much you advance, O believer, you never advance beyond this; whatever your experience, or your information, or your ripeness for glory, it is needful still to sit at Jesus' feet. You shall never get into a higher class in the school of wisdom than is the class which Christ teaches; his is the infant class in the school, but it is the highest class also. It is always needful, every moment needful, that we sit at Jesus' feet.

It is needful, I have already said, to the sinner. Life, and health, and peace will come to him when he becomes a disciple of the Crucified. Would God that he might be made so this very morning. There is life in a look at the Crucified One. To depend entirely upon the sinner's Saviour is the sinner's salvation. God bring you to his feet, dear hearers.

But it is equally needful for the saint. Covered with the fruits of righteousness, his root must still cling to the riven rock. You must never imagine, whatever you have done or whatever you have attained, that you are to leave Mary's seat; still must you abide there.

It is the one thing needful for the backslider. If you have fallen never so much, you will rise again if you come to the Master submissively and abide with him. It was the mark of the man who had the devil cast out of him, that he was clothed and in his right mind, sitting at the feet of Jesus; it shall show that you, too, are restored when you learn of your Lord. A seat at Jesus' feet is the place for all Christians to die in, they shall sleep sweetly with their heads in Jesus' bosom: it is the place for them to live in, for joy and bliss are there.

Beloved, I desire for myself never again to be worried with the cares of this church, but to take them all to my Master, and wait at his feet. I desire not to be troubled about my preaching, nor to be cumbered about anything beneath the sun, but to leave all these, as he would have me leave them, in his hands. You who are working in the classes, in the school, or anywhere else, I pray you look well to your fellowship with Jesus. You cannot slay the enemy by throwing away your sword, and nearness to Christ is your battle-axe and weapons of war; you have lost your power when you have left your Lord. One thing is needful--let the rest go. What if we have not learning?--what if we have not eloquence? If we live near to Christ, we have something better than all these; if we abide in him, and he abides in us, we shall go and bring forth fruit, and our fruit shall remain; if he abides in us, we shall enjoy heaven on earth, and be daily preparing of that eternal heaven which is to be our portion. "One thing is needful." God grant it to every one of us!--Amen.

PORTION OF SCRIPTURE READ BEFORE SERMON--Luke 10.

Beauty for Ashes

A Sermon (No. 1016)
Delivered by
C. H. SPURGEON,
At the Metropolitan Tabernacle, Newington

"To appoint unto them that mourn in Zion, to give unto them beauty for ashes the oil of joy for mourning, the garment of praise for the spirit of heaviness, that they might be called trees of righteousness, the planting of the Lord, that he might be glorified." - Isaiah 61:3.

WHEN SOLDIERS ARE ON THE MARCH, or advancing to the battle, military men think it wise to let the trumpet sound, that the warriors may be stimulated by the thrilling music. Many a weary soldier has tramped on with new vigor when the band has struck up a lively march, or a soul-moving tune. In the midst of our present Christian service, my brethren, when I trust all of you have resolved to come to the help of the Lord--to the help of the Lord against the mighty--we would bid the silver trumpets of gospel promise sound aloud, that the hosts of God as they march on in battle array may feel their pulses quickened and their souls cheered. May times of revival be also seasons of refreshing. In times of great toil and eminent service much extra refreshment may with wisdom be dealt out. Harvest men require substantial meals amid their exhausting toil; and, as I feel that the Lord of the harvest would not have his laborers treated niggardly, I have to regale each of you with a portion of bread, a good piece of flesh, and a flagon of wine. Melchisedek met Abraham with bread and wine--not on some fine holiday when he had been musing in the plains of Mamre, but when he returned from the slaughter of the kings. After hard fighting comes sweet refreshment, and any here who have striven diligently to serve the Master, and have been pursuing their sacred calling even unto faintness, will be entitled to come and sit down, and partake of the nourishing bread and wine, which such a text as this prepares for all the sons of the Father of the faithful. Elijah ate of bread brought by angelic hands, for a forty days' journey was before him; such a trial of strength may be ordained for brethren to whom this word shall come. Precious promises are for poverty-stricken saints. The strong drink of divine consolation is for the heavy of heart, as saith Solomon--"Let him drink and forget his poverty, and remember his misery no more." May he who uttered the words which are now open before us speak them with power to the heart of each one here present. They came from the lips of Jesus; may they drop again into our hearts fresh from his mouth (that well of comfort undefiled), and fall with all their ancient life-giving power.

We will read our text again, and then meditate thereon. "To appoint unto them that mourn in Zion, to give unto them beauty for ashes, the oil of joy for mourning, the garment of praise for the spirit of heaviness; that they might be called trees of righteousness, the planting of the Lord, that he might be glorified."

Our first consideration will be, who gives this word? Secondly, to whom doth he give it? Thirdly, what saith he in it? And, fourthly, what will come of it?

I. First then, WHO GIVES THIS WORD? It is a word to mourners in Zion, meant for their consolation. But who gives it? The answer is not far to seek. It comes from him who said, "The Spirit of the Lord God is upon me," "he hath sent me to bind up the broken-hearted." Now, in a very inferior and subordinate sense, Christian ministers have the Spirit of God resting upon them, and they are sent to bind up the broken-hearted; but they can only do so in the name of Jesus, and in strength given from him. This word is not spoken by them, nor by prophets or apostles either, but by the great Lord and Master of apostles and prophets, and ministers, even by Jesus Christ himself. If he declares that he will comfort us, then we may rest assured we shall be comforted! The stars in his right hand may fail to penetrate the darkness, but the rising of the Sun of Righteousness effectually scatters the gloom. If the consolation of Israel himself comes forth for the uplifting of his downcast people, then their doubts and fears may well fly apace, since his presence is light and peace.

But, who is this anointed one who comes to comfort mourners? He is described in the preface to the text as a preacher. "The Spirit of the Lord God is upon me; because the Lord hath appointed me to preach good tidings unto the meek." Remember what kind of preacher Jesus was. "Never man spake like this man." He was a son of consolation indeed. It was said of him, "A bruised reed shall he not break, and the smoking flax shall he not quench." He was gentleness itself: his speech did not fall like a hail shower, it dropped like the rain, and distilled as the dew, as the small rain upon the tender herb. He came down like the soft vernal shower upon the new-mown grass, scattering refreshment and revival wherever his words were heard. The widow at the gates of Nain dried her eyes when he spake, and Jairus no longer mourned for his child. Magdalene gave over weeping, and Thomas ceased from doubting, when Jesus showed himself. Heavy hearts leaped for joy, and dim eyes sparkled with delight at his bidding. Now, if such be the person who declares he will comfort the broken-hearted, if he be such a preacher, we may rest assured he will accomplish his work.

In addition to his being a preacher, he is described as a physician. "He hath sent me to bind up the broken-hearted." Some hearts want more than words. The choicest consolations that can be conveyed in human speech will not reach their case; the wounds of their hearts are deep, they are not flesh cuts, but horrible gashes which lay bare the bone, and threaten ere long to kill unless they be skilfully closed. It is, therefore, a great joy to know that the generous friend who, in the text, promises to deal with the sorrowing, is fully competent to meet the most frightful cases. Jehovah Rophi is the name of Jesus of Nazareth; he is in his own person the Lord that healeth us. He is the beloved physician of men's souls. "By his stripes we are healed." Himself took our infirmities, and bare our sicknesses, and he is able now with a word to heal all our diseases, whatever they may be. Joy to you, ye sons of mourning; congratulation to you, ye daughters of despondency: he who comes to comfort you can not only preach with his tongue, but he can bind up with his hand. "He healeth the broken in heart, and bindeth up their wounds. He telleth the number of the stars; he calleth them all by their names."

As if this were not enough, our gracious helper is next described as a liberator. "He hath sent me to proclaim liberty to the captives, and the opening of the prison to them that are bound." There were many downcast persons in Israel in the olden times--persons who had become bankrupt, and, therefore, had lost their estates, and had even sunk yet further into debt, till they were obliged to sell their children into slavery, and to become themselves bondsmen. Their yoke was very heavy, and their trouble was very sore. But the fiftieth year came round, and never was there heard music so sweet in all Judea's land, as when the silver trumpet was taken down on the jubilee morn, and a loud shrill blast was blown in every city, and hamlet, and village, in all Israel, from Dan even to Beer-sheba. What meant that clarion sound? It meant this: "Israelite, thou art free. If thou hast sold thyself, go forth without money for the year of jubilee has come." Go back, go back, ye who have lost your lands; seek out the old homestead, and the acres from whence ye have been driven: they are yours again. Go back, and plough, and sow, and reap once more, and sit each man under his vine and his fig-tree, for all your heritages are restored. This made great joy among all the tribes, but Jesus has come with a similar message. He, too, publishes a jubilee for bankrupt and enslaved sinners. He breaks the fetters of sin, and gives believers the freedom of the truth. None can hold in captivity the souls whom Jesus declares to be the Lord's free men.

Surely, if the Savior has power, as the text declares, to proclaim liberty to the captive, and if he can break open prison doors, and set free those convicted and condemned, he is just the one who can comfort your soul and mine, though we be mourning in Zion. Let us rejoice at his coming, and cry Hosanna, blessed is he that cometh in the name of the Lord. Happy are we that we live in an age when Jesus breaks the gates of brass and cuts the bars of iron in sunder.

As if this were not all and not enough, one other matter is mentioned concerning our Lord, and he is pictured as being sent as the herald of good tidings of all sorts to us the sons of men. Read the second verse: "To proclaim the acceptable year of the Lord." God has taken upon himself human flesh. The infinite Jehovah came down from heaven and became an infant, lived among us, and then died for us. Behold in the person of the incarnate God the sure pledge of divine benevolence. "He that spared not his own Son, but freely delivered him up for us all, how shall he not with him also freely give us all things?" Beloved, the very fact that a Savior came to the world should be a source of hope to us, and when we think what a Savior he was, how he suffered, how he finished the work that was given him to do, and what a salvation it is which he has wrought out for us, we may well feel that the comfort of mourners is work for which he is well suited, and which he can execute most effectually. How beautiful upon Olivet and Calvary are the feet of him that bringeth, in his person and his world "good tidings, that publisheth peace, that bringeth good tidings of good, that publisheth salvation." But I must not linger. I have spoken of you enough to lead your thoughts to the blessed person who here declares that he will comfort the mourner. May the Holy Ghost reveal him unto you in all the power of his arm, the love of his heart, the virtue of his blood, the prevalence of his plea, the majesty of his exaltation, and the glory of his character.

II. Secondly, TO WHOM IS THIS WORD SPOKEN? It is spoken to those who mourn in Zion. They are in Zion. They are the Lord's people, but they mourn. To mourn is not always a mark of grace. Nature mourns. Fallen human nature will have to mourn for ever, except grace shall change it. But the mourning here meant is a mourning in Zion--a mourning of gracious souls. Let me try and describe what kind of mourning it is. It assumes various shapes. It begins in most hearts with lamentation over past sin. I have broken God's just commandments, I have done evil against my God, I have destroyed my soul; my heart feels this, and bitterly mourns. It is one thing to say formally, "I am a miserable sinner;" it is a very different thing to be one. To say it may be gross hypocrisy, to feel it is a mark of grace. Oh that every one of us, if we have never felt mourning for sin may feel it at this hour. May we mourn to think that we have pierced the Savior, that we have transgressed against a God so good, and a Redeemer so generous. Those who mourn for the guilt of past sin, before long, reach a higher point. Mourners are not suffered long to tarry; grace takes their load of guilt away. Their transgressions are covered. Do they leave off mourning then? Oh, no, they mourn in another way. There is a sweet mourning concerning my past sin which I would never wish to lose. It is forgiven, every sin of mine is blotted out, and my soul, therefore, with a sweet bitterness, would mourn over it more and more.

"My sins, my sins, my Savior!
How sad on thee they fall,
Seen through thy gentle patience
I tenfold feel them all.
I know they are forgiven;
But still their pain to me
Is all the grief and anguish
They laid, my Lord, on thee."

This is a kind of mourning which may accompany us even to heaven's gates, and we might almost regret to have to part with such a friend even there.

"Lord, let me weep, for nought but sin,
And after none but thee.
And then I would--oh that I might--
A constant weeper be."

True hearts, however, mourn not only for their past transgressions, but they also sorrow over their present imperfections. If you are what you should be, dear friend, I am quite certain you see a great deal in yourself to grieve over. You cannot live as you would live. Whenever I meet with a person who feels that he is perfect, I conceive at once that he has not yet attained even a remote conception of what true perfection must be. The savage of Australia is satisfied with his weapons of war so long as he has never seen a rifle or heard of a cannon: to him his hovel is a model of architecture, for he has never heard of a cathedral or a palace. I have no doubt that a barn-door fowl would be quite surprised at the complaint which an eagle might make about its inability to mount as high as it desires to do. The fowl is perfect--perfect up to the condition of its barn-door, barley-scratching life, it knows nothing higher than its roosting place, and so it concludes itself absolutely perfect and fit for all that is desirable in flight. But oh, could it know where the thunders dwell, and sail above the clouds where the callow lightnings wait the bidding of the Lord, then would the creature feel something of the aspirations and the griefs which torment the heart of the royal bird. Men know not what God is, nor the infinity of his perfections, nor the majesty of his purity, else, when highest would they cry, "Higher, higher, higher," and mourn because they have not yet attained, and need still to mount as on eagle's wings. Brethren, I speak for you all when I say, there is not a day in which our service satisfies us, not a deed we have ever performed that contents us. We see our spots, and would fain wash them out with tears if we could, though we bless God they are removed by the precious blood of Jesus. Those are among the blessed who mourn because they cannot live a perfect life as they desire. To mourn after more holiness is a sign of holiness, to mourn after greater conformity to the image of Christ proves that we are already in a measure conformed thereunto; to sigh after more complete subordination of our entire life to the will of God is a mourning for which Jesus Christ will bring rich comfort.

The Christian mourner laments, also, because he cannot be more continually in communion with God. He knows the sweetness of fellowship with the Father and with the Son. He cannot bear to have it broken. If but the thinnest cloud pass between him and the sun of God's love, he is distressed directly, for he is sensitive lest he should lose the delights of communion. A native of sunny Italy deplores the absence of heaven's bright blue, when made to dwell in this land of the fleecy clouds; and he who has dwelt in unclouded fellowship with the Lord bemoans his hard lot, if even for awhile he beholds not that face which is as the sun shining in its strength. Love cannot endure absence, much less, coldness. True grace finds its life in fellowship, and pines if it be denied it.

The real Christian mourns, again, because he cannot be more useful. He wishes he were like a pillar of fire and light, so that he might evermore by day and by night enlighten the ignorant, and inspire the dull and laggard. He wishes not so much for more talent as for more grace to make use of the talent which he has. He would fain bring in a great rental to the owner of the vineyard who has placed him as a husbandman among the vines. He longs to bring up priceless pearls from the deep seas of sin, wherewith to adorn the diadem of his Lord and king. He sighs because thorns and thistles will spring up where he looked for a hundred-fold harvest: this makes him groan out, "Who hath believed our report, and to whom is the arm of the Lord revealed?"

Moreover, like his Lord, he mourns for others. He mourns in Zion because of the deadness of the Christian church, its divisions, its errors, its carelessness towards the souls of sinners. He cries with Jeremiah, "How is the gold become dim! How is the much fine gold changed!" But, he mourns most of all for the unconverted. He sees their state of alienation from God, and knowing the danger of it, his heart shrinks within him, as with prophetic glance he sees what their end will be: when "there shall be wailing and gnashing of teeth." His heart breaks for the sins and sorrows of others, and, like his Savior, he could weep over the cities that reject divine love; he could say like Moses that he was almost willing to have his name blotted out of the Book of Life if others might be saved: he feels such sorrow and heaviness of heart for his kinsmen according to the flesh who are strangers to Christ, that he has no rest in his death concerning them. Dear brethren, he that is quickened by the new life obtains an enlarged heritage of mourning; but, let it not be forgotten, he wins tenfold more joy as well; and, meanwhile, such weeping is in itself sweet--tears not too briny, and griefs not too bitter; such griefs we would wish to feel as long as we live, especially if the Lord Jesus alternates them with the fulfilling of that most excellent promise, to which I now direct you.

III. What is that, then, in the third place, WHICH IS SPOKEN in the text to those that mourn? I would draw particular attention to the words here, "To appoint unto them that mourn in Zion, to give unto them beauty for ashes." Come, mourning souls, who mourn in the way described, come ye gladly hither: there is comfort appointed for you, and there is also comfort given to you. It is the prerogative of King Jesus both to appoint and to give. How cheering is the thought that as our griefs are appointed, so also are our consolations. God has allotted a portion to every one of his mourners, even as Joseph allotted a mess to each of his brethren at the feast. You shall have your due share at the table of grace, and if you are a little one, and have double sorrows, you shall have a double portion of comfort. "To appoint unto them." This is a word full of strong consolation; for if God appoints me a portion, who can deprive me of it? If he appoints my comfort, who dare stand in the way? If he appoints it, it is mine by right. But then, to make the appointment secure, he adds the word "To give." The Holy One of Israel in the midst of Zion gives as well as appoints. The rich comforts of the gospel are conferred by the Holy Spirit, at the command of Jesus Christ, upon every true mourner in the time when he needs them; they are given to each spiritual mourner in the time when he would faint for lack of them. He can effectually give the comfort appointed for each particular case. All I can do is to speak of the comfort for God's mourners. I can neither allot it, nor yet distribute it; but our Lord can do both. My prayer is that he may do so at this moment; that every holy mourner may have a time of sweet rejoicing while siting at the Master's feet in a waiting posture. Did you never feel, while cast down, on a sudden lifted up, when some precious promise has come home to your soul? This is the happy experience of all the saints.

"Sometimes a light surprises
The Christian while he sings:
It is the Lord who rises
With healing in his wings.
When comforts are declining,
He grants the soul again,
A season of clear shining
To cheer it, after rain."

Our ever gracious and almighty Lord knows how to comfort his children, and be assured he will not leave them comfortless. He who bids his ministers again and again attend to this duty, and says, "Comfort ye, comfort ye my people," will not himself neglect to give them consolation. If you are very heavy, there is the more room for the display of his grace in you, by making you very joyful in his ways. Do not despair; do not say, "I have fallen too low, my harp has been so long upon the willows that it has forgotten Zion's joyful tunes." Oh, no, you shall lay your fingers amongst the old accustomed strings, and the art of making melody shall come back to you, and your heart shall once more be glad. He appoints and he gives--the two words put together afford double hope to us--he appoints and he gives comfort to his mourners.

Observe, in the text, the change Christ promises to work for his mourners. First, here is beauty given for ashes. In the Hebrew there is a ring in the words which cannot be conveyed in the English. The ashes that men put upon their head in the East in the time of sorrow made a grim tiara for the brow of the mourner; the Lord promises to put all these ashes away, and to substitute for them a glorious head dress--a diadem of beauty. Or, if we run away from the word, and take the inner sense, we may look at it thus:--mourning makes the face wan and emaciated, and so takes away the beauty; but Jesus promises that he will so come and reveal joy to the sorrowing soul, that the face shall fill up again: the eyes that were dull and cloudy shall sparkle again, and the countenance, yea, and the whole person shall be once more radiant with the beauty which sorrow had so grievously marred. I thank God I have sometimes seen this change take place in precious saints who have been cast down in soul. There has even seemed to be a visible beauty put upon them when they have found peace in Jesus Christ, and this beauty is far more lovely and striking, because it is evidently a beauty of the mind, a spiritual lustre, far superior to the surface comeliness of the flesh. When the Lord shines full upon his servants' faces, he makes them fair as the moon, when at her full she reflects the light of the sun. A gracious and unchanging God sheds on his people a gracious and unfading loveliness. O mourning soul, thou hast made thine eyes red with weeping, and thy cheeks are marred with furrows, down which the scalding tears have burned their way; but the Lord that healeth thee, the Lord Almighty who wipeth all tears from human eyes, shall visit thee yet; and, if thou now believes "in Jesus, he shall visit thee now, and chase these cloudy griefs away, and thy face shall be bright and clear again, fair as the morning, and sparkling as the dew. Thou shalt rejoice in the God of thy salvation, even in God, thy exceeding joy. Is not this a dainty promise for mourning souls?

Then, it is added, "He will give the oil of joy for mourning." Here we have first beauty, and then unction. The Orientals used rich perfumed oils on their persons--used them largely and lavishly in times of great joy. Now, the Holy Spirit comes upon those who believe in Jesus, and gives them an anointing of perfume, most precious, more sweet and costly than the herd of Araby. An unction, such as royalty has never received, sheds its costly moisture over all the redeemed when the Spirit of the Lord rests upon them. "We have an unction from the Holy One," saith the apostle. "Thou anointest my head with oil, my cup runneth over." Oh, how favored are those who have the Spirit of God upon them! You remember that the oil which was poured on Aaron's head went down to the skirts of his garment, so that the same oil was on his skirts that had been on his head. It is the same Spirit that rests on the believer as that which rests on Jesus Christ, and he that is joined unto Christ is one Spirit. What favor is here! instead of mourning, the Christian shall receive the Holy Spirit, the Comforter who shall take of the things of Christ, and reveal them unto him, and make him not merely glad, but honored and esteemed.

Then, it is added, to give still greater fullness to the cheering promise, that the Lord will give "the garment of praise for the spirit of heaviness." The man is first made beautiful, next he has the anointing, then afterwards he is arrayed in robes of splendor. What garments these are! Surely Solomon in all his glory wore not such right royal apparel. "The garment of praise." what a dress is this! Speak of wrought gold, or fine linen, or needlework of divers colors, or taffeta, or damasks, or gorgeous silks most rich and rare which come from far off lands--where is anything compared with "the garment of praise?" When a man wraps himself about, as it were, with psalmody, and lives for ever a chorister, singing not with equal voice, but with the same earnest heart as they do who day and night keep up the never ending hymn before the throne of the infinite! As, what a life is his, what a man is he! O mourner, this is to be your portion; take it now; Jesus Christ will cover you, even at this hour, with the garment of praise; so grateful shall you be for sins forgiven, for infirmity overcome, for watchfulness bestowed, for the church revived, for sinners saved, that you shall undergo the greatest conceivable change, and the sordid garments of your woe shall be put aside for the brilliant array of delight. It shall not be the spirit of praise for the spirit of heaviness, though that were a fair exchange, but as your heaviness you tried to keep to yourself, so your praise you shall not keep to yourself, it shall be a garment to you, external and visible, as well as inward and profound. Wherever you are it shall be displayed to others, and they shall see and take knowledge of you that God has done great things for you whereof you are glad. I wish I had power to speak fitly on such a theme as this; but, surely, it needs him upon whom the Spirit rested without measure to proclaim this joyful promise to the mourners in Zion.

We must close, by noticing what will be the result of this appointment, and text concludes, by saying, "That they might be called trees of righteousness, the planting of the Lord, that he might be glorified." We learn, here, that those mourning souls who are cast down, and have put ashes on their heads, shall, when Jesus Christ in infinite mercy comes to them, be made like trees--like "oaks;" the original is, like "oaks of righteousness," that is, they shall become strong, firmly rooted, covered with verdure; they shall be like a well-watered tree for pleasantness and delight. Thou sayest, "I am a dry tree, a sere branch, I am a cast off, fruitless bough; Oh that I were visited of God and saved! I mourn because I cannot be what I would." Mourner, thou shalt be all thou wouldst be, and much more if Jesus visits thee. Breathe the prayer to him now; look to him, trust him. He can change thee from a withered tree that seems twice dead into a tree standing by the rivers of water, whose leaf is unwithering, and whose fruit ripens in its season. Only have confidence in an anointed Savior, rely upon him who came not here to destroy but to bless, and thou shalt yet through faith become a tree of righteousness, the planting of the Lord, that he may be glorified.

But, the very pith of the text lies in a little word to which you must look. "Ye shall be called trees of righteousness." Now, there are many mourning saints who are trees of righteousness, but nobody calls them so, they are so desponding that they give a doubtful idea to others. Observers ask, "Is this a Christian?" And those who watch and observe them are not at all struck with their Christian character. Indeed, I may be speaking to some here who are true believers in Jesus, but they are all their lifetime subject to bondage; they hardly know themselves whether they are saved, and, therefore, they cannot expect that others should be very much impressed by their godly character and fruitful conversation. But, O mourners! if Jesus visits you, and gives you the oil of joy, men shall call you "trees of righteousness," they shall see grace in you, they shall not be able to help owning it, it shall be so distinct in the happiness of your life, that they shall be compelled to see it. I know some Christian people who, wherever they go, are attractive advertisements of the gospel. Nobody could be with them for a half an hour without saying, "Whence do they gain this calm, this peace, this tranquility, this holy delight and joy?" Many have been attracted to the cross of Christ by the holy pleasantness and cheerful conversation of those whom Christ has visited with the abundance of his love. I wish we were all such. I would not discourage a mourner; no, but encourage him to seek after the garments of praise; nevertheless, I must say that it is a very wretched thing for so many professors to go about the world grumbling at what they have and at what they have not, murmuring at the dispensations of providence, and at the labors of their brethren. They are more like wild crab-trees than the Lords fruit-trees. Well may people say, "If these are Christians, God save us from such Christianity." But, when a man is contented--more than that, when he is happy under all circumstances, when "his spirit doth rejoice in God his Savior" in deep distress, when he can sing in the fires of affliction, when he can rejoice on the bed of sickness, when his shout of triumph grows louder as his conflict waxes more and more severe, and when he can utter the sweetest song of victory in his departing moments, then all who see such people call them trees of righteousness, they confess that they are the people of God.

Note, still, the result of all this goes further, "They shall he called trees of righteousness, the planting of the Lord," that is to say, where there is joy imparted, and unction given from the Holy Spirit, instead of despondency, men will say, "It is God's work, it is a tree that God has planted, it could not grow like that if anybody else had planted it; this man is a man of God's making, his joy is a joy of God's giving." I feel sure that in the case of some of us we were under such sadness of heart before conversion, through a sense of sin, that when we did find peace, everybody noticed the change there was in us, and they said one to another, "Who has made this man so happy, for he was just now most heady and depressed?" And, when we told them where we lost our burden, they said, "Ah, there is something, in religion after all." "Then said they among the heathen the Lord hath done great things for them." Remember poor Christian in Pilgrim's Progress. Mark what heavy sighs he heaved, what tears fell from his eyes, what a wretched man he was when he wrung his hands, and said, "The city wherein I dwell is to be burned up with fire from heaven, and I shall be consumed in it, and, besides, I am myself undone by reason of a burden that lieth hard upon me. Oh that I could get rid of it!" Do you remember John Bunyan's description of how he got rid of the burden? He stood at the foot of the cross, and there was a sepulcher hard by, and as he stood and looked, and saw one hanging on the tree, suddenly the bands that bound his burden cracked, and the load rolled right away into the sepulcher, and when he looked for it, it could not be found. And what did he do? Why, he gave three great leaps for joy, and sang,

"Bless'd cross! bless'd sepulcher! bless'd rather
be the man that there was put to shame for me."

If those who knew the pilgrim in his wretchedness had met him on the other side of that never-to-be-forgotten sepulcher, they would have said, "Are you the same man?" If Christiana had met him that day, she would have said, "My husband, are you the same? What a change has come over you;" and, when she and the children marked the father's cheerful conversation, they could have been compelled to say, "It is the Lord's doing, and it is wondrous in our eyes." Oh live such a happy life that you may compel the most wicked man to ask where you learned the art of living. Let the stream of your life be so clear, so limpid, so cool, so sparkling, so like the river of the water of life above, that men may say, "Whence came this crystal rivulet? We will trace it to its source," and so may they be led to the foot of that dear cross where all your hopes began.

Another word remains, and when we have considered it, we will conclude. That other word is this, "The planting of the Lord, that he might be glorified." That is the end of it all, that is the great result we drive at, and that is the object even of God himself, "that he might be glorified." For when men see the cheerful Christian, and perceive that this is God's work, then they own the power of God; not always, perhaps, with their hearts as they should, but still they are obliged to confess "this is the finger of God." Meanwhile, the saints, comforted by your example, praise and bless God, and all the church lifts up a song to the Most High. Come, my brethren and sisters, are any of you down; are you almost beneath the enemy's foot? Here is a word for you, "Rejoice not over me, O mine enemy, though I fall yet shall I rise again." Are any of you in deep trouble--very deep trouble? Another word then for you; "When thou passeth through the waters, I will be with thee, and through the rivers, they shall not overflow thee: when thou walkest through the fire, thou shalt not be burned; neither shall the flame kindle upon thee." Are you pressed with labors and afflictions? "As thy days so shall thy strength be," "All things work together for good to them that love God, to them that are the called according to his purpose." Are you persecuted? Here is a note of encouragement for you: "Blessed are ye, when men shall revile you, and persecute you, and shall say all manner of evil against you falsely, for my sake. Rejoice, and be exceeding glad; for great is your reward in heaven: for so persecuted they the prophets which were before you." Whatever your circumstances are, "Rejoice in the Lord always, and again I say rejoice." Think what Jesus has given you, your sins are pardoned for his name sake, your heaven is made secure to you, and all that is wanted to bring you there; you have grace in your hearts, and glory awaits you; you have already grace within you, and greater grace shall be granted you; you are renewed by the Spirit of Christ in your inner man the good work is begun, and God will never leave it till he has finished it; your names are in his book, nay, graven on the palms of his hands; his love never changes, his power never diminishes, his grace never fails, his truth is firm as the hills, and his faithfulness is like the great mountains. Lean on the love of his heart, on the might of his arm, on the merit of his blood, on the power of his plea, and the indwelling of his Spirit. Take such promises as these for your consolation, "Strengthen ye the weak hands, and confirm the feeble knees. Say to them that are of a fearful heart, be strong, fear not." "Fear not, thou worm Jacob, and ye men of Israel; I will help thee, saith the Lord, and thy Redeemer, the Holy One of Israel." "For a small moment have I forsaken thee; but with great mercies will I gather thee. In a little wrath I hid my face from thee for a moment; but with everlasting kindness will I have mercy on thee, saith the Lord thy Redeemer. For this is as the waters of Noah unto me: for as I have sworn that the waters of Noah should no more go over the earth; so have I sworn that I would not be wroth with thee, nor rebuke thee. For the mountains shall depart, and the hills be removed; but my kindness shall not depart from thee, neither shall the covenant of my peace be removed, saith the Lord that hath mercy on thee." "My grace is sufficient for thee, for my strength is made perfect in weakness." "He giveth power to the faint; and to them that have no might he increaseth strength." "The eternal God is thy refuge, and underneath are the everlasting arms: and he shall thrust out the enemy from before thee; and shall say, destroy them." "I am God, I fail not, therefore ye sons of Jacob are not consumed." One might continue for ever quoting these precious passages, but may the Lord apply one or other of them to every mourner's soul; and, especially if there be a mourning sinner here, may he get a grip of that choice word, "Him that cometh to me I will in no wise cast out;" or, that other grand sentence, "All manner of sin and blasphemy shall be forgiven unto men;" or, that other, "The blood of Jesus Christ, his Son, cleanseth us from all sin:" or, that equally encouraging word, "Come now, and let us reason together; though your sins be as scarlet they shall be as wool, though they be red like crimson they shall be as snow." The Lord bring us all into comfort and joy by the way of the cross.

Peradventure, I speak to some for whom the promises of God have no charm; let me, then, remind them that his threatenings are as sure as his promises. He can bless, but he can also curse. Be appoints mourning for those who laugh now with sinful merriment; he will give to his enemies vengeance for all their rebellions. He has himself said, "And it shall come to pass, that instead of sweet smell there shall be stink; and instead of a girdle a rent; and instead of well set hair baldness; and instead of a stomacher a girding of sackcloth; and burning instead of beauty." Beware, then, ye that forget God, lest he overthrow you in his hot displeasure. Seek ye the Savior now, lest the acceptable year of the Lord be closed with a long winter of utter despair.

"Ye who spurn his righteous sway,
Yet, oh yet, he spares your breath;
Yet his hand, averse to slay,
Balances the bolt of death.
Ere that dreadful bolt descends,
Haste before his feet to fall,
Kiss the scepter he extends,
And adore him, Lord of all.'"

PORTION OF SCRIPTURE READ BEFORE SERMON--Isaiah 61.

The Talking Book

A Sermon (No. 1017)
Delivered on Lord's-day Morning, October 22nd, 1871 by
C. H. SPURGEON,
At the Metropolitan Tabernacle, Newington

"When thou awakest, it shall talk with thee" - Proverbs 6:22.

IT IS A VERY HAPPY CIRCUMSTANCE when the commandment of our father and the law of our mother are also the commandment of God and the law of the Lord. Happy are they who have a double force to draw them to the right--the bonds of nature, and the cords of grace. They sin with a vengeance who sin both against a father on earth and the great Father in heaven, and they exhibit a virulence and a violence of sin who do despite to the tender obligations of childhood, as well as to the demands of conscience and God. Solomon, in the passage before us, evidently speaks of those who find in the parents' law and in God's law the same thing, and he admonishes such to bind the law of God about their heart, and to tie it about their neck; by which he intends inward affection and open avowal. The law of God should be so dear to us, that is should be bound about the most vital organ of our being, braided about our heart. That which a man carries in his hand he may forget and lose, that which he wears upon his person may be torn from him, but that which is bound about his heart will remain there as long as life remains. We are to love the Word of God with all our heart, and mind, and soul, and strength; with the full force of our nature we are to embrace it; all our warmest affections are to be bound up with it. When the wise man tells us, also, to wear it about our necks, he means that we are never to be ashamed of it. No blush is to mantle our cheek when we are called Christians; we are never to speak with bated breath in any company concerning the things of God. Manfully must we take up the cross of Christ; cheerfully must we avow ourselves to belong to those who have respect unto the divine testimonies. Let us count true religion to be our highest ornament; and, as magistrates put upon them their gold chains, and think themselves adorned thereby, so let us tie about our neck the commands and the gospel of the Lord our God.

In order that we may be persuaded so to do, Solomon gives us three telling reasons. He says that God's law, by which I understand the whole run of Scripture, and, especially the gospel of Jesus Christ, will be a guide to us:--"When thou goest, it shall lead thee." It will be a guardian to us: "When thou sleepest"--when thou art defenceless and off thy guard--"it shall keep thee." And it shall also be a dear companion to us: "When thou awakest, it shall talk with thee." Any one of these three arguments might surely suffice to make us seek a nearer acquaintance with the sacred word. We all need a guide, for "it is not in man that walketh to direct his steps." Left to our own way, we soon excel in folly. There are dilemmas in all lives where a guide is more precious than a wedge of gold. The Word of God, as an infallible director for human life, should be sought unto by us, and it will lead us in the highway of safety. Equally powerful is the second reason: the Word of God will become the guardian of our days; whoso hearkeneth unto it shall dwell safely, and shall be quiet from fear of evil. Unguarded moments there may be; times, inevitable to our imperfection, there will be, when, unless some other power protect us, we shall fall into the hands of the foe. Blessed is he who has God's law so written on his heart, and wears it about his neck as armour of proof, that at all times he is invulnerable, kept by the power of God through faith unto salvation.

But I prefer, this morning, to keep to the third reason for loving God's word. It is this, that is becomes our sweet companion: "When thou awakest, it shall talk with thee." The inspired law of God, which David in the hundred and nineteenth Psalm calls God's testimonies, precepts, statutes, and the like, is the friend of the righteous. Its essence and marrow is the gospel of Jesus, the law-fulfiller, and this also is the special solace of believers. Of the whole sacred volume it may be said, "When thou awakest, it shall talk with thee." I gather four or five thoughts from this expression, and upon these we will speak.

I. We perceive here that THE WORD IS LIVING. How else could it be said: "It shall talk with thee"? A dead book cannot talk, nor can a dumb book speak. It is clearly a living book, then, and a speaking book: "The word of God, which liveth and abideth for ever." How many of us have found this to be most certainly true! A large proportion of human books are long ago dead, and even shrivelled like Egyptian mummies; the mere course of years has rendered them worthless, their teaching is disproved, and they have no life for us. Entomb them in your public libraries if you will, but, henceforth, they will stir no man's pulse and warm no man's heart. But this thrice blessed book of God, though it has been extant among us these many hundreds of years, is immortal in its life, unwithering in its strength: the dew of its youth is still upon it; its speech still drops as the rain fresh from heaven; its truths are overflowing founts of ever fresh consolation. Never book spake like this book; its voice, like the voice of God, is powerful and full of majesty.

Whence comes it that the word of God is living? Is it not, first, because it is pure truth? Error is death, truth is life. No matter how well established an error may be by philosophy, or by force of arms, or the current of human thought, the day cometh that shall burn as an oven, and all untruth shall be as stubble before the fire. The tooth of time devours all lies. Falsehoods are soon cut down, and they wither as the green herb. Truth never dies, it dates its origin from the immortals. Kindled at the source of light, its fame cannot be quenched; if by persecution it be for a time covered, it shall blaze forth anew to take reprisals upon its adversaries. Many a once venerated system of error now rots in the dead past among the tombs of the forgotten; but the truth as it is in Jesus knows no sepulchre, and fears no funeral; it lives on, and must live while the Eternal fills His throne.

The word of God is living, because it is the utterance of an immutable, self-existing God. God doth not speak to-day what He meant not yesterday, neither will He to-morrow blot out what He records to-day. When I read a promise spoken three thousand years ago, it is as fresh as though it fell from the eternal lips to-day. There are, indeed, no dates to the Divine promises; they are not of private interpretation, nor to be monopolised by any generation. I say again, as fresh to-day the eternal word drops from the Almighty's lips as when He uttered it to Moses, or to Elias, or spake it by the tongue of Esaias or Jeremiah. The word is always sure, steadfast, and full of power. It is never out of date. Scripture bubbles up evermore with good matters, it is an eternal Geyser, a spiritual Niagara of grace, for ever falling, flashing, and flowing on; it is never stagnant, never brackish or defiled, but always clear, crystal, fresh, and refreshing; so, therefore, ever living.

The word lives, again, because it enshrines the living heart of Christ. The heart of Christ is the most living of all existences. It was once pierced with a spear, but it lives on, and yearns towards sinners, and is as tender and compassionate as in the days of the Redeemer's flesh. Jesus, the Sinner's Friend, walks in the avenues of Scripture as once He traversed the plains and hills of Palestine: you can see Him still, if you have opened eyes, in the ancient prophecies; you can behold Him more clearly in the devout evangelists; He opens and lays bare His inmost soul to you in the epistles, and makes you hear the footsteps of His approaching advent in the symbols of the Apocalypse. The living Christ is in the book; you behold His face almost in every page; and, consequently, it is a book that can talk. The Christ of the mount of benedictions speaks in it still; the God who said, "Let there be light," gives forth from its pages the same divine fiat; while the incorruptible truth, which saturated every line and syllable of it when first it was penned, abides therein in full force, and preserves it from the finger of decay. "The grass withereth, and the flower thereof falleth away: but the word of the Lord endureth for ever."

Over and above all this, the Holy Spirit has a peculiar connection with the word of God. I know that He works in the ministries of all His servants whom He hath ordained to preach; but for the most part, I have remarked that the work of the Spirit of God in men's hearts is rather in connection with the texts we quote than with our explanations of them. "Depend upon it," says a deeply spiritual writer, "it is God's word, not man's comment on it, which saves souls." God does save souls by our comment, by still it is true that the majority of conversions have been wrought by the agency of a text of Scripture. It is the word of God that is living, and powerful, and sharper than any two-edged sword. There must be life in it, for by it men are born again. As for believers, the Holy Spirit often sets the word on a blaze while they are studying it. The letters were at one time before us as mere letters, but the Holy Ghost suddenly came upon them, and they spake with tongues. The chapter is lowly as the bush at Horeb, but the Spirit descends upon it, and lo! it glows with celestial splendour, God appearing in the words, so that we feel like Moses when he put off his shoes from his feet, because the place whereon he stood was holy ground. It is true, the mass of readers understand not this, and look upon the Bible as a common book; but if they understand it not, as least let them allow the truthfulness of our assertion, when we declare that hundreds of times we have as surely felt the presence of God in the page of Scripture as ever Elijah did when he heard the Lord speaking in a still small voice. The Bible has often appeared to us as a temple God, and the posts of its doors have moved at the voice of Him that cried, whose train also has filled the temple. We have been constrained adoringly to cry, with the seraphim. "Holy, holy, holy, is the Lord God of Hosts." God the Holy Spirit vivifies the letter with His presence, and then it is to us a living word indeed.

And now, dear brethren, if these things be so--and our experience certifies them--let us take care how we trifle with a book which is so instinct with life. Might not many of you remember your faults this day were we to ask you whether you are habitual students of holy writ? Readers of it I believe you are; but are you searchers; for the promise is not to those who merely read, but to those who delight in the law of the Lord, and meditate therein both day and night. Are you sitting at the feet of Jesus, with His word as your school-book? If not, remember, though you may be saved, you lacked very much of the blessing which otherwise you might enjoy. Have you been backsliding? Refresh your soul by meditating in the divine statues, and you will say, with David, "Thy word hath quickened me." Are you faint and weary? Go and talk with this living book: it will give you back your energy, and you shall mount again as with the wings of eagles. But are you unconverted altogether? Then I cannot direct you to Bible-reading as being the way of salvation, nor speak of it as though it had any merit in it; but I would, nevertheless, urge upon you unconverted people great reverence for Scripture, an intimate acquaintance with its contents, and a frequent perusal of its pages, for it has occurred ten thousand times over that when men have been studying the word of life, the word has brought life to them. "The entrance of thy word giveth light." Like Elijah and the dead child, the word has stretched itself upon them, and their dead souls have been made to live. One of the likeliest places in which to find Christ is in the garden of the Scriptures, for there He delights to walk. As of old, the blind men were wont to sit by the wayside begging, so that, if Jesus passed by, they might cry to Him, so would I have you sit down by the wayside of the Holy Scriptures. Hear the promises, listen to their gracious words; they are the footsteps of the Saviour; and, as you hear them, may you be led to cry, "Thou Son of David, have mercy upon me!" Attend most those ministries which preach God's Word most. Do not select those that are fullest of fine speaking, and that dazzle you with expressions which are ornamental rather than edifying; but get to a ministry that is full of God's own Word, and, above all, learn God's Word itself. Read it with a desire to know its meaning, and I am persuaded that, thereby, many of you who are now far from God will be brought near to him, and led to a saving faith in Jesus, for "the Word of the Lord is perfect, converting the soul." "Faith cometh by hearing, and hearing by the word of God."

II. If the text says, "When thou awakest, it shall talk with thee," then it is clear THE WORD IS PERSONAL. "It shall talk with thee." It is not written, "It shall speak to the air, and thou shalt hear its voice," but, "It shall talk with thee." You know exactly what the expression means. I am not exactly talking with any one of you this morning; there are too many of you, and I am but one; but, when you are on the road home, each one will talk with his fellow: then it is truly talk when man speaks to man. Now, the word of God has the condescending habit of talking to men, speaking personally to them; and, herein, I desire to commend the word of God to your love. Oh! that you might esteem it very precious for this reason!

"It shall talk with thee," that is to say, God's word talks about men, and about modern men; it speaks of ourselves, and of these latter days, as precisely as if it had only appeared this last week. Some go to the word of God with the idea that they shall find historical information about the ancient ages, and so they will, but that is not the object of the Word. Others look for facts upon geology, and great attempts have been made either to bring geology round to Scripture, or Scripture to geology. We may always rest assured that truth never contradicts itself; but, as nobody knows anything yet about geology--for its theory is a dream and an imagination altogether--we will wait till the philosophers settle their own private matters, being confident that when they find out the truth, it will be quite consistent with what God has revealed. At any rate, we may leave that. The main teachings of Holy Scripture are about men, about the Paradise of unfallen manhood, the fall, the degeneracy of the race, and the means of its redemption. The book speaks of victims and sacrifices, priests and washings, and so points us to the divine plan by which man can be elevated from the fall and be reconciled to God. Read Scripture through, and you shall find that its great subject is that which concerns the race as to their most important interests. It is a book that talks, talks personally, for it deals with things not in the moon, nor in the planet Jupiter, nor in the distant ages long gone by, nor does it say much of the periods yet to come, but it deals with us, with the business of to-day; how sin may be to-day forgiven, and our souls brought at once into union with Christ.

Moreover, this book is so personal, that it speaks to men in all states and conditions before God. How it talks to sinners--talks, I say, for its puts it thus: "Come, now, and let us reason together; though your sins be as scarlet, they shall be as wool; though they be red like crimson, they shall be as snow." It has many very tender expostulations for sinners. It stoops to their condition and position. If they will not stoop to God, it makes, as it were, eternal mercy stoop to them. It talks of feasts of fat things, of fat things full of marrow; and the book, as it talks, reasons with men's hunger, and bids them eat and be satisfied. In all conditions into which the sinner can be cast, there is a word that precisely meets his condition.

And, certainly, when we become the children of God the book talks with us wondrously. In the family of heaven it is the child's own book. We no sooner know our Father than this dear book comes at once as a love letter from the far-off country, signed with our own Father's hand, and perfumed with our Father's love. If we grow in grace, or if we backslide, in either case Scripture still talks with us. Whatever our position before the eternal God, the book seems to be written on purpose to meet that position. It talks to you as you are, not only as you should be, or as others have been, but with you, with you personally, about your present condition.

Have you never noticed how personal the book is as to all your states of mind, in reference to sadness or to joy? There was a time with some of us when we were very gloomy and sore depressed, and then the book of Job mourned to the same dolorous tune. I have turned over the Lamentations of Jeremiah wrote. It mourns unto us when we lament. On the other hand, when the soul gets up to the exceeding high mountains, to the top of Amana and Lebanon, when we behold visions of glory, and see our Beloved face to face, lo! The word is at our side, and in the delightful language of the Psalms, or in the yet sweeter expressions of the Song of Solomon, it tells us all that is in our heart, and talks to us as a living thing that has been in the deeps, and has been on the heights, that has known the overwhelmings of affliction, and has rejoiced in the triumphs of delight. The word of God is to me my own book: I have no doubt, brother, it is the same to you. There could not be a Bible that suited me better: it seems written on purpose for me. Dear sister, have not you often felt as you have put your finger on a promise, "Ah, that is my promise; if there be no other soul whose tearful eyes can bedew that page and say, It is mine,' yet I, a poor afflicted one, can do so!" Oh, yes; the book is very personal, for it goes into all the details of our case, let our state be what it may.

And, how very faithful it always is. You never find the word of God keeping back that which is profitable to you. Like Nathan it cries, "Thou art the man." It never allows our sins to go unrebuked, nor our backslidings to escape notice till they grow into overt sin. It gives us timely notice; it cries to us as soon as we begin to go aside, "Awake thou that sleepest," "Watch and pray," "Keep thine heart with all diligence," and a thousand other words of warning does it address personally to each one of us.

Now I would suggest, before I leave this point, a little self-examination as healthful for each of us. Does the word of God after this fashion speak to my soul? Then it is a gross folly to lose by generalisations that precious thing which can only be realised by a personal grasp. How sayest thou, dear hearer? Dost thou read the book for thyself, and does the book speak to thee? Has it ever condemned thee, and has thou trembled before the word of God? Has it ever pointed thee to Christ, and has thou looked to Jesus the incarnate Saviour? Does the book now seal, as with the witness of the Spirit, the witness of thine own spirit that thou art born of God? Art thou in the habit of going to the book to know thine own condition, to see thine own face as in a glass? Is it thy family medicine? Is it thy test and tell-tale to let thee know thy spiritual condition? Oh, do not treat the book otherwise than this, for if thou dost thus unto it, and takest it to be thy personal friend, happy art thou, since God will dwell with the man that trembles at His word; but, if you treat it as anybody's book rather than your own, then beware, lest you be numbered with the wicked who despise God's statutes.

III. From the text we learn that HOLY SCRIPTURE IS VERY FAMILIAR. "When thou awakest, it shall talk with thee. To talk signifies fellowship, communion, familiarity. It does not say, "It shall preach to thee." Many persons have a high esteem for the book, but they look upon it as though it were some very elevated teacher speaking to them from a lofty tribunal, while they stand far below. I will not altogether condemn that reverence, but it were far better if they would understand the familiarity of God's word; it does not so much preach to us as talk to us. It is not, "When thou awakest, it shall lecture thee," or, it shall scold thee;" no, no, "it shall talk with thee." We sit at its feet, or rather at the feet of Jesus, in the Word, and it comes down to us; it is familiar with us, as a man talketh to his friend. And here let me remind you of the delightful familiarity of Scripture in this respect that it speaks the language of men. If God had written us a book in His own language, we could not have comprehended it, or what little we understood would have so alarmed us, that we should have besought that those words should not be spoken to us any more; but the Lord, in His Word, often uses language which, though it be infallibly true in its meaning, is not after the knowledge of God, but according to the manner of man. I mean this, that the word uses similes and analogies of which we may say that they speak humanly, and not according to the absolute truth as God Himself sees it. As men conversing with babes use their broken speech, so doth the condescending word. It is not written in the celestial tongue, but in the patois of this lowland country, condescending to men of low estate. It feeds us on bread broken down to our capacity, "food convenient for us". It speaks of God's arm, His hand, His finger, His wings, and even of His feathers. Now, all this is familiar picturing, to meet our childish capacities; for the Infinite One is not to be conceived of as though such similitudes were literal facts. It is an amazing instance of divine love, that He puts those things so that we may be helped to grasp sublime truths. Let us thank the Lord of the word for this.

How tenderly Scripture comes down to simplicity. Suppose the sacred volume had all been like the book of the prophet Ezekiel, small would have been its service to the generality of mankind. Imagine that the entire volume had been as mysterious as the Book of Revelation: it might have been our duty to study it, but if its benefit depended upon our understanding it, wew should have failed to attain it. But how simple are the gospels, how plain these words, "He that believeth and is baptised shall be saved"; how deliciously clear those parables about the lost piece of money, the lost sheep, and the prodigal son. Wherever the word touches upon vital points, it is as bright as a sunbeam. Mysteries there are, and profound doctrines, deeps where Leviathan can swim; but, where it has to do immediately with what concerns us for eternity, it is so plain that the babe in grace may safely wade in its refreshing streams. In the gospel narrative the wayfaring man, though a fool, need not err. It is familiar talk; it is God's great mind brought down to our littleness, that it may lift us up.

How familiar the book is too--I speak now as to my own feelings--as to all that concerns us. It talks about my flesh, and my corruptions, and my sins, as only one that knew me could speak. It talks of my trials in the wisest way; some, I dare not tell, it knows all about. It talks about my difficulties; some would sneer at them and laugh, but this book sympathises with them, knows my tremblings, and my fears, and my doubts, and all the storm that rages within the little world of my nature. The book has been through all my experience; somehow or other it maps it all out, and talks with me as if it were a fellow-pilgrim. It does not speak to me unpractically, and scold me, and look down on me from an awful height of stern perfection, as if it were an angel, and could no sympathise with fallen men; but like the Lord whom it reveals, the book seems as if it were touched with a feeling of my infirmities, and had been tempted in all points like as I am. Have you not often wondered at the human utterances of the divine word: it thunders like God and yet weeps like man. It seems impossible that anything should be too little for the word of God to notice, or too bitter, or even too sinful for that book to overlook. It touches humanity at all points. Everywhere it is a personal, familiar acquaintance, and seems to say to itself, "Shall I hide this thing from Abraham my friend?"

And, how often the book has answered enquiries! I have been amazed in times of difficulties to see how plain the oracle is. You have asked friends, and they could not advise you; but you have gone to your knees, and God has told you. You have questioned, and you have puzzled, and you have tried to elucidate the problem, and lo! In the chapter read at morning prayer, or in a passage of Scripture that lay open before you, the direction has been given. Have we not seen a text, as it were, plume its wings, and fly from the word like a seraph, and touch our lips with a live altar coal? It lay like a slumbering angel amidst the beds of spices of the sacred word, but it received a divine mission, and brought consolation and instruction to your heart.

The word of God, then, talks with us in the sense of being familiar with us. Do we understand this? I will close this point by another word of application. Who, then, that finds God's word so dear and kind a friend would spurn or neglect it? If any of you have despised it, what shall I say to you? If it were a dreary book, written within and without with curses and lamentations, whose every letter flashed with declarations of vengeance, I might see some reason why we should not read it; but, O precious, priceless companion, dear friend of all my sorrows, making my bed in my sickness, the light of my darkness, and the joy of my soul, how can I forget thee--how can I forsake thee? I have heard of one who said that the dust on some men's Bibles lay there so thick and long that you might write "Damnation" on it. I am afraid that such is that case with some of you. Mr. Rogers, of Dedham, on one occasion, after preaching about the preciousness of the Bible, took it away from the front of the pulpit, and, putting it down behind him, pictured God as saying, "You do not read the book: you do not care about it; I will take it back--you shall not be wearied with it any more." And then he portrayed the grief of wise men's hearts when they found the blessed revelation withdrawn from men; and how they would besiege the throne of grace, day and night, to ask it back. I am sure he spoke the truth. Though we too much neglect it, yet ought we to prize it beyond all price, for, if it were taken from us, we should have lost our kindest comforter in the hour of need. God grant us to love the Scriptures more!

IV. Fourthly, and with brevity, our text evidently shows that THE WORD IS RESPONSIVE. "When thou awakest, it shall talk with thee," not to thee. Now, talk with a man is not all on one side. To talk with a man needs answering talk from him. You have both of you something to say when you talk together. It is a conversation to which each one contributes his part. Now, Scripture is a marvellously conversational book; it talks, and makes men talk. It is ever ready to respond to us. Suppose you go to the Scriptures in a certain state of spiritual life: you must have noticed, I think, that the word answer to that state. If you are dark and gloomy, it will appear as though it had put itself in mourning, so that it might lament with you. When you are on the dunghill, there sits Scripture, with dust and ashes on its head, weeping side by side with you, and not upbraiding like Job's miserable comforters. But suppose you come to the book with gleaming eyes of joy, you will hear it laugh; it will sing and play to you as with psaltery and harp, it will bring forth the high-sounding cymbals. Enter its goodly land in a happy state, and you shall go forth with you and be led forth with peace, its mountains and its hills shall break before you into singing, and all the trees of the field shall clap their hands. As in water the face is reflected, so in the living stream of revealed truth a man sees his own image.

If you come to Holy Scripture with growth in grace, and with aspirations for yet higher attainments, the book grows with you, grows upon you. It is ever beyond you, and cheerily cries, "Higher yet; Excelsior!" Many books in my library are now behind and beneath me; I read them years ago, with considerable pleasure; I have read them since, with disappointment; I shall never read them again, for they are of no service to me. They were good in their way once, and so were the clothes I wore when I was ten years old; but I have outgrown them I know more than these books know, and know wherein they are faulty. Nobody ever outgrows Scripture; the book widens and deepens with our years. It is true, it cannot really grow, for it is perfect; but it does so to our apprehension. The deeper you dig into Scripture, the more you find that it is a great abyss of truth. The beginner learns four or five points of orthodoxy, and says, "I understand the gospel, I have grasped all the Bible." Wait a bit, and when his soul grows and knows more of Christ, he will confess, "Thy commandment is exceeding broad, I have only begun to understand it."

There is one thing about God's word which shows its responsiveness to us, and that is when you reveal your heart to it, it reveals its heart to you. If, as you read the word, you say, "O blessed truth, thou art indeed realised in my experience; come thou still further into my heart. I give up my prejudices, I assign myself, like the wax, to be stamped with thy seal,"--when you do that, and open your heart to Scripture, Scripture will open its heart to you; for it has secrets which it does not tell to the casual reader, it has precious things of the everlasting hills which can only be discovered by miners who know how to dig and open the secret places, and penetrate great veins of everlasting riches. Give thyself up to the Bible, and the Bible will give itself up to thee. Be candid with it, and honest with thy soul, and the Scripture will take down its golden key, and open one door after another, and show to thy astonished gaze ingots of silver which thou couldst not weigh, and heaps of gold which thou couldst not measure. Happy is that man who, in talking with the Bible, tells it all his heart, and learns the secret of the Lord which is with them that fear Him.

And how, too, if you love the bible and talk out your love to it, the Bible will love you! Its wisdom says, "I love them that love me." Embrace the word of God, and the word of God embraces you at once. When you prize its every letter, then it smiles upon you graciously, greets you with many welcomes, and treats you as an honoured guest. I am always sorry to be on bad terms with the Bible, for then I must be on bad terms with God. Whenever my creed does not square with God's word, I think it is time to mould my creed into another form. As for God's words, they must not be touched with hammer or axe. Oh, the chiselling, and cutting, and hammering in certain commentaries to make God's Bible orthodox and systematic! How much better to leave it alone! The word is right, and we are wrong, wherein we agree not with it. The teachings of God's word are infallible, and must be reverenced as such. Now, when you love it so well that you would not touch a single line of it, and prize it so much that you would even die for the defence of one of its truths, then, as it is dear to you, you will be dear to it, and it will grasp you and unfold itself to you as it does not to the world.

Dear brethren and sisters, I must leave this point, but it shall be with this remark--Do you talk to God? Does God talk to you? Does your heart go up to heaven, and does His Word come fresh from heaven to your soul? If not, you do not know the experience of the living child of God, and I can earnestly pray you may. May you this day be brought to see Christ Jesus in the word, to see a crucified Saviour there, and to put your trust in Him, and then, from this day forward, the word will echo to your heart--it will respond to your emotions.

V. Lastly, SCRIPTURE IS INFLUENTIAL. That I gather from the fact that Solomon says, "When thou wakest, it shall talk with thee"; and follows it up with the remark that it keeps man from the strange woman, and from other sins which he goes on to mention. When the word of God talks with us, it influences us. All talk influences more or less. I believe there more done in this world for good or bad by talk than there is by preaching; indeed, the preacher preaches best when he talks; there is no oratory in the world that is equal to simple talk; it is the model of eloquence; and all your rhetorician's action and verbiage are so much rubbish. The most efficient way of preaching is simply talking; the man permitting his heart to run over at his lips into other men's hearts. Now, this book, as it talks with us, influences us, and it does so in many ways.

It soothes our sorrows, and encourages us. Many a warrior has been ready to steal away from God's battle, but the word has laid its hand on him, and said, "Stand on thy feet, be not discouraged, be of good cheer, I will strengthen thee, I will help thee; yea, I will uphold thee with the right hand of my righteousness." Brave saints we have read of, but we little know how often they would have been arrant cowards only the good word came and strengthened them, and they went back to be stronger than lions and swifter than eagles.

While the book thus soothes and cheers, it has a wonderfully elevating power. How you never felt it put fresh life-blood into you? You have thought, "How can I continue to live at such a dying rate as I have lived, something nobler must I gain?" Read that part of the word which tells of the agonies of your Master, and you will feel--

"Now for the love I bear His name,
What was my gain I count my loss;
My former pride I call my shame,
And nail my glory to His cross."

Read of the glories of heaven which this book reveals, and you will feel that you can run the race with quickened speed, because a crown so bright is glittering in your view. Nothing can so lift a man above the gross considerations of carnal gain or human applause as to have his soul saturated with the spirit of truth. It elevates as well as cheers.

Then, too, how often it warns and restrains. I had gone to the right or to the left if the law of the Lord had not said, "Let thine eyes look right on, and let thine eyelids look straight before thee."

This book's consecrated talk sanctifies and moulds the mind into the image of Christ. You cannot expect to grow in grace if you do not read the Scriptures. If you are not familiar with the word, you cannot expect to become like Him that spake it. Our experience is, as it were, the potter's wheel on which we revolve; and the hand of God is in the Scriptures to mould us after the fashion and image which He intends to bring us to. Oh, be much with the holy word of God, and you will be holy. Be much with the silly novels of the day, and the foolish trifles of the hour, and you will degenerate into vapid wasters of your time; but be much with the solid teaching of God's word, and you will become solid and substantial men and women: drink them in, and feed upon them, and they shall produce in you a Christ-likeness, at which the world shall stand astonished.

Lastly, let the Scripture talk with you, and it will confirm and settle you. We hear every now and then of apostates from the gospel. hey must have been little taught in the truth as it is in Jesus. A great outcry is made, every now and then, about our all being perverted to Rome. I was assured the other day by a good man with a great deal of alarm, that all England was going over to Popery. I told him I did not know what kind of God he worshipped, but my God was a good deal bigger than the devil, and did not intend to let the devil have his way after all, and that I was not half as much afraid of the Pope at Rome as of the Ritualists at home. But mark it, there is some truth in these fears. There will be a going over to one form of error or another unless there be in the Christian church a more honest, industrious, and general reading of Holy Scripture. What if I were to say most of you church members do not read your Bibles, should I be slandering you? You hear on Sabbath day a chapter read, and you perhaps read a passage at family prayer, but a very large number never read the Bible privately for themselves, they take their religion out of the monthly magazine, or accept it from the minister's lips. Oh, for the Berean spirit back again, to search the Scriptures whether these things be so. I would like to see a huge pile of all the book, good and bad that were ever written, prayer-books, and sermons, and hymn-books, and all, smoking like Sodom of old, if the reading of those books keeps you away from the reading of the Bible; for a ton weight of human literature is not worth an ounce of Scripture; one single drop of the essential tincture of the word of God is better than a sea full of our commenting and sermonisings, and the like. The word, the simple, pure, infallible word of God, we must live upon if we are to become strong against error, and tenacious of truth. Brethren, may you be estalished in the faith rooted, grounded, built up; but I know you cannot be except ye search the Scriptures continually.

The time is coming when we shall all fall asleep in death. Oh, how blessed it will be to find when we awake that the word of God will talk with us then, and remember its ancient friendship. Then the promise which we loved before shall be fulfilled; the charming intimations of a blessed future shall be all realised, and the face of Christ, whom we saw as through a glass darkly, shall be all uncovered, and He shall shine upon us as the sun in its strength. God grant us to love the word, and feed thereon, and the Lord shall have the glory for ever and ever. Amen and amen.

PORTION OF SCRIPTURE READ BEFORE SERMON--Psalm 119:161-179; Proverbs 6:1-23.

Pleading

A Sermon (No. 1018)
Delivered on Lord's-day Morning, October 29th, 1871 by
C. H. SPURGEON,
At the Metropolitan Tabernacle, Newington

"But I am poor and needy: make haste unto me, O God: Thou art my help and my deliverer; O Lord, make no tarrying." - Psalm 70:5

YOUNG painters were anxious, in olden times, to study under the great masters. They concluded that they should more easily attain to excellence if they entered the schools of eminent men. Men have paid large premiums that their sons may be apprenticed or articled to those who best understood their trades or professions; now, if any of us would learn the sacred art and mystery of prayer, it is well for us to study the productions of the greatest masters of that science. I am unable to point out one who understood it better than did the psalmist David. So well did he know how to praise, that his psalms have become the language of good men in all ages; and so well did he understand how to pray, that if we catch his spirit, and follow his mode of prayer, we shall have learned to plead with God after the most prevalent sort. Place before you, first of all, David's Son and David's Lord, that most mighty of all intercessors, and, next to Him, you shall find David to be one of the most admirable models for your imitation.

We shall consider our text, then, as one of the productions of a great master in spiritual matters, and we will study it, praying all the while that God will help us to pray after the like fashion.

In our text we have the soul of a successful pleader under four aspects: we view, first, the soul confessing: "I am poor and needy." You have next, the soul pleading, for he makes a plea out of his poor condition, and adds, "Make haste unto me, O God!" You see, thirdly, a soul in it's urgency, for he cries, "Make haste," and he varies the expression but keeps the same idea: "Make no tarrying." And you have in the fourth and last view, a soul grasping God, for the psalmist puts it thus: "Thou art my help and my deliverer"; thus with both hands he lays hold upon His God, so as not to let Him go till a blessing is obtained.

I. To begin with, then, we see in this model of supplication, A SOUL CONFESSING. The wrestler strips before he enters upon the contest, and confession does the like for the man who is about to plead with God. A racer on the plains of prayer cannot hope to win, unless, by confession, repentance, and faith, he lays aside every weight of sin.

Now, let it be ever remembered that confession is absolutely needful to the sinner when he first seeks a Saviour. It is not possible for thee, O seeker, to obtain peace for thy troubled heart, till thou shalt have acknowledged thy transgression and thine iniquity before the Lord. Thou mayest do what thou wilt, ay, even attempt to believe in Jesus, but thou shalt find that the faith of God's elect is not in thee, unless thou art willing to make a full confession of thy transgression, and lay bare thy heart before God. We do not usually think of giving charity to those who do not acknowledge that they need it: the physician does not send his medicine to those who are not sick. The blind man in the gospels had to feel his blindness, and to sit by the wayside begging; if he had entertained a doubt as to whether he were blind of not, the Lord would have passed him by. He opens the eyes of those who confess their blindness, but of others, He says, "Because ye say we see, therefore, your sin remaineth." He asks of those who are brought to Him, "What wilt thou that I should do unto thee?" in order that their need may be publicly avowed. It must be so with all of us: we must offer the confession, or we cannot gain the benediction.

Let me speak especially to you who desire to find peace with God, and salvation through the precious blood: you will do well to make your confession before God very frank, very sincere, very explicit. Surely you have nothing to hide, for there is nothing that you can hide. He knows your guilt already, but He would have you know it, and therefore He bids you confess it. Go into the details of your sin in your secret acknowledgments before God; strip yourself of all excuses, make no apologies; say, "Against thee, thee only have I sinned, and done this evil in thy sight: that thou mightest be justified when thou speakest, and be clear when thou judgest." Acknowledge the evil of sin, ask God to make you feel it; do not treat it as a trifle, for it is none. To redeem the sinner from the effect of sin Christ Himself must needs die, and unless you be delivered from it you must die eternally. Therefore, play not with sin; do not confess it as though it were some venial fault, which would not have been noticed unless God had been too severe; but labour to see sin as God sees it, as an offence against all that is good, a rebellion against all that is kind; see it to be treason, to be ingratitude, or be a mean and base thing. Do not think that you can improve your condition before God by painting your case in brighter colours than it should be. Blacken it: if it were possible blacken it, but it is not possible. When you feel your sin most you have not half felt it; when you confess it most fully you do not know a tithe of it; but oh, to the utmost of your ability make a clean breast of it, and say, "I have sinned against heaven, and before thee." Acknowledge the sins of your youth and your manhood, the sins of your body and of your soul, the sins of omission and of commission, sins against the law and offenses against the gospel; acknowledge all; neither for a moment seek to deny one portion of the evil with which God's law, your own conscience, and his Holy Spirit justly charge you.

And oh, soul, if thou wouldst get peace and approval with God in prayer, confess the ill desert of thy sin. Submit thyself to do whatever divine justice may sentence thee to endure: confess that the deepest hell is thy desert, and confess this not with thy lips only, but with thy soul. Let this be the doleful ditty of thine inmost heart--

"Should sudden vengeance seize my breath,
I must pronounce thee just in death
And, if my soul were sent to hell,
Thy righteous law approves it well."

If thou wilt condemn thyself, God will acquit thee; if thou wilt put the rope about thy neck, and sentence thyself, then he who otherwise would have sentenced thee will say, "I forgive thee, through the merit of my son." But never expect that the King of heaven will pardon a traitor, if he will not confess and forsake his treason. Even the tenderest father expects that the child should humble himself when he has offended, and will not withdraw his frown from him till with tears he has said, "Father, I have sinned." Darest thou expect God to humble Himself to thee, and would it not be so if He did not constrain thee to humble thyself to Him? Wouldst thou have Him connive at thy faults and wink at thy transgressions? He will have mercy, but He must be holy. He is ready to forgive, but not to tolerate sin; and, therefore, He cannot let thee be forgiven if thou huggest thy sins, or if thou presumest to say, "I have not sinned." Hasten, then, O seeker, hasten I pray thee, to the mercy seat with this upon thy lips: "I am poor and needy, I am sinful, I am lost; have pity on me." With such an acknowledgment thou beginnest thy prayer well, and through Jesus thou shalt prosper in it.

Beloved hearers, the same principle applies to the church of God. We are praying for a display of the Holy Spirit's power in this church, and, in order to successful pleading in this matter, it is necessary that we should unanimously make the confession of our text, "I am poor and needy." We must own that we are powerless in this business. Salvation is of the Lord and we cannot save a single soul. The Spirit of God is treasured up in Christ, and we must seek Him of the great head of the church. We cannot command the Spirit, and yet we can do nothing without Him. He bloweth where He listeth. We must deeply feel and honestly acknowledge this. Will you not heartily assent to it my brethren and sisters at this hour. May I not ask you unanimously to renew the confession this morning? We must also acknowledge that we are not worthy that the Holy Spirit should condescend to work with us and by us. There is no fitness in us for his purposes, except he shall give us that fitness. Our sins might well provoke him to leave us: he has striven with us, he has been tender towards us, but he might well go away and say, "I will no more shine upon that church, and no more bless that ministry." Let us feel our unworthiness, it will be a good preparation for earnest prayer; for mark you, brethren, God will have His church before He blesses it know that the blessing is altogether from Himself. "Not by might nor by power, but by my Spirit, saith the Lord." The career of Gideon was a very remarkable one, and it commenced with two most instructive signs. I think our heavenly Father would have all of us learn the very same lesson which He taught to Gideon, and when we have mastered that lesson, He will use us for His own purposes. You remember Gideon laid a fleece upon the barn floor, and in the morning all round was dry and the fleece alone was wet. God alone had saturated the fleece so that he could wring it out, and its moisture was not due to its being placed in a favourable situation, for all around was dry. He would have us learn, that, if the dew of His grace fills any one of us with its heavenly moisture, it is not because we lie upon the barn-floor of a ministry which God usually blesses, or because we are in a church which the Lord graciously visits; but we must be made to see that the visitations of His Spirit are fruits of the Lord's sovereign grace, and gifts of His infinite love, and not of the will of man, neither by man. But then the miracle was reversed, for, as old Thomas Fuller says, "God's miracles will bear to be turned inside out and look as glorious one way as another." The next night the fleece was dry and all around was wet. For sceptics might have said, "Yes, but a fleece would naturally attract moisture, and if there were any in the air, it would be likely to be absorbed by the wool." But, lo, on this occasion, the dew is not where it might be expected to be, even though it lies thickly all around. Damp is the stone and dry is the fleece. So God will have us know that He does not give us His grace because of any natural adaptation in us to receive it, and even where He has given a preparedness of heart to receive, He will have us understand that His grace and His Spirit are most free in action, and sovereign in operation: and that He is not bound to work after any rule of our making. If the fleece be wet He bedews it, and that not because it is a fleece, but because He chooses to do so. He will have all the glory of all His grace from first to last. Come then, my brethren, and become disciples to this truth. Consider that from the great Father of lights every good and perfect gift must come. We are His workmanship, he must work all our works in us [Isaiah 26:12]. Grace is not to be commanded by our position or condition: the wind bloweth where it listeth, the Lord works and no man can hinder; but if He works not, the mightiest and most zealous labour is but in vain.

It is very significant that before Christ fed the thousands, He made the disciples sum up all their provisions. It was well to let them see how low the commissariat had become, for then when the crowds were fed they could not say the basket fed them nor that the lad had done it. God will make us feel how little are our barley loaves, and how small our fishes, and compel us to enquire, "What are they among so many?" When the Saviour bade His disciples cast the net on the right side of the ship, and they dragged such a mighty shoal to land, He did not work the miracle till they had confessed that they had toiled all the night and had taken nothing. They were thus taught that the success of their fishery was dependent upon the Lord, and that it was not their net, nor the way of dragging it, nor their skill and art in handling their vessels, but that altogether and entirely their success came from their Lord. We must get down to this, and the sooner we come to it the better.

Before the ancient Jews kept the passover, observe what they did. The unleavened bread is to be brought in, and the paschal lamb to be eaten; but there shall be no unleavened bread and no paschal lamb, till they have purged out the old leaven. If you have any old strength and self-confidence; if you have anything that is your own, and is, therefore, leavened, it must be swept right out; there must be a bare cupboard before there can come in the heavenly provision, upon which the spiritual passover can be kept. I thank God when He clears us out; I bless His name when He brings us to feel our soul poverty as a church, for then the blessing will be sure to come.

One other illustration will show this, perhaps, more distinctly still. Behold Elijah with the priests of Baal at Carmel. The test appointed to decide Israel's choice was this--the God that answereth by fire let him be God. Baal's priests invoked the heavenly flame in vain. Elijah is confident that it will come upon his sacrifice, but he is also sternly resolved that the false priests and the fickle people shall not imagine that he himself had produced the fire. He determines to make it clear that there is no human contrivance, trickery, or maneuver about the matter. The flame should be seen to be of the Lord, and of the Lord alone. Remember the stern prophet's command, "Fill four barrels with water, and pour it on the burnt sacrifice, and on the wood. And he said, Do it a second time; and they did it a second time. And he said, Do it a third time; and they did it a third time. And the water ran round about the altar; and he filled the trench also with water." There could be no latent fire there. If there had been any combustibles or chemicals calculated to produce fire after the manner of the cheats of the time, they would all have been damped and spoiled. When no one could imagine that man could burn the sacrifice, then the prophet lifted up his eyes to heaven, and began to plead, and down came the fire of the Lord, which consumed the burnt sacrifice and the wood, and the altar stones and the dust, and even licked up the water that was in the trench. Then when all the people saw it they fell on their faces, and they said, "Jehovah is the God; Jehovah is the God." The Lord in this church, if He means greatly to bless us, may send us trial of pouring on the water once, and twice, and thrice; He may discourage us, grieve us, and try us, and bring us low, till all shall see that it is not of the preacher, it is not of the organization, it is not of man, but altogether of God, the Alpha and the Omega, who workest all things according to the council of His will.

Thus I have shown you that for a successful season of prayer the best beginning is confession that we are poor and needy.

II. Secondly, after the soul has unburdened itself of all weights of merit and self-sufficiency, it proceeds to prayer, and we have before us A SOUL PLEADING. "I am poor and needy, make haste unto me, O God. Thou art my help and my deliverer: O Lord, make no tarrying." The careful reader will perceive four pleas in this single verse.

Upon this topic I would remark that it is the habit of faith, when she is praying, to use pleas. Mere prayer sayers, who do not pray at all, forget to argue with God; but those who would prevail bring forth their reasons and their strong arguments and they debate the question with the Lord. They who play at wrestling catch here and there at random, but those who are really wrestling have a certain way of grasping the opponent--a certain mode of throwing, and the like; they work according to order and rule. Faith's art of wrestling is to plead with God, and say with holy boldness, "Let it be thus and thus, for these reasons." Hosea tells us of Jacob at Jabbok, "that there he spake with us"; from which I understand that Jacob instructed us by his example. Now, the two pleas which Jacob used were God's precept and God's promise. First, he said, "Thou saidst unto me, Return unto thy country and to thy kindred": as much as if he put it thus:--"Lord, I am in difficulty, but I have come here through obedience to thee. Thou didst tell me to come hither, into the very teeth of my brother Esau, who comes to meet me like a lion, Lord, Thou canst not be so unfaithful as to bring me into danger and then leave me in it." This was sound reasoning, and it prevailed with God. Then Jacob also urged a promise: "Thou saidst, I will surely do thee good." Among men, it is a masterly way of reasoning when you can challenge you opponent with his own words: you may quote other authorities, and he may say, "I deny their force"' but, when you quote a man against himself, you foil him completely. When you bring a man's promise to his mind, he must either confess himself to be unfaithful and changeable, or if he holds to being the same, and being true to his word, you have him, and you have won your will of him. Oh brethren, let us learn thus to plead the precepts, the promises, and whatever else may serve our turn; but let us always have something to plead. Do not reckon you have prayed unless you have pleaded, for pleading is the very marrow of prayer. He who pleads well knows the secret of prevailing with God, especially if he pleads the blood of Jesus, for that unlocks the treasury of heaven. Many keys fit many locks, but the master-key is the blood and the name of Him that died but rose again, and ever lives in heaven to save unto the uttermost.

Faith's pleas are plentiful, and this is well, for faith is placed in diverse positions, and needs them all. She hath many needs, and having a keen eye she perceives that there are pleas to be urged in every case. I will not, therefore, tell you all faith's pleas, but I will just mention some of them, enough to let you see how abundant they are. Faith will plead all the attributes of God. "Thou art just, therefore spare thou the soul for whom the Saviour died. Thou art merciful, blot out my transgressions. Thou art good, reveal thy bounty to thy servant. Thou art immutable--thou hast done thus and thus to others of thy servants, do thus unto me. Thou art faithful, canst thou break thy promise, canst thou turn away from thy covenant?" Rightly viewed, all the perfections of Deity become pleas for faith.

Faith will boldly plead all God's gracious relationships. She will say to Him, "Art Thou not the creator? Wilt Thou forsake the work of thine own hands? Art Thou not the Redeemer, Thou hast redeemed thy servant, wilt Thou cast me away?" Faith usually delights to lay hold upon the fatherhood of God. This is generally one of her master points: when she brings this into the field she wins the day. "Thou art a Father, and wouldst Thou chasten us [as] though thou wouldst kill? A Father, and hast Thou no sympathy and no bowels of compassion? A Father, and canst Thou deny what Thine own child asks of Thee?" Whenever I am impressed with the divine majesty, and so, perhaps, a little dispirited in prayer, I find the short and sweet remedy is to remember that, although He is a great King, and infinitely glorious, I am His child, and no matter who the father is, the child may always be bold with his father. Yes, faith can plead any and all of the relationships in which God stands to His chosen.

Faith too, can ply heaven with the Divine Promises. If you were to go to one of the banks in Lombard Street, and see a man go in and out and lay a piece of paper on the tables and take it up again and nothing more; if he did that several times a day, I think there would soon be orders issued to the porter to keep the man out, because he was merely wasting the clerk's time, and doing nothing to purpose. Those city men who come to the bank in earnest present their cheques, they wait till they receive their money and then they go, but not without having transacted real business. They do not put the paper down, speak about the excellent signature and discuss the correctness of the document, but they want their money for it, and they are not content without it. These are the people who are always welcome at the bank, and not the triflers. Alas, a great many people play at praying, it is nothing better. I say they play at praying, they do not expect God to give them an answer, and thus they are mere triflers, who mock the Lord. He who prays in a businesslike way, meaning what he says, honours the Lord. The Lord does not play at promising, Jesus did not sport at confirming the word by His blood, and we must not make a jest of prayer by going about it in a listless unexpecting spirit.

The Holy Spirit is in earnest, and we must be in earnest also. We must go for a blessing, and not be satisfied till we have it; like the hunter, who is not satisfied because he has run so many miles, but is never content till he takes his prey.

Faith, moreover, pleads the performances of God, she looks back on the past and says, "Lord, thou didst deliver me on such and such an occasion; wilt thou fail me now?" She, moreover, takes her life as a whole, and pleads thus:--

"After so much mercy past,
Wilt thou let me sink at last?"

"Hast thou brought me so far that I may be put to shame at the end?" She knows how to bring the ancient mercies of God, and make them arguments for present favours. But your time would all be gone if I tried to exhibit, even a thousandth part of faith's pleas.

Sometimes, however, faith's pleas are very singular. As in this text, it is by no means according to the proud rule of human nature to plead: "I am poor and needy, make haste unto me, O God." It is like another prayer of David: "Have mercy upon mine iniquity, for it is great." It is not the manner of men to plead so, they say, "Lord, have mercy on me, for I am not so bad a sinner as some. But faith reads things in a truer light, and bases her pleas on truth. "Lord, because my sin is great, and thou art a great God, let Thy great mercy be magnified in me." You know the story of the Syrophenician woman; that is a grand instance of the ingenuity of faith's reasoning. She came to Christ about her daughter, and He answered her not a word. What do you think her heart said? Why, she said in herself, "It is well, for He has not denied me: since He has not spoken at all, He has not refused me." With this for an encouragement, she began to plead again. Presently Christ spoke to her sharply, and then her brave heart said, "I have gained words from Him at last, I shall have deeds from Him by-and-by." That also cheered her; and then, when He called her a dog. "Ah," she reasoned, "but a dog is a part of the family, it has some connection with the master of the house. Though it does not eat meat from the table, it gets the crumbs under it, and so I have thee now, great Master, dog as I am; the great mercy that I ask of Thee, great as it is to me, is only a crumb to Thee; grant it then I beseech Thee." Could she fail to have her request? Impossible! When faith hath a will, she always finds a way, and she will win the day when all things forebode defeat.

Faith's pleas are singular, but, let me add, faith's pleas are always sound; for after all, it is a very telling plea to urge that we are poor and needy. Is not that the main argument with mercy? Necessity is the very best plea with benevolence, either human or divine. Is not our need the best reason we can urge? If we would have a physician come quickly to a sick man, "Sir," we say, "it is no common case, he is on the point of death, come to him, come quickly!" If we wanted our city firemen to rush to a fire, we should not say to them, "Make haste, for it is only a small fire"; but, on the contrary, we urge that it is an old house full of combustible materials, and there are rumours of petroleum and gunpowder on the premises; besides, it is near a timber yard, hosts of wooden cottages are close by, and before long we shall have half the city in a blaze." We put the case as bad as we can. Oh for wisdom to be equally wise in pleading with God, to find arguments everywhere, but especially to find them in our necessities.

They said two centuries ago that the trade of beggary was the easiest one to carry on, but it paid the worst. I am not sure about the last at this time, but certainly the trade of begging with God is a hard one, and undoubtedly it pays the best of anything in the world. It is very noteworthy that beggars with men have usually plenty of pleas on hand. When a man is hardly driven and starving, he can usually find a reason why he should ask aid of every likely person. Suppose it is a person to whom he is already under many obligations, then the poor creature argues, "I may safely ask of him again, for he knows me, and has been always very kind." If he never asked of the person before, then he says, "I have never worried him before; he cannot say he has already done all he can for me; I will make bold to begin with him." If it is one of his own kin, then he will say, "Surely you will help me in my distress, for you are a relation"; and if it be a stranger, he says, "I have often found strangers kinder than my own blood, help me, I entreat you." If he asks of the rich, he pleads that they will never miss what they give; and if he begs of the poor, he urges that they know what want means, and he is sure they will sympathize with him in his great distress. Oh that we were half as much on the alert to fill our mouths with arguments when we are before the Lord. How is it that we are not half awake, and do not seem to have any spiritual senses aroused. May God grant that we may learn the art of pleading with the eternal God, for in that shall rest our prevalence with Him, through the merit of Jesus Christ.

III. I must be brief on the next point. It is A SOUL URGENT: "Make haste unto me, O God. O Lord, make no tarrying." We may well be urgent with God, if as yet we are not saved, for our need is urgent; we are in constant peril, and the peril is of the most tremendous kind. O sinner, within an hour, within a minute, thou mayest be where hope can never visit thee; therefore , cry, "Make haste, O God, to deliver me: make haste to help me, O Lord!" Yours is not a case that can bear lingering: you have not time to procrastinate; therefore, be urgent, for your need is so. And, remember, if you really are under a sense of need, and the Spirit of God is at work with you, you will and must be urgent. An ordinary sinner may be content to wait, but a quickened sinner wants mercy now. A dead sinner will lie quiet, but a living sinner cannot rest till pardon is sealed home to his soul. If you are urgent this morning, I am glad of it, because your urgency, I trust, arises from the possession of spiritual life. When you cannot live longer without a Saviour, the Saviour will come to you, and you shall rejoice in Him.

Brethren, members of this church, as I have said on anoher point, the same truth holds good with you. God will come to bless you, and come speedily, when your sense of need becomes deep and urgent. Oh, how great is this church's need! We shall grow cold, unholy and worldly; there will be no conversions, there will be no additions to our numbers; there will be diminutions, there will be divisions, there will be mischief of all kinds; Satan will rejoice, and Christ will be dishonoured, unless we obtain a larger measure of the Holy Spirit. Our need is urgent, and when we feel that need thoroughly, then we shall get the blessing which we want. Does any melancholy spirit say, "We are in so bad a state that we cannot expect a large blessing"? I reply, perhaps if we were worse, we should obtain it all the sooner. I do not mean if we were really so, but if we felt we were worse, we should be nearer the blessing. When we mourn that we are in an ill state, then we cry the more vehemently to God, and the blessing comes. God never refused to go with Gideon because he had not enough valiant men with him; but he paused because the people were too many. He brought them down from thousands to hundreds, and he diminished the hundreds before he gave them victory. When you feel that you must have God's presence, but that you do not deserve it, and when your consciousness of this lays you in the dust, then shall the blessing be vouchsafed.

For my part, brethren and sisters, I desire to feel a spirit of urgency within my soul as I plead with God for the dew of His grace to descend upon this church. I am not bashful in this matter, for I have a license to pray. Mendicancy is forbidden in the streets, but, before the Lord I am a licensed beggar. Jesus has said, "men ought always to pray and not to faint." You land on the shores of a foreign country with the greatest confidence when you carry a passport with you, and God has issued passports to His children, by which they come boldly to His mercy seat; He has invited you, He has encouraged you, He has bidden you come to Him, and He has promised that whatsoever ye ask in prayer, believing, ye shall receive. Come, then, come urgently, come importunately, come with this plea, "I am poor and needy; make no tarrying, O my God," and a blessing shall surely come; it will not tarry. God grant we may see it, and give Him the glory of it.

IV. I am sorry to have been so brief where I had need to have enlarged, but I must close with the fourth point. Here is another part of the art and mystery of prayer--THE SOUL GRASPING GOD. She has pleaded, and she has been urgent, but now she comes to close quarters; she grasps the covenant angel with one hand, "Thou art my help." and with the other, "Thou art my deliverer." Oh, those blessed "my's," those blessed potent "my's." The sweetness of the Bible lies in the possessive pronouns, and he who is taught to use them as the psalmist did, shall come off a conqueror with the eternal God. Now sinner, I pray God thou mayest be helped to say this morning to the blessed Christ of God, "Thou art my help and my deliverer." Perhaps you mourn that you cannot get that length, but, poor soul, hast thou any other help? If thou hast, then thou canst not hold two helpers with the same hand. "Oh, no," say you, "I have no help anywhere. I have no hope except in Christ." Well, then, poor soul, since thy hand is empty, that empty hand was made on purpose to grasp thy Lord with: lay hold on Him! Say to Him, this day, "Lord, I will hang on thee as poor lame Jacob did; now I cannot help myself, I will cleave to Thee: I will not let Thee go except Thou bless me." "Ah, it would be too bold," says one. But the Lord loves holy boldness in poor sinners; He would have you be bolder than you think of being. It is an unhallowed bashfulness that dares not trust a crucified Saviour. He died on purpose to save such as thou art; let Him have His way with thee, and do thou trust Him. "Oh," saith one, "but I am so unworthy." He came to seek and save the unworthy. He is not the Saviour of the self-righteous: He is the sinners' Saviour--"friend of sinners" is His name. Unworthy one, lay hold on Him! "Oh," saith one, "but I have no right." Well, since you have no right, your need shall be your claim: it is all the claim you want. Methinks I hear one say, "It is too late for me to plead for grace." It cannot be: it is impossible. While you live and desire mercy, it is not too late to seek it. Notice the parable of the man who wanted three loaves. I will tell you what crossed my mind when I read it: the man went to his friend at midnight; it could not have been later; for if he had been a little later than midnight, it would have been early in the morning, and so not late at all. It was midnight, and it could not be later; and so, if it is downright midnight with your soul, yet, be of good cheer, Jesus is an out of season Saviour; many of His servants are "born out of due time." Any season is the right season to call upon the name of Jesus; therefore, only do not let the devil tempt thee with the thought that it can be too late. Go to Jesus now, go at once, and lay hold on the horns of the altar by the venturesome faith, and say, "Sacrifice for sinners, Thou art a sacrifice for me. Intercessor for the graceless, Thou art an intercessor for me. Thou Who distributest gifts to the rebellious, distribute gifts to me, for a rebel I have been." When we were yet without strength, in due time Christ died for the ungodly. "Such am I, Master; let the power of Thy death be seen in me to save my soul."

Oh, you that are saved and, therefore love Christ, I want you, dear brethren, as the saints of

God, to practice this last part of my subject; and be sure to lay hold upon God in prayer. "Thou art my help and my deliverer." As a church we throw ourselves upon the strength of God, and we can do nothing without Him; but we do not mean to be without Him, we will hold Him fast. "Thou art my help and my deliverer." There was a boy at Athens, according to the old story, who used to boast that he ruled all Athens, and when they asked him how, he said, "Why, I rule my mother, my mother rules my father, and my father rules the city." He who knows how to be master of prayer will rule the heart of Christ, and Christ can and will do all things for His people, for the Father hath committed all things into His hands. You can be omnipotent if you know how to pray, omnipotent in all things which glorify God. What does the Word itself say? "Let him lay hold of my strength." Prayer moves the arm that moves the world. Oh for grace to grasp Almighty love in this fashion. We want more holdfast prayer; more tugging, and gripping, and wrestling, that saith, "I will not let thee go." That picture of Jacob at Jabbok shall suffice for us to close with. The covenant angel is there, and Jacob wants a blessing from him: he seems to put him off, but no put-offs will do for Jacob. Then the angel endeavours to escape from him, and tugs and strives; so he may, but no efforts shall make Jacob relax his grasp. At last the angel falls from ordinary wrestling to wounding him in the very seat of his strength; and Jacob will let his thigh go, and all his limbs go, but he will not let the angel go. The poor man's strength shrivels under the withering touch, but in his weakness he is still strong: he throws his arms about the mysterious man, and holds him as in a death-grip. Then the other says, "Let me go, for the day breaketh." Mark, he did not shake him off, he only said, "Let me go"; the angel will do nothing to force him to relax his hold, he leaves that to his voluntary will. The valiant Jacob cries, "No, I am set on it, I am resolved to win an answer to my prayer. I will not let thee go except thou bless me." Now, when the church begins to pray, it may be, at first, the Lord will make as though he would have gone further [Luke 24:28], and we may fear that no answer will be given. Hold on, dear brethren. Be ye steadfast, unmovable, notwithstanding all. By-and-by, it may be, there will come discouragements where we looked for a flowing success; we shall find brethren hindering, some will be slumbering, and others sinning; backsliders and impenitent souls will abound; but let us not be turned aside. Let us be all the more eager. And if it should so happen that we ourselves become distressed and dispirited, and feel we never were so weak as we are now; never mind, brethren, still hold on, for when the sinew is shrunk the victory is near. Grasp with a tighter clutch than ever. Be this our resolution, "I will not let thee go except thou bless me." Remember the longer the blessing is coming the richer it will be when it arrives. That which is gained speedily by a single prayer is sometimes only a second rate blessing; but that which is gained after many a desperate tug, and many an awful struggle, is a full weighted and precious blessing. The children of importunity are always fair to look upon. The blessing which costs us the most prayer will be worth the most. Only let us be persevering in supplication, and we shall gain a broad far-reaching benediction for ourselves, the churches, and the world. I wish it were in my power to stir you all to fervent prayer; but I must leave it with the great author of all true supplication, namely, the Holy Spirit. May He work in us mightily, for Jesus' sake. Amen.

PORTION OF SCRIPTURE READ BEFORE SERMON--Genesis 32; Luke 11:1-13.

Household Salvation

A Sermon (No. 1019)
Delivered on Lord's-day Morning, November 5th, 1871 by
C. H. SPURGEON,
At the Metropolitan Tabernacle, Newington

"And they spake unto him the word of the Lord, and to all that were in his house. And he took them the same hour of the night, and washed their stripes, and was baptized, he and all his, straightway. And when he had brought them into his house, he set meat before them, and rejoiced, believing in God with all his house." - Acts 16:32-34.

IT SOMETIMES HAPPENS that a good man has to go alone to heaven: God's election has separated him from the midst of an ungodly family, and, notwithstanding his example and his prayers, and his admonitions, they still remain unconverted, and he himself, a solitary one, a speckled bird amongst them, has to pursue his lonely flight to the skies. Far oftener, however, it happens that the God who is the God of Abraham becomes the God of Sarah, and then of Isaac, and then of Jacob, and though grace does not run in the blood, and regeneration is not of blood nor of birth, yet doth it very frequently--I was about to say almost always--happen that God, by means of one of a household, draws the rest to himself. He calls an individual, and then uses him to be a sort of spiritual decoy to bring the rest of the family into the gospel net. John Bunyan, in the first part of his "Pilgrim's Progress," describes Christian as a lonely traveler, pursuing his road to the Celestial City alone; occasionally he is attended by Faithful, or he meets with a Hopeful; but these are casual acquaintances, and are not of his kith or kin: brother or child after the flesh he has none with him. The second part of Bunyan's book exhibits family piety, for we see Christiana, and the children, and many friends, all travelling in company to the better land; and, though it is often said that the second part of Bunyan's wondrous allegory is somewhat weaker than the former, and probably it is so, yet many a gentle spirit has found it sweeter than the former, and it has given to many a loving heart great delight to feel that there is a possibility, beneath the leadership of one of the Lord's Greathearts, to form a convoy to the skies, so that a sacred caravan shall traverse the desert of earth, and women and children shall find their way, in happy association, to the City of Habitations. We rejoice to think of whole families enclosed within the lines of electing grace, and entire households, redeemed by blood, devoting themselves to the service of the God of love. I am sure any of you, who yourselves have tasted that the Lord is gracious, are most anxious to bring others into reconciliation with God. It is an instinct with the Christian to desire that his fellow-men should, as he has done, both taste and see that the Lord is good. Judaism wraps itself up within itself, and claims a monopoly of blessing for the chosen nation. The heir after the flesh gnashes with his teeth when we declare that the true heirs of Abraham are born after the Spirit and are found in every land. They would reserve all heavenly privileges to the circumcised, and keep up the ancient middle wall of partition. It is the very genius of Christianity to embrace all mankind in its love. If there be anything true, let all believe it: if there be anything good, let all receive it. We desire no gates of brass to shut out the multitude; and if there be barriers, we would throw them down, and pray eternal mercy to induce the teeming millions to draw near to the fountain of life. It will not be wrong, but, on the contrary, most natural and proper, that your desire for the salvation of others should, first of all, rest upon your own families. If charity begins at home, so, assuredly, piety will. They have special claims upon us who gather around our table and our hearth. God has not reversed the laws of nature, but he has sanctified them by the rules of grace; it augurs nothing of selfishness that a man should first seek to have his own kindred saved. I will give nothing for your love for the wide world, if you have not a special love for your own household. The rule of Paul may, with a little variation, be applied here; we are to "do good unto all men, but specially unto such as be of the household of faith;" so are we to seek the good of all mankind, but specially of those who are of our own near kindred. Let Abraham's prayer be for Ishmael, let Hannah pray for Samuel, let David plead for Solomon, let Andrew find first his brother Simon, and Eunice train her Timothy: they will be none the less large or prevalent in their pleadings for others, because they were mindful of those allied to them by ties of blood.

To allure and encourage you to long for family religion, I have selected this text this morning. God grant it may answer the purpose designed. May many here have a spiritual hunger and thirst, that they may receive the blessing which so largely rested upon the Philippian jailer.

Note in our text five things. We have a whole household hearing the word, a whole household believing it, a whole household baptized, a whole household working for God, and then, a whole household rejoicing.

I. Observe, first, in the passage before us, A WHOLE HOUSEHOLD HEARING THE WORD. I do not know whether they had ever heard the Gospel before: perhaps they had. We have no certain proof that the jailer heard the name of Jesus Christ for the first time amidst the tumult of the earthquake; he may have listened to Paul in the streets, and so have known something of the Gospel and of the name of Jesus Christ; but this is hardly probable, as he would then have scarcely treated the apostle so harshly. Most likely the word of God sounded at midnight in the ears of the jailer and his household for the first time, and, on that remarkable occasion, they all heard it together. The father first, in his alarm, asked the question, "What must I do to be saved?" and received personally the answer, "Believe in the Lord Jesus Christ and thou shalt be saved, and thy house;" and then it appears that all the family gathered around their parent, and the two holy men, while Paul and Silas spake unto him the word of the Lord, and also to all that were in his house. We do not know whether there were children there, but if so, and we will assume it for this occasion, all were hearers that night. There was not a solitary exception, no one was away from that sermon in a jail. His wife, his children, his servants, all that were in his house, listened to the heavenly message. It is true, he who preached was a prisoner, but that made the word none the less powerful, for he was to them an ambassador in bonds. Prisoner as he was, he preached to them a free gospel, and a gospel of divine authority. He erred not from the truth in what he taught; he preached unto them the "word of God." Would to God that all preachers would keep to the word of God, and, above all things, would exalt The Incarnate Word of God. This were infinitely better than to delude men's minds with those "germs of thought," those strikingly new ideas, those metaphysical subtleties, and speculations, and theories, and discoveries of science, falsely so called, which are now-a-days so fashionable. If all ministers could preach the word, the revealed mind and will of God, then hearers would in larger numbers become converts; for God will bless his own word, but he will not bless anything else. The jailor's household all heard God's word faithfully declared, and there was the main cause of blessing, for, alas! with many hearers, the Sabbath is utterly wasted; for, though they are attentive listeners, they are left without a blessing, because that which they hear is not the gospel of Jesus Christ.

I have myself heard sermons which, I am persuaded, God Almighty himself could not bless to the conversion of anybody. He could not, because it would have been a denial of himself. The discourses were not true, nor according to his word; they were not such as were calculated to honor himself, and how can he bless that which is not to his own honor? and how can he set his seal to a lie? The word of God must be preached, and then the place, the hour, or the garb of the preacher will matter nothing. The minister may have been led up from a prison, and the smell of the dungeon may be upon him, but when he opens his mouth with the glad tidings, the name of Jesus will be as ointment poured forth.

I began my remarks on this point by noting that they all heard Paul; and observe the need of this, as a starting-point, for "faith cometh by hearing, and hearing by the word of God." It is not all who hear theft will be saved, but the ordinary way with God is for men first to hear, then to believe, and so to be saved. "Being in the way, God met with me," said Obadiah; and the road which a soul should follow to be met with by God is the way of hearing. Though it may seem a very trite thing to say, it is nevertheless exceedingly important, if we are to have household conversion, that there should be a household hearing of the word. This is the chosen instrumentality, and we must bring all under the instrumentality if we wish them to obtain the blessing. Now, in this City, many fathers never hear the word of God, because they regard the Sabbath Day as a day of laziness. They work so hard all the week, they say, that they are not fit to rise from their beds in the morning, and then, after a heavy dinner, the evening must be spent in loitering about, and chatting away time. Brethren, if you want to see your fellow-workmen saved, you should earnestly endeavor to bring them under the sound of the gospel. Here is a very useful occupation for many of you. You cannot preach, but you can gather a congregation for those who do. A little persuasion would succeed in many cases, and once bring them here, we would hope to hold them. If I could not be the instrument of converting a soul by preaching the gospel myself, I would habitually addict myself to the bringing of strangers to listen to those whom God has owned to the conversion of souls. Why, our congregations need never be thin--I speak not now for myself, for I have no need--but in no place where the gospel is preached need there be a thin audience, if those who already appreciate the Gospel would feel it to be a Christian duty to bring others to hear it. Do this, I pray you. I believe it to be one of the most important efforts which a Christian man can make, to endeavor to bring the working men of London, and, indeed, all classes of men everywhere, to listen to the Gospel of Christ. The men, the fathers, the heads of households, we must have.

If we are to have the household saved, however, the mothers must hear the word as well as the fathers. Many of them do, but I know cases, and, perhaps, there may be such present, and I wish to speak what is practical; where a man comes to hear the word himself, but his wife is detained at home with the children. Perhaps she is not converted, and has not much care to go to the service; perhaps she is a Christian woman, and though she would wish to go she must look after the children; in either case it is the duty of every such father, if he does not keep a servant to attend to the children, to take his turn with the wife and let her have her fair share of opportunity for hearing the gospel. He meanly shirks the duty of a husband, who, being a working man, does not take his turn at home and give his wife as good an opportunity of learning the way of salvation as himself. This may be a new suggestion to some, I only hope they will carry it out. It is plain that if we are to have whole households saved, we must have whole households hearing the word, and if the mother cannot hear the word, we cannot rationally expect the blessing to come to her.

Then the children also must be thought of. We desire to see them converted as children. There is no need that they should wait until they are grown up, and have run into sin as their fathers did, that they may be afterwards brought back; it would be infinitely better if they were preserved from such wanderings, and early brought into the fold of Jesus. The blessing which God gave to the jailor's children by hearing, he gives in the same way to other children. Let the little ones be brought to hear the Gospel. They can hear it in the Sabbath School, end there are special services adapted to them; but, for my part, I like also so to preach that boys and girls shall be interested, and I shall feel that I am very faulty in my style if children cannot understand much that I teach in the congregation. Bring all who have reached years of understanding with you. Suffer none to be at home, except for good reasons. Bring each young Samuel to the house of the Lord. Let it be said of you, as it is written in the Book of Chronicles, "And all Judah stood before the Lord, with their little ones, their wives, and their children." If nothing else shall come from children's attending our worship, the holy habit of going up to God's house will be a perpetual heritage to them; and who knows but while they are yet young their hearing the word shall be the means of their salvation.

Then there are the servants, and by no means are they to be overlooked. To have all that are in the house saved, all that are in the house must hear the Gospel. Do you all make such opportunities for your servants on the Sabbath as you should? I do not know, of course, how you conduct your family arrangements; but I know of some who do not think enough of their servants' hearing the Gospel. Servants frequently are sent out in the afternoon, when there is no preaching worth the hearing. It may be unavoidable in many cases; but I would ask, What is the use of their going out at an hour warn no preaching is to be found? If we give them only opportunities of going out when there is nothing to hear, we certainly have not given them a fair portion of the Lord's-day. By some contrivance or other, perhaps with a little pinch and self-sacrifice, our servants might hear our own minister. You cannot pray God to save your household, and be honest, unless you give the whole household an opportunity of being saved, and God's way of saving souls, we repeat it, is by the preaching and the hearing of the word. Oh! let every one of us be able to say, as masters and as parents, "I cannot save my children, and I cannot save my servants, but this I have done, I have directed them to a man of God who preaches the gospel faithfully; I do not send them to a place merely because there is talent or fashion there, but I have selected for them a ministry which God blesses, and I do my best to put them all in the way of the blessing, praying and beseeching the Lord to call them all by his grace." I anticipate the many difficulties you will urge, but would again say, if we love souls, we should try to meet these difficulties, and if we cannot do all we would, we should at least do all we can, that we may have all our households every Sabbath-day hearing the glorious gospel of the blessed God.

II. We now turn to the next, which is a most comfortable and cheering sight. Here is A WHOLE HOUSEHOLD BELIEVING. We know that the whole household believed, for we are told so in the thirty-fourth verse; "Believing in God with all his house:"--all, all, all were powerfully affected, savingly affected by the gospel which Paul preached to them. I have already remarked, that they were very probably new hearers. Certainly, if they had heard the word before, it could not have been many times; and yet they all believed. Is it not a most sad fact that many of my old hearers have not believed? The battering-ram has beaten often on their walls, but it leas not shaken them yet; wooing invitations of the gospel have been presented to them again and again, accompanied by the soul-piercing music of a Savior's dying cries; and yet, for all that, they remain unconverted still. Oh I the responsibilities that are heaped up upon gospel-hardened sinners! Take home to yourselves that warning word, I pray you. This household heard the gospel probably but once, certainly only once or twice, yet they believed, and here are some of us who have heard it from our youth up, and remain rebellious still.

Of this family it may be said that as they were new hearers, so they were most unlikely hearers. The Romans did not select for jailers the most tender hearted of men. Frequently they were old legionaries who had seen service in bloody wars, and been inured to cruel fights; and, when these men settled down as, in a measure, pensioners of the empire, they were allotted such offices as that which the jailer held. In the society and associations of a jail there was very little that could be likely to improve the mother, to benefit the children, or elevate the servants. They were, then, most unpromising hearers. Yet how often are the most unlikely persons convinced of sin, and led to the Savior. How true is it still of many who are most moral and excellent, and even outwardly religious, that "the publicans and harlots enter into the kingdom of heaven before them." This is an encouragement to you who work in lodginghouses and in the slums of this vast city, to bring all kinds of people to hear the word, for if a jailer and his household were numbered among the first fruits unto God at Philippi, may we not hope that others of an unlikely class may be converted too? Who are you, that you should say, "It is of no use to invite such a man to hear, for he would not be converted?" The more improbable it seems to be in your judgment, perhaps the more likely it is that God will look upon him with an eye of love. How happy a thing it was for the jailer that, in the providence of God, his hardened but probably honest spirit was brought under the influence of the earnest apostle. Bring others, like him, into the place of worship, for who can tell?

Note, that though they were thus unlikely hearers, yet they were immediately converted, there and then. It took but a short time. I do not know how long Paul's sermon was; he was a wise man, and I should not think he would preach a long sermon in the dead of the night, just after an earthquake. I have no doubt it was a simple exposition of the doctrine of the cross. And then Silas talked too; perhaps, when Paul had done, Silas gave a little exhortation, a brief address to finish up with, and fill up anything which Paul had left out. The teaching was soon over, and at its close the jailer, his wife, his children (if he had any), his servants, and indeed all that were in the house, avowed themselves to be believers. It does not take a month to convert a soul. Glory be to God, if he wills to do it, he can convert all here this morning, in a moment. Once hearing the gospel may be sufficient to make a man a Christian. When the eternal word of God comes forth with omnipotent energy, it turns lions into lambs, and that in a single instant of time. As the lightning flash can split the oak from its loftiest bough to the earth in a single second, so the ever blessed lightning of God's Spirit can cleave the heart of man in a moment. Our text shows us a whole family saved at once.

It is said particularly of them all that "they believed." Was that the only thing? Could it not be said that they all prayed? I dare say it could, and many other good things; but then faith was at the root of them all. It was the sneer of an old Greek philosopher against the Christians his day: "Faith," he said, "is your only wisdom." Yes, and we rejoice in the same wisdom now--faith; for the moment we receive faith we are saved. It is the one essential grace;--"Believe on the Lord Jesus Christ, and thou shalt be saved." The moment God gives a man faith--and that he can do at any time--the instant the heart casts itself into the arms of Jesus crucified, and rests there, whoever it is, he is saved in an instant: effectually and infallibly saved; he is, in all respects, a new creature in Christ Jesus. Faith is an instantaneous act at its beginning, and then it remains as an abiding grace; its first act, by the power of God, puts a man into the present possession of immediate salvation. I wonder if we preachers fully believe this as a matter of fact. If I were to go into a jail to-morrow evening, and were to preach to the jailer and his household, should I expect to see all saved there and then? And if they were, should I believe it? Most likely I should not see it, and the reason would lie because I should not have faith enough to expect it. We preach the gospel, no doubt, but it is with the slender hope that some may be converted, and they are converted, here and there; but if God would clothe us with the faith of the apostles, we should see far greater things. When he works in us a larger faith, he will also restore to us the hundredfold harvest, which, alas! is so rare in these days.

Notice very particularly, that these persons though converted thus suddenly, all of them were, nevertheless, very hearty converts. They did that night, as I shall show you soon, abundantly prove how thoroughly converted they were. They were quick to do all that in them lay for the apostle, and for the good cause. They were not half converted, as many people are. I like to see a man renewed all over from head to foot. It is delightful to meet your hearty Christian, who, when he gave his heart to Jesus, meant it, and devoted his whole body, soul, and spirit to the good Lord who had bought him with his blood. Some of you have only got a little finger conversion, just enough to wear the ring of profession, and look respectable, but oh! to have hand and foot, lungs, heart, voice, and soul, all saturated with the Spirit's influence and consecrated to the cause of God. We have a few such men, full of the Holy Ghost, but, alas, we have too many other converts, who are rather tinctured with grace, than saturated with it, and to whom sprinkling is a very significant ordinance, for it would appear that they never have received anything but a sprinkling of grace. Oh, for saints in whom there will be a thorough death and burial to the world, and a new life, in the resurrection image of the Lord Jesus Christ, which is the true baptism of the Holy Ghost.

However, I must return on this head to the point, that they all believed. What a sweet picture for you to look upon. The father is a believer in Jesus, but he has not to kneel down and pray, "Lord, save my dear wife;" for see, and rejoice as you see it, she is a believer too. And then there is the elder son and the daughters; we know not, and we must not guess, how many there might be, but there they are all rejoicing in their father's God. And then there are the servants, the old nurse who brought up the little ones, and the little maid, and the warders who have to look after the prisoners, they are all of them ready to sing the psalm of praise, and all delighted to look upon those who were once their prisoners as now their instructors and their fathers in the faith. O brethren, if some of us should ever see all our children and our servants saved, we would cry like Simeon of old, "Lord, now lettest thou thy servant depart in peace according to thy word." Many have seen it; the jailor's case is by no means an exceptional one, and I hope all of us are earnestly crying to God that we may gain the same unspeakable privilege.

III. We have, in the third place, in our text, A WHOLE HOUSEHOLD BAPTIZED. "He was baptized, he and all his straightway." In almost every case in Scripture where you read of a household baptism, you are distinctly informed that they were also a believing household. In the case of Lydia it may not be so; but then there are remarkable circumstances about her case which render that information needless. In this instance they were all believers, and, therefore, they were all of them baptized. First, "HE" was baptised,--the jailor; he was ready first to submit himself to the ordinance in which he declared himself to be dead to the world, and risen anew in Christ Jesus. Then "all his" followed. What a glorious baptism, amidst the glare of the torches that night! perhaps in the prison hath, or in the impluvium which was usually in the center of most oriental houses, or perhaps the stream that watered Philippi ran by the prison wall, and was used for the occasion. It matters not, but into the water they descended, one after another, mother, children, servants; and Paul and Silas stood there delighted to aid them in declaring themselves to be on the Lord's side, "buried with him in baptism."

And this was done, mark you, straightway. There was not one who wished to have it put off till he had tried himself a little, and seen whether he was really regenerated. In those days no one had any scruple or objection to obey; none advocated the following of some ancient and doubtful tradition; all were obedient to the divine will. No one shrank from baptism for fear that water might damage his health, or in some way cause him inconvenience; but he and all his, wishing, to follow the plain example of our Lord Jesus Christ, were baptized, and that straightway,--at once, and on the spot. No minister has any right to refuse to baptise any person who professes faith in Jesus Christ, unless there be some glaring fact to cast doubt upon the candidate's sincerity. I, for one, would never ask from any person weeks and months of delay, in which the man should prove to me that he was a believer; but I would follow the example of the apostle. The gospel of Christ was preached, the people were converted, and they were baptized, and all perhaps in the space of an hour. The whole transaction may not have taken up so much time as I shall occupy in preaching about it this morning. How, then, is it with you, who wait so long? Where is the precept or example to warrant your hesitation? Permit me to remind you that duties delayed are sins. Will you take that home with you, you who have been believers for years and yet are not baptised? Permit me to remind you, also, that privileges postponed are losses. Put the two together, and where duty and privilege meet do not incur the sin and the loss, but, like David, "make haste and delay not" to keep the divine command.

"Why say so much about baptism?" says somebody. Much about baptism! Never was a remark more ungenerous, if it is made against me. I might, far more justly, be censured for saying so little about it. Much about baptism! I call you all to witness that, unless it comes across my path in the Scriptures, I never go away from the text to drag it in. I am no partisan: I never made baptism my main teaching, and God forbid I should; but I will not be hindered from preaching the whole truth, and, I dare say, no less than I am now saying. The Holy Ghost has recorded the baptism here: will you think little of what he chooses to record? Paul and Silas, an apostle and his companion, dared not neglect the ordinance: how dare you despise it?

It was the dead of the night, it was in a prison; if it might have been put off, it surely might have been then: it was not a reputable place to dispense baptism, some would have said; it was hardly a seasonable hour, but they thought it so important that there and then, and at once, they baptised the whole household. If this be God's command--and I solemnly believe it to be so--do not despise it, I beseech you; as you love Christ, do not talk about its being non-essential. If the Lord command, shall his servant talk about its being non-essential? It is essential in all things to do my Master's will, and to preach it; for hath he not said, "He that shall break one of the least of these my commandments, and shall teach men so, the same shall be least in the kingdom of heaven"? I hope it may be our privilege here to see whole families baptized. Come along with you, beloved father, if you are a believer in Jesus: come with him, mother: come with him, daughters: come with your mother, ye godly sons, and come ye servants too. If you have come to the cross, and all your hope is placed there, then come and declare that you are Christ's. Touch not the ordinance till you believe in Jesus Christ: it may work you mighty mischief if you do. The sacramentarianism, which is so rampant in this age, is of all lies I think the most deadly, and you encourage sacramentarianism if you give a Christian ordinance to an unconverted person. Touch it not, then, until you are saved. Until you are believers, ordinances are not for you, and it is a sacrilege for you to intrude yourselves into them. How I long to see whole households believe, for then I may safely rejoice at seeing them baptised!

IV. Next, we have A WHOLE HOUSEHOLD AT WORK FOR GOD. Read the passage, and you will see that they all did something. The father called for a light, the servants bring the torches, and the lamps such as were used in the prisons. He took his prisoners the same hour of the night, and washed their stripes. Here is work for himself, and work for gentle hands to do, to assuage the pains of those poor bleeding backs; to wash out the grit that had come there through their lying on their backs on the dungeon floor, and to mollify and bind up their wounds. There was suitable occupation for the mother and for the servants, for they set meat before the holy men. The kitchen was sanctified to supply the needs of the ministers of Christ. Everything was done for their comfort. They were hungry, and they gave them meat; they were bleeding and they bathed their wounds. The whole household was astir that night. They had all believed and been baptised, and their very first enquiry is, "What can we do for Jesus?" It was clear to them that they could help the two men who had brought them to Christ, and they did so affectionately. No Martha had to complain that her sister left her to serve alone. I am persuaded there was not one of the family who shirked the pleasant duty of hospitality, though it was at dead of night. They soon had a meal ready; and how pleased they felt when they saw the two holy men reclining at their ease at the table, instead of lying with their feet fast in the stocks in the prison. They did not take the food down to the prison to them, or wash them, and send them back to the dungeon; but they brought them up from the cell into their own house, and accommodated them with the best they had. Now, beloved, it is a great mercy when you have a family saved and baptized, if the whole household sets to work to serve God, for there is something for all to do. Is there a lazy church member here? Friend, you miss a great blessing. Is there a mother here whose husband is very diligent in serving God, but she neglects to lead her children in the way of truth? Ah, dear woman, you are losing what would be a great comfort to your own soul. I know you are; for one of the best means for a soul to be built up in Christ is for it to do something for Christ. We cease to grow when we cease either to labor or to suffer for the Lord. Bringing forth fruit unto God is, unto ourselves, a most pleasant and profitable operation. Even our children when they are saved can do something for the Master. The little hand that drops its halfpence into the offering box, out of love to Jesus, is accepted of the Lord. The young child trying to tell its brother or sister of the dear Savior who has loved it is a true missionary of the cross. We should train our children as the Spartans trained their sons early for feats of war. We must have them first saved, but after that we must never think that they may be idle till they come to a certain period of life. I have known a little boy take his young companion aside, and kneel down in a field and pray with him, and I have heard of that young lad's being now, in the judgment of his parents, a believer in Christ. I have seen it, and my heart has been touched when I have seen it--two or three boys gathered round another to seek that boy's salvation, and praying to God as heartily and earnestly as their parents could have done. There is room for all to work to help on the growing kingdom; and blessed shall that father be who shall see all his children enlisted in the brand army of God's elect, and all striving together for the promotion of the Redeemer's kingdom.

V. That brings me to the fifth sight, which is A FAMILY REJOICING, for he rejoices in God with all his home. According to the run of the text the object of their joy was that they had believed. Believing obtains the pardon of all sin, and brings Christ's righteousness into our possession, it declares us to be the sons of God, gives us heirship with Christ, and secures us his blessing here and glory hereafter: who would not rejoice at this? If the family had been left a fortune they would have rejoiced, but they had found more than all the world's wealth at once in finding a Savior, therefore were they glad.

But though their joy sprang mainly from their believing, it also arose from their being baptized, for do we not read of the Ethiopian of old after he was baptised that he "went on his way rejoicing." God often gives a clearing of the skies to those who are obedient to his command. I have known persons habitually the subjects of doubts and fears, who have suddenly leaped into joy and strength when they have done as their Lord commanded them. Not for keeping, but "in keeping his commandments there is great reward."

They rejoiced, no doubt, also because they had enjoyed an opportunity of serving the church in waiting upon the apostle. They felt glad to think that Paul was at their table; very sorry that he had been imprisoned, but glad that they were his jailers; sorry that he had been beaten, but thankful that they could wash his stripes. And Christian people are never so happy as when they are busy for Jesus. When you do most for Christ you shall feel most of His love in your hearts. Why it makes my heart tingle with joy when I feel that I can honor my God. Rejoice, my brethren, that you have doors of usefulness set open before you, and say, now we can glorify the Savior's name; now we can visit the sick; now we can teach the ignorant; now we can bring sinners to the Savior. Why, there is no joy except the joy of heaven itself, which excels the bliss of serving the Savior who has done so much for us!

I have no doubt that their joy was permanent and continued. There would not be any quarrelling in that house now, no disobedient children, no short tempered father, no fretful mother, no cruel brother, no exacting sister, no purloining servants, or eyeservers; no warders who would exceed their duty, or be capable of receiving bribes from the prisoners. The whole house would become a holy house, and a happy house hence forth. It is remarkable they should be so happy, because they might have thought sorrowfully of what they had been. They had fastened the apostle's feet in the stocks. Ah! but that was all gone, and they were happy to know that it was all forgiven. The father had beers a rough soldier, and perhaps his sons had been little better; but it was all blotted out, Christ's blood had covered all their sin, they were happy though they were penitent. It is true, they had a poor prospect before them, as the world would say, for they would be likely to be persecuted, and to suffer much. Here were two of the great ones of the church who had been scourged and put in prison: the humble members could not expect to fare better. Ah, never mind, they rejoiced in God. If they had known they would have to die for it, they would have rejoiced, for to have a Savior is such a source of thankfulness to believing souls, that if we had to burn to-morrow, we would rejoice to-day; if we had to die a thousand deaths in the course of the next month, yet, to find a Savior such as Jesus Christ is, is joy enough to make us laugh at death itself. They were a rejoicing family because they were a renewed family.

In closing, regard these two words. That household is now in glory: they are all there--the jailer, and his spouse, and his children, and his servants; they are all there, for is it not written, "He that believeth and is baptized shall be saved?" They were obedient to that word, and they are saved. Now, with some of you the father is in heaven, and the mother is on the road, but the children, ah, the children! With others of you, your little ones have gone before you, snatched away from the mother's breast; and your grandsire is also in glory; but, ah! husband and wife, your faces are turned towards the ways and wages of sin, and you will never meet your children and your parents. There will be broken households around the throne, and if it could mar their joy--if anything could--it would be the thought that there is a son in hell, or perhaps a husband in the flames, while the wife and mother sings the endless song. O God, grant it never may be so. May no child of our loins die an heir of wrath; none that have slept in our bosoms be banished from Jehovah's presence. By the bliss of a united family, I beseech you seek after it that you may have that united family in heaven. For this is the last question, "Will my family be there?" Will yours be there? Turn it over in your minds, my brothers and sisters, and if you can give the happy answer, and say, "Yes, by the blessing of God, I believe we shall all be there," then, I will ask you to serve God very much, for you owe him very much. You are deep debtors to the mercy of God, you parents who have godly children. You ought to do twice as much; nay, seven times as much for Jesus as any other Christians. But on the other hand, if you have to give a painful answer, then let this day be a day of prayer, and I would say to you, could not you, fathers, who love the Lord, call your children together this afternoon, and tell them what I have been talking about. Say to the boy, "My dear boy, our minister this morning has been speaking about a household in heaven, and a household being baptized because they believed; I pray that you may be a believer." Pray with the boys, pray with the girls, pray with the mother; and I do not know but what this very afternoon your whole household may be brought to the Savior. Who can tell?

You, dear boys, just below me, who are a few out of my large family at the Orphanage, some of you have fathers in heaven, I hope you will follow them in the right way. The church of God tries to take care of you because you are orphans, and God has promised to be the father of the fatherless: O dear boys give him your hearts. Some of you have godly mothers, I know them, and I know that they pray for you. May their prayers be heard for you. I hope you will trust the Savior, and grow up to serve him. May it not be long before you profess your faith in baptism; and may we all of us meet in glory above, everyone without exception. The Lord grant it, for Christ's sake. Amen.

PORTION OF SCRIPTURE READ BEFORE SERMON--Acts 16:6-40.

"The Sun of Righteousness"

A Sermon (No. 1020)
Delivered on Lord's-day Morning, November 12th, 1871 by
C. H. SPURGEON,
At the Metropolitan Tabernacle, Newington

"In them hath he set a tabernacle for the sun, which is as a bridegroom coming out of his chamber, and rejoiceth as a strong man to run a race. His going forth is from the end of the heaven, and his circuit unto the ends of it: and there is nothing hid from the heat thereof." - Psalm 19:4-6.

"The Sun of righteousness." - Malachi 4:2.

WE SHOULD FEEL QUITE JUSTIFIED in applying the language of the 19th Psalm to our Lord Jesus Christ from the simple fact that he is so frequently compared to the sun; and especially in the passage which we have given you as our second text, wherein he is called "the Sun of Righteousness." But we have a higher justification for such a reading of the passage, for it will be in your memories that, in the 10th chapter of the Epistle to the Romans, the Apostle Paul, slightly altering the words of this psalm, applies them to the gospel and the preachers thereof. "Have they not heard?" said he, "Yea, verily, their sound went into all the earth, and their words unto the ends of the world." So that what was here spoken of the sun by David, is referred by Paul to the gospel, which is the light streaming from Jesus Christ, "the Sun of Righteousness." We can never err if we allow the New Testament to interpret the Old: comparing spiritual things with spiritual is a good mental and spiritual exercise for us; and I feel, therefore, that we shall not be guilty of straining the text at all when we take the language of David in relation to the sun, and use it in reference to our Lord Jesus Christ.

Do not your hearts often say, "What shall we do, or what shall we say to render honor unto our Redeemer?" Have you not often felt confounded as to what offering you shall bring to him? If you had been Possessor of all the worlds, you would have laid them at his feet; if the universe had been your heritage, you would cheerfully have resigned it to him, and felt happy in stripping yourself of everything, that he might be rendered the more glorious by your sacrifice. Since you have not all this wealth, have you not again and again asked of your soul,

"Oh what shall I do,
My Savior to praise?"

I would write the best of poems if so I could extol him, but the faculty is not in me; I would sing the sweetest of songs, and compose the most melting music, if I could, and count art, and wit, and music exalted by being handmaidens to him; but, wherewithal shall I adore him, before whom the best music on earth must be but discord; and how shall I set him forth, the very skirts of whose garments are bright with insufferable light? At such times you have looked the whole world through to find metaphors to heap upon him; you have culled all the fair flowers of nature, and made them into garlands to cast at his feet, and you have gathered all earth's gems and precious things wherewith to crown his head, but you have been disappointed with the result, and have cried out with our poet:--

"The whole creation can afford
But some faint shadows of my Lord;
Nature, to make his beauties known,
Must mingle colors not her own."

At such times, while ransacking land, and sea, and sky for metaphors, you have probably looked upon the sun, and have said: "This great orb, the lord of light and lamp of day, is like my Savior; it is the faint image of his excellent glory whose countenance thineth as the sun in its strength." You have done well to seize on such a figure. What Milton calls the golden-tressed sun is the most glorious object in creation, and in Jesus the fullness of glory dwells; the sun is at the same time the most influential of existences, acting upon the whole world, and truly our Lord is, in the deepest sense, "of this great world both eye and soul; he "with benignant ray sheds beauty, life, and joyance from above. The sun is, moreover, the most abiding of creatures; and therein it is also a type of him who remaineth from generation to generation, and is the same yesterday, to-day, and for ever. The king of day is so vast and so bright that the human eye cannot bear to gaze upon him; we delight in his beams, but we should be blinded should we continue to peer into his face; even yet more brilliant is our Lord by nature, for as God he is a consuming fire, but he deigns to smile upon us with milder beams as our brother and Redeemer. Jesus, like the sun, is the center and soul of all things, the fullness of all good, the lamp that lights us, the fire that warms us, the magnet that guides and controls us; he is the source and fountain of all life, beauty, fruitfulness, and strength; he is the fosterer of tender herbs of penitence, the quickener of the vital sap of grace, the ripener of fruits of holiness, and the life of everything that grows within the garden of the Lord. Whereas to adore the sun would be idolatry; it were treason not to worship ardently the divine Sun of Righteousness.

Jesus Christ is the great, the glorious, the infinitely blessed; even the sun fails to set hire forth; but, as it is one of the best figures we can find, be it ours to use it this day. We will think of Jesus as the Sun this morning; first as in the text; secondly, as he is to us; and then, thirdly, for a few minutes, we will bask in his beams.

I. First, then, we will contemplate Jesus AS THE SUN IN THE TEXT.

Note how the passage begins: "In them hath he set a tabernacle for the sun." Kings were accustomed in their pompous progresses through their dominions to have canopies of splendor borne aloft over them, so that marching in the midst of their glittering soldiery they were themselves the main attraction of the gorgeous pageant. Our Lord Jesus Christ in his church is, as it were, traversing the heavens in a majestic tabernacle, and, like the sun, scattering his beams among men. The Redeemer is canopied by the adoration of his saints, for he "inhabiteth the praises of Israel." He is from day to day advancing in his glorious matchings through the universe, conquering and to conquer, and he will journey onward till the dispensation shall terminate, and the gospel age shall be closed by his second advent. When the text saith that there is a tabernacle set for the sun in the firmament, we are reminded of Christ as dwelling in the highest heavens. He is not alone the Christ of ancient history, but he is the Christ of to-day. Think not always of him as the lowly man despised and rejected, as nailed to the cross, or buried in the tomb; he is not here, for he is risen, but he still exists, not as a dream or phantom, but as the real Christ. Doubt it not, for up yonder, in the seventh heaven, the Lord has set a tabernacle for the Sun of Righteousness. There Jesus abides in splendor inconceivable, the joy and glory of all those blessed spirits who, having believed in him on the earth, have come to behold him in the heavens.

"Bright, like a sun, the Savior sits,
And spreads eternal noon;
No evenings there, nor gloomy nights,
To want the feeble moon."

That Jesus lives is a deep well of consolation to the saints, and did we always remember it our hearts would not be troubled. If we always remembered that Jesus both lives and reigns; our joys would never wither. We worship him, it is true, as one who was slain and hath redeemed us unto God by his blood; but we also extol him as one who is "alive for evermore, and hath the keys of death and of hell."

Let your faith to-day behold Jesus sitting at the right hand of God, even the Father. He sits there because his atoning work is done, and he is receiving the infinite reward which his Father promised him. He is exalted as a king upon his throne, expecting until his enemies are made his footstool. He dwells within his tabernacle of praise, adored and admired by angels and glorified spirits. He sits there, not as a weary one, feeble and exhausted, but with the keys of universal monarchy at his girdle, for "the government is upon his shoulder, and his name is called Wonderful, Counsellor, the mighty God." I want you fully to grasp the thought of the living Savior,--of the Sun in his tabernacle in the highest heavens, for this must be the fulcrum upon which we shall work this morning. We shall get our leverage here: the living Savior, the mighty Savior, the reigning Savior; he is the church's joy and hope in the present and for all years to come.

The text proceeds to speak of Jesus as the sun, and describes him first as a bridegroom coming out of his chamber. A beautiful description indeed of the sun when he rises in the early morning. He comes forth from the vast obscure, as from within a secret chamber. He withdraws the veil of night, and floods the earth with fluid gold. From curtains of purple and vermillion, he looks forth, and scatters orient pearl around him. Clad with a blaze of glory, he begins the race of day.

Thus our Lord Jesus Christ when he rose from the dead, was as the sun unveiling itself. He came forth from the sepulcher as a bridegroom from his chamber. Observe that dear name of bridegroom. The Lord of heaven and earth, between whom and us there was an infinite distance, has deigned to take our humanity into union with himself of the most intimate kind. Among men, there is no surer mode of making peace between two contending parties, than for a marriage to be established between them. It has often so been done, and thus wars have been ended, and alliances have been established. The Prince of Peace on heaven's side condescends to be married to our nature, that henceforth heaven and earth may be as one. Our Lord came as the bridegroom of his church out of his chamber, when he was born of the virgin and was revealed to the shepherds and the wise men of the east; yet, in a certain sense, he still continued in his chamber as a bridegroom all his life, for he was hidden and veiled, the Jewish world knew not their king; though he spake openly in their streets and sought not mystery, yet he was unknown, they did not discern him; and in some respects he did not then desire to be discerned, for he often bade his disciples to tell no man what was done. That was the time when the bridegroom was in his chamber, being made perfect through suffering and perfectly conformed unto his church, hearing her sicknesses and her sorrows, suffering her wants, enduring her shame, and thus completing the marriage union between the two. To this end, he actually descended by dark steps of anguish into the silent inner room of the grace, and there he slept in his chamber, perfectly wedded to his church. Come and look at him, you who admire the lover of your souls; he stooped to death and the sepulcher, because manhood had fallen under their yoke; his church was subject to death, and he must die. She deserved to stiffer the penally due to God's insulted law, and, therefore, Jesus bowed his head to the stroke.

"Yea, said the Son, with her I'll go
Through all the depths of sin and woe;
And on the cross will even dare
The bitter pains of death to bear."

And he did bear them, and in the darksome chamber of the tomb, he proved how true a bridegroom he was to his church. Before his great race began, of which we are soon to speak, it behaved our mighty champion to descend into the lowest parts of the earth, and sleep among the dead. Before every day there is a night wherein darkness seems to triumph. It behaved Christ to suffer, and then to rise again. His descent was necessary to his ascent; his sojourn in the chamber to his race and victory.

Thus I have introduced to you the prelude of the race, the bridegroom in his chamber. Now observe the coming out of it. The sun comes forth, at the appointed hour, from the gates of day, and begins to gladden the earth; even so on the third day, early in the morning, Jesus, our Lord, arose from his sleep, and there was a great earthquake, for the angel of the Lord descended from heaven and rolled back the stone from the door of the sepulcher. Then did the Sun of Righteousness arise. Then did the great Bridegroom come forth from his chamber, and begin his joyful race. It must have been a ravishing sight to have beheld the risen Savior; well might the disciples hold him by the feet and worship him. Methinks, if ever angels sung more sweetly at one time than another, it must have been on that first Easter morning, when they saw the divine champion break his bonds of death asunder, and rise into the glorious resurrection life. Then was he revealed to the sons of men; and, no longer hidden: he began to tell his disciples the meaning of those enigmas which had been dark to them; things which they had not understood, which seemed inexplicable, were all opened up by him, for now was his time to come out of his chamber. His words, though plain enough, had aforetime hidden him even from those who loved him; but now he speaketh no more in proverbs, but showeth them openly concerning himself and the Father. He hath laid aside the incognito in which he traversed the earth as a stranger, and he is now divinely familiar with his friends, bidding them even touch his hands and his side. In his death the veil was rent, and in his resurrection the High Priest came forth in his robes of glory and beauty. A little while he was gone away, but he returned from the secret chambers of the ivory palaces, and showed himself unto his disciples. Blessed were the eyes that saw him in that day.

Though during the forty days in which our Lord lingered among his followers upon earth we may truly say that he had come out of his chamber, we perceive that he more fully did so when, after the forty days had been accomplished, he took his disciples to the top of Olivet, and there ascended into heaven, out of their sight. Then had the sun indeed ascended above the horizon to make his glories stream along the heavens. See ye not the angelic bands poising themselves upon the wing in mid-air, waiting until he shall return all gloving with the victory non in long and deadly fight. Mark ye well that matchless spectacle as he is "seen of angels."

"The helmed cherubim
And sworded seraphim
Are seen in glittering ranks, with wings displayed."

They have hastened to meet the Prince of Glory, and attend him to his ancient patrimony. Right glad are an the heavenly band to welcome back the Captain of the Lord's host, and, therefore, they harp in loud and solemn quire to Heaven's triumphant Heir. As for the glorified of mortal race, redeemed of old by his blood which in the fullness of time was shed, they hail him with gladdest hymn, and lift up their sweetest symphonies to extol him who finished transgression, made an end of sin, and brought in everlasting righteousness. Then the bridegroom came out of his chamber with fit marriage music: his beauties hidden awhile in the chamber, where he vies regarded as without form or comeliness, blazed forth with renewed splendor, such as confounded both sun and moon.

In another respect, Christ came out of his chamber at his ascension, because, when he ascended on high, leading captivity captive, he received and gave gifts for men. The gifts were intended for the manifestation of himself. His church, which is his body, was by his own command sitting still in the chamber, tarrying till power was given. But, on a sudden, the bridegroom's power was felt, for there was heard the sound as of a rushing mighty wind, which filled all the place, and then descending upon each favored head came the cloven tongue, and, straightway, you could see that the bridegroom had come out of his chamber, for the multitude in the street began to hear his voice. It was Peter that spake, we say, but far rather was it Christ, the bridegroom, who spake by Peter. It was the sun, from the chambers of the east, bursting through the clouds, and beginning to shine on Parthians, and Medes, and Elamites, and the dwellers in Mesopotamia, and Rome, and Egypt, and making the multitudes in far off lands to see the day which prophets and kings had waited for, but which had never visited their eyes. Do you hear the joyful motion among the people, the joy mingled with the sorrows of repentance? This is the singing of birds, and these the dewdrops which hail the rising sun. The people cry, "What must we do to be saved?"--the shadows are fleeing. They believe in Jesus, and are baptized into his name,--the true light is shining. Three thousand souls are added in one day to the church, for truly the bridegroom is awaked as one out of sleep, and like a mighty man that shouteth by reason of wine (Psalm 78:65). Then was the gospel race commenced with a glorious burst of strength, such as only our champion could have displayed. Meditate at your leisure upon this first general manifestation of our Lord to the general multitude. He had not gone out of Israel before. "I am not sent," said he, "save to the lost sheep of the House of Israel." Palestine was his chamber: he went to the windows of it, and looked forth on Tyre and Sidon wistfully; but he had not come forth of his chamber till that day, when the gospel began to be preached to the Gentiles also, and in fulfillment of the gift of Pentecost, when the Spirit was poured out upon all flesh, the apostles vent everywhere preaching the word. When even we, the dwellers in the far off northern isles, received the gospel, then, indeed, had the bridegroom come forth out of his chamber.

But enough of this, or time will fail me. After the coming forth, we have to consider in the text his course. The course of Jesus has been as that of the sun, or like that of a mighty champion girded for running.

Notice, under this head, his continuance. Our Lord's gospel has been no meteor that flashed for a while and then passed away, but it has remained as the sun in the heavens. What systems of philosophy have come and none since on Calvary the Christ of God was lifted up! What speculations, what lo-heres and lo-theres have shone forth, have dazzled fools, and have been quenched in night, since he left the chamber of his marriage! Yet he continues still the same; nor, brethren, are there any marks of decrepitude either in him or in his gospel. They tell us that the idolatry of Hindostan is evidently crumbling: it falls not yet, but it is worm-eaten through and through. Equally sure is it that the false prophet holds but a feeble swats among his followers, and we can all see that though popery makes desperate efforts, and its extremities are vigorous, yet it is paralyzed at its heart, and the Vatican is made to feel than its time of power is short.

As for the gospel, it wears the dew of its youth after eighteen centuries of struggles; and it predominates most in those young nations which have evidently a history before them. The old systems are now most favored by those nations which are left behind in the race of civilisation, but the peoples whom God has made quick by nature are those to whom he has given to be receptive of his grace. There are grand days coming for the church of God. Voltaire said that he lived in the twilight of Christianity; and so he did, but it was the twilight of the morning, not the twilight of the evening. Glory be unto God, the little cloud the size of a man's hand is spreading; it begins to cover the heavens, and the day is not far distant when the sound of abundance of rain shall be heard. Christ was not a strong man, who bounded forth at a leap, and then put forth no more strength, but he rejoiced to continue his work, and to run his race. He was not a shooting star that sparkles for a moment, but a sun that shall thine throughout the livelong day.

Note next in this metaphor the unity of our Lord's course, for it is clear in the text: "Rejoicing as a strong man to run the race." A race is one thing; there is the one goal, and the man gathers up his strength to reach it. He has nothing else to think of. They may throw the golden apples in his road, but he does not observe them; they may sound harp and sackbut to the right, and breathe the lute or sweeter instruments of music to the left, but he is deaf to all; he has a race to run, and he throws his whole strength into it. This is a fit image of our Lord; he has never turned aside, he has never been compelled to retrace his steps, to revise his doctrine, to amend his system, or change his tactics. On, on, on has the course of Jesus been, shining more and more unto the perfect day.

A certain people now-a-days who yet dare to call themselves Christians, are always hankering after something new, pining for novelties, and boasting of their fresh discoveries, though, forsooth, their fresh things are only fragments of broken images of heresies, which our fathers dashed to shivers centuries ago. The great thinkers of the present day are nothing more than mere translators--you know the London meaning of that word--buyers of old shoes who patch then up, and send them forth again as if they were something new. Old shoes and clouted are common enough among those Gibeonites who would deceive Israel, and whose boast is that they have come from far, and bring us treasures of wisdom from remote regions. Sirs, we want not your new things, for our Lord's race is the same as of old, and as he continues in one course so also will we. To spread righteousness and, in so doing, to save sinners and to glorify God, this is the one purpose of Christ; from it he will never cease, and nothing shall ever tempt him from the pursuit of it. Look, I pray you, with pleasure and see how our Lord, from his first coming out of his chamber until now, has continued still in the gospel to thine forth with rays of glory, without variableness or shadow of a turning. Though we believe not, he abideth faithful, he cannot deny himself; he changes not in work or way. For Zion's sake he worketh hitherto, and the pleasure of the Lord prospers in his hand.

But now, observe next, the notable idea of strength which the text conveys to us. "Rejoicing as a strong man to run his race." It is no drudgery the ascended Lord to carry on his cause;

"The baffled prince of hell
In lain new efforts tries,
Truth's empire to repel
By cruelty and lies;
Th' infernal gates shall rage in vain
Conquest awaits the Lamb once slain."

There is a race to be run but Jesus is strong enough for it; he does not come panting up to the starting place, and thence go creeping on, but like a strong man he surveys the course. He knows that he is equal to it, and, therefore, he delights in it. When he began his race he was opposed, but the opposition only made him triumph the more readily, for "they that were scattered abroad went everywhere preaching the word." When our Lord arose like the sun, the clouds were thick and heavy, but he painted their fleecy skirts with gold; persecution hung over the eastern horizon, but he turned it into the imperial purple of his sovereignty. As he pursued his course the ice of centuries melted, the dense gloom of ages disappeared. No chains could bind him, and no bonds could hold him. He dashed on with undiminished energy, and the gates of hell could not prevail.

As no cloud has ever stayed the sun as he has "whirled his car along the ethereal plain," so no difficulties impeded the onward course of the gospel in the days of its dawning. To the first days of the church Thomson's lines to the sun are fully applicable--

"Now, flaming up the heavens, the potent sun
Melts into limpid air the high-raised clouds,
And morning fogs, that hover'd round the hills,
In party-coloured bands; till wide, unveiled,
The face of nature shines, from where earth seems
Far stretch'd around, to meet the bending sphere."

The gospel soon shed its light in every land, and all nations felt its benign power. Men ceased to persecute, and bowed before the cross.

Anon fresh clouds arose, and the church passed through them. Errors and heresies multiplied, filthy dreamers led away a huge apostacy, Rome became the mother of harlots and abominations, but the true church, and the true Christ within her, went right on. The church was not less triumphant in her second trial than in her first. Rome Papal was overcome as, surely as Rome Pagan. Popes were no more her conquerors than bloody emperors had been of yore. To the thoughtful eye the sun of Christ is not less bright over the valleys of Piedmont than over the waves of the sea which bore Paul and his fellow apostles. The champion's race was as eager and as triumphant as before.

Since then, dense banks of spiritual deadness and false teaching have barred the visible heavens, and have appeared to mortal sight an ebon wall impenetrable as steel, but the Lord reigneth. He that sitteth in the heavens doth laugh, the Lord doth have them in derision. Strong is his right hand, and his enemies shall be broken. On goes the Sun of Righteousness, nothing impedes him, his tabernacle is above them all, he rideth on the heavens, yea, he rideth on the wings of the wind. Trust ye in the Lord for ever, for in the Lord Jehovah there is everlasting strength. Christ has failed in nothing, the decrees have been executed, the eternal purposes have been fulfilled, the elect have been saved, his kingdom is established, and shall continue as long as the sun. Who shall stay his hand? Who shall resist his will?

Observe, therefore, how the force is coupled with joy. Weakness brings sorrow, but strength begets joy. Christ is always glad, and he would have his people rejoice, for his cause goeth right on and he shall not fail nor be discouraged. He rejoices as he divides the spoil with the strong. When a man has a task to do which is easy to him, and which he can readily perform, he sings at his work; and so this day doth Christ rejoice over his church with joy, and triumph over her with singing. His cause goes on in spite of foes, and his strength is so great, that even the battle fills him with delight. I remember to have heard a Welsh preacher make use of the following simile. He was speaking of the joy of Christ in heaven, and he said, "You tell me that the church is sorrowful on earth and I tell you that Christ is joyous in heaven; and then you ask me how this can be? You see yonder mother with her babe, and she is washing the child; its face is foul and she desires to see it shine with brightness, she would see it white as the marble mingled with the redness of the rose. Therefore she washes it; but the child cries, it is fretful and knows not what is good for it, so it whines and struggles; the mother does not cry, or share its sorrow, she keeps on singing because she knows that all is right, and that her darling will smile like a cherub when all is over; she sees the good results coming, while the babe only feels the present discomfort, so she sings her song and never stops, let the child cry as it may." And so the Lord Jesus has pleasure in his work; he is purifying his church, and making her fit to be presented to himself, and though she winces and laments, it is the flesh that makes her so to do. The Lord sings still joyously, because he sees the end from the beginning! Earth may be swathed in mist, but the sun is never so, he shines gloriously evermore.

The text mentions one other fact connected with Jesus as the sun,--"There is nothing hid from the heat thereof;" by which is meant, nothing is able to escape the powerful influence of Christ Jesus. His own chosen people must, in due season, feel his power to save. They may wander as they do, and sin as they may, but when the time appointed comes, they shall be redeemed out of the land of the enemy. The sun's power is felt in the darkest and deepest mines; that there is a sun still shining might be discoverable even in the bowels of the earth! and so, in the darkest haunts of sin, God's elect shall be made to feel the sovereign power and omnipotent grace of our Lord Jesus Christ. When you and I shall die, and when we shall be buried in the grave, we shall not there be hid from the heat of this Sun of Righteousness, by-and-by he shall kindle life within our bones again; he shall create a soul within the ribs of death, and we shall spring upward as the grass, and as the willows by the watercourses, when the sun renewers the year. Our dry bones shall live, and in our flesh shall we see God. Meanwhile, while the gracious operations of Christ thus fall on all his elect, and there is nothing hid from the heat thereof, other operations are at work on all the sons of men. He rules in providence over all people, whether they believe in him or not, and if men do not accept the gospel, yet they are affected by it, in some way or other. Even the darkest parts of the world feel something of the presence of the Christ of God. Responsibility is heaped on those that hear of him and reject him; he becomes a savor of death unto death where he is not a savor of life unto life. There is nothing hid from the heat thereof. Oh, how this ought to encourage you Christian people to work! The Lord has gone before you; there is nothing hid from the heat of his presence. Jesus is King of the darkest settlements of the heathen, and he reigns in the lowest haunts of London's vice. Go there, for you are not intruders; you have a right to go any there in your Master's dominions; and the earth is the Lord's, and the fullness thereof. Be not afraid to face the vilest blasphemer, or the most foul-mouthed infidel, for Christ is Master, and if you bring the gospel before his enemy, he will be made to feel its power, either so as to yield to it a willing submission, or else to be condemned by it, In either case, you shall have done your part, and uttered your testimony, and freed your head of his blood.

In these thoughts combined, we see Christ Jesus, the risen Savior, pursuing his ever glorious course till he shall descend again the second time to take his people to himself to reign with him.

II. Very briefly indeed in the second place. Let us think for a moment of JESUS AS A SUN TO US. Worship and bless our Savior, it is ever meet and right to do so. Let him be extolled and be very high. Some would give him a secondary place, let it never be so with us. As the sun is the center, so is Christ; as the sun is the great motor, the first source of motive power, so is Christ to his people; as the sun is the fountain from which light, life, and heat perpetually flow, so is the Savior;

as the sun is the fructifier by which fruits multiply and ripen, so is Christ: and as the sun is the regulator and rules the day, and marks the seasons, even so is Jesus owned as Lord to the glory of God the Father.

Think these thoughts over in the following respects. When you take the Bible remember that Christ is the center of the Scriptures. Do not put election in the center; some do, and they make a one-sided system. Do not put man in the center,--some do, and they fall into grievous errors. Christ is the center of the entire system of the gospel, and all will be seen to move with regularity when you perceive that he is the chief fixed point; you cannot be right in the rest unless you think rightly of him. He is the center and King of all truth.

He is the center of the Church too. Not the pastor, not the church itself, not any rule or government, no bishop, no priest, and no Pope can be our center, Christ alone is our central sun. We follow as planets where he leads the way: around him we revolve, but we own no other Lord.

Let it be so in the world that even there Christ governs and is the center of all history. You will understand history better when you know this, for this is the key of the world's story, the reason for the rise and fall of empires. You shall understand all things when you know Immanuel, God with us.

And let him have this place in your hearts. There enthrone him! Establish him as the central sun, and let him rule your entire being, enlightening your understanding, warming your hearts, filling all your powers, passions, and faculties with the fullness of his presence. To have Christ in us, the hope of glory--oh, what blessedness! But let us take care that it is so, for we know not Christ aright unless we give him such a place in our hearts as the sun occupies in God's world.

III. But time fails me, and we must now pass on to the last point, and let us for a minute or two BASK IN HIS BEAMS. How shall we do it?

First, we must realize that he is. Sinner, saint, Christ lives: he who trod the wave of Galilee lives on. He who was marked with the nails rules on. Oh, sinner, does not that comfort you? The Savior lives, the redeemer lives; he who forgives sins still lives. Saint, does not this comfort you? The man of the tender heart still lives, with a bosom still to be leaned upon, and with lips still ready to speak endearing words. There is a tabernacle for the sun; he is not extinct; he thineth still, he blesses still. Bask in his beams, then, by realising that he is.

Then come and lay your souls beneath his divine influence. O my soul, if thou art guilty come and rest in his atonement, if thou art unrighteous come and take his righteousness. If thou art feeble lay hold upon his strength. If thou canst not pray accept him as thine intercessor. If thou art in thyself nothing, take him to be thy all in all. Some creatures delight to warm themselves in the sun, but oh, what a pleasure it is to sun ones self in the presence of Christ. Never mind how little I am, how nothing I am, how vile I am, how foul I am; all I am he has taken to himself, and all he has belongs to me. I sin, but he has taken all my sin: he is righteous and all his righteousuess is mine. I am feeble, he is mighty; his mightiness is mine, I wrap myself in his omnipotence. Christ is all and Christ is mine. Why, I utterly fail when trying to talk about such things as these; talking is but stuttering on such a theme. Faith must enjoy rather than express her delight. Come, plunge ye all into this sea of sweetness, dive deep into this abyss of happiness--Christ Jesus is yours for ever and for ever. The sun is very great but it is all for me, and Christ is very bright and glorious, but he is all my own.

Then next, if you would sun yourself in his beams, imbibe the joy of his strength. He is like a bridegroom rejoicing to run his race. Now, brethren and sisters, I am often afraid lest in serving God, we should grow dispirited and downcast, and think that things are not going on as they should, the joy of the Lord is your strength. If you begin to say, "Our cause is very feeble, the gospel will not prevail among us, you will slacken your efforts." Do not so, but remember that Jesus Christ does not fret or sadden himself about his kingdom. He runs on full of strength and rejoices as he runs; and I bid you in the power of the Holy-Spirit, do the same. Cast away your doubts and fears, the kingdom is the Lord's, and he will deliver his adversaries, into your hands. I fret and worry myself sometimes about these inventors of new doctrines, and those ritualists who bring up the old rates and stale tallow of the past ages. Let us fret no more, but think that these are only like the clouds to the great sun; the gospel will still proceed in its career. Let us laugh the enemies of God to scorn and defy them to their faces. They defy the Lord God of Israel as did the Philistine of old, but God himself is mightier than they, and the victory is sure to the true church and to the gospel of his Son. Be ye very courageous! Be not alarmed with sudden fear! Trust in Jehovah, for the Lord will surely give unto his own servants the victory in the day of battle.

And brethren, if you would sun yourselves in Christ's beams, let me bid you reflect his light whenever you receive it. He is the sun, and you are the planet, but every planet shines, shines with borrowed light. It conceals no light, but sends back to other worlds what the sun has given to it. Cast back on men the light which Jesus gives you. Triumph in Christ's circuit, that it is so broad as to comprehend the world, and compass all time. Enlarge your oven hearts, and let your light thine far and wide, believing that the power of God which gives you light will go with the light which you reflect. Comfort your hearts! "Be ye stedfast, unmoveable, always abounding in the work of the Lord, forasmuch as ye know that your labor is not in vain in the Lord." Who shall stop the Christ of God in his race? Let him first go pluck the sun from his sphere. Who shall stay the champion of God who has girt himself for his race? Whosoever cometh in his way woe unto him, for if Samson smote a thousand men hip and thigh, what shall our immortal Samson do? Let all the armies of pope and devil come against him, he will utterly defy them, and drive them like chaff before the wind.

Sing ye unto his name, for he hath triumphed gloriously! Begin the everlasting song, for he is the Lord and God, and to the uttermost ages shall he reign; yea, for ever and ever is he priest and King.

God bless you, for Christ's sake. Amen.

PORTION OF SCRIPTURE READ BEFORE SERMON--Psalm 19.

Heaven's Nurse Children

A Sermon (No. 1021)
Delivered by
C. H. SPURGEON,
At the Metropolitan Tabernacle, Newington

"I taught Ephraim also to go, taking them by their arms." - Hosea 11:3.

IF you note well the opening part of this chapter, you will find that it consists of a wonderful chain of mercies; every one single line is a rare jewel, and the whole passage is a casket unspeakably precious. The chapter begins with love; ancient, sovereign, electing love. "When Israel was a child, then I loved him." When the Israelitish nation was in a very low and poor estate, and was brought into slavery and subjection in Egypt, God had set his love upon it, and called it his own inheritance. Not for their numbers or greatness as a nation were they chosen, but when they were little and despised they were yet beloved of God. Distinguishing grace had written the name of Israel upon Jehovah's heart. Spiritually we who have believed are in the same favored condition, and our hearts rejoice this day at the memory of "His great love, wherewith he loved us, even when we were dead in trespasses and sins." This is the river-head, from which all the streams of after-mercy flow,--"I have loved thee with an everlasting love, therefore with lovingkindness have I drawn thee." Like the golden-sanded river which had its rise in Eden, electing love branches off into many streams, and waters all the garden of the Lord. This is the root from which the tree of blessing springs. "He hath blessed us with all spiritual blessings in heavenly places in Christ Jesus: according as he hath chosen us in him before the foundation of the world." Ephesians 1:3, 4. Let others say what they will, electing love will always be most precious to us; for it is the foundation blessing, the first of all favors, the mother of mercies. We nail to our mast the old flag of free grace, and believe with the apostle (Ephesians 1:11) that we were "predestinated according to the purpose of him who worketh all things after the counsel of his own will."

The next sweet word in the chapter is sonship; "When Israel was a child, then I loved him, and called my son out of Egypt." We are, according to the inspired apostle, "predestinated unto the adoption of children by Jesus Christ to himself, according to the good pleasure of his will." Ephesians 1:5. Adoption follows hard upon the heels of election, and is another messenger of good tidings. Innumerable blessings come to us by this door. "Because ye are sons, God hath sent forth the Spirit of his Son into your hearts, crying, Abba, Father. Wherefore thou art no more a servant, but a son." "Behold what manner of love the Father hath bestowed upon us, that we should be called the sons of God." "Beloved, now are we the sons of God, and it doth not yet appear what we shall be: but we know that, when he shall appear, we shall be like him; for we shall see him as he is." Sonship with God is a dignity unspeakable, and yet it is reserved for such poor dust and ashes as we are: what shall we say concerning this? Are we not swallowed up with adoring gratitude? Unto which of the angels hath he said at any time, "Thou art my son"? but this hath been said to us; and we are thus favored above all creatures that the Lord God has made. Boundless blessings are included in sonship: it is no light thing to be a child of the Lord of Hosts, the Prince of the kings of the earth. "If a son, then an heir of God through Christ." This opens up before us far-reaching views of present covenant provision, and of future infinite bliss. To be, indeed, born into the family of God is a dignity to which the descent of an imperial prince bears no more comparison than a spark in the tinder to the sun in the heavens.

And, because we have in this chapter love and sonship, we see immediately after, in the same verse, calling, salvation, and deliverance: "I called my son out of Egypt." The Lord doth not leave his chosen people for ever in the bondage of sin; when the day of their jubilee dawns, they go forth without price or reward, with a high hand and an outstretched arm. They cannot remain for ever under guilt, nor abide heirs of wrath, even as others; out of Egypt they must come when the years are accomplished. They are his, and he will call them by his effectual grace, and separate them to himself. Their calling is something more than the common and universal gospel invitation: it is a persuasive, convincing, conquering call. They only know it whom the Lord has set apart for himself: "Whom he did predestinate them he also called." This call is like Joseph's invitation to his venerable father to come and see him: it was accompanied by the waggons in which the old man could ride. It was not only an entreating call, but an enabling call. "All that the Father giveth me shall come to me," says the Saviour; and he speaks to purpose, because he helps them to come--nay, he brings them himself, carrying them, like lost sheep, "upon his shoulders rejoicing." There is no violence done to the will, but it is set free, and then, being acted upon by a graciously enlightened understanding, it yields to the call, and follows Jesus. "My sheep hear my voice, and I know them, and they follow me." Israel would never have come out of Pharaoh's country, if the Lord had not fetched them; but none can say that he drove them out --nay, rather, "as for his people, he led them forth like sheep." Every step of their exodus from bondage under the divine call was the result of divine leading and influence. Even thus spiritually a peculiar but delightful stress is put upon the chosen of God, and, therefore, they come out of the Egypt of sin. The grace to eat the paschal lamb, to strike the blood upon the lintel, and to gird up the loins, and leave the land of leeks, and garlic, and onions, is given only to the heirs of the promised possession.

Then we come upon the blessing of holy rearing and education, which we have in our text: "I taught Ephraim also to go, taking them by their arms," as they do who have to teach little children to walk, supporting their tottering footsteps, and instructing them how to put one foot before the other, until they are able, at last, to run alone. Calvin says it means, "I have led him on foot. As a child who cannot yet walk with a firm foot is, by degrees, accustomed to do so, and the nurse, or the father, or the mother, who leads him, has a regard for his infancy; so, also, have I led Israel, as much as his feet could bear." And, as if this mercy and condescension of God, in thus comparing himself to a woman with her babe, were not sufficient, in addition to this he becomes a physician too, and grants healing; he says, "I healed them." They had not only weakness that needed to be supported, and ignorance that needed to be tutored; but they had, in addition, sickness and infirmity that needed medicine. "I healed them." He who had carried them as Shaddai--the Lord All-sufficient, became to them Jehovah Rophi --the Lord that healeth them. Who shall tell how much we all owe to heavenly pharmacy? Our diseases are deep-seated and most dangerous; how happy are we in having an omnipotent Physician, whose word alone is more than a match for all our maladies. Surely we have a sickness for every day in the year, but the Beloved Physician has a remedy for every complaint. Glory be unto him who forgiveth all our iniquities, and healeth all our diseases. Then, as if all this were not enough, we find him drawing them on in the paths of obedience and holiness--not with ropes and chains, that would compel against their will, overhauling them roughly-- but with forces suited for minds and hearts. "I drew them with cords of a man, with bands of love." Thus does the gracious Spirit of God work in us to will and to do of his own good pleasure. "The love of Christ constraineth us:" "As many as are led by the Spirit of God, they are the sons of God:" "The Spirit also helpeth our infirmities."

Thus we have in a few lines unostentatiously opened up before us a cabinet of covenant gems, rivalling those which adorned the high priest of old. Here is a holy education for the nursling that was taunt to walk; here is exercise of the strength which the physician had restored.

As if this had not completed it, there come unburdening and rest-giving: "I was to them as they that take off the yoke on their jaws." They had been like oxen, with a heavy yoke upon them, and God had come and taken the yoke away; and there they stood, as we see horses stand when they are made to rest, when the bearing-rein is loosened, and they stand at ease. And this God has as surely done for us as for his ancient people. He has fulfilled that word unto us, "Take my yoke upon you, and learn of me, and ye shall find rest unto your souls." We enjoy the peace of God, which passeth all understanding: it keeps our hearts and minds by Christ Jesus. Nor is this all for the gracious Redeemer takes care to fill his people's mouths with good things; hence, he does not forget the feeding, and it is added, "I laid meat unto them." The Lord refreshed his weary people with "food convenient for them." As the oxen, after the yoke was removed, were fed, so God, when had removed our yoke of guilty bondage, fed us with the finest of the wheat, as he made us understand the gospel of his Son. The doctrines and promises of his word are substantial meat for hungry souls. "My soul shall be satisfied with marrow and fatness, and my mouth shall praise thee with joyful lips." Certain under-shepherds are afraid of laying too much doctrinal food before the Lord's people, but it is a great mistake. Truth never surfeits, though it always satisfies. The Good Shepherd does not stint his sheep, but he gives them so much, that they lie down amid the exceeding plenty of the green pastures. They cannot eat it all, and they lie down in the midst of a superabundance, which infinite mercy has provided. See, then, how God's boundless love piles mountain upon mountain, as the old classics used to say, Pelion upon Ossa, that we, up from the depths of our distress, may climb to the heights of his blessedness, and enjoy the fullness of the glory which God has treasured up for us in the person of Christ Jesus our Lord. One is tempted, with such a preface to our text, to linger in it, and to be like the man who made the porch of his house larger than the house itself. You can but be fed, and it matters not whether the barley loaves and fishes are in my basket, or whether I carry them loosely in my hand: so long as you are refreshed by them you will not quarrel with my disorderly serving. However, I restrain my loitering heart, and proceed to the text.

Here is the figure of a nurse and a child. "I taught Ephraim to go, taking them by their arms." Let us look at this in reference to the children of Israel; then let us view it in reference to ourselves.

Take Israel's case first. They were in Egypt, and God was about to bring them forth, and make them a nation, and give them a country of their own. He began to deal with them as little children, for he selected as his ambassador and as the mediator between him and them, not a man of imperious disposition, not an Elijah with fire at his beck, or a John the Baptist with an axe in his hand, but "the man Moses, who was very meek, above all men that were upon the face of the earth." They were childish, vain, foolish, and their leader must be very gentle and full of pity. It requires a patient disposition to deal with such grownup children, for what you could bear from children, who are children in years, you cannot so well endure from those who, though they have reached the age of maturity, have not reached the age of discretion, and seem as if they never would. You can teach a child of six; but who shall be tutor to a child of sixty? The great God, the Father of Israel, selected as a tutor for these grown up children, the meekest man that lived, and, in so doing, he dealt tenderly with them, as a mother with her child. Then, though he meant them ultimately and finally to come out of Egypt, he did not uproot them from their adopted land all at once, roughly and without previous loosening. No unexpected command was given them that they were at once to sever all the ties that connected them with the people of Egypt. They were not forced in an unlooked-for moment to leave the leeks, and garlic, and onions, and to go forth into the desert; but a long series of miracles was exhibited before their eyes, not only that Pharaoh's power might be broken, but that they might be encouraged to venture themselves upon the providence of God, and trust themselves with him. They ought to have been strong enough have marched out of Egypt at once, at the first word of their leader. Had they forgotten the old covenant which had been made with their fathers, that, the Lord would give them a land that flowed with milk and honey? But they were little children and could not perform manly exploits; they needed to be taught courage, and manliness, and faith in the unseen God of their father Abraham. All those plagues which God wrought in the fields of Zoan, while they had a dark side to Egypt, had a bright side to Israel; it was a "teaching them to go;" a gently persuading them to trust in God, and go forth at his call. Yet, after having seen all Jehovah's wonders, when at last they did take the first step, and found themselves at Succoth, and by-and-by came to Pi-hahiroth by the sea, they trembled like babes who totter and are ready to fall. Was it not tender mercy on the part of God that he put forth his hand, and held them up, and drowned all their fears at once? They had been alarmed, when they heard the whip of their taskmasters, and the rattling of the war chariots behind them; but God made, as it were with one sweep, an end of every thing that need give them distress. I do not find, whatever were their foolish fears, that the children of Israel in the wilderness were ever again afraid of the Egyptians pursuing them and attempting to drive them back as slaves. The old fear was slain at once; they had been slaves, and dreaded their masters, but the strength of Egypt had been so terribly broken at the Red Sea, that Israel, who before tottered, even began to dance to the music of the triumphant timbrel. Infinite tenderness removed the stumbling block out of their way, lest their infant faith should be tripped up.

When they were fairly in the wilderness they were still treated as children, and they needed it. They had many sensible manifestations of the presence of God with them. A truly spiritual faith does not expect any manifestation to the senses. God treats us to-day as men, compared with the way in which he nursed the Israelites. We have no pillar of glory shining over a visible tabernacle; no shekinah above a material mercy-seat. We have now no holy places whatsoever; and no symbolic worship:--

"Where'er we seek Him He is found,
And every place is hallowed ground."

Our service of the spiritual God is spiritual; we walk by faith and not by sight; we worship God in the spirit and have no confidence in the flesh. The tribes of Israel, as being in their religious childhood, had manifestations of different kinds. They saw not God, for who shall behold the invisible? but the bright light shone between the wings of the cherubim, the glory of the Lord at times burst forth from the tabernacle, and on an ever memorable occasion they heard a voice speaking out of the thick darkness from the top of Sinai, when the Lord came from Paran with ten thousand of his holy ones. We have not heard the voice, neither have we seen the glory, nor need are wish for either, since we have a sure word of testimony, and the abiding of the Holy Ghost: but the Lord treated the tribes in the wilderness as children--their faith and spirituality were so feeble that, like the young church of Christ in the upper room, which needed the rushing wind, and cloven tongues, and miraculous power, they were favored with signs and wonders to confirm their faith:

"He taught them to go, taking them by their arms."

Another part of this spiritual nursing, which the Lord condescendingly gave to his people, was their instruction by symbols. He did not give to them, as he gives to us, the clear vision of the glorious gospel in the face of Jesus Christ, but as they were not capable of reading the plain sense, and they needed pictures in their books, he gave them many and most instructive symbols. They saw the morning and the evening lamb. How full of instruction must that double offering have been. They ate the passover; they saw the doors besprinkled with blood; here was a sort of kindergarten infant school teaching for them. The high priest in his white garments, or in his glorious robes of beauty, with the Urim and Thummim glistening on his breast, the altar, the censor, the candlestick, the table of the shewbread, the laver--all these were pictures in the first A B C book for children. The gentle Father was teaching them to go. There are some childish lovers of the first covenant who would like to get the child's books back again: like big babies they cry for the horn-books of infancy, and would put aside the glory book which God has given to his children to read in the day of the open manifestation of his Holy Spirit. We need not imitate their example. We desire not go back to the rudiments, when the Lord hath revealed himself in the person of the Only-begotten. Yet to Israel type and symbol was the main instruction, and in that respect the Lord taught them to go. Yea, and it was not only instruction by a few chosen symbols, but everything was a symbol to them. They were always being instructed and helped. The bread they ate was food from heaven, and the water they drank leaped from the living rock; they were covered from the heat by the cloud; they were lighted at night in their encampment by the fiery pillar; everything about them was fitted for a people that needed something tangible, something to be felt, something to be seen and perceived of the senses, a people in childhood who required to have everything represented to the eye as well as spoken to the ear.

The whole of that forty years' journey in the wilderness was a long "teaching them to go." They were not a people able to have formed a well-regulated state. They were no better than a mob of slaves, they were not fit for self-government; and, therefore, they were led about, trained, taught, educated by the space of forty years, before they were able to go, as they did at last, when the Lord settled them in Canaan. And note--and here I will not continue the story longer, because there are ten thousand various ways in which we can illustrate the truth--how he treated them as children even in the conquest of Canaan. Before they came up to the country to conquer it, a pestilence had destroyed many of the people. The spies said, "It is a land that eateth up the inhabitants thereof". The Lord had also sent the hornet before them--some terrible and deadly insect which had distressed and driven out the Canaanites, and, in addition to these two scourges, the fear of them and the dread of them had very much weakened their adversaries, and prepared the whole land to submit to them. That marvellous passage of the Jordan, and that miraculous falling, down of the walls of Jericho without their needing to strike a blow--were not these all the means of teaching them to go?--were they not thus gently led on till at last they became men enough to drive out the Canaanites and to settle in the land, and sit every man beneath his own vine and figtree?

We will now leave the seed of Israel, and think of ourselves a while. How very graciously has the meaning of our text been fulfilled in us. The Lord has treated us as a nurse treats a little child.

To begin with, the first step the child takes--its first introduction to the art of locomotion--is caused by the nurse's holding it up. Do we not remember the first uplifting that the Lord gave to some of us? We were grovelling in the dust, and should have been content to be there still, but, under a gracious word that he sent to us, through the ministry, or by some other means, he lifted us up, and we began to feel that there was something better for us than to be always creeping about on the earth, or lying still in supine worldliness. The nurse's hand is first put out before the child thinks of walking, and the divine power of the Holy Ghost was first exerted upon us (we being then passive under it for a while) before we felt a desire for better things. We crawled upon the earth like beasts till God taught us to stand erect in uprightness like grace-born men. We owe all to him who has taught us from our youth.

The nurse, when the child begins to walk, soon teaches it to know its own weakness. It has a fall or two, and a few bruises and tears; but the falls are necessary to its learning to walk. We, also, had many slips and falls. Oh, how often did we resolve in the most admirable manner, but our resolutions ended in smoke! How frequently did we make attempts in our own strength, and these were failures, till at last we said, "We must give it up," and we were compelled to lean wholly upon our Lord. We became more active in the right way after we were weaned from our natural self-reliant activities, which had been so dear to us; but we were very long in the weaning. Falls into sin are terrible things, and these are not what I speak of here, but I mean those broken resolutions, and those aspirations to which we did not attain, those many disappointing tumbles which we encountered when we tried to walk. It is a part of the nurse's art to let the child feel its weakness: and it is a part of our heavenly Father's wisdom to let us know how feeble we are. We are never wise, till we discover that we are fools: we are never strong, till we confess that we are weak. True enough are the Apostle's words, "When I am weak, then am I strong."

The nurse regulates the child's exertions, and allows it to take a step or two at first, and only a step or two. Do we remember how tottering were our first steps? We limped very sadly. Our walking was comparable to the seeing of the man to whom men looked like trees. Our state of mind was a mixture of light and darkness. We cried, "Lord, I believe; help thou mine unbelief." There were only one or two promises in God's word which I could get any hold of when I first came to him. My soul was stayed a little while on that word, "Whosoever calleth upon the name of the Lord shall be saved." Only that could I grasp. I have known some who could get consolation from nothing but this sweet word, "Him that cometh unto me, I will in no wise cast out." They could believe only a little; it hardly amounted to believing: they reached as far as hoping and trusting, intermittently mixed up with a world of doubting and fearing, but they could stir no further. Very delightful to the Christian pastor is it to see a young convert begin to take the first step or two. We have seen them fall down with doubts and fears, but we have been so pleased that they could walls even a little in the way of faith, and believe even a portion of the word of God. What a mercy it is that the Lord reveals to us his own truth by slow degrees! We ought never to expect our young converts to understand the doctrine of election, and to be able to split hairs in orthodoxy. It is vain to overload them with such a precious truth as union with Christ, or so deep a doctrine as predestination. Do they know Christ as the Saviour, and themselves as sinners? Well, then, do not try to make a child run; it will never walk if you do. Do not try to teach the babe gymnastics; first let it totter on and tremble forward a little way. "I have many things to say unto you," said the Saviour, "but ye cannot hear them now." Now, had certain reputedly wise men been there they would have said, "Lord, let us hear it all; make full proof of it all; bring it all out: we can hear it--only try us." But our Lord knew what was in man, and, therefore, he only little by little, line upon line, precept upon precept, brought out the truth, and he does so experimentally with his children still. We do not know our own depraved hearts so well at first as we do afterwards. The disease and the remedy have both of them to be more fully revealed to us by-and-by. Did we know at the first all we shall know hereafter, we should be so overwhelmed with the abundance of the revelation that we should not be able to endure it; the Lord, therefore, lets in the light by degrees. If a person had been long famished, and you were to find him hungry, and faint, and ready to die, your instincts would say, "Put food before him at once, and let him have all he wants." Yet this would be a ready enough way to kill him. If you are wise, you will give him nutriment slowly, as he is able to bear it. If you have been long in the dark, and come into the light at once, your eyes smart, and you cannot bear it, you need to come to it by degrees, and thus is it with the Lord's children. By little and by little he introduces them into the glory of his kingdom, preparing them for its fullness as children are prepared for their manhood. Have you not seen how the nurse will tempt the child to take a little longer walk, by holding out a pleasant thing to allure it? And how often has our blessed Lord tempted us to some bolder deed of service, to something that required more faith than we had before, by giving us choice signs of his presence, and ravishing our hearts with his love. Some of us know what it is to have seen such sweet results from our little faith, that we could not but desire to try what stronger faith would do. God so rewarded the weak faith we had, that we felt we must rely upon him, and venture still further. Kindly hath the Lord conducted us onward in this respect.

The nurse does not let the child put too much weight upon its little legs at first, for it might be to its lasting injury. It shall have a little trial of walking: but she will put her hands under its arms, and hold it up that it shall not be tried too long, lest it be strained and injured; so does our heavenly Father try our faith by little and by little. When we shall have become men in Christ Jesus, we shall be tested by stronger trials, for the Lord loveth to put stress upon faith; he sends forth his knights of the cross upon desperate battles, knowing that he intends to glorify himself in their natural weakness, by granting them strength: but to the little babe, he sets no such stern tasks. He tempereth the wind to the shorn lamb, and deals tenderly with those that are but tender. "He carrieth the lambs in his bosom, and doth gently lead those that are with young." Can you not look back, beloved brethren and sisters, to your own experience, and confirm all I have said, only feeling that you could say very much more about it if you could speak out your own heart?

The Lord has dealt with us, in other respects as children, as, for instance, in not chiding us for our many mistakes. If the nurse were to scold the child for not walking as she does; if she were to be angry with it because it is not as strong as she is; the poor thing might be long before it came to walk at all. God sometimes does with his people as Apelles did with Alexander when he painted him--he did not draw the scar on Alexander's face, but placed his finger over it. Note how the Holy Spirit describes Sarah. There was not much good in what Sarah said on that day when she lied; but she called her husband "lord," and the Holy Spirit lights on that, and mentions it to her honor. He has often accepted our poor service, and given us sweetly to feel that it was so, though now we look back upon it, we wonder how it could have been accepted at all.

Many of us who preach the gospel, had God's blessing on our early preachings. Our knowledge was dreadfully scant, and our ability slender. We wonder how God could have blessed us, but he did. If he were to let us know how badly we do his work even now, we should despair, and do no more; but in his great mercy, he lets the light thine on the brighter spots, and lets us see what his Spirit is doing; and so we take courage and go on, and learn to walk after all. With all our tremblings, and tumblings, and failings down, we do at length learn to stand upright, and even to run in his ways.

Dear brethren and sisters, do you not feel that God has had great patience with you? Do you not wonder that he has endured you? Could you have had so much patience with another as God has had with you? Impossible. You can hardly run alone yet, can scarcely take a step without slipping or sliding, you need still to be carried in the everlasting arms like babes, and yet you are persuaded that his patience will hold out till there shall be no more need of it. He will bear us as on eagle's wings, that is, with unwearied perseverance and strength of love he will uphold us even to the end.

We must remind you, however, before we leave this, that there are some respects in which the figure before us does not come up to the full point. God has been very gracious to us, beyond what a nurse is to a child. Let us unfold this fact for a moment or two. The nurse, with the child, has not the disadvantages that God has with us, for we are full of the notion that we can walk, and thus there are two battles in our case--the first, is to get us out of our bad walking, and the next is, to teach us to walk rightly. It is sometimes more difficult to instruct a man who has been educated wrongly, than it would have been if he knew nothing. He has both to learn and to unlearn. So with us: we have a notion that we can do so much, until the Lord shows us thee without him we can do nothing. We are very strong in our own opinion: we are blown out with pride and self-sufficiency, and that has to be taken from us; so that there is a double task for infinite mercy to perform--not merely to plant a tree, but to cut down the old tree and root it up--to get rid of our former way of walking, and then to teach us to walk in the Spirit, and not in the fancied energy of the flesh.

Moreover, you never found a babe anxious to use stilts; but every one of us, when God's Spirit has begun to teach us to walk, have been seeking to use crutches. "Cursed is he that trusteth in man. And how many of us must have deserved that curse; for trusting in man is very very common. Resting on an arm of flesh seems to be the hereditary disease of God's people. They fly first to this and then to that, but forget their true and only resting-place. The simple walk of faith, trusting and leaning alone upon the Invisible, how difficult it into bring ourselves to it! We would have some favourite child to lean upon, or husband, or wife, or friend. Our abilities, or something or other that we can see and handle, shall be the golden calf which we set up and say, "These be thy gods, O Israel!" Here is a great difficulty, then, to wean us from crutches, which are promoters of spiritual lameness.

I have never met with a child that had any fear about the nurse's power to hold it up. She puts her arms about it, and it trusts itself with her, leaning wholly upon her. But we appear to be afraid of leaning hard upon God: we cannot leave ourselves with him: we don't throw ourselves right back on the divine bosom. Yet is there no true rest to ourselves till we do. As long as we are trying to support ourselves in some measure or degree, we have not yet come to the rest of faith. I have known people who went in the sea to learn to swim, but they never dare take their feet off the bottom, and I do not see how they can swim while they also endeavor to stand on their feet. Standing and swimming cannot be managed at the same time. So there am souls that would fain trust themselves to the goodness of God, but they cannot be content without an earthly prop. They cannot quite cast themselves upon God and trust in the stream of his abundant faithfulness. This, then, is another difficulty which is not with the nurse, but which is with our God in reference to us.

One more remark let us make, and that is, that we are, many of us, most unwilling to try to walk. Though we are believers, after a fashion, it may be said of us at this day as of those in the Saviour's time: "If the Son of Man cometh, shall he find faith on the earth?" Why, entire portions of the Christian church are afraid to trust God with the maintenance of their ministers and the support of their worship; they enter into an adulterous alliance with the State sooner than trust in God and rely upon the faithfulness of his people. And as it is with large masses of the people, so is it with separate Christians.; they cannot walk by faith; they must have some way or other of clinging to the flesh. Oh, for grace to be willing to believe in God! Oh, for power to cut the moorings, and have done with the signs, and the evidences, and the marks, and come to look upon Christ and his finished work; upon the covenant, and upon the faithful God, who breaketh not his promise and cannot turn away from his decree. May he who teacheth us to profit make us to walk in his ways. Our prayer is like that of quaint old Quarles:--

"Great ALL IN ALL, that art my rest, my home;
My way is tedious, and my steps are slow:
Reach forth thy helping hand: or bid me come;
I am thy child, O teach thy child to go:
Conjoin thy sweet commands to my desire,
And I will venture, though I fall or tire."

Now, why is it that mothers take so much pains in teaching their children to walk? I suppose the reason is, because they are their own offspring. And the reason why the Lord has been so patient with us, and will be so still, is because we are his children, still his children, still, his children! Ah there is wondrous power in that--still his children! I was sitting at table once, and I heard a mother expatiating upon her son. She said a very great deal about him; and some one sitting near me said, "I wish that good woman would be quiet." I said, "What's the matter? May she not speak of her son?" "Why," he said, "he's been transported. He was as bad a fellow as ever fired, and yet she always sees something wonderful in him." So I ventured, some little time after, when I had gained her acquaintance, to say something about this son; and I remember her remark: "If there is nobody else to speak up for him his mother always will." Just so; she loved him so that if she could not be altogether blind to his faults, yet she would also see all that was hopeful in him, Our blessed God does not bring into the foreground what we are, so much as what he means to make us. "Their sins and their iniquities will I remember no more for ever." He puts our blackness away; and he sees us as we shall be when we shall bear the image of the heavenly, and shall be like our Lord. For Christ's sake, beholding our shield and looking upon the face of his anointed, he loves us and goes on to instruct us still. It seems at times as if there were a conflict in the divine bosom, and he felt he must surely give us up, but then his love rushes to the rescue, and it comes to this: "How shall I make thee as Admah? how shall I set thee as Zeboim? mine heart is turned within me, my repentings are kindled together." He returns to us with such a word as this: "I have betrothed thee unto me in righteousness, and in mercy, and in judgment." He declares that he hates putting away: "Turn, O backsliding children, saith the Lord, for I am married unto you." We are his own children. Oh! I have found it such a blessed thing, in my own experience, to plead before God that I am his child. When I was racked some months ado with pain, to an extreme degree, so that I could no longer bear it without crying out, I asked all to go from the room, and leave me alone; and then I had nothing I could say to God but this, "Thou art my Father and I am thy child; and thou, as a Father, art tender and full of mercy. I could not bear to see my child suffer as thou makest me suffer, and if I saw him tormented as I am now, I would do what I could to help him, and put my arms under him to sustain him. Wilt thou hide thy face from me, my Father? Wilt thou still lay on a heavy hand, and not give me a smile from thy countenance?" I held the Lord to that. I talked to him as Luther would have done, and pleaded his Fatherhood in right down earnest. "Like as a father pitieth his children, even so the Lord pitieth them that fear him." If he be a Father, let him show himself a Father--so I pleaded, and I ventured to say, when I was quiet, and they came back who watched me: "I shall never have such pain again from this moment, for God has heard my prayer." I bless God that ease came and the racking pain never returned. Faith mastered the pain by laying hold upon God in his own revealed character, that character in which in our darkest hour we are best able to appreciate him. I think that is why that prayer, "Our Father which art in heaven," is given to us, because, when we are lowest, we can still say, "Our Father," and when it is very dark, and we are very weak, our childlike appeal can go up, "Father, help me! Father rescue me!" He teacheth us still to go, taking us by the arms, because he is our parent still. If any one fears God may leave him, let him enquire whether a mother can forget her sucking child, that she should not have compassion on the son of her womb, for even if it be so, God will not forget his people. He has graven you upon the palms of his hands. There is a relationship between you and him so familiar that it never can be forgotten, so firm that it can never be dissolved. Be of good confidence; he will teach you to go, till you shall run without weariness, and walk without fainting. I would that all here had committed themselves to this good Father's hand; I pray that they may do so. The Holy Spirit grant it, for whosoever believeth in the Lord Jesus Christ shall be saved. Amen.

PORTION OF SCRIPTURE READ BEFORE SERMON--Hosea 11.

Sleep Not

A Sermon (No. 1022)
Delivered by
C. H. SPURGEON,
At the Metropolitan Tabernacle, Newington

"Let us not sleep, as do others." - 1 Thessalonians 5:6.

WE DO NOT usually sleep towards the things of this world. We rise up early, and sit up late, and eat the bread of carefulness, for Mammon's sake. In this age of competition, most men are wide enough awake for their temporal interests; but, so is it, partly through our being in this body, and partly through our dwelling in a sinful world, that we are all of us very apt to sleep concerning the interests of our souls. We drive like Jehu for this present world, but loiter for the world to come. Nothing so much concerns us as eternity, and yet nothing so little affects us. We work for the present world, and we play with the world to come. Quaint old Quarles long ago likened us to roebucks as to earth, and snails as to hearer; and then he oddly enough rebuked this fault in rugged verse:--

"Lord, when we leave the world and come to thee,
How dull, how slur, are we!
How backward! How prepost'rous is the motion
Of our ungain devotion!
Our thoughts are millstones, and our souls are lead,
And our desires are dead:
Our vows are fairly promis'd, faintly paid,
Or broken, or not made.

***

Is the road fair, we loiter; clogged with mire,
We stick or else retire;
A lamb appeals a lion, and we fear
Each bush we see's a bear.
When our dull souls direct our thoughts to thee,
As slow as snails are we;
But at the earth we dart our winged desire,
We burn--we burn like fire!"

A piece of news about a fire in another continent makes a sensation in all our homes, but the fire that never shall be quenched is heard of almost without emotion. The discovery of a gold-field will affect half the markets in the world, and send a thrill through the public pulse; but when we speak of that blessed city where the streets are of gold, how coolly men take it all, regarding it as though it were a pretty fiction, and as it only the things which are seen were worthy of their notice.

We sleep when heavenly things and eternal things are before us. Alas! that it should be so. Even those choice spirits which have been awakened by the Holy Ghost, and not only awakened into life, but aroused into ardor, have to complain that their fervor very frequently is chilled. I was recommended to try a pillow of hops to obtain sleep during my late illness, but I find now that I want a waking pillow rather than a sleeping pillow; and I am of the same mired as that ancient saint who preferred a roaring devil to a sleepy devil. How earnest, how diligent, how watchful, how heavenly ought he to be, but how much are we the reverse of all this. When in this respect we would do good, evil is present with us. We would have our hearts like a furnace for Christ, and, behold, the coals refuse to burn. We would be living pillars of light and fire, but we rather resemble smoke and mist. Alas! alas! alas! that when we would mount highest, our wings are clipped, and when we would serve God best, the evil heart of unbelief mars the labor. I knew it would be seasonable--I hoped it might be profitable if I spake a little to you to-night, and to myself in so doing, concerning the need that there is, that we shake ourselves from slumber, and leave the sluggard's couch.

I intend to take the text in reference first to those who are born again from the dead, and secondly, in reference to those who are still in the terrors slumber of their sin; and I shall gather my illustrations to-night from no remote region, but from the self-same Word of God, from which I take the text. The text says, "Let Us not sleep, as do others." We will mention some "others," whose histories are recorded in Scripture, who have slept to their own injury, and I pray you let them be warnings to you.

I. First, to those of you who are THE PEOPLE OF GOD, let me say, "Let us not sleep, as do others."

1. First, let us not sleep as those disciples did who went with their Lord to the garden, and fell a slumbering while he was agonizing. Let us not be as the eight who slept at a distance, nor as the highly-favored three, who were admitted into the more secret chamber of our Lord's woes, and were allowed to tread the precincts of the most holy place where he poured out his soul, and sweat as it were great drops of blood. He found them sleeping, and though he awakened them, they slept again and again. "What, could ye not watch with me one hour?" was his gentle expostulation. They were slumbering for sorrow. Though our Lord might in our case make an excuse for us as he did for them--"The spirit truly is willing, but the flesh is weak,"--let us endeavor by his grace not to need such an apology, by avoiding their fault. "Let us not sleep, as do others." But, beloved fellow Christians, are not the most of us sleeping as the apostles did? Behold our Master's zeal for the salvation of the sons of men! Throughout all his life, he seemed to have no rest. From the moment when his ministry began he was ever toiling, laboring, denying himself. It was his meat and his drink to do the will of him that sent him. Truly he might have taken for his life's motto,--"Wist ye not that I must be about my Father's business?" So intent was he on saving souls, that he counted not his life dear unto him. He would lay it down, and that amidst circumstances of the greatest pain and ignominy; anything and everything would he do to seek and to save that which was lost. Zeal for his chosen church, which was God's house, had eaten him up: for his people's sakes he could bear all the reproaches of them that reproached God, and though that reproach broke his heart, yet still he persevered and ceased not till salvation's work was done. He was incessant in toil and suffering, but, what are we?

There is our Lord, our great Exemplar, before us now. Behold him in Gethsemane! imagination readily sees him amid the olives. I might say, that his whole life was pictured in that agony in the garden, for in a certain sense it was all an agony. It was all a sweating, not such as distils from those who purchase the staff of life by the sweat of their face, but such as he must feel who purchased life itself with the agony of his heart. The Saviour, as I see him throughout the whole of his ministry, appears to me on his knees pleading, and before his God agonising--laying out his life for the sons of men. But, brethren, do I speak harshly when I say that the disciples asleep are a fit emblem of our usual life? As compared or rather contrasted with our Master, I fear it is so. Where is our zeal for God? Where is our compassion for men? Do we ever feel the weight of souls as we ought to feel it? Do are ever melt in the presence of the terrors of God which we know to be coming upon others? Have we realised the passing away of an immortal spirit to the judgment bar of God? Have we felt pangs and throes of sympathy when we have remembered that multitudes of our fellow creatures have received, as their eternal sentence, the words-- "Depart ye cursed into everlasting fire in hell, prepared for the devil and his angels?" Why, if these thoughts really possessed us, we should scarce sleep; if they became as real to us as they were to him, we should wrestle with God for souls as he did, and become willing to lay down our lives, if by any means we might save some. I see by the we of faith, at this moment, Jesus pleading at the mercy-seat. "For Zion's sake," he saith, "I will not hold my peace, and for Jerusalem's sake I will not rest;" and yet, we around him lie asleep, without self-denying activity, and almost without prayer, missing opportunities, or, when opportunities for doing good have been seized, using them with but a slothful hand, and doing the work of the Lord, if not deceitfully, yet most sluggishly. Brethren, "let us not sleep, as do others." If it be true that the Christian Church is to a great extent asleep, the more reason why we should be awake; and, if it be true, as I fear it is, that we have ourselves slumbered and slept, the more reason now that we should arise and trim our lamps, and go forth to meet the Bridegroom. Let us from this moment begin to serve our Master and his church more nearly after the example which he himself has set us in his consecrated life and blessed death. Let us not sleep then, as did the disciples at Gethsemane.

"O thou, who in the garden's shade,
Didst wake thy weary ones again,
Who slumbered at that fearful hour,
Forgetful of thy pain;
Bend o'er us now, as over them
And set our sleep-bound spirits free;
Nor leave us slumbering in the watch
Our souls should keep with thee!"

2. A second picture we select from that portion of the inspired page which tells us of Samson. Let us not sleep, as that ancient Hebrew hero did, who, while he slept, lost his locks, lost his strength, by-and-by lost his liberty, lost his eyes, and ultimately lost his life. I have spoken under the first head of our slumbering in respect to others; but, here, I come to ourselves. In our slumbering with respect to ourselves, Samson is the sad picture of many professors. We are about to sketch a portrait of one whom we knew in years gone by. He was "strong in the Lord, and in the power of his might." Years ago, the man we picture--and it is no fancy portrait, for we have seen many such--when the Spirit of the Lord came upon him, did mighty things, and we looked on and wondered, yea, we envied him, and we said, "Would God we had an hour of such strength as has fallen upon him." He was the leader among the weak, and often infused courage into faint hearts; but where is he now? All our Israel knew him, for his name was a tower of strength; and our enemies knew him too, for he was a valiant man in battle. Where is this hero now? We hear little of him now in the fields of service where once he glorified his God and smote the enemies of Israel; we do not meet him now at the prayermeeting, or in the Sunday-school, or at the evangelist station. We hear nothing of his seeking for souls. Surely, he has gone to sleep. He thinks that he has much spiritual goods laid up for many years, and he is now taking his rest. He has had his share, he says, of labor, and the time has come now for him to take a little ease. It is our loss and his peril that he has allowed himself to fall into such a drowsy condition. O that we could bestir him!

"Break his bonds of sleep asunder--
Rouse him with a peal of thunder."

Alas! carnal security is a Delilah always. It gives us many a dainty kiss, and lulls us into tranquil slumbers which we imagine to be God's own peace, whereas the peace of fascination and of satanic enchantment is upon us. Yes, we have seen the good man: we could not doubt that he had been both good and great: yet we have seen him lying asleep. And, perhaps, some of us who have never been so distinguished or done so much, though, nevertheless, in our own small way we have done something for God, and yet we too lie in Delilah's lap. Blessed be his name who has not suffered us to lead quite a useless life; but possibly we are degenerating and getting now to take things more easily than we did. In our fancied wisdom, we half rebuke what we call our "juvenile zeal." We are prudent now and wise; would God we were not prudent and not wise, and were as foolish as we used to be when we loved our God with zeal so great, that nothing was hard and nothing was difficult, if we were called upon to do it for his name's sake. Now, what do I see in Samson while he lies asleep in Delilah's lap. I see peril of the deadliest sort. The Philistines are not asleep. When the good man slumbers and ceases to watch, Satan does not slumber, and temptations do not cease to waylay him. There are the Philistines looking on, while you see the razor softly stealing over the champion's head. Those locks, bushy end black as a raven, fall thickly on the ground; one by one the razor shears them all away till the Nazarite has lost the hair of his consecration. I am terribly fearful lest this should happen to ourselves. Our strength lies in our faith. That is our Samsonian lock. Take that away, and we are as weak as other men, ay, and weaker still; for Samson was weaker than the weakest when his hair was gone, though aforetime stronger than the strongest. By degrees, it may be, Satan is stealing away all our spiritual strength. Oh! if it be my case, I shall come up into this pulpit and I shall preach to you, and shake myself, as I have done aforetime, and perhaps expect to see sinners saved, but there will be none. And, possibly, some of you also, when you awake a little, will go forth to preach in the streets or to seek after men's souls as you have done before, but, alas, you will find the Philistines will bind you, and that your strength has passed away while you slept; your glory has gone--gone amidst the deluding dreams which lulled you--gone not to come back except with bitterest grief, with eyes, perhaps, put out for ever. Many backsliders will die thanking God, if ever their strength returns to them, and perhaps it never may till their dying hour. Oh, brethren! warned by what has happened, not to Samson only, but to many of the Lord's greatest champions, "Let us not sleep, as do others."

3. Now we change the picture again. It is the same subject under other forms. You remember our Saviour's parable concerning the tares and the wheat. There was an enclosure which was

reserved for wheat only, but, while men slept, the enemy came and sowed tares among the good corn. Now, you who are members of the Church of Christ need not that I should enter into a full explanation of the parable; neither is this the time, but it will suffice to say that when false doctrines and unholy practices have crept into a church, the secret cause of the mischief has usually been that the church itself was asleep. Those who ought to have been watchmen, and to have guarded the field, slept, and so the enemy had ample time to enter and scatter tares among the wheat.

Now, my last illustration spoke to you of your own dangers, this ought to appeal to you with equal force, because it concerns dangers incident to that which is dearest to you, I hope, of anything upon earth, namely, the church of the living God. An unwatchful church will soon become an unholy church. A church which does not carefully guard the truth as it is in Jesus, will become an unsound church, and, consequently, a degenerate church. It will grieve the Holier Spirit, and cause him to remove his power from the ministry and his presence from the ordinances. It will open the door for Satan, and he is quite sure to avail himself of every opportunity of doing mischief. I believe that the only way after all in any church, to purge out heresy in it, is by having more of the inner life; by this fire in Zion shall the chaff be burned up. When the constitution of a man is thoroughly sound, it throws out many of those diseases which otherwise would have lingered in his system; and good physicians sometimes do not attempt to touch the local disease but they do their best to strengthen the general constitution' and when that is right, then the cure is wrought. So, here and there, there may be a defalcation in the one point--that of doctrine, or in the other-- as to an affair of practice; and so it may be necessary to deal with the disordered limb of doctrine, or you may have to cut out the cancer of an evil custom; but, as a rule, the main cure of a church comes by strengthening its inner life. When we live near to Jesus, when we drink from the fountain-head of eternal truth and purity, when we become personally true and pure, then our watchfulness is, under God, our safeguard, and heresy, false doctrine, and unclean profession are kept far away. Sleeping guards invite the enemy. He who leaves his door unlocked asks the thief to enter. Watchfulness is always profitable, and slothfulness is always dangerous.

Members of this church, I speak to you in particular, and forget for the moment that any others are present. We have enjoyed these many years the abiding dew of God's Spirit, shall we lose it? God has been in our midst, and thousands of souls, By, tens of thousands of souls have been brought to Jesus, and God has never taken away his hand, but it has been stretched out still; shall we by sinful slumber sin away this blessing? I am jealous over you with a holy jealousy. Trembling has taken hold on me, lest ye lose your first love. "Hold fast," O church, "that which thou hast received, that no man take thy crown." Our sins will grieve the Spirit; our sleepiness will vex the Holy One of Israel. Unless we wake up to more earnest prayerfulness and to closer fellowship with Christ, it may be we shall hear the sound such as Joseph us tells us was observed at the destruction of Jerusalem, when there was heard the rustling of wings and the voice that said "Let Us go hence." O Lord, though our sins deserve that thou shouldst forsake us, yet turn not away from us, for thy mercy sake! Tarry, Jehovah, for the sake of the precious blood! Tarry with us still! Depart not from us. We deserve that thou shouldst withdraw, but, oh! forsake not the people whom thou hast chosen! By all the love thou hast manifested towards us, continue thy lovingkindness to thine unworthy servants still. Is not that your prayer, you that love the Church of God? I know it is, not for this church only, but for all others where the power and presence of God have been felt. Pray continually for the church, but remember this is the practical exhortation arising out of it all--"Let us not sleep, as do others," lest in our case too, the enemy come and mar the harvest of our Master by sowing, tares among the wheat.

4. Only one other picture, and a very solemn one, still addressing myself to God's people. We are told that while the bridegroom tarried, the virgins who had gone out to meet him slumbered and slept. O virgin hearts! "Let us not sleep, as do others." When the cry was heard--"Behold, the bridegroom cometh," they were all slumbering, wise and foolish alike, O ye wise virgins who have oil in your vessels your lamps, "sleep not, as do others," lest the midnight cry come upon you unawares. The Lord Jesus may come in the night. He may come in the heavens with exceeding great power and glory, before the rising of another sun; or, he may tarry awhile, and yet though it should seem to us to be long, he will come quickly, for one day is with the Lord as a thousand years, and a thousand years as one day. Suppose, however, he were to come to-night; if now, instead of going along to your homes and seeing once more the streets busy with traffic, the sign of the Son of Man should be revealed in the air, because the king had come in his glory, and his holy angels with him, would you be ready? I press home the question. The Lord may suddenly come; are you ready? Are you ready? You who profess to be his saints--are your loins girt up, and your lamps trimmed? Could you go in with him to the supper, as guests who have long expected him, and say, "Welcome, Welcome Son of God?" Have you not much to set in order? are there not still many things undone? Would you not be afraid to hear the midnight cry? Happy are those souls who live habitually with Jesus, who have given themselves up completely to the power of his indwelling

Spirit--who follow the Lamb whithersoever he goeth. "They shall walk with him in white for they are worthy." Wise are they who live habitually beneath the influence of the Second Advent, looking for and hasting unto the coming of the Son of God. We would have our window opened towards Jerusalem; we would sit as upon our watch-tower whole nights; we would be ready girt to go out of this Egypt at a moment's warning. We would be of that host of God who shall go out harnessed, in the time appointed, when the signal is given. God grant us grace to be found in that number in the day of his appearing; but, "Let us not sleep, as do others." I might say, let us not sleep as we have done ourselves. God forgive us and arouse us from this good hour.

I feel as if I did not want to go on to the second part of my subject at all, but were quite content to stand here and speak to you who love the Lord. Brethren and sisters, we must have an awakening among us. I feel within my soul that I must be awakened myself, and my oven necessities are, I believe, a very accurate gauge of what is wanted by the most of you. Shall our season of triumph, our march of victory, come to an end? Will you turn back after all that God has done for you? Will you limit the Holy One of Israel? Will you cease from the importunities of prayer? Will you pause in the labors of zeal? Will you bring dishonor upon Christ and upon his cross? By the living God who sleepeth not, neither is weary in his deeds of love, I beseech you, slumber not, and be not weary nor faint in your mind. "Be ye steadfast, immovable, always abounding in the work of the Lord.'

II. But I must pass on to the second part of our subject. I have now to speak TO THOSE OF YOU WHO ARE NOT CONVERTED; and if I felt as I ought to feel, it would be sorrowful work even to remember that any of you are yet unsaved. I like to see these little children here. I pray God they may grow up to fear and love him, and that their young hearts may be given to our dear Lord and Master while they are yet boys and girls. But I overlook them just now, and speak to some of you who have had many years of intelligent hearing of the word, and are still unsaved. Pitiable objects! You do not think so; but I repeat the word, Pitiable objects! The tears which flood my eyes almost prevent my seeing you. You fancy you are very merry and happy, but you are to be pitied, for "the wrath of God abideth on you." "He that believeth not is condemned already, because he hath not believed on the Son of God." You will soon be where no pity can help you, and where the Lord himself will not help you. May God give you ears to hear the words of affectionate warning which I address to you now! "Let us not sleep, as do others."

I beg you not to sleep, as did Jonah. He was in the vessel, you remember, when it was tossed with the tempest, and all the rest in the vessel were praying, but Jonah was asleep. Every man called upon his God except the man who had caused the storm. He was the most in danger, but he was the most careless. The ship-master and mate, and crew, all prayed, every man to his god, but Jonah carelessly slept on. Now, do you not some of you here live in houses where they all pray but you? You have a godly mother, but are yourself godless. John, you have a Christian father, and brothers and sisters, too, whom Christ has looked upon in love, and they pray for you continually. But the strange thing is, that your soul is the only one in the house which remains unblest, and yet you are the only one who feels no anxiety or fear about the matter. There are many of us in this house who can honestly say that we would give anything we have, if we could save your souls we do not know what we would not do, but we know we would do all in our power, if we could but reach your consciences and your hearts. I stand often in this pulpit almost wishing that I had never been born, because of the burden and distress it brings upon my soul to think of some of you who will die and be lost for ever. Lost, though you love to listen to the preacher! Lost, though you sometimes resolve to be saved! We are praying for you daily, but you,--you are asleep! What do you, while we are preaching but criticise our words, as if we discoursed to you as a piece of display, and did not mean to plead as for life and death with you, that you would escape from the wrath to come. Observations will be made by the frivolous among you during the most solemn words, about some-one's dress or personal appearance. Vain minds will be gadding upon the mountains of folly, while those, who are not, by far, so immediately concerned, are troubled and have deep searchings of heart about those very souls. I believe God is going to send a revival into this place; I have that conviction growing upon me, but it may be that though the gracious wave may sweep over the congregation, it will miss you. It has missed you up to this hour. Around you all the door is wet, but you, like Gideon's fleece, are dry, and you sleep though the blessing comes not upon you,--sleep though sleep involves a certain and approaching curse. O slumbering Jonah, in the name of the Host High, I would say to thee, "Awake thou that steepest, and call upon thy God. Peradventure, he shall deliver thee, and this great tempest shall yet be stayed." Yea, I would put it above a peradventure, for they that seek the Lord shall find him, if they seek him with full purpose of heart.

Let us change the illustration now, and take another. You remember Solomon's sluggard. What did he? It was morning, and the sun was up; ay, the dawning of the day had passed some hours, and he had not yet gone forth to labor. There was a knock at his door, and he opened his eyes a little; he listened and he said, "Leave me alone." "But will you never get up?" "Yes, I will be up soon; but I want a little more sleep--only a little." Then came another knock, for his master would have him in the field at work; but he turned over again, and he grumbled within himself, and said, "A little more slumber." He slept hour after hour. Yes, but he did not mean to sleep hours; all he intended was to sleep five minutes; but minutes fly rapidly to men who dream. If at the first onset he had known that if he fell asleep he would slumber till noon, he would have been shocked at such abominable laziness. But what harm could it be just to turn over once more? Who would deny him another wink or two? Surely there can be no fault found with one more delicious doze? Now, there are in this congregation persons who have said to themselves many times, "That appeal is right. My conscience gives assent to that gospel demand, it shall be attended to very soon. I must, however, enjoy a little pleasure first-- not much. I do not mean to risk my soul another twelve months, but we will stay till next Sunday; then I shall have got over certain engagements which now stand in my way." Well, sirs, you know, some of you, that it has been Sabbath after Sabbath, and then it has grown to be year after year; and still you are saying a little more sleep and a little more slumber. I met one the other day: I do not see him here to-night, but I generally see him on the Sabbath. I think he heard the first sermon I preached in London; that is many years alto now. And that man loves me: I know he does; and I can say I love him; but if he dies as he is, he is a lost man. He knows it. He has told me so, and he has said, "Pray for me." But, oh! what is the benefit of my praying for him if he never prays for himself! It is grievous to know that many of you are in the same dreadful way of procrastinating and putting off. You would do anything to help the church, too; and if you knew that I needed anything you would be among the first to do it for me, such is your kindness. You are kind to your minister, but you are cruel to your souls. You have held your soul over hell's mouth for these twenty years by your continual delays and indecisions. Yet you never meant it. No, you thought long ago that you would have given your hearts to Christ. One of these days I shall have to bury you, and it will be with no hope of your future happiness, for it has always been, "A little more sleep, and a little more slumber, and a little more folding of the hands," till your "poverty shall come upon you as one that travelleth, and your want like an armed man." Alas! it shall be eternal poverty, and the armed man shall be the arch-destroyer from whom none can escape! O young man and young woman, do not procrastinate. Delay is the devil's great net, and it is filled wish exceeding great fishes; yet doth not the net break. Oh that you could break through it. May God help you to do it, for to you I would say, "Let us not," in this respect, "sleep, as do others."

Again, the picture changes. Do you remember the story in the Acts of the Apostles of the young man who sat in the third loft while Paul was preaching? It could not have been a dull sermon, I should think; but Paul preached till midnight. That was rather long. You do not allow me such liberal time. And when Paul preached on, Eutychus went to sleep, until he fell from the third loft, and was taken up dead. It is true that Paul prayed, and he was restored to life by miracle; but I have known many a Eutychus fall dead under the word, but he was never known to live again. I do not mean that I have known many go to sleep in the house of God, and fall from the third loft; but this, that they have heard the word, and heard the word, till they have been preached into sleep of the deepest kind, and at last preached into hell. If we by our preaching do not wake you, we rock your cradles, and make you more insensible every time we warn you. The most startling preaching in a certain time ceases to arouse the hearers. You know the great boiler factories over here in Southwark. I am told that when a man goes inside the boiler to hold the hammer, when they are fixing rivets, the sound of the copper deafens him so that he cannot bear it, it is so horrible; but, after he has been a certain number of months in that employment, he hardly notices the hammering: he does not care about it. It is just so under the word. People go to sleep under that which once was like a thunderbolt to them. As the blacksmith's dog will lie under the anvil, where the sparks fly into his face, and yet go to sleep, so will many sinners sleep while the sparks of damnation fly into their faces. Horrible that it should be so. It would need an earthquake and a hurricane to move some of you stolid ones. I wish they would come if they would stir you; but even such terrors would be of no avail, only the trumpet which will arouse the dead will ever awaken you. Oh, dear hearers, remember that to perish under the gospel ministry is to perish with a vengeance. If I must be lost, let it be as a Zulu Kaffir, or as a Red Indian, who has never listened to the truth; but it is dreadful to go down to the pit with this as an aggravation: "You knew your duty, but you did it not; you heard the warning, but you would not receive it; the medicine was put to your lip, but you preferred to be diseased; the bread was placed before you, and the living water, but you would not take them. Your blood be on your own heads." Oh, may this never be said of any of us! May we never sleep under the word as do others, lest we die in our sins; and, as I told you the other Sunday night, I think that is one of the most dreadful words in the Bible where Christ said twice, one time after another--"If ye believe not that I am he, ye shall die in your sins." To die on a dunghill, or in a ditch, or on the rack, or on the gallows, is nothing compared with this--to die in your sins! to die in your sins! And yet this will be your lot if you continue much longer to sleep, as do others.

Another picture; not to detain you too long. Do you remember in David's life when he went with one of his mighty men at night into Saul's camp, and found the king and his guards all asleep? There were certain men of war who ought to have watched at Saul's bed head to take care of their master who lay in the trench, but no one was awake at all; end David and his friend went all among the sleepers, treading gently end softly lest they should wake one of them; till, by-and-by, they came to the center of the circle where lay the king, with a cruse of water at his bolster, and his spear stuck in the ground. Little did he know as he slept so calmly there that Abishai was saying to David: "Let me strike him; it shall be but this once." How easily that strong hand with that sharp javelin would have pinned the king to the ground. One only stroke, and it would be done, and David's enemy would pursue him no more for ever. Methinks I see you, O ye sleeping sinners, lying in the same imminent peril. At this moment the evil one is saying: "Let me smite him; I will smite him but this once; let me prevent his hearing the gospel this night; let me thrust the javelin of unbelief into his soul but this once; and then the harvest will be past, the summer will be ended, and he will not be saved." Slumbering sinner, I would fain shout as the thunder of God, if thereby I could arouse you. Man, the knife is at your throat, and can you sleep? The spear is ready to smite you, and will you still doat and dream? I think I see the angel of justice who has long been pursuing the sinner who is rejecting Christ, and he cries: "Let me smite him! he has had time enough; let me smite him!" Or, as Christ puts it in the parable, there has come one into the vineyard who has looked at you, the barren tree, and seen no fruit; and he has come these three years, and now he is saying: "Cut it down! why cumbereth it the ground?" O mercy, stay the axe! O God, bid the enemy put by the spear, and let the sleeper wake, not in hell, but still on mercy's plains, where there is a Christ to forgive him and a Spirit to sanctify him! Imploringly, I, your brother, beseech you tonight to turn unto the living God. Even now in this your day, attend to the things which make for your peace:--

"To-day, a pardoning God
Will hear the suppliant pray
To-day, a Saviour's cleansing blood
Will wash thy guilt away.
But, grace so dearly bought
If yet thou wilt despise,
Thy fearful doom with vengeance fraught,
Will fill thee with surprise."

The last picture is this (may it never be seen in you)--there Vent once into a tent, which he thought to be friendly, a mighty man who had fought a battle and lost the day. Hot of foot and full of fear, Sisera came into the tent of Jael to ask for water, and she gave him milk; she brought forth butter in a lordly dish. He drank, and then, all weary, he threw himself along in the tent. He is a photograph of many ungodly men who have gone where they thought they had friends; for sinners think sinners their friends, and think sin their friend, and they have asked for pleasure, and they have had it; and, now, after having had their fill, and eaten butter in a lordly dish, they are tonight in contentment, sleeping in supposed security. They have gone into the house of the evil one to find pleasure, and they are going there again to-night, and they will continue there, and try to find rest in the house of their enemies. Sometimes it is the house of the strange woman, often the settle of the drunkard, or the chair of the scorner, where men think to rest in peace, Oh, hark thee, man, and beware! Fly the ways of the destroyer: fly the haunt of the strange woman, as for thy very life every den of sin; for, lo! she cometh stealthily, the tent pin is in her left hand, and in her right hand the workman's hammer. Many mighty has she slain aforetime, for she hunts for the precious life, and her chambers lead down to death. If thou sleepest on but another night, or even another hour, the destroyer may have done the deed, and thou mayst be fastened to the earth for ever, the victim of thine own delusions. I may be in error, but I think I spear; to some man to-night who must now immediately change his ways, or else the jaws of hell will close upon him. I do not desire to speak my own words, or my own thoughts, but to speak as the divine wind blows through my soul; and I think I am warning some one to-night of whom, if he turn not, it will soon be written, as of another in the Book of Proverbs, "He goeth after her straightway, as an ox goeth to the slaughter, or as a fool to the correction of the stocks; till a dart strike through his liver; as a bird hasteth to the snare, and knoweth not that it is for his life." In the name of the Ever Blessed and Most Merciful, "turn thee! sinner, turn thee! Why wilt thou die?" Thy course is destruction, and is near its end. Awake! Why sleepest thou? Sleep to others is dangerous; to thee it is damnable. Awake, arise, or be for ever ruined. May God's grace bestir thee! Some of you to-night are like Lot and his daughters in the burning city. You must flee; you must flee at once out of Sodom, or you will perish in it. Behold, we would put our hand upon you to-night, and press you to flee, the Lord being merciful unto you.

His servants and his Spirit constrain you to make haste. Linger not; look not back; hesitate not. To your knees! to your knees! "Seek ye the Lord while he may be found; call ye upon him while he is near." To the cross! to the cross! There is your shelter, the mountain where the only refuge can be found from the vengeance of God. Behold the wounds of Jesus, God's beloved Son given for the guilty, slaughtered for the sinful--

"There is life in a look at the crucified One;
There is life at this moment for thee!"--

and for all who look. But it may be that if this night ye look not to Jesus, his cross may never appear before your eyes again, for they will be sealed in death. Ere long, Jael's tent-pin shall have passed through Sisera's skull; the sin shall have destroyed the sinner: the sin that is unto death shall have shut up the spirit in despair. Oh, may God, who is mighty to save, turn you to himself at this moment.

"Sound the trumpet in Zion: sound an alarm in my holy mountain," seems to ring in my ears; and I would fain sound that alarm to God's saints, and to sinners too. May he call many by his grace, and awaken us all; and his shall be the glory for ever and ever! Amen.

PORTION OF SCRIPTURE READ BEFORE SERMON --1 Thessalonians 5.

Praises and Vows Accepted in Zion

A Sermon (No. 1023)
Delivered by
C. H. SPURGEON,
At the Metropolitan Tabernacle, Newington

"Praise waiteth for thee, O God, in Sion: and unto thee shall the vow be performed. O thou that hearest prayer, unto thee shall all flesh more." - Psalm 65:1-2.

UPON Zion there was erected an altar dedicated to God for the offering of sacrifices. Except when prophets were commanded by God to break through the rule, burnt offering was only to be offered there. The worship of God upon the high places was contrary to the divine command: "Take heed to thyself that thou offer not thy burnt offerings in every place that thou seest: but in the place which the Lord shall choose in one of thy tribes, there thou shalt offer thy burnt offerings, and there thou shalt do all that I command thee." Hence the tribes on the other side of Jordan, when they erected a memorial altar, disclaimed all intention of using it for the purpose of sacrifice, and said most plainly, "God forbid that we should rebel against the Lord, and turn this day from following the Lord, to build an altar for burnt offerings, for meat offerings, or for sacrifices, beside the altar of the Lord our God that is before his tabernacle."

In fulfillment of this ancient type, we also "have an altar whereof they have no right to eat that serve the tabernacle." Into our spiritual worship, no observers of materialistic ritualism may intrude; they have no right to eat at our spiritual altar, and there is no other at which they can eat and live for ever. There is but one altar Jesus Christ our Lord. All other altars are impostures and idolatrous inventions. Whether of stone, or wood, or brass, they are the toys with which those amuse themselves who have returned to the beggarly elements of Judaism, or else the apparatus with which clerical jugglers dupe the sons and daughters of men. Holy places made with hands are now abolished; they were once the figures of the true, but now that the substance has come, the type is done away with. The all-glorious person of the Redeemer, God and Man, is the great center of Zion's temple, and the only real altar of sacrifice. He is the church's head, the church's heart, the church's altar, priest, and all in all. "To him shall the gathering of the be." Around him we all congregate even as the tribes around the tabernacle of the Lord in the wilderness.

When the church is gathered together, we may liken it to the assemblies upon Mount Zion, whither the tribes go up, even the tribes of the Lord, unto the testimony of Israel. There the song went up, not so much from each separate worshipper as from all combined; there the praise as it rose to heaven was not only the praise of each one, but the praise of all. So where Christ is the center, where his one sacrifice is the altar whereon all offerings are laid; and where the church unites around that common center, and rejoices in that one sacrifice, there is the true Zion. If we this evening --gathering in Christ's name, around his one finished sacrifice, present our prayers and praises entirely to the Lord through Jesus Christ, we are "come unto Mount Zion, and unto the city of the living God, the heavenly Jerusalem, and to an innumerable company of angels, to the general assembly and church of the firstborn, whose names are written in heaven." This is Zion, even this house in the far-off islands of the Gentiles, and we can say indeed and of a truth, "Praise waiteth for thee, O God, in Zion; and unto thee shall the vow be performed."

We shall, with devout attention, notice two things: the first is our holy worship, which we desire to render; and then the encouragement, the stimulative encouragement, which God provides for us: "O thou that hearest prayer, unto thee shall all flesh come."

I. First, let us consider the HOLY OFFERING OF WORSHIP WHICH WE DESIRE TO PRESENT TO GOD. It is twofold: there is praise, and there is also a vow, a praise that waiteth, and a vow of which performance is promised.

Let us think, first of all, of the praise. This is the chief ingredient of the adoration of heaven; and what is thought to be worthy of the world of glory, ought to be the main portion of the worship of earth. Although we shall never cease to pray as long as we live here below, and are surrounded by so many wants, yet we should never so pray as to forget to praise. "Thy kingdom come. Thy will be done on earth, as it is heaven," must never be left out because we are pressed with want, and therefore hasten to cry, "Give us this day our daily bread." It will be a sad hour when the worship of the church shall be only a solemn wail. Notes of exultant thanksgiving should ever ascend from her solemn gatherings. "Praise the Lord O Jerusalem; praise thy God, O Zion." "Praise ye the Lord. Sing unto the Lord a new song, and his praise in the congregation of saints. Let Israel rejoice in him that made him: let the children of Zion be joyful in their King." Let it abide as a perpetual ordinance, while sun and moon endure, "Praise waiteth for thee, O God, in Zion." Never think little of praise, since holy angels and saints made perfect count it their life-long joy, and even the Lord himself saith, "Whoso offereth praise, glorifieth me." The tendency, I fear, among us has been to undervalue praise as a part of public worship, whereas it should be second to nothing. We frequently hear of prayer-meetings, and but seldom of praise-meetings. We acknowledge the duty of prayer by setting apart certain times for it; we do not always so acknowledge the duty of praise. I hear of "family prayer;" do I always hear of "family praise?" I know you cultivate private prayer: are you as diligent also in private thanksgiving and secret adoration of the Lord? In everything we are to give thanks; it is as much an apostolic precept as that other, "In everything, by prayer and supplication, make your requests known unto God." I have often said to you, dear brethren, that prayer and praise are like the breathing in and out of the air, and make up that spiritual respiration by which the inner life is instrumentally supported. We take in an inspiration of heavenly air as we pray: we breathe it out again in praise unto God, from whom it came; if, then, we would be healthy in spirit, let us be abundant in thanksgiving. Prayer, like the root of a tree, seeks for and finds nutriment; praise, like the fruit, renders a revenue to the owner of the vineyard. Prayer is for ourselves, praise is for God; let us never be so selfish as to abound in the one and fail in the other. Praise is a slender return for the boundless favors we enjoy; let us not be slack in rendering it in our best music, the music of a devout soul. "Praise the Lord; for the Lord is good: sing praises unto his name; for it is pleasant."

Let us notice the praise which is mentioned in our text, which is to be so large a matter of concern to the Zion of God whenever the saints are met together.

You will observe, first, that it is praise exclusively rendered to God. "Praise waiteth for thee, O God, in Zion." "Praise for thee, and all the praise for thee," and no praise for man or for any other who may be thought to be, or may pretend to be, worthy of praise. Have I not sometimes gone into places called houses of God where the praise has waited for a woman--for the Virgin, where praise has waited for the saints, where incense has smoked to heaven, and songs and prayers have been sent up to deceased martyrs and confessors who are supposed to have power with God? In Rome it is so, but in Zion it is not so. Praise waiteth for thee, O Mary, in Babylon; but praise waiteth for thee, O God, in Zion. Unto God, and unto God alone, the praise of his true church must ascend. If Protestants are free from this deadly error, I fear they are guilty of another, for in our worship, we too often minister unto our own selves. We do so when we make the tune and manner of the song to be more important than the matter of it. I am afraid that where organs, choirs, and singing men and singing women are left to do the praise of the congregation, men's minds are more occupied with the due performance of the music, than with the Lord, who alone is to be praised. God's house is meant to be sacred unto himself, but too often it is made an opera-house, and Christians form an audience, not an adoring assembly. The same thing may, unless great care be taken, happen amid the simplest worship, even though everything which does not savor of gospel plainness is excluded, for in that case we may drowsily drawl out the words and notes, with no heart whatever. To sing with the soul, this only is to offer acceptable song! We come not together to amuse ourselves, to display our powers of melody or our aptness in creating harmony we come to pay our adoration at the footstool of the Great King, to whom alone be glory for ever and ever. True praise is for God--for God alone.

Brethren, you must take heed lest the minister, who would, above all, disclaim a share of praise, should be set up as a demi-god among you. Refute practically the old slander that presbyter is only priest writ large. Look higher than the pulpit, or you will be disappointed. Look far above an arm of flesh, or it will utterly fail you. We may say of the best preacher upon the earth, "Give God the praise, for we know that this man is a sinner." If we thought that you paid superstitious reverence to us, we would, like Paul and Silas at Lystra, rend our clothes, and cry, "Sirs, why do ye these things? We also are men of like passions with you, and preach unto you that ye should turn from these vanities unto the living God, which made heaven, and earth, and the sea, and all things that are therein." It is not to any man, to any priest, to any order of men, to any being in heaven or earth beside God, that we should burn the incense of worship. We would as soon worship cats with the Egyptians, as popes with the Romanists: we see no difference between the people whose gods grew in their gardens and the sect whose deity is made by their baker. Such vile idolatry is to be loathed. To God alone shall all the praise of Zion ascend.

It is to be feared that some of our praise ascends nowhere at all, but it in as though it were scattered to the winds. We do not always realize God. Now, "he that cometh to God must believe that he is, and that he is the rewarder of them that diligently seek trim;" this is as true of praise as of prayer. "God is a Spirit," and they that praise him must praise him "in spirit and in truth," for "the Father seeketh such" to praise him, and only such; and, if we do not lift our eyes and our hearts to him, we are but misusing words and wasting time. Our praise is not as it should be, if it be not reverently and earnestly directed to the Lord of Hosts. Vain is it to shoot arrows without a target: we must aim at God's glory in our holy songs, and that exclusively.

Note, next, that it should be continual. "Praise waiteth for thee, O God, in Zion." Some translators conceive that the main idea is that of continuance. It remains; it abides; for Zion does loot break up when the assembly is gone. We do not leave the holiness in the material house, for it never was in the stone and the timber, but only in the living amenably of the faithful.

"Jesus, where'er thy people meet,
There they behold thy mercy-seat;
Where'er they seek thee, thou art found,
And every place is hallow'd ground,
For thou within no walls confined,
Inhabitest the humble mind;
Such ever bring thee where they come,
And going, take thee to their home."

The people of God, as they never cease to be a church, should maintain the Lord's praise perpetually as a community. Their assemblies should begin with praise and end with praise, and ever be conducted in a spirit of praise. There should be in all our solemn assemblies a spiritual incense altar, always smoking with "the pure incense of sweet spices, mingled according to the art of the apothecary": the thanksgiving which is made up of humility, gratitude, love, consecration, and holy joy in the Lord. It should be for the Lord alone, and it should never go out day nor night. "His mercy endureth for ever:" let our praises endure for ever. He makes the outgoings of the morning to rejoice, let us celebrate the rising of the sun with holy psalm and hymn. He makes the closing in of the evening to be glad, let him have our vesper praise. "One generation shall praise thy works to another, and shall declare thy mighty acts." Could his mercy cease, there might be some excuse for staying our praises: but, even should it seem to be so, men who love the Lord would say with Job, "Shall we receive good at the hand of the Lord, and shall we not also receive evil? The Lord gave, end the Lord hath taken away; and blessed be the name of the Lord." Let our praise abide, continue, remain, and be perpetual. It was a good idea of Bishop Farrar, that, in his own house he would keep up continual praise to God, and as, with a large family and household, he numbered just twenty-four, he set apart each one for an hour in the day to be engaged specially in prayer and praise, that he might girdle the day with a circle of worship. We could not do that. To attempt it might on our part be superstition; but to fall asleep blessing God, to rise in the night to meditate on him, and when we wake in the morning to feel our hearts leap in the prospect of his presence during the day, this is attainable, and we ought to reach it. It is much to be desired that all day long, in every avocation, and every recreation, the soul should spontaneously pour forth praise, even as birds sing, and flowers perfume the air, and sunbeams cheer the earth. We would be incarnate psalmody, praise enshrined in flesh and blood. From this delightful duty we would desire no cessation, and ask no pause. "Praise waits for thee, O God, in Zion;" thy praise may come and go, from the outside world, where all things ebb and flow, for it lies beneath the moon, and there is no stability in it; but amidst thy people, who dwell in thee, and who possess eternal life--in them thy praise perpetually abides.

A third point, however, is clear upon the surface of the words. "Praise waiteth for thee"--as though praise must always be humble. The servants "wait" in the king's palace. There the messengers stand girt for any mission; the servitors wait, prepared to obey; and the courtiers surround the throne, all eager to receive the royal smile and to fulfill the high command. Our praises ought to stand, like ranks of messengers, waiting to hear what God's will is; for this is to praise him, Furthermore, true praise lies in the actual doing of the divine will, even this,--to pause in sacred reverence until God the Lord shall speak, whatever that will may be; it is true praise to wait subserviently on him. Praises may be looked upon as servants who delight to obey their master's bidding. There is such a thing as an unholy familiarity with God; this age is not so likely to fall into it as some ages have been, for there is little familiarity with God of any sort now; public worship becomes more formal, and stately, and distant. The intense nearness to God which Luther enjoyed--how seldom do we meet with it! But, however near we come to God, still he is God, and we are his creatures. He is, it is true, "our Father," but be it ever remembered that he is "our Father which art in heaven." "Our Father"--therefore near and intimate: "our Father in heaven," therefore we humbly, solemnly bow in his presence. There is a familiarity that runs into presumption: there is another familiarity, is so sweetly tempered with humility that it doth not intrude. "Praise waiteth for thee" with a servant's livery on, a servant's ear to hear, and a servant's heart to obey. Praise bows at thy foot-stool, feeling that it is still an unprofitable servant.

But, perhaps, you are aware, dear friends, that there are other translations of this verse. "Praise waiteth for thee," may be read, "Praise is silent unto thee"--"is silent before thee." One of the oldest Latin commentators reads it, "Praise and silence belong unto thee;" and Dr. Gill tells us, that in the King of Spain's Bible, it runs "The praise of angels is only silence before thee, O Jehovah," so that when we do our best our highest praise is but silence before God, and we must praise him with confession of shortcomings. Oh, that we too, as our poet puts it, might,

"Loud as his thunders speak his praise,
And sound it lofty as his throne!"

But we cannot do that, and when our notes are most uplifted, and our hearts most joyous, we have not spoken all his praise. Compared to what his nature and glory deserve, our most earnest praise has been little more than silence. Oh, brethren, have you not often felt it to be so? Those who are satisfied with formal worship, think that they have done well when the music has been correctly sung; but those who worship God in spirit, feel that they cannot magnify him enough. They blush over the hymns they sing, and retire from the assembly of the saints mourning that they have fallen far short of his glory. O for an enlarged mind, rightly to conceive the divine majesty; next fur the gift of utterance to clothe the thought in fitting language; and then for a voice like many waters, to sound forth the noble strain. Alas! as yet, we are humbled at our failures to praise the Lord as we would.

"Words are but air, and tongues but clay,
And his compassions are divine;

How, then, shall we proclaim to men God's glory? When we have done our best, our praise is but silence before the merit of his goodness, and the grandeur of his greatness.

Yet it may be well to observe here, that the praise which God accepts, presents itself under a variety of forms. There is praise for God in Zion, and it is often spoken; but there is often praise for God in Zion, and it is silence. There are some who cannot sing vocally, but perhaps, before God, they sing best. There are some, I know, who sing very harshly and inharmoniously--that is to say, to our ears; and yet God may accept them rather than the noise of stringed instruments carefully touched. There is a story told of Rowland Hill's being much troubled by a good old lady who would sit near him and sing with a most horrible voice, and very loudly-- as those people generally do who sing badly--and he at last begged her not to sing so loudly. But when she said, "It comes from my heart," the honest man of God retracted his rebuke, and said, "Sing away, I should be sorry to stop you." When praise comes from the heart, who would wish to restrain it. Even the shouts of the old Methodists, their "hallelujahs" and "glorys," when uttered in fervor, were not to be forbidden; for if these should hold their peace, even the stones would cry out. But there are times when those who sing, and sing well, have too much praise in their soul for it to enclose itself in words. Like some strong liquors which cannot use a little vent, but foam and swell until they burst each hoop that binds the barrel; so, sometimes, we want a larger channel for our soul than that of mouth and tongue, and we long to have all our nerves and sinews made into harpstrings, and all the pores of our body made mouths of thankfulness. Oh, that we could praise with our whole nature, not one single hair of our heads, or drop of blood in our veins, keeping back from adoring the Most High! When this desire for praise is most vehement, we fall back upon silence, and quiver with the adoration which we cannot speak. Silence becomes our praise.

"A sacred reverence cheeks our songs,
And praise sits silent on our tongues."

It would be well, perhaps, in our public service, if we had more often the sweet relief of silence. I am persuaded that silence, ay, frequent silence, is most beneficial; and the occasional unanimous silence of all the saints when they bow before God would, perhaps, better express, and more fully promote, devout feeling than any hymns which have been composed or songs that could be sung. To make silence a part of worship habitually might be affectation and formalism, but to introduce it occasionally, and even frequently into the service, would be advantageous and profitable. Let us, then, by our silence, praise God, and let us always confess that our praise, compared with God's deserving, is but silence.

I would add that there is in the text the idea that praise waits for God expectantly. When we praise God, we expect to see more of him by and by, and therefore wait for him. We bless the King, but we desire to draw nearer to him. We magnify him for what we have seen, and we expect to see more. We praise him in his outer courts, for we shall soon be with him in the heavenly mansions. We glorify him for the revelation of himself in Jesus, for we expect to be like Christ, and to be with him where he is. When I cannot praise God for what I am, I will praise him for what I shall be. When I feel dull and dead about the present, I will take the words of our delightful hymn and say,

"And a near song is in my mouth,
To long-loved music set;
Glory to thee for all the grace
I have not tasted yet."

My praise shall not only be the psalmody of the past, which is but discharging a debt of gratitude, but my faith shall anticipate the future, and wait upon God to fulfill his purposes; and I will begin to pay my praise even before the mercy comes.

Dear brethren and sisters, let us for a moment present our praise to God, each one of us on his own account. We have our common mercies. We call them common, but, oh, how priceless they are. Health to be able to come here and not to be stretched on a bed of sickness, I count this better than bags of gold. To have our reason, and not to be confined in yonder asylum; to have our children still about us and dear relatives spared still to us--to have bread to eat and raiment to put on--to have been kept from defiling our character--to have been preserved to-day from the snares of the enemy! These are godlike mercies, and for all these our praises shall wait upon God.

But oh! take up the thoughts suggested by the psalm itself in the next verse, and you will doubly praise God. "Iniquities prevail against me. As for our transgressions, thou shalt purge them away." Infinite love has made us clean every whit!--though we were black and filthy. We are washed --washed in priceless blood. Praise him for this! Go on with the passage, "Blessed is the man whom thou choosest and causest to approach unto thee." Is not the blessing of access to God an exceeding choice one? Is it a light thing to feel that, though once far off, we are made nigh through the blood of Christ; and this because of electing love! "Blessed is the man whom thou choosest." Ye subjects of eternal choice, can you be silent? Has God favored you above others, and can your lips refuse to sing? No, you will magnify the Lord exceedingly, because he hath chosen Jacob unto himself, and Israel for his peculiar treasure. Let us read on, and praise God that we have an abiding place among his people--"That he may dwell in thy courts."--Blessed be God we are not to be cast forth and driven out after a while, but we have an entailed inheritance amongst the sons of God. We praise him that we have the satisfaction of dwelling in his house as children. "We shall be satisfied with the goodness of thy house, even of thy holy temple." But I close the psalm, and simply say to you, there are ten thousand reasons for taking down the harp from the willows; and I know no reason for permitting it to hang there idle. There are ten thousand times ten thousand reasons for speaking well of "him who loved us, and gave himself for us." "The Lord hath done great things for us whereof we are glad." I remember hearing in a prayer-meeting this delightful verse mutilated in prayer, "The Lord hath done great things for us, whereof we desire to be glad." Oh, brethren, I dislike mauling, and mangling, and adding to a text of Scripture. If we are to have the Scriptures revised, let it be by scholars, and not by every ignoramus. "Desire to be glad," indeed? This is fine gratitude to God when he hath done great things for us." If these great things have been done, our souls must be glad, and cannot help it; they must overflow with gratitude to God for all his goodness.

2. So much on the first part of our holy sacrifice. Attentively let us consider the second, namely, the vow. "Unto thee shall the vow be performed."

We are not given to vow-making in these days. Time was when it was far oftener done. It may be that had we been better men we should have made more vows; it may possibly be that had we been more foolish men we should have done the same. The practice was so abused by superstition, that devotion has grown half-ashamed of it. But we have, at any rate, most of us bound ourselves with occasional vows. I do confess to-day a vow I have not kept as I should desire; the vow made on my first conversion. I surrendered myself, body, soul, and spirit, to him that bought me with a price, and the vow was not made by way of excess of devotion or supererogation, it was but my reasonable service. You have done that. Do you remember the love of your espousals, the time when Jesus was very precious, and you had just entered into the marriage bond with him? You gave yourselves up to him, to be his for ever and for ever. O brethren and sisters, it is a part of worship to perform that vow. Renew it to-night, make another surrender of yourselves to him whose you are and whom you serve. Say to-night, as I will, with you, "Bind the sacrifice with cords, even with cords to the horns of the altar." Oh, for another thong to strap the victim to the altar-horn! Does the flesh struggle? Then let it be more fastly bound, never to escape from the altar of God.

Beloved, many of us did, in effect, make a most solemn vow at the time of our baptism. We were buried with Christ in baptism unto death, and, unless we were greatly dissembling, we avowed that we were dead in Christ and buried with him; wherein, also, we professed that we were risen with him. Now, shall the world live in those who are dead to it, and shall Christ's life be absent from those who are risen with him? We gave ourselves up there and then, in that solemn act of mystic burial. Recall that scene, I pray you; and as you do it blush, and ask God that your vow may yet be performed, as Doddridge well expresses it:--

"Baptised into your Saviour's death
Your souls to sin must die;
With Christ your Lord ye live anew,
With Christ ascend on high."

Some such vow we made, too, when we united ourselves to the church of God. There was an understood compact between us and the church, that we would serve it, that we would seek to honor Christ by holy living, increase the church by propagating the faith, seek its unity, its comfort, by our own love and sympathy with the members. We had no right to join with the church if we did not mean to give ourselves up to it, under Christ, to aid in its prosperity and increase. There was a stipulation made, and a covenant understood, when we entered into communion and league with our brethren in Christ. How about that? Can we say that, as unto God and in his sight, the vow has been performed? Yes, we have been true to our covenant in a measure, brethren. Oh, that it were more fully so! Some of us made another vow, when we gave ourselves, as I trust, under divine call, altogether to the work of the Christian ministry; and though we have taken no orders, and received no earthly ordination, for we are no believers in man-made priests, yet tacitly it is understood that the man who becomes a minister of the church of God is to give his whole time to his work--that body, soul, and spirit should be thrown into the cause of Christ. Oh, that this vow were more fully performed by pastors of the church! You, my brethren, elders and deacons, when you accepted office, you knew what the church meant. She expected holiness and zeal of you. The Holy Ghost made you overseers that you might feed the flock of God. Your office proves your obligation. You are practically under a vow. Has that vow been performed? Have you performed it in Zion unto the Lord?

Besides that, it has been the habit of godly men to make vows occasionally, in times of pain, and losses, and affliction. Did not the psalm we just now sang it so?--

"Among the saints that fill thine house,
My offerings shall be paid;
There shall my zeal perform the vows
My soul in anguish made.
Now I am thine, for ever thine,
Nor shall my purpose move!
Thy hand hath loosed my bands of pain,
And bound me with thy love.
Here in thy courts I leave my vow,
And thy rich grace record;
Witness, ye saints, who hear me now,
If I forsake the Lord."

You said, "If I am ever raised up, and my life is prolonged, it shall be better spent." You said, also, "If I am delivered out of this great trouble, I hope to consecrate my substance more to God." Another time you said, "If the Lord will return to me the light of his countenance, and bring me out of this depressed state of mind, I will praise him more than ever before." Have you remembered all this? Coming here myself so lately from a sick bed, I at this time preach to myself. I only wish I had a better hearer; I would preach to myself in this respect, and say, "I charge thee, my heart, to perform thy vow." Some of us, dear friends, have made vows in time of joy, the season of the birth of the first-born child, the recovery of the wife from sickness, the merciful restoration that we have ourselves received, times of increasing goods, or seasons when the splendor of God's face has been unveiled before our wondering eye. Have we not made vows, like Jacob when he woke up from his wondrous dream, and took the stone which had been his pillow, and poured oil on its top, and made a vow unto the Most High? We have all had our Bethels. Let us remember that God has heard us, and let us perform unto him our vow which our soul made in her time of joy. But I will not try to open the secret pages of your private note-books. You have had tender passages, which you would not desire me to read aloud: the tears start at their memory. If your life were written, you would say,

"Let these not be told; they were only between God and my soul"--some chaste and blessed love passages between you and Christ, which must not be revealed to men. Have you forgotten how then you said, "I am my beloved's, and he is mine," and what you promised when you saw all his goodness made to pass before you. I have now to stir up your pure minds by way of remembrance, and bid you present unto the Lord to-night the double offering of your heart's praise and of your performed vow. "O magnify the Lord with me, and let us exalt his name together."

II. And now, time will fail me, but I must have a few words upon THE BLESSED ENCOURAGEMENT afforded us in the text for the presentation of these offerings unto God. Here it is,--"O thou that hearest prayer, unto thee shall all flesh come?"

Observe, here, that God hears prayer. It is, in some aspects, the lowest form of worship, and yet he accepts it. It is not the worship of heaven, and it is, in a measure, selfish. Praise is superior worship, for it is elevating; it is the utterance of a soul that has received good from God, and is returning its love to him in acknowledgment. Praise has a sublime aspect. Now, observe, if praiser is heard, then praise will be heard too. If the lower form, on weaker wing as it were, reaches the throne of the majesty on high, how much more shall the seraphic wing of praise bear itself into the divine presence. Prayer is heard of God: therefore our praises and vows will be. And this is a very great encouragement, because it seems terrible to pray when you are not heard, and discouraging to praise God if he will not accept it. What would be the use of it? But if prayer and yet more praise be most surely heard, ah, brethren, then let us continue and abide in thanksgiving. "Whoso offereth praise glorifieth me, saith the Lord."

Observe too according to the text, that all prayer, if it be true prayer, is heard of God, for so it is put--"Unto thee shall all flesh come." Oh, how glad I am at that word. My poor prayer--shall God reject it? Yes, I might have feared so if he had said, "Unto thee shall all spirits come." Behold, my brethren, he takes the grosser part as it were, and looks at prayer in his infinite compassion, perceiving it to be what it is--a feeble thing--a cry coming from poor fallen flesh, and yet he puts it, "Unto thee shall all flesh come. My broken prayer, my groaning prayer shall get to thee, though it seems to me a thing of flesh, it is nevertheless wrought in me by thy Spirit. And, O my God, my song, though my voice be hoarse and oftentimes my notes most feeble, shall reach thee. Though I groan because it is so imperfect, yet even that shall come to thee. Prayer, if true, shall be received of God, notwithstanding all its faultiness, through Jesus Christ. Then so it will be with our praises and our vows.

Again, prayer is always and habitually received of God. "O thou that hearest prayer." Not that didst hear it or on a certain occasion may have heard it, but thou that ever hearest prayer. If he always hears prayer, then he always hears praise. Is not this delightful to think of my praise, though it be but that of a child or a poor unworthy sinner--God does hear it, does accept it, in spite of its imperfections, and does accept it always? Oh, I will have another hymn to-morrow, I will sing a new song to-morrow. I will forget my pain, I will forget for a moment all my care, and if I cannot sing aloud by reason of those that are with me, yet will I set the bells of my heart ringing, I will make my whole soul full of praise. If I cannot let it out of my mouth, I will praise him in my soul, because he always hears me. You know it is hard to do things for one who never accepts what you do. Many a wife has said, "Oh! it is hard. My husband never seems pleased. I have done all I can, but he takes no notice of little deeds of kindness." But how easy it is to serve a person who, when you have done any little thing, saw, "How kind it was of you" and thinks much of it. Ah, poor child of God, the Lord thinks much of thy praises, much of thy vows, much of thy prayers. Therefore, be not slack to praise and magnify him unceasingly.

And this all the more, because we have not quite done with that word, "Unto thee shall all flesh come." All flesh shall come because the Lord hears prayer. Then all my praises will be heard and all the praises of all sorts of men, if sincere, come unto God. The great ones of the earth shall present praise, and the poorest of the poor also, for thou shalt not reject them.

And, Lord, wilt thou put it so; "Unto thee shall all flesh come," and wilt thou say, "but not such a one?" Wilt thou exclude me? Brethren, fear not that God will reject you. I remind you of what I told you the other night concerning a good earnest believing woman, who in prayer said, "Lord, I am content to be the second thou shalt forsake, but I cannot be the first." The Lord says all flesh shall come to him, and it is implied that he will receive them when they come--all sorts of men, all classes and conditions of men. Then he cannot reject me if I go, nor my prayers if I pray, nor my praise if I praise him, nor my vows if I perform them. Come then, let us praise the Lord, let us worship and bow down, let us kneel before the Lord our maker, for we are the people of his pasture and the sheep of his hand.

I have done when I have said this. Dear brethren and sisters, there may be difficulties in your way; iniquities may hinder you, or infirmities; but there is the promise, "thou shalt purge them away." Infirmities may check you, but note the word of divine help, "Blessed is the man whom thou causest to approach unto thee." He will come to your aid, and lead you to himself. Infirmities, therefore, are overcome by divine grace. Perhaps your emptiness hinders you: "He shall be satisfied with the goodness of thy house." It is not your goodness that is to satisfy either God or you, but God's goodness is to satisfy. Come, then, with thine iniquity, come with thine infirmity; come with thy emptiness. Come, dear brethren, if you have never come to God before. Come and confess your sin to God, and ask for mercy; you can do no less than ask. Come and trust his mercy, which endures for ever; it has no limit. Think not hardly of him, but come and lay yourself down at his feet. If you perish, perish there. Come and tell your grief; pour out your hearts before him. Bottom upwards turn the vessel of your nature, and drain out the last dreg, and pray to be filled with the fullness of his grace. Come unto Jesus; he invites you, he enables you. A cry from that pew will reach the sacred ear: "You have not prayed before," you say. Everything must have a beginning. Oh that that beginning might come now. It is not because you pray well that you are to come, but because the Lord hears prayer graciously, therefore, all flesh shall come. You are welcome; none can say you nay. Come! tis mercy's welcome hour. May the Lord's bands of love be cast about you; may you be drawn now to him. Come by way of the cross; come resting in the precious atoning sacrifice, believing in Jesus; and he has said, "Him that cometh unto me, I will in no wise cast out." The grace of our Lord be with you. Amen.

PORTION OF SCRIPTURE READ BEFORE SERMON--Psalm 65.

The Throne of Grace

A Sermon (No. 1024)
Delivered on Lord's-Day Morning, November 19th, 1871, by
C. H. SPURGEON,
At the Metropolitan Tabernacle, Newington

"The throne of grace." - Hebrews 4:16

THESE words are found embedded in that gracious verse, "Let us therefore come boldly unto the throne of grace, that we may obtain mercy, and find grace to help in time of need"; they are a gem in a golden setting. True prayer is an approach of the soul by the Spirit of God to the throne of God. It is not the utterance of words, it is not alone the feeling of desires, but it is the advance of the desires to God, the spiritual approach of our nature towards the Lord our God. True prayer is not a mere mental exercise, nor a vocal performance, but it is deeper far than that--it is spiritual commerce with the Creator of heaven and earth. God is a Spirit unseen of mortal eye, and only to be perceived by the inner man; our spirit within us, begotten by the Holy Ghost at our regeneration, discerns the Great Spirit, communes with him, prefers to him its requests, and receives from him answers of peace. It is a spiritual business from beginning to end; and its aim and object end not with man, but reach to God himself.

In order to such prayer, the work of the Holy Ghost himself is needed. If prayer were of the lips alone, we should only need breath in our nostrils to pray: if prayer were of the desires alone, many excellent desires are easily felt, even by natural men: but when it is the spiritual desire, and the spiritual fellowship of the human spirit with the Great Spirit, then the Holy Ghost himself must be present all through it, to help infirmity, and give life and power, or else true prayer will never be presented, but the thing offered to God will wear the name and have the form, but the inner life of prayer will be far from it.

Moreover, it is clear from the connection of our text, that the interposition of the Lord Jesus Christ is essential to acceptable prayer. As prayer will not be truly prayer without the Spirit of God, so it will not be prevailing prayer without the Son of God. he, the Great High Priest, must go within the veil for us; nay, through his crucified person the veil must be entirely taken away; for, until then, we are shut out from the living God. The man who, despite the teaching of Scripture, tries to pray without a Saviour insults the Deity; and he who imagines that his own natural desires, coming up before God, unsprinkled with the precious blood, will be an acceptable sacrifice before God, makes a mistake; he has not brought an offering that God can accept, any more than if he had struck off a dog's neck, or offered an unclean sacrifice. Wrought in us by the Spirit, presented for us by the Christ of God, prayer becomes power before the Most High, but not else.

In order, dear friends, that I may stir you up to prayer this morning, and that your souls may be led to come near to the Throne of Grace, I purpose to take these few words and handle them as God shall give me ability. You have begun to pray; God has begun to answer. This week has been a very memorable one in the history of this church. Larger numbers than ever before at one time have come forward to confess Christ,--as plain an answer to the supplications of God's people, as though the hand of the Most High had been stretched out of heaven handing down to us the blessings for which we asked. Now, let us continue in prayer, yea, let us gather strength in intercession, and the more we succeed, the more earnest let us be to succeed yet more and more. Let us not be straitened in our own bowels, since we are not straitened in our God. This is a good day, and a time of glad tidings, and seeing that we have the King's ear, I am most anxious that we should speak to him for thousands of others; that they also, in answer to our pleadings, may be brought nigh unto Christ.

In trying to speak of the text this morning, I shall take it thus: First, here is a throne; then, secondly, here is grace; then we will put the two together, and we shall see grace on a throne; and putting them together in another order, we shall see sovereignty manifesting itself, and resplendent in grace.

II. Our text speaks of A THRONE:--"The Throne of Grace." God is to be viewed in prayer as our Father; that is the aspect which is dearest to us; but still we are not to regard him as though he were such as we are; for our Saviour has qualified the expression "Our Father," with the words "who art in heaven"; and close at the heels of that condescending name, in order to remind us that our Father is still infinitely greater than ourselves, he has bidden us say, "Hallowed be thy name; thy kingdom come"; so that our Father is still to be regarded as a King, and in prayer we come, not only to our Father's feet, but we come also to the throne of the Great Monarch of the universe. The mercy-seat is a throne, and we must not forget this.

If prayer should always be regarded by us as an entrance into the courts of the royalty of heaven; if we are to behave ourselves as courtiers should in the presence of an illustrious majesty, then we are not at a loss to know the right spirit in which to pray. If in prayer we come to a throne, it is clear that our spirit should, in the first place, be one of lowly reverence. It is expected that the subject in approaching to the king should pay him homage and honour. The pride that will not own the king, the treason which rebels against the sovereign will should, if it be wise, avoid any near approach to the throne. Let pride bite the curb at a distance, let treason lurk in corners, for only lowly reverence may come before the king himself when he sits clothed in his robes of majesty. In our case, the king before whom we come is the highest of all monarchs, the King of kings, the Lord of lords. Emperors are but the shadows of his imperial power. They call themselves kings by right divine, but what divine right have they? Common sense laughs their pretensions to scorn. The Lord alone hath divine right, and to him only doth the kingdom belong. He is the blessed and only potentate. They are but nominal kings, to be set up and put down at the will of men, or the decree of providence, but he is Lord alone, the Prince of the kings of the earth.

"He sits on no precarious throne,
Nor borrows leave to be."

My heart, be sure that thou prostrate thyself in such a presence. If he be so great, place thy mouth in the dust before him, for he is the most powerful of all kings; his throne hath sway in all worlds; heaven obeys him cheerfully, hell trembles at his frown, and earth is constrained to yield to him homage willingly or unwillingly. His power can make or can destroy. To create or to crush, either is easy enough to him. My soul be thou sure that when thou drawest nigh to the Omnipotent, who is as a consuming fire, thou put thy shoes from off thy feet, and worship him with lowliest humility.

Besides, he is the most Holy of all kings. His throne is a great white throne, unspotted, and clear as crystal. "The heavens are not pure in his sight, and he charged his angels with folly." And thou, a sinful creature, with what lowliness shouldst thou draw nigh to him. Familiarity there may be, but let it not be unhallowed. Boldness there should be, but let it not be impertinent. Still thou art on earth and he in heaven; still thou art a worm of the dust, a creature crushed before the moth, and he the Everlasting: before the mountains were brought forth, he was God, and if all created things should pass away again, yet still were he the same. My brethren, I am afraid we do not bow as we should before the Eternal Majesty; but, henceforth, let us ask the Spirit of God to put us in a right frame, that every one of our prayers may be a reverential approach to the Infinite Majesty above.

A throne, and therefore, in the second place, to be approached with devout joyfulness. If I find myself favoured by divine grace to stand amongst those favoured ones who frequent his courts, shall I not feel glad? I might have been in his prison, but I am before his throne: I might have been driven from his presence for ever, but I am permitted to come near to him, even into his royal palace, into his secret chamber of gracious audience, shall I not then be thankful? Shall not my thankfulness ascend into joy, and shall I not feel that I am honoured, that I am made the recipient of great favours when I am permitted to pray? Wherefore is thy countenance sad, O suppliant, when thou standest before the throne of grace? If thou wert before the throne of justice to be condemned for thine iniquities, thy hands might well be on thy loins; but now thou art favoured to come before the King in his silken robes of love, let thy face shine with sacred delight. If thy sorrows be heavy, tell them unto him, for he can assuage them; if thy sins be multiplied, confess them, for he can forgive them. O ye courtiers in the halls of such a monarch, be ye exceeding glad, and mingle praises with your prayers.

It is a throne, and therefore, in the third place, whenever it is approached, it should be with complete submission. We do not pray to God to instruct him as to what he ought to do, neither for a moment must we presume to dictate the line of the divine procedure. We are permitted to say unto God, "Thus and thus would we have it," but we must evermore add, "But, seeing that we are ignorant and may be mistaken--seeing that we are still in the flesh, and, therefore, may be actuated by carnal motives--not as we will, but as thou wilt." Who shall dictate to the throne? No loyal child of God will for a moment imagine that he is to occupy the place of the King, but he bows before him who has a right to be Lord of all; and though he utters his desire earnestly, vehemently, importunately, and pleads and pleads again, yet it is evermore with this needful reservation: "Thy will be done, my Lord: and, if I ask anything that is not in accordance therewith, my inmost will is that thou wouldst be good enough to deny thy servant; I will take it as a true answer if thou refuse me, if I ask that which seemeth not good in thy sight." If we constantly remembered this, I think we should be less inclined to push certain suits before the throne, for we should feel, "I am here in seeking my own ease, my own comfort, my own advantage, and peradventure, I may be asking for that which would dishonour God; therefore will I speak with the deepest submission to the divine decrees."

But, brethren, in the fourth place, if it be a throne, it ought to be approached with enlarged expectations. Well doth our hymn put it:

"Thou art coming to a king:
Large petitions with thee bring."

We do not come, as it were, in prayer, only to God's almonry where he dispenses his favours to the poor, nor do we come to the back-door of the house of mercy to receive the broken scraps, though that were more than we deserve; to eat the crumbs that fall from the Master's table is more than we could claim; but, when we pray, we are standing in the palace, on the glittering floor of the great King's own reception room, and thus we are placed upon a vantage ground. In prayer we stand where angels bow with veiled faces; there, even there, the cherubim and seraphim adore, before that selfsame throne to which our prayers ascend. And shall we come there with stunted requests, and narrow and contracted faith? Nay, it becomes not a King to be giving away pence and groats, he distributes pieces of broad gold; he scatters not as poor men must, scraps of bread and broken meat, but he makes a feast of fat things, of fat things full of marrow, of wines on the lees well refined. When Alexander's soldier was told to ask what he would, he did not ask stintedly after the nature of his own merits, but he made such a heavy demand, that the royal treasurer refused to pay it, and put the case to Alexander, and Alexander in right kingly sort replied: "He knows how great Alexander is, and he has asked as from a king; let him have what he requests." Take heed of imagining that God's thoughts are as thy thoughts, and his ways as thy ways. Do not bring before God stinted petitions and narrow desires, and say, "Lord, do according to these," but, remember, as high as the heavens are above the earth, so high are his ways above your ways, and his thoughts above your thoughts, and ask, therefore, after a God-like sort, ask for great things, for you are before the throne of grace, for then he would do for us exceeding abundantly above what we ask or even think.

And, beloved, I may add, in the fifth place, that the right spirit in which to approach the throne of grace, is that of unstaggering confidence. Who shall doubt the King? Who dares impugn the Imperial word? It was well said that if integrity were banished from the hearts of all mankind besides, it ought still to dwell in the hearts of kings. Shame on a king if he can lie. The veriest beggar in the streets is dishonoured by a broken promise, but what shall we say of a king if his word cannot be depended upon? Oh, shame upon us, if we are unbelieving before the throne of the King of heaven and earth. With our God before us in all his glory, sitting on the throne of grace, will our hearts dare to say we mistrust him? Shall we imagine either that he cannot, or will not, keep his promise? Banished be such blasphemous thoughts, and if they must come, let them come upon us when we are somewhere in the outskirts of his dominions, if such a place there be, but not in prayer, when we are in his immediate presence, and behold him in all the glory of his throne of grace. There, surely, is the place for the child to trust its Father, for the loyal subject to trust his monarch; and, therefore, far from it be all wavering or suspicion. Unstaggering faith should be predominant before the mercy-seat.

Only one other remark upon this point, and that is, that if prayer be a coming before the throne of God, it ought always to be conducted with the deepest sincerity, and in the spirit which makes everything real. If you are disloyal enough to despise the King, at least, for your own sake, do not mock him to his face, and when he is upon his throne. If anywhere you dare repeat holy words without heart, let it not be in Jehovah's palace. If a person should ask for audience with royalty, and then should say, "I scarce know why I have come, I do not know that I have anything very particular to ask; I have no very urgent suit to press;" would he not be guilty both of folly and baseness? As for our great King, when we venture into his presence, let us have an errand there. As I said the other Sabbath, let us beware of playing at praying. It is insolence toward God. If I am called upon to pray in public, I must not dare to use words that are intended to please the ears of my fellow-worshippers, but I must realize that I am speaking to God himself, and that I have business to transact with the great Lord. And, in my private prayer, if, when I rise from my bed in the morning, I bow my knee and repeat certain words, or when I retire to rest at night go through the same regular form, I rather sin than do anything that is good, unless my very soul doth speak unto the Most High. Dost thou think that the King of heaven is delighted to hear thee pronounce words with a frivolous tongue, and a thoughtless mind? Thou knowest him not. He is a Spirit, and they that worship him must worship him in spirit and in truth. If thou hast any empty forms to prate, go and pour them out into the ears of fools like thyself, but not before the Lord of Hosts. If thou hast certain words to utter, to which thou dost attach a superstitious reverence, go and say them in the bedizened courts of the harlot Rome, but not before the glorious Lord of Zion. The spiritual God seeks spiritual worshipers, and such he will accept, and only such; but the sacrifice of the wicked is an abomination unto the Lord, and only a sincere prayer is his delight.

Beloved, the gathering up of all our remarks is just this,--prayer is no trifle. It is an eminent and elevated act. It is a high and wondrous privilege. Under the old Persian Empire a few of the nobility were permitted at any time to come in unto the king, and this was thought to be the highest privilege possessed by mortals. You and I, the people of God, have a permit, a passport to come before the throne of heaven at any time we will, and we are encouraged to come there with great boldness; but still let us not forget that it is no mean thing to be a courtier in the courts of heaven and earth, to worship him who made us and sustains us in being. Truly, when we attempt to pray, we may hear the voice saying out of the excellent glory: "Bow the knee." From all the spirits that behold the face of our Father who is in heaven, even now, I hear a voice which saith, "Oh, come let us worship and bow down, let us kneel before the Lord our Maker; for he is our God, and we are the people of his pasture and the sheep of his hand. O worship the Lord in the beauty of holiness; fear before him all the earth."

II. Lest the glow and brilliance of the word "throne" should be too much for mortal vision, our text now presents us with the soft, gentle radiance of that delightful word--"GRACE." We are called to the throne of grace, not to the throne of law. Rocky Sinai once was the throne of law, when God came to Paran with ten thousand of his holy ones. Who desired to draw near to that throne? Even Israel might not. Bounds were set about the mount, and if but a beast touched the mount, it was stoned or thrust through with a dart. O ye self-righteous ones who hope that you can obey the law, and think that you can be saved by it, look to the flames that Moses saw, and shrink, and tremble, and despair. To that throne we do not come now, for through Jesus the case is changed. To a conscience purged by the precious blood there is no anger upon the divine throne, though to our troubled minds--

"Once twas a seat of burning wrath,
And shot devouring flame;
Our God appeared consuming fire,
And jealous was his name."

And, blessed be God, we are not this morning to speak of the throne of ultimate justice. Before that we shall all come, and as many uf us as have believed will find it to be a throne of grace as well as of justice; for, he who sits upon that throne shall pronounce no sentence of condemnation against the man who is justified by faith. But I have not to call you this morning to the place from whence the resurrection-trumpet shall ring out so shrill and clear. Nor yet do we see the angels with their vengeful swords come forth to smite the foes of God; not yet are the great doors of the pit opened to swallow up the enemies who would not have the Son of God to reign over them. We are still on praying ground and pleading terms with God, and the throne to which we are bidden to come, and of which we speak at this time, is the throne of grace. It is a throne set up on purpose for the dispensation of grace; a throne from which every utterance is an utterance of grace; the scepter that is stretched out from it is the silver sceptre of grace; the decrees proclaimed from it are purposes of grace; the gifts that are scattered down its golden steps are gifts of grace; and he that sits upon the throne is grace itself. It is the throne of grace to which we approach when we pray; and let us for a moment or two think this over, by way of consolatory encouragement to those who are beginning to pray; indeed, to all of us who are praying men and women.

If in prayer I come before a throne of grace, then the faults of my prayer will be overlooked. In beginning to pray, dear friends, you feel as if you did not pray. The groanings of your spirit, when you rise from your knees are such that you think there is nothing in them. What a blotted, blurred, smeared prayer it is. Never mind; you are not come to the throne of justice, else when God perceived the fault in the prayer he would spurn it,--your broken words, your gaspings, and stammerings are before a throne of grace. When any one of us has presented his best prayer before God, if he saw it as God sees it, there is no doubt he would make great lamentation over it; for there is enough sin in the best prayer that was ever prayed to secure its being cast away from God. But it is not a throne of justice I say again, and here is the hope for our lame, limping supplications. Our condescending King does not maintain a stately etiquette in his court like that which has been observed by princes among men, where a little mistake or a flaw would secure the petitioner's being dismissed with disgrace. Oh, no; the faulty cries of his children are not severely criticized by him. The Lord High Chamberlain of the palace above, our Lord Jesus Christ, takes care to alter and amend every prayer before he presents it, and he makes the prayer perfect with his perfection, and prevalent with His own merits. God looks upon the prayer, as presented through Christ, and forgives all its own inherent faultiness. How this ought to encourage any of us who feel ourselves to be feeble, wandering, and unskillful in prayer. If you cannot plead with God as sometimes you did in years gone by, if you feel as if somehow or other you had grown rusty in the work of supplication, never give over, but come still, yea and come oftener, for it is not a throne of severe criticism, it is a throne of grace to which you come.

Then, further, inasmuch as it is a throne of grace, the faults of the petitioner himself shall not prevent the success of his prayer. Oh, what faults there are in us! To come before a throne how unfit we are--we, that are all defiled with sin within and without! Dare any of you think of praying were it not that God's throne is a throne of grace? If you could, I confess that I could not. An absolute God, infinitely holy and just, could not in consistency with his divine nature answer any prayer from such a sinner as I am, were it not that he has arranged a plan by which my prayer comes up no longer to a throne of absolute justice, but to a throne which is also the mercy-seat, the propitiation, the place where God meets sinners, through Jesus Christ. Ah, I could not say to you, "Pray," not even to you saints, unless it were a throne of grace, much less could I talk of prayer to you sinners; but now I will say this to every sinner here, though he should think himself to be the worst sinner that ever lived, cry unto the Lord and seek him while he may be found. A throne of grace is a place fitted for you: go to your knees; by simple faith go to your Saviour, for he, he it is who is the throne of grace. It is in him that God is able to dispense grace unto the most guilty of mankind. Blessed be God, neither the faults of the prayer nor yet of the suppliant shall shut out our petitions from the God who delights in broken and contrite hearts.

If it be a throne of grace, then the desires of the pleader will be interpreted. If I cannot find words in which to utter my desires, God in his grace will read my desires without the words. He takes the meaning of his saints, the meaning of their groans. A throne that was not gracious would not trouble itself to make out our petitions; but God, the infinitely gracious One, will dive into the soul of our desires, and he will read there what we cannot speak with the tongue. Have you never seen the parent, when his child is trying to say something to him, and he knows very well what it is the little one has got to say, help him over the words and utter the syllables for him, and if the little one has half-forgotten what he would say, you have seen the father suggest the word: and so the ever-blessed Spirit, from the throne of grace, will help us and teach us words, nay, write in our hearts the desires themselves. We have in Scripture instances where God puts words into sinners' mouths. "Take with you words," saith he, "and say unto him, Receive us graciously and love us freely." He will put the desires, and put the expression of those desires into your spirit by his grace; he will direct your desires to the things which you ought to seek for; he will teach you your wants, though as yet you know them not; he will suggest to you his promises that you may be able to plead them; he will, in fact, be Alpha and Omega to your prayer, just as he is to your salvation; for as salvation is from first to last of grace, so the sinner's approach to the throne of grace is of grace from first to last. What comfort is this. Will we not, my dear friends, with the greater boldness draw near to this throne, as we suck out the sweet meaning of this precious word, "the throne of grace"?

If it be a throne of grace, then all the wants of those who come to it will be supplied. The King from off such a throne will not say, "Thou must bring to Me gifts, thou must offer to Me sacrifices." It is not a throne for receiving tribute; it is a throne for dispensing gifts. Come, then, ye who are poor as poverty itself; come ye that have no merits and are destitute of virtues, come ye that are reduced to a beggarly bankruptcy by Adam's fall and by your own transgressions; this is not the throne of majesty which supports itself by the taxation of its subjects, but a throne which glorifies itself by streaming forth like a fountain with floods of good things. Come ye, now, and receive the wine and milk which are freely given, yea, come buy wine and milk without money and without price. All the petitioner's wants shall be supplied, because it is a throne of grace.

And so, all the petitioner's miseries shall be compassionated. Suppose I come to the throne of grace with the burden of my sins; there is one on the throne who felt the burden of sin in ages long gone by, and has not forgotten its weight. Suppose I come loaded with sorrow; there is One there who knows all the sorrows to which humanity can be subjected. Am I depressed and distressed? Do I fear that God himself has forsaken me? There is One upon the throne who said, "My God, my God, why hast thou forsaken me?" It is a throne from which grace delights to look upon the miseries of mankind with tender eye, to consider them and to relieve them. Come, then; come, then; come, then, ye that are not only poor, but wretched, whose miseries make you long for death, and yet dread it. Ye captive ones, come in your chains; ye slaves, come with the irons upon your souls; ye who sit in darkness, come forth all blindfold as you are. The throne of grace will look on you if you cannot look on it, and will give to you, though you have nothing to give in return, and will deliver you, though you cannot raise a finger to deliver yourself.

"The throne of grace." The word grows as I turn it over in my mind, and to me it is a most delightful reflection that if I come to the throne of God in prayer, I may feel a thousand defects, but yet there is hope. I usually feel more dissatisfied with my prayers than with anything else I do. I do not believe that it is an easy thing to pray in public so as to conduct the devotions of a large congregation aright. We sometimes hear persons commended for preaching well, but if any shall be enabled to pray well, there will be an equal gift and a higher grace in it. But, brethren, suppose in our prayers there should be defects of knowledge: it is a throne of grace, and our Father knoweth that we have need of these things. Suppose there should be defects of faith: he sees our little faith and still doth not reject it, small as it is. He doth not in every case measure out his gifts by the degree of our faith, but by the sincerity and trueness of faith. And if there should be grave defects in our spirit even, and failures in the fervency or in the humility of the prayer, still, though these should not be there and are much to be deplored; grace overlooks all this, forgives all this, and still its merciful hand is stretched out to enrich us according to our needs. Surely this ought to induce many to pray who have not prayed, and should make us who have been long accustomed to use the consecrated art of prayer, to draw near with greater boldness than ever to the throne of grace.

III. But, now regarding our text as a whole, it conveys to us the idea of GRACE ENTHRONED. It is a throne, and who sits on it? It is grace personified that is here installed in dignity. And, truly, to-day grace is on a throne. In the gospel of Jesus Christ grace is the most predominant attribute of God. How comes it to be so exalted? We reply, well, grace has a throne by conquest. Grace came down to earth in the form of the Well-beloved, and it met with sin. Long and sharp was the struggle, and grace appeared to be trampled under foot of sin; but grace at last seized sin, threw it on its own shoulders, and, though all but crushed beneath the burden, grace carried sin up to the cross and nailed it there, slew it there, put it to death for ever, and triumphed gloriously. For this cause at this hour grace sits on a throne, because it has conquered human sin, has borne the penalty of human guilt, and overthrown all its enemies.

Grace, moreover, sits on the throne because it has established itself there by right. There is no injustice in the grace of God. God is as just when he forgives a believer as when he casts a sinner into hell. I believe in my own soul that there is as much and as pure a justice in the acceptance of a soul that believes in Christ as there will be in the rejection of those souls who die impenitent, and are banished from Jehovah's presence. The sacrifice of Christ has enabled God to be just, and yet the justifier of him that believeth. He who knows the word "substitution," and can spell its meaning aright, will see that there is nothing due to punitive justice from any believer, seeing that Jesus Christ has paid all the believer's debts, and now God would be unjust if he did not save those for whom Christ vicariously suffered, for whom his righteousness was provided, and to whom it is imputed. Grace is on the throne by conquest, and sits there by right.

Grace is enthroned this day, brethren, because Christ has finished his work and gone into the heavens. It is enthroned in power. When we speak of its throne, we mean that it has unlimited might. Grace sits not on the footstool of God; grace stands not in the courts of God, but it sits on the throne; it is the regnant attribute; it is the king to-day. This is the dispensation of grace, the year of grace: grace reigns through righteousness unto eternal life. We live in the era of reigning grace, for seeing he ever liveth to make intercession for the sons of men, Jesus is able also to save them to the uttermost that come unto God by him. Sinner, if you were to meet grace in the by-way, like a traveller on his journey, I would bid you make its acquaintance and ask its influence; if you should meet grace as a merchant on the exchange, with treasure in his hand, I would bid you court its friendship, it will enrich you in the hour of poverty; if you should see grace as one of the peers of heaven, highly exalted, I would bid you seek to get its ear; but, oh, when grace sits on the throne, I beseech you close in with it at once. It can be no higher, it can be no greater, for it is written "God is love," which is an alias for grace. Oh, come and bow before it; come and adore the infinite mercy and grace of God. Doubt not, halt not, hesitate not. Grace is reigning; grace is God; God is love. Oh that you, seeing grace is thus enthroned, would come and receive it. I say, then, that grace is enthroned by conquest, by right, and by power, and, I will add, it is enthroned in glory, for God glorifies his grace. It is one of his objects now to make his grace illustrious. He delights to pardon penitents, and so to show his pardoning grace; he delights to look upon wanderers and restore them, to show his reclaiming grace; he delights to look upon the broken-hearted and comfort them, that he may show his consoling grace. There is a grace to be had of various kinds, or rather the same grace acting different ways, and God delights to make his grace glorious. There is a rainbow round about the throne like unto an emerald, the emerald of his compassion and his love. O happy souls that can believe this, and believing it can come at once and glorify grace by becoming instances of its power.

IV. Lastly, our text, if rightly read, has in it SOVEREIGNTY RESPLENDENT IN GLORY,--THE GLORY OF GRACE. The mercy seat is a throne; though grace is there, it is still a throne. Grace does not displace sovereignty. Now, the attribute of sovereignty is very high and terrible; its light is like unto a jasper stone, most precious, and like unto a sapphire stone, or, as Ezekiel calls it, "the terrible crystal." Thus saith the King, the Lord of hosts: "I will have mercy on whom I will have mercy, and I will have compassion on whom I will have compassion." "Who art thou, O man, that repliest against God? Shall the thing formed say to him that formed it, Why hast thou made me thus?" "Hath not the potter power over the clay to make of the same lump one vessel unto honour and another unto dishonour?" These are great and terrible words, and are not to be answered. He is a King, and he will do as he wills. None shall stay his hand, or say unto him, What doest thou? But, ah! lest any of you should be downcast by the thought of his sovereignty, I invite you to the text. It is a throne,--there is sovereignty; but to every soul that knows how to pray, to every soul that by faith comes to Jesus, the true mercy seat, divine sovereignty wears no dark and terrible aspect, but is full of love. It is a throne of grace; from which I gather that the sovereignty of God to a believer, to a pleader, to one who comes to God in Christ, is always exercised in pure grace. To you, to you who come to God in prayer, the sovereignty always runs thus: "I will have mercy on that sinner; though he deserves it not, though in him there is no merit, yet because I can do as I will with my own, I will bless him, I will make him my child, I will accept him; he shall be mine in the day when I make up my jewels." On the mercy seat God never executed sovereignty otherwise than in a way of grace. He reigns, but in this case grace reigns through righteousness unto eternal life by Jesus Christ our Lord.

There are these two or three things to be thought of, and I have done. On the throne of grace sovereignty has placed itself under bonds of love. I must speak with words choice and picked here, and I must hesitate and pause to get the right sentences, lest I err while endeavouring to speak the truth in plainness. God will do as he wills; but, on the mercy seat, he is under bonds--bonds of his own making, for he has entered into covenant with Christ, and so into covenant with his chosen. Though God is and ever must be a sovereign, he never will break his covenant, not alter the word that is gone out of his mouth. He cannot be false to a covenant of his own making. When I come to God in Christ, to God on the mercy seat, I need not imagine that by any act of sovereignty God will set aside his covenant. That cannot be: it is impossible.

Moreover, on the throne of grace, God is again bound to us by his promises. The covenant contains in it many gracious promises, exceeding great and precious. "Ask and it shall be given you; seek and ye shall find; knock and it shall be opened unto you." Until God had said that word or a word to that effect, it was at his own option to hear prayer or not, but it is not so now; for now, if it be true prayer offered through Jesus Christ, his truth binds him to hear it. A man may be perfectly free, but the moment he makes a promise, he is not free to break it; and the everlasting God wants not to break his promise. He delights to fulfil it. He hath declared that all his promises are yea and amen in Christ Jesus; but, for our consolation when we survey God under the high and terrible aspect of a sovereign, we have this to reflect on, that he is under covenant bonds of promise to be faithful to the souls that seek him. His throne must be a throne of grace to his people.

And, once more, and sweetest thought of all, every covenant promise has been endorsed and sealed with blood, and far be it from the everlasting God to pour scorn upon the blood of his dear Son. When a king has given a charter to a city, he may before have been absolute, and there may have been nothing to check his prerogatives, but when the city has its charter, then it pleads its rights before the king. Even thus God has given to his people a charter of untold blessings, bestowing upon them the sure mercies of David. Very much of the validity of a charter depends upon the signature and the seal, and, my brethren, how sure is the charter of covenant grace. The signature is the hand-writing of God himself, and the seal is the blood of the Only-begotten. The covenant is ratified with blood, the blood of his own dear Son. It is not possible that we can plead in vain with God when we plead the blood-sealed covenant, ordered in all things and sure. Heaven and earth shall pass away, but the power of the blood of Jesus with God can never fail. It speaks when we are silent, and it prevails when we are defeated. Better things than that of Abel doth it ask for, and its cry is heard. Let us come boldly, for we hear the promise in our hearts. When we feel alarmed because of the sovereignty of God, let us cheerfully sing--

"The gospel bears my spirit up,
A faithful and unchanging God
Lays the foundation for my hope
In oaths, and promises, and blood."

May God the Holy Spirit help us to use aright from this time forward "the throne of grace." Amen.

Rome, Dec. 7, 1871.

TO MY BELOVED CHURCH AND FRIENDS IN GENERAL,

Beloved in the Lord, having felt it to be my duty to leave England for a short time to prevent a return of my former complaint, I am bound gratefully to acknowledge the good hand of the Lord upon me during my sojourn abroad. I hope to return in a brief season, so strengthened as to continue to labour on for a considerable period without another pause. I take this opportunity of thanking my affectionate church and kind friends, for their innumerable acts of generous sympathy, in aiding our College and Orphanage, and especially for those many prayers which were turned to my comfort and healing in my late illness, and are the means of my upholding in my ever-growing service for the Lord. The Lord return into their bosoms a thousandfold the good which faithful friends have implored for me, and make me more than ever the means of blessing to them by ministry.

Just now I implore a renewal of those prayers with increased earnestness, for a revival of religion is greatly needed; and it would be a sure evidence of its speedy coming, if believers united in prayer for it. Already the flame is kindled at the Tabernacle, but it needs to be fanned into a mighty conflagration. Our country requires a divine visitation, and the promise of it only needs to be pleaded to be fulfilled. Brethren, as one man, cry mightily to the God of our Lord Jesus Christ, the Father of glory, beseeching him to put his hand to the work, and magnify his Son in the eyes of all the people. Standing where Satan's seat is, in the midst of ten thousand idols, I beseech those who worship God in the spirit to wrestle in prayer for times of refreshing, that all lands may know that Jesus Christ is Lord. How long shall the name of Jesus be blasphemed by the idolatries of Antichrist? It may be that the times of darkness will last till the children of light cry out bitterly, day and night, by reason of soul anguish. Then will God avenge his own elect, and that speedily.

As I have trodden the Appian way I have rejoiced that Jesus, whom Paul preached, is yet alive, and is certain in due season to put down his enemies. Already he has desolated the Colosseum where his faithful martyrs poured forth their blood; the pagan power has fallen, and so also shall the papal, and all other which opposes his kingdom. Let us proclaim a spiritual crusade, and set up our banners by redoubled prayer. It is certain that supplication produces marvellous results in heaven and earth; its power is proven in our own personal experience, and throughout the history of the church. Brethren, LET US PRAY.

Yours, for Jesus' sake,

C.H. SPURGEON.

A Visit to the Harvest Field

A Sermon (No. 1025)
Delivered by
C. H. SPURGEON,
At the Metropolitan Tabernacle, Newington

"Be patient therefore, brethren, unto the coming of the Lord. Behold, the husbandman waited for the precious fruit of the earth, and hath long patience for it, until he receive the early and latter rain. Be ye also patient; stablish your hearts: for the coming of the Lord draweth nigh."
- James 5:7-8.

THE EARTH THAT YIELDS seed to the sower and bread to the eater has received its constitution from God; and it is governed through his wise providence by fixed laws that are infinitely reliable; and yet, at the same time, with such diversified conditions and minute peculiarities as may well convince us that the Almighty intended the operations of nature to supply us with spiritual instruction as well as with material good. He who ordained the seed time and the harvest meant to teach us by them. Nor has he left us in vague uncertainty as to the lessons we should learn! In metaphor and parable he has interpreted them to us. The author of the Bible is also the architect of the universe. The book that is writ and the things that are made alike bear witness to his eternal power and Godhead. He who shall study them both will see clearly the idioms of one author. In the two masterpieces the hand of the same great artist may be discerned. We are all so dependent upon the labors of the field, that we ought at the season of harvest to remember how much we owe to the God of harvest. It is but common gratitude that we should go to the field awhile, and there hear what God the Lord may have to say to us among the waving sheaves. No matter what our business may be, the wealth of the country must after all, to a large extent, depend upon the crops that are produced, and the well being of the whole state has a greater dependence upon the harvest than many of you could probably imagine. We will not forget the bounties of God. We will not fail at least to endeavor to learn the lesson which this bountiful season is intended to teach us. Our Lord Jesus often preached of the sowing and of the reaping. His were the best of sermons and his the choicest of illustrations: therefore, we shall do well if are repair to the field, mark the scattering of the corn, and the ingathering of it, to enforce the exhortation of the text.

Our subject, to-night, will involve three or four questions: How does the husbandman wait? What does he wait for? What is has encouragement? What are the benefits of his patient waiting? Our experience is similar to his. We are husbandmen, so we have to toil hard, and we have to wait long: then, the hope that cheers, the fruit that buds and blossoms, and verily, too, the profit of that struggle of faith and fear incident to waiting will all crop up as we proceed.

I. First, then, HOW DOES THE HUSBANDMAN WAIT? He waits with a reasonable hope for the precious fruit of the earth, and hath long patience for it until he receive the early and latter rain. He expects the harvest because he has ploughed the fields and sown the grain. If he had not, he would not be an example for our imitation. Had he left his fields fallow, never stirred the clods, and never cast in among them the golden seed, he would be an idiot were he expecting the soil to produce a harvest. Thorns and thistles would it bring forth to him--nothing more. Out on the folly of those, who flatter their souls with a prospect of good things in time to come while they neglect the opportunity of sowing good things in the time present. They say they hope it will be well with them at the end; but, since it is not well with them now, why should they expect any change--much less a change contrary to the entire order of Providence? Is it not written "He that soweth to the flesh shall of the flesh reap corruption"? Do you expect to sow to the flesh and reap salvation? That is a blessing reserved for him who soweth to the spirit; for he that soweth to the spirit shall of the spirit reap life everlasting. As for the man who scatters nothing but the wild oats of sin, who simply lives to indulge his own passions, and determinately resolves to neglect the things that make for his peace,--he can but upbraid himself if he collect to reap anything good of the Lord. They that sow to the wind shall reap the whirlwind, they that sow nothing shall reap nothing, they that sow sparingly shall reap also sparingly. It is only those who by God's grace have been enabled to sow abundantly, though they have gone forth weeping, who shall afterwards come again rejoicing, bringing their sheaves with them. Patience by all means, but not that foolish patience which expects something good to turn up in spiritual things, as some fools do in business when they turn aside from legitimate trade to foster bubble schemes. Thou shalt have, my brother, after all according to what thou art, and to what thou art fairly going for. If thou art a believer, to thee shall be the promise--thou shalt share the victories and spoils of thy Lord. If thou art a careless, godless worldling, to thee shall be the fruit of thy deeds, and sad and bitter shall be those grapes of Gomorrah that thou shalt have to eat. The husbandman waits with a reasonable hope; he does not look for grain where he has cast in garlic. Save then that thou art a fool, thou wilt like him count only on the fruit of thine own sowing.

While he waits with a patient hope, he is no doubt all the more patient of the issue, because his hope is so reasonable. And not only does he wait with patience, but some stress is put upon the length of it; "and hath long patience for the precious fruit of the earth." Now, brethren in Christ, our waiting, if it be the work of the Holy Spirit, must have this long patience in it. Are you a sufferer? There are sweet fruits to come from suffering! "Not for the present seemeth it to be joyous but grievous, nevertheless, afterward it yieldeth the peaceable fruits of righteousness unto them that are exercised thereby." Have long patience for those peaceable fruits. You shall be brought out of your trouble, deliverance will be found for you out of your affliction when the discipline for which you were brought into it has been fulfilled. Have lot patience, however, for not the first month does the husbandman find a harvest. If he has sown in the winter, he does not expect he will reap in the early spring: he does not go forth with his sickle in the month of May and expect to find golden sheaves. He waits. The moons wax and wane; suns rise and set; but the husbandman waits till the appointed time is come. Wait thou, O sufferer, till the night be over. Watch after watch thou hast already passed through; the morning breaketh. Tarry thou a little longer, for if the vision tarry it shall come. "Thou shalt stand in thy lot in the end of the days." Ere long thou shalt have a happy exit out of thy present trials. Are you a worker? Then you need as much patience in working as you do in suffering. We must not expect to see immediate results in all cases from the preaching of the Gospel, from the teaching of Scripture in our classes, from distributing religious literature, or from any other kind of effort. Immediate results may come. Sometimes they do, and they greatly cheer the worker; but it is given to some to wait long, like the husbandman, ere the fruit reaches maturity. Truth, like the grain of mustard seed, does not wax into a tree tomorrow being sown to-day: it takes its leisure. Or, like the leaven in the measure, it doth not work in the next moment; it must have its time. If you have some principle to teach that is now obnoxious, go on with it. Perhaps, you may never see it popular in your day. Do not mind the fickle winds or fret yourself because of the nipping frosts. Truth is mighty and it will prevail, though it may have a hard fight before it wins the victory. Souls may not be won to God the first time you pray for them, nor the first time you exhort them, nay, nor the twentieth time. If thou hast gone to a sinner once on Christ's errand and he has rejected thee, go again seven times; nay, go again seventy times seven; for if thou shouldst at last succeed by thy master's gracious help, it will well repay thee. The long, tedious winter of thy waiting will appear as a short span to look back upon when thou hast reaped the field of thy labor. The little patience that thou hadst to exert for a while will seem as nothing, like the travail of the mother when the man-child is born into the world. Hush, then, your sad complaints, and still your petulant wailings.

"O dreary life! we cry, O dreary life!
And still the generations of the birds
Sing thro' our sighing; and the flocks and herds
Serenely live while we are keeping strife."

Be patient, O worker, for impatience sours the temper, chills the blood, sickens the heart, prostrates the vigor of one's spirit, and spoils the enterprise of life before it is ripe for history. Wait thou, clothed with patience, like a champion clad in steel. Wait with a sweet grace, as one who guards the faith and sets an example of humility. Wait in a right spirit, anxious, prayerful, earnest submissive to the ways of God, not doubtful of his will. Disciple of Jesus, "learn to labor and to wait."

With regard to the result of Christian obedience, the lesson is no less striking. The first thing that a farmer does by way seeking gain on his farm is to make a sacrifice which could seem immediately to entail on him a loss. He has some good wheat in the granary, and he takes out sacks full of it and buries it. He is so much the poorer, is not he? At any rate, there is so much the less to make bread for his household. He cannot get it again; it is under the clod, and there too it must die; for except it die, it bringeth not forth fruit. You must not expect as soon as you become a Christian, that you shall obtain all the gains of your religion, perhaps you may lose all that you have for Christ's sake. Some have lost their lives; they have sown their house and land, relatives, comfort, ease, and at last they have sown life itself in Christ's field, and they seemed for the time to be losers; but, verily I say unto you, this day, if you could see them in their white robes before the throne of God, rejoicing, you would see how rich a harvest they have reaped, and how the sowing which seemed a loss at first has ended, through God's abundant grace, in the greatest eternal gain. Have patience, brother, have patience. That is a false religion that aims at present worldly advantage. He who becomes religious for the loaves and fishes, when he hath eaten his loaves and fishes, hath devoured his religion. There is nothing in such piety but pretension. If thou canst be bought, thou canst be sold: if thou hast taken it up for gain, thou wilt lay it down for what promises thee a better bargain. Be willing to be a loser for Christ, and so prove thou art his genuine follower. The husbandman, I say, does not expect immediate reward, but reckons upon being a loser for a while. He waits, waits with long patience, for the precious fruit of the earth. It is a reasonable waiting on the outset, and not regretful when wearied and worried with delay.

And, while the husbandman waits, you observe in the text he waits with his eye upward, he waits until God shall send him the early and the latter rain. He has wit enough for this; even if he be a worldly man he knows that the harvest depends not only on the seed he sows and on the soil he cultivates, but upon the rain which he cannot control; the rain that cometh at the bidding of the Almighty. If the skies be brass, the clods will be iron. Unless God shall speak to the clouds, and the clouds shall speak to the earth, the earth will not speak to the corn, and the corn will not make us speak the words of rejoicing. Every husbandman is aware of this, and every Christian must remember it. "I am to wait," says a sufferer, "for God's help and for the graces that come by affliction, but I must wait with my eye upward, for all the ploughing of affliction will not profit me, and all the sowing of meditation will not speed me, unless God send his gracious Spirit like showers of heavenly rain. If I am a worker, I must work. When I wait, I must wait always looking upward." The keys of the rain-clouds which water the earth hang at the girdle of Jehovah. None but the eternal Father can send the Holy Spirit like showers on the church. He can send the comforter, and my labor will prosper; it will not be in vain in the Lord; but if he deny, if he withold this covenant blessing, ah me! work is useless, patience is worthless, and all the cost is bootless: it is in vain. In spiritual, as in temporal things, "it is vain to rise up early and sit up late, and eat the bread of carefulness." "Except the Lord build the house, they labor in vain that build it." We must have the dew, O God, or else our seed shall rot under the clod. We must wait, and wait with our eye upwards, or else our expectation will perish as a still-born child. So with regard to the comfort, and joy, and ultimate fruit of our faith, we must have our eye upward looking for the coming of the Lord from heaven, for the day of his appearing will be the day of our manifestation. Our life is hid with Christ now; when he shall appear we shall appear with him. When he shall be revealed in glory before the eyes of the assembled multitude, we shall be conspicuous in glory too. Not till then shall the fullness of the reward be bestowed, but the risen saints shall be glorified in the glorification of their coming Lord. Oh, for more of this living with the eyes upward, less minding of earthly things, and more looking for and hasting unto the coming of the Son of God!

Note, however, that while the husbandman waits with his eye upward, he waits with his hands at work, engaged in restless toil. He sows, and it is a busy time. When he sees the green blade, what then? He has to work. Those weeds must not be suffered to outgrow the wheat and choke it. Up and down the field the laborer must go, and the husbandman must be at the expense of this, and all along until the wheat is ripened there is sure to be something to do in this field, so his eyes must be keen, his skill must be taxed, and no drudgery must be disdained. In all labor there is profit, but nothing is gained without pains. We look up to God. He will not accept the look of a sluggard. The eye that looks up to God must be attended with the hand that is ready for work. So if I suffer and expect the blessing for the suffering, I must spend solitary hours in my chamber seeking and searching; to wit, seeking in prayer, and searching God's Word for the blessing. If I am a worker, I must look to God for the result, but then I must also use all the means. In fact, the Christian should work as if all depended upon him, and pray as if it all depended upon God. He should be always nothing in his own estimation; yet he should be one of those gloriously active nothings of which God makes great use, for he treats the things that are not as though they were, and gets glory out of them. Yes, the husbandman waits. He cannot push on the months; he cannot hasten the time of the harvest home; but he does not wait in silence; in sluggishness and negligence; he keeps to his work and waits too. So do you, O Christian men! wait for the coming of your Lord, but let it be with your lamps trimmed and your lights burning, as good servants attending to the duties of the house, until the master of the house returns to give you the reward.

The husbandman waits under changeful circumstances, and various contingences. At one time he sees the fair prospect of a good crop. The wheat has come up well. He has never seen more green springing from the ground; but, peradventure, it may be too-strong, and may need even to be put back. By-and-by, after long showers and cold nights, the wheat looks yellow, and he is half afraid about it. Anon there comes, or he fancies there is a blight or a black smut. Nobody knows what may happen. Only a farmer knows how his hopes and fears alternate and fluctuate from time to time. It is too hot, too cold; it is too dry; it is too wet; it is hardly ever quite right, according to his judgment, or rather according to his unbelief. He is full of changes in his mind because the season is full of changes. Yet he waits, he waits with patience. Ah dear friends, when we work for God, how often will this happen! I speak from no inconsiderable experience. There are always changes in the field of Christian labor. At one time we see many conversions, and we bless God that there are so many seals to our testimony. But some of the converts after a while disappoint us. There was the blossom, but it produced no fruit. Then there will come a season when many appear to backslide. The love of many waxes cold. Perhaps we have found in the church the black smut of heresy. Some deadly heresy creeps in, and the anxious husbandman fears there will be no harvest after all. Oh, patience, sir, patience. Ten thousand farmers' fears have been disappointed this year. Many a fretful expression and murmuring word need to be repented of, as the farmer has looked at last upon the well-filled ear, and the heavy wheat sheaf. So, too, mayhap, O evangelical worker, it will be with you. When God shall give you a rich return for all you have done for him, you will blush to think you ever doubted; you will be ashamed to think you ever grew weary in his service. You shall have your regard. Not to-morrow, so wait: not the next day perhaps, so be patient. You may be full of doubts one day, your joys sink low. It may be rough windy breather with you in your spirit. You may even doubt whether you are the Lord's, but if you have rested in the name of Jesus, if by the grace of God you are what you are, if he is all your salvation, and all your desire,--have patience; have patience, for the reward will surely come in God's good time. Now this is how the husbandman waits, and becomes to us the model of patience.

II. Very briefly, in the second place, we have to ask, WHAT DOES THE HUSBANDMAN WAIT FOR? for we are in this respect like him. He waits for results, for real results; right results; he hopes also rich results. And this is just what we are waiting for--waiting as sufferers for the results of sanctified affliction. May those results be read; may they be right; may they be rich. Oh that we might have every virtue strengthened, every grace refined, by passing through the furnace. There are great blessings connected with patient endurance as in Job's case. He had a plenteous harvest, may we have the same. And you workers, you must work for results, for, though conversion is the work of God, it is in many cases as clearly a product of the holy living, the devout teaching, and the fervent praying of his servants, as any collect can be the result from a cause. Go on, go on, and may you have real conversions--not pretended conversions--not such as are sometimes chronicled in newspapers-- "fifty-one conversions of an evening"--as if anybody knew! May there be real conversions, and ripe fruits for Jesus, in the growth and advance of those who are converted, and may many of them turn out to be such fruit-bearing Christians when they are matured in, grace, that the richest result in the prosperity of the Church may come to you from all your work. You are waiting for results. And you are, also, dear brethren, like the husbandman, waiting for a reward. All the while till the harvest comes, he has nothing but outlay. From the moment he sows, it is all outgoing until he sells his crops, and then, recovering at once the principal and the interest, he gets his reward. In this world, look not for a recompense. You may have a grateful acknowledgment in the peace, and quiet, and contentment of your own spirit, but do not expect even that from your fellow-men. The pure motive of any man who serves his generation well is generally misrepresented. As a rule the lounger looks on at the laborer not to praise but to blame him: not to cheer him but to chide him. The less he does, the less he will be open to rebuke, and the more he does oftentimes, and the more vigorously, the more he shall be upbraided. Look not for your reward here. Suppose men praise you, what is their praise worth? It would not fill your nostrils if you were about to die. The approbation of those who have neither skill nor taste--what pleasure can it afford the artist? Should one stoop for it, or, having it, lift his head the higher? Our reward is the approbation of God, which he will give of his abundant grace. He first gives us good works, as one observes, and then rewards us for those good works, as if they were altogether our own. He gives rewards though they are not a debt, but altogether of grace. Look for the reward hereafter. Wait a bit, man, wait a bit; your reward is not yet. Wait till the week is over, and then shall come the wage. Wait until the sun is gone down, and then there will be the penny for every laborer in the vineyard. Not yet, not yet, not yet. The husbandman waiteth for the precious fruit of the earth. This is what we wait for.

III. Thirdly, WHAT IS THE HUSBANDMAN'S ENCOURAGEMENT IN WAITING? Well, he has many.

The first is, that the fruit he waits for is precious. He waiteth for the precious fruit of the earth. It is worth waiting for. Who that walks through a corn field, such corn fields as we have seen this year, where the crops are plentiful, but will say, "Well, this was, after all, worth all the trouble and all the expense, and all the long patience of that winter which is over and gone?" If the Lord should draw you near unto himself by your affliction, if he should make his image in you more clear, it will be worth waiting for. And if, after your labors he should give you some soul for your reward, oh, will it not repay you? Mother, if your dear child should after all be brought back from his sinful ways to love his Saviour! Sunday-school teacher, if some of those little girls should love the name of Jesus, and you should live to see them honored members of the Church of God, will it not be worth waiting for? It there worth while to preach every Sabbath for a million years, if but one soul were brought in at last. I remember Mr. Richard Knill saying, if there were one unconverted person, and he were in Siberia, and God had ordained that he should only be saved by all the Christians in all the world (and that would be a vast number), all of them making a journey to Siberia to talk with him, it would be worth all the trouble if the soul were at length brought in. And so it would. We may wait, therefore, with patience, because the reward of our labor will be precious. Above all, the reward of hearing the master say, "Well done, good and faithful servant," is worth waiting for! Even now to get a word from him is quite enough to cheer us on, though he a soft, still voice that speaks it, but oh, the joy of that loud voice "Well done.

It were worth going through a thousand perils by land and by sea to come out and win that "Well done." We might count it worth while to face the lions of hell and do battle with Apollyon himself, to snatch but one poor lamb from between their jaws. It were worth while to do all that I say, if we might hear the Master say to us, "Well done," at the last. This then encourages us, as well as the husbandman--the preciousness of the fruit.

A godly husbandman waits with patience, again, because he knows God's covenant. God has said "seed time and harvest, summer and winter, shall not cease," and the Christian farmer knowing, this is confident. But oh, what strong confidences have we who have looked to Christ, and who are resting on the faithful word of a covenant God. He cannot fail us. It is not possible that he should suffer our faith to be confounded. "Heaven and earth may pass away," and they shall, but his word shall not fail. They that sow in faith shall reap abundantly. The glory shall be theirs. And, brother workers, if we do not for a time see all the results we expect, yet the Lord has said, "Surely all flesh shall see the salvation of God." The day must come when the dwellers in the wilderness shall bow before him and lick the dust. "He has set his king upon his holy hill of Zion," and they that said, "Let us break their bands asunder, and cast their cords from us," will have to submit themselves and lick the dust at his feet. Have courage, therefore. The covenant stands good, the harvest must come as surely as the seed time has come.

Moreover, every husbandman is encouraged by the fact, that he has seen other harvests. I suppose if the farmer had never heard of a harvest, and had never seen one, it would take some considerable persuasion to get him to sow his seed. But then he knows his father sowed seed and his grandsire, and that the race of men in all generations have put their seed under the clods as an act of faith, and God has accepted their faith, and sent them a return. And, O brethren, have not we multitudes of instances to confirm our confidence? Let us cheerfully resign ourselves to the Lord's will in suffering, for as others of his saints who went before us have reaped the blessing, So shall we. Let us work on for our Lord and Master, knowing that apostles and confessors, and a great cloud of witnesses who have gone before, have seen great results, and so shall we. Let us patiently tarry till the Lord come, for as in the first coming those that waited for him rejoiced, so shall those who are found watching and waiting at his second advent. We have not only the promise of God, but that promise fulfilled to tens of thousands who have preceded us, therefore, we should be ashamed to be impatient, rather let us patiently wait and work on, till the day breaketh, and the harvest cometh.

IV. And now, brethren, do you ask, WHAT ARE THE BENEFITS OF PATIENCE? To patiently wait God's appointed time is our business. I have shown you how we are to wait, but note this, whatever benefit there may be in patience, it is very clear there is none in impatience. Suppose a man should be impatient under suffering. Will it diminish his suffering? Will it increase the probabilities of his restoration? We all know that the irritability of temper which is caused by impatience, is one of the difficulties which the physician has to battle with. When the patient is calm there is a better chance of his recovery. If we were near impatient till there was any good to be derived from our fretfulness, we should not be impatient just yet. There is a story told of Mr. Hill being on board a vessel once. It is said he heard the mate swear, and afterwards he heard the captain use a profane oath. I think Mr. Hill interposed as the captain was about to swear again, and said, "No, no, let us be fair, let us have everything turn and turn about. Your mate has sworn, and you have had an oath. Now it is my turn--my turn to swear." The captain looked at him somewhat astonished, and could not but admit that there was a degree of rightness and propriety in every man having his turn. However, Mr. Hill did not swear, and the captain said, "I suppose, sir, you don't mean to take your turn, you don't mean to swear." "Oh, yes," said the good old man, "I mean to swear as soon as ever I can see the good of it." We might do the same by our impatience brethren. Let us be impatient as soon as ever we can see the use it will serve. If the farmer should want rain just now, his impatience would not influence the clouds and make them pour out their torrents. If your child happened to be very petulant, and have a very noisy tongue, and a mischievous disposition, the mother's impatience would not calm the child, control its temper, still its fitful passion, or subdue its stubborn humor. Whatever happens to you, there is nothing can happen to you worse than your being impatient, for of all troubles in the world that one can be troubled with, an impatient spirit is about the worst. O that ye would endeavor to conquer impatience. It cast Satan out of heaven, when he was impatient at the honor and dignity of the Son of God. He was impatient at being a servant to his Maker, and was driven from his high estate. Let us be rid of impatience which made Cain kill his brother, and which has done a thousand mischievous things since. May God grant us like the husbandman patiently to watch and wait.

But the benefits of patience are too many for me to hope to enumerate them. Suffice it to say, patience saves a man from great discouragement. If I expect that God will bless my labors to a large extent the first month, and so strain every nerve and toil with every sinew till my strength is ready to yield, and my spirit begins to flag; and the blessing does not come at the time I looked for; I shall be disheartened. But, if I expect some result, a great result in God's appointed week of harvest, even though I may not count on seeing it myself at once; I shall keep on renewing my labors, reviving my hopes, and encouraging myself in the Lord my God. Surely a farmer would give up his farm in sheer despair if he expected a harvest in a month's time after sowing. He would be month after month in a very sad way, if waiting to see it were not a condition for which he was thoroughly prepared. If you expect an interval during which your patience will be tried, you will not grow discouraged, because it is absolutely requisite that you should wait. Expect to wait for the glory; expect to wait for the reward which God hath promised; and, while you are waiting on the Lord your bread shall be certain, and your water shall be sure: you shall often eat meat, thank God, and take courage. The short days and long nights shall not be all charged with gloom, but full often they shall be tempered with good cheer. When we patience it keeps us in good heart for service. A man to whom it is given to wait for a reward keeps up his courage, and when he has to wait, he says, "It is no more than I expected. I never reckoned that I was to slay my enemy at the first blow. I never imagined that I was to capture the city as soon as ever I had digged the first trench; I reckoned upon waiting, and now that is come, I find that God gives me the grace to fight on and wrestle on, till the victory shall come." And patience saves a man from a great deal of haste and folly. A hasty man never is a wise man. He is wise that halts a little, and ponders his ways, especially when adversity crosses his path. I have known brethren in the ministry get discouraged and leave their pulpits, and repent as long as ever they lived that they left a sphere of labor, where they ought to have toiled on. I have known Christian people get discouraged, and touchy, and angry, fall out with the church of which they were members, go out in the wilderness, and leave the fat pastures behind them. They have only had to regret all their lives, that they had not a little more patience with their brethren, and with the circus stances which surrounded them. Whenever you are about to do anything in a great hurry, pause and pray. The hot fever in your own system ill fits you to act discreetly. While you tarry for a more healthy temperature of your own feelings, there may be a great change in the thermometer outside as to the circumstances that influence you. Great haste makes little speed. He that believeth shall not make haste; and as the promise runs, he shall never be confounded.

Above all, patience is to be commended to you because it glorifies God. The man that can wait, and wait calmly, astonishes the worlding, for the worldling wants it now. You remember John Bunyan's pretty parable (as you all know it, I will only give the outline)--of Passion and Patience. Passion would have all his best things first, and one came in, and lavished before him out of a bag all that the child could desire. Patience would have his best things last, and Patience sat and waited, so when Passion had used up all his joy, and all he sought for, Patience came in for his portion, and as John Bunyan very well remarked, there is nothing to come after the last, and so the portion of Patience lasted for ever. Let me have my best things last, my Lord, and my worst things first. Be they what they may, they shall be over, and then my best things shall last for ever and for ever. He that can wait has faith, and it is faith that marks the true Christian. He that can wait hath grace, and it is grace that marks the child of God. O that the Lord would grant to every one of you more and more of this excellent grace of patience, to the praise and glory of his name.

I have well nigh done. Yet there is one other respect in which our case is like that of the husbandman. As the season advances, his anxieties are prone to increase rather than to abate. If he has had long need of patience while the seasons have succeeded each other, and while organic chances have been in course of development, surely there is a stronger denoted on his patience as the crisis approaches when he shall reap the produce. How anxiously at this season will he observe the skies, watch the clouds, and wait the opportune time to get in his crops and garner them in good condition! Is there no peril that haunts him lest, after all, the blast or the mildew should cheat his hopes; lest fierce winds should lay the full-grown stems prostrate on the ground; lest then the pelting showers of rain should drench the well-filled ears of corn? I might almost call this the husbandman's last fear, and yet the most nervous fear that agitates his mind. In like manner, beloved, we have a closing scene in prospect which may, and will in all probability, involve a greater trial of faith, and a sterner call for patience, than any or all of the struggles through which we have already passed. Perhaps I can best describe it to you by quoting two passages of Scripture, one specially addressed to workers, the other more particularly to sufferers. For the first of these texts; you will find it in Hebrews 10:35-36. "Cast not away therefore your confidence, which hath great recompence of reward. For ye have need of patience, What, after ye have done the will of God, ye may receive the promise." This is sweet counsel for thee, O pilgrim, to Zion's city bound. When thou wast young and strong, thou didst walk many a weary mile with that staff of promise. It helped thee over the ground. Don't throw it aside as useless, now that thou art old and infirm. Lean upon it. Rest upon that promise, in thy present weakness, which lightened thy labor in the days of thy vigor. "Cast not away your confidence." But, brethren, there is something more. The Apostle says, "Ye have need of patience, after ye have done the will of God." But, why, you will say, is patience so indispensable at this juncture of experience? Doubtless you all know that we are never so subject to impatience as when there is nothing we can do. All the while the farmer is occupied with ploughing, harrowing, tilling, drilling, hoeing, and the like, he is too busy to be fretful. It is when the work is done, and there is nothing more to occupy his hands, that the very leisure he has to endure gives occasion to secret qualms and lurking cares. So it ever is with us. While "we are laborers together with God," our occupation is so pleasant that we little heed the toil and moil of hard service. But when it comes to a point where we have no province, for it is "God that giveth the increase," we are apt to be grievously distrustful; our unbelief finds full play. Hence it is, brethren, that after our fight is fought, after our race is run, after our allotted task is finished, there is so much need of patience, of such patience as waits only on God and watches unto prayer, that we may finish our course with joy and the ministry we have received of the Lord Jesus. And what about the second text? Where is that to be found? It is in the early part of this epistle of James. Turn to James 1:4. "Let patience have her perfect work, that ye may be perfect and entire, wanting nothing." Oh, how indisposed we all of us are to take this advice! Methinks I see Paul retiring thrice to wrestle with God in prayer, that he would remove the thorn from his flesh. He felt the rankling, and he craved for relief. He had hardly thought of it as a seton that must irritate before it could relieve, or as a medicine that must gripe before it could head. But oh, patience is then wrought up to its climax, when the soul so accepts the chastisement from the hand of God that she cannot, and will not, ask him to change his treatment or alter his discipline.

Seemeth it not as though patience were a virtue par excellence which puts the last polish on Christian chastity? We will hie us back to the cornfields again: I am afraid we were forgetting them. But this time we will not talk so much with the farmer as with the crops. Knowest thou then what it is that gives that bright yellow tinge of maturity to those blades which erst were green and growing? What, think you, imparts that golden hue to the wheat? How do you suppose the husbandman judges when it is time to thrust in the sickle? I will tell you. All the while the corn was growing, those hollow stems served as ducts that drew up nourishment from the soil. At length the process of vegetation is fulfilled. The fibres of the plant become rigid; they cease their office; down below there has been a failure of the vital power which is the precursor of death. Henceforth the heavenly powers work quick and marvellous changes; the sun paints his superscription on the ears of grain. They have reached the last stage: having fed on the riches of the soil long enough, they are only influenced from above. The time of their removal is at hand, when they shall be cut down, carried away in the team, and housed in the garners. So, too, beloved in the Lord, it is with some of you. Do I speak as a prophet? Do I not rather echo a trite observation? "The fall of the year is most thickly strewn with the fall of human life." You have long been succoured with mercies that have come up from mother-earth; you have been exposed to cold dews, chilling frosts, stormy blasts; you have had the trial of the vapory fog, the icy winter, the fickle spring, and the summer drought; but it is nearly all over now. You are ready to depart. Not yet for a brief space has the reaper come. "Ye have need of patience." Having suffered thus far, your tottering frame has learnt to bend. Patience, man--patience! A mighty transformation is about to be wrought on you in a short space. Wait on the Lord. Holiness shall now be legibly, more legibly than ever, inscribed on your forefront by the clear shining of the Sun of Righteousness. The heavenly husbandman has you daily, hourly, in his eye, till he shall say to the angel of his presence, "Put in your sickle." Then, as we pronounce your obituary with the meed of praise due to one in whom God has wrought a perfect work, we shall record that you were patient under affliction, resigned to the will of the Lord, and ready to depart and to be with Christ, which is far better. Patience has had her perfect work: you lack nothing. God grant unto you this gracious "nunc dimittis" when your time for ingathering has come!

Now, I have only spoken to believers, because as I have already said, the unbeliever cannot wait with patience, for he has nothing to wait for. There is nothing for him but a fearful looking for of judgment. Oh, it must be an awful thing to go from a life of poverty, or of suffering, or of drudgery here, into the world where the wrath of God abideth for ever. It matters not what your position here may be, if at the end you enter into rest. Equally little does it matter what joys or wealth you have here, if after all you are driven from the Lord's presence. May you be led to believe in Jesus. There lies safety. May you rest in his precious blood. There is pardon; there is salvation. God grant it, for Christ's sake Amen.

Joy Born at Bethlehem

A Sermon (No. 1026)
Delivered on Lord's-Day Morning, December 24th, 1871, by
C. H. SPURGEON,
At the Metropolitan Tabernacle, Newington

"And the angel said unto them, Fear not: for, behold, I bring you good tidings of great joy, which shall be to all people. For unto you is born this day in the city of David a Saviour, which is Christ the Lord. And this shall be a sign unto you; Ye shall find the babe wrapped in swaddling clothes, lying in a manger." - Luke 2:10-12.

WE HAVE NO superstitious regard for times and seasons. Certainly we do not believe in the present ecclesiastical arrangement called Christmas: first, because we do not believe in the mass at all, but abhor it, whether it be said or sung in Latin or in English; and, secondly, because we find no Scriptural warrant whatever for observing any day as the birthday of the Saviour; and, consequently, its observance is a superstition, because not of divine authority. Superstition has fixed most positively the day of our Saviour's birth, although there is no possibility of discovering when it occurred. Fabricius gives a catalogue of 136 different learned opinions upon the matter; and various divines invent weighty arguments for advocating a date in every month in the year. It was not till the middle of the third century that any part of the church celebrated the nativity of our Lord; and it was not till very long after the Western church had set the example, that the Eastern adopted it. Because the day is not known, therefore superstition has fixed it; while, since the day of the death of our Saviour might be determined with much certainty, therefore superstition shifts the date of its observance every year. Where is the method in the madness of the superstitious? Probably the fact is that the holy days were arranged to fit in with heathen festivals. We venture to assert, that if there be any day in the year, of which we may be pretty sure that it was not the day on which the Saviour was born, it is the twenty-fifth of December. Nevertheless since, the current of men's thoughts is led this way just now, and I see no evil in the current itself, I shall launch the bark of our discourse upon that stream, and make use of the fact, which I shall neither justify nor condemn, by endeavoring to lead your thoughts in the same direction. Since it is lawful, and even laudable, to meditate upon the incarnation of the Lord upon any day in the year, it cannot be in the power of other men's superstitions to render such a meditation improper for to-day. Regarding not the day, let us, nevertheless, give God thanks for the gift of his dear son.

In our text we have before us the sermon of the first evangelist under the gospel dispensation. The preacher was an angel, and it was meet it should be so, for the grandest and last of all evangels will be proclaimed by an angel when he shall sound the trumpet of the resurrection, and the children of the regeneration shall rise into the fullness of their joy. The key-note of this angelic gospel is joy--"I bring unto you good tidings of great joy." Nature fears in the presence of God--the shepherds were sore afraid. The law itself served to deepen this natural feeling of dismay; seeing men were sinful, and the law came into the world to reveal sin, its tendency was to make men fear and tremble under any and every divine revelation. The Jews unanimously believed that if any man beheld supernatural appearances, he would be sure to die, so that what nature dictated, the law and the general beliefs of those under it also abetted. But the first word of the gospel ended all this, for the angelic evangelist said, "Fear not, behold I bring you good tidings." Henceforth, it is to be no dreadful thing for man to approach his Maker; redeemed man is not to fear when God unveils the splendor of his majesty, since he appears no more a judge upon his throne of terror, but a Father unbending in sacred familiarity before his own beloved children.

The joy which this first gospel preacher spoke of was no mean one, for he said, "I bring you good tidings"--that alone were joy: and not good tidings of joy only, but "good tidings of great joy." Every word is emphatic, as if to show that the gospel is above all things intended to promote, and will most abundantly create the greatest possible joy in the human heart wherever it is received. Man is like a harp unstrung, and the music of his soul's living strings is discordant, his whole nature wails with sorrow; but the son of David, that mighty harper, has come to restore the harmony of humanity, and where his gracious fingers move among the strings, the touch of the fingers of an incarnate God brings forth music sweet as that of the spheres, and melody rich as a seraph's canticle. Would God that all men felt that divine hand.

In trying to open up this angelic discourse this morning, we shall note three things: the joy which is spoken of; next, the persons to whom this joy comes; and then, thirdly, the sign, which is to us a sign as well as to these shepherds--a sign of the birth and source of joy.

I. First, then, THE JOY, which is mentioned in our text--whence comes it, and what is it?

We have already said it is a "great joy"--"good tidings of great joy." Earth's joy is small, her mirth is trivial, but heaven has sent us joy immeasurable, fit for immortal minds. Inasmuch as no note of time is appended, and no intimation is given that the message will ever be reversed, we may say that it is a lasting joy, a joy which will ring all down the ages, the echoes of which shall be heard until the trumpet brings the resurrection; aye, and onward for ever and for ever. For when God sent forth the angel in his brightness to say, "I bring you good tidings of great joy, which be to all people," he did as much as say, "From this time forth it shall be joy to the sons of men; there shall be peace to the human race, and goodwill towards men for ever and for ever, as long as there is glory to God in the highest." O blessed thought! the Star of Bethlehem shall never set. Jesus, the fairest among ten thousand, the most lovely among the beautiful, is a joy for ever.

Since this joy is expressly associated with the glory of God, by the Words, "Glory to God in the highest," we may be quite clear that it is a pure and holy joy. No other would an angel have proclaimed, and, indeed, no other joy is joy. The wine pressed from the grapes of Sodom may sparkle and foam, but it is bitterness in the end, and the dregs thereof are death; only that which comes from the clusters of Eschol is the true wine of the kingdom, making glad the heart of God and man. Holy joy is the joy of heaven, and that, be ye sure, is the very cream of joy. The joy of sin is a fire-fountain, having its source in the burning soil of hell, maddening and consuming those who drink its fire-water; of such delights we desire not to drink. It were to be worse than damned to be happy in sin, since it is the beginning of grace to be wretched in sin, and the consummation of grace to be wholly escaped from sin, and to shudder even at the thought of it. It is hell to live in sin and misery, it is a deep lower still when men could fashion a joy in sin. God save us from unholy peace and from unholy joy! The joy announced by the angel of the nativity is as pure as it is lasting, as holy as it is great. Let us then always believe concerning the Christian religion that it has its joy within itself, and holds its feasts within its own pure precincts, a feast whose viands all grow on holy ground. There are those who, to-morrow, will pretend to exhibit joy in the remembrance of our Saviour's birth, but they will not seek their pleasure in the Saviour: they will need many additions to the feast before they can be satisfied. Joy in Immanuel would be a poor sort of mirth to them. In this country, too often, if one were unaware of the name, one might believe the Christmas festival to be a feast of Bacchus, or of Ceres, certainly not a commemoration of the Divine birth. Yet is there cause enough for holy joy in the Lord himself, and reasons for ecstasy in his birth among men. It is to be feared that most men imagine that in Christ there is only seriousness and solemnity, and to them consequently weariness, gloom, and discontent; therefore, they look out of and beyond what Christ allows, to snatch from the tables of Satan the delicacies with which to adorn the banquet held in honor of a Saviour. Let it not be so among you. The joy which the gospel brings is not borrowed but blooms in its own garden. We may truly say in the language of one of our sweetest hymns--

"I need not go abroad for joy,
I have a feast at home,
My sighs are turned into songs,
My heart has ceased to roam.
Down from above the Blessed Dove
Has come into my breast,
To witness his eternal love,
And give my spirit rest."

Let our joy be living water from those sacred wells which the Lord himself has digged; may his joy abide in us, that our joy may be full. Of Christ's joy we cannot have too much; no fear of running to excess when his love is the wine we drink. Oh to be plunged in this pure stream of spiritual delights!

But why is it that the coming of Christ into the world is the occasion of joy? The answer is as follows:--First, because it is evermore a joyous fact that God should be in alliance with man, especially when the alliance is so near that God should in very deed take our manhood into union with his godhead; so that God and man should constitute one divine, mysterious person. Sin had separated between God and man; but the incarnation bridges the separation: it is a prelude to the atoning sacrifice, but it is a prelude full of the richest hope. From henceforth, when God looks upon man, he will remember that his own Son is a man. From this day forth, when he beholds the sinner, if his wrath should burn, he will remember that his own Son, as man, stood in the sinner's place, and bore the sinner's doom. As in the case of war, the feud is ended when the opposing parties intermarry, so there is no more war between God and man, because God has taken man into intimate union with himself. Herein, then, there was cause for joy.

But there was more than that, for the shepherds were aware that there had been promises made of old which had been the hope and comfort of believers in all ages, and these were now to be fulfilled. There was that ancient promise made on the threshold of Eden to the first sinners of our race, that the seed of the woman should bruise the serpent's head; another promise made to the Father of the faithful that in his seed should all the nations of the earth be blessed, and promises uttered by the mouths of prophets and of saints since the world began. Now, the announcement of the angel of the Lord to the shepherds was a declaration that the covenant was fulfilled, that now in the fullness oftime God would redeem his word, and the Messiah, who was to be Israel's glory and the world's hope; was now really come. Be glad ye heavens, and be joyful O earth, for the Lord hath done it, and in mercy hath he visited his people. The Lord hath not suffered his word to fail, but hath fulfilled unto his people his promises. The time to favor Zion, yea the set time, is come. Now that the scepter is departed from Judah, behold the Shiloh comes, the Messenger of the covenant suddenly appears in his temple!

But the angel's song had in it yet fuller reason for joy; for our Lord who was born in Bethlehem came as a Saviour. "Unto you is born this day a Saviour." God had come to earth before, but not as a Saviour. Remember that terrible coming when there went three angels into Sodom at night-fall, for the Lord said, "I will go now and see whether it be altogether according to the cry thereof." He had come as a spy to witness human sin, and as an avenger to lift his hand to heaven, and bid the red fire descend and burn up the accursed cities of the plain. Horror to the world when God thus descends. If Sinai smokes when the law is proclaimed, the earth itself shall melt when the breaches of the law are punished. But now not as an angel of vengeance, but as a man in mercy God has come; not to spy out our sin, but to remove it; not to punish guilt, but to forgive it. The Lord might have come with thunderbolts in both his hands he might have come like Elias to call fire from heaven; but no, his hands are full of gifts of love, and his presence is the guarantee of grace. The babe born in the manger might have been another prophet of tears, or another son of thunder, but he was not so: he came in gentleness, his glory and his thunder alike laid aside.

"Twas mercy filled the throne,
And wrath stood silent by,
When Christ on the kind errand came
To sinners doomed to die."

Rejoice, ye who feel that ye are lost; your Saviour comes to seek and save you. Be of good cheer ye who are in prison, for be comes to set you free. Ye who are famished and ready to die, rejoice that he has consecrated for you a Bethlehem, a house of bread, and he has come to be the bread of life to your souls. Rejoice, O sinners, everywhere for the restorer of the castaways, the Saviour of the fallen is born. Join in the joy, ye saints, for he is the preserver of the saved ones, delivering them from innumerable perils, and he is the sure prefecter of such as he preserves. Jesus is no partial Saviour, beginning a work and not concluding it; but, restoring and upholding, he also prefects and presents the saved ones without spot or wrinkle, or any such thing before his Father's throne. Rejoice aloud all ye people, let your hills and valleys ring with joy, for a Saviour who is mighty to save is born among you.

Nor was this all the holy mirth, for the next word has also in it a fullness of joy:--"a Saviour, who is Christ," or the Anointed. Our Lord was not an amateur Saviour who came down from heaven upon an unauthorized mission; but he was chosen, ordained, and anointed of God; he could truly say, "the Spirit of the Lord is upon me, because the Lord hath anointed me." Here is great comfort for all such as need a Saviour; it is to them no mean consolation that God has himself authorized Christ to save. There can be no fear of a jar between the mediator and the judge, no peril of a nonacceptance of our Saviour's work; because God has commissioned Christ to do what he has done, and in saving sinners he is only executing his Fathers own will. Christ is here called "the anointed." All his people are anointed, and there were priests after the order of Aaron who were anointed, but he is the anointed, "anointed with the oil of gladness above his fellows;" so plenteously anointed that, like the unction upon Aaron's head, the sacred anointing of the Head of the church distils in copious streams, till we who are like the skirts of his garments are made sweet with the rich perfume. He is "the anointed" in a threefold sense: as prophet to preach the gospel with power; as priest to offer sacrifice; as king to rule and reign. In each of these he is preeminent; he is such a teacher, priest, and ruler as was never seen before. In him was a rare conjunction of

glorious offices, for never did prophet, priest, and king meet in one person before among the sons of men, nor shall it ever be so again. Triple is the anointing of him who is a priest after the order of Melchisedec, a prophet like unto Moses, and a king of whose dominion there is no end. In the name of Christ, the Holy Ghost is glorified, by being seen as anointing the incarnate God. Truly, dear brethren, if we did but understand all this, and receive it into our hearts, our souls would leap for joy on this Sabbath day, to think that there is born unto us a Saviour who is anointed of the Lord.

One more note, and this the loudest, let us sound it well and hear it well-- "which is Christ the Lord." Now the word Lord, or Kurios, here used is tantamount to Jehovah. We cannot doubt that, because it is the same word used twice in the ninth verse, and in the ninth verse none can question that it means Jehovah. Hear it, "And, lo, the angel of the Lord came upon them, and the glory of the Lord shone round about them." And if this be not enough, read the 23rd verse, "As it is written in the law of the Lord, every male that openeth the womb shall be called holy to the Lord." Now the word Lord here assuredly refers to Jehovah, the one God, and so it must do here. Our Saviour is Christ, God, Jehovah. No testimony to his divinity could be plainer; it is indisputable. And what joy there is in this; for suppose an angel had been our Saviour, he would not have been able to bear the load of my sin or yours; or if anything less than God had been set up as the ground of our salvation, it might have been found too frail a foundation. But if he who undertakes to save is none other than the Infinite and the Almighty, then the load of our guilt can be carried upon such shoulders, the stupendous labor of our salvation can be achieved by such a worker, and that with ease: for all things are possible with God, and he is able to save to the uttermost them that come unto God by him. Ye sons of men perceive ye here the subject of your joy. The God who made you, and against whom you have offended, has come down from heaven and taken upon himself your nature that he might save you. He has come in the fullness of his glory and the infinity of his mercy that he might redeem you. Do you not welcome this news? What! will not your hearts be thankful for this? Does this matchless love awaken no gratitude? Were it not for this divine Saviour, your life here would have been wretchedness, and your future existence would have been endless woe. Oh, I pray you adore the incarnate God, and trust in him. Then will you bless the Lord for delivering you from the wrath to come, and as you lay hold of Jesus and find salvation in his name, you will tune your songs to his praise, and exult with sacred joy. So much concerning this joy.

II. Follow me while I briefly speak of THE PEOPLE to whom this joy comes. Observe how the angel begins, "Behold, I bring you good tidings of great joy, for unto you is born this day." So, then, the joy began with the first who heard it, the shepherds. "To you," saith he; "for unto you is born." Beloved hearer, shall the joy begin with you to-day?--for it little avails you that Christ was born, or that Christ died, unless unto you a child is born, and for you Jesus bled. A personal interest is the main point. "But I am poor," saith one. So were the shepherds. O ye poor, to you this mysterious child is born. "The poor have the gospel preached unto them." "He shall judge the poor and needy, and break in pieces the oppressor." But I am obscure and unknown," saith one. So were the watchers on the midnight plain. Who knew the men who endured hard toil, and kept their flocks by night? But you, unknown of men, are known to God: shall it not be said, that "unto you a child is born?" The Lord regardeth not the greatness of men, but hath respect unto the lowly. But you are illiterate you say, you cannot understand much. Be it so, but unto the shepherds Christ was born, and their simplicity did not hinder their receiving him, but even helped them to it. Be it so with yourself: receive gladly the simple truth as it is in Jesus. The Lord hath exalted one chosen out of the people. No aristocratic Christ have I to preach to you, but the Saviour of the people, the friend of publicans and sinners. Jesus is the true "poor men's friend;" he is "a covenant for the people," given to be "a leader and commander to the people." To you is Jesus given. O that each heart might truly say, to me is Jesus born; for it I truly believe in Jesus, unto me Christ is born, and I may be as sure of it as if an angel announced it, since the Scripture tells me that if I believe in Jesus He is mine.

After the angel had said "to you," he went on to say, "it shall be to all people." But our translation is not accurate, the Greek is, "it shall be to all the people." This refers most assuredly to the Jewish nation; there can be no question about that; if any one looks at the original, he will not find so large and wide an expression as that given by our translators. It should be rendered "to all the people." And here let us speak a word for the Jews. How long and how sinfully has the Christian church despised the most honorable amongst the nations! How barbarously has Israel been handled by the so-called church! I felt my spirit burn indignantly within me in Rome when I stood in the Jew's quarter, and heard of the cruel indignities which Popery has heaped upon the Jews, even until recently. At this hour there stands in the Jew's quarter a church built right in front of the entrance to it, and into this the unhappy Jews were driven forcibly on certain occasions. To this church they were compelled to subscribe--subscribe, mark you, as worshippers of the one invisible God, to the support of a system which is as leprous with idolatry as were the Canaanites whom the Lord abhorred. Paganism is not more degrading than Romanism. Over the door of this church is placed, in their own tongue in the Hebrew, these words: --"All day long have I stretched out my hands to a disobedient and gainsaying generation;" how, by such an insult as that, could they hope to convert the Jew. The Jew saw everywhere idols which his soul abhorred, and he loathed the name of Christ, because he associated it with idol worship, and I do not wonder that he did. I praise the Jew that he could not give up his own simple theism, and the worship of the true God, for such a base, degrading superstition as that which Rome presented to him. Instead of thinking it a wonder of unbelief that the Jew is not a Christian, I honor him for his faith and his courageous resistance of a fascinating heathenism. If Romanism be Christianity I am not, neither could I be, a Christian. It were a more manly thing to be a simple believer in one God, or even an honest doubter upon all religion, than worship such crowds of gods and goddesses as Popery has set up, and to bow, as she does, before rotten bones and dead men's winding sheets. Let the true Christian church think lovingly of the Jew, and with respectful earnestness tell him the true gospel; let her sweep away superstition, and set before him the one gracious God in the Trinity of his divine Unity; and the day shall yet come when the Jews, who were the first apostles to the Gentiles, the first missionaries to us who were afar off; shall be gathered in again. Until that shall be, the fullness of the church's glory can never come. Matchless benefits to the world are bound up with the restoration of Israel; their gathering in shall be as life from the dead. Jesus the Saviour is the joy of all nations, but let not the chosen race be denied their peculiar share of whatever promise holy writ has recorded with a special view to them. The woes which their sins brought upon them have fallen thick and heavily; and even so let the richest blessings distil upon them.

Although our translation is not literally correct, it, nevertheless, expresses a great truth, taught plainly in the context; and, therefore, we will advance another step. The coming of Christ is a joy to all people. It is so, for the fourteenth verse says: "On earth peace," which is a wide and even unlimited expression. It adds, "Good will towards"--not Jews, but "men" --all men. The word is the generic name of the entire race, and there is no doubt that the coming of Christ does bring joy to all sorts of people. It brings a measure of joy even to those who are not Christians. Christ does not bless them in the highest and truest sense, but the influence of his teaching imparts benefits of an inferior sort, such as they are capable of receiving; for wherever the gospel is proclaimed, it is no small blessing to all the population. Note this fact: there is no land beneath the sun where there is an open Bible and a preached gospel, where a tyrant long can hold his place. It matters not who he be, whether pope or king; let the pulpit be used properly for the preaching of Christ crucified, let the Bible be opened to be read by all men, and no tyrant can long rule in peace. England owes her freedom to the Bible; and France will never possess liberty, lasting and well-established, till she comes to reverence the gospel, which too long she has rejected. There is joy to all mankind where Christ comes. The religion of Jesus makes men think, and to make men think is always dangerous to a despot's power. The religion of Jesus Christ sets a man free from superstition; when he believes in Jesus, what cares he for Papal excommunications, or whether priests give or withhold their absolution? The man no longer cringes and bows down; he is no more willing, like a beast, to be led by the nose; but, learning to think for himself and becoming a man, he disdains the childish fears which once held him in slavery. Hence, where Jesus comes, even if men do not receive him as the Saviour, and so miss the fullest joy, yet they get a measure of benefit; and I pray God that everywhere his gospel may be so proclaimed, and that so many may be actuated by the spirit of it, that it may be better for all mankind. If men receive Christ, there will be no more oppression: the true Christian does to others as he would that they should do to him, and there is no more contention of classes, nor grinding of the faces of the poor. Slavery must go down where Christianity rules, and mark you, if Romanism be once destroyed, and pure Christianity shall govern all nations, war itself must come to an end; for if there be anything which this book denounces and counts the hugest of all crimes, it is the crime of war. Put up thy sword into thy sheath, for hath not he said, "Thou shalt not kill," and he meant not that it was a sin to kill one but a glory to kill a million, but he meant that bloodshed on the smallest or largest scale was sinful. Let Christ govern, and men shall break the bow and cut the spear in sunder, and burn the chariot in the fire. It is joy to all nations that Christ is born, the Prince of Peace, the King who rules in righteousness.

But, beloved, the greatest joy is to those who know Christ as a Saviour. Here the song rises to a higher and sublimer note. Unto us indeed a child is born, if we can say that he is our "Saviour who is Christ the Lord." Let me ask each of you a few personal questions. Are your sins forgiven you for his name's sake? Is the head of the serpent bruised in your soul? Does the seed of the woman reign in sanctifying power over your nature? Oh then, you have the joy that is to all the people in the truest form of it; and, dear brother, dear sister, the further you submit yourself to Christ the Lord, the more completely you know him, and are like him, the fuller will your happiness become. Surface joy is to those who live where the Saviour is preached; but the great deeps, the great fathomless deeps of solemn joy which glisten and sparkle with delight, are for such as know the Saviour, obey the anointed one, and have communion with the Lord himself. He is the most joyful man who is the most Christly man. I wish that some Christians were more truly Christians: they are Christians and something else; it were much better if they were altogether Christians. Perhaps you know the legend, or perhaps true history of the awakening of St. Augustine. He dreamed that he died, and went to the gates of heaven, and the keeper of the gates said to him, "Who are you?" And he answered, "Christianus sum," I am a Christian. But the porter replied, "No, you are not a Christian, you are a Ciceronian, for your thoughts and studies were most of all directed to the works of Cicero and the classics, and you neglected the teaching of Jesus. We judge men here by that which most engrossed their thoughts, and you are judged not to be a Christian but a Ciceronian." When Augustine awoke, he put aside the classics which he had studied, and the eloquence at which he had aimed, and he said, "I will be a Christian and a theologian;" and from that time he devoted his thoughts to the word of God, and his pen and his tongue to the instruction of others in the truth. Oh I would not have it said of any of you, "Well, he may be somewhat Christian, but he is far more a keen money-getting tradesman." I would not have it said, "Well, he may be a believer in Christ, but he is a good deal more a politician." Perhaps he is a Christian, but he is most at home when he is talking about science, farming, engineering, horses, mining, navigation, or pleasure-taking. No, no, you will never know the fullness of the joy which Jesus brings to the soul, unless under the power of the Holy Spirit you take the Lord your Master to be your All in all, and make him the fountain of your intensest delight. "He is my Saviour, my Christ, my Lord," be this your loudest boast. Then will you know the joy which the angel's song predicts for men.

III. But I must pass on. The last thing in the text is The SIGN. The shepherds did not ask for a sign, but one was graciously given. Sometimes it is sinful for us to require as an evidence what God's tenderness may nevertheless see fit to give as an aid to faith. Wilful unbelief shall have no sign, but weak faith shall have compassionate aid. The sign that the joy of the world had come was this,--they were to go to the manger to find the Christ in it, and he was to be the sign. Every circumstance is therefore instructive. The babe was found "wrapped in swaddling clothes." Now, observe, as you look at this infant, that there is not the remotest appearance of temporal power here. Mark the two little puny arms of a little babe that must be carried if it go. Alas, the nations of the earth look for joy in military power. By what means can we make a nation of soldiers? The Prussian method is admirable; we must have thousands upon thousands of armed men and big cannon and ironclad vessels to kill and destroy by wholesale. Is it not a nation's pride to be gigantic in arms? What pride flushes the patriot's cheek when he remembers that his nation can murder faster than any other people. Ah, foolish generation, ye are groping in the flames of hell to find your heaven, raking amid blood and bones for the foul thing which ye call glory. A nation's joy can never lie in the misery of others. Killing is not the path to prosperity; huge armaments are a curse to the nation itself as well as to its neighbors. The joy of a nation is a golden sand over which no stream of blood has ever rippled. It is only found in that river, the streams whereof make glad the city of God. The weakness of submissive gentleness is true power. Jesus founds his eternal empire not on force but on love. Here, O ye people, see your hope; the mild pacific prince, whose glory is his self-sacrifice, is our true benefactor.

But look again, and you shall observe no pomp to dazzle you. Is the child wrapped in purple and fine linen? Ah, no. Sleeps he in a cradle of gold? The manger alone is his shelter. No crown is upon the babe's head, neither does a coronet surround the mother's brow. A simple maiden of Galilee, and a little child in ordinary swaddling bands, it is all you see.

"Bask not in courtly bower,
Or sunbright hall of power,
Pass Babel quick,
and seek the holy land.
From robes of Tyrian dye,
Turn with undazzled eye
To Bethlehem's glade, and by the manger stand."

Alas, the nations are dazzled with a vain show. The pomp of empires, the pageants of kings are their delight. How can they admire those gaudy courts, in which too often glorious apparel, decorations, and rank stand in the stead of virtue, chastity, and truth. When will the people cease to be children? Must they for ever crave for martial music which stimulates to violence, and delight in a lavish expenditure which burdens them with taxation? These make not a nation great or joyous. Bah! how has the bubble burst across yon narrow sea. A bubble empire has collapsed. Ten thousand bayonets and millions of gold proved but a sandy foundation for a Babel throne. Vain are the men who look for joy in pomp; it lies in truth and righteousness, in peace and salvation, of which yonder new-born prince in the garments of a peasant child is the true symbol.

Neither was there wealth to be seen at Bethlehem. Here in this quiet island, the bulk of men are comfortably seeking to acquire their thousands by commerce and manufactures. We are the sensible people who follow the main chance, and are not to be deluded by ideas of glory; we are making all the money we can, and wondering that other nations waste so much in fight. The main prop and pillar of England's joy is to be found, as some tell us, in the Three per Cents., in the possession of colonies, in the progress of machinery, in steadily increasing our capital. Is not Mammon a smiling deity? But, here, in the cradle of the world's hope at Bethlehem, I see far more of poverty than wealth; I perceive no glitter of gold, or spangle of silver. I perceive only a poor babe, so poor, so very poor, that he is in a manger laid; and his mother is a mechanic's wife, a woman who wears neither silk nor gem. Not in your gold, O Britons, will ever lie your joy, but in the gospel enjoyed by all classes, the gospel freely preached and joyfully received. Jesus, by raising us to spiritual wealth, redeems us from the chains of Mammon, and in that liberty gives us joy.

And here, too, I see no superstition. I know the artist paints angels in the skies, and surrounds the scene with a mysterious light, of which tradition's tongue of falsehood has said that it made midnight as bright as noon. This is fiction merely; there was nothing more there than the stable, the straw the oxen ate, and perhaps the beasts themselves, and the child in the plainest, simplest manner, wrapped as other children are; the cherubs were invisible and of haloes there were none. Around this birth of joy was no sign of superstition: that demon dared not intrude its tricks and posturings into the sublime spectacle: it would have been there as much out of place as a harlequin in the holy of holies. A simple gospel, a plain gospel, as plain as that babe wrapped in the commonest garments, is this day the only hope for men. Be ye wise and believe in Jesus, and abhor all the lies of Rome, and inventions of those who ape her detestable abominations.

Nor does the joy of the world lie in philosophy. You could not have made a schoolmen's puzzle of Bethlehem if you had tried to do so; it was just a child in the manger and a Jewish woman looking on and nursing it, and a carpenter standing by. There was no metaphysical difficulty there, of which men could say, "A doctor of divinity is needed to explain it, and an assembly of divines must expound it." It is true the wise men came there, but it was only to adore and offer gifts; would that all the wise had been as wise as they. Alas, human subtlety has disputed over the manger, and logic has darkened counsel with its words. But this is one of man's many inventions; God's work was sublimely simple. Here was "The Word made flesh" to dwell among us, a mystery for faith, but not a football for argument. Mysterious, yet the greatest simplicity that was ever spoken to human ears, and seen by mortal eyes. And such is the gospel, in the preaching of which our apostle said, "we use great plainness of speech." Away, away, away with your learned sermons, and your fine talk, and your pretentious philosophies; these never created a jot of happiness in this world. Fine-spun theories are fair to gaze on, and to bewilder fools, but they are of no use to practical men, they comfort not the sons of toil, nor cheer the daughters of sorrow. The man of common sense, who feels the daily rub and tear of this poor world, needs richer consolation than your novel theologies, or neologies, can give him. In a simple Christ, and in a simple faith in that Christ, there is a peace deep and lasting; in a plain, poor man's gospel there is a joy and a bliss unspeakable, of which thousands can speak, and speak with confidence, too, for they declare what they do know, and testify what they have seen.

I say, then, to you who would know the only true peace and lasting joy, come ye to the babe of Bethlehem, in after days the Man of Sorrows, the substitutionary sacrifice for sinners. Come, ye little children, ye boys and girls, come ye; for he also was a boy. "The holy child Jesus" is the children's Saviour, and saith still, "Suffer the little children to come unto me, and forbid them not. Come hither, ye maidens, ye who are still in the morning of your beauty, and, like Mary, rejoice in God your Saviour. The virgin bore him on her bosom, so come ye and bear him in your hearts, saying, "Unto us a child is born, onto us a son is given." And you, ye men in the plenitude of your strength, remember how Joseph cared for him, and watched with reverent solicitude his tender years; be you to his cause as a Father and a helper; sanctify your strength to his service. And ye women advanced in years, ye matrons and widows, come like Anna and bless the Lord that you have seen the salvation of Israel, and ye hoar heads, who like Simeon are ready to depart, come ye and take the Saviour in your arms, adoring him as your Saviour and your all. Ye shepherds, ye simple hearted, ye who toil for your daily bread, come and adore the Saviour; and stand not back ye wise men, ye who know by experience and who by meditation peer into deep truth, come ye, and like the sages of the East bow low before his presence, and make it your honor to pay honor to Christ the Lord. For my own part, the incarnate God is all my hope and trust. I have seen the world's religion at the fountain head, and my heart has sickened within me; I come back to preach, by God's help, yet more earnestly the gospel, the simple gospel of the Son of Man. Jesus, Master, I take thee to be mine for ever! May all in this house, through the rich grace of God, be led to do the same, and may they all be thine, great Son of God, in the day of thine appearing, for thy love's sake. Amen.

The Joy of the Lord, the Strength of His People

A Sermon (No. 1027)
Delivered on Lord's Day Morning, December 31st, 1871, by
C. H. SPURGEON,
At the Metropolitan Tabernacle, Newington

"The joy of the Lord is your strength." - Nehemiah 8:10.

"And the singers sang aloud, with Jezrahiah their overseer. Also that day they offered great sacrifices, and rejoiced: for God had made them rejoice with great joy: the wives also and the children rejoiced: so that the joy of Jerusalem was heard even afar off." - Nehemiah 12:42-43.

LAST Sabbath day in the morning I spoke of the birth of our Saviour as being full of joy to the people of God, and, indeed, to all nations. We then looked at the joy from a distance; we will now in contemplation draw nearer to it, and perhaps as we consider it, and remark the multiplied reasons for its existence, some of those reasons may operate upon our own hearts, and we may go out of this house of prayer ourselves partakers of the exceeding great joy. We shall count it to have been a successful morning if the people of God are made to rejoice in the Lord, and especially if those who have been bowed down and burdened in soul shall receive the oil of joy for mourning. It is no mean thing to comfort the Lord's mourners; it is a work specially dear to the Spirit of God, and, therefore, not to be lightly esteemed. Holy sorrow is precious before God, and is no bar to godly joy. Let it be carefully noted in connection with our first text that abounding mourning is no reason why there should not speedily be seen an equally abundant joy, for the very people who were bidden by Nehemiah and Ezra to rejoice were even then melted with penitential grief, "for all the people wept when they heard the words of the law." The vast congregation before the watergate, under the teaching of Ezra, were awakened and cut to the heart; they felt the edge of the law of God like a sword opening up their hearts, tearing, cutting, and killing, and well might they lament: then was the time to let them feel the gospel's balm and hear the gospel's music, and, therefore, the former sons of thunder changed their note, and became sons of consolation, saying to them, "This day is holy unto the Lord your God; mourn not, nor weep. Go your way eat the fat, and drink the sweet, and send portions unto them for whom nothing is prepared: for this day is holy unto our Lord: neither be ye sorry; for the joy of the Lord is your strength." Now that they were penitent, and sincerely turned to their God, they were bidden to rejoice. As certain fabrics need to be damped before they will take the glowing colours with which they are to be adorned, so our spirits need the bedewing of repentance before they can receive the radiant colouring of delight. The glad news of the gospel can only be printed on wet paper. Have you ever seen clearer shining than that which follows a shower? Then the sun transforms the rain-drops into gems, the flowers look up with fresher smiles and faces glittering from their refreshing bath, and the birds from among the dripping branches sing with notes more rapturous, because they have paused awhile. So, when the soul has been saturated with the rain of penitence, the clear shining of forgiving love makes the flowers of gladness blossom all around. The steps by which we ascend to the palace of delight are usually moist with tears. Grief for sin is the porch of the House Beautiful, where the guests are full of "The joy of the Lord." I hope, then, that the mourners, to whom this discourse shall come, will discover and enjoy the meaning of that divine benediction in the sermon on the mount, "Blessed are they that mourn, for they shall be comforted."

From our text we shall draw several themes of thought, and shall remark: first, there is a joy of divine origin,-- "The joy of the Lord;" and, secondly, that joy is to all who partake of it a source of strength-- "The joy of the Lord is your strength." Then we shall go on to show that such strength always reveals itself practically--our second text will help us there: and we shall close by noticing, in the fourth place, that this joy, and, consequently, this strength, are within our reach today.

I. THERE IS A JOY OF DIVINE ORIGIN--"The joy of the Lord." Springing from the Lord as its source, it will necessarily be of a very elevated character. Since man fell in the garden, he has too often sought for his enjoyments where the serpent finds his. It is written, "upon thy belly shalt thou go and dust shalt thou eat all the days of thy life," this was the serpent's doom; and man, with infatuated ambition, has tried to find his delight in his sensual appetites, and to content his soul with earth's poor dust. But the joys of time cannot satisfy an undying nature, and when a soul is once quickened by the eternal Spirit, it can no more fill itself with worldly mirth, or even with the common enjoyments of life than can a man snuff up wind and feed thereon. But, beloved, we are not left to search for joy; it is brought to our doors by the love of God our Father; joy refined and satisfying, befitting immortal spirits. God has not left us to wander among those unsatisfactory things which mock the chase which they invite; he has given us appetites which carnal things cannot content, and he has provided suitable satisfaction for those appetites; he has stored up at his right hand pleasures for evermore, which even now he reveals by his Spirit to those chosen ones whom he has taught to long for them.

Let us endeavour to analyze that special and peculiar pleasure which is here called "The joy of the Lord." It springs from God, and has God for its object. The believer who is in a spiritually healthy state rejoices mainly in God himself; he is happy because there is a God, and because God is in his person and character what he is. All the attributes of God become well-springs of joy to the thoughtful, contemplative believer; for such a man says within his soul, "All these attributes of my God are mine: his power, my protection; his wisdom, my guidance; his faithfulness, my foundation; his grace, my salvation." He is a God who cannot lie, faithful and true to his promise; he is all love, and at the same time infinitely just, supremely holy. Why, the contemplation of God to one who knows that this God is his God for ever and ever, is enough to make the eyes overflow with tears, because of the deep, mysterious, unutterable bliss which fills the heart. There was nothing in the character of Jupiter, or any of the pretended gods of the heathen, to make glad a pure and holy spirit, but there is everything in the character of Jehovah both to purify the heart and to make it thrill with delight. How sweet is it to think over all the Lord has done; how he has revealed himself of old, and especially how he has displayed his glory in the covenant of grace, and in the person of the Lord Jesus Christ. How charming is the thought that he has revealed himself to me personally, and made me to see in him my Father, my friend, my helper, my God. Oh, if there be one word out of heaven that cannot be excelled, even by the brightness of heaven itself, it is this word, "My God, my Father," and that sweet promise, "I will be to them a God, and they shall be to me a people." There is no richer consolation to be found: even the Spirit of God can bring nothing home to the heart of the Christian more fraught with delight than that blessed consideration. When the child of God, after admiring the character and wondering at the acts of God, can all the while feel "he is my God; I have taken him to be mine; he has taken me to be his; he has grasped me with the hand of his powerful love; having loved me with an everlasting love, with the bands of lovingkindness has he drawn me to himself; my beloved is mine and I am his;" why, then, his soul would fain dance like David before the ark of the Lord, rejoicing in the Lord with all its might.

A further source of joy is found by the Christian, who is living near to God, in a deep sense of reconciliation to God, of acceptance with God, and yet, beyond that, of adoption and close relationship to God. Does it not make a man glad to know that though once his sins had provoked the Lord they are all blotted out, not one of them remaineth; though once he was estranged from God, and far off from him by wicked works, yet he is made nigh by the blood of Christ. The Lord is no longer an angry judge pursuing us with a drawn sword, but a loving Father into whose bosom we pour our sorrows, and find ease for every pang of heart. Oh, to know, beloved, that God actually loves us! I have often told you I cannot preach upon that theme, for it is a subject to muse upon in silence, a matter to sit by the hour together and meditate upon. The infinite to love an insignificant creature, an ephemera of an hour, a shadow that declineth! Is not this a marvel? For God to pity me I can understand, for God to condescend to have mercy upon me I can comprehend; but for him to love me, for the pure to love a sinner, for the infinitely great to love a worm, is matchless, a miracle of miracles! Such thoughts must comfort the soul. And then, add to this, that the divine love has brought us believers into actual relationship with God, so that we are his sons and daughters, this again is a river of sacred pleasure. "Unto which of the angels said he at any time, Thou art my Son." No minister of flame, though perfect in obedience, has received the honour of adoption; to us, even to us frail creatures of the dust, is given a boon denied to Gabriel, for through Jesus Christ the firstborn, we are members of the family of God. Oh! The abyss of joy which lies in sonship with God, and joint heirship with Christ! Words are vain here. Moreover, the joy springing from the spirit of adoption is another portion of the believer's bliss. He cannot be an unhappy man who can cry, "Abba, Father." The spirit of adoption is always attended by love, joy, and peace, which are fruits of the Spirit; for we have not received the spirit of bondage again to fear, but we have received the spirit of liberty and joy in Christ Jesus. "My God, my Father." Oh how sweet the sound. But all men of God do not enjoy this, say you. Alas! we grant it, but we also add that it is their own fault. It is the right and portion of every believer to live in the assurance that he is reconciled to God, that God loves him, and that he is God's child, and if he doth not so live he has himself only to blame. If there be any starving at God's table, it is because the guest stints himself, for the feast is superabundant. If however, a man comes, and I pray you all may, to live habitually under a sense of pardon through the sprinkling of the precious blood, and in a delightful sense of perfect reconciliation with the great God, he is the possessor of a joy unspeakable and full of glory.

But, beloved, this is not all. The joy of the Lord in the spirit springs also from an assurance that all the future, whatever it may be, is guaranteed by divine goodness, that being children of God, the love of God towards us is not of a mutable character, but abides and remains unchangeable. The believer feels an entire satisfaction in leaving himself in the hands of eternal and immutable love. However happy I may be today, if I am in doubt concerning tomorrow, there is a worm at the root of my peace; although the past may now be sweet in retrospect, and the present fair in enjoyment, yet if the future be grim with fear, my joy is but shallow. If my salvation be still a matter of hazard and jeopardy, unmingled joy is not mine, and deep peace is still out of my reach. But when I know that he whom I have rested in hath power and grace enough to complete that which he hath begun in me, and for me; when I see the work of Christ to be no half-way redemption, but a complete and eternal salvation; when I perceive that the promises are established upon an unchangeable basis, and are yea and amen in Christ Jesus, ratified by oath and sealed by blood, then my soul hath perfect contentment. It is true, that looking forward there may be seen long avenues of tribulation, but the glory is at the end of them; battles may be foreseen, and woe unto the man who does not expect them, but the eye of faith perceives the crown of victory. Deep waters are mapped upon our journey, but faith can see Jehovah fording these rivers with us, and she anticipates the day when we shall ascend the banks of the hither shore and enter into Jehovah's rest. When we have received these priceless truths into our souls we are satisfied with favour and full of the goodness of the Lord. There is a theology which denies to believers this consolation, we will not enter into controversy with it, but sorrowfully hint that a heavy chastisement for the errors of that system of doctrine, lies in the loss of the comfort which the truth would have brought into the soul. For my part, I value the gospel not only for what it has done for me in the past, but for the guarantees which it affords me of eternal salvation. "I give unto my sheep eternal life, and they shall never perish, neither shall any pluck them out of my hand."

Now, beloved, I have not yet taken you into the great deeps of joy, though these streams are certainly by no means shallow. There is an abyss of delight for every Christian when he comes into actual fellowship with God. I spoke of the truth that God loved us, and the fact that we are related to him by ties most near and dear; but, oh, when these doctrines become experiences, then are we indeed anointed with the oil of gladness. When we enter into the love of God, and it enters into us; when we walk with God habitually, then our joy is like Jordan at harvest time, when it overfloweth all its banks. Do you know what it means--to walk with God--Enoch's joy; to sit at Jesus' feet--Mary's joy; to lean your head upon Jesus' bosom--John's familiar joy? Oh yes, communion with the Lord is no mere talk with some of us. We have known it in the chamber of affliction; we have known it in the solitude of many a night of broken rest; we have known it beneath discouragements and under sorrows and defamations, and all sorts of ills; and we reckon that one dram of fellowship with Christ is enough to sweeten an ocean full of tribulation, and that only to know that he is near us, and to see the gleaming of his dear eye, would transform even hell itself into heaven, if it were possible for us to enjoy his presence there. Alas! Ye do not and cannot know this bliss, ye who quaff. Your foaming bowls, listening to the sound of stringed instruments, ye do not know what this bliss means--ye have not dreamed of it, nor could ye compass it though a man should tell it unto you. As the beast in the meadow knows not the far-reaching thoughts of him who reads the stars and threads the spheres, so neither can the carnal man make so much as a guess of what are the joys which God hath prepared for them that love him, which any day and every day, when our hearts seek it, he revealeth unto us by his Spirit. This is "the joy of the Lord," fellowship with the Father and with his Son Jesus Christ. Beloved, if we reach this point, we must labour to maintain our standing, for our Lord saith to us "abide in me." The habit of communion is the life of happiness.

Another form of "the joy of the Lord" will visit us practically every day in the honour of being allowed to serve him. It is a joy worth worlds to be allowed to do good. To teach a little child his letters for Christ, will give a true heart some taste of the joy of the Lord, if it be consciously done for the Lord's sake alone. To bear the portion to those for whom nothing is prepared, to visit the sick, to comfort the mourner, to aid the poor, to instruct the ignorant, any, and all of such Christian works, if done in Jesus' name, will in their measure array us in Jehovah's joy. And happy are we, brethren, if when we cannot work we are enabled to lie still and suffer, for acquiescence is another silver pipe through which "the joy of the Lord" will come to us. It is sweet to smart beneath God's rod, and feel that if God would have us suffer it is happiness to do so, to fall back with the faintness of nature, but at the same time with the strength of grace, and say, "Thy will be done." It is joy, when between the millstones crushed like an olive, to yield nothing but the oil of thankfulness; when bruised beneath the flail of tribulation, still to lose nothing but the chaff, and to yield to God the precious grain of entire submissiveness. Why, this is a little heaven upon earth. To glory in tribulations also, this is a high degree of up-climbing towards the likeness of our Lord. Perhaps, the usual communions which we have with our Beloved, though exceeding precious, will never equal those which we enjoy when we have to break through thorns and briars to be at him; when we follow him into the wilderness then we feel the love of our espousals to be doubly sweet. It is a joyous thing when in the midst of mournful circumstances, we yet feel that we cannot mourn because The Bridegroom is with us. Blessed is that man, who in the most terrible storm is driven--not from his God, but even rides upon the crest of the lofty billows nearer towards heaven. Such happiness is the Christian's lot. I do not say that every Christian possesses it, but I am sure that every Christian ought to do so. There is a highway to heaven, and all in it are safe; but in the middle of that road there is a special way, an inner path, and all who walk therein are happy as well as safe. Many professors are only just within the hedge, they walk in the ditch by the road side, and because they are safe there, they are content to put up with all the inconveniences of their walk; but he who takes the crown of the causeway, and walks in the very centre of the road that God has cast up, shall find that no lion shall be there, neither shall any ravenous beast go up thereon, for there the Lord himself shall be his companion, and will manifest himself to him. You shallow Christians who do but believe in Christ, and barely that, whose bibles are unread, whose closets are unfrequented, whose communion with God is a thing of spasms, you have not the joy of the Lord, neither are you strong. I beseech you, rest not as you are, but let your conscious feebleness provoke you to seek the means of strength: and that means of strength is to be found in a pleasant medicine, sweet as it is profitable--the delicious and effectual medicine of "the joy of the Lord."

II. But time would fail me to prolong our remarks upon this very fruitful subject, and we shall turn to our second head, which is this: that THIS JOY IS A SOURCE OF GREAT STRENGTH.

Very rapidly let us consider this thought. It is so because this joy arises from considerations which always strengthen the soul. Very much of the depth of our piety will depend upon our thoughtfulness. Many persons, after having received a doctrine, put it by on the shelf; they are orthodox, they have received the truth, and they are content to keep that truth on hand as dead stock. Sirs, of what account can this be to you, to store your garners with wheat if you never grind the corn for bread, or sow it in the furrows of your fields? He is the joyful Christian who uses the doctrines of the gospel for spiritual meat, as they were meant to be used. Why, some men might as well have a heterodox creed as an orthodox one for all the difference it makes to them. Having the notion that they know, and imagining that to know sufficeth them, they do not consider, contemplate, or regard the truths which they profess to believe, and, consequently, they derive no benefit from them. Now, to contemplate the great truths of divine election, of eternal love, of covenant engagements, of justification by faith through the blood of Christ, and the indwelling and perpetual abiding of the Holy Ghost in his people, to turn over these things is to extract joy from them; and this also is strengthening to the mind. To press the heavenly grapes by meditation, and make the red wine flow forth in torrents, is an exercise as strengthening as it is exhilarating. Joy comes from the same truths which support our strength, and comes by the process of meditation.

Again, "the joy of the Lord" within us is always the sign and symbol of strong spiritual life. Holy vivacity betokens spiritual vigour. I said that he who had spiritual joy gained it by communion with God, but communion with God is the surest fosterer of strength. You cannot be with a strong God without getting strength yourself, for God is always a transforming God; regarding and looking upon him our likeness changes till we become in our measure like our God. The warmth of the South of France, of which you often hear so much, does not spring from soft balmy winds, but from the sun; at sunset the temperature falls. You shall be on one side of the street in Italy and think it May, cross the street into the shade and it is cold as January. The sun does it all. A man who walks in the sunlight of God's countenance, for that very reason is warm and strong. The sunlight of joy usually goes with the warmth of spiritual life. As the light of joy varies so does the warmth of holy strength; he who dwells in the light of God is both happy and strong. He who goes into the shade and loses the joy of the Lord becomes weak at the same time. So the joy of the Lord becomes our strength, as being an indicator of its rise or fall. When a soul is really vigorous and active, it is like the torrent which dashes down the mountain side, which scorns in winter to own the bonds of frost: in a few hours the stagnant pools and slowly moving streams are enchained in ice; but the snow king must bring forth all his strength ere he can manacle the rushing torrent. So when a soul dashes on with the sacred force of faith, it is hard to freeze it into misery, its vigour secures its joy.

Furthermore, the man who possesses "the joy of the Lord," finds it his strength in another respect, that it fortifies him against temptation. What is there that he can be tempted with? He has more already than the world can offer him as a reward for treachery. He is already rich; who shall ensnare him with the wages of unrighteousness? He is already satisfied; who is he that can seduce him with pleasing baits? "Shall such a man as I flee?" The rejoicing Christian is equally proof against persecution. They may well afford to be laughed at who win at such a rate as he does. "You may scoff," saith he, "but I know what true religion is within my soul, and your scoffing will not make me relinquish the pearl of great price." Such a man is, moreover, made strong to bear affliction; for all the sufferings put upon him are but a few drops of bitterness cast into his cup of bliss, to give a deeper tone to the sweetness which absorbs them.

Such a man becomes strong for service, too. What can he not do who is happy in his God? By his God he leaps over a wall, or breaks through a troop. Strong is he, too, for any kind of self-sacrifice. To the God who gives him all, and remains to him as his perpetual portion, such a man gives up all that he hath, and thinks it no surrender. It is but laying up his treasure in his own peculiar treasure house, even in the God of his salvation.

A joyous man, such I have now in my mind's eye, is to all intents and purposes a strong man. He is strong in a calm restful manner. Whatever happens he is not ruffled or disturbed. He is not afraid of evil tidings, his heart is fixed, trusting in the Lord. The ruffled man is ever weak. He is in a hurry, and doth things ill. The man full of joy within is quiet, he bides his time and croucheth in the fulness of his strength. Such a man, though he is humble, is firm and steadfast; he is not carried away with every wind, or bowed by every breeze, he knows what he knows, and holds what he holds, and the golden anchor of his hope entereth within the veil, and holds him fast. His strength is not pretentious but real. The happiness arising from communion with God breeds in him no boastfulness; he does not talk of what he can do, but he does it; he does not say what he could bear, but he bears all that comes. He does not himself always know what he could do; his weakness is the more apparent to himself because of the strength which the Holy Ghost puts upon him; but when the time comes, his weakness only illustrates the divine might, while the man goes calmly on, conquering and to conquer. His inner light makes him independent of the outward sun; his secret granaries make him independent of the outer harvest; his inward fountains place him beyond dread though the brook Cherith may dry Up; he is independent of men and angels, and fearless of devils; all creatures may turn against him if they please, but since God himself is his exceeding joy, he will not miss their love or mourn their hate. He standeth where others fall, he sings where others weep, he wins where others fly, he glorifies his God where others bring dishonour on themselves and on the sacred name. God grant us the inward joy which arises from real strength and is so linked with it as to be in part its cause.

III. But now I must hasten on to notice in the third place that THIS STRENGTH LEADS TO PRACTICAL RESULTS. I am sure I shall have your earnest attention to this, because in many of you I have seen the results follow of which I now speak. I would not flatter any one, but my heart has been full of thanksgiving to the God of all grace when I have seen many of you rejoicing in the Lord under painful circumstances and producing the fruits of a gracious strength. Turn then to our second text, and there you shall observe some of the fruits of holy joy and pious strength.

First, it leads to great praise. "The singers sang aloud," their ministrelsy was hearty and enthusiastic. Sacred song is not a minor matter. Quaint George Herbert has said--

"Praying's the end of preaching."

Might he not have gone further and have said, praising's the end of praying? After all, preaching and praying are not the chief end of man, but the glorifying of God, of which praising God vocally is one form. Preaching is sowing, prayer is watering, but praise is the harvest. God aims at his own glory so should we; and "whoso offereth praise glorifieth me saith the Lord." Be ye diligent then to sing his praises with understanding. We have put away harps and trumpets and organs, let us mind that we really rise above the need of them. I think we do well to dispense with these helps of the typical dispensation; they are all inferior even in music to the human voice, there is assuredly no melody or harmony like those created by living tongues; but let us mind that we do not put away an atom of the joy. Let us be glad when in the congregation we unite in psalmody. It is a wretched thing to hear the praises of God rendered professionally, as if the mere music were everything. It is horrible to have a dozen people in the table-pew singing for you, as if they were proxies for the whole assembly. It is shocking to me to be present in places of worship where not a tenth of the people ever venture to sing at all, and these do it through their teeth so very softly, that one had need to have a mircroscope invented for his ears, to enable him to hear the dying strain. Out upon such mumbling and murdering of the praises of God; if men's hearts were joyous and strong, they would scorn such miserable worship. In this house we all try to sing, but might we not have more praise services? We have had a praise meeting every now and then. Ought we not to hold a praise meeting every week? Should not the prayer meeting be more than ever cheered by praise. The singing of God's people should be, and if they were more full of divine strength would be, more constant and universal. How sinners chant the praise of Baechus in the streets! You can hardly rest in the middle of the night, but what unseemly sounds of revelry startle you. Shall the votaries of wine sing so lustily, and shall we be silent? We are not often guilty of disturbing the world with our music; the days in which Christian zeal interfered with the wicked seem to have gone by; we have settled down into more orderliness, and I am afraid also into more lukewarmness. Oh for the old Methodistic shout. Brethren, wake up your singing again. May the Lord give us again a singing-time, and make us all praise him with heart, and with voice, till even the adversaries shall say, "The Lord hath done great things for them;" and we shall reply, "Ay, ye speak the truth; he hath done great things for us, whereof we are glad." Perhaps there has not been so large a blessing upon the churches of England, because they have not rendered due thanksgiving. In all the time in which we are in trouble we are anxious and prayerful; when a prince is sick bulletins are issued every hour or so; but ah, when the mercy comes but few bulletins are put out, calling upon us to bless and praise the name of God for his mercies. Let us praise the Lord from the rising of the sun unto the going down of the same, for great is the Lord, and greatly is he to be praised.

The next result is great sacrifice. "That day they offered great sacrifices and rejoiced." What day is that in which the church of God now makes great sacrifices? I have not seen it in the calendar of late; and, alas! If men make any sacrifice they very often do so in a mode which indicates that they would escape the inflection if they could. Few make great sacrifices and rejoice. You can persuade a man to give a considerable sum; a great many arguments at last overcome him, and he does it because he would have been ashamed not to do it, but in his heart he wishes you had not come that way, and had gone to some other donor. That is the most acceptable gift to God which is given rejoicingly. It is well to feel that whatever good your gift may do to the church, or the poor, or the sick, it is twice as much benefit to you to give it. It is well to give, because you love to give; as the flower which pours forth its perfume because it never dreamed of doing otherwise; or like the bird which quivers with song, because it is a bird and finds a pleasure in its notes; or like the sun which shines, not by constraint, but because, being a sun, it must shine; or like the waves of the sea which flash back the brilliance of the sun, because it is their nature to reflect and not to hoard the light. Oh, to have such grace in our hearts that we shall joyfully make sacrifices unto our God. The Lord grant that we may have much of this; for the bringing of the tithes into the storehouse is the way to the blessing; as saith the Scripture: "Bring ye all the tithes into the storehouse, that there may be meat in thine house, and prove me now herewith, saith the Lord of hosts, if I will not open you the windows of heaven, and pour you out a blessing, that there shall not be room enough to receive it."

Next to that, there are sure to follow other expressions of joy. They "rejoiced, for God had made them to rejoice with great joy." It was not all singing and giving. When the wheels of the machine are well oiled the whole machine goes easily; and when the man has the oil of joy, then in his business, and in his family, the wheels of his nature glide along sweetly and harmoniously, because he is a glad and a happy man. There are some professors who imagine the sorrow of the Lord to be their strength; they glory in the spirit of bondage and in an unbelieving experience, having great acquaintance with the corruption of their hearts, sometimes of a rather too practical character. They make the deformities of the saints to be their beauty-spots, and their faults to be their evidences. Such men denounce all who rejoice in the Lord, and only tolerate the unbelieving. Their strength lies in being able to take you through all the catacombs of nature's darkness, and to show you the rottenness of their evil hearts. Well, such strength as that let those have who will, but we are persuaded that our text is nearer to wisdom: "The joy of the Lord is your strength." While we know something of our corruption, and mourn it, know something of the world's troubles, and sometimes lament as we bear them; yet there is a joy in the perfect work of Christ, and a joy in our union to him which uplifts us far above all other considerations. God becomes to us such a strength that we cannot help showing our joy in our ordinary life.

But then the text tells us that holy joy leads to family happiness. "The wives also and the children rejoiced." It is so in this church. I have lately seen several children from households which God has blessed, and I have rejoiced to see that father and mother know the Lord, and that even the last of the family has been brought to Jesus. O happy households where the joy is not confined to one, but where all partake of it. I dislike much that Christianity which makes a man feel, "If I go to heaven it is all I care for." Why, you are like a German stove which I found in the room of an hotel the other day--a kind of stove which required all the wood they could bring up merely to warm itself, and then all the heat went up the chimney. We sat around it to make it warm, but scarce a particle of heat came forth from it to us. Too many need all the religion they can get to cheer their own hearts, and their poor families and neighbours sit shivering in the cold of ungodliness. Be like those well constructed stoves of our own houses, which send out all the heat into the room. Send out the heat of piety into your house, and let all the neighbours participate in the blessing, for so the text finishes, "The joy of Jerusalem was heard afar off." The joy of the Lord should be observed throughout our neighbourhood, and many who might otherwise have been careless of true religion will then enquire, "What makes these people glad, and creates such happy households?" Your joy shall thus be God's missionary.

IV. And now I have to close. THIS JOY, THIS STRENGTH, ARE BOTH WITHIN OUR REACH! "For the Lord had made them glad with great joy." God alone can give us this great joy. Then it is within the reach of any, for God can give it to one as well as to another. If it depended upon our good works or our natural abilities, some of us could never reach it; but if God is the source and giver of it he may give it to me as well as to thee, my brother, and to thee as well as to another. What was the way in which God gave this joy? Well first, he gave it to these people by their being attentive hearers. They were not only hearers, but they heard with their ears, their ears were into the word; it was read to them and they sucked it in, receiving it into their souls. An attentive hearer is on the way to being a joyous receiver. Having heard it they felt the power of it, and they wept. Did that seem the way to joy? It was. They received the threatenings of the law with all their terrors into their soul, they allowed the hammer of the word to break them in pieces, they submitted themselves to the word of reproof. Oh! That God would incline you all to do the same, for this, again, is the way in which God gives joy. The word is heard, the word is felt. Then after this, when they had felt the power of the word, we see that they worshipped God devoutly. They bowed the head. Their postures indicated what they felt within. Worshippers who with penitent hearts really adore God, will never complain of weary Sabbaths; adoration helps us into joy. He who can bow low enough before the throne shall be lifted as high before that throne as his heart can desire.

We read also that these hearers and worshippers understood clearly what they heard. Never be content with hearing a sermon unless you can understand it, and if there be a truth that is above you, strain after it, strive to know it. Bible-reader, do not be content with going through the words of the chapter: pray the Holy Ghost to tell you the meaning, and use proper means for finding out that meaning; ask those who know, and use your own enlightened judgment to discover the sense. When shall we have done with formalism of worship and come into living adoration? Sometimes, for all the true singing that there is, the song might as well be in Latin or in Greek. Oh! To know what you are singing, to know what you are saying in prayer, to know what you are reading, to get at it, to come right into it, to understand it--this is the way to holy joy.

And one other point. These people when they had understood what they had devoutly heard, were eager to obey. They obeyed not only the common points of the law in which Israel of old had furnished them with examples, but they found out an old institution which had been buried and forgotten. What was that to them; God had commanded it, and they celebrated it, and in so doing this peculiar joy came upon them. Oh, for the time when all believers shall search the word of God, when they shall not be content with saying, "I have joined myself with a certain body of Christians, and they do so; therefore I do so." May no man say to himself any longer, "Such is the rule of my church;" but may each say, "I am God's servant and not the servant of man, not the servant of thirty-nine articles, of the Prayer-book, or the Catechism; I stand to my own Master, and the only law book I acknowledge is the book of his word, inspired by his Spirit." Oh, blessed day, when every man shall say, "I want to know wherein I am wrong; I desire to know what I am to do; I am anxious to follow the Lord fully." Well, then, if your joy in God leads you to practical obedience, you may rest assured it has made you strong in the very best manner.

Beloved brethren and sisters, we had, before I went away for needed rest, a true spirit of prayer among us. I set out for the continent joyfully, because I left with you the names of some eighty persons proposed for church-membership. My beloved officers, with great diligence, have visited these and others, and next Lord's-day we hope to receive more than a hundred, perhaps a hundred and twenty fresh members into the church. Blessed be God for this. I should not have felt easy in going away if you had been in a barren, cold, dead state; but there was a real fire blazing on God's altar, and souls were being saved. Now, I desire that this gracious zeal should continue, and be renewed. It has not gone out in my absence, I believe, but I desire now a fresh blast from God's Spirit to blow the flame very vehemently. Let us meet for prayer tomorrow, and let the prayer be very earnest, and let those wrestlers who have been moved to agonizing supplication renew the ardour and fervency of their desires, and may we be a strong people, and consequently a joyous people in the strength and joy of the Lord. May sinners in great numbers look unto Jesus and be saved. Amen, and Amen.

PORTION OF SCRIPTURE READ BEFORE SERMON--Nehemiah 8.

www.ingramcontent.com/pod-product-compliance
Lightning Source LLC
Chambersburg PA
CBHW060322100426
42812CB00003B/853

* 9 7 8 1 7 7 3 5 6 1 6 9 1 *